BUSINESS
and
SOCIETY

BUSINESS and SOCIETY

A Strategic Approach to Social Responsibility & Ethics

Sixth Edition

O. C. Ferrell
Auburn University

Debbie Thorne
Texas State University

Linda Ferrell
Auburn University

CHICAGO
BUSINESS PRESS

CHICAGO
BUSINESS PRESS

BUSINESS & SOCIETY:
A STRATEGIC APPROACH TO SOCIAL RESPONSIBILITY & ETHICS

© 2018 Chicago Business Press

For product information or assistance, contact us at
www.chicagobusinesspress.com

Paperback ISBN: 978-0-9971171-4-1
Loose-Leaf ISBN: 978-0-9971171-7-2

Brief Table of Contents

Table of Contents

4 LEGAL, REGULATORY, AND POLITICAL ISSUES   110

12   SOCIAL RESPONSIBILITY IN A GLOBAL ENVIRONMENT   402

Preface

This is the sixth edition of *Business and Society: A Strategic Approach to Social Responsibility*. Our text has become widely used and the Chicago Business Press has facilitated adding value by providing the book at a significantly lower cost than other business and society textbooks. We were one of the first business and society textbooks to use a strategic framework that integrates business and society into organizational strategies. Today in corporate America, social responsibility has become a major consideration in strategic planning. Most boards of directors face issues related to sustainability, legal responsibilities, employee well-being, consumer protection, corporate governance, philanthropy, as well as emerging social issues. Social responsibility has been linked to financial performance, and business and society courses are as important as other functional areas in preparing students for their careers.

In this text, we demonstrate and help the instructor prove that social responsibility is a theoretically grounded yet highly actionable and practical field of interest. The relationship between business and society is inherently controversial and complex, yet the intersection of its components, such as corporate governance, workplace ethics, community needs, and technology, is experienced in every organization. For this reason, we developed this text to effectively assist decision-making and inspire the application of social responsibility principles to a variety of situations and organizations.

Because of this transformation of corporate responsibility, the fifth edition of *Business and Society: A Strategic Approach to Social Responsibility* is designed to fully reflect these changes. We have been diligent in this revision about discussing the most current knowledge and describing best practices related to social responsibility. The innovative text, cutting-edge cases, and comprehensive teaching and learning package for *Business and Society* ensure that business students understand and appreciate concerns about philanthropy, employee well-being, corporate governance, consumer protection, social issues, and sustainability.

Business and Society is a highly readable and teachable text that focuses on the reality of social responsibility in the workplace. We have revised the fifth edition to be the most practical and applied business and society text available. A differentiating feature of this book is its focus on the role that social responsibility takes in strategic business decisions. We demonstrate that studying social responsibility provides knowledge and insights that positively contribute to organizational performance and professional success. This text prepares students for the social responsibility challenges and opportunities they will face throughout their careers. We provide the latest examples, stimulating cases, and unique learning tools that capture the reality and complexity of social responsibility. Students and instructors prefer this book because it presents examples, tools, and practices needed to develop and implement a socially responsible business strategy. Finally, this book makes the assumption that students will be working in an organization trying to improve social responsibility and not just critics of business.

In this revision, we have tried to capture emerging trends in the social and economic environment. For example, one trend impacting business and society involves the rise of companies offering sharing services, including Uber, Airbnb, Lyft, Instacart, and more. These firms offer services through independent contractors rather than employees. They have become such a large part of our daily lives that a new term was developed to describe their impact on business and society—the sharing economy. The sharing economy allows for consumers to be their own boss as an independent contractor and make use of underutilized resources, such as cars or lodging, to earn extra income. The entire concept of ownership is being challenged. In addition, the regulatory issues necessary to deal with various risks have not moved fast enough to address many economic and social issues. Throughout the book, we attempt to deal with this and other emerging trends.

IMPORTANT CHANGES TO THE SIXTH EDITION

The sixth edition has been revised to include new examples, vignettes, and cases. Each chapter of the text has been updated to include recent social responsibility issues related to the economy, ethical decision-making, and concerns about corporate governance. Chapter 4 has been updated to include recent legislation that impacts business, including the most recent amendment to the Federal Sentencing Guidelines for Organizations. In Chapter 5, we introduce new normative terms and concepts that contribute toward ethical decision making.

Opening cases at the start of each chapter address a variety of issues related to the chapter content, including greenwashing, fracking, and childhood obesity. Companies featured in these cases include Warby Parker, CarMax, General Motors, and Uber. Two boxed inserts focus on social responsibility. One relates to ethical challenges in different areas of business, including human resources, marketing, accounting, and finance. Topics discussed in these vignettes include minimum wages, integrated reporting, and cooperative banking. Another boxed insert entitled "Earth in the Balance" focuses on social responsibility related to sustainability issues. These vignettes discuss green initiatives at companies such as Google, Unilever, and SodaStream.

The "Responsible Business Debate" feature at the end of each chapter introduces a real-world issue and presents two competing perspectives. The debate is positioned so that class teams can defend a position and analyze topics, giving students the opportunity to engage in active learning. Topics discussed include controversies over clearance pricing, performance reviews, business's influence on society, and the use of genetically engineered pesticides. We have also provided 15 cutting-edge cases, all of which are new or significantly updated.

CONTENT AND ORGANIZATION

Professors who teach business and society courses come from diverse backgrounds, including law, management, marketing, philosophy, and many others. Such diversity affords great opportunities to the field of business and society and showcases the central role that social responsibility occupies within various academic, professional, work, and community circles. Because of the widespread interest and multiplicity of stakeholders, the philosophy and practice of social responsibility is both exciting and debatable; it is in a constant state of discussion and refinement—just like all important business concepts and practices.

We define social responsibility in Chapter 1, "Social Responsibility Framework," as *the adoption by a business of a strategic focus for fulfilling the economic, legal, ethical, and philanthropic responsibilities expected of it by its stakeholders.* To gain the benefits of social responsibility, effective and mutually beneficial relationships must be developed with customers, employees, investors, government, the community, and others who have a stake in the company. We believe that social responsibility must be fully valued and championed by top managers and granted the same planning time, priority, and management attention as any company initiative. Therefore, the framework for the text reflects a process that begins with the social responsibility philosophy, includes the four types of responsibilities, involves many types of stakeholders, and ultimately results in both short- and long-term performance gains. We also provide a strategic orientation, so students will develop the knowledge, skills, and attitudes for understanding how organizations achieve many benefits through social responsibility.

Chapter 2, "Strategic Management of Stakeholder Relationships," examines the types and attributes of stakeholders, how stakeholders become influential, and the processes for integrating and managing their influence on a firm. The chapter introduces the stakeholder interaction model and examines the impact on global business, corporate reputation, and crisis situations on stakeholder relationships.

Because both daily and strategic decisions affect a variety of stakeholders, companies must maintain a governance structure for ensuring proper control and responsibility for their actions. Chapter 3, "Corporate Governance," examines the rights of shareholders, the accountability of top management for corporate actions, executive compensation, and strategic-level processes for ensuring that economic, legal, ethical, and philanthropic responsibilities are satisfied. Corporate governance is an integral element for social responsibility, which, until the recent scandals, had not received the same level of emphasis as issues such as environment and human rights.

Chapter 4, "Legal, Regulatory, and Political Issues," explores the complex relationship between business and government. Every business must be aware of and abide by the laws and regulations that dictate required business conduct. This chapter also examines how business can participate in the public policy perspective to influence government. A strategic approach for legal compliance, based on the Federal Sentencing Guidelines for Organizations, is also provided.

Chapter 5, "Business Ethics and Ethical Decision-Making," and Chapter 6, "Strategic Approaches to Improving Ethical Behavior," are devoted to exploring the role of ethics and ethical leadership in business decision-making. Business ethics relates to responsibilities and expectations that exist beyond legally prescribed levels. We examine the factors that influence ethical decision-making and consider how companies can apply this understanding to improve ethical conduct. We fully describe the components of an organizational ethics program and detail the implementation plans needed for effectiveness.

Chapter 7, "Employee Relations," and Chapter 8, "Consumer Relations," explore relationships with two pivotal stakeholders—consumers and employees. These constituencies, although different by definition, have similar expectations of the economic, legal, ethical, and philanthropic responsibilities that must be addressed by business.

Chapter 9, "Community Relations and Strategic Philanthropy," examines companies' synergistic use of organizational core competencies and resources to address key stakeholders' interests and achieve both organizational and social benefits. While traditional benevolent philanthropy involves donating a percentage of sales to social causes, a strategic approach aligns employees and organizational resources and expertise with the needs and concerns of stakeholders. Strategic philanthropy involves both financial and nonfinancial contributions to stakeholders, but it also directly benefits the company.

Due to the internet and other technological advances, communication is faster than ever, information is readily available, people are living longer and healthier lives, and consumer expectations of businesses continue to rise. Chapter 10, "Technology Issues," provides cutting-edge information on the unique issues that arise as a result of enhanced technology in the workplace and business environment, including its effects on privacy, intellectual property, and health. The strategic direction for technology depends on the government's and businesses' ability to plan, implement, and audit the influence of technology on society.

Chapter 11, "Sustainability Issues," explores the significant environmental issues business and society face today, including air pollution, global warming, water pollution and water quantity, land pollution, waste management, deforestation, urban sprawl, biodiversity, genetically modified foods, and alternative energy. This chapter also considers the impact of government environmental policy and regulation and examines how some companies are going beyond these laws to address environmental issues and act in an environmentally responsible manner.

Chapter 12, "Social Responsibility in a Global Environment," is a chapter that addresses the unique issues found in a global business environment. Emerging trends and standards are placed in a global context.

SPECIAL FEATURES

Examples

Company examples and anecdotes from all over the world are found throughout the text. The purpose of these tools is to take students through a complete strategic planning and implementation perspective on business and society concerns by incorporating an active and team-based learning perspective. Every chapter opens with a vignette and includes examples that shed more light on how social responsibility works in today's business. In this edition, all boxed features focus on managerial and global dimensions of social responsibility. Chapter opening objectives, a chapter summary, boldfaced key terms, and discussion questions at the end of each chapter help direct students' attention to key points.

Experiential Exercises

Experiential exercises at the end of each chapter help students apply social responsibility concepts and ideas to business practice. Most of the exercises involve research on the activities, programs, and philosophies that companies and organizations are using to implement social responsibility today. These exercises are designed for higher-level learning and require students to apply, analyze, synthesize, and evaluate knowledge, concepts, practices, and possibilities for social responsibility. At the same time, the instructor can generate rich and complex discussions from student responses to exercises. For example, the experiential exercise for Chapter 1 asks students to examine *Fortune* magazine's annual list of the Most Admired Companies. This exercise sets the stage for a discussion on the broad context in which stakeholders, business objectives, and responsibilities converge.

"What Would You Do?" exercises depict people in real-world scenarios who are faced with decisions about social responsibility in the workplace. One exercise (see Chapter 9) discusses the dilemma of a newly named vice president of corporate philanthropy. His charge over the next year is to develop a stronger reputation for philanthropy and social responsibility with the company's stakeholders, including employees, customers, and community. At the end of the scenario, students are asked to help the VP develop a plan for gaining internal support for the office and its philanthropic efforts.

A new debate issue is located at the end of each chapter. The topic of each debate deals with a real-world company or dilemma that is both current and controversial. Many students have not had the opportunity to engage in a debate and to defend a position related to social responsibility. This feature highlights the complexity of ethical issues by creating a dialog on advantages and disadvantages surrounding issues. The debates also help students develop their critical-thinking, research, and communication skills.

Cases

So that students learn more about specific practices, problems, and opportunities in social responsibility, 15 cases are provided at the end of the book. The cases represent a comprehensive collection for examining social responsibility in a multidimensional way. The 15 cases allow students to consider the effects of stakeholders and responsibility expectations on larger and well-known businesses. These cases represent the most up-to-date and compelling issues in social responsibility. All of the cases used in this book are original and have been updated with all developments that have occurred through 2014. Students will find these cases to be pivotal to their understanding of the complexity of social responsibility in practice. The following provides an overview of the 15 cases:

- Case 1: Uber Faces Ethical and Regulatory Challenges. This case discusses the success of Uber and the regulatory challenges it faces as it expands globally. One of the biggest controversies is the fact that Uber drivers do not always have to be licensed, unlike taxi companies. This has led several cities worldwide to place bans on certain Uber services.
- Case 2: The Mission of CVS: Corporate Social Responsibility and Pharmacy Innovation. This case examines the corporate social responsibility initiatives of CVS as well as ethical challenges it has faced. Of particular interest is CVS's decision to drop profitable tobacco products from stores to better align itself as a health services company.
- Case 3: Belle Meade Plantation: The First Non-Profit Winery Engages in Social Entrepreneurship. We discuss the Nashville plantation, Belle Meade's background, and the challenges it has faced as a nonprofit. To support itself instead of having to rely solely on donations or tour tickets, Belle Meade has become a social entrepreneur by developing and selling wine from the plantation's vineyards on the premises. Proceeds go to support the plantation. This endeavor in social entrepreneurship has led to the nation's first non-profit winery.
- Case 4: Multilevel Marketing Under Fire: Herbalife Defends Its Business Model. This case considers the accusations levied against Herbalife by

activist investor William Ackman charging Herbalife's business model as being a pyramid scheme. We differentiate between a pyramid scheme and a multilevel marketing compensation model and apply this to Herbalife's business.

- Case 5: Hobby Lobby: Balancing Stakeholders and Religious Freedom in Business Decisions. We investigate the landmark decision in *Burwell v. Hobby Lobby* and its impact on the religious rights of closely held private companies. This victory for Hobby Lobby is likely to have major implications for the government's ability to require certain benefits if they conflict with a closely held company's religious principles.

- Case 6: Starbucks' Mission: Social Responsibility and Brand Strength. This case examines Starbucks' foundation for a socially responsible culture. It also describes how Starbucks strives to meet the needs of different stakeholders and how this stakeholder emphasis has led to the development of successful products and a strong brand image.

- Case 7: Lululemon: Encouraging a Healthier Lifestyle. We demonstrate Lululemon's success in its mission to help consumers live a healthier lifestyle. Additionally, we look at some of the controversies that have hit Lululemon in recent years, including the remarks and subsequent resignation of Board Chairman and founder Chip Wilson.

- Case 8: The Hershey Company and West African Cocoa Communities.

- Case 9: The Coca-Cola Company Struggles with Ethical Crises. We look at the many ethical issues that have challenged Coca-Cola's dominancy in the late 1990s to the first decades of the twenty-first century. In particular, we focus on how Coca-Cola has reacted to these crises and its initiatives to become a socially responsible company.

- Case 10: Enron: Questionable Accounting Leads to Collapse. This case describes the well-known example of Enron, one of the biggest bankruptcies of the time that shocked the world with its far-reaching effects. We examine the different players in the Enron crisis as well as the lessons that the Enron debacle can teach the business world.

- Case 11: The Complexity of Intellectual Property. This case takes an in-depth look at different types of intellectual property as well as how common violations occur. The lawsuit between Apple and Samsung is discussed to show that even large well-established companies deal with this issue.

- Case 12: Salesforce.com: Responsible Cloud Computing. We examine the success of Salesforce.com's cloud computing model. In particular, we focus on its 1-1-1 model to give back to the communities in which it does business.

- Case 13: Mattel Responds to Ethical Challenges. This case goes over Mattel's corporate social responsibility initiatives with a particular emphasis on its supplier code of conduct. Two major controversies Mattel has faced are discussed. The first is the lead paint and magnet scandal that forced Mattel to undergo a massive recall and damaged its reputation. A more recent example is the intellectual property dispute it has had with rival company MGA over the ownership of the Bratz dolls.

- Case 14: Home Depot Implements Stakeholder Orientation. Although Home Depot faced a decrease in customer satisfaction in the past, it has implemented a number of initiatives to restore its ethical reputation with stakeholders. Some major initiatives include its diversity supplier program, its use of wood certified by the Forest Stewardship Council, and its philanthropic involvement with Habitat for Humanity. Above all, Home Depot has adopted a stakeholder orientation that considers how it can best meet the needs of all its various stakeholders.
- Case 15: New Belgium Brewing: Engaging in Sustainable Social Responsibility. This case examines the background of New Belgium Brewing and its social responsibility initiatives. Its strong emphasis on sustainability and employee involvement are discussed as examples of how the craft brewery has been able to maintain its corporate values since its founding.

Role-Play Exercises

In addition to many examples, end-of-chapter exercises, and the cases, we provide three role-play exercises in the *Instructor's Manual*. The role-play exercises built around a fictitious yet plausible scenario or case support higher-level learning objectives, require group decision-making skills, and can be used in classes of any size. Implementation of the exercises can be customized to the time frame, course objectives, student population, and other unique characteristics of a course. These exercises are aligned with trends in higher education toward teamwork, active learning, and student experiences in handling real-world business issues. For example, the National Farm & Garden exercise places students in a crisis situation involving a product defect that requires an immediate response and consideration of changes over the long term. The Soy-Dri exercise requires students to come up with an action plan for how to deal with customer confusion over the appropriate use of different products. The Shockvolt exercise places students in a situation in which they must determine the ethics and potential legal implications for marketing an energy drink. The role-play simulations (1) give students the opportunity to practice making decisions that have consequences for social responsibility, (2) utilize a team-based approach, (3) recreate the pressures, power, information flows, and other factors that affect decision-making in the workplace, and (4) incorporate a debriefing and feedback period for maximum learning and linkages to course objectives. We developed the role-play exercises to enhance more traditional learning tools and to complement the array of resources provided to users of this text. Few textbooks offer this level of teaching support and proprietary learning devices.

A SUPPLEMENTS PACKAGE

The comprehensive *Instructor's Manual* includes chapter outlines, answers to the discussion questions at the end of each chapter, comments on the experiential exercises at the end of each chapter, comments on each case, and a sample syllabus. The role-play exercises are included in the manual along with specific suggestions for using and implementing them in class.

The Test Bank provides multiple choice and essay questions for each chapter and includes a mix of descriptive and application questions.

A PowerPoint slide program is available for easy downloading and provides a recap of the highlights in each chapter.

Visit www.chicagobusinesspress.com to request access to the instructor supplements

AUTHORS' PERSONAL WEBSITE

O. C. Ferrell and Linda Ferrell have established a teaching resource website based on their participation in the Daniels Fund Ethics Initiative. Their publicly accessible website contains original cases, debate issues, videos, interviews, and PowerPoint modules on select business and society topics as well as other resources such as articles on ethics and social responsibility education. It is possible to access this website at http://danielsethics.mgt.unm.edu.

ACKNOWLEDGMENTS

A number of individuals provided reviews and suggestions that helped improve the text and related materials, specifically, Patricia Smith at North Carolina Wesleyan College, Velvet Landingham at Kent State University, Martha Broderick at the University of Maine, Kathryn Coulter at Mount Mercy University, and William Ferris at Western New England University. We sincerely appreciate their time, expertise, and interest in this project.

We wish to acknowledge the many people who played an important role in the development of this book. Jennifer Sawayda played a key role in research, writing, editing, and project management. We would like to thank Paul Ducham and the Chicago Business Press for their leadership and support of this edition. We wish to thank Vitaly Nishanov at the University of Washington for his insightful review of chapters 5 and 6. Finally, we express much appreciation to our colleagues and the administration at Texas State University-San Marcos and the Belmont University.

Our goal is to provide materials and resources that enhance and strengthen teaching, learning, and thinking about social responsibility. We invite your comments, concerns, and questions. Your suggestions will be sincerely appreciated and utilized.

O. C. Ferrell
Debbie M. Thorne
Linda Ferrell

CHAPTER ONE

Social Responsibility Framework

Chapter Objectives

- To define the concept of social responsibility
- To trace the development of social responsibility
- To examine the global nature of social responsibility
- To discuss the benefits of social responsibility
- To introduce the framework for understanding social responsibility

Chapter Outline

Social Responsibility Defined

Development of Social Responsibility

Global Nature of Social Responsibility

Benefits of Social Responsibility

Framework for Studying Social Responsibility

Warby Parker: Socially Responsible Vision

Consumers may be surprised to realize that one company controls much of the industry for eyewear, including manufacturing, distribution. Critics claim this has resulted in excessive prices for quality eyewear. Among these critics was Neil Blumenthal. In 2008 Neil Blumenthal partnered with David Gilboa, and three classmates to develop a plan for a business to compete against the industry giant and eyewear affordable for the masses. The idea was developed for Wharton Business School's business plan competition. Unfortunately, the school did not see their idea as a promising endeavor. The business plan did not even reach the final round.

Nearly a decade later, this business plan has developed into a successful firm that has now sold more than 1 million pairs of glasses. The founders founded their firm—Warby Parker—on the premise that designing and manufacturing glasses in-house and selling them on the Internet would significantly reduce costs. These costs could then be passed onto the consumer so they would be able to afford designer glasses at a fraction of their competitor's costs. Because of its ability to save on costs, consumers can purchase eyeglasses for as little as $95 each from Warby Parker. Today this $1.2 billion company has expanded beyond selling solely online and has been able to open up 27 retail locations.

Warby Parker is known for more than just making eyeglasses affordable for the masses. The foundation of the business was also built on making eyewear available for people in developing countries who could not normally afford glasses. Enter Visionspring, a nonprofit charity that provides glasses to individuals in developing countries. Warby Parker partnered with Visionspring to donate one pair of eyeglasses to an individual in a developing country for every pair of eyeglasses it sells. Each month Warby Parker determines how many glasses it sold and then makes a donation to Visionspring that handles the costs of sourcing the eyeglasses. The reason why Warby Parker does not simply donate the glasses is because Visionspring trains consumers in the country—particularly women—to be entrepreneurs and sell the glasses to tradespeople for approximately $4 each. This is much more affordable for tradespeople while also providing more economic opportunities for women to own their own small businesses and generate income. Glasses have been found to make a world of difference for people who require eye care in developing countries. It is estimated that these tradespeople see their earning power rise by 20 percent after they have purchased glasses. Warby Parker demonstrates how a company can effect positive change in this world while simultaneously earning a profit. Its strategic social responsibility results in high-quality products at lower prices as well as the ability for those in developing countries to obtain the eyewear they need.

B usinesses today must cope with challenging decisions related to their interface with society. Consumers, as well as others, are increasingly emphasizing the importance of companies' reputations, which are often based on ethics and social responsibility. The meaning of the term "social responsibility" goes beyond being philanthropic or environmentally sustainable. Seventy-six percent of Americans think the meaning now extends to how employees are treated and the values a company holds.[2] In an era of intense global competition and increasing media scrutiny, consumer activism, and government regulation, all types of organizations need to become adept at fulfilling these expectations. Like Warby Parker, many companies are trying, with varying results, to meet the many economic, legal, ethical, and philanthropic responsibilities they now face. Satisfying the expectations of social responsibility is a never-ending process of continuous improvement that requires leadership from top management, buy-in from employees, and good relationships across the community, industry, market, and government. Companies must properly plan, allocate, and use resources to satisfy the demands placed on them by investors, employees, customers, business partners, the government, the community, and others. Those who have an interest or stake in the company are referred to as stakeholders.

In this chapter, we examine the concept of social responsibility and how it relates to today's complex business environment. First, we define social responsibility. Next, we consider the development of social responsibility, its benefits to organizations, and the changing nature of expectations in our increasingly global economy. Finally, we introduce the framework for studying social responsibility used by this text, which includes such elements as strategic management for stakeholder relations; legal, regulatory, and political issues; business ethics; corporate governance; consumer relations; employee relations; philanthropy and community relations; technology issues; sustainability issues; and global relations.

SOCIAL RESPONSIBILITY DEFINED

Business ethics, corporate volunteerism, philanthropic activities, going green, sustainability, corporate governance, reputation management—these are terms you may have heard used, or even used yourself, to describe the various rights and responsibilities of business organizations. You may have thought about what these terms actually mean for business practice. You may also have wondered how businesses engage in these behaviors or contribute to these outcomes. In this chapter, we clarify some of the confusion that exists in the terminology that people use when they talk about expectations for business. To this end, we begin by defining social responsibility.

In most societies, businesses are granted a license to operate and the right to exist through a combination of social and legal institutions. Businesses are expected to provide quality goods and services, abide by laws and regulations, treat employees fairly, follow through on contracts, protect the natural environment, meet warranty obligations, and adhere to many other standards of good business conduct. Companies that continuously meet and exceed these standards are rewarded with customer satisfaction, employee dedication, investor loyalty, strong relationships in the community, and the time and energy to continue focusing on business-related concerns. Firms that fail to meet these responsibilities can face penalties, both formal and informal, and may have their attention diverted away from core business practice. For example, Volkswagen received a number of penalties and criticisms for installing "defeat devices" into its diesel vehicles. These defeat devices were intended to fool regulators. While the cars were undergoing emissions testing, the cars ran below performance to meet requirements. However, when on the road they emitted 40 times the allowable limit of emissions in the United States. Perhaps most damaging to the firm is that this scandal was a deliberate attempt to bypass environmental rules. German prosecutors launched an investigation to determine whether top executives also mislead investors by failing to inform them about complaints filed against the company in a timely manner.[3] The goal is to prevent these negative outcomes in the future.

In contrast, a large multinational corporation may be faced with protestors who use illicit means to destroy or deface property. More firms are seeing their websites hacked and/or sabotaged by those who are protesting specific issues. For instance, the Japan External Trade Organization's website crashed after hackers attacked the site to protest against Japan's stance toward whale hunting.[4] Whether the attacks are physical or virtual, they can cost companies significant resources in having to rebuild.

Finally, a company engaged in alleged deceptive practices may face formal investigation by a government agency. For instance, a group of prominent authors and booksellers are demanding that the Justice Department investigate Amazon for engaging in anticompetitive practices. According to the group, Amazon, which holds 40 percent of the market for new books, has used below-cost pricing to put competitors out of business and blocked the sale of books to force publishers for more favorable deals.[5] Investigations such as this could lead to legal charges and penalties, perhaps severe enough to significantly alter the company's products and practices or close the business. For example, The Scooter Store, a company that sold motorized wheelchairs all over the United States, filed for Chapter 11 bankruptcy after a federal investigation determined the company had deceptively overcharged Medicare and Medicaid between $47 million and $88 million over the course of two years. The company was found to have engaged in deceptive tactics, such as continually contacting doctors to prescribe the motorized wheelchairs whether or not a patient was in need of one; claiming the wheelchairs were free in advertisements when taxpayers were paying for them; and contributing to political campaigns to avoid any changes to Medicare and Medicaid. In addition, the city of New Braunfels, Texas, the home of the company's headquarters, sued the company for the more than $2 million that was given to them from an economic development fund to build their headquarters. To make matters worse, consumers remarked they made purchases from the company because they claimed their goal was to "Always Do the Right Thing."[6]

Businesses today are expected to look beyond self-interest and recognize that they belong to a larger group, or society, that expects responsible participation. Therefore, if any group, society, or institution is to function, there must be a delicate interplay between rights (i.e., what people expect to get) and responsibilities (i.e., what people are expected to contribute) for the common good. Research indicates that the most ethical and socially responsible companies are the most profitable.[7] Therefore, responsible conduct and policies yield significant benefits to society as well as shareholders. While the media provides much coverage of misconduct and illegal activities in business, most businesses try to act in an ethical and socially responsible manner.

The term *social responsibility* came into widespread use in the business world during the 1970s. It has evolved into an emphasis on the following areas: social issues, consumer protection, sustainability, and corporate governance. Social issues are linked with the idea of the "common good." The common good is associated with the development of social conditions that allow for societal welfare and fulfillment to be achieved. In other words, social issues involve the ethical responsibilities a firm owes to society. Equal rights, gender roles, marketing to vulnerable populations, data protection, and internet tracking are examples of social issues common in business. Social issues can become so significant that they warrant legislation to protect consumers. For the Federal Trade Commission's Bureau of Consumer Protection, leading consumer protection issues include misleading advertising, product safety, and advertising to children.

Sustainability has also become a growing area of concern in society. In the United States, sustainability is used to refer more to the environmental impact on stakeholders. Green marketing practices, consumption of resources, and greenhouse gas emissions are important sustainability considerations that socially responsible businesses will have to address. Corporate governance will be described in more detail in Chapter 3. It refers to formal systems of accountability, oversight, and control. Corporate governance is becoming an increasingly important topic in light of business scandals over the last 10–15 years. Issues in corporate governance include concerns over executive compensation, internal control mechanisms, and risk management.[8] Figure 1.1 discusses the social responsibility issues that we will be covering in this text.

These four areas of social responsibility tend to conflict with the traditional or neoclassical view of a business's responsibility to society. The traditional view of social responsibility, articulated in the famous economist Milton Friedman's 1962 *Capitalism and Freedom,* asserts that business has one purpose, satisfying its investors or shareholders, and that any other considerations are outside its scope.[9] Although this view still exists today, it has lost credibility as more and more companies have assumed a social responsibility orientation.[10] Companies see social responsibility

FIGURE 1.1 Major Emphases of Social Responsibility

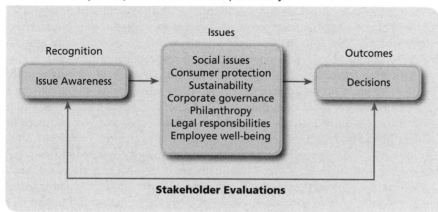

as a part of their overall corporate strategy and a benefit that directly increases the bottom line. We define **social responsibility** as the adoption by a business of a strategic focus for fulfilling the economic, legal, ethical, and philanthropic responsibilities expected of it by its stakeholders. This definition encompasses a wide range of objectives and activities, including both historical views of business and perceptions that have emerged in the last decade. Let's take a closer look at the parts of this definition.

social responsibility
The adoption by a business of a strategic focus for fulfilling the economic, legal, ethical, and philanthropic responsibilities expected of it by its stakeholders.

Social Responsibility Applies to All Types of Businesses

It is important to recognize that all types of businesses—small and large, sole proprietorships and partnerships, as well as large corporations—implement social responsibility initiatives to further their relationships with their customers, their employees, and their community at large. For example, Altered Seasons, a candle retailer in Buffalo, New York, operates on a one-for-one model, where the company gives a meal to the hungry for every candle that it sells. The company's candles are made from environmentally friendly materials and are manufactured in the United States.[11] Thus, the ideas advanced in this book are equally relevant and applicable across a wide variety of businesses and nonprofits.

Nonprofit organizations are expected to be socially responsible. Relationships with stakeholders—including employees, those that are served, and the community—affect their reputation. For example, the Southern California chapter of the Better Business Bureau was expelled from the organization after evidence emerged in 2010 that it had been operating a pay-for-play scheme. The Better Business Bureau is a nonprofit self-regulatory organization that objectively rates businesses on how they treat consumers and handle consumer complaints. Investigations revealed that employees at the Southern California bureau were awarding businesses high rankings only if they paid to become members. The bureau is the largest ever expelled for misconduct.[12] This example demonstrates that nonprofit organizations must also develop strategic plans for social responsibility. In addition, government agencies are expected to uphold the common good and act in an ethical and responsible manner.

Although the social responsibility efforts of large corporations usually receive the most attention, the activities of small businesses may have a greater impact on local communities.[13] Owners of small businesses often serve as community leaders, provide goods and services for customers in smaller markets that larger corporations are not interested in serving, create jobs, and donate resources to local community causes. Medium-sized businesses and their employees have similar roles and functions on both a local and a regional level. Although larger firms produce a substantial portion of the gross national output of the United States, small businesses employ about half of the private sector workforce and produce roughly half of the private sector output. In addition to these economic outcomes, small business presents an entrepreneurial opportunity to many people, some of whom have been shut out of the traditional labor force. Women, minorities, and veterans are increasingly interested in self-employment and other forms of small business activity.[14] It is vital that all businesses consider the relationships and expectations that our definition of social responsibility suggests.

Social Responsibility Needs a Strategic Focus

Social responsibility is an important business concept and involves significant planning and implementation. Our definition of social responsibility requires a formal commitment, or a way of communicating the company's social responsibility philosophy. For example, Herman Miller, a multinational provider of office, residential, and healthcare furniture and services, established a set of values that create a culture of community both within and outside of the company (shown in Table 1.1). This statement declares Herman Miller's philosophy and the way it will fulfill its responsibilities to its customers, its shareholders, its employees, the community, and the natural environment. Because this statement takes into account all of Herman Miller's constituents and applies directly to all of the company's operations, products, markets, and business relationships, it demonstrates the company's strategic focus on social responsibility. Other companies that embrace social responsibility have incorporated similar elements into their strategic communications, including mission and vision statements, annual reports, and websites. For example, Hershey Entertainment & Resorts focuses upon four pillars of CSR: (1) the environment and the goal to reduce the ecological footprint; (2) the community and being a positive, productive, and informed

TABLE 1.1 Herman Miller, Inc.'s, Corporate Culture Values of Community

- Curiosity and Exploration
- Performance
- Engagement
- Design
- Relationships
- Inclusiveness
- A Better World
- Transparency
- Foundations

Source: "Things That Matter to Us," Herman Miller, Inc., http://www.hermanmiller.com/about-us/things-that-matter-to-us.html (accessed June 17, 2016). Courtesy of Herman Miller, Inc.

partner; (3) the workplace, in fostering one that is safe, inclusive, desirable, and respectful; and (4) a marketplace and guest focus that considers the ethical treatment of all stakeholders.[15]

In addition to a company's verbal and written commitment to social responsibility, our definition requires action and results. To implement its social responsibility philosophy, Herman Miller has developed and implemented several corporate-wide strategic initiatives, including research on improving work furniture and environments, innovation in the area of ergonomically correct products, progressive employee development opportunities, volunteerism, and an environmental stewardship program.[16] These efforts have earned the company many accolades, such as being named the "Most Admired" furniture manufacturer in America by *Fortune* magazine, and a place on many prestigious lists, including *Fortune* magazine's "100 Best Companies to Work for in America," *Forbes* magazine's "Platinum List" of America's 400 best-managed large companies, *Business Ethics* magazine's "100 Best Corporate Citizens," *Diversity Inc.* magazine's "Top 10 Corporations for Supplier Diversity," and *The Progressive Investor*'s "Sustainable Business Top 20."[17] As this example demonstrates, effective social responsibility requires both words and action.

If any such initiative is to have strategic importance, it must be fully valued and championed by top management. Leaders must believe in and support the integration of stakeholder interests and economic, legal, ethical, and philanthropic responsibilities into every corporate decision. For example, company objectives for brand awareness and loyalty can be developed and measured from both a marketing and a social responsibility standpoint because researchers have documented a relationship between consumers' perceptions of a firm's social responsibility and their intentions to purchase that company's brands.[18] Likewise, engineers can integrate consumers' desires for reduced negative environmental impact in product designs, and marketers can ensure that a brand's advertising campaign incorporates this product benefit. Finally, consumers' desires for an environmentally sustainable product may stimulate a stronger company interest in assuming environmental leadership in all aspects of its operations. Home Depot, for example, responded to demands by consumers and environmentalists for environmentally friendly wood products by launching a new initiative that gives preference to wood products certified as having been harvested responsibly over those taken from endangered forests.[19] With this action, the company—which has long touted its environmental principles—has chosen to take a leadership role in the campaign for environmental responsibility in the home improvement industry. Although social responsibility depends on collaboration and coordination across many parts of the business and among its constituencies, it also produces effects throughout these same groups. We discuss some of these benefits in a later section of this chapter.

Because of the need for coordination, a large company that is committed to social responsibility often creates specific positions or departments to spearhead the various components of its program. For example, Starbucks has a Global Responsibility Department that focuses on responsible and ethical behaviors regarding the environment, employee relations, customer interactions, suppliers, and communities. The company's Environmental Starbucks Coffee Company Affairs team works to develop environmentally responsible policies and minimize the company's "footprint." CEO Howard Schultz considers the creation of a good work environment a top priority. Some of the results of this philosophy include offering one of the best healthcare programs in the coffee shop industry and the institution of wellness programs. Starbucks also practices conservation with its Starbucks Coffee and Farmer Equity Practices (CAFE), which is a set of socially responsible coffee-buying guidelines. Finally, the company is philanthropic and engages the community on how well the company is doing from their perspective. In the table of contents page of the company's annual report, CSR (corporate social responsibility) is listed as a key feature.[20] A smaller firm may give an executive, perhaps in human resources or the business owner, the ability to make decisions regarding community involvement, ethical standards, philanthropy, and other areas. Regardless of the formal or informal nature of the structure, this department or executive should ensure that social responsibility initiatives are aligned with the company's corporate culture, integrated with companywide goals and plans, fully communicated within and outside the company, and measured to determine their effectiveness and strategic impact. In sum, social responsibility must be given the same planning time, priority, and management attention that is given to any other company initiative, such as continuous improvement, cost management, investor relations, research and development, human resources, or marketing research.

Social Responsibility Fulfills Society's Expectations

Another element of our definition of social responsibility involves society's expectations of business conduct. Many people believe that businesses should accept and abide by four types of responsibility: financial, legal, ethical, and philanthropic (see Table 1.2). To varying degrees, the four types are required, expected, and/or desired by society.[21]

At Stage 1, businesses have a responsibility to be financially viable so that they can provide a return on investment for their owners, create jobs for the community, and contribute goods and services to the economy. The economy is influenced by the ways organizations relate to their shareholders, their customers, their employees, their suppliers, their competitors, their community, and even the natural environment. For example, in nations with corrupt businesses and industries, the negative effects often pervade the entire society. Transparency International, a German organization dedicated to curbing national and international corruption, conducts an annual survey on the effects of business and government corruption on a country's economic growth and prospects.

TABLE 1.2 Social Responsibility Requirements

Stages	Examples
Stage 1: Financial Viability	Starbucks offers investors a healthy return on investment, including paying dividends.
Stage 2: Compliance with Legal and Regulatory Requirements	Starbucks specifies in its code of conduct that payments made to foreign government officials must be lawful according to the laws of the United States and the foreign country.
Stage 3: Ethics, Principles, and Values	Starbucks offers healthcare benefits to part-time employees and supports coffee growers so they get a fair price.
Stage 4: Philanthropic Activities	Starbucks created the Starbucks Foundation to award grants to eligible nonprofits and to give back to their communities.

The organization reports that corruption reduces economic growth, inhibits foreign investment, and often channels investment and funds into "pet projects" that may create little benefit other than high returns to the corrupt decision makers. Many of the countries with the highest levels of perceived corruption also report the highest levels of poverty in the world. These countries include Somalia, Chad, Iraq, Haiti, Afghanistan, and Myanmar. Transparency International also notes that some relatively poor countries, including Bulgaria, Colombia, and Estonia, have made positive strides in curbing corruption. However, Canada and Iceland have started to experience higher levels of perceived corruption, yet maintain relatively strong economies. The organization encourages governments, consumers, and nonprofit groups to take action in the fight against corruption.[22] Although business and society may be theoretically distinct, there are a host of practical implications for the four levels of social responsibility, business, and its effects on society.

At Stage 2, companies are required to maintain compliance with legal and regulatory requirements specifying the nature of responsible business conduct. Society enforces its expectations regarding the behavior of businesses through the legal system. If a business chooses to behave in a way that customers, special-interest groups, or other businesses perceive as irresponsible, these groups may ask their elected representatives to draft legislation to regulate the firm's behavior, or they may sue the firm in a court of law in an effort to force it to "play by the rules." For example, the New York attorney general's office is questioning the legality of making new hires sign noncompete agreements. A noncompete agreement stipulates that the employee cannot work for a competitor for a certain amount of time after leaving the organization. New York authorities believes this placed undue hardships on employees. Jimmy John's settled with the attorney general's office by agreeing to no longer make employees sign these agreements. It is estimated that 15 percent of workers without college degrees are subject to these noncompete agreements. Criticisms have emerged from other states as well.[23]

Beyond financial viability and legal compliance, companies must decide what they consider to be just, fair, and right—the realm of ethics, principles, and values. Business ethics refers to the principles and standards that guide behavior in the world of business. Principles are specific and universal boundaries for behavior that should never be violated. Principles such as fairness and honesty are determined and expected by the public, government regulators, special-interest groups, consumers, industry, and individual organizations. The most basic of these principles have been codified into laws and regulations to require that companies conduct themselves in ways that conform to society's expectations. Ethical issues exist in most managerial decisions. A firm needs to create an ethical culture with values and norms that meet the expectations of stakeholders. Values are enduring beliefs and ideals that are socially enforced. Freedom of speech, for example, is a strong value in the Western world. At the Marriott, values include putting people first, pursuing excellence, embracing change, acting with integrity, and serving our world.[24]

Many firms and industries have chosen to go beyond these basic laws in an effort to act responsibly. The Direct Selling Association (DSA), for example, has established a code of ethics that applies to all individual and company members of the association. Because direct selling involves personal contact with consumers, there are many ethical issues that can arise. For this reason, the DSA code directs the association's members to go beyond legal standards of conduct in areas such as product representation, appropriate ways of contacting consumers, and warranties and guarantees. In addition, the DSA actively works with government agencies and consumer groups to ensure that ethical standards are pervasive in the direct selling industry. The World Federation of Direct Selling Associations (WFDSA) also maintains two codes of conduct, one for dealing with consumers and the other for interactions within the industry, that provide guidance for direct sellers around the world in countries as diverse as Argentina, Canada, Finland, Taiwan, and Poland.[25]

At Stage 4 are philanthropic activities, which promote human welfare and goodwill. By making philanthropic donations of money, time, and other resources, companies can contribute to their communities and society and improve the quality of life. For example, the UPS Foundation has been active in the global community since 1951. The foundation offers programs in philanthropy and humanitarian relief. Donations total approximately $100 million worldwide. In addition to the monetary contributions, 1.9 million annual volunteer hours have also been given. The foundation focuses its efforts on education, disaster preparedness and resiliency, urgent response to unexpected disasters, post-disaster recovery, in-kind disaster relief, skill-based volunteering, partnerships with humanitarian organizations, and thought leadership.[26]

When these dimensions of social responsibility were first introduced, many people assumed that there was a natural progression from financial viability to philanthropic activities, meaning that a firm had to be financially

FIGURE 1.2 Social Responsibility Continuum

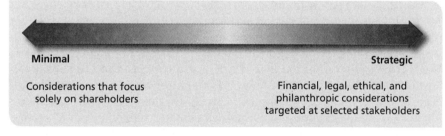

Minimal

Considerations that focus
solely on shareholders

Strategic

Financial, legal, ethical, and
philanthropic considerations
targeted at selected stakeholders

viable before it could properly consider the other three elements. Today, social responsibility is viewed in a more holistic fashion, with all four dimensions seen as related and integrated, and this is the view we will use in this book.[27] In fact, companies demonstrate varying degrees of social responsibility at different points in time. Figure 1.2 depicts the social responsibility continuum. Companies' fulfillment of their responsibilities can range from a minimal to a strategic focus that results in a stakeholder orientation. Firms that focus only on shareholders and the bottom line operate from a legal or compliance perspective. Firms that take minimal responsibility view such activities as a "cost of doing business." Some critics believe that pharmaceutical manufacturers take the minimal approach with respect to the advertising and sale of certain drugs. A court case involving pharmaceutical company GlaxoSmithKline revealed a string of pharmaceutical companies engaging in aggressive and deceptive marketing to encourage doctors to prescribe psychotropic drugs to children. It was found that over the course of 20 years, many companies—including Pfizer, Johnson & Johnson, and Eli Lilly—targeted academic leaders, wrote articles, suppressed data, and seduced doctors with gifts to sell these drugs for pediatric use. Further, the children who were prescribed these drugs were mainly foster children from low-income backgrounds.[28]

Strategic responsibility is realized when a company has integrated a range of expectations, desires, and constituencies into its strategic direction and planning processes. In this case, an organization considers social responsibility an essential component of its vision, mission, values, and practices. BT, formerly known as British Telecom, is communicating its commitment to strategic responsibility with the theme of "Responsible Business," where BT is focused on tackling climate change, helping create a more inclusive society, and enabling sustainable economic growth. BT has been reporting on its social responsibility activities for nearly 20 years, which makes the company a leader in accountability disclosure. Finally, firms may be forced to be more socially responsible by government, nongovernmental organizations, consumer groups, and other stakeholders. In this case, any expenditures are considered a "tax" that occurs outside the firm's strategic direction and resource allocation process.[29] Executives with this philosophy often maintain that customers will be lost, employees will become dissatisfied, and other detrimental effects will occur because of forced social responsibility.[30]

In this book, we will give many examples of firms that are at different places along this continuum to show how the pursuit of social responsibility is never ending. For example, ConocoPhillips was nominated to the 100 Best Corporate Citizens list in 2015. It was also named to the Dow Jones Sustainability North America Index for a number of years. ConocoPhillips even has a sustainable development group that considers the company's impact on environmental issues such as climate change and biodiversity. However, in 2016 it was dropped from the 100 Best Corporate Citizens list. In 2015 it settled a lawsuit in California accusing the firm of violating the state's anti-pollution laws since 2006. It also spent money to resolve spill-related claims in China.[31]

Social Responsibility Requires a Stakeholder Orientation

stakeholders
Constituents who have an interest or stake in a company's products, industry, markets, and outcomes.

The final element of our definition involves those to whom an organization is responsible, including customers, employees, investors and shareholders, suppliers, governments, communities, and many others. These constituents have a stake in, or claim on, some aspect of a company's products, industry, markets, and outcomes and are thus known as **stakeholders**. We explore the roles and expectations of stakeholders in Chapter 2. Companies that consider the diverse perspectives of these constituents in their daily operations and strategic planning are said to have a stakeholder orientation, meaning that they are focused on stakeholders' concerns. Adopting this orientation is part of the social responsibility philosophy, which implies that business is fundamentally connected to other parts of society and must take responsibility for its effects in those areas.

R. E. Freeman, a developer of stakeholder theory, maintains that business and society are "interpenetrating systems," in that each affects and is affected by the other.[32] For the common good to be achieved, cross-institutional and -organizational interactions must move society toward shared partnerships. For example, Kingfisher, the operator of more than 1,150 home improvement retail stores in nine countries, embarked on a new corporate responsibility initiative called "Kingfisher Net Positive." The four components to this plan included timber, energy, innovation, and communities. The company has nearly reached its goal of sourcing 100 percent of timber from responsible sources, with 96 percent responsibly sourced. Kingfisher has expanded energy-efficient product lines in its stores to help customers reduce energy consumption. In terms of innovation, the company is focusing on designing products with closed loop systems and determining ways of producing materials from in-store recycling. Finally, the company impacts its communities through education, volunteering, and partnering with other organizations.[33]

DEVELOPMENT OF SOCIAL RESPONSIBILITY

In 1959, Harvard economist Edward Mason asserted that business corporations are "the most important economic institutions."[34] His declaration implied that companies probably affect the community and society as much, or perhaps more, in social terms as in monetary, or financial, terms. Employment and the benefits associated with a living wage are necessary to develop a sustainable economy. The opportunity for individuals and businesses to attain economic success is necessary to create a society that can address social issues. Today some question our economic system, but without economic resources little progress can be made in developing society.

Although some firms have more of a social impact than others, companies do influence many aspects of our lives, from the workplace to the natural environment. This influence has led many people to conclude that companies' actions should be designed to benefit employees, customers, business partners, and the community as well as shareholders. Social responsibility has become a benchmark for companies today.[35] However, these expectations have changed over time. For example, the first corporations in the United States were granted charters by various state governments because they were needed to serve an important function in society, such as transportation, insurance, water, or banking services. In addition to serving as a "license to operate," these charters specified the internal structure of these firms, allowing their actions to be more closely monitored.[36] During this period, corporate charters were often granted for a limited period of time because many people, including legislators, feared the power that corporations could potentially wield. It was not until the mid 1800s and early 1900s that profit and responsibility to stockholders became major corporate goals.[37]

After World War II, as many large U.S. firms came to dominate the global economy, their actions inspired imitation in other nations. The definitive external characteristic of these firms was their economic dominance. Internally, they were marked by the virtually unlimited autonomy afforded to their top managers. This total discretion meant that these firms' top managers had the luxury of not having to answer for some of their actions.[38] In the current business mindset, such total autonomy would be viewed as a hindrance to social responsibility because there is no effective system of checks and balances. In Chapter 3, we elaborate on corporate governance, the process of control and accountability in organizations that is necessary for social responsibility.

In the 1950s, the 130 or so largest companies in the United States provided more than half of the country's manufacturing output. The top 500 firms accounted for almost two-thirds of the country's nonagricultural economic activity.[39] U.S. productivity and technological advancements dramatically outpaced those of global competitors, such as Japan and Western Europe. For example, the level of production in the United States was twice as high as that in Europe and quadruple that in Japan. The level of research and development carried out by U.S. corporations was also well ahead of overseas firms. For these reasons, the United States was perceived as setting a global standard for other nations to emulate.

During the 1950s and 1960s, these companies provided benefits that are often overlooked. Their contributions to charities, the arts, culture, and other community activities were beneficial to the industry or to society rather than simply to the companies' own profitability. For example, the lack of competition meant that companies had the profits to invest in higher quality products for consumer and industrial use. Although the government passed laws that required companies to take actions to protect the natural environment, make products safer, and promote equity and diversity in the workplace, many companies voluntarily adopted responsible practices rather than constantly fighting government regulations and taxes. These corporations once provided many of the services that are now provided by the government in the United States. For example, during this period, the U.S. government spent less than the government of any other industrialized nation on such things as pensions and health benefits, as these were provided by companies rather than by the government.[40] In the 1960s and 1970s, however, the business landscape changed.

Economic turmoil during the 1970s and 1980s changed the role of corporations. Venerable firms that had dominated the economy in the 1950s and 1960s became less important as a result of bankruptcies, takeovers, mergers, or other threats, including high energy prices and an influx of foreign competitors. The stability experienced by the U.S. firms of midcentury dissolved. During the 1960s and 1970s, the Fortune 500 had a relatively low turnover of about 4 percent. By 1990, however, one-third of the companies in the Fortune 500 of 1980 had disappeared, primarily as a result of takeovers and bankruptcies. The threats and instability led companies to protect themselves from business cycles by becoming more focused on their core competencies and reducing their product diversity. To combat takeovers, many companies adopted flatter organizational hierarchies. Flatter organizations meant workforce reduction but also entailed increasing empowerment of lower-level employees.

Thus, the 1980s and 1990s brought a new focus on profitability and economies of scale. Efficiency and productivity became the primary objectives of business. This fostered a wave of downsizing and restructuring that left some people and communities without financial security. Before 1970, large corporations employed about one of every five Americans, but by the 1990s, they employed only one in ten. The familial relationship between employee and employer disappeared, and along with it went employee loyalty and company promises of lifetime employment. Companies slashed their payrolls to reduce costs, and employees changed jobs more often. Workforce reductions and "job hopping" were almost unheard of in the 1960s but had become commonplace two decades later. These trends made temporary employment and contract work the fastest growing forms of employment throughout the 1990s.[41]

Along with these changes, top managers were largely stripped of their former freedom. Competition heated up, and both consumers and stockholders grew more demanding. The increased competition led business managers to worry more and more about the bottom line and about protecting the company. Escalating use of the internet provided unprecedented access to information about corporate decisions and conduct, and fostered communication among once unconnected groups, furthering consumer awareness and shareholder activism. Consumer demands put more pressure on companies and their employees. The education and activism of stockholders had top management fearing for their jobs. Throughout the last two decades of the twentieth century, legislators and regulators initiated more and more regulatory requirements every year. These factors resulted in difficult trade-offs for management.

Corporate responsibilities were renewed in the 1990s. Partly as a result of business scandals and Wall Street excesses in the 1980s, many industries and companies decided to pursue and expect more responsible and respectable business practices. Many of these practices focused on creating value for stakeholders through more effective processes and decreased the narrow and sole emphasis on corporate profitability. At the same time, consumers and employees became less interested in making money for its own sake and turned toward intrinsic rewards and a more holistic approach to life and work.[42] This resulted in increased interest in the development of human and intellectual capital; the installation of corporate ethics programs; the development of programs to promote employee volunteerism in the community; strategic philanthropy efforts and trust in the workplace; and the initiation of a more open dialog between companies and their stakeholders.

Despite major advances in the 1990s, the sheer number of corporate scandals at the beginning of the twenty-first century prompted a new era of social responsibility. The downfall of Enron, WorldCom, and other corporate stalwarts caused regulators, former employees, investors, nongovernmental organizations, and ordinary citizens to question the role and integrity of big business and the underlying economic system. Federal legislators passed the Sarbanes–Oxley Act to overhaul securities laws and governance structures. The new Public Company Accounting Oversight Board was implemented to regulate the accounting and auditing profession after Enron and WorldCom failed due to accounting scandals. Newspapers, business magazines, and news websites devoted entire sections—often labeled Corporate Scandal, Year of the Apology, or Year of the Scandal— to the trials and tribulations of executives, their companies and auditors, and stock analysts.

In 2007 and 2008, a housing boom in the United States collapsed, setting off a financial crisis. Homeowners could not afford to pay their mortgages. Because of the housing boom, in many cases the mortgages were higher than the houses were worth. People all across the United States began to walk away from their mortgages, leaving banks and other lenders with hundreds of thousands of houses that had decreased in value.

Meanwhile, companies such as AIG were using complex financial instruments known as derivatives to transfer the risks of securities such as mortgages, almost as a type of insurance policy. The housing collapse created a number of demands on financial firms who had sold these derivatives to pay their insurance contracts on the defaulted debt securities, but financial firms did not have enough of a safety net to cover so many defaults. The housing collapse created a chain reaction that led to the worst recession since the Great Depression. The government was forced to step in to bail out financial firms in order to keep the economy going and prevent the economy from collapsing further. Many established organizations such as Bear Stearns, Lehman Brothers, and Countrywide went bankrupt or were acquired by other firms at a fraction of what they were originally worth. Table 1.3 describes some of the corporations and banks that collapsed in the financial crisis.

In 2010, Congress passed the Dodd–Frank Wall Street Reform and Consumer Protection Act, the most sweeping legislation since Sarbanes–Oxley. Dodd–Frank is intended to protect the economy from similar financial crises in the future by creating more transparency in the financial industry. This complex law required legislators to develop hundreds of laws to increase transparency and create financial stability. The Dodd–Frank Act will be discussed in more detail in Chapter 4. The financial crisis and the collapse of many well-known institutions has led to a renewed interest in business ethics and social responsibility.

In the last five years, the economy has stabilized and the stock market has recovered. Even though many banks failed during the financial crisis,

TABLE 1.3 Corporations and Banks Involved in the Financial Crisis

Organization	Outcome
General Motors	Declared bankruptcy and required a government bailout of $49.5 billion to reorganize. The government sold their last shares in GM in 2013 and is estimated to have lost more than $10 billion on its investment.
AIG	Received a government bailout of $182 million and was criticized for using bailout money to pay executives large bonuses. AIG repaid the last of its loans in 2013.
Bank of America	Received $42 billion in bailout money as part of the Troubled Asset Relief Program. It paid back its loans in 2009.
Washington Mutual	Its banking subsidiaries were sold by the Federal Deposit Insurance Corporation to J.P. Morgan for $1.9 billion.
Chrysler	Declared bankruptcy and required a government bailout of $12.5 billion. By 2011 Chrysler had repaid most of the debt, and Fiat agreed to purchase the rest of the U.S. Treasury's shares in Chrysler for $500 million.
Countrywide Financial	Acquired by Bank of America for $4.1 billion. Bank of America inherited many of the lawsuits against Countrywide claiming it had engaged in fraudulent and discriminatory lending practices.

today banks and the other financial institutions are much larger. The largest five banks are twice as large as they were a decade ago.[43] Rather than getting rid of too-big-to-fail financial institutions, they seem to be growing much larger despite recent legislation.

GLOBAL NATURE OF SOCIAL RESPONSIBILITY

Although many forces have shaped the debate on social responsibility, the increasing globalization of business has made it an international concern. A common theme is criticism of the increasing power and scope of business and income differences among executives and employees. Questions of corruption, environmental protection, fair wages, safe working conditions, and the income gap between rich and poor were posed. Many critics and protesters believe that global business involves exploitation of the working poor, destruction of the planet, and a rise in inequality.[44] After the financial crisis, global trust in business dropped significantly. More recent polls indicate that trust is rebounding in certain countries, but companies are still vulnerable to the ramifications of distrust. Approximately 50 percent of the general public among global consumers indicate they trust business. This is even lower in the United States, where only 49 percent trust business overall.[45] In an environment where consumers distrust business, greater regulation and lower brand loyalty are the likely results. We discuss more of the relationship between social responsibility and business outcomes later in this chapter.

The globalization of business has critics who believe the movement is detrimental because it destroys the unique cultural elements of individual countries, concentrates power within developed nations and their corporations, abuses natural resources, and takes advantage of people in developing countries. Multinational corporations are perhaps most subject to criticism because of their size and scope. Table 1.4 shows 25 multinational companies that are more powerful than many of the countries in which they do business. For instance, Apple's cash exceeds the gross domestic product of two-thirds of the world's countries. Because of the economic and political power they potentially wield, the actions of large, multinational companies are under scrutiny by many stakeholders. Most allegations by antiglobalization protestors are not extreme, but the issues are still of consequence. For example, the pharmaceutical industry has long been criticized for excessively high pricing, interference with clinical evaluations, some disregard for developing nations, and aggressive promotional practices. Critics have called on governments, as well as public health organizations, to influence the industry in changing some of its practices.[46]

Advocates of the global economy counter these allegations by pointing to increases in overall economic growth, new jobs, new and more effective products, and other positive effects of global business. Although these differences of opinion provide fuel for debate and

TABLE 1.4 Top 25 Corporate Nations

Company	Type of Company	Annual Revenue (in billions)
Walmart	Retailer	$486
ExxonMobil	Oil and Gas	269
Royal Dutch Shell	Oil and Gas	265
Apple	Tech Company	234
Glencore	Commodity Trading and Mining Company	221
Samsung	Tech Company	163
Amazon	E-Commerce Company	107
Microsoft	Tech Company	94
Nestle	Food and Beverage Producer	93
Alphabet	Tech Conglomerate	75
Uber	Ride-Hailing Service	62.5
Huawei Technologies	Telecommunications Company	60
Vodafone	Telecommunications Provider	60
Anheuser-Busch InBev	Beverage Company	47
Maersk	Shipping Company	40
Goldman Sachs	Investment Banking Firm	34
Halliburton	Multinational Conglomerate	33
Accenture	Consulting Firm	31
McDonald's	Fast-Food Restaurant	25
Emirates	Airline	24
Facebook	Social Media Company	18
Alibaba	E-Commerce Company	12
BlackRock	Investment Manager	11
McKinsey & Company	Consulting Firm	8
Twitter	Social Media Company	2.2

Sources: David Francis, "The Top 25 Corporate Nations," *Foreign Policy*, March 15, 2016, http://foreignpolicy.com/2016/03/15/these-25-companies-are-more-powerful-than-many-countries-multinational-corporate-wealth-power/ (accessed June 17, 2016).

discussion, the global economy probably "holds much greater potential than its critics think, and much more disruption than its advocates admit. By definition, a global economy is as big as it can get. This means that the scale of both the opportunity and the consequences are at an apex."[47] In responding to this powerful situation, companies around the world are increasingly implementing programs and practices that strive to achieve a balance between economic responsibilities and other social responsibilities. The Nestlé Company, a global foods manufacturer and marketer, published the Nestlé Corporate Business Principles in 1998 and has continually revised them (2002, 2004, and 2010). These principles serve as a management tool for decision making at Nestlé and have been translated into over 50 languages. The updated principles are consistent with the United Nations' Global Compact, an accord that covers environmental standards, human rights, and labor conditions.[48] We explore the global context of social responsibility more fully in Chapter 12.

In most developed countries, social responsibility involves stakeholder accountability and the financial, legal, ethical, and philanthropic dimensions discussed earlier in the chapter. However, a key question for implementing social responsibility on a global scale is: "Who decides on these responsibilities?" Many executives and managers face the challenge of doing business in diverse countries while attempting to maintain their employers' corporate culture and satisfy their expectations. Some companies have adopted an approach in which broad corporate standards can be adapted at a local level. For example, a corporate goal of demonstrating environmental leadership could be met in a number of different ways depending on local conditions and needs. The Coca-Cola Company releases sustainability and social responsibility reports for each region in which it conducts business. In Eurasia and Africa, the company highlights initiatives and progress achieved regarding women's empowerment, water conservation, and improvement of communities. In Greece, the company contributed toward reforestation and to active lifestyles for youth in the Netherlands. While some of the sustainability and social responsibility initiatives are similar among countries, Coca-Cola's focus on each individual region allows them to make the most relevant contributions to their stakeholders.[49]

Global social responsibility also involves the confluence of government, business, trade associations, and other groups. For example, countries that belong to the Asia-Pacific Economic Cooperation (APEC) are responsible for half the world's annual production and trade volume. As APEC works to reduce trade barriers and tariffs, it has also developed meaningful projects in the areas of sustainable development, clean technologies, workplace safety, management of human resources, and the health of the marine environment. This powerful trade group has demonstrated that financial, social, and ethical concerns can be tackled simultaneously.[50] Like APEC, other trade groups are also exploring ways to enhance economic productivity within the context of legal, ethical, and philanthropic responsibilities.

Another trend involves business leaders becoming "cosmopolitan citizens" by simultaneously harnessing their leadership skills, worldwide business connections, access to funds, and beliefs about human and social rights. Bill Gates, the founder of Microsoft, is no longer active day-to-day in the company, as he and his wife spearhead the Bill and Melinda Gates Foundation to tackle AIDS, poverty, malaria, and the need for educational resources. Golfer Jack Nicklaus and his business partner Jack Milstein designed a line of golf balls whose proceeds are designated to children's health care.[51] SurveyMonky has a platform called SurveyMonkey Contribute that allows survey takers to earn rewards for taking surveys. Every week for each survey completed, SurveyMonkey will donate to a participating charity of the survey taker's choice.[52] Patagonia donates 1 percent of its profits to environmental organizations. These business leaders are acting as agents to ensure the economic promises of globalization are met with true concern for social and environmental considerations. In many cases, such efforts supplant those historically associated with government responsibility and programs.[53]

In sum, progressive global businesses and executives recognize the "shared bottom line" that results from the partnership among business, communities, government, customers, and the natural environment. In a Nielsen survey of more than 28,000 citizens in 56 countries, 76 percent of the respondents indicated that they consult others online regarding the social responsibility of companies before they make a purchase. The top three issues that are most important to consumers include environmental sustainability, advancements in STEM (science, technology, engineering, mathematics) education, and relieving hunger and poverty.[54] Thus, our concept of social responsibility is applicable to businesses around the world, although adaptations of implementation and other details on the local level are definitely required. In companies around the world, there is also the recognition of a relationship between strategic social responsibility and benefits to society and organizational performance.

BENEFITS OF SOCIAL RESPONSIBILITY

The importance of social responsibility initiatives in enhancing stakeholder relationships, improving performance, and creating other benefits has been debated from many different perspectives.[55] Many business managers view such programs as costly activities that provide rewards only to society at the expense of the bottom line. Another view holds that some costs of social responsibility can be recovered through improved performance. If social responsibility is strategic and aligned with a firm's mission and values, then improved performance can be achieved. It is hard to measure the reputation of a firm, but it is important to build trust and achieve success. Moreover, ample research evidence demonstrates that companies that implement strategic social responsibility programs are more profitable.

Some of the specific benefits include increased efficiency in daily operations, greater employee commitment, higher product quality, improved decision making, increased customer loyalty, as well as improved financial performance. In short, companies that establish a reputation for trust, fairness, and integrity develop a valuable resource that fosters success, which then translates to greater financial performance

FIGURE 1.3 The Role of Social Responsibility in Performance

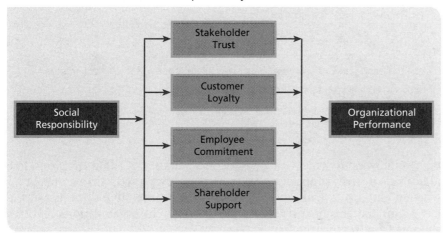

(see Figure 1.3). This section provides evidence that resources invested in social responsibility programs reap positive outcomes for both organizations and their stakeholders.

Trust

Trust is the glue that holds organizations together and allows them to focus on efficiency, productivity, and profits. According to Stephen R. Covey, author of *The 7 Habits of Highly Effective People,* "Trust lies at the very core of effective human interactions. Compelling trust is the highest form of human motivation. It brings out the very best in people, but it takes time and patience, and it doesn't preclude the necessity to train and develop people so their competency can rise to that level of trust." When trust is low, organizations decay and relationships deteriorate, resulting in infighting, playing politics within the organization, and general inefficiency. Employee commitment to the organization declines, product quality suffers, employee turnover skyrockets, and customers turn to more trustworthy competitors.[56] Any stakeholder that loses trust can create a missing link necessary for success.

In a trusting work environment, however, employees can reasonably expect to be treated with respect and consideration by both their peers and their superiors. They are also more willing to rely and act on the decisions and actions of their coworkers. Thus, trusting relationships between managers and their subordinates and between peers contribute to greater decision-making efficiencies. Research by the Ethics Resource Center indicates that this trust is pivotal for supporting an ethical climate. Employees of an organization with a strong ethical culture are much more likely to report misconduct but are much less likely to observe misconduct

TABLE 1.5 Indicators of Support, Trust, and Transparency

Supervisor gives positive feedback for ethical behavior
Satisfied with information from senior leadership about what is going on in company
Supervisor supports following company's ethics standards
Believe that senior leadership is transparent about critical issues that impact our company
Trust coworkers will keep their promises and commitments

Source: Ethics Resource Center, *National Business Ethics Survey of the U.S. Workforce* (Arlington, Virginia: Ethics Resource Center, 2014), p. 33.

than employees in firms with a weak ethical culture.[57] Table 1.5 shows five indicators of trust, support, and transparency that have a strong impact on whether employees will report ethical issues. As the table demonstrates, a key factor that inspires trust and transparency in organizations involves support from senior leadership.

Trust is also essential for a company to maintain positive long-term relationships with customers. A study by Cone Communications reported that 42 percent of consumers have boycotted or refused to purchase from companies that have demonstrated irresponsible behavior in the last 12 months.[58] For example, after the *Deepwater Horizon* oil spill in 2010, certain groups and individual citizens aggressively boycotted BP due to the vast environmental damage in the Gulf of Mexico. Communities and regulators that lose trust in a company can damage the firm's reputation and relationships with other stakeholders.

Customer Loyalty

The prevailing business philosophy about customer relationships is that a company should strive to market products that satisfy customers' needs through a coordinated effort that also allows the company to achieve its own objectives. It is well accepted that customer satisfaction is one of the most important factors for business success. Although companies must continue to develop and adapt products to keep pace with consumers' changing desires, it is also crucial to develop long-term relationships with customers. Relationships built on mutual respect and cooperation facilitate the repeat purchases that are essential for success. By focusing on customer satisfaction, a business can continually strengthen its customers' trust in the company, and as their confidence grows, this in turn increases the firm's understanding of their requirements.

In a Cone survey of consumer attitudes, 89 percent of consumers indicated they would be likely to switch to brands associated with a good cause if price and quality were equal. These results show that consumers take for granted that they can buy high-quality products at low prices; therefore, companies need to stand out as doing something—something that demonstrates their commitment to society.[59] A study by Harris

Interactive Inc. and the Reputation Institute reported that one-quarter of the respondents had boycotted a firm's products or lobbied others to do so when they did not agree with the firm's policies or activities.[60] Another way of looking at these results is that irresponsible behavior could trigger disloyalty and refusals to buy, whereas good social responsibility initiatives could draw customers to a company's products. For example, many firms use cause-related marketing programs to donate part of a product's sales revenue to a charity that is meaningful to the product's target market. Among the best known cause-related marketing programs is Avon's "pink ribbon."

Employee Commitment

Employee commitment stems from employees who are empowered with training and autonomy. Sir Richard Branson, founder of the Virgin Group, has one of the most committed groups of employees in business for these reasons, as well as many others. He has created a culture wherein he personally asks employees for their input, writes their ideas down, and incorporates them when relevant. He is a very visible and approachable authority and inspires a "passion of commitment" for customer service. Virgin Airlines is ranked as the highest in quality for domestic airlines. In the end, empowered employees keep customers happy and coming back for more.[61] For instance, service quality is positively related to employee loyalty. This, in turn, leads to higher customer satisfaction and customer loyalty.[62] Evidence also suggests that corporate social responsibility initiatives are a good way to retain and attract employees.[63]

When companies fail to provide value for their employees, loyalty and commitment suffer. A survey by Gallup found low levels of employee loyalty and commitment worldwide. The study, which surveyed thousands of employees in 142 countries, found that only 13 percent of workers indicated feeling engaged in their jobs.[64] Employees spend many of their waking hours at work; thus, an organization's commitment to goodwill and respect of its employees usually results in increased employee loyalty and support of the company's objectives.

Shareholder Support

Investors look at a corporation's bottom line for profits or the potential for increased stock prices. To be successful, relationships with stockholders and other investors must rest on dependability, trust, and commitment. But investors also look for potential cracks or flaws in a company's performance. Companies perceived by their employees as having a high degree of honesty and integrity had an average three-year total return to shareholders of 101 percent, whereas companies perceived as having a low degree of honesty and integrity had a three-year total return to shareholders of just 69 percent.[65] After hackers broke into Target's databases and stole customers' credit card numbers and other information, stock fell 46 percent.[66] Target has been criticized for its lack of sufficient internal controls.

Many shareholders are also concerned about the reputation of companies in which they invest. Investors have even been known to avoid buying the stock of firms they view as irresponsible. For example, Warren Buffet sold 25 percent of his holdings in General Motors after a series of recalls was initiated following a federal investigation. The investigation concluded that the company was at fault in several injuries and deaths resulting from negligence of a faulty ignition switch.[67] Many socially responsible mutual funds and asset management firms are available to help concerned investors purchase stock in responsible companies. These investors recognize that corporate responsibility is the foundation for efficiency, productivity, and profits. In contrast, investors know that fines or negative publicity can decrease a company's stock price, customer loyalty, and long-term viability. Consequently, many chief executives spend a great deal of time communicating with investors about their firms' reputations and financial performance and trying to attract them to their stock.

The issue of drawing and retaining investors is a critical one for CEOs, as roughly 50 percent of investors sell their stock in companies within one year, and the average household replaces 80 percent of its common stock portfolio each year.[68] This focus on short-term gains subjects corporate managers to tremendous pressure to boost short-term earnings, often at the expense of long-term strategic plans. The resulting pressure for short-term gains deprives corporations of stable capital and forces decision makers into a "quarterly" mentality.

Conversely, those shareholders willing to hold onto their investments are more willing to sacrifice short-term gains for long-term income. Attracting these long-term investors shields companies from the vagaries of the stock market and gives them flexibility and stability in long-term strategic planning. In the aftermath of the Enron scandal, however, trust and confidence in financial audits and published financial statements were severely shaken. Membership in grassroots investment clubs declined, retail stock investments declined, and investors called for increased transparency in company operations and reports.[69] Gaining investors' trust and confidence is vital for sustaining a firm's financial stability.

The Bottom Line: Profits

Social responsibility is positively associated with return on investment, return on assets, and sales growth.[70] A company cannot continuously be socially responsible and nurture and develop an ethical organizational culture unless it has achieved financial performance in terms of profits.

Businesses with greater resources—regardless of their staff size—have the ability to promote their social responsibility along with serving their customers, valuing their employees, and establishing trust with the public. As mentioned before, the stock returns of the world's most ethical companies are often higher than that of companies listed on the S&P 500.

Many studies have identified a positive relationship between social responsibility and financial performance.[71] For example, a survey of the 500 largest public corporations in the United States found that those that commit to responsible behavior and emphasize compliance with codes of conduct show better financial performance.[72] A managerial focus on stakeholder interests can affect financial performance, although the relationships between stakeholders and financial performance vary and are very complex.[73] A meta analysis of 25 years of research identified 33 studies (63 percent) demonstrating a positive relationship between corporate social performance and corporate financial performance, 5 studies (about 10 percent) indicating a negative relationship, and 14 studies (27 percent) yielding an inconclusive result or no relationship.[74] Research on the effects of legal infractions suggests that the negative effect of misconduct does not appear until the third year following a conviction, with multiple convictions being more harmful than a single one.[75]

In summary, a company with strong efforts and results in social responsibility is generally not penalized by market forces, including the intention of consumers to purchase the firm's products. Social responsibility efforts and performance serve as a reputational lever that managers may use to influence stakeholders. A high-performing company may also receive endorsements from governmental officials or other influential groups, and these are more believable than company messages. A company with a strong social responsibility orientation often becomes quite proactive in managing and changing conditions that yield economic benefits, including avoiding litigation and increased regulation. Finally, corporate social performance and corporate financial performance are positively correlated. These findings subjugate the belief that social responsibility is just a "cost factor" for business and has no real benefits to the firm.[76]

National Economy

An often asked question is whether business conduct has any bearing on a nation's overall economic performance. Many economists have wondered why some market-based economies are productive and provide a high standard of living for their citizens, whereas other market-based economies lack the kinds of social institutions that foster productivity and economic growth. Perhaps a society's economic problems can be explained by a lack of social responsibility. Trust stems from principles of morality and serves as an important "lubricant of the social system."[77] Many descriptions of market economies fail to take into account the role of such institutions as family, education, and social systems in explaining standards of living and economic success. Perhaps some countries do a better job of developing economically and socially because of the social structure of their economic relationships.

Social institutions, particularly those that promote trust, are important for the economic wellbeing of a society.[78] Society has become economically successful over time "because of the underlying institutional framework persistently reinforcing incentives for organizations to engage in productive activity."[79] In some developing countries, opportunities for political and economic development have been stifled by activities that promote monopolies, graft, and corruption and by restrictions on opportunities to advance individual, as well as collective, wellbeing. L. E. Harrison offers four fundamental factors that promote economic wellbeing: "(1) The degree of identification with others in a society— the radius of trust, or the sense of community; (2) the rigor of the ethical system; (3) the way authority is exercised within the society; and (4) attitudes about work, innovation, saving, and profit."[80]

Countries with institutions based on strong trust foster a productivity-enhancing environment because they have ethical systems in place that reduce transaction costs and make competitive processes more efficient and effective. In market-based systems with a great degree of trust, such as Germany, Sweden, Switzerland, Canada, and the United Kingdom, highly successful enterprises can develop through a spirit of cooperation and the ease in conducting business.[81]

Superior financial performance at the firm level within a society is measured as profits, earnings per share, return on investment, and capital appreciation. Businesses must achieve a certain level of financial performance to survive and reinvest in the various institutions in society that provide support. But, at the institutional or societal level, a key factor distinguishing societies with high standards of living from those with lower standards of living is whether the institutions within the society are generally trustworthy. The challenge is to articulate the process by which institutions that support social responsibility can contribute to firm-level superior financial performance.[82]

A comparison of countries that have high levels of corruption and underdeveloped social institutions with countries that have low levels of corruption reveals differences in the economic wellbeing of the country's citizens. Transparency International, an organization discussed earlier, publishes an annual report on global corruption that emphasizes the effects of corruption on the business and social sectors. Table 1.6 lists the countries with the most and least corrupt public sectors, as perceived by Transparency International. Eighteen countries are perceived to be more ethical than the United States.[83] As stated several times in this chapter, conducting business in an ethical and responsible manner generates trust and leads to relationships that promote higher productivity and a positive cycle of effects.[84]

TABLE 1.6 Perceptions of Countries as Least/Most Corrupt

Country Rank	CPI Score*	Least Corrupt	Country Rank	CPI Score*	Most Corrupt
1	91	Denmark	167	8	Somalia
2	90	Finland	167	8	North Korea
3	89	Sweden	166	11	Afghanistan
4	88	New Zealand	165	12	Sudan
5	87	Netherlands	163	15	South Sudan
5	87	Norway	163	15	Angola
7	86	Switzerland	161	16	Libya
8	85	Singapore	161	16	Iraq
9	83	Canada	158	17	Venezuela
10	81	Germany	158	17	Guinea-Bissau
10	81	Luxembourg	158	17	Haiti
10	81	United Kingdom	154	18	Yemen
13	79	Australia	154	18	Turkmenistan
13	79	Iceland	154	18	Syria
15	77	Belgium	154	18	Eritrea

* CPI score relates to perceptions of the degree of public sector corruption as seen by businesspeople and country analysts and ranges between 10 (highly clear) and 0 (highly corrupt). The United States is perceived as the 16th least-corrupt nation.

Source: © Transparency International, *Corruption Perceptions Index 2015* (Berlin, Germany, 2016). All rights reserved.

FRAMEWORK FOR STUDYING SOCIAL RESPONSIBILITY

The framework we have developed for this text is designed to help you understand how businesses fulfill social expectations. It begins with the social responsibility philosophy, includes the four levels of social responsibilities, involves many types of stakeholders, and ultimately results in both short and long-term performance benefits. As we discussed earlier, social responsibility must have the support of top management—both in words and in deeds—before it can become an organizational reality. Like many organizations, Cummins Engine Company has faced a number of challenges over the past several decades. Cummins is currently the world leader in the design and manufacture of diesel engines and was the largest employer in Columbus, Indiana, for many years. Cummins's drive to build positive relationships with employees, customers, and community led *Business Ethics* to rank the firm on the magazine's list of the "100 Best Corporate Citizens." The company received the highest possible rating for its corporate governance practices from Governance Metrics International (GMI), even during the global recession of 2009. In addition, *Ethisphere* named the company as one of the "World's Most Ethical Companies" for seven years in a row.[85]

Once the social responsibility philosophy is accepted, the four aspects of corporate social responsibility are defined and implemented through programs that incorporate stakeholder input and feedback. Cummins, like other companies, is aware of the potential costs associated with addressing social responsibility issues and stakeholder requirements. When social responsibility programs are put into action, they have both immediate and delayed outcomes.

Figure 1.4 depicts how the chapters of this book fit into our framework. This framework begins with a look at the importance of working with stakeholders to achieve social responsibility objectives. The framework also includes an examination of the influence on business decisions and actions of the legal, regulatory, and political environment; business ethics; and corporate governance. The remaining chapters of the book explore the responsibilities associated with specific stakeholders and issues that confront

FIGURE 1.4 An Overview of This Book

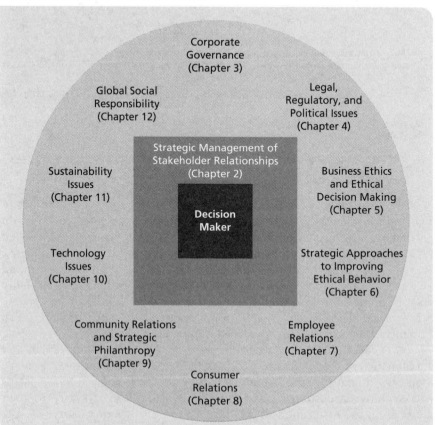

business decision makers today, including the process of implementing a social responsibility audit.

Strategic Management of Stakeholder Relationships

Social responsibility is grounded in effective and mutually beneficial relationships with customers, employees, investors, competitors, government, the community, and others who have a stake in the company. Increasingly, companies are recognizing that these constituents both affect and are affected by their actions. For this reason, many companies attempt to address the concerns of stakeholder groups, recognizing that failure to do so can have serious long-term consequences. For example, the Better Business Bureau of the Alaska, Oregon, and Western Washington region revoked the membership of 12 businesses in a period of three months for not meeting the organization's standards.[86] Chapter 2 examines the types of stakeholders and their attributes, how stakeholders become influential, and the processes for integrating and managing stakeholders' influence on a firm. It also examines the impact of corporate reputation and crisis situations on stakeholder relationships.

Corporate Governance

Because both daily and strategic decisions affect a variety of stakeholders, companies must maintain a governance structure to ensure proper control of their actions and assign responsibility for those actions. In Chapter 3, we define corporate governance and discuss its role in achieving strategic social responsibility. Key governance issues addressed include the rights of shareholders, the accountability of top management for corporate actions, executive compensation, and strategic-level processes for ensuring that financial, legal, ethical, and philanthropic responsibilities are satisfied.

Legal, Regulatory, and Political Issues

In Chapter 4, we explore the complex relationship between business and government. Every business must be aware of and abide by the laws and regulations that dictate acceptable business conduct. This chapter also examines how business can influence government by participating in the public policy process. A strategic approach for legal compliance is also provided.

Business Ethics and Strategic Approaches to Improving Ethical Behavior

Because individual values are a component of organizational conduct, these findings raise concerns about the ethics of future business leaders. Chapters 5 and 6 are devoted to exploring the role of ethics in business decision making. These chapters explore business responsibilities that go beyond the conduct that is legally prescribed. We examine the factors that influence ethical decision making and consider how companies can apply this understanding to increase their ethical conduct. We also examine ethical leadership and how it contributes to an ethical corporate culture.

Employee Relations

In today's business environment, most organizations want to build long-term relationships with a variety of stakeholders, but particularly with employees—the focus of Chapter 7. Employees today want fair treatment, excellent compensation and benefits, and assistance in balancing work and family obligations. This is increasingly important as employee privacy issues have become a major concern in recent years. Raytheon developed a computer program called SilentRunner that can detect patterns of data activity that may reflect employee fraud, insider trading, espionage, or other unauthorized activity.[87] Critics, however, question whether the use of such software contributes to an environment of trust and commitment. Research has shown that committed and satisfied employees are more productive, serve customers better, and are less likely to leave their employers. These benefits are important to successful business performance, but organizations must be proactive in their human resources programs if they are to receive them.

Consumer Relations

Chapter 8 explores companies' relationships with consumers. This constituency is part of a firm's primary stakeholder group, and there are a number of financial, legal, ethical, and philanthropic responsibilities that companies must address. Chapter 8 therefore considers the obligations that companies have toward their customers, including health and safety issues, honesty in marketing, consumer rights, and related responsibilities.

Community and Philanthropy

Chapter 9 examines community relations and strategic philanthropy, the synergistic use of organizational core competencies and resources to address key stakeholders' interests and to achieve both organizational and social benefits. Whereas traditional benevolent philanthropy involves donating a percentage of sales to social causes, a strategic approach aligns employees and organizational resources and expertise with the needs and concerns of stakeholders, especially the community. Strategic philanthropy involves both financial and nonfinancial contributions (employee time, goods and services, technology and equipment, and facilities) to stakeholders and reaps benefits for the community and company.

Technology Issues

In Chapter 10, we examine the issues that arise as a result of enhanced technology in the business environment, including the effects of new technology on privacy, intellectual property, and health. The strategic direction for technology depends on government as well as on business's ability to plan the implementation of new technology and to assess the influence of that technology on society.

Thanks to the internet and other technological advances, we can communicate faster than ever before, find information about just about anything, and live longer, healthier lives. However, not all of the changes that occur as a result of new technologies are positive. For example, because shopping via the internet does not require a signature to verify transactions, online credit card fraud is significantly greater than fraud through mail-order catalogs and traditional storefront retailers. A major identity theft ring in New York affected thousands of people. Members of the theft ring illegally obtained the credit records of consumers and then sold them to criminals for about $60 per record. The criminals used the credit records to obtain loans, drain bank accounts, and perform other fraudulent activities.[88]

Sustainability Issues

In Chapter 11, we dedicate an entire chapter to issues of sustainability, including the interdependent nature of economic development, social development, and environmental impact. Sustainability has become a watchword in business and community circles, and this chapter explores the ways in which companies define and develop goals, implement programs, and contribute to sustainability concerns. The Dow Jones Sustainability Index (DJSI) makes an annual assessment of companies' economic, environmental, and social performance, based on more than 50 general and industry specific criteria. The DJSI includes 2,500 companies from 20 countries and is used by investors who prefer to make financial investments in companies engaged in socially responsible and sustainable practices.[89]

Global Social Responsibility

Finally, in order for many businesses to remain competitive, they must continually evolve to reach global markets and anticipate emerging world trends. Chapter 12 delves into the complex and intriguing nature of social responsibility in a global economy. Building on key concepts discussed throughout the book, we examine the forces that make overseas business plans and activities of paramount concern to host countries, local and national governments, nongovernmental organizations, and other members of society. The chapter covers a wide range of challenges and opportunities, such as outsourcing, environmental protection, living wages, labor standards, and trade restrictions.

We hope this framework provides you with a way of understanding the range of concepts, ideas, and practices that are involved in an effective social responsibility initiative. So that you can learn more about the

Earth in the Balance: BUSINESS SUSTAINABILITY

Automakers Develop Lighter Cars to Meet Fuel-Efficient Standards

Today, many consumers are using sustainability criteria in their purchase decisions. This has had a major impact on the automotive industry. Automobile makers such as Ford are investigating new ways to increase the sustainability of their vehicles. Vehicles have started evolving into lighter versions of themselves as lighter materials increase fuel efficiency.

Although automobile makers have a market incentive to increase the fuel-efficiency of vehicles, they also have a legal incentive. In the United States it has been mandated that vehicles must reach 35.5 miles per gallon (mpg) by 2016. The government plans to extend this to 54.5 mpg by 2025. In Europe, cars must reduce emissions 40 percent 2007 levels by 2021. This is requiring automakers to be innovative in investigating ways to make their vehicles lighter. Materials for these lighter cars include aluminum, carbon fiber, and high-strength steel, which can decrease a vehicle's weight by 200 pounds. Automakers are optimistic that developing these lighter vehicles will cut fuel emissions in half.

Unfortunately, these criteria create a challenge for carmakers developing electric vehicles (EVs). Although EVs reduce greenhouse gas emissions, the batteries needed for the EV are often expensive and heavy. EV maker Tesla Motor is dealing with these issues by using less costly, lighter batteries. Its Giga Factory is estimated to produce 30 gigawatt hours worth of batteries each year—what is needed to power approximately 400,000 vehicles. BMW is spending nearly $3 billion to completely reinvent the car. It is producing a new brand of light hybrid luxury vehicle with a carbon-neutral supply chain. Its i3 EV utilizes light carbon-fiber thread and aluminum to make it incredibly lightweight for a car, at 2,680 pounds. This enables it to get 81 mpg.

Automakers are also increasing their use of sustainable materials in their vehicles' interiors. The i3, for instance, has an interior made from eucalyptus. Another EV firm called Fisker is using reclaimed wood for the interior of its sedans. These often lighter materials contribute to a more fuel-efficient vehicle. The Ford Fusion's use of kenaf leaves instead of oil-based resins in its doors reduces door bolsters by 25 percent.

All of these changes will entail challenges, not only for automakers but also for consumers. While consumers might desire more socially responsible and sustainable products, many do not like to sacrifice convenience or cost. It is estimated that repair costs for vehicles made of aluminum will increase due to the lightness of the materials. In countries such as Germany, consumers enjoy driving quickly on the roads, requiring vehicles that use a lot of gas. More fuel-efficient vehicles may be more limited in speed. Both businesses and consumers will have to make trade-offs in the quest for a more sustainable industry. However, these trade-offs have the potential to significantly reduce the negative impact of vehicle emissions on the environment.

Sources: Gary Witzenburg, "Future Fuel Economy Mandates, Part I: 54.5 mpg Is Going to Be Hard to Reach," *Green Auto Blog*, January 26, 2012, http://green.autoblog.com/2012/01/26/future-fuel-economy-mandates-part-i-54-5-mpg-is-going-to-be-ha/ (accessed June 5, 2014); Chris Woodyard, "If a Tree Falls in the Forest, Does It End Up in a Car?" *USA Today*, June 28, 2013, 3B; Bill Esler, "Real Wood Preferred in Eco Car Interiors," Wood Working Network, July 8, 2013, http://www.woodworkingnetwork.com/wood/component-sourcing/Reclaimed-Wood-Dresses-Car-Interiors-214604411.html#sthash.cuo9IOEi.dpbs (accessed July 26, 2013); Ford, "Ford Uses Kenaf Plant Inside Doors in the All-New Escape, Saving Weight and Energy," http://media.ford.com/article_display.cfm?article_id=35895 (accessed July 26, 2013); Chris Woodyard, "Lighter Cars Add Weight to Repair," *USA Today*, September 16, 2013, 1B; Brad Plumer, "Why Cars Will Keep Getting Lighter," *Washington Post,* January 12, 2012, http://www.washingtonpost.com/blogs/wonkblog/post/why-cars-will-keep-getting-lighter/2012/01/12/gIQARefVtP_blog.html (accessed October 15, 2013); Mark Rogowsky, "Musk: 'We Hope The Big Car Companies Do Copy Tesla,'" *Forbes*, February 5, 2014, http://www.forbes.com/sites/markrogowsky/2014/02/05/musk-we-hope-the-big-car-companies-do-copy-tesla/ (accessed June 5, 2014); Jennifer Collins, "For Germans, Need for Speed Clashes with Eco-Friendly Ideals," *USA Today*, May 26, 2014, http://www.usatoday.com/story/news/world/2014/05/24/german-autobahn-speed-limits-emissions/9387539/ (accessed June 5, 2014); Dan Neil, "BMW Plots Sustainable Supercar with the i8 Project," *The Wall Street Journal*, May 2, 2014, http://online.wsj.com/news/articles/SB10001424052702304677904579535612915387656 (accessed June 5, 2014).

practices of specific companies, a number of cases are provided at the end of the book. In addition, every chapter includes an opening vignette and other examples that shed more light on how social responsibility works in today's businesses. Every chapter also includes a real-life scenario entitled "What Would You Do?," a contemporary debate issue, and another exercise to help you apply concepts and examine your own decision-making process. As you will soon see, the concept of social responsibility is both exciting and controversial; it is in a constant state of development—just like all important business concepts and practices.

A recent survey of thought leaders in the area of social responsibility found that a majority believes social responsibility has made steady progress into conventional business thinking. Much like the social responsibility continuum introduced in this chapter, the thought leaders described several stages of commitment to corporate social responsibility. These stages range from light, where companies are concerned about responding to complaints, to deep, where companies are founded on a business model of improving social or environmental circumstances. Many companies fall somewhere in between, with a focus on complying with new standards and surviving in a climate of increasing social responsibility expectations.[90] We encourage you to draw on current news events and your own experiences to understand social responsibility and the challenges and opportunities it poses for your career, profession, role as a consumer, leadership approach, and the business world.

SUMMARY

The term *social responsibility* came into widespread use during the last several decades, but there remains some confusion over the term's exact meaning. This text defines social responsibility as the adoption by a business of a strategic focus for fulfilling the economic, legal, ethical, and philanthropic responsibilities expected of it by its stakeholders.

All types of businesses can implement social responsibility initiatives to further their relationships with their customers, their employees, and the community at large. Although the efforts of large corporations usually receive the most attention, the actions of small businesses may have a greater impact on local communities.

The definition of social responsibility involves the extent to which a firm embraces the social responsibility philosophy and follows through with the implementation of initiatives. Social responsibility must be fully valued and championed by top managers and given the same planning time, priority, and management attention as is given to any other company initiative.

Many people believe that businesses should accept and abide by four types of responsibilities: financial, legal, ethical, and philanthropic. Companies have a responsibility to be financially or economically viable so that they can provide a return on investment for their owners, create jobs for the community, and contribute goods and services to the economy. They are also expected to obey laws and regulations that specify what is responsible business conduct. Business ethics refers to the principles and standards that guide behavior in the world of business. Philanthropic activities promote human welfare or goodwill. These responsibilities can be viewed holistically, with all four related and integrated into a comprehensive approach. Social responsibility can also be expressed as a continuum.

Because customers, employees, investors and shareholders, suppliers, governments, communities, and others have a stake in or claim on some aspect of a company's products, operations, markets, industry, and outcomes, they are known as stakeholders. Adopting a stakeholder orientation is part of the social responsibility philosophy.

The influence of business has led many people to conclude that corporations should benefit their employees, their customers, their business partners, and their community as well as their shareholders. However, these responsibilities and expectations have changed over time. After World War II, many large U.S. firms dominated the global economy. Their power was largely mirrored by the autonomy of their top managers. Because of the relative lack of global competition and stockholder input during the 1950s and 1960s, there were few formal governance procedures to restrain management's actions. The stability experienced by midcentury firms dissolved in the economic turmoil of the 1970s and 1980s, leading companies to focus more on their core competencies and reduce their product diversity. The 1980s and 1990s brought a new focus on efficiency and productivity, which fostered a wave of downsizing and restructuring. Concern for corporate responsibilities was renewed in the 1990s. In the 1990s and beyond, the balance between the global market economy and an interest in social justice and cohesion best characterizes the intent and need for social responsibility. Despite major advances in the 1990s, the sheer number of corporate scandals at the beginning of the twenty-first century prompted a new era of social responsibility.

The increasing globalization of business has made social responsibility an international concern. In most developed countries, social responsibility involves economic, legal, ethical, and philanthropic responsibilities to a variety of stakeholders. Global social responsibility also involves responsibilities to a confluence of governments, businesses, trade associations, and other groups. Progressive global businesses recognize the "shared bottom line" that results from the partnership among businesses, communities, governments, and other stakeholders.

The importance of social responsibility initiatives in enhancing stakeholder relationships, improving performance, and creating other benefits has been debated from many different perspectives. Many business managers view such programs as costly activities that provide rewards only to society at the expense of the bottom line. Others hold that some costs of social responsibility can be recovered through improved performance. Although it is true that some aspects of social responsibility may not accrue directly to the bottom line, we believe that organizations benefit indirectly over the long run from these activities. Moreover, ample research and anecdotal evidence demonstrate that there are many rewards for companies that implement such programs.

The process of social responsibility begins with the social responsibility philosophy, includes the four responsibilities, involves many types of stakeholders, and ultimately results in both short and long-term performance benefits. Once the social responsibility philosophy is accepted, the four types of responsibility are defined and implemented through programs that incorporate stakeholder input and feedback.

Responsible Business Debate

How to Regulate Global Business

Issue: *Are less formal systems and agreements likely to be more successful than a formal legal and regulatory system?*

A key lesson learned from recent business scandals is that responsible, transparent, and ethical leadership is needed in order for companies to develop and maintain a long-term commitment to social responsibility for the benefit of multiple stakeholders. This is especially true of multinational corporations (MNCs) because of the power and influence these businesses and their executives represent. MNCs operate in multiple environments and contexts where laws, rules, expectations, and mores are divergent. In addition, the enforcement and monitoring mechanisms to oversee these expectations range from the barely existent to well-resourced government agencies.

The failure to have a global legal and regulatory scheme has resulted in environmental disasters, child labor, financial fraud, antitrust violations, tainted food products, and other problems. For example, in 2008 Mattel paid a $12 million settlement to 39 U.S. states for shipping Chinese-made toys containing unsafe amounts of lead. The country's largest toy maker also agreed to new standards for lead content in its toys. Apple Inc. was later criticized for workplace disasters and worker suicides at one of its Chinese suppliers, Foxconn. To save on manufacturing costs, many U.S. companies make products where wages are lower and regulatory standards often differ.

Despite the new coverage of corporate wrongdoing and questionable decision-making, there are many firms making the commitment to social responsibility through self-regulation. Over 12,000 participants in 145 countries are signatories to the United Nation's (UN) Global Compact, signaling their agreement to 10 principles on human rights, anticorruption, environment, and labor. The Global Reporting Initiative (GRI) provides a framework for companies developing social responsibility reports that discuss key standards, are comparable to peers, and capture performance over time. The new ISO 26000 standards assist in voluntary organizational self-analysis, media review, investor due diligence, and other reviews of social responsibility efforts.

There Are Two Sides to Every Issue

1. Defend the need for a legal and regulatory system that would oversee international and multination business operations. How would the system be developed? How would the system enact its responsibility for enforcing legal and regulatory standards?

2. Defend the efficacy of assurance systems and agreements, such as the UN Global Compact and ISO 26000 standards. Why are these less formal systems and agreements likely to be more successful than a formal legal and regulatory system?

KEY TERMS

social responsibility (p. 7)   stakeholders (p. 14)

DISCUSSION QUESTIONS

1. Define social responsibility. How does this view of the role of business differ from your previous perceptions? How is it consistent with your attitudes and beliefs about business?

2. If a company is named to one of the "best in social responsibility" lists, what positive effects can it potentially reap? What are the possible costs or negative outcomes that may be associated with being named to one of these lists?

3. What historical trends have affected the social responsibilities of business? How have recent scandals affected the business climate, including any changes in responsibilities and expectations?

4. How would you respond to the statement that this chapter presents only the positive side of

the argument that social responsibility results in improved organizational performance?

5. On the basis of the social responsibility model presented in this chapter, describe the philosophy, responsibilities, and stakeholders that make up a company's approach to social responsibility. What are the short and long-term outcomes of this effort?

6. Consider the role that various business disciplines, including marketing, finance, accounting, and human resources, have in social responsibility. What specific views and philosophies do these different disciplines bring to the implementation of social responsibility?

EXPERIENTIAL EXERCISE

Evaluate *Fortune* magazine's annual list of the most admired companies found on the magazine's website (www.fortune.com). These companies as a group have superior financial performance compared to other firms. Go to each company's website and try to assess its management commitment to the welfare of

stakeholders. If any of the companies have experienced legal or ethical misconduct, explain how this may affect specific stakeholders. Rank the companies on the basis of the information available and your opinion on their fulfillment of social responsibility.

WHAT WOULD YOU DO?

Jamie Ramos looked out her window at the early morning sky and gazed at the small crowd below. The words and pictures on their posters were pretty tame this time, she thought. The last protest group used pictures of tarred lungs, corpses, and other graphic photos to show the effects of smoking on a person's internal organs. Their words were also hateful, so much so that employees at the Unified Tobacco headquarters were afraid to walk in and out of the main building. Those who normally took smoking breaks on the back patio decided to skip the break and eat something instead at the company-subsidized cafeteria. By midday, Unified hired extra security to escort employees in and out of the building and to ensure that protestors followed the state

guideline of staying at least 15 feet from the company's entrance. The media picked up on the story—and the photos—and it caused quite a stir in the national press.

At least this protest group seemed fairly reasonable. Late yesterday, a state court provided a reduced judgment to the family of a lifelong smoker, now deceased. This meant that Unified was going to owe millions less than originally expected. The length and stress of the lawsuit had taken its toll, especially on top management, although all employees were certainly affected. After two years of being battered in the media, learning of a huge settlement, and then continuing on with the appeals process, emotions were wearing thin with the continued criticism.

Jamie wondered what this day would bring. As the manager of community relations, her job was to represent Unified in the community, manage the employee volunteer program, create a quarterly newsletter, serve as a liaison to the company's philanthropic foundation, develop solid relationships, and serve on various boards related to social welfare and community needs. The company's foundation donated nearly $1.5 million a year to charities and causes. Over one-quarter of its employees volunteered ten hours a month in their communities.

Jamie reported to a vice-president and was pleased with the career progress she had made since graduating from college eight years earlier. Although some of her friends wondered out loud how she could work for a tobacco company, Jamie was steadfast in her belief that even a tobacco firm could contribute something

meaningful to society. She had the chance to affect some of those contributions in her community relations role.

Jamie's phone rang and she took a call from her vice-president. The VP indicated that, although the protestors seemed relatively calm this time, he was not comfortable with their presence. Several employees had taped signs in office windows telling the protestors to "Go away." Other VPs had dropped by his office to discuss the protest and thought that the responsibility for handling these issues fell to his group. He went on to say that he needed Jamie's help, and the assistance of a few others, in formulating a plan to (1) deal with the protest today and (2) strengthen the strategy for communicating the company's message and goodwill in the future. Their meeting would begin in one hour, so Jamie had some time to sketch out her recommendations on both issues. What would you do?

CHAPTER TWO

Strategic Management of Stakeholder Relationships

Childhood Obesity: A Weighty Issue in Our Society

America's children are growing, not in height or intellectual capacity but in weight. Advertising of fast food and highly processed, corn syrup–laced foods is at the heart of the controversy. While TV advertising of food and restaurants has dropped 34 percent from 1977 to 2004, the use of the internet, promotions, school advertising and vending machines, and sponsored sports stadiums is on the rise. Childhood obesity has become such a concern that First Lady Michelle Obama has created the movement Let's Move! to encourage the development of a healthier generation of children. Regulators, parents, and our society in general are concerned about the health of our children. It is estimated that medical costs associated with childhood obesity will total $19,000 over a person's lifetime.

Studies conducted by the Kaiser Family Foundation have found that the average child sees around 40,000 advertisements per year on television—most of these encourage children to consume candy, cereal, fast food, and soft drinks. What seems to be particularly problematic is the use of popular licensed children's cartoon characters (e.g., SpongeBob SquarePants and Scooby Doo) to advertise these unhealthy foods. Critics believe food manufacturers are not being socially responsible by encouraging children to eat food that is detrimental to their health. Companies are choosing to do something about this problem.

A study over a five-year period revealed that 16 major food and beverage companies—including PepsiCo, Coca-Cola, and Bumble Bee Foods—have reduced calories in foods amounting to an average of 78 calories a day from the American diet. For instance, Nestlé used new technology to reduce fat by half and calories by one-third in their "Slow Churned" Edy's and Dreyer's ice cream. What is especially important is that these 16 companies account for about 36 percent of calories in packaged foods.

Changes are also being made in advertising. The Walt Disney Company mandated that the company will no longer allow sponsorships or advertisements on its networks for foods that do not meet certain nutritional criteria. It also pledged to reduce the calories in foods sold at its theme parks. Coca-Cola has pledged to eliminate advertising targeted toward children in markets where more than 35 percent of viewers are under the age of 12. These companies' actions demonstrate sensitivity and concern for consumer health and stakeholder interests.[1]

As this example illustrates, most organizations have a number of constituents and a web of relationships that interface with society. In this case, the food industry and its member companies are facing the complex task of balancing the concerns of government, special-interest groups, parents, children, and corporate. These stakeholders are increasingly expressing opinions and taking actions that have an effect on the industry's reputation, relationships, and products. Today, many organizations are learning to anticipate such issues and to address them in their strategies long before they become the subject of media stories of negative attention.

In this chapter, we examine the concept of stakeholders and explore why these groups are important for today's businesses. First, we define stakeholders and examine primary, secondary, and global stakeholders. Then, we examine the concept of a stakeholder orientation to enhance social responsibility. Next, we consider the impact of corporate reputation and crisis situations on stakeholder relationships. Finally, we examine the development of stakeholder relationships implementing a stakeholder perspective and the link between stakeholder relationships and social responsibility.

STAKEHOLDERS DEFINED

In Chapter 1, we defined stakeholders as those people and groups to whom an organization is responsible—including customers, shareholders, employees, suppliers, governments, communities, and many others—because they have a "stake" or claim in some aspect of a company's products, operations, markets, industry, or outcomes. These groups not only are influenced by businesses, but they also have the ability to affect businesses.

Responsibility issues, conflicts, and successes revolve around stakeholder relationships. Building effective relationships is considered one of the more important areas of business today. The stakeholder framework is recognized as a management theory that attempts to balance stakeholder interests. Issues related to indivisible resources and unequal levels of stakeholder influence and importance constrain managers' efforts to balance stakeholder interests.[2] A business exists because of relationships among employees, customers, shareholders or investors, suppliers, and managers that develop strategies to attain success. In addition, an organization usually has a governing authority, often called a board of directors, which provides oversight and direction to make sure the organization stays focused on objectives in an ethical, legal, and socially responsible manner. Corporate governance is discussed in Chapter 3. When misconduct is discovered in organizations, it is often found that in most instances there is knowing cooperation or compliance that facilitates the acceptance and perpetuation of unethical conduct.[3] Therefore, relationships are associated not only with organizational success but also with organizational failure to assume responsibility.

These perspectives take into account both market and nonmarket constituencies that may interact with a business and have some effect on the firm's policies and strategy.[4] Market constituencies are those who are directly involved and affected by the business purpose, including investors, employees, customers, and other business partners. Nonmarket groups include the general community, media, government, special-interest groups, and others who are not always directly tied to issues of profitability and performance.

The historical assumption that the foremost objective of business is profit maximization led to the belief that business is accountable primarily to shareholders and others involved in the market and economic aspects of an organization. Because shareholders and other investors provide the financial foundation for business and expect something in return, managers and executives naturally strive to maintain positive relationships with them.[5]

In the latter half of the twentieth century, perceptions of business accountability evolved toward an expanded model of the role and responsibilities of business in society. The expansion included questions about the normative role of business: "What is the appropriate role for business to play in society?" and "Should profit be the sole objective of business?"[6] Many businesspeople and scholars have questioned the role of social responsibility in business. Legal and economic responsibilities are generally accepted as the most important determinants of performance: "If this is well done," say classical economic theorists, "profits are maximized more or less continuously and firms carry out their major responsibilities to society."[7] Some economists believe that if companies address economic and legal issues, they are satisfying the demands of society, and trying to anticipate and meet additional needs would be almost impossible. Milton Friedman has been quoted as saying that "the basic mission of business [is] thus to produce goods and services at a profit, and in doing this, business [is] making its maximum contribution to society and, in fact, being socially responsible."[8] Even with the business ethics scandals of the twenty-first century, Friedman suggests that, although individuals guilty of wrongdoing should be held accountable, the market is a better deterrent than new laws and regulations that discourage firms from wrongdoing.[9] Thus, Friedman would diminish the role of stakeholders such as the government and employees in requiring that businesses demonstrate responsible and ethical behavior.

This form of capitalism has unfortunately been exported to many less developed and developing countries without the appropriate concerns for ethics and social responsibility. Friedman's capitalism is a far cry from Adam Smith's, one of the founders of capitalism. Smith created the concept of the invisible hand and spoke about self-interest; however, he went on to explain that this common good is associated with psychological motives and that each individual has to produce for the common good "with values such as Propriety, Prudence, Reason, Sentiment and promoting the happiness of mankind."[10] These values could be associated with the needs and concerns of stakeholders.

In the twenty-first century, Friedman's form of capitalism is being replaced by Smith's original concept of capitalism (or what is now called enlightened capitalism), a notion of capitalism that reemphasizes stakeholder concerns and issues. The acceptance of enlightened capitalism may be occurring faster in developed countries than in those still developing. Theodore Levitt, a renowned business professor, once wrote that although profits are required for business just like eating is required for living, profit is not the purpose of business any more than eating is the purpose of life.[11] Norman Bowie, a well-known philosopher, extended Levitt's sentiment by noting that focusing on profit alone can create an unfavorable paradox that causes a firm to fail to achieve its objectives. Bowie contends that when a business also cares about the well-being of stakeholders, it earns trust and cooperation that ultimately reduce costs and increases productivity.[12] This in turn results in increased profits and success of the organization.

Some critics of business believe there is a tradeoff between profits and social responsibility. They believe that to increase profits a firm must view social responsibility as a cost that reduces profits. However, there is much evidence that social responsibility is associated with increased profits. For example, one survey indicates that half of all consumers are willing to pay more for goods and services from socially responsible companies. This rate of response is up by 10 percent from a few years ago and relates to a range of demographic groups.[13] An important academic study found that there is a direct relationship between social responsibility and profitability. The study also found that social responsibility contributes to employee commitment and customer loyalty—vital concerns of any firm trying to increase profits.[14] As mentioned earlier, the Ethisphere Institute has found that the world's most ethical companies outperform the companies on the Standard & Poor's index. This clearly demonstrates that social responsibility decisions are good for business.

STAKEHOLDER ISSUES AND INTERACTION

Stakeholders provide resources that are more or less critical to a firm's long-term success. These resources may be both tangible and intangible. Shareholders, for example, supply capital; suppliers offer material resources or intangible knowledge; employees and managers grant expertise, leadership, and commitment; customers generate revenue and provide loyalty and positive or negative word-of-mouth promotion; local communities provide infrastructure; and the media transmits positive or negative corporate images. When individual stakeholders share similar expectations about desirable business conduct, they may choose to establish or join formal communities that are dedicated to better defining and advocating these values and expectations. Stakeholders' ability to withdraw—or threatening to withdraw—these needed resources gives them power over businesses.[15]

New reforms to improve corporate accountability and transparency also suggest that stakeholders such as suppliers—including banks, law firms, and public accounting firms—can play a major role in fostering responsible decision making.[16] Stakeholders apply their values and standards to many diverse issues, such as working conditions, consumer rights, environmental conservation, product safety, and proper information disclosure. These are issues that may or may not directly affect an individual stakeholder's own welfare. We can assess the level of social responsibility an organization bears by scrutinizing its efforts and communication on the issues of concern to its stakeholders. Table 2.1 provides examples of common stakeholder issues along with indicators of businesses' impacts on these issues.[17]

TABLE 2.1 Examples of Stakeholder Issues and Associated Measures of Corporate Impacts

Stakeholder Groups and Issues	Potential Indicators of Corporate Impact on These Issues
Employees	
1. Compensation and benefits	1. Average wage paid versus industry averages
2. Training and development	2. Changes in average training dollars spent per year per employee. Resources for ethics training versus industry averages.
3. Employee diversity	3. Percentages of employees from different genders and races, especially in leadership roles
4. Occupational health and safety	4. Standard injury rates and absentee rates
5. Communications with management	5. Availability of open-door policies or ombudsmen management
Customers	
1. Product safety and quality	1. Number of product recalls over time
2. Management of customer	2. Number of customer complaints and availability of complaint procedures to answer them
3. Services to customers with disabilities	3. Availability and nature of measures taken to ensure services to customers with disabilities
Investors	
1. Transparency of shareholder	1. Availability of procedures to inform shareholders about corporate activities
2. Shareholder rights	2. Frequency and type of litigation involving violations of shareholder rights
Suppliers	
1. Encouraging suppliers in developing countries	1. Prices offered to suppliers in developed countries and developing countries in comparison to other suppliers
2. Encouraging minority suppliers	2. Percentage of minority suppliers
Community	
1. Public health and safety	1. Availability of emergency response plan protection
2. Conservation of energy and materials	2. Data on reduction of waste produced and materials comparison to industry

(Continued)

TABLE 2.1 (*Continued*)

Stakeholder Groups and Issues	Potential Indicators of Corporate Impact on These Issues
3. Donations and support of local organizations	3. Annual employee time spent in community service organizations
Environmental Groups	
1. Minimizing the use of energy	1. Amount of electricity purchased; percentage of "green" electricity
2. Minimizing emissions and waste	2. Type, amount, and designation of waste generated
3. Minimizing adverse environmental effect of products	3. Percentage of product weight reclaimed after the product has been used

Identifying Stakeholders

primary stakeholders
They are fundamental to a company's operations and survival; these include shareholders and investors, employees, customers, suppliers, and public stakeholders, such as government and the community.

We can identify two different types of stakeholders, primary and secondary. **Primary stakeholders** are those whose continued association is absolutely necessary for a firm's survival; these include employees, customers, suppliers, and shareholders, as well as the governments and communities that provide necessary infrastructure. For example, many large companies decided to eliminate health care plans in light of the implementation of the Affordable Care Act, which requires all U.S. citizens to be enrolled in a healthcare plan whether or not their employer offers such benefits. This has a direct impact on a primary stakeholder—employees. However, more than half of all employees indicate that they value the fact that their employers offer healthcare plans, especially those plans that can be customized to their health needs.[18] These benefits can enhance the relationship between employer and employee. Other primary stakeholders such as customers are directly impacted by the quality of products and the integrity of communication and relationships. Shareholders depend on transparency regarding financial information as well as forward-looking statements about sales and profits.

secondary stakeholders
They do not typically engage in direct transactions with a company and thus are not essential for its survival; these include the media, trade associations, and special-interest groups.

Secondary stakeholders do not typically engage in direct transactions with a company and thus are not essential for its survival; these include the media, trade associations, and special-interest groups. For example, the American Association of Retired People (AARP), a special-interest group, works to support the rights of retirees in areas such as healthcare benefits. Both primary and secondary stakeholders embrace specific values and standards that dictate what constitutes acceptable or unacceptable corporate behaviors. It is important for managers to recognize that primary groups may present more day-to-day concerns, but secondary groups cannot be ignored or given less consideration. Sometimes a secondary stakeholder, such as the media, can have more of an impact than a primary stakeholder.

Ethical Responsibilities in Human Resources

Cashing in on Minimum Wage: Can and Should We Do More?

In 2014, Seattle passed the largest minimum wage law to date. Seattle's city council unanimously voted to raise the minimum wage to $15 over the next several years. Cities in California and New York have since followed suit.

There are many reasons why raising the minimum wage might be a good idea. One major issue is that the minimum wage rates have not kept up with inflation over the years. A report by the Congressional Office Budget claims that a federal minimum wage increase to $10.10 per hour could raise as many as 900,000 people out of poverty. This could add $31 billion to the paychecks of American families. The biggest argument in support of a minimum wage increase is that greater purchasing power will stimulate the economy.

On the other hand, critics believe raising the minimum wage has disadvantages. Many veteran workers have also expressed discontent. They feel it is unfair that new hires get paid a higher wage than they received when they started. They also believe that if newcomers get paid higher wages, then they should get raises as well. They feel the government and businesses should focus more on increasing employment.

The impact on stakeholders is less clear. Although some studies have concluded that a minimum wage increase increases unemployment, others claim that it has little discernible effect. According to economists, this is because labor markets react differently to increases. As an alternative to laying off employees, economists claim that some businesses choose to cut benefits, cut wages for employees who already make beyond the minimum wage, settle for less profit, or raise prices. On the contrary, some economists claim that minimum wage increases can be beneficial because it causes business owners to be more efficient and increases positive relationships between employee and employer, reducing turnover and motivating employees to work harder.

Because the minimum wage issue stalled in Congress, supporters are encouraging states and cities to raise the minimum wage themselves. Oklahoma responded by passing a law forbidding individual towns and cities to raise the minimum wage. The governor of Oklahoma claimed raising minimum wages would destroy Oklahoma jobs, cause business owners to move to other states, and raise prices for consumers. Supporters of a minimum wage increase are likely to challenge this law.

Seattle could also experience difficulties based upon how it chooses to implement the increase. The International Franchise Association filed a lawsuit based upon what they see as unequal treatment. For instance, Seattle is giving businesses with fewer than 500 employees more time to comply with the law. However, franchises that have more than 500 employees anywhere in the United States are currently not given this extension, even though many franchisees are independently owned.

Walmart claims that it does not oppose a minimum wage increase. In fact, it recently increased wages for many of its workers. How an increase affects a business will likely depend on the size, nature, and operations of the company. Not only employee stakeholders but communities as well as customers and suppliers will be affected by the decisions on minimum wages.

Sources: Katie Lobosco, "Coping with $15 Minimum Wage in Seattle," *CNN Money,* June 4, 2014, http://money.cnn.com/2014/06/03/smallbusiness/seattle-business-minimum-wage/ (accessed June 23, 2016); Brad Plumer, "Economists Disagree on Whether the Minimum Wage Kills Jobs. Why?" *The Washington Post,* February 14, 2013, http://www.washingtonpost.com/blogs/wonkblog/wp/2013/02/14/why-economists-are-so-puzzled-by-the-minimum-wage/ (accessed June 23, 2016); Jeanne Sahadi, "Minimum Wage: Congress Stalls, States Act," *CNN Money,* April 28, 2014, http://money.cnn.com/2014/04/28/news/economy/states-minimum-wage/ (accessed June 23, 2016); Gregory Wallace, "Oklahoma Bans Minimum Wage Hikes," *CNN Money,* April 15, 2014, http://money.

cnn.com/2014/04/15/news/economy/oklahoma-minimum-wage-ban/ (accessed June 23, 2016); Shelly Banjo, "Wal-Mart Says It Won't Oppose Increase in Minimum Wage," *The Wall Street Journal,* May 15, 2014, http://online.wsj.com/news/articles/SB1000142405270 23049083045795637634056799116 (accessed June 23, 2016); Editorial Board, "The Clear Benefits of a Higher Wage," *The New York Times,* February 19, 2014, http://www.nytimes.com/2014/02/20/opinion/the-clear-benefits-of-a-higher-wage.html (accessed June 23, 2016). Rachel Feintzeig and Lauren Weber, "New Wage Laws Raise Pay--And Tensions," *The Wall Street Journal*, May 6, 2016, A1-A2.

stakeholder interaction model
A model that conceptualizes the two-way relationships between a firm and a host of stakeholders.

Figure 2.1 offers a conceptualization of the relationship between businesses and stakeholders. In this **stakeholder interaction model,** there are two-way relationships between the firm and a host of stakeholders. In addition to the fundamental input of investors, employees, and suppliers, this approach recognizes other stakeholders and explicitly acknowledges the dialog and interaction that exists between a firm's internal and external environments.

FIGURE 2.1 Stakeholder Model for Implementing Social Responsibilities

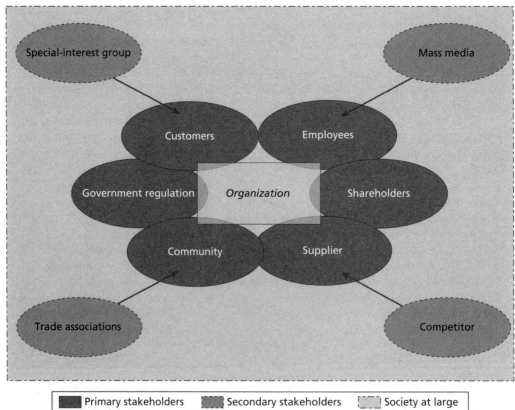

Source: Adapted from Isabelle Maignan, O. C. Ferrell, and Linda Ferrell, "A Stakeholder Model for Implementing Social Responsibility in Marketing," *European Journal of Marketing* 39 (September/October 2005): 956–977.

A Stakeholder Orientation

The degree to which a firm understands and addresses stakeholder demands can be referred to as a **stakeholder orientation**. This orientation comprises three sets of activities: (1) the organization-wide generation of data about stakeholder groups and assessment of the firm's effects on these groups, (2) the distribution of this information throughout the firm, and (3) the organization's responsiveness as a whole to this intelligence.[19]

Generating data about stakeholders begins with identifying the stakeholders that are relevant to the firm. Relevant stakeholder communities should be analyzed on the basis of the power each enjoys, as well as by the ties between them. Next, the firm should characterize the concerns about the business's conduct that each relevant stakeholder group shares. This information can be derived from formal research, including surveys, focus groups, internet searches, or press reviews. For example, Ford Motor Company obtains input on social and environmental responsibility issues from company representatives, suppliers, customers, and community leaders. Shell has an online discussion forum where website visitors are invited to express their opinions on the company's activities and their implications. Employees and managers can also generate this information informally as they carry out their daily activities. For example, purchasing managers know about suppliers' demands, public relations executives about the media, legal counselors about the regulatory environment, financial executives about investors, sales representatives about customers, and human resources advisors about employees. Finally, the company should evaluate its impact on the issues that are important to the various stakeholders it has identified.[20] To develop effective stakeholder dialogs, management needs to appreciate how others perceive the risks of a specific decision. A multiple stakeholder perspective must take into account communication content and transparency when communicating with specific stakeholders.[21]

Given the variety of the employees involved in the generation of information about stakeholders, it is essential that this intelligence be circulated throughout the firm. This requires that the firm facilitate the communication of information about the nature of relevant stakeholder communities, stakeholder issues, and the current impact of the firm on these issues to all members of the organization. The dissemination of stakeholder intelligence can be organized formally through activities such as newsletters and internal information forums.[22]

A stakeholder orientation is not complete unless it includes activities that actually address stakeholder issues. For example, Cloetta, an international confectionary company, has taken stakeholder orientation seriously. A page on their website is dedicated to the topic and clearly identifies all of its stakeholders, the issues that are important to them, and how the company interacts with consumers to address these issues. Cloetta engages with all stakeholders through various media: social media, face-to-face meetings, virtual meetings, surveys, and influential leaders in the community. This allows for a free flow of information

stakeholder orientation
The degree to which a firm understands and addresses stakeholder demands.

between stakeholders and the company.[23] The responsiveness of the organization as a whole to stakeholder intelligence consists of the initiatives the firm adopts to ensure that it abides by or exceeds stakeholder expectations and has a positive impact on stakeholder issues. Such activities are likely to be specific to a particular stakeholder group (e.g., family-friendly work schedules) or to a particular stakeholder issue (e.g., pollution-reduction programs). These responsiveness processes typically involve the participation of the concerned stakeholder groups. Kraft, for example, includes special-interest groups and university representatives in its programs to become sensitized to present and future ethical issues.

Stakeholder orientation can be viewed as a continuum in that firms are likely to adopt the concept to varying degrees. To gauge a given firm's stakeholder orientation, it is necessary to evaluate the extent to which the firm adopts behaviors that typify both the generation and dissemination of stakeholder intelligence and responsiveness to it. A given organization may generate and disseminate more intelligence about certain stakeholder communities than about others and, as a result, may respond to that intelligence differently.[24]

Stakeholder Attributes[25]

Traditionally, companies have had an easier time understanding the issues stakeholders raise than their attributes and the tactics they use to affect organizational decision making. It is therefore necessary to understand both the content (specific issues) and process (actions, tactics) of each stakeholder relationship. For example, animal rights activists sometimes use an unreasonable process to communicate the content of their beliefs. Although they are controversial, animal rights issues do have solid support from a number of citizens. One mechanism for understanding stakeholders and their potential salience to a firm involves assessing three stakeholder attributes: power, legitimacy, and urgency. Table 2.2 describes these three attributes. This assessment provides one analytical tool to help managers uncover the motivations and needs of stakeholders and how they relate to the company and its interests. In addition, stakeholder actions may also sensitize the firm to issues and viewpoints not previously considered.[26]

TABLE 2.2 Stakeholder Attributes

Attributes	Example
Power	A well-established employee in a specialized field has power if replacing the employee would require extensive training and resources.
Legitimacy	Special-interest groups that are against genetically modified foods encourage protests after legislation favorable to biotechnology companies is passed.
Urgency	A company that has discovered a serious product defect that can cause injury must immediately implement a product recall.

Power, legitimacy, and urgency are not constant, meaning stakeholder attributes can change over time and context. For example, there was a very strong "Buy American" sentiment in the United States in the 1980s, a time when Japanese manufacturers were making steady market share gains. As globalization increased and overseas manufacturing became the norm, consumer activism or retailer strategy on activism toward this nationalistic buying criterion waned. In the late 1990s and the first decade of the twenty-first century, there was increased urgency concerning Chinese manufacturers and legitimate claims concerning market share gains. However, nationalism, as it relates to retail purchasing, seems to contribute to the intensity of the power gained in the stakeholder environment. This was largely due to the fact that the U.S. economy was strong, so products from other countries were not seen as threatening. The "Buy American" sentiment rose again after the advent of the Great Recession in 2008–2009, as Americans felt the sting of job loss. American manufacturing came to the forefront of consumer consciousness through organizations and movements promoting American-made products and activists pressuring companies to bring manufacturing back to the United States. More recently, although controversial, the use of hydraulic fracturing (fracking) of shale has significantly increased American gas and oil production, making the country more energy independent. The signing of the American Recovery and Investment Act also put pressure on domestic sourcing, investment, and reinvestment in the United States. Some companies have taken this sentiment to heart and are investing in American manufacturing.[27]

Power A stakeholder has **power** to the extent that it can gain access to coercive, utilitarian, or symbolic means to impose or communicate its views to an organization.[28] *Coercive power* involves the use of fear, suppression, punishment, or some type of restraint. *Utilitarian power* involves financial or material control or based on a decision's utility or usefulness. Finally, *symbolic power* relies on the use of symbols that connote social acceptance, prestige, or some other attribute.

power
The extent to which a stakeholder can gain access to coercive, utilitarian, or symbolic means to impose or communicate its views to an organization.

Symbolism contained in letter-writing campaigns, advertising messages, and websites can be used to generate awareness and enthusiasm for more responsible business actions. In fact, the internet has conferred tremendous power on stakeholder groups in recent years. Disgruntled stakeholders, especially customers and former employees, may share their concerns or dissatisfaction on social media sites. Even current employees are increasingly expressing their job frustrations over the internet. Symbolic power is the least threatening of the three types.

Utilitarian measures, including boycotts and lawsuits, are also fairly prevalent, although they often come about after symbolic strategies fail to yield the desired response. For example, the government, an important stakeholder for most firms, banned the importation of goods made by children under the age of 15 through indentured or forced labor.[29] This action came about after the media and activist groups exposed widespread abuses in the apparel industry. This law carries financial—utilitarian—repercussions for firms that purchase products manufactured under unacceptable labor conditions. Utilitarian power can be exerted over the fear that profits will fall if too much is spent on managing labor or sustainability.

Finally, some stakeholders use coercive power to communicate their message, especially when the issue is emotionally charged and somewhat controversial. Many protests around the world over hydraulic fracturing or fracking, a method of extracting natural gas from the earth by means of fluid and other substances, have become violent. For example, a protest in Denton, Texas resulted in several fracking protesters being arrested by police. According to police, the protesters broke the law by trespassing on private property.[30]

legitimacy
The perception or belief that a stakeholder's actions are proper, desirable, or appropriate within a given context.

Legitimacy The second stakeholder attribute is **legitimacy**, which is the perception or belief that a stakeholder's actions are proper, desirable, or appropriate within a given context.[31] This definition suggests that stakeholder actions are considered legitimate when claims are judged to be reasonable by other stakeholders and by society in general. Legitimacy is gained through the stakeholder's ability and willingness to explore the issue from a variety of perspectives and then to communicate in an effective and respectful manner on the desire for change. Legitimacy is also linked to compliance with regulations, values, and norms that support ethical conduct.

Thus, extremist views are less likely to be considered legitimate because these groups often use covert and inflammatory measures that overshadow the issues and create animosity. For example, extreme groups have destroyed property, threatened customers, and committed other acts of violence that ultimately discredit their legitimacy.[32] Opponents of fracking are at risk of delegitimizing their efforts if the main theme of their communication is violent. It is important to remember that this issue is highly controversial, and it is in the best interest of companies engaged in this activity to be sensitive to the requests of stakeholders. After many years of stakeholders requesting acknowledgement and measurement of the risks of fracking from various oil and energy companies, ExxonMobil has agreed to become the first to disclose such information. Their report will address fracking's effects on air and water quality, roads, and any potential effects of the chemicals used in the process. While some stakeholders are not completely satisfied with the details of this report, as they think many more issues need to be addressed, ExxonMobil is taking a step in the right direction toward becoming more transparent in addressing stakeholder concerns. The pressure that stakeholders in this example have exerted on the industry was seen as a legitimate concern to ExxonMobil. This report may spur other energy companies to follow their lead. Although an issue may be legitimate, such as environmental sensitivity, it is difficult for the claim to be evaluated independently of the way the stakeholder group communicates on it.[33]

Urgency Stakeholders exercise greater pressures on managers and organizations when they stress the urgency of their claims. **Urgency** is based on two characteristics: time sensitivity and the importance of the claim to the stakeholder. Time sensitivity usually heightens the stakeholder's effort and may compress an organization's ability to research and react to a claim. For example, hundreds of protesters in Bangladesh took to the streets after a major garment factory fire killed over 100 workers. This fire came after a string of similar incidents in the region, which caused the death of over 600 workers in a period of 6 years. The aim of the protest was to obtain justice for the death of the workers. Factory owners and managers had known the factory was deemed an unsafe workplace, but allowed work to continue despite this knowledge. The urgency of the protestors resulted in the arrest of factory managers, investigations into the safety practices for factories in the region, and a refocusing of multinational companies that used the factories in their operations.[34]

urgency
The time sensitivity and the importance of the claim to the stakeholder.

In another example, labor and human rights are widely recognized as critical issues because they are fundamental to the well-being of people around the world. These rights have become a focal point for college student associations that criticized Nike, the world's leading shoe company, for its failure to improve the working conditions of employees of suppliers and in not making information available to interested stakeholders. Nike experienced a public backlash from its use of offshore subcontractors to manufacture its shoes and clothing. When Nike claimed no responsibility for the subcontractors' poor working conditions and extremely low wages, some consumers demanded greater accountability and responsibility by engaging in boycotts, letter-writing campaigns, public-service announcements, and so forth. Nike ultimately responded to the growing negative publicity by changing its practices and becoming a model company in managing offshore manufacturing.

Overall, stakeholders are considered more important to an organization when their issues are legitimate, their claims are urgent, and they can make use of their power on the organization. These attributes assist the firm and employees in determining the relative importance of specific stakeholders and making resource allocations for developing and managing the stakeholder relationship.

PERFORMANCE WITH STAKEHOLDERS

Effectively managing stakeholder relationships requires careful attention to a firm's reputation and the effective handling of crisis situations. Boeing's release of the acclaimed 787 Dreamliner was grounded when the plane's lithium ion battery began to overheat. The company had outsourced production of many components of the aircraft, one of which was the battery to Japanese manufacturer GS Yuasa. Although the 787 Dreamliner had undergone many tests, the company learned that excessive outsourcing could cause coordination issues as well as some unforeseen quality issues. Boeing is a company known for its safety standards, but lack of coordination with third parties can result in the failure for safety standards to be emphasized.[35] On the other hand, CVS made the strategic decision to drop tobacco products from its offerings, forgoing $2 billion in tobacco sales. The pharmacy believes selling a harmful and addictive substance is contrary to its goal of becoming a healthcare firm. Despite its short-term losses, CVS believes it will gain long-term stakeholder relationships. Other pharmacies have not followed CVS's lead.[36]

Reputation Management

There are short- and long-term outcomes associated with positive stakeholder relationships. One of the most significant of these is a positive reputation. Because a company's reputation has the power to attract or repel stakeholders, it can be either an asset or a liability in developing and implementing strategic plans and social responsibility initiatives.[37] Reputations take a long time to build or change, and it is far more important to monitor reputation than many companies believe. Whereas a strong reputation may take years to build, it can be destroyed seemingly overnight if a company does not handle crisis situations to the satisfaction of the various stakeholders involved.

Corporate reputation, image, and brands are more important than ever and are among the most critical aspects of sustaining relationships with constituents, including investors, customers, financial analysts, media, and government watchdogs. It takes companies decades to build a great reputation, yet just one slip can cost a company dearly. Although an organization does not control its reputation in a direct sense, its actions, choices, behaviors, and consequences do influence the reputation that exists in perceptions of stakeholders. A 2009 corporate reputation poll taken during the financial crisis showed that misconduct and the failure to manage properly lowered the overall reputation of American corporations. In a more recent reputation poll of American companies, respondents indicated that while they are still skeptical of businesses, they are confident that their reputations are improving. Even the percentage of those who are most skeptical has decreased significantly.[38]

reputation management
The process of building and sustaining a company's good name and generating positive feedback from stakeholders.

Reputation management is the process of building and sustaining a company's good name and generating positive feedback from stakeholders. A company's reputation is affected by every contact with a stakeholder.[39] Various trends may affect how companies manage their reputations. These trends include market factors, such as increased consumer knowledge and community access to information, and workplace factors, including technological advances, closer vendor relationships, and more inquisitive employees. These factors make companies more cautious about their actions because increased scrutiny in this area requires more attention from management. A company needs to understand these factors and how to properly address them to achieve a strong reputation. These factors have also helped companies recognize a link between reputation and competitive advantage. If these trends are dealt with wisely and if internal and external communication strategies are used effectively, a firm can position itself positively in stakeholders' minds and thus create a competitive advantage. Intangible factors related to reputation can account for as much as 50 percent of a firm's market valuation.[40]

The importance of corporate reputation has created a need for accurate reputation measures. As indicated in Table 2.3, business publications, research

TABLE 2.3 Reputation Measures

Reputation List	Conducted By	Groups Surveyed	Primary Purpose
100 Best Companies to Work for in America	*Fortune* magazine, Great Place to Work Institute	Companies that are at least five years old and employ at least 1,000 employees; employees and top managers are surveyed	Publication
100 Best Corporate Citizens	*Corporate Responsibility* Magazine, Corporate Responsibility Officers Association (CROA)	Russell 1000 companies	Publication
America's Most Admired Companies	*Fortune* magazine, Hay Group	*Fortune 1000* companies and *Fortune's Global 500* with revenues at or over $10 billion; company executives, directors, and analysts are surveyed	Publication
Best and Worst: Social Responsibility	*Fortune* magazine, Hay Group	*Fortune 1000* companies and *Fortune's Global 500* with revenues at or over $10 billion; company executives, directors, and analysts are surveyed	Publication
Corporate Branding Index	CoreBrand, LLC	Business executives responsible for purchasing and strategic relationship decisions from the top brands with over $50 million as well as high-level customers	Customized for clients
Global Reputation Pulse	Reputation Institute	All of the company's stakeholders	Customized for clients
Reputation Quotient	Reputation Institute and Harris Interactive	General public	Customized for Clients
World's Most Respected Companies	Barron's	Professional money managers	Publication

firms, consultants, and public relations agencies have established a foothold in the new field of reputation management through research and lists of "the most reputable" firms. However, some questions have arisen as to who can best determine corporate reputation. For example, some measures survey only chief executives, whereas others also elicit perceptions from the general public. Although executives may be biased toward a firm's financial performance, the general public may lack experience or data on which to evaluate a company's reputation. Regardless of how it is measured, reputation is the result of a process involving an organization and various constituents.[41]

The process of reputation management involves four components that work together: organizational identity, image, performance, and ultimately, reputation.[42] Organizational performance involves the actual interaction between the company and its stakeholders.

To build and manage a good reputation, these four areas must be aligned. Companies must manage identity and culture by pinpointing those standards and responsibilities that will allow them to achieve their objectives, work with stakeholders effectively, and continuously monitor and change for effectiveness.[43] The Corporate Citizens list provides recognition and publicity for outstanding performance using corporate responsibility criteria. AT&T ranked number 16 in 2015. The company has implemented a widespread and comprehensive approach to sustainability and social responsibility, and the results are significant. One of the company's points of pride is in their "It Can Wait" program, which encourages its customers to make a pledge on their website not to text while driving. So far there have been over 9 million pledges. AT&T also entered into a partnership with the Environmental Defense Fund (EDF), and together they have found ways of conserving millions of gallons of water each year. Another partnership in which AT&T contributed $4.5 million to Communities in Schools (CIS), the leading dropout prevention organization in the United States, was noted as a reason for recognition.

Additionally, the Guinness Book of World Records entered the company into their records for the highest number of cell phones recycled each week. The company received other recognitions in 2013, including placement on the Carbon Disclosure Leadership Index, Vigeo's U.S. 50 (the 50 most advanced companies) for its contributions to environmental, social, and governance performance, as well as the FTSE4Good Index. These are only a few of the accomplishments the company has achieved over the last few years. AT&T's vice-president of Sustainability and Philanthropy credits the success of the company's social responsibility endeavors to the commitment of the leadership, strength of the collaboration among the various partnerships the company holds, as well as to the dedication of the company's employees.[44] Table 2.4 lists ten socially responsible companies known for their CSR initiatives. Salesforce.com, for instance, has developed a model called the 1-1-1 model that contributes 1 percent of the company's time, 1 percent of equity, and 1 percent of company products to

TABLE 2.4 Ten Socially Responsible Companies

AT&T	Patagonia
Bueno Foods	Salesforce.com
Cummins	SC Johnson
Eaton	Starbucks
Marriott	Whole Foods

worthy causes, such as significantly discounting its products for nonprofit organizations.

Thus, all these elements must be continually implemented to ensure that the company's reputation is maximized through community relations. However, most firms will, at one time or another, experience crisis situations that threaten or harm this reputation. How a company reacts, responds, and learns from the situation is indicative of its commitment and implementation of social responsibility.

Reputation management is becoming a key consideration for corporations around the world. Several years ago German firms invested resources into building, maintaining, and strengthening their reputations. A survey showed that roughly two-thirds of company executives felt that reputation management was of "very high" or "high" importance to their companies. This focus has paid off: An Edelman poll measuring trust among foreign firms ranked Germany at the top of the list. In addition, when the American Chamber of Commerce asked American business executives which foreign business environment they preferred to conduct business in, 73 percent marked Germany as their first choice. Many other surveys measuring various aspects of reputation have placed Germany at or near the top of the list. Furthermore, the emphasis on building a good reputation is extending beyond corporations to business schools. For example, the European University in Munich offers students an MBA in Reputation Management.[45]

Crisis Management[46]

Organizational crises are far-reaching events that can have dramatic effects on both the organization and its stakeholders. Along with the industrialization of society, companies and their products have become ever more complex and therefore more susceptible to crisis. As a result, disasters and crisis situations are increasingly common events from which few organizations are exempt. General Motors CEO Mary Barra's response to the scrutiny associated with the 2014 recall of certain GM automobiles with faulty ignition switches is an example of effective crisis management. At the time of the disaster, she had only been CEO for several weeks. Barra addressed the problem quickly and straightforwardly. She took responsibility for the incidents and issued a recall of millions of vehicles. Barra also directly addressed victims injured or affected by death due to the faulty switches by meeting with them personally at their request. Finally, she addressed the state of the corporate culture that allowed the ignition switch problem to go unaddressed for such a long period of time. She also announced that she intended to change that culture under her leadership.[47]

An ethical misconduct disaster (EMD) can be an unexpected organizational crisis that results from employee misconduct, illegal activities such as fraud, or unethical decisions that significantly disrupts operations and threatens or is perceived to threaten the firm's continuity of operations. An EMD can even be more devastating than natural disasters such as a

TABLE 2.5 Ethical Misconduct Disasters

Company	Disaster
FIFA	Engaged in widespread corruption by top FIFA officials, including bribery, racketeering, and fraud.
Credit Suisse	Pleaded guilty to helping Americans evade taxes and agreed to pay $2.5 billion in penalties.
Target	Appeared to ignore warnings of potential hacking activity, resulting in the theft of millions of customers' personal information.
Air Force	Discovered a massive cheating scandal at its Air Force base in Montana among officers involved in the launching of intercontinental ballistic missiles.
GlaxoSmithKline	Paid $3 billion to settle allegations that it had marketed different medications for uses that were unapproved by the Food and Drug Administration.
Volkswagen	Purposefully installed defeat devices in diesel vehicles to fool regulators during emissions testing.
Barclay's Bank	Rigged the Libor rate—used as the benchmark for trillions of loans—to benefit the company.

hurricane or technology disruptions.[48] Table 2.5 discusses some recent ethical misconduct disasters that happened due to lapses in leadership and the failure to manage risks properly.

As organizations plan for natural disasters and insure against traditional risks, so too should they prepare for ethical crises. An EMD can be managed by organizational initiatives to recognize, avoid, discover, answer, and recover from the misconduct. The potential damage of an ethical disaster can affect both business and society. The costs of an EMD from both a financial and reputation perspective can be assessed, as well as the need for planning to avoid an EMD. The role of leadership in preventing a crisis relates to a contingency plan to develop effective crisis management programs.

The risks facing organizations today are significant, and the reputational damage caused can be far greater for companies that find themselves unprepared. The key is to recognize that the risks associated with misconduct are real and that, if insufficient controls are in place, the company can suddenly find itself the subject of an EMD. Although it is hard to predict an ethical disaster, companies can and must prepare for one.

The Deepwater Horizon oil spill of 2010, involving oil company BP, is a prominent example of an EMD. The disaster occurred due to "negligent misinterpretation" of pressure readings on the oil rig. Although the company was aware of the potential issues, they did not fully disclose the issue or make efforts to ensure its function. As a result, an explosion occurred, the rig sank, and an oil leak lasting over three months spewed over 206 million gallons of oil into the Gulf of Mexico. Among many injuries, 11 deaths are attributed to the disaster as well as severe destruction to the environment and economy. The company pleaded guilty to various charges, including manslaughter, negligence, and obstruction of Congress. Six years later the company continued to experience fallout from the scandal. It paid more than $56 billion in legal and cleanup costs. Additionally, the company has to contend with continual governmental and civil litigations. This incident was not the first the company faced as a result of ethical lapses, but it was, and continues to be, one of the most egregious in its history. Many regulations have been instituted or changed in order to prevent such an occurrence, and BP is having difficulty reestablishing a good reputation.[49]

Of course, not every unethical decision relates to negligence. Many often begin as a marketing effort, and only in retrospect is it revealed to be unethical. And clearly not every decision becomes a crisis. Lord & Taylor, for instance, settled charges that it deceived consumers when it paid for an ad in the magazine *Nylon* without disclosing that it had paid for the content. It also paid 50 fashion influencers to wear one of its dresses without disclosing that it had done so. This was found to be deceptive because consumers were not aware of the company's direct connections to these promotions.[50]

It is critical for companies to manage crises effectively because research suggests that these events are a leading cause of organizational mortality. What follows are some key issues to consider in **crisis management**, the process of handling a high-impact event characterized by ambiguity and the need for swift action. In most cases, the crisis situation will not be handled in a completely effective or ineffective manner. Thus, a crisis usually leads to both success and failure outcomes for a business and its stakeholders and provides information for making improvements to future crisis management and social responsibility efforts.[51]

crisis management
The process of handling a high-impact event characterized by ambiguity and the need for swift action.

Organizational crises are characterized by a threat to a company's high-priority goals, surprise to its membership, and stakeholder demands for a short response time. The nature of crises requires a firm's leadership to communicate in an often stressful, emotional, uncertain, and demanding context. Crises are very difficult on a company's stakeholders as well. For this reason, the firm's stakeholders, especially its employees, shareholders, customers, government regulators, competitors, creditors, and the media, will closely scrutinize communication after a crisis. Hence, crises have widespread implications not only for the organization but also for each group affected by the crisis. To better understand how crises develop and move toward resolution, some researchers use a medical analogy. Using the analogy, the organization proceeds through chronological stages similar to a person with an illness. The prodromal stage is a pre-crisis period during which warning signs may exist. Next is the acute stage, in which the actual crisis occurs. During the third (or chronic) stage, the business is required to sufficiently explain its actions to move to the final stage, crisis resolution. Figure 2.2 illustrates these stages. Although the stages are conceptually distinct, some crises happen so quickly and without warning that the organization may move from the prodromal to acute stage within

FIGURE 2.2 Crisis Management Process

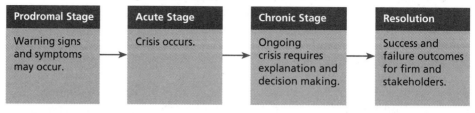

Prodromal Stage	Acute Stage	Chronic Stage	Resolution
Warning signs and symptoms may occur.	Crisis occurs.	Ongoing crisis requires explanation and decision making.	Success and failure outcomes for firm and stakeholders.

minutes. Many organizations faced this situation after Hurricane Katrina crashed into New Orleans and the Mississippi Gulf Coast, disrupting all business and social activity for years.

One of the fundamental difficulties that a company faces is how to communicate effectively to stakeholders during and after a disaster. Once a crisis strikes, the firm's stakeholders need a quick response in the midst of the duress and confusion. They need information about how the company plans to resolve the crisis as well as what each constituent can do to mitigate its own negative effects. If a company is slow to respond, stakeholders may feel that the company does not care about their needs or is not concerned or remorseful, if the company is at fault, about the crisis. Furthermore, a delayed response may in fact increase the suffering of particular stakeholder groups. For instance, some stakeholders may take on considerable debt due to medical expenses as a result of the crisis. Therefore, a rapid response to stakeholders is central to any crisis resolution strategy so that these groups can plan their recovery.

Ironically, crisis events are often so chaotic that a company's leadership may not be certain of the cause of the situation before the media and other relevant groups demand a statement. Thus, it is not surprising for organizations to begin their crisis response with some degree of ambiguity in their statements. In fact, some crisis theorists advise companies to avoid too much detail in their initial response due to the embarrassment that results from changing positions later in the crisis when more information is available. Still, stakeholder groups want and, as a matter of safety in some cases, need access to whatever information the firm can share. Although tensions between the public's needs and the organization's fear of litigation can hamper an organization's willingness to communicate, the demand for information in such situations is unyielding.

Not only should the firm's leadership make a public statement quickly, but it is also necessary for the organization to communicate about specific issues to stakeholder groups. First, leadership should express concern and/ or remorse for the event. Second, the organization should delineate guidelines regarding how it intends to address the crisis so that stakeholders can be confident that the situation will not escalate or reoccur. Finally, the company should provide explicit criteria to stakeholders regarding how each group will be compensated for any negative effects it experiences as a result of the crisis. Many companies, however, overlook these three essential conditions of crisis management. More often, they focus on minimizing harm to the organization's image, denying responsibility for the crisis, and shifting blame away from the organization and toward other stakeholder groups. Although this may be an appropriate strategy when the firm is not actually responsible, too often companies choose this course of action under the stress of the crisis when they are responsible or partially responsible for the crisis without expressing sufficient remorse for their involvement or concern for their stakeholders.

The varying communication needs and levels of concern of stakeholders during and after a crisis often hamper effective communication. The firm's leadership should try to communicate as much accurate information to these groups as possible to minimize their uncertainty. When a firm fails to do so, its credibility, legitimacy, and reputation in the eyes of stakeholders often suffer. Adding to the complexity of communication challenges, the needs of various stakeholder groups may conflict. For instance, the needs of customers who become ill as a result of a contaminated product and their desire to have medical bills paid may be at odds with the company's ability to bolster its stock price to satisfy shareholders. Some stakeholders will obviously have more opportunities than others to voice their concerns after a crisis. Victims and the general public rarely have an opportunity to meet with the organization's leadership after a crisis. Conversely, the organization's stockholders and employees will likely have a greater opportunity to express their views about the crisis and therefore may have their ideas accepted by management. Some researchers suggest that, due to this ability to communicate directly with leadership, internal stakeholder needs often take precedence over those of external stakeholders. Organizations have a responsibility to manage the competing interests of stakeholders to ensure that all stakeholder groups are treated fairly in the aftermath of a crisis. Responsible companies try to balance the needs of their stakeholders rather than favoring some groups over others. The Walt Disney Corporation experienced a major crisis when an alligator killed a two-year-old boy who was wading in a lake at one of Disney's resorts. Although Disney had posted do not swim signs around the lake and had worked with Florida wildlife officials to remove alligators from the lake in the past, it did not have signs posted warning about alligators, despite the fact that they were likely to be present. While Disney may face legal repercussion for not warning consumers about the possibility of alligators, crisis-communication experts praised the response of Disney's CEO who personally contacted the parents to offer condolences from Shanghai. Other experts, however, thought Disney could have done a better job of placing a public statement of regret on their websites. Disney has since put up signs warning about the possibility of dangerous wildlife.[53] Organizations that fail to accomplish effective crisis communication alienating stakeholder groups and intensifying the negative media attention toward the company. For many reasons, including effective crisis management, organizations need to understand and pursue solid and mutually beneficial relationships with stakeholders.

DEVELOPMENT OF STAKEHOLDER RELATIONSHIPS

Relationships of any type, whether they involve family, friends, coworkers, or companies, are founded on principles of trust, commitment, and transparent communication. They also are associated with a certain degree of time, interaction, and shared expectations. For instance, we do not normally speak of "having a relationship" with someone we have just met. We even differentiate between casual acquaintances, work colleagues, and close friends.

In business, the concept of relationships has gained much acceptance. Instead of just pursuing one-time transactions, companies are now searching for ways to develop long-term and collaborative relationships with their customers and business partners.[54] Many companies focus on relationships with suppliers, buyers, employees, and others directly involved in economic exchange. These relationships involve investments of several types. Some investments are tangible, such as buildings, equipment, new tools, and other elements dedicated to a particular relationship. Apple made an unprecedented move in this regard when it launched an iPhone trade-in day in select retail locations. Some owners of older iPhones were sent an email invitation to upgrade to a new device.[55] Other investments are less tangible, such as the time, effort, trust, and commitment required to develop a relationship. Southwest Airlines develops the intangible aspect of relationships through the level of customer service they provide as well as the enjoyable experience they give to their customers.[56]

Whereas tangible investments are often customized for a specific business relationship, intangible efforts have a more lucid and permeable quality. Although social responsibility involves tangible activities and other communication signals, the key to good stakeholder relationships resides in trust, communication quality, and mutual respect. As a company strives to develop a dialog and a solid relationship with one stakeholder, investments and lessons learned through the process should add value to other stakeholder relationships. For example, Starbucks provides excellent benefits, including healthcare for part-time employees, and supports fair trade or a fair income for farmers growing its coffee.

social capital
An asset that resides in relationships and is characterized by mutual goals and trust.

These efforts result in **social capital**, an asset that resides in relationships and is characterized by mutual goals and trust.[57] Social capital include the social connections that can provide economic benefits that are mutually advantageous. Social capital provides social networks that have value. Like financial and intellectual capital, social capital facilitates internal and external transactions and processes. This is especially true as more businesses become part of the sharing economy. Companies such as Airbnb, a rental sharing company, and Uber, a car reservation company, are prime examples of businesses whose level of social capital is necessary for their success. These business models depend upon building and reinforcing transparency and accountability among users as well as between users and the company.[58]

Unlike financial and intellectual capital, however, social capital is not tangible or the obvious property of one organization. In this same regard, social responsibility is not compartmentalized or reserved for a few issues or stakeholders but should have the companywide strategic focus discussed in Chapter 1.

IMPLEMENTING A STAKEHOLDER PERSPECTIVE IN SOCIAL RESPONSIBILITY[59]

An organization that develops effective corporate governance and understands the importance of business ethics and social responsibility in achieving success should develop some processes for managing these important concerns. Although there are many different approaches, we provide some steps that have been found effective to utilize the stakeholder framework in managing responsibility and business ethics. The steps include: (1) assessing the corporate culture, (2) identifying stakeholder groups, (3) identifying stakeholder issues, (4) assessing the organization's commitment to social responsibility, (5) identifying resources and determining urgency, and (6) gaining stakeholder feedback. The importance of these steps is to include feedback from relevant stakeholders in formulating organizational strategy and implementation. Table 2.6 summarizes these six steps.

TABLE 2.6 Six Steps for Utilizing a Stakeholder Framework

Steps	Example
Assess the corporate culture	New Belgium Brewing decides to invest in wind power because it aligns with its mission of environmental responsibility.
Identify stakeholder groups	Whole Foods recognizes the importance of working with animal activist organizations to ensure the animals supplying its meat products are treated humanely.
Identify stakeholder issues	Chevron identifies sustainability and the increasing concern over greenhouse gas emissions as important stakeholder considerations impacting the industry.
Assess the organization's commitment to social responsibility	CVS determines that eliminating cigarette sales will reinforce its commitment toward becoming a health services company.
Identify resources and determine urgency	Home Depot provides emergency supplies in areas that are struck by natural disasters.
Gain stakeholder feedback	Best Buy asked consumers for feedback and realized that the recycling of electronic waste was a major concern.

Step 1: Assessing the Corporate Culture

To enhance organizational fit, a social responsibility program must align with the corporate culture of the organization. The purpose of this first step is to identify the organizational mission, values, and norms that are likely to have implications for social responsibility. In particular, relevant existing values and norms are those that specify the stakeholder groups and stakeholder issues that are deemed most important by the organization. Very often, relevant organizational values and norms can be found in corporate documents such as the mission statement, annual reports, sales brochures, or websites. For example, Keurig Green Mountain (formerly known as Green Mountain Coffee) is a pioneer in helping struggling coffee growers by paying them fair trade prices. The company also offers microloans to coffee-growing families to underwrite business ventures that diversify agricultural economies.[60]

Step 2: Identifying Stakeholder Groups

In managing this stage, it is important to recognize stakeholder needs, wants, and desires. There are many important issues that gain visibility because key constituencies such as consumer groups, regulators, or the media express an interest. When agreement, collaboration, or even confrontations exist on an issue, there is a need for a decision-making process. A model of collaboration to overcome the adversarial approaches to problem solving has been suggested. Managers can identify relevant stakeholders that may be affected by or may influence the development of organizational policy.

Stakeholders have some level of power over a business because they are in the position to withhold, or at least threaten to withhold, organizational resources. Stakeholders have most power when their own survival is not really affected by the success of the organization and when they have access to vital organizational resources. For example, most consumers of shoes do not have a specific need to buy Nike shoes. Therefore, if they decide to boycott Nike, they have to endure only minor inconveniences. Nevertheless, their loyalty to Nike is vital to the continued success of the sport apparel giant. The proper assessment of the power held by a given stakeholder community also requires an evaluation of the extent to which that community can collaborate with others to pressure the firm.

Step 3: Identifying Stakeholder Issues

Together, Steps 1 and 2 lead to the identification of the stakeholders who are both the most powerful and legitimate. The level of power and legitimacy determines the degree of urgency in addressing their needs. Step 3 consists then in understanding the nature of the main issues of concern to these stakeholders. Conditions for collaboration exist when problems are so complex that multiple stakeholders are required to resolve the issue and the weaknesses of adversarial approaches are understood.

For example, obesity in children continues to be a concern across groups and stakeholders. In recent years special interest groups and government programs have been directed toward alleviating this issue; however, recent reports have shown that more progress has yet to be made. The rate of childhood obesity is still up from 15 years ago, and statistics comparing more recent years show little change. The rate of obesity in children ages 2–5 years has decreased, but overall the rate is stagnating. This is important for businesses to remember when designing and marketing new products for children's use.[61]

Step 4: Assessing the Organization's Commitment to Social Responsibility

Steps 1 through 3 consist of generating information about social responsibility among a variety of influencers in and around the organization. Step 4 brings these three first stages together to arrive at an understanding of social responsibility that specifically matches the organization of interest. This general definition will then be used to evaluate current practices and to select concrete social responsibility initiatives. Firms such as Starbucks have selected activities that address stakeholder concerns. Starbucks has formalized its initiatives in official documents such as annual reports, webpages, and company brochures. They have a website devoted to social responsibility. Starbucks is concerned with the environment and integrates policies and programs throughout all aspects of operations to minimize their environmental impact. They also have many community building programs that help them be good neighbors and contribute positively to the communities where their partners and customers live, work, and play.[62]

Step 5: Identifying Resources and Determining Urgency

The prioritization of stakeholders and issues along with the assessment of past performance provides for allocating resources. Two main criteria can be considered. First, the levels of financial and organizational investments required by different actions should be determined. A second criterion when prioritizing social responsibility challenges is urgency. When the challenge under consideration is viewed as significant and when stakeholder pressures on the issue could be expected, then the challenge can be treated as urgent. For example, the White House and the Department of Agriculture are considering banning advertising for junk food in schools. This would have a major impact on food and beverage companies, as they spend approximately $149 million to market in schools. Laws in California have already made it more difficult to have junk food in elementary schools.[63]

Step 6: Gaining Stakeholder Feedback

Stakeholder feedback can be generated through a variety of means. First, stakeholders' general assessment of the firm and its practices can be obtained through satisfaction or reputation surveys. Second, to gauge stakeholders' perceptions of the firm's contributions to specific issues, stakeholder-generated media such as blogs, websites, podcasts, and newsletters can be assessed. Third, more formal research may be conducted using focus groups, observation, and surveys. Websites can be both positive and negative; for example, user review sites such as Yelp have both generated and decreased sales based on reviews left on the site. Because so many consumers refer to these websites before visiting a business, many companies are focusing on good customer service to ensure good reviews. However, these reviews can be misleading and do harm to a business. For example, a small salon owner expressed concern over the effect of one negative review left by a customer who never set foot in her location. The customer perceived the salon owner as rude and rushed in a telephone call and wrote about it. The owner has seen a decrease in business that she attributes to the review.[64]

In the process of developing stakeholder relationships, most strategies are focused on increasing the trust that a stakeholder has in a particular company. Of course, there is not a "one size fits all" approach for building and sustaining trusting relationships with stakeholders. As we discussed earlier in the chapter, not all stakeholders engage with a company with the same level of intensity or locus of control, whether internal or external. For example, employees are highly engaged internal stakeholders while suppliers may be considered low intensity external stakeholders. Depending on the specific issues at hand, historical interactions, relationships intensity, and other factors, managers must understand the relative importance of transparency, competence, benevolence, integrity, values, and other factors.[65]

LINK BETWEEN STAKEHOLDER RELATIONSHIPS AND SOCIAL RESPONSIBILITY

You may be wondering what motivations companies have for pursuing stakeholder relationships. As the previous section indicates, a great deal of time, effort, and commitment goes into the process of developing and implementing a stakeholder perspective. Sometimes, however, these efforts do not have the desired effect. Coca-Cola and PepsiCo have received criticism regarding the messages of their social responsibility initiatives when compared with their perceived role in the obesity issue. For example, Coca-Cola partnered with the Rwandan government and other organizations to open EKOCENTER, a site that will provide Internet services, Coca-Cola products, clean water, and other basic goods for people in the local community. Despite Coca-Cola's impact on communities, some critics accuse the firm of promoting soft drinks in low-income areas that would benefit more from nutritious items rather than sugary unhealthy drinks.[66] As was discussed in Chapter 1, social responsibility is a relational approach and involves the views and stakes of a number of groups. Stakeholders are engaged in the relationships that both challenge and support a company's efforts. Thus, without a solid understanding of stakeholders and their interests, a firm may miss important trends and changes in its environment and not achieve strategic social responsibility.

Rather than holding all companies to one standard, our approach to evaluating performance and effectiveness resides in the specific expectations and actual results that develop between each organization and its stakeholders. Max Clarkson, an influential contributor to our understanding of stakeholders, sums up this view:

> *Performance is what counts. Performance can be measured and evaluated. Whether a corporation and its management are motivated by enlightened self-interest, common sense or high standards of ethical behavior cannot be determined by empirical methodologies available today. These are not questions that can be answered by economists, sociologists, psychologists, or any other kind of social scientist. They are interesting questions, but they are not relevant when it comes to evaluating a company's performance in managing its relationships with its stakeholder groups.[67]*

Although critics and some researchers may seek answers and evidence as to the motivations of business for social responsibility, we are interested in what companies are actually doing that is positive, negative, or neutral for their stakeholders and their stakeholders' interests. The Reactive–Defensive–Accommodative–Proactive Scale (see Table 2.7) provides a method for assessing a company's strategy and performance with each stakeholder. This scale is based on a continuum of strategy options

TABLE 2.7 The Reactive–Defensive–Accommodative–Proactive Scale

Rating	Strategy	Performance	Example
Reactive	Deny responsibility	Doing less than required	Exxon's refusal to continue oil spill cleanup after a certain date
Defensive	Admit responsibility, but fight it	Doing the least that is required	Valero Energy claims it meets federal regulation; therefore community complaints are not legitimate
Accommodative	Accept responsibility	Doing all that is required	General Motors promised job security if productivity gains were realized
Proactive	Anticipate responsibility	Doing more than is required	Xerox shares product blueprints with suppliers and takes suggestions before production

Source: Adapted from Max B. E. Clarkson, "A Stakeholder Framework for Analyzing and Evaluating Corporate Social Performance," *Academy of Management Review* 20 (January 1995): 92–117; I. M. Jawahar and Gary McLaughlin, "Toward a Descriptive Stakeholder Theory: An Organizational Life Cycle Approach," *Academy of Management Review* 26 (July 2001): 397–414; Ian Wilson, "What one company is doing about today's demands on business," in G. A. Steiner (Ed.), *Changing business-society interrelations*, Los Angeles, CA: Graduate School of Management, UCLA, 1975.

and performance outcomes with respect to stakeholders.[68] This evaluation can take place as stakeholder issues arise or are identified. Therefore, it is possible for one company to be rated at several different levels because of varying performance and transitions over time. For example, a poorly handled crisis situation may provide feedback for continuous improvement that creates more satisfactory performance in the future. Or a company may demonstrate a proactive stance toward employees yet be defensive with consumer activists.

The reactive approach involves denying responsibility and doing less than is required. This approach can be characterized as "fighting it all the way."[69] A firm that fails to invest in safety and health measures for employees is denying its responsibilities. An organization with a defensive strategy acknowledges reluctantly and partially the responsibility issues that may be raised by its stakeholders. A firm in this category fulfills basic legal obligations and demonstrates the minimal responsibility discussed in Chapter 1. With an accommodative strategy, a company attempts to satisfy stakeholder demands by doing all that is required and may be seen as progressive because it is obviously open to this expanded model of business relationships.[70] Today, many organizations are giving money and other resources to community organizations as a way of demonstrating social responsibility. Finally, the proactive approach not only accepts but also anticipates stakeholder interests. In this case, a company sincerely aligns legitimate stakeholder views with its responsibilities and will do more than is required to meet them.[71] Hoechst, a German life sciences company now part of Aventis, gradually assumed the proactive orientation with communities in which it operates. The initiation of a community discussion group led to information sharing and trust building and helped transform Hoechst into a society-driven company.[72]

The Reactive–Defensive–Accommodative–Proactive Scale is useful because it evaluates real practice and allows an organization to see its strengths and weaknesses within each stakeholder relationship. SABMiller, the second largest brewer in the world, uses a risk assessment program to understand the stakeholders and issues that may pose a potential risk to its reputation. These risks are prioritized, planned for, monitored, and if necessary, responded to if SABMiller cannot predict, preempt, or avoid the concern.[73] Results from a stakeholder assessment like the one at SABMiller should be included in the **social audit**, the process of assessing and reporting a firm's performance in adopting a strategic focus for fulfilling the economic, legal, ethical, and philanthropic social responsibilities expected of it by its stakeholders. Because stakeholders are so important to the concept of social responsibility, as well as to business success, Chapters 3–12 are devoted to exploring significant stakeholder relationships and issues.

social audit
The process of assessing and reporting a firm's performance in adopting a strategic focus for fulfilling the economic, legal, ethical, and philanthropic social responsibilities expected of it by its stakeholders.

SUMMARY

Stakeholders refer to those people and groups who have a "stake" in some aspect of a company's products, operations, markets, industry, or outcomes. The relationship between organizations and their stakeholders is a two-way street.

The historical assumption that the key objective of business is profit maximization led to the belief that business is accountable primarily to investors and others involved in the market and economic aspects of the organization. In the latter half of the twentieth century, perceptions of business accountability evolved to include both market constituencies that are directly involved and affected by the business purpose (e.g., investors, employees, customers, and other business partners) and nonmarket constituencies that are not always directly tied to issues of profitability and performance (e.g., the general community, media, government, and special-interest groups).

In the stakeholder model, relationships, investors, employees, and suppliers provide inputs for a company to benefit stakeholders. This approach assumes a relatively mechanistic, simplistic, and non-stakeholder view of business. The stakeholder model assumes a two-way relationship between the firm and a host of stakeholders. This approach recognizes additional stakeholders and acknowledges the two-way dialog and effects that exist with a firm's internal and external environment.

Primary stakeholders are fundamental to a company's operations and survival and include shareholders and investors, employees, customers, suppliers, and public stakeholders, such as government and the community. Secondary stakeholders influence and/or are affected by the company but are neither engaged in transactions with the firm nor essential for its survival.

As more firms conduct business overseas, they encounter the complexity of stakeholder issues and relationships in tandem with other business operations and decisions. Although general awareness of the concept of stakeholders is relatively high around the world, the importance of stakeholders varies from country to country.

A stakeholder has power to the extent that it can gain access to coercive, utilitarian, or symbolic means to impose or communicate its views to the organization. Such power may be coercive, utilitarian, or symbolic. Legitimacy is the perception or belief that a stakeholder's actions are proper, desirable, or appropriate within a given context. Stakeholders exercise greater pressures on managers and organizations when they stress the urgency of their claims. These attributes can change over time and context.

The degree to which a firm understands and addresses stakeholder demands can be referred to as a stakeholder orientation. This orientation comprises three sets of activities: (1) the organization-wide generation of data about stakeholder groups and assessment of the firm's effects on these groups, (2) the distribution of this information throughout the firm, and (3) the organization's responsiveness as a whole to this intelligence.

Reputation management is the process of building and sustaining a company's good name and generating positive feedback from stakeholders.

The process of reputation management involves the interaction of organizational identity (how the firm wants to be viewed), organizational image (how stakeholders initially perceive the firm), organizational performance (actual interaction between the company and stakeholders), and organizational reputation (the collective view of stakeholders after interactions with the company). Stakeholders will reassess their views of the company on the basis of how the company has actually performed.

Crisis management is the process of handling a high-impact event characterized by ambiguity and the need for swift action. Some researchers describe an organization's progress through a prodromal, or precrisis, stage to the acute stage, chronic stage, and finally, crisis resolution. Stakeholders need a quick response with information about how the company plans to resolve the crisis, as well as what they can do to mitigate negative effects to themselves. It is also necessary to communicate specific issues to stakeholder groups, including remorse for the event, guidelines as to how the organization is going to address the crisis, and criteria regarding how stakeholder groups will be compensated for negative effects.

Companies are searching for ways to develop long-term, collaborative relationships with their stakeholders. These relationships involve both tangible and intangible investments. Investments and lessons learned through the process of developing a dialog and relationship with one stakeholder should add value to other stakeholder relationships. These efforts result in social capital, an asset that resides in relationships and is characterized by mutual goals and trust.

The first step in developing stakeholder relationships is to acknowledge and actively monitor the concerns of all legitimate stakeholders. A firm should adopt processes and modes of behavior that are sensitive to the concerns and capabilities of each stakeholder. Information should be communicated consistently across all stakeholders. A firm should be willing to acknowledge and openly address potential conflicts. Investments in education, training, and information will improve employees' understanding of and relationships with stakeholders. Relationships with stakeholders need to be periodically assessed through both formal and informal means. Sharing feedback with stakeholders helps establish the two-way dialog that characterizes the stakeholder model.

An organization that develops effective corporate governance and understands the importance of business ethics and social responsibility in achieving success should develop some processes for managing these important concerns. Although there are many different approaches, we provide some steps that have been found effective to utilize the stakeholder framework in managing responsibility and business ethics. The steps include (1) assessing the corporate culture, (2) identifying stakeholder groups, (3) identifying stakeholder issues, (4) assessing the organization's commitment to social responsibility, (5) identifying resources and determining urgency, and (6) gaining stakeholder feedback. The importance of these steps is to include feedback from relevant stakeholders in formulating organizational strategy and implementation.

The Reactive–Defensive–Accommodative–Proactive Scale provides a method for assessing a company's strategy and performance with one stakeholder. The reactive approach involves denying responsibility and doing less than is required. The defensive approach acknowledges only reluctantly and partially the responsibility issues that may be raised by the firm's stakeholders. The accommodative strategy attempts to satisfy stakeholder demands. The proactive approach accepts and anticipates stakeholder interests. Results from this stakeholder assessment should be included in the social audit, which assesses and reports a firm's performance in fulfilling the economic, legal, ethical, and philanthropic social responsibilities expected of it by its stakeholders.

Responsible Business Debate

Prioritizing Stakeholder Concerns

Issue: *A stakeholder or shareholder orientation—whose company is it?*

For decades, the question of "Whose company is it?" has permeated discussions of the role of business in society. Famously, some economists have long argued for the primacy of profit, noting that without economic stability and prospects for growth, a firm cannot continue to pay employees, buy from suppliers, pay taxes, and meet other economic and legal expectations. Adam Smith made this point succinctly, "It is not from the benevolence of the butcher, the brewer, or the baker that we expect our dinner, but from their regard to their own interest." In the United States and United Kingdom, the belief is that shareholders are the owners of firms and managers have a fiduciary responsibility to act in the interests of shareholders. The shareholder orientation is dominant in most business and investment communities, although this mind-set is shifting.

In other countries, a stakeholder, not shareholder, orientation is the norm. Several European countries operate under a system of "co-determination," where both employees and shareholders in large companies hold seats on the oversight board and are required to consider multiple interests in decision making. In Denmark,

employees in firms with more than 35 workers elect one-third of the firm's board members, with a minimum of two. In Sweden, companies with more than 25 employees have two labor representatives appointed to the board. In large German corporations, employees and shareholders hold an equal number of seats. Finally, in Japan, executives can be liable for managerial negligence, but do not have fiduciary duties to shareholders and are expected to meet an array of stakeholder expectations.

There Are Two Sides to Every Issue

1. Defend the belief that companies exist first and foremost for the benefit of shareholders and investors. For what reasons should the maximization of shareholder value be the accepted corporate paradigm?
2. Defend the belief that companies, in addition to shareholders and investors, have equally important stakeholders, such as employees, customers and suppliers. What about responsibilities to the community, society, and the natural environment?

Sources: "Whose Company Is It?: New Insights into the Debate over Shareholders vs. Stakeholders," http://knowledge.wharton.upenn.edu/article.cfm?articleid=1826 (accessed July 7, 2016). Tibor R. Machan, "Stakeholder vs. Shareholder Theory of the Ethics of Corporate Management," *International Journal of Economics and Business Research* 1 (2009): 12–20.

KEY TERMS

primary stakeholders (p. 46)
secondary stakeholders (p. 46)
stakeholder interaction model
    (p. 48)

stakeholder orientation (p. 49)
power (p. 51)
legitimacy (p. 52)
urgency (p. 53)

reputation management (p. 54)
crisis management (p. 59)
social capital (p. 62)
social audit (p. 68)

DISCUSSION QUESTIONS

1. Define stakeholder in your own terms. Compare your definition with the definition used in this chapter.
2. What is the difference between primary and secondary stakeholders? Why is it important for companies to make this distinction?
3. How do legitimacy, urgency, and power attributes positively and negatively affect a stakeholder's ability to develop relationships with organizations?
4. What is reputation management? Explain why companies are concerned about their reputation and its effects on stakeholders. What are the four

elements of reputation management? Why is it important to manage these elements?
5. Define crisis management. What should a company facing a crisis do to satisfy its stakeholders and protect its reputation?
6. Describe the process of developing stakeholder relationships. What parts of the process seem most important? What parts seem most difficult?
7. How can a stakeholder orientation be implemented to improve social responsibility?
8. What are the differences between the reactive, defensive, accommodative, and proactive approaches to stakeholder relationships?

EXPERIENTIAL EXERCISE

Choose two companies in different industries and visit their respective websites. Peruse these sites for information that is directed at three company stakeholders: employees, customers, and the media. For example, a company that places its annual reports online may be

appealing primarily to the interests of investors. Make a list of the types of information that are on the site and indicate how the information might be used and perceived by these three stakeholder groups. What differences and similarities did you find between the two companies?

THAI DIE...ENVIRONMENTAL EXPLOITATION OR ECONOMIC DEVELOPMENT: WHAT WOULD YOU DO?

Literally hundreds of buildings dotted the ground below and the thousands of cars on highways looked like ants on a mission. The jet airliner made its way to the Bangkok International Airport and eased into the humid afternoon. The group of four passed through customs control and looked for the limousine provided by Suvar Corporation, their Thai liaison in this new business venture. Representing Global Amusements were the vice-president of corporate development, director of Asian operations, vice-president of global relations, and director of governmental relations for Southeast Asia.

Global Amusements, headquartered in London, was considering the development of a Thai cultural amusement center on the island of Phuket. Phuket is a tourist destination known for its stunning beaches, fine resorts, and famous Thai hospitality. Both Global Amusements and Suvar Corporation believed Phuket was a great candidate for a new project. The amusement center would focus on the history of Thailand and include a variety of live performances, rides, exhibits, and restaurants. Domestic and international tourists who visited Phuket would be the primary target market.

Global Amusements had been in business for nearly 20 years and currently used a joint venture approach in establishing new properties. Suvar was its Thai partner, and the two firms had been successful two years ago in developing a water amusement park outside Bangkok. Phuket could hold much promise, but there were likely to be questions about the potential destruction of its beauty and the exploitation of this well-preserved island and cultural reserve. These concerns had been heightened as the island slowly recovered from the 2004 tsunami and set a course for managing future development.

Following a day to adjust to the time zone and refine the strategy for the visit, the next three days would be spent in Bangkok, meeting with various company and governmental officials who had a stake in the proposed amusement facility. After a short flight to Phuket, the group would be the guest of the Southern Office of the Tourism Authority of Thailand for nearly a week. This part of the trip would involve visits to possible sites as well as meetings with island government officials and local interest groups.

After arriving at the hotel, the four employees of Global Amusement agreed to meet later that evening to discuss their strategy for the visit. One of their main concerns was the development of an effective stakeholder analysis. Each member of the group was asked to bring a list of primary and secondary stakeholders and indicate the various concerns or "stakes" that each might have with the proposed project. What would you do?

CHAPTER THREE

Corporate Governance

Chapter Objectives

- To define corporate governance
- To describe the history and practice of corporate governance
- To examine key issues to consider in designing corporate governance systems
- To describe the application of corporate governance principles around the world
- To provide information on the future of corporate governance

Chapter Outline

Corporate Governance Defined

History of Corporate Governance

Corporate Governance and Social Responsibility

Issues in Corporate Governance Systems

Corporate Governance Around the World

Future of Corporate Governance

Credit Suisse: A Case of Bankrupt Leadership

Credit Suisse is the first bank in more than a decade to admit to a crime in the United States. The company was charged with conspiring to aid American clients in tax evasion. Government officials claim that hundreds of Credit Suisse employees, including managers, helped American clients evade taxes to the Internal Revenue Service by concealing funds, destroying records, and failing to accurately disclose financial information. Approximately 22,000 Americans had accounts with Credit Suisse, owning assets worth between $10 and $20 billion.

The crime was discovered through an investigation involving 100,000 internal documents. Some of the documents revealed that Credit Suisse bankers had helped Americans evade taxes through such entities as secret offshore accounts. Such systemic misconduct demonstrates that Credit Suisse not only lacked effective risk management but was also deficient in its oversight responsibilities.

Credit Suisse maintains that its internal investigation did not discover any leadership failures that led to the scandal. However, the Federal Sentencing Guidelines for Organizations (FSGO) clearly places the burden of knowledge on the company's leadership. According to the FSGO, the board of directors and company leaders are responsible for maintaining an effective ethics and compliance program with internal control measures. This scandal seems to indicate a failure to have strong values and enforce the spirit of the laws of the customers' home countries.

The U.S. government believes this guilty plea will help demonstrate that nobody, even MNCs, is above the law. However, the impact this will have on Credit Suisse is questionable. In addition to its guilty plea, Credit Suisse must pay a fine of $2.6 billion and agree to independent monitoring for two years. Although a guilty plea would generally mean that Credit Suisse would have to give up its investment-adviser license, the Securities and Exchange Commission (SEC) has granted the bank a temporary exemption.

Some have called for the resignation of Credit Suisse's American CEO for corporate governance failures. Others point to the fact that Credit Suisse is not being forced to disclose the names of American tax evaders. Credit Suisse claims that this is due to Swiss law, which has traditionally valued the privacy of clients. This brings up the issue of corporate governance in Switzerland. The laws of Switzerland regarding this issue are different than those in the United States, which makes it more difficult to effectively prosecute a Swiss company. Finally, critics have also accused U.S. law enforcement of a lack of governance controls, as they appeared less than eager to pursue the matter for many years.[1]

Business decisions today are increasingly placed under a microscope by stakeholders and the media, especially those made by high-level personnel in publicly held corporations. Stakeholders are demanding greater transparency in business, meaning that company motives and actions must be clear, open for discussion, and subject to scrutiny. Recent scandals and the associated focus on the role of business in society have highlighted a need for systems that take into account the goals and expectations of various stakeholders, as the example of Credit Suisse's guilty plea illustrates. To respond to these pressures, businesses must effectively implement policies that provide strategic guidance on appropriate courses of action. This focus is part of corporate governance, the system of checks and balances that ensures that organizations are fulfilling the goals of social responsibility.

Governance procedures and policies are typically discussed in the context of publicly traded firms, especially as they relate to corporations' responsibilities to investors.[2] However, the trend is toward discussing governance within many industry sectors, including nonprofits, small businesses, and family-owned enterprises. Corporate governance deserves broader consideration because there is evidence of a link between good governance and strong social responsibility. Corporate governance and accountability are key drivers of change for business in the twenty-first century. The corporate misconduct at firms such as Credit Suisse, J.P. Morgan, and Walmart represent fundamental failures in corporate governance systems that provide oversight. Investors and other stakeholders must be able to trust management while boards of directors oversee managerial decisions. In the most recent recession, some of the nation's oldest and most respected financial institutions teetered on the brink of failure and were either bailed out or acquired by other firms. Many problems in the financial sector come from boards of directors allowing excessive risk taking.

In this chapter, we define corporate governance and integrate the concept with the other elements of social responsibility. Then, we examine the corporate governance framework used in this book. Next, we trace the evolution of corporate governance and provide information on the status of corporate governance systems in several countries. We look at the history of corporate governance and the relationship of corporate governance to social responsibility. We also examine primary issues that should be considered in the development and improvement of corporate governance systems, including the roles of boards of directors, shareholder activism, internal control and risk management, and executive compensation. Finally, we consider the future of corporate governance and indicate how strong governance is tied to corporate performance and economic growth. Our approach in this chapter is to demonstrate that corporate governance is a fundamental aspect of social responsibility.

CORPORATE GOVERNANCE DEFINED

In a general sense, the term *governance* relates to the exercise of oversight, control, and authority. For example, most institutions, governments, and businesses are organized so that oversight, control, and authority are clearly delineated. These organizations usually have an owner, president, chief executive officer, and a board of directors that serves as the ultimate authority on decisions and actions. The board of directors should have final authority on decisions, including the ability to approve corporate strategy, provide financial oversight, and even remove the CEO. Nonprofit organizations, such as homeowners associations, have a president and a board of directors to make decisions in the interest of a community of homeowners. A clear delineation of power and accountability helps stakeholders understand why and how the organization chooses and achieves its goals. This delineation also demonstrates who bears the ultimate risk for organizational decisions. Legally, Sarbanes-Oxley and the FGSO places responsibility and accountability on top officers and the board of directors. Although many companies have adopted decentralized decision-making, empowerment, team projects, and less hierarchical structures, governance remains a required mechanism for ensuring accountability to regulatory authorities. Even if a company has adopted a consensus approach for its operations, there has to be authority for delegating tasks, making tough and controversial decisions, and balancing power throughout the organization. Governance also provides oversight to uncover and address mistakes, risks, as well as ethical and legal misconduct. Consider the failure of boards at Enron and AIG to address risks and provide internal controls to prevent misconduct. More recently, boards at J.C. Penney and J.P. Morgan have been criticized for issues such as failing to have a solid succession plan in place and not exerting enough oversight to prevent misconduct. On the other hand, corporate governance consultants have praised the boards of Eaton Corporation and Abbott Laboratories for strong benchmarking and incentive pay systems.[3]

We define **corporate governance** as the formal system of oversight, accountability, and control for organizational decisions and resources. Oversight relates to a system of checks and balances that limit employees' and managers' opportunities to deviate from policies and codes of conduct. Accountability relates to how well the content of workplace decisions is aligned with a firm's stated strategic direction. Control involves the process of auditing and improving organizational decisions and actions. The philosophy that is embraced by a board or firm regarding oversight, accountability, and control directly affects how corporate governance works. Table 3.1 describes some examples of important corporate governance decisions.

corporate governance
Formal system of oversight, accountability, and control for organizational decisions and resources.

Corporate Governance Framework

The majority of businesses and many courses taught in colleges of business operate under the belief that the purpose of business is to maximize profits for shareholders. In 1919, the Michigan Supreme Court in the case of *Dodge v. Ford Motor Co.*[4] ruled that a business exists for the profit of shareholders, and the board of directors should focus on that objective. On the other hand, the stakeholder model places the board of directors

TABLE 3.1 Corporate Governance Decisions

Decisions	Examples
Ethical and legal risks	Approve ethics and compliance program
Regulatory financial reporting	Audit committee oversees financial reporting
Compensation	Committee approves compensation for top officers
Strategic	Approves decisions related to strategies, mergers, and acquisitions
Financial	Major decisions related to the use of financial assets, including issuing stocks and bonds
Stakeholder	Decisions regarding employee benefits, shareholder rights, and contributions to society

in the central position to balance the interests and conflicts of the various constituencies. As we will see, there should be no conflict between maximizing profits and maintaining a stakeholder orientation. External control of the corporation includes government regulation but also includes key stakeholders such as employees, consumers, and communities, who exert pressures for responsible conduct. Many of the obligations to balance stakeholder interest have been institutionalized in legislation that provides incentives for responsible conduct. It is not correct to assume that it is necessary to take advantage of or ignore stakeholders to maximize profits. There is much evidence that a stakeholder orientation maximizes profits in the long run. By taking preventive action against misconduct, a company may avoid onerous penalties should a violation occur. Top officers and the board of directors are legally responsible for accurate financial reporting, as well as providing oversight to manage ethical decision-making. Today, most companies understand that ethical decision-making supports the firm's reputation and the cooperation of stakeholders.

Therefore, the failure to balance stakeholder interests can result in a failure to maximize shareholders' wealth. Sometimes the issue is so major that fines and serious penalties occur as a result. For instance, the manager of a home health-care company was convicted of Medicare fraud for directing employees to visit patients who were physically capable of leaving their homes and having them bill at the highest level. This lack of ethical leadership demonstrated a true failure in corporate governance.[5] Most firms are moving more toward a balanced stakeholder model, as they see that this approach will sustain the relationships necessary for long-run success.

Both directors and officers of corporations are fiduciaries for the shareholders. Fiduciaries are persons placed in positions of trust who use due care and loyalty in acting on behalf of the best interests of the organization. There is a duty of care, also called a *duty of diligence*, to make informed and prudent decisions.[6] Directors have an obligation to avoid ethical misconduct in their role and to provide leadership in decisions to prevent ethical misconduct in the organization. Directors are not held responsible for negative outcomes if they are informed and diligent in their decision-making. For example, the directors of General Motors (GM) must remain diligent in ensuring that financial reporting is accurate to the best of their knowledge. Manufacturing cars that lose market share is a serious concern, although it is not a legal issue. On the other hand, if the directors know that the firm is covering up a safety concern, then they can be held responsible. This means directors have an obligation to request information, research, and use accountants, attorneys, and obtain the services of consultants in matters where they need assistance or advice.

The duty of loyalty means that all decisions should be in the interests of the corporation and its stakeholders. Conflicts of interest exist when a director uses the position to obtain personal gain, usually at the expense of the organization. Two hedge funds opposed United Continental Holdings Inc.'s decision to appoint the CEO the additional role of Chairman and questioned the amount of compensation he received. The hedge funds asked shareholders to consider six new directors for the board. Many corporate governance experts have criticized appointing the same person as both CEO and Chairman, although it is common occurrence in U.S. companies.[7]

Officer compensation packages challenge directors, especially those on the board who are not independent. Directors have an opportunity to vote for others' compensation in return for their own increased compensation. Opportunities to know about the investments, business ventures, and stock market information create issues that could violate the duty of loyalty. Insider trading of a firm's stock is illegal and violations can result in serious punishment. A probe of Samsung involving several employees, including president-level executives, was launched to investigate whether the employees used insider trading tips to profit from an upcoming purchase. The employees allegedly purchased $43 million in a Samsung de facto holding company before it disclosed plans to purchase an affiliate firm. This knowledge would have provided them with an unfair advantage that other shareholders did not have. If found guilty, employees could face fines and jail time.[8] The ethical and legal obligations of directors and officers interface with their fiduciary relationships to the company. Ethical values should guide decisions and buffer the possibility of illegal conduct. With increased pressure on directors to provide oversight for organizational ethics and compliance, there is a trend toward director training to increase their competence in ethics program development as well as other areas, such as accounting.

Corporate governance establishes fundamental systems and processes for oversight, accountability, and control. This requires investigating, disciplining, and planning for recovery and continuous improvement. Effective corporate governance creates compliance and values so that employees feel that integrity is at the core of competitiveness.[9] Even if a company has adopted a consensus approach to decision-making, there should be oversight and authority for delegating tasks, making difficult and sometimes controversial decisions, balancing power throughout the firm, and maintaining social responsibility. Governance also provides mechanisms for identifying risks and planning for recovery when mistakes or problems occur.

The development of a stakeholder orientation should interface with the corporation's governance structure. Corporate governance is also part of a firm's corporate culture that establishes the integrity of all relationships. A governance system that does not provide checks and balances creates opportunities for top managers to put their own self-interests before those of important stakeholders. Medical products distributor McKesson Corp. announced changes in corporate governance at the behest of stakeholders. CEO John H. Hammergren's compensation has been called into question for reaching unprecedented levels, and the restructuring addressed these issues. The company reevaluated other aspects of governance and plans to implement more changes in phases.[10] Concerns about the need for greater corporate governance are not limited to the United States. Reforms in governance structures and issues are occurring all over the world.[11] In many nations, companies are being pressured to implement stronger corporate governance mechanisms by international investors; by the process of becoming privatized after years of unaccountability as state companies; or by the desire to imitate successful governance movements in the United States, Japan, and the European Union (EU).[12] As the business world becomes more global, standardization of governance becomes important in order for multinational and international companies to maintain standards and a level of control.

Table 3.2 lists examples of major corporate governance issues. These issues normally involve strategic-level decisions and actions taken by boards of directors, business owners, top executives, and other managers

TABLE 3.2 Corporate Governance Issues

Shareholder rights
Executive compensation
Composition and structure of the board of directors
Auditing and control
Risk management
CEO selection and termination decisions
Integrity of financial reporting
Stakeholder participation and input into decisions
Compliance with corporate governance reform
Role of the CEO in board decisions
Organizational ethics programs

with high levels of authority and accountability. Although these people have often been relatively free from scrutiny, changes in technology, consumer activism, government attention, recent ethical scandals, and other factors have brought new attention to such issues as transparency, executive pay, risk and control, resource accountability, strategic direction, stockholder rights, and other decisions made for the organization.

HISTORY OF CORPORATE GOVERNANCE

In the United States, a discussion of corporate governance draws on many parallels with the goals and values held by the U.S. Founding Fathers.[13] As we mentioned earlier in the chapter, governance involves a system of checks and balances, a concept associated with the distribution of power within the executive, judiciary, and legislative branches of the U.S. government. The U.S. Constitution and other documents have a strong focus on accountability, individual rights, and the representation of broad interests in decision-making and resource allocation.

In the late 1800s and early 1900s, corporations were headed by such familiar names as Carnegie, DuPont, and Rockefeller. These "captains of industry" had ownership investment and managerial control over their businesses. Thus, there was less reason to talk about corporate governance because the owner of the firm was the same individual who made strategic decisions about the business. The owner primarily bore the consequences—positive or negative—of decisions. During the twentieth century, however, an increasing number of public companies and investors brought about a shift in the separation of ownership and control. By the 1930s, corporate ownership was dispersed across a large number of individuals. This raised new questions about control and accountability for organizational resources and decisions.

One of the first known anecdotes that helped shape our current understanding of accountability and control in business occurred in the 1930s. In 1932, Lewis Gilbert, a stockholder in New York's Consolidated Gas Company, found his questions repeatedly ignored at the firm's annual shareholders' meeting. Gilbert and his brother took the problem to the federal government and pushed for reform, which led to the creation of the U.S. Securities and Exchange Commission, which requires corporations to allow shareholder resolutions to be brought to a vote of all stockholders. Because of the Gilbert brothers' activism, the SEC formalized the process by which executives and boards of directors respond to the concerns and questions of investors.[14]

Since the mid-1900s, the approach to corporate governance has involved a legal discussion of principals and agents to the business relationship. Essentially, owners are "principals" who hire "agents," the executives, to run the business. A key goal of businesses is to align the interests of principals and agents so that organizational value and viability are maintained. Achieving this balance has been difficult, as evidenced by these business terms coined by media—*junk bonds, empire building, golden parachute*, and *merger madness*—all of which have negative connotations. In these cases, the long-term value and competitive stance of organizations were traded for short-term financial gains or rewards. The results of this short-term view included workforce reduction, closed manufacturing plants, struggling communities, and a generally negative perception of corporate leadership. In our philosophy of social responsibility, these long-term effects should be considered alongside decisions designed to generate short-run gains in financial performance.

The Sarbanes-Oxley Act was the most significant piece of corporate governance reform at the time since the 1930s. Under these rules, both CEOs and CFOs are required to certify that their quarterly and annual reports accurately reflect performance and comply with the requirements of the SEC. Among other changes, the act also required more independence of boards of directors, protected whistle-blowers, and established a Public Company Accounting Oversight Board. The New York Stock Exchange (NYSE) and NASDAQ also overhauled the governance standards required for listed firms. Business ethics, director qualifications, unique concerns of foreign firms, loans to officers and directors, internal auditing, and many other issues were part of the NYSE and NASDAQ reforms.[15]

Despite the implementation of Sarbanes-Oxley, corporate misconduct and the quest for short-term profits led the U.S. financial system to a near collapse during the last recession. The cause was a pervasive use of instruments like credit default swaps, risky debt like subprime lending, and corruption in major corporations. The government was forced to step in and bail out many financial companies. Later on, because of the weak financial system and reduced consumption, the government also had to step in to help major automotive companies GM and Chrysler. The U.S. government became a majority shareholder in GM, an unprecedented move (it has since divested itself of its final shares). Not since the Great Depression and President Franklin Delano Roosevelt has the United States seen such widespread government intervention and regulation—something that most deem necessary but is nevertheless worrisome to free market capitalists. The basic assumptions of capitalism are under debate as countries around the world work to stabilize markets and question those that managed the money of individual corporations and nonprofits. The latest recession caused many to question government institutions that provide oversight and regulation. As changes are made, there is a need to address issues related to law, ethics, and the required level of compliance necessary for government and business to serve the public interest.

Finance Reforms

The lack of effective control and accountability mechanisms prompted a strong interest in corporate governance. In 2010, the Dodd-Frank Wall Street Reform and Consumer Protection Act was passed to protect consumers from overly complex financial instruments, better regulate the financial industry, and prevent too-big-to-fail financial institutions. (One of the reasons why the government had to intervene during the financial meltdown was that allowing large institutions such as Bank of America or AIG to fail would devastate the economy at a much higher rate.) The Dodd-Frank Act established a Consumer Financial Protection Bureau (CFPB), among other agencies. The CFPB is similar to the Bureau of Consumer Protection in that its purpose is to protect consumers from being deceived by institutions selling high-risk financial products. The Dodd-Frank Act will be discussed in detail in the following chapter. Boards of directors have the responsibility to provide oversight and compliance with regulation.

Beyond the legal issues associated with governance, there has also been interest in the board's role in social responsibility and stakeholder engagement. Table 3.3 provides a list of companies with good corporate governance. The board of directors should provide leadership for social responsibility initiatives. It is apparent that some boards have been assuming greater responsibility for strategic decisions and have decided to focus on building more effective social responsibility.

TABLE 3.3 Companies with Good Corporate Governance

| The Allstate Corporation |
| AMN Healthcare |
| CVS Health Corporation |
| General Electric |
| Graybar |
| Lockheed Marting |
| Marsh & McLennan Companies |
| Microsoft |
| Splunk |
| Westpac Banking Corporation |

Source: IR Media Group Ltd., "Corporate Governance Awards 2015," *Corporate Secretary*, November 4, 2015, http://www.corporatesecretary.com/events/corporate-governance-awards/corporate-governance-awards-2015/research/ (accessed June 17, 2016).

CORPORATE GOVERNANCE AND SOCIAL RESPONSIBILITY

Corporate social responsibility can be a difficult concept to define. While there is broad agreement among professionals, academics, and policy makers that being socially responsible does pay, corporate social responsibility always involves trade-offs, and most businesses have yet to formulate an idea of what social responsibility really entails for their organization.[16] Interpreted narrowly, a company can consider itself socially responsible if it generates returns for shareholders and provides jobs for employees (called the shareholder model). A broad definition of social responsibility interprets the corporation as a vehicle for stakeholders and for public policy (called the stakeholder model). A company that takes the latter view would be more concerned with the public good as well as with profitability and shareholder return. Because most firms have so many potential stakeholders, a key to developing a socially responsible agenda involves determining which of these groups are most important for your business. Social responsibility should seek to help a firm's principal stakeholders. For example, a line of high-end organic soaps might seek to source its ingredients from sustainable sources, avoid products that have been tested on animals, and hire workers at living wages.

To understand the role of corporate governance in business today, it is also important to consider how it relates to fundamental beliefs about the purpose of business organizations. Some people believe that as long as a company is maximizing shareholder wealth and profitability, it is fulfilling its core responsibility. Although this must be accomplished in accordance with legal and ethical standards, the primary focus is on the economic dimension of social responsibility. Thus, this belief places the philanthropic dimension beyond the scope of business. Other people, however, take the view that a business is an important member, or citizen, of society and must assume broad responsibilities. This view assumes that business performance is reflexive, meaning it both affects and is influenced by internal and external factors. In this case, performance is often considered from a financial, social, and ethical perspective. From these assumptions, we can derive two major conceptualizations of corporate governance: the shareholder model and the stakeholder model.

shareholder model of corporate governance
Founded in classic economic precepts, it focuses on improving the formal system of performance accountability between the top management and the shareholders.

The **shareholder model of corporate governance** is founded in classic economic precepts, including the maximization of wealth for investors and owners. For publicly traded firms, corporate governance focuses on developing and improving the formal system of performance accountability between top management and the firms' shareholders.[17] Thus, the shareholder orientation should drive management decisions toward what is in the best interests of investors. Underlying these decisions is a classic agency problem, where ownership (i.e., investors) and control (i.e., managers) are separate. Managers act as agents for investors, and their primary goal is to generate value for shareholders. However, investors and managers are distinct parties with unique insights, goals, and values with respect to the business. Managers, for example, may have motivations beyond shareholder value, such as market share, personal compensation, or attachment to particular products and projects. Because of these potential differences, corporate governance mechanisms are needed to ensure an alignment between investor and management interests.

For example, Deutsche Bank was investigated for questionable practices including possible manipulation of worldwide benchmark interest rates and legality of payment processing in various countries. These activities generated profits and raised the company's stock price. As a result of alleged misconduct, numerous employees have been fired, at least $6.9 billion has been paid in fines and penalties, and former senior executive William Broeksmit committed suicide apparently owing to the pressure and stress of the investigations. In addition, regulators have indicated that these investigations will continue for an unforeseen amount of time. The investigations have forced the bank to set aside billions of dollars for legal fees and more potential fines. This is now causing harm to investors as these costs are driving down the stock price.[18] The shareholder model has been criticized for its somewhat singular purpose and focus because there are other ways of "investing" in a business. Suppliers, creditors, customers, employees, business partners, the community, and others also invest their resources in the success of the firm.

In the **stakeholder model of corporate governance,** the purpose of business is conceived in a broader fashion. Although a company has a responsibility for economic success and viability, it must also answer to other parties, including employees, suppliers, government agencies, communities, and groups with which it interacts. This model presumes a collaborative and relational approach to business and its constituents. Because management time and resources are limited, a key decision within the stakeholder model is to determine which stakeholders are primary. Once primary groups have been identified, appropriate corporate governance mechanisms are implemented to promote the development of long-term relationships.[19] As we discussed in Chapter 2, primary stakeholders include stockholders, suppliers, customers, employees, the government, and the community. Governance systems that consider stakeholder welfare in tandem with corporate needs and interests characterize this approach. For instance, several companies including Google, Inc., J. Crew Group, Inc., and Deere & Co. have discovered that some of their materials have been supplied through suppliers that may have engaged in unethical and illegal conduct. Questionable market channels can damage a firm's reputation and social responsibility agenda. Conflict minerals, sourced from the Congo whose profits benefit armed militias, may have been used to make some of the companies' products. While determining the origin of all materials is a difficult and sometimes even impossible process, it is important for companies to do everything in their power to most positively impact all stakeholders. This discovery came as a result of one of the mandates of the 2010 Dodd-Frank Act that requires companies to fully understand their supply chains.[20]

Although these two approaches seem to represent ends of a continuum, the reality is that the shareholder model is often a precursor to the stakeholder model. Many businesses have evolved into the stakeholder model as a result of government initiatives, consumer activism, industry activity, and other external forces. In the aftermath of corporate scandals, it became clear how the economic accountability of corporations could not be detached from other responsibilities and stakeholder concerns. Although this trend began with large, publicly held firms, its aftereffects are being felt in other types of organizations and industries as well. Figure 3.1 illustrates a continuum of stakeholder concerns. One end demonstrates the shareholder model. The other end demonstrates a stakeholder model with concern for various company stakeholders.

The shareholder model focuses on a primary stakeholder—the investor—whereas the stakeholder model incorporates a broader philosophy toward internal and external constituents. According to the World Bank, a development institution whose goal is to reduce poverty by promoting sustainable economic growth around the world, corporate governance is defined by both internal (i.e., long-term value and efficient operations) and external (i.e., public policy and economic development) factors.[21] We are concerned with the broader conceptualization of corporate governance in this chapter.

stakeholder model of corporate governance
A model where the business is accountable to all its stakeholders, not just the shareholders.

FIGURE 3.1 Stakeholder Continuum

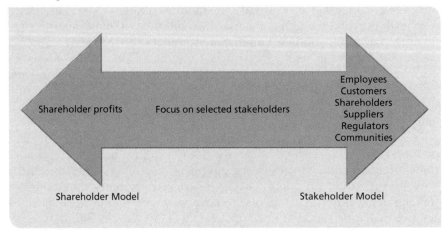

In the social responsibility model that we propose, governance is the organizing dimension for keeping a firm focused on continuous improvement, accountability, and engagement with stakeholders. Although financial return, or economic viability, is an important measure of success for all firms, the legal dimension of social responsibility is also a compulsory consideration. The ethical and philanthropic dimensions, however, have not been traditionally mandated through regulation or contracts. This represents a critical divide in our social responsibility model and associated governance goals and systems because there are some critics who challenge the use of organizational resources for concerns beyond financial performance and legalities. This view was summarized in an editorial in *National Journal,* a nonpartisan magazine on politics and government: "Corporations are not governments. In the everyday course of their business, they are not accountable to society or to the citizenry at large.... Corporations are bound by the law, and by the rules of what you might call ordinary decency. Beyond this, however, they have no duty to pursue the collective goals of society."[22] This type of philosophy, long associated with the shareholder model of corporate governance, prevailed throughout the twentieth century. However, as the consequences of neglecting the stakeholder model of corporate social responsibility have become clearer, fewer firms persist in adhering to such a narrow view.

ISSUES IN CORPORATE GOVERNANCE SYSTEMS

Organizations that strive to develop effective corporate governance systems consider a number of internal and external issues. In this section, we look at four areas that need to be addressed in the design and improvement of governance mechanisms. We begin with boards of directors, which have the ultimate responsibility for ensuring governance. Then,

Earth in the Balance

SodaStream: Bubbling Up with Socially Responsible Products

Daniel Birnbaum, CEO of SodaStream, sees plastic bottles as a thing of the past. SodaStream manufactures home carbonation systems that allow consumers to make their own sodas. The home carbonation systems include a reusable bottle, which cuts back on plastic ending up in landfills. Although SodaStream controls less than 1 percent of the global soda market, Birnbaum hopes that one day SodaStream will become its leader. The company sells its products through retailers ranging from Sears and Walmart to Bloomingdale's and Williams-Sonoma.

The first rendition of SodaStream was introduced in 1903 and became a big hit in Europe. After several acquisitions over a period of time, SodaStream began selling products globally. SodaStream became a public corporation in 2010 with an initial public offering of $109 million in the United States. Its share price has fluctuated greatly as the firm continues to be the underdog in a fierce competition between the two heavyweight corporations—PepsiCo and Coca-Cola.

SodaStream's success is the result of CEO Daniel Birnbaum's promotion of the product as a healthier and greener alternative to prepackaged sodas. As consumers become increasingly concerned about their health and about the firm's impact on the environment, SodaStream is becoming a household name. As SodaStream has grown in recent years, it has had to increase its corporate governance efforts to maintain its position as an ethical and sustainable company. The firm has established a corporate governance committee for its board of directors to ensure adherence to its responsibilities. Additionally, it has a number of governance documents to provide guidelines for managers and employees, including a conflict minerals policy, a social media policy, a code of ethics for executives, and a code of conduct for employees.

The company's promotion efforts focus on the amount of plastic, glass, and aluminum bottles that are thrown away every year. SodaStream continues to be visibly critical of the amount of waste created by beverage companies and was even given a cease-and-desist order by Coca-Cola regarding one of its marketing campaigns. The campaign featured a cage full of discarded plastic and canned sodas collected from dumpsites—which included Coca-Cola products. Birnbaum's response was to point to the massive amounts of litter Coca-Cola has produced worldwide. He also hinted that if Coke wants to claim any of its discarded trademark waste, it should be forced to claim all of it.

Some might question whether it is a smart corporate move to challenge such major competitors. Yet, because SodaStream is governed by sustainable values and practices, it seems appropriate to challenge firms it believes are violating these values. This does not always mean SodaStream receives support. In 2013, SodaStream created an ad to be aired on Super Bowl Sunday. It was estimated that over 500 million plastic bottles would be discarded on that day alone. The television networks refused to air the ad as many of their sponsors and advertisers were large beverage companies, but SodaStream posted the ad online and received over 2 million views on YouTube. In 2014, a censored SodaStream advertisement with endorser Scarlett Johansson aired during the Super Bowl. Again, the commercial was edited to remove a barb at Coke and Pepsi but remained popular on the internet.

Source: Michal Lev-Ram, "SodaStream's Bubbly Rise," *CNN Money*, March 21, 2013, http://fortune.com/2013/03/21/sodastreams-bubbly-rise/ (accessed July 12, 2016); Emily Jane Fox, "Super Bowl Showdown: SodaStream vs. Pepsi and Coke," *CNN Money*, February 3, 2013, http://money.cnn.com/2013/02/03/news/companies/sodastream-coke-pepsi-super-bowl/ (accessed July 12, 2016); SodaStream website, http://www.sodastream.com/ (accessed July 12, 2016), http://sodastream.investorroom.com/index.php?s=116#.U58iAXnQe70 (accessed July 12, 2016); "Governance Documents," *SodaStream*, http://sodastream.investorroom.com/index.php?s=116#.U58ncXnQe73 (accessed July 12, 2016).

TABLE 3.4 Challenges in Corporate Governance

Challenge	Example
Independence	Increasing the percentage of independent directors who do not own shares or otherwise have a material interest in the company
Quality	Tracking quality control issues and ensuring that the organization meets benchmarks for product quality
Performance	Ensuring that performance meets shareholder expectations
Shareholder Activism	Dealing with shareholder demands such as calls for limiting executive compensation
Internal Controls	Appointing an ethics officer to oversee the company's ethics and compliance program
Audits	Periodically auditing different areas of the company to determine areas of improvement
Risk Management	Understanding major risks the company faces and developing controls to limit these risks

we discuss shareholder activism, internal control and risk management, and executive compensation within the governance system. These issues affect most organizations, although individual businesses may face unique factors that create additional governance questions. For example, a company operating in several countries will need to resolve issues related to international governance policy. Table 3.4 discusses major areas of risk in corporate governance that organizational leaders are facing across various corporations.

Boards of Directors

A company's board of directors assume responsibility for the firm's resources and legal and ethical compliance. The board appoints top executive officers and is responsible for overseeing their performance. This is also true of a university's board of trustees, and there are similar arrangements in the nonprofit sector. In each of these cases, board members have a fiduciary duty, which was discussed earlier in this chapter. These responsibilities include acting in the best interests of those they serve. Thus, board membership is not designed as a vehicle for personal financial gain; rather, it provides the intangible benefit of ensuring the success of the organization and the stakeholders affected and involved in the fiduciary arrangement.

In the case of public corporations, boards of directors hold the ultimate responsibility for their firms' ethical culture and legal compliance. This governing authority is held responsible by the 2004 and 2007 amendments to the Federal Sentencing Guidelines for creating an ethical culture that provides leadership, values, and compliance. The members of a company's board of directors assume legal responsibility for the firm's resources and decisions, and they appoint its top executive officers. In an effort to revamp the company after the last recession, Citigroup appointed new directors to its board. This overhauled board now includes financial experts from government, the banking industry, and academia—all in an effort to increase transparency and accountability.[23]

The traditional approach to directorship assumed that board members managed the corporation's business. Research and practical observation have shown that boards of directors rarely, if ever, perform the management function.[24] Because boards usually meet four to six times a year, there is no way that time allocation would allow for effective management. In small nonprofit organizations, the board may manage most resources and decisions. The complexity of large organizations requires full attention on a daily basis. Today, boards of directors are concerned primarily with monitoring the decisions made by managers on behalf of the company. This includes choosing top executives, assessing their performances, helping to set strategic direction, evaluating company performance, developing CEO succession plans, communicating with stakeholders, maintaining legal and ethical practices, ensuring that control and accountability mechanisms are in place, and evaluating the board's own performance. In sum, the board members assume the ultimate authority for organizational effectiveness and subsequent performance.

Independence Just as social responsibility objectives require more employees and executives, boards of directors are also experiencing increasing accountability and disclosure mandates. The desire for independence is one reason that a few firms have chosen to split the powerful roles of chair of the board and CEO. Although the practice is common in the United Kingdom and activists have called for this move for years, the idea is newer to the United States and is sometimes met with resistance. The past couple of years have placed pressure on J.P. Morgan Chase Chairman and CEO James Dimon. After a number of regulatory hearings concerning the London Whale Fiasco, lack of oversight in the Bernard Madoff Ponzi scheme incident, and risky loans before the Great Recession, shareholders at J.P. Morgan requested that the chairman and CEO roles be divided. The request was met with resistance and did not pass a board vote, but Dimon did relinquish his role as chairman of the bank business. Some think this is an acknowledgement of responsibility and a step in the right direction concerning better corporate governance.[25]

Traditionally, board members were retired company executives or friends of current executives, but the trend since the corporate scandals associated with Enron, WorldCom, and more recently Countrywide Financial and J.P. Morgan has been toward independent directors who have valuable expertise yet little vested interest in the firm before assuming the director role. According to Rule 303A.01 of the NYSE corporate governance guidelines, the boards of listed companies must be comprised of a majority of independent directors.[26] However, a listed company in which more than 50 percent of the voting power for the election of directors is held by a group or individual does not have to abide by Rule 303A.01.[27]

Thus, directors today are more likely chosen for their competence, motivation, and ability to bring enlightened and diverse perspectives to strategic discussions. Outside directors are thought to bring more independence to the monitoring function because they are not bound by past allegiances, friendships, a current role in the company, or some other matter that may create a conflict of interest. However, independent directors who sit on a board for a long time may eventually lose some of the outsider perspective. While they are more likely to be impartial, independent directors are not always guaranteed to avoid conflict of interest issues. For example, hedge fund management firm The Galleon Group had independent directors on its board, but this did not stop massive misconduct at the firm. Founder Raj Rajaratnam was convicted of insider trading and was sentenced to 11 years in prison, the longest sentencing to date for the crime. Directors have to avoid 'groupthink' and be competent enough to understand risks. They must also be willing to ask for information relevant to avoiding organizational misconduct.

Quality Finding board members who have some expertise in the firm's industry or who have served as chief executives at similar-sized organizations is a good strategy for improving the board's overall quality. Directors with competence and experiences that reflect some of the firm's core issues should bring valuable insights to bear on discussions and decisions. Directors without direct industry or comparable executive experience may bring expertise on important issues, such as auditing, executive compensation, succession planning, and risk management, to improve decision-making. Board members must understand the company's strategy and operations; this suggests that members should limit the number of boards on which they serve. Directors need time to read reports, attend board and committee meetings, and participate in continuing education that promotes strong understanding and quality guidance. For example, directors on the board's audit committee may need to be educated on new accounting and auditing standards. Experts recommend that fully employed board members sit on no more than four boards, whereas retired members should limit their memberships to seven boards. Directors should be able to attend at least 75 percent of the meetings. Thus, many of the factors that promote board quality are within the control of directors.[28]

Performance An effective board of directors can serve as a type of insurance against the business cycle and the natural highs and lows of the economy. A company with a strong board free from conflicts of interest and clearly stated corporate governance rules will be more likely to weather a storm if something bad does happen.[29] As federal regulations increase and the latitude afforded boards of directors shrinks, boards are going to be faced with greater responsibility and transparency.

Board independence, along with board quality, stock ownership, and corporate performance, are often used to assess the quality of corporate boards of directors. Many CEOs have lost their jobs because the board of directors is concerned about performance, ethics, and social responsibility. The main reason for this is the boards' fear of losing their personal assets. This fear comes from lawsuits by shareholders who sued the directors of financial firms over their roles in the collapse on Wall Street. These events make it clear that board members are accountable for oversight.

Just as improved ethical decision-making requires more of employees and executives, so too are boards of directors feeling greater demands for ethics and transparency. Directors today are increasingly chosen for their proficiency and ability to bring different perspectives to strategic discussions. As mentioned earlier, outside directors are thought to bring more independence to the monitoring function because they are not bound by past allegiances and other issues that may create a conflict of interest. The chair of the board audit committee must be an outside independent director with financial expertise.

Many of the corporate scandals uncovered in recent years might have been prevented if each of the companies' boards of directors had been better qualified, more knowledgeable, and less biased. The institution of the Volcker Rule, one component of the Dodd-Frank Wall Street Reform and Consumer Protection Act, provides stricter rules on financial management and controls on hedge funds and money-market mutual funds. The aim is to ensure that banks will have more liquid assets than before. It also aims to provide increased openness and transparency, greater oversight and enforcement, and clearer, more common-sense language in the financial system.[30] Board members are being asked to understand changes in regulations and participate in providing better oversight on risk-taking in their firms.

Rules promulgated by the Sarbanes-Oxley Act and various stock exchanges now require a majority of independent directors on the board with no material relationship to the firm; regular meetings between non-management board members; audit, compensation, governance, and nominating committees either fully made up of or with a majority of independent directors; no more than $120,000 in compensation for independent directors per year; and a financial expert on the audit committee. The governance area will continue to evolve as corporate scandals are resolved and the government and companies begin to implement and test new policies and practices. Regardless of the size and type of business for which boards are responsible, a system of governance is needed to ensure effective control and accountability. As a corporation grows, matures, enters international markets, and takes other strategic directions, it is likely that the board of directors will evolve to meet its new demands. Sir Adrian Cadbury, former president of the Centre for Board Effectiveness at the Henley Business School in Reading, England, and an architect of corporate governance changes around the world, outlined responsibilities of strong boards:

- Boards are responsible for developing company purpose statements that cover a range of aims and stakeholder concerns.
- Annual reports and other documents include more nonfinancial information.

- Boards are required to define their role and implement self-assessment processes better.
- Selection of board members will become increasingly formalized, with less emphasis on personal networks and word of mouth.
- Boards need to work effectively as teams.
- Serving on boards will require more time and commitment than in the past.[31]

These trends are consistent with our previous discussion of social responsibility. In all facets of organizational life, greater demands are being placed on business decisions and people. Many of these expectations emanate from those who provide substantial resources in the organization—namely, shareholders and other investors.

Shareholder Activism

Shareholders, including large institutional ones, have become more active in articulating their positions with respect to company strategy and executive decision-making. *Activism* is a broad term that can encompass engaging in dialog with management, attending annual meetings, submitting shareholder resolutions, bringing lawsuits, and other mechanisms designed to communicate shareholder interests to the corporation. Table 3.5 lists characteristics of effective shareholder activism campaigns.

TABLE 3.5 Characteristics of a Successful Shareholder Activism Campaign

Alliances	Alliances with social movements or public interest groups, where shareholder concerns and activity mesh with and play a part in a larger, multifaceted campaign
Grass-roots pressure	Letter writings or phone-ins to public investors to generate support for the resolution
Communications	Media outreach, public and shareholder education, etc.
High-level negotiations with senior decision-makers	Company executives and directors
Support and active involvement from large institutional investors	Financial firms such as Goldman Sachs and JP Morgan
A climate that makes it difficult for the company not to make the "right decision"	If you have a plainly compelling financial argument, you have a better chance of getting company management and other shareholders on board with your proposal.
Persistence	Shareholders don't go away. They own the company and have a right to be heard. Often shareholder activists stick with issues for years.

Source: "Characteristics of a Successful Shareholder Activism Campaign," *Friends of the Earth*, http://www.foe.org/international/shareholder/characteristics.html (accessed April 25, 2006). Courtesy Friends of the Earth © 2006.

Shareholder resolutions are nonbinding, yet important, statements about shareholder concerns. A shareholder that meets certain guidelines may bring one resolution per year to a proxy vote of all shareholders at a corporation's annual meeting. Recent resolutions brought forth relate to auditor independence, executive compensation, independent directors, environmental impact, human rights, and other social responsibility issues. In some cases, the company will modify its policies or practices before the resolution is ever brought to a vote. In other situations, a resolution will receive less than a majority vote, but the media attention, educational value, and other stakeholder effects will cause a firm to reconsider, if not change, its original position to meet the resolution's proposal. The accounting scandals prompted many resolutions about executive compensation among shareholders who believe that improper compensation structures are often a precursor to accounting mismanagement.[32] The resolution process is regulated by the SEC in the United States and by complementary offices in other countries; some claim this to be more favorable to the corporation than to shareholders.

Although labor and public pension fund activists have waged hundreds of proxy battles in recent years, they rarely have much effect on the target companies. Now shareholder activists are attacking the process by which directors themselves are elected. After a poor performance leading up to the latest recession, Bank of America shareholders voted to oust six board members. The move got rid of entrenched directors with possible conflicts of interest and replaced them with qualified financial experts.[33] Although shareholders and investors want their resources used efficiently and effectively, they are increasingly willing to take a stand to encourage companies to change for reasons beyond financial return.

Investor Confidence

Shareholders and other investors must have assurance that their money is being placed in the care of capable and trustworthy organizations. These primary stakeholders are expecting a solid return for their investment, but as illustrated earlier, they have additional concerns about social responsibility. When these fundamental expectations are not met, the confidence that investors and shareholders have in corporations, market analysts, investment houses, stockbrokers, mutual fund managers, financial planners, and other economic players and institutions can be severely tested. In Chapter 1, we discussed the importance of investor trust and loyalty to organizational and societal performance. Part of this trust relates to the perceived efficacy of corporate governance. Table 3.6 shows the characteristics of a well-governed board of directors.

Internal Control and Risk Management

Controls and a strong risk management system are fundamental to effective operations, as they allow for comparisons between the actual performance and the planned performance and goals of the organization. Controls are

TABLE 3.6 Attributes of a Highly Functioning Board

Attributes	A Highly Functioning Board Exhibits the Following
Skills and knowledge	The board understands the attributes of successful leaders and how to apply them to the organization and its strategic plans; has experience developing leadership pipelines in organizations of similar size and scale; understands the mechanics of the company's compensations plans and the risks inherent in the plans.
Process	• Appoints the CEO and oversees the CEO's development, goal-setting, and compensation • Approves and monitors compensation performance metrics for the CEO • Oversees CEO compensation and transparent disclosure of executive compensation to stakeholders • Ensures development of executive succession plans that contemplate various scenarios • Collaborates with management to develop and adopt a compensation philosophy for the organization • Meets periodically with executive leadership, including risk and HR, to understand organizational compensation plans, talent pipeline, and underlying risks • Monitors external stakeholder considerations related to executive management and compensation
Information	Obtains independent views and peer company benchmarks of compensation plans proposed by management; has access to and receives periodic reports related to compensation plans, including internal audit and other reports; monitors marketplace developments.
Behavior	Board leadership takes responsibility for the development of the CEO; appropriately supports and mentors the CEO; develops and maintains relationships with other key executives, especially those with potential to succeed the CEO.

Source: "Framing the Future of Corporate Governance," *Deloitte*, 2015, http://www2.deloitte.com/content/dam/Deloitte/us/Documents/risk/us-aers-framing-the-future-of-corporate-governance-09262014.pdf (accessed June 17, 2016).

used to safeguard corporate assets and resources, protect the reliability of organizational information, and ensure compliance with regulations, laws, and contracts. Risk management is the process used to anticipate and shield the organization from unnecessary or overwhelming circumstances while ensuring that executive leadership is taking the appropriate steps to move the organization and its strategy forward.

Internal and External Audits Auditing, both internal and external, is the linchpin between risk and controls and corporate governance. Boards of directors must ensure that the internal auditing function of the company is provided with adequate funding, up-to-date technology, unrestricted access, independence, and authority to carry out its audit plan. To ensure these characteristics, the internal audit executive should report to the board's audit committee and, in most cases, the chief executive officer.[34]

The external auditor should be chosen by the board and must clearly identify its client as the board, not the company's chief financial officer. Under Sarbanes-Oxley, the board audit committee should be directly responsible for the selection, payment, and supervision of the company's external auditor. The act also prohibits an external auditing firm from performing some non-audit work for the same public company, including bookkeeping, human resources, actuarial services, valuation services, legal services, and investment banking. However, even with regulations in place, many auditors failed to do their jobs properly. For example, trustees of New Century Financial Corporation sued its auditor, KPMG, for "reckless and grossly negligent audits" that hid the company's financial problems and sped its collapse. New Century was one of the early casualties of the subprime mortgage crisis but was once one of the country's largest mortgage lenders to those with poor credit histories. After it disclosed accounting errors not discovered by KPMG, the company collapsed.[35] Part of the problem relates to the sheer size and complexity of organizations, but these factors do not negate the tremendous responsibility that external auditors assume.

Control Systems The area of internal control covers a wide range of company decisions and actions, not just the accuracy of financial statements and accounting records. Controls also foster understanding when discrepancies exist between corporate expectations and stakeholder interests and issues. Internal controls effectively limit employee or management opportunism or the use of corporate assets for individualistic or nonstrategic purposes. Controls also ensure the board of directors has access to timely and quality information that can be used to determine strategic options and effectiveness. For these reasons, the board should have ultimate oversight of the integrity of the internal control system.[36] Although board members do not develop or administer the control system, they are responsible for ensuring that an effective system exists. The need for internal controls is rarely disputed, but implementation can vary. The CEO or chair appears to be the key decision-maker relating to public and political debates that have an impact on shareholder value. Thus, internal control represents a set of tasks and resource commitments that require high-level attention. See Table 3.7 for an integrated framework for implementing internal controls.

Although most large publicly traded corporations have designed internal controls, smaller private companies and nonprofit organizations are less likely to have invested in a complete system. For example, electric car company Green Tech Automotive came under investigation by the SEC for questionable practices in recruiting foreign investors. The claims that the company overstated guaranteed returns on investment and accepted investment from investors that may compromise national security are highlighted in the investigation.[37] Such questionable behaviors are common in private businesses because they often lack effective internal controls. The framework in Table 3.7, while developed for large corporations,

TABLE 3.7 Integrated Framework for Internal Control

Control Environment	• The organization demonstrates a commitment to integrity and ethical values
	• The board of directors demonstrates independence from management and exercises oversight of the development and performance of internal control
	• Management establishes, with board oversight, structures, reporting lines, and appropriate authorities and responsibilities in the pursuit of objectives
	• The organization demonstrates a commitment to attract, develop, and retain competent individuals in alignment with objectives
	• The organization holds individuals accountable for their internal control responsibilities in the pursuit of objectives
Risk Assessment	• The organization specifies objectives with sufficient clarity to enable the identification and assessment of risks relating to objectives
	• The organization identifies risks to the achievement of its objectives across the entity and analyzes risks as a basis for determining how the risks should be managed
	• The organization considers the potential for fraud in assessing risks to the achievement of objectives
	• The organization identifies and assesses changes that could significantly impact the system of internal control
Control Activities	• The organization selects and develops control activities that contribute to the mitigation of risks to the achievement of objectives to acceptable levels
	• The organization selects and develops general control activities over technology to support the achievement of objectives
	• The organization deploys control activities through policies that establish what is expected and procedures that put policies into action
Information and Communication	• The organization obtains or generates and uses relevant, quality information to support the functioning of internal control
	• The organization internally communicates information, including objectives and responsibility for internal control, necessary to support the functioning of internal control
	• The organization communicates with external parties regarding matters affecting the functioning of internal control
Monitoring Activities	• The organization selects, develops, and performs ongoing and/or separate evaluations to ascertain whether the components of internal control are present and functioning
	• The organization evaluates and communicates internal control deficiencies in a timely manner to those parties responsible for taking corrective action, including senior management and the board of directors, as appropriate

Source: "Internal Control—Integrated Framework Executive Summary," *Committee of Sponsoring Organizations of the Treadway Commission,* May 2013, http://www.coso.org/documents/coso%20 2013%20icfr%20executive_summary.pdf (accessed June 17, 2016).

can be used in all types of organizations. These techniques are not always costly, and they conform to best practices in the prevention of ethical and legal problems that threaten the efficacy of governance mechanisms.

Amendments to the Federal Sentencing Guidelines for Organizations make it clear that a corporation's governing authority must be well informed about its control systems with respect to implementation and effectiveness. This places the responsibility squarely on the shoulders of the firm's leadership, usually the board of directors. The board must ensure that there is a high-ranking officer accountable for the day-to-day operational responsibility of the control systems. The board must also provide for adequate authority, resources, and access to the board or an appropriate subcommittee of the board. The guidelines further call for confidential mechanisms whereby the organization's employees and agents may report or seek guidance about potential or actual misconduct without fear of retaliation. Finally, the board is required to oversee the discovery of risks and to design, implement, and modify approaches to deal with those risks. Thus, the board of directors is clearly accountable for discovering risks associated with a firm's specific industry and assessing the firm's ethics program to ensure that it is capable of uncovering misconduct.[38]

Risk Management A strong internal control system should alert decision-makers to possible problems, or risks, that may threaten business operations, including worker safety, company solvency, vendor relationships, proprietary information, environmental impact, and other concerns. As we discussed in Chapter 2, having a strong crisis management plan is part of the process for managing risk. The term *risk management* is normally used in a narrow sense to indicate responsibilities associated with insurance, liability, financial decisions, and related issues. Kraft General Foods, for example, has a risk management policy for understanding how prices of commodities, such as coffee, sugar, wheat, and cocoa, will affect its relationships throughout the supply chain.[39]

Most corporate leaders' greatest fear is discovering serious misconduct or illegal activity somewhere in their organization. The fear is that a public discovery can immediately be used by critics in the mass media, competitors, and skeptical stakeholders to undermine a firm's reputation. Corporate leaders worry that something will be uncovered outside their control that will jeopardize their careers and their organizations. Fear is a paralyzing emotion. Of course, maybe even organizational leaders such as Raj Rajaratnam experienced fear as they participated in misconduct. The former chairman of Satyam Computer Services, Ramalinga Raju, said it was a terrifying experience to watch a small act of fudging some numbers snowball out of control. He compared knowingly engaging in misconduct for years to "riding a tiger, not knowing how to get off without being eaten."[40] These leaders were the captains of their respective ships, and they made a conscious decision to steer their firms into treacherous waters with a high probability of striking an iceberg.[41]

Corporate leaders do fear the possibility of damage to reputation, financial loss, or a regulatory event that could potentially end their careers and even threaten their personal lives through fines or prison sentences. Indeed, the whole concept of risk management involves recognizing the possibility of a misfortune that could jeopardize or even destroy the corporation.[42] Organizations face significant risks and threats from financial misconduct. There is a need to identify potential risks that relate to misconduct that could devastate the organization. If risks and misconduct are discovered and disclosed, they are more likely to be resolved before they become front page news.

Risk is always present within organizations, so executives must develop processes for remedying or managing its effects. A board of directors will expect the top management team to have risk management skills and plans in place. There are at least three ways to consider how risk poses either a potentially negative or positive concern for organizations.[43] First, risk can be categorized as a hazard. In this view, risk management is focused on minimizing negative situations, such as fraud, injury, or financial loss. Second, risk may be considered an uncertainty that needs to be hedged through quantitative plans and models. This type of risk is best associated with the term *risk management,* which is used in financial and business literature. Third, risk also creates the opportunity for innovation and entrepreneurship. Just as management can be criticized for taking too much risk, it can also be subject to concerns about not taking enough risk. All three types of risk are implicitly covered by our definition of corporate governance because there are risks for both control (i.e., preventing fraud and ensuring accuracy of financial statements) and accountability (i.e., innovation to develop new products and markets). For example, the internet and electronic commerce capabilities have introduced new risks of all types for organizations. Privacy, as we discuss in Chapter 10, is a major concern for many stakeholders and has created the need for policies and certification procedures. A board of directors may ensure that the company has established privacy policies that are not only effective but can also be properly monitored and improved as new technology risks and opportunities emerge in the business environment.[44]

Executive Compensation

Executive compensation has been a topic rife with controversy. In the midst of government bailouts of corporations and financial institutions and loss of jobs and life savings, top executives continued to receive incredibly high bonuses. This brought attention to the manner in which executives are paid, which had largely been left uninvestigated until this point. The Dodd-Frank Act included measures to rein in overcompensation including a "say-on-pay" mandate requiring shareholders to vote on their company's compensation policies, and "compensation committee independence" requiring board members in charge of determining compensation to be independent from the company's management. Other mandates, which have been proposed by the SEC, but are not yet approved, include requiring companies to disclose the ratio between CEO and employee pay, the disclosure of pay as it relates to performance, the process of recovering of compensation that was wrongly awarded, and disclosure of any hedging activities conducted by directors or employees.[45]

Executive compensation is such an important matter that many boards spend more time deciding how much to compensate top executives than they do perhaps in ensuring the integrity of the company's financial reporting systems. Because of the large government bailouts during the last recession, many people became enraged because they felt that the government was sponsoring corporate excess with taxpayer money. This was a major contributor to the Occupy Wall Street protests of 2011. Even many boards of directors—which are responsible for setting executive pay—feel that the United States has a problem in that executive pay is not in line with performance or demonstration of stewardship to the company.[46] According to the AFL-CIO, average executive pay is $13.5 million, which is 373 times the pay of the average U.S. worker.[47]

An increasing number of corporate boards are imposing performance targets on the stock and stock options they include in their CEOs' pay package. The SEC proposed that companies disclose how they compensate lower-ranking employees as well as top executives. This was part of a review of executive pay policies that addresses the belief that many financial corporations have historically taken on too much risk. The SEC believes that compensation may be linked to excessive risk-taking.[48] Another issue is whether performance-linked compensation encourages executives to focus on short-term performance at the expense of long-term growth.[49] Shareholders today, however, may be growing more concerned about transparency than short-term performance and executive compensation.

Some people argue that executives deserve the rewards that follow from strong company performance, because they assume so much risk on behalf of the company. In addition, many executives' personal and professional lives meld to the point that they are "on call" 24 hours a day. Because not everyone has the skill, experience, and desire to become an executive, with the accompanying pressure and responsibility, market forces dictate a high level of compensation. When the pool of qualified individuals is limited, many corporate board members feel that offering large compensation packages is the only way to attract and retain top executives and thereby ensure that their firms are not left without strong leadership. In an era when top executives are increasingly willing to "jump ship" to other firms that offer higher pay, potentially lucrative stock options, bonuses, and other benefits, such thinking is not without merit.[50]

Executive compensation is a difficult but important issue for boards of directors and other stakeholders to consider because it receives much attention in the media, sparks shareholder concern, and is hotly debated in discussions of corporate governance. One area for board members to consider is the extent to which executive compensation is linked to company performance. Corporate plans that base compensation on the achievement of several performance goals, including profits and revenues, are intended to align the interests of owners with management. For example, General Electric CEO Jeff Immelt missed his five-year performance target and lost out on a stock award that was valued at more than $3 million.[51]

TABLE 3.8 Examples of Chief Executive Officer Compensation

Executive	Company	Pay ($millions)
Dara Khosrowshahi	Expedia	94.6
Robert Iger	Walt Disney	43.5
AT&T	Randall L. Stephenson	22.6
James Gorman	Morgan Stanley	22.1
Kenneth I. Chenault	American Express	21.7
Virginia Rometty	IBM	19.8
Meg Whitman	Hewlett-Packard	17.1
Muhtar Kent	Coca-Cola	14.6
Jeff Bezos	Amazon	1.7
Larry Page	Alphabet	1

Source: Equilar Inc., "Equilar/Associated Press S&P 500 CEO Pay Study 2016," *Equilar*, 2016, http://www.equilar.com/reports/37-2-associated-press-pay-study-2016.html (accessed June 17, 2016).

Table 3.8 shows CEO compensation at some of the world's largest companies. While still hundreds of times higher than what the average worker makes, overall CEOs' compensation is decreasing, indicating a possible change in the way executives are compensated. On the other hand, critics still believe there is a mismatch between the compensation of Wall Street CEOs and performance. In 2015 Wall Street CEOs saw their pay rise about 10 percent even though shares of major banks fell.[52]

CORPORATE GOVERNANCE AROUND THE WORLD

Increased globalization, enhanced electronic communications, economic agreements and zones, and the reduction of trade barriers have created opportunities for firms around the world to conduct business with both international consumers and industrial partners. These factors propel the need for greater homogenization in corporate governance principles. Standard & Poor's has a service called Corporate Governance Scores, which analyzes four macro-forces that affect the general governance climate of a country, including legal infrastructure, regulation, information infrastructure, and market infrastructure. On the basis of these factors, a country can be categorized as having strong, moderate, or weak support for effective governance practices at the company level. Institutional investors are very interested in this measure, as it helps determine possible risk.[53] As financial, human, and intellectual capital cross borders, a number of business, social, and cultural concerns arise. Institutional investors in companies based in emerging markets claim to be willing to pay more for shares in companies that are well governed. Global shareholders also would like companies in their countries to disclose more financial data, to adopt CEO pay plans that reward only strong performance, and to use independent boards with no ties to management.

In response to this business climate, the Organisation for Economic Co-operation and Development (OECD), a forum for governments to discuss, develop, and enhance economic and social policy, issued a set of principles intended to serve as a global model for corporate governance.[54] After years of discussion and debate among institutional investors, business executives, government representatives, trade unions, and nongovernmental organizations, 30 OECD member governments signaled their agreement with the principles by signing a declaration to integrate them within their countries' economic systems and institutions. The purpose of the OECD Corporate Governance Principles (see Table 3.9) is to formulate minimum standards of fairness, transparency, accountability, disclosure, and responsibility for business practice. The principles

TABLE 3.9 OECD Principles of Corporate Governance

Principle	Explanation
1. Ensuring the basis for an effective corporate governance framework	The corporate governance framework should promote transparent and efficient markets, be consistent with the rule of law and clearly articulate the division of responsibilities among different supervisory, regulatory and enforcement authorities.
2. The rights of shareholders and key ownership functions	The corporate governance framework should protect and facilitate the exercise of shareholders' rights.
3. The equitable treatment of shareholders	The corporate governance framework should ensure the equitable treatment of all shareholders, including minority and foreign shareholders. All shareholders should have the opportunity to obtain effective redress for violation of their rights.
4. The role of stakeholders in corporate governance	The corporate governance framework should recognize the rights of stakeholders as established by law and encourage active cooperation between corporations and stakeholders in creating wealth, jobs, and the sustainability of financially sound enterprises.
5. Disclosure and transparency	The corporate governance framework should ensure that timely and accurate disclosure is made on all material matters regarding the corporation, including the financial situation, performance, ownership, and governance of the company.
6. The responsibilities of the board	The corporate governance framework should ensure the strategic guidance of the company, the effective monitoring of management by the board, and the board's accountability to the company and the shareholders.

Source: ComplianceOnline.com, "OECD Principles of Corporate Governance," 2014, http://www.complianceonline.com/dictionary/OECD_Principles_of_Corporate_Governance.html (accessed June 17, 2016).

focus on the board of directors, which the OECD says should recognize the impact of governance on the firm's competitiveness. In addition, the OECD charges boards, executives, and corporations with maximizing shareholder value while responding to the demands and expectations of their key stakeholders.

The OECD Corporate Governance Principles cover many specific best practices, including (1) (ensuring) the basis for an effective corporate governance framework; (2) rights of shareholders to vote and influence corporate strategy; (3) greater numbers of skilled, independent members on boards of directors; (4) fewer techniques to protect failing management and strategy; (5) wider use of international accounting standards; and (6) better disclosure of executive pay and remuneration. Although member governments of the OECD are expected to uphold the governance principles, there is some room for cultural adaptation.

Best practices may vary slightly from country to country because of unique factors such as market structure, government control, role of banks and lending institutions, labor unions, and other economic, legal, and historical factors. Both industry groups and government regulators moved quickly in the United Kingdom after the Enron crisis. Because some British bankers were indicted in the scandal, corporate governance concerns increased. Several British reforms resulted, including annual shareholders' votes on board compensation policies and greater supervision of investment analysts and the accounting profession.

Corporate governance, or lack of it, was one of the reasons for the financial crisis that occurred in Southeast Asia in the late 1990s. For example, the government structure of some Asian countries created greater opportunities for corruption and nepotism. Banks were encouraged to extend credit to companies favored by the government. In many cases, these companies were in the export business, which created an imbalance in financing for other types of businesses. The concentration of business power within a few families and tycoons reduced overall competitiveness and transparency. Many of these businesses were more focused on size and expanded operations than profitability. Foreign investors recognized the weakening economies and pulled their money out of investments. India has experienced a decrease in foreign investment for this reason. Despite the government's maneuvers to improve the economy, by easing restrictions on joint ventures in certain sectors, foreign firms decided against investing as this was not enough incentive in light of the nation's weakening currency.[55]

FUTURE OF CORPORATE GOVERNANCE

As the issues discussed in the previous section demonstrate, corporate governance is primarily focused on strategic-level concerns for accountability and control. Although many discussions of corporate governance still revolve around responsibility in investor-owned companies, good governance is fundamental to effective performance in all types of organizations. As you have gleaned from history and government classes, a system of checks and balances is important for ensuring a focus on multiple perspectives and constituencies; proper distribution of resources, power, and decision authority; and the responsibility for making changes and setting direction.

To pursue social responsibility successfully, organizations must consider issues of control and accountability. As we learned earlier, the concept of corporate governance is in transition from the shareholder model to one that considers broader stakeholder concerns and inputs to financial performance. A number of market and environmental forces, such as the OECD and shareholder activism, have created pressures in this direction. This evolution is consistent with our view of social responsibility. Although some critics deride this expanded focus, a number of external and internal forces are driving business toward the stakeholder orientation and the formalization of governance mechanisms. One concern centers on the cost of governance. Companies like Nike have had problems in the past and have implemented strong ethics and compliance systems. However, many of the largest firms on Wall Street, which were overleveraged and did not have strong ethics and compliance programs in place, either failed or had to be bailed out to prevent failure.[56]

Most businesspeople and academicians agree that the benefits of a strong approach to corporate governance outweigh its costs. However, the positive return on governance goes beyond organizational performance to benefit the industrial competitiveness of entire nations, something which was discussed in Chapter 1. For example, corrupt organizations often fail to develop competitiveness on a global scale and can leave behind financial ruin, thus negating the overall economic growth of the entire region or nation. At the same time, corrupt governments usually have difficulty sustaining and supporting the types of organizations that can succeed in global markets. Thus, a lack of good governance can lead to insular and selfish motives because there is no effective system of checks and balances. In today's interactive and interdependent business environment, most organizations are learning the benefits of a more cooperative approach to commerce. It is possible for a company to retain its competitive nature while seeking a "win-win" solution for all parties to the exchange.[57] Furthermore, as nations with large economies embrace responsible governance principles, it becomes even more difficult for nations and organizations that do not abide by such principles to compete in these lucrative and rich markets. There is a contagion effect toward corporate governance among members of the global economy, much like peer pressure influences the actions and decisions of individuals. Portugal is a good example of this effect.

Because governance is concerned with the decisions made by boards of directors and executives, it has the potential for far-reaching positive—and negative—effects. A recent study by the OECD found that stronger financial performance is the result of several governance factors and practices, including (1) large institutional shareholders that are active monitors of company decisions and boards, (2) owner-controlled firms, (3) fewer mergers, especially between firms with disparate corporate values and business lines, and (4) shareholders', not board of directors', decisions on executive remuneration.[58] The authors of the study note that these practices may not hold true for a strong performance in all countries and economic systems. However, they also point out that a consensus view is emerging, with fewer differences among OECD countries than among all other nations. Similarities in organizational-level accountability and control should lead to smoother operations between different companies and countries, thereby bolstering competitiveness on many levels.

The future of corporate governance is directly linked to the future of social responsibility. Because governance is the control and accountability process for achieving social responsibility, it is important to consider who should be involved in the future. First and most obviously, business leaders and managers will need to embrace governance as an essential part of effective performance. Some of the elements of corporate governance, particularly executive pay, board composition, and shareholder rights, are likely to stir debates for many years. However, business leaders must recognize the forces that have brought governance to the forefront as a precondition of management responsibility. Thus, they may need to accept the "creative tension" that exists among managers, owners, and other primary stakeholders as the preferable route to mutual success.[59]

Second, governments have a key role to play in corporate governance. National competitiveness depends on the strength of various institutions, with primacy on the effective performance of business and capital markets. Strong corporate governance is essential to this performance, and thus, governments will need to be actively engaged in affording both protection and accountability for corporate power and decisions. Just like the corporate crises in the United States, the Asian economic crisis discussed earlier prompted companies and governments around the world to consider tighter governance procedures. Finally, other stakeholders may become more willing to use governance mechanisms to influence corporate strategy or decision-making. Investors—whether shareholders, employees, or business partners—have a stake in decisions and should be willing to take steps to align various interests for long-term benefits. There are many investors and stakeholders willing to exert great influence on underperforming companies.

Until recently, governance was one area in the business literature that had not received the same level of attention as other issues, such as environmental impact, diversity, and sexual harassment. Over the next few years, however, corporate governance will emerge as the operational centerpiece to the social responsibility effort. The future will require that business leaders have a different set of skills and attitudes, including the ability to balance multiple interests, handle ambiguity, manage complex systems and networks, create trust among stakeholders, and improve processes so that leadership is pervasive throughout the organization.[60]

In the past, the primary emphasis of governance systems and theory was on the conflict of interests between management and investors.[61] Governance today holds people at the highest organizational levels accountable and responsible to a broad and diverse set of stakeholders. Although top managers and boards of directors have always assumed responsibility, their actions are now subject to greater accountability and transparency. A *Wall Street Journal* writer put the shift succinctly, indicating, "Boards of directors have been put on notice." A key issue going forward will be the board's ability to align corporate decisions with various stakeholder interests.[62] Robert Monks, the activist money manager and leader in corporate governance issues, wrote that effective corporate governance requires understanding that the "indispensable link between the corporate constituents is the creation of a credible structure (with incentives and disincentives) that enables people with overlapping but not entirely congruent interests to have a sufficient level of confidence in each other and the viability of the enterprise as a whole."[63] We will take a closer look at some of these constituents and their concerns in the next few chapters.

SUMMARY

To respond to stakeholder pressures for companies to be more accountable for organizational decisions and policies, organizations must implement policies that provide strategic guidance on appropriate courses of action. Such policies are often known as corporate governance, the formal system of accountability and control for organizational decisions and resources. Accountability relates to how well the content of workplace decisions is aligned with the firm's stated strategic direction, whereas control involves the process of auditing and improving organizational decisions and actions.

Both directors and officers of corporations are fiduciaries for the shareholders. Fiduciaries are persons placed in positions of trust who are loyal and take due care in acting on behalf of the best interests of the organization. There is a duty of care, also called a duty of diligence, to make informed and prudent decisions. As directors, they too have a duty to avoid ethical misconduct and to provide leadership in decisions to prevent ethical misconduct in the organization. Directors are not held responsible for negative outcomes if they are informed and diligent in their decision-making. The duty of loyalty means that all decisions should be in the interests of the corporation and its stakeholders. Conflicts of interest exist when a director uses the position to obtain personal gain, usually at the expense of the organization.

There are two major conceptualizations of corporate governance. The shareholder model of corporate governance focuses on developing and improving the formal system of performance accountability between the top management and the firm's shareholders. The stakeholder model of corporate governance views the purpose of business in a broader fashion in which the organization not only has a responsibility for economic success and viability but also must answer to other stakeholders. The shareholder model focuses on a primary stakeholder—the investor—whereas the stakeholder model incorporates a broader philosophy that focuses on internal and external constituents.

Governance is the organizing dimension that keeps a firm focused on continuous improvement, accountability, and engagement with stakeholders. Although financial return, or economic viability, is an important measure of success for all firms, the legal dimension of social responsibility is also a compulsory consideration. The ethical and philanthropic dimensions, however, have not been traditionally mandated through regulation or contracts. This represents a critical divide in our social responsibility model and associated governance goals and systems because there are some critics who challenge the use of organizational resources for concerns beyond financial performance and legalities.

In the late 1800s and early 1900s, corporate governance was not a major issue because company owners made strategic decisions about their businesses. By the 1930s, ownership was dispersed across many individuals, raising questions about control and accountability. In response to shareholder activism, the Securities and Exchange Commission required corporations to allow shareholder resolutions to be brought to a vote of all shareholders. Since the mid-1900s, the approach to corporate governance has involved a legal discussion of principals (owners) and agents (managers) in the business relationship. The lack of effective control and accountability mechanisms in years past has prompted a current trend toward boards of directors playing a greater role in strategy formulation than they did in the early 1990s. The board of directors assumes legal responsibility and a fiduciary duty for organizational resources and decisions. Boards today are concerned primarily with monitoring the decisions made by managers on behalf of the company. The trend today is toward boards composed of external directors who have little vested interest in the firm. Shareholder activism is helping to propel this trend, as they seek better representation from boards that are less likely to have conflicts of interest.

Another significant governance issue is internal control and risk management. Controls allow for comparisons between actual performance and the planned performance and goals of the organization. They are used to safeguard corporate assets and resources, protect the reliability of organizational information, and ensure compliance with regulations, laws, and contracts. Controls foster understanding when discrepancies exist between corporate expectations and stakeholder interests and issues. A strong internal control system should alert decision-makers to possible problems or risks that may threaten business operations. Risk can be categorized (1) as a hazard, in which case risk management focuses on minimizing negative situations, such as fraud, injury, or financial loss; (2) as an uncertainty that needs to be hedged through quantitative plans and models; or (3) as an opportunity for innovation and entrepreneurship.

How executives are compensated for their leadership, service, and performance is another governance issue. Many people believe the ratio between the highest paid executives and median employee wages in the company should be reasonable. Others argue that because executives assume so much risk on behalf of the organization, they deserve the rewards that follow from strong company performance. One area for board members to consider is the extent to which executive compensation is linked to company performance.

The Organisation for Economic Co-operation and Development has issued a set of principles from which to formulate minimum standards of fairness, transparency, accountability, disclosure, and responsibility for business practice. These principles help guide companies around the world and are part of the convergence that is occurring with respect to corporate governance.

Most businesspeople and academicians agree that the benefits of a strong approach to corporate governance outweigh its costs. Because governance is concerned with the decisions taken by boards of directors and executives, it has the potential for far-reaching positive, and negative, effects. The future of corporate governance is directly linked to the future of social responsibility. Business leaders and managers will need to embrace governance as an essential part of effective performance. Governments also have a role to play in corporate governance. National competitiveness depends on the strength of various institutions, with primacy on the effective performance of business and capital markets. Other stakeholders may become more willing to use governance mechanisms to affect corporate strategy or decision-making.

Responsible Business Debate

Corporate Governance at CVS

Issue: *Should pharmacies sell harmful products?*

CVS is discontinuing sales of cigarettes and other tobacco products. In a risky move that cost it $2 billion, CVS claimed that selling cigarettes was incompatible with its intention to position itself as a healthcare provider. By the end of 2014, it was estimated that the number of insured Americans increased by 11–13 million. Pharmacies are competing with one another to capture a share of this growing market, and they are attempting to move away from their position as drugstores toward becoming healthcare providers.

CVS believes that the move, although costly in the short-term, will provide it with a long-term advantage. It has partnered with about two dozen health systems in its quest toward gaining leadership in healthcare services. CVS believes discontinuing sales of its tobacco products will increase its standing with its healthcare partners, providing it with a competitive advantage over rival pharmacies that continue to sell cigarettes.

This creates an ethical dilemma for CVS's rivals. Walgreen's has argued that selling cigarettes is necessary for remaining competitive. Rite Aid has stated it will continue selling cigarettes based on the demands of its customers. Both firms offer smoking-cessation products and clinics.

From a stakeholder orientation, this issue can be examined a variety of ways. Those that believe Walgreen's, Rite Aid, and other pharmacies should follow CVS's lead feel that it is the most ethical response if they want to position themselves as health services companies since it is hypocritical to offer customers access to harmful products while promoting that they care about consumer health. Possible advantages also exist for pharmacies choosing to discontinue tobacco-related product sales. For instance, it is possible that healthcare partners will be more inclined to do business with CVS over other pharmacies who continue to sell cigarettes.

On the other hand, there are potential downsides for companies that follow CVS's lead. One of the most obvious would be loss of profits. CVS acknowledges that it will lose revenue from cigarette sales, and other companies too would face similar losses should they choose to discontinue tobacco products. In fact, CVS's stock went down after the announcement that it was eliminating cigarette sales. Conversely, the stock of Walgreen's and Rite Aid increased. This shows that investors believe selling cigarettes is more beneficial financially in the short-term. From a stakeholder perspective, it is necessary to consider the needs of investors as well as customers because the firm also has a duty to work toward profitability. Finally, tobacco products might be harmful, but they are not illegal. While many customers might applaud CVS for taking a stand, cigarette smokers lose out.

There Are Two Sides to Every Issue:

1. Major pharmacies should stop selling cigarettes because they are harmful products that are not consistent with their healthcare focus.
2. Major pharmacies should not stop selling cigarettes because they are legal, highly profitable for the company, and offer consumers choice.

Sources: Marilyn Alva, "Walgreen, Rite Aid Rise as CVS Falls on Tobacco Ban," *Investors.com*, http://news.investors.com/business/020514-688934-walgreen-and-rite-aid-rise-as-cvs-falls.htm (accessed July 12, 2016); Aaron Blake, "Obama praises CVS's Decision to Stop Selling Cigarettes," *The Washington Post*, February 5, 2014, https://www.washingtonpost.com/news/post-politics/wp/2014/02/05/obama-praises-cvss-decision-to-stop-selling-cigarettes/ (accessed July 12, 2016); Peter Frost, "CVS Cigarette Move urges Action by Walgreens, Rivals," *Chicago Tribune,* February 5, 2014, http://articles.chicagotribune.com/2014-02-05/business/chi-walgreen-cigarettes-20140205_1_tobacco-sales-cvs-caremark-walgreen-co (accessed July 12, 2016); Timothy W. Martin and Mike Esterl, "CVS to Stop Selling Cigarettes," *The Wall Street Journal,* February 5, 2014, http://online.wsj.com/news/articles/SB10001424052702304851104579363520905849600 (accessed July 12, 2016); Staff, "Rite Aid Gives Generic Response to Decision by CVS to Stop Selling Cigarettes," *MEDCity News,* February 6, 2014, http://medcitynews.com/2014/02/rite-aid-gives-generic-response-decision-cvs-stop-selling-cigarettes/ (accessed February 6, 2014).

KEY TERMS

corporate governance (p. 77)
shareholder model of corporate
   governance (p. 84)

stakeholder model of corporate
   governance (p. 85)

DISCUSSION QUESTIONS

1. What is corporate governance? Why is it an important concern for companies pursuing the social responsibility approach? How does it improve or change the nature of executive and managerial decision-making?
2. Compare the shareholder and stakeholder models of corporate governance. Which one seems to predominate today? What implications does this have for businesses in today's complex environment?
3. What role does executive compensation play in risk taking and accountability? Why do some people partially blame compensation for the failures of the subprime mortgage and financial industries in 2008–2009?
4. What is the role of the board of directors in corporate governance? What responsibilities does the board have?
5. What role do shareholders and other investors play in corporate governance? How can investors effect change?
6. Why are internal control and risk management important in corporate governance? Describe three approaches organizations may take to manage risk.

7. Why is the issue of executive compensation controversial? Are today's corporate executives worth the compensation packages they receive?
8. In what ways are corporate governance practices becoming standardized around the world? What differences exist?

9. As corporate governance becomes a significant aspect of social responsibility, what new skills and characteristics will managers and executives need to possess? Consider how pressures for governance require managers and executives to relate and interact with stakeholders in new ways.

EXPERIENTIAL EXERCISE

Visit the website of the Organisation for Economic Co-operation and Development (http://www.oecd.org). Examine the origins of the organization and its unique role in the global economy. After visiting the site, answer the following questions:

1. What are the primary reasons that OECD exists?
2. How would you describe OECD's current areas of concern and focus?

3. What role do you think OECD will play in the future with respect to corporate governance and related issues?

CORE-TEX CREATES A VORTEX AROUND AGGRESSIVE ACCOUNTING: WHAT WOULD YOU DO?

The statewide news carried a story about Core-Tex that evening. There were rumors swirling that one of the largest manufacturers in the state was facing serious questions about its social responsibility. A former accountant for Core-Tex, whose identity was not revealed, made allegations about aggressive accounting methods and practices that overstated company earnings. He said he left Core-Tex after his supervisor and colleagues did not take his concerns seriously. The former accountant hinted that the company's relationship with its external auditor was quite close, since Core-Tex's new CFO had once been on the external auditing team. Core-Tex had recently laid off 270 employees—a move that was not unexpected given the turbulent financial times. However, the layoffs hit some parts of the site's community pretty hard. Finally, inspectors from the state environmental protection agency had just issued a series of citations to Core-Tex for improper disposal methods and high emissions at one of its larger manufacturing plants. A television station had run an exposé on the environmental citations a week ago.

CEO Kelly Buscio clicked off the television set and thought about the company's next steps. Core-Tex's attorney had cautioned the executive group earlier that

week about communicating too much to the media and other constituents. The firm's vice president for marketing countered the attorney by insisting that Core-Tex needed to stay ahead of the rumors and assumptions that were being made about the company. He said that suppliers and business partners were starting to question Core-Tex's financial viability. The vice president of information technology and the vice president of operations were undecided on the next step, while the vice president of manufacturing had not attended the meeting. Buscio wondered what tomorrow could bring.

To her surprise, the newspapers had gone easy on Core-Tex the next day, owing to a shift in the media attention on a major oil spill, the retirement of a *Fortune* 500 CEO, and a major league baseball championship game the night before. The company's stock price, which averaged around $11.15, was down $0.35 by midmorning. The vice-president of marketing suggested that employees needed to hear from the CEO and be reassured about Core-Tex's strong future. Her first call after lunch came from a member of the board asking Buscio what the board could do to help the situation. What would you do?

CHAPTER FOUR

Legal, Regulatory, and Political Issues

Apple vs Samsung: Which Came First…the Chicken or the Egg?

In the technology industry, protecting one's intellectual property through patents is crucial to the survival of a company. A patent gives an organization such as Microsoft a temporary monopoly over a new technology. Patents are intended to reward firms for the risks they take in developing new products. They not only allow the firms to recoup their investment but also give them the chance to earn a significant profit. This prompts technology firms to constantly innovate and stay ahead of the competition by patenting new items.

Companies will often file lawsuits seeking damages from those they believe violated their intellectual property rights. One well-publicized case occurred between two titans of the cell phone industry, Apple and Samsung. After Apple introduced its iconic iPhone, Samsung came out with its own smartphone called Galaxy S. Apple filed a lawsuit against Samsung, accusing it of violating its iPhone patent by copying many components of the iPhone, including the rectangular shape; the black color of the phone; the tap to zoom, the flip to rotate, the slide to scroll features; and so on. It also claimed that Samsung copied features of its iPad product.

Samsung countersued, claiming that many of these components had already been patented by Samsung; thus, Samsung—and not Apple—held the intellectual property rights. The lawsuit soon snowballed, with suits being filed in the United States, South Korea, Germany, Japan, and other areas. Many of these countries came to different conclusions. For instance, the United States found Samsung guilty of intellectual property violations and ordered Samsung to pay Apple $1 billion in damages (this was later reduced). However, South Korea determined that Apple violated two of Samsung's patents, while Samsung violated one of Apple's. The United Kingdom ruled in favor of Samsung, while Germany banned sales of the Galaxy Tab 2.0 because of its similarities to Apple's iPad 2.

The different court rulings demonstrate the complexities of international regulations. The ethical and legal standards of intellectual property vary from country to country, making it difficult for firms to protect their intellectual property. Samsung appealed the ruling in the United States. In 2012, Apple filed another lawsuit against Samsung in the United States alleging that it had violated another five of its patents. The United States ordered Samsung to pay Apple $119.6 million. Apple requested that Samsung be banned from sales in the United States, but this was not granted, and legal experts say a direct ban is unlikely.

With so many different verdicts, it can be hard to determine which, if any, of the companies is at fault. Samsung has encountered price-fixing allegations in the past and has been accused by more than one competitor of copying its technology. However, Apple has also been involved in lawsuits. Apple recently paid to settle a lawsuit that it engaged in no-hiring agreements with competitors in the tech industry. Both companies have had to deal with past issues of legal misconduct. Whoever is at fault, the current ruling on intellectual property will have a major impact on the technology industry as a whole.[1]

The government has the power through laws and regulations to structure how businesses and individuals achieve their goals. The purpose of regulating firms is to create a fair competitive environment for businesses, consumers, and society. All stakeholders need to demonstrate a commitment to social responsibility through compliance with relevant laws and proactive consideration of social needs. The law is one of the most important business subjects in terms of its effect on organizational practices and activities. Thus, compliance with the law is a fundamental expectation of social responsibility. Because the law is based on principles, norms, and values found within society, the law is the foundation of responsible decision-making.

This chapter explores the complex relationship between business and government. First, we discuss some of the laws that structure the environment for the regulation of business. Major legislation relating to competition and regulatory agencies is reviewed to provide an overview of the regulatory environment. We also consider how businesses can participate in the public policy process through lobbying, political contributions, and political action committees. Finally, we offer a framework for a strategic approach to managing the legal and regulatory environment.

GOVERNMENT'S INFLUENCE ON BUSINESS

The government has a profound influence on business. Most Western countries have a history of elected representatives working through democratic institutions to provide the structure for the regulation of business conduct. For example, one of the differences that have long characterized the two major parties of the U.S. political system involves the government's role with respect to business. In general terms, the Republican Party tends to favor smaller central government with less regulation of business, while the Democratic Party is more open to government oversight, federal aid program, and sometimes higher taxes. From the start, President Obama worried some businesspeople, as he has promised more oversight of many different areas of the economy. For example, he promised to be tough on antitrust violations and has followed through by reversing a Bush-era policy that made it more difficult for the government to pursue antitrust violations.[2]

President Obama has brought U.S. policy regarding antitrust cases more in line with Europe's model.[3] Third-party and independent candidates typically focus on specific business issues or proclaim their distance from the two major political parties. However, the power and freedom of big business have resulted in conflicts among private businesses, government, private interest groups, and even individuals as businesses try to influence policy makers.

In the United States, the role that society delegates to government is to provide laws that are logically deduced from the Constitution and the Bill of Rights and to enforce these laws through the judicial system. Individuals and businesses, therefore, live under a rule of law designed to protect society and support an acceptable quality of life. Ideally, by limiting the influence and force by some parties, the overall welfare and freedom of all participants in the social system will be protected.

The provision of a court system to settle disputes and punish criminals, both organizational and individual, provides for justice and order in society. Both Google (renamed Alphabet) and Microsoft have come under numerous ongoing investigations for alleged antitrust activity in Europe, where the companies have been accused of engaging in behavior that prevents smaller companies from competing. In just over a year, the EU's antitrust regulator filed four charges against Alphabet that, among other allegations, Google favors its search functions more than rival sites, it restricts how a website can show advertisements from other companies, and it forces smartphone makers into pre-installing its search engine as the default on mobile devices.[4] The European Union is famous for being tough on companies suspected of antitrust cases, igniting the ire of many multinational corporations that feel as if they are being punished for being successful. Being aware of antitrust laws is important for all large corporations around the world, because judicial systems can punish businesses that fail to comply with laws and regulatory requirements.

The legal system is not always accepted in some countries as insurance that business will be conducted in a legitimate way. For example, after generations of being known for its top-secret bank accounts, Swiss banks were ordered by the United States Internal Revenue Service to disclose information about some of their clients because of concerns over illegal activities. In many places around the world, the business climate has become less tolerant of illegal and immoral actions, and countries like Switzerland, Liechtenstein, and Luxembourg now are being pressured to share information on potential tax dodgers with government agencies like the IRS. Credit Suisse pleaded guilty to aiding wealthy Americans in tax evasion and was ordered to give the Justice Department all records concerning American clients and was charged a fine of $2.6 billion for criminal misconduct.[5] This case illustrates the complexity of complying with international business laws.

While many businesses may object to regulations aimed at maintaining ethical cultures and preserving stakeholder welfare, businesses' very existence is based on laws permitting their creation, organization, and dissolution. From a social perspective, it is significant that a corporation has the same legal status as a "person" who can sue, be sued, and be held liable for debts. Laws may protect managers and stockholders from being personally liable for a company's debts, but individuals as well as organizations are still responsible for their conduct. Because corporations have a perpetual life, larger companies like ExxonMobil, Ford, and Sony take on an organizational culture, including social responsibility values, that extends beyond a specific time period, management team, or geographical region. Organizational culture plays an important role in the ability of corporations to outlive individual executives—it sets the tone for the business and allows for continuity even during times of leadership turnover.

Most, generally smaller, companies are owned by individual proprietors or operated as partnerships. However, large incorporated firms like those just mentioned often receive more attention because of their size, visibility, and impact on so many aspects of the economy and society. In a pluralistic society, diverse stakeholder groups such as business, labor, consumers, environmentalists, privacy advocates, and others attempt to influence public officials who legislate, interpret laws, and regulate business. The public interest is served through open participation and debate that result in effective public policy. Because no system of government is perfect, legal and regulatory systems are constantly evolving and changing in response to changes in the business environment and social institutions. For example, increasing use of the internet for information and business created a need for legislation and regulations to protect the owners of creative materials from unauthorized use and consumers from fraud and invasions of privacy. The line between acceptable and illegal activity on the internet is increasingly difficult to discern and is often determined by judges and juries and discussed widely in the media.

In response, the Better Business Bureau (BBB), a self-regulatory association supported by businesses, offers an Online Accredited Business certification to retailers, which certifies their high ethical standards and safety for online shoppers. The BBB lists the companies on its website and directs consumers to approved businesses' websites.[6] Over a million times a month, web users click on the BBBOnline seals to check a firm's credibility and high standards.[7]

Like the companies that have pursued and received the BBB accreditation, firms that adopt a strategic approach to the legal and regulatory system develop proactive organizational values and compliance programs that identify areas of risks and include formal communication, training, and continuous improvement of responses to the legal and regulatory environment.

In the next section, we take a closer look at why and how the government affects businesses through laws and regulation, the costs and benefits of regulation, and how regulation may affect companies doing business in foreign countries.

The Rationale for Regulation

The United States was established as a capitalist system, but the prevailing capitalistic theory has changed over time. Adam Smith published his critical economic ideas in *The Theory of Moral Sentiments* and *Inquiry into the Nature and Causes of the Wealth of Nations* during the late 1700s, which are still considered important today. Smith observed the supply and demand, contractual efficiency, and division of labor of various companies within England. Smith's writings formed the basis of modern economics.

Smith's idea of *laissez faire*, or "the invisible hand," is critical to capitalism in that it assumes the market, through its own inherent mechanisms, will keep commerce in equilibrium.

A second form of capitalism gained support at the beginning of the Great Depression. During the 1930s, John Maynard Keynes argued that the state could stimulate economic growth and improve stability in the private sector—through, for example, controlling interest rates, taxation and public projects.[8]

Keynes argued that government policies could be used to increase aggregate demand, thus increasing economic activity and reducing unemployment and deflation. He argued that the solution to depression was to stimulate the economy through some combination of a reduction in interest rates or government investment in infrastructure. President Franklin D. Roosevelt employed Keynesian economic theories to pull the United States out of the Great Depression.

The third and most recent form of capitalism was developed by Milton Friedman and represented a swing to the right on the political spectrum. Friedman had lived through the Great Depression but rejected the Keynesian conclusion that the market sometimes needs some intervention in order to function most efficiently. Friedman instead believed in deregulation because he thought that the system could reach equilibrium without government intervention.[9] Friedman's ideas were the guiding principles for government policy making in the U.S., and increasingly throughout the world, starting in the second half of the twentieth century, especially during the presidencies of Ronald Reagan, George H.W. Bush, Bill Clinton, and George W. Bush. However, President Barack Obama's policies moved back in the direction of Keynesian capitalism with higher taxes and more spending on healthcare, as well as other public projects related to stabilizing the economy after the financial crisis.

Many communist countries too are adopting components of capitalism. State capitalism occurs when the government runs commercial activity in a capitalist manner. In China, for instance, many of the largest for-profit firms are owned in some capacity by the government. Despite this ownership, the day-to-day workings of the companies operate in a capitalist manner. This gives them the ability to compete against global firms. Table 4.1 gives a brief overview of the different forms of capitalism.

Although the opinions of which form of capitalism is the better option has changed over time, the federal and state governments in the United States have always stepped in to enact legislation and create regulations to address particular issues and restrict the behavior of business in accordance with society's wishes. Many of the issues used to justify business regulation can be categorized as economic or social.

Economic and Competitive Reasons for Regulation A great number of regulations have been passed by legislatures over the last 100 years in an effort "to level the playing field" on which businesses operate. When the

TABLE 4.1 Forms of Capitalism

Type of Capitalism	Description	Example
Adam Smith's *laissez faire*	The market, through its own inherent mechanisms, will keep commerce in equilibrium	Popular in the United States during the nineteenth century
Keynesian capitalism	Government policies could be used to stimulate growth	Popular in the United States after the Great Depression
Friedman capitalism	Emphasizes deregulation and significantly less government intervention	Popular in the second half of the twentieth century
State capitalism	Major organizations are owned by the government but run in a capitalist manner	China's economic system

United States became an independent nation in the eighteenth century, the business environment consisted of many small farms, manufacturers, and cottage industries operating on a primarily local scale. With the increasing industrialization of the United States after the Civil War, "captains of industry" like John D. Rockefeller (oil), Andrew Carnegie (railroads and steel), Andrew Mellon (aluminum), and J.P. Morgan (banking) began to consolidate their business holdings into large national trusts.

trusts
Organizations established to gain control of a product market or industry by eliminating competition.

Trusts are organizations generally established to gain control of a product market or industry by eliminating competition. Such organizations are often considered detrimental because, without serious competition, they can potentially charge higher prices and provide lower quality products to consumers. Thus, as these firms grew in size and power, public distrust of them likewise grew because of often-legitimate concerns about unfair competition. This suspicion and the public's desire to require these increasingly powerful companies to act responsibly spurred the first antitrust legislation. If trusts are successful in eliminating competition, a monopoly can result.

monopoly
A market type in which just one business provides a good or service in a given market.

A **monopoly** occurs when just one business provides a good or service in a given market. Utility companies that supply electricity, natural gas, water, or cable television are recent examples of monopolies, but that is starting to change. The government tolerates these monopolies because the cost of supplying the good or providing the service is so great that few companies would be willing to invest in new markets without some protection from competition. Monopolies may also be allowed by patent laws that grant the developer of a new technology a period of time (usually 20 years) during which no other firm can use the same technology without the patent holder's consent. Patent protections are permitted to encourage businesses to engage in riskier research and development by allowing them time to recoup their research, development, and production expenses and to earn a reasonable profit.

Because trusts and monopolies lack serious competition, there are concerns that they may either exploit their market dominance to restrict their output and raise prices or lower quality to gain greater profits. This concern is the primary rationalization for their regulation by the government. Public utilities, for example, are regulated by state public utility commissions and, where they involve interstate commerce, are subject to federal regulation as well. In recent years, some of these industries have been deregulated with the idea that greater competition will police the behavior of individual firms. However, in areas like utilities it is difficult to develop perfect competition because of the large sunk costs required. Oftentimes, deregulation has led to increased costs to stakeholders. For example, Maryland deregulated the state's residential energy market in the late 1990s, and when rate caps came off in 2004, residences were hit with skyrocketing utilities costs. The problem has been market prices—when petroleum costs are high, so are the costs to generate energy. In a deregulated privatized market, these costs are passed on to consumers. The governor has tried numerous tactics to relieve the burden, including a one-time handout, but stakeholders remain concerned.[10]

Related to the issue of regulation of trusts and monopolies is the society's desire to restrict destructive or unfair competition. What is considered unfair varies with the standard practice of the industry, the impact of specific conduct, and the individual case. When one company dominates a particular industry, it may engage in destructive competition or employ anticompetitive tactics. For example, it may slash prices in an effort to drive competitors out of the market and then raise prices later. It may conspire with other competitors to set, or "fix," prices so that each firm can ensure a certain level of profit. Other examples of unfair competitive trade practices are stealing trade secrets or obtaining confidential information from a competitor's employees, trademark and copyright infringement, false advertising, and deceptive selling methods such as "bait and switch" and false representation of products.

Regulation is also intended to protect consumers from unethical business practices. For instance, the government has been scrutinizing large-scale increases in the price of pharmaceuticals. Although businesses generally have freedom to determine their pricing strategies, pharmaceuticals are a hot-button issue because of their impact on people's health. The nation was outraged when Turing Pharmaceuticals raised the price of an old generic drug 5,000%. Even though most pharmaceutical firms do not implement such massive price increases, many are increasing their prices. There is some concern among drug makers that Congress might implement controls on the amount that pharmaceutical companies can raise the prices of their drugs.[11]

Social Reasons for Regulation Regulation may also occur when marketing activities result in undesirable consequences for society. Many manufacturing processes, for example, create air, water, or land pollution.

Such consequences create uncounted "costs" in the form of contamination of natural resources, illness, and so on that neither the manufacturer nor the consumer "pays" for directly, although consumers may end up paying for these costs nevertheless. Because few companies are willing to shoulder these costs voluntarily, regulation is necessary to ensure that all firms within an industry do their part to minimize damages and pay their fair share. Likewise, regulations have proven necessary to protect natural (e.g., forests, fishing grounds, and other habitats) and social resources (e.g., historical and architecturally or archeologically significant structures). We will take a closer look at some of these environmental protection regulations and related issues in Chapter 11 on sustainability.

Other regulations have come about in response to social demands for equality in the workplace, especially after the 1960s. Such laws and regulations require that companies ignore race, ethnicity, gender, religion, and disabilities in favor of qualifications that more accurately reflect an individual's capacity for performing a particular job. Likewise, deaths and injuries because of employer negligence resulted in regulations designed to ensure that people can enjoy a safe working environment. The airline industry has become a prime example of how tough economic times result in overworked, under-trained employees. Many pilots receive low compensation, poor health benefits, and are forced to work long hours—all factors that contribute to a weak and careless organizational culture. It is thought that the crash of a FlyDubai plane might have occurred partially due to overwork. Although there may have other factors involved, colleagues claim the pilot was going to leave the airline because of fatigue. Crew members have claimed acute fatigue is common in the industry.[12]

Still other regulations have resulted from special-interest group crusades for safer products. For example, Ralph Nader's *Unsafe at Any Speed*, published in 1965, criticized the automobile industry as a whole, and General Motors specifically, for putting profit and style ahead of lives and safety. Nader's consumer protection organization, popularly known as Nader's Raiders, successfully campaigned for legislation that required automakers to provide safety belts, padded dashboards, stronger door latches, head restraints, shatterproof windshields, and collapsible steering columns in automobiles. As we will see in Chapter 8, consumer activists also helped secure passage of several other consumer protection laws, such as the Wholesome Meat Act of 1967, the Clean Water Act of 1972, and the Toxic Substance Act of 1976.

Issues arising from the increasing use of the internet have led to demands for new laws protecting consumers and business. Laws such as the Stop Online Piracy Act (SOPA) and the Protect Intellectual Property Act (PIPA) were proposed to prevent copyright infringement over the internet. Under these provisions companies could be penalized for posting pirated content over the internet. However, Google, Yahoo, and other internet companies protested the bills, saying that it gave the government too much power to shut down websites and infringe on freedom of speech.[13] Wikipedia, Google, and other websites underwent a service blackout for an entire day to protest the bills. The proposed laws were defeated, much to the frustration of content providers who hoped the bills would help protect their intellectual property. Intellectual property protection versus freedom of speech is a tricky balance that requires legislators to research solutions that respects both of these rights.

As we shall see in Chapter 10, the technology associated with the internet has generated a number of issues related to privacy, fraud, and copyrights. For instance, creators of copyrighted works such as movies, books, and music are calling for new laws and regulations to safeguard their ownership of these works. In response to these concerns, Congress enacted the Digital Millennium Copyright Act in 1998, which extended existing copyright laws to better protect "digital" recordings of music, movies, and the like. While other countries have implemented similar measures, copyright violations continue to plague many global industries, which to some critics calls into question the effectiveness of legal action. A team of security specialists recommends technological, not legal, solutions as most effective in the fight against piracy and copyright infringement.[14]

Concerns about the collection and use of personal information, especially regarding children, resulted in the passage of the Children's Online Privacy Protection Act of 2000 (COPPA). The Federal Trade Commission (FTC) enforces the act by levying fines against non-complying website operators. For example, Singapore-based mobile advertising firm InMobi paid $950,000 in civil penalties for tracking the locations of hundreds of millions of consumers, many of them children, for the geo-targeting of ads.[15]

Internet safety among children is a major topic of concern. This is true for children of all ages. Studies have shown that approximately 50 percent of children between the ages of six and nine use social media, and over 90 percent of children under the age of two have accessible information online, including photos and other personal information. Many are urging parents to encourage their children to practice safe online behaviors such as using privacy restrictions and not posting information or photos that contain too much personal information.[16]

Another major concern is online fraud. According to the Internet Crime Complaint Center (IC3), online fraudsters are becoming more and more creative by making use of over 20 listed types of scams. These scams are designed to target all age groups and together contribute to the loss of nearly $200 million a year. While online fraud is a major concern, it is only a small portion of the entirety of online crimes committed. It is estimated that there are 25 million fraudulent log-in attempts per month.[17]

Ethical Responsibilities in Marketing

Ackman vs. Herbalife: It's Multilevel War!

Herbalife International is the third largest direct-selling company in the world, with independent contractors in 90 countries. Its product line consists of weight-management and nutrition products. Like many direct selling companies, Herbalife employs a multilevel marketing compensation system. Multilevel marketing is a compensation system wherein contractors earn income from their own sales of products as well as commissions from sales made by those they have recruited. However, sales are never forced, and independent contractors do not receive additional compensation unless their recruits make sales.

Multilevel marketing is a legal activity. However, pyramid schemes are illegal. These schemes occur when investors are promised large profits based primarily on recruiting others to join their program. The promise is not based on profits from any real investment or sale of goods. The reason why this scheme is illegal is because it is unsustainable—the scheme falls apart once new recruits dry up, and investors often lose their investments.

Because of the similarities between the two, many people mistake legal multilevel marketing with illegal pyramid schemes. China, in fact, has banned multilevel marketing in the belief that it too closely resembles a pyramid scheme. However, U.S. courts have determined multiple times that multilevel marketing is a legitimate way of doing business.

Like other direct selling companies, Herbalife has faced accusations of operating pyramid schemes. However, one of its biggest challenges occurred when a famous hedge fund manager tried to discredit the company. In 2012, Herbalife was accused of being an elaborate pyramid scheme by hedge fund manager William Ackman. Ackman had bet $1 billion in a short sale off

Herbalife's stock. Short selling occurs when an investor sells shares borrowed from a lender in the belief that the stock will decrease. If the stock decreases, the investor profits.

Ackman's accusations against Herbalife included the following: (1) the majority of contractors for Herbalife lose money, (2) Herbalife pays more for recruiting new contractors than selling actual products, and (3) only the top 1 percent of contractors earn most of the money. Herbalife defended its business model and pointed out that many people become contractors to get a 25 percent discount on their purchases. Often they are not trying to make money. Also, independent contractors who decide not to sell products have the option of returning merchandise to Herbalife. A respected Nielsen survey found that 7.9 million consumers, or 3.3 percent of the U.S. population, had purchased a Herbalife product in the last three months. This supports the fact that Herbalife uses a valid and successful business model, which is producing profits directly related to product sales.

Although Herbalife's stock initially dropped due to the allegations, it has now recovered. Many have criticized Ackman, claiming that his short against the company created an incentive for him to try to discredit Herbalife. In 2014 the Federal Trade Commission claimed they were investigating Herbalife's operations. It believed Herbalife was misrepresenting opportunities as "get-rick-quick" schemes and did not have adequate disclosures. Herbalife disagreed with the FTC but paid $200 million to settle and promised to improve disclosures with distributors. The main issue involved accurately reporting retail sales. However, the FTC did not rule that the firm was a pyramid scheme, a great victory for Herbalife and a blow for Ackman.

Sources: Adapted from the case "Multilevel Marketing Under Fire: Herbalife Defends Its Business Model," developed by Michelle Urban and Jennifer Sawayda for the UNM Daniels Fund Ethics Initiative; David Benoit, "Herbalife to Pay $200 Million Over Claims of Misrepresentation," *The Wall Street Journal,* July 15, 2016, http://www.wsj.com/articles/herbalife-to-pay-200-million-over-claims-of-misrepresentation-1468584397 (accessed July 15, 2016).

Laws and Regulations

As a result of business abuses and social demands for reform, the federal government began to pass legislation to regulate business conduct in the late nineteenth century. In this section, we will look at a few of the most significant of these laws. Table 4.2 summarizes many more laws that affect business operations.

TABLE 4.2 Major Federal Legislation Regulating Business

Sherman Antitrust Act, 1890	Prohibits monopolies
Clayton Act, 1914	Prohibits price discrimination, exclusive dealing, and other efforts to restrict competition
Federal Trade Commission Act, 1914	Created the Federal Trade Commission (FTC) to help enforce antitrust laws
Robinson-Patman Act, 1936	Prohibits price discrimination between retailers and wholesalers
Wheeler-Lea Act, 1938	Prohibits unfair and deceptive acts regardless of whether competition is injured
Lanham Act, 1946	Protects and regulates brand names, brand marks, trade names, and trademarks
Celler-Kefauver Act, 1950	Prohibits one corporation from controlling another when the effect substantially lessens competition
Consumer Goods Pricing Act, 1975	Prohibits price maintenance agreements among manufacturers and resellers in interstate commerce
Antitrust Improvements Act, 1976	Strengthens earlier antitrust laws; gives Justice Department more investigative authority
Federal Corrupt Practices Act, 1977	Makes it illegal to pay foreign government officials to facilitate business or to use third parties such as agents and consultants to provide bribes to such officials
Trademark Counterfeiting Act, 1984	Provides penalties for individuals dealing in counterfeit goods
Trademark Law Revision Act, 1988	Amends the Lanham Act to allow brands not yet introduced to be protected through patent and trademark registration
Federal Trademark Dilution Act, 1995	Provides trademark owners the right to protect trademarks and requires them to relinquish those that match or parallel existing trademarks
Digital Millennium Copyright Act, 1998	Refines copyright laws to protect digital versions of copyrighted materials, including music and movies
Sarbanes-Oxley Act, 2002	Made securities fraud a criminal offense; stiffened penalties for corporate fraud; created an accounting oversight board; and instituted numerous other provisions designed to increase corporate transparency and compliance

(Continued)

TABLE 4.2 (*Continued*)

Controlling the Assault of Non-solicited Pornography and Marketing Act (CAN-SPAM), 2003	Bans fraudulent or deceptive unsolicited commercial email and requires senders to provide information on how recipients can opt out of receiving additional messages
Fraud Enforcement and Recovery Act, 2009	Strengthens provisions to improve the criminal enforcement of fraud laws, including mortgage fraud, securities fraud, financial institutions fraud, and fraud related to the federal assistance relief program
Dodd-Frank Wall Street Reform and Consumer Protection Act (2010)	Increases accountability and transparency in the financial industry, protects consumers from deceptive financial practices, and establishes the Consumer Financial Protection Bureau

Sherman Antitrust Act The Sherman Antitrust Act, passed in 1890, is the principal tool employed by the federal government to prevent businesses from restraining trade and monopolizing markets. Congress passed the law, almost unanimously, in response to public demands to curtail the growing power and abuses of trusts in the late nineteenth century. The law outlaws "every contract, combination in the form of trust or otherwise, or conspiracy, in restraint of trade or commerce."[18] The law also makes a violation a felony crime, punishable by a fine of up to $10 million for corporate violators and $350,000 and/or 3 years in prison for individual offenders.[19]

The Sherman Antitrust Act applies to all firms operating in interstate commerce as well as to U.S. firms engaged in foreign commerce. The law has been used to break up some of the most powerful companies in the United States, including the Standard Oil Company (1911), the American Tobacco Company (1911), and AT&T (1984). There was also an attempt to break up Microsoft. In the Microsoft case, a U.S. district court judge ruled that the software giant inhibited competition by using unlawful tactics to protect its Windows monopoly in computer operating systems and by illegally expanding its dominance into the market for internet Web-browsing software. However, the ruling to break up Microsoft was appealed, and the order overturned. Microsoft agreed to adhere to a consent decree, where it complied with stricter remedies to prevent non-competitive business practices through 2010. The Sherman Act remains the primary source of antitrust law in the United States, although it has been supplemented by several amendments and additional legislation.

Clayton Antitrust Act Because the provisions of the Sherman Antitrust Act were vague, the courts have interpreted the law in different ways. To rectify this situation, Congress enacted the Clayton Antitrust Act in 1914 to limit mergers and acquisitions that have the potential to stifle competition.[20] The Clayton Act also specifically prohibits price discrimination, tying agreements (when a supplier furnishes a product to a buyer with the stipulation that the buyer must purchase other products as well), exclusive agreements (when a supplier forbids an intermediary to carry products of competing manufacturers), and the acquisition of stock in another corporation where the effect may be to substantially lessen competition, or tend to create a monopoly. In addition, the Clayton Act prohibits members of one company's board of directors from holding seats on the boards of competing corporations. The law also exempts farm corporations and labor organizations from antitrust laws.

Federal Trade Commission Act In the same year the Clayton Act was passed, Congress also enacted the Federal Trade Commission Act to further strengthen the antitrust provisions of the Sherman Act. Unlike the Clayton Act, which prohibits specific practices, the Federal Trade Commission Act more broadly prohibits unfair methods of competition. More significantly, this law created the Federal Trade Commission (FTC) to protect consumers and businesses from unfair competition. Of all the federal regulatory agencies, the FTC has the greatest influence on business activities.

When the FTC receives a complaint about a business or finds reason to believe that a company is engaging in illegal conduct, it issues a formal complaint stating that the firm is in violation of the law. If the company continues the unlawful practice, the FTC can issue a cease-and-desist order, which requires the offender to stop the specified behavior. The weight loss industry has been a target for complaints in recent years. Lunada Biomedical, Inc. and three of its principals settled with the FTC after it filed a lawsuit over misleading claims regarding its dietary supplement Amberen. According to the FTC, the health and efficacy claims of Amberen, a dietary supplement for women over 40, were unsubstantiated.[21]

Although a firm can appeal to the federal courts to have the order rescinded, the FTC can seek civil penalties in court, up to a maximum penalty of $10,000 a day for each infraction, if a cease-and-desist order is ignored. The commission can also require businesses to air corrective advertising to counter previous ads the commission considers misleading. For example, Lasik surgery providers were required by the FTC to run corrective advertising to inform consumers of the risks of undergoing the irreversible surgery along with the benefits.[22]

In addition, the FTC helps to resolve disputes and makes rulings on business decisions. The FTC ruled that POM Wonderful LLC, maker of a pomegranate juice product, made unsubstantiated claims about the product's health benefits. The FTC mandated that POM could not claim its product helped fight disease unless backed up by two pharmaceutical clinical trials. A federal appeals court upheld the FTC's finding but questioned whether the need for two clinical trials in order to make health claims could be a free speech violation.[23] In this case, the FTC helped to reinforce truthfulness in advertising, but some question whether its requirements for POM are too stringent.

Proposed Financial Reforms In response to the 2008–2009 financial crisis, government leaders proposed sweeping reforms to increase consumer protection. This proposed legislation has been a step away from the deregulation practices of the last several decades, instead giving government a freer hand in regulating the financial industry. The Obama administration has given the Federal Reserve more power over the financial industry and established a new Consumer Financial Protection Bureau that aids in regulating banks and other financial institutions. More specifically, the agency monitors financial instruments like subprime mortgages and other high-risk lending practices. The problems leading up to the financial crisis included inaction on the part of federal regulators to protect consumers from fraud and predatory lending practices, lack of responsibility on the part of mortgage brokers taking large risks, conflicts of interest among credit rating industries, and complex financial instruments that investors did not understand.

To prevent these problems from leading to future financial crises, the Obama administration proposed legislation that would include the following reforms among others: removing some of the FTC's powers and creating a Consumer Financial Protection Bureau; creating a Financial Stability Oversight Council to identify and address key risks to the financial industry; requiring loan bundlers to retain a percentage of what they sell (a proposal also being considered by the EU); providing new powers for the Securities and Exchange Commission to monitor credit rating industries for objectivity; and requiring complex financial instruments to be traded on a regulated exchange.

Enforcement of the Laws Because violations of the Sherman Antitrust Act are felony crimes, the Antitrust Division of the U.S. Department of Justice enforces it. The FTC enforces antitrust regulations of a civil, rather than criminal, nature. There are many additional federal regulatory agencies (see Table 4.3) that oversee the enforcement of other laws and regulations. Most states also have regulatory agencies that make and enforce laws for individuals and businesses. In recent years, cooperation among state attorneys general, regulatory agencies, and the federal government has increased, particularly in efforts related to the control of drugs, organized crime, and pollution.

The 2008–2009 financial meltdown revealed the need for better enforcement of the financial industry. Institutions took advantage of loopholes in the regulation system to make quick profits. For example, some adjustable mortgage rates offered low "teaser" rates that did not even cover the monthly interest on loans. This ended up increasing the principal balances on mortgages, resulting in debt that many consumers could not pay off. Unethical actions such as these led to the financial crisis. However, since these institutions were not as carefully monitored as other institutions, such as banks, regulators did not catch them until it was too late.[24]

TABLE 4.3 Federal Regulatory Agencies

Food and Drug Administration, 1906	Enforces laws and regulations to prevent distribution of adulterated or misbranded foods, drugs, medical devices, cosmetics, veterinary products, and potentially hazardous consumer products
Federal Reserve Board, 1913	Regulates banking institutions; protects the credit rights of consumers; maintains the stability of the financial system; conducts the nation's monetary policy; and serves as the nation's central bank
Federal Trade Commission, 1914	Enforces laws and guidelines regarding business practices; takes action to stop false and deceptive advertising and labeling
Federal Deposit Insurance Corporation, 1933	Insures deposits in banks and thrift institutions for at least $250,000; identifies and monitors risks related to deposit insurance funds; and limits the economic effects when banks or thrift institutions fail
Federal Communications Commission, 1934	Regulates communication by wire, radio, and television in interstate and foreign commerce
Securities and Exchange Commission, 1934	Regulates the offering and trading of securities, including stocks and bonds
National Labor Relations Board, 1935	Enforces the National Labor Relations Act; investigates and rectifies unfair labor practices by employers and unions
Equal Employment Opportunity Commission, 1970	Promotes equal opportunity in employment through administrative and judicial enforcement of civil rights laws and through education and technical assistance
Environmental Protection Agency, 1970	Develops and enforces environmental protection standards and conducts research into the adverse effects of pollution
Occupational Safety and Health Administration, 1971	Enforces the Occupational Safety and Health Act and other workplace health and safety laws and regulations; makes surprise inspections of facilities to ensure safe workplaces
Consumer Product Safety Commission, 1972	Ensures compliance with the Consumer Product Safety Act; protects the public from unreasonable risk of injury from any consumer product not covered by other regulatory agencies
Commodity Futures Trading Commission, 1974	Regulates commodity futures and options markets. Protects market users from fraud and abusive trading practices
Federal Housing Finance Industry, 2008	Combined the agencies of the Office of the Federal Housing Enterprise Oversight, the Federal Housing Finance Board, and the GSE mission office of the Department of Housing and Urban Development to oversee the country's secondary mortgage markets
Consumer Financial Protection Bureau, 2010	Created as part of the Dodd-Frank Act to educate consumers and protect them from deceptive financial products

New enforcement aims to require brokers to display a greater fiduciary duty to their clients, requiring them to put their clients' interests above their own and eliminating any conflicts of interest. This could cause them to offer products that are less costly and more tax-efficient for consumers rather than promoting products that would benefit their companies at consumers' expense.[25]

In addition to enforcing stricter regulations for financial institutions, the Obama administration has taken steps to protect consumers. This includes encouraging consumers to manage credit cards, savings, and mortgages more carefully; providing cardholders with warnings about how long it will take to pay off their debt if they only pay the minimum on their credit cards each month; and preventing certain credit card issuers from offering credit cards to people under the age of 21.

In addition to enforcement by state and federal authorities, lawsuits by private citizens, competitors, and special-interest groups are used to enforce legal and regulatory policy. Through private civil actions, an individual or organization can file a lawsuit related to issues such as antitrust, price fixing, or unfair advertising. An organization can even ask for assistance from a federal agency to address a concern. For example, broadcasting companies gained the assistance of the Department of Justice in fighting the start-up service Aereo, which used equipment to stream local television content to consumers for a fee. The case was eventually taken to the Supreme Court, where it was ruled that Aereo needed to secure permission from content providers.[26]

Apple has been under an antitrust investigation for fixing prices on electronic books as a means to block competition with Amazon. A U.S. District Court Judge ruled that the company colluded with five e-book publishers on pricing. Apple denies any wrongdoing and claims its pricing is due to natural competitive pressures that resulted as they entered the market. The company filed an appeal to the ruling that was denied. Apple was forced to pay $400 million in compensation. Consumers who purchased e-books from the *New York Times* bestseller lists received $6.93 credit for every purchase.[27]

Global Regulation

The twentieth century brought a number of regional trade agreements that decreased the barriers to international trade. The North American Free Trade Agreement (NAFTA) and the EU are two such agreements that were formed with the intention of enhancing regional competitiveness and decreasing inequalities. NAFTA, which eliminates virtually all tariffs on goods produced and traded between the United States, Canada, and Mexico, makes it easier for businesses of each country to invest in the other member countries. The agreement also provides some coordination of legal standards governing business transactions among the three countries. NAFTA promotes cooperation among various regulatory agencies to encourage effective law enforcement in the free trade area. Within the framework of NAFTA, the United States and Canada have developed many agreements to enforce each other's antitrust laws. The agreement provides for cooperation in investigations, including requests for information and the opportunity to visit the territory of the other nation in the course of conducting investigations.

The European Union was established in 1958 to promote free trade among its members and now includes 28 European nations, with more expected to join in coming years.[28] However, in 2016 the United Kingdom voted to leave the EU. If the separation takes place, it will some years for it to occur. These changes will likely have a profound impact on both the U.K. and the EU economy. To facilitate trade among its members, the EU standardized business laws and trade barriers, eliminated customs checks among its members, and introduced the euro as a standard currency. Moreover, the Commission of the European Communities has entered into an agreement with the United States, similar to NAFTA, regarding joint antitrust laws. The European Union is in favor of tighter financial-market regulation in the wake of the financial crisis. Proposals discussed by the European Commission include laws restricting proprietary trading at large banks, revisions on rules regulating occupational pension funds, and improving benchmarks used as reference prices for financial instruments.[29] However, not all countries in the EU agree on which reforms to adopt. Citizens in the United Kingdom disagreed on certain policies such as immigration and disliked the impact the EU's financial struggles were having on the economy. This likely contributed to the vote to leave the EU. It is noteworthy that the vote only won by a slim margin.[30]

A company that engages in commerce beyond its own country's borders must contend with the potentially complex relationship among the laws of its own nation, international laws, and the laws of the nation in which it will be trading, as well as various trade restrictions imposed on international trade. International business activities are affected to varying degrees by each nation's laws, regulatory agencies, courts, the political environment, and special-interest groups. The European Union, for example, has been tough on large businesses, leaving some critics in the United States to call the EU anti-competitive and anti-innovative. However, as regulations in the United States and the EU continue to be modified as a result of the 2008–2009 financial crisis, incongruences from each side can be seen. For example, as part of the Dodd-Frank Act, the United States mandated that large banks rely more upon liquid capital for financing rather than debt. While this mandate seems to reduce risks in the financial industry, those banks in the EU see this mandate as creating a competitive disadvantage. Financial firms have historically been held to local standards of the country where business is conducted. EU regulators fear that this new capital requirement will restrict economic growth and give U.S. firms an advantage over those in the EU. They also cite potential issues regarding international trade.[31]

This example demonstrates how companies can experience major barriers when doing business in foreign countries. In addition to stricter regulations, countries can also establish import barriers, including tariffs, quotas, minimum price levels, and port-of-entry taxes that affect the

TABLE 4.4 Signs of Possible Antitrust Violation

- Any evidence that two or more competing sellers of similar products have agreed to price their products a certain way, to sell only a certain amount of their product or to sell only in certain areas or to certain customers;

- Large price changes involving more than one seller of very similar products of different brands, particularly if the price changes are of an equal amount and occur at about the same time;

- Suspicious statements from a seller suggesting that only one firm can sell to a particular customer or type of customer;

- Fewer competitors than normal submit bids on a project;

- Competitors submit identical bids;

- The same company repeatedly has been the low bidder on contracts for a certain product or service or in a particular area;

- Bidders seem to win bids on a fixed rotation;

- There is an unusual and unexplainable large dollar difference between the winning bid and all other bids; or

- The same bidder bids substantially higher on some bids than on others, and there is no logical cost reason to explain the difference.

Source: U.S. Department of Justice, "Antitrust Enforcement and the Consumer," http://www.justice.gov/atr/public/div_stats/antitrust-enfor-consumer.pdf (accessed June 17, 2016).

importation of products. Other laws govern product quality and safety, distribution methods, and sales and advertising practices.

Although there is considerable variation in focus among different nations' laws, many countries have laws that are quite similar to those in the United States. Indeed, the Sherman Act has been copied throughout the world as the basis for regulating fair competition. Antitrust issues, such as price fixing and market allocation, have become a major area of international cooperation in the regulation of business.[32] Table 4.4 provides a list of situations and signs indicating that antitrust may become a concern.

Costs and Benefits of Regulation

Costs of Regulation Regulation results in numerous costs for businesses, consumers, and society at large. Although many experts have attempted to quantify these costs, it is quite difficult to find an accurate measurement tool. To generate such measurements, economists often classify regulations as economic (applicable to specific industries or businesses) or social (broad regulations pertaining to health, safety, and the environment). One yardstick for the direct costs of regulation is the administrative spending patterns of federal regulatory agencies. The 2013 estimated cost of regulatory activities was over $58 billion, which was up by approximately 8 percent from 2011. Many people in the business world and beyond are concerned about the upward trajectory of regulatory costs. Another way to measure the direct cost of regulation is to look at the staffing levels of federal regulatory agencies. The expenditures and staffing of state and local regulatory agencies also generate direct costs to society. Federal regulatory agency jobs have been on the rise in recent years, growing to 290,690 full-time jobs in 2013, indicating a 2.5 percent increase or approximately 7,000 new employees each year.[33]

Still another way to approach the measurement of the costs of regulation is to consider the burden that businesses incur in complying with regulations. Various federal regulations, for example, may require companies to change their manufacturing processes or facilities (e.g., smokestack "scrubbers" to clean air and wheelchair ramps to make facilities accessible to customers and employees with disabilities). Companies also must keep records to document their compliance and to obtain permits to implement plans that fall under the scope of specific regulatory agencies. Again, state regulatory agencies often add costs to this burden. Regulated firms may also spend large amounts of money and other resources to prevent additional legislation and to appear responsible. Of course, businesses generally pass these regulatory costs on to their consumers in the form of higher prices, a cost that some label a "hidden tax" of government. Additionally, some businesses contend that the financial and time costs of complying with regulations stifle their ability to develop new products and make investments in facilities and equipment. Moreover, society must pay for the cost of staffing and operating regulatory agencies, and these costs may be reflected in federal income taxes. Table 4.5 describes the primary drivers to the cost of regulation, including those associated with administering, enforcing, and complying with the regulation.

Benefits of Regulation

Despite business complaints about the costs of regulation, it provides many benefits to business, consumers, and society as a whole. These benefits include greater equality in the workplace, safer workplaces, resources

TABLE 4.5 Cost of Regulation

Type of Cost	Description
1. Administration and Enforcement	Expenditures by government to develop and administer regulatory requirements, including the salaries of government workers, hiring inspectors, purchasing office supplies, and other overhead expenses
2. Compliance	Expenditures by organizations, both private and public, to meet regulatory requirements, such as reporting activities and establishing an ethics and compliance program
3. Costs of Legal Consultants	Expenditures by organizations for company or outside legal consultants to deal with legal accusations or issues associated with regulation
4. Additional Costs to Operation	Additional costs to the operations of an organization related to improved safety, sustainability, communication, product requirements, and more

for disadvantaged members of society, safer products, more information about and greater choices among products, cleaner air and water, and the preservation of wildlife habitats to ensure that future generations can enjoy their beauty and diversity.

Companies that fail to respond to consumer desires or that employ inefficient processes are often forced out of the marketplace by more efficient and effective firms. Truly competitive markets also spur companies to invest in researching and developing product innovations as well as new, more efficient methods of production. These innovations benefit consumers through lower prices and improved goods and services. For example, companies such as Apple, Samsung, and Lenovo continue to engineer smaller, faster, and more powerful computers and mobile devices that help individuals and businesses to be more productive.

Regulatory Reform Many businesses and individuals believe that the costs of regulation outweigh its benefits. They argue that removing regulation will allow Adam Smith's "invisible hand of competition" to more effectively and efficiently dictate business conduct. Some people desire complete **deregulation,** or removal of all regulatory authority. Proponents of deregulation believe that less government intervention allows business markets to work more effectively. For example, many businesses want their industries deregulated to decrease their costs of doing business. Many industries have been deregulated to a certain extent since the 1980s, including trucking, airlines, telecommunications (long-distance telephone and cable television), and more recently, electric utilities. In many cases, this deregulation has resulted in lower prices for consumers as well as in greater product choice.

deregulation
Removal of all regulatory authority.

However, the onset of the 2008–2009 financial crisis slowed the call for deregulation. After the economy plummeted, the United States and other countries around the world saw the need for greater regulation, particularly of the financial industry, and began to reverse the deregulatory trend of the previous two or three decades. Although the economic crisis stemmed from a variety of factors, many perceived that much of it stemmed from a lack of appropriate governmental oversight and a lack of ethical leadership in businesses. However, governments' reactions and plans have many worrying that governments will assume too much control. There has always been considerable debate on the relative merits and costs of regulation, and these new changes resulting from the worst financial crisis since the Great Depression are not likely to lessen this controversy.

Self-Regulation Many companies attempt to regulate themselves in an effort to demonstrate social responsibility, to signal responsibility to stakeholders, and to preclude further regulation by federal or state government. Many firms choose to join trade associations that have self-regulatory programs, often established as a preventative measure to stop or delay the development of laws and regulations that would restrict the associations' business practices. Some trade associations establish codes of conduct by which their members must abide or risk discipline or expulsion from the association. The Direct Marketing Association in the United Kingdom expelled Reactiv Media from its membership after its own investigation upheld consumer complaints regarding the company's telemarketing practices.[34]

Perhaps the best-known self-regulatory association is the Better Business Bureau. Founded in 1912, today there are more than 110 bureaus in the United States, parts of Canada, Puerto Rico, and the Caribbean territories. The bureaus have accredited over 375,000 local and national businesses and charities and resolve problems for millions of consumers and businesses each year.[35] Each bureau also works to champion good business practices within a community, although it usually does not have strong tools for enforcing its business conduct rules. When a company violates what the BBB believes to be good business practices, the bureau warns consumers through local newspapers or broadcast media.

If the offending organization is a member of the BBB, it may be expelled from the local bureau. For example, the Better Business Bureau revoked accreditation for two Texas businesses for not adhering to BBB standards. One firm agreed to arbitration with the customer but failed to honor the arbitrator's decison.[36]

Self-regulatory programs like the Better Business Bureau have a number of advantages over government regulation. Establishment and implementation of such programs are usually less costly, and their guidelines or codes of conduct are generally more practical and realistic. Furthermore, effective self-regulatory programs reduce the need to expand government bureaucracy. However, self-regulation also has several limitations. Nonmember firms are under no obligation to abide by a trade association's industry guidelines or codes. Moreover, most associations lack the tools or authority to enforce their guidelines. Finally, these guidelines are often less strict than the regulations established by government agencies.

THE CONTEMPORARY POLITICAL ENVIRONMENT

During the 1960s, a significant "antiestablishment" movement manifested in the form of hostile protests toward businesses. These efforts spurred a 15-year wave of legislation and regulation to address a number of issues of the day, including product safety, employment discrimination, human rights, energy shortages, environmental degradation, and scandals related to bribery and payoffs. During the 1980s, the pendulum swung back in favor of business, and the economic prosperity of the 1990s was driven by technological advances and the self-regulation of business. In addition, business priorities were beginning to be focused on protecting competition and the natural environment. These policies continued through 2008, with continued self-regulation of industries and the rolling back of environmental laws that businesses deemed detrimental. However, the regulatory climate changed again in 2009 toward more regulation of environmental and health issues, resulting in higher taxes and increased social services. The onset of the financial crisis created an even greater need for stricter legislation, such as the Troubled Assets Recovery Program (TARP) that authorized the U.S. Treasury to purchase up to $700 billion of troubled assets like mortgage-backed securities. It has also resulted in support for entirely new regulation and regulatory agencies like the Consumer Financial Protection Bureau. These new regulations have had wide-sweeping effects over the financial industry. Other organizations such as the Environmental Protection Agency and the Food and Drug Administration also began to regulate with the aim of protecting stakeholders with renewed vigor.

Such changes in the political environment over the last 50 years shaped the political environment in which businesses operate and created new avenues for businesses to participate in the political process. Among the most significant factors shaping the political environment were changes in Congress and the rise of special-interest groups. As the Obama administration sought to revive and increase oversight of the finance industry, more companies became interested in hiring lobbyists to campaign on behalf of their interests in Washington.

Changes in Congress Among the calls for social reform in the 1960s were pressures for changes within the legislative process of the U.S. Congress itself. Bowing to this pressure, Congress enacted an amendment to the Legislative Reorganization Act in 1970, which ushered in a new era of change for the political process. This legislation significantly revamped the procedures of congressional committees, most notably stripping committee chairpersons of many of their powers, equalizing committee and chair assignments, and requiring committees to record and publish all roll-call votes taken in the committee. By opening up the committee process to public scrutiny and reducing the power of senior members and committee leaders, the act reduced the level of secrecy surrounding the legislative process and effectively brought an end to an era of autonomous committee chairs and senior members.[37]

Another significant change occurred in 1974 when Congress amended the Federal Election Campaign Act to limit contributions from individuals, political parties, and special-interest groups organized to get specific candidates elected or policies enacted.[38] Around the same time, many states began to shift their electoral processes from the traditional party caucus to primary elections, further eroding the influence of the party in the political process. These changes ultimately had the effect of reducing the importance of political parties by decreasing members' dependence on their parties. Many candidates for elected offices began to turn to special-interest groups to raise enough funds to mount serious campaigns and reelection bids.

In 2002, Congress passed the Bipartisan Campaign Reform Act (BRCA), sponsored by Senators John McCain and Russell Feingold.

This new act limited the amount of contributions parties could donate to political campaigns, and it implemented rules for how corporate and labor treasury funds could be used in federal elections. The act also forbade national party committees from raising or spending unregulated funds. Though the act outraged certain legislators, who appealed to the Supreme Court over its constitutionality, the Supreme Court upheld it.[39]

However, the Supreme Court decision popularly referred to as *Citizens United* grants more powers to organizations regarding corporate contributions. *Citizens United* gives corporations the right to spend as much as they want in independent political expenditures to support governmental candidates. These independent political expenditures are provided through political action committees. **Political action committees (PACs)** are organizations that solicit donations from individuals and then contribute these funds to candidates running for political office. Companies can organize PACs to which their executives, employees, and stockholders can make significant donations as individuals. PACs operate independently of business and are usually incorporated. Labor unions and other special-interest groups, such as teachers and medical doctors, can also establish PACs to promote their goals.

political action committees (PACs) Organizations that solicit donations from individuals and contribute these funds to candidates running for political office.

The *Citizens United* decision enabled the creation of what has been termed Super PACs. Before *Citizens United,* individuals were able to contribute $2,500 to PACs, and unions and corporations were not allowed to contribute. The Supreme Court ruled that these prohibitions violated the First Amendment. After the Supreme Court decision, many PACs were dubbed Super PACs because of what is seen as their unlimited ability to receive political donations.[40] The Federal Election Committee has rules to restrict PAC donations to $5,000 per candidate for each election. However, many PACs exploit loopholes in these regulations by donating so-called soft money to political parties that do not support a specific candidate for federal office. Under the current rules, these contributors can make unlimited donations to political parties for general activities.

Rise of Special-Interest Groups The success of activists' efforts in the 1960s and 1970s marked the rise of special-interest groups. The movements to promote African American and women's rights and to protest the Vietnam War and environmental degradation evolved into well-organized groups working to educate the public about significant social issues and to crusade for legislation and regulation of business conduct they deemed irresponsible. These progressive groups were soon joined on Capitol Hill by more conservative groups working to further their agendas on issues such as business deregulation, restriction of abortion and gun control, and promotion of prayer in schools. Businesses joined in by forming industry and trade associations. These increasingly powerful special-interest groups now focused on getting candidates who could further their own political agendas elected. Common Cause, for example, is a nonprofit, nonpartisan organization working to fight corrupt government and special interests backed by large sums of money. Since 1970, Common Cause, with nearly

475,000 members, has campaigned for greater openness and accountability in government. Some of its self-proclaimed "victories" include reform of presidential campaign finances, tax systems, congressional ethics, open meeting standards, and disclosure requirements for lobbyists. Table 4.6 lists the dates and subject matter of Common Cause's major accomplishments over the past three decades.

TABLE 4.6 Accomplishments of Common Cause

1971: Helps pass the Twenty-Sixth Amendment, giving 18-year olds the right to vote
1974: Leads efforts to pass presidential public financing, contribution limits, and disclosure requirements
1974–1975: Helps pass Freedom of Information Act (FOIA) and open meetings laws at federal, state, and local levels
1978: Leads efforts to pass the historic Ethics in Government Act of 1978, requiring financial disclosure for government officials and restricting the "revolving door" between business and government
1982: Works to pass extension of the Voting Rights Act
1989: Successfully lobbies for passage of the Ethics in Government Act
1990: Works to help pass the Americans with Disabilities Act, guaranteeing civil rights for the disabled
1995: Lobbies for limits on gifts in the House and Senate and for passage of the Lobby Reform Act, providing disclosure of lobbyists' activity and spending
2000: Successfully works for legislation to unmask and require disclosure of "527" political groups
2001: Lobbies successfully with a coalition for the Help America Vote Act, which provided funding to states for improvement of the nation's system of voting
2002: Leads successful multiyear campaign to enact the Bipartisan Campaign Reform Act, banning soft money in federal campaigns. In 2003, in a landmark decision, the U.S. Supreme Court upheld the law
2004: Launches major voter mobilization and election monitoring programs for presidential election
2005: Wins the fight against efforts to cut federal funding for the Corporation for Public Broadcasting, and gathers 150,000 petition signatures calling for the resignation of CPB Chairman Ken Tomlinson for partisan and unethical behavior
2005/2006: Leads the charge against disgraced Majority Leader Tom DeLay and fights for major ethics reform
2007: Fights successfully for passage of the Honest Leadership and Open Government Act of 2007, making major improvements in ethics and lobby laws and rules
2008: Leads successful campaign to create the first-ever independent ethics commission in the U.S. House of Representatives
2010: Spurred by the U.S. Supreme Court's Citizens United decision that lifted the decades-old ban on corporate and union spending around elections, Common Cause redoubles efforts to pass the Fair Elections Now Act, which would allow candidates to run competitive campaigns on small donations and fair elections funds

Source: Common Cause, "History and Accomplishments," http://www.commoncause.org/site/pp.asp?c=dkLNK1MQIwG&b=4860205 (accessed June 11, 2014).

Corporate Approaches to Influencing Government

Although some businesses view regulatory and legal forces as beyond their control and simply react to conditions arising from those forces, other firms actively seek to influence the political process to achieve their goals. In some cases, companies publicly protest the actions of legislative bodies. More often, companies work for the election of political candidates who regard them positively. Lobbying, political action committees, and campaign contributions are some of the tools businesses employ to influence the political process.

Lobbying Among the most powerful tactics business can employ to participate in public policy decisions is direct representation through full-time staff who communicate with elected officials. **Lobbying** is the process of working to persuade public and/or government officials to favor a particular position in decision-making. Organizations may lobby officials either directly or by combining their efforts with other organizations.

Many companies concerned about the threat of legislation or regulation that may negatively affect their operations employ lobbyists to communicate their concerns to officials on their behalf. Google, for example, has recently expanded its Washington office to one the size of the White House. Less than a decade ago, the company had a small presence in Washington but today they are within the top five of the companies with the largest lobbying activities. With all of the controversy over data collection and privacy concerns, both of which are core aspects of Google's business, the company has learned to be an active member in shaping the political conversation.[41] Table 4.7 provide examples of organizations that spend money on lobbying.

lobbying
The process of working to persuade public and/or government officials to favor a particular position in decision-making.

TABLE 4.7 Organizations that Engage in Lobbying

Lobbying Organization	Total
U.S. Chamber of Commerce	$1,248,040,680
National Association of Realtors	$363,246,628
American Medical Association	$338,642,500
General Electric	$336,680,000
American Hospital Association	$301,548,726
Pharmaceutical Research and Manufacturers of America	$294,890,300
Blue Cross/Blue Shield	$277,811,849
AARP	$257,951,064
Northrop Grumman	$236,102,213
Boeing Co.	$230,403,310

Source: The Center for Responsive Politics, "Top Spenders," *Open Secrets*, 2016, https://www.opensecrets.org/lobby/top.php?showYear=a&indexType=s (accessed June 17, 2016).

The financial industry has long employed lobbyists to push for increased deregulation so that it can pursue riskier and more profitable avenues. However, changes in regulation and compensation practices in the financial sector are making this a more difficult task. In the past, bank officials have often been awarded for the quantity of business they do, rather than the quality, which encouraged employees to engage in riskier business practices to increase their compensation packages. Some changes in bank compensation packages include adjusting pay to account for any risks taken in the process of generating profits and changing the system of awarding bonuses from a more individualistic focus to one that is more encompassing of the entire organization. Additionally, new Treasury rules mandate banks to better inform borrowers about the costs of certain loans, create greater supervision of bank practices, and even establish a capital surcharge for certain banks. Banks and other financial organizations voiced their opinions on these financial reforms through discreet lobbying and industry groups.[42]

Companies may attempt to influence the legislative or regulatory process more indirectly through trade associations and umbrella organizations that represent collective business interests of many firms. Virtually every industry has one or more trade associations that represent the interests of their members to federal officials and provide public education and other services for their members. Examples of such trade associations include the National Association of Home Builders, the Tobacco Institute, the American Booksellers Association, and the Pet Food Institute. Additionally, there are often state trade associations, such as the Hawaii Coffee Association and the Michigan Beer and Wine Wholesalers Association, which work on state- and regional-level issues. Umbrella organizations such as the National Federation of Independent Businesses and the U.S. Chamber of Commerce also help promote business interests to government officials. The U.S. Chamber of Commerce takes positions on many political, regulatory, and economic questions. With more than 3 million member companies, its goal is to promote its members' views of the ideal free enterprise marketplace. The cozy relationship between corporations and the government has been a growing concern for years, and was a topic of serious discussion after the 2008–2009 financial industry meltdown. For example, 48 members of the House Energy and Commerce Committee that were at the forefront of climate change legislation owned stock in energy, oil, and natural gas companies. This was a concern to some citizens as these investments could create a conflict of interest among legislators. However, House and Senate ethics do not forbid Congress from having a stake in companies unless they pass a law that would benefit only their own interests.[43]

Campaign Contributions Corporate money can also be channeled into candidates' campaign coffers as corporate executives' or stockholders' personal contributions. A sizable contribution to a candidate may carry with it an implied understanding that the elected official will perform some favor, such as voting in accordance with the contributor's desire on a particular law. Occasionally, some businesses find it so important to ensure favorable treatment that they make illegal corporate contributions to campaign funds. As mentioned earlier, it is also common for businesses and other organizations to make donations to political parties through PACs. Critics are concerned that decisions such as *Citizens United* will give organizations unfettered power to allow large corporations to effectively "buy" elections.[44]

THE GOVERNMENT'S STRATEGIC APPROACH FOR LEGAL AND ETHICAL COMPLIANCE

Thus far, we have seen that, although legal and regulatory forces have a strong influence on business operations, businesses can also affect these forces through the political process. In addition, socially responsible firms strive to comply with society's wishes for responsible conduct through legal and ethical behavior. Indeed, the most effective way for businesses to manage the legal and regulatory environment is to establish values and policies that communicate and reward appropriate conduct. Most employees will try to comply with an organization's leadership and directions for responsible conduct. Therefore, top management must develop and implement a highly visible strategy for effective compliance. This means that top managers must take responsibility and be accountable for assessing legal risks and developing corporate programs that promote acceptable conduct.

Federal Sentencing Guidelines for Organizations

Companies are increasingly establishing organizational compliance programs to ensure that they operate legally and responsibly, as well as to generate a competitive advantage based on a reputation for responsible citizenship. There are also strong legal incentives to establish such programs. The **Federal Sentencing Guidelines for Organizations (FSGO)** was developed by the U.S. Sentencing Commission and approved by Congress in November 1991. These guidelines streamline sentencing and punishment for organizational crimes and holds companies, as well as their employees, responsible for misconduct. The guidelines codified into law incentives to reward organizations for implementing controls to prevent misconduct, such as developing effective internal legal and ethical compliance programs.[45] The commission describes seven steps that companies must implement to demonstrate due diligence. These steps are discussed in Table 4.8.

The assumption underlying the FSGO is that good, socially responsible organizations maintain compliance systems and internal governance controls that deter misconduct by their employees. Thus, these guidelines provide guidance for both organizations and courts regarding program

Federal Sentencing Guidelines for Organizations (FSGO)
Developed by the U.S. Sentencing Commission and approved by Congress in November 1991 to streamline sentencing and punishment for organizational crimes and holds companies and employees responsible for misconduct.

TABLE 4.8 Seven Steps to Effective Compliance and Ethics Programs

1. Establish codes of conduct (identify key risk areas).
2. Appoint or hire high-level compliance manager (ethics officer).
3. Take care in delegating authority (background checks on employees).
4. Institute a training program and communication system (ethics training).
5. Monitor and audit for misconduct (reporting mechanisms).
6. Enforce and discipline (management implementation of policy).
7. Revise program as needed (feedback and action).

Source: U.S. Federal Sentencing Guidelines for Organizations.

effectiveness. Organizations have flexibility about the type of program they develop; the seven steps are not a checklist requiring that legal procedures be followed to gain certification of an effective program. Organizations implement the guidelines through effective core practices that are appropriate for their firms. The programs they put into effect must be capable of reducing the opportunity for organizational misconduct.

The guidelines pertain to all felonies and class A misdemeanors committed by employees regarding their work. Organizations demonstrating due diligence in developing effective compliance programs can avoid or reduce organizational penalties if an employee commits a crime.[46] When it was discovered that bribery had occurred at Ralph Lauren's Argentine operations, the company took immediate action. Its thorough investigation generated praise from the Securities and Exchange Commission (SEC). Although the company paid $882,000 in penalties to the Department of Justice and $735,000 to the Securities and Exchange Commission, for the first time the SEC entered into a non-prosecution agreement with Ralph Lauren. This was a clear demonstration that the company was being rewarded for its due diligence in handling the misconduct.[47]

Overall, the spirit behind the FSGO is that legal violations can be prevented through organizational values and a commitment to ethical conduct. The law develops new amendments almost every year. Table 4.9 shows all of the amendments made to date.

In 2004, an amendment to the FSGO placed responsibility on the business's governing authority, requiring them to be knowledgeable about the company's ethics program regarding content, implementation, and effectiveness. Usually the governing authority in an organization is the board of directors. The board must make certain there is a high-ranking manager responsible for the daily oversight of the ethics program; provide for sufficient authority, resources, and access to the board or an appropriate board subcommittee; and ensure that there are confidential mechanisms so the organization's employees and agents may ask questions or report concerns without fear of retaliation. The board is also required to oversee the discovery of risks and to design, apply, and modify approaches to deal with

TABLE 4.9 Institutionalization of Ethics through the U.S. Sentencing Guidelines for Organizations

1991	*Laws:* U.S. Sentencing Guidelines for Organizations were created for federal prosecutions of organizations. These guidelines provide for just punishment, adequate deterrence, and incentives for organizations to prevent, detect, and report misconduct. Organizations need to have an effective ethics and compliance program to receive incentives in the case of misconduct.
2004	*Amendments:* The definition of an effective ethics program now includes the development of an ethical organizational culture. Executives and board members must assume the responsibility of identifying areas of risk, providing ethics training, creating reporting mechanisms, and designating an individual to oversee ethics programs.
2007–2008	*Additional definition of a compliance and ethics program:* Firms should focus on due diligence to detect and prevent misconduct and to promote an organizational culture that encourages ethical conduct. More details are provided, encouraging the assessment of risk and outlining appropriate steps in designing, implementing, and modifying ethics programs and training that will include all employees, top management, and the board or governing authority. These modifications continue to reinforce the importance of an ethical culture in preventing misconduct.
2010	*Amendments:* Chief compliance officers are directed to make their reports to their firm's board rather than to the general counsel. Companies are encouraged to create hotlines, perform self-audit programs, and adopt controls to detect misconduct internally. More specific language has been added to the word *prompt* in regards to what it means to promptly report misconduct. The amendment also extends operational responsibility to all personnel within a company's ethics and compliance program
2014	The Commission investigated how the sentencing guidelines could be used by regulatory and law enforcement agencies to recommend effective ethics and compliance programs. The Commission assessed its efforts to encourage corporations, nonprofits, government agencies, and other organizations to form institutional cultures that discourage misconduct.

Sources: "U.S. Sentencing Guidelines Changes Become Effective November 1," *FCPA Compliance and Ethics Blog*, November 2, 2010, http://fcpacompliancereport.com/2010/11/us-sentencing-guidelines-changes-become-effective-november-1/ (accessed June 17, 2016). United States Sentencing Commission, "Amendments to the Sentencing Guidelines," April 30, 2012, http://www.ussc.gov/Legal/Amendments/Reader-Friendly/20120430_RF_Amendments.pdf (accessed June 17, 2016); Paula Desio, Deputy General Counsel, *An Overview of the Organizational Guidelines*, http://www.ussc.gov/sites/default/files/pdf/training/organizational-guidelines/ORGOVERVIEW.pdf (accessed June 17, 2016).

those risks. If board members do not understand how to execute an ethics program, the organization risks insufficient oversight and misconduct that can snowball into a crisis.[48]

In 2005, the Supreme Court held that the federal sentencing guidelines were not mandatory but would act as recommendations for judges to use in their decisions. Some legal experts thought that this might weaken the effectiveness of the FSGO, but the majority of federal sentences have remained similar to what they had been before the Supreme Court decision. Thus, the guidelines are important in developing a successful ethics and compliance program.[49]

The 2007–2008 amendments to the FSGO extend the necessary ethics training to board members or the governing authority, managers, employees, and the organizations' agents. This change pertains to mandatory training at all organizational levels. Simply disseminating a code of ethics is not enough to meet training requirements. The new amendments compelled most governmental contractors to implement ethics and compliance training.

In 2010, the FSGO adopted four new amendments. The first amendment simplified reporting relationships by recommending that chief compliance officers report misconduct directly to the board or to a board committee, rather than simply to the general counsel. The second amendment encouraged organizations to strengthen internal controls through hotlines, self-auditing programs, and other mechanisms to increase the chances that misconduct will be detected internally instead of externally. The third amendment adopted more specific wording to clarify what it means to report an ethical violation promptly. Finally, a fourth amendment extended operational responsibility to all personnel within a company's ethics and compliance program. This means that everyone in an organization has a responsibility to ensure ethical conduct.[50]

In 2014, the Federal Sentencing Commission reiterated the importance of best practices in organizations. The commission advocated the sharing of best practices among regulatory and law enforcement agencies. Agencies such as the Department of Justice's Antitrust Division are using the FSGO's seven steps for ethics programs to develop their own compliance programs. The Commission also encourages the sharing of best practices among industry associations. The FSGO does not believe this sharing of best practices should be limited to for-profit organizations, however. It also assessed the success of nonprofit organizations, businesses, regulators, and other organizations in creating effective organizational cultures that will work toward preventing misconduct. The emphasis of the FSGO is increasingly geared toward best practices, principles, and values over formal regulations in which organizations do the bare minimum to comply with the law.[51]

The Department of Justice also recommended general principles to apply in cases of corporate misconduct. Ethics and compliance programs are essential in discovering the types of misconduct common in a particular organization's industry. If an organization does not have an effective ethics and compliance program in place, a firm convicted of misconduct will likely not be treated lightly, particularly as the prosecutor has a large amount of freedom in determining when, whom, and whether to prosecute illegal conduct. Even minor misconduct could result in significant penalties if committed by a large number of employees or approved by upper management. Without an effective ethics and compliance program to identify misconduct, a firm can face severe consequences from legal issues, enforcement, and sentencing.[52] Legal and administrative policies mostly agree that an effective ethics and compliance program is required to prevent misconduct and reduce legal repercussions should it occur.

Sarbanes-Oxley (SOX) Act

The **Sarbanes-Oxley Act** was enacted to restore stakeholder confidence and provide a new standard of ethical behavior for U.S. businesses in the wake of Enron and WorldCom in the early 2000s. During probes into financial reporting fraud at many of the world's largest companies, investigators learned that hundreds of public corporations were not reporting their financial results accurately. Accounting firms, lawyers, top corporate officers, and boards of directors had developed a culture of deception in an attempt to gain investor approval and competitive advantage. The downfall of many of these companies resulted in huge losses to thousands of investors, and employees even lost much of their savings from 401ks.

The Sarbanes-Oxley Act (SOX) legislation protects investors by improving the accuracy and reliability of corporate disclosures. The act had almost unanimous support by Congress, government regulatory agencies, and the general public. When President Bush signed the act, he emphasized the need for the standards it provides, especially for top management and boards of directors responsible for company oversight. Table 4.10 details the requirements of the act.

Sarbanes-Oxley Act
Enacted to restore stake-holder confidence and provide a new standard of ethical behavior for U.S. businesses in the wake of Enron and WorldCom in the early 2000s.

TABLE 4.10 Major Provisions of the Sarbanes-Oxley Act

1. Requires the establishment of an Independent Accounting Oversight Board in charge of regulations administered by the Securities and Exchange Commission.

2. Requires CEOs and CFOs to certify that their companies' financial statements are true and without misleading statements.

3. Requires that corporate board of directors' audit committees consist of independent members with no material interests in the company.

4. Prohibits corporations from making or offering loans to officers and board members.

5. Requires codes of ethics for senior financial officers; code must be registered with the SEC.

6. Prohibits accounting firms from providing both auditing and consulting services to the same client.

7. Requires company attorneys to report wrongdoing to top managers and, if necessary, to the board of directors; if managers and directors fail to respond to reports of wrongdoing, the attorney should stop representing the company.

8. Mandates "whistle-blower protection" for persons who disclose wrongdoing to authorities.

9. Requires financial securities analysts to certify that their recommendations are based on objective reports.

10. Requires mutual fund managers to disclose how they vote shareholder proxies, giving investors information about how their shares influence decisions.

11. Establishes a ten-year penalty for mail/wire fraud.

12. Prohibits the two senior auditors from working on a corporation's account for more than five years; other auditors are prohibited from working on an account for more than seven years; in other words, accounting firms must rotate individual auditors from one account to another from time to time.

The section of SOX that initially caused the most concern for companies was compliance with section 404. Section 404 comprises three central issues: (1) it requires that management create reliable internal financial controls; (2) it requires that management attest to the reliability of those controls and the accuracy of financial statements that result from those controls; and (3) it requires an independent auditor to further attest to the statements made by management. Because the cost of compliance was so high for many companies, some publicly traded companies considered de-listing themselves from the U.S. Stock Exchange. However, although compliance costs were high after Sarbanes–Oxley, they have decreased over the years. Compliance costs have decreased 50 percent from their level when the laws were put into effect. The current costs of compliance range from between $100,000 and $500,000.[53]

To address fraudulent occurrences, SOX required the creation of the Public Company Accounting Oversight Board, which provides oversight of the accounting firms that audit public companies and sets standards for the auditors in these firms. The board has investigatory and disciplinary power over accounting firm auditors and securities analysts who issue reports about companies. Specific duties include: (1) registration of public accounting firms; (2) establishment of auditing, quality control, ethics, independence, and other standards relating to preparation of audit reports; (3) inspection of accounting firms; (4) investigations, disciplinary proceedings, and imposition of sanctions; and (5) enforcement of compliance with accounting rules of the board, professionals standards, and securities laws relating to the preparation and issuance of audit reports and obligations and liabilities of accountants.

SOX also requires corporations to take more responsibility and to provide principles-based ethical leadership. Enhanced financial disclosures are required, including certification by top officers that audit reports are complete and that nothing has been withheld from auditors. For example, registered public accounting firms are now required to identify all material correcting adjustments to reflect accurate financial statements. Also, all material off-balance sheet transactions and other relationships with unconsolidated entities that affect current or future financial conditions of a public company must be disclosed in each annual and quarterly financial report. In addition, public companies must also report "on a rapid and current basis" material changes in the financial condition or operations. Section 201 of SOX prohibits registered public accounting firms from providing both audit and non-audit services to a public company, a major issue with the now defunct accounting firm Arthur Andersen in its relationship with Enron.

Other provisions of the act include whistle-blower protection and changes in the attorney-client relationship so that attorneys are now required to report wrongdoing to top managers or to the board of directors. Employees of public companies and accounting firms, in general, are also accountable to report unethical behavior. SOX intends to motivate employees through "whistle-blower" protection that would prohibit the employer from taking certain actions against employees who lawfully disclose private employer information to, among others, parties in a judicial proceeding involving a fraud claim. Whistle-blowers are also granted a remedy of special damages and attorney's fees. This protection is designed to encourage whistleblowers to come forward when detecting business misconduct, as much of the fraud that eludes audits or other controls may be detected by employees. According to a 2008 report published by the Association of Certified Fraud Examiners, data compiled on 959 cases of occupational fraud between 2006 and 2008 revealed that 46 percent of the cases were detected by tipsters such as employees or vendors.[54] Acts of retaliation that harm informants, including interference with the lawful employment or livelihood of any person, shall result in fines and/or imprisonment for ten years. Table 4.11 lists the benefits of the act.

Dodd-Frank Wall Street Reform and Consumer Protection Act

In 2010, the **Dodd–Frank Wall Street Reform and Consumer Protection Act** was passed. The act was hailed as "a sweeping overhaul of the financial regulatory system...on a scale not seen since the reforms that followed the Great Depression."[55] Dodd-Frank seeks to prevent financial crisis through improved financial regulation, additional oversight of the industry, and preventative measures to reduce the types of risk-taking, deceptive practices, and lack of oversight that led to the financial fallout in 2007–2008.[56] Its provisions include increasing the transparency of financial institutions, creating a bureau to educate consumers about financial

Dodd–Frank Wall Street Reform and Consumer Protection Act
Passed in 2010 to prevent financial crisis by increased financial deregulation, additional oversight of the industry, and preventative measures against unhealthy risk-taking and deceptive practices.

TABLE 4.11 Benefits of Sarbanes-Oxley

1. Greater accountability by top management and board of directors to employees, communities, and society. The goals of the business will be to provide stakeholders with a return on their investment rather than providing a vehicle for management to reap excessive compensation and other benefits.
2. Renewed investor confidence providing managers and brokers with the information they need to make solid investment decisions, which will ultimately lead to a more stable and solid growth rate for investors.
3. Clear explanations by CEOs about why their compensation package is in the best interest of the company. It eliminates certain traditional senior management perks, including company loans, and requires disclosures about stock trades, thus making executives more like other investors.
4. Greater protection of employee retirement plans. Employees can develop greater trust that they will not lose savings tied to such plans.
5. Improved information from stock analysts and rating agencies.
6. Greater penalties and accountability of senior managers, auditors and board members. The penalties now outweigh the rewards of purposeful manipulation and deception.

products and protect them from deceptive financial practices, implementing added incentives for whistle-blowers, increasing oversight of the financial industry, and regulating the use of derivatives.

Unlike Sarbanes-Oxley, there was not a clear consensus on the Dodd-Frank Act. Opponents of the act expressed many concerns, asserting that the rules on derivatives would be too difficult to follow, the changes would create chaos in the financial system, and the government could gain too much power.[57] J.P. Morgan claimed that they supported the law but were against certain provisions.[58] Included in these provisions was the creation of new financial regulatory agencies that would increase government oversight of the financial system.

The Office of Financial Research was developed with the responsibility to improve the quality of financial data accessible to government officials and construct an improved system of analysis for the finance industry.[59] The Financial Stability Oversight Council (FSOC) has been given the responsibility to keep the financial system stabilized through market monitoring, threat identification, the promotion of market discipline among public constituents, and responses to risks that threaten stability.[60] FSOC can limit or supervise financial risks, create more stringent rules for banking and nonbanking financial organizations, and break up financial organizations that present major risks to market stability.[61] The purpose of these two new agencies is to eliminate loopholes that allowed financial companies to commit risky and deceptive actions leading up to the financial crisis.

Consumer Financial Protection Bureau (CFPB) Established by the Dodd–Frank Act to regulate banks and other financial institutions by monitoring financial instruments like subprime mortgages and high-risk lending practices.

The Dodd-Frank Act also developed the **Consumer Financial Protection Bureau (CFPB)**. The CFPB is an independent agency within the Federal Reserve System that "regulate[s] the offering and provision of consumer financial products or services under the Federal consumer financial laws."[62] A major problem leading up to the financial meltdown was that average investors usually did not understand the complex financial products in which they were trading. The federal government has granted the CFPB supervisory power over credit markets and the ability to monitor lenders to ensure they are in legal compliance.[63] The CFPB also has authority to restrict unfair lending and credit card practices, enforce consumer financial protection laws, and ensure the safety of financial products before their release onto the market.[64]

Some have major concerns about the extent of the agency's powers. For instance, critics are concerned that this increased power could lead to severe sanctions or heavy regulations.[65] Goldman Sachs was one financial organization affected by the regulation. In order to comply with part of the Dodd-Frank Act, it was forced to limit investing in its own private-equity funds. This provision restricts financial organizations from using their own money to make large bets.[66] The CFPB has oversight powers over organizations that tend to be accused of questionable conduct, such as payday lenders and debt collectors.[67] The CFPB's goal is to maintain a more transparent financial environment for consumers.

Finally, the Dodd–Frank law created a whistle-blower bounty program. Whistle-blowers who report financial fraud to government agencies are eligible to receive 10–30 percent of fines and settlements if their reports result in convictions of more than $1 million in penalties.[68] In 2012, the government awarded its first payout of $50,000 to a whistleblower who assisted regulators in convicting a company of fraud.[69]

SUMMARY

In a pluralistic society, many diverse stakeholder groups attempt to influence the public officials who legislate, interpret laws, and regulate business. Companies that adopt a strategic approach to the legal and regulatory system develop proactive organizational values and compliance programs that identify areas of risks and include formal communication, training, and continuous improvement of responses to the legal and regulatory environment.

Economic reasons for regulation often relate to efforts to level the playing field on which businesses operate. These efforts include regulating trusts, which are generally established to gain control of a product market or industry by eliminating competition, and eliminating monopolies, which occur when just one business provides a good or service in a given market. Another rationale for regulation is society's desire to restrict destructive or unfair competition. Social reasons for regulation address imperfections in the market that result in undesirable consequences and the protection of natural and social resources. Other regulations are created in response to social demands for safety and equality in the workplace, safer products, and privacy issues.

The Sherman Antitrust Act is the principal tool used to prevent businesses from restraining trade and monopolizing markets. The Clayton Antitrust Act limits mergers and acquisitions that could stifle competition and prohibits specific activities that could substantially lessen competition or tend to create a monopoly. The Federal Trade Commission Act prohibits unfair methods of competition and created the Federal Trade Commission (FTC). Legal and regulatory policy is also enforced through lawsuits by private citizens, competitors, and special-interest groups.

A company that engages in commerce beyond its own country must contend with the complex relationship among the laws of its own nation, international laws, and the laws of the nation in which it will be trading. There is considerable variation and focus among different nations' laws, but many countries' antitrust laws are quite similar to those of the United States.

Regulation creates numerous costs for businesses, consumers, and society at large. Some measures of these costs include administrative spending patterns, staffing levels of federal regulatory agencies, and costs businesses incur in complying with regulations. The cost of regulation is passed on to consumers in the form of higher prices and may stifle product innovation and investments in new facilities and equipment. Regulation also provides many benefits, including greater equality in the workplace, safer workplaces, resources for disadvantaged members of society, safer products, more information about and greater choices among products, cleaner air and water, and the preservation of wildlife habitats. Antitrust laws and regulations strengthen competition and spur companies to invest in research and development. Many businesses and individuals believe that the costs of regulation outweigh its benefits. Some people desire complete deregulation, or removal of regulatory authority.

Because government is a stakeholder of business (and vice versa), businesses and government can work together as both legitimately participate in the political process. Business participation can be a positive or negative force in society's interest, depending not only on the outcome but also on the perspective of various stakeholders.

Changes over the last 40 years have shaped the political environment in which businesses operate. Among the most significant of these changes were amendments to the Legislative Reorganization Act and the Federal Election Campaign Act, which had the effect of reducing the importance of political parties. Many candidates for elected offices turned to increasingly powerful special-interest groups to raise funds to campaign for elected office. Until the *Citizens United* decision, corporations were restricted in giving contributions to political action committees. However, the Supreme Court decision gives corporations the right to spend as much as they want in political independent expenditures to support governmental candidates.

Some organizations view regulatory and legal forces as beyond their control and simply react to conditions arising from those forces; other firms seek to influence the political process to achieve their goals. One way they can do so is through lobbying, the process of working to persuade public and/or government officials to favor a particular position in decision-making. Companies can also influence the political process through political action committees, which are organizations that solicit donations from individuals and then contribute these funds to candidates running for political office. Corporate funds may also be channeled into candidates' campaign coffers as corporate executives' or stockholders' personal contributions, although such donations can violate the spirit of corporate campaign laws. It is also common for businesses and other organizations to make donations to political parties.

More companies are establishing organizational compliance programs to ensure that they operate legally and responsibly as well as to generate a competitive advantage based on a reputation for good citizenship. Under the Federal Sentencing Guidelines for Organizations (FSGO), a company that wants to avoid or limit fines and other penalties as a result of an employee's crime must be able to demonstrate that it has implemented a reasonable program for deterring and preventing misconduct. To implement an effective compliance program, an organization should develop a code of conduct that communicates expected standards, assign oversight of the program to high-ranking personnel who abide by legal and ethical standards, communicate standards through training and other mechanisms, monitor and audit to detect wrongdoing, punish individuals responsible for misconduct, and take steps to continuously improve the program. A strong compliance program acts as a buffer to keep employees from committing crimes and to protect a company's reputation should wrongdoing occur despite its best efforts.

Enacted after many corporate financial fraud scandals, the Sarbanes-Oxley Act created the Public Company Accounting Oversight Board to provide oversight and set standards for the accounting firms that audit public companies. The board has investigatory and disciplinary power over accounting firm auditors and securities analysts. The act requires corporations to take responsibility to provide principles-based ethical leadership and holds CEOs and CFOs personally accountable for the credibility and accuracy of their company's financial statements.

However, the 2008–2009 recession, collapse of the subprime mortgage market, and troubles on Wall Street all pointed to systemic flaws and gaps in the regulatory system. In 2010, the Obama administration passed the Dodd-Frank Wall Street Reform and Consumer Protection Act. Dodd-Frank seeks to prevent financial crisis through the improvement of financial regulation, the increase in oversight of the industry, and preventative measures to reduce types of risk-taking, deceptive practices, and lack of oversight. It established several new agencies, including the Consumer Financial Protection Bureau to protect consumers from complex financial instruments. It also established a whistle-blower bounty program, in which whistle-blowers are eligible to receive 10–30 percent of fines and settlements if their reports result in convictions of more than $1 million in penalties

Responsible Business Debate

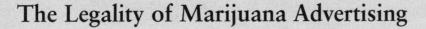

The Legality of Marijuana Advertising

Issue: *Should marijuana be advertised where it is legally sold?*

Marketers in any vice industry face political, legal, and sociocultural challenges when communicating the message of their brand or product. Marijuana is no exception. The legalization of cannabis for recreational use in Colorado and Washington has created both opportunities in a new market as well as uncertainties associated with advertising to this market. The media industry as a whole is averse to promoting recreational

marijuana use due to its controversial nature. While two states have legalized this activity and others are planning on putting the issue to a vote, federal law still considers it to be illegal. Marijuana retailers are technically considered to be narcotics traffickers, and marketers for the substance can be held as accomplices to criminal activity.

Google, one of the main online advertising outlets, has long restricted searches related to drugs out of its own conviction. Other advertising channels, such as newspapers and billboards, are legally restricted from accepting advertising money related to drugs. This is true in cities where the substance is legal for both recreational and medicinal use. These laws work to protect underage individuals from seeing the advertisements and sparking their interest in drug use. For example, Colorado laws state that any kind of mass media advertising that has the potential to reach 30 percent or more individuals under the age of 21 is restricted. Online content that does not block minors' access cannot contain marijuana advertising. Signage, flyers, and leaflets are also restricted as their reach cannot be controlled. Similar advertising regulations apply in Washington as well.

However, some startup advertising agencies are emerging to help marijuana retailers with their advertising. Seattle-based Mirsky Media is one such company, whose services include search engine optimization, Web page design, marketing consulting, and obtaining advice on how to get good feedback on the review website Yelp. There are other methods that marijuana retailers use to promote themselves as well. Sponsoring charity walks, sporting events, and live concerts have been an effective means of public relations for some dispensaries.

Despite these legal restrictions in advertising, the question as to whether marijuana dispensaries should advertise their products remains. On the one hand, they are a legal business in Colorado and Washington, and it is their legal right to generate a profit. But is this profit generated to the detriment of society? Some argue that the legality of the issue does not mean that it should be promoted. The use of marijuana is linked to side effects, including memory loss, a tendency toward depression, and a lack of motivation. It is also linked to more positive side effects such as slowing the progression of Alzheimer's, reducing the spread of cancer, and controlling epileptic seizures. Despite these linkages, research has not been adequate to make any definitive claims.

There Are Two Sides to Every Issue:

1. Advertising for recreational marijuana should be legal in states where its use has been legalized.

2. Because recreational marijuana use can be a detriment to society, advertising for recreational marijuana should be prohibited.

Sources: Bruce Kennedy, "Ad Agencies Prepare for the Legal Marijuana Market," *CBS News,* January 6, 2014, http://www.cbsnews.com/news/ad-agencies-prepare-for-the-legal-marijuana-market/ (accessed July 15, 2016); Eleazar David Melendez, "Marijuana Doesn't Just Sell Itself, as Marketers Face Resistance from Google, Media Companies," *The Huffington Post,* August 30, 2013, http://www.huffington-post.com/2013/08/30/marijuana-marketers_n_3832448.html (accessed July 15, 2016); Melanie Williamson, "Legalized Weed Means Changes for Digital Marketing Strategies," *Josic,* January 14, 2014, http://www.josic.com/legalized-weed-means443-changes-for-digital-marketing-strategies (accessed July 15, 2016); Anne Holland, "Recreational Marijuana Retailers to Face Major Advertising Restrictions in Colorado," *Marijuana Business Daily,* September 17, 2013, http://mmj-businessdaily.com/recreational-marijuana-retailers-to-face-significant-advertising-constrictions-in-colorado/ (accessed July 15, 2016); Jacob Sullum, "6 Ways Washington's Marijuana Rules Are Looser Than Colorado's," *Reason,* July 5, 2013, http://reason.com/blog/2013/07/05/6-ways-washingtons-marijuana-rules-are-l (accessed July 15, 2016) Jennifer Welsh, Dina Spector, and Randy Astaiza, "The Positives and Negatives: How Marijuana Affects Your Brain and Body," *thejournal.ie,* January 11, 2014, http://www.thejournal.ie/marijauan-health-effects-legalised-medical-negative-positve-1256236-Jan2014/ (accessed July 15, 2016).

KEY TERMS

trusts (p. 116)
monopoly (p. 116)
deregulation (p. 130)
political action committee (PAC)
    (p. 133)
lobbying (p. 135)

Federal Sentencing Guidelines for
    Organizations (FSGO) (p. 137)
Sarbanes-Oxley Act (SOX) (p. 141)
Dodd-Frank Wall Street Reform
    and Consumer Protection Act
    (p. 143)

Consumer Financial Protection
    Bureau (CFPB) (p. 144)

DISCUSSION QUESTIONS

1. Discuss the existence of both cooperation and conflict between government and businesses concerning the regulation of business.
2. What is the rationale for government to regulate the activities of businesses? How is our economic and social existence shaped by government regulations?
3. What was the historical background that encouraged the government to enact legislation such as the Sherman Antitrust Act and the Clayton Act? Do these same conditions exist today?
4. What is the role and function of the Federal Trade Commission in the regulation of business? How does the FTC engage in proactive activities to avoid government regulation?
5. How do global regulations influence U.S. businesses operating internationally? What are the major obstacles to global regulation?
6. Compare the costs and benefits of regulation. In your opinion, do the benefits outweigh the costs or do the costs outweigh the benefits? What are the advantages and disadvantages of deregulation?
7. Name three tools that businesses can employ to influence government and public policy. Evaluate the strengths and weaknesses of each of these approaches.
8. How do political action committees influence society, and what is their appropriate role in a democratic society?
9. Why should an organization implement the Federal Sentencing Guidelines for Organizations (FSGO) as a strategic approach for legal compliance?
10. What is the significance of Sarbanes-Oxley and the Dodd-Frank Act to business operations in the United States?

EXPERIENTIAL EXERCISE

Visit the website of the Federal Trade Commission (FTC) (http://www.ftc.gov/). What is the FTC's current mission? What are the primary areas for which the FTC is responsible? Review the press releases of the last two months: on the basis of these releases, what appear to be major issues of concern at this time?

THE TAXING ROLE OF BEING A POLITICIAN: WHAT WOULD YOU DO?

The election of a new governor brings many changes to any state capital, including the shuffling of a variety of appointed positions. In most cases, political appointees have contributed a great deal to the governor's election bid and have expertise in a specific area related to the appointed post. Joe Barritz was in that position when he became assistant agricultural commissioner in January 2010. He was instrumental in getting the governor elected, especially through his fundraising efforts. Joe's family owned thousands of acres in the state and had been farming and ranching since the 1930s. Joe earned a bachelor's degree in agricultural economics and policy and a law degree from one of the state's top institutions. He worked as an attorney in the state's capital city for over 18 years and represented a range of clients, most of whom were involved in agriculture. Thus, he possessed many characteristics that made him a strong candidate for assistant commissioner. After about six months

on the job, Joe had lunch with a couple of friends he had known for many years. During that June lunch, they had a casual conversation about the fact that Joe never did have a true "celebration" after being named assistant agricultural commissioner. His friends decided to discuss with others and plan a celebration in a few months. Before long, eight of Joe's friends were busy planning to hold a reception in his honor on October 5. Two of these friends were currently employed as lobbyists. One represented the beef industry association, and the other worked for the cotton industry council. They asked Joe if they could hold the celebration at his lake home in the capital city. Joe talked with the commission's ethics officer about the party and learned that these types of parties, between close friends, were common for newly appointed and elected officials. The ethics officer told Joe that the reception and location were fine, but only if his lobbyist friends paid for the reception with personal funds. The state's ethics rules did not allow a standing government official to take any type of gift, including corporate dollars, that might influence his or her decision-making. Joe communicated this information to his friends.

During the next few months, Joe was involved in a number of issues that could potentially help or harm agriculture-based industries. Various reports and policy statements within the Agricultural Commission were being used to tailor state legislation and regulatory proposals. The beef and cotton councils were actively supporting a proposal that would provide tax breaks to farmers and ranchers. Staff on the Agricultural Commission were mixed on the proposal, but Joe was expected to deliver a report to a legislative committee on the commission's preferences. His presentation was scheduled for October 17.

On October 5, nearly 60 of Joe's friends gathered at the catered reception to reminisce and congratulate him on his achievements. Most were good friends and acquaintances, so the mood and conversation were relatively light that evening. A college football game

between two big rivals drew most people to the big-screen TV. By midnight, the guests were gone. Back at the office the following week, Joe began working on his presentation for the legislative committee. Through a series of economic analyses, long meetings, and electronic discussions, he decided to support the tax benefits for farmers and ranchers. News reports carried information from his presentation.

It was not long before some reporters made a "connection" between the reception in Joe's honor and his stand on the tax breaks for agriculture industries. An investigation quickly ensued, including reports that the beef and cotton industry associations had not only been present but also financially supported the reception on October 5. The small company used to plan and cater the party indicated that checks from the cotton industry council and beef industry association were used to cover some of the expenses. A relationship between the "gift" of the reception and Joe's presentation to the legislative committee would be a breach of his oath of office and state ethics rules. If you were Joe, what would you do?

CHAPTER FIVE

Business Ethics and Ethical Decision-Making

Greenwashing: Don't Be 'Taken to the Cleaners'

As concerns about the environment grow among consumers and stakeholder groups, more companies are trying to portray themselves in an eco-friendly light. This can lead to a form of deception called *greenwashing,* which occurs when companies market products as environmentally friendly when they are actually not. It is a way for companies to appeal to green consumers while avoiding the costs of developing truly "green" products.

Businesses accused of greenwashing can be exposed as misguiding the public and face the possibility of negative publicity and resulting sales declines. In the United States, firms that label or advertise products as organic or environmentally friendly are supposed to abide by the Federal Trade Commission's revised "Green Guides," which provides guidelines to help companies make sure that their green claims are truthful. Those found to be misleading consumers risk fines, negative publicity and the possibility of consumer reimbursement.

Both the Federal Trade Commission and consumer advocates are beginning to hold companies to stricter standards. The FTC levied a $450,000 fine against AJM Packaging Corporation for violating a 1994 order not to represent its products or packaging as being biodegradable without reliable evidence to back it up. A lawsuit was filed against PepsiCo because critics found synthetic vitamins in the drink despite its claims to be all-natural. PepsiCo paid to settle the lawsuit and agreed not to use the all-natural label.

The problem is that terms such as "natural" and "green" can be hard to define. Is a product eco-friendly if most, but not all, of its components are made from sustainable materials? What about companies that still give off carbon emissions but which have improved their products over the years? The automobile industry faces this problem as vehicles continue to negatively impact the environment. Even hybrids, electric vehicles, and fuel-efficient cars impact the environment. Norway actually banned all green claims in car advertising after concerns about greenwashing in the auto industry.

To not become a victim of greenwashing, ask the right questions. When buying green, investigate what materials the products use and how the company obtained those materials. Always look for evidence to back up a green product's claims. Also, beware of ambiguous claims. For instance, the phrase "lower carbon emissions" in and of itself does not explain much if it does not have a point of comparison. Third-party certification including the Forest Stewardship Council and Green Globes offer some assurance that certified products adhere to certain green guidelines. However, consumers must exert caution with certification firms as well. The FTC sent warning letters to five marketers of green certifications and seals warning them that their criteria for the certifications fail to meet the guidelines set forth in its "Green Guides." With greenwashing incidents increasing, consumers need to use caution and verify that the products they buy are truly eco-friendly.[1]

Key business ethics concerns relate to questions about whether various stakeholders consider specific business practices acceptable. A reputation as an ethical firm takes a long time to earn but just minutes to lose. Once lost, it can take considerable time to restore goodwill with stakeholders. For example, banks and financial institutions have had major reputational damage. The financial services industry ranks the lowest in consumer and investor trust. However, the financial services industry has begun to rebound slowly. About 51 percent of the global population claims they trust the financial services industry.[2] Business ethics is important to build trust and create an organizational culture that establishes a good reputation.

By its very nature, the field of business ethics is complex because organizational issues often require subject matter knowledge. For example, accounting ethics is embedded with principles, rules, and regulatory requirements. Most businesses are establishing initiatives that include the development and implementation of ethics programs designed to deter misconduct. Raytheon Company, a long-established defense and security company employing 63,000 people worldwide, has a comprehensive ethics and compliance program. The company's ethics education program has been ranked by 82 percent of employees as relevant and useful in making ethical decisions. The strength of the program has contributed to a strong organizational culture of integrity. Employees engage in annual peer meetings called "Ethics Checkpoint" sessions where all have an opportunity to reflect on and provide solutions to real life ethical dilemmas. Video vignettes and other online educational materials on supplier relations, product integrity, and labor issues are also utilized. The company displays an outward focus on ethics by supporting education and proper conduct in defense and university programs.[3]

The definition of social responsibility that appears in Chapter 1 incorporates society's expectations and includes four levels of concern: economic, legal, ethical, and philanthropic. Because ethics is becoming an increasingly important issue in business today, this chapter and Chapter 6 are devoted to exploring this dimension of social responsibility. First, we define business ethics, examine its importance from an organizational perspective, and review its foundations. Next, we define ethical issues in business to help understand areas of risk. We then look at the individual, organizational, and opportunity factors that influence ethical decision-making in the workplace. We conclude by examining requirements for developing an ethical organizational culture.

THE NATURE OF BUSINESS ETHICS

Business decisions can be both acceptable and beneficial to society. It is necessary to examine business ethics to understand decisions made in the context of an organizational culture. The term *ethics* relates to choices and judgments about acceptable standards of conduct that guide the behavior of individuals and groups. These standards require both organizations and individuals to accept responsibility for their actions and to comply with established principles, values, and norms. Without a shared view of which values and norms are appropriate and acceptable, companies will not have consistency in decisions, with individuals differing in how they resolve issues. Building an ethical culture results in shareholder loyalty and can contribute to success that supports even broader social causes and concerns. Director of Sustainability at the Verdigris Group, Garratt Hasenstab, has stated regarding its corporate social responsibility initiatives that "the true value we receive from our ongoing initiatives is that of social good will—we believe that setting a good example is the greatest benefit."[4] Society has developed rules—both legal and implied—to guide companies in their efforts to earn profits through means that do not bring harm to individuals or to society at large.

Business ethics comprises the principles and standards that guide the behavior of individuals and groups in the world of business. Most definitions of business ethics relate to rules, standards, and principles regarding what is right or wrong in specific situations. **Principles** are specific and pervasive boundaries for behavior that are universal and absolute. Principles often become the basis for rules. Some examples of principles include freedom of speech, principles of justice, and equal rights to civil liberties. **Values** are used to develop norms that are socially enforced. Integrity, accountability, and trust are examples of values. Investors, employees, customers, interest groups, the legal system, and the community often determine whether a specific action is right or wrong, ethical or unethical. Although these groups are not necessarily "right," their judgments influence society's acceptance or rejection of a business and its activities.

Managers, employees, consumers, industry associations, government regulators, business partners, and special interest groups all contribute to these conventions, and they may change over time. The most basic of these standards have been codified as laws and regulations to encourage companies to conform to society's expectations of business conduct. As we said in Chapter 4, public concerns about accounting fraud and conflicts of interest in the securities industry led to the passage of the Sarbanes-Oxley Act to restore the public's trust in the stock market.

It is vital to recognize that business ethics goes beyond legal issues. Ethical business decisions foster trust in business relationships, and as we discussed in Chapter 1, trust is a key factor in improving productivity and achieving success in most organizations. When companies deviate from the prevailing standards of industry and society, the result is customer dissatisfaction, lack of trust, and lawsuits.

Some businesspeople choose to behave ethically because of enlightened self-interest, or the expectation that "ethics pays." They want to act responsibly and assume that the public and customers will reward the company for its ethical actions. For example, Patagonia began donating one percent of their sales to environmental causes and encourages customers not to buy their products if they do not need them. While these

business ethics
The principles and standards that guide the behavior of individuals and groups in the world of business.

principles
Specific and pervasive boundaries for behavior that are universal and absolute and often form the basis for rules.

values
Norms that are socially enforced, such as integrity, accountability, and trust.

activities have the potential to negatively affect the company's sales, consumers value Patagonia's responsible message and opt to support them over other outdoor retailers, which could increase long-run profitability.[5]

FOUNDATIONS OF BUSINESS ETHICS

Because all individuals and groups within a company may not have embraced the same set of values, there is always the possibility of ethical conflict. Most ethical issues in an organizational context are addressed openly whenever a policy, code, or rule is questioned. Even then, it may be hard to distinguish between the ethical issue and the legal means used to resolve it. Because it is difficult to draw a boundary between legal and ethical issues, all questionable issues need an organizational mechanism for resolution.

The legal ramifications of some issues and situations may be obvious, but questionable decisions and actions more often result in disputes that must be resolved through some type of negotiation or even litigation. Companies that sell e-cigarettes, for instance, may be subject to such risks similar to traditional tobacco firms. The FDA has issued tough new rules for e-cigarettes that bans selling to minors, requires warning labels on packaging, and having all e-cigarette products undergo government approval. Some argue that these restrictions are too cumbersome in terms of cost for businesses, particularly in light of the fact that many tobacco users have reduced or eliminated their dependence on the drug as a result of switching to e-cigarettes. On the other hand, many say these devices are targeted toward youth since they offer flavors such as chocolate and bubblegum, which are likely to attract this demographic and get them dabbling with tobacco products.[6] Such highly publicized issues strengthen the perception that ethical standards in business need to be raised.

When ethical disputes wind up in court, the costs and distractions associated with litigation can be devastating to a business. In addition to the compensatory or nominal damages actually incurred, punitive damages may be imposed on a company that is judged to have acted improperly to punish the firm and to send an intimidating message to others. The legal system, therefore, provides a formal venue for businesspeople to resolve ethical as well as legal disputes; in fact, many of the examples we cite in this chapter had to be resolved through the courts. To avoid the costs of litigation, companies should develop systems to monitor complaints, suggestions, and other feedback from stakeholders. In many cases, issues can be negotiated or resolved without legal intervention. Strategic responsibility entails systems for listening to, understanding, and effectively managing stakeholder concerns.[7]

A high level of personal morality may not be sufficient to prevent an individual from violating the law in an organizational context in which even experienced attorneys debate the exact meaning of the law. Because it is impossible to train all the members of an organization as lawyers, the identification of ethical issues and the implementation of standards of conduct that incorporate both legal and ethical concerns are the best approaches to preventing crime and avoiding civil litigation. Codifying ethical standards into meaningful policies that spell out what is and is not acceptable gives businesspeople an opportunity to reduce the probability of behavior that could create legal problems. Without proper ethical training and guidance, it is impossible for the average business manager to understand the exact boundaries for illegal behavior in the areas of product safety, price fixing, fraud, collusion, copyright violations, and so on. For example, the largest technology companies, including Google, Apple, Intel, and Adobe, were charged in a class-action suit regarding collusion on employee wages. The claim stated that the executives of all companies agreed not to recruit the others' employees for a number of years, the effect of which was a suppression of wages. The companies settled the lawsuit for $415 million.[8]

Although the values of honesty, respect, and trust are often assumed to be self-evident and universally accepted, business decisions involve complex and detailed discussions in which correctness may not be so clear-cut. Both employees and managers need experience within their specific industry to understand how to operate in gray areas or to handle close calls in evolving areas. Warren Buffett and his company Berkshire Hathaway command significant respect from investors because of their track record of financial returns and the integrity of their organizations. Buffett says, "I want employees to ask themselves whether they are willing to have any contemplated act appear the next day on the front page of their local paper—to be read by their spouses, children and friends—with the reporting done by an informed and critical reporter." The high level of accountability and trust Buffett places in employees translates into investor trust and confidence.[9]

Many people with limited business experience suddenly find themselves required to make decisions about product quality, advertising, pricing, sales techniques, hiring practices, privacy, and pollution control. For example, how do advertisers know when they are making misleading statements in advertising versus "puffery"? Bayer is "the world's best aspirin," Snapple "made from the best stuff on earth," and Firestone (before recalling 6.5 million tires) promised "quality you can trust."[10] The personal values learned through non-work socialization from family, religion, and school may not provide specific guidelines for these complex business decisions. In other words, a person's experiences and decisions at home, in school, and in the community may be quite different from the experiences and the decisions he or she has to make at work. Moreover, the interests and values of individual employees may differ from those of the company in which they work, from industry standards, and from the society in general. When personal values are inconsistent with the configuration of values held by the work group, ethical conflict may ensue. It is important that a shared vision of acceptable behavior develop from an organizational perspective to cultivate consistent and reliable relationships with all concerned stakeholders. A shared vision of ethics that is part of an organization's culture can be questioned, analyzed, and modified as new issues develop. However, business ethics should relate to work environment decisions and should not control or influence personal ethical issues.

Recognizing an Ethical Issue

Although we have described a number of relationships and situations that may generate ethical issues, it can be difficult to recognize specific ethical issues in practice. Failure to acknowledge ethical issues is a great danger in any organization, particularly if business is treated as a game in which ordinary rules of fairness do not apply. Sometimes, people who take this view do things that are not only unethical but also illegal to maximize their own position or boost the profits or goals of the organization.

Figure 5.1 identifies the frequency of misconduct observed by employees in different countries. In the 2016 global survey on workplace misconduct, 30 percent of U.S. employees noted observing misconduct at work. This is down from 55 percent in 2007. This figure shows how important it is to have a comprehensive ethics and compliance program in place to assess risk and to reduce instances of personal misconduct. These data provide evidence that the institution of an ethical organizational culture has a positive impact on business.

However, just because an unsettled situation or activity is an ethical issue does not mean the behavior is necessarily unethical. An ethical issue

FIGURE 5.1 Employee Observed Misconduct in the Workplace

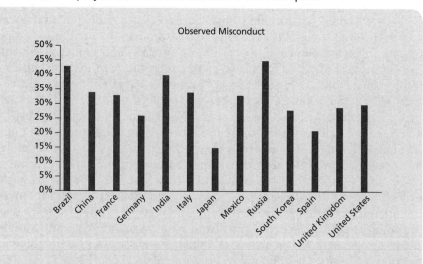

Source: Ethics and Compliance Initiative, *2016 Global Business Ethics Survey™: Measuring Risk and Promoting Workplace Integrity* (Arlington, VA: Ethics and Compliance Initiative, 2016), p. 31-43.

may relate to a situation, a problem, or even an opportunity that requires thought, discussion, or investigation to determine the potential impact of the decision. Because the business world is dynamic, new ethical issues are emerging all the time.

One way to determine whether a specific behavior or situation has an ethical component is to ask other individuals in the business for feedback and guidance, or approval/disapproval of your decision. Another way is to determine whether the organization has adopted specific policies or whether there are legal ramifications. An activity approved of by most members of an organization, if it is also customary in the industry, is probably ethical. An issue, activity, or situation that can withstand open discussion between many stakeholders, both inside and outside the organization, and survive untarnished probably does not pose a threat. For instance, it is a common legal practice for medical device manufacturers to have close relationships with medical practitioners, which often include monetary transactions. However, the nature of these relationships may concern outside stakeholders, especially when devices are found to malfunction and cause patients harm. Johnson & Johnson had such an experience with one of their medical devices, and it was found that some internal conversations about the language of marketing materials were changed to increase sales, potentially misleading physicians.[11]

ETHICAL ISSUES IN BUSINESS

An **ethical issue** is a problem, situation, or opportunity requiring an individual, group, or organization to choose among several actions that must be evaluated as right or wrong, ethical or unethical. Surveys can render a useful overview of the many unsettled ethical issues in business. A constructive step toward identifying and resolving ethical issues is to classify the issues relevant to most business organizations. In this section, we examine ethical issues related to abusive behavior, misuse of company resources, conflict of interest, bribery, discrimination and sexual harassment, fraud, and privacy issues.

Although not all-inclusive or mutually exclusive, these classifications provide an overview of some major ethical issues that business decision-makers face. Table 5.1 provides statistics on organizational misconduct in the United States. Putting one's own interests ahead of the organization, abusive behavior, and lying to employees are all personal in nature. Abusive behavior, lying to employees, and conflict of interest are three major issues that directly relate to the firm's agenda.

Although Table 5.1 documents some ethical issues that exist in global organizations, due to the almost infinite number of ways that misconduct can occur, we cover only the major organizational ethical issues. Any type of manipulation, deceit, or the absence of transparency in decision-making can create harm to others.

ethical issue
A problem, situation, or opportunity requiring an individual, group, or organization to choose among several actions that must be evaluated as right or wrong, ethical or unethical.

TABLE 5.1 Organizational Misconduct in the United States

Misconduct Facts	Percentages
Observed misconduct	30%
Abusive behavior	22%
Lying to stakeholders	22%
Conflict of interest	19%
Pressure to compromise standards	22%
Report observed misconduct	76%
Experience retaliation for reporting	53%

Source: Ethics and Compliance Initiative, *2016 Global Business Ethics Survey™: Measuring Risk and Promoting Workplace Integrity* (Arlington, VA: Ethics and Compliance Initiative, 2016), p. 43.

Abusive or Intimidating Behavior

Abusive or intimidating behavior is the most common ethical problem for employees, but what does it mean to be abusive or intimidating? The concepts can mean anything from physical threats, false accusations, annoying a coworker, profanity, insults, yelling, harshness, and ignoring someone to the point of being unreasonable, and the meaning of these words are subjective and can vary from person to person. It is important to understand that each term falls along a continuum. For example, what one person may define as yelling might be another's definition of normal speech. Civility in our society has been a concern, and the workplace is no exception. The productivity level of many organizations has declined on account of the time spent unraveling abusive relationships.

Within the concept of abusive behavior, intent should be a consideration. If the employee was trying to convey a compliment when the comment was considered abusive, then it was probably a mistake. The way a word is spoken (voice inflection) can be important. Add to this the fact that we now live in a multicultural environment doing business and working with many different cultural groups and the businessperson soon realizes the depth of the ethical and legal issues that may arise. There are problems of word meanings across different age-groups and cultures. For example, an expression such as, "Did you guys hook up last night?" can have various meanings, including some that could be considered offensive in a work environment.

Misuse of Company Time and Resources

Theft of time is estimated to cost companies hundreds of billions of dollars annually. It is estimated that the average employee "steals" more than ten hours per week with late arrivals, long lunch breaks, leaving early, daydreaming, excessive socializing, engaging in personal activities, and using social networking sites such as Facebook.[12] The misuse of time and resources has been identified by the Ethics Resource Center as a major form of observed misconduct. In one survey, 31 percent of respondents observed others misusing company time, and 17 percent observed company resource abuse such as theft of office supplies. Therefore, nearly 50 percent noted misconduct related to resource issues. When enforcement is lax or non-existent, employees may get the impression that they are entitled to certain company resources.

Using company computer equipment for personal business is a common way employees engage in time theft. While employees might recognize that spending the workday talking with friends and relatives is unacceptable, they might not hesitate to go online and do the same thing. Typical examples of misusing company computers include sending personal emails, socializing on Facebook, shopping on Amazon or eBay, downloading music, doing personal banking, or watching sporting events online. Many employees, for instance, engage in time theft during March Madness during the NCAA basketball tournament. As a result, many organizations block websites where employees can watch sports events. Some even block sites such as Netflix and Pandora to prevent employees from watching video clips or streaming music.

To deter this type of misconduct, many organizations implement policies describing the acceptable use of such resources. For example, Boeing's code of ethics states that resource use is acceptable when it does not result in "significant added costs, disruption of business processes, or any other disadvantage to the company." The policy states that use of company resources for non-company purposes is only acceptable when an employee receives permission to do so.[13]

Conflict of Interest

A **conflict of interest** exists when an individual must choose whether to advance his or her own interests, those of his or her organization, or those of some other group. Investment manager BlackRock agreed to pay $12 million after failing to report a conflict of interest. One of its portfolio managers was running an energy company that partnered with a coal firm. The coal firm eventually became the largest holding in a fund the manager ran for BlackRock. BlackRock also agreed to allow an independent compliance consultant to conduct a review of its policies.[14]

To avoid conflicts of interest, employees must be able to separate their private interests from their work roles. Organizations, too, must avoid potential conflicts of interest in providing goods or services. Environmental organization Sierra Club requested documents from the U.S. State Department regarding the hiring of Environmental Resources Management, a contractor set to work on the Keystone XL pipeline. The documents reveal several conflicts of interest as many of its consultants also work for companies that benefit greatly from the completion of the pipeline. It was found that the company did not disclose these issues nor did it appear that the U.S. government investigated them.[15]

conflict of interest
An issue that arises when an individual must choose whether to advance his or her own interests, those of his or her organization, or those of some other group.

Bribery

Bribery is the practice of offering something, such as money, gifts, entertainment, and travel, in order to gain an illicit advantage from someone in authority. The definition of bribery depends upon whether the illicit payment or favor is used to gain an advantage in a relationship. In many developed countries, society generally recognizes that employees should not accept bribes or special favors from people who could influence the outcome of a decision. However, bribery is an acceptable way of doing business in other countries. The U.S. Securities and Exchange Commission has cracked down on cases of bribery involving hundreds of companies. One investigation resulted in pharmaceutical firm Novartis agreeing to pay $25 million to settle allegations that it bribed health care providers in China.[16]

Bribery can be considered an unlawful act, but in some cultures bribing business or government officials with fees is considered standard practice. In this case, bribery becomes a business ethics issue. Bribes have led to the downfall of many managers, legislators, and government officials. The World Bank estimates that more than $1 trillion is paid annually in bribes.[17]

When a government official accepts a bribe, it is usually from a business that seeks some advantage, perhaps to obtain business or the opportunity to avoid regulation. Giving bribes to legislators or public officials, then, is both a legal and a business ethics issue. It is a legal issue in the United States under the U.S. Foreign Corrupt Practices Act (FCPA). This act maintains that it is illegal for individuals, firms, or third parties doing business in American markets to "make payments to foreign government officials to assist in obtaining or retaining business."[18] Companies have paid billions of dollars in fines to the Department of Justice for bribery violations. The law applies not only to American firms but to all firms transacting business with operations in the United States. This also means that firms do not necessarily have to commit bribery in the United States to be held accountable.

The United Kingdom Bribery Act passed in 2010 is similar to the FCPA but more encompassing. For instance, while the FCPA applies to bribing foreign government officials, the U.K. Bribery Act holds people or businesses responsible for commercial bribery as well. The first cases convicted under the U.K. Bribery Act were acts of commercial bribery committed largely by individuals, such as a student who tried to bribe a professor to pass him. The Act also does not allow for facilitation payments or small payments to get normal services performed. Like the FCPA, any organization is subject to the U.K. Bribery Act if it has operations in the United Kingdom, no matter where the bribery occurred.

Discrimination and Sexual Harassment

Discrimination remains a significant ethical issue in business despite nearly 50 years of legislation to outlaw it. Once dominated by white men, today's

U.S. workforce includes significantly more women, African Americans, Hispanics, and other minorities, as well as workers with disabilities and older workers. Experts project that within the next 30 years, Hispanics will represent 30 percent of the population, while African Americans and Asians/Pacific Islanders will make up 15 and 9.2 percent, respectively.[19] These groups have traditionally faced discrimination and higher unemployment rates and have been denied opportunities to assume leadership roles in corporate America.

The most significant piece of legislation against discrimination is Title VII of the Civil Rights Act of 1964, which prohibits employment discrimination on the basis of race, national origin, color, religion, and gender, and applies to employers with 15 or more employees, including state and local governments. This law is fundamental to employees' rights to join and advance in an organization according to merit rather than one of the characteristics just mentioned. As a result of racial discrimination class-action settlements, some companies, such as Coca-Cola, were required to establish an independent task force to monitor and modify company practices to combat racial discrimination.

Additional laws passed in the 1970s, 1980s, and 1990s were designed to prohibit discrimination related to pregnancy, disabilities, age, and other factors. The Americans with Disabilities Act, for example, prohibits companies from discriminating on the basis of physical or mental disability in all employment practices and requires them to make facilities accessible to and usable by persons with disabilities. The Age Discrimination in Employment Act specifically outlaws hiring practices that discriminate against people ages 40 or older, but it also bans policies that require employees to retire before the age of 70. Despite this legislation, charges of age discrimination persist in the workplace. Currently, about half of the United States workforce is 40 or older. This is a large segment of the workplace, and naturally age discrimination lawsuits are prevalent. In a 5-4 split ruling, the U.S. Supreme Court ruled to make it more difficult for workers to claim age discrimination in lawsuits. Now employees must be able to prove that their employers terminated them for age-related reasons. Because this is a difficult thing to prove for certain, the ruling signaled a major coup for employers. The ruling was part of a case brought to trial by Jack Gross, who at 54 was demoted from a director position by his employer FBL Financial Group.[20] Given that more than 25 percent of the nation's workers will be 55 years old or over by 2020, many companies need to change their approach toward older workers.[21]

Sexual harassment is a form of sex discrimination that violates Title VII of the Civil Rights Act of 1964. **Sexual harassment** can be defined as any repeated, unwanted behavior of a sexual nature perpetrated upon one individual by another. It may be verbal, visual, written, or physical and can occur between people of different genders or those of the same gender. Displaying sexually explicit materials "may create a hostile work environment or constitute harassment, even though the private possession, reading, and consensual sharing of such materials is protected under

sexual harassment
Any repeated, unwanted behavior of a sexual nature perpetrated upon one individual by another; it may be verbal, visual, written, or physical and can occur between people of different genders or those of the same gender.

the Constitution."[22] The Equal Employment Opportunity Commission (EEOC), the institution that monitors compliance with Title VII, in one year received 6,822 charges of sexual harassment, of which men filed over 17 percent. In the same year, the EEOC resolved 7,289 sexual harassment charges and recovered $46 million in penalties.[23]

To establish sexual harassment, an employee must understand the definition of a **hostile work environment,** for which three criteria must be met: (1) the conduct was unwelcome; (2) the conduct was severe, pervasive, and regarded by the claimant as so hostile or offensive as to alter his or her conditions of employment; and (3) the conduct was such that a reasonable person would find it hostile or offensive. To assert a hostile work environment, an employee need not prove that it seriously affected his or her psychological well-being or that it caused an injury; the decisive issue is whether the conduct interfered with the claimant's work performance.[24]

hostile work environment
A kind of work environment where the conduct is: unwelcome; severe and hostile as to affect conditions of employment; and offensive to a reasonable person.

Fraud

fraud
Any false communication that deceives, manipulates, or conceals facts to create a false impression when others are damaged or denied a benefit.

When an individual engages in deceptive practices to advance his or her own interests over those of the organization or some other group, charges of illegal fraud may result. In general, **fraud** is any false communication that deceives, manipulates, or conceals facts to create a false impression when others are damaged or denied a benefit. It is considered a crime, and convictions may result in fines, imprisonment, or both. Employee expense fraud alone is estimated to cost businesses more than $2.8 billion annually.[25] Among the most common fraudulent activities reported by 40 percent of employees are embezzlement, offshore financial accounts, and stealing money or products.[26] Table 5.2 indicates what fraud examiners view as the biggest risks to companies. In recent years, accounting fraud has become a major ethical issue, but fraud can also relate to marketing and consumer issues as well. Online fraud is also a large concern and is growing as internet use expands.[27]

Privacy

privacy issues
Issues that businesses must address that include the monitoring of employees' use of available technology, consumer privacy, and online marketing.

The final category of ethical issues relates to privacy, especially within the health-care and internet industries. Some **privacy issues** that businesses must address include the monitoring of employees' use of available technology, consumer privacy, and online marketing. Companies often use cookies or other devices to engage in online tracking, and many websites use consumer information to improve services. Although this can benefit consumers in the form of better marketing and tailored searches, it is also controversial because many consumers do not want their information being tracked. Others are still willing to provide personal information despite the potential risks.[28]

The challenge for today's firms is balancing their need for consumer or employee information with the desire for privacy. In terms of employees, there are few legal protections for their right to privacy, giving businesses flexibility in establishing policies regarding employee privacy while using company equipment on company property. Some common ways that an employer might track employee use of equipment is through computer monitoring, telephone monitoring, video surveillance, and GPS satellite tracking. Although employers have the right to make sure their resources are being used for appropriate purposes, the ability to gather and use data about employee behavior creates the need for trust and responsibility.

There are two issues involving consumer privacy: consumer awareness of information collection and a growing lack of consumer control with respect to how organizations use their personal information. For example, many are not aware that Google, Inc., reserves the right to track each time you click on a link from one of its searches.[29] Online purchases and random web surfing can be tracked without a consumer's knowledge. The Progress and Freedom Foundation found that 96 percent of popular commercial websites collect personally identifying information from visitors.[30]

However, consumer information is valuable not only to businesses but to criminals as well. An identity is stolen approximately once every three seconds.[31] Criminals may try to steal personal consumer information and sell it online. Some of this information comes from publicly accessible sources such as social networking profiles, but poorly protected corporate files are another major source for criminals. In one year, 90 percent of large U.K. organizations reported security breaches.[32]

To reassure consumers that their information will be protected, an increasing number of companies are displaying an online seal from the Better Business Bureau available to sites that subscribe to certain standards. A similar seal is provided through TRUSTe, a nonprofit global initiative. These seals assure customers that the websites adhere to certain policies meant to protect their privacy.

TABLE 5.2 Greatest Fraud Risk to Companies

Corruption 35.4%
Conflicts of interrest
Purchasing schemes
Sales schemes
Bribery
Invoice kickbacks
Bid rigging
Illegal gratuities
Economic Extortion
Asset Misappropriation 83.5%
Theft of cash on hand
Theft of cash receipts
Skimming
Cash larceny
Fraudulent disbursements
Billing schemes
Payroll schemes
Expense reimbursement schemes
Expense reimbursement schemes
Check tampering
Register disbursements
Inventory and all other assets
Misuse
Larceny
Financial Statement Fraud 9.6%
Net worth/net income overstatements
Net worth/net income understatements

Source: Association of Certified Fraud Examiners, *Report to the Nations on Occupational Fraud and Abuse,* 2016, https://s3-us-west-2.amazonaws.com/acfepublic/2016-report-to-the-nations.pdf (accessed June 17, 2016). .

UNDERSTANDING THE ETHICAL DECISION-MAKING PROCESS

To grasp the significance of ethics in business decision-making, it is important to understand how ethical decisions are made within the context of an organization. Understanding the ethical decision-making process can help individuals and businesses design strategies to deter misconduct. Our

FIGURE 5.2 Factors That Influence the Ethical Decision-Making Process

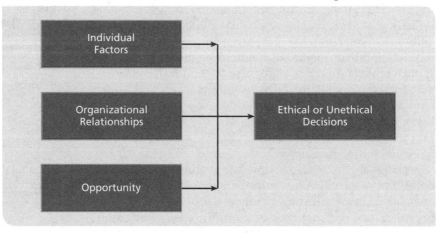

descriptive approach to understanding ethical decision-making does not prescribe what to do but, rather, provides a framework for managing ethical behavior in the workplace. Figure 5.2 depicts this framework, which shows how individual factors, organizational relationships, and opportunities interact to determine ethical decisions in business.

Individual Factors

Individuals make ethical choices on the basis of their own concepts of right or wrong, and they act accordingly in their daily lives. Studies suggest that individual ethics are reaching a new low. A Josephson Institute Center for Youth Ethics survey of teens showed that 95 percent feel trust and honesty are necessary in the workplace. In addition to this, 36 percent of those surveyed feel it is sometimes necessary to lie and cheat in order to succeed. More than one-fourth of the respondents confessed to cheating on a test more than once. While this survey indicates teens are more concerned about ethics when compared with a similar survey from two years prior, these results show that more needs to be done to teach teens about the importance of ethical decision-making.[33] If today's students are tomorrow's leaders, there is likely to be a correlation between acceptable behavior today and tomorrow, adding to the argument that the leaders of today must be prepared for the ethical risks associated with acceptance of unethical behavior.

Significant factors that affect the ethical decision-making process include an individual's personal moral philosophy, motivation, and other personal factors such as gender, age, and experience.

Ethical Theories Many people have justified difficult decisions by citing the golden rule ("Do unto others as you would have them do unto you") or some other principle. Such principles, or rules, which individuals apply in deciding what is right or wrong, are often referred to as **moral philosophies.** Morals refers to the individuals' philosophies about what is right or wrong. It is important to understand the distinction between moral philosophies and business ethics. A moral philosophy is a person's principles and values that define what is moral or immoral. Moral philosophies are person-specific, whereas business ethics is based on decisions in groups or those made when carrying out tasks to meet business objectives. In the context of business, ethics refers to what the group, firm, or strategic business unit (SBU) defines as right or wrong actions pertaining to its business operations and the objective of profits, earnings per share, or some other financial measure of success. Socialization by family members, social groups, religion, and formal education teaches moral philosophies. This concept is particularly important to the concept of **social exchange theory,** which states that social behavior is determined by social exchanges between different parties. Most moral philosophies can be classified as consequentialism, ethical formalism or deontology, or justice.

Consequentialism is a class of moral philosophy that considers a decision right or acceptable if it accomplishes a desired result, such as career growth, the realization of self-interest, or utility in a decision. This looks at the moral outcome based on the consequences associated with decision-making. Egoism and utilitarianism are two important consequentialist philosophies that often guide decision-making in business.

Egoism is a philosophy that defines right or acceptable conduct in terms of the consequences for the individual. Egoists believe they should make decisions that maximize their own self-interest, which, depending on the individual, may be defined as career success, power, fame, a satisfying career, a good family life, wealth, and so forth. In a decision-making situation, the egoist will probably choose the alternative that most benefits his or her self-interest. Many people feel that egoists are inherently unethical, that they focus on the short term, and that they will take advantage of any opportunity to exploit consumers or employees.

Utilitarianism is another consequentialist philosophy that is concerned with seeking the greatest good for the greatest number of people. Using a cost-benefit analysis, a utilitarian decision-maker calculates the utility of the consequences of all possible alternatives and then chooses the one that achieves the greatest utility.

In contrast with consequentialism, **ethical formalism** or deontology is a class of moral philosophy that focuses on the rights of individuals and on the intentions associated with a particular behavior rather than on its consequences. This theory falls under what is known as the rights-based ethics. Deontologists regard certain behaviors as inherently right, and their determination of rightness focuses on the individual actor, not on society. Thus, these perspectives are sometimes referred to as nonconsequentialism and the ethics of respect for persons. Contemporary ethical formalism has been greatly influenced by German philosopher Immanuel Kant, who developed the so-called categorical imperative: "Act as if the maxim of thy action were to become by thy will a universal law of nature."[34] Unlike utilitarians, ethical formalists contend that there are some things that people should not do,

moral philosophies
Principles, or rules, which individuals apply in deciding what is right or wrong; morals refers to the individuals' philosophies about what is right or wrong.

social exchange theory
This concept is particularly important to the concept of social exchange theory, which states that social behavior is determined by social exchanges between different parties.

consequentialism
A class of moral philosophy that considers a decision right or acceptable if it accomplishes a desired result, such as career growth, the realization of self-interest, or utility in a decision.

egoism
A philosophy that defines right or acceptable conduct in terms of the consequences for the individual.

utilitarianism
A consequentialist philosophy that is concerned with seeking the greatest good for the greatest number of people.

ethical formalism
A class of moral philosophy that focuses on the rights of individuals and on the intentions associated with a particular behavior rather than on its consequences.

even to maximize utility. For example, an ethical formalist would consider it unacceptable to allow a coalmine to continue to operate if some workers became ill and died of black lung disease. A utilitarian, however, might consider some disease or death an acceptable consequence of a decision that resulted in large-scale employment and economic prosperity.

Justice theory is a class of moral philosophy that relates to evaluations of fairness, or the disposition to deal with perceived injustices of others. Justice demands fair treatment and due reward in accordance with ethical or legal standards. A similar concept is the **Principle of Equal Freedom**, which asserts that all persons must have equality under the law. In business, this requires that the rules an individual uses to determine justice be based on the perceived rights of individuals and on the intentions associated with a business interaction. Justice, therefore, is more likely to be based on non-consequentialist moral philosophies than on consequentialist philosophies. Justice primarily addresses the issue of what individuals feel they are due based on their rights and performance in the workplace. For example, the U.S. Equal Employment Opportunity Commission exists to help employees who suspect the injustice of discrimination in the workplace.

There are three types of justice that can be used to assess fairness in different situations. Distributive justice evaluates the outcomes or results of a business relationship. For example, if an employee feels that she is paid less than her coworkers for the same work, she has concerns about distributive justice. Procedural justice assesses the processes and activities employed to produce an outcome or results. Procedural justice concerns about compensation would relate to the perception that salary and benefit decisions are consistent and fair to all categories of employees. Procedural justice is associated with group cohesiveness and helping behaviors.[35] Interactional justice evaluates the communication processes used in the business relationship. Being untruthful about the reasons for missing work is an example of an interactional justice issue.[36]

It is important to recognize that there is no one "correct" moral philosophy to apply in resolving ethical and legal issues in the workplace. It is also important to acknowledge that each philosophy presents an ideal perspective and that most people seem to adapt a number of moral philosophies as they interpret the context of different decision-making situations. Each philosophy could result in a different decision in a situation requiring an ethical judgment. And depending on the situation, people may even change their value structure or moral philosophy when making decisions.[37]

Strong evidence shows that individuals use different moral philosophies depending on whether they are making a personal decision outside the work environment or making a work-related decision on the job.[38] Two possible reasons may explain this. First, in the business arena, some goals and pressures for success differ from the goals and pressures in a person's life outside of work. As a result, an employee might view a specific action as "good" in the business sector but "unacceptable" in the non-work environment. Business has two variables that are absent from other situations: the profit motive and the influence of managers and coworkers

justice theory
A class of moral philosophy that relates to evaluations of fairness, or the disposition to deal with perceived injustices of others.

Principle of Equal Freedom
A similar concept is the Principle of Equal Freedom, which asserts that all persons must have equality under the law.

(corporate culture). The weights on the various factors that make up a person's moral philosophy are shifted in a business (profit) situation. The statement "it's not personal, it's just business" demonstrates the conflict businesspeople can have when their personal values do not align with utilitarian or profit-oriented decisions. In extreme cases, this mentality could become Machiavellian in nature. **Machiavellianism** in business is the use of duplicity or cunning to achieve business goals. The second reason people change moral philosophies could be the corporate culture where they work. When a child enters school, for example, he or she learns certain rules such as raising your hand to speak or asking permission to use the restroom. So it is with a new employee. Rules, personalities, and historical precedence exert pressure on the employee to conform to the new firm's culture. As this occurs, the individual's moral philosophy may change to be compatible with the work environment. The employee may alter some or all of the values within his or her moral philosophy as he or she shifts into the firm's different moral philosophy. There are many examples of people who are known for their goodness at home or in their communities making unethical decisions in the workplace.

machiavellianism
In extreme cases, this mentality could become Machiavellian in nature. Machiavellianism in business is the use of duplicity or cunning to achieve business goals.

Ethical Diversity It is obvious that not everyone holds the same ethical values. One person may have values that another person does not have, or that person might value a certain trait more highly than another. Additionally, individuals can have significantly different values than those of the organization.[39] This concept is referred to as ethical diversity. **Ethical diversity** refers to the fact that employee values often differ from person to person. Every employee has developed his or her personal values over a lifetime, and these values are not likely to disappear just because they differ from others or the organization. However, it also means that employees cannot be allowed to bring their individual values to the workplace as they see fit. Imagine the chaos that would happen if each employee acted in a way that was appropriate in his or her eyes. Instead, members need to accept that some values are superior to others and handle the organizational need to develop consensus among employees. This may result in possible tensions and conflicts that must be figured out between individual and organizational values.[40] However, it is best to follow a consensus approach rather than just having managers assign and enforce their own individual values to the organization. There should be group discussions, negotiations, and modifications to determine how organizational values are implemented.[41]

ethical diversity
Refers to the fact that employee values often differ from person to person.

Organizational Relationships

Although individuals can and do make ethical decisions, they do not operate in a vacuum.[42] Ethical choices in business are most often made jointly in committees and work groups or in conversations with coworkers. Moreover, people learn to settle ethical issues not only from their individual backgrounds but also from others with whom they associate in the business environment. The outcome of this learning process depends on

organizational, or corporate, culture
A set of values, beliefs, and artifacts shared by members or employees of an organization.

the strength of each individual's personal values, opportunity for unethical behavior, and exposure to others who behave ethically or unethically. Consequently, the culture of the organization, as well as superiors, peers, and subordinates, can have a significant impact on the ethical decision-making process.

Organizational Culture Organizational, or corporate, culture can be defined as a set of values, norms, and artifacts shared by members or employees of an organization. It answers questions such as "What is important?" "How do we treat each other?" and "How do we do things around here?" Culture may be conveyed formally in employee handbooks, codes of conduct, memos, and ceremonies, but it is also expressed informally through dress codes, extracurricular activities, and anecdotes. A firm's culture gives its members meaning and offers direction as to how to behave and deal with problems within the organization. The corporate culture at American Express, for example, includes numerous anecdotes about employees who have gone beyond the call of duty to help customers out of difficult situations. This strong tradition of customer service might encourage an American Express employee to take extra steps to help a customer who encounters a problem while traveling overseas.

Organizational culture depends on company strategy because it prioritizes stakeholders. For example, Marriott prioritizes employees to provide exceptional service for customers. Therefore, its strategic priority is keeping Marriott as one of the best companies to work for. Walmart, on the other hand, values customers and therefore places a priority on a low cost, efficient operating environment. Amazon has developed a culture that focuses on competitors and is making extreme inroads into traditional markets for durable goods sold in stores. Therefore, the company strategy will help shape stakeholder relationships and the ethical culture.

On the other hand, an organization's culture can also encourage employees to make decisions that others may judge as unethical, or it can encourage actions that may be viewed as socially irresponsible. Some misconduct comes from employees trying to attain the performance objectives of the firm. ethicaWhile high performance objectives are not a bad thing, it is important for managers to ensure these objectives can be reached without cutting corners or engaging in questionable conduct. Derivatives used in financial markets to transfer risk are so complex, difficult to value, poorly regulated, and have been so widely used that they can bring down a company. They also contributed a great deal to the severity of the most recent recession, challenging our financial systems. To make ethical decisions when using derivatives, one requires a great deal of transparency, financial expertise and competence, and responsibility.[43] Because of their complexity, derivatives provide openings for manipulation and misconduct. When a corporation uses certain compensation systems, employees striving for financial success could be inadvertently rewarded for their sales of dangerous derivatives. The corporate culture may drive decisions on developing and selling derivatives because of the difficulty in applying moral reasoning.

Earth in the Balance

Unilever Opens Opportunity in Sustainability Initiatives

Unilever is working toward full sustainability when it comes to palm oil production. The process of extracting palm oil has gained global attention because of unsustainable practices such as deforestation, which has led to the destruction of native animal habitats. Because Unilever is a large company that works with an extensive supply chain, maintaining ethical sourcing practices can be a bit of a burden and are hard to track. Yet as the buyer, Unilever is responsible for any unethical sourcing practices in its supply chain.

Unilever is attempting to monitor its supply chain in two ways. First, it has invested $100 million to build a palm oil processing plant in Indonesia, the source of much of its palm oil, to ensure responsible practices. This plant represents a $130 million investment on Unilever's part. Second, Unilever is purchasing GreenPalm certificates from the Roundtable on Sustainable Palm Oil (RSPO) when it purchases palm oil from other processing companies. Unilever helped to found the RSPO, which monitors the practices of palm oil processing companies and issues them certificates when they meet sustainable, environmentally-responsible standards. Belonging to the RSPO is a signal to consumers that Unilever is adhering to a set of strict environmental standards. These certificates can then be purchased by companies like Unilever in an attempt to ensure ethically sourced supply chains. This alleviates some of the skepticism about the origins of the palm oil.

Unilever announced that it had reached its target of purchasing all palm oil from credible sustainable sources by the end of 2012. Unilever was three years ahead of schedule on this projection. The certification was issued through GreenPalm Certificates. However, this method is not entirely dependable because the processing of all palm oil is not completely traceable. Additionally, some have criticized GreenPalm certificates for their confusing language, calling them a type of greenwashing.

However, Unilever is still determined to improve its palm oil sourcing practices. It has developed a Sustainable Palm Oil Sourcing Policy based on three principles: (1) halt deforestation, (2) protect peat land, and (3) drive economic and social impact. It also announced a few sustainability goals it aims to attain in the near future. By 2019 Unilever plans to have all its palm oil and derivatives physically certified. The company has announced that by 2020 all Unilever palm oil will come from sustainable, traceable, and certified sources.

To continue achieving the company's sustainability goals, Unilever is working directly with producers to purchase segregated supplies of sustainable palm oil to ensure customers they are delivering a sustainable product. The company also wants to ensure that its suppliers are being ethical in other ways. For instance, the company has partnered with leading Asian agribusiness group Wilmar International in an agreement to ensure that the company's farming efforts are free from deforestation and human rights abuses. With such a large global supply chain, it is important for Unilever to make certain that their suppliers are following other ethical practices as well, such as treating farmers fairly. Despite the difficulty in tracking the sustainability of its palm oil, Unilever's initiative demonstrates a commitment toward reducing its environmental impact.

Sources: Paul Sonne, "Unilever Takes Palm Oil in Hand," *The Wall Street Journal*, April 24, 2012, http://online.wsj.com/article/SB100014240 52702303978104577362160223536388.html (accessed August 4, 2016); "How It Works," *Green Palm Sustainability*, http://www.greenpalm. org/en/what-is-greenpalm/how-it-works (accessed July 1, 2014); "Unilever's Europe-wide Palm Oil Covered Sustainably," *Unilever*, July 4, 2010, http://www.unilever.com/mediacentre/pressreleases/2010/UnileversEuropewidepalmoilcoveredsustainably.aspx (accessed July 1, 2014); Samantha Neary from Triple Pundit, "Unilever Reaches Sustainable Palm Oil Goal Three Years Early," *TodayEco*, August 2, 2012, http:// www.triplepundit.com/2012/08/unilever-reaches-sustainable-palm-oil-goal-three-years-early/ (accessed August 4, 2016); Unilever, "Working with Suppliers," http://www.unilever.com/sustainable-living-2014/reducing-environmental-impact/sustainable-sourcing/sustainable-palm-oil/ working-with-suppliers/index.aspx (accessed July 1, 2014); Voices for Biodiversity, "Consumer Group Slams Greenwashing in Sustainable Palm Oil Marketing," *National Geographic*, August 8, 2013, http://newswatch.nationalgeographic.com/2013/08/08/consumer-groups-slamgreenwashing-in-sustainable-palm-oil-marketing/ (accessed August 4, 2016); Unilever, "Roundtable on Sustainable Palm Oil," http://www.unilever.com/sustainable-living-2014/reducing-environmental-impact/ sustainable-sourcing/sustainable-palm-oil/roundtable-on-sustainable-palm-oil/index.aspx (accessed July 1, 2014); Unilever, "Sustainable Palm Oil," http://www.unilever.com/sustainable-living-2014/reducing-envi-ronmental-impact/sustainable-sourcing/sustainable-palm-oil/ (accessed July 1, 2014); Unilever, "Unilever Sustainable Palm Oil Sourcing Policy -- 2016," https://www.unilever.com/Images/unilever-palm-oil-poli-cy-2016_tcm244-479933_en.pdf (accessed August 4, 2016).

ethical climate
That part of the firm's culture that focuses specifically on issues of right and wrong.

Whereas a firm's overall culture establishes ideals that guide a wide range of behaviors for members of the organization, its **ethical climate** focuses specifically on issues of right and wrong. We think of ethical climate as the part of a corporate culture that relates to an organization's expectations about appropriate conduct. To some extent, ethical climate is the character component of an organization. Corporate policies and codes, the conduct of top managers, the values and moral philosophies of coworkers, and opportunity for misconduct all contribute to a firm's ethical climate. When top managers strive to establish an ethical climate based on responsibility and citizenship, they set the tone for ethical decisions.

New Belgium Brewing (NBB) is an example of a company in which the top leaders set the tone for the rest of the organization. Former CEO and current Executive Chair Kim Jordan helped co-found the company with her former husband Jeff Lebesch. Before starting the company, the two carefully considered the values they wanted to use as the foundation for the company. These values included sustainability and employee empowerment. Under Jordan's leadership, New Belgium's ethical climate placed a great deal of emphasis on these two values. Among a number of sustainability initiatives, New Belgium became the first brewery to use 100 percent wind power. Over the years, NBB has become a 100 percent employee-owned company, giving employees the ability to make crucial decisions regarding company operations. Ethical climate also determines whether an individual perceives an issue as having an ethical component. Recognizing ethical issues and generating alternatives to address them are manifestations of ethical climate.

significant others
Include superiors, peers, and subordinates in the organization who influence the ethical decision-making process.

Significant Others **Significant others** include superiors, peers, and subordinates in the organization who influence the ethical decision-making process. Although people outside the firm, such as family members and friends, also influence decision-makers, organizational structure and culture operate through significant others to influence ethical decisions. Ethics and Compliance Initiative, 2016 Global Business Ethics SurveyTM: Measuring Risk and Promoting Workplace Integrity (Arlington, VA: Ethics and Compliance Initiative, 2016), p. 43.[44] Reporting misconduct is most likely to come from upper levels of management compared to lower level supervisors and non-management employees. Employees in lower level positions have a greater tendency to not understand misconduct or to be complacent about the misconduct they observe. While other options like ethics officers

FIGURE 5.3 Employees Most Likely to Engage in Bribery Globally

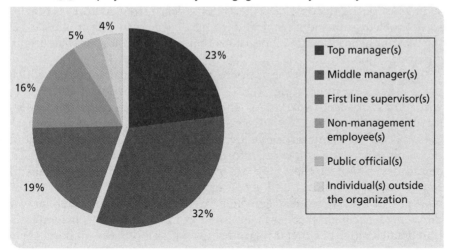

SOURCE: Ethics and Compliance Initiative, 2016 *Global Business Ethics Survey™: Measuring Risk and Promoting Workplace Integrity* (Arlington, VA: Ethics and Compliance Initiative, 2016), p. 17.

and ethics hotlines exist, the vast majority of employees surveyed prefer to report to supervisors and other higher management.

Most experts agree that the CEO establishes the ethical tone for the entire firm. This can be problematic when managers are more likely to engage in certain forms of misconduct. For instance, Figure 5.3 shows that managers are more likely to engage in bribery globally than lower-level employees. Lower level managers obtain their cues from top managers, and they in turn impose some of their personal values on the company. This interaction between corporate culture and executive leadership helps determine the ethical value system of the firm. However, obedience to authority can also explain why many people resolve workplace issues by following the directives of a superior. An employee may feel obligated to carry out the orders of a superior even if those orders conflict with the employee's values of right and wrong. If that decision is later judged to have been wrong, the employee may justify it by saying, "I was only carrying out orders" or "My boss told me to do it this way."

Coworkers' influence on ethical decision-making depends on the person's exposure to unethical behavior in making ethical decisions. The more a person is exposed to unethical activity by others in the organization, the more likely it is that he or she will behave unethically, especially in (ethically) "gray" areas. Thus, a decision maker who associates with others who act unethically is more likely to behave unethically as well. Within work groups, employees may be subject to the phenomenon of "groupthink," going along with group decisions even when those decisions run counter to their own values. They may rationalize the decision with "safety in numbers" when everyone else appears to back a particular decision. Most businesspeople take their cues or learn from coworkers how to solve problems—including ethical dilemmas.[45] Close friends at work exert the most influence on ethical decisions that relate to roles associated with a particular job.

Superiors and coworkers can create organizational pressure, which plays a key role in creating ethical issues. Although power differences will exist between supervisors and their employees, ethical leaders attempt to reduce these differences when communicating with employees. It is not uncommon for leaders within the organization to adopt the habit of viewing employee information as unimportant.[46] However, employees who feel that they are not being heard are less likely to report concerns and more likely to ignore questionable conduct in the workplace. Ethical leaders can help to reduce these perceived power differences through frequent employee communication. This interaction creates more beneficial relationships with employees, making them more comfortable in bringing up issues of concern to their supervisors. Leader–follower congruence occurs when leaders and followers share the same organizational vision, ethical expectations, and objectives. A crucial way to communicate ethical values to employees is through codes of ethics and training to familiarize employees with the ethical decision-making process.

Nearly all businesspeople face difficult issues where solutions are not obvious or where organizational objectives and personal ethical values may conflict. For example, a salesperson for a Web-based retailer may be asked by a superior to lie to a customer over the telephone about a late product shipment. A study by the Ethics Resource Center found that 22 percent of U.S. employees said they felt pressure from other employees or managers to compromise standards. In addition, 76 percent of employees reported misconduct after they observed it and 53 percent of these were met with some type of retailiation.[47]

Opportunity

opportunity
A set of conditions that limits barriers or provides rewards.

Together, organizational culture and the influence of coworkers may foster conditions that either hinder or permit misconduct. **Opportunity** is a set of conditions that limits barriers or provides rewards. When these conditions provide rewards—be it financial gain, recognition, promotion, or simply the good feeling from a job well done—the opportunity for unethical conduct may be encouraged or discouraged. For example, a company policy that fails to specify the punishment for employees who violate the rules provides an opportunity for unethical behavior because it allows individuals to engage in such behavior without fear of consequences. Thus, company policies, processes, and other factors may create opportunities to act unethically. Advancing technology associated with the internet is challenging companies working to limit opportunities to engage in unethical and illegal behavior. Individual factors as well as organizational relationships may influence whether an individual becomes opportunistic and takes advantage of situations in an unethical or even illegal manner.

Opportunity usually relates to employees' immediate job context—where they work, with whom they work, and the nature of the work. This context includes the motivational "carrots and sticks," or rewards and punishments, that superiors can use to influence employee behavior. Rewards, or positive reinforcers, include pay raises, bonuses, and public recognition, whereas reprimands, pay penalties, demotions, and even firings act as negative reinforcers. For example, a manager who decides to sell customers' personal data may be confident that such behavior is an easy way to boost revenue because other companies sell customer account information. Even if this activity violates the employee's personal value system, it may be viewed as acceptable within the organization's culture. This manager may also be motivated by opportunities to thereby improve his or her performance standing within the organization. A survey by Kessler International indicates that 52 percent of employees take office supplies for personal use. As Table 5.3 shows, many employees pilfer office supply rooms for matters unrelated to the job. It is possible that the opportunity is provided for small-scale theft in the company; in some cases, there are no concerns if employees take pens, Post-its, envelopes, notepads, and paper. Printing large documents at work for their own or spouse's use, or even for their children's school assignments, is a common form of misconduct. Additionally, some indicated that they take more expensive items such as USB drives, blank disks, and computer accessories.[48] If there is no policy against this practice, employees will not learn where to draw the line and will get into the habit of taking even more expensive items for personal use.

Often, opportunity can arise from someone whose job is to create opportunities for others. Barbara Toffler, an ethics consultant and professor, learned firsthand how difficult it can be to follow one's own moral compass when she worked as a consultant at Arthur Andersen creating ethics programs for Andersen clients (the firm itself had no internal ethics program). After charging a client $1 million for developing an ethics program that should have cost $500,000, the praise Toffler earned from Andersen "was the only day in four years that I felt truly valued by Arthur Andersen." Despite her expertise, she learned that "unethical or illegal behavior happens when decent people are put under the unbearable pressure to do their jobs and meet ambitious goals without the resources to get the job done right."[49]

General Electric has taken steps to place itself at the head of the ethical pack. Its "ecomagination" campaign is designed to "build innovative solutions for today's environmental challenges while driving economic growth." It also has an initiative called "healthymagination," which aims to improve the quality of healthcare. As part of its

TABLE 5.3 Most Common Office Supplies Stolen by Employees

1	Post-It notes
2	Paper clips
3	Toilet paper
4	Copier paper
5	Scissors
6	Tape
7	Notepads
8	Staplers
9	Highlighters
10	Pens and pencils

Source: Bryan Johnston, "Top 10 Most Stolen Office Supplies," *CareerAddict*, October 10, 2015, http://www.careeraddict.com/top-10-most-stolen-office-supplies (accessed June 17, 2016).

investment, GE focuses on investigating clean-tech research, releasing products that are more eco-friendly, partnering with community health organizations, and continuing employee healthcare efforts.[50]

If an employee takes advantage of an opportunity to act unethically and is rewarded or suffers no penalty, he or she may repeat such acts as other opportunities arise. Dov Charney, founder and former CEO of American Apparel, was pushed out of his position by the board after allegations concerning sexual misconduct and sexual harassment. These allegations had persisted for more than a decade before he was eventually terminated.[51] His removal as CEO demonstrates the effectiveness of good corporate governance and the duty of the board of directors to maintain an ethical organizational culture. When company managers get away with unethical conduct, their behavior is reinforced and a culture of manipulation and misconduct can develop. Indeed, the opportunity to engage in unethical conduct is often a better predictor of unethical activities than personal values.[52]

In addition to rewards and the absence of punishment, other elements in the business environment tend to create opportunities. Professional codes of conduct and ethics-related corporate policies also influence opportunity by prescribing what behaviors are acceptable. Compliance programs are necessary to provide internal controls to prevent situations just discussed. The larger the rewards and the milder the punishment for unethical behavior, the greater is the probability that unethical behavior will be practiced.

DEVELOPING AN ETHICAL CULTURE

ethical culture
Refers to the character of the decision-making process employees use to determine if their responses to ethical issues are right or wrong.

Organizational ethics and compliance initiatives are developed to establish appropriate conduct and core values. The term **ethical culture** refers to the character of the decision-making process employees use to determine if their responses to ethical issues are right or wrong. Ethical culture is that part of corporate culture that encompasses the values and norms an organization defines as appropriate conduct. The goal of an ethical culture is to curtail the need for enforced compliance of rules and amplify the use of principles that contribute to ethical reasoning in complex or new situations. Ethical culture is positively related to organizations with hotlines and with employees who confront ethics issues in the workplace and/or report observed misconduct to management.[53] Developing an ethical culture involves communicating organizational values and norms to employees throughout the organization, developing effective ethics programs, and appointing ethics officers to run them. An ethical culture creates shared values and managerial commitment for ethical decisions.

Organizational Values

Organizational values are abstract ideals distinct from individual values. Values can evolve over time. They are more subjective and are viewed by societal members as ethical or unethical. Values-based practices become the end results and are separate from organizational practices based on technical or efficiency considerations.[54]

Both stakeholders and the organizational culture impact the development of organizational values. As mentioned earlier, New Belgium Brewing has adopted sustainability as an organizational value. The organizational culture strongly supports this value through initiatives aimed at reducing energy, recycling, and providing employees with mountain bikes after one year of employment. Because values are more subjective, they are influenced by firm, industry, country, and global specific factors.[55] For instance, firms from countries that stress individualism might encourage the ability to work independently, whereas firms from more collectivist nations might place more value on teamwork. Additionally, core values might differ depending upon the industry. Although safety is a core value of many firms, it is more likely to be emphasized in a factory environment than in an office environment. For instance, organizations from countries that value risk may value innovative risk taking, while organizations from countries more averse to risk may have a different opinion. Table 5.4 provides an example of the organizational values of Marriot. From its organizational values one can determine that Marriot tries to deliver exceptional customer service and operate with high ethical standards. Marriott's values reinforce its vision "to be the #1 hospitality company in the world."[56] These types of organizational values are critical to organizational ethical decision-making. Organizations that have ethics programs based upon values tend to make a greater contribution than those based simply on compliance, or obeying rules.[57]

TABLE 5.4 Organizational Values of Marriott

| 1. Put people first |
| 2. Pursue excellence |
| 3. Embrace change |
| 4. Act with integrity |
| 5. Serve our world |

Source: Marriott, "Core Values & Heritage," http://www.marriott.com/culture-and-values/core-values.mi (accessed June 17, 2016).

Normative Considerations of Ethical Decision-Making

Earlier in the chapter, we described how ethical decision-making occurs in an organization. Understanding what impacts the ethical decision-making process is necessary for developing and managing an ethical culture within an organization. However, understanding how ethical decisions are made is different from determining what ought to guide ethical decisions. **Normative approaches** are concerned with how organizational decision-makers *should* approach an ethical issue. It is concerned with providing a vision and recommendations for improving ethical decision-making. Concepts like fairness, justice, and moral philosophies such as deontology and utilitarianism are important to a normative approach. Strong normative approaches in organizations have a positive relationship to ethical decision-making. Besides values, norms provide more specific beliefs about expected behaviors in a specific context. Norms may exist about expected behavior in work groups and teams throughout the organization. Examples of norms could relate to expected professionalism and how to resolve a reoccurring ethical issue.

normative approaches Provide a vision and recommendations for improving ethical decision-making; they are concerned with how organizational decision-makers *should* approach an ethical issue.

Managing the Ethical Culture: Variations of Employee Conduct

Despite the creation and implementation of shared organizational values, organizations must recognize that employee behavior will still vary. Overall, it is up to the organization to take responsibility for an ethical culture and implementation. However, research indicates that there are major differences in the values and philosophies influencing how individuals that comprise organizations make ethical decisions.[58] Due to ethical diversity, employees will often interpret situations differently and will vary in their responses to an ethical issue.

Table 5.5 reflects a study that measures variation in employee conduct. It demonstrates that approximately 10 percent of employees will take advantage of situations to further their own personal interests. These employees are often referred to as "bad apples" and are more likely to manipulate, cheat, or be self-serving when the benefits gained from misconduct are greater than the penalties. These employees are more likely to steal office supplies or engage in other forms of misconduct. The lower the risk of penalties, the higher the likelihood that these 10 percent of employees will commit unethical activities.

Approximately 40 percent of workers go along with the work group on most decisions. These employees are most concerned about the social implications of their actions and desire to be accepted in the organization. They have their own personal opinions but are easily impacted by other employees around them. For instance, they might be well aware that using office supplies for personal use is improper. However, if it is common for other employees to take office supplies for personal use, than these employees are likely to do the same just to fit in. These employees tend to rationalize, claiming that the use of office supplies is one of the benefits and that because there is no company policy prohibiting it, then it must be acceptable. Coupled with this is the belief of safety in numbers. These employees feel that they will not get into trouble since everybody is doing it.

On the other hand, approximately 40 percent of a company's employees always try to follow company policies and rules. These workers have

TABLE 5.5 Variation in Employee Conduct

10 Percent	40 Percent	40 Percent	10 Percent
Follow their own values and beliefs; believe that their values are superior to those of others in the company	Always try to follow company policies	Go along with the work group	Take advantage of situations if the penalty is less than the benefit—the risk of being caught is low

Source: These percentages are based on a number of studies in the popular press and data gathered by the authors. The percentages are not exact and represent a general typology that may vary by organization. The 10 percent that will take advantage is adapted from John Fraedrich and O. C. Ferrell, "Cognitive Consistency of Marketing Managers in Ethical Situations," *Journal of the Academy of Marketing Science* 20 (Summer 1992): 243–252.

a strong understanding of how their corporate culture defines acceptable behavior and try to comply with organizational codes of ethics, ethics training, and other communications about ethical conduct. In the office supply example, if the company has a policy that prohibits taking office supplies from work for personal use, these employees would most likely obey the policy. However, they probably would not tell anyone about the 40 percent who go along with the work group, for these employees prefer to focus on their jobs and avoid any conflicts or organizational misconduct. These employees rely heavily on organizational communication and expectations. If the organization fails to communicate standards for ethical conduct, then members of this group will devise their own.

The final 10 percent of employees attempt to uphold formal ethical standards focusing on rights, duties, and rules. They adopt values that support certain inalienable rights and actions. From their perspective, these actions are always ethically correct if they protect inalienable rights. Overall, these employees believe that their values are correct and superior to the values of other employees in the organization, or even to the organization's own value system, when an ethical issue arises. These employees tend to report observed misconduct or report when they view activities within the organization that they believe are unethical. As a result, these employees would most likely report coworkers who steal office supplies.

It should be clear by now that employees use different approaches when making ethical decisions. Because of the probability that a large percentage of employees will take advantage of a situation or go along with the rest of employees, it is important that companies provide communication and internal controls to support an ethical culture. Organizations that do not monitor activities and enforce ethical policies provide a low-risk environment for employees inclined to take advantage of situations to accomplish their own personal objectives.

Although the percentages in Table 5.5 are only estimates, the specific percentages are not as important as the fact that research has identified these employee variations as existing within most organizations. Organizations should pay particular attention to managers who monitor the daily operations of employees. They should also provide ethics training and communication to make certain that the business operates in an ethical manner, misconduct is caught before it becomes a major issue, and risk to stakeholders is eliminated or minimized.

Maintaining ethical conduct is a business goal that should be no different from increasing profits. If progress in maintaining an ethical culture stalls, then the organization must determine the reason and take corrective action through the enforcement of existing standards or setting higher standards. If the code of ethics is strongly enforced and becomes part of the corporate culture, it can lead to strong improvements in the ethical conduct within the organization. On the other hand, if the code of ethics and managerial commitment are merely window-dressing and not truly a part of the corporate culture, it will not be effective.

SUMMARY

Business ethics comprises principles and standards that guide individual and work group behavior in the world of business. Principles are specific and pervasive boundaries that are absolute, while values are used to develop norms that are socially enforced. Stakeholders determine these conventions, and they may change over time. The most basic of these standards have been codified as laws and regulations. Business ethics goes beyond legal issues.

Because individuals and groups within a company may not have embraced the same set of values, ethical conflict may occur. An ethical issue is a problem, situation, or opportunity requiring an individual, group, or organization to choose among several actions that must be evaluated as right or wrong, ethical or unethical. Questionable decisions and actions may result in disputes that must be resolved through some type of negotiation or even litigation. Codifying ethical standards into meaningful policies that spell out what is and is not acceptable gives businesspeople an opportunity to reduce the possibility of behavior that could create legal problems. Business decisions involve complex and detailed discussions in which correctness may not be clear-cut. It is important that a shared vision of acceptable behavior develops from an organizational perspective to create consistent and reliable relationships with all concerned stakeholders. Common ethical issues faced by businesses include abusive or intimidating behavior, misuse of company time and resources, conflicts of interest, bribery, discrimination and sexual harassment, fraud, and privacy issues.

Understanding the ethical decision-making process can help individuals and businesses design strategies to prevent misconduct. Three of the important components of ethical decision-making are individual factors, organizational relationships, and opportunity.

Significant individual factors that affect the ethical decision-making process include personal moral philosophy, stage of moral development, motivation, and other personal factors such as gender, age, and experience. Moral philosophies are the principles or rules that individuals apply in deciding what is right or wrong. Most moral philosophies can be classified as consequentialism, ethical formalism, or justice. Consequentialist philosophies consider a decision to be right or acceptable if it accomplishes a desired result such as pleasure, knowledge, career growth, the realization of self-interest, or utility. Consequentialism may be further classified as egoism and utilitarianism. Ethical formalism focuses on the rights of individuals and on the intentions associated with a particular behavior rather than on its consequences. Justice theory relates to evaluations of fairness or the disposition to deal with perceived injustices of others.

The culture of the organization, as well as superiors, peers, and subordinates, can have a significant impact on the ethical decision-making process. Organizational, or corporate, culture can be defined as a set of values, beliefs, goals, norms, and rituals shared by members or employees of an organization. Whereas a firm's overall culture establishes ideals that guide a wide range of behaviors for members of the organization, its ethical climate focuses specifically on issues of right and wrong. Significant others include superiors, peers, and subordinates in the organization who influence the ethical decision-making process. Interaction between corporate culture and executive leadership helps determine the ethical value system of the firm, but obedience to authority can also explain why many people resolve workplace issues by following the directives of a superior. The more exposed a person is to unethical activity in the organization, the more likely it is that he or she will behave unethically. Superiors and coworkers can create organizational pressure, which plays a key role in creating ethical issues.

Opportunity is a set of conditions that limit barriers or provide rewards. If an individual takes advantage of an opportunity to act unethically and escapes punishment or gains a reward, that person may repeat such acts when circumstances favor them.

To develop an ethical culture, it is crucial for the organization to develop strong organizational values to guide the organization. The values often form the basis of a normative structure. A normative approach is concerned with how organizational decision makers *should* approach an ethical issue.

Finally, studies have shown that employee ethical behavior in the workplace tends to vary. While 10 percent are bad apples who will take advantage of the organization, 40 percent of employees are estimated to go along with the majority in ethical decision-making. Another 40 percent are likely to obey policies and procedures themselves but will not often report the misconduct of others. The final 10 percent view their values as superior to others. They adhere to their high ethical values and will report those employees that they consider to be unethical. Organizations should pay particular attention to managers who monitor the daily operations of employees.

Responsible Business Debate

Should the FDA Protect Consumers from the Potential Harm Caused by Antibacterial Soap?

Issue: *Are Consumers Being Harmed by Antibacterial Soap?*

The Food and Drug Administration (FDA) has proposed that antibacterial soap and body wash manufacturers provide additional evidence that their products are more effective than other soap products and safe for long-term use. A chemical commonly found in antibacterial products has raised concerns. It is estimated that approximately 75 percent of liquid antibacterial soaps contain triclosan. Studies have revealed the presence of triclosan in urine samples of a shocking 75 percent of respondents.

If the proposal of the FDA passes, it will have significant implications for soap manufacturers. Antibacterial soap is a strong business within the United States. If antibacterial soap manufacturers cannot prove their claims of effectiveness, they might have to relabel their products, reformulate them, or even remove them completely once they are deemed unsafe.

There are three major concerns over triclosan. First, there is the question of whether triclosan is actually effective in killing more bacteria than other soap products. If it is not more effective, then the benefits of antibacterial soap are untrue. Secondly, consumer advocates are concerned that triclosan might interfere with hormones, making long-term use harmful. Finally, there is the possibility that too much use of triclosan could lead to bacteria that are not only resistant to triclosan but to other antibiotics as well.

Since 2005, some scientists have been calling for the FDA to get involved. Tests on animals have suggested that prolonged triclosan use could act as endocrine disrupters, negatively impacting a person's hormone system. So far these tests have been performed largely on animals, so there is still the question of how this would affect humans. Research has also revealed the presence of triclosan in breast milk and umbilical cord blood. Canada has requested that companies within the country voluntarily phase out triclosan from products.

The American Cleaning Institute counteracts these claims, stating that triclosan has helped fight against bacteria for decades. More than 600 firms support this claim, citing studies that have revealed there are fewer microbes on the hands of those who use antibacterial soap than on those who do not. There is not much evidence suggesting that triclosan-resistant bacteria exist outside of labs. Many studies have found that relationships between antibiotic-resistant bacteria and triclosan are not statistically significant. Even the FDA admits there is no evidence suggesting that triclosan is harmful to humans.

The soap industry amounts to about $5.5 billion in sales of soaps, shower products, and body washes. Forcing the industry to reformulate or relabel their products would be highly costly. Additionally, many other industries, including cosmetics, use triclosan in products as well. Growing concern is causing some firms to voluntarily remove triclosan. Johnson and Johnson and Reckitt Benckiser have already begun phasing out triclosan from their products.

There Are Two Sides To Every Issue:

1. There is enough evidence to support the FDA's concerns about the negative impacts of antibacterial soap.
2. There is not enough evidence to support the FDA's concerns about the effects of antibacterial soap.

Source: Thomas M. Burton and Serena Ng, "FDA Seeks Stricter Rules on Antibacterial Soaps," *The Wall Street Journal*, December 16, 2013, http://www.nytimes.com/2011/08/20/business/triclosan-an-antibacterial-chemical-in-consumer-products-raises-safety-issues.html?pagewanted=all&_r=0 (accessed August 4, 2016); Brian Clark Howard, "Avoid Antibacterial Soaps, Say Consumer Advocates," *National Geographic,* http://news.nationalgeographic.com/news/2013/12/131217-antibacterial-soaps-triclosan-fda-hygiene-safety-health/?rptregcta=reg_free_np&rptregcampaign=20131016_rw_membership_r1p_us_se_w# (accessed December 18, 2013); Allison E. Aiello, Bonnie Marshall, Stuart B. Levy, Phyllis Della-Latta, and Elaine Larson, "Relationship between Triclosan and Susceptibilities of Bacteria Isolated from Hands in Community," *Antimicrob Agents Chemother* 48 (8), American Society for Microbiology, 2004, pp. 2973–2979; Elizabeth Weise, "FDA: Antibacterial Soaps Could Pose Health Risks," *USA Today*, December 16, 2013, http://www.usatoday.com/story/news/nation/2013/12/16/fda-antibacterial-soap/4038907/ (accessed August 4, 2016); Andrew Martin, "Antibacterial Chemical Raises Safety Issues," *The New York Times,* August 19, 2011, http://www.nytimes.com/2011/08/20/business/triclosan-an-antibacterial-chemical-in-consumer-products-raises-safety-issues.html?pagewanted=all&_r=0 (accessed August 4, 2016). Laura Landro, "Are Antibacterial Soaps Safe?" *The Wall Street Journal*, February 15, 2016, http://www.wsj.com/articles/are-antibacterial-soaps-safe-1455592023 (accessed August 4, 2016); Alexandra Sifferlin, "The Case Against Antibacterial Soap Is Getting Stronger," *Time*, May 18, 2016, http://time.com/4339866/triclosan-antibacterial-soap-safety/ (accessed August 4, 2016).

KEY TERMS

business ethics (p. 155)
principles (p. 155)
values (p. 155)
ethical issue (p. 159)
conflict of interest (p. 161)
bribery (p. 162)
sexual harassment (p. 163)
hostile work environment (p. 164)
fraud (p. 164)

privacy issues (p. 164)
moral philosophies (p. 167)
social exchange theory (p. 167)
consequentialism (p. 167)
egoism (p. 167)
utilitarianism (p. 167)
ethical formalism (p. 167)
justice theory (p. 168)
Principle of Equal Freedom (p. 168)

machiavellianism (p. 169)
ethical diversity (p. 169)
organizational, or corporate, culture (p. 170)
ethical climate (p. 172)
significant others (p. 172)
opportunity (p. 174)
ethical culture (p. 176)
normative approaches (p. 177)

DISCUSSION QUESTIONS

1. Why is business ethics a strategic consideration in organizational decisions?
2. How do individual, organizational, and opportunity factors interact to influence ethical or unethical decisions?
3. How do moral philosophies influence the individual factor in organizational ethical decision-making?
4. How can ethical formalism be used in organizational ethics programs and still respect diversity and the right for individual values?
5. What are the potential benefits of an emphasis on procedural justice?
6. Describe the importance of normative approaches to ethical decision making.
7. How do organizations create an ethical climate?
8. Why are we seeing more evidence of widespread ethical dilemmas within organizations?
9. Describe the importance of organizational values to the development of an ethical culture.
10. Why is it important for managers to take ethical diversity into account?

EXPERIENTIAL EXERCISE

Visit www.bbb.org, the home page for the Better Business Bureau. Locate the International Marketplace Ethics award criteria. Find recent winners of the award and summarize what they did to achieve this recognition. Describe the role of the BBB in supporting self-regulatory activities and business ethics.

MOONLIGHTING MONICA: WHAT WOULD YOU DO?

On Sunday, Armando went to work to pick up a report he needed to review before an early Monday meeting. While at work, he noticed a colleague's light on and went over to her cubicle for a short visit. Monica was one of the newest systems designers on the department's staff. She was hired six weeks ago to assist with a series of human resources (HR) projects for the company. Before joining the firm, she had worked as an independent consultant to organizations trying to upgrade their HR systems that track payroll, benefits, compliance, and other issues. Monica was very well qualified, detail oriented, and hard working. She was the only female on the systems staff.

In his brief conversation with Monica, Armando felt that he was not getting the full story of her reason for being at work on a Sunday. After all, the systems team completed the first HR systems proposal on Thursday and was prepared to present its report and recommendations on Monday. Monica said she was "working on a few parts" of the project but did not get more specific. Her face turned red when Armando joked, "With the beautiful sunshine outside, only someone hoping to earn a little extra money would be at work today."

Armando and another coworker, David, presented the systems team's report to the HR staff on Monday. The HR team was generally pleased with the recommendations but wanted a number of changes in specifications. This was normal and the systems designers were prepared for the changes. Everyone on the team met that afternoon and Tuesday morning to develop a plan for revamping the HR system. By Tuesday afternoon, each member was working on his or her part of the project again.

On Friday afternoon, David went up and down the hall, encouraging everyone to go to happy hour at the pub down the street. About ten people, including Monica and Armando, went to the pub. The conversation was mainly about work and the new HR project. On several occasions, Monica offered ideas about other systems and companies with which she was familiar. Most of the systems designers listened, but a few were quick to question her suggestions. Armando assumed her suggestions were the result of work with previous clients. Over the weekend, however, Armando began to wonder whether Monica was talking about current clients. He remembered their conversation on Sunday and decided to look into the matter.

On Monday, Armando asked Monica directly whether she still had clients. Monica said yes and that she was finishing up on projects with two of them. She went on to say that she worked late hours and on the weekends and was not skimping on her company responsibilities. Armando agreed that she was a good colleague but was not comfortable with her use of company resources on personal, moneymaking projects. He was also concerned that the team's intellectual capital was being used. What would you do?

CHAPTER SIX

Strategic Approaches to Improving Ethical Behavior

Chapter Objectives

- To provide an overview of the need for an organizational ethics program

- To consider crucial keys to development of an effective ethics program

- To demonstrate the elements of a corporate culture.

- To examine leadership and its importance to an ethical corporate culture.

- To discuss the requirements for ethical leadership.

Chapter Outline

Scope and Purpose of Organizational Ethics Programs

Codes of Conduct

Ethics Officers

Ethics Training and Communication

Establishing Systems to Monitor and Enforce Ethical Standards

Continuous Improvement of the Ethics Program

Institutionalization of Business Ethics

Ethical Leadership

Requirements for Ethical Leadership

NiSource—A Top Firm in Social Responsibility

For NiSource, social responsibility involves actively living its four core values: fairness, honesty, integrity, and trust. NiSource is a Fortune 500 company that owns a portfolio of energy businesses. Headquartered in Merrillville, Indiana, NiSource is involved in natural gas and electric transmission, storage, generation, and distribution in seven states.

The company's mission reflects its emphasis on social responsibility. It seeks to deliver "safe, reliable, clean and affordable energy" that benefits all stakeholders. As a profitable company complying with all applicable laws, NiSource achieves the economic and legal levels of social responsibility. It also exhibits strong ethical and philanthropic initiatives, leading it to be named one of the "World's Most Ethical Companies". Its code of ethics encourages employees to take responsibility for the company's success and ethical conduct.

NiSource demonstrates a strong commitment to employees, customers, the environment, and communities. For instance, NiSource has taken a strong stance on improving employee safety and has become an industry leader in this area. NiSource incentivizes employees by offering them rewards for safe behavior. As a result, vehicle and safety-related accidents have decreased.

NiSource also recognizes the dangers that consumers might face, especially in situations such as potentially hitting an underground utility line when digging in their yards. NiSource invests $3.2 million on public and safety awareness programs for consumers. As part of its awareness campaign, it created the mascot Digger Dog to appeal to children and educate them about calling the number 811 to receive information about the location of utility lines before digging.

Environmental sustainability is a strong component of NiSource's corporate culture. In 2014 the company completed a project estimated to reduce harmful sulfur dioxide emissions significantly. The company maintains a Board of Directors' Environmental Health and Safety Committee that evaluates and approves NiSource's environmental policy, including policies concerning climate change. NiSource also helps its customers save energy by developing energy efficiency programs such as its Customer CHOICE® program. This program allows customers to reduce energy costs by purchasing natural gas from non-utilities suppliers.

Finally, NiSource recognizes its responsibilities toward communities. It has established the NiSource Charitable Foundation to provide funds to nonprofits who it believes contribute toward its mission to help create "strong and sustainable communities." NiSource has contributed more than $5 million toward nonprofit organizations.

NiSource invests resources in social responsibility and has been recognized for its many benefits. Because of its sustainability initiatives, NiSource was named to the Dow Jones Sustainability Index in 2012. It was also named among the top 25 Socially Responsible Dividend Stocks by the Dividend Channel. These awards are beneficial in attracting investors interested in investing in socially responsible companies. This has significantly impacted NiSource's bottom line—its stock experienced a 19 percent annual return at a time when the average return in the utilities sector of the Standard and Poor's index was -8. NiSource clearly proves that social responsibility helps stakeholders and the bottom line.[1]

A strategic approach to ethical decisions will contribute to both business and society. This chapter provides a framework that is consistent with research, best practices, and regulatory requirements for improving ethical conduct within the organization. Some companies have not implemented effective business ethics programs, but they should because ethics and compliance programs create good systems to manage organizational misconduct. Our framework for developing effective ethics programs is consistent with the ethical decision-making process described in Chapter 5. In addition, the strategic approach to an ethics program presented here is consistent with the Federal Sentencing Guidelines for Organizations, the Sarbanes-Oxley Act, and the Dodd-Frank Act described in Chapter 4. These legislative reforms require managers to assume responsibility and ensure that ethical standards are implemented properly on a daily basis. Ethics programs include not only the need for top executive leadership but also responsibility by boards of directors for corporate governance.

Unethical and illegal business conduct occurs, even in organizations that have ethics programs. For example, although Enron had a code of ethics and was a member of the Better Business Bureau, the company was devastated by unethical activities and corporate scandal. Many business leaders believe that personal moral development and character are all that is needed for corporate responsibility. There are those who feel that ethics initiatives should arise inherently from a company's culture and that hiring good employees will limit unethical behavior within the organization. Many executives and board members do not understand how organizational ethical decisions are made nor how to develop an ethical corporate culture. Customized ethics programs may help many organizations provide guidance for employees from diverse backgrounds to gain an understanding of acceptable behavior within the organization. Many ethical issues in business are complex and include considerations that require organizational agreement regarding appropriate action. Top executives and boards of directors must provide leadership, a system to resolve these issues, and support for an ethical corporate culture.

In this chapter, we provide an overview of why businesses need to develop an organizational ethics program. Next, we consider the factors that are crucial for the development of such a program: a code of conduct, an ethics officer and appropriate delegation of authority, effective ethics training, a system to monitor and support ethical compliance, and continual efforts to improve the ethics program. Next we discuss the institutionalization of business ethics through mandated and voluntary programs. We discuss the importance of ethical leadership to a company's ethics program. Finally, we examine the requirements of ethical leadership and its impact on organizational culture, including the different forms of communication an ethical leader must master.

SCOPE AND PURPOSE OF ORGANIZATIONAL ETHICS PROGRAMS

Usually, an organization is held accountable for the conduct of its employees. Companies must assess their ethical risks and develop values and compliance systems to avoid legal and ethical mistakes that could damage the organization. The Federal Sentencing Guidelines for Organizations hold corporations responsible for conduct engaged in as an entity. Some corporate outcomes cannot be tied to one individual or even a group, and misconduct can result from a collective pattern of decisions supported by a corporate culture. Therefore, corporations can be held accountable, fined, and even ordered to close their doors when they are operating in a manner inconsistent with major legal requirements. Organizations are sensitive to avoid infringing on employees' personal freedoms and ethical beliefs. In cases where an individual's personal beliefs and activities are inconsistent with company policies on ethics, conflict may develop. If the individual feels that ethics systems in the organization are deficient or directed in an inappropriate manner, some type of open conflict resolution may be needed to deal with the differences.

Understanding the factors that influence how individuals make decisions to resolve ethical issues, as discussed in Chapter 5, can help companies encourage ethical behavior and discourage undesirable conduct. Fostering ethical decisions within an organization requires eliminating unethical behavior and improving the firm's ethical standards. Some people will always do things in their own self-interest regardless of organizational goals or accepted standards of conduct. For example, professional athletes know that use of steroids is prohibited, yet some players still choose to use them in order to gain an edge. Professional tennis star Maria Sharapova, who had been selected to participate in the Rio de Janeiro Olympics, was banned for two years from the sport after failing a drug test.[2] Eliminating inappropriate or abnormal behavior through screening techniques and enforcement of the firm's ethical standards can help improve the firm's overall ethical conduct.

Organizations can foster unethical corporate cultures not because individuals within them are bad but because the pressures to succeed create opportunities that reward unethical decisions. In the case of an unethical corporate culture, the organization must redesign its ethical standards to conform to industry and stakeholder standards of acceptable behavior. Most businesses attempt to improve ethical decision making by establishing and implementing a strategic approach to improving organizational ethics. Companies such as Texas Instruments, Starbucks, and Levi's take a strategic approach to organizational ethics but monitor their programs on a continuous basis and make improvements when problems occur.

To be socially responsible and promote legal and ethical conduct, an organization should develop an organizational ethics program by establishing, communicating, and monitoring ethical values and legal requirements that characterize its history, culture, industry, and operating environment. Without such programs and uniform standards and policies of conduct, it is difficult for employees to determine what behaviors are acceptable within a company. As discussed earlier, in the absence of such programs and standards, employees generally will make decisions based on their observations of how their coworkers and managers behave. A strong ethics program includes a written code of conduct, an ethics officer to oversee the program, careful delegation of authority, formal ethics training, auditing, monitoring, enforcement, and periodic revision of program standards. Without a strong customized program, problems are much more likely to arise. Figure 6.1 outlines what employees identified as the causes of organizational misconduct.

Trust in top management and business is low. An analysis of trustworthy companies revealed three characteristics that CEOs have implemented that resulted in trust and confidence in business. These include involving those directly affected by company decisions in the decision-making process, being transparent and consistent in actions, and nurturing relationships.[3] This is a recurring theme among primary stakeholders. Consumers are looking for clear, creative, and constructive leadership from CEOs that demonstrates trust is a priority.

FIGURE 6.1 Employee Assessment of the Causes of Misconduct

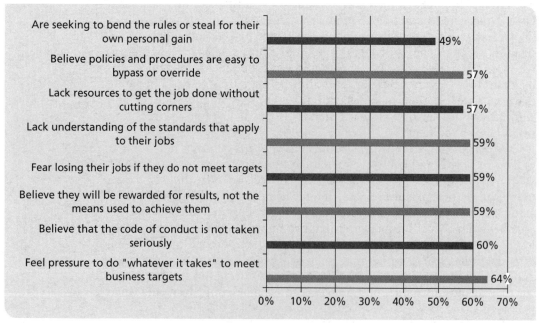

Source: "Integrity Survey 2013," *KPMG*, 2013, p. 13, http://www.kpmg.com/CN/en/IssuesAndInsights/ArticlesPublications/Documents/Integrity-Survey-2013-O-201307.pdf (accessed June 21, 2016).

No universal standards exist that can be applied to organizational ethics programs in all organizations, but most companies develop codes, values, or policies for guidance about business conduct. The majority of companies that have been in ethical or legal trouble usually have stated ethics codes and programs. Often, the problem is that top management, as well as the overall corporate culture, has not integrated these codes, values, and standards into daily decision making. For example, Priceline CEO Darren Huston resigned after it was discovered that he had a personal relationship with an employee in violation of the company's ethics policies.[4] If a company's leadership fails to provide the vision and support needed for ethical conduct, then an ethics program will not be effective. Ethics is not something to be delegated to lower-level employees while top managers break the rules. Excellent leaders must lead by example and reinforce the integrity of the organizational culture.

No matter what their specific goals, ethics programs are developed as organizational control systems, the aim of which is to create predictability and consistency in employee behavior. There are two types of organizational control systems. A compliance orientation creates order by requiring that employees identify with and commit to specific required conduct. It uses legal terms and statutes that teach employees the rules and penalties for noncompliance. The other type of system is a values orientation, which strives to develop shared values. Although penalties are attached, the focus is more on an abstract core of principles such as respect and responsibility. The goal is to create an environment where employees are compelled and willing to support an ethical organizational culture. More than half of employees in the KPMG Forensic Ethics Survey stated that they had observed misconduct that could cause 'a significant loss of public trust if discovered.' The industries in which this type of misconduct increased the most include electronics, chemicals and diversified industrials, consumer markets, and aerospace and defense.[5] The goal of an effective ethics program is to get employees to report wrongdoing when they become aware of it and seek guidance when they are uncertain as to how to respond in ambiguous circumstances.

Research into compliance- and values-based approaches reveals that both types of programs can interact or work toward the same end, but a values orientation tends to have a stronger influence on employees. Values-based programs increase employees' awareness of ethics at work, their integrity, their willingness to deliver bad news to supervisors, and the perception that better decisions are made. Compliance-based programs are linked to employees' awareness of ethical issues at work and their perception that decision making is better because of the expectations of its employees.

To meet the public's escalating demands for ethical decision making, companies need to develop plans and structures for addressing ethical considerations. Some directions for the improvement of ethics have been mandated through regulations, but companies must be willing to have a values and ethics implementation system in place that exceeds the minimum regulatory requirements. In addition, companies that have experienced reputational damage in the past are much further along compared to their peers in establishing ethics and compliance programs.[6]

CODES OF CONDUCT

Because people come from diverse family, educational, and business backgrounds, it cannot be assumed that they know how to behave appropriately when they enter a new organization or job. Most companies begin the process of establishing organizational ethics programs by developing **codes of conduct** (also called codes of ethics), which are formal statements that describe what an organization expects of its employees. Table 6.1 depicts elements of an effective ethics and compliance program (such as codes and training). Codes of ethics address risk areas that organizations face and which employees may experience in the workplace.

A code of ethics has to reflect the board of directors' and senior management's desire for organizational compliance with the values and

codes of conduct
Formal statements that describe what an organization expects of its employees; also called codes of ethics.

TABLE 6.1 Elements of an Effective Ethics Program

1	Standards and Codes	Used to prevent and detect criminal conduct by expressing what the right thing is, how it can be accomplished, and the expectations to which the employee is held. They should be communicated and written in a concise, clear language in codes of ethics.
2	Leadership and the Ethics Officer	The company's board of directors usually oversees the implementation of the program, and a senior executive or committee of executives should be given overall responsibility for its compliance. Many ethics officers report to the chief executive and interact with the board of directors on a regular basis.
3	Communication and Effective Training	The company must effectively implement the program through education and training. Training should be focused on industry-specific areas of risk, and should not merely recite the law, but should explicitly explain the company's policies and ask employees to think through complex "gray areas" they may encounter in their day-to-day tasks.
4	Monitoring and Disclosure	The ethics and compliance program should be implemented. Employees should be asked about the "unwritten rules" within the company to determine whether the program's goals match its actual operation. Employees must be provided with effective mechanisms through which to anonymously or confidentially report potential misconduct or seek guidance on compliance issues, protect such individuals against retaliation, and adequately follow up on their reports.

(Continued)

TABLE 6.1 (*Continued*)

5	Observation and Reinforcement	Appropriate incentives must be provided to encourage employees to comply with the program and impose appropriate disciplinary measures if audits reveal that employees fail to do so. It is important for the company to enforce these rules consistently to maintain the credibility of the program.
6	Corrective Action	Misconduct must be addressed after it occurs including, at times, self-reporting to the authorities. Reasonable steps must be taken to prevent similar misconduct in the future. In addition, the company's board or audit committee must receive regular and meaningful reports on audit results and the status of corrective action.

Source: Adapted from U.S. Federal Sentencing Guidelines, Chapter 8; 2012 Amendments to the U.S. Federal Sentencing Guidelines; Kristin Graham Koehler and Brian P. Morrissey, "Seven Steps for Developing an Effective Compliance and Ethics Program," *Chain Store Age*, January 3, 2013, http://chainstoreage.com/article/seven-steps-developing-effective-compliance-and-ethics-program (accessed June 21, 2016).

principles, mission, rules, and policies that support an ethical climate. Development of a code of ethics should involve the board of directors, president, ethics officer, and senior managers who will be implementing the code. Legal staff should be called on to ensure that the code has correctly assessed key areas of risk and that potential legal problems are buffered by standards in the code. A code of ethics that does not address specific high-risk activities within the scope of daily operations is inadequate for maintaining standards that can prevent misconduct. Table 6.2 shows considerations in developing and implementing a code of ethics.

A large multinational firm, Texas Instruments (TI), manufactures computers, calculators, and other high-technology products. Its code of ethics has some of the elements listed in the table above as its base. The code addresses issues relating to policies and procedures; government laws and regulations; acceptance of gifts, travel, and entertainment; handling of proprietary information and trade secrets; and more.[7] To ensure that its

TABLE 6.2 Developing and Implementing a Code of Ethics

1. Consider areas of risk and state values as well as conduct necessary to comply with laws and regulations. Values and principles are an important buffer in preventing serious misconduct.
2. Identify values and principles that specifically address current ethical issues.
3. Consider values and principles that link the organization to a stakeholder orientation. Attempt to find overlaps in organizational and stakeholder values.
4. Make the code understandable by providing examples that reflect values.
5. Communicate the code frequently and in language that employees can understand.
6. Revise the code every year with input from organizational members and stakeholders.

employees understand the nature of business ethics and the ethical standards they are expected to follow, TI provides the "Ethics Quick Test" to help employees when they have doubts about the ethics of specific situations and behaviors. It urges employees to reflect upon the following questions and statements:

Is the action legal?

Does it comply with our values?

If you do it, will you feel bad?

How will it look in the newspaper?

If you know it's wrong, don't do it!

If you're not sure, ask.

Keep asking until you get an answer.[8]

Texas Instruments explicitly states what it expects of its employees and what behaviors are unacceptable. When such standards of behavior are not made explicit, employees sometimes base ethical decisions on their observations of the behavior of peers and management. The use of rewards and punishments to enforce codes and policies controls the opportunity to behave unethically and increases employees' acceptance of ethical standards.

As we stated, codes of conduct may address a variety of situations, from internal operations to sales presentations and financial disclosure practices. Research has found that corporate codes of ethics often have five to seven core values or principles, in addition to more detailed descriptions and examples of appropriate conduct.[9] The six values that have been suggested as desirable to appearing in the codes of ethics include: (1) trustworthiness, (2) respect, (3) responsibility, (4) fairness, (5) caring, and (6) citizenship. These values will not be effective without distribution, training, and the support of top management in making the values a part of the corporate culture. Employees need specific examples of how the values can be implemented and guide ethical decision making.

Codes of conduct will not resolve every ethical issue encountered in daily operations, but they help employees and managers deal with ethical dilemmas by prescribing or limiting specific actions. Many companies have a code of ethics, but is it communicated effectively? According to the Ethics Resource Center, the number of companies developing and implementing effective ethics and compliance programs is increasing each year.[10] A code that is placed on a website or in a training manual is useless if it is not reinforced on a daily basis. By communicating to employees both what is expected of them and what punishments they face if they violate the rules, codes of conduct curtail opportunities for unethical behavior and thereby improve ethical decision making. Wells Fargo Bank offers a comprehensive code of conduct that specifies: "If you violate any provision of the Code or fail to cooperate fully with any inquiries or investigations, you will be subject to corrective action, which may include termination of your employment."[11] Codes of conduct do not have to be so detailed that they take into account every situation, but they should provide guidelines and principles that are capable of helping employees achieve organizational ethical objectives and address risks in an accepted manner.

ETHICS OFFICERS

Organizational ethics programs also must have oversight by a high-ranking person known to respect and understand legal and ethical standards. This person is often referred to as an **ethics officer** but can also be the general counsel, the vice-president of human resource management, or any other officer. Corporate wrongdoings and scandal-grabbing headlines have a profound negative impact on public trust. To ensure compliance with state and federal regulations, many corporations are now appointing chief compliance officers and ethics and business conduct professionals to develop and oversee corporate compliance programs.

ethics officer
A high-ranking person known to respect and understand legal and ethical standards.

Consistent enforcement and necessary disciplinary action are essential to a functional ethics and compliance program. The ethics or compliance officer is usually responsible for companywide disciplinary systems, implementing all disciplinary actions the company takes for violations of its ethical standards. Many companies are including ethics and compliance in employee performance appraisals. During performance appraisals, employees may be asked to sign an acknowledgment that they have read the company's current guidelines on its ethics policies. The company must also promptly investigate any known or suspected misconduct. The appropriate company official, often the ethics officer, needs to make a recommendation to senior management on how to deal with a particular ethics infraction.

The Ethics and Compliance Association consists of front line managers of ethics programs in dozens of industries worldwide.[12] Ethics and compliance officers are instrumental in managing ethics programs and have the attention of top managers and boards of directors.[13] The ethics officer position has existed for decades, but its importance increased tremendously when the Federal Sentencing Guidelines for Organizations were passed in 1991. The guidelines gave companies that faced federal charges for misconduct the incentive of fine reductions up to 95 percent if they had an effective comprehensive ethics program in place. The financial reporting requirements of the Sarbanes-Oxley Act put more pressure on ethics officers to monitor financial reporting, as well as reporting of sales and inventory movements, to prevent fraud in reporting revenue and profits. While not always deemed to be most effective, it is recommended that ethics officers report directly to the board of directors.

Building an ethics program and hiring an ethics officer to avoid fines alone will not be effective. Only with the involvement of top management and the board can an ethics officer earn the trust and cooperation of all key decision makers. Ethics officers should be knowledgeable about the industry's laws and regulations as well as adept at communicating and reinforcing values that build an ethical corporate culture.

ETHICS TRAINING AND COMMUNICATION

Instituting a training program and a system of communication to disseminate the firm's ethical standards is a major step in developing an effective ethics program. Such training can educate employees about the firm's policies and expectations, relevant laws and regulations, and general social standards. Training programs can make employees aware of available resources, support systems, and designated personnel who can assist them with ethical and legal advice. Training also can help empower employees to ask tough questions and make ethical decisions.

Ethics officers provide the oversight and management of most ethics training. Although training and communication should reinforce values and provide learning opportunities about rules, risks, and acceptable behavior, it is only one part of an effective ethics program. The employee's capacity to exercise judgments that result in ethical decisions must be reinforced and developed. Ethics training should be customized to the specific risk areas they face. If ethical evaluations are not a part of regular performance appraisals, the message employees will receive is that ethics is not an important component of decision making. For ethics training to make a difference, employees must understand why it is conducted, how it fits into the organization, and what their role is in its implementation.

Top corporate executives must communicate with managers at the operations level (e.g., in production, sales, and finance) and enforce overall ethical standards within the organization. Table 6.3 lists the factors crucial to successful ethics training. It is most important to help employees identify ethical issues and give them the means to address and resolve such

TABLE 6.3 Factors Crucial to Ethics Training

1. Identify the key ethical risk areas.
2. Relate ethical decisions to the organization's values, principles, and culture.
3. Communicate company codes, policies, and procedures regarding ethical business conduct.
4. Provide leadership training to model desired behavior.
5. Provide directions for internal questions and non-retaliatory reporting mechanisms.
6. Engage in regular training events using a variety of educational tools.
7. Establish manuals, websites, social media, and other communication to reinforce ethics training.
8. Evaluate and use feedback to improve training.

Source: © O. C Ferrell 2018.

issues in ambiguous situations. In addition, employees must be offered direction on seeking assistance from managers or other designated personnel in resolving ethical problems. An effective ethics program can reduce criminal, civil, and administrative consequences, including fines, penalties, judgments, debarment from government contracts, and court control of the organization. An ineffective ethics program that results in many unethical acts may cause negative publicity, a decrease in organizational financial performance, and lowered stakeholder trust. An ethical disaster can be more damaging to an organization than a natural disaster because of the damage that occurs to organizational reputation.

Companies can implement ethical principles in their organizations through training programs. Discussions conducted in ethics training programs sometimes break down into personal opinions about what should or should not be done in particular situations. To be successful, business ethics programs need to educate employees about how to identify and deal with business ethics issues. Employees are then able to base ethical decisions on their knowledge of appropriate actions, from an organizational perspective, rather than on emotions.

Training and communication initiatives should reflect the unique characteristics of an organization: its size, culture, values, management style, and employee base. It is important for the ethics program to differentiate between personal and organizational ethics. If ethics training is to be effective, it must start with a foundation, a code of ethics, commitment from all levels of the organization, and executive priorities on ethics that are communicated to employees. Managers from every department must be involved in the development of an ethics training program.

Most experts agree that one of the most effective methods of ethics training involves resolving ethical dilemmas that relate to actual situations employees may encounter while performing their jobs. For example, Lockheed Martin developed a training game called *Gray Matters*. This training device includes dilemmas that can be resolved by teams. Each member of the team can offer his or her perspective and understand the ramifications of the decision for coworkers and the organization.

Another training device is the behavioral simulation or role-play exercise in which participants are given a short hypothetical ethical issue scenario to review. The participants are assigned roles within the hypothetical organization and are provided with varying levels of information about the issue. They then must interact to provide recommended courses of action representing short-term, midrange, and long-term considerations. The simulation recreates the complexities of organizational relationships and of having to address a situation without complete information. Learning objectives of the simulation exercise include (1) increased awareness by participants of the ethical, legal, and social dimensions of business decision making; (2) development of analytical skills for resolving ethical issues; and (3) exposure to the complexity of ethical decision making in organizations. Simulations help teach students about why ethics is important as well as how to handle ethics conflict situations.[14]

A growing number of small businesses deliver "learning-management" systems software and content to train and certify employees on a variety of topics. In addition to streamlined training, the systems provide real-time records of instruction that increasingly are the first line of defense for companies facing litigation or questions about whether they are accountable for an employee's actions. The e-learning market is growing very rapidly both in education and business. For multinational companies, the computerized training elements of such systems provide consistency of content and delivery to all locations and allow for customization of languages and to cultures. Some of the goals of an ethics training program might be to improve employee understanding of ethical issues and the ability to identify them, to inform employees of related procedures and rules, as well as to identify the contact person who could help in resolving ethical problems. In keeping with these goals, the purpose of Boeing's Code of Ethics and Business Conduct program is to:

- Communicate the Boeing Values and standards of ethical business conduct to employees.
- Inform employees of company policies and procedures regarding ethical business conduct.
- Establish company-wide processes to assist employees in obtaining guidance and resolving questions regarding compliance with the company's standards of conduct and the Boeing Values.
- Establish company-wide criteria for ethics education and awareness programs.[15]

Ethical decision making is influenced by organizational culture, by coworkers and supervisors, and by the opportunity to engage in unethical behavior. All three types of influence can be affected by ethics training. Full awareness of the philosophy of management, rules, and procedures can strengthen both the organizational culture and the ethical stance of peers and supervisors. Such awareness also arms employees against opportunities for unethical behavior and reduces the likelihood of misconduct. Thus, the existence and enforcement of company rules and procedures limit unethical practices in the organization. The primary goals of ethics training are to make employees aware of the risks associated with their jobs, industry, and stakeholders; provide an understanding of the culture and expectations within the organization; create accountability for individual actions; and inform employees not only of the behavior that is unacceptable but also that which is acceptable and supported in the organization.

ESTABLISHING SYSTEMS TO MONITOR AND ENFORCE ETHICAL STANDARDS

Ethics and compliance programs also involve comparing employee ethical performance with the organization's ethical standards. Ethics programs can be measured through employee observation, internal audits, surveys, reporting systems, and investigations. An effective ethics program uses a variety of resources to effectively monitor ethical conduct. Sometimes, external auditing and review of company activities are helpful in developing benchmarks of compliance and identifying areas for improvement.

Systems to Monitor and Enforce Ethical Standards

Many companies set up ethics assistance lines, also known as 'hotlines', to provide support and give employees the opportunity to ask questions or report concerns. The most effective ethics hotlines operate on an anonymous basis and are supported 24 hours a day, 365 days a year. Approximately 52 percent of the employees who report concerns indicated using their company's hotline to do so. In addition, 15 percent use the company's website to report misconduct and 32 percent use other traditional methods such as face-to-face reporting to supervisors or managers, email, fax, and direct mail.[16]

It is interesting that most of the issues reported do not relate to serious ethical and legal issues. Nearly 70 percent of the issues raised on help lines relate to human resources and complaints such as coworker abuse, failure of management to intervene in such abuse, and inappropriate language. Other top issues reported include business integrity at 17 percent; environment, health, and safety at 7 percent; misuse or misappropriation of assets at 6 percent; and accounting, auditing, and financial reporting at 3 percent.[17]

A help line or desk is characterized by ease of accessibility and simple procedures, and it serves as a safety net that facilitates monitoring and reporting. Companies such as Global Compliance provide automated case management systems which collect, categorize, and provide alerts to the appropriate manager for dealing with ethics issues in the organization. Companies are increasingly using case management services and software to track employees and issues throughout their entire organization. These programs provide reports of employee concerns, complaints, or observations of misconduct. Systems such as these allow the company to track investigations, analysis, resolutions, documentation, emerging/declining issues, and the time required for resolution.

Observation and Feedback

To determine whether a person is performing his or her job adequately and ethically, observation might focus on how the person handles an ethically charged situation. For example, during role-plays in the training sessions of salespeople and managers, ethical issues can be introduced into the discussion, and the decisions can be videotaped and outcomes evaluated by managers.

Questionnaires that survey employees' ethical perceptions of their company, their superiors, their coworkers, and themselves, as well as ratings of ethical or unethical practices within the firm and industry, can serve as benchmarks in an ongoing assessment of ethical performance. Then, if unethical behavior is perceived to increase, management will have a better understanding of what types of unethical practices may be occurring and why. A change in the ethics training within the company may be necessary. In addition, organization-wide risk management systems identify new and emerging risks employees face and to which management must respond.

Appropriate action involves rewarding employees who comply with company policies and standards and punishing those who do not. When employees comply with organizational standards, their efforts may be acknowledged and rewarded through public recognition, bonuses, raises, or some other means. Conversely, when employees deviate from organizational standards, they may be reprimanded, transferred, docked, suspended, or even fired.

Whistle-blowing

Interpersonal conflict ensues when employees think they know the right course of action in a situation, yet their work group or company promotes or requires a different, possibly unethical decision. In such cases, employees usually follow the organizational values. If they conclude that they cannot discuss what they are doing or what should be done with their coworkers or immediate supervisors, these employees may go outside the organization to publicize and correct the unethical situation. **Whistle-blowing** means exposing an employer's wrongdoing to outsiders, such as the media or government regulatory agencies.

whistle-blowing
Exposing an employer's wrongdoing to outsiders such as the media or government regulatory agencies.

Whistle-blowers have provided pivotal evidence documenting corporate wrongdoing at a number of companies. Since the institution of the Whistleblower Protection Act, many employees are coming forward to reveal company misdeeds to government authorities. Bradley Birkenfeld of UBS reported a tax evasion scheme to the Internal Revenue Service and was awarded $104 million for the revelation. The SEC awarded one whistleblower $17 million, the second largest award under the Dodd-Frank whistleblower bounty program, because his information was a substantial help to the SEC in its investigation.[18] Another whistleblower, Keith Edwards, was awarded over $63 million for providing information regarding J. P. Morgan's plan to hide findings from internal reviews about faulty mortgage loans from the government. It is estimated that the SEC paid out $37 million to whisteblowers in the security industry in 2015.[19] Despite these large monetary rewards, the fortunes of whistleblowers are peppered with negative pushback. Most are labeled traitors, many lose their jobs, and some find it difficult to gain new employment afterward.

Critics have stated that the potential for large monetary sums related to whistleblowing encourage employees to come forward regardless of whether their claims are valid. However, a survey by the Ethics Resource Center showed that only 14 percent of employees are motivated by such incentives. Rather, the majority of external reporting is a result of other factors such as lack of trust in company authorities, experience of retaliation from prior internal reporting, and the fear of losing one's job.[20] Because of the risks involved in being a whistleblower, Table 6.4 provides a checklist of questions an employee should ask before blowing the whistle.

TABLE 6.4 Questions to Ask Before Engaging in External Whistle-Blowing

1. Have I exhausted internal anonymous reporting opportunities within the organization?
2. Have I examined company polices and codes that outline acceptable behavior and violations of standards?
3. Is this a personal issue that should be resolved through other means?
4. Can I manage the stress that may evolve from exposing potential wrongdoing in the organization?
5. Can I deal with the consequences of resolving an ethical or legal conflict within the organization?

Source: © O. C. Ferrell 2016.

CONTINUOUS IMPROVEMENT OF THE ETHICS PROGRAM

Improving the system that encourages employees to make more ethical decisions is not very different from implementing other types of business strategies. Implementation means putting strategies into action. Implementation in ethics and compliance means the design of activities to achieve organizational objectives using available resources and given existing constraints. Implementation translates a plan for action into operational terms and establishes a means by which organizational ethical performance will be monitored, controlled, and improved.

A firm's ability to plan and implement ethical business standards depends in part on the organization's structuring of resources and activities to achieve its ethical objectives in an effective and efficient manner. Some U.S. companies are setting up computer systems that encourage whistle-blowing. For instance, Marvin Windows (one of the world's largest custom manufacturers of wood windows and doors) was concerned about employees feeling comfortable reporting violations of safety conditions, bad management, fraud, or theft. It established an anonymous system that allows for reporting in native country languages. This system is used to alert management to potential problems in the organization and facilitate an investigation.[21] Systems such as these help alleviate employee concerns when reporting observed misconduct.

Once a company determines that its ethical performance has not been satisfactory, the company's management may want to reorganize the way certain ethical decisions are made. For example, a decentralized organization may need to centralize key decisions, if only for a time, so that top-level managers can ensure improved organizational decision-making. Centralization may reduce the opportunity for lower-level managers and employees to make unethical decisions. Top management can then focus on improving the corporate culture and infusing more ethical values throughout the organization. Dell Computer is an example of a centralized organization, possibly because of its focus on manufacturing processes.

In other companies, decentralization of important decisions may be a better way to attack ethical problems so that lower-level managers, familiar with the forces of the local business environment and local culture and values, can make more decisions. Coca-Cola is a more decentralized company due to its use of independent distributors and unique localized cultures. Whether the ethics function is centralized or decentralized, the key need is to delegate authority in such a way that the organization can achieve ethical performance.

INSTITUTIONALIZATION OF BUSINESS ETHICS[22]

To successfully implement an ethics program, managers should be aware of the core, legally mandated, and voluntary elements of organizational business practices. All three should be incorporated into an organization's ethics program. This generates an ethical culture that successfully controls and manages ethical risks. Institutionalization involves the legal and social forces that provide organizational rewards and punishments based upon stakeholder assessments of an organization's behavior. In business ethics, institutionalization is associated with the establishment of laws, regulations, norms, and organizational programs. A refusal to conform to what is believed to be ethical conduct is often perceived to be an ethical issue and a concern to stakeholders. Institutions involve obligations, structures, and social expectations that reward and limit ethical decisions. Federal agencies, for instance, are institutions that mandate laws for appropriate conduct. They may even recommend core practices for developing an ethical organizational culture.

Voluntary, Core Practices, and Mandatory Dimensions of Ethics Programs[23]

voluntary practices
The beliefs, values, and voluntary responsibilities of an organization.

Table 6.5 summarizes the three elements of institutionalization. **Voluntary practices** are the beliefs, values, and voluntary responsibilities of an organization. All organizations engage in some level of voluntary activities to

TABLE 6.5 Voluntary Boundary, Core Practices, and Mandated Boundaries of Ethical Decisions

Voluntary boundary	A management-initiated boundary of conduct (beliefs, values, voluntary polices, and voluntary responsibilities)
Core practice	A highly appropriate and common practice that helps ensure compliance with legal requirements, industry self-regulation, and societal expectations
Mandated boundary	An externally imposed boundary of conduct (laws, rules, regulations, and other requirements)

Source: Adapted from the "Open Compliance Ethics Group (OCEG) Foundation Guidelines," v1.0, Steering Committee Update, December 2005, Phoenix, AZ.

help different stakeholders. These responsibilities often manifest themselves through **philanthropy**, which occurs when businesses give back to communities and causes. Home Depot strongly supports the nonprofit organization Habitat for Humanity and encourages employees to volunteer. Evidence suggests that a sense of the law and ethical behavior increases voluntary responsibility activities. Research has also confirmed that when a company's core practices support ethical and legal responsibilities, they enhance economic performance.[24]

Core practices are recognized best practices that are often encouraged by regulatory forces and industry trade associations. As we mentioned in the previous chapter, the Better Business Bureau provides guidance for managing customer conflicts and reviewing advertising disputes. Core practices are appropriate practices often common to the industry. They guarantee compliance with legal requirements and social expectations. Core practices align the expectations of the consumer with a business to create satisfying exchanges.[25]

Although core practices are not enforced on a legal basis, businesses can face consequences for not engaging in them when misconduct occurs. For example, the Federal Sentencing Guidelines for Organizations provide incentives for firms that effectively implement core practices. If misconduct occurs, firms that have demonstrated best practices may be able to avoid serious penalties. However, if the board took no initiative to oversee ethics and compliance in the organization, its failure could increase the level of punishment the company experiences. In institutionalizing core practices, the government allows organizations to structure their own methods and takes action only if violations occur. **Mandated boundaries** are externally imposed boundaries of conduct, such as laws, rules, regulations, and other requirements. Laws regulating business competition are examples of mandated boundaries.

Organizations manage stakeholder expectations for ethical conduct through corporate governance mechanisms, compliance, risk management, and voluntary activities. Government initiatives and stakeholder demands have helped to institutionalize these drivers of an ethical organizational culture. For instance, the governing authority of an organization structures corporate governance to provide oversight, checks, and balances to ensure the organization meets its ethical objectives. Compliance represents areas that must follow laws and regulations. Risk management examines the chance that misconduct may occur based on the type of business and the risk areas it commonly faces. Voluntary activities often involve the values and responsibilities organizations adopt in contributing to stakeholder expectations.

philanthropy
The act of businesses giving back to communities and causes.

core practices
Recognized best practices that are often encouraged by regulatory forces and industry trade associations.

mandated boundaries
Externally imposed boundaries of conduct, such as laws, rules, regulations, and other requirements.

ETHICAL LEADERSHIP[26]

A company's leaders provide the blueprint for an organization's corporate culture.[27] If organizational leaders do not display ethical conduct, the corporate culture will evolve on its own to exhibit the organization's norms and

Ethical Responsibilities in Accounting

Integrated Financial Reporting Paints an Accurate Picture

Most people believe that financial statements such as income statements and balance sheets provide the entire picture of a firms' financial standing. In reality, however, this is not the case. It has been estimated that about 80 percent of a firm's value is not found on the balance sheet. One of the least understood areas involves sustainability. For instance, how much does violating an environmental law truly cost a firm, not only monetarily but also in terms of its reputation? Some socially responsible businesses have adopted a triple bottom line approach in which the organization reports its financial results, its impact on society, and its impact on the planet. Yet even these companies find it difficult to take three different dimensions and add them up to provide an overall report.

A pilot program consisting of about 100 global companies in 25 countries is investigating ways to overcome these challenges. This program, monitored by the International Integrated Reporting Council, seeks to create an integrated reporting model giving investors the opportunity to gain a holistic view of the company's operations and business strategies. Integrated reporting combines both financial and non-financial information. According to the Chartered Institute of Management Accountants, integrated reporting is meant to examine how organizations "really create value." Companies testing this program include Microsoft, Unilever, Clorox, and Coca-Cola. Although most of these firms already develop sustainability or social responsibility reports, these reports are separate from the company's financial information. Such an endeavor requires the active participation of both company financial officers and accountants.

Companies in the pilot program have different ways of reporting, but all focus on the true cost of capital and resources. For instance, U.K. global support and construction firm Interserve developed an integrated report focused upon four dimensions, including financial, natural/environmental, knowledge, and social capital. This reporting system recognizes the value of intangible assets such as knowledge as well as the firm's societal impact. The point of such reports is not to report more information, but to provide more thorough information so both investors and consumers receive a more complete view of the company. Whereas financial reports focus on short-term numbers, it is hoped that integrated reporting will allow firms to adopt a more long-term orientation by taking an in-depth look at their resources and their impacts.

Proponents of integrated reporting hope that integrated reports will become the primary reports of the organization. In other words, integrated reporting may become the new norm for investor reports such as the annual report. Additionally, the demand for integrated reporting metrics seems to be growing. For instance, stock exchanges such as the Nasdaq are beginning to require more information on a firm's corporate governance and environmental activities.

Sources: "Integrated Reporting," http://www.theiirc.org/ (accessed August 4, 2016); Kathleen Hoffelder, "What Does Sustainability *Really* Cost?" *CFO,* August 28, 2012, http://ww2.cfo.com/cash-flow/2012/08/what-does-sustainability-really-cost/ (accessed August 4, 2016); "Triple Bottom Line," *The Economist,* November 17, 2009, http://www.economist.com/node/14301663 (accessed August 4, 2016); IIRC Pilot Programme Yearbook, *Business and Investors Explore the Sustainability Perspective of Integrated Reporting,* 2013, http://www.theiirc.org/wp-content/uploads/2013/12/IIRC-PP-Yearbook-2013_PDF4_PAGES.pdf (accessed August 4, 2016); "Integrated Reporting," *The Prince's Accounting for Sustainability Project,* http://www.accountingforsustainability.org/connected-reporting (accessed August 4, 2016); Chartered Institute of Management Accountants, "Integrated Reporting <IR>," http://www.cimaglobal.com/Thought-leadership/Integrated-reporting/ (accessed August 4, 2016).

values. Consider the infamous accounting firm Arthur Andersen, once one of the "Big Five" accounting firms (they were reduced to the "Big Four" after Arthur Andersen's demise). Arthur Andersen, who founded the company, valued ethical behavior. In one situation, he refused to improperly record an accounting entry for a major client.[28] Contrast this to the firm Arthur Andersen a few years before its demise and you can see what could happen when an organization strays from ethical leadership. Without ethical leadership, an organizational culture cannot be maintained for long periods of time.

Organizational leaders are important to ethical decision making because they have the ability to motivate employees and enforce the organization's norms, policies, and procedures. Ethical leaders make certain that operational goals are achieved in an ethical manner. They do not simply allow employees to follow their individual moral codes, but enforce shared organizational values to support an ethical organizational culture. Ethical leaders also take the responsibility to model acceptable conduct for employees.[29] Ethical leadership is positively related to employee organizational citizenship; conversely, it is negatively related to employee misconduct. In other words, ethical leaders are more likely to have employees that support the organization's ethical culture and less likely to have employees that deviate from organizational values.[30]

In addition to CEOs and managers, the board of directors is important in whether the organization displays ethical leadership. Legally, the board has a fiduciary duty to stakeholders to manage in the best interests of the organization. However, it is not always easy to determine what is in the best interests of the organization. A good example would be whether to engage in a risky activity that would result in short-term gains but which could cost the organization significantly in the long-run. To determine the appropriate course of action, board members must consider the impact a decision will have on different stakeholders.[31]

So far we have discussed individuals in a position of authority within an organization. However, ethical leadership is not limited to authority figures. It should also be practiced by employees at all levels of the organization. Often, the actions of fellow employees significantly influence the ethical decision making of an individual.[32] Thus, both leaders as well as employees within an organization have the responsibility to demonstrate ethical leadership characteristics when making decisions.

If stakeholders are dissatisfied with an organizational leader, the leader will not remain in that position. Ethical leaders must have the trust and respect of their followers. For instance, Martin Winterkorn, former CEO of Volkswagen, stepped down after it was discovered that Volkswagen had installed defeat devices into its diesel vehicles to fool regulators. Although initially is was unclear whether Winterkorn knew about the misconduct, as the leader of the company, the misconduct occurred during his watch.[33] The nature of the relationship was found to violate Best Buy ethical policies. Ineffective tone at the top generates the perception that managers do not care about the organization's ethics program or that they feel they are above the ethical requirements that everyone else in the organization must follow.

Just as strong ethical leadership plays a key role in guiding employee behavior, so does a strong corporate culture of support. A KPMG Forensic Integrity Survey asked employees whether the leaders of their companies displayed personal integrity and ethical leadership traits. Approximately 68 percent of employees indicated that leaders emphasized ethics and integrity in the organization.[34] These types of responses are becoming more common as organizations continue strengthening their ethics programs. The results of having an ethical focus are proving to be beneficial toward business operations. Challenges persist, however, and ethical leaders must be vigilant in nurturing the corporate culture of their organizations.

Leadership Power

As we have shown, organizational leaders use their power and influence to shape corporate culture. Power refers to the influence that leaders and managers have over the behavior and decisions of subordinates. An individual has power over others when his or her presence causes them to behave differently. Exerting power is one way to influence the ethical decision-making framework we described in Chapter 5 (especially significant others and opportunity).

The status and power of leaders are directly related to the amount of pressure they can exert on employees to conform to their expectations. A superior in a position of authority can put strong pressure on employees to comply, even when their personal ethical values conflict with the superior's wishes. For example, a manager might say to a subordinate, "I want the confidential data about our competitor's sales on my desk by Monday morning, and I don't care how you get it." A subordinate who values his or her job or who does not realize the ethical questions involved may feel pressured to do something unethical to obtain the data.

There are five power bases from which one person may influence another: (1) reward power, (2) coercive power, (3) legitimate power, (4) expert power, and (5) referent power.[35] These five bases of power can be used to motivate individuals either ethically or unethically.

Reward Power Reward power refers to a person's ability to influence the behavior of others by offering them something desirable. Typical rewards might be money, status, or promotion. Consider, for example, a retail salesperson who has two watches (a Timex and a Casio) for sale. Let us assume that the Timex is of higher quality than the Casio but is priced about the same. In the absence of any form of reward power, the salesperson would logically attempt to sell the Timex watch. However, if Casio gave him an extra 10 percent commission, he would probably focus his efforts on selling the Casio watch. This "carrot dangling" and incentives have been shown to be very effective in getting people to change their behavior in the long run. In the short run, however, it is not as effective as coercive power.

Coercive Power Coercive power is essentially the opposite of reward power. Instead of rewarding a person for doing something, coercive power penalizes actions or behavior. As an example, suppose a valuable client asks an industrial salesperson for a bribe and insinuates that he will take his business elsewhere if his demands are not met. Although the salesperson believes bribery is unethical, her boss has told her that she must keep the client happy or lose her chance at promotion. The boss is also imposing a negative sanction if certain actions are not performed. Every year, 20 percent of Enron's workforce was asked to leave because they were ranked as "needs improvement," or because of other issues. Employees not wanting to fall into the bottom 20 percent engaged in corruption or exhibited complacency toward corruption.[36]

Coercive power relies on fear to change behavior. For this reason, it has been found to be more effective in changing behavior in the short run than in the long run. Coercion is often employed in situations where there is an extreme imbalance in power. However, people who are continually subjected to coercion may seek a counterbalance by aligning themselves with other more powerful persons or simply by leaving the organization. In firms that use coercive power, relationships usually break down in the long run. Power is an ethical issue not only for individuals but also for work groups that establish policy for large corporations.

Legitimate Power Legitimate power stems from the belief that a certain person has the right to exert influence and that certain others have an obligation to accept it. The titles and positions of authority that organizations bestow on individuals appeal to this traditional view of power. Many people readily acquiesce to those who wield legitimate power, sometimes committing acts that are contrary to their beliefs and values. Betty Vinson, an accountant at WorldCom, objected to her supervisor's requests to produce improper accounting entries in an effort to conceal WorldCom's deteriorating financial condition. She finally gave in to their requests, however, after being told that this was the only way to save the company. She and other WorldCom accountants eventually pleaded guilty to conspiracy and fraud charges.[37]

Such loyalty to authority figures can also be seen in corporations that have strong charismatic leaders and centralized structures. In business, if a superior tells an employee to increase sales "no matter what it takes" and that employee has a strong affiliation to legitimate power, the employee may try anything to fulfill that order.

Expert Power Expert power is derived from a person's knowledge (or the perception that the person possesses knowledge). Expert power usually stems from a superior's credibility with subordinates. Credibility, and thus expert power, is positively related to the number of years a person has worked in a firm or industry, the person's education, or the honors he or she has received for performance. Expert power can also be conferred on a person by others who perceive him or her as an expert on a specific topic.

A relatively low-level secretary may have expert power because he or she knows specific details about how the business operates and can even make suggestions on how to inflate revenue through expense reimbursements.

Expert power may cause ethical problems when it is used to manipulate others or to gain an unfair advantage. Physicians, lawyers, or consultants can take unfair advantage of uninformed clients, for example. Accounting firms may gain extra income by ignoring concerns about the accuracy of financial data they are provided in an audit.

Referent Power Referent power may exist when one person perceives that his or her goals or objectives are similar to another's. The second person may attempt to influence the first to take actions that will lead both to achieve their objectives. Because they share the same objectives, the person influenced by the other will perceive the other's use of referent power as beneficial. For this power relationship to be effective, however, some sort of empathy must exist between the individuals. Identification with others helps to boost the decision maker's confidence when making a decision, thus increasing his or her referent power.

Consider the following situation: Lisa Jones, a manager in the accounting department of a manufacturing firm, has asked Michael Wong, a salesperson, to speed up the delivery of sales contracts, so the revenue can be reported in the current quarter. Michael protests that he is not to blame for the slow process. In this case, Lisa makes use of referent power. She invites Michael to lunch, and they discuss some of their work concerns. They agree to speed up document processing, and Lisa suggests that Michael start asking for contracts that he expects in the next quarter. He agrees to give it a try, and within several weeks, the contracts are moving faster and revenue has increased in the current quarter. Lisa's job is made easier, and Michael gets his commission checks a little sooner. (On the other hand, they may be engaging in channel stuffing, which in some cases can be considered revenue fraud.)

The five bases of power are not mutually exclusive. People typically use several power bases to effect change in others. Although power in itself is neither ethical nor unethical, its use can raise ethical issues. Sometimes, a leader uses power to manipulate a situation or a person's values in a way that creates a conflict with the person's value structure. For example, a manager who forces an employee to choose between staying home with his sick child and keeping his job is using coercive power, which creates a direct conflict with the employee's values.

The Role of an Ethical Corporate Culture

Top management sets the tone for the ethical culture of an organization. If executives and CEOs do not explicitly address ethics issues, a culture may emerge where unethical behavior is sanctioned and rewarded. To be most successful, ethical standards and expected behaviors should be integrated throughout every organizational process from hiring, training, compensating, and rewarding to firing. This requires ethical leadership.

An ethical organizational culture is important to employees. A fair, open, and trusting organizational climate supports an ethical culture and can be attributed to lower turnover and higher employee satisfaction. Southwest Airlines has a very strong organizational culture that has remained consistent from the days of its key founder Herb Kelleher. All Southwest employees have heard the stories of Kelleher engaging employees and emphasizing loyalty, teamwork, and the creation of a fun environment. Kelleher strove to treat employees like family. Today, Southwest continues that legacy and culture. Pilots willingly support the 'Adopt a Pilot' program that allows students in classrooms countrywide to adopt a Southwest pilot for its four-week educational and mentoring program.[38]

Some leaders assume that hiring or promoting good, ethical managers will automatically produce an ethical organizational climate. This ignores the fact that an individual may have limited opportunity to enforce his or her own personal ethics on management systems and informal decision making that occurs in the organization. The greatest influence on employee behavior is that of peers and coworkers.[39] Many times, workers do not know what constitutes specific ethical violations such as price fixing, deceptive advertising, consumer fraud, and copyright violations. The more ethical the culture of the organization is perceived to be, the less likely it is that unethical decision making will occur. Over time, an organization's failure to monitor or manage its culture may foster questionable behavior. FedEx maintains a strong ethical culture and has woven its values and expectations throughout the company. FedEx's open-door policy specifies that employees may bring up any work issue or problem with any manager in the organization.[40]

REQUIREMENTS OF ETHICAL LEADERSHIP[41]

Ethical leaders develop their skills through years of training, experience, and learning. In identifying what makes an effective leader, there is no clear consensus of the exact skills needed. However, there are certain skills that seem to be common to ethical organizational leaders. To be an ethical organizational leader, individuals should model corporate values, place the organization's own interests above their own, understand their employees, develop tools for reporting, and recognize the limitations of organizational rules and values.[42] Additionally, ethical leaders should never ignore issues of misconduct.

Ethical leaders do not live in a vacuum but are constantly interacting with others to encourage them to develop ethical leadership skills. Perhaps the best ethical leaders recognize their own limitations and establish strong support networks within the organization to help them in the decision making process. In so doing, they motivate employees toward reaching their full potential and emphasize their importance to the organization.[43] They also establish incentives for those in the organization who train new leaders.[44] Developing effective ethical leaders should be a never-ending process within an organization.

Archie Carroll developed a list of characteristics called the "7 Habits of Highly Moral Leaders," based on Stephen Covey's *The 7 Habits of Highly Effective People*.[45] We have adapted Carroll's work[46] to develop "The 7 Habits of Strong Ethical Leaders." These characteristics include (1) having a strong personal character, (2) having a passion to do what is right, (3) being proactive, (4) considering stakeholder interests, (5) modeling the organization's values, (6) being transparent and actively involved in organizational decision making, and (7) being a competent manager who takes a holistic view of the firm's ethical culture. Ethical leadership requires holistic thinking—one that is willing to take on the challenging issues organizations face every day. Strong ethical leaders have the knowledge and courage to put together important information in order to make the most ethical decision. Various stakeholder demands and conflicts make this a major challenge, but ethical leaders are up to the task. Above all, ethical leaders abide by their principles. This might even require the leader to leave the organization if he or she feels that the culture is too unethical to change.

Additionally, effective ethical leaders are so passionate about the organization and its success that they place the organizations' interests above their own.[47] It also requires them to align employees behind a shared vision.[48] Ethical leaders are concerned with the legacy of their companies, desiring for the company's success to continue long after they are gone. For example, Milton Hershey's legacy has continued at Hershey Foods long after his death, and the firm's ethical culture remains a role model for other companies.

Ethical leaders must be proactive in anticipating, planning, and acting to avoid potential ethical crises.[49] They shoulder the important responsibility of developing effective ethics programs to guide employees in their ethical decision making. Ethical leaders understand social needs and develop core practices of ethical leadership. Vice Chairman Tom Mendoza at NetApp tells managers to let him know when an employee is "doing something right." Mendoza then calls the employees to thank them. His personal "thank you" calls average approximately 10–20 calls per day.[50] Recognizing employee accomplishments in promoting ethical conduct is a great way to make employees feel appreciated and reinforce an ethical organizational culture.

Finally, ethical leaders should be role models. If leaders do not model the values that they advocate, then those values become little more than window dressing. Behavioral scientist Brent Smith claims that leaders acting as role models are the primary influence on individual ethical behavior. On the other hand, leaders whose decisions go against the organization's values signal to employees that the organization's ethical values are meaningless.[51] Whole Foods is an example of a company that strongly supports its core values. In addition to providing quality products, Whole Foods establishes employee well-being through the creation of a transparent workplace. To reduce the power gap between executives and employees, a salary cap has been placed on executive compensation. Each Whole Foods store donates at least 5 percent of profits to its communities.[52] Table 6.6 displays Whole Foods' core values.

TABLE 6.6 Whole Food's Core Values

- Sell the highest quality natural and organic products
- Satisfy, delight, and nourish our customers
- Support team member happiness and excellence
- Create wealth through profits and growth
- Serve and support our global and local communities
- Practice and advance environmental stewardship
- Create ongoing win-win partnerships with our suppliers
- Promote the health of our stakeholders through healthy eating education

Source: "Our Core Values," Whole Foods Markets, http://www.wholefoodsmarket.com/company/cor-evalues.php (accessed June 21, 2016).

Benefits of Ethical Leadership[53]

Perhaps the most important influence of ethical leadership is its impact on organizational culture. Because ethical leaders communicate and oversee the implementation of an organization's values, they make certain that employees are familiarized with core beliefs.[54] Some may provide incentives for ethical conduct, such as rewards for making ethical decisions. These incentives have a positive impact on ethical conduct among employees.[55] Teaching employees to value integrity is a key component in creating an ethical organization.

Research has shown that ethical leadership tends toward higher employee satisfaction and commitment.[56] Employees seem to like working for ethical companies and are more likely to stay with ethical organizations.[57] This saves the firm money and leads to higher productivity. Employees at The Container Store are provided with 263 hours of training, receive higher pay than at competing stores, and are shown appreciation through events like We Love Our Employees Day. This strong organizational culture has resulted in a turnover rate of 10 percent for The Container Store. This is compared to 100 percent for other retailers in the industry.[58]

In addition to employee satisfaction and productivity, ethical leadership also creates strong connections with stakeholders external to the organization. Studies have revealed that customers are willing to pay higher prices for products from companies they consider to be ethical.[59] Consumer trust for businesses still has a long way to go after the latest recession, and organizations that can establish trust are likely to receive a large and loyal customer following.

Ethical leadership also impacts an organization's long-term value. Evidence shows that the ethical commitment of organizational members is positively associated with the organization's value on the stock market.[60] This is because reputation has a profound influence on whether an investor will even invest. Investors consider the risk of an investment as a major factor in their decision, and because social responsibility programs are negatively related to long-term risks,[61] ethical conduct is likely to improve reputation and consequently lower the risks of investment. As we already discussed in the previous chapters, from a regulatory standpoint, organizations demonstrated as having strong ethics programs are more likely to see reduced penalties if misconduct should happen.[62] By creating strong relationships with a variety of stakeholders, ethical leaders are able to develop major competitive advantages for their organizations.

Leadership Styles[63]

Leadership styles impact not only how a leader leads but also how employees accept and/or adhere to organizational norms and values. Clearly, leadership styles that reinforce the development of organizational values are beneficial. These styles of leadership affect the organization's communication and oversight of values, norms, and ethics codes.[64] The challenge that leaders face is earning employee trust. This trust is imperative if a leader hopes to guide employees into ethical decision making. Trustworthy leaders tend to be seen as ethical stewards.[65] Employees often look to their organizational leaders to determine how to respond to a situation, even when that response may be ethically questionable.

Effective ethical leadership requires the leader to understand the organization's vision and values, ethical challenges, and the risks involved in accomplishing organizational objectives. One of the biggest assumptions is that those who fail in ethical leadership do not have an ethical character. This is a fallacy. In reality, there are a number of examples of people implicated in misconduct who appeared to have good character. Rajat Gupta, who was convicted for passing on insider trading tips, has been recognized for his strong philanthropic endeavors and exceptional kindness.[66]

Ethical leaders must learn from their experiences and gain knowledge about appropriate practices. They display transparency in their leadership and have the ability to understand both current ethical issues as well as to anticipate future issues. These leaders often adopt a stakeholder orientation approach to management. It is also important to note that even the most ethical leaders are human; they will make ethical mistakes, but how they acknowledge these mistakes is what often separates them from other leaders.

One important characteristic that many ethical leaders appear to possess is **emotional intelligence**, or the skills to manage themselves and their relationships with others effectively. Emotionally intelligent leaders are characterized by self-awareness, self-control, and relationship building. They see their efforts as achieving "something greater than themselves."[67] Warren Buffett and Howard Schultz are examples of emotionally intelligent leaders. These leaders are able to motivate employees to support a common vision, making them feel that their efforts matter in the successful operation of the organization.[68] Because emotionally intelligent leaders exhibit self-control and self-awareness, they are more proficient in tackling

emotional intelligence
An important characteristic possessed by ethical leaders referring to the skills to manage themselves and their relationships with others effectively.

stressful and challenging situations. Because of the impact of emotional intelligence on the success of the organization, some employers have begun viewing emotional intelligence as more important than IQ.[69]

Daniel Goleman examined leadership styles based upon emotional intelligence. He came up with the following six styles:[70]

1. The coercive leader requires complete obedience and focuses on achievement, initiative, and self-control. This style can be highly effective during times of crisis but tends to be detrimental to long-term performance.
2. The authoritative leader motivates employees to follow a shared vision, embraces change, and creates a strongly positive performance climate.
3. The affiliative leader values people and their needs. This leader depends upon friendship and trust to encourage flexibility and innovation.
4. The democratic leader values participation and teamwork to develop collaborative decisions. This style focuses heavily on communication and creating a positive work climate.
5. The pacesetting leader sets high standards of performance. This style works well for achieving quick results from motivated, achievement-oriented employees but can have negative results due to its stringent performance standards.
6. The coaching leader creates a positive work climate by developing skills to promote long-term success, delegating responsibility, and assigning challenging assignments.

Using Goleman's research, Richard Boyatzis and Annie McKee came up with the idea of a resonant leader. Resonant leaders are mindful of their emotions, believe that goals can be achieved, and display a caring attitude toward other employees. This leads to resonance within the organization, enhancing collaboration and the ability of employees to work toward shared goals.[71] Resonant leaders are highly effective in creating an ethical corporate culture as well as strong relationships with employees.

The most successful leaders tend to adapt their styles based upon the situation. Leadership style relies heavily on how the leader measures risks as well as his or her desire to attain a positive corporate culture. Like other leadership characteristics, many emotional intelligence skills can be learned. Starbucks places great importance on emotional intelligence. New employees at the company undergo a training program called the "Latte Method" to learn how to detect negative emotions from their customers and the best ways of responding to them.[72]

Two dominant leadership styles in an organization are transactional and transformational. Transactional leadership attempts to create employee satisfaction through negotiating for levels of performance or "bartering" for desired behaviors. Transformational leadership, in contrast, tries to raise the level of commitment of employees and creates greater trust and motivation.[73] Transformational leaders attempt to promote activities and behavior through a shared vision and common learning experiences. Both transformational and transactional leaders can positively influence the organizational climate.

Transformational leaders communicate a sense of mission, stimulate new ways of thinking, and enhance as well as generate new learning experiences. Transformational leadership considers the employees' needs and aspirations in conjunction with organizational needs. Therefore, transformational leaders have a stronger influence on coworker support and the building of an ethical culture than transactional leaders. Transformational leaders also build a commitment and respect for values that provide agreement on how to deal with ethical issues. Transformational ethical leadership is best suited for higher levels of ethical commitment among employees and strong stakeholder support for an ethical climate. A number of industry trade associations, such as the American Institute of Certified Public Accountants, Defense Industry Initiative on Business Ethics and Conduct, and the Ethics and Compliance Officer Association, are assisting companies in providing transformational leadership.[74] Research suggests that organizations with transformational leadership are more likely to be involved in corporate social responsibility (CSR) activities.[75]

Transactional leadership focuses on ensuring that the required conduct and procedures are implemented. The "barter" aspects of negotiations to achieve the desired outcomes result in a dynamic relationship between lenders and employees where reactions, conflicts, and crises influence the relationship more than ethical concerns. Transactional leaders produce employees who achieve a negotiated level of required ethical performance or compliance. As long as employees and leaders find the exchange mutually rewarding, the compliance relationship is likely to be successful. However, transactional leadership is best suited to quickly changing ethical climates or reacting to ethical problems or issues. After a major leadership scandal at Tyco resulted in the conviction of CEO Dennis Kozlowski and the removal of its board members, the need for quick action to pull up the struggling company was apparent. Without a quick turnaround—both in leadership and in the company's ethical conduct—Tyco may not have survived. Eric Pillmore was hired to be the senior vice president of corporate governance at Tyco. Pillmore had to institute ethics and corporate governance decisions quickly to aid in the turnaround. He helmed a new ethics program that changed leadership policies and gave him direct communications with the board of directors.[76]

Other leadership experts are classifying leaders into a new category based on how they model organizational values. Authentic leadership includes individuals who are passionate about the organization, display corporate values in their daily behavior at work, and establish enduring relationships with stakeholders. Kim Jordan, former CEO of craft brewery New Belgium Brewing (NBB), is an example of an authentic leader. Jordan constantly attempts to embody NBB's mission to "operate a profitable company which makes our love and talent manifest."[77] Jordan has also successfully aligned employees at NBB toward a shared goal of providing high quality products, improving sustainability, and embracing a stakeholder orientation.

Authentic leadership can also be learned. In fact, authentic leaders often learn by observing the successful leadership habits of other strong leaders.[78] Authentic leaders possess principle-centered power, meaning that they can handle difficult situations and are extremely dedicated toward their organizations.[79] They also exhibit organizational core values and incorporate these values into daily operations. This type of leadership should be the aim for all ethical leaders in an organization.

Leader-Follower Relationships[80]

Communication is the key toward establishing strong relationships between organizational leaders and employees. Leader–follower congruence takes place when leaders and their followers (employees) share the same organizational vision, ethical expectations, and objectives. It is important for ethical leaders to get employees to adopt shared organizational goals and values. If employees feel that the organizational leaders are unapproachable, this will create a major obstacle toward the achievement of the organization's vision and objectives.

On the other hand, leaders may take the opposite approach by micromanaging employees. Managing employees too closely will make them feel stifled and give them the feeling that the management does not trust them. Micromanagement in organizations is associated with lower morale, decreased productivity, and greater tendency to leave the company.[81] These disadvantages can be avoided when ethical leaders use communication to develop respectful relationships with employees. These more positive relationships tend to increase job satisfaction and employee commitment.[82]

Because organizational leaders are often managers or executives, they may not work very much with lower-level employees. This could create a sense of isolation in which the leader feels cut off from other employees. The more isolated organizational leaders are, the less connected they will be with employees—and the less likely they will be to detect organizational misconduct. Instead, ethical leaders must frequently interact with employees. This takes the form of not only speaking with employees but also listening to them and encouraging them to provide feedback. Often employees tend to want to avoid discussing ethical issues in the workplace. To get past this hesitation, ethical leaders must proactively communicate the firm's ethical values and develop a transparent workplace in which employees can feel comfortable expressing concerns.[83] We discuss communication in more detail in the next section. When organizational leaders and employees are on the same page, they are able to advance the organization's goals and culture more effectively.

Ethical Leadership Communication[84]

The development of an ethical culture is impossible without strong communication in the organization. If an organizational leader communicates through highly controlling speech that tolerates little criticism, employees will be reluctant to bring up any ethical issues or problems. However,

TABLE 6.7 Communication Skills for Becoming an Ethical Leader

1. Tell employees the truth about their conduct.
2. Listen to employee concerns about ethical issues they observe.
3. Engage in direct personal communication about appropriate conduct.
4. Use coaching to provide expectations about behavior.
5. Include performance feedback on ethical evaluations.
6. Be sure your feedback on ethical conduct is correct.
7. Always ask for feedback from employees.
8. Continue to develop your leadership skills.

ethical leaders understand the importance of frequent communication and interaction with employees. Table 6.7 shows how leaders can use communication to become better leaders.

An ethical culture must contain both transparency and strong mechanisms for reporting. Ethical leaders in the organization must create a transparent environment where ethics is frequently discussed. This helps remove the idea that discussing issues is a "taboo" topic. Reporting occurs when organizational leaders and their employees communicate. Most of the time, employees report to the leaders. However, ethical leaders should also be responsible for reporting crucial information to employees to promote an ethical workplace and advance organizational goals.

Reporting can be either formal or informal. Formal reports occur in contexts such as conferences and meetings. An important tool for formal reporting is an anonymous ethics hotline employees can use to report concerns. Informal reporting is no less important. It happens when ethical leaders interact with their employees on a less formal basis to keep them apprised of organizational policies, expectations, and decisions.[85] Informal discussions are incredibly important in identifying ethical risk areas as concerns are frequently expressed through casual conversations. Ethical leaders must recognize the importance of both formal and informal communication mechanisms.

Just as individuals can learn leadership skills, they can also learn how to communicate effectively. Effective communication skills are often developed and honed through training and experience. Organizational communication necessary for the establishment of an ethical culture includes the following: interpersonal communication, small group communication, nonverbal communication, and listening. Table 6.8 summarizes the four categories of communication.

Interpersonal Communication. Interpersonal communication is the most common form of communication. It occurs when two or more people communicate with one other.[86] A meeting between an employee and her supervisor is an example of interpersonal communication. Interpersonal communication (versus small group communication) is more intimate because fewer people are involved. This type of communication should

TABLE 6.8 Four Categories of Communication

Communication	Description
Interpersonal	When two or more people communicate with one another
Small Group	Communication that occurs in small groups
Nonverbal	Expressed through body language, actions, expressions, tone of voice, proximity, volume, rhythm, or any other way that is not oral or written
Listening	Actively listening to the other person's verbal or nonverbal behavior

occur often within an organization because it gives ethical leaders a greater chance to uncover ethical risk areas, create better employee relationships, and encourage feedback about the organization's ethical climate. For interpersonal communication to be effective, ethical leaders must show the employee respect and dignity to maintain a positive relationship—even during disciplinary procedures. Respecting the employee demonstrates that the leader cares about what the employee has to say. On the other hand, this does not mean that ethical leaders should ignore or compromise unethical employee conduct. It is less about placating an employee and more about showing him or her dignity as a person.

It is not uncommon for employees to feel intimidated by their superiors due to power differences.[87] An ethical leader can use communication to reassure employees as well as balance the interests of all relevant stakeholders.[88] A good way to reduce perceived power distances is for the ethical leader to be open and respectful to the employee instead of judgmental. This approach helps make employees feel more comfortable about bringing up ethical concerns.[89]

Communication is not always black-and-white. Like many ethical issues, there are times when the ethical leader will have different options on what to communicate, with some being more or less ethical than others. For instance, lying to a customer is clearly unacceptable, but white lies that do not damage stakeholders (such as complimenting an employee on a haircut despite the fact that it looks awful) may be permissible in some instances. Additionally, as the Rajat Gupta example from earlier demonstrates, communication that is not thought out carefully can have serious consequences. For Rajat Gupta, giving his friend Raj Rajaratnam from The Galleon Group nonpublic information directly violated the law. Ethical leaders will encounter numerous situations in which they must consider the ethical consequences of communication with stakeholders. Ethical leaders who strongly support ethical interpersonal communication can empower employees while promoting the organization's ethical objectives.

Small Group Communication. Small group communication is becoming increasingly important to ethical decision making.[90] Because ethical decision making does not occur in a silo, small group communication is often necessary to investigate and select the most ethical course of action. Small group communication has an advantage over interpersonal communication because it increases collaboration, explores more options, and allows employees to participate more in ethical decision making. Small groups generate a variety of perspectives on a particular issue, enabling ethical leaders to look at an issue from a number of different angles. This diversity of perspectives can lead to better solutions than if the leader had tried to arrive at the outcome individually.

Small groups also help to create checks and balances through accountability. An effective team holds individual members accountable for their contributions. For effective small group communication to take place, all small group members should feel comfortable with contributing input, understand the organization's ethical values, be trained in ethical communication, know how to listen to the input of other members, try to understand the other person's point of view, demonstrate a readiness to seek common agreement, investigate different alternatives, and commit to choosing the most ethical solution.[91]

However, ethical leaders should also recognize the limitations of small group communication. Sometimes routine group decision making can cause the group to overlook possibilities. It is also not uncommon for teams to experience groupthink or group polarization. Group polarization is the tendency to decide on a more extreme solution than an individual might choose on his or her own. A small group, for instance, might choose to pursue a riskier decision than would normally be chosen.[92] Groupthink is when group members feel pressured to conform to the group consensus, even if they personally disagree with it. This could result in a less-than-optimal ethical decision.

Nonverbal Communication. Non-spoken communication is a dimension of ethical communication that is just as important as spoken forms. Nonverbal communication is expressed through body language, actions, expressions, tone of voice, proximity, volume, rhythm, or any other way that is not oral or written. Nonverbal communication is important because it provides clues to an individual's emotional state.[93] Paralanguage, which includes the way we talk, can indicate whether a person is angry, sad, happy, etc. Often nonverbal communication is more trustworthy than spoken communication. For instance, although a person might say one thing, if his or her body language communicates something else, then the nonverbal communication is often a better indicator of what the person really means. This is because nonverbal communication is harder to control than the spoken word as it occurs in the subconscious.

Nonverbal communication helps to clarify ambiguous or confusing language, alerting the communicator about whether the recipient understands the communication. Because nonverbal communication provides important insights into a person's feelings, ethical leaders should pay careful attention to their employees' nonverbal cues. Sometimes permission to engage in unethical activities is granted by an expression or nodding of the head. They should also be careful to monitor their own nonverbal cues so they do not give off the wrong impression to employees.

Listening. Ethical communication is not limited to speaking or communicating nonverbally. It also involves actively listening to the other person's verbal or nonverbal behavior.[94] Communication between stakeholders cannot occur without listening. Organizational leaders who fail to listen can overlook ethical issues and fail to stop them before they snowball into a crisis. In fact, many employees have cited the failure to listen as one of their top complaints in the workplace,[95] so listening to employee concerns is crucial in advancing an ethical organizational culture. Without listening ethical leaders cannot learn important information from employee reports necessary in understanding the ethical climate of the firm.

On the other hand, listening to employees increases morale as well as their willingness to participate in the ethical decision making process. Effective listening skills create a sense of credibility and trustworthiness.[96] This supports a transparent organizational culture in which ethical concerns can be discussed freely. Because ethical leaders act as role models, their ability to listen encourages employees to do the same, further promoting the acceptance of the organization's ethical values.

SUMMARY

A strategic approach to ethical decisions will contribute to both business and society. To be socially responsible and promote legal and ethical conduct, an organization should develop an organizational ethics program by establishing, communicating, and monitoring ethical values and legal requirements that characterize its history, culture, industry, and operating environment. Most companies begin the process of establishing an organizational ethics program by developing a code of conduct, a formal statement that describes what the organization expects of its employees. A code should reflect senior management's desire for organizational compliance with values, rules, and policies that support an ethical climate. Codes of conduct help employees and managers address ethical dilemmas by prescribing or limiting specific activities.

Organizational ethics programs must be overseen by high-ranking persons reputed for their legal and ethical standards. Often referred to as ethics officers, these persons are responsible for assessing the needs and risks to be addressed in an organization-wide ethics program, developing and distributing a code of conduct, conducting training programs for employees, establishing and maintaining a confidential service to answer questions about ethical issues, making sure the company is in compliance with government regulations, monitoring and auditing ethical conduct, taking action on possible violations of the organization's code, and reviewing and updating the code. Instituting a training program and a system to communicate and educate employees about the firm's ethical standards is a major step in developing an effective ethics program.

Ethical compliance involves comparing the employee's ethical performance with the organization's ethical standards. Ethical compliance can be measured through employee observation, internal audits, reporting systems, and investigations. An internal system for reporting misconduct is especially useful. Employees who conclude that they cannot discuss current or potential unethical activities with co-workers or superiors and go outside the organization for help are known as whistle-blowers.

Consistent enforcement and necessary disciplinary action are essential to a functional ethical compliance program. Continuous improvement of the ethics program is necessary. Ethical leadership and a strong corporate culture in support of ethical behavior are required to implement an effective organizational ethics program.

Ethical leadership is particularly important to the organization's ethical culture. The most effective leaders are able to adapt their leadership styles—reward, coercive, legitimate, expert, and referent power—to the type of situation. These styles also have a major impact on the organization's corporate culture. Emotional intelligence is also an important component of ethical leadership.

There are many requirements for ethical leadership, including a passion for doing right, being competent and proactive, taking a holistic view of the ethics program, considering stakeholder interests, and acting as a role model. Ethical leadership leads to several benefits for the organization, including higher employee satisfaction and productivity as well as the promotion of ethical values. Leaders have different methods of leading. These methods, including transactional, transformational, and authentic, have different impacts on the organization's ethical culture. To promote an ethical culture, it is necessary for leaders to have strong positive relationships with the employees. An important way of maintaining these relationships is through communication. Ethical leaders should master interpersonal, small group, and nonverbal communication as well as listening. Being an effective communicator helps the ethical leader to develop positive employee relationships, uncover ethical issues, address employee concerns, and include employees in the ethical decision-making process.

Responsible Business Debate

Enron: The Capitalist Manifesto?

Issue: *Was it greed, corporate culture, or something else that caused the downfall of Enron?*

"Greed is good," said Gordon Gekko in the movie *Wall Street*—a mind-set that permeated the financial firms of Wall Street for decades. If this phrase is the capitalist manifesto, Enron is the archetype of this philosophy. The company marked both the height and the beginning of the end of that kind of corporate mentality.

Ken Lay, former CEO of Enron, has become the ultimate symbol of unethical conduct. He was the key executive involved in a massive fraud that destroyed thousands of jobs, life savings, as well as billions in shareholder value. Lay was put on trial and found guilty of "consciously avoiding knowing about wrongdoing" at Enron. Yet even after his conviction, Lay maintained that "with 30,000 employees in 30 countries and 200 executives at the vice president level," the corruption had existed without his knowledge. Most experts believe that ethical corporate cultures are a top-down phenomenon, and after the fall of Enron, most people felt Lay had to be held responsible.

Enron whistle blower Sherron Watkins asserted that Lay was indeed some distance from the fraud, and that Jeff Skilling, also CEO for a short time, was the one who had created a strong culture of greed where bad behavior was rewarded as long as it delivered profits for the company. Aggressive business practices included finding loopholes in regulation, extreme pressure to perform, periodic firing of the lowest performing employees, paying huge salaries and bonuses to those who did perform well (regardless of what ethical corners they may have cut), and bribing lawyers, bankers, accountants, and other so-called gatekeepers.

A culture of greed evolved where everyone took risks and expected a big reward. And yet, until his death Key Lay claimed the firm had strong values of respect, integrity, communication, and excellence, including a detailed code of ethics. How could these two corporate cultures—the greedy one created by Skilling and the ethical one Lay believed Enron had—exist in the same company? In the end, Lay stated internal controls

were not effective and that he believed the frauds of Andy Fastow, the former CFO, were what brought down the company. Sherron Watkins, although a key whistleblower, did not blame Lay. She thought that Jeff Skilling's charismatic and intimidating leadership had been the central problem. Watkins believes that if Skilling had been out of the picture, the fraud would not have happened. The Enron disaster created more new regulatory legislation and incited an ongoing debate about the nature of capitalism and what is an effective business ethics program.

There Are Two Sides To Every Issue:

1. Ethical misconduct was caused by the corporate culture at Enron.
2. Ethical misconduct at Enron was caused by Ken Lay's and Jeff Skilling's leadership.

Sources: Gerard Beenen and Jonathan Pinto, "Resisting Organizational Level Corruption: An Interview with Sherron Watkins," *Academy of Management Learning and Education* 8, no. 2 (June 2009): 275–289; O. C Ferrell and Linda Ferrell, "The Responsibility and Accountability of CEOs: The Last Interview with Ken Lay," *Journal of Business Ethics* 100, no. 2 (May 2011): 209–219; Fareed Zakaria, "Greed is Good (to a point)," *Newsweek,* June 22, 2009, p.41.

KEY TERMS

codes of conduct (p. 190)
ethics officer (p. 193)
whistle-blowers (p. 198)

voluntary practices (p. 200)
philanthropy (p. 201)
core practices (p. 201)

mandated boundaries (p. 201)
emotional intelligence (p. 210)

DISCUSSION QUESTIONS

1. How can an organization be socially responsible and promote legal and ethical conduct?
2. What are the elements that should be included in a strong ethics program?
3. What is a code of conduct and how can a code be communicated effectively to employees?
4. How and why are a training program and a communications system important in developing an effective ethics program?
5. What does ethical compliance involve and how can it be measured?
6. What role does leadership play in influencing organizational behavior?
7. Describe some of the skills needed to be an ethical leader.
8. List some of the benefits of ethical leadership.
9. Compare transformational leadership and transactional leadership.
10. Describe the four different types of communication.

EXPERIENTIAL EXERCISE

Visit the website of the Ethics and Compliance Officer Association (http://www.theecoa.org). What is the association's current mission and membership composition? Review the website to determine the issues and concerns that comprise the ECOA's most recent programs, publications, and research. What trends do you find? What topics seem most important to ethics officers today?

UP-CHARGING THE GOVERNMENT: WHAT WOULD YOU DO?

Robert Rubine flipped through his messages and wondered which call he should return first. It was only 3:30 P.M., but he felt as though he had been through a week's worth of decisions and worries. Mondays were normally busy, but this one was anything but normal. Robert's employer, Medic-All, is in the business of selling a wide array of medical supplies and equipment. The company's products range from relatively inexpensive items, like bandages, gloves, and syringes, to more costly items, such as microscopes, incubators, and examination tables. Although the product line is broad, it represents the "basics" required in most healthcare settings. Medic-All utilizes an inside sales force to market its products to private hospitals, elder care facilities, government healthcare institutions, and other similar organizations. The company employs 275 people and is considered a small business under government rules.

The inside sales force has the authority to negotiate on price, which works well in the highly competitive market of medical supplies and equipment. The salespeople are compensated primarily on a commission basis. The sales force and other employees receive legal training annually. All employees are required to sign Medic-All's code of ethics each year and attend an ethics training session. Despite the importance of the inside sales force, Medic-All has experienced a good deal of turnover in its sales management team. A new lead manager was hired about four months ago. Robert oversees the sales division in his role as vice president of marketing and operations.

Late Friday afternoon last week, Robert received word that two employees in the company's headquarters were selling products to the government at a higher price than they were selling them to other organizations. Both employees have been on the job for over two years and seem to be good performers. A few of their sales colleagues have complained to the lead sales manager about the high quarterly commissions that the two employees recently received. They insinuated that these commissions were earned unfairly by charging government-run hospitals high prices. A cursory review of their accounts showed that, in many instances, the government was paying more than other organizations. Under procurement rules, the government is supposed to pay a fair price, one that other cost-conscious customers would pay. When asked about the situation, the two employees said that the price offered was based on volume, so the pricing always varied from customer to customer.

Robert took the information to his boss, the president. The two of them discussed how these employees received legal and ethics training, signed the company code of ethics, and should have been knowledgeable about rules related to government procurement. The president said that these two salespeople sounded like "rogue employees," who committed acts without the approval of the management to increase their commissions. They also discussed many issues and scenarios, such as how to deal with the two salespeople, whether to continue the investigation and inform the government, what strategies to put in place for preventing similar problems in the future, how to protect the firm's good name, whether the company could face suspension from lucrative government business, and others. What would you do?

CHAPTER SEVEN

Employee Relations

Chapter Objectives

- To discuss employees as stakeholders

- To examine the economic, legal, ethical, and philanthropic responsibilities related to employees

- To describe an employer of choice and the employer of choice's relationship to social responsibility

Chapter Outline

Employee Stakeholders

Responsibilities to Employees

Strategic Implementation of Responsibilities to Employees

Beep Beep: CarMax is an Admired 'Road Runner'

In 1991 a few executives from Circuit City decided to test-launch a new business idea for a used car company termed Project X. Two years later CarMax was officially launched. CarMax makes it a priority to develop satisfied employees. The company has a decentralized structure where employees are encouraged to submit recommendations and develop leadership skills. Over the past 20 years, CarMax has grown to 150 stores with 22,000 employees. CarMax has been listed as one of Fortune magazine's "Best Companies to Work For" for over a decade.

CarMax uses RFID technology to track how long cars sit in the lot, extensive sales data to determine inventory needs accurately, and a flat commission compensation system so salespeople will promote the cars that best meet customer needs rather than trying to sell the most expensive car. Unlike other dealerships, CarMax offers no-haggle prices to consumers in order to simplify the car-buying process. It also reduces pressure on the salesperson. Employees at CarMax receive many benefits, including health benefits, paid time off, life insurance, and retirement savings plans. They also offer more non-traditional benefits, including smoking cessation assistance, tuition assistance, weight loss programs, and discounts on company products. CarMax's time away policy allows salaried associates to take as much time off as they deem necessary to meet work/life obligations.

Tom Folliard, the CEO of CarMax, learned that developing a decentralized corporate culture focusing on teamwork and employee empowerment generates positive results. CarMax uses teams to implement corporate strategies. It has a Consumer Insights team that focuses on improving customer experiences, an Operations Team that focuses on repair work, and an Inventory Strategy Team to focus on using data to improve purchasing in car auctions. CarMax also encourages teams for volunteerism. Its Volunteer Team-Builders who volunteer at nonprofits make those organizations eligible for grants from the CarMax Foundation.

CarMax prides itself on being founded on fundamental principles by which every store must abide. Values include respect, communication, customer focus, and teamwork. CarMax believes that employees who work together are able to place the customer first and serve their best interests. CEO Folliard stays accessible for employees through town hall meetings. He also visits sites that meet their sales goals and rewards them with steak dinners. Approximately 95 percent of employees claim that their workplace is friendly, 87 percent claim that management is easy to approach with concerns or other issues, and 80 percent say that they consistently look forward to going to work.

This type of culture enables employees to feel a sense of ownership in the company. Employees hold themselves to higher standards, resulting in higher work performance. In an industry that has a certain stigma about car salespeople and tactics, CarMax's focus on empowering employees to provide quality customer service and take ownership of the company has revolutionized the used car industry.[1]

CarMax illustrates the extent to which some firms consider the needs, wants, and characteristics of employees and other stakeholders in designing various business processes and practices. Although it is widely understood that employees are of great importance, beliefs about the extent and types of responsibilities that organizations should assume toward employees are likely to vary. For example, some managers are primarily concerned with economic and legal responsibilities, whereas proponents of the stakeholder interaction model would advocate for a broader perspective. As this chapter will show, a delicate balance of power, responsibility, and accountability resides in the relationships a company develops with its employees.

Because employee stakeholders are so important to the success of any company, this chapter is devoted to the employer-employee relationship. We explore the many issues related to the social responsibilities employers have to their employees, including the employee-employer contract, workforce reduction, wages and benefits, labor unions, health and safety, equal opportunity, sexual harassment, whistle-blowing, diversity, and work/life balance. Along the way, we discuss a number of significant laws that affect companies' human resources programs. Finally, we look at the concept of employer of choice and what it takes to earn that reputation and distinction.

EMPLOYEE STAKEHOLDERS

Think for a minute about the first job or volunteer position you held. What information were you given about the organization's strategic direction? How were you managed and treated by supervisors? Did you feel empowered to make decisions? How much training did you receive? The answers to these questions may reveal the types of responsibilities that employers have toward employees. If you worked in a restaurant, for example, training should have covered safety, cleanliness, and other health issues mandated by law. If you volunteered at a hospital, you may have learned about the ethical and economic considerations in providing healthcare for the uninsured or poor and the philanthropic efforts used to support the hospital financially. Although such issues may have seemed subtle or even unimportant at the time, they are related to the responsibilities that employees, government, and other stakeholders expect of employing organizations.

RESPONSIBILITIES TO EMPLOYEES

In her book *The Working Life: The Promise and Betrayal of Modern Work*, business professor Joanne B. Ciulla writes about the different types of work, the history of work, the value of work to a person's self-concept, the relationship between work and freedom, and as the title implies, the rewards and pitfalls that exist in the employee-employer relationship. Ciulla contends that two common phrases—"Get a job!" and "Get a life!"—are antithetical in today's society, meaning they seem diametrically opposed goals or values.[2] For the ancient Greeks, work was seen as the gods' way of punishing humans. Centuries later, Benedictine monks, who built farms, church abbeys, and villages, were considered the lowest order of monks because they labored. By the eighteenth century, the Protestant work ethic had emerged to imply that work was a method for discovering and creating a person.[3] Today, psychologists, families, and friends lament how work has become the primary source of many individuals' fulfillment, status, and happiness. Just as in the complicated history of work, the responsibilities, obligations, and expectations between employees and employers are also fraught with challenges and debates. In this section, we review the four levels of corporate social responsibilities as they relate to employees. Although we focus primarily on the responsibilities of employers to employees, we also acknowledge the role that employees have in achieving strategic social responsibility.

Economic Issues

The significance of the economic realm of employment is evidenced in the story of Malden Mills Industries. In 1995, just a few weeks before the winter holidays, the factory and office space at Malden Mills burned to the ground, injuring many workers. In an unusual move, CEO Aaron Feuerstein paid full wages, year-end bonuses, and benefits to employees while the buildings were reconstructed. Human resource managers set up a temporary job-training center, collected Christmas gifts for employees' children, and worked with community agencies to support employees and their families.[4] When economic factors forced Malden Mills through several employee layoffs in the late 1990s, employees were offered jobs at another plant and received career transition assistance. Feuerstein believed in an unwritten contract that considers the economic prospects of both employer and employees.

Several years later, Malden Mills filed for bankruptcy protection. Malden Mills' assets were sold and the company name was changed to Polartec, LLC. Polartec started with the original synthetic fleece developed by Malden and today offers 300 different fabrics. Customers include the U.S. military, L.L. Bean, Patagonia, and a number of small businesses. While Feuerstein is no longer at the company, his original product invention and commitment to social responsibility continues to exist at Polartec.[5]

Employee-Employer Contract As we discussed in Chapter 1, the recent history of social responsibility has brought many changes to bear on stakeholder relationships. One of the more dramatic shifts has been in the "contract" and mutual understanding that exist between employee and employer. At the beginning of the twenty-first century, many companies had to learn and accept new rules for recruiting, retaining, and compensating employees. For example, although employers held the position of power for many years, the new century brought record employment rates and the tightest job market in years. Huge salaries, signing bonuses, multiple offers, and flexible, not seniority-based, compensation plans became commonplace throughout the late 1990s. However, the first decade of the 2000s reversed this trend. Business scandals in the early 2000s, the World Trade Center attacks, and the latest recession brought a decline in lucrative employment opportunities and forced many firms to implement layoffs and other cost-cutting measures. At one point unemployment in the United States reached 10 percent. Pay raises, healthcare benefits, mental health coverage, retirement funding, paid maternity leave, and other benefits were reduced or costs were shifted to employees.[6] The Affordable Care Act shifted aspects of healthcare to the government.

psychological contract
Largely unwritten, it includes beliefs, perceptions, expectations, and obligations that make up the agreement between individuals and the organizations that employ them.

Regardless of salary, perks, and specific position, a **psychological contract** exists between an employee and employer. This contract is largely unwritten and includes the beliefs, perceptions, expectations, and obligations that make up the agreement between individuals and the organizations that employ them.[7] Details of the contract develop through communications, via interactions with managers and coworkers, and through perceptions of the corporate culture often formed by watching management and leadership. These interactions are especially important for new employees, who are trying to make sense of their new roles.[8] This contract, though informal, has a significant influence on the way employees act. When promises and expectations are not met, a psychological contract breach occurs, and employees may become less loyal, less trusting, inattentive to work, or otherwise dissatisfied with their employment situation.[9] On the other hand, when employers present information in a credible, competent, and trustworthy manner, employees are more likely to be supportive of and committed to the organization. Therefore, employers and employees are the two groups that contribute to the development, maintenance, and evolution of the psychological contract at work. Table 7.1 provides an overview of what is needed for employee commitment to the firm and employer promises to the employee.

TABLE 7.1 Psychological Contract between Employee and Employer

Employee Commitment	Employer Promises
Loyalty to the company	Respect from management
Teamwork and cooperation	Training opportunities
Compliance with policies	Opportunity to advance
Ethical leadership	Adequate benefits
Protection of company resources	Fairness in work assignments
Volunteer to address challenges	Ethical culture
Solve problems independently	Financial rewards
Trust and confidentiality	Work and family balance

An employee's perception of how well employer promises are kept provides for an ongoing psychological assessment of the employment relationship, including whether the employee will choose to leave the organization. The promises, or inducements, made by the organization are valuable to nearly all employees, but one study of over 5,000 employees indicates this rank order for their importance to employees: (1) social atmosphere, (2) career development opportunities, (3) job content, (4) work/life balance, and (5) financial rewards. This same sample ranked the organizational fulfillment of these promises as: (1) job content, (2) social atmosphere, (3) work/life balance, (4) career development opportunities, and (5) financial rewards. Based on these results, it is clear that career development opportunities deserve more attention from managers to strengthen the psychological contract and provide incentives for employee retention. Organizations that are able to implement the key promises so that employees view them as fulfilled reap rewards in terms of increased employee loyalty and decreased intentions to leave and/or search for a new employer.[10] Strong employee commitment is then revealed through their positive interactions with key stakeholders, especially customers, and ultimately has a positive influence on organizational success, as we discussed in Chapter 1.[11]

Just as in other stakeholder relationships, expectations in the employment psychological contract are subject to a variety of influences. This section discusses how the contract has ebbed and flowed over the last 100 years. Table 7.2 describes some examples of ways companies fulfill the psychological contract.

Until the early 1900s, the relationship between employer and employee was best characterized as a master-servant relationship.[12] In this view, there was a natural imbalance in power that meant employment was viewed as a privilege that included few rights and many obligations. Employees were expected to work for the best interests of the organization, even at the expense of personal and family welfare. At this time,

TABLE 7.2 Examples of Psychological Contracts

Company	Employee Promise
Google	Child care
Starbucks	Two years of college tuition
The Container Store	Extensive employee training and higher pay
SAS	Free on-site healthcare clinic
REI	Provides annual surveys to employees to get feedback on employee engagement
Salesforce.com	Employee recognition and reward programs for the company's salespeople
Wegman's Market	Strong growth opportunities in the company
W.L. Gore and Associates	Flat non-hierarchical business structure

most psychologists and management scholars believed that good leadership required aggressive and domineering behavior.[13] Images from Upton Sinclair's novel *The Jungle,* which we discuss briefly in the next chapter, characterized the extreme negative effects of this employment contract.[14]

In the 1920s and 1930s, employees assumed a relationship with an employer that was more balanced in terms of power, responsibilities, and obligations. This shift meant that employees and employers were coequals, and in legal terms, employees had many more rights than under the master-servant model.[15] Much of the employment law in the United States was enacted in the 1930s, when legislators passed laws related to child labor, wages, working hours, and labor unions.[16] Throughout the twentieth century, the employee-employer contract evolved along the coequals model, although social critics began to question the influence large companies had on employees.

In the 1950s, political commentator and sociologist C. Wright Mills criticized white-collar work as draining on employees' time, energy, and even personalities. He also believed that individuals with business power were apt to keep employees happy in an attempt to ward off the development of stronger labor unions and unfavorable government regulations.[17] A few years later, the classic book *The Organization Man* by William H. Whyte was published. This book examined the social nature of work, including the inherent conflict between belonging and contributing to a group on the job while maintaining a sense of independence and identity.[18] Organizational researchers and managers in the 1960s began to question authoritarian behavior and consider participatory management styles that assumed employees were motivated and eager to assume responsibility for work. A study by the U.S. Department of Health, Education, and Welfare in the early 1970s confirmed that employees wanted interesting work and a chance to demonstrate their skills. The report also recommended job redesign and managerial approaches that increased participation, freedom, and democracy at work.[19] By the 1980s, a family analogy was being used to describe the workplace. This implied strong attention to employee welfare and prompted the focus on business ethics that we explored in previous chapters. At the same time, corporate mission statements touted the importance of customers and employees, and *In Search of Excellence,* a best-selling book by Thomas J. Peters and business consultant Robert H. Waterman Jr., profiled companies with strong corporate cultures that inspired employees toward better work, products, and customer satisfaction.[20] The total quality management (TQM) movement increased empowerment and teamwork on the job throughout the 1990s and led the charge toward workplaces simultaneously devoted to employee achievement at work and home.[21]

Although there were many positive initiatives for employees in the 1990s, the confluence of economic progress with demands for global competitiveness convinced many executives of the need for cost cutting. For individuals accustomed to messages about the importance of employees to organizational success, workforce reduction was both unexpected and traumatic. These experiences effectively ended the loyalty- and commitment-based contract that employees had developed with employers. A study of young employees showed that their greatest psychological need in the workplace is security but that they viewed many employers as "terminators."[22] By the time Barack Obama became President of the United States in 2009, his administration was facing an economy in terrible condition. By mid-2009, over 8 million employees had been laid off and recessionary effects loomed large. The Conference Board, which publishes the Employment Trend Index (ETI) monthly, announced the index was declining faster than at any other time in the 35-year history of the ETI. Eight indicators contribute to the index, including claims for unemployment insurance, number of part-time workers due to economic reasons, consumer confidence, industrial production, manufacturing and trade sales, among others.

Although unemployment went as high as 10 percent during the last recession, the economy slowly began to recover. In 2015, unemployment had decreased to 5.3 percent, and the number of long-term unemployed individuals had been reduced. According to economists, it had been the slowest recovery in 55 years.[23] Unfortunately, recovery has proven slower for minorities and individuals between the ages of 18 and 29 years old. In the same year, unemployment for younger adults was 12.2 percent, more than double the national average.[24] There are concerns that the opportunities for employment based on education and skills has diminished. For example, many college graduates are underemployed in their first job.

Workforce Reduction At different points in a company's history, there are likely to be factors that beg the question, "How can we decrease our overall costs?"[25] In a highly competitive business environment, where new companies, customers, and products emerge and disappear every day, there is a continuous push for greater organizational efficiency and effectiveness. This pressure often leads to difficult decisions, including ones that require careful balance and consideration for the short-run survival and long-term vision of the company. This situation can create the need for **workforce reduction,** the process of eliminating employment positions. This process places considerable pressure on top management, causes speculation and tension among employees, and raises public ire about the role of business in society.[26]

workforce reduction
The process of eliminating employment positions.

There are several strategies that companies use to reduce overall costs and expenditures. For example, organizations may choose to reduce the number of employees, simplify products and processes, decrease quality and promises in service delivery, or develop some other mechanism for eliminating resources or nonperforming assets. Managers may find it difficult to communicate about cost reductions, as this message carries both emotional and social risk. Employees may wonder, "What value do I bring to the company?" and "Does anyone really care about my years of service?" Customers may inquire, "Can we expect the same level of service and product quality?" Governments and the community may ask, "Is this really necessary? How will it affect our economy?" For all of these questions, company leadership must have a clear answer. This response should be based on a thorough analysis of costs within the organizational system and how any changes are likely to affect business processes and outcomes. Intel reduced its global workforce by 11 percent. This is a decision many large technology companies are facing as newcomers in the industry gain more market share.[27]

In the last two decades, many firms chose to adopt the strategy that also creates the most anxiety and criticism—the reduction of the workforce. Throughout the 1990s, the numbers were staggering, as Sears eliminated 50,000 jobs and Kodak terminated nearly 17,000 people. Economic decline and financial scandals in the first decade of the twenty-first century also created a wave of layoffs. General Motors cut thousands of jobs and needed government assistance just to stay afloat. These actions effectively signaled the "end of the old contract" that employees had with employers.[28] This strategy, sometimes called *downsizing* or *rightsizing,* usually entails employee layoffs and terminations. In other cases, a company freezes new hiring, hopes for natural workforce attrition, offers incentives for early retirement, or encourages job sharing among existing employees. There are three different tactics for downsizing. We have already discussed workforce reduction through layoffs, retirement incentives, buyout packages, transfers, etc. Another tactic is organization redesign to eliminate organizational layers or functions and/or merge units. The third tactic is systemic redesign, which necessitates a major culture change, the simplification of processes, an emphasis on continuous improvement, and changes in employee responsibility.[29] The reality is that some employees will lose their current positions one way or another. Thus, although workforce reduction may be the strategy chosen to control and reduce costs, it may have profound implications for the welfare of employees, their families, and the economic prospects of a geographical region and other constituents, as well as for the corporation itself.

As with other aspects of business, it is difficult to separate financial considerations for costs from other obligations and expectations that develop between a company and its stakeholders. Depending on a firm's resource base and current financial situation, the psychological contract that exists between an employer and employee is likely to be broken through layoffs, and the social contract between employers, communities, and other groups may also be threatened. Downsizing makes the private relationship between employee and employer a public issue that affects many stakeholders and subsequently draws heavy criticism.[30] Fundamentally, top managers must recognize the many different types of "costs" that occur through workforce reduction. These include costs associated with future talent and leadership, company morale, perceptions on Wall Street, and rehiring needs.[31]

The impact of the workforce reduction process depends on a host of factors, including corporate culture, long-term plans, and creative calculations on both quantitative and qualitative aspects of the workplace.

Because few human resource directors and other managers have extensive experience in restructuring the workforce, there are several issues to consider before embarking on the process.[32] First, a comprehensive plan must be developed that takes into account the financial implications and qualitative and emotional toll of the reduction strategy. This plan may include a systematic analysis of workflow so that management understands how tasks are currently completed and how they will be completed after restructuring. Second, the organization should commit to assisting employees who must make a career transition as a result of the reduction process. To make the transition productive for employees, this assistance should begin as soon as management is aware of possible reductions. Through the Worker Adjustment and Retraining Notification Act (WARN), U.S. employers are required to give at least 60 days' advance notice if a layoff will affect 500 or more employees or more than one-third of the workforce.[33] Offering career assistance and other services is beneficial over the long term, as it demonstrates a firm's commitment to social responsibility.

External factors also play a role in how quickly employees find new work and affect perceptions of a firm's decision to downsize. Michigan launched an initiative called Community Ventures to connect the long-term unemployed with jobs. The initiative worked with individuals for up to one year, providing services such as literacy training, networking connections, and transportation. Since its beginning, the initiative has linked 3,000 hard-core unemployed to new jobs.[34] Those unemployed for long periods of time are likely to experience feelings of discouragement and low morale. On the other hand, individuals who are reemployed quickly, whether through company efforts or market circumstances, experience fewer negative economic and emotional repercussions. In addition, employees who are kept well informed of the downsizing decision process are more likely to retain positive attitudes toward the company, even if they experience job loss.[35]

Companies must be willing to accept the consequences of terminating employees. Although workforce reduction can improve a firm's financial performance, especially in the short run, there are costs to consider, including the loss of intellectual capital.[36] The years of knowledge, skills, relationships, and commitment that employees develop cannot be easily replaced or substituted, and the loss of one employee can cost a firm between $50,000 and $100,000.[37] So although workforce reduction lowers costs, it often results in lost intellectual capital, strained customer relationships, negative media attention, and other issues that drain company resources. Employees who retain their jobs may suffer guilt, depression, or stress as a result of the reduction in the workforce. Thus, a long-term understanding of the qualitative and quantitative costs and benefits should guide downsizing decisions.[38]

Although workforce reduction is a corporate decision, it is also important to recognize the potential role of employees in these decisions. Whereas hiring and job growth reached a frantic pace by the late 1990s, a wave of downsizings in the early 1990s and 2000s meant that some individuals had embraced the reality of having little job security. Instead of becoming cynical or angry, employees may have reversed roles and began asking, "What is this company doing for me?" and "Am I getting what I need from my employer?" Employees of all types began taking more responsibility for career growth, demanding balance in work and personal responsibilities, and seeking opportunities in upstart firms and emerging industries. Thus, although workforce reduction has negative effects, it has also shifted the psychological contract and power between employee and employer. The following suggestions examine how individuals can potentially mitigate the onset and effects of downsizing.

First, all employees should understand how their skills and competencies affect business performance. Not recognizing and improving this relationship makes it more difficult to prove their worth to managers faced with workforce reduction decisions. Second, employees should strive for cost-cutting and conservation strategies regardless of the employer's current financial condition. This is a workforce's first line of defense against layoffs—assisting the organization in reducing its costs before drastic measures are necessary. Third, today's work environment requires that most employees fulfill diverse and varying roles. For example, manufacturing managers must understand the whole product development and introduction process, ranging from engineering to marketing and distribution activities. Thus, another way of ensuring worth to the company, and to potential employers, is through an employee's ability to navigate different customer environments and organizational systems. It is now necessary to "cross-train," show flexibility, and learn the entire business, even if a company does not offer a formal program for gaining this type of experience and exposure. Although this advice may not prevent workforce reduction, it does empower employees against some of its harmful effects. Through laws and regulations, the government has also created a system for ensuring that employees are treated properly on the job. The next section covers the myriad of laws that all employers and employees should consider both in daily and strategic decisions.

Legal Issues

Employment law is a very complex and evolving area. Most large companies and organizations employ human resource managers and legal specialists who are trained in the detail and implementation of specific statutes related to employee hiring, compensation, benefits, safety, and other areas. Smaller organizations often send human resource managers to workshops and conferences to keep abreast of legal imperatives in the workplace. Table 7.3 lists the major federal laws that cover employer responsibilities with respect to wages, labor unions, benefits, health and safety, equal opportunity, and other areas. Until the early 1900s, employment was primarily governed by the concept of **employment at will,** a common-law doctrine that allows either the employer or the employee to terminate the relationship at any time as long as it does not violate an employment

employment at will
A common-law doctrine until the early 1900s that allows either the employer or the employee to terminate the relationship at any time as long as it does not violate an employment contract.

TABLE 7.3 Major Employment Laws

Act (Date Enacted)	Purpose
National Labor Relations Act (1935)	Established the rights of employees to engage in collective bargaining and to strike.
Fair Labor Standards Act (1938)	Established minimum wage and overtime pay standards, recordkeeping, and child labor standards for most private and public employers.
Equal Pay Act (1963)	Protects women and men who perform substantially equal work in the same establishment from gender-based wage discrimination.
Civil Rights Act, Title VII (1964)	Prohibits employment discrimination on the basis of race, national origin, color, religion, and gender.
Age Discrimination in Employment Act (1967)	Protects individuals aged 40 or older from age-based discrimination.
Occupational Safety and Health Act (1970)	Ensures safe and healthy working conditions for all employees by providing specific standards that employers must meet.
Employee Retirement Income Security Act (1974)	Sets uniform minimum standards to assure that employee benefit plans are established and maintained in a fair and financially sound manner.
Americans with Disabilities Act (1990)	Prohibits discrimination on the basis of physical or mental disability in all employment practices and requires employers to make reasonable accommodation to make facilities accessible to and usable by persons with disabilities.
Family and Medical Leave Act (1993)	Requires certain employers to provide up to 12 weeks of unpaid, job-protected leave to eligible employees for certain family and medical reasons.
Uniformed Services Employment and Reemployment Rights Act (1994)	The pre-service employer must reemploy service members returning from a period of service in the uniformed services if those service members meet five criteria.
Patient Protection and Affordable Care Act (2010)	Makes healthcare affordable and universal so all employees can have access to it.

Source: U.S. Department of Labor, "Employment Law Guide," http://www.dol.gov/compliance/guide/index.htm (accessed June 21, 2016).

contract. Today, many states still use the employment-at-will philosophy, but laws and statutes may limit total discretion in this regard.[39] The following discussion highlights employment laws and their fundamental contribution to social responsibility.[40]

Wages and Benefits After the Great Depression, the U.S. Congress enacted a number of laws to protect employee rights and extend employer responsibilities. The Fair Labor Standards Act (FLSA) of 1938 prescribed minimum wage and overtime pay, recordkeeping, and child labor standards for most private and public employers. The minimum wage is set by the federal government and is periodically revised, although states have the option to adopt a higher standard. For example, the federal minimum wage was raised from $6.55 per hour to $7.25 per hour in 2009. In 2013, the Fair Minimum Wage Act was introduced and it proposed that the minimum wage be raised to $10.10 per hour but has not been passed yet. Various members of Congress, including the U.S. Chamber of Commerce, have proposed a $15 per hour minimum wage. On the other hand, Republicans in Congress and other opponents are worried that a substantial minimum wage increase would lead to job loss or higher prices for consumers. The nonprofit Empire Center for New York State Policy has concerns that increasing the minimum wage too much will lead to increased costs for businesses, therefore having a major detrimental impact on smaller businesses.[41]

As demonstrated, minimum wage remains a highly debated topic. Many workers are not earning enough to make ends meet. Critics of the proposal say that it is not the most effective way to address the plight of those workers living in poverty. The bill did not receive enough votes from Congress, and the debate continues.[42] The majority of states abide by the federal standard, although Alaska, California, Oregon, Vermont, Washington, and several others have adopted a higher minimum wage. Most employees who work more than 40 hours per week are entitled to overtime pay in the amount of one and a half times their regular pay. There are exemptions to the overtime pay provisions for four classes of employees: executives, outside salespeople, administrators, and professionals.[43]

The FLSA also affected child labor, including the provision that individuals under the age of 14 are allowed to do only certain types of work, such as delivering newspapers and working in their parents' businesses. Children under age 16 are often required to get a work permit, and their work hours are restricted so that they can attend school. Persons between the ages of 16 and 18 are not restricted in terms of number of work hours, but they cannot be employed in hazardous or dangerous positions. Although passage of the FLSA was necessary to eliminate abusive child labor practices, its restrictions became somewhat problematic during the booming economy of the late 1990s, when unemployment rates were extremely low in the United States. Some business owners may have even considered lobbying for relaxed standards in very restrictive states so that they could hire more teens. In addition, general FLSA restrictions have created problems in implementing job-sharing and flextime arrangements with employees who are paid on an hourly basis.[44]

Two other pieces of legislation relate to employer responsibilities for benefits and job security. The Employee Retirement Income Security Act (ERISA) of 1974 set uniform minimum standards to assure that employee benefit plans are established and maintained in a fair and financially sound manner. ERISA does not require companies to establish retirement pension plans; instead, it developed standards for the administration of plans that management chooses to offer employees. A key provision relates to **vesting,** the legal right to pension plan benefits. In general, contributions an employee makes to the plan are vested immediately, whereas company

vesting
The legal right to pension plan benefits.

contributions are vested after five years of employment. ERISA is a very complicated aspect of employer responsibilities because it involves tax law, financial investments, and plan participants and beneficiaries.[45]

The Family and Medical Leave Act (FMLA) of 1993 requires certain employers to provide up to 12 weeks of unpaid, job-protected leave to eligible employees for certain family and medical reasons. However, if the employee is paid in the top 10 percent of the entire workforce, the employer does not have to reinstate him or her in the same or comparable position.[46] Typical reasons for this type of leave include the birth or adoption of a child, personal illness, or the serious health condition of a close relative. The FMLA applies to employers with fifty or more employees, which means that its provisions do not cover a large number of U.S. employees. In addition, employees must have worked at least one year for the firm and at least 25 hours per week during the past year before the FMLA is required.

Labor Unions In one of the earliest pieces of employment legislation, the National Labor Relations Act (NLRA) of 1935 legitimized the rights of employees to engage in collective bargaining and to strike. This law was originally passed to protect employee rights, but subsequent legislation gave more rights to employers and restricted the power of unions. Before the NLRA, many companies attempted to prohibit their employees from creating or joining labor organizations. Employees who were members of unions were often discriminated against in terms of hiring and retention decisions. This act sought to eliminate the perceived imbalance of power between employers and employees. Through unions, employees gained a collective bargaining mechanism that enabled greater power on several fronts, including wages and safety.[47] For example, in a series of strikes against Walmart, members of the Organization for United Respect at Walmart (OUR Walmart), founded by the United Food and Commercial Workers (UFCW) union, called for the retailer to offer employees $25,000 per year, plenty of hours for workers to support their families, no more retaliation against those making these requests, and fair treatment to pregnant workers. When the strikes were ongoing, they had the following results: Walmart agreed to a $21 million settlement regarding wages in one of its warehouses, the U.S. government initiated prosecutions regarding illegal firing of workers, and the city of Portland cut ties with the retailer. In order to avoid continuous labor strikes, the company will have to address employees' needs more completely.

Health and Safety In 1970, the Occupational Safety and Health Act (OSHA) sought to ensure safe and healthy working conditions for all employees by providing specific standards that employers must meet. This act led to the development of the Occupational Safety and Health Administration, also known as OSHA, the agency that oversees the regulations intended to make U.S. workplaces the safest in the world. In its more than 40 years of existence, OSHA has made great strides to improve and maintain the health and safety of employees. For example, since the 1970s, the workplace death rate in the United States has been reduced by more than 65 percent, and the agency's initiatives in cotton dust and lead standards have reduced disease in several industries. The agency continues to innovate and uses feedback systems for improving its services and standards. As more Spanish-speaking workers entered the workforce, officials were concerned about their understanding of the agency and their rights in the workplace. In response, OSHA translated a variety of its documents into Spanish and posted them onto a prominent place on its website.[48] OSHA has the authority to enter and make inspections of most employers. Because of its far-reaching power and unwarranted inspections made in the 1970s, the agency's relationship with business has not always been positive. For example, OSHA proposed rules to increase employer responsibility for **ergonomics,** the design, arrangement, and use of equipment to maximize productivity and minimize fatigue and physical discomfort. Without proper attention to ergonomics, employees may suffer injuries and long-term health issues as a result of work motion and tasks. Many business and industry associations opposed the proposal, citing enormous costs and unsubstantiated claims. A federal ergonomics rule was established under the Clinton presidency but was repealed by President George W. Bush. However, the issue continues to be raised on the regulatory agenda. OSHA has focused its ergonomics efforts by developing guidelines for each industry, while individual states, such as Alaska, Washington, and California, have implemented their own ergonomics rules.[49] Despite differences between this federal agency and some states and companies on a number of regulations, most employers are required to display the poster shown in Figure 7.1 or one required by their state safety and health agency. Gildan Activewear Inc., a manufacturer and marketer of clothing, developed a program to improve ergonomic practices and reduce injuries. This is particularly important since repetitive actions in the sewing industry are common and prolonged repetitive actions can lead to injury over time.[50]

ergonomics
The design, arrangement, and use of equipment to maximize productivity and minimize fatigue and physical discomfort.

An emerging issue in the area of health and safety is the increasing rate of violence in the workplace. According to OSHA, 2 million workers are assaulted and over 400 are murdered in the workplace every year.[51] A recent survey of Fortune 1000 companies indicates that workplace violence is one of the most important security issues they face, costs up to $36 billion annually, and results in three deaths daily and thousands of injuries each year. The fourth leading cause of all occupational fatalities is homicide.[52]

The Society for Human Resource Management (SHRM) has identified four types of workplace violence: (1) crimes committed by strangers and intruders in the workplace; (2) acts committed by nonemployees, such as customers, patients, students, and clients; (3) violence committed by coworkers; and (4) incidences involving those with a personal relationship with an employee.[53] Taxi drivers and clerks working late-night shifts at convenience stores are often subject to the first type of violence. Airline attendants are increasingly experiencing the second category of workplace

FIGURE 7.1 Job Safety and Health Protection Poster

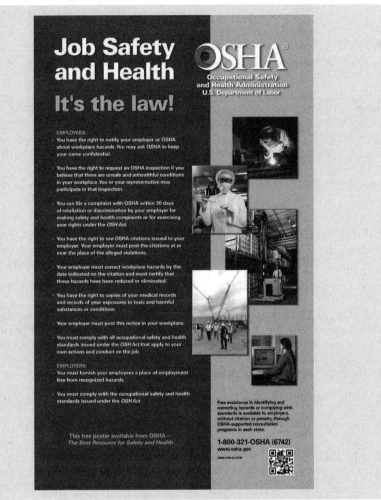

Source: Occupational Safety and Health Administration, "OSHA's Free Workplace Poster," http://www.osha.gov/Publications/osha3165low-res.pdf (accessed June 28, 2014).

violence when passengers become unruly, drunk, or otherwise violent while in flight. Nurses and customer service associates also experience verbal and sometimes physical violence from angry patients and customers.

Many instances abound of employee-related workplace violence. A worker at a lawn care company in Kansas opened fire, killing three people and injuring an additional 16. The shooter himself was shot by a policeman.[54] Today, many organizations are conducting workplace shooter trainings in order to decrease the number of fatalities in these types of violent situations. Although crimes reflect general problems in society, employers have a responsibility to assess risks and provide security, training, and safeguards to protect employees and other stakeholders from such acts. Companies often purchase insurance policies to cover the costs of workplace violence, including business interruption, psychological counseling, informant rewards, and medical claims related to injuries. One expert suggests that all organizations publish and communicate an anti-violence policy and make employees and managers aware of antecedents to workplace violence.[55]

Equal Opportunity Title VII of the Civil Rights Act of 1964 prohibits employment discrimination on the basis of race, national origin, color, religion, and gender. This law is fundamental to employees' rights to join and advance in an organization according to merit rather than one of the characteristics just mentioned. For example, employers are not permitted to categorize jobs as only for men or women unless there is a reason gender is fundamental to the tasks and responsibilities. Additional laws passed in the 1970s, 1980s, and 1990s were also designed to prohibit discrimination related to pregnancy, disabilities, age, and other factors. The Americans with Disabilities Act prohibits companies from discriminating on the basis of physical or mental disability in all employment practices and requires them to make facilities accessible to and usable by persons with disabilities. The Pregnancy Discrimination Act, now 30 years old, was created to help protect the rights of mothers and mothers-to-be in the workplace. The act has been modified many times since its inception. As a result, the number of pregnancy discrimination complaints filed with the Equal Employment Opportunity Commission (EEOC) has continually decreased over the years.[56] Figure 7.2 depicts the number of complaints and resolutions on pregnancy discrimination cases from 2012 through 2015.

These legal imperatives require that companies formalize employment practices to ensure that no discrimination is occurring. Thus, managers must be fully aware of the types of practices that constitute discrimination and work to ensure that hiring, promotion, annual evaluation, and other procedures are fair and based on merit. The spread of HIV and AIDS has prompted multinational firms with operations in Africa to distribute educational literature and launch prevention programs. Some companies work with internal and external stakeholders and even fund medical facilities that help prevent the disease and treat HIV/AIDS patients. Another component to their initiatives involves education on fair treatment of employees with the disease. Multinational companies in Mexico produced a written commitment to eliminate the stigma and discrimination often surrounding HIV/AIDS in the workplace.[57]

To ensure that they build balanced workforces, many companies have initiated affirmative action programs, which involve efforts to recruit, hire, train, and promote qualified individuals from groups that have traditionally been discriminated against on the basis of race, sex, or other characteristics. Coca-Cola established a program to create a level foundation for all employees to have access to the same information and

FIGURE 7.2 Growth in Filings and Resolutions of Pregnancy Discrimination Act Complaints to the EEOC

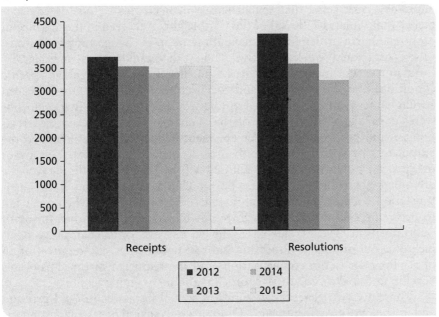

Source: U.S. Equal Employment Opportunity Commission, "Pregnancy Discrimination Charges," http://www.eeoc.gov/eeoc/statistics/enforcement/pregnancy_new.cfm (accessed June 21, 2016).

development opportunities.[58] A key goal of these programs is to reduce any bias that may exist in hiring, evaluating, and promoting employees. A special type of discrimination, sexual harassment, is also prohibited through Title VII.

Sexual Harassment The flood of women into the workplace during the last half of the twentieth century brought new challenges and opportunities for organizations. Although harassment has probably always existed in the workplace, the presence of both genders in roughly equal numbers changed norms and expectations of behavior. When men dominated the workplace, photos of partially nude women or sexually suggestive materials may have been posted on walls or in lockers. Today, such materials could be viewed as illegal if they contribute to a work environment that is intimidating, offensive, or otherwise interferes with an employee's work performance. The U.S. government indicates the nature of this illegal activity: unwelcome sexual advances, requests for sexual favors, and other verbal or physical conduct of a sexual nature constitutes **sexual harassment** when submission to or rejection of this conduct explicitly or implicitly affects an individual's employment, unreasonably interferes with an individual's work performance, or creates an intimidating, hostile, or offensive work environment.[59]

sexual harassment
Unwelcome sexual advances, requests for sexual favors, and other verbal or physical conduct of a sexual nature which when submitted to or rejected explicitly or implicitly affects an individual's employment, unreasonably interferes with an individual's work performance, or creates an intimidating, hostile, or offensive work environment.

Prior to 1986, sexual harassment was not a specific violation of federal law in the United States. In *Meritor Savings Bank v. Vinson,* the U.S. Supreme Court ruled that sexual harassment creates a "hostile environment" that violates Title VII of the Civil Rights Act, even in the absence of economic harm or demand for sexual favors in exchange for promotions, raises, or related work incentives.[60] In other countries, sexual harassment in the workplace is considered an illegal act, although the specific conditions may vary by legal and social culture. Until recently, Mexican sexual harassment law protected public sector employees only if their jobs were jeopardized on the basis of the exchange of sexual favors or relations. A bill proposed by former President Felipe Calderon expanded the parameters of such an offense to include private businesses. Employees of Mexican public and private entities will be fired if found guilty of the offending behavior.[61] In the European Union (EU), sexual harassment legislation focuses on the liability that employers carry when they fail to promote a workplace culture free of harassment and other forms of discrimination. The EU has strengthened its rules on sexual harassment, including definitions of direct and indirect harassment, the removal of an upper limit on victim compensation, and the requirement that businesses develop and make "equality reports" available to employees.[62]

There are two general categories of sexual harassment: quid pro quo and hostile work environment.[63] **Quid pro quo sexual harassment** is a type of sexual extortion where there is a proposed or explicit exchange of job benefits for sexual favors. For example, telling an employee, "You will get the promotion if you spend the weekend with me in Las Vegas," is a direct form of sexual harassment. Usually, the person making such a statement is in a position of authority over the harassed employee, and thus, the threat of job loss is real. One incident of quid pro quo harassment may create a justifiable legal claim. **Hostile work environment sexual harassment** is less direct than quid pro quo harassment and can involve epithets, slurs, negative stereotyping, intimidating acts, graphic materials that show hostility toward an individual or group, and other types of conduct that affect the employment situation. For example, at one automobile manufacturing plant, male employees drew inappropriate sexually explicit pictures on cars before they were painted. This was found to be sexual harassment. An e-mail message containing sexually explicit jokes that is broadcast to employees could be viewed as contributing to a hostile work environment. Some hostile work environment harassment is nonsexual, meaning the harassing conduct is based on gender without explicit reference to sexual acts. For example, in *Campbell v. Kansas State University* (1991), the courts found repeated remarks about women "being intellectually inferior to men" to be part of a hostile environment. Unlike quid pro quo cases, one incident may not justify a legal claim. Instead, the courts will examine a range of acts and circumstances to determine if the work environment was intolerable and the victim's job performance was impaired.[64] From a social responsibility perspective, a key issue in both types of sexual harassment is the employing organization's knowledge and tolerance for these

quid pro quo sexual harassment
A type of sexual extortion where there is a proposed or explicit exchange of job benefits for sexual favors.

hostile work environment sexual harassment
Less direct than quid pro quo harassment, it involves epithets, slurs, negative stereotyping, intimidating acts, graphic materials that show hostility toward an individual or group, and other types of conduct that affect the employment situation.

types of behaviors. A number of court cases have shed more light on the issues that constitute sexual harassment and organizations' responsibility in this regard.

In *Harris v. Forklift Systems* (1993), Teresa Harris claimed that her boss at Forklift Systems made suggestive sexual remarks, asked her to retrieve coins from his pants pocket, and joked that they should go to a motel to "negotiate her raise." Courts at the state level threw out her case because she did not suffer major psychological injury. The U.S. Supreme Court overturned these decisions and ruled that employers can be forced to pay damages even if the worker suffered no proven psychological harm. This case brought about the "reasonable person" standard in evaluating what conduct constitutes sexual harassment. From this case, juries now evaluate the alleged conduct with respect to commonly held beliefs and expectations.[65]

Several firms have been embroiled in sexual harassment suits. For example, Sterling Jewelers, parent company of Kay Jewelers and Jared the Galleria of Jewelry, is being accused of discrimination and sexual harassment for a period of over ten years. If the class-action suit involving over 40,000 women is approved, the company may have to pay thousands in punitive damages and fines. At least 12 women claim they were underpaid in comparison to men and faced lewd harassment that became unbearable.[66] In another case, a jury awarded the victim $95 million in damages due to years of experiencing severe sexual harassment by a manager at furniture rent-to-own store, Aarons Inc. The manager's behavior encouraged other male employees to harass the victim, creating a hostile workplace. To make matters worse, the company neglected to respond to the victim when she left a message on their hotline.[67]

U.S. Supreme Court decisions on sexual harassment cases indicate that (1) employers are liable for the acts of supervisors; (2) employers are liable for sexual harassment by supervisors that culminates in a tangible employment action (loss of job, demotion, etc.); (3) employers are liable for a hostile environment created by a supervisor but may escape liability if they demonstrate that they exercised reasonable care to prevent and promptly correct any sexually harassing behavior and that the plaintiff employee unreasonably failed to take advantage of any preventive or corrective measures offered by the employer; and (4) claims of hostile environment sexual harassment must be severe and pervasive to be viewed as actionable by the courts.[68]

Much like the underlying philosophy of the Federal Sentencing Guidelines for Organizations that we discussed in earlier chapters, these decisions require top managers in organizations to take the detection and prevention of sexual harassment seriously. To this end, many firms have implemented programs on sexual harassment. To satisfy current legal standards and set a higher standard for social responsibility, employees, supervisors, and other close business partners should be educated on the company's zero-tolerance policy against harassment. Employees must also be educated on the policy prohibiting harassment, including the types of behaviors that constitute harassment, how offenders will be punished, and what employees should do if they experience harassment. Just like an organizational compliance program, employees must be assured of confidentiality and no retaliation for reporting harassment.

Training on sexual harassment should be balanced in terms of legal definitions and practical tips and tools. Although employees need to be aware of the legal issues and ramifications, they also may need assistance in learning to recognize and avoid behaviors that may constitute quid pro quo harassment, create a hostile environment, or appear to be retaliatory in nature. In fact, retaliation claims have more than doubled since the early 1990s, prompting many companies to incorporate this element into sexual harassment training. Finally, employees should be aware that same-sex conduct may also constitute sexual harassment.[69] Sexual harassment from women to their male subordinates is yet another issue. One law enforcement officer in Texas won a lawsuit against his female boss after claiming that she frequently wanted sexual favors and touched him inappropriately.[70] Table 7.4 lists facts about sexual harassment that should be used in company communication and training on this workplace issue.

TABLE 7.4 Sexual Harassment in the Workplace

Sexual harassment is a form of sex discrimination that violates Title VII of the Civil Rights Act of 1964.
Unwelcome sexual advances, requests for sexual favors, and other verbal or physical conduct of a sexual nature constitute sexual harassment when submission to or rejection of this conduct explicitly or implicitly affects an individual's employment, unreasonably interferes with an individual's work performance, or creates an intimidating, hostile, or offensive work environment.
Sexual harassment can occur in a variety of circumstances including but not limited to the following: • The victim as well as the harasser may be a woman or a man. The victim does not have to be of the opposite sex.   • The harasser can be the victim's supervisor, an agent of the employer, a supervisor in another area, a coworker, or a nonemployee.   • The victim does not have to be the person harassed but could be anyone affected by the offensive conduct.   • Unlawful sexual harassment may occur without economic injury to or discharge of the victim.   • The harasser's conduct must be unwelcome.
It is helpful for the victim to inform the harasser directly that the conduct is unwelcome and must stop. The victim should use any employer complaint mechanism or grievance system available.   When investigating allegations of sexual harassment, the Equal Employment Opportunity Commission looks at the whole record: the circumstances, such as the nature of the sexual advances, and the context in which the alleged incidents occurred. A determination of the allegations is made from the facts on a case-by-case basis.

Source: U.S. Equal Employment Opportunity Commission, "Facts About Sexual Harassment," http://www.eeoc.gov/eeoc/publications/fs-sex.cfm (accessed June 21, 2016).

Whistle-blowing An employee who reports individual or company wrong-doing to either internal or external sources is considered a whistle-blower.[71] Whistle-blowers usually focus on issues or behaviors that need corrective action, although managers and other employees may not appreciate reports that expose company weaknesses, raise embarrassing questions, or otherwise detract from organizational tasks. Although not all whistle-blowing activity leads to an extreme reaction, whistle-blowers have been retaliated against, demoted, fired, and subject to even worse consequences as a result of their actions.[72] For example, Eddie Garcia, energy specialist at Santa Fe County in New Mexico, was accused of grand larceny and was fired from his job after pointing out improper conduct on the part of an exclusive government contractor. Garcia revealed to his supervisors that the contractor had double billed the county and was failing to obtain required permits for work. When they did not respond, he expressed his concerns to the media, which spurred retaliation from his employer. In the end, the charges against Garcia were dropped and he was awarded $180,000 in settlement fees, but he suffered personal and professional hardship for five years as a result.[73]

As discussed in Chapter 4, whistle-blowers have legal protections. The federal government and most state governments in the United States have enacted measures to protect whistle-blowers from retaliation. If you recall, the Whistleblower Protection Act of 1986 shields federal employees from retaliatory behavior; the Sarbanes-Oxley Act provides solid protection to whistle-blowers and strong penalties for those who retaliate against them; and other legislation such as the Dodd-Frank Act has provisions to reward whistle-blowers for revealing illegal behavior. Even with this protection, most reported misconduct to the government does not result in an investigation. Most internal and external whistle-blowers are not legal experts and use their own judgment about an issue. Therefore, it is important to know the facts and conduct research before reporting.

Ethical Issues

Laws are imperative for social responsibility. The ethical climate of the workplace, however, is more values-driven and dependent on top management leadership and corporate culture. In this section, we examine several trends in employment practices that have not fully reached the legal realm. Company initiatives in these areas indicate a corporate philosophy or culture that respects and promotes certain ethical values.

Training and Development As discussed in the business ethics chapter, organizational culture and the associated values, beliefs, and norms operate on many levels and affect a number of workplace practices. Organizations should value employees as individuals, not just functional units to do work. Firms with this ethical stance fund initiatives to develop employees' skills, knowledge, and other personal characteristics. Although this development is linked to business strategy and aids the employer, it also demonstrates a commitment to the future of the employee and his or her interests. Jiffy

Lube has been listed as number one for *Training Magazine's* list of top 125 employee training programs. It was selected for focused approach on training on topics including customer service, leadership, and new services. Its training program is credited with helping the organization increase stores by 900 percent and approval ratings by 93 percent.[74]

Professionals also appreciate and respect a training and development focus from their employers. For example, the University of California, Berkeley incorporates an Individual Development Plan (IDP) component to their professional employee training program. The IDP is a one-on-one mentoring process between the employee and supervisor in which they discuss setting specific goals, how to reach them, and overcoming obstacles.[75] These organizations are finding many benefits from employee training and development, including stronger employee recruitment and retention strategies. Indeed, there is a link between investments in employees and the amount of commitment, job satisfaction, and productivity demonstrated by them. Happier employees tend to stay with their employer and to better serve coworkers, customers, and other constituents, which has a direct bearing on the quality of relationships and financial prospects of a firm. Leadership training is also critical, as the main reason employees leave a company is because of poor or unskilled management and leadership, not salary, benefits, or related factors. In exit interviews, departing employees often mention their desire for more meaningful feedback and steady communication with managers.[76]

Employees recognize when a company is diligently investing in programs that not only improve operations but also increase empowerment and provide new opportunities to improve knowledge and grow professionally. Through formal training and development classes, workers get a better sense of where they fit and how they contribute to the overall organization. This understanding empowers them to become more responsive, accurate, and confident in workplace decisions. Training also increases ethical decision-making skills, accountability, and responsibility, a situation most employees prefer to micromanaging or "hand-holding." All these effects contribute to the financial and cultural health of an organization.[77] Thus, a commitment to training enables a firm to enhance its organizational capacity to fulfill stakeholder expectations.

Training and development activities require resources and the commitment of all managers to be successful. For example, a departmental manager must be supportive of an employee using part of the workday to attend a training session on a new software package. At the same time, the organization must pay for the training, regardless of whether it uses inside or outside trainers and develops in-house materials or purchases them from educational providers. A study by the American Society for Training and Development indicates that, on average, employers in the U.S. spend about $1,182 per employee on training every year, and employees engaged in approximately 31 hours of annual learning. The survey also tracked the major topics offered to employees. Over 35 percent of material accounted for three main topics: managerial and supervisory; industry or profession; and processes, procedures, and business practices.[78] Another area that has received much attention in the United States involves support for outside education. For example, Starbucks partnered with Arizona State University to offer tuition coverage for eligible employees to earn their bachelor's degrees.[79]

Diversity Whereas Title VII of the Civil Rights Act grants legal protection to different types of employees, initiatives in **workplace diversity** focus on recruiting and retaining a diverse workforce as a business imperative.[80] With diversity programs, companies assume an ethical obligation to employ and empower individuals regardless of age, gender, ethnicity, physical or mental ability, or other characteristics. These firms go beyond compliance with government guidelines to develop cultures that respect and embrace the unique skills, backgrounds, and contributions of all types of people. Thus, legal statutes focus on removing discrimination whereas diversity represents a leadership approach for cultivating and appreciating employee talent.[81] Firms with an effective diversity effort link their diversity mission statement with the corporate strategic plan, implement plans to recruit and retain a diverse talent pool, support community programs of diverse groups, hold management accountable for various types of diversity performance, and have tangible outcomes of the diversity strategy. Each firm must tailor its diversity initiative to meet unique employee, market, and industry conditions.[82]

> **workplace diversity**
> Focuses on recruiting and retaining a diverse workforce as a business imperative.

Many firms embrace employee diversity to deal with supplier and customer diversity. Their assumption is that to effectively design, market, and support products for different target groups, a company must employ individuals who reflect its customers' characteristics.[83] Organizations and industries with a population-wide customer base may use national demographics for assessing their diversity effort. Kaiser Permanente uses a dashboard to assess the links between its senior-executive compensation and diversity. It is mandatory for company recruiters to have diversity slates that are viewed by human resources. Kaiser Permanente's strong emphasis on diversity began in 1989 after the company developed the Minority Recruitment and Development Task Force to address racial inequalities.[84] As demographics in the United States continue to shift, companies are faced with reconsidering their marketing and hiring strategies, including the link between employee and customer characteristics. The sharp growth in the Hispanic population is one of the most important shifts recorded. This has prompted firms to hire Hispanic employees and consultants and tailor their offerings to this demographic. Clorox and General Mills, for instance, are appealing to Hispanics with bilingual advertisements via mobile applications.[85]

As we discussed in Chapter 1, there are opportunities to link social responsibility objectives with business performance, and many firms are learning the benefits of employing individuals with different backgrounds and perspectives. For example, at New York Life, diversity is treated like all other business goals. The company employs a chief diversity officer to create accountability and inclusion strategies with employees, suppliers, community members, and other stakeholders.[86] Hewlett-Packard (HP), a multinational information technology company, is committed to including people with disabilities into the workplace. The company was recently named Private-Sector Employer of the Year by *CAREERS & the disABLED magazine*, a publication that provides career advice for people with disabilities. HP was chosen by readers for providing a positive environment in which to work. The company values diversity and believes that this component of their culture allows them to innovate in ways that less diverse companies are not able. In addition, HP designs goods and services that are informed by its diverse workforce.[87]

Conflicting views and voices of different generations abound in the workplace, and this is the first time in history that the workforce has been composed of so many generations at one time. Generations have worked together in the past, but these groups were usually divided by organizational stratification. Many workplaces now include members of multiple generations working shoulder to shoulder. The result may be greater dissension among the age groups than when they were stratified by the organizational hierarchy. Because employees serve an important role in the social responsibility framework, managers need to be aware of generational differences and their potential effects on teamwork, conflict, and other workplace behaviors. Table 7.5 lists the three generations in today's workplace as well as their key characteristics.

Baby boomers are service oriented, good team players, and want to please. However, they are also known for being self-centered, overly sensitive to feedback, and not budget minded. People in Generation X are adaptable, technologically literate, independent, and not intimidated by authority. However, their liabilities include impatience, cynicism, and inexperience. The latest generation to enter the workforce, Generation Y, or the Millennials, is technologically savvy. They also bring the assets of collective action, optimism, multitasking ability, and tenacity to the workplace. However, they bring the liabilities of inexperience, especially with difficult people issues, and a need for supervision and structure.

Although generational issues existed in the workforce in the 1920s and the 1960s, there are some new twists today. The older generations no

TABLE 7.5 Profiles of Generations at Work

Generation Name	Birth Years	Key Characteristics
Baby boomers	1946–1964	Rejection of traditional values, optimistic, achievement-oriented
Generation X	1965–1983	Family-oriented, impatient, individualistic
Millennials (Generation Y)	After 1983	Technologically savvy, greater expectations for workplace, optimistic

longer have all the money and power. Times of anxiety and uncertainty can aggravate differences and generational conflict, and these conflicts need to be handled correctly when they occur. Understanding the different generations and how they see things is a crucial part of handling this conflict. The authors of *Generations at Work: Managing the Clash of Veterans, Boomers, Xers, and Nexters in Your Workplace* developed the ACORN acronym to describe five principles that managers can use to deal with generational issues. Accommodating employee differences entails treating employees as customers and giving them the best service that the company can give. Creating workplace choices as to what and how employees work can allow for change and satisfaction. Operating from a sophisticated management style requires that management be direct but tactful. Respecting competence and initiative assumes the best from the different generations and responds accordingly. Nourishing retention means keeping the best employees. When combined with effective communication skills, the ACORN principles can help managers mend generational conflicts for the benefit of everyone in the company.[88]

Although workplace diversity reaps benefits for both employees and employers, it also brings challenges that must be addressed. For example, diverse employees may have more difficulty communicating and working with each other. Although differences can breed innovation and creativity, they can also create an atmosphere of distrust, dissatisfaction, or lack of cooperation.[89] Today many companies are seizing the opportunity for discussing diversity and creating stronger bonds among employees of different ethnicities, religions, beliefs, and experiences. Other firms engage employees in community service projects and similar initiatives that promote teamwork and cohesion and help to minimize any negative effects of diversity.

Finally, the diversity message will not be taken seriously unless top management and organizational systems fully support a diverse workforce. After Home Depot settled a gender-discrimination lawsuit, it developed an automated hiring and promotion computer program. Although the Job Preference Program (JPP) was originally intended as insurance against discrimination, the system opens all jobs and applicants to the companywide network, eliminates unqualified applications, and enables managers to learn employee aspirations and skills in a more effective manner. JPP has also brought a positive change to the number of female and minority managers within Home Depot.[90] On the other hand, Silicon Valley has been highly criticized for its apparent lack of diversity. Although many tech firms are setting more diversity goals, companies like Facebook have made only minimal gains. Facebook claims that there is simply not enough available talent.[91] In addition, some employees of companies with diversity training programs have viewed such training as intended to blame or change white men only. Other training has focused on the reasons diversity should be important, though not the actual changes in attitudes, work styles, expectations, and business processes that are needed for diversity to work.[92]

Work/Life Balance Just as increasing numbers of women in the workplace have changed the norms of behavior at work and prompted attention to sexual harassment, they have also brought challenges in work/life balance. This balance is not just an issue for women, as men also have multiple roles that can create the same types of stress and conflict.[93] The work/life balance may be described otherwise, such as people who are torn between work and home on a regular basis. An employee thinking about work (or actually working) when he is at home and vice versa is ultimately struggling with multiple responsibilities.[94]

Because employees have roles within and outside the organization, there is increasing corporate focus on the types of support that employees have in balancing these obligations. Deloitte & Touche (now part of Deloitte Touche Tohmatsu), an international professional services firm, was forced to address issues of work/life balance when it discovered the alarming rate at which women were leaving the firm. In the early 1990s, only four of the 50 employees being considered for partner status were women, despite the company's heavy recruitment of women from business schools. The company convened the Initiative for the Retention and Advancement of Women task force and soon uncovered cultural beliefs and practices that needed modification. The task force found that younger employees—both male and female—wanted a balanced life, were willing to forgo some pay for more time with family and less stress, and had similar career goals. Therefore, Deloitte & Touche developed a major work/life balance initiative that included reduced travel schedules and flexible work arrangements to benefit both men and women employed at the firm. According to a survey, issues related to work/life balance such as telecommuting, flexible scheduling, and assistance with child care and elder care are almost equally important to male and female employees. Whereas men rarely utilized these benefits in the past, this is no longer the case. Many midlevel executives, both male and female, are part of dual-earner couples "sandwiched" between raising children and caring for aging parents.[95]

work/life programs
Assist employees in balancing work responsibilities with personal and family responsibilities.

Such **work/life programs** assist employees in balancing work responsibilities with personal and family responsibilities. A central feature of these programs is flexibility so that employees of all types are able to achieve their own definition of balance. For example, a single parent may want child care and consistent work hours, whereas another employee may need assistance in finding elder care for a parent with Alzheimer's disease. A working mother may need access to "just-in-time" care when a child is sick or school is out of session. Employees of all types appreciate flextime arrangements, which allow them to work 40 hours per week on a schedule they develop within a range of hours specified by the company. Other employees work some hours at home or in a location more conducive to their personal obligations. SAS Institute, the world's largest private software company, has been recognized by Glassdoor.com for its exceptional work/life balance program. The company offers employees and their families many perks supporting a balanced life, such as free access to a gymnasium, a healthcare clinic on company grounds, discounted child care, free "work-life" counseling, and more.[96] Work/life balance not only enhances employee productivity, but it is also an imperative to attracting and maintaining a healthy workforce.

More than 80 million Americans suffer from symptoms of stress at work, including headaches, sleeplessness, and other physical ailments.[97] To remedy these concerns, Americans spend more than $20 billion per year on stress-reducing goods, services, and strategies.[98] Compared to Japanese and Chinese workers, however, the U.S. figures are moderate. The term "karoshi," which means, "death from overwork," became widely used in Japan. Thousands of deaths per year are attributed to overwork, such as brain hemorrhages, heart attacks, suicides, etc. The Japanese government passed legislations to establish support centers, assist businesses in reducing the number of deaths, and conduct more research into the phenomenon. China, as its economy continues to grow, is beginning to experience the same issue. The death toll is estimated at 600,000 employees per year, or 1,600 per day.[99]

Managers must become sensitive to cues that employees need to create a stronger work/life balance. Frustration, anger, moodiness, a myopic focus, and physiological symptoms are often present when an employee needs to take vacation, work fewer hours, utilize flexible scheduling, or simply reduce his or her workload. One manager of a telecommunications firm in California returned to the workplace around 11:30 P.M. every night to send people home. Otherwise, she knew many of them would sleep on the floor in the office. Not only do some employees work too many hours, but they may largely ignore nutrition and fitness, friendships, community involvement, and other aspects of work/life balance.[100]

There is no generic work/life program. Instead, companies need to consider their employee base and the types of support their employees are likely to need and appreciate. James Goodnight, SAS's founder, believes that dinnertime should be spent with family and friends, not in the office. Most employees leave by 5:00 P.M., and others participate in flextime or job-sharing arrangements. This, among other characteristics listed earlier, have resulted in the company receiving honors such as its high ranking on *Fortune* magazine's annual list of the 100 Best Companies to Work For and one of *Working Mother* magazine's 100 Best Companies for Working Mothers.[101]

Successful work/life programs, like that developed by the SAS Institute, are an extension of the diversity philosophy so that employees are respected as individuals in the process of contributing to company goals. Thus, connecting employees' personal needs, lives, and goals to strategic business issues can be fruitful for both parties. This perspective is in contrast to the "employee goals versus business goals" trade-off mentality that has been pervasive. IBM implemented a work/life strategy over two decades ago and periodically conducts employee surveys to see if changes or additions are needed.[102]

The Silk Road Survey found that 55 percent of all applicants consider work/life balance the most important consideration in identifying potential employers and considering job offers.[103] For this reason, companies have become quite innovative in their approach to work/life balance. Agilent Technologies, for example, not only offers flexible work schedules and employee discounts, but also has organized sports teams, massages on location, and yoga sessions.[104] Nokia is known for making employees feel cared for. Employees have noted that beyond flexible work schedules and the ability to work from home, the company encourages them to take time off and recharge.[105] Such efforts demonstrate the company's willingness to accommodate employee needs and concerns beyond the workplace.

Philanthropic Issues

In later chapters, we examine the philanthropic efforts of companies and the important role that employees play in the process of selecting and implementing projects that contribute time, resources, and human activity to worthy causes. In social responsibility, philanthropic responsibilities are primarily directed outside the organization, so they are not directly focused on employees. However, employees benefit from participating in volunteerism and other philanthropic projects. Employee volunteerism increases the level of engagement the employee feels, which not only contributes to their performance but also to the company's performance. The engagement is a result of many factors including gaining a sense of purpose through volunteering, having the ability to work in positions of leadership, and gaining new skills. In addition, engaged employees are more likely to stay with the company for longer periods of time.[106]

Many employers help organize employees to participate in walkathons, marathons, bikeathons, and similar events. For example, Blue Cross Blue Shield companies hold an annual event called National Walk@Lunch Day. The event challenges employees and community members to put on their shoes and walk at lunch. Over a six-week period, participants log their steps on the company's Facebook page. At the end of the event, Blue Cross Blue Shield donates up to $1 per mile reported to the American Diabetes Association.[107] Thus, the benefits of corporate philanthropy in the community reflect positively on the organization. There are many strategies for demonstrating community involvement and care. CA Technologies holds a month-long volunteer program in which employees from all over the world spend time volunteering at nonprofits in their local communities.[108]

STRATEGIC IMPLEMENTATION OF RESPONSIBILITIES TO EMPLOYEES

As this chapter has demonstrated, responsibilities toward employees are varied and complex. Legal issues alone require full-time attention from lawyers and human resource specialists. These issues are also emotional because corporate decisions have ramifications on families and communities as well as on employees. In light of this complexity, many companies

Earth in the Balance

Google to Employees: Go Green!

For employees at Alphabet's Google, it pays to be green. In addition to the extensive benefits Google offers, the company provides incentives for employees to increase their sustainability habits. Google recognizes that becoming a sustainable company requires support both from external and internal stakeholders. As a result, the company takes great pains to make being sustainable easy for employees. Google employees can save money, donate to charities, and receive discounts on eco-friendly technology by taking advantage of the company's green incentives. For instance, employees can save fuel costs by riding to work on Google's biodiesel shuttles. Approximately 6,400 Google employees use the company's shuttles to commute to work.

Google's GFleet car-sharing program, a car sharing program employees can use to get around on Google's campus, consists of electric vehicles including Nissan LEAFs and Chevrolet Volts. To power these vehicles Google has installed the largest electric vehicle charging station in the country. Approximately 1,000 charging sessions occur every day at Google headquarters. Together Google's shuttle and GFleet programs save 29,000 metric tons of carbon dioxide emissions. Google has also invested in car sharing programs Sidecar and Uber.

Employees can also use Google's bike-sharing program to get around campus. The company encourages employees to bike to work and holds an annual Google Bike to Work Day. Approximately 3,700 Google employees at 26 offices participated in the event.

Others have been known to adopt more unusual ways to get around campus, including pogo jumping. For employees who choose to bike, walk, or pogo to work, the company provides them with digital stamps. These stamps can be redeemed for company donations to the employee's favorite charity.

Many of Google's green initiatives help both employees and society. For example, Google developed a $300 million fund for SolarCity in a partnership to support the installation of solar panels on residential homes. While it may be difficult to convince the average consumer to adopt solar technology, Google offers its employees discounts on SolarCity products. This encourages employees to adopt sustainable practices outside of work. Google has also invested in additional solar companies as well as wind power.

It appears that Google's concerns with sustainability are successfully catching on with employees. At Google's EMEA Engineering facility in Zurich, Google surveyed employees on ways to redesign a local brewery building into office space for the company. The result was a uniquely designed work space that emphasizes innovation, creativity, and sustainability. One major feature in the construction was the use of transparent glass to section space in the building. This design increases daylighting, which cuts back on the building's energy consumption. It is clear that Google seeks to make a difference in the field of sustainability—starting with its employees.

Sources: Brian Dumaine, "Google's Zero-Carbon Quest," *Fortune Tech*, http://fortune.com/2012/07/12/googles-zero-carbon-quest/ (accessed July 18, 2016); Bill Weihl, "Reducing Our Carbon Footprint," *Google*, May 6, 2009, http://googleblog.blogspot.com/2009/05/reducing-our-carbon-footprint.html#!/2009/05/reducing-our-carbon-footprint.html (accessed July 18, 2016); Taflin Laylin, "Gallery: Google Employees in Zurich (Zooglers) Have the World's Coolest Re-Purposed Office," September 27, 2011, http://inhabitat.com/google-employees-in-zurich-zooglers-have-the-worlds-coolest-re-purposed-office/emea-engineering-hub-zurich-camenzind-evolution-1/?extend=1 (accessed July 18, 2016); Joseph Stomberg, "Google's Rick Needham is Feeling Lucky About the Future of Sustainable Energy," *Smithsonian*, September 2, 2013, http://www.smithsonianmag.com/innovation/googles-rick-needham-is-feeling-lucky-about-the-future-of-sustainable-energy-3415041/?page=1 (accessed July 18, 2016); Robert McMillan, "Inside the Cycleplex: The Weird, Wild World of Google Bikes," *Wired*, April 25, 2013, http://www.wired.com/2013/04/google-bikes/ (accessed July 18, 2016); Google, "Campus Operations," *Google Green*, https://www.google.com/green/efficiency/oncampus/ (accessed July 18, 2016); SolarCity Creates Fund to Finance $750 Million in Residential Solar Projects with Investment from Google," February 26, 2015, http://www.solarcity.com/newsroom/press/solarcity-creates-fund-finance-750-million-residential-solar-projects-investment (accessed July 18, 2016). Alison van Diggelen, "Working @ Google: Green Carrots & Pogo Sticks," *Fresh Dialogues*, August 23, 2011, http://www.freshdialogues.com/2011/08/23/working-google-green-carrots-pogo-sticks/ (accessed July 18, 2016).

have chosen to embrace these obligations to benefit both employee and organizational goals. This philosophy stands in stark contrast to the master-servant model popular more than 100 years ago. Today, companies are using distinctive programs and initiatives to set themselves apart and to become known as desirable employers. Low unemployment levels before the last recession, along with diversity, work/life balance, outsourcing, and generational differences, prompted companies to use marketing strategy and business insight normally applied to customer development in the employee recruitment and retention realm. Even in a time of economic downturn, employers will need to be mindful of keeping top talent and maintaining employee satisfaction. For example, Patagonia encourages its employees to stay physically fit. It places so much emphasis on employee satisfaction and physical fitness, in fact, that employees are allowed to go surfing in the middle of the workday.[109]

employer of choice
An organization of any size in any industry that is able to attract, optimize, and retain the best employee talent over the long term.

An **employer of choice** is an organization of any size in any industry that is able to attract, optimize, and retain the best employee talent over the long term. ENSR, a European environmental consulting firm, created a cross-functional and geographically diverse committee to provide guidance for maintaining and strengthening the company's positive culture. The committee focuses on ways in which ENSR's top management can ensure that integrity, respect, open communications, flexibility and balance are the key values and defining qualities of every ENSR career.[110] Advertising, websites, and other company communications often use the term to describe and market the organization to current and potential employees. These messages center on the various practices that companies have implemented to create employee satisfaction. Firms with this distinction value the human component of business, not just financial considerations, ensure that employees are engaged in meaningful work, and stimulate the intellectual curiosity of employees. These businesses have strong training practices, delegate authority, and recognize the link between employee morale, customer satisfaction, and other performance measures.[111] Thus, becoming an employer of choice is an important manifestation of strategic social responsibility. Potential employees may look for signs that social responsibility is a top concern. College graduates often evaluate a potential employer's socially responsible and ethical behavior when deciding on a career path. Table 7.6 shows the percentage of college graduates who indicated the top characteristics of a job they considered to be the most important. The table provides results from college graduates and demonstrates the kind of culture companies should cultivate to attract employees.

Despite the negative effects that certain actions may have on perceptions of a company's social responsibility, there are strategies and programs

TABLE 7.6 What Graduates Consider Most Important for Employment

Employer Action	Graduates (%)
1. Opportunity for personal growth	60.7%
2. Job security	46.0%
3. Friendly coworkers	43.7%
4. Good benefits package	39.2%
5. Ability to improve community	34.7%

Source: National Association of Colleges and Employers, "Student Survey: The Job/Employer Preferences of the Class of 2014," July 23, 2014, http://www.naceweb.org/s07232014/job-preferences-graduating-class-2014.aspx (accessed June 21, 2016).

that demonstrate a proactive approach to employee relations. One traditional way to strengthen trust is through employee stock ownership plans (ESOPs), which provide the opportunity both to contribute to and gain from organizational success. Such programs confer not only ownership but also opportunities for employees to participate in management planning, which foster an environment that many organizations believe increases profits. Several studies of companies with ESOPs cast a positive light on these plans. ESOPs appear to increase sales by about 2.3–2.4 percent over what would have been expected without an ESOP. ESOP companies were also found to pay better benefits, higher wages, and provide nearly twice the retirement income for employees than their non-ESOP counterparts. Under these plans, employees must take on an ownership perspective, work as a team in an environment that forges trust, and provide excellent interactions and service to customers. Some of the 7,000 "employee-owned" firms include Dunn-Edwards Paints, Publix Supermarkets, and Round Table Pizza.[112] Of *Fortune* magazine's 100 Best Companies to Work For, more than half are employee-owned.[113] Research has shown that the decision to become an employee-owned company enhances company performance and provides higher wealth accumulation for employee owners. Despite the advantages of ESOPs, experts also warn that some plans are potentially risky for employees, as in the case of Enron.[114] Just like any other company initiative, management must take responsibility for managing an ESOP well.

Becoming an employer of choice has many benefits, including an enhanced ability to hire and retain the best people, who in turn offer strong commitment to the company mission and its stakeholders. The expectations of such businesses are very high because employee stakeholders often have specific criteria in mind when assessing the attractiveness of a particular employer. Some people may be focused on specific environmental issues, whereas others may be searching for a company that markets healthy and helpful products. Although top managers must decide on how the firm will achieve strategic social responsibility with employees, Table 7.7 provides guidance on eight key principles that are typically exhibited and managed by employers of choice. Although most companies have long understood the importance of attracting and keeping customers through strong branding efforts, many are relatively new to the idea and implementation of similar strategies to create an employer brand.[115]

Finally, the global dimensions of today's workplace shape an organization's ability to effectively work with employee stakeholders and to become an employer of choice. Firms with offices and sites around the world must deal with a complexity of norms and expectations, all of which can affect its reputation at home. For example, when Nike was first accused of dealing with suppliers that used child labor in the mid-1990s, the company claimed that it was not in the business of manufacturing shoes and that it could therefore not be blamed for the practices of Asian manufacturers. Following media criticism, Nike publicized a report claiming that the employees of its Indonesian and Vietnamese suppliers were living quite well. The veracity of this report was tarnished by contradictory evidence

TABLE 7.7 Key Principles of Employers of Choice

Principle	Explanation
1. Organizational reputation	Employees desire to work in an organization that maintains a good reputation among stakeholders.
2. Organizational culture	Employees want to work in an ethical organizational culture that maintains integrity and encourages employee contributions.
3. Strong leadership	Employees want to work in an environment that has strong ethical leaders who care passionately about the company.
4. Interesting work	Employees want their jobs to be challenging and rewarding, not mundane or too difficult.
5. Opportunities for Growth	Employees want to work in a job or industry where there are significant opportunities for career advancement.
6. Employee recognition	Employees appreciate being recognized for their contributions to the company and are encouraged to continue serving.
7. Employee well-being	Employees expect fair compensation, appropriate benefits, and an adequate work/life balance from their employers.
8. Social Responsibility	Studies have demonstrated that employees enjoy working for a company that considers the needs of stakeholders and contributes toward improving society.

Sources: Barbara J. Bowen, "Being an Employer of Choice has Bottom-Line Benefits," *CMA Management* 82 (November 2008): 14–15; "Main Page," *Employer of Choice.net,* http://www.employerofchoice.net/ (accessed July 1, 2014); Roger E. Herman and Joyce L. Gioia, *How to Become an Employer of Choice* (Winchester, VA: Oakhill Press, 2000); Jody Ordioni, "How to Become an Employee of Choice," *ere.net,* July 15, 2013, http://www.eremedia.com/ere/how-to-become-an-employer-of-choice/ (accessed June 21, 2016).

produced by activists. Next, Nike started introducing workers' rights and environmental guidelines for its suppliers. Yet some company representatives explained that any additional social responsibility initiative would damage the competitive position of the firm.

In the late 1990s, Nike designed a suppliers' auditing process that invited student representatives along with other activists to visit manufacturing plants and provide recommendations for better practice. Before the company's shift, many media reports discussed Nike's manufacturing practices, and it is likely that some consumers and potential employees turned their attention away from Nike. Nike actually settled the legal case that rose all the way to the Supreme Court. Nike agreed to pay $1.5 million to the Fair Labor Association to help fund worker development programs. In this case, Nike's relationships with its manufacturing suppliers and their employees affected its ability to achieve strategic social responsibility.[116] Today, Nike's supply chain practices have improved considerably. The company has been awarded the Corporate Register Reporting Award for excellence in global reporting, demonstrating that its auditing and ethical programs for supply chains have significantly increased the transparency and accountability of the company.[117]

SUMMARY

Throughout history, people's perceptions of work and employment have evolved from a necessary evil to a source of fulfillment. The relationship between employer and employee involves responsibilities, obligations, and expectations as well as challenges.

On an economic level, many believe there is an unwritten, informal psychological contract that includes the beliefs, perceptions, expectations, and obligations that make up the agreement between individuals and their employers. This contract has evolved from a primarily master-servant relationship, in which employers held the power, to one in which employees assume a more balanced relationship with employers. Workforce reduction, the process of eliminating employment positions, breaches the psychological contract that exists between an employer and employee and threatens the social contract among employers, communities, and other groups. Although workforce reduction lowers costs, it often results in lost intellectual capital, strained customer relationships, negative media attention, and other issues that drain company resources.

Employment law is a complex and ever-evolving area. In the past, employment was primarily governed by employment at will, a common-law doctrine that allows either the employer or employee to terminate the relationship at any time as long as it does not violate an employment contract. Many laws have been enacted to regulate business conduct with regard to wages and benefits, labor unions, health and safety, equal employment opportunity, sexual harassment, and whistle-blowing. Title VII of the Civil Rights Act, which prohibits employment discrimination on the basis of race, national origin, color, religion, and gender, is fundamental to employees' rights to join and advance in an organization according to merit. Sexual harassment is defined as unwelcome sexual advances, requests for sexual favors, and other verbal or physical conduct of a sexual nature when submission to or rejection of this conduct explicitly or implicitly affects an individual's employment, unreasonably interferes with an individual's work performance, or creates an intimidating, hostile, or offensive work environment. Sexual harassment may take the form of either quid pro quo harassment or hostile work environment harassment. An employee who reports individual or corporate wrongdoing to either internal or external sources is considered a whistle-blower.

Although legal compliance is imperative for social responsibility, the ethical climate of the workplace is more subjective and dependent on top management support and corporate culture. Companies with a strong ethical stance fund initiatives to develop employees' skills, knowledge, and other personal characteristics. With diversity programs, companies assume an ethical obligation to employ and empower individuals regardless of age, gender, physical and mental ability, and other characteristics. Work/life programs assist employees in balancing work responsibilities with personal and family responsibilities.

Employees may play an important role in a firm's philanthropic efforts. Employees benefit from such initiatives through participation in volunteerism and other projects.

In light of the complexity of and emotions involved with responsibilities toward employees, many companies have chosen to embrace these obligations to benefit both employee and organizational goals. An employer of choice is an organization of any size in any industry that is able to attract, optimize, and retain the best employee talent over the long term. One traditional way to strengthen trust is through ESOPs, which provide the opportunity both to contribute to and gain from organizational success. Finally, the global dimensions of today's workplace shape an organization's ability to effectively work with employee stakeholders and to become an employer of choice.

Responsible Business Debate

The Usefulness of Performance Reviews

Issue: *Should companies get rid of the performance review?*

The beginning of the year brings with it something dreaded by employees: the performance review. Performance reviews are meant to measure employees' progress over the year and determine whether their performance meets job expectations. The theory behind performance reviews is that they help employees enhance their strengths and improve on their weaknesses. Performance reviews are often used in promotion or compensation decisions.

Performance reviews act as an important benchmark for employees. Supporters argue that it helps employees realize how they are doing compared to others in the company. The ability to measure an employee's performance is essential in determining how he or she fits in with the firm. Performance reviews also provide the manager with the ability to help employees improve on their strengths and weaknesses, improving employee skill sets and giving them more of an opportunity to advance in their careers. Managers who genuinely care about their subordinates can work with employees more closely to enhance their performance.

However, organizations including Adobe, Juniper, and Kelly Services have begun to scrap the traditional performance review due to perceived weaknesses. Critics of performance reviews believe they have so many flaws that the time it takes to implement a review in no way equals the benefits. Instead, it creates tension between employees and supervisors. There are many disadvantages to performance reviews that could hinder their usefulness. For instance, managers are not unbiased. It has been shown that managers tend to give higher ratings to employees that they have hired and lower ratings to employees who are different from them.

Critics suggest that the performance review harms employee relations with their managers because they have different intentions. Employees are more concerned with compensation or promotion, while employers are more interested in employee improvement. Also, because the performance review is a one-way form of communication, it places the boss in a powerful position. Additionally, many performance reviews have criteria that may or may not be specific to that employee's job. Opponents argue that employees cannot possibly be fit into a box of predetermined criteria.

A recent study suggests that it is often a company's best employees that dislike criticism the most. Additionally, high achievers who are rated below the highest rating are often crushed, even if they receive a high score. Contrary to popular opinion, this research study seems to demonstrate that those who want to improve do not like the negative feedback given in a performance review and—like many people—will often zone out once a supervisor begins providing negative feedback.

Some alternatives to the traditional performance review have been suggested. One alternative is to make the performance review more of a two-way form of communication. Instead of the manager simply evaluating the employee's performance, employees could also be provided with the opportunity to share their thoughts about their superiors or the company. This would help keep the managers accountable in working toward employee progress. REI, for instance, has an independent firm conduct an annual employee survey to gather employee feedback about the company, its benefits, engagement, and more.

There Are Two Sides to Every Issue

1. Traditional performance reviews act as important indicators of employee progress and productivity.

2. Traditional performance reviews should be completely eliminated due to their disadvantages.

Sources: Josh Bersin, "Time to Scrap Performance Appraisals?" *Forbes*, May 6, 2013, http://www.forbes.com/sites/joshbersin/2013/05/06/time-to-scrap-performance-appraisals/ (accessed July 18, 2016); Samuel A. Colbert, "Get Rid of the Performance Review!" *The Wall Street Journal*, October 20, 2008, http://online.wsj.com/news/articles/SB122426318874844933 (accessed July 18, 2016); Rose Johnson, "Advantages & Disadvantages of Performance Evaluation," *Chron*, http://smallbusiness.chron.com/advantages-disadvantages-performance-evaluation-21143.html (accessed July 18, 2016); Jena McGregor, "Study Finds That Basically Every Single Person Hates Performance Reviews," *The Washington Post*, January 27, 2014, https://www.washingtonpost.com/news/on-leadership/wp/2014/01/27/study-finds-that-basically-every-single-person-hates-performance-reviews/ (accessed July 18, 2016); REI, "Employee Engagement & Retention," https://www.rei.com/stewardship/report/2013/workplace/employee-engagement-retention.html (accessed July 18, 2016); Derek Thompson, "The Case Against Performance Reviews," *The Atlantic,* January 29, 2014, http://www.theatlantic.com/business/archive/2014/01/the-case-against-performance-reviews/283402/ (accessed July 18, 2016).

KEY TERMS

psychological contract (p. 226)
workforce reduction (p. 229)
employment at will (p. 232)
vesting (p. 234)
ergonomics (p. 236)

sexual harassment (p. 239)
quid pro quo sexual harassment (p. 240)
hostile work environment sexual harassment (p. 240)

workplace diversity (p. 245)
work/life programs (p. 248)
employer of choice (p. 252)

DISCUSSION QUESTIONS

1. Review Table 7.1, Psychological Contract between Employee and Employer. Indicate the positive effects associated with the contract's characteristics. For example, what is positive about an employee's ability to solve problems independently?

2. What is workforce reduction? How does it affect employees, consumers, and the local community? What steps should a company take to address these effects?

3. What responsibilities do companies have with respect to workplace violence? Using the three categories of violence presented in the chapter,

describe the responsibilities and actions that you believe are necessary for an organization to demonstrate social responsibility in this area.

4. Describe the differences between workplace diversity and equal employment opportunity. How do these differences affect managerial responsibilities and the development of social responsibility programs?

5. Why is it important to understand the profiles of different generations at work? How can managers use the ACORN principles to develop a strong sense of community and solidarity among all employee groups?

6. What trends have contributed to work/life programs? How do work/life programs help employees and organizations?

7. What is an employer of choice? Describe how a firm could use traditional marketing concepts and strategies to appeal to current and potential employees.

8. Review the best practices in Table 7.7 for becoming an employer of choice. What are some potential drawbacks to each practice? Rank the eight practices in terms of their importance to you.

EXPERIENTIAL EXERCISE

Develop a list of five criteria that describe your employer of choice. Then, visit the websites of three companies in which you have some employment interest. Peruse each firm's website to find evidence on how it fulfills your criteria. On the basis of this evidence, develop a chart to show how well each firm meets your description and criteria of your employer of choice. Finally, provide three recommendations on how these companies can better communicate their commitment to employees and the employer of choice criteria.

X, Y, & MILLENIAL: WHAT WOULD YOU DO?

Dawn Burke, director of employee relations, glanced at her online calendar and remembered her appointment at 3:00 p.m. today. She quickly found the file labeled "McCullen and Aranda" and started preparing for the meeting. She recalled that this was essentially an employee-supervisor case, where the employee had been unwilling or unable to meet the supervisor's requests. The employee claimed that the supervisor was too demanding and impatient. Their conflict had escalated to the point that both were unhappy and uncomfortable in the work environment. Other employees had noticed, and overheard, some of the conflict.

In her role, Dawn was responsible for many programs, including a new mediation initiative to resolve workplace conflict. The program was designed to help employees develop stronger communication and conflict resolution skills. In this case, the program was also providing an intermediary step between informal and formal discipline. Today, she was meeting with both parties to discuss mediation guidelines, a time line, their goal, and their general points of conflict.

John McCullen, 51, a buyer in the facilities department, and Terry Aranda, the director of facilities procurement, arrived separately. John had been with the company for 32 years and had started his career with the company right out of high school. Terry, 31, was hired from another firm to oversee the procurement area a year ago and had recently graduated from a prestigious M.B.A. program. Dawn started the meeting by reviewing the mediation guidelines and time line. She reminded John and Terry that their goal was to develop a workable and agreeable solution to the current situation. Dawn then asked for each party to explain his or her position on the conflict.

John began, "Ms. Aranda is a very smart lady. She seems to know the buying and procurement area, but she knows less about the company and its history. I am not sure she has taken the time to learn our ways and values. Ms. Aranda is impatient with our use of the new software and computer system. Some of us don't have college degrees, and we haven't been using computers since we were young. I started working at this company about the time she was born, and I am not sure that her management style is good for our department. Everything was going pretty well until we starting changing our systems."

Terry commented, "John is a valuable member of the department, as he knows everyone at this company. I appreciate his knowledge and loyalty. On the other hand, he has not completed several tasks in a timely manner nor has he asked for an extension. I feel that I must check up on his schedule and proof all of his work. John has attended several training classes, and I asked that he use an electronic calendar so that projects are completed on time. He continues to ignore my advice and deadlines. We've had several conversations, but John's work has not substantially improved. We have many goals to achieve in the department, and I need everyone's best work in order to make that happen."

Dawn thanked them for their candor and told them she would meet with them next week to start the mediation process. As she contemplated what each had said, she remembered an article that discussed how people born in different generations often have contrasting perceptions about work. Dawn started to jot a few notes about the next steps in resolving their conflict. What would you do?

CHAPTER EIGHT

Consumer Relations

Chapter Objectives

- To describe customers as stakeholders
- To investigate consumer protection laws
- To examine six consumer rights
- To discuss the implementation of responsibilities to consumers

Chapter Outline

Consumer Stakeholders

Responsibilities to Consumers

Strategic Implementation of Responsibilities to Consumers

Not Your Grandparents' Bar: The Protein Bar

It is not uncommon to see long lines stretching out the door during lunchtime at the Protein Bar. Protein Bar specializes in healthy, high-protein food options that appeal to busy consumers on the go. The Protein Bar was founded in Chicago by Matt Matros. Although it was founded in 2009, Matros got the idea for the restaurant two years earlier while working as an associate brand manager for Kraft Foods. Matros used his life savings to open his original restaurant, which at first focused solely on protein shakes. The restaurant was later expanded to include healthy burritos, salads, and breakfast items. Today Protein Bar locations can be found in Chicago, Washington D.C., Denver, and Boulder, Colorado.

Matros's journey to healthy living was not easy. After losing his father to a sudden heart attack at a young age, Matros struggled with his weight throughout his youth. At 22, he decided to drastically change his lifestyle. He adopted an exercise regimen and a high-protein diet. He lost 50 pounds and from then on became committed toward living healthy. Matros learned that trying to eat healthy on the go was expensive, requiring him to bring some of his own ingredients to make high-protein shakes. He began to recognize that other consumers were having similar problems.

It was then he conceived of a convenient casual dining restaurant that would offer healthy options. Two years later, he founded Protein Bar. Protein Bar offers bar-ritos (burritos), gluten-free food bowls, blended drinks, chilis and side dishes, breakfast items, salads, and raw juices. Common ingredients include quinoa, a grain high in protein, tofu, chicken, and kale. Protein Bar was founded with the mission "to change the way people eat on the go." Service is an important principle at Protein Bar, and employees aim to serve high-quality, healthy food quickly so consumers can resume their busy lives.

Protein Bar is concerned with consumer satisfaction and uses this as a competitive advantage. Restaurants that compete on health are increasingly popular and Protein Bar knows it must cater to the customers' right to choose to remain competitive. Customers choose to patronize the restaurant due to its quality service and unique mix of high-protein food options. Additionally, they know they will not be misled, as Protein Bar is transparent about the nutrition of its products. Under each menu item listed on its website, information is provided regarding carbohydrates, protein, calorie, and fat content. This allows consumers to make informed choices, meeting their right to be informed.

Because service is so important at Protein Bar, the restaurant takes any concerns consumers may have seriously. Protein Bar urges any dissatisfied customer to contact the restaurant and promises that a member of its corporate team will respond to any complaints within 48 hours. This emphasizes the consumers' right to be heard and demonstrates how Protein Bar is living its values of service and quality. Protein Bar's actions demonstrate the importance it places on consumer relations. As for Matt Matros, he went on to found another company Limitless High Definition Coffee and Tea. However, he remains on Protein Bar's board.[1]

Protein Bar illustrates how organizations are able to meet customer needs and satisfy stakeholder groups. From a social responsibility perspective, the key challenge is how an organization assesses its stakeholders' needs, integrates them with company strategy, reconciles differences between stakeholders' needs, strives for better relationships with stakeholders, achieves mutual understandings with them, and finds solutions for problems. In this chapter, we explore relationships with consumers and the expectations of the economic, legal, ethical, and philanthropic responsibilities that must be addressed by business.

CONSUMER STAKEHOLDERS

For the past 20 years, "green marketing," the promotion of more environmentally friendly products, has become a much-discussed strategy in the packaged goods industry. Procter & Gamble (P&G), the venerable manufacturer of soap, paper goods, and other household products, feared that increasing environmental consciousness among consumers would lead to a resurgence in the use of cloth diapers, which would have had a negative effect on its disposable diaper business. P&G launched a marketing campaign touting the benefits of disposables, including the fact that their use does not require hot water for laundering or fuel for diaper service trucks. P&G also initiated a pilot project for composting disposable diapers. Today, the debate over cloth versus disposables has largely faded, and the P&G marketing campaign has disappeared.

The dawn of the twenty-first century brought many new products, including disposable tableware, food containers that can be used repeatedly or thrown away, and electrostatic mops with cloths that are disposed of after one use. Although these product introductions suggest a decline in environmental consciousness among consumers, other initiatives counter this assumption. Whole Foods Markets, a grocery chain that specializes in organic and environmentally friendly items, reports $940 of sales per square foot versus the $496 of sales per square foot earned by Kroger.[2] Today, the company utilizes a wide variety of approaches to reinforce its green philosophy, including blogs, store projects, loans for local producers, selling organic foods, and the use of biodiesel for its trucks.[3] Indeed, environmental and related social initiatives have become a global concern. One goal of the annual International Buy Nothing Day, sponsored by consumer associations around the world, is to encourage consumers to consider the environmental consequences of their buying habits. The event's organizers remind consumers that the richest 20 percent of people consume 80 percent of the world's resources.[4]

Although the future of different marketing strategies can be debated, the real test of effectiveness lies in the expectations, attitudes, and ultimate buying patterns of consumers. The preceding examples illustrate that there is no true consensus around issues such as environmental responsibility and companies therefore face complex decisions about how to respond to them. This is true for all types of expectations, including the ones we explore in this chapter. In the sections that follow, we examine the economic, legal, ethical, and philanthropic responsibilities that businesses have to **consumers**, those individuals who purchase, use, and dispose of products for themselves and their homes.

consumers
Those individuals who purchase, use, and dispose of products for themselves and their homes.

RESPONSIBILITIES TO CONSUMERS

Not too long ago, the emphasis of marketing was on investors and competitors. However, as marketers began to develop a stakeholder orientation, the importance of consumers as a primary stakeholder became apparent. Consumers are necessary for the success of a business; any business that does not consider the impact its operations will have on consumers will likely not be in business very long. As such, organizations must consider their responsibilities to meet consumer needs. The following sections illustrate how the different components to social responsibility are applied to consumers.

Economic Issues

As discussed in Chapter 2, consumers are primary stakeholders because their awareness, purchase, use, and repurchase of products are vital to a company's existence. Fundamentally, therefore, consumers and businesses are connected by an economic relationship. This relationship begins with an exchange, usually of a good or service for money, which often leads to deeper attachments or affiliation. A well-known advertising campaign slogan, "Delivering Happiness," typifies the close relationship that Zappos customers develop with the shoes they purchase. Other consumers may choose to shun particular brands or opt for the environmentally sensitive products described earlier. In all of these cases, however, consumers expect the products they purchase to perform as guaranteed by their sellers. Remember from our opening example, a member of Protein Bar's executive team responds to dissatisfied customers within 48 hours. Thus, a firm's economic responsibilities include following through on promises made in the exchange process. Although this responsibility seems basic today, business practices have not always been directed in this way. In the early part of the 1900s, the caveat "Let the buyer beware" typified the power that business—not consumers—wielded in most exchange relationships.[5] In some parts of the world, this phrase often accurately describes the consumer marketplace. For example, although Indonesia has consumer protection laws, consumers often feel like they have to test products in stores before purchasing them. It is not uncommon for them to take electronics out of the packaging and plug them in to see if they work. Many Indonesian consumers do not appear to be fully aware of their rights in the exchange process.[6]

Fulfillment of economic responsibilities depends on interactions with the consumer. However, there are situations in which the consumer does

consumer fraud

Intentional deception to derive an unfair economic advantage over an organization.

not act as a fair participant in the exchange.[7] **Consumer fraud** involves intentional deception to derive an unfair economic advantage over an organization. Examples of fraudulent activities include shoplifting, collusion or duplicity, and guile. Collusion typically involves an employee who assists the consumer in fraud. For example, a cashier may not scan all merchandise or may give an unwarranted discount. Duplicity may involve a consumer staging an accident in a grocery store and then seeking damages against the store for its lack of attention to safety. A consumer may purchase, wear, and then return an item of clothing for a full refund. In other situations, the consumer may ask for a refund by claiming a defect that either is nonexistent or was caused by consumer misuse.[8] Although some of these acts warrant legal prosecution, they can be very difficult to prove, and many companies are reluctant to accuse patrons of a crime when there is no way it can be verified. Businesses that operate with the "customer is always right" philosophy have found that some consumers will take advantage of this promise and have therefore modified return policies to curb unfair use. REI, for instance, modified its 100 percent satisfaction guarantee so consumers now have a year to return defective or unwanted products (previously there was no limit). Other companies, especially electronic firms, charge a "restocking fee" if goods are not returned within a specified time period. Table 8.1 describes different types of consumer fraud.

Because of the vague nature of some types of consumer fraud, its full financial toll is somewhat difficult to tally. However, rough estimates indicate that the average inventory shrinkage—which occurs when inventory is lost through shoplifting, vendor fraud, employee error, or other means—costs U.S. businesses more than $45 billion per year globally.[9] While shrinkage is most often considered in the context of brick-and-mortar establishments, companies in many industries have problems with fraud and related issues that raise costs and lower profitability. The internet has complicated matters as it can be harder for consumers to determine which

TABLE 8.1 Types of Consumer Fraud

Motivation	Example
Shoplifting	A teenager steals a flash drive from an office supply store
Collusion	An employee provides a consumer with substantial company discounts because of their friendship
Duplicity	A consumer stages an accident with the intent to file false claims against a retailer
Tag switching	A customer switches the tags of a higher priced item with that of a lower priced item
Credit card fraud	A consumer uses a credit card he or she got through fraudulent means

TABLE 8.2 Ways to Avoid Credit Card Fraud on the Internet

1. Don't give out your credit card number unless the site is secure and reputable!
2. Before using the site, check out security software/encryption software it uses.
3. Obtain a physical address and phone number rather than settling for a post office box number. Call the telephone number to ensure the company is legitimate.
4. Check out the email address to make sure it is active.
5. Check out the Better Business Bureau from the seller's area.
6. Check out other websites about this person/company.
7. When possible, purchase items with your credit card because you can dispute the charges if something goes wrong.
8. Keep a list of all your credit cards as well as the seller's information. If anything looks suspicious, immediately report to your credit card issuer.

Source: Federal Bureau of Investigations, "Common Fraud Schemes: Internet Fraud," http://www.fbi.gov/scams-safety/fraud/internet_fraud (accessed June 21, 2016).

online retailers are legitimate. Table 8.2 shows some effective tools that individuals can use to combat credit card fraud over the internet.

Many consumers, of course, do not engage in such activities. However, there are cases when buyers and sellers disagree on whether or how well companies have satisfied their economic responsibilities. Thus, a consumer may believe that a product is not worth the price paid, perhaps because he or she believes the product's benefits have been exaggerated by the seller. For example, although some marketers claim that their creams, pills, special massages, and other techniques can reduce or even eliminate cellulite, most medical experts and dermatologists believe that only exercise and weight loss can reduce the appearance of this undesirable condition. Products for reducing cellulite remain on the market, but many consumers have returned these products and complained about the lack of results. In the United Kingdom, a number of cosmetics companies have been reprimanded by the Advertising Standards Authority for making misleading claims in advertising and packaging.[10] If a consumer believes that a firm has not fulfilled its basic economic responsibilities, he or she may ask for a refund, tell others about the bad experiences, discontinue patronage, post a complaint to a website, contact a consumer agency, and even seek legal redress. Many consumer and government agencies keep track of consumer complaints. For example, every year the Federal Trade Commission (FTC) reports the top consumer complaints across the nation. Problems related to identity theft, debt collection, fraud involving bankers and lenders, imposter scams, and scams involving telephone and mobile services have been at the top of the list in recent years.[11] To protect consumers and provide businesses with guidance, a number of laws and regulations have been enacted to ensure that economic responsibility is met in accordance with institutionalized standards.

Legal Issues

As we discussed earlier, legal issues with respect to consumers in the United States primarily fall under the domain of the FTC, which enforces federal antitrust and consumer protection laws. Within this agency, the Bureau of Consumer Protection works to protect consumers against unfair, deceptive, and fraudulent practices. The bureau is further organized into eight divisions, including those focused on marketing practices, privacy and identity protection, advertising practices, and international consumer protection.[12] For example, the FTC charged Lumosity for claiming that its brain training devices could help with brain trauma and cognitive decline. The FTC claims the firm does not have sufficient evidence to back this up. The FTC claims that it is cracking down on firms that claim they can improve cognitive ability without substantiation, especially since many ads for these products tend to be geared toward more elderly people more likely to suffer from dementia or other cognitive issues.[13]

In addition to the FTC, several other federal agencies regulate specific goods, services, or business practices to protect consumers. The Food and Drug Administration, for example, enforces laws and regulations enacted to prevent distribution of adulterated or misbranded foods, drugs, medical devices, cosmetics, veterinary products, and potentially hazardous consumer products. The Consumer Product Safety Commission enforces laws and regulations designed to protect the public from unreasonable risk of injury from consumer products. Many states also have regulatory agencies that enforce laws and regulations regarding business practices within their states. Most federal agencies and states have consumer affairs or information offices to help consumers. The Federal Communications Commission's Consumer Affairs and Outreach Division educates consumers on issues related to cable and satellite service, telecommunications, wireless technology, and other areas under the FCC's domain.[14] In Montana, the Department of Justice's Consumer Protection Division publishes information on their website to assist consumers in complaining effectively, recognizing scams, and avoiding identity theft. They also post information specific to the region such as farming and oil and gas industry concerns.[15]

In this section, we focus on U.S. laws related to exchanges and relationships with consumers. Table 8.3 summarizes some of the laws that are likely to affect a wide range of companies and consumers. State and local laws can be more stringent than federal statutes, so it is important that businesses fully investigate the laws applicable to all markets in which they operate. In Texas, for example, the Deceptive Trade Practices Act prohibits a business from selling anything to a consumer that he or she does not need or cannot afford.[16] In Colorado, the Colorado Consumer Protection Act is a broad law protecting consumers from damages associated with fraud.

Health and Safety One of the first consumer protection laws in the United States came about in response to public outrage over a novel.

TABLE 8.3 Major Consumer Laws

Act (Date Enacted)	Purpose
Pure Food and Drug Act (1906)	Established the Food and Drug Administration; outlaws the adulteration or mislabeling of food and drug products sold in interstate commerce.
Cigarette Labeling and Advertising Act (1965)	Requires manufacturers to add to package labels warnings about the possible health hazards associated with smoking cigarettes.
Fair Packaging and Labeling Act (1966)	Outlaws unfair or deceptive packaging or labeling of consumer products.
Truth in Lending Act (1968)	Requires creditors to disclose in writing all finance charges and related aspects of credit transactions.
Child Protection and Toy Safety Act (1969)	Requires childproof devices and special labeling.
Fair Credit Reporting Act (1970)	Promotes accuracy, fairness, and privacy of credit information; gives consumers the right to see their personal credit reports and to dispute any inaccurate information therein.
Consumer Product Safety Act (1972)	Established the Consumer Product Safety Commission to regulate potentially hazardous consumer products.
Equal Credit Opportunity Act (1974)	Outlaws denial of credit on the basis of race, color, religion, national origin, sex, marital status, age, or receipt of public assistance and requires creditors to provide applicants, on request, with the reasons for credit denial.
Magnuson-Moss Warranty (FTC) Act (1975)	Establishes rules for consumer product warranties, including minimum content and disclosure standards; allows the FTC to prescribe interpretive rules in policy statements regarding unfair or deceptive practices.
Consumer Goods Pricing Act (1975)	Prohibits the use of price maintenance agreements among manufacturers and resellers in interstate commerce.
Fair Debt Collection Practices Act (1977)	Prohibits third-party debt collectors from engaging in deceptive or abusive conduct when collecting consumer debts incurred for personal, family, or household purposes.
Toy Safety Act (1984)	Authorizes the Consumer Product Safety Commission to recall products intended for use by children when they present substantial risk of injury.
Nutrition Labeling and Education Act (1990)	Prohibits exaggerated health claims and requires all processed foods to contain standardized labels with nutritional information.
Home Ownership and Equity Protection Act (1994)	Requires home equity lenders to disclose to borrowers in writing the payment amounts, the consequences of default, and the borrowers' right to cancel the loan within a certain time period.
Telemarketing and Consumer Fraud and Abuse Prevention Act (1994)	Authorizes the FTC to establish regulations for telemarketing, including prohibiting deceptive, coercive, or privacy-invading telemarketing practices; restricting the time during which unsolicited telephone calls may be made to consumers; and requiring telemarketers to disclose the nature of the call at the beginning of an unsolicited sales call.

(Continued)

TABLE 8.3 (*Continued*)

Identity Theft Assumption and Deterrence Act (1998)	Makes the FTC a central clearinghouse for identity theft complaints and requires the FTC to log and acknowledge such complaints, provide victims with relevant information, and refer their complaints to appropriate entities (e.g., the major national consumer reporting agencies and other law enforcement agencies).
Children's Online Privacy Protection Act (1998)	Protects children's privacy by giving parents the tools to control what information is collected from their children online.
Do-Not-Call Registry Act (2003)	Allows the FTC to implement and enforce a do-not-call registry.
Fair and Accurate Credit Transactions Act (2003)	Amends the Fair Credit Reporting Act (FCRA), gives consumers the right to one free credit report a year from the credit reporting agencies, adds provisions designed to prevent and mitigate identity theft, and grants consumers additional rights with respect to how information is used.
Bankruptcy Abuse Prevention and Consumer Protection Act (2005)	Amends the Truth in Lending Act including requiring certain creditors to disclose on the front of billing statements a minimum monthly payment warning for consumers and a toll-free telephone number, established and maintained by the Commission, for consumers seeking information on the time required to repay specific credit balances.
Credit Card Accountability Responsibility and Disclosure Act (2009)	Amends the Truth in Lending Act to prescribe fair practices regarding the extension of credit under an open-end consumer credit plan.
Dodd-Frank Wall Street Reform and Consumer Protection Act, Titles X and XIV (2010)	Established a Bureau of Consumer Financial Protection to protect consumers from complex and deceptive financial products.

Sources: Federal Trade Commission, "Statutes Relating to Consumer Protection Mission," http://www .ftc.gov/enforcement/statutes?title=&field_mission_tid%5B%5D=2973 (accessed June 21, 2016).

In *The Jungle,* Upton Sinclair exposed atrocities, including unsanitary conditions and inhumane labor practices, by the meat-packing industry in Chicago at the turn of the twentieth century. Appalled by the unwholesome practices described in the book, the public demanded reform. Congress responded by passing the Pure Food and Drug Act in 1906, just six months after *The Jungle* was published.[17] In addition to prohibiting the adulteration and mislabeling of food and drug products, the new law also established one of the nation's first federal regulatory agencies, the Food and Drug Administration.

Since the passage of the Pure Food and Drug Act, public health and safety have been major targets of federal and state regulation. For example, the Consumer Product Safety Act established the Consumer Product Safety Commission to enforce rules relating to product safety. IKEA recalled 36 million dressers after three children were killed after the dressers fell on them.[18] Companies that provide defective or faulty products resulting in customer harm must respond quickly to avoid government penalties.

They will still probably face civil litigation from those who were harmed or killed by the defective products. Other laws attempt to protect children from harm, including the Child Protection and Toy Safety Act and the Children's Online Privacy Protection Act.

Credit and Ownership Abuses and inequities associated with loans and credit have resulted in the passage of laws designed to protect consumers' rights and public interests. The most significant of these laws prohibits discrimination in the extension of credit, requires creditors to disclose all finance charges and related aspects of credit transactions, gives consumers the right to dispute and correct inaccurate information on their credit reports, and regulates the activities of debt collectors. For example, the Home Ownership and Equity Protection Act requires home equity lenders to disclose, in writing, the borrower's rights, payment amounts, and the consequences of defaulting on the loan. Together, the U.S. Department of Justice and Department of Housing and Urban Development (HUD) enforce laws that ensure equal access to sale and rental housing. Every April, the government sponsors Fair Housing Month to educate property owners, agents, and consumers on rights with respect to housing.

While home ownership is often considered part of the American Dream, specific business practices in the banking and finance industry have been questioned. During our last recession, the alarming number of mortgage foreclosures arose from a combustible situation involving risky lending practices, subprime mortgage disasters, and a general economic downturn. Many Americans assumed high interest rate loans or bought a house they could not really afford and eventually could no longer make mortgage payments. In many cases, individuals or institutions bought or sold financial products they did not fully understand. The response included Titles X and XIV of the Dodd-Frank Act, which established a Bureau of Consumer Financial Protection to oversee the finance industry and help prevent financial practices that could deceive consumers.

Marketing, Advertising, and Packaging Legal issues in marketing often relate to sales and advertising communications and information about product content and safety. Abuses in promotion can range from exaggerated claims, concealed facts, and deception to outright lying. Such misleading information creates ethical issues because the communicated messages do not include all the information consumers need to make sound purchasing decisions. Sketchers paid consumers $40 million after it was found to have engaged in deceptive advertising. Sketchers claimed that its Shape-Up Shoes as well as other shoe lines would help women lose weight and shape their posteriors. This settlement came a year after Reebok was forced to pay $25 million to settle deceptive advertising claims stating its EasyTone and RunTone shoes would help to tone the body. The FTC determined that there was no evidence to support either of these claims.[19]

Although a certain amount of exaggeration and puffery is tolerated, deceptive claims or claims that cannot be substantiated are likely to invite legal action from the FTC. For example, the FTC levied a $26.5 million fine against the marketers of Sensa, a supposed weight loss company, for marketing campaigns that used unsupported claims and misleading endorsements. The FTC also sued L'Occitane over claims that their skin cream had slimming properties. Cases such as these prompted the FTC to develop a list of phrases that should alert both consumers and marketers to unsubstantiated or false claims about weight loss products (see Figure 8.1).[20]

Since the FTC Act of 1914 outlawed all deceptive and unfair trade practices, additional legislation has further delineated which activities are permissible and which are illegal. For example, the Telemarketing and Consumer Fraud and Abuse Prevention Act requires telemarketers to disclose the nature of the call at the beginning of an unsolicited sales call and restricts the times during which such calls may be made to consumers. Another legal issue in marketing has to do with the promotion of products that involve health or safety. Numerous laws regulate the promotion of alcohol and tobacco products, including the Public Health Cigarette Smoking Act (1970) and the Cigarette Labeling and Advertising Act (1965). The 18th Amendment to the U.S. Constitution prohibited the manufacture and sale of alcoholic beverages in 1919; the prohibition was repealed in 1933 by the 21st Amendment. However, this amendment gave states the power to regulate the transportation of alcoholic beverages across state lines. Today, each state has unique regulations, some of which require the use of wholesalers and retailers to limit direct sales of alcoholic beverages to final consumers in other states. In this case, a law aimed at protecting consumers by promoting temperance in alcohol consumption now affects wine sellers' ability to implement e-commerce and subsequent interstate sales. Currently, roughly 19 states prohibit the interstate sale of wine, another 19 states allow interstate sales on a limited basis, and

FIGURE 8.1 Red Flags: Inaccurate Weight Loss Claims

- Cause weight loss of 2 pounds or more a week for a month or more without dieting or exercise
- Cause substantial weight loss no matter what or how much the consumer eats
- Cause permanent weight loss (even when the consumer stops using product)
- Block the absorption of fat or calories to enable consumers to lose substantial weight
- Cause substantial weight loss for all users
- Cause substantial weight loss by wearing it on the body or rubbing it into the skin

Source: Federal Trade Commission, "FTC Releases Guidance to Media on False Weight-Loss Claims," December 9, 2003, https://www.ftc.gov/news-events/press-releases/2003/12/ftc-releases-guidance-media-false-weight-loss-claims (accessed June 21, 2016).

12 states provide for reciprocal transactions only (e.g., between the states of Colorado and New Mexico).[21]

Sales and Warranties Another area of law that affects business relationships with consumers has to do with warranties. Many consumers consider the warranty behind a product when making a purchase decision, especially for expensive durable goods such as automobiles and appliances. One of the most significant laws affecting warranties is the Magnuson-Moss Warranty (FTC) Act of 1975, which established rules for consumer product warranties, including minimum content and standards for disclosure. All 50 states have enacted "lemon laws" to ensure that automobile sales are accompanied by appropriate warranties and remedies for defects that impair the safety, use, or value of the vehicle. Courts have ruled that consumers who lease instead of purchase automobiles are also entitled to warranty protection under Magnuson-Moss.[22]

Product Liability One area of law that has a profound effect on business and its relations with consumers is **product liability,** which refers to a business's legal responsibility for the performance of its products. This responsibility, which has evolved through both legislation and court interpretation (common law), may include a legal obligation to provide financial compensation to a consumer who has been harmed by a defective product. To receive compensation, a consumer who files suit in the United States must prove that the product was defective, that the defect caused an injury, and that the defect made the product unreasonably dangerous. Under the concept of *strict liability,* an injured consumer can apply this legal responsibility to any firm in the supply chain of a defective product, including contractors, suppliers of component parts, wholesalers, and retailers. Companies with operations in other countries must understand the various forms of product liability law that exist. For example, China passed a new law providing parameters for product liability. The law, which was passed as a result of many consumer injuries and deaths, covers medical devices, environmental pollution, and automobiles. Prior to this legislation, victims could file civil suits, but many claimed they were insufficient. Now, consumers have a more effective means of retribution through the courts and a chance to receive monetary compensation for their distress.[23]

Because the law typically holds businesses liable for their products' performance, many companies choose to recall potentially harmful products; such recalls may be required by legal or regulatory authorities as well. However, critics believe the FTC's recall process is too slow. For instance, it took 165 days for a nut butter manufacturer to recalls its products after salmonella was detected. Part of the delay may come from the firm's chance to issue a voluntary recall. The FDA would prefer the firm to voluntarily recall a dangerous product rather than having it be mandatory.[24]

Product liability lawsuits have increased dramatically in recent years, and many suits have resulted in huge damage awards to injured consumers or their families. In a much-publicized case, a jury awarded a McDonald's

product liability
A business's legal responsibility for the performance of its products.

customer $2.9 million after she was scalded when she spilled hot coffee on her lap. Although that award was eventually reduced on appeal, McDonald's and other fast-food restaurants now display warning signs that their coffee is hot to eliminate both further injury and liability. Most companies have taken steps to minimize their liability, and some firms—such as medical technology company C.R. Bard—have stopped making products or withdrawn completely from problematic markets because of the high risk of expensive liability lawsuits. Johnson & Johnson discontinued its power morcellator, used to remove uterine fibroids in women, because it could spread undetected cancers. Several wrongful death and product liability lawsuits have been filed against Johnson & Johnson, which will likely spend millions in resolving these cases.[25] Although some states have limited damage awards and legislative reform is often on the agenda, the issue of product liability remains politically sensitive.

International Issues Concerns about protecting consumers' legal rights are not limited to the United States. Most developed nations have laws and offices devoted to this goal. For example, the Chinese government enacted tougher safety standards for automobiles, bringing Chinese expectations in line with safety standards in the United States and Europe.[26] In the European Union (EU), the health and consumer protection directorate general oversees efforts to increase consumer confidence in the unified market. Its initiatives center on health, safety, economic, and public-health interests. One EU directive establishes minimum levels of consumer protection in member states. For example, EU consumers now have a legal guarantee of two years on all consumer goods. If they find a defective product, they may choose repair or replacement or, in special circumstances, ask for a price reduction or rescind the contract altogether.[27]

In Japan, unlike in the United States, product liability lawsuits are much less common. In the early 1990s, Chikara Minami filed one of the first such lawsuits against Japanese automaker Mitsubishi. Minami's suit alleged a defect in the Mitsubishi Pajero. Although the court sided with the automaker in the said case, ten years later Mitsubishi was accused of deliberately covering up consumer complaints. Despite this revelation and an enhanced product liability law in 1995, consumer rights are often subverted to preserve the power and structure of big business in Japan.[28] Much like Japan, China's consumer rights movement is also relatively new and resulted from economic policy changes away from isolationism and central economic planning. The China Consumers' Association was established in 1984 and has helped create consumer expectations and company responses that are starting to resemble those found in Western economies. Despite this action, however, there have been numerous consumer scares surrounding products manufactured in China and other countries. Table 8.4 discloses a number of cases involving food products, medicine, and toys.[29]

As we have discussed in this section, there are many laws that influence business practices with respect to consumers all over the world. Every year, new laws are enacted, and existing rules are modified in response to

TABLE 8.4 Notable Cases Involving Recalls

Year	Recall	Description
2007	Lead paint toys	It was discovered that many Mattel toys had been painted using lead paint, which is poisonous if ingested
2007	Pet food	Contaminated pet food from China resulted in the sickness and death of many pets
2010	Children's medicines	Johnson & Johnson issued a massive recall on children's medicines such as Tylenol due to product contamination
2012	Peanut Butter	Salmonella bacteria was detected in many peanut products
2013	Chobani yogurt	Mold was detected in some Chobani yogurt products
2014	General Motors	GM issued a recall on several car models because of faulty ignition switches
2016	Samsung	Samsung recall its Galaxy Note 7 due to overheating and fire risk

the changing business environment, including the incidence of consumer product concerns. Although companies must monitor and obey all laws and regulations, they also need to keep abreast of the ethical obligations and standards that exist in the marketplace.

Ethical Issues

In 1962, President John F. Kennedy proclaimed a Consumer Bill of Rights that includes the rights to choose, to safety, to be informed, and to be heard. Kennedy also established the Consumer Advisory Council to integrate consumer concerns into government regulations and processes. These four rights established a philosophical basis on which state and local consumer protection rules were later developed.[30] Around the same time, Ralph Nader's investigations of auto safety and his publication of *Unsafe at Any Speed* in 1965 alerted citizens to the dangers of a common consumer product. Nader's activism and Kennedy's speech provided support for **consumerism,** the movement to protect consumers from an imbalance of power on the side of business and to maximize consumer welfare in the marketplace.[31] The consumer movement is a global phenomenon, as is indicated by the annual celebration of World Consumer Rights Day.

Over the last five decades, consumerism has affected public policy through a variety of mechanisms. Early efforts were aimed primarily at advocating for legislation and regulation, whereas more recent efforts have shifted to education and protection programs directed at consumers.[32] The Consumers Union (CU), for example, works with regional and federal legislators and international groups to protect consumer interests, sponsors conferences and research projects, tests consumer products, and publishes the results in its *Consumer Reports* magazine. The magazine details business practices that the CU deems unfair to consumers, such as predatory lending, the poor value of some life insurance products, and advertisements

consumerism
The movement to protect consumers from an imbalance of power on the side of business and to maximize consumer welfare in the marketplace.

aimed at vulnerable groups, like children and senior citizens.[33] The internet and electronic communication have become main vehicles for consumer advocacy, education, and protection. Visitors to the National Consumers League website at www.nclnet.org or www.consumerworld. org find publications on many consumer issues, research and campaign reports, product reviews, updates on legal matters, and many other types of services. Thus, consumer groups and information services have shifted the balance of power between consumer and business because consumers are able to compare prices, read independent rankings, communicate with other buyers, and have greater knowledge about products, companies, and competitors.[34]

Despite the opportunities to exert more power, some researchers question whether most consumers take the time and energy to do so. For example, although the internet provides a great deal of information and choices, access to the internet partly depends on educational level and income. In addition, the volume of information available online may actually make it more difficult to analyze and assimilate. Even with these issues, consumer groups have developed a legion of e-activists who e-mail legislators and regulators and work to get consumer protection legislation passed. These consumer activists hope to use their campaigns to spur policy changes in the area of consumer protection. Some major accomplishments include lower credit card rates, improved card services, and higher security of financial information.[35] The CU provides a number of consumer advocacy tools on its website, such as recommendations for writing letters to government agencies and corporations.

All U.S. presidents since Kennedy have confirmed the four basic consumer rights and added new ones in response to changing business conditions. President William J. Clinton, for example, appointed a commission to study the changing healthcare environment and its implications for consumer rights. The result was the proposal of a Patient's Bill of Rights and Responsibilities to ensure rights to confidentiality of patient information, to participate in healthcare decisions, to access emergency services, and other needs.[36] During the same period, a Financial Consumer's Bill of Rights Act was proposed in the U.S. House of Representatives to curb high bank fees, automated teller machine surcharges, and other practices that have angered consumers.[37]

Consumer rights were first formalized through a presidential speech and subsequent affirmations, resulting in the legal establishment of specific elements of these rights. However, the relatively broad nature of the rights means they must be interpreted and implemented on a company-by-company basis. Table 8.5 lists six consumer rights that have become part of the ethical expectations of business. Although these rights are not necessarily provided by all organizations, our social responsibility philosophy requires their attention and implementation.

Right to Choose The right to choose implies that, to the extent possible, consumers have the opportunity to select from a variety of products at competitive prices. This right is based on the philosophy of the competitive

TABLE 8.5 Basic Consumer Rights

Right	General Issues
To choose	Consumers have the opportunity to select from a variety of products at reasonable prices
To safety	All products should be safe for their intended use, include instructions for proper and safe use, and have been sufficiently tested to ensure reliability
To be informed	Information is accurate, adequate, and free of deception so consumers can make a sound decision
To be heard	Provides opportunities for consumers to communicate or voice their concerns in the public policy process
To redress	The right for consumers to express dissatisfaction and seek restitution from a business when a product does not meet their expectations
To privacy	Relates to consumers' awareness of how personal data are collected and used and places a burden on firms to protect this information

nature of markets, which should lead to high-quality products at reasonable prices. Antitrust activities that reduce competition may jeopardize this right. This right has been called into question with respect to safety in some parts of the United States. The right has manifested itself differently in recent times. Google, for example, was ordered by an EU ruling dubbed the "right to be forgotten" to erase consumers' information in search results. This gives consumers in the EU more power to choose how their information will be used. While the rule only applies in the EU, the effects of this mandate may be far-reaching.[38]

Right to Safety The right to safety also implies that all products should be safe for their intended use, include instructions for proper and safe use, and have been sufficiently tested to ensure reliability. Companies must take great care in designing warning messages about products with potentially dangerous or unsafe effects. These messages should take into account consumers' ability to understand and respond to the information. Warnings should be relevant and meaningful to every potential user of the product. Some warnings use symbols or pictures to communicate. Companies that fail to honor the right to safety risk expensive product liability lawsuits. In an instance of unfortunate timing, McDonald's announced its response to media allegations of serving unsafe food items in China soon before World Consumer Rights Day. Claims involved the serving of chicken an hour past the suggested time period after being cooked as well as the serving of unsanitary beef. The incident damaged the company's reputation as they had launched a marketing campaign highlighting their commitment to food quality and safety only weeks before.[39]

Right to Be Informed Consumers also have the right to be informed. Any information, whether communicated in written or verbal format, should be accurate, adequate, and free of deception so that consumers can make a sound decision. This general assertion has also led to specific legislation, such as the Nutrition Labeling and Education Act of 1990, which requires certain nutrition facts on food labels. This right can be associated with safety issues if consumers do not have sufficient information to purchase or use a product effectively. Other types of violations include companies charging customers for unrequested products or not providing them with enough information. The Federal Communications Commission fined AT&T $100 million because it did not inform customers with unlimited plans that after using 5 gigabytes of data per month, the carrier would slow transmission speeds. This slower speed interfered with the functionality of mobile apps and appeared to contradict the network speeds that AT&T advertised. AT&T did not tell its customers that their transmission speed would go slower after 5 gigabytes of data usage, and the FCC believed this violated consumer rights.[40]

In an age of rapid technological advances and globalization, the degree of complexity in product marketing is another concern related to consumers' right to information. This complexity may relate to the ways in which product features and benefits are discussed in advertising, how effective salespeople are in answering consumer questions, the expertise needed to operate or use the product, and the ease of returning or exchanging the product. To help consumers make decisions based on adequate and timely information, some organizations sponsor consumer education programs. For example, pharmaceutical companies and health maintenance organizations sponsor free seminars, health screenings, websites, and other programs to educate consumers about their health and treatment options. Nonprofit organization URAC is committed to promoting healthcare quality and provides a "seal of approval" that lets consumers know that the website's content is trustworthy and reliable.[41]

Right to Be Heard The right to be heard relates to opportunities for consumers to communicate or voice their concerns in the public policy process. This also implies that governments have the responsibility to listen and take consumer issues and concerns into account. One mechanism for fulfilling this responsibility is through the FTC and state consumer affairs offices. Another vehicle includes congressional hearings held to educate elected officials about specific issues of concern to consumers. At the same time, consumers are expected to be full participants in the process, meaning they must be informed and willing to take action against misconduct in the marketplace.

Right to Seek Redress In addition to the rights described by Kennedy, consumers also have the right to express dissatisfaction and seek restitution from a business when a good or service does not meet their expectations. However, consumers need to be educated in the process for seeking redress and to recognize that the first course of action in such cases should be with the seller. At the same time, companies need to have explicit and formal processes for dealing with customer dissatisfaction. Although some product problems lead to third-party intervention or legal recourse, the majority of issues should be resolvable between the consumer and the business. One third party that consumers may consult in such cases is the Better Business Bureau (BBB), which promotes self-regulation of business. To gain and maintain membership, a firm must agree to abide by the ethical standards established by the BBB. This organization collects complaints on businesses and makes this information, along with other reports, available for consumer decision-making. The BBB also operates the dispute resolution division to assist in out-of-court settlements between consumers and businesses. For example, the division has a program, BBB Auto Line, to handle disputes between consumers and automobile manufacturers.[42] This self-regulatory approach not only provides differentiation in the market but can also minimize or prevent new laws and regulations.

Right to Privacy The advent of new information technology and the internet has prompted increasing concerns about consumer privacy. This right relates to consumers' awareness of how personal data are collected and used, and it places a burden on firms to protect this information. How information is used can create concerns for consumers. Although some e-commerce firms have joined together to develop privacy standards for the internet, many websites do not meet the FTC's criteria for fair information practices, including notice, choice, access, and security.[43] We will take a closer look at the debate surrounding privacy rights in Chapter 10.

A firm's ability to address these consumer rights can serve as a competitive advantage. Service Line Warranties of America (SLWA), a utility service company and a past recipient of the National Torch Award for Marketplace Ethics given by the BBB, is highly regarded for their ethical approach to consumers. They help consumers understand their responsibilities with respect to utility maintenance so that they are not charged extra fees by their utility companies. The company's mission is to take care of the complexities of home ownership, so consumers can enjoy more free time.[44]

When consumers believe a firm is operating outside ethical or legal standards, they may be motivated to take some type of action. As we discussed earlier, there are a number of strategies consumers can employ to communicate their dissatisfaction, such as complaining or discontinuing the relationship. For example, some people believe Walmart's presence has contributed to the demise of locally owned pharmacies and variety stores in many small towns. The chain's buying power ensures lower prices and wider product variety for consumers but also makes it difficult for some smaller retailers to compete. Other consumers and community leaders worry about the traffic congestion and urban sprawl that accompany new retail sites. Some Walmart critics have taken their discontent with the retailer to the internet. Disgruntled customers and others share complaints about the retail chain, provide updates about legal action, and promote campaigns against the retailer on makingchangeatwalmart.org.[45]

Stakeholders may use the three types of power—symbolic, utilitarian, and coercive—discussed in Chapter 2 to create organizational awareness of important issues. For example, wealthy Thai consumers who support military rule asked consumers to avoid purchasing European brands after the EU criticized a Thai government coup. In particular, the EU criticized the decisions to make it harder to express dissent as well as delays in elections. Brussels announced it was suspending official visits to Thailand and would not sign an agreement with the country. Wealthy Thai consumers felt betrayed by a region with which they extensively trade.[46] While this response is not a result of a company's action, the situation highlights the lingering contention between the two countries. These consumers are engaging in another form of consumer action, a **boycott**, by abstaining from using, purchasing, or dealing with an organization.

boycott
A form of consumer action in which consumers abstain from using, purchasing, or dealing with an organization.

Many groups choose to boycott certain businesses or products because of disagreements over beliefs or governmental policies. Famous celebrities and organizations boycotted the Beverly Hills Hotel because of the actions of its owner, Sultan Hassanal Bolkiah of Brunei, a country located on the north coast of the island of Borneo. The boycott occurred after the sultan stated he was enforcing Sharia law in the country. Boycotters protested against some of the harsher punishments levied against certain people groups committed of crimes under Sharia law.[47] Protests are also a common consumer method of showing displeasure with an organization's policies.

Philanthropic Issues

Although relationships with consumers are fundamentally grounded in economic exchanges, the previous sections demonstrate that additional levels of expectations exist. Research continues to show that the majority of consumers would be likely to switch to brands associated with a good cause, as long as price and quality were equal. These results suggest that today's consumers take for granted that they can obtain high-quality products at reasonable prices, so businesses need to do something to differentiate themselves from the competition. More firms are therefore investigating ways to link their philanthropic efforts with consumer interests. Starbucks, for example, has contributed to environmental programs, sustainable farming initiatives, and investment in employee well-being and happiness. These programs not only form a link between the company's possible effects and its interest in the natural environment but also provide a service to its customers and other stakeholders.

From a strategic perspective, a firm's ability to link consumer interests to philanthropy should lead to stronger economic relationships. As we shall see in Chapter 9, philanthropic responsibilities to consumers usually entail broader benefits, including those that affect the community. For example, large pharmaceutical and health insurance firms provided financial support to the Foundation for Accountability (FACCT), a nonprofit organization that assists healthcare consumers in making better decisions. FACCT initiated an online system for patients to evaluate their physician on several quality indicators. Although FACCT ceased its operations, the Markle Foundation continues to host the nonprofit's legacy with

Ethical Responsibilities in Marketing

General Motors Recall: We Know Something You Don't Know

General Motors (GM) faced immense criticism as it dealt with the fallout from the faulty ignition switch scandal in 2014. As the story unfolded, it appeared that GM had violated many of the rights outlined in Kennedy's Consumer Bill of Rights. These failures had major repercussions for GM, including massive recalls, lawsuits, testimonies before Congress, and reputational damage.

Earlier GM issued a recall of 2.6 million Chevrolet Cobalts. The problem involved faulty ignition switches that could inadvertently switch to a position that could cause the car to stall and the air bags to be disabled. Soon, recalls were issued on other models for the same reason, bringing the number of vehicles recalled in North America to 30 million. At least 15 deaths have been attributed to faulty ignition switches in GM vehicles (actual deaths are believed to be about 124).

A product recall is a serious issue by itself. However, the situation for GM worsened when it was revealed that certain employees in the company knew about the defective component since 2004. Although GM developed a snap-on cover to prevent the problem, it did not issue a recall. Instead, it provided the snap-on covers to dealers and told them to install them if customers complained.

GM's failure to address the problem violated consumers' rights to safety and to be informed. The ignition switch defect made vehicles unsafe for consumers. As a company selling a product that could be deadly if it failed to work properly, GM had an obligation to ensure customer safety to the best of its ability. Owners of the vehicles were not informed of the potential dangers,

even though GM had found a way to fix the problem through a snap-on cover. These failures on GM's part suggest an indifferent attitude toward consumer well-being.

According to some employees, the GM culture also had the tendency to punish or ignore those with bad news. One whistleblower claims he was demoted after discovering vehicle defects and pressing for recalls. However, a lawsuit he filed against the company was dismissed. Others claim that this type of retaliation dissuaded them from reporting product quality issues. It appears that the right to be heard was also ignored at GM.

This debacle prompted Congress to require testimony from GM CEO Mary Barra about why it took GM so long to issue the recalls. An internal investigation that GM conducted concluded that knowledge about the defects had existed for a decade and that GM was negligent in its responsibility to customers. This led to the dismissal of 15 employees for failing to take action after discovering the product defect.

Due to this serious safety issue, consumers sought their right for redress by filing lawsuits against GM. GM lawyers argued that their previous bankruptcy should mitigate depreciation claims that occurred before then. Although initially a bankruptcy judge ruled in GM's favor, a federal court overruled the ruling and claimed that GM's bankruptcy cannot protect it from lawsuits involving accidents from before its bankruptcy filing. Despite these challenges, General Motors resolved these major legal issues and rebounded with record profitability in 2016.

Sources: Jeff Bennett, "New Set of GM Recalls Involves Pickups, SUVs," *The Wall Street Journal*, June 9, 2014, p. B3; Ashby Jones, "Plaintiff Lawyers Take Aim At GM," *The Wall Street Journal*, June 9, 2014, p. A1; Tim Higgins and Nick Summers, "If Only They Had Listened," *Bloomberg Businessweek*, June 18, 2014, pp. 48–53; Bill Vlasic, "G. M. Inquiry Cites Years of Neglect Over Fatal Defect," *The New York Times*, June 5, 2014, http://www.nytimes.com/2014/06/06/business/gm-ignition-switch-internal-recall-investigation-report.html (accessed July 20, 2016); Max Blau, "No Accident: Inside GM's deadly ignition switch scandal," *Atlanta Magazine*, January 2016, http://www.atlantamagazine.com/great-reads/no-accident-inside-gms-deadly-ignition-switch-scandal/ (accessed July 20, 2016); Nathan Bomey, "Court: Ignition-switch lawsuits against GM can proceed," *USA Today*, July 14, 2016, http://www.usatoday.com/story/money/cars/2016/07/13/general-motors-bankruptcy-ignition-switch-lawsuit/87029916/ (accessed July 20, 2016).

TABLE 8.6 Top Ten Philanthropic Companies

Corporate Foundation	Annual Giving ($)
Novartis Patient Assistance Foundation, Inc.	456,825,176
Wells Fargo Foundation	189,380,780
The Bank of America Charitable Foundation, Inc.	175,729,430
The Wal-Mart Foundation, Inc.	168,582,621
The JPMorgan Chase Foundation	130,855,483
GE Foundation	108,401,652
The Coca-Cola Foundation, Inc.	90,518,700
Citi Foundation	78,000,000
ExxonMobil Foundation	75,212,563
Bayer U.S. Patient Assistance Foundation	58,474,547

Source: Foundation Center, "50 Largest Corporate Foundations by Total Giving," http://foundationcenter.org/findfunders/topfunders/top50giving.html (accessed June 21, 2016).

documents and white papers. The foundation partners with other organizations to improve the role of technology in addressing critical public health needs.[48]

Companies will have more successful philanthropic efforts when the cause is a good fit with the firm's product category, industry, customer concerns, and/or location. This alignment is an important contributor to the long-term relationships that often develop between specific companies and cause-related organizations. Many firms involved in medicine and pharmaceuticals will contribute to causes that improve access to proper healthcare and medication, provide stronger patient support and outcomes, decrease accidents and injuries, and respond to emergency or critical needs of a community. Table 8.6 describes the philanthropic contribution levels of 10 firms, all of which rank in the top 50 corporate foundations in terms of annual giving. These companies have established corporate foundations with large endowments, which means that annual contributions are relatively unaffected by corporate profitability and the economic cycle. Nonprofits prefer consistent donations rather than wide variance from year to year.

STRATEGIC IMPLEMENTATION OF RESPONSIBILITIES TO CONSUMERS

As this chapter has demonstrated, social responsibility entails relationships with many stakeholders—including consumers—and many firms are finding creative ways to meet these responsibilities. Just as in other aspects of social responsibility, these relationships must be managed,

TABLE 8.7 Business in the Community Marketplace Responsibility

The Marketplace Responsibility Principles:

- Respect your customers
- Support vulnerable customers
- Seek potential customers within excluded groups
- Manage the impact of product or service
- Actively discourage product misuse
- Actively manage responsibility in your supply chain
- Treat suppliers as partners
- Work with the rule makers
- Have consistent standards

Best Practice for Marketplace Responsibility:

- Be consistent
- Anticipate trends
- Aim to deliver quality results
- Put at the heart of business strategy
- Part of the culture
- Encourage and motivate responsible behaviour
- Mainstream not niche
- Share best practice within the business

Source: Business in the Community, "The Marketplace Responsibility Principles," http://www.bitc.org.uk/our-resources/report/marketplace-responsibility-principles (accessed June 21, 2016).

nurtured, and continuously assessed. Resources devoted to this effort may include programs for educating and listening to consumers, surveys to discover strengths and weaknesses in stakeholder relationships, hiring consumer affairs professionals, the development of a community relations office, and other initiatives. Business in the Community, a coalition of companies in the United Kingdom, developed nine marketplace responsibility principles to guide its members and other businesses in dealing with consumers and the supply chain. Table 8.7 lists these principles, along with eight best practices for effectively putting them into action.

Understanding consumer and stakeholder issues can be especially complex in the global environment. For example, PUMA intended to honor the United Arab Emirates (UAE) as it celebrated its 40th National Day by developing a limited edition shoe with the colors of the UAE flag. However, when it was released UAE consumers were outraged. They viewed it as putting a respected symbol on something perceived to be unclean in Middle Eastern culture. PUMA had to apologize and remove the shoes.[49] Organizations must understand the importance of integrating all stakeholders into their social responsibility efforts, including employees, as we explored in Chapter 7, and the general community, which we examine in Chapter 9.

SUMMARY

Companies face complex decisions about how to respond to the expectations, attitudes, and buying patterns of consumers—those individuals who purchase, use, and dispose of products for personal and household use. Consumers are primary stakeholders because their awareness, purchase, use, and repurchase of products are vital to a company's existence.

Consumers and businesses are fundamentally connected by an economic relationship. Economic responsibilities include following through on promises made in the exchange process. Consumer fraud involves intentional deception to derive an unfair economic advantage over an organization. If consumers believe that a firm has not fulfilled its economic responsibility, they may ask for a refund, tell others about the bad experience, discontinue their patronage, contact a consumer agency, or seek legal redress.

In the United States, legal issues with respect to consumers fall under the jurisdiction of the FTC, which enforces federal antitrust and consumer protection laws. Other federal and state agencies regulate specific goods, services, or business practices. Among the issues that may have been addressed through specific state or federal laws and regulations are consumer health and safety, credit and ownership, marketing and advertising, sales and warranties, and product liability. Product liability refers to a business's legal responsibility for the performance of its products. Concerns about protecting consumers' legal rights are not limited to the United States.

Ethical issues related to consumers include the Consumer Bill of Rights enumerated by President Kennedy. Consumerism refers to the movement to protect consumers from an imbalance of power with business and to maximize consumer welfare in the marketplace. Some specific elements of consumer rights have been mandated by law, but the relatively broad nature of the rights means they must be interpreted and implemented on a company-by-company basis. Consumer rights have evolved to include the right to choose, the right to safety, the right to be informed, the right to be heard, the right to seek redress, and the right to privacy. When consumers believe a firm is operating outside ethical or legal standards, they may be motivated to take action, including boycotting—abstaining from using, purchasing, or dealing with an organization.

More firms are investigating ways to link their philanthropic efforts with consumer interests. From a strategic perspective, a firm's ability to link consumer interests to philanthropy should lead to stronger economic relationships.

Many companies are finding creative ways to satisfy their responsibilities to consumers. Much like employee relationships, these responsibilities must be managed, nurtured, and continuously assessed. Resources devoted to this effort may include programs for educating and listening to consumers, surveys to discover strengths and weaknesses in stakeholder relationships, hiring consumer affairs professionals, working with industry groups, and the development of other initiatives that engage consumers.

Responsible Business Debate

The Use of Clearance Pricing as A Price Signal

Issue: *Should the use of clearance pricing be regulated?*

Sales are price discounts that are designed to encourage purchase of a particular item. Sometimes the term clearance is used, but not with the term sale, since the use of the term sale is regulated in most states. According to the American Marketing Association, clearance is "an end-of-season sale to make room for more goods." While retailers can offer sales for temporary time periods, items in a clearance do not return to their original prices. Rather, the product is discounted until it is sold. Clearance events are often short in duration, and items under clearance are not advertised.

Studies have demonstrated that many view the word "clearance" as a price signal indicating substantial discounts. Yet unlike other forms of sales promotion, clearance events are less regulated. Many retailers, including Macy's and clothing stores, use the word clearance extensively. By 2004, more than 30 percent of merchandise was sold at clearance. Consumers may be attracted to clearance pricing due to the following factors: (1) fear that the product will be discontinued before they purchase it, (2) belief that others will get to the item first, (3) perceived value of the product, (4) the belief that they are saving money, and (5) escalation of commitment due to time spent searching for sales.

It has generally been ruled that the term "clearance" is an example of puffery, an exaggerated promotional claim that should not be taken seriously by a reasonable person. In 1985, the state of Wisconsin filed a lawsuit against American TV & Appliance alleging that the retailer's claims of offering "a clearance sale on the finest washers and dryers you can buy" was deceptive due to the following factors: (1) the products were not deemed to be of the finest quality, (2) the store was using the advertisement to get people in the store and then tried to up-sell them higher priced products, and (3) the merchandise was purchased exclusively for the event and therefore did not qualify as clearance. Although at first the courts ruled against the retailer, a later court overturned the ruling, stating that the term "clearance" in the ad was an example of puffery.

However, do consumers themselves view the term clearance as an exaggerated claim they should not accept at face value? Critics argue no. It has been generally accepted that clearance indicates substantial price discounts, so using the term "clearance" inappropriately can be deceptive. Without regulation, they argue, retailers can use this term to make consumers think they are receiving a substantial deal. In fact, research has shown that less than 15 percent of consumers know the amount of the associated price discount.

On the other hand, regulating how the term "clearance" is used could have negative implications. Like any form of business regulation, regulation of the word clearance would limit what a business can and cannot do. Placing limits on how clearance sales can be used will likely mean that retailers will display the term "clearance sale" less due to the fear of violating FTC regulations. Yet clearance sales can be important strategies for retailers in selling products, particularly for firms that face much demand uncertainty for a product.

There Are Two Sides to Every Issue:

1. Retailers should be able to use the term clearance without having to qualify or justify the amount of the discount.
2. Because the term clearance is potentially misleading, usage of the term should be regulated and not used unless there are substantial price discounts.

Sources: State of Wisconsin v. American TV & Appliance of Madison, Inc., 430 N.W.2d 709 (Wisc. App. Ct. 1988); Cullen Goretzke, *The Resurgence of Caveat Emptor: Puffery Undermines the Pro-Consumer Trend in Wisconsin's Misrepresentation Doctrine,* 2003 Wis. L. Rev. 171, 222; Kit Yarrow, "Why Shoppers Just Can't Resist Clearance Sales," *Time,* http://business.time.com/2013/01/07/why-shoppers-just-cant-resist-clearance-sales/ (accessed July 20, 2016). Volker Nocke and Martin Peitz, "A Theory of Clearance Sales," *Economic Journal* 117, no. 522 (July 2007): 964; American Marketing Association, "Dictionary," *Marketing Power,* http://www.marketingpower.com/_layouts/dictionary.aspx?dletter=c (accessed July 20, 2016); Kenneth C. Manning, O.C. Ferrell, and Linda K. Ferrell, "Toward Understanding 'Clearance' Promotions," Working paper; J. Jeffrey Inman, Leigh McAlister, and Wayne D. Hoyer, "Promotion Signal: Proxy for a Price Cut?" *Journal of Consumer Research* 17 (June 1990): 74–81.

KEY TERMS

consumers (p. 263)
consumer fraud (p. 264)

product liability (p. 271)
consumerism (p. 273)

boycott (p. 278)

DISCUSSION QUESTIONS

1. List and describe the consumer rights that have become social expectations of business. Why have some of these rights been formalized through legislation? Should these rights be considered ethical standards?

2. Look at Southwest Airline's Customer Service Commitment at http://www.southwest.com/assets/pdfs/corporate-commitments/customer-service-commitment.pdf. Describe how different elements of its commitment relate to specific economic, legal, ethical, or philanthropic responsibilities that the airline has to its customers.

3. What is the purpose of a boycott? Describe the characteristics of companies and consumers that are likely to be involved in a boycott situation. What circumstances would cause you to consider participating in a boycott?

4. How can companies strive for successful relationships with consumers, including meeting their economic, legal, ethical, and philanthropic expectations?

5. How will consumer rights and activism change over the next decade? Will the movement strengthen or decline? Why?

EXPERIENTIAL EXERCISE

Visit the website of Consumers International (http://www.consumersinternational.org//). What is the purpose of this website? Select a current issue and read the information provided by CI on that issue. How useful is this information to you? With what information do you agree and/or disagree? How could a business manager use this site to understand and improve a company's relationship and reputation with consumers?

THERE'S A RINGING IN MY EARS: WHAT WOULD YOU DO?

Justin Thompson was excited. He really enjoyed his job at the Kingston's department store downtown. This location housed Kingston's first store and still had many of its original features. As he rode the subway into the city center, Justin thought about the money he would earn this summer and the great car he hoped to buy before school started. He was lucky to have secured this type of job, since many of his friends were working early or late hours at fast-food chains or out in the summer heat. The management team at Kingston's had initiated a program with his high school counselors, hoping to attract top high school seniors into retail management throughout their college career and beyond. Justin was a strong student from a single-parent background, and his counselor was highly complimentary of his work ethic and prospects for professional employment.

Justin's first week was consumed with various training sessions. There were eight students in the special high school program. They watched a company video that discussed Kingston's history, ethics policy, current operations, and customer service philosophy. They met with staff from Human Resources to fill out paperwork. They learned how to scan merchandise and operate the computer software and cash register. They toured the store's three levels and visited with each department manager. Justin was especially excited about working in the electronics department, but he was assigned to men's clothing.

Justin worked alongside several employees during the first few weeks on the store floor. He watched the experienced employees approach customers, help them, and ring up the sale. He noticed that some employees took personal telephone calls and that others did not clean up the dressing rooms or restock items very quickly. On slower days, he eventually worked alone in the department. Several times when he came to work in the afternoon, he had to clean up the mess left behind by the morning shift. When he spoke to various colleagues about it in the break room, they told him it was best to keep quiet. After all, he was a high school student earning money for a car, not a "real employee" with kids to feed and bills to pay. Justin assumed that retail work was much like team projects in school—not everyone pulled their weight but it was hard to be the tattletale.

One Saturday morning was extremely busy, as Kingston's was running a big sale. People were swarming to the sales racks, and Justin was amazed at how fast the time was passing. In the late afternoon, several friends of one of his coworkers dropped by the men's section. Before long, their hands were filled with merchandise. The crowd was starting to wane, so Justin took a few minutes to clean up the dressing room. When he came out of the dressing room, his coworker was ringing up the friends' merchandise. Justin saw two ties go into the bag, but only one was scanned into the system. He saw an extra discount provided on an expensive shirt. Justin was shocked to see that not every item was scanned or that improper discounts were applied, and his mind was racing. Should he stop his coworker? Should he "take a break" and get security? Was there another alternative? What would you do?

CHAPTER NINE

Community Relations and Strategic Philanthropy

Chapter Objectives

- To describe the community as a stakeholder
- To discuss the community relations function
- To distinguish between strategic philanthropy and cause-related marketing
- To examine how social entrepreneurship relates to social responsibility.
- To identify the benefits of strategic philanthropy
- To explain the key factors in implementing strategic philanthropy

Chapter Outline

Community Stakeholders

Responsibilities to the Community

Philanthropic Contributions

Strategic Philanthropy Defined

Strategic Philanthropy and Social Responsibility

Social Entrepreneurship and Social Responsibility

Benefits of Strategic Philanthropy

Implementation of Strategic Philanthropy

TOMS Walks into the Eyewear Business

Although many organizations try to incorporate cause-related marketing into their business operations, TOMS Shoes takes the concept of philanthropy one step further. TOMS blends a for-profit business with social entrepreneurship in what it terms the one for one model. For every pair of shoes sold, another pair is provided to a child in need. TOMS has also expanded into eyewear and the coffee business. For every pair of sunglasses sold, a person with vision problems in developing countries receives surgery, prescription glasses, or medical treatment to help restore his or her sight. For every TOMS coffee product sold, clean water is donated to a person in need. Unlike many nonprofits, TOMS' for-profit business enables the company to support its philanthropic component, which keeps the company from having to solicit donations.

The idea for TOMS Shoes occurred after founder Blake Mycoskie witnessed the immense poverty in Argentinean villages—poverty so bad that many families could not afford to purchase shoes for their children. As a result, Mycoskie decided to create a business that would consist of two parts: TOMS Shoes, a for-profit business that would sell the shoes, and Friends of TOMS, the company's nonprofit subsidiary that would distribute shoes to those in need.

For his original product, Mycoskie decided to adopt the *alpargata* shoe worn in Argentina. The *alpargata* is a slip-on shoe made from canvas or fabric with rubber soles. After a *Los Angeles Times* article featured Mycoskie's new business, demand for the shoes exploded. Today TOMS is a thriving business.

After distributing its 1-millionth pair of shoes in 2010, TOMS began to consider other products that could be used in the one-to-one model. Because 80 percent of vision impairment in developing countries is preventable or curable, TOMS decided that for every pair of sunglasses it sold, the company would provide treatment or prescription glasses for those in need. TOMS chose Nepal as the first country to apply its one-to-one model. TOMS also recognized that many people in developing countries lack access to clean water. Polluted water is one of the biggest causes of disease. Therefore, TOMS has also expanded into the coffee business, once again applying its one for one model. With every TOMS Roasting Co. product sold, the organization provides clean water to a person in need.

TOMS takes its obligations for social responsibility seriously. The company builds the cost of the extra pair of shoes and eye care into the price of the products it sells. TOMS also works closely with local humanitarian organizations so they can understand the communities to which they are donating.

Customers who do business with TOMS feel committed to the company because they know that their purchases are going toward a good cause, even if they might pay a bit more in the process. TOMS goes to great lengths to educate the public about the importance of its mission. For instance, the company provides internship opportunities and engages brand ambassadors at universities to spread the TOMS message. Every year the company promotes the One Day Without Shoes campaign, in which participants spend one day without shoes to understand what children in developing countries must undergo daily. These events have been supported by celebrities such as Charlize Theron, Kris Ryan, and the Dallas Cowboys Cheerleaders.

Despite its success, TOMS' mission is far from complete. As its expansion into eyewear and coffee demonstrates, the company is looking for new opportunities for applying its one for one model to address social issues. TOMS demonstrates how an innovative concept and the ability to engage in social entrepreneurship can create a successful company that can make a difference.[1]

TOMS Shoes, like most organizations with operational expertise and other core competencies, can also focus on implementing social responsibility and satisfying stakeholder groups. From a social responsibility perspective, the key challenge is how an organization assesses its stakeholders' needs, integrates them with company strategy, reconciles differences between stakeholders' needs, strives for better relationships with stakeholders, achieves mutual understandings with them, and finds solutions for problems. In this chapter, we explore community stakeholders and how organizations deal with stakeholder needs through philanthropic initiatives. We explore the relationship with communities and the economic, legal, ethical, and philanthropic responsibilities that must be addressed by business. We define strategic philanthropy and integrate this concept with other elements of social responsibility. Next, we trace the evolution of corporate philanthropy and distinguish the concept from cause-related marketing. We also provide examples of best practices of addressing stakeholders' interests that meet our definition of strategic philanthropy. From there, we define social entrepreneurship and explain how it relates to strategic philanthropy and social responsibility. Then we consider the benefits of investing in strategic philanthropy to satisfy both stakeholders and corporate objectives. Finally, we examine the process of implementing strategic philanthropy in business. Our approach in this chapter is to demonstrate how companies can link strategic philanthropy with economic, legal, and ethical concerns for the benefit of all stakeholders.

COMMUNITY STAKEHOLDERS

The concept of *community* has many varying characteristics that make it a challenge to define. The community does not always receive the same level of acceptance as other stakeholders. Some people even wonder how a company determines who is in the community. Is a community defined by city or county boundaries? What if the firm operates in multiple locations? Or is a community prescribed by the interactions a firm has with various constituents who do not fit neatly into other stakeholder categories? For a small restaurant in a large city, the owner may define the community as the immediate neighborhood where most patrons live. The restaurant may demonstrate social responsibility by hiring people from the neighborhood, participating in the neighborhood crime watch program, donating food to the elementary school's annual parent-teacher meetings, or sponsoring a neighborhood Little League team. For example, J.P. Morgan Chase & Co. has instituted a program called Corporate Challenge, a global initiative that invites employees to participate in running events for charity. One of the latest events, which took place in Syracuse, New York, hosted over 28,000 runners and walkers from more than 350 companies. The proceeds supported local nonprofit Hillside Work-Scholarship Connection. Each year, this series of events brings in over $500,000 for causes around the world.[2] For a corporation with facilities in North and South America, Europe, and Africa, the community may be viewed as virtually the entire world. To focus its social responsibility efforts, the multinational corporation might employ a community relations officer in each facility who reports to and coordinates with the company's head office.

Under our social responsibility philosophy, the term *community* should be viewed from a global perspective, beyond the immediate town, city, or state where a business is located. Thus, we define **community** as those members of society who are aware of, concerned with, or in some way affected by the operations and output of an organization. With information technology, high-speed travel, and the emergence of global business interests, the community as a constituency can be geographically, culturally, and attitudinally quite diverse. Issues that could become important include pollution of the environment, land use, economic advantages to the region, and discrimination within the community, as well as exploitation of workers or consumers.

From a positive perspective, an organization can significantly improve the quality of life through employment opportunities, economic development, and financial contributions for educational, health, artistic, and recreational activities. Through such efforts, a firm may become a **neighbor of choice,** an organization that builds and sustains trust with the community.[3] To become a neighbor of choice, a company should strive for positive and sustainable relationships with key individuals, groups, and organizations; demonstrate sensitivity to community concerns and issues; and design and implement programs that improve the quality of community life while promoting the company's long-term business strategies and goals.[4] Merck's Neighbor of Choice program interacts with organizations and initiatives that are in line with the company's mission on well-being. Finding solutions to health and social issues where the company is located and bringing results to stakeholders or neighbors is the top goal of each initiative. The company made contributions in grants awarded to local nonprofit organizations in health, education, social services, environment, the arts, and civic and international issues.[5]

Similar to other areas of life, the relationship between a business and the community should be symbiotic. A business may support educational opportunities in the community because the owners feel it is the right thing to do, but it also helps develop the human resources and consumer skills necessary to operate the business. Customers and employees are also community members who benefit from contributions supporting recreational activities, environmental initiatives, safety, and education. Many firms rely on universities and community colleges to provide support for ongoing education of their employees. The Dow Chemical Company, for example, committed to an annual investment of $25 million over the course of ten years to universities for research purposes. Beyond that, they have working relationships with faculty, students, and other academicians to apply the research and create useful solutions to pressing issues.[6]

community
Members of society who are aware of, concerned with, or in some way affected by the operations and output of an organization.

neighbor of choice
An organization that builds and sustains trust with the community through employment opportunities, economic development, and financial contribution to education, health, artistic, and recreational activities of the community.

community relations
The organizational function dedicated to building and maintaining relationships and trust with the community.

To build and support these initiatives, companies may invest in **community relations,** the organizational function dedicated to building and maintaining relationships and trust with the community. In the past, most businesses have not viewed community relations as strategically important or associated them with the firm's ultimate performance. Although the community relations department interacted with the community and often doled out large sums of money to charities, it essentially served as a buffer between the organization and its immediate community. Today, community relations activities have achieved greater prominence and responsibility within most companies, especially due to the rise of stakeholder power and global business interests. The function has gained strategic importance through linking to overall business goals, professionalizing its staff and their knowledge of business and community issues, assessing its performance in quantitative and qualitative terms, and recognizing the breadth of stakeholders to which the organization is accountable.[7] Community relations also assist in short-term crisis situations, such as disaster relief. Humanitarian aid organization Direct Relief was given an Excellence Award by the Committee Encouraging Corporate Philanthropy (CECP) for its collaboration with FedEx to bring health services to people and places stricken by disaster. When the typhoon hit the Philippines, more than 250,000 people received needed medical supplies. Additionally, the partnership has provided over 10 million Americans with approximately $400 million in necessary medications.[8] Progressive companies manage community relations with partnership in mind. They seek out community partners for a range of interests and activities—philanthropy, volunteerism, quality educational system and qualified workforce, appropriate roads and infrastructure, quality housing, and other community assets.

Over the past two decades, corporate support for philanthropy has been steadily growing. According to Giving USA Foundation, corporate giving totaled $18.45 billion in 2015. This number increased by 3.9 percent from the year before. The sluggish recovery of the economy since the Great Recession had an effect on corporate giving, but as the economy recovers corporate giving has begun to increase once more. PepsiCo, for instance, has a matching gifts program and is involved in a number of sustainability initiatives. The company donated a $1 million grant to Kiva, a nonprofit organization that provides small loans to entrepreneurs in developing countries to start their own businesses.[9] Even before the economic downtown, corporate giving was becoming more effective and strategic. Companies are working to align their stakeholder interests and develop partnerships that are more closely aligned to business goals, community interests, and sustainable activities.[10]

In a diverse society, however, there is no general agreement as to what constitutes the ideal model of business responsibility to the community. Businesses are likely to experience conflicts among stakeholders as to what constitutes a real commitment to the community. Therefore, the community relations function should cooperate with various internal and external constituents to develop community mission statements and assess opportunities and develop priorities for the types of contributions it will make to the community. Table 9.1 provides several examples of company missions and programs with respect to community involvement. As you can see, these missions are specific to the needs of the people and areas in which the companies operate and are usually aligned with the competencies of the organizations involved and their employees.

TABLE 9.1 Community Mission Statements

Organization	Community Mission
The Advisory Board Company	With an EVP mission to serve hospitals, health systems, and universities by helping them tackle their most pressing challenges, The Advisory Board Company helps them achieve their highest calling: improving health and educational outcomes for their partners, and in turn, for their communities. The gift of empowering an organization to achieve efficient protocols enables them to reach and serve more individuals they set out to help. As with many non-profits, resources and capital are not abundant. The Advisory Board Company realizes this and has taken on the challenge to empower their community partners with the tools needed to meet their service goals.
Capital One	At Capital One, we have always believed that as business leaders we have a unique opportunity to create value in the communities where we live and work. One of the most impactful ways Capital One serves the community is through the volunteer efforts of its thousands of talented associates.
Eli Lilly and Company	Lilly's commitment to corporate responsibility is not new—it's a fundamental part of the corporate culture. Through its Lilly Hands and Hearts Employee Volunteer Program, employees have committed to building healthier communities where they live and work, looking beyond operations to address significant societal challenges. Lilly and its employees are creating communities that are healthier in the traditional sense—as well as cleaner, more vibrant and prosperous, and with citizens who are better educated.
Pinnacol Assurance	Pinnacol's community involvement program, Pinnacol in Action, is an integral part of the company's culture. Employees receive paid time off to participate in volunteer activities such as youth mentoring and education, human services programs, community beautification and promoting health awareness.
Salesforce.com	Salesforce.com established the Salesforce.com Foundation soon after the company was founded in 1999 to ensure that community service was a central part of the corporate culture. To formalize this vision, salesforce.com implemented "1/1/1 Model" to harnesses the power of Salesforce.com's people, resources and technology through 1 percent Time, 1 percent Equity and 1 percent Product to improve its communities, inspire youth to be more successful, support the world during times of extreme need, and promote compassionate capitalism.

(Continued)

TABLE 9.1 (*Continued*)

UnitedHealth Group	UnitedHealth Group's comprehensive approach to employee volunteering begins with an analysis of skills-based volunteer needs, followed by the creation of strategic programs that offer rich and rewarding opportunities for UnitedHealth Group employees. This holistic approach has provided valuable insight on volunteering and health and contributed to UnitedHealth Group's leadership in corporate service as a resource and advocate for the benefits of employee volunteer programs.

Sources: Eli Lilly, "Points of Light Institute Honors Corporate America's Renewed Call to Service," Lilly, June 24, 2009, https://investor.lilly.com/releasedetail.cfm?releaseid=391819 (accessed June 22, 2016); "2014 Corporate Engagement Award of Excellence Honorees," Hands On Network, http://www.handsonnetwork.org/corporateawards (accessed July 30, 2014).

Community mission statements are likely to change as needs are met and new issues emerge. For example, as Japan-based Takeda Pharmaceutical Company Limited continues to expand operations throughout the world, their community involvement also expands to meet the needs of each community. In Brazil, the company focuses on renovating orphanages, while in South Africa, they have initiatives teaching children to make blankets. When global communities experience unexpected disasters, such as flooding in Australia, Takeda has been there to assist with the recovery.[11] Thus, as stakeholder needs and concerns change, the organization will need to adapt its community relations efforts. To determine key areas that require support and to refine the mission statement, a company should periodically conduct a community needs assessment like the one presented in Table 9.2.[12]

RESPONSIBILITIES TO THE COMMUNITY

It is important for a company to view community stakeholders in a trusting manner, recognizing the potential mutual benefit to each party. In a networked world, much about a company can be learned with a few clicks of a mouse. Activists and disgruntled individuals have used websites to publicize the questionable activities of some companies. Target and Ryanair have been the focus of "hate" websites that broadcast concerns about the company's treatment of employees, pricing strategies, and marketing and advertising tactics.[13] Because of the visibility of business activities and the desire for strategic social responsibility, successful companies strive to build long-term mutually beneficial relationships with relevant communities. Achieving these relationships may involve some trial and error. Table 9.3 illustrates some of the common mistakes organizations make in planning for and implementing community responsibilities. A positive example, on the other hand, is Eli Lilly Pharmaceuticals' strong support for the Indianapolis Symphony Orchestra. In return, the orchestra stages private concerts for Eli Lilly employees. Dell Computer has a similar

TABLE 9.2 Community Needs Assessment

For each of the questions in the survey, circle the number that corresponds to your assessment:

Community Issues	Exceptional	Adequate	Inadequate	Don't Know
Parks	3	2	1	0
Culinary water system	3	2	1	0
Street maintenance	3	2	1	0
Garbage collection	3	2	1	0
Snow removal	3	2	1	0
Fire protection	3	2	1	0
Police protection	3	2	1	0
Ambulance service	3	2	1	0
Building inspection	3	2	1	0
Animal control	3	2	1	0
Other code enforcement (weeds, junk cars, etc.)	3	2	1	0
Arts	3	2	1	0
Street lighting	3	2	1	0

Other issues that can be evaluated: grocery stores, pharmacies, clothing stores, fast-food restaurants, entertainment, hardware/lumber stores, auto services, banking/financial services, affordable housing, business offices, warehouses, convenience stores, community colleges, higher education satellite campuses.

Source: Utah State University Extension, "Community Needs Assessment Survey Guide," http://extension.usu.edu/files/uploads/surveyguide.pdf (accessed June 22, 2016).

relationship with the Round Rock Express, a minor league (Texas League) baseball team. A community focus can be integrated with concerns for employees and consumers. Chapter 1 provided evidence that satisfied customers and employees are correlated with improved organizational performance.

TABLE 9.3 Common Myths About Community Relations

1. Support of political and regulatory officials is not needed
2. We will cause a problem for our company if we engage in community relations
3. The community has no expertise on our decisions and actions
4. Engaging the community will delay us in finding the right solution
5. Community officials have no concern for the cost of solutions to issues
6. We serve the community simply through employment opportunities and paying taxes
7. Our only focus is national and global relationships
8. Community relationships involve only public relations
9. The local community does not impact our success
10. Spending time with the community distracts from the economic success of the firm

Economic Issues

From an economic perspective, business is absolutely vital to a community. Companies play a major role in community economic development by bringing jobs to the community and allowing employees to support themselves and their families. These companies also buy supplies, raw materials, utilities, advertising services, and other goods and services from area firms; this in turn produces more economic effects. In communities with few employers, an organization that expands in or moves to the area can reduce some of the burden on community services and other subsidized support. Even in large cities with many employers, some companies choose to address social problems that tax the community. In countries with developing economies, a business or industry can also provide many benefits. A new company brings not only jobs but also new technology, related businesses, improvements to infrastructure, and other positive factors. Conversely, globalization has incited criticism regarding the effects of U.S. businesses on other parts of the world, namely developing countries. For example, Nestlé has been criticized for marketing baby formula to nursing mothers in Turkey, claiming that their offspring will receive more nutrition from the formula than from their mothers; aggressive selling of bottled water in developing parts of the world, which is said to be expensive for consumers and works as a deterrent to governments to solve water sanitation issues; and for child labor accusations in African cocoa farms. The company has committed to "The Nestlé Cocoa Plan" which involves building schools and providing cocoa trees to farmers with the aim of contributing to the betterment of the local community.[14]

Interactions with suppliers and other vendors also stimulate the economy. Some companies are even dedicated to finding local or regional business partners in an effort to enhance their economic responsibility. For example, Starbucks, in an unprecedented move for the company, began franchising locations in Europe. By having locals run the coffee chains' stores, the company hopes to further its influence in the region.[15] Furthermore, there is often a contagion effect when one business moves into an area: by virtue of its prestige or business relationships, such a move can signal to other firms that the area is a viable and attractive place for others to locate. There are parts of the United States that are highly concentrated with automotive manufacturing, financial services, or technology. Local chambers of commerce and economic development organizations often entice new firms to a region because of the positive reputation and economic contagion it brings. Finally, business contributions to local health, education, and recreation projects not only benefit local residents and employees but also may bring additional revenue into the community from tourism and other businesses that appreciate the region's quality of life. AT&T, for example, hosts the Pebble Beach National Pro-Am golf tournament. The annual event has raised more than $110 million for local charities and honors different influential groups each year.[16]

Just as a business brings positive economic effects by expanding in or relocating to an area, it can also cause financial repercussions when it exits a particular market or geographical location. Thus, workforce reduction, or downsizing—a topic discussed in Chapter 7—is a key issue with respect to economic responsibility. The impact of layoffs due to plant closings and corporate restructuring often extends well beyond the financial well-being of affected employees. Laid-off employees typically limit their spending to basic necessities while they look for new employment, and many may ultimately leave the area altogether. Even employees who retain their jobs in such a downsizing may suffer from poor morale, distrust, guilt, and continued anxiety over their own job security, further stifling spending in a community.

Because companies have such a profound impact on the economic viability of the communities in which they operate, firms that value social responsibility consider both the short- and long-term effects on the community of changes in their workforce. Today, many companies that must reduce their workforce—regardless of the reasons—strive to give both employees and the community advance notice and offer placement services to help the community absorb employees who lose their jobs. Quad/Graphics, the second largest printer in the United States, closed plants in Illinois and Minnesota. The company offered to transfer affected employees to other plants in the nation. However, for those who did not want to transfer, Quad/Graphics agreed to offer a severance package including pay, career placement assistance, and extension of benefits.[17] Depending on economic circumstances and business profitability, companies may choose to offer extra compensation commensurate with an employee's length of employment that gives laid-off employees a financial cushion while they find new work. However, the realities of economic turmoil mean that many employees receive little compensation.

Legal Issues

To conduct business, a company must be granted a "license to operate." For many firms, a series of legal and regulatory matters must be resolved before the first employee is hired or the first customer is served. If you open a restaurant, for example, most states require a business license and sales tax number. These documents require basic information, such as business type, ownership structure, owner information, number of expected employees, and other data.

On a fundamental level, society has the ability to dictate what types of organizations are allowed to operate. In exchange for the license to operate, organizations are expected to uphold all legal obligations and standards. We have discussed many of these laws throughout this book, although individual cities, counties, and municipalities will have additional laws and regulations that firms must obey. For example, a construction company in Destin, Florida, was charged with repeated safety violations that have endangered employees. The leading cause of fatality in construction work is falling, and the company has been found liable for neglecting to provide employees with protections against this danger.[18]

Other communities have concerns about whether and how businesses fit into existing communities, especially those threatened by urban sprawl and small towns working to preserve a traditional way of life. Some states, cities, and counties have enacted legislation that limits the square footage of stores in an effort to deter "big-box stores," such as Walmart and Home Depot, unless local voters specifically approve their being allowed to build. In most cases, these communities have called for such legislation to combat the noise and traffic congestion that may be associated with such stores, to protect neighborhoods, and to preserve the viability of local small businesses.[19] Thus, although living wages and store location may be ethical issues for business, some local governments have chosen to move them into the legal realm.

Ethical Issues

As more companies view themselves as responsible to the community, they will contemplate their role and the impact of their decisions on communities as they make managerial ethical decisions. Many companies have opted to be proactive on important issues, such as minimum wages and benefits for employees. While legislative bills have been proposed on raising the minimum wage, it may take time before any changes to the law are made in this respect. Ikea, however, raised the minimum wage for employees in all U.S. locations to $10.76 per hour because they believe it is the right thing to do. Other companies such as Gap and Costco have followed suit, raising their minimum wages to $9 and $11.50 per hour, respectively.[20] Walmart raised wages so that new employees will receive $9 per hour and move up to $10 per hour after completing training.[21]

Business leaders are increasingly recognizing the significance of the role their firms play in the community and the need for their leadership in tackling community problems. Bill Daniels, founder of Cablevision, was an extremely successful entrepreneur. His approach to ethical decision-making in Cablevision had a positive impact on the communities. He established The Daniels Fund, which has a significant impact on business ethics education and other social concerns in the states of Wyoming, Colorado, New Mexico, and Utah. Millions of dollars have been donated to causes such as ethics and integrity, education, youth development, and amateur sports.[22]

These examples demonstrate that the ethical dimension of community responsibility can be multifaceted. This dimension and related programs are not legally mandated but emanate from the particular philosophy of a company and its top managers. Since many cities have not mandated a living wage, the actions of Ikea, Gap, and Costco are based on an ethical obligation felt toward employees and the community. There are many ways that a company can demonstrate its ethical commitment to the community. As Bill Daniels's commitment to business ethics illustrates, a common extension of "doing the right thing" ethically provides a role model for all political and civic leaders.

Philanthropic Issues

The community relations function has always been associated with philanthropy, as one of the main historical roles of community relations was to provide gifts, grants, and other resources to worthy causes. Today, that thinking has shifted. Although businesses have the potential to help solve social issues, the success of a business can be enhanced from the publicity generated by and through stakeholder acceptance of community activities. For example, Colorado-based New Belgium Brewing Company donates $1 for every barrel of beer brewed the prior year to charities within the markets it serves. The brewery tries to divide the funds among states in proportion to interests and needs, considering environmental, social, drug and alcohol awareness, and cultural issues. Donation decisions are made by the firm's philanthropy committee, which is a volunteer group of diverse employees; employees are encouraged to bring philanthropy suggestions to the committee.[23] However, New Belgium belongs to an industry that some members of society believe contributes to social problems. Thus, regardless of the positive contributions such a firm makes to the community, some members will always have a negative view of the business.

One of the most significant ways that organizations are exercising their philanthropic responsibilities is through volunteer programs. **Volunteerism** in the workplace, when employees spend company-supported time in support of social causes, has been increasing among companies of all sizes. Approximately 62.8 million Americans spend nearly 8 billion hours supporting formal volunteer activities. The four main activities that volunteers perform are fundraising, collecting and distributing food, helping with general labor needs, and tutoring or teaching. These activities are performed for a variety of organizations, with religious, education, and social service agencies topping the list.[24] Figure 9.1 shows the states, large cities, and mid-sized cities with the highest rates of volunteerism.

volunteerism
When employees spend company-supported time in support of social causes.

People who volunteer feel more connected to other people and society and ultimately have lower mortality rates, greater functional ability, and lower rates of depression later in life than those who do not volunteer. When volunteering is a result of employment, benefits of volunteering accrue to both the individual, in terms of greater motivation, enjoyment, and satisfaction, and to the organization through employee retention and productivity increases.[25] Communities benefit from the application of new skills and initiatives toward problems, better relations with business, a greater supply of volunteers, assistance to stretch limited resources, and social and economic regeneration.[26] Philanthropic issues are just another dimension of voluntary social responsibility and relate to business's contributions to stakeholders.

FIGURE 9.1 States with Highest Volunteerism

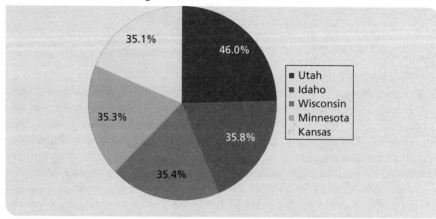

Source: Corporation for National and Community Service, "Volunteering and Civic Life in America 2015–National, State, and City Information," http://www.volunteeringinamerica.gov/rankings.cfm (accessed June 22, 2016).

Chicago-based Exelon Energy, for example, instituted their Energy for the Community volunteer engagement program that offers incentives to encourage employees to volunteer. One of the incentives is the Dollars for Doers program in which an employee can volunteer either 10, 20, or 40 hours per year at an organization of his or her choice, and Exelon awards a corresponding grant to the organization. Employees who volunteer more than 50 hours per year are nominated for the Exelon Employee Volunteer Award, who are recognized during National Volunteer Week. In the most recent year, employees volunteered for over 129,000 hours, Exelon contributed $2.19 million in matching gifts, and employees contributed over $6.3 million dollars to the annual United Way.[27]

There are several considerations in deciding how to structure a volunteer program. Attention must be paid to employee values and beliefs; therefore, political or religious organizations should be supported on the basis of individual employee initiative and interest. Some companies will partner with nonprofit organizations as a means to give their employees more options for volunteerism. For example, WorldVision humanitarian organization partners with corporations for financial, volunteer hour, and product donations as well as opportunities for cause-related marketing. Volunteer opportunities exist in education, sanitation, economic development, etc. all over the globe.[28]

Another issue is what to do when some employees do not wish to volunteer. If the company is not paying for the employees' time to volunteer and volunteering is not a condition of employment or an aspect of the job description, it may be difficult to convince a certain percentage of the workforce to participate. If the organization is paying for one day a month, on the other hand, to allow the employee exposure to volunteerism, then individual compliance is usually expected.

PHILANTHROPIC CONTRIBUTIONS

Philanthropy provides four major benefits to society. First, it improves the quality of life and helps make communities places where people want to do business, raise families, and enjoy life. Thus, improving the quality of life in a community makes it easier to attract and retain employees and customers. Second, philanthropy reduces government involvement by providing assistance to stakeholders. Third, philanthropy develops employee leadership skills. Many firms, for example, use campaigns by the United Way and other community service organizations as leadership- and skill-building exercises for their employees. Philanthropy helps create an ethical culture and promotes the values that can act as a buffer to organizational misconduct.[29] In the United States, charitable giving has stagnated at 2 percent of gross domestic product annually.[30]

The most common way that businesses demonstrate philanthropy is through donations to local and national charitable organizations. Corporations gave more than $18.5 billion to environmental, educational, and social causes in a recent year. Individual giving, which is always the largest component of charitable contributions, was an estimated $264.6 billion, or 71 percent of the total. Figure 9.2 displays the sources of charitable giving. Figure 9.3 displays the major recipients of the $373.25 billion in philanthropic donations made. Religious organizations received 33 percent of all contributions, with educational causes collecting 16 percent of the funds.[31]

philanthropy
Acts such as donations to charitable organizations to improve the quality of life, reduce government involvement, develop employee leadership skills, and create an ethical culture to act as buffer to organizational misconduct.

FIGURE 9.2 Sources of Charitable Giving ($ in billions)

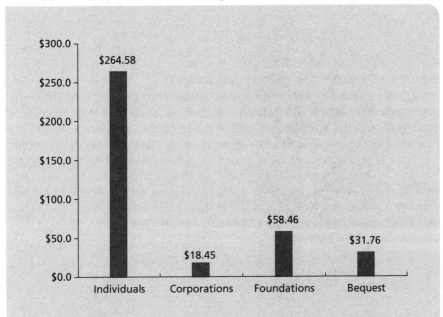

Source: "Giving Statistics," Charity Navigator, 2016, http://www.charitynavigator.org/index.cfm?bay=content.view&cpid=42#.U7q_BhZX9g0 (accessed June 22, 2016).

FIGURE 9.3 Recipients of Charitable Giving ($ in billions)

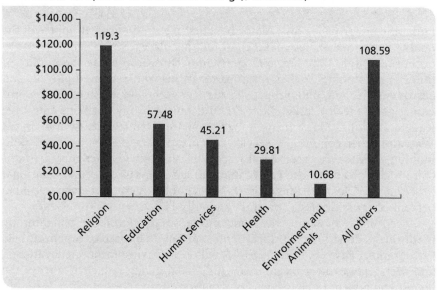

Source: "Giving Statistics," Charity Navigator, 2016, http://www.charitynavigator.org/index.cfm?bay=content.view&cpid=42#.U7q_BhZX9g0 (accessed June 22, 2016).

In a general sense, philanthropy involves any acts of benevolence and goodwill, such as making gifts to charities, volunteering for community projects, and taking action to benefit others. For example, your parents may have spent time on non-work projects that directly benefited the community or a special population. Perhaps you have participated in similar activities through work, school groups, or associations. Have you ever served Thanksgiving dinner at a homeless shelter? Have you ever raised money for a neighborhood school? Have you ever joined a social club that volunteered member services to local charities?

Most religious organizations, educational institutions, and arts programs rely heavily on philanthropic donations from both individuals and organizations. Philanthropy is a major driver of the nonprofit sector of the economy, as these organizations rely on the time, money, and talents of both individuals and organizations to operate and fund their programs. Consider the partnership between Pampers and UNICEF. These two organizations have had a successful decade-long partnership in which Pampers donates a portion of its proceeds to UNICEF to provide tetanus shots for babies around the world. This partnership fits well with Pampers' core product.[32]

strategic philanthropy
The synergistic use of an organization's core competencies and resources to address key stakeholders' interests and to achieve both organizational and social benefits.

STRATEGIC PHILANTHROPY DEFINED

Our concept of corporate philanthropy extends beyond financial contributions and explicitly links company missions, organizational competencies, and various stakeholders. Thus, we define **strategic philanthropy** as the synergistic use of an organization's core competencies and resources to address key stakeholders' interests and to achieve both organizational and social benefits. Strategic philanthropy goes well beyond the traditional benevolent philanthropy of donating a percentage of sales to social causes by involving employees (utilizing their core skills), organizational resources and expertise (equipment, knowledge, and money), and the ability to link employees, customers, suppliers, and social needs with these key assets. Strategic philanthropy involves both financial and nonfinancial contributions to stakeholders (employee time, goods and services, and company technology and equipment as well as facilities), but it also benefits the company.

Organizations are best suited to deal with social or stakeholder issues in areas with which they have some experience, knowledge, or expertise. From a business perspective, companies want to refine their intellectual capital, reinforce their core competencies, and develop synergies between business and philanthropic activities. The process of addressing stakeholder concerns through philanthropy should be strategic to a company's ongoing development and improvement. For example, SAP, a global software company, has made financial and product investments in developing economies such as Mexico and Swaziland. These investments are beneficial to both parties as the technology aids economic, educational, and health advancements for the communities. However, it also allows the company to identify emerging talent and become established in these economies for their own growth.[33] Some critics would argue that this is not true philanthropy because SAP will receive business benefits. However, social responsibility takes place on many levels, and effective philanthropy depends on the synergy between stakeholder needs and business competencies and goals. Thus, the fact that each partner receives unique benefits does not diminish the overall good that results from a project. As global competition escalates, companies are increasingly responsible to stakeholders in justifying their philanthropic endeavors. This ultimately requires greater planning and alignment of philanthropic efforts with overall strategic goals. Table 9.4 provides additional examples of philanthropic activities.

TABLE 9.4 Examples of Strategic Philanthropy

- The Target Corporation donates 5 percent of its pretax income to charities.
- Patagonia donates 1 percent of profits to 1 Percent for the Planet, a global movement that donates the proceeds to environmental organizations.
- Salesforce.com donates 1 percent of its technology, 1 percent of its resources, and 1 percent of its people (employees can take off six days a year to volunteer) to nonprofits and to their communities.
- Home Depot has a strong partnership with the nonprofit Habitat for Humanity, spending significant time and resources in its mission to build homes for those in need.
- New Belgium Brewing engages in extensive philanthropy grants, product donations, and sponsorships to support the community.
- Whole Foods holds a number of community giving days in which 5 percent of the day's net revenue goes toward nonprofits or education.

STRATEGIC PHILANTHROPY AND SOCIAL RESPONSIBILITY

It is important to place strategic philanthropy in the context of organizational responsibilities at the economic, legal, ethical, and philanthropic levels. Most companies understand the need to be economically successful for the benefit of all stakeholders and to comply with the laws required within our society and others in which they do business. Additionally, through the establishment of core values and ethical cultures, most firms are recognizing the many benefits of good ethics. As we saw in Chapter 1, evidence is accumulating that there is a positive relationship between social responsibility and performance, especially with regard to customer satisfaction, investor loyalty, and employee commitment. Strategic social responsibility can reduce the cost of business transactions, establish trust among stakeholders, improve teamwork, and preserve the social capital necessary for an infrastructure for doing business. In sum, these efforts improve the context and environment for corporate operations and performance.[34]

When Daniel Lubetzky founded Kind Healthy Snacks, he had transparency and kindness in mind. Transparency is demonstrated in the fact that the company's bars and snacks contain ingredients that are easily pronounced (meaning they are natural), and come in clear packaging where those ingredients can be seen. The company initiated a charitable campaign where it donated $10,000 per month to a different charity through a program called "Do the Kind Thing." Each charity was crowdsourced, meaning that people would visit the company's website to vote for the charity they thought should get that month's donation. The self-described "not-only-for-profit" company has become the fastest growing energy and nutrition bar in the United States.[35] In this way, Kind Healthy Snacks has linked philanthropic contributions to revenue generation.

Many companies consider philanthropy only after they have met their financial, legal, and ethical obligations. As companies strive for social responsibility, their ability to meet each obligation lays the foundation for success with other responsibilities. In addition, there is synergy in corporate efforts directed at the four levels of responsibility. As one of the most voluntary dimensions of social responsibility, philanthropy has not always been linked to profits or business ethics. In fact, the traditional approach to philanthropy disconnects giving from business performance and its impact on stakeholders. Before the evolution of strategic philanthropy, most corporate gift programs separated the company from the organizations, causes, and individuals that its donations most benefited.[36]

Research has begun to highlight organizations' formalization of philanthropic activities and their efforts to integrate philanthropic goals with other business strategies and implementation. U.S. companies are adopting a more businesslike approach to philanthropy and experiencing a better image, increased employee loyalty, and improved customer ties.[37] Philanthropy involves using organizational resources, and specific methods are used to measure its impact on key stakeholders. In this case, philanthropy is an investment from which a company can gain some type of value. For instance, J.P. Morgan and other wealthy entities and individuals engage in impact investing. Impact investing is the investment of a significant amount of money toward finding solutions for a social problem, with the promise of financial return that depends upon the achievement of a stated goal. This measured activity is becoming increasingly popular because not only is it drawing in millions of dollars to be invested, but many hurdles are being overcome in environmental and social issues. Examples of some initiatives include sustainable farming in East Africa and banking options to low-income communities in Mexico. J.P. Morgan has spent $68 million in impact investing across 11 funds.[38] Indeed, there are numerous examples of companies supporting community involvement. Although these actions are noble, they are not always considered in tandem with organizational goals and strengths.

In some cases, corporate contributions may be made to nonprofit organizations in which top managers have a personal interest. When Unilever acquired Ben and Jerry's Homemade, they agreed to support the causes and initiatives that are extremely important to founders Ben Cohen and Jerry Greenfield. Unilever agreed to maintain the Vermont employment and manufacture base, pay workers a livable wage with complete benefits, buy milk from Vermont dairy farmers who do not use bovine growth hormones, contribute over $1.1 million annually to the Ben and Jerry's Foundation, open more Partner Shops owned by nonprofit organizations providing employment opportunities for disadvantaged persons, and maintain relationships with alternate suppliers.[39] Finally, many companies will match employees' personal gifts to educational institutions. Although gift-matching programs instill employee pride and assist education, they are rarely linked to company operations and competencies.[40] In the traditional approach to corporate philanthropy, then, companies have good intentions, but there is no solid integration with organizational resources and objectives.

In the social responsibility model that we propose, philanthropy is only one focal point for a corporate vision that includes both the welfare of the firm and benefits to stakeholders. This requires support from top management as well as a strategic planning structure that incorporates stakeholder concerns and benefits. Corporate giving, volunteer efforts, and other contributions should be considered and aligned not only with corporate strategy but also with financial, legal, and ethical obligations. The shift from traditional benevolent philanthropy to strategic philanthropy has come about as companies struggled in the 1990s and 2000s to redefine their missions, alliances, and scope, while becoming increasingly accountable to stakeholders and society.

Strategic Philanthropy versus Cause-Related Marketing

The first attempts by organizations to coordinate organizational goals with philanthropic giving emerged with cause-related marketing in the early 1980s. Whereas strategic philanthropy links corporate resources and knowledge to address broader social, customer, employee, and supplier problems and needs, **cause-related marketing** ties an organization's product(s) directly to a social concern. Table 9.5 compares cause-related marketing and strategic philanthropy.

Cause-related marketing donates a percentage of a product's sales to a cause appealing to the relevant target market. The Avon Breast Cancer Crusade, for example, generates proceeds for the breast cancer cause through several fundraising efforts, including the sale of special "pink ribbon" products by Avon independent sales representatives nationwide. Gifts are awarded by the Avon Products Foundation, Inc., a nonprofit 501(c)(3) accredited public charity, to support six vital areas of the breast cancer cause. Both the cause and Avon Crusade "pink ribbon" products appeal to Avon's primary target market: women. The Avon Breast Cancer Crusade generated more than $800 million net in total funds raised worldwide to fund access to care and in finding a cure for breast cancer.[41]

American Express was the first company to use cause-related marketing widely, when it began advertising in 1983 that it would give a percentage of credit-card charges to the Statue of Liberty and Ellis Island Restoration Fund.[42] As is the case with Avon, American Express companies generally prefer to support causes that are of interest to their target markets. In a single year, organizations raised roughly $1.92 billion for causes through marketing efforts.[43] Thus, a key feature of cause-related marketing is the promise of donations to a particular social cause based on customer sales or involvement. Whereas strategic philanthropy is tied to the entire organization, cause-related marketing is linked to a specific product and marketing program. The program may involve in-store promotions, messages on packages and labels, and other marketing communications.[44]

cause-related marketing
Ties an organization's product(s) directly to a social concern.

TABLE 9.5 Strategic Philanthropy Contrasted with Cause-Related Marketing

	Strategic Philanthropy	Cause-Related Marketing
Focus	Organizational	Product or product line
Goals	Improvement of organizational competence or tying organizational competence to social need or charitable cause Builds brand equity	Increase of product sales
Time frame	Ongoing	Traditionally of limited duration
Organizational members involved	Potentially all organizational employees	Marketing department and related personnel
Cost	Moderate—alignment with organizational strategies and mission	Minimal—alliance development and promotion expenditures

Although cause-related marketing has its roots in the United States, the marketing tool is gaining widespread usage in other parts of the world. Population Services International (PSI) was founded with marketing for social issues as its base. After traveling to Africa in the 1990s and witnessing the devastating effects of HIV/AIDS on the population, founder Kate Roberts decided to use her marketing expertise to address the problem. She established YouthAIDS as an education and prevention program for young people using media, celebrity partnerships, and music to relay messages to the target group. Over the years, YouthAIDS became a recognizable brand. This success led to the organization's involvement with other social issues such as malaria, sanitary water, and tuberculosis in over 50 countries.[45]

Cause-related marketing activities have real potential to affect buying patterns. For cause-related marketing to be successful, consumers must have awareness and affinity for the cause, the brand and cause must be associated and perceived as a good fit, and consumers should be able to transfer feelings toward the cause to their brand perceptions and purchase intentions. Studies have found that a majority of consumers said that, given equal price and product quality, they would be more likely to buy the product associated with a charitable cause. More than 80 percent of customers say they have more positive perceptions of firms that support causes about which they personally care. These surveys have also noted that most marketing directors felt that cause-related marketing would increase in importance over the coming years.[46] Through cause-related marketing, companies first become aware that supporting social causes, such as environmental awareness, health and human services, education, and the arts, can support business goals and help bolster a firm's reputation, especially those with an ethically neutral image. However, firms that are perceived as unethical may be suspected of ulterior motives in developing cause-related campaigns.[47]

One of the main weaknesses with cause-related marketing is that some consumers cannot link specific philanthropic efforts with companies.[48] Consumers may have difficulty recalling exact philanthropic relationships because many cause-related marketing campaigns have tended to be of short duration and have not always had a direct correlation to the sponsoring firm's core business. Because strategic philanthropy is more pervasive and relates to company attributes and skills, such alliances should have greater stakeholder recognition and appreciation

SOCIAL ENTREPRENEURSHIP AND SOCIAL RESPONSIBILITY

While social philanthropy and cause-related marketing are important ways for businesses to demonstrate social responsibility, some entrepreneurs are taking this a step further by structuring their entire business model around creating positive social change. Traditionally, organizations that structured themselves around the creation of social value chose to become nonprofit organizations. Nonprofits are organizations that are formed to meet some public purpose rather than making profits. Unlike for-profit companies, non-profits must reinvest any additional earnings into their operations.[49] While some non-profits sell their goods or perform services to raise funds, many depend upon stakeholder donations to support their causes.

However, a new type of organizational structure is emerging that spans across or within nonprofit, business, and government industries. The social enterprise is an organization that uses entrepreneurial principles to create positive social change. Because it is an emerging field, researchers have not yet come up with a consensus on how to define it. For our purposes, we define **social entrepreneurship** as what occurs when an entrepreneur founds a business with the purpose of creating social value. This means that unlike a traditional for-profit business, the main goal of a social entrepreneur is not to earn profits but to provide a solution to a social problem.[50]

As mentioned earlier, because the overarching purpose of social entrepreneurship is creating social value, social enterprises can be organized as a nonprofit, business, or government form of an organization—as well as a combination of any of these. Many social enterprises are set up with a nonprofit organizational structure. However, social enterprises differ from more traditional nonprofits as they pursue business-led strategies to achieve social objectives.[51] While a social enterprise might be a nonprofit, it operates more like an entrepreneurial business venture in its strategy, structure, norms, values, and its approach to finding innovative solutions to social problems.[52] Like a business entrepreneur, social entrepreneurs seek to be change agents by seizing upon opportunities and finding solutions that others missed to solve challenges in society.[53] We go into further detail about nonprofit and for-profit types of social enterprises in the following sections.

social entrepreneurship
When an entrepreneur founds a business with the purpose of creating social value.

History of Social Entrepreneurship

Social entrepreneurship as a concept is relatively new, but its precursors go back hundreds of years. Using entrepreneurial practices as a means to support a social mission is not new. For instance, monasteries sold surplus wine and cheese and used the money to further their mission.[54] Early social entrepreneurs included historical figures such as Florence Nightingale, John Muir, Susan B. Anthony, and Maria Montessori.[55] The concept itself was first widely used in the 1960s and 1970s. In 1980, entrepreneur Bill Drayton made major inroads in popularizing the concept when he founded Ashoka as an enterprise to encourage and support social entrepreneurs throughout the world.[56]

Probably the most famous social entrepreneurship success story is Muhammad Yunus' establishment of micro-lending organization Grameen Bank in Bangladesh. Micro-lending occurs when investors provide small loans to local entrepreneurs to start their own businesses, cutting out the middlemen and avoiding predatory lending rates that are often common in developing countries. The inspiration for Grameen Bank occurred in 1974 during a famine when Yunus lent $27 to a woman and her neighbors to help them earn a living. After he was paid back in full, Yunus realized the difference these small amounts of money could have in the lives of poor people. The Grameen Bank Project was founded in 1976, and in 1983 a government ordinance allowed Yunus to turn his micro-lending project into an independent bank.[57]

Grameen Bank adopted an innovative approach to lending. It would have borrowers take out loans in groups of five, and each borrower would guarantee the other's debts.[58] Interest rates are around 16 percent, which is lower than bank rates in many other countries. Grameen's model places pressure upon the borrowers to repay their loans or risk being shamed in front of their community members. Grameen Bank has had a high repayment rate, with 95 percent of borrowers paying back their loans.[59]

Grameen Bank has successfully changed the business environment in Bangladesh. Not only did it develop an innovative model to help villagers get out of poverty, but because 97 percent of loans are made to women, Grameen's micro-lending model promoted respect for women entrepreneurs.[60] Grameen also established training programs to replicate its micro-lending model in other countries.

Approximately 95 percent of the bank is owned by the borrowers themselves, giving them the incentive to see the bank succeed.[61] In 2006, Yunus and Grameen Bank won the Nobel Peace Prize.[62] The bank's emphasis on joint accountability and ownership has led to a successful lending model to address a major economic problem. Grameen Bank has also been sustainable; with the exception of a couple of years, the bank has earned a profit.[63] Today, similar micro-finance organizations include Kiva.org, BRAC, Accion, and FINCA International.

Types of Social Entrepreneurship

Many social enterprises tend to organize themselves as nonprofits. The Delancey Street Foundation is a nonprofit based in San Francisco. Founded by Mimi Silbert in 1971, the purpose of the Delancey Foundation is to assist homeless people, drug addicts, felons, and others into changing their lives. The Delancey Street Foundation acts as a residential education center that trains people in skills and expertise so they can become productive members of society. Approximately 65 percent of the Delancey Street's operating costs are paid for by operating over 20 small businesses, including the Delancey Street Restaurant, which are staffed by the people using Delancey's services. Thus far, Delancey Street has helped more than 14,000 people change their lives.[64]

Other social entrepreneurs decide to organize as a for-profit organization or as hybrid between the two. Blake Mycoskie's Toms, for instance, was created with the mission to provide a pair of shoes to children in need throughout the world. However, the model was incorporated into a for-profit business that builds the cost of the free pair of shoes into shoe sales. Another for-profit firm, Sseko Designs, provides internships to women in Uganda. The women make leather bags and ribbon sandals to sell in the United States. The intention of the internships is to help these Ugandan women save enough to go to college. A certain amount of the women's earnings go toward a college fund. At the end of their internships, Sseko Designs matches the savings so that the women will have enough to attend college.

It is clear that social entrepreneurship does not encompass any particular type of business structure. Rather, it is distinguished from traditional organizations—both for-profit and non-profit—by its emphasis on innovative solutions and entrepreneurial principles to solve social problems.

Social Entrepreneurship and Strategic Philanthropy

There are many distinct similarities among social entrepreneurship, cause-related marketing, and strategic philanthropy. All of these concepts emphasize social responsibility and a desire to support positive change. The delineation occurs more in how they achieve their goals. Businesses with cause-related marketing initiatives have not incorporated philanthropy into their business models. Rather, they use programs to strongly support initiatives to benefit society, such as Yoplait's support of the Susan G. Komen Foundation or Avon's support for breast cancer research. Strategic philanthropy uses organizational core competencies to achieve both organizational and social benefits. Strategic philanthropy in business occurs when organizations incorporate these causes into their overall strategies. As part of its strategy to support environmental awareness, Patagonia donates 1 percent of its profits to a global movement of companies called 1 Percent for the Planet, which in turn donates to environmental organizations.

Like social entrepreneurship, strategic philanthropy implements strategies to support solutions for societal challenges. Companies incorporating strategic philanthropy, however, usually outsource the execution of their program and its goals to other organizations, often nonprofits. Home Depot, for instance, strongly supports Habitat for Humanity but its operations are not centered around building houses for people in need. In contrast, the social entrepreneur executes the organization's program for change directly.[65] The business objectives of these organizations are to create social value; Grameen, therefore, is in the business of microlending, while Sseko Designs was founded to increase Ugandan women's access to a college education. Cause-related marketing, strategic philanthropy, and social entrepreneurship are all innovative and socially responsible ways to meet the organization's obligations to society.

Earth in the Balance

Heal the World & Make It a Better Place

Many companies worldwide have become increasingly concerned with the society and communities in which they operate. This new breed of business is concerned about bettering the lives of the surrounding community while providing a profitable good or service at the same time. This new type of business is called *social entrepreneurship*. Leaders in organizations from the United States to Egypt are becoming social entrepreneurs.

Social entrepreneurs typically follow a four-stage process. In the first stage of envisioning, a clear need, gap, and opportunity are identified. The second stage is engaging in the opportunity and doing something about it. Enabling something to happen is the third stage. The final stage is enacting and leading the project to completion.

The Institute of PATH, based in San Francisco, has been a leader in social entrepreneurship. PATH's focus is on creating medicines to cure diseases that affect Third World countries. The nonprofit organization is currently working with partners in biotechnology, pharmaceutical, and academic industries to increase the availability of artemisinin-based combination therapy through improving the manufacturing process of the drug. Artemisinin-based combination therapy is effective against malaria, but the supply of this drug, which comes from a plant, varies. By improving the manufacturing process, PATH and its partners hope to help the 200 million people each year that become victims of malaria.

The nonprofit status offers many advantages to PATH. Most of its funding comes from the government or philanthropic organizations. Biotech companies have gained a channel for intellectual property that might normally have gone unused because of lack of profit potential. Many members of the scientific community are donating time and effort to help fight disease in Third World countries.

Social entrepreneurs are present all over the world. Take, for example, Sekem, located just north of Cairo, Egypt. Sekem was founded in 1977 by Dr. Ibrahim Abouleish. Since 1977, the organization has grown from one person to several business firms. Sekem produces several organic products on its farms. Some of its long-term goals include the following:

- We endeavor to build our economic, social, and cultural activities so that they invigorate each other.

- We nurture the development of all coworkers by facilitating the possibility to learn through their work, to commit themselves to their task and to practice agriculture.

- We intend to restore the earth through implementing and developing biodynamic agriculture.

- We provide Primary Health Care and therapy using holistic medicine.

- We strive through our research to meet the questions of all aspects of life for the present age.

Sekem developed an alternative method for using pesticides to protect cotton crops. This new system led to a ban on crop dusting in Egypt. In 2011, Sekem won the IMPACT Business Award in recognition of their innovative contributions to preventing climate change. In 2013, Dr. Abouleish won the "Award for Excellence in Positive Change" by the Global Thinker Forum.

Sekem has also opened a school for holistic education. The profits earned by Sekem help fund medical centers and education for both children and adults. They are committed to helping the community break away from the poverty that has taken control of their lives. Sekem is continually expanding operations to help the community achieve a higher quality of life.

Sources: Anonymous, "Two Awards for the Institute of OneWorld Health," *Appropriate Technology*, June 2005, p. 26; Christian Seelos and Johanna Mair, "Social Entrepreneurship," *Business Horizons 48*, no. 3 (May–June 2005): 241–246; "Global Initiatives," *VIVALEAP*, http://www.vivaleap.com/global.html (accessed July 28, 2016); Skoll Foundation, http://skoll.org/ (accessed July 28, 2016); John L. Thompson, "The World of the Social Entrepreneur," *The International Journal of Public Sector Management* 15 (2002): 412–432; Sekem website, http://www.sekem.com/index.html (accessed July 28, 2016); PATH website, http://sites.path.org/drugdevelopment/ (July 28, 2016); "Innovative Models Promoting Adaptation and Climate Technologies (IMPACT) Business Award: Call for Submissions," FANRPAN, http://www.fanrpan.org/documents/d01233/ (accessed July 28, 2016).

BENEFITS OF STRATEGIC PHILANTHROPY

To pursue strategic philanthropy successfully, organizations must weigh both the costs and benefits associated with planning and implementing it as a corporate priority. Companies that assume a strategic approach to philanthropy are using an investment model with respect to their charitable acts and donations. In other words, these firms are not just writing checks; they are investing in solutions to stakeholder problems and corporate needs. Such an investment requires the commitment of company time, money, and human talent to succeed. Companies often need to hire staff to manage projects, communicate goals and opportunities throughout the firm, develop long-term priorities and programs, handle requests for funds, and represent the firm on other aspects of philanthropy. In addition, philanthropy consumes the time and energy of all types of employees within the organization. Thus, strategic philanthropy involves real corporate costs that must be justified and managed.

Most scholars and practitioners agree that the benefits of strategic philanthropy ultimately outweigh its costs. The positive return on strategic philanthropy is closely aligned with benefits obtained from strong social responsibility. First, in the United States, businesses can declare up to 10 percent of pretax profits as tax-deductible contributions. Most firms do not take full advantage of this benefit, as 10 percent is viewed as a very generous contribution level. In fact, corporate giving has dipped to 0.7 percent of pretax profits in the last year.[66] Second, companies with a strategic approach to philanthropy experience rewards in the workplace. Employees involved in volunteer projects and related ventures not only have the opportunity to refine their professional skills but also develop a stronger sense of loyalty and commitment to their employer. A national survey of employees demonstrated that corporate philanthropy is an important driver in employee relations. Those who perceive their employer as strong in philanthropy were four times as likely to be very loyal as those who believed their employer was less philanthropic. Employees in firms with favorable ratings on philanthropy are also more likely to recommend the company and its products to others and have intentions to stay with the employer. Positive impressions of the executives' role in corporate philanthropy also influenced employees' affirmative attitudes toward their employer.[67] Results such as these lead to improved productivity, enhanced employee recruitment practices, and reduced employee turnover, each contributing to the overall effectiveness and efficiency of the company.

As a third benefit, companies should experience enhanced customer loyalty as a result of their strategic philanthropy. By choosing projects and causes with links to its core business, a firm can create synergies with its core competencies and customers. Consider the Pampers partnership with UNICEF described earlier. Pampers has developed a partnership to donate a portion of proceeds to help improve the health of babies throughout the world. This resonates well with the target market for Pampers: parents of

TABLE 9.6 Benefits of Socially Responsible Strategic Corporate Philanthropy

- Consumer trust
- Stakeholder loyalty
- Employee engagement
- Reputation
- Enhance brand image
- Increase share value
- Positive publicity

infants and newborns. Another example is Home Depot's partnership with Habitat for Humanity.

Finally, strategic philanthropy should improve a company's overall reputation in the community and ease government and community relations. Research indicates a strong negative relationship between illegal activity and reputation, whereas firms that contribute to charitable causes enjoy enhanced reputations. Moreover, companies that contribute to social causes, especially to problems that arise as a result of their actions, may be able to improve their reputations after committing a crime.[68] If a business is engaged in a strategic approach to contributions, volunteerism, and related activities, a clear purpose is to enhance and benefit the community. By properly implementing and communicating these achievements, the company will "do well by doing good." Essentially, community members and others use cues from a strategic philanthropy initiative, along with other social responsibility programs, to form a lasting impression—or reputation—of the firm. These benefits, together with others discussed in this section, are consistent with research conducted on European firms. Table 9.6 highlights the perceived benefits of corporate philanthropy. The table suggests that companies believe that their charitable activities generally have a positive effect on goodwill, public relations, community relations, employee motivation, and customer loyalty.[69]

IMPLEMENTATION OF STRATEGIC PHILANTHROPY

Attaining the benefits of strategic philanthropy depends on the integration of corporate competencies, business stakeholders, and social responsibility objectives to be fully effective. However, fruitfully implementing a strategic philanthropy approach is not simple and requires organizational resources and strategic attention. In this section, we examine some of the key factors associated with implementing strategic philanthropy.

Although some organizations and leaders see beyond economic concerns, other firms are far less progressive and collaborative in nature. To the extent that corporate leaders and others advocate for strategic philanthropy, planning and evaluation practices must be developed just as with any other business process. Almost all effective actions taken by a company are well-thought-out business plans. However, although most large organizations have solid plans for philanthropy and other community involvement, these activities typically do not receive the same attention that other business forays garner. A study by the American Productivity and Quality Center found that many organizations are not yet taking a systematic or comprehensive approach in evaluating the impact of philanthropy on the business and other stakeholders.[70]

Top Management Support

The implementation of strategic philanthropy is impossible without the endorsement and support of the chief executive officer and other members of top management. Although most executives care about their communities and social issues, there may be debate or confusion over how their firms should meet stakeholder concerns and social responsibility. Under CEO Jean-Laurent Bonnafé, BNP Paribas has partnered with the Chair of Philanthropy at ESSEC Business School in order to collaborate and contribute to the development of philanthropy itself. This is in addition to the Individual Philanthropy Offering program established by the seventh largest bank and the social activities of the BNP Paribas Foundation.[71]

Top managers often have unique concerns with respect to strategic philanthropy. For example, chief executive officers may worry about having to defend the company's commitment to charity. Some investors may see these contributions as damaging to their portfolios. A related concern involves the resources required to manage a philanthropy effort. Top managers must be well versed in the performance benefits of social responsibility that we discussed in Chapter 1. Additionally, some executives may believe that less philanthropic-minded competitors have a profit advantage. If these competitors have any advantage at all, it is probably just a short-term situation. The tax benefits and other gains that philanthropy provides should prevail over the long run.[72] In today's environment, there are many positive incentives and reasons that strategic philanthropy and social responsibility make good business sense.

Planning and Evaluating Strategic Philanthropy

As with any initiative, strategic philanthropy must prove its relevance and importance. For philanthropy and other stakeholder collaborations to be fully diffused and accepted within the business community, a performance benefit must be evident. In addition, philanthropy should be treated as a corporate program that deserves the same professionalism and resources as other strategic initiatives. Thus, the process for planning and evaluating strategic philanthropy is integral to its success.

To make the best decisions when dealing with stakeholder concerns and issues, there should be a defensible, workable strategy to ensure that every donation is wisely spent. Author Curt Weeden, President of Business & Nonprofit Strategies, Inc., has developed a multistep process for ensuring effective planning and implementation of strategic philanthropy.

1. **Research** If a company has too little or inaccurate information, it will suffer when making philanthropic decisions. Research should cover the internal organization and programs, organizations, sponsorship options, and events that might intersect with the interests and competencies of the corporation.

2. **Organize and Design** The information collected by research should be classified into relevant categories. For example, funding opportunities can be categorized according to the level of need and alignment with organizational competencies. The process of organizing and designing is probably the most crucial step in which management should be thoroughly involved.

3. **Engage** This step consists of engaging management early on so as to ease the approval process in the future. Top managers need to be co-owners of the corporate philanthropy plan. They will have interest in seeing the plan receive authorization, and they will enrich the program by sharing their ideas and thoughts.

4. **Spend** Deciding what resources and dollars should be spent where is a very important task. A skilled manager who has spent some time with the philanthropy program should preferably handle this. If the previous steps were handled appropriately, this step should go rather smoothly.[73]

Evaluating corporate philanthropy should begin with a clear understanding of how these efforts are linked to the company's vision, mission, and resources. As our definition suggests, philanthropy can only be strategic if it is fully aligned with the values, core competencies, and long-term plans of an organization. Thus, the development of philanthropic programs should be part of the strategic planning process.

Assuming that key stakeholders have been identified, organizations need to conduct research to understand stakeholder expectations and their willingness to collaborate for mutual benefit. Although many companies have invested time and resources to understand the needs of employees, customers, and investors, fewer have examined other stakeholders or the potential for aligning stakeholders and company resources for philanthropic reasons. Philanthropic efforts should be evaluated for their effects on and benefits to various constituents.[74] Although philanthropists have always been concerned with results, the aftermath of September 11 brought not only widespread contributions but also a heightened sensitivity to accountability. For example, the American Red Cross suffered intense scrutiny after its leaders initially decided to set aside a portion of donations received in response to the terrorist strikes. The rationale for setting aside $200 million was that a long-term program on terrorism response needed to be developed and funded. Many donors rejected this plan, and the Red Cross reversed its decision. A survey in late 2002 indicated that 42 percent of Americans have less confidence in charities than they did before the September 11 attacks. Major philanthropists are also stepping up their expectations for accountability, widespread impact, strategic thinking, global implications, and results. A recent report by The Panel on the Nonprofit Sector discusses four major areas that all non-profit organizations need to address in order to demonstrate solid governance and ethical practices. Table 9.7 lists these areas, along with specific recommendations on how charitable organizations can go about preserving the soundness and integrity of the nonprofit

TABLE 9.7 Principles for Sound Practice for Charities and Foundations

| 1. Legal Compliance and Public Disclosure |
| 2. Effective Governance |
| 3. Strong Financial Oversight |
| 4. Responsible Fundraising |

Source: Independent Sector, "Principles for Good Governance and Ethical Practice: A Guide for Charities and Foundations," https://www.independentsector.org/principles (accessed June 22, 2016).

Table 9.8 A Donor Bill of Rights

Philanthropy is based on voluntary action for the common good. It is a tradition of giving and sharing that is primary to the quality of life. To assure that philanthropy merits the respect and trust of the general public and that donors and prospective donors can have full confidence in the not-for-profit organizations and causes they are asked to support, we declare that all donors have these rights:

1. To be informed of the organization's mission, of the way the organization intends to use donated resources, and of its capacity to use donations effectively for their intended purposes

2. To be informed of the identity of those serving on the organization's governing board and to expect the board to exercise prudent judgment in its stewardship responsibilities

3. To have access to the organization's most recent financial statements

4. To be assured their gifts will be used for the purposes for which they were given

5. To receive appropriate acknowledgment and recognition

6. To be assured that information about their donations is handled with respect and with confidentiality to the extent provided by law

7. To expect that all relationships with individuals representing organizations of interest to the donor will be professional in nature

8. To be informed whether those seeking donations are volunteers, employees of the organization, or hired solicitors

9. To have the opportunity for their names to be deleted from mailing lists that an organization may intend to share

10. To feel free to ask questions when making a donation and to receive prompt, truthful, and forthright answers

Source: Association of Fundraising Professionals, "A Donor Bill of Rights," http://www.aps.org/about/support/upload/bill-rights.pdf (accessed June 22, 2016). The Donor Bill of Rights was created by the Association of Fundraising Professionals (AFP), the Association for Healthcare Philanthropy (AHP), the Council for Advancement and Support of Education (CASE), and the Giving Institute: Leading Consultants to Non-Profits. It has been endorsed by numerous organizations.

community.[75] Table 9.8 lists ten guidelines that potential donors should use in evaluating and choosing organizations with which to partner or provide funding. Both types of input are important to individuals and companies in the process of deciding where to donate time and money.

Methods to evaluate strategic philanthropy should include an assessment of how these initiatives are communicated to stakeholders. It is recommended that organizations develop an overall evaluation framework to be used to measure the initiative's success. This evaluation framework provides guidelines for how the organization will view the evaluation as well as descriptions of the evaluation type, standards to demonstrate successful implementation, and methods for communicating results.[76] Such reporting mechanisms not only improve stakeholder knowledge but also lead to improvements and refinements. Although critics may deride organizations for communicating their philanthropic efforts, the strategic philanthropy model is dependent on feedback and learning to create greater value for the organization and its stakeholders, as we shall see in the next chapter.

SUMMARY

More firms are investigating ways to link their philanthropic efforts with consumer interests. From a strategic perspective, a firm's ability to link consumer interests to philanthropy should lead to stronger economic relationships. Community relations are the organizational functions dedicated to building and maintaining relationships and trust with the community. To determine the key areas that require support and to refine the mission statement, a company should periodically conduct a community needs assessment.

Companies play a major role in community economic development by bringing jobs to the community, interacting with other businesses, and making contributions to local health, education, and recreation projects that benefit residents and employees. When a company leaves an area, financial repercussions may be devastating. Because they have such a profound impact on the economic viability of their communities, firms that value social responsibility consider both the short- and long-term effects of changes in their workforce on the community.

For many firms, a series of legal and regulatory matters must be resolved before launching a business. On a basic level, society has the ability to dictate what types of organizations are allowed to operate. As more companies view themselves as responsible to the community, they consider their role and the impact of their decisions on communities from an ethical perspective.

The success of a business can be enhanced by the publicity generated from and through stakeholder acceptance of community activities. One way that organizations are exercising their philanthropic responsibilities is through volunteerism, the donation of employee time by companies in support of social causes. In structuring volunteer programs, attention must be paid to employee values and beliefs.

Many companies are finding creative ways to satisfy their responsibilities to consumers and the community. These relationships must be managed, nurtured, and continuously assessed. Resources devoted to this effort may include programs for educating and listening to consumers, surveys to discover strengths and weaknesses in stakeholder relationships, hiring consumer affairs professionals, the development of a community relations office, and other initiatives.

Generally, philanthropy involves any acts of benevolence and goodwill. Strategic philanthropy is defined as the synergistic use of organizational core competencies and resources to address key stakeholders' interests and to achieve organizational and social benefits. Strategic philanthropy involves both financial and nonfinancial contributions to stakeholders, but it also benefits the company. As such, strategic philanthropy is part of a broader philosophy that recognizes how social responsibility can help an organization improve its overall performance. Research suggests that companies that adopt a more businesslike approach to philanthropy will experience a better image, increased employee loyalty, and improved customer ties.

Corporate giving, volunteer efforts, and other philanthropic activities should be considered and aligned with corporate strategy and financial, legal, and ethical obligations. The concept of strategic philanthropy has evolved since the middle of the twentieth century, when contributions were prohibited by law, to emerge as a management practice to support social responsibility in the 1990s. Whereas strategic philanthropy links corporate resources and knowledge to address broader social, customer, employee, and supplier problems and needs, cause-related marketing ties an organization's product(s) directly to a social concern. By linking products with charities and social causes, organizations acknowledge the opportunity to align philanthropy to economic goals and to recognize stakeholder interests in organizational benevolence.

Social entrepreneurship occurs when an entrepreneur founds a business with the purpose of creating social value. There are many distinct similarities among social entrepreneurship, cause-related marketing, and strategic philanthropy. All of these concepts emphasize social responsibility and a desire to support positive change. The delineation occurs more in how they achieve their goals. Like social entrepreneurship, strategic philanthropy implements strategies to support solutions for societal challenges. Companies incorporating strategic philanthropy, however, usually outsource the execution of their program and its goals to other organizations, often nonprofits. The social entrepreneur executes the organization's program for change directly. The business objectives of these organizations are to create social value.

Many organizations have skillfully used their resources and core competencies to address the needs of employees, customers, business partners, the community and society, and the natural environment. To pursue strategic philanthropy successfully, organizations must weigh the costs and benefits associated with planning and implementing it as a corporate priority. The benefits of strategic philanthropy are closely aligned with benefits obtained from social responsibility. Businesses that engage in strategic philanthropy often gain a tax advantage. Research suggests that they may also enjoy improved productivity, stronger employee commitment and morale, reduced turnover, and greater customer loyalty and satisfaction. In the future, many companies will devote more resources to understand how strategic philanthropy can be developed and integrated to support their core competencies.

The implementation of strategic philanthropy is impossible without the support of top management. To integrate strategic philanthropy into the organization successfully, the efforts must fit with the company's mission, values, and resources. Organizations must also understand stakeholder expectations and the propensity to support such activities for mutual benefit. This process relies on the feedback of stakeholders in improving and learning how to better integrate the strategic philanthropy objectives with other organizational goals. Finally, companies will need to evaluate philanthropic efforts and assess how these results should be communicated to stakeholders.

Responsible Business Debate

The Influence of Business on Society

Issue: *Does business owe anything to society?*

For decades, there have been two clear and opposing responses when answering the question, "What is the role of business in society?" One camp argues that the business of business is business, and therefore, there ought to be little consideration beyond profit and shareholder return. Milton Friedman was a supporter of this belief. He believed businesses only owed responsibility to shareholders and worried that any concern for the general public would lead to a totalitarian state.

There is also the fear that big businesses could have too much power over our daily lives. Critics believe that if society relinquishes its decision-making authority and power to businesspeople, then negative consequences are likely to result. Businesses might try to make decisions that some people believe should be a personal choice. The marketing of unhealthy food to children is a good example. While many societal members are calling for companies to increase their healthy food offerings or decrease their marketing of unhealthy food, critics believe this decision belongs to the parents and it is their job to oversee what their children eat. For this reason, they claim that business is about making a profit and business ideas probably won't work for confronting societal issues.

The other group focuses on the prospects for social responsibility and for business to play a critical and positive role in society. Because business has such a major impact, it should be responsible for reducing the negative impact of its decisions. Pollution is one example. It is not uncommon for business operations to result in the emission of greenhouse gases or unusable chemical runoff. A common belief is that this pollution should belong to the business, and it should carry the costs of disposing of it. Others also point out that business is in a unique position to make a significant positive difference. While government regulation takes a long time to pass, businesses can make the conscious decision to give back to their communities, take action to reduce their harmful impact on stakeholders, and promote objectives that would benefit society. Businesses have the financial resources and human talent that can be effectively applied to community needs and problems. Supporters of this mentality argue that in so doing, businesses build a positive relationship with customers, investors, and other stakeholders, leading to more business and increased profits for the firm.

Beyond the theoretical question, however, emerges the reality of the funds, time, and ideas that business contributes to a host of charitable, social, and quasi-governmental platforms. Implied in these activities is that business has a role to play beyond its own industry, products, and employees. Clearly, if society expects business to make these contributions, then there ought to be consideration to the level and type of influence that business will have on society over the long-term.

There Are Two Sides to Every Issue:

1. Big business should be concerned solely with profits and leave societal concerns out of the equation.
2. Businesses operate in society and therefore have a social responsibility to effect positive change.

Source: Milton Friedman, "The Social Responsibility of Business Is To Increase Its Profits," *The New York Times Magazine*, September 13, 1970.

KEY TERMS

community (p. 289)
neighbor of choice (p. 289)
community relations (p. 290)

volunteerism (p. 297)
philanthropy (p. 299)
strategic philanthropy (p. 300)

cause-related marketing (p. 304)
social entrepreneurship (p. 306)

DISCUSSION QUESTIONS

1. What are some of the issues you might include in a defense of strategic philanthropy to company stockholders?
2. Describe your personal experiences with philanthropy. In what types of activities have you participated? Which companies that you do business with have a philanthropic focus? How did this focus influence your decision to buy from those companies?
3. How have changes in the business environment contributed to the growing trend of strategic philanthropy?

4. Compare and contrast cause-related marketing with strategic philanthropy. What are the unique benefits of each approach?
5. Compare social entrepreneurship to cause-related marketing and strategic philanthropy.
6. What role does top management play in developing and implementing a strategic philanthropy approach?
7. Describe the four-stage process for planning and implementing strategic philanthropy.

EXPERIENTIAL EXERCISE

Choose one major corporation and investigate how closely its philanthropic efforts are strategically aligned with its core competencies. Visit the company's website, read its annual reports, and use other sources to justify your conclusions. Develop a chart or table to depict how the company's core competencies are linked to various philanthropic projects and stakeholder groups. Finally, provide an analysis of how these efforts have affected the company's performance.

CREATING 'BUY IN' FOR VOLUNTEERISM: WHAT WOULD YOU DO?

As a new vice president of corporate philanthropy, Jack Birke was looking forward to the great initiatives and partnerships the company could create through his office. During his 18-year career, Jack worked for several large nonprofit organizations and earned an excellent reputation for his ability to raise funds, develop advisory boards, and in general, work well with the business community.

About a year ago, Jack decided to investigate other opportunities within the fundraising industry and started looking at companies that were formalizing their philanthropy efforts. He was hired as vice president less than a month ago and was in the process of developing an office structure, getting to know the organization, and creating a strategic plan. His charge over the next year was to develop a stronger reputation for philanthropy and social responsibility with the company's stakeholders, including employees, customers, and the community. An executive assistant, director of volunteerism, and director of community relations were already on board, and Jack was looking for additional staff.

The position and office were new to the company, and Jack had already heard dissent from other employees, who openly questioned how important philanthropy was to the business. After all, the economy was slowing, and it seemed that customers were more concerned about price and value than any "touchy feely" program. About half of the company's employees worked on the manufacturing line, and the other half was employed in administrative or professional positions. Both groups seemed to be equally suspicious of Jack and his office. The company developed an employee volunteer program two years ago, but it was never very successful. A program to gather food, gifts, and money to support needy families at Christmas, however, drew strong support. The firm had fairly good relationships in the community, but these were primarily the top executives' connections through the chamber of commerce, industry associations, nonprofit boards, and so forth. In sum, while Jack had the support of top management, many employees were unsure about philanthropy and its importance to the company. Jack was starting to think about short-term policies and long-term strategy for "marketing" his office and goals to the rest of the organization. What would you do?

CHAPTER TEN

Technology Issues

Chapter Objectives

- To examine the nature and characteristics of technology

- To explore the economic impact of technology

- To examine technology's influence on society

- To provide a framework for the strategic management of technology issues

Chapter Outline

The Nature of Technology

Technology's Influence on the Economy

Technology's Influence on Society

Strategic Implementation of Responsibility for Technology

Responding to Business Challenges

Uber Disrupts the Transportation Industry

Uber, Airbnb, Instacar, Lyft—while these names were unheard of a few years ago, today they are recognized worldwide. The advent of mobile technology—combined with economic conditions such as wide-scale unemployment—has led to an entirely new economic model: the sharing economy. The sharing economy involves the sharing of underutilized assets. Private individuals with resources such as cars or houses can "rent" these resources, becoming their own entrepreneurs. This allows consumers to make extra money off underutilized resources as well as be their own boss.

Riding high on the success of the sharing economy is Uber, founded in 2009 as a ride sharing service. Uber is a disruptive technology that has revolutionized the transportation industry. It operates via a mobile phone app that connects drivers – everyday people with cars– with passengers that want to get somewhere. The passenger's credit card is automatically charged, and the driver gets a commission. Uber has operations in 300 cities worldwide and has an estimated $60 billion value.

Uber offers convenience to customers who are looking for a quick way to get to their destination. Using the app on their phone gives customers the ability to contact a local Uber driver in their area. The Uber driver operates as independent contractors, meaning they drive their own cars. For many consumers Uber proves to be cheaper than taxi services, although this depends upon the time and distance. Uber operates with surge-based pricing, meaning it uses an algorithm to determine pricing based on demand. In periods of higher demand, Uber charges higher pricing.

Uber has upended the transportation industry, and many traditional transportation firms are unhappy about it. Taxi companies argue that the ride-sharing model should be held to the same rules as taxies. Global governments have begun limiting Uber from operating until they can determine how to regulate it. In France an attempt was made to ban an Uber service because drivers do not have to be licensed. Calls for Uber regulations occur when a driver commits a crime, even when not driving for Uber at the time.

However, it is also facing challenges on its home front. For instance, both Uber and its competitor Lyft left Austin, Texas because unfavorable regulation requires drivers to have fingerprint background checks. The taxi industry claimed Uber puts them at a competitive disadvantage because of its advantage on saving costs on licensing, insurance, and other fees. Regulators are considering regulations that will deal with obstacles necessary to level the competitive playing field.

Despite these challenges, Uber's success has popularized a number of sharing services, from transportation to lodging, chores to doctor visits. Some of these firms, such as Lyft, and Didi Kuaidi in China, are competing against Uber directly. Others have taken on totally different industries. For instance, TaskRabbit uses its digital site to connect independent contractors with clients who need chores performed, and DogVacay focuses on dog watching. Companies are finding that with technology, the possibilities for offering services through the sharing models are nearly endless.

In this chapter, we explore the nature of technology and its positive and negative effects on society. Technology's influence on the economy is very powerful, especially with regard to growth, employment, and working environments. This influence on society includes issues related to the internet, privacy, intellectual property, health, and the general quality of life. The strategic direction for technology depends on government as well as on business's ability to plan, implement, and audit the influence of technology on society.

THE NATURE OF TECHNOLOGY

technology
Relates to the application of knowledge, including the processes and applications to solve problems, perform tasks, and create new methods to obtain desired outcomes.

Technology relates to the application of knowledge, including the processes and applications to solve problems, perform tasks, and create new methods to obtain desired outcomes. It includes intellectual knowledge as well as the physical systems devised to achieve business and personal objectives. The evolution of civilization is tied to developments in technology. Through technological advances, humans have moved from a hunter-gatherer existence to a stable agricultural economy to the Industrial Revolution. Today, our economy is based more on information technology and services than on manufacturing. This technology is changing the way we take vacations, shop for groceries, do homework, track criminals, navigate to places, and maintain friendships. Technology has made it possible to go to work or attend meetings without leaving the house. Our new economy is based on these dynamic technological changes in our society.

Characteristics of Technology

Some of the characteristics of technology include the dynamics, reach, and self-sustaining nature of technological progress. The dynamics of technology relate to the constant change that often challenges the structure of social institutions. The automobile, airplane, and personal computer all created major changes and influenced government, the family, social relationships, education, the military, and leisure. These changes can happen so fast that they require significant adjustments in the political, religious, and economic structures of society. Some societies have difficulty adjusting to this rate of change to the point that they even attempt to legislate against new technologies to isolate themselves. China tried to isolate its citizens from the internet and the social trends resulting from the application of new technology to music, movies, and other carriers of culture. But eventually they eased restrictions, allowing for limited and monitored use. Since then, internet use in China has grown, with the number of regular users totaling more than 700 million, usually on mobile devices. However, the government still utilizes a number of strategies for reminding Chinese citizens that their internet activity is being monitored. Often, the Chinese government will completely shut down the use of instant messaging or social media applications to limit the potential of groups to organize protests or other anti-government activities.[2]

The dynamics of technology are not only changing many traditional products, such as books and music, but also the way in which we conduct everyday activities. The proliferation of e-readers and smartphones prepared consumers for the introduction of iPads. These devices changed the way people accomplish both work-related and personal tasks, as well as the way we store data. As the capacity for cloud storage of data increases, other storage devices such as USB drives will likely become a thing of the past. Today we can conduct banking transactions without going to a bank, draft a document while riding the bus to work and save it to our Dropbox account, and share information with others with a touch of a button. Each advance in technology seems to lead to new developments across industries, sometimes making things more convenient, while at other times raising serious concerns about privacy, protection of digital property, and other issues.

Reach relates to the broad nature of technology as it moves through society. For instance, every community in both developed and developing countries has been influenced by cellular and wireless telephones. The ability to make a call from almost any location has many positive effects, but negative side effects include increases in traffic accidents and noise pollution as well as fears about potential health risks. Through telecommunications, businesses, families, and governments have been linked from far distances. Satellites allow instant visual and voice electronic connections almost anywhere in the world. These technologies have reduced the need for in-person meetings via business travel. Web conferencing and video conferencing are becoming more popular alternatives, although it may be difficult for technology to fully replace the nature of face-to-face encounters. Even though collaboration technology continues to grow in lieu of business travel, companies recognize that some occasions demand face-to-face interaction, such as meeting a new client for the first time, dealing with certain cultures, and discussing significant financial and legal transactions.

The self-sustaining nature of technology relates to the fact that technology acts as a catalyst to spur even faster development. As innovations are introduced, they stimulate the need for more technology to facilitate further development. For example, the internet created the need for broadband transmission of electric signals through phone lines (DSL), satellites, and cable. Broadband allows connections to the internet to be 50 times faster than through a traditional telephone modem. It also allows users to download large files and creates the opportunity for a rich multimedia experience. Today, most people refer to it as Wi-Fi, and many restaurants and coffee shops offer it as a feature to attract customers. The latest discussion in the advancement of internet transmission is through fiber optic cables. Many developed countries are heavily investing in building and utilizing fiber optic infrastructure for faster internet connections, and we are seeing adoption among consumers rapidly increase. Google Fiber, the company's fiber optic internet connection, claims to run 100 times faster than broadband.[3]

Effects of Technology

Civilizations must harness and adapt to changes in technology to maintain a desired quality of life. The cell phone, for example, has dramatically altered communication patterns, particularly in developing countries where there are few telephone lines. Innovations can also change entire industries. Companies and governments are creating supercomputers that are millions of times more powerful than personal computers. The computers are making use of "big data," which is the accumulation of large volumes of varied data that need to be transmitted at very fast speeds. The concept of big data is a result of the continual use of the internet via computers and mobile devices.[4] Such examples illustrate how technology can provide new methods to accomplish tasks that were once thought impossible. These advancements create new processes, new products, and economic progress and ultimately have profound effects on society.

The global economy experienced the greatest acceleration of technological advancement that ever occurred, propelling increased productivity, output, corporate profits, and stock prices, over the last decade.[5] Among the positive contributions of these advances were reductions in the number of worker hours required to generate the nation's output. At the same time, the economic conditions that accompanied this period of technical innovation resulted in increased job opportunities. But in the early 2000s, with the fall of the dot-coms and the integrity meltdown of major U.S. corporations, the economy had taken a downturn, along with the falling stock market. Many information technology firms expanded too rapidly and misreported revenue and earnings to hold onto stock prices and please executives and investors. The result was incidences of massive accounting fraud that damaged confidence and the economy. Earlier chapters dealt with many of these cases and their effect on social responsibility expectations. The traditional work environment has changed because telecommunications (e.g., e-mail and video conferencing) reduce the need for face-to-face interaction. Through online shopping, the internet can also reduce the need for trips to a shopping center and has increased the amount of business done by UPS and FedEx. In addition, the ease and number of business-to-business transactions have expanded.

However, there are concerns that dramatic shifts in the acceleration and innovations derived from technology may be spurring imbalances not only in the economy but also in our social existence. The flow of technology into developing countries can serve as a method to jump-start economic development. In Kenya many residents use the mobile phone payment service M-Pesa to quickly and securely transfer funds to merchants and family members, reducing the need to travel long distances to banks. The service has also allowed many to start their own businesses, contributing to the growth of the local economy.[6] However, a failure to share technology or provide methods to disseminate technology could cause a major divide in the quality of life. Limited resources in underdeveloped countries and the lack of a technology infrastructure may lead to many social, political, and economic problems in the future.

In the United States, the federal government implemented plans to subsidize computers, mobile phones, and internet access for low-income households and individuals across the nation. Although this initiative was somewhat controversial, proponents argued it had the potential to raise the standard of living for low-income families.[7] Some companies are also trying to help bridge the technology gap that exists between those who can afford technology and those who are on the other side of the so-called digital divide. Comcast Corporation established a program called Internet Essentials where people can sign up to see if they qualify for low-cost internet connection, computers for $150, and free internet training.[8] Other internet providers offer programs similar to Comcast's and serve as examples of a corporate attempt to keep the positive effects of the reach of technology available to all segments of society.

There are concerns about the way information technology can improve the quality of life for society. In addition, there are concerns about the negative consequences of the reduction of privacy and the emergence of cyber-crime. It is becoming common for hackers to install malware into company and government computer systems to steal secrets or consumer data. If higher security measures are not taken, significant changes in our economy and individual lifestyles could occur, causing the roles of business, government, and technology to be questioned. Public advocacy organizations are helping by participating in charting the future of computer networks to integrate these technological innovations into the way we live.[9]

TECHNOLOGY'S INFLUENCE ON THE ECONOMY

Technology has had an enormous influence on the global economy. In many ways, technology has contributed to significant economic growth through new business opportunities, better ways to connect across long distances, and more efficient processes. For example, the widespread growth of companies like Uber and Airbnb have led to a new economic term called the sharing economy. In the sharing economy, independent contractors can "rent out" underutilized resources such as cars or lodging to earn extra income. Companies like Uber act as agents. Their technology links the buyer and seller, but they do engage in the distribution process directly. The sharing economy has led to a number of opportunities for both buyers and sellers. However, technology has also given rise to concerns as well. The following sections document technology's overall impact on the economy.

Economic Growth and Employment

Technological advancements have had a profound impact on economic growth and employment. Over the past several decades, technology has been a major factor in the economic growth of the United States. Investments in educational technologies, increased support for basic government research, and continued commitment to the mission of research and development (R&D) in both the public and private sectors

TABLE 10.1 Leading Technology Firms

Company	Number of Employees
Google	57,100
Intel	107,300
Microsoft	112,689
Apple Inc.	115,000
Sony	131,700
Amazon.com	230,800
Samsung	319,000
IBM	377,757

have become major drivers of economic growth. Through lower interest rates, tax credits, and liberalization of export controls, the government established the economic infrastructure for using technology to drive economic development. The expansion of industry-led technology partnerships among corporations, governments, and non-profit organizations has also been a key component of growth. Table 10.1 shows some leading technology firms and their number of employees.

Investments in research and development are among the highest return investments a nation can make. Technological innovation has been a key contributor to the nation's growth in productivity.[10] For example, the ability to access information in real time through the electronic data interface among retailers, wholesalers, and manufacturers has reduced the time it takes to produce and deliver products. Likewise, product design times and costs have declined because computer modeling has minimized the need for architectural drafters and some engineers required for building projects. Medical diagnoses have become faster, more thorough, and more accurate thanks to the accessibility of information and records over the internet, which has hastened treatment and eliminated unnecessary procedures.[11]

The relationship between businesses and consumers has been transformed through e-commerce, as more people turn to the internet to make all type of purchases from one-time purchases to everyday purchases. The sharing of information has led to greater transparency, and social media has facilitated closer communication and greater customer loyalty. Business-to-business (B2B) e-commerce involving companies buying from and selling to each other online is also growing in popularity as it is the preferred method of purchase for more than half of all businesses. Certain aspects of internet transactions are particularly important in B2B relationships, where the improved quantity, reliability, and timeliness of information have reduced uncertainties. It has also facilitated supply chain management as more companies outsource purchasing over the internet.[12]

Walmart and Amazon are two companies that have not only mastered the management and integration of their supply chains over the years but have also used the internet to establish further efficiencies within the supply chain. Walmart's technology infrastructure is among the largest in the world and informs operations regarding accurate forecasting of demand and inventory, the most efficient transportation routes, and management of customer relationships and service response logistics. Amazon has fulfillment centers strategically located in areas where customers can be reached quickly. A technology known as sortation allows Amazon to determine how different items can be combined to efficiently fit into boxes. The software instructs employees on where to store the item in the warehouse and how large a package will be needed when it comes time to ship. Amazon's expertise at supply chain management has earned it strong accolades and saved it billions of dollars in costs.[13]

Science and technology are powerful drivers of economic growth and improvements in the quality of life in the United States. Advancements in technology have created millions of new jobs, better health and longer lives, new opportunities, and more. Public and private investment in R&D contributes to these advancements and continues to produce more jobs and improve living standards. Industries that have grown as a result of innovations in technology include biotechnology, computers, communications, software, aerospace, and semiconductors. Retailing, wholesaling, and other commercial institutions have also been transformed by technology as we can tell from the examples of Amazon and Dell above.

Economic Concerns about the Use of Technology

Despite the staggering economic growth fostered by technological advancements, there are some economic downsides to technology. For instance, some people have lost their jobs because of technology. Technology makes it easier to outsource business activities to other countries with less expensive labor, leading to a loss in domestic jobs. Also, many factories have increasingly invested in robotics, which can be used to replace factory workers at a lower cost. Although technology also creates numerous job opportunities, this is little consolation for those who lose their jobs and do not have the technological skills to get new jobs in the growing technological emerging field.

Small businesses in particular may have difficulty taking advantage of certain opportunities such as digital supply chain management systems or other large-scale information technology (IT) applications. The ability to purchase technology may affect the nature of competition and the success of various types of businesses. Limited resources and tough economic times may cause small businesses to cancel, modify, or delay IT projects; decrease IT budgets; and reduce staffing and training levels. Experts recommend several solutions to IT problems in small business:

1. Focus on core competencies while seeking to explore outsourcing options.
2. Take advantage of free software and other offerings.
3. Explore the benefits of "cloud computing" where applications are utilized and maintained on a subscription basis.
4. Consider IT infrastructure alternatives to capital expenditures through hosted hardware, software, and services.[14]

As mentioned earlier, a key concern today with advancing technology is the digital divide that occurs when certain groups have limited access to the latest technology. Also, part of the debate involves access issues for certain populations, such as persons with disabilities, people who are barely literate, the distribution of technology among low-income and high-income households, and accommodations for senior citizens.[15]

There are several ways to address these inevitable consequences of accelerating change in the technology drivers of the new economy. One way to address the negative consequences of accelerating new technology is to assess problems related to its impact on competition. Restraining competition, domestic or international, to suppress competitive turmoil is a major concern of governments. Allowing anticompetitive practices, price fixing, or other unfair methods of competition would be counterproductive to rising standards of living.[16]

TECHNOLOGY'S INFLUENCE ON SOCIETY

Information and telecommunications technology minimizes the borders between countries, businesses, and people and allows people to overcome the physical limitations of time and space. Technological advances also enable people to acquire customized goods and services that cost less and are of higher quality than ever imagined.[17]

For example, airline passengers can purchase tickets online and either print out boarding passes on their home or office printers or download them to their mobile devices so that they can go straight to their plane on arrival at the airport after clearing security.[18] Cartographers and geologists can create custom maps—even in three dimensions—that aid experts in managing water supplies, finding oil, and pinpointing future earthquakes.[19] In this section, we explore four broad issues related to technology and its impact on society, including the internet, privacy, intellectual property, and health and biotechnology. Although there are many other pressing issues related to technology, these seem to be the most widely debated at this time.

The Internet

The internet, the global information system that links many computer networks together, has profoundly altered the way people communicate, learn, do business, and find entertainment. Although many people believe the internet began in the early 1990s, its origins can be traced to the late 1950s (see Table 10.2). Over five decades, the network evolved from a system for government and university researchers into an information and entertainment tool used by millions around the globe. With the development of the World Wide Web, which organizes the information on the internet into interconnected "pages" of text, graphics, audio, and video, use of the internet exploded in the 1990s.

Today, more than 3.2 billion people around the world utilize the internet. In the United States alone, nearly 287 million access the internet via computers or mobile devices. Internet use by consumers in other countries, especially Japan (115 million users), the United Kingdom (60 million), Germany (71 million), Brazil (139 million) and France (56 million), has escalated rapidly.[20] Figure 10.1 shows the pattern of active internet usage around the world. To keep up with the growing demand for new e-mail and website addresses, the Internet Corporation for Assigned Names and Numbers has added over 300 domain name suffixes to allow for the creation of millions of new addresses. In addition, recent petitions have been approved to allow for hundreds more

TABLE 10.2 History of the Internet

Year	Event
1969	The first node is connected to Advanced Research Projects Agency Network (ARPANET), the initial version of the internet. ARPANET was a government project created to serve as a communications network during the Cold War.
1972	Email is invented by adapting an internal messaging program and extending it to use the ARPANET to send messages between sites. Within a year, three quarters of ARPANET traffic is email.
1989	The World Wide Web is invented to make information easier to publish and access on the internet.
1993	The first Web-browser, Mosaic, is launched. It introduced proprietary HTML tags and more sophisticated image capabilities. The browser is a massive success and businesses start to notice the web's potential.
1994	Internet Magazine launches, reporting on London's first cybercafe and reviewing 100 websites. It was known as the 'most extensive' list of websites ever to appear in a magazine. A 28.8Kbps modem costs £399 (plus VAT). Jerry and David's Guide to the World Wide Web is renamed Yahoo! and receives 100,000 visitors. In 1995, it begins displaying advertisements.
1995	Search engine Alta Vista is launched, which can store and index the HTML from every internet page. It also introduces the first multilingual search. Amazon.com, an online bookseller that pioneers ecommerce, is launched. eBay is launched to enable internet users to trade with each other.
1998	Google launches and pioneers a ranking system that uses links to assess a website's popularity. The site's simple design is soothing while existing search engines cram their pages with animated advertisements.
2000	The infamous dotcom bust occurs after several years of venture capitalists investing in internet business proposals that do not have a viable business model.
2004	Media companies start selling music and video online. Napster and iTunes are the major players. Facebook launches at Harvard University. The social networking site gained 30 million members by 2007 and over 200 million active users in 2009. Photo sharing website Flickr launches, coinciding with the rise in digital photography. (Kodak discontinues reloadable film cameras in Western Europe and North America in this year.)
2006	Twitter is launched.
2010	The industry of big data, or the accumulation of large volumes of varied data that need to be transmitted at very fast speeds, is estimated to be worth more than $100 billion.
2013	Media reports reveal the extent to which national security agencies monitor the online activities of citizens without search warrants.
2015	The Internet of Things, in which consumer or industrial devices are connected to the internet for management and monitoring, became a popular concept in our connected environment. Facebook has 1.6 billion active users

Sources: Adapted from "A Short History of the Internet," http://www.sean.co.uk/a/science/history_of_the_internet.shtm (accessed June 22, 2015); Economist staff, "Data, data everywhere," *The Economist,* February 25, 2010, http://www.economist.com/node/15557443 (accessed June 22, 2016).

to come into existence. These new suffixes will differ from the traditional website endings such as .com (for companies), .edu (schools and universities), .gov (government agencies and offices), .mil (military use), .net (networks), etc., and will be more descriptive of the website's purpose or content. For example, a clothing retailer may have the suffix .clothes, while a plumber may have a website ending in .plumbing.[21]

The interactive nature of the internet has created tremendous opportunities for businesses to forge relationships with consumers and business

FIGURE 10.1 Use of the Internet around the Globe

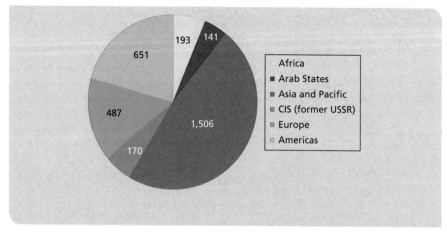

Note: *Commonwealth of Independent States (CIS) is a regional organization whose participants are former Soviet Republics.

Source: ITU, "Key 2005-2015 ICT data for the world, by by geographic regions and by level of development," *Interntional Telecommunication Union (ITU)*, http://www.itu.int/en/ITU-D/Statistics/Pages/stat/default.aspx (accessed June 22, 2016).

customers, target markets more precisely, and even reach previously inaccessible markets. The internet also facilitates supply chain management, allowing companies to network with manufacturers, wholesalers, retailers, suppliers, and outsource firms to serve customers more efficiently.[22] However, widespread use of the internet has also led to the storing of mass amounts of information that hackers and other cybercriminals can take advantage of. Online fraud has become a major issue for businesses and consumers, with U.S. business losing $32 billion in a one year period.[23] Interestingly, the rate of online fraud targeting businesses is decreasing, while the rate for consumer online fraud increases. This is largely due to the fact that companies are using more sophisticated methods of tracking abnormal credit and debit transactions. Many are making use of data by analyzing trends such as average amount spent per month and locations where the money is spent. Automated systems quickly keep track of these behaviors and notify customers when there are any abnormalities from the trends.[24] However, the methods by which cybercriminals and other hackers infiltrate payment and information systems all across the internet are also becoming increasingly sophisticated. It is often hard for the average consumer to spot malware or other viruses created by hackers, which can lead to unknowing participation in scams and significant monetary losses.

Consumers, companies, and governments alike are having difficulty keeping up with the fast pace of cybercriminal technology, and are increasingly worried about becoming victims of online fraud. The newspapers have been filled with examples of this over the past few years. Sometimes, consumers and companies can become victims of online fraud without making a purchase from a personal computer or mobile device. Credit card transactions occur by means of the internet even when a purchase is made in a physical location. Target's credit card system was hacked during the holiday season, and personal information from approximately 40 million customers was stolen. This shows that online fraud can include information as well as money. In addition, some say that the fraudulent methods employed by the cyber-criminals were not especially complex, indicating the commonality of such activities.[25] Consumers, government agencies, and merchants are exploring options, including regulation, to protect the security of online transactions.[26]

It is estimated that by the end of this decade, up to 50 billion things, including cars, household items such as refrigerators, and medical devices, will be hooked up to web connections. Known as the Internet of Things, this phenomenon is already being extensively pursued in countries such as South Korea. The Internet of Things has the potential to greatly enhance our ability to do activities and make devices more efficient. For instance, a doctor with smart medical devices can monitor patients from far away. On the other hand, with cybersecurity risks increasing, many are worried that criminals will use these connections to sabotage or hack into devices. Just as a hacker hacks into a computer, so a criminal might be able to hack into a smart car. The risks are worse because hacking into a smart car or smart medical device could endanger lives. Technology firms such as Cisco and IBM are setting up consortiums to identify innovative ways to prevent these attacks. They believe that the sharing of information will help alert both people and companies to risks, prompting them to take action to prevent cybercrimes before they strike.[27]

Privacy

The extraordinary growth of the internet has generated issues related to privacy. As instances of hacking become more commonplace and severe, consumers are realizing the responsibility they have to protect their own privacy. However, while a large percentage of online shoppers are concerned about their privacy, many are not taking appropriate measures to protect their information. This is largely a result of consumers feeling like this problem is beyond their control. Table 10.3 describes top privacy concerns for consumers.

Because of the ease of access to personal information, however, unauthorized use of this information may occur.[28] Information can be collected on the internet with or without a person's knowledge. Many websites follow users' tracks through their site by storing a "cookie," or identifying string of text, on their computers. These cookies permit website operators to track how often a user visits the site, what he or she looks at while there, and in what sequence. Cookies also allow website visitors to customize services, such as virtual shopping carts, as well as the particular content they see when they log on to a webpage. However, if a website operator can exploit cookies to link a visitor's interests to a name and address, that information could be sold to advertisers and other parties without the visitor's consent or knowledge. The potential for misuse has left many consumers rather uncomfortable with this technology.[29]

TABLE 10.3 Top Privacy Concerns

Privacy Issue	Concern	Example
Cookies (tracking)	Companies can track where I have been on the internet	Many well-known companies, including Amazon.com, use cookies to track activity
Seizures of cloud data	Whatever information I put on cloud sourcing sites belongs to the online service I am using	Government authorities can seize data on crowd sourcing sites such as Google Drive
Location data	Companies will know where I am at all times	Based on the location of a person's cell phone, digital coupons could be sent for neighboring businesses
Facial recognition software	Online photos can be picked up by an online facial recognition database	Photos posted on Flickr could easily be used in facial recognition
Cybersecurity scanning	Government authorities may monitor my online activity in the name of cybersecurity	Government authorities are increasing their scanning to try and detect cyber risks before they hit—possibly leading to monitoring of consumer posts in the process
Marketing research	My data on social networks will be used for advertising, marketing research, and other purposes	Facebook conducted a study which involved manipulating the news feeds of some users to monitor how they react
Hacking	My personal identifying data such as credit card and social security numbers are not safe	Criminals hacked into Target's system and stole the personal information of millions of customers

Source: Adapted from Melissa Riofrio, "The 5 Biggest Online Privacy Threats of 2013," *PC World,* April 8, 2013, http://www.pcworld.com/article/2031908/the-5-biggest-online-privacy-threats-of-2013.html (accessed June 22, 2016).

Identity theft, the access and theft of personal information, is a top crime in the nation, with 300,000 identity theft complaints submitted to the Federal Trade Commission (FTC) annually. Fraud is another major type of misconduct. The most common types of theft and fraud include government documents/benefits fraud, the misuse of credit card information, phone or utilities fraud, bank fraud, employment-related fraud, and loan fraud.[30] Identity fraud is defined as the use of someone's personal information to access money. The infraction affects about one person every two seconds in the United States, and the rate of increase is growing rapidly. Data breaches, like the one Target experienced, are the most common source of identity theft and identity fraud. Over 45 percent of those whose information was collected in a data breach experienced fraud in later months, while 28 percent of identity theft victims experienced takeovers of their bank accounts. Internal data breaches are also becoming a problem. It is estimated that 27 percent of attacks on organizations come from within the organization from disgruntled employees. New tools such as Scout are being developed that can be used to analyze the language in employee emails and flag anything that seems suspicious or that indicates the employee is unhappy. However, this too generates privacy concerns as employees may not realize the language in their emails is being examined.[31]

Nearly all internet websites require visitors to register and provide information about themselves to access some or all of their content. How this information is used is generating concern. This is another aspect of the big data concept mentioned earlier in the chapter. A variety of organizations have been collecting and storing information on consumers for years and are now able to see trends and behaviors. This information is valuable to companies that want to better target people's buying behaviors and interests, and it is becoming a multi-billion dollar industry. For example, Facebook is generating revenue by allowing companies to access users' email addresses and phone numbers in order to better target their advertising efforts, while Barclays announced that it would begin selling information to third parties. The bank assured customers that their information would be presented along with many others to show trends rather than distinctive personal information. However, because there are no current regulations regarding the selling of customer information, many people are concerned about the practice.[32]

Privacy issues remain at the forefront of the FTC's investigative and enforcement activities. Snapchat, a mobile messaging service, settled a case with the FTC regarding misstatements of privacy measures. The messaging service distinguished itself on the basis of privacy concerns by allowing users to send messages that would disappear within seconds of being opened. They promised users that their messages would not be stored in databases nor would they collect any personal information. The FTC found otherwise. Not only were the message contents stored, an unsecure feature in the app allowed hackers to steal information from more than 4 million users.[33]

Privacy issues related to children are generating even more debate, as well as laws to protect children's interests. The U.S. Children's Online Privacy Protection Act (COPPA) prohibits websites and internet providers from seeking personal information from children under age 13 without parental consent.[34] The law was recently amended to protect children's privacy in using social media sites and mobile devices. However, issues still exist. For example, photosharing app Instagram has received criticism for allowing children under the age of 13 to join the site. The company's policy is that only users above the age of 13 are allowed to join, but entering a date of birth upon registering is not required, making it difficult to track underage users. A Pew poll indicated that Instagram is the third most popular site among teens, and this concerns parents because their children are posting pictures of themselves and their friends along with the locations they frequent. This can make them vulnerable to predators or create other dangerous situations. This is an issue that many social networking sites, including Facebook, Tumblr, and Twitter, are also dealing with. Parents are calling for tighter company controls and monitoring of user ages.[35] Table 10.4 provides recommendations for improving child safety on the internet.

TABLE 10.4 Six Tips to Improve Child Safety on the Internet

1. Know what your children are doing online.
2. Get to know the technologies your children are using.
3. Discuss the risks with your children and agree on some rules for internet use.
4. Install an internet content filter.
5. Make sure your children know not to share personal information or photos.
6. Report inappropriate, harmful, or criminal activities that occur online or on a mobile device.

Source: "Protect Your Children," *Stay Smart Online*, http://www.staysmart online.gov.au/home_users/protect_your_children (accessed July 14, 2014).

Ethical Responsibilities in Human Resources

Big Brother IS Watching You

With the explosion of social media sites, a person's private details are increasingly becoming public information. Individuals like to share their lives through postings, photos, videos, and other content with friends or acquaintances. However, due to the public nature of social media, much of what a person puts up about him or herself could be viewed by individuals that the user did not anticipate—including employers. According to a survey, 39 percent of employers research potential job candidates using social media. Employers recognize that an employee's online presence speaks volumes about his or her character; 43 percent of employers who research job candidates' online profiles have reported that they have eliminated candidates from consideration because of what they found out about them online.

Many users of social media place privacy controls on their pages to keep unauthorized people from seeing their activities. However, employers have a way of getting beyond these controls by asking employees or candidates for hire for their login and password information. In most states, this is not yet illegal. There is currently legislation pending in 23 states to address this issue. While some states have barred private employers from asking employees this question, public employers are not necessarily covered. Needless to say, many employees and regulators believe that requiring employee information to monitor their personal social media activities is an invasion of privacy.

However, with so many people engaging in social media, work life and personal life have become blurred. It is not uncommon for an employee who might have once kept something private, such as a complaint about a job, to post it online for others to see. Carelessly posting something regarding company product introductions or financials could be devastating for a firm if it gets out beforehand. For this reason, the Financial Industry Regulatory Authority and Wall Street are asking regulators to make an exception for employees in the financial industry. Worries of insider trading, potential Ponzi schemes, and influencing stock activity on the market are at the heart of this request. For instance, one CFO was fired after venting on social media using confidential financial information. Such information could negatively impact the firm if released early.

Regulators allow financial firms to communicate information through social media outlets as long as they disclose to the investor where, when, and how they plan to divulge this information. This could lead employees to believe it is also all right to discuss non-public information on social media. Financial firms are concerned that by protecting employees' privacy on social media, they become vulnerable to potential scandals involving the misappropriation of financial information, which could harm investors. While the requested amendment to the privacy laws will only be put to use if an employee is suspected of releasing unwarranted information, critics believe that such an exception will erode employee privacy altogether.

Sources: Jean Eaglesham and Michael Rothfeld, "Wall Street vs. Its Employees' Privacy," *The Wall Street Journal*, April 22, 2013, p. A1; Jennifer Van Grove, "Securities Regulators Balk at Employee Social Media Privacy," *CNet*, April 22, 2013, http://news.cnet.com/8301-1023_3-57580814-93/securities-regulators-balk-at-employee-social-media-privacy/ (accessed August 5, 2016); Rachel Emma Silverman, "Facebook and Twitter Postings Cost CFO His Job," *The Wall Street Journal*, May 14, 2012, http://online.wsj.com/article/SB1000142405270230350550457740454216806 1590.html (accessed August 5, 2016); National Conference of State Legislators, "Employer Access to Social Media Usernames and Passwords," http://www.ncsl.org/research/telecommunications-and-information-technology/employer-access-to-social-media-passwords-2013.aspx (accessed August 5, 2016); John Weber, Nancy Flynn, and Lewis Maltby, "Should Companies Monitor Their Employees' Social Media?" *The Wall Street Journal*, May 11, 2014, http://online.wsj.com/news/articles/SB10001424052702303825604579514471793116740 (accessed August 5, 2016); Marcia Heroux Pounds, "Does your boss have a right to know your Facebook password?" *Sun Sentinel*, November 13, 2015, http://www.sun-sentinel.com/business/fl-facebook-employers-legislation-20151113-story.html (accessed August 5, 2016).

Some measure of protection for personal privacy is already provided by the U.S. Constitution as well as Supreme Court rulings and federal laws (see Table 10.5). The FTC also regulates, enforces privacy standards, and monitors websites to ensure compliance. Similar laws are coming into existence to address privacy issues resulting from mobile device use. The Location Privacy Protection Act addresses the use of GPS devices in the following areas: companies are required to obtain users' permission before collecting location information, mobile apps created explicitly for stalking are prohibited, and companies that collect location information of more than 1,000 devices must post the details of what is collected and how it is used on the website. These are just a few provisions of the law.[36]

Unsurprisingly, many other issues regarding mobile and internet privacy exist. For example, company privacy statements are often lengthy and filled with legal jargon that the average consumer will not understand if they take the time to read them. The FTC has set out some best practices for mobile companies to be more transparent. Some of these principles include creating "just-in-time" permission requests for the company to collect location, personal information, photos, etc., and instituting a "Do Not Track" feature on devices and websites so the user has a choice as to the data being collected.[37] The Commission has also addressed best practices for mobile payment security and children's use of mobile applications.[38] These best practices are important guidelines for companies to follow to avoid litigation and protect the privacy of customers.

International Initiatives on Privacy The European Union (EU) has made great strides in protecting the privacy of its citizens. The 1998 European Union Directive on Data Protection specifically requires companies that want to collect personal information to explain how the information will be used and to obtain the individual's permission. Companies must make customer data files available on request, just as U.S. credit-reporting firms must grant customers access to their personal credit histories. The law also bars website operators from selling e-mail addresses and using cookies to track visitors' movements and preferences without first obtaining permission. Because of this legislation, no company may deliver personal information about EU citizens to countries whose privacy laws do not meet EU standards.[39] In an effort to further protect citizens' privacy, the EU instituted the "right to be forgotten" rule, which mandates that internet companies erase search results of individuals who make such a request. This has sparked some controversy in the United States. Critics claim the law will hinder the sharing of information and law enforcement activities. EU legislators are also working on making data collection a choice of the user rather than the company offering the service. One proposal will require that companies specifically detail each data item that they will collect and how it will be used. Also, they would not be allowed to begin the process of collecting data until they have received permission from the user. Such regulations highlight the differences in how Europeans and Americans approach online privacy.[40]

TABLE 10.5 Privacy Laws

Act (Date Enacted)	Purpose
Privacy Act (1974)	Requires federal agencies to adopt minimum standards for collecting and processing personal information; limits the disclosure of such records to other public or private parties; requires agencies to make records on individuals available to them on request, subject to certain conditions.
Right to Financial Privacy Act (1978)	Protects the rights of financial institution customers to keep their financial records private and free from unjust government investigation.
Computer Security Act (1987)	Brought greater confidentiality and integrity to the regulation of information in the public realm by assigning responsibility for the standardization of communication protocols, data structures, and interfaces in telecommunications and computer systems to the National Institute of Standards and Technology (NIST), which also announced security and privacy guidelines for federal computer systems.
Computer Matching and Privacy Protection Act (1988)	Amended the Privacy Act by adding provisions regulating the use of computer matching, the computerized comparison of individual information for purposes of determining eligibility for federal benefits programs.
Video Privacy Protection Act (1988)	Specifies the circumstances under which a business that rents or sells videos can disclose personally identifiable information about a consumer or reveal an individual's video rental or sales records.
Telephone Consumer Protection Act (1991)	Regulates the activities of telemarketers by limiting the hours during which they can solicit residential subscribers, outlawing the use of artificial or prerecorded voice messages to residences without prior consent, prohibiting unsolicited advertisements by telephone facsimile machines, and requiring telemarketers to maintain a "do not call list" of any consumers who request not to receive further solicitation.
Driver Privacy Protection Act (1993)	Restricts the circumstances under which state departments of motor vehicles may disclose personal information about any individual obtained by the department in connection with a motor vehicle record.
Fair Credit Reporting Act (amended in 1997)	Promotes accuracy, fairness, and privacy of information in the files of consumer reporting agencies (e.g., credit bureaus); grants consumers the right to see their personal credit reports, to find out who has requested access to their reports, to dispute any inaccurate information with the consumer reporting agency, and to have inaccurate information corrected or deleted.
Children's Online Privacy Protection Act (amended in 2013)	Regulates the online collection of personally identifiable information (name, address, e-mail address, hobbies, interests, or information collected through cookies) from children under age 13 by specifying what a website operator must include in a privacy policy, when and how to seek consent from a parent, and what responsibilities an operator has to protect children's privacy and safety online.

Sources: "Computer Matching and Privacy Protection Act," *Internal Revenue Service*, http://www.irs.gov/irm/part11/irm_11-003-039.html (accessed June 22, 2016); "United States Privacy Laws," *Information Shield*, http://www.informationshield.com/usprivacylaws.html (accessed July 14, 2014).

In Canada, private industry has taken the lead in creating and developing privacy policies through the Direct Marketing Association of Canada (DMAC). The DMAC's policies resulted in the proposal of legislation to protect personal privacy. The Personal Information Protection and Electronic Documents Act established a right of personal privacy for information collected by Canadian businesses and organizations. The law instituted rules governing the collection, use, and disclosure of personal information in the private sector. It also works in conjunction with other legislation that protects personal information collected by federal and/or provincial governments. The Canadian Standards Association (CSA) was also instrumental in bringing about privacy protection guidelines in Canada. The CSA Model Code for the Protection of Personal Information requires organizations to protect personal information and to allow individuals access to their own personal information, allowing for correction if necessary.[41]

In Japan, the Ministry of International Trade and Industry established the Electronic Network Consortium (ENC) to resolve issues associated with the internet. The ENC (which comprises 93 organizations) has prepared guidelines for protecting personal data gathered by Japanese online service providers. These guidelines require websites to obtain an individual's consent before collecting personal data or using or transferring such data to a third party. The guidelines also call for organizations to appoint managers who understand the ENC guidelines to oversee the collection and use of personal data and to utilize privacy information management systems such as the Platform for Privacy Protection (P3P).[42] P3P is a set of standards recommended by the World Wide Web Consortium that would permit websites to translate their privacy statements and standards into a uniform format that Web-browsing software could access to supply users with relevant information about a particular firm's policies. Website visitors could then decide what information, if any, they are willing to share with websites.[43] However, P3P has not been widely implemented, and Internet Explorer is the only major browser to make use of P3P. Critics maintain that P3P makes it too difficult for consumers to protect their privacy online. Google has claimed P3P privacy protection features are "impractical" for the modern Web. These sites have adopted alternative tools for their websites' privacy policies.[44]

Protection of citizens' privacy on the internet is not a major public concern in Russia. For many years, internet activity was largely left unmonitored, and citizens and companies were able to do what they wanted with data. However, the Russian parliament passed legislation requiring internet companies to store Russian users' data within the country's borders. The country will put restrictions on how the companies can use the data if they do not comply with these storage measures, and will most likely ask them to stop doing business in the country. In addition, the government granted themselves the authority to block websites. In conjunction with this law, another deemed the "bloggers law" requires influential bloggers (those whose site is visited more than 3,000 times per day) to register with the state. This limits the amount of outspoken writers who have previously been able to anonymously voice their opinions without fear. While the government claims to be doing this for the sake of protecting people's privacy, ensuring national security and protecting against piracy, many conclude that it is for the purpose of controlling free speech and censorship.[45]

Privacy Officers and Certification Businesses are beginning to recognize that the only way to circumvent further government regulation with respect to privacy is to develop systems and policies to protect consumers' interests.

In addition to creating and posting policies regarding the gathering and use of personal information, more companies—including American Express, AT&T, and Citigroup—employ chief privacy officers (CPOs). The International Association of Privacy Professionals (IAPP) was established as a result of this movement, and is responsible for developing and launching the first broad-based credentialing program in information privacy. This program is known as the Certified Information Privacy Professional (CIPP). Most healthcare related businesses must appoint a privacy official to safeguard patient data. High-level executives are typically given broad powers to establish policies to protect consumer privacy and, in so doing, to protect their companies from negative publicity and legal scrutiny. Table 10.6 lists the major provisions of the FTC's Fair Information Practices, which can be used as a starting point in developing a corporate privacy policy.

Several organizations have also stepped in to help companies develop privacy policies. Among the best known are TRUSTe and Guardian. TRUSTe is a for-profit organization devoted to promoting global trust in internet technology by providing a standardized, third-party oversight program that addresses the privacy concerns of consumers, website operators, and government regulators. Companies that agree to abide by TRUSTe's privacy standards may display a "trustmark" on their websites. These firms must disclose their personal information collection and privacy policies in a straightforward privacy statement. TRUSTe is supported by a network of corporate, industry, and nonprofit sponsors.[46] For example, eBay's website is TRUSTe certified, which means that its online privacy practices fulfill TRUSTe's requirements. The online auction company's privacy policy promises that eBay will not share any personal information gathered from customers with any third parties and specifies how it will

TABLE 10.6 Fair Information Practice Principles

Notice	Websites would be required to provide consumers clear and conspicuous notice of their information practices, including what information they collect, how they collect it, how they use it, how they provide Choice, Access, and Security to consumers, whether they disclose the information collected to other entities, and whether other entities are collecting information through the site.
Choice	Websites would be required to offer consumers choices as to how their personal identifying information is used beyond the use for which the information was provided. Such choice would encompass both internal secondary uses and external secondary uses.
Access	Websites would be required to offer consumers reasonable access to the information a Web site has collected about them, including a reasonable opportunity to review information and to correct inaccuracies or delete information.
Security	Websites would be required to take reasonable steps to protect the security of the information they collect from consumers.

Source: Federal Trade Commission, "Privacy Online: Fair Information Practices In The Electronic Marketplace," May 2000, https://www.ftc.gov/reports/privacy-online-fair-information-practices-electronic-marketplace-federal-trade-commission (accessed June 22, 2016).

use the information it obtains. TRUSTe maintains the largest privacy seal program, with thousands of websites certified throughout the world. The organization is very active in educating and encouraging companies to improve privacy, security, and related aspects of business.

The mission of Guardian is to promote trust and confidence in e-commerce by encouraging ethical business practices. The Guardian eCommerce SSL Privacy Seal Program provides verification of trustworthy sites, as companies that receive the seal must abide by Guardian's code of ethics. The code of ethics is comprised of seven sections outlining the following important practices: honesty and integrity; disclosure of information; terms of sale; trust, online privacy, and e-commerce security; customer satisfaction; the protection of children; and abiding by the law. Guardian's strong oversight and evaluation methods ensure that seal-bearing websites are operating legally and truthfully, according to the code of ethics. For example, websites are checked for accuracy and functionality regarding description of services and contact information, the establishment and enforcement of privacy policies, and reputation among other online businesses.[47]

Intellectual Property

In addition to protecting personal privacy, many are concerned about protecting their rights to property they create, including songs, movies, books, and software. Such **intellectual property** (IP) consists of the ideas and creative materials developed to solve problems, carry out applications, educate, and entertain others. It is the result, or end product, of the creative process. Intellectual property is most commonly protected by patents and copyrights; however, technological advancements are increasingly challenging the ownership of such property. Online advertising is one of these challenging areas, as Google has experienced. The company has been sued by several companies regarding the selling of trademarked keywords in Google AdWords. For instance, Rosetta Stone filed a lawsuit against Google for allowing other companies—including competitors—to purchase Rosetta Stone's trademarked names to use as key search words. These keyword searches would generate "sponsored links" advertisements on search results Web pages. The two companies eventually reached a settlement.[48] While this may be considered a general competitive practice, intellectual property protections complicate the matter and require clear guidelines internet firms can use to deal with this issue.

Intellectual property losses in the United States total more than $300 billion a year in lost revenue from the illegal copying of computer programs, movies, compact discs, and books. IP losses also relate to stolen business plans, customer-related information, basic research reports, manufacturing process plans, product specifications, and many other proprietary documents. IP and other intangible assets typically represent about 70 percent of a company's value and source of revenue creation. Some experts estimate that companies lose several billions of dollars in

Intellectual property (IP) Consists of the ideas and creative materials developed to solve problems, carry out applications, educate, and entertain others.

proprietary information and intellectual property each year through a variety of channels.[49] Most cases involve one of the following scenarios:

1. *Inadvertent actions by current or former employees,* such as oral seminar presentations, discussions at an exhibit booth, and electronically misdirected fax and/or e-mail.
2. *Deliberate actions by current or former employees,* such as unauthorized physical access to information and deliberate disclosure to unauthorized parties.
3. *Deliberate actions by individuals/entities in trusted relationships other than employee relationships,* such as the exploitation of vendor-client relationships, subcontractor knowledge, joint ventures, and other relationships.
4. *Deliberate actions or activities by outsiders—those without a trusted relationship,* such as data mining of open-source data and public information and the practice of hiring away employees and placing them in a position where they must use trade secrets from a former employer.[50]

This issue has become a global concern because of disparities in enforcement of laws throughout the world. For example, a report by the IP Commission revealed an instance wherein an American software company's software was downloaded illegally onto 30 million Chinese computers—a multibillion-dollar infraction.[51] The Business Software Alliance says 39 percent of software installed on computers worldwide is unlicensed. Chief information officers believe that 15 percent of employees install unlicensed software on work computers. This is particularly concerning because malware attacks are greater with unlicensed software. It is estimated that cyberattacks cost companies $400 million annually. Russia and China are the two worst countries in terms of piracy violations. It is predicted that the trade-related aspects of intellectual property rights disputes will make countries more accountable for adhering to copyright standards.[52] Former U.S Attorney General Eric Holder indicted five Chinese military officials after discovering they had hacked into the systems of several American organizations. The allegations included stealing thousands of emails in order to obtain trade secrets and other intellectual property. Those companies whose systems were infiltrated included U.S. Steel Corp., Westinghouse Electric Co., and Alcoa Inc. Other cases of foreign IP theft are being investigated against Russia, Syria, and Iran.[53]

Microsoft has been particularly aggressive in battling software piracy. In one year alone, the company settled 3,265 cases related to copyright infringement worldwide. Only 35 of these cases took place in the United States, while 3,230 were international cases encompassing 42 countries. The company's efforts to stamp out piracy have been facilitated by customers reporting the illegal activity.[54] Microsoft is working to transform the economics of the software business, allowing cheaper, more innovative software to be available for legitimate, paying customers, as well as some free online software options.[55] Microsoft has even opened up a howto-tell.com website for people to consult when loading software onto their computers. The website helps educate customers on how to tell if their software is genuine.

U.S. copyright laws protect original works in text form, pictures, movies, computer software, musical multimedia, and audiovisual work. Owners of copyrights have the right to reproduce, derive from, distribute, and publicly display and perform the copyrighted works. Copyright infringement is the unauthorized execution of the rights reserved by a copyright holder. Congress passed the Digital Millennium Copyright Act (DMCA) in 1998 to protect copyrighted materials on the internet and to limit the liability of online service providers (OSPs). The DMCA provides a "safe harbor" provision that limits judgments that can be levied against OSPs for copyright infringement by their customers. To limit their liability, service providers must pay a nominal fee and comply with the act's reporting requirements.[56]

Digital copyright violations are not always clear cut and often involve lengthy lawsuits that can progress all the way to the higher courts. Streaming technology company Aereo Inc. sold equipment that captured broadcast signals from major broadcasting networks. Aereo's service allowed customers to download television shows onto their mobile devices the day after they aired for $8 per month. Broadcasters sued Aereo for copyright infringement since it was not licensing the content to resell. Aereo claimed it was simply a provider of equipment similar to a cable company. The Supreme Court ruled against Aereo Inc. and ordered Aereo to halt its services.[57] Table 10.7 provides additional facts about copyrights.

The internet has created other copyright issues for some organizations that have found that the web addresses (URLs) of other online firms either match or are very similar to their own trademarks. In some cases, "cybersquatters" have deliberately registered web addresses that match or relate to other firms' trademarks and then have attempted to sell the registration to the trademark owners. A number of companies, including Taco Bell, MTC, and KFC, have paid thousands of dollars to gain control of names that match or parallel company trademarks.[58] Registering a domain name involves filling out an online form to automatically reserve a domain name. This process makes it easy for cybersquatters or other scammers looking to defraud businesses and consumers. The Federal Trademark Dilution Act of 1995 was enacted to help companies resolve this conflict. The law gives trademark owners the right to protect their trademarks, prevents the use of trademark-protected entities by others, and requires cybersquatters to relinquish trademarked names.[59] However, this does not always hold up in foreign countries that do not have strict intellectual property laws. Starbucks first filed for a trademark in Russia in the 1990s, but because it did not open any stores, a Russian lawyer used a loophole to convince the government to annul Starbucks' trademark registration. He then registered the company name and offered to relinquish it to Starbucks for $600,000. Although Starbucks eventually prevailed in a lawsuit, the legal entanglements kept the firm from opening Starbucks locations in Russia for three years.[60]

TABLE 10.7 Facts About Copyrights

- No registration is required to acquire copyright ownership of original works. No registration is required to place copyright notice on works [© Year Name of Owner]. (No "innocent infringers" if there is notice on the work.). Copyright registration is required before a lawsuit may be brought. (See U.S. Copyright Office)

- Works in public domain are free to use. The copyright duration may have expired, the creator of works may have relinquished his or her rights, or it may not be copyright protectable.

- An exception for seeking copyright permission to use a work, called the "fair use doctrine," involves weighing four factors (See US Copyright Office Publication) and the use of a work for criticism, comment, news reporting, teaching, scholarship, research, or parody.

- The "right of first sale" occurs when an owner of a copyrighted work sells a copy of it; the new owner does not now possess the copyright but can sell the copy or give it away without the copyright owner's permission.

- Derivative works are works that are derived from other copyrighted sources or works. With the exception of works that fall under the "fair use doctrine," derivative works cannot be sold without permission from the original copyright holders.

- Courts consider remedies for copyright infringement of one work in the range of $750 (for "innocent infringers") up to $150,000 for intentional, willful violations. Remedies can go up or down depending upon whether the copyright violation was intentional or not.

Source: Derived and paraphrased with permission from Willow Misty Parks, ©Copyrights and Businesses, PPT presentation on UNM Daniels Fund Ethics Initiative website, http://danielsethics.mgt. unm.edu/teaching-resources/presentations.asp (accessed June 22, 2016); "The U.S. Copyright Office," http://copyright.gov.

The Internet Corporation for Assigned Names and Numbers (ICANN), a nonprofit organization charged with overseeing basic technical matters related to addresses on the internet, has had success, including the introduction of a competitive domain registrar and registration market, the Uniform Dispute Resolution Policy (UDRP), and the creation of seven new top-level domains.[61] Many trademark holders immediately turn to the Internet Corporation for Assigned Names and Numbers' Uniform Dispute Resolution Policy as a vehicle for combating cybersquatters. However, remedies available in federal court under the Anti-Cybersquatting Consumer Protection Act may better protect the rights of trademark holders. All ICANN-authorized registrars of domain names in the .com, .net, and .org top-level domains must agree to abide by the UDRP. Under the terms of the UDRP, a domain name will be transferred between parties only by agreement between them or by order of a court of competent jurisdiction or a UDRP-authorized dispute resolution provider.[62]

Since ICANN is overseen by the U.S. Department of Commerce, leaders in other countries have begun to question whether the United States has too much control of the internet. Under the philosophy that the internet is above the domain of any one government, these leaders pose several concerns. First, ICANN controls the master root file that provides users with access to the internet. Some countries have threatened to develop a competing master root file, which would create parallel internets. China has already developed a competing file and is encouraging other countries to join its effort. Second, ICANN has the power to affect selective parts of the internet. For example, ICANN delayed adoption of a new .xxx top-level domain (TLD) for adult content because of pressure from U.S. government agencies. It went into operation in 2011.[63] Third, because ICANN is a private corporation performing a significant public service, critics point to a lack of transparency and effectiveness in its operations and decisions. Finally, some leaders worry that ICANN will serve as a social and cultural gatekeeper, since all new TLD names and other requests must be approved by ICANN. The debate over governance of the internet is related to a number of significant issues, including intellectual property, privacy, security, and other top-level concerns of the public and government.[64]

Health and Biotechnology

The advance of life-supporting technologies has raised a number of medical and health issues related to technology. **Bioethics** refers to the study of ethical issues in the fields of medical treatment and research, including medicine, nursing, law, philosophy, and theology, though today medical ethics is also recognized as a separate discipline.[65] All of these fields have been influenced by rapid changes in technology that require new approaches to solving issues. Genetic technologies have shown promise in giving medical ethics an even greater role in social decision-making. For example, the Human Genome Project, a program to decode the entire human genetic map, identified a number of genes that may contribute to particular diseases or traits.

Because so many of our resources are spent on healthcare, the role of the private sector in determining the quality of healthcare is an important consideration to society. The pharmaceutical industry, for example, has been sharply criticized by politicians, health-care organizations, and consumers because of escalating drug costs. Investigators from federal and state agencies all over the nation have initiated legal action over allegations that Medicare and Medicaid overpaid for drugs by $1 billion or more a year.[66] T. Mark Jones, founder of Ven-A-Care, a company that acts as a whistleblower on account of taxpayers, built a business on stopping pharmaceutical companies from overcharging Medicare. Since 1995, Ven-A-Care has restored $3 billion back to the taxpayers, and was awarded $597.6 million in awards, making it the most successful whistleblower in the United States.[67] On the other hand, pharmaceutical companies claim that the development of new lifesaving drugs and tests requires huge expenditures in research and development. The pharmaceutical industry is among the most profitable U.S. industries and spends billions each year in marketing, including drug samples provided to doctors, advertising in medical journals, and other strategies. More than $5 billion is spent by the pharmaceutical industry on direct-to-consumer advertising.[68] The visibility of pharmaceutical advertising and promotion prompted Pharmaceutical Research & Manufacturers of America, an industry association, to develop its Guiding Principles on Direct-to-Consumer (DTC) Advertising. The voluntary guidelines are

bioethics
Refers to the study of ethical issues in the fields of medical treatment and research, including medicine, nursing, law, philosophy, and theology.

TABLE 10.8 Preamble to PhRMA Guiding Principles for Direct-to-Consumer Advertisements

Preamble
Given the progress that continues to be made in society's battle against disease, patients are seeking more information about medical problems and potential treatments so they can better understand their healthcare options and communicate effectively with their physicians. An important benefit of direct-to-consumer (DTC) advertising is that it fosters an informed conversation about health, disease and treatments between patients and their healthcare practitioners.
A strong empirical record demonstrates that DTC communications about prescription medicines serve the public health by:
• Increasing awareness about diseases;
• Educating patients about treatment options;
• Motivating patients to contact their physicians and engage in a dialogue about health concerns;
• Increasing the likelihood that patients will receive appropriate care for conditions that are frequently under-diagnosed and under-treated; and
• Encouraging compliance with prescription drug treatment regimens.

Source: Pharmaceutical Research and Manufacturers of America, "PhRMA Guiding Principles: Direct-to-Consumer Advertisements About Prescription Medicines," http://www.phrma.org/sites/default/files/pdf/phrmaguidingprinciplesdec08final.pdf (accessed June 22, 2016).

designed to ensure that DTC advertising is accurate, accessible, and useful. Table 10.8 shows the preamble that accompanies the association's booklet on the guiding principles.

Biotechnology The biotechnology industry emerged over 40 years ago when Stanley Cohen and Herbert Boyer published a new recombinant DNA technique, a method of making proteins, such as human insulin, in cultured cells under controlled manufacturing conditions. Boyer went on to co-found Genentech, which is one of the most well-known biotechnology companies. From these insights, other scientists set out to map the human genome, a 13-year project to discover all of the estimated 20,000–25,000 human genes and make them accessible for further biological study. The ability to map the human genome has spurred over 250 new vaccines and medicines, and many more are being tested in product trials. These innovations are changing the way that cancer, diabetes, AIDS, arthritis, and multiple sclerosis are treated. Biotech innovations in other fields, such as manufacturing, have led to cleaner processes that produce less waste and use less energy and water. Most laundry detergents marketed in the United States contain biotechnology-based enzymes that combine better with bleach, are biodegradable, and reduce the need for hot water. Law enforcement officials used DNA finger printing, a biotech process, to catch criminals, increase conviction rates, and perform stronger investigations and forensic science.[69] There are over 1,300 biotechnology companies in the United States in a variety of sectors including health, agriculture, and industrial.[70] Finally, the biotechnology industry invests approximately $50 billion per year in research and development activities.[71]

The government and the private sector often partner with academic researchers and nonprofit institutes to develop new technologies in health and biotechnology. Research ranges from mapping the human genetic code to finding drugs that cure cancer to genetically modifying food products. Many of these collaborative efforts to improve health involve scientists, funded globally by a variety of sources. For example, the Avon Foundation donated more than $800 million through its Avon Breast Cancer Crusade, which supports virtually every facet of the cause by funding five critical areas: breast cancer biomedical research, clinical care, support services, education, and early detection programs.[72] National Institutes of Health scientists created great excitement when they reported that embryonic stem cells had been coaxed to form pancreatic cells that make insulin, a potential treatment for diabetes. But another study suggests that the cells didn't really make insulin and instead just absorbed it from the culture medium they were grown in and later released it.[73] Using cell-engineering techniques, scientists may have found a way to generate unlimited supplies of brain cells for transplanting into patients with ALS, Parkinson's disease, epilepsy, and stroke. Other advances have revealed ways to slow the progression of Alzheimer's disease and provide treatments for blindness.[74] These examples illustrate technology advances that could result in commercially viable products that save and/or prolong life.

Cloning, the replication of organisms that are genetically identical to the parent, has become a highly controversial topic in biotechnology and bioethics. Human cloning has raised unanswered questions about the future of human reproduction. Since Scottish scientists first cloned Dolly the sheep, scientists have also successfully cloned mice, cows, pigs, goats, and cats but with mixed reports about the health of the cloned progeny. While cloning humans would appear to be the final step of scientific reproduction, indisputable proof of the first human clone will actually serve as a starting point for many years of research. Like in vitro fertilization, human clones will need to grow up before scientists know the effects that this process will have on a person's physical, mental, and emotional states.[75] Cloning has the potential to revolutionize the treatment of diseases and conditions such as Parkinson's disease and cancer. Stem cell technology has allowed doctors to create replacement organs, thereby restoring infected organs and lengthening human lives.[76] The ability to create and modify life processes is often generated through collaborative research involving businesses, universities, and government. The results of such research have already contributed to life-altering products of the future, and more progress is expected for years to come.

Despite the potential of this technology, many people have negative views about cloning. Some contend that it is unethical to "meddle with nature," whereas others believe that cloning is wrong because every time it is used to treat a patient, a cloned human embryo is destroyed.[77] New processes in cloning and stem cell research have reduced the need for embryos since cells can be taken from consenting adults without invasive procedures. Nevertheless, ethical concerns exist.[78] The cloning of a miniature pig, named Goldie, lacking both copies of a gene involved in immediate immune rejection has brought the prospect of transplanting pig organs into people a little closer. The small pig's organs are similar in size to those of humans, and the missing genes make the organs less likely to be rejected. But although Goldie's creation may have solved the problem of immediate transplant rejection, there is a slower rejection in which the transplant is attacked by the recipient's white blood cells.[79] Some people argue that cloning of human beings should be banned, and several bills have been introduced in Congress and various state legislatures to do just that. Additionally, 19 European nations have signed an agreement prohibiting the genetic replication of humans. Harvesting stem cells from surplus in vitro fertilization (IVF) embryos is allowed by the Australian government, and the United Kingdom allows researchers to harvest stem cells from surplus IVF embryos and to conduct therapeutic cloning. In the past, the United States restricted federally funded researchers from pursuing therapeutic cloning or harvesting stem cells from discarded embryos. However, today the ban is lifted, allowing both public and private entities to conduct research.[80]

Genetic research holds the promise to revolutionize how many diseases are diagnosed and treated. However, consumer advocates urged the World Trade Organization (WTO) to place limits on gene patents, which they claim are tantamount to "ownership of life." As patents dealing with human DNA increased, worries about the limitations on ownership also increased. These worries came to the forefront of a Supreme Court decision that stated natural DNA cannot be patented as it does not fit within the characteristics of things that can be patented ("novel, useful, and non-obvious"), but complementary DNA (a copy of the original) can be patented. While this may seem a straightforward solution to the advocates' concerns, these definitions are not as distinct as they sound. There are times when complementary DNA contains components that are both natural and synthetic. Many other issues arise from patents relating to genetics whether they belong to humans, animals, or even plants. For example, Monsanto has been involved in many lawsuits regarding the patents of their genetically modified seeds. As more discoveries are made in the field, more complexities in the realm of laws and ethics will be made manifest.[81]

A final concern with genetics is the increasing availability of direct-to-consumer testing kits. With these kits, consumers can proactively manage their health, including gaining access to knowledge about predispositions to cancer, diseases, and illnesses. Most specialists agree that the results of such tests are best delivered in a professional medical setting, not via the internet or mail. A consumer could receive a positive finding on a DNA-based prostate cancer screening test through a mail-order kit, and may take measures to self-treat rather than consult a doctor. Other dangerous situations may ensue, as receiving the news of potentially having cancer is hard to hear. In addition, the result of the test may not be straightforward. For instance, the consumer may have cancerous growths that can be removed, cancer that has spread, or neither because the test is a false positive. Medical advice is warranted at this point because the consumer has no way of determining the appropriate course of action. Genetic testing company 23andMe was ordered by the FTC to stop selling their tests for these reasons.[82]

Genetically Modified Foods More than 800 million people around the world don't have enough to eat. Increasing food production to satisfy the growing demand for food without increasing land use will require farmers to achieve significant increases in productivity. Genetically modified (GM) foods offer a way to quickly improve crop characteristics such as yield, pest resistance, or herbicide tolerance, often to a degree not possible with traditional methods. GM crops can be manipulated to produce completely artificial substances, from the precursors of plastics to consumable vaccines.[83] Also discussed in Chapter 11, genetically modified, or transgenic, crops are created when scientists introduce a gene from one organism to another. Scientists believe that genetically engineered crops could raise overall crop production in developing countries by as much as 25 percent.[84] The idea that GM crops can significantly reduce world hunger is hotly debated. Some say it will make all the difference, while others point out issues with these claims. For example, a large population of the developing world suffers from hunger and malnourishment. A new development called "golden rice" is said to be high in vitamin A and can serve as a food source for these people. However, it has been noted that the "golden rice" will require fertilizer, pesticides, significant amounts of water, and corresponding irrigation systems that are too expensive for these areas. Further, because of the severe state of the populations' malnutrition, the vitamin A cannot be absorbed into their bodies.[85]

Others are concerned about potential health and environmental risks of GM foods. The European public has been known to call GM products "Frankenfood" for fear it could pose a health threat or create an environmental disaster. It is presumed that genes may jump from GM crops to wild plants and reduce biodiversity or create superweeds. For a time, Europe held up approvals of U.S. exports of GM foods, until parliament voted to require extensive labeling and traceability of food containing genetically modified organisms. Only those foods that meet these standards are accepted into the EU. However, regulations still restrict the growing of GM crops. Over 20 years have passed since countries have begun growing GM crops all over the world, and there has not been significant evidence showing that these foods or the presence of crops are actually harmful. For this reason, many advocates, scientists, and others in the EU are pressing the regulatory agencies to rethink and update the GM crop and food laws to better reflect evidence-based research.[86]

Many people do not realize that some of the foods they eat are made from genetically engineered crops. Consumer groups are increasingly concerned that these foods could be unhealthy and harmful to the environment. The power of genetic modification techniques raises the possibility of human health, environmental, and economic problems, including unanticipated allergic responses to novel substances in foods, the spread of pest resistance or herbicide tolerance to wild plants, inadvertent toxicity to benign wildlife, and increasing control of agriculture by biotechnology corporations.[87] Many consumers are boycotting products made from genetically modified materials, and several countries have opposed trade in GM foods through the World Trade Organization. In addition, Japan has asked U.S. corn producers not to include genetically modified corn in animal feed exported to Japan.[88] Insects and birds transport seeds from one field to the next, allowing cross-pollination geneticists never intended. Unlike chemical or nuclear contamination, gene pollution can never be cleaned up. Advocates in the United States are urging regulators to mandate that GM foods be labeled. Vermont had already signed such a law into action. Under pressure from states, Congress passed a requirement for labeling products containing GM ingredients. However, in a blow to Vermont the new requirement, which supersedes its law, gives manufacturers years to comply and allows them the option to use straightforward language, digital codes, or symbols to indicate the presence of GM ingredients.[89] Table 10.9 demonstrates the millions of hectares that are being used to cultivate GM crops across the world. There has been solid growth of GM crops since 1996.[90]

A number of companies have responded to public concerns about genetically modified food products by limiting or avoiding their use altogether, while others have responded on the basis of transparency. Unilever and General Mills, for example, state on their websites that they are committed to following regulations regarding GM labeling while at the same time maintaining their belief in the benefits of GM products to alleviate hunger and reduce the amounts of energy and water needed to maintain traditional crops. They also state that their organic product lines will be packaged with non-GM labels as appropriate. Whole Foods Market and Allegro Coffee, on the other hand, are committed to mandatory GM labeling. Whole Foods has committed to ensuring all GM products are labeled in their Canada and U.S. stores by 2018, while Allegro Coffee has many products already approved by the Non-GMO Project and several others in the process of being approved.[91]

Ethical questions about the use of some types of genetically modified products have also been raised. For example, Monsanto and other companies had begun developing so-called terminator technology to create plants that are genetically engineered to produce sterile seeds. Other plants in development will

TABLE 10.9 Commercial Cultivation of Genetically Modified Crops (in millions of hectares)

	Hectares (Million)	Acres (Million)
1998	27.8	69.5
1999	39.9	98.6
2000	44.2	109.2
2001	52.6	130.0
2002	58.7	145.0
2003	67.7	167.2
2004	81.0	200.0
2005	90.0	222.0
2006	102.0	250.0
2007	114.3	282.0
2008	125.0	308.8
2009	134.0	335.0
2010	148.0	365.0
2011	160.0	395.0
2012	170.3	420.8
2013	175.2	433.2
2014	181.5	448.0
2015	179.7	444.0
TOTAL	1,964.6	4,854.6

Source: Clive James, 2015. "Pocket K No. 16: Biotech Crop Highlights in 2015," *International Service for the Acquisition of Agri-Biotech Applications*, 2016, http://www.isaaa.org/resources/publications/pocketk/16/ (accessed June 22, 2016).

require spraying with chemicals supplied by the seed companies to produce desired traits, such as resistance to certain pests or disease. Farmers say the issue isn't the technology itself but, rather, who controls the technology—in most cases, the multinational seed companies. In response to global concerns about this issue, Monsanto halted commercial development of the terminator technology.[92] Control over who owns the seeds after purchase continues to be an issue with GM crops. In one case, Indiana soybean farmer Vernon Hugh Bowman purchased seeds from Monsanto and continued to use them for eight seasons. When Monsanto discovered this, they sued Bowman for patent infringement. The court ruled in favor of Monsanto, and some worry that the incident would renew interest in terminator technology so companies can further protect their patents.[93]

Defenders of biotechnology say consumer health fears about genetically modified foods have not been substantiated by research.[94] As the U.S. agriculture industry is eager to point out, the technology has been a big success: it has reduced the amount of pesticides farmers have had to spray on their cornfields, with happy consequences for the environment and human health. U.S. health regulators have not been able to find anything wrong with eating Bwt (*Bacillus thuringiensis)* corn. It is now found in roughly 90 percent of all corn, beet, and soybean products on U.S. store shelves.[95] One disturbing trend that is occurring, however, is growing resistance to certain GM crops. Rootworms once vulnerable to GM crops containing a gene called Bt are now developing a resistance against it, making the gene ineffective. As resistance grows, some farmers are beginning to turn to older pesticides.[96] The issue of resistance to herbicides and pesticides is a significant issue that Monsanto and other biotechnology companies are working to address.

STRATEGIC IMPLEMENTATION OF RESPONSIBILITY FOR TECHNOLOGY

To accrue the maximum benefits from the technologies driving the new economy, many parties within society have important roles to play. While many continue to debate the issues associated with technology, the government must take steps to provide support for continued technological advancements and to ensure the benefits of technology apply to as many people as possible. The challenge is to establish regulations as needed in order to minimize any potential for harm to competition, the environment, and human welfare while not stifling innovation. Stakeholders, including employees, customers, special-interest groups, and the general public, can influence the use and control of technology through the public policy process. Businesses also have a significant role to play in supporting technology. New technologies are developed, refined, and introduced to the market through the research and development and marketing activities of business. Businesses that aspire to be socially responsible must monitor the impact of technology and harness it for the good of all.

The Role of Government

An economy that is increasingly driven by technology requires a government that maintains the basic infrastructure and support for technology in our society. The Department of Defense, for example, explores ways that technology can improve the quality of life. The government also serves as a watchdog to ensure that technology benefits society, not criminals. However, as the pace of technology continues to escalate, law enforcement agencies ranging from the FBI to local police forces are struggling to recruit and retain officers and prosecutors who are knowledgeable about the latest technology and the ways criminals can exploit it. High-caliber forensic computer experts are often lured away to technology firms and private security outfits by salaries more than twice their government paychecks.[97] Computer crimes currently share sentencing guidelines with larceny, embezzlement, and theft, where the most significant sentencing factor is the amount of financial loss inflicted, and additional points are awarded for using false IDs or ripping off more than ten victims. "Cyberterrorism," in which a foreign power sabotages another country's computer system, has been declared a potential act of war by the U.S. government. The government believes cyberattacks represent a significant threat toward U.S. security and therefore requires serious action in response. This decision came after a major cyberattack was launched against Google and its computer servers—which included the accounts of some government officials.[98]

Digital copyright lawsuits illustrate a significant difference in opinion in the interpretation of existing laws when exploiting the evolving multimedia potential of the internet. Although the government's strategy thus far has been not to interfere with the commercial use of technology, disputes and differing interpretations of current laws increasingly bring technology into the domain of the legal system. New laws related to breakthrough technologies that change the nature of competition are constantly being considered. Usually, the issues of privacy, ownership of intellectual property, health and safety, environmental impact, competition, or consumer welfare are the legislative platforms for changing the legal and regulatory system.

The Role of Business

Business, like government, is involved in both reactive and proactive attempts to market and make effective use of technology. Reactive concerns relate to issues that have legal and/or ethical implications as well as issues of productivity, customer welfare, or other stakeholder concerns. Many large firms have suffered public embarrassment, legal bills, compensation claims, and clean-up costs when employees seek inappropriate material online, send e-mail to people they shouldn't, accidentally circulate confidential information outside a business, or spread a computer virus. As a result, some companies are purchasing software that assists employees in managing the internet time they spend on personal activities.

On the other hand, a strategic, proactive approach to technology will consider its impact on social responsibility. Proactive management of technology requires developing a plan for utilizing resources to take advantage of competitive opportunities. For instance, many companies address the proper use of computers and other technology in their codes of ethics. Addressing these risk areas beforehand allows employees to understand what is and is not acceptable. These policies inform employees about corporate expectations regarding company technology and the potential penalties for misuse.

With competition increasing, companies are spending more time and resources to establish technology-based competitive advantages. The strategic approach to technology requires an overall mission, strategy, and coordination of all functional activities, including a concern for social responsibility, to have an effective program. To promote the responsible use of technology, a firm's policies, rules, and standards must be integrated into its corporate culture. Reducing undesirable behavior in this area is a goal that is no different from reducing costs, increasing profits, or improving quality that is aggressively enforced and integrated into the corporate culture to be effective in improving appropriate behavior within the organization.

Top managers must consider the social consequences of technology in the strategic planning process. When all stakeholders are involved in the process, everyone can better understand the need for and requirements of responsible development and use of technology. There will always be conflicts in making the right choices, but through participation in decision-making, the best solutions can be found. Individual participants in this process should not abdicate their personal responsibility as concerned members of society. Organizations that are concerned about the consequences of their decisions create an environment for different opinions on important issues.

Strategic Technology Assessment

To calculate the effects of new technologies, companies can employ a procedure known as a **technology assessment** to foresee the effects new products and processes will have on their firm's operations, on other business organizations, and on society in general. This assessment is a tool that managers can use to evaluate their firm's performance and to chart strategic courses of action to respond to new technologies. With information obtained through a technology assessment or audit, managers can estimate whether the benefits of adopting a specific technology outweigh costs to the firm and to society at large. The assessment process can also help companies ensure compliance with government regulations related to technology. Remember that one of the four components of social responsibility is legal compliance. A strategic technology assessment or audit can help organizations understand these issues and develop appropriate and responsible responses to them (see Table 10.10).[99]

technology assessment
A procedure used by companies to calculate the effects of new technologies by foreseeing the effects new products and processes will have on their firm's operations, on other business organizations, and on society in general.

TABLE 10.10 Strategic Technology Assessment Issues

Yes	No	Checklist
O	O	Are top managers in your organization aware of the federal, state, and local laws related to technology decisions?
O	O	Does your organization have an effective system for monitoring changes in the federal, state, and local laws related to technology?
O	O	Is there an individual, committee, or department in your organization responsible for overseeing government technology issues?
O	O	Does your organization do checks on technology brought into the organization by employees?
O	O	Are there communications and training programs in your organization to create an effective culture to protect employees and organizational interests related to technology?
O	O	Does your organization have monitoring and auditing systems to determine the impact of technology on key stakeholders?
O	O	Does your organization have a method for reporting concerns about the use or impact of technology?
O	O	Is there a system to determine ethical risks and appropriate ethical conduct to deal with technology issues?
O	O	Do top managers in your organization understand the ramifications of using technology to communicate with employees and customers?
O	O	Is there an individual or department in your organization responsible for maintaining compliance standards to protect the organization in the areas of privacy and intellectual property?

If the assessment process indicates that the company has not been effective at utilizing technologies or is using them in a way that raises questions, changes may be necessary. Companies may need to consider setting higher standards, improving reporting processes, and improving communication of standards and training programs, as well as participating in aboveboard discussions with other organizations. If performance has not been satisfactory, management may want to reorganize the way certain kinds of decisions are made. Table 10.10 contains some issues to assess for proactive and reactive technology responsibility issues. Some social concerns might relate to a technology's impact on the environment, employee health and working conditions, consumer safety, and community values.

Finally, the organization should focus on the positive aspects of technology to determine how it can be used to improve the work environment, its products, and the general welfare of society. Technology can be used to reduce pollution, encourage recycling, and save energy. Also, information can be made available to customers to help them maximize the benefits of products. Technology has been and will continue to be a major force that can improve society.

SUMMARY

Technology relates to the application of knowledge, including the processes and applications to solve problems, perform tasks, and create new methods to obtain desired outcomes. The dynamics of technology relate to the constant change that requires significant adjustments in the political, religious, and economic structures of society. Reach relates to the far-reaching nature of technology as it moves through society. The self-sustaining nature of technology relates to the fact that technology acts as a catalyst to spur even faster development. Civilizations must harness and adapt to changes in technology to maintain a desired quality of life. Although technological advances have improved our quality of life, they have also raised ethical, legal, and social concerns.

Advances in technology have created millions of new jobs, better health and longer lives, new opportunities, and the enrichment of lives. Without greater access to the latest technology, however, economic development could suffer in underserved areas. The ability to purchase technology may affect the nature of competition and business success. Information and telecommunications technology minimizes borders, allows people to overcome the physical limitations of time and space, and enables people to acquire customized goods and services that cost less and are of higher quality.

The internet, a global information system that links many computer networks together, has altered the way people communicate, learn, do business, and find entertainment. The growth of the internet has generated issues never before encountered and that social institutions, including the legal system, have been slow to address.

Because current technology has made it possible to collect, share, and sell vast quantities of personal information, often without consumers' knowledge, privacy has become a major concern associated with technology. Many websites follow users' tracks through their site by storing a cookie, or identifying string of text, on the users' computers. What companies do with the information about consumers they collect through cookies and other technologies is generating concern. Privacy issues related to children are generating even more debate and laws to protect children's interests. Identity theft occurs when criminals obtain personal information that allows them to impersonate someone else to use that individual's credit to obtain financial accounts and to make purchases. Some measure of protection of personal privacy is provided by the U.S. Constitution as well as by Supreme Court rulings and federal laws. Europe and other regions of the world are also addressing privacy concerns. In addition to creating and posting policies regarding the gathering and use of personal information, more companies are beginning to hire chief privacy officers.

Intellectual property consists of the ideas and creative materials developed to solve problems, carry out applications, educate, and entertain others. Copyright infringement is the unauthorized execution of the rights reserved by a copyright holder. Technological advancements are challenging the ownership of intellectual property. Other issues relate to "cybersquatters" who deliberately register Web addresses that match or relate to other firms' trademarks and then attempt to sell the registration to the trademark owners.

Bioethics refers to the study of ethical issues in the fields of medical treatment and research, including medicine, nursing, law, philosophy, and theology. Genetic research, including cloning, may revolutionize how diseases are diagnosed and treated. Genetically modified crops are created when scientists introduce a gene from one organism to another. However, these technologies are controversial because some people believe they are immoral, unsafe, or harmful to the environment.

To accrue the maximum benefits from the technology driving the new economy, many parties within society have important roles to play. With an economy that is increasingly driven by technology, the government must maintain the basic infrastructure and support for technology in our society. The government also serves as a watchdog to ensure that technology benefits society, not criminals.

Business is involved in both reactive and proactive attempts to make effective use of technology. Reactive concerns relate to issues that have legal or ethical implications as well as to productivity, customer welfare, or other stakeholder issues. Proactive management of technology requires developing a plan for utilizing resources to take advantage of competitive opportunities. The strategic approach to technology requires an overall mission, strategy, and coordination of all functional activities, including a concern for social responsibility, to produce an effective program. To calculate the effects of new technologies, companies can employ a procedure known as technology assessment to foresee the effects of new products and processes on their firm's operation, on other business organizations, and on society in general.

Responsible Business Debate

Is Technology Detrimental for Society?

Issue: *What are the benefits and drawbacks of technology to social interaction?*

While technology has brought advancements, conveniences, and efficiencies to our lives, some critics wonder if the benefits outweigh the costs, especially those that are transforming the ways we communicate, connect with other people, solve problems, and generally interact as human beings. In other words, are

we losing the relationships that have made the United States a great place to live and work?

In 1831, Alexis de Tocqueville visited the United States on behalf of the French government. He set out to study the prison system, but ended up writing a grand treatise, *Democracy in America*. In his book, Tocqueville noted how Americans were dedicated to social cohesion, equality, common purpose, and concern for both individuals and the community. Years later, writers on the topic of social capital, mentioned in Chapter 2, drew from Tocqueville's work to describe the American approach to community service, active neighborhood associations, and other types of civic engagement. Recent studies, however, indicate civic engagement is declining. Is technology part of the problem?

Consider these daily occurrences: students do not talk to classmates after class, as they are quick to begin texting people they already know. With autocorrect features on their phones that correct their writing, they do not even have to know how to spell correctly. People on the subway rarely acknowledge the riders they see every day, because they are busy checking their smartphones and getting a jumpstart on the day. Many children spend more time on the internet or playing video games than they do playing outside with other children. Coworkers send each other emails, rather than walk 30 steps to the next office for a brief conversation. Studies show that younger generations do not even realize that you need to dial "1" first to call long-distance on a landline. Finally, handwriting is so passé that a hand-written envelope will be opened much sooner than any other piece of mail.

On the other hand, technology has opened up new avenues for research and business activities. Because of the internet, researchers literally have libraries of knowledge at their fingertips. Marketers use social media and other digital channels to connect on a more one-on-one basis with customers. Southwest even has a Twitter team to answer customer concerns quickly, making for a smoother customer service process. Small business owners now have the ability to use technology to sell their products across the world without needing the infrastructure required to set up a large company. Online chat forums can help people connect from different parts of the country who never would have met otherwise. Additionally, many people have used social networks like Facebook to reconnect with friends they had known from long ago.

There Are Two Sides to Every Issue:

1. Defend the changes that technology has brought to society's communication patterns, such as the expediency of email and texting, reduced costs, and access to people around the world.

2. Defend the need for society to rely less on technology and more on traditional communication patterns, such as face-to-face meetings, verbal conversations, and hand-written correspondence.

KEY TERMS

technology (p. 322)
intellectual property (p. 339)

bioethics (p. 343)

technology assessment (p. 351)

DISCUSSION QUESTIONS

1. Define technology and describe three characteristics that can be used to assess it.
2. What effect has technology had on the United States and global economies? Have these effects been positive or negative?
3. Many people believe that the government should regulate business with respect to privacy online, but companies say self-regulation is more appropriate. Which approach would benefit consumers most? Businesses?
4. What is intellectual property? How can owners of intellectual property protect their rights?
5. What is bioethics? What are some of the consequences of biomedical research?
6. Should genetically modified foods be labeled as "genetically modified"? Why or why not?
7. How can a strategic technology assessment help a company?

EXPERIENTIAL EXERCISE

Visit three websites that are primarily designed for children or that focus on products of interest to children under age 13. For example, visit the websites for new movies, games, action figures, candy, cereal, or beverages. While visiting these sites, put yourself in the role and mind-set of a child. What type of language and persuasion is used? Is there a privacy statement on the site that can be understood by children? Are there any parts of the site that might be offensive or worrisome to parents? Provide a brief evaluation of how well these sites attend to the provisions of the Children's Online Privacy Protection Act.

THE EMAIL POLICE: WHAT WOULD YOU DO?

James Kitling thought about his conversation with Ira Romero earlier that day. He was not really surprised that the human resources (HR) department was concerned about the time employees were spending on personal issues during the workday. Several departments were known for their rather loose management approach. Internet access for personal tasks, like shopping, using Instant Messaging services, and answering nonwork e-mails, had been a concern for several months. Recent news reports indicated that over 50 percent of large companies now filter or monitor e-mail. Companies are also monitoring Web browsing, file downloads, chat room use, and group postings. A survey published in the media reported that workers spend an average of eight hours a week looking at nonwork internet sites.

As the director of information technology, James was very dedicated to the effective use of technology to enhance business productivity. Although he was knowledgeable about technology, James was equally attuned to the ways in which technology can be abused in a work setting. He knew that some employees were probably using too much internet time on personal tasks.

On the other hand, his company mainly employed professionals, administrative staff, and customer service personnel. All 310 employees were expected to use the computer a great deal throughout the day. At present, the company had a skeleton code of ethics and policy on the use of company resources, including the internet.

A couple of managers and now HR had spoken with James about the prospects of monitoring employee computer and internet use. Ira's inquiry about the software, however, was a bit more serious. An employee had recently been formally reprimanded for downloading and printing nonwork documents from the internet. These documents were designed to help the employee's spouse in a new business venture. Although the employee did most of the searching and downloading during lunch, the supervisor felt this was an improper use of company resources. Other employees had been informally spoken with about their use of the internet for personal matters. Ira believed this was a growing problem that definitely affected productivity. He had read the news reports and believed that monitoring software was becoming a necessary tool in today's workplace.

So far, James had been hesitant to purchase and implement one of these systems. The employee internet management software was somewhat expensive, running approximately $25 per computer. He felt that the software could cause employee trust to sharply decline, resulting in even greater problems than currently existed. After all, employees engage in some personal tasks during work hours, including making personal telephone calls, getting coffee, chatting with coworkers, and so forth. James wondered if the internet was that much different from these other personal activities. He recalled a discussion in a management class in his MBA program, where they learned that employees in the early 1900s were only allowed to use the telephone to call the police. Thus, the telephone was once thought of as a great distracter, much like the internet today.

Ira and a few other managers were pretty firm in their beliefs about the internet monitoring system. James was still not convinced that it was the best route to curbing the problem. In his role, however, he was expected to provide leadership in developing a solution. What would you do?

CHAPTER ELEVEN

Sustainability Issues

Chapter Objectives

- To define sustainability

- To examine the nature of sustainability as it relates to social responsibility

- To explore a variety of global environmental issues faced by business and society

- To examine the impact of environmental policy and regulations

- To gain an understanding of different types of alternative energy

- To examine business responses to sustainability

- To discuss a strategic approach to respond to environmental responsibility

Chapter Outline

Defining Sustainability

How Sustainability Relates to Social Responsibility

Global Environmental Issues

Environmental Policy and Regulation

Alternative Energy

Business Response to Sustainability Issues

Strategic Implementation of Environmental Responsibility

Keep Calm and Frack On?

Hydraulic fracturing, known as fracking, has the potential to reduce the United States' dependence on foreign oil. Fracking forces water, sand, and chemicals into underground tunnels of shale rock, bringing natural gas to the surface. Because of fracking, energy prices are lowering and the United States is becoming more self-sufficient in generating their own energy. The United States is now the world's second leading producer of natural gas after Russia.

Natural gas releases half the carbon dioxide of oil, and the United States has the potential to produce more than 30 percent more than currently consumed. Natural gas releases fewer sulfur dioxide, nitrogen oxide, and mercury emissions than coal. Lower-income towns have benefited economically from fracking because the drilling creates jobs and inserts money into the community. For instance, fracking is growing in North Dakota, and the state has the lowest unemployment rate in the nation.

However, fracking does have some negative impacts on the environment. There have been instances where fracking chemicals have contaminated drinking water and increased levels of methane in water wells. Currently, fracking is exempt from elements of the Safe Drinking Water Act. Gas companies can declare their chemical formulas as proprietary trade secrets (although this may be changing). Oil from fracking operations is also more volatile, making it more difficult and risky to transport it. Studies have also suggested links between fracking and minor earthquakes.

Many fear that the energy crisis and economic benefits will overshadow environmental concerns. Natural gas is a critical component of the government's plan for the country to run on 70 percent clean energy by 2035. Yet this has not stopped a number of states, provinces, and even countries from banning fracking operations within their borders. France as well as Quebec and New York have placed moratoriums on fracking.

On the other hand, many believe that the dangers of fracking will be significantly reduced if certain safety precautions are taken. Wells that are properly cemented and well-built can keep fracking chemicals from infiltrating groundwater. Any leaks discovered must be fixed immediately. Because the effects of fracking on groundwater are still somewhat unknown, studies could be conducted to determine if fracking negatively affects groundwater, as well as the extent. The Environmental Protection Agency (EPA) has mandated that fracking wells must have pollution control mechanisms to catch methane and volatile organic compound emissions.

Gas and oil companies themselves can adopt socially responsible practices when fracking. Some are looking for alternatives, such as trying to engage in hydraulic fracking without the use of chemicals. Others are able to recycle contaminated water used in the fracking process. It is important for gas and oil companies to safely dispose of chemicals and train all employees in appropriate safety procedures.

Fracking remains a controversial topic. It could very well lead the United States on its quest toward energy independence, but its environmental impact is uncertain. Gas and oil companies must find a balance between the economic benefits and the potential costs to the environment and worker safety.[1]

A s concerns over fracking, global warming, erratic weather patterns, and diminished quality of life continue to rise, public and business support for environmental causes has increased a great deal since the first Earth Day was held in 1970. Most Americans claim that they have made changes in their lifestyles, like switching to energy efficient light bulbs or recycling, to help the environment. One survey indicated that 78 percent of Americans purchase green products in certain circumstances, with Millennials more likely to purchase green products than other age groups. Nearly half of those who purchase green products indicate they do so because it is better for the environment.[2] Many businesses have adopted environmental policies in their operations, and 77 Fortune 500 corporations are using nearly 14.6 billion kWh of green power each year.[3]

In this chapter, we explore the concept of sustainability in the context of social responsibility in today's complex business environment. First, we define sustainability and explore some of the significant environmental issues that businesses and society face. Next, we consider the impact of government environmental policy and regulation on business and examine how some companies are going beyond the scope of these laws to address environmental issues and act in an environmentally responsible manner. We also examine different types of alternative energy. Finally, we highlight a strategic approach to environmental issues, including risk management and strategic audits.

DEFINING SUSTAINABILITY

Most people probably associate the term *environment* with nature, including wildlife, trees, oceans, rivers, mountains, and prairies. Until the twentieth century, people generally thought of the environment solely in terms of how these resources could be harnessed to satisfy their needs for food, shelter, transportation, and recreation. As Earth's population swelled and technology advanced, however, humans began to use more of these resources with greater efficiency. Although these conditions have resulted in an improved standard of living, they come at a cost. Plant and animal species, along with wildlife habitats, are disappearing at an accelerated rate; water use has become a critical issue in many parts of the globe; and pollution has rendered the skies of some cities a gloomy haze. How to deal with these issues has become a major concern for business and society in the twenty-first century.

Although the scope of the word sustainability is broad—including plants, animals, human beings, oceans and other waterways, land, and the atmosphere—in this book, we discuss the term from a strategic business perspective. Thus, we define **sustainability** as the potential for long-term well-being of the natural environment, including all biological entities, as well as the interaction among nature and individuals, organizations, and business strategies. Sustainability includes the assessment and improvement of business strategies, economic sectors, work practices, technologies, and lifestyles while maintaining the natural environment. It meets the

sustainability
The potential for long-term well-being of the natural environment, including all biological entities, as well as the interaction among nature and individuals, organizations, and business strategies.

needs of the present without compromising the ability of future generations to meet their own needs.[4]

However, it is important to realize that sustainability means different things to different cultures. Europeans use both environmental and economic variables when considering the sustainability of an organization. In the United States, sustainability is used more often in relation to environmental concerns. Others still believe the term is too broad; some researchers want the term sustainability in business to only emphasize human sustainability with a customer focus.[5] This lack of a clear consensus complicates the matter for businesses, especially when trying to evaluate ways to broaden the sustainable footprint of their operations.[6] For the purposes of this chapter, we use the U.S. concept of sustainability to describe how organizations interact with the natural environment.

HOW SUSTAINABILITY RELATES TO SOCIAL RESPONSIBILITY

Sustainability does not mean the same thing as social responsibility.[7] Rather, sustainability is a domain of social responsibility. Social responsibility is an attempt to maximize an organization's positive impact and minimize its negative impact on stakeholders. Sustainability according to our definition seeks to minimize a business's negative impact on the natural environment while maximizing its positive impact. Like any social concern, organizations should respond to consumer concerns over sustainability by addressing the issue in their strategies, policies, and objectives. This involves the process of assessing risks, monitoring ethical and legal compliance, and developing policies to minimize unethical conduct.

Although social responsibility and sustainability are not the same things, many socially responsible organizations display sustainable behaviors. Social responsibility meets the needs of stakeholders, including both environmental stakeholders and consumers concerned about the impact of business operations on the earth. Sustainability requires the organization to make ethical decisions on how it will implement, monitor, and improve upon sustainability initiatives. Figure 11.1 re-illustrates the major emphases of social responsibility featured in Chapter 1 to demonstrate sustainability's role.

Stakeholders are demanding that businesses become more sustainable. At the very least, organizations are expected to minimize their negative effects on the environment through such activities as the proper disposal of chemicals, recycling, or keeping greenhouse gas emissions down to a minimum. Organizations such as Best Buy have been responding by including sustainability as a key factor in annual corporate social responsibility reports. These reports are mandatory for publicly held corporations in Europe.

Sustainability has become a major issue for organizations for different reasons. First, sustainable business practices can result in competitive advantages. Sustainable practices are beneficial to stakeholder relationships

FIGURE 11.1 Major Emphases of Social Responsibility

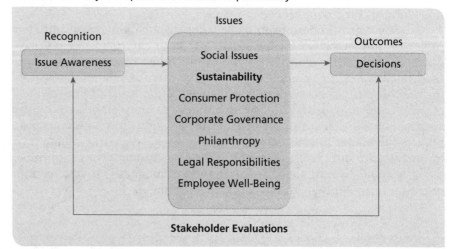

© O.C. and Linda Ferrell, 2016.

and can even lower costs in areas such as energy in the long-term. Second, as consumers become more aware of environmental issues, their power over organizations in this area is increasing.[8] Third, sustainable organizations are more likely to have their brand associated with positive concepts such as social value and product quality. Fourth, organizations are using sustainability to differentiate themselves from competitors and to market their goods and services. Patagonia has adopted the unique campaign of encouraging consumers not to buy products from the company that they do not need. They also want customers to return used products that the customer no longer wants so the organization can reuse it. This positions Patagonia as a sustainable company truly desiring to live its mission.

Sustainability not only involves best practices, but it is increasingly becoming an issue of concern to lawmakers. Companies that recognize this are investing in sustainable practices before laws are passed that may limit their activities. For instance, in anticipation of stricter miles per gallon standards, automakers like Ford are investing in ways to increase the gas mileage of its cars. Oil and gas companies are some of the biggest investors in renewable energy technologies. Total, Shell, Statoil and ExxonMobil are investing billions of dollars in alternative energy projects.[9] Many stakeholders respond positively to these changes.

GLOBAL ENVIRONMENTAL ISSUES

The protection of air, water, land, biodiversity, and renewable natural resources emerged as a major issue in the twentieth century in the face of increasing evidence that pollution, uncontrolled use of natural resources, and population growth were putting increasing pressure on the long-term sustainability of these resources. As the environmental movement sounded the alarm over these issues, governments around the globe responded with environmental protection laws during the 1970s. In recent years, companies have been increasingly incorporating these issues into their overall business strategies. Most have been the focus of concerned citizens as well as government and corporate efforts. Some nonprofit organizations have stepped forward to provide leadership in gaining the cooperation of diverse groups in responsible environmental activities. For example, the Coalition for Environmentally Responsible Economies (CERES), a union of businesses, consumer groups, environmentalists, and other stakeholders, has established a set of goals for environmental performance.

In the following section, we examine some of the most significant environmental issues facing business and society today, including air pollution, acid rain, global warming, water pollution and water quantity, land pollution, waste management, deforestation, urban sprawl, biodiversity, and genetically modified foods.

Atmospheric Issues

Among the most far-reaching and controversial environmental issues are those that relate to the air we breathe. These include air pollution, acid rain, global warming, and pollution emitted by coal.

Air Pollution Air pollution typically arises from three different sources: stationary sources such as factories and power plants; mobile sources such as cars, trucks, planes, and trains; and natural sources such as windblown dust and volcanic eruptions.[10] These sources discharge gases, as well as particulates, that can be carried long distances by surface winds or linger on the surface for days if there is a lack of winds or if geographical conditions permit.

The World Health Organization (WHO) has issued standardized safe levels of particulate matter (PM), which are used to determine whether a city's pollution is considered dangerous. Particulates measuring 2.5 are the most dangerous to public health, as these particles are small enough to enter the bloodstream and cause ailments such as cancer and emphysema. China has long been considered the country with the most air polluted cities. However, India has since taken the lead, and it is estimated that half a million people in India die premature deaths annually as a result of pollution.[11] Such conditions can cause markedly shorter life spans, along with chronic respiratory problems (e.g., asthma, bronchitis, and allergies) in humans and animals, especially in the elderly and the very young. Some of the chemicals associated with air pollution may contribute to birth defects, cancer, and brain, nerve, and respiratory system damage. Air pollution can also harm plants, animals, and water bodies. Haze caused by air pollution can reduce visibility, interfering with aviation, driving, and recreation.[12] As a result of experiencing the detrimental effects of pollution on the population and the economy, China has "declare[d] a war on pollution" by reducing energy levels, closing factories, and minimizing the amount of cars driving on the roads.[13]

Acid Rain In addition to the health risks posed by air pollution, when nitrous oxides and sulfur dioxides emitted from manufacturing facilities react with air and rain, the result is acid rain. This phenomenon has contributed to the deaths of many valuable forests and lakes in North America and Europe. It also corrodes paint and deteriorates stone, leaving automobiles, buildings, and cultural resources such as architecture and outside art vulnerable unless they are protected from its effects.[14] While we have made great strides since the passing of the Clean Air Act in 1963, some of our forests and lakes are still recovering from the damage caused by acid rain.[15] In addition, we have not yet been able to eliminate this phenomenon, although implementing more environmentally conscious practices has been successful in reducing emissions that cause acid rain. Today the United States emits around 5.7 million tons of sulfur dioxide emissions and 2.0 million tons of nitrogen oxide into the atmosphere each year—a significant decrease from previous years. Cleaning up emissions from factories and cars is one way to help reduce acid rain.

Global Warming When carbon dioxide and other gases collect in Earth's atmosphere, they trap the sun's heat like a greenhouse and prevent Earth's surface from cooling. Without this process, the planet becomes too cold to sustain life. However, during the twentieth century, the burning of fossil fuels—gasoline, natural gas, oil, and coal—accelerated dramatically, increasing the concentration of "greenhouse" gases like carbon dioxide and methane in Earth's atmosphere. Chlorofluorocarbons—from refrigerants, coolants, and aerosol cans—also harm Earth's ozone layer. A hole, measuring nine miles high and several hundred miles wide, was discovered in the lowest layer of the atmosphere and is believed to be caused by the presence of chlorofluorocarbons. The protective layer of the ozone, that protects the earth from the sun's harmful ultraviolet rays, is said to be stripped away. These harmful rays not only damage the environment but also humans' eyesight and skin health.[16]

World carbon dioxide emissions are currently around 31 billion metric tons and are expected to rise to 45 billion metric tons by 2040.[17] The United States and China are the two largest greenhouse gas emitters in the world.[18] As noted above, India, as well as other developing countries, are going to make up an increasing percentage of overall emissions, since they are most likely to use coal—the dirtiest of all fossil fuels in terms of emissions. Figure 11.2 below shows emissions outputs by countries in the Organisation for Economic Co-operation and Development (OECD), excluding the BRIICS (Brazil, Russia, India, Indonesia, China, and South Africa) and the rest of the world (ROW). To cut greenhouse gas emissions, the EPA has written rules providing stricter standards for new cars to cut the amount of greenhouse gases emitted from new cars by 25 percent. Large trucks and power plants will also have standards that will contribute to a 17 and 30 percent reduction, respectively.[19]

Most scientists believe that concentrations of greenhouse gases like methane and carbon dioxide in the atmosphere are accelerating a warming of the

FIGURE 11.2 GHG Emissions Per Capita

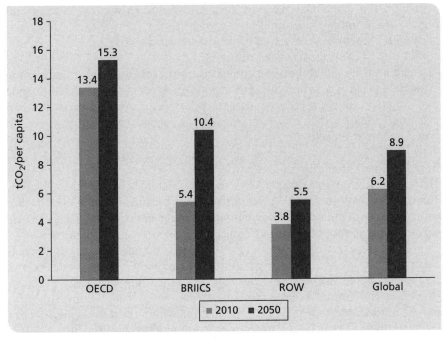

Note: ROW short for Rest of the World

Source: Organisation for Economic Co-operation and Development, "OECD Environmental Outlook to 2050," OECD, November 2011, http://www.oecd.org/env/cc/49082173.pdf (accessed June 22, 2016).

planet. Accumulations of greenhouse gases have increased dramatically in the past century. The year 2015 is the hottest year on record. The second hottest year on record was 2014, and 2010 was recorded as the third hottest around the world.[20] The accumulation of gases appears to have increased average temperatures by 1.4°F over the last century. Although this does not sound like much of a change, it is sufficient to increase the rate of polar ice sheet melting, which is occurring at unprecedented rates.[21] The years 2008 and 2009 marked record years for severity of summer ice cap melting. Climate change has caused such dramatic melting of glaciers along the Italian/Swiss border in the Alps that mapmakers were forced to redraw the border between the two countries to follow the new glacial boundaries.[22] Climate change has also affected weather in this region—making Switzerland to the north more prone to flooding and Italy to the south more drought-ridden.

As the polar ice caps melt, scientists fear that rising sea levels will flood many coastal areas and even submerge low-lying island nations. With less snow and ice cover to reflect the sun's rays, Earth absorbs even more of the sun's heat, accelerating the warming process. Some scientists also think that global warming may alter long-term weather patterns, causing drought in some parts of the world while bringing floods to others—something that many believe we are already witnessing in the form of extreme weather patterns. For example, many claim that the effects of Hurricane Sandy on the east coast were so devastating due to warmer waters and higher coast lines. Additionally, record-breaking heat waves, droughts, and winter storms are also said to be a result of the changing atmospheric conditions caused by global warming.[23]

The concept of global warming has been controversial among some groups, especially in the United States. Critics of global warming argue that apparent temperature increases are part of a natural cycle of temperature variation that the planet has experienced over millions of years. Some people even like the sound of global warming, as it brings to mind warmer temperatures and longer growing seasons. Many companies and organizations have also maligned the theory because reducing emissions and tightening environmental laws means greater expenses at the outset. Nevertheless, most nations, scientists, and businesses now agree that something must be done about climate change. Failure to act may create extreme climate conditions that could have negative consequences.

Hydraulic fracturing (fracking), discussed in the opening vignette, is controversial due to its effects on global warming. While supporters claim fracking is better for the environment and is leading to energy independence for the United States, critics say otherwise. They claim the burning of natural gas releases harmful methane into the atmosphere. They estimate methane to be 21 times more potent than carbon dioxide over a period of 100 years. The Intergovernmental Panel on Climate Change claims the estimate is closer to 34 times. Since the rise of fracking, the EPA has issued rules for production and consumption and will continue to do so as more information on its effects on the climate become known.[24]

Kyoto Protocol
A treaty among industrialized nations aimed at slowing global warming.

The **Kyoto Protocol** is a treaty among industrialized nations aimed at slowing global warming. The United States did not ratify the treaty and therefore was not bound to it. Since its creation in 1997, the Kyoto Protocol was highly unpopular amongst polluting multinational corporations. At the time, signing the treaty required reducing levels of greenhouse gas emissions by five percent that of 1990 levels. However, only 37 countries as well as the European Union (EU) signed the protocol, leaving out the largest polluters such as Canada, the United States, Australia, and developing countries including China and India. The United States has adopted a voluntary U.S. Global Climate Initiative for reporting greenhouse gases, as outlined in Table 11.1. Many leaders worried that compliance would jeopardize businesses and the economy.[25] The treaty went into effect in 2005 and instituted its first commitment period for years 2008–2012. The second commitment period (2013–2020) has goals to reduce emissions by 18 percent of the 1990 levels, with 192 signatory nations.[26] Also in 2012, another attempt to develop a legally binding international agreement to reduce greenhouse gas emissions was discussed. The Doha Gateway Agreement calls for both developed and developing countries to decrease greenhouse gas emissions. The global agreement is expected to be implemented in 2020. As of 2016, 66 countries have signed the amendment.[27]

TABLE 11.1 Elements of the U.S. Global Climate Change Initiative

- Enhancement of the 1605(b) Voluntary Reporting of Greenhouse Gases Program
- Significantly expanded funding for basic scientific research and advanced technology development
- Tax incentives, such as credits for renewable energy, cogeneration, and new technology
- Challenges for business to undertake voluntary initiatives and commit to greenhouse gas intensity goals, such as through recent agreements with the semiconductor and aluminum industries
- Transportation programs, including technology research and development and fuel economy standards
- Carbon sequestration programs, which include increased funding for U.S. Department of Agriculture conservation programs under the Farm Bill
- Investments in climate observation systems in developing countries
- Funding for "debt-for-nature" forest conservation programs
- Use of economic incentives to encourage developing countries to participate in climate change initiatives
- Expanding technology transfer and capacity building in the developing world
- Joint research with Japan, Italy, and Central America

Sources: Energy Information Administration, U.S. Department of Energy, "Voluntary Reporting of Greenhouse Gases—Summary," http://www.eia.doe.gov/oiaf/1605/vrrpt/summary/special_topic.html (accessed June 22, 2016); USAID, "U.S. Global Climate Change Initiative," https://www.usaid.gov/climate (accessed June 22, 2016).

Many U.S. businesses are responding to stakeholder pressure and are committing to self-regulatory standards with respect to global warming and related areas, even in the absence of federal mandates. States like California have worked hard to gain the right to issue their own environmental legislation. After many years of making arguments to the federal government, the EPA granted California the right to impose tough emissions standards on cars and trucks. California had wanted to re-implement the toughest reading of the Clean Air Act legislation in over 40 years. This change in ruling opened the door for other states to pass similar emissions legislation and demonstrated a willingness on the part of the EPA to let states decide how strict they want to be on polluters.[28] A host of energy-efficient designations now exist to help consumers make more environmentally friendly choices. For example, Energy Star, a joint program between the U.S. EPA and the U.S. Department of Energy, helped Americans and businesses reduce greenhouse gas emissions by 2.5 billion metric tons—all while saving them more than $362 billion on utility bills.[29] Table 11.2 describes some ways companies and governments are adopting climate change strategies.

Coal and Carbon Emissions As already mentioned, coal is an area of debate among different countries and is considered to be one of the dirtiest forms of energy.[30] The consumption of coal pollutes the air by releasing large amounts of gaseous and particulate matter into the atmosphere. Many governments believe that their intervention is needed to bring down

TABLE 11.2 Climate Change Strategy

Climate Change Strategy	Description	Example
Greenhouse Gas Reduction	A commitment to reduce carbon emissions by a certain percentage	To reduce greenhouse gas emissions, the U.S. government is requiring automobiles to get 35.5 miles per gallon (mpg) by 2016
Cap-and-Trade Program	Set emissions limits (caps) for businesses, countries, or individuals	The United States used a cap-and-trade program for acid rain, requiring fossil-fueled power plants to reduce levels of sulfur oxide and nitrogen oxide emissions
Proactive Business Practices	Occurs when businesses proactively adopt business practices to address sustainability before there is a call for them	Walmart has worked on adopting a sustainability index that will allow customers to determine how eco-friendly a product is

levels of greenhouse gas emissions. Some countries are intervening with cap-and-trade programs, which set emissions limits (caps) for businesses, countries, or individuals. Companies are given a certain amount of carbon they are allowed to emit, and to legally emit anything beyond that limit, a company must purchase carbon credits from another company that did not pollute as much. The EU has been at the forefront of mandated emissions reductions and has implemented a cap-and-trade program on carbon emissions known as the European Union Emission Trading Scheme.

When the EU signed the Kyoto Protocol, it committed to collectively reduce its greenhouse gas emissions by 8 percent. The EU does this by issuing a fixed number of permits to businesses and other parties that limits the amount of emissions their companies can give off. A carbon emissions cap can strain many businesses, especially manufacturing companies, which emit large amounts of carbon in the process of operating. Opponents of this scheme argue that a single cap puts certain companies at a financial disadvantage, as they can only reduce their carbon footprint by so much before they begin sacrificing productivity. To solve this problem, a cap-and-trade system allows for businesses to sell the carbon permits they do not use. In other words, companies that do not release as much carbon emissions can sell their permits to companies that do. Companies that pollute less are therefore rewarded with extra income, while companies that produce more are allowed to continue working. In order to give companies time to adapt more efficient technologies, governments impose progressively smaller caps over the years.[31]

The cap-and-trade program has gained some support in the United States. For several years, ten states, including California, New York, and Maryland, have implemented these programs to reduce emissions. Cap-and-trade has also been used to reduce acid rain by restricting the amount of sulfur dioxide and nitrogen oxides released by fossil-fired power plants.[32] However, opposition has been fierce, and federal legislation has not focused on mandating cap-and-trade programs. Instead, the government is more concerned with providing collective goals that must be met. The EPA works with companies and states on implementing rules to meet these goals. One initiative supported by the Obama administration is to reduce emissions 30 percent from 2005 levels by the year 2030. The EPA has suggested market-based programs, investment in existing or new energy efficiency programs, or expansion of renewable energy initiatives to state legislators, who will decide what methods work best for their states.[33] However, opposition to this proposed rule remains high, particularly as it would significantly impact the nation's 600 coal-fired plants. As a result, the Supreme Court temporarily put a hold on the initiative in 2016.[34]

Proactive businesses do not have to wait for legislation to be passed to reduce their carbon footprint. Many companies have created best practices programs which utilize cleaner energy over dirty forms of energy like gasoline or coal, as well as more efficient building codes. These codes have been shown to cut energy consumption by a significant amount. As these codes are implemented and reevaluated, drafters are able to revise the codes, making them all the more effective.[35] However, most companies have a long way to go. According to a report compiled by the EPA, nearly half of all U.S. emissions are produced by businesses across all industries.[36] A business needs to know the size of its carbon footprint before it can effectively reduce emissions and other environmental pollutants. Companies including Walmart, Coca-Cola, and Nestlé have actively monitored their carbon output and have set ambitious goals, such as eventually becoming net zero when it comes to emissions.

Water Issues

Water is emerging as the most important and contested resource of the twenty-first century. Nothing is more important to human survival, yet water is being polluted and consumed at an unprecedented rate. An estimate published by the United Nations suggests that 1.8 billion people will be living in conditions of absolute water scarcity by 2025, and that approximately 75 percent of the global population may be living with limited access to potable water. There are many reasons for this—including industrial waste, 70 percent of which pollutes water supplies in developing countries; human waste, which accounts for 2 million tons per day; and agricultural waste, which pollutes 40 percent of water in high income areas and 54 percent in low income areas.[37] In order to remain viable, all businesses must think about water conservation, purification, and allocation.

Water Pollution Water pollution results from the dumping of sewage and toxic chemicals from manufacturing into rivers and oceans; from oil and gasoline spills; and from the burial of trash and industrial waste in the ground where it can contaminate underground water supplies. Fertilizers and pesticides used in farming and grounds maintenance also drain into water supplies with each rainfall. These chemicals are harmful to all life that depends on oceans and streams. Fertilizers upset algae balances in rivers causing fish to die. Mercury contaminates the oceans and therefore human food supplies. Overuse of water can lead to shortages; deforestation and climate change are contributing to desertification of sections of China and even the United States; and various chemical and methane leaks associated with fracking are seeping into water supplies.[38] Additionally, one in ten people lack access to safe water, and every 90 seconds one child dies from a disease obtained from unsafe water.[39]

From the passage of the Clean Water Act in 1972 to 2001 the United States made significant strides to clean up and protect water sources. However, the water preservation movement lost federal backing in the early 2000s. According to the Natural Resources Defense Council (NRDC), 10 percent of U.S. beaches are highly polluted, causing them to be closed or on advisory for most of the year. Six of these beaches are located in the Great Lakes area, as water pollution problems are especially notable in heavily industrialized areas.[40] A large percentage of streams, lakes, and other American waterways are not fit for fishing or swimming, and pollution from agriculture and organic decomposition are significant enough to have created "dead zones" in large bodies of water. The Gulf of Mexico is known to have a dead zone the size of the state of New Jersey.[41]

While the United States has one of the safest drinking water supplies in the world, pollution remains a problem. Flint, Michigan experienced a state of emergency after it switched its water supply from Lake Huron to the Flint River. The Flint River was known for being filthy. Soon iron and lead was leaking into the water supply, creating a toxic supply that could cause long-term effects to residents who drank or bathed in it. However, the problem of lead is not limited to Flint, Michigan. Safety experts are warning that only nine states in the United States claim to have safe levels of lead in their drinking water.[42] Many of these have unknown side effects on people and wildlife. The EPA released a study on the quality of water coming from 50 wastewater treatment plants all over the nation, and found over 25 types of pharmaceuticals present in the water supply. Pharmaceutical companies have released the drugs into the water supply, but consumers who take the drugs are the largest contributor to the problem. Pharmaceuticals have also been found in water sources in Europe, Asia, and Australia. Although the concentrations found have been small, scientists worry about the long-term health effects they could have upon humans. Effects have already been found in male frogs that have ingested small amounts of estrogen and developed eggs.[43] Tougher regulations are needed globally to address pollution from activities such as dumping waste into the ocean, large animal-feeding operations, logging sites, public roads, parking lots, and industrial waste created by production operations.

Water Quantity In addition to concerns about the quality of water, some parts of the globe are increasingly worried about its quantity. Over the last two decades, water use has soared, resulting in serious consequences for the global water supply. This creates issues for businesses in various industries that consume large amounts of water in their operations. For example, it takes approximately 20 gallons of water to brew a pint of beer, 132 gallons to make a two-liter bottle of soda, and 500 gallons to make a pair of Levi's jeans. In light of the decreasing amount of water on the planet, companies are taking a responsible approach by measuring their water footprints. Levi Strauss & Co. partnered with several organizations to develop assessments for the lifecycle impact of their jeans. As a result, the company has been able to determine ways to use up to 96 percent less water to make their jeans without compromising the quality.[44]

Record-breaking years of heat and below-average precipitation result in costly and dangerous droughts across the nation. About 15 percent of the United States experienced a moderate to extreme drought during July of 2014. These conditions put added pressure on facility managers to conserve water. The nation's supply of accessible fresh water is decreasing drastically, in no small part because of consumption rates. The average American uses 100 gallons of water per day, and it is estimated that up to 10 percent of American homes are fitted with leaking water pipes, faucets, and toilets that waste 90 gallons of water each day. As a result, at least 40 states are preparing for or experiencing water shortages. There are many small things companies and individuals can do to slow down water consumption rates. For example, switching to low-flow toilets could save as much as 640 billion gallons of water.[45]

Land Issues

Land sustainability is diverse and encompasses some of the issues already discussed, such as pollution and waste as well as loss of biodiversity and genetically modified foods. Our land is becoming less viable for human and animal habitation due to the impact of these activities. Because businesses generate waste and require natural resources, stakeholders believe they have the responsibility to minimize their harmful impact on the environment.[46]

Land Pollution Land pollution results from the dumping of residential and industrial waste, strip mining, and poor forest conservation. Such pollution causes health problems in humans, jeopardizes wildlife habitats, causes erosion, alters watercourses (leading to flooding), and can eventually poison groundwater supplies. China is at the epicenter of a debate over pollution. The country's rapid development as manufacturer to the world has exposed hundreds of millions of people to the ill effects of pollution. A report released by Chinese officials indicated the extent to which their land is polluted. Of the 3.7 million square miles of land, at least 16 percent is polluted with heavy metals, including cadmium, nickel and arsenic. An additional 19 percent of farmland has been deemed polluted, which necessarily infects a large portion of food grown in the country. The government announced an investment of $4.8 billion to clean polluted land and prevent these levels from recurring. However, these efforts will take time and significant damage has already been done.[47] In order to reduce pollution around the planet, businesses are all going to have to be aware of and accept responsibility for the problem of pollution.

Determining responsibility for environmental degradation is not always easy, especially on a global scale involving different countries. In 2015 Shell was sued by a community in the Niger River Delta for oil spills that contaminated the land and settled the claim for $84 million. A year later more communities in Nigeria sued Shell for destruction caused by leaking oil. The communities claim that Shell does not have the proper technology to detect and shut off leaks in the area. Shell maintains that the pollution occurs mainly because of thieves who are trying to steal oil from the pipelines.[48] Ecuador sued Chevron for environmental damage that occurred years earlier with oil and gas firm Texaco. Chevron later acquired Texaco, and the country claimed that Chevron was responsible for the environmental damage. After many court battles, a U.S. court ruled in favor of Chevron citing an agreement Texaco had signed with Ecuador absolving it of liability.[49]

Fracking has also led to concerns over land pollution. Fracking often occurs in rural areas where trees are cut down to make way for roads, well pads, and other infrastructure specific to fracking. Wyoming, for example, has experienced habitat fragmentation, a reduction in hunting, and a depopulation of wildlife; sections of forests in Pennsylvania have been cut down; and Alberta, Canada, has reported serious detrimental effects to land and other natural resources in the area believed to be caused by fracking.[50]

Waste Management Improper or irresponsible disposal of waste is another aspect of the land pollution problem. American consumers are by far the world's biggest wasters. In one year, they contributed 254 million tons of waste, which strains declining landfill space. The United States has over 3,000 active landfills and more than 10,000 abandoned landfills. Often left untreated, these abandoned landfills result in hazardous leakage. Methane gas makes up the largest emissions given off from landfills, which is 20 times more powerful than carbon dioxide in terms of atmospheric heating. Some organizations have learned to convert that gas into power.[51] The EPA established the Landfill Methane Outreach Program (LMOP), with partners consisting of landfill owners and operators, industry organizations, energy providers and marketers, state agencies, communities, end users, and other stakeholders to convert landfill methane gas into power. Europe also has thousands of biogas plants that convert methane from farm waste and trash into electricity, which in a 15-year period has reduced methane emissions from landfills by 3.1 million tons annually.[52]

Plastics in landfills are a major concern as they can take up to 1,000 years to biodegrade. A large contributor is plastic bags, of which Americans use 1 billion per year. Twelve cities have passed legislation either prohibiting the use of plastic bags in stores or charging a fee for their use. Many countries have passed similar legislation in various regions.[53] Stores like Whole Foods banned plastic bags voluntarily, and offer incentives for consumers to use more recyclable materials such as canvas grocery bags. The United States recycles more than 34 percent of waste produced, while other countries such as Germany, Austria, and Belgium recycle at least half of their waste.[54]

Electronic waste (e-waste) in landfills has been proven to release harmful toxins into the air and water. It is estimated that the United States generated 3.14 million tons of e-waste, and only 16 percent of the world's e-waste is recycled.[55] Increasingly, electronics firms are pressured to take back used electronics for recycling. Large chains such as Best Buy offer e-recycling, as does Dell and Sprint. Sprint takes a slightly different approach with their buyback program, wherein customers may receive up to a $300 buyback value for qualifying devices.[56] The EPA established its own electronics recycling program, and a host of state governments have passed laws to encourage the recycling of electronic devices. Many stakeholders, including environmental groups and some politicians, believe that companies that produce the goods should be responsible for their proper disposal and recycling.[57]

Deforestation Rainforests serve to regulate temperatures and weather patterns, absorb carbon dioxide, and maintain water supplies. Before deforestation became a common occurrence, there was approximately 6 million square miles of rainforests, whereas today rainforests cover a little over 2 million square miles. It is estimated that the global tree count has fallen to 46 percent of what it was at the dawn of human civilization.[58] The reasons for deforestation are varied. The boom in biofuels in Southeast Asia and the Pacific regions have resulted in the cutting down of trees to make room for palm oil plantations. Brazil cuts down the Amazon rainforests for farming or for raising sugarcane. The amount of deforestation that occurred in Brazil's rain forests last year covers an area the size of Rhode Island.[59]

A competitive global economy drives the need for money in economically challenged tropical countries. In the short term, logging and converting forestlands to other uses seems the profitable thing to do. However, the profits from deforestation are generally short lived due to the poor quality in rainforest soil. While initially it can create a boom of prosperity, farming and other activities are only sustainable by moving and cutting down more trees.[60] Deforestation began largely out of need that sprang from poverty in these areas. However, those involved in the activity are more commonly large corporations. Many see this as an advantage because it is easier to put pressure on these entities to be more responsible. In addition, this pressure can come from many stakeholder groups, which can increase the response time.[61]

Companies are obtaining certifications like the one granted by the Forest Stewardship Council (FSC), a nonprofit organization comprised of loggers, environmentalists, and sociologists. The FSC seeks to coordinate forest management around the world and to develop a uniform set of standards. FSC-certification helps companies indicate to consumers and stakeholders that they are committed to preserving forest resources, are focused on social responsibility, and hold a long-term perspective of environmental management. Table 11.3 lists some facts about deforestation.

TABLE 11.3 Facts about Global Deforestation

- One and a half acres of forest is cut down every second.
- Loss of forests contributes between 12 and 17 percent of annual global greenhouse gas emissions.
- If the current rate of deforestation continues, it will take less than 100 years to destroy all the rainforests on the earth.
- 20 percent of the world's oxygen is produced in the Amazon forest.
- Poverty, over-population and unequal land access are the main causes of man-made deforestation.
- Industrialized countries consume 12 times more wood and its products per person than the non-industrialized countries.
- Soil erosion, floods, wildlife extinction, increase in global warming, and climate imbalance are a few of the effects of deforestation.
- Deforestation affects water cycle. Trees absorb groundwater and release the same into the atmosphere during transpiration. When deforestation happens, the climate automatically changes to a drier one and also affects the water table.
- On an average, a person in the United States uses more than 700 pounds of paper every year.
- Fuel wood in sub Saharan African countries is consumed up to 200 percent times more than the annual growth rates of the trees. This is causing deforestation, lack of timber resources and loss of habitat for the species living in it.

Source: "Deforestation Facts," *Conserve Energy Future,* http://www.conserve-energy-future.com/various-deforestation-facts.php (accessed June 22, 2016).

Urban Sprawl Urban sprawl began in the United States with the post–World War II building boom that transformed the nation from primarily low-density communities designed to accommodate one-car households, bicyclists, and pedestrians to large-scale suburban developments at the edges of established towns and cities. Downtowns and inner cities deteriorated as shopping malls, office parks, corporate campuses, and residential developments sprang up on what was once forest, prairie, or farmland. As the places where people live, work, and shop grew further apart, people began spending more time in automobiles, driving ever greater distances. Urban sprawl consumed wildlife habitat, wetlands, and farmland, and has also contributed to land, water, and air pollution. Lack of urban planning means that these places grow without reason, contributing to uneven development of services. In an age of erratic gas prices, traffic congestion, and obesity, it has become increasingly expensive, in both dollars and health, to live in sprawling cities. Large companies with many locations, such as Walmart and Starbucks, have been criticized for contributing to urban sprawl.

Some urban areas fight to limit sprawl. Portland, Oregon, for example, established an Urban Growth Boundary to restrict growth and preserve open space and rural land around the city. The California legislature passed a bill that limits urban sprawl through better transportation and more efficient land use. Adding to the appeal of returning to cities is a movement to increase urban parks. Rather than allowing loggers to profit from forests, more cities are buying forested land to convert to park space. Stemming sprawl also preserves natural spaces outside of the city. Additionally, people realize that living near their place of employment is more convenient, cheaper, and better for their health. Although limiting urban sprawl creates disadvantages for car and oil companies, many businesses can benefit from urban renewal movements that reduce sprawl.

Biodiversity

Deforestation, pollution, development, and urban sprawl put increasing pressure on wildlife, plants, and their habitats. Many plants and animals have become extinct, and thousands more are threatened. For example, in the Brazilian Savannah, scientists examined 163 tree species and determined that 70 of them would eventually become nonexistent.[62] Experts' fears that over-utilization of natural resources will cause catastrophic imbalance to the environment are becoming realized. Because each biological species plays a unique role in its ecosystem and is part of a complex chain of events, the loss of any one of them may threaten the entire ecosystem.

Decrease in Bees, Bats, and Frogs An alarming rate of decline in the populations of bees, bats, and frogs are at the forefront of this issue. Pollinators play a significant role in that they help fruits and vegetables grow by spreading pollen from plant to plant. Increasing development and widespread use of pesticides have reduced populations of bees, insects, and bats needed for plant reproduction. The population of domestic honeybees, the primary pollinators of food-producing plants, has declined by at least one-third, and many wild honeybees have become virtually extinct in many places around the world. This decline has become so widespread that the phenomenon has been termed Colony Collapse Disorder (CCD), and organizations are working to stop the decline before complete extinction occurs. Declines in pollinating species not only threaten the success of their relevant ecosystems but also may harm long-term global food production because significant portions of all food products require pollinators to reproduce.[63]

Bat populations are also on the decline, due mainly to a fungus disease called White Nose Syndrome. Many believe that this epidemic is due to environmental and habitat changes resulting from human-related activities. Bats aid the environment in a number of ways, such as feeding on insects, which reduces the need for pesticide use.[64] The same is true for amphibians such as toads, salamanders, and frogs, which are declining at an annual rate of 3.7 percent. Scientists claim that if this rate continues, frog extinction will occur within the next 20 years. Frogs are especially vulnerable to environmental changes including habitat modification, urban sprawl, pollution, and depletion of the ozone layer because their skin is made to absorb the water wherein they live. Any changes in frog populations immediately inform us of negative changes in the environment.[65]

Genetically Modified Organisms

genetically modified (GM) organisms
Organisms created through manipulating plant and animal DNA so as to produce a desired effect like resistance to pests and viruses, drought resistance, or high crop yield.

Depending on whom you ask, genetically modified foods are either going to save impoverished areas from starvation and revolutionize agriculture, or they will destroy biodiversity and make us all sick. **Genetically modified (GM) organisms** are created through manipulating plant and animal DNA so as to produce a desired effect like resistance to pests and viruses, drought resistance, or high crop yield. This process generally involves transferring genes from one organism to another in a way that would never occur naturally, in order to create a new life form that has unique traits. Companies like Monsanto and DuPont develop genetically modified corn, soybeans, potatoes, canola oil seeds, and cotton plants they claim are more resistant to weeds and insects, sometimes require fewer chemicals to produce, and produce higher yields. However, studies show that certain GM crops are losing their effectiveness as insects become increasingly resistant. More farmers have reverted to using pesticides, which also damages the environment.[66]

Many people also fear that these unnatural genes will have negative effects on nature, somewhat like how invader species of plants and animals can wipe out native ones, or even have negative effects on humans. Other concerns result from the fact that these seeds are patented, restricting farmers from keeping and replanting the seeds and requiring them to purchase new seeds each year. Nevertheless, considerable interest in GM products remains. In countries where malnutrition is a problem, the prospect of higher yields is very appealing, even if the seed itself is more expensive. Monsanto, the world's largest agricultural biotechnology company, has released GM seeds that can withstand drought, which could make a major difference in many regions.[67]

GM foods may be controversial, but some researchers and scientists see the technology as a valuable way to develop drugs in the future. The U.S. Food and Drug Administration (FDA) approved the first GMO drug, ATryn, created to treat people who suffer from the blood-clotting condition antithrombin deficiency. The drug comes from goats that were genetically engineered to produce human antithrombin in their milk.[68] As with GM plants, the problem with the genetic engineering of animals or animal products is that the long-run effects are unknown. Large numbers of genetically altered animals could upset the balance in relationships among various species with undetermined effects, such as the ability to reproduce or fight diseases and pests. Additionally, if genetically modified plant seeds are carried by wind or pollinators to areas with native plants, it is possible that genetic contamination could take place among native plants, thus reducing biological diversity. Further research is needed to address public concerns about the safety and long-term environmental effects of these technologies.

The long-term impact of this genetic tinkering is a question that concerns many, despite the fact that the FDA has deemed GM food safe to consume and many scientific research studies have shown no dangers to human health. Today, more than 75 percent of all processed food contains GM ingredients.[69] The United States does not require labeling. Because

Earth in the Balance

Organic and Natural: Labeling Lies?

There is a general belief that organic and natural foods are healthier because of their lack of additives and pesticide use. The fears over issues such as genetically modified food have driven more people to embrace organic and natural food claims. For this reason, companies such as Whole Foods and Trader Joe's have become popular among grocery shoppers. Even Walmart is capitalizing on this trend by offering organic food products in stores.

However, the idea that organic and natural labels automatically means healthier could be misleading. The FDA has determined that there is no proof that organic food is healthier than genetically modified food. Additionally, the word "organic" does not necessarily mean totally pesticide-free. Organic farmers are allowed to use organic pesticides on their crops and still be considered organic.

One benefit is that organic farmers must meet strict criteria developed by the U.S. Department of Agriculture to be able to label their crops as such. Products can adopt this label if at least 95 percent of the content is organic. However, the costs of growing organic food are not cheap. On average, organic fruit costs 13–36 cents more per pound for fruits and vegetables. Hormone- and antibiotic-free milk averages approximately $6 per gallon versus $3.50 for regular milk.

The word natural is more vague than organic because there is no single definition of what is meant by "natural." This makes it easier for companies to come under criticism when consumers dispute their "natural" claims. For instance, a lawsuit was filed against PepsiCo for labeling its Naked Juice brand as natural. Consumer groups had found that synthetic vitamins had been added to the juice as well as manmade fibers. "Natural" is generally thought to mean a food product that has not been processed. However, even the FDA admits this is difficult because the majority of products have been processed in some way. While there is certification for use of the word "organic," companies can use "natural" more freely—although not necessarily without consequences. Companies cannot use this term to mislead consumers. The Federal Trade Commission charged five companies with falsely promoting skin products, shampoo, and sunscreen as natural when they actually contained synthetic ingredients. This was the first time the FTC took action against natural claims.

Supporters, however, claim that there may be unrealized benefits of organic and natural food. Genetically modified food is still under suspicion in many countries, and the long-term health effects are not readily known. Because organic farmers use more organic techniques to grow their crops, this reduces the negative impact of farming on the environment. Additionally, many consumers simply enjoy the feeling of consuming more natural products and are therefore willing to pay a higher price.

The choice of whether to eat organic or natural foods is up to the consumer. However, it is important that the consumer realize that the label organic or natural does not necessarily mean healthier. Natural potato chips, for instance, still contain fats and sugars. Consumers should still look at the ingredients to analyze the nutrition of the product.

Sources: Manoj Hastak and Michael B. Mazis, "Deception by Implication: A Typology of Truthful but Misleading Advertising and Labeling Claims," *Journal of Public Policy & Marketing* 30, no. 2 (Fall 2011: 157–167; David Biello, "Is Organic Really Better?" *Scientific American*, http://www.scientificamerican.com/podcast/episode.cfm?id=is-organic-really-better-09-05-28 (accessed August 8, 2016); "Organic Pesticides Not Always Greener Choice," *Science Daily*, June 23, 2010, http://www.sciencedaily.com/releases/2010/06/100622175510.htm (accessed August 8, 2016); Associated Press, "Pepsi Co. To No Longer Call Naked Juices 'Natural'," *USA Today*, July 26, 2013, http://www.usatoday.com/story/money/business/2013/07/26/pepsi-co-naked-juice-not-natural/2589717/ (accessed August 8, 2016); Ethan Huff, "Pepsi Forks Over $9 Million Settlement, Agrees to Stop Calling Naked Juice 'Natural'," *Natural News*, July 30, 2013, http://www.naturalnews.com/041412_Naked_Juice_food_labeling_all_natural.html (accessed August 8, 2016); Rachel Tepper, "Naked Juice Class-Action Lawsuit Settlement Over Health Claims Means $9 Million for Consumers," *The Huffington Post*, September 24, 2013, http://www.huffingtonpost.com/2013/08/28/naked-juice-class-action-lawsuit_n_3830437.html (accessed August 8, 2016); Mayo Clinic staff, "Organic Food: Are They Safer? More Nutritious?" *Mayo Clinic*, http://www.mayoclinic.org/healthy-living/nutrition-and-healthy-eating/in-depth/organic-food/art-20043880 (accessed August 8, 2016); United States Environmental Protection Agency, "Pesticides and Food: What 'Organically Grown' Means," May 9, 2012, http://www.epa.gov/pesticides/food/organics.htm (accessed July 25, 2014); U.S. Department of Agriculture, "What is Organic?" *USDA website*, October 17, 2012, http://www.ams.usda.gov/AMSv1.0/ams.fetchTemplateData.do?template=TemplateC&leftNav=NationalO rganicProgram&page=NOPConsumers&description=Consumers (accessed August 8, 2016) Serena Ng, "FTC Charges Five 'Natural' Products Firms Over Claims," *The Wall Street Journal*, April 13, 2016, http://www.wsj.com/articles/ftc-charges-five-natural-products-firms-over-claims-1460500050 (accessed July 20, 2016).

many consumers demand to know what is in their food, organic and all-natural grocery chains like Whole Foods have take advantage of this market opportunity by implementing their own policies regarding labeling or the elimination of GM ingredients.

Another example of the backlash against GM organisms is in the dairy industry. Many large dairy producers use hormones, called recombinant bovine growth hormones, or rBGH, to increase milk production in cows. Many cows get sick from the hormones and are also given antibiotics. Even in America, where government bans are not in place and GM food is more accepted, many Americans refuse to buy milk that has come from cows given these drugs because it is perceived as less healthy. Companies such as Walmart, Starbucks, Kroger, and Safeway grocery store chains stopped carrying rBGH milk after strong consumer backlash.[70] While this has had some effect on the milk market, 40 percent of dairy products in stores still contain rBGH.[71]

Countries Against GM Food All of these concerns have prompted consumers around the world, particularly in Europe and Japan, to boycott products made from GM crops. Moreover, 60 countries—including all of the European Union, Australia and Japan—have imposed bans or restrictions on GM products.[72] However, as more GM crops are grown and more GM foods are consumed without detrimental effects, some countries are becoming open to the technology. However slowly it may be, countries in Africa are adopting the crops in order to combat hunger and ecological changes. Egypt and Sudan have cultivated small crops, while South Africa has lessened restrictions on GM crop imports due to a prolonged drought. Additionally, Nigeria has proposed a bill to lessen the restrictions on GM crops.[73]

GM Trout and Other Living Organisms Researchers have created GM rainbow trout having up to 20 percent more muscle mass that non-GM trout. By injecting 20,000 eggs with different myostatin-supressing DNA (a protein that controls muscle growth), 300 eggs were found to carry the gene, resulting in muscular trout. These fish carry the potential benefit of increasing food supply, although concerns about them being released into water streams are high. The effects of them breeding with native fish are unknown, as their new genes will be transferred to offspring. In addition, their size will require them to consume more food, which may cause shortages, and birds that typically feed on small fish may eventually find their food supply lacking. In effect, releasing these muscular fish into the wild could upset the entire ecosystem.[74]

There are over 30 types of GM animals under development for the purpose of selling commercially as food. AquaBounty Technologies is the leading company that has fully developed GM salmon for the dinner table. These salmon are twice the size and grow twice as fast as original salmon. In addition, they are able to be grown year round, which will increase the food supply. The FDA has issued studies citing no harm in ingesting these GM foods and is expected to approve these foods for commercialization. If approved, the salmon will be the first fully GM food to make its way to dinner plates. The Food and Drug Administration approved the genetically-modified salmon, but fishing and environmental groups filed lawsuits against the agency claiming that it did not sufficiently examine environmental impact or consider the opinions of other stakeholders.[75]

Supreme Court Ruling About Seed Contamination Seed contamination is described as the cross pollination of natural seeds with GM seeds. This has become an issue for several reasons. First, the crops of farmers who are committed to producing natural and/or organic foods have been compromised when GM seeds are blown into their fields. One Oregon farmer's wheat was found to contain GM seeds developed by Monsanto, which were still in the experimental phase and had not yet achieved USDA approval. This discovery had international impact, as wheat shipments in Japan and South Korea had to be put on hold until the issue was resolved. Another organic farmer in Australia lost his organic certification due to GM seeds infiltrating his crops. Several more complex instances abound from seed contamination, and many court cases have been initiated.

However, because the GM seeds are patent protected, there is little recourse farmers can take in this regard. In fact, they are likely to be charged with patent infringement if GM seeds are found in their fields without them purchasing them. Monsanto has been known for enforcing their patents on farmers whose fields are found with their seeds, as well as farmers who have purchased their seeds and reused them in succeeding years. In a Supreme Court ruling regarding seed contamination, the verdict was in favor of Monsanto, mainly because of the patented nature of the seeds. Monsanto has said that it will not sue farmers whose fields end up with the protected seeds by accidental means, but farmers whose livelihood depends on the organic or all-natural quality of food could be compromised by the presence of these seeds.[76]

ENVIRONMENTAL POLICY AND REGULATION

The United States, like most other nations, has passed numerous laws and established regulatory agencies to address environmental issues. Most of these efforts have focused on the activities of businesses, government agencies, and other organizations that use natural resources in providing goods and services.

Environmental Protection Agency

The most influential regulatory agency that deals with environmental issues and enforces environmental legislation in the United States is the **Environmental Protection Agency (EPA)**. The EPA's founding in 1970 was the culmination of a decade of growing protests over the deterioration of environmental quality. This movement reached a significant climax with the publication of Rachel Carson's *Silent Spring*, an attack on the indiscriminate use of pesticides, which rallied scientists, activists, and citizens from around the country to crusade to protect the environment from abuses of the time. Twenty million Americans joined together on April 22, 1970, for the first Earth Day, a nationwide demonstration for environmental reforms. The EPA was formed in response to these events. The EPA is an independent agency that establishes and enforces environmental protection standards, conducts environmental research, provides assistance in fighting pollution, and assists in developing and recommending new policies for environmental protection. The agency is also charged with ensuring the following:

- Protecting Americans from significant risks to their health and to the environment.
- Managing environmental risks based on the best scientific information available.
- Enforcing federal laws protecting human health and the environment fairly and effectively.
- Ensuring environmental protection is an integral consideration in U.S. policies.
- Ensuring access to accurate information sufficient to all parts of society.
- Ensuring environmental protection contributes to diverse, sustainable, and economically productive communities and ecosystems.[77]

To fulfill its primary mission to protect human health and sustainability into the twenty-second century, the EPA established five long-term strategic goals to define its planning, budgeting, analysis, and accountability processes (see Table 11.4). To determine these goals, the agency solicited and evaluated significant stakeholder input on priority areas related to

Environmental Protection Agency (EPA) The most influential regulatory agency that deals with environmental issues and enforces environmental legislation in the United States.

TABLE 11.4 Strategic Goals of the Environmental Protection Agency

1	Taking action on climate change and improving air quality
2	Protecting America's waters
3	Cleaning up communities and advancing sustainable development
4	Ensuring the safety of chemicals and preventing pollution
5	Enforcing environmental laws

Source: "FY 2011–2015 EPA Strategic Plan," Environmental Protection Agency, http://nepis.epa.gov/Exe/ZyPDF.cgi?Dockey=P1008YOS.PDF (accessed June 22, 2016).

human health and environmental protection activities. Thus, these goals reflect public priorities as voiced by Congress in the form of statutes and regulations designed to achieve clean air and water, proper waste management, and other important concerns.[78]

To achieve these goals and carry out its public mission, the EPA is empowered to file civil charges against companies that violate the law. For years, many companies involved in the mining and extraction industries were not forced to pay for cleanup of environmental damage. However, the EPA has taken steps to ensure that companies are financially responsible for future environmental damage, rather than taxpayers and other stakeholders.[79]

Environmental Legislation

A number of laws have been passed to address both general and specific environmental issues, including public health, threatened species, toxic substances, clean air and water, and natural resources. For instance, leaded gasoline was phased out during the 1990s because catalytic converters, which are used to reduce pollution and required by law on most vehicles, do not work properly with leaded gasoline. In addition, lead exposure is harmful to people. The automobile industry is responding to increased Corporate Average Fuel Economy (or CAFE) standards by determining methods to increase gas mileage. Federal regulation requires automobiles to get 35.5 miles per gallon (mpg) by 2016 and 54.5 mpg by 2025, and car makers have devised alternative ways of building their cars to achieve these goals.[80] Strategies include incorporating lighter materials like aluminum, increased production and sales of hybrid vehicles, and improving electric cars and hydrogen fuel-cell technology.[81] Table 11.5 summarizes some significant laws related to environmental protection.

Clean Air Act The Clean Air Act is a comprehensive federal law that regulates atmospheric emissions from a variety of sources.[82] The law established national air quality standards as well as standards for significant new pollution sources emitting hazardous substances. These maximum pollutant standards, called National Ambient Air Quality Standards (NAAQS), are federally mandated to protect public health and the environment. States have the responsibility of developing implementation plans to meet the NAAQS by restricting emissions of criteria pollutants from stationary sources (industries) within the state.

The Clean Air Act mandates that states are responsible for their air quality. The majority of people appear to overwhelmingly agree with the purpose of the Clean Air Act. For instance, a survey conducted by the American Lung Association indicated that 75 percent view clean air as very or extremely important.[83] This means that clean air should be a primary concern for businesses in order to maintain good relationships with stakeholders.[84]

TABLE 11.5 Major Environmental Laws

Act (Date Enacted)	Purpose
National Environmental Policy Act (1969)	Established national environmental policy, set goals, and provided a means for implementing the policy; promotes efforts to prevent damage to the biosphere and to stimulate human health and welfare, established a Council on Environmental Quality.
Occupational Safety and Health Act (1970)	Ensures worker and workplace safety by requiring employers to provide a place of employment free from health and safety hazards.
Clean Air Act (1970)	Regulates emissions from natural, stationary, and mobile sources; authorized the EPA to establish National Ambient Air Quality Standards (NAAQS) to protect public health and the environment.
Federal Insecticide, Fungicide, and Rodenticide Act (1972)	Provides for federal control of pesticide distribution, sale, and use; requires users to register when purchasing pesticides.
Endangered Species Act (1973)	Established a conservation program for threatened and endangered plants and animals and their habitats; prohibits the import, export, interstate, and foreign commerce or any action that results in a "taking" of a listed species or that adversely affects habitat.
Safe Drinking Water Act (1974)	Protects the quality of drinking water in the United States; authorized the EPA to establish water purity standards and required public water systems to comply with health-related standards.
Toxic Substances Control Act (1976)	Empowered the EPA to track industrial chemicals currently produced or imported into the United States; authorized the EPA to require reporting or testing of chemicals and to ban the manufacture and import of chemicals that pose an unreasonable risk.
Resource Conservation Recovery Act (1976)	Empowered the EPA to control the generation, transportation, treatment, storage, and disposal of hazardous waste.
Clean Water Act (1977)	Authorized the EPA to set effluent standards on an industry-wide basis and to continue to set water quality standards for all contaminants in surface waters; made it unlawful for any person to discharge any pollutant from a point source into navigable waters without a permit.
Comprehensive Environmental Response, Compensation, and Liability Act (1980)	Established prohibitions and requirements concerning closed and abandoned hazardous waste sites; authorized a tax on the chemical and petroleum industries to establish a "superfund" to provide for cleanup when no responsible party could be identified.
Superfund Amendments Reauthorization Act (1986)	Amended the Comprehensive Environmental and Response, Compensation, and Liability Act to increase the size of the superfund; required superfund actions to consider the standards and requirements found in other state and federal environmental laws and regulations; provided new enforcement authorities and tools.
Emergency Planning and Community Right-to-Know Act (1986)	Enacted to help local communities protect public health and safety and the environment from chemical hazards; requires each state to appoint a State Emergency Response Commission (SERC) and to establish Emergency Planning Districts.
Oil Pollution Act (1990)	Requires oil storage facilities and vessels to submit plans detailing how they will respond to large spills; requires the development of area contingency plans to prepare and plan for responses to oil spills on a regional scale.

(Continued)

TABLE 11.5 (*Continued*)

Pollution Prevention Act (1990)	Promotes pollution reduction through cost-effective changes in production, operation, and use of raw materials and practices that increase efficiency and conserve natural resources, such as recycling, source reduction, and sustainable agriculture.
Food Quality Protection Act (1996)	Amended the Federal Insecticide, Fungicide, and Rodenticide Act and the Federal Food, Drug, and Cosmetic Act to change the way the EPA regulates pesticides; applies a new safety standard—reasonable certainty of no harm—to all pesticides used on foods.
Beaches Environmental Assessment and Coastal Health Act (2000)	Amended the Clean Water Act to include provisions decreasing the risks of illness due to using the nation's recreational waters.
Energy Policy Act (2005)	Addresses the way energy is produced in the United States in terms of energy efficiency, renewable energy, oil and gas, coal, Tribal energy, nuclear matters and security, vehicles and motor fuels, hydrogen, electricity, energy tax incentives, hydropower and geothermal energy, and climate change technology.
American Clean Energy Act (2009)	Seeks to create clean energy jobs; more energy independence; reduce greenhouse gas emissions; and lay the groundwork for a clean energy economy

Sources: Environmental Protection Agency, "Major Environmental Laws," http://www.epa.gov/pahome/laws.htm (accessed June 22, 2016); Environmental Protection Agency, "Summary of the Energy Policy Act," http://www2.epa.gov/laws-regulations/summary-energy-policy-act (accessed June 22, 2016); Environmental Protection Agency, "About the BEACH Act," https://www.epa.gov/beach-tech/about-beach-act (accessed June 22, 2016).

Endangered Species Act The Endangered Species Act established a program to protect threatened and endangered species as well as the habitats in which they live.[85] An endangered species is one that is in danger of extinction, whereas a threatened species is one that may become endangered without protection. The U.S. Fish and Wildlife Service of the Department of the Interior maintains the list of endangered and threatened species, which currently includes 1,229 endangered species (732 are plants) and 367 threatened species (166 are plants).[86] The Endangered Species Act prohibits any action that results in the harm to or death of a listed species or that adversely affects endangered species habitat. It also makes the import, export, and interstate and foreign commerce of listed species illegal. Protected species may include birds, insects, fish, reptiles, mammals, crustaceans, flowers, grasses, cacti, and trees.

The Endangered Species Act is highly controversial because some threatened or endangered species are a nuisance to ranchers and farmers, and have been harmed or killed by landowners seeking to avoid the hassle or expense of complying with the law. Concerns about the restrictions and costs associated with the law are not entirely unfounded. For example, a man was charged with unlawfully killing a grizzly bear (a species listed as threatened under the Endangered Species Act) when it and her two cubs showed up on his property. Several of the man's children were playing outside when the bears appeared, and he shot at them in order to protect his family. At the time of trial, the man was facing two years in prison, a $50,000 fine, and one year probation. In the end, the man was not convicted, but this example shows the kind of issues that can arise from this law.[87]

Toxic Substances Control Act Congress passed the Toxic Substances Control Act to empower the EPA with the ability to track the 75,000 industrial chemicals currently produced or imported into the United States. The agency repeatedly screens these chemicals and requires reporting or testing of those that may pose an environmental or human health hazard. It can also ban the manufacture and import of chemicals that pose an unreasonable risk. The EPA tracks the thousands of new chemicals developed by industry each year with either unknown or dangerous characteristics. It also controls these chemicals as necessary to protect human health and the environment.[88] For instance, new rules for bisphenol A (BPA), a toxic chemical found in some plastics, were implemented under this law. Today, the chemical can no longer be used in the manufacturing of plastic baby bottles or children's sippy cups.[89]

Clean Water Act The Federal Water Pollution Control Act was renamed as the Clean Water Act in 1977. The law grants the EPA the authority to establish effluent standards on an industry basis and continue the earlier law's requirements to set water quality limits for all contaminants in surface waters. The Clean Water Act makes it illegal for anyone to discharge any pollutant from a point source into navigable waters without a permit.[90] This includes the pouring of contaminates down the drain. Duke Energy pleaded guilty to nine violations of the Clean Water Act. For many years, the company had polluted four North Carolina rivers with toxic coal ash from its power plants. The firm was fined $102 million for these violations. It was also put on a five-year probation for environmental crimes.[91]

Food Quality Protection Act The Food Quality Protection Act amended the Federal Insecticide, Fungicide, and Rodenticide Act and the Federal Food, Drug, and Cosmetic Act to fundamentally change the way the EPA regulates pesticides. The law included a new safety standard—reasonable certainty of no harm—that must be applied to all pesticides used on foods.[92] The legislation establishes a more consistent, science-based regulatory environment and mandates a single health-based standard for all pesticides in all foods. The law also provides special protections for infants and children, expedites approval of safer pesticides, provides incentives for the development and maintenance of effective crop protection tools for farmers, and requires periodic reevaluation of pesticide registrations and tolerances to ensure that they are up-to-date and based on good science.

Energy Policy Act The Energy Policy Act focuses the nation's priorities on alternative forms of energy in the hopes to lessen U.S. dependence on foreign oil. The bill offered tax breaks and loan guarantees to alternative energy companies, like nuclear power plants, solar companies, and wind energy farms, and also requires utilities to comply with federal reliability standards for the electricity grid. Consumers who purchased hybrid gasoline-electric cars and other energy-saving measures were rewarded with tax benefits. Tax credits were also provided for plug-in electric drive conversion kits.[93] The bill also extended daylight savings time by one month to save energy.[94]

ALTERNATIVE ENERGY

Ongoing plans to reduce global carbon emissions are spurring countries and companies alike toward alternative energy sources. Traditional fossil fuels are problematic because of their contribution to climate change and global warming, as well as because of the increasing depletion of resources. Foreign fossil fuels are often imported from politically and economically unstable regions, often making it unsafe or unseemly to conduct business there. About 24 percent of petroleum consumed in the United States came from foreign sources. This is the lowest level since 1970.[95] This decrease is largely due to the recognition by the U.S. government of the need to look toward alternative forms of energy as a source of fuel and electricity. These sources include wind power, solar power, nuclear power, biofuels, and hydro and geothermal power. Table 11.6 provides some examples of companies and/or countries that use these alternative power sources.

TABLE 11.6 Alternative Energy

Energy Source	Examples
Wind	SC Johnson uses wind power to power its largest manufacturing facility
Geothermal	The largest complex of geothermal plants, known as the Geysers in Northern California, produces 60 percent of the average electricity demand in the North Coast region of California
Solar	Kohl's has begun installing solar panels at some of its locations
Nuclear	75 percent of France's electricity comes from nuclear power
Biofuels	Boeing is partnering with South African Airways and Dutch company SkyNRG to work on developing jet fuel from a type of tobacco plant
Hydropower	Yahoo uses hydropower at its New York facilities

Sources: Chad Garland, "Boeing, South African Airways to Develop Jet Fuel From Tobacco," *Los Angeles Times,* August 6, 2014, http://www.latimes.com/business/la-fi-tn-boeing-biofuel-tobacco-20140806-story.html (accessed June 22, 2016); Calpine Corporation, "About Geyser Energy," http://www.geysers.com/geothermal.aspx (accessed June 22, 2016); Yevgeniy Sverdlik, "Yahoo Launches Second 'Computing Coop' Data Center in New York State," *Data Center Knowledge,* April 27, 2015, http://www.datacenterknowledge.com/archives/2015/04/27/second-yahoo-data-center-comes-online-in-new-york-state/ (accessed June 22, 2016).; SC Johnson, "SC Johnson Powers Up Wind Energy at Company's Largest Manufacturing Facility," December 18, 2012, http://www.scjohnson.com/en/press-room/press-releases/12-18-2012/sc-johnson-powers-up-wind-energy-at-largest-mfg-facility.aspx (accessed June 22, 2016).

Wind Power

The Great Plains of the United States is one of the greatest sources of wind energy in the world, and many people believe that harnessing this energy will go a long way toward providing the United States' energy needs in the future. In fact, wind power is the fastest growing form of renewable energy worldwide. It consists of nearly 4 percent of total electricity generation capacity in the United States, and some states—including Iowa and South Dakota—generate more than 25 percent of their electricity needs through this method.[96] However, there are a number of roadblocks standing between taking abundant wind and turning it into affordable energy. First of all, restructuring the nation's power grids to efficiently transmit wind, solar, and other forms of renewable energy will require a large investment. Widespread adoption of wind power has been slowed by the high cost of the turbines and limitations on an outdated national power grid. The technology is more expensive and less efficient than fossil fuels currently, but advances are being made all of the time. Many people believe that the United States will be a wind power hot spot in the future, and more Americans than ever are supporting the movement. The United States is a close second to China, the largest producer of wind power.[97]

Wind energy has long been popular in other countries such as the Netherlands and Denmark and is becoming a lucrative business for many companies. Danish Company Vestas Wind Systems is the world's largest producer of wind turbines. It has 19 percent of the U.S. wind energy market. It has even expanded production to the United States in order to take advantage of the growing interest in wind energy.[98]

Mexico also has goals to become one of the top producers of wind power. Energy in Mexico has long relied on oil. However, new legislation serves to dissolve that monopoly and open the market to new forms of energy—including wind power. Two gigawatts of wind power per year will be installed, enabling the country to achieve its goal of 35 percent electricity generated from renewable sources by 2024.[99] However, some setbacks are present. Mexico's Isthmus of Oaxaca was one of the proposed areas for a wind farm, because of the vast landscape and presence of winds. Indigenous residents oppose the wind farm because of its unknown and possibly detrimental effects to the ecosystem, upon which their livelihood depends. The strong opposition resulted in the cancellation of the wind farm in this area, and highlights some obstacles Mexico will have to overcome in implementing renewable energy initiatives.[100]

Geothermal Power

Geothermal energy comes from the natural heat inside the Earth, which is extracted by drilling into steam beds. Although initial costs to build geothermal plants are high, savings in the long-term are well worth the investment. For example, Lipscomb University in Nashville, Tennessee, utilizes a geothermal heating and cooling system in many of their campus buildings, saving the University up to 70 percent annually.[101] Carbon dioxide emissions are less than those produced by efficient natural gas power plants, and geothermal plants use less water than coal power plants. Geothermal power also provides a steady flow of electricity every day of the year, unlike wind or solar energy.

Despite these advantages, the extraction of fluids from the ground causes pollution and can sometimes cause the land to subside if careful environmental measures are not implemented. Additionally, geothermal drilling sites are not readily available everywhere because of certain factors such as the permeability of rock. This—along with the high cost—has resulted in slow adoption, as geothermal power represents less than 10 percent of global energy. The United States, France, Russia, Mexico, Costa Rica, Indonesia, New Zealand, the Philippines, Iceland, Portugal, Japan, and Lithuania are the countries where the most geothermal energy is generated.[102] Research has shown that geothermal energy could become cheaper than fossil fuels as research and development receive more investment.

Solar Power

Solar power is a 100 percent renewable, passive energy source that can be converted into electricity through the use of either photovoltaic cells (solar cells) on homes and other structures or solar power plants. The major disadvantages of solar power are that the technology remains expensive and inefficient compared to traditional fossil fuel-generated energy and that the infrastructure for mass production of solar panels is not in place in many locations. Cloudy days, a seeming disadvantage, are not necessarily a problem as the UV rays required to generate power filter through clouds. Germany, a country not exactly known for its abundant sunshine, is number one in the world for solar power implementation.

Given the strong sunshine in places like the U.S. Southwest and California, solar power has gained a lot of support in the United States. For example, the world's largest solar power plant was completed in California, having the capacity to power nearly 95,000 American homes.[103] Additionally, the United States is adopting solar power at a record-breaking rate which will outpace Germany if it continues.[104] Solar energy is becoming an increasingly viable alternative for businesses to cut their pollution and emissions. Many Walmart facilities, with their huge flat roofs perfect for solar panels, now use solar power to generate the electricity of some stores.

Nuclear Power

Countries throughout Europe have managed to greatly reduce their emissions through the implementation of nuclear power plants, yet this form of power remains controversial. Because of the danger associated with nuclear meltdowns and radioactive waste disposal, nuclear power has some significant disadvantages. On the one hand, nuclear power is pollution-free and cost-competitive. Uranium is abundant enough that generating even 60 times more energy than what is produced today would not be a problem. The United States is the leader in nuclear power generation. The U.S. government provided $319 million in nuclear research and development for new power plant design.[105]

On the other hand, concerns over the safety of nuclear power plants and the disposal of waste are prevalent. Radiation output of nuclear power can be harmful to workers and the areas where transport of nuclear waste occurs. The Chernobyl accident in the Ukraine resulted in deaths, sickness, and birth defects. The crisis that occurred in Japan after nuclear reactors were damaged in the 2011 earthquake and tsunami was disturbing to many people as Japan is a developed country that has significant infrastructure. The fact that a natural disaster could lead to a nuclear emergency has led some to question our abilities to ensure the complete safety of nuclear power.

Biofuels

Biofuels are derived from organic materials like corn, sugarcane, vegetable oil, even trash. Ethanol made from sugarcane has been widely used in Brazil for decades, and the United States has adopted the use of ethanol made mostly from corn. This has become especially popular with those who want to reduce their car's carbon output or who are concerned with the nation's addiction to foreign oil. Automobile makers have responded by creating flex fuel and hybrid vehicles that can run on biofuels or gasoline. General Motor's Chevrolet Volt is an electric car with a backup motor for distances over 40 miles. When it uses gasoline, the Volt is designed to run mostly on E85, a blend of 85 percent ethanol (a type of alcohol that can be used as a biofuel) and a small percentage of gasoline.

Legal mandates to incorporate biofuels have been passed in some countries. This is a major reason for Brazil's widespread use, as they made it a requirement to blend gasoline with ethanol. There is some controversy over the use of biofuels in the United States, however, because it is made from corn, which is highly energy intensive to produce. Another point of criticism is that they currently use food crops, which with widespread adoption, could lead to food shortages.

Researchers have been hard at work developing new technologies that could produce biofuels without deforestation of land or compromising food supplies. Cellulosic ethanol would be made from non-edible plants like grasses, sugarcane waste, algae, and wood waste. Euglena Company, based in Japan, makes biofuel using algae. Japan's largest airline, ANA Holdings, has partnered with Euglena to use a mix of fuel in which 10 percent is algae-based.[106]

Hydropower

Throughout history people have used water as a power source and a means of transportation. From the water-powered mills of centuries past to modern hydroelectric dams, water is a powerful renewable energy source. Although in the United States, hydroelectric power only provides 2.8 percent of total output, hydropower provides 16 percent of total electricity production worldwide, making it the largest form of renewable energy. As with all other forms of energy production, hydropower has benefits and downsides. One of the major downsides is the destruction of wildlife habitats and sometimes even human habitations, when valleys are flooded due to dams. Hydroelectricity also disrupts the lifecycles of aquatic life. Damming the Columbia River between Washington and Oregon States decimated the region's salmon industry, for example. Benefits of hydroelectric energy include little pollution and inexpensive maintenance costs, once the infrastructure is in place.[107]

BUSINESS RESPONSE TO SUSTAINABILITY ISSUES

Many businesses have adopted a triple-bottom line approach that takes into consideration social and environmental performance in addition to economic performance. Firms are learning that being environmentally friendly and sustainable has numerous benefits—including increased goodwill from stakeholders and even money savings from being more efficient and less wasteful. Positions such as vice president of environmental affairs have been created to help companies achieve their business goals in an environmentally responsible manner. Businesses like Walmart and Nike have also developed environmental scorecards for their suppliers.[108] Corporate efforts to respond to environmental issues focus on green marketing, recycling, emissions reductions, and socially responsible buying.

Yet despite the importance of the environment, companies are in business to make a profit. Economic performance is still a necessary bottom line for most businesses. This begs the question: is going green cost-effective for companies? Studies suggest that improving a company's environmental performance can in fact increase revenues and reduce costs. Table 11.7 provides examples of how companies have used sustainability opportunities to impact performance.

Better environmental performance can increase revenue in three ways: through better access to certain markets, differentiation of products, and the sale of pollution-control technology. A firm's innovation in sustainability can be based on applying existing knowledge and technology or creating a completely new approach. Improving a firm's reputation for environmental stewardship may help companies capture this growing market niche.

Supply Chain Issues

An important aspect of building a corporate reputation is ensuring the sustainability of the supply chain. Walmart, for instance, is requiring their

TABLE 11.7 Sustainability Opportunities for Economic Performance

Sustainability Opportunity	Example
Differentiation of products	Method successfully used sustainability to differentiate its cleaning products from the competition
Cost of energy	Walmart lowers its energy costs through the use of solar power
Relationship with customers	Customers that purchase a Preserve Products recycled toothbrush are given a mailer that they can use to mail the toothbrush back to the company for recycling at the end of their use
Employee loyalty	New Belgium Brewing motivates employees to be sustainable by providing them with a mountain bike after they have worked there for one year
Community relations	Patagonia has a Common Threads Initiative that encourages people to reduce their consumption and help the environment by refraining from buying items they do not need

suppliers to be more environmentally friendly. Walmart has developed a Sustainability Index that it uses to track the environmental impact of its products. So far the index has been applied to 700 product categories.[109] These kinds of activities should go a long way toward helping consumers make 'greener' choices.[110] Improving a supply chain's environmental performance may be key to attracting more business from the retail industry.

Better environmental performance can also reduce costs by improving risk management and stakeholder relationships, reducing the amount of materials and energy used, and reducing capital and labor costs. Improved environmental standards should help prevent some major environmental disasters in the future. For those disasters that cannot be avoided, the firm can at least show that it applied due diligence with its environmental performance, which may reduce the company's culpability in the public's eye. Companies can also decrease the costs of compliance with governmental regulations and reduce fines if they become more energy efficient.

Green Marketing

green marketing
A strategic process involving stakeholder assessment to create meaningful long-term relationships with customers while maintaining, supporting, and enhancing the natural environment.

Green marketing is a strategic process involving stakeholder assessment to create meaningful long-term relationships with customers, while maintaining, supporting, and enhancing the natural environment. One company that is known for its commitment to being green is New Belgium Brewing in Fort Collins, Colorado. From its conception, New Belgium has been a company committed to sustainability. Its facilities use natural lighting and evaporative coolers to save on energy costs, and the buildings themselves were constructed of pine trees that were killed by invasive beetles (a growing problem in the Rockies). The brewery has been wind powered for over a decade and uses waste from the brewing process to produce on-site methane gas for energy as well. The company encourages its employees to bike to work, and actively engages in benchmarking and setting ambitious goals for reducing energy and waste even further.[111]

Many products are certified as "green" by environmental organizations such as Green Seal and carry a special logo identifying them as such. In Europe, companies can voluntarily apply for an Eco-label (see Figure 11.3) to indicate that their product is less harmful to the environment than competing products based on scientifically determined criteria. The European Union supports the Eco-label program, which has been utilized in product categories as diverse as refrigerators, mattresses, vacuum cleaners, footwear, and televisions. Certification does not include food and medicine.[112]

Greenwashing

Businesses must approach their green marketing tactics with caution so as not to mislead consumers.[113] **Greenwashing** involves misleading a consumer into thinking that a good or service is more environmentally friendly than it is. It occurs when companies want to attract environmentally-conscious consumers and can range from making environmental claims that are required by law and are therefore irrelevant (CFC-free) to puffery, or exaggerating environmental claims, to fraud. Researchers compared claims on products sold in ten countries, including the United States, to labeling guidelines established by the International Organization for Standardization (ISO), which prohibit vague and misleading claims as well as unverifiable ones such as "environmentally friendly" and "non-polluting." The study found that many products' claims are too vague or misleading to meet ISO standards.[114] For example, some products will be labeled as "chemical-free," when in fact everything contains chemicals, including plants and animals. Products with the highest number of misleading or unverifiable claims were laundry detergents, household cleaners, and paints. Advocates agree there is still a long way to go to ensure that shoppers are adequately informed about the environmental impact of the products they buy.[115]

Often, consumers do not find out about these false claims until after the purchase. [116] So while greenwashing may increase sales in the short-term and build the appearance of a company's sustainability reputation, it will cause serious repercussions when consumers learn they have been misled. This leads to poor long-term financial performance, which negatively affects all stakeholders of the company.[117] At the same time, the terms "green" and "sustainability" can be hard to define, resulting in unintentional greenwashing. The FTC issued green guidelines to help marketers determine the truthfulness of "green" claims in order to reduce this confusion.[118]

FIGURE 11.3 The European Eco-label

Source: "European Union Eco-label Logo," *Europa,* European Union, http://ec.europa.eu/environment/ecolabel/ (accessed June 22, 2016).

greenwashing
Misleading a consumer into thinking that a product is more environmentally friendly than it is.

STRATEGIC IMPLEMENTATION OF ENVIRONMENTAL RESPONSIBILITY

Businesses have responded to the opportunities and threats created by environmental issues with varying levels of commitment. Some companies, like New Belgium Brewing, consider sustainability a core component of the business. Other companies engage in greenwashing and do not actively seek to be more sustainable at all. As Figure 11.4 indicates, a low-commitment business attempts to avoid dealing with environmental issues and hopes that nothing bad will happen or that no one will ever find out about an environmental accident or abuse. Such firms may try to protect themselves against lawsuits. If you recall the example of Chevron earlier in the chapter, you will notice this is also an example of a low-commitment company in terms of sustainability. Other firms are more proactive in anticipating risks and environmental issues. Such firms develop strategic management programs, which view the environment as an opportunity for advancing organizational interests. These companies respond to stakeholder interests, assess risks, and develop a comprehensive environmental strategy. Home Depot, for example, has established a set of environmental principles that include selling responsibly marketed products, eliminating unnecessary packaging, recycling and encouraging the use of products with recycled content, and conserving natural resources by using them wisely. The company also makes contributions to many environmental organizations.

FIGURE 11.4 Strategic Approaches to Environmental Issues

Low Commitment	Medium Commitment	High Commitment
Deals only with existing problems	Attempts to comply with environmental laws	Has strategic programs to address environmental issues
Makes only limited plans for anticipated problems	Deals with issues that could cause public relations problems	Views environment as an opportunity to advance the business strategy
Fails to consider stakeholder environmental issues	Views environmental issues from a tactical, not a strategic, perspective	Consults with stakeholders about their environmental concerns
Operates without concern for long-term environmental impact	Views environment as more of a threat than an opportunity	Conducts an environmental audit to assess performance and adopts international standards

Recycling Initiatives

Many organizations engage in **recycling**, the reprocessing of materials, especially steel, aluminum, paper, glass, rubber, and some plastics, for reuse. In fact, recycling is one of the country's greatest sustainability success stories. Sixty-seven percent of all newspaper and mechanical paper used in the United States is now recycled. About 63 percent of paper and paperboard is recovered.[119] Paper is not the only thing that is recyclable, however. New Belgium Brewing engages in a type of recycling by using waste from beer production to generate methane gas that powers its facilities. Gills, the largest onion processor in the country, uses onion waste to make electricity and cattle feed. Starbucks makes coffee grounds available free to those who wish to use them for compost to add nutrition to their gardens.

Sometimes companies join partnerships and become members of organizations like WasteWise, which aims to reduce municipal solid waste and industrial waste.[120] These collaborations help companies save money through reducing waste, receiving positive publicity, and tracking how they reduce waste over time. Local and regional governments are also finding ways to recycle water to avoid discharging chemicals into rivers and streams and to preserve diminishing water supplies. After decades of siphoning water from surrounding regions, the city of Dallas, Texas, had to change their behaviors due to dwindling resources. Many conservationists see city-dwellers' love of green lawns and golf courses in a drought-prone region as simply wasteful and irresponsible. Part of the plan to address this thirst for water is the installation of more and larger water recycling facilities.[121]

recycling
The reprocessing of materials, especially steel, aluminum, paper, glass, rubber, and some plastics, by many organizations for reuse.

Stakeholder Assessment

Stakeholder analysis is an important part of a high-commitment approach to environmental issues. This process requires acknowledging and actively monitoring the environmental concerns of all legitimate stakeholders. Thus, a company must have a process in place for identifying and prioritizing the many claims and stakes on its business and for dealing with trade-offs related to the impact on different stakeholders. Although no company can satisfy every claim, all risk-related claims should be evaluated before a firm decides to take action on or ignore a particular issue. To make accurate assumptions about stakeholder interests, managers need to conduct research, assess risks, and communicate with stakeholders about their respective concerns.

However, not all stakeholders are equal. There are specific regulations and legal requirements that govern some aspects of stakeholder relationships, such as air and water quality. A business cannot knowingly harm the water quality of other stakeholders in order to generate a profit. Additionally, some special-interest groups take extreme positions that, if adopted, would undermine the economic base of many other stakeholders (e.g., fishing rights, logging, and hunting). Regardless of the final decision a company makes with regard to particular environmental issues, information should be communicated consistently across all stakeholders. This is especially important when a company faces a crisis or negative publicity about a decision. Another aspect of strong relationships is the willingness to acknowledge and openly address potential conflicts. Some degree of negotiation and conciliation will be necessary to align a company's decisions and strategies with stakeholder interests.

Risk Analysis

The next step in a high-commitment response to environmental concerns is assessing risk. Through industry and government research, an organization can usually identify environmental issues that relate to manufacturing, marketing, consumption, and use patterns associated with its products. Through risk analysis, it is possible to assess the environmental risks associated with business decisions. The difficulty is measuring the costs and benefits of environmental decisions, especially in the eyes of interested stakeholders. Research often conflicts, adding to the confusion and controversy over sustainability.

Debate surrounding environmental issues will force corporate decision-makers to weigh the evidence and take some risks in final decisions. The important point for high-commitment organizations is to continue to evaluate the latest information and to maintain communication with all stakeholders. For example, if the millions of sport utility vehicles (SUVs) on U.S. roads today were replaced with fuel-efficient electric-powered cars and trucks, there would be a tremendous reduction of greenhouse gas emissions. However, the cooperation and commitment needed to gain the support of government, manufacturers, consumers, and other stakeholders to accomplish this would be impossible to achieve. Although SUVs may contribute to the detriment of the environment, many of their owners prefer them because they provide greater protection in an accident than smaller vehicles.

The issue of environmental responsibility versus safety in SUVs illustrates that many environmental decisions involve tradeoffs for various stakeholders' risks. Through risk management, it is possible to quantify these tradeoffs in determining whether to accept or reject environmentally related activities and programs. Usually, the key decision is between the amount of investment required to reduce the risk of damage and the amount of risk acceptable in stakeholder relationships. A company should assess these relationships on an ongoing basis. Both formal and informal methods are needed to get feedback from stakeholders. For example, the employees of a firm can use formal methods such as exit interviews, an open-door policy, and toll-free telephone hotlines. Conversations between employees could provide informal feedback. But it is ultimately the responsibility of the business to make the best decision possible after processing all available research and information. Then, if it is later discovered that a mistake has been made, change is still possible through open disclosure and thoughtful reasoning. Finally, a high-commitment organization will incorporate new information and insights into the strategic planning process.

The Strategic Environmental Audit

Organizations that are highly committed to environmental responsibility may conduct an audit of their efforts and report the results to all interested stakeholders. Table 11.8 provides a starting point for examining environmental sensitivity. Such organizations may also wish to use globally accepted standards, such as ISO 14000, as benchmarks in a strategic environmental audit. The International Organization for Standardization developed **ISO 14000** as a comprehensive set of environmental standards that encourage a cleaner, safer, and healthier world. There is considerable variation among the environmental laws and regulations of nations and regions, making it difficult for high-commitment organizations to find acceptable solutions on a global scale. The goal of the ISO 14000 standards is to promote a common approach to environmental management and to help companies attain and measure improvements in environmental performance. Companies that choose to abide by the ISO standards must review their environmental management systems periodically and identify all aspects of their operations that could impact the environment.[122] Other performance benchmarks available for use in environmental audits come

ISO 14000
A comprehensive set of environmental standards that encourage a cleaner, safer, and healthier world developed by the International Organization for Standardization.

TABLE 11.8 Strategic Sustainability Audit

Yes	No	Checklist
O	O	Does the organization show a high commitment to a strategic environmental policy?
O	O	Do employees know the environmental compliance policies of the organization?
O	O	Do suppliers and customers recognize the organization's stand on environmental issues?
O	O	Are managers familiar with the environmental strategies of other organizations in the industry?
O	O	Has the organization compared its environmental initiatives with those of other firms?
O	O	Is the company aware of the best practices in environmental management regardless of industry?
O	O	Has the organization developed measurable performance standards for environmental compliance?
O	O	Does the firm reconcile the need for consistent responsible values with the needs of various stakeholders?
O	O	Do the organization's philanthropic efforts consider environmental issues?
O	O	Does the organization comply with all laws and regulations that relate to environmental impact?

from nonprofit organizations such as CERES, which has also developed standards for reporting information about environmental performance to interested stakeholders. The Green Globe program also offers environmental auditing and benchmarking services along with worldwide environmental certification for businesses.[123]

As this chapter has demonstrated, social responsibility entails responding to stakeholder concerns about the environment, and many firms are finding creative ways to address environmental challenges. Although many of the companies mentioned in this chapter have chosen to implement strategic environmental initiatives to capitalize on opportunities and achieve greater efficiency and cost savings, most also believe that responding to stakeholders' concerns about environmental issues will both improve relationships with stakeholders and make the world a better place.

SUMMARY

Although the scope of sustainability is quite broad, we define it as the potential for long-term well-being of the natural environment, including all biological entities, as well as the interaction among nature and individuals, organizations, and business strategies. Sustainability includes the assessment and improvement of business strategies, economic sectors, work practices, technologies, and lifestyles while maintaining the natural environment. Sustainability does not mean the same thing as social responsibility. Rather, sustainability is a domain of social responsibility.

A major part of achieving sustainability is reducing sources of pollution. Air pollution arises from stationary sources such as factories and power plants; mobile sources such as cars, trucks, planes, and trains; and natural sources such as windblown dust and volcanic eruptions. Acid rain results when nitrous oxides and sulfur dioxides emitted from manufacturing facilities react with air and rain. Scientists believe that increasing concentrations of greenhouse gases in the atmosphere are warming the planet, although this theory is still controversial. The Kyoto Protocol is a treaty among industrialized nations to slow global warming. However, major polluters such as the United States and China were not signatories of the Kyoto Protocol. The second commitment phase is currently in place. Europe has instituted a cap-and-trade program, which places a limit (cap) on carbon emissions, but allows businesses to purchase carbon permits from other companies. The United States is avoiding a wide-scale cap-and-trade program but is placing limits on carbon emissions that will impact coal plants.

Water pollution results from the dumping of raw sewage and toxic chemicals into rivers and oceans; from oil and gasoline spills; from the burial of industrial waste in the ground where it can reach underground water supplies; and from the runoff of fertilizers and pesticides used in farming and grounds maintenance. The amount of clean water available is also a concern and the topic of political disputes.

Land pollution results from the dumping of residential and industrial waste, strip mining, and poor forest conservation. How to dispose of waste in an environmentally responsible manner is an important issue. Deforestation to make way for agriculture and development threatens animal and plant species, as well as humans. Urban sprawl, the result of changing human development patterns, consumes wildlife habitat, wetlands, and farmland.

Deforestation, pollution, and urban sprawl threaten wildlife, plants, and their habitats and have caused many species to become endangered or even extinct. Biodiversity is threatened by all these activities, and should be an important topic of consideration for organizations and businesses. Scientists poorly understand rainforests and other biologically diverse environments, yet we do know that they still hold many important discoveries.

Genetically modified (GM) organisms are created through manipulating plant and animal genes so as to produce a desired effect like resistance to pests and viruses, drought resistance, or high crop yield. Many farmers now plant GM crops that are more pest and insecticide resistant, require fewer chemicals to produce, and have higher yields. The long-term consequences of these scientific innovations are unknown. Some fear that, because GM food is not naturally occurring, it could harm biodiversity or cause health problems in humans. Even so, there is a continued interest in GM products as a way to solve problems such as world hunger, drought, and pest invasions.

The U.S. Environmental Protection Agency (EPA) is an independent regulatory agency that establishes and enforces environmental protection standards, conducts environmental research, provides assistance in fighting pollution, and assists in developing and recommending new policies for environmental protection.

To reduce greenhouse gas emissions and dependence on fossil fuels, many countries and businesses are investigating in alternative forms of renewable energy. Wind power utilizes large turbines to convert wind into electricity. It has long been popular in windy regions such as northern Europe and is catching on in places like the United States and Mexico. Geothermal power harnesses the heat trapped inside the earth to generate power. While not feasible everywhere, it is an attractive option because energy is available all of the time, unlike with wind or solar power. Solar power can also be converted to electricity. Sunny places like the American Southwest are the sites of intensive solar power research. Nuclear power is another possible, albeit controversial, form of alternative energy. Countries in Europe and Asia continue to use nuclear power a great deal, but concerns remain over possible meltdowns and how to dispose of the waste. Biofuels have gained in popularity as a way to reduce the consumption of gasoline. However, adopting corn ethanol in the United States has been more problematic as it involves using a key food source. Hydropower is the most common alternative fuel used in the world but is expensive to initially set up and can have detrimental effects on river systems and surrounding areas.

Businesses are applying creativity, technology, and business resources to respond to environmental issues. Some firms have a vice president of environmental affairs position to help them achieve their business goals in an environmentally responsible manner. Green marketing is a strategic process involving stakeholder assessment to create meaningful long-term relationships with customers, while maintaining, supporting, and enhancing the natural environment. While green marketing has become more popular, companies must be careful not to engage in greenwashing. Greenwashing involves misleading a consumer into thinking that a product is more environmentally friendly than it really is.

There is growing agreement among environmentalists and businesses that companies should work to protect and preserve sustainability. Many organizations engage in recycling, the reprocessing of materials—especially steel, aluminum, paper, glass, rubber, and some plastics—for reuse. Businesses have responded to the opportunities and threats created by environmental issues with varying levels of commitment. A high-commitment business develops strategic management programs, which view the environment as an opportunity for advancing organizational interests. Stakeholder analysis requires a process for identifying and prioritizing the many claims and stakes on its business and for dealing with trade-offs related to the impact on different stakeholders. Risk analysis tries to assess the environmental risks and trade-offs associated with business decisions. Organizations that are highly committed to environmental responsibility may conduct an audit of their efforts and report the results to all interested stakeholders. Such organizations may use globally accepted standards, such as ISO 14000, as benchmarks in a strategic environmental audit.

Responsible Business Debate

The Pros and Cons of GM Crops

Issue: *Are seeds that have been genetically modified a better alternative than pesticides?*

In the United States, GM food has become a way of life. More than half of the crops grown in the country are genetically modified, including 70 percent of corn. While the European Union has largely resisted GM crops, biotechnology firms such as Monsanto see opportunities to expand in places such as Africa and India. However, new findings have cast a cloud over GM seed. Despite the numerous benefits, their extensive use in agriculture has created controversy.

GM crops offer a number of benefits. Because they are able to develop their own toxins to kill pests, they have enabled farmers to use fewer pesticides on crops. One study indicates that GM crops have prevented the use of 965 million pounds of pesticide. Because fuel is needed for farmers to operate machinery in spraying pesticides, GM crops have been estimated to save on carbon dioxide emissions to the equivalent of 8.6 million cars. GM crops are also beneficial because they have been modified to target certain types of pests. Pesticides, on the other hand, tend to kill a number of insects without differentiating which ones are harmful to the crop. Finally, GM crops result in greater crop yields. Corn crop yields are approximately 31 million tons larger worldwide. This increase in crop yields is important as the world's population grows.

Despite these benefits, obstacles to GM crops remain. Although the FDA has studied the impact of GM crop consumption and have determined it to be safe, many consumers are still skeptical. Because they are relatively new, critics argue, it is impossible to gauge their long-term health effects. Biodiversity is also an issue since wind and pollinators can transport GM seeds into areas with non-GM plants, leading to the contamination of native vegetation.

Another major problem is insect resistance. The more a pesticide—or a GM crop that produces its own toxins—is used, the more likely insects are to develop resistance. Insects that become resistant to these toxins are harder to kill. While companies like Monsanto have advised farmers to rotate their crops every year to keep resistance at bay, many farmers do not follow these guidelines. Consequently, certain GM crops are starting to lose their effectiveness, and resistant super bugs are emerging. For example, rootworms have been attacking crops after becoming resistant to a rootworm-targeting gene called Bt. This is causing some U.S. farmers to once again turn toward pesticides. An increase in pesticide use not only exposes the environment to potential harm but also eliminates one of the biggest benefits of using GM seeds.

Biotechnology companies are working on a solution to the problem of resistance. Monsanto is working on seeds that possess multiple traits for killing rootworms, which should increase the GM seed's effectiveness. Monsanto also plans to release new technology to combat pests. However, some scientists believe that even multiple trait seeds might not solve the problem for long as rootworms resistant to one trait are more likely to become resistant to the other traits also.

There Are Two Sides to Every Issue:

1. Genetically modified crops are more effective in combating pests and are therefore more beneficial than pesticide use.

2. Genetically modified crops are not a permanent solution to pesticides and are therefore not a more beneficial alternative.

Sources : "Monsanto Attempts to Balance Stakeholder Interests," in *Business Ethics*: *Ethical Decision Making and Cases*, 9th ed. (pp. 308–318), ed. O.C. Ferrell, John Fraedrich, and Linda Ferrell (Mason, OH: South-Western Cengage Learning, 2013);
Ian Berry, "Pesticides Make a Comeback," *The Wall Street Journal*, May 21, 2013, http://online.wsj.com/article/SB10001424127887323463704578496923254944066.html (accessed August 8, 2016);
"The Perils of Always Ignoring the Bright Side," *The Wall Street Journal*, http://online.wsj.com/article/SB100008723963904440047045780303403222277954.html (accessed August 8, 2016).

KEY TERMS

DISCUSSION QUESTIONS

1. Define sustainability in the context of social responsibility. How does adopting this concept affect the way businesses operate?
2. Describe the controversy surrounding GM foods.
3. Discuss renewable energy initiatives such as wind, solar, and geothermal. Which do you think are most feasible and most important for businesses to focus on?
4. Think of instances of greenwashing that you have encountered. What is the harm of greenwashing?
5. What is the role of the EPA in U.S. environmental policy? What impact does this agency have on businesses?
6. What federal laws seem to have the greatest

impact on business efforts to be environmentally responsible?
7. What role do stakeholders play in a strategic approach to environmental issues? How can businesses satisfy the interests of diverse stakeholders?
8. What is environmental risk analysis? Why is it important for an environmentally conscious company?
9. What is ISO 14000? What is its potential impact on key stakeholders, community, businesses, and global organizations concerned about environmental issues?
10. How can businesses become more sustainable? What are the advantages and disadvantages of striving to become more sustainable?

EXPERIENTIAL EXERCISE

Visit the website of the U.S. EPA (http://www.epa.gov/newsroom/). What topics and issues fall under the authority of the EPA? Peruse the agency's most recent news releases. What themes, issues, regula-tions, and other areas is the EPA most concerned with today? How can this site be useful to consumers and businesses?

THE 'SUSTAINABILITY' OF SUSTAINABILITY: WHAT WOULD YOU DO?

The Sustainability Committee's first meeting was scheduled for Thursday afternoon. Although it was only Tuesday, several people had already dropped by committee members' offices to express their opinions and concerns about the company's new focus on sustainability. Some colleagues had trouble with the broad definition of sustainability—"to balance the economic, environmental, and social needs of today's world while planning for future generations." Others worried the sustainability project was just another passing fad. A small group of colleagues believed the company should be most concerned with performance and should forget about trying to become a leader in the social responsibility movement. In general, however, most employees were either supportive or neutral on the initiative.

As the committee's meeting started, the committee chair reminded the group that the company's CEO was very committed to sustainability for several reasons. First, the company was engaged in product development and manufacturing processes that had environmental effects. Second, most companies in the industry were starting initiatives on sustainable development. Third, recent scandals had negatively affected public opinion about business in general. Finally, the company was exploring markets in Europe where environmental activism and rules were often more stringent. With these reasons in mind, the committee set out to develop plans for the next year.

For an hour, the committee discussed the general scope of sustainability in the company. They agreed that sustainability was concerned with increasing positive results while reducing negative effects on a variety of stakeholders. They also agreed that sustainability focused on the "triple bottom line" of financial, social, and environmental performance. For example, a company dedicated to sustainability could design and build a new facility that used alternative energy sources, minimized impact on environmentally sensitive surrounding areas, and encouraged recycling and composting. Another firm might implement its sustainability objectives by requiring suppliers to meet certain standards for environmental impact, business ethics, economic efficiency, community involvement, and others.

After this discussion, the committee made a list of current and potential projects that were likely to be affected by the company's new sustainability focus. These projects included

Energy consumption	Philanthropy
Manufacturing emissions and waste	Product development
Employee diversity	Technology
Community relations	Supplier selection
Corporate governance	Employee health and safety
Regulations and compliance	Volunteerism

After much discussion, the committee agreed that each member would take one of these 12 projects and prepare a brief report on its link to the environmental component of sustainability. This report should review the ways environmental issues can be discussed, changed, improved, or implemented within that area to demonstrate a commitment to sustainability. What would you do?

CHAPTER TWELVE

Social Responsibility in a Global Environment

The 10,000 Pound Gorilla in the Room Lives in Amazon

From its humble founding in a Bellevue, Washington garage in 1994, Amazon.com has risen to become a global player in the e-commerce industry. Although it started out as a bookstore, today Amazon is known for being a retailer that "sells everything." In the United States, Amazon sells approximately 488 million items. A top seller in Japan and Europe, Amazon is currently the world's eighth largest retailer. In terms of market value, however, Amazon has surpassed the world's biggest retailer, Walmart.

Amazon sees great opportunities for expansion in other countries. It tripled the rate of fulfillment centers in Europe, Asia, and America between 2010 and 2013. With approximately 100 fulfillment centers across the world, Amazon is well poised to have its products delivered to customers from all over. In Great Britain, Amazon is even testing with making last-minute deliveries itself.

Amazon is making a very small profit, and most of this profit comes from vendors selling on the Amazon site. This means Amazon can use its pricing to crush the competition or force them to sell out to Amazon. There are also complaints that Amazon pushes its workers in warehouses too hard. These are important considerations in analyzing whether Amazon is acting fairly on a global level.

Despite Amazon's worldwide success, it has come across a number of unique challenges in expansion—both at home and abroad. Amazon has been heavily criticized for destroying small businesses such as bookshops. To give bookshops more of an edge, the French government banned free shipping that Amazon offered to its customers on book orders. Amazon responded to the ban by charging shipping fees of only a penny, thereby adhering to the letter—if not the spirit—of the law.

Another more recent dispute occurred in Germany. Unionized workers at some of Amazon's logistics centers went on strike to protest what they believed to be unfair pay. The union maintains that Amazon pays less than comparable industries, whereas Amazon claims it pays more. Germany is a lucrative market for Amazon, with sales growing 21 percent in one year. Amazon responded to the situation by claiming it would work with employee-works councils rather than the union.

Amazon is growing faster than any other retailing format and is challenging many traditional retailers. Most durable goods can be purchased through Amazon, often at lower prices than at traditional stores. Amazon is starting its own delivery fleet. Through Amazon Prime, consumers can receive their products in one or two days, depending on their location. While Alibaba, a large Chinese online retailer, is attempting to challenge Amazon on a global basis, it has had a number of ethical and legal issues, especially involving counterfeit products. Walmart, in order to protect itself in the online market, purchased Jet.com, a shopping site that is trying to compete against Amazon.

It is likely Amazon will have to make concessions on things in some countries that it would not necessarily have to make in other countries. However, Amazon's relentless pursuit of satisfying the customer and sustaining growth is likely to increase its popularity on a global scale.[1]

T he expanding global marketplace requires that executives and managers develop the ability to conduct business effectively and in a socially responsible manner in different regions of the world. As Amazon.com is learning, values and expectations can differ from country to country. In this chapter, we elaborate on key topics and concepts discussed in Chapters 1 through 11, by examining the unique nature of issues in the global environment and trends around the world. We discuss the importance of cultural intelligence, delve into the complexities of working with stakeholders, provide emerging trends with primary stakeholders, and point to global standards of social reporting.

CULTURAL INTELLIGENCE

The movement of people across cities and continents means that ideas, values, traditions, languages, and customs have also migrated. While managers in different parts of the world may have unique and even contrasting perspectives, they also identify with a number of similar problems and opportunities, such as employee turnover, new business development, environmental protocols, and product innovation plans. Therefore, any culturally diverse work group will have a set of common experiences and another set of differences that must be recognized and managed. The potential for the group to achieve positive outcomes is largely based on each member's level of cultural intelligence. **Cultural intelligence** (CQ) is the ability to interpret and adapt successfully to different national, organizational, and professional cultures.[2] There are three components to the development and use of cultural intelligence:

cultural intelligence (CQ) The ability to interpret and adapt successfully to different national, organizational, and professional cultures.

1. Cognitive—Knowledge of economic, legal, ethical, and social systems prevalent in different cultures and subcultures.
2. Motivational—Intrinsic desire to learn about different cultures and subcultures and the confidence to function effectively in situations where differences are present.
3. Behavioral—Ability to use appropriate verbal and nonverbal actions when interacting with people from different cultures and subcultures.[3]

Cultural intelligence is desired of all employees but is necessary for those who work in different countries, manage diverse groups, and in general, have responsibilities that require the ability to interpret unfamiliar gestures, behaviors, and situations. These employees must be comfortable suspending immediate judgment and practice thinking before acting. For example, when an American businesswoman made multiple presentations to potential partners in Bangkok, Thailand, she was surprised there were so many side discussions while she presented. Since she did not speak Thai, she did not know the content of their discussions and wondered if they were bored, disinterested, or even disrespectful. She decided to relax, continue, and accept the chatter. It occurred to her that these side discussions were likely a cultural norm, or perhaps simply the act of translating key points to a colleague who had less familiarity with English. In this example, this businesswoman demonstrated strong cultural intelligence and in so doing, ensured her company established a strong market presence in Thailand and Southeast Asia. If she had shown anger or frustration, the potential partners may have decided to take their business elsewhere. Figure 12.1 provides a short self-assessment of your CQ.

FIGURE 12.1 Self-Assessment of CQ

Quick CQ Self-Assessment Tool

Think about your cultural intelligence in each of the following areas.

Select the answer (1 – 5) that BEST describes you as you really are.
1 – None of the description fits me.
2 – Only some of this fits me.
3 – Half of the description fits me.
4 – Most of the description fits me.
5 – The statements describe me perfectly.

CQ-Strategy 1 2 3 4 5

I plan carefully before I meet with someone who is from a different cultural background. After one of these experiences, I reflect carefully and try to make sense of the interaction.

CQ-Knowledge 1 2 3 4 5

I generally understand other cultures and cultural values. I know about the basic ways in which cultural are similar and the ways they are different.

CQ-Motivation 1 2 3 4 5

I am very interested in other cultures, and I enjoy meeting people who have different cultural backgrounds. I am confident that I can live in different cultures and that I can adapt to different parts of the world.

CQ-Behavior 1 2 3 4 5

I modify my behavior to make others more comfortable when I interact with people who are from different cultural backgrounds. I change the way I speak and act when I am in cross cultural settings. I mimic others to make sure that I follow local conventions so that my speech patterns and body language are not offensive.

Copyright © 2006 VanDyne and Ang

Interpreting Your Quick CQ Self-Assessment Responses

Sum your answers to the four questions in the Quick CQ Assessment Tool. Your score can range from 4 to 20.

4–7 points You see yourself as low in Cultural Intelligence. A CQ personal development plan could help you to become more capable of functioning effectively in culturally diverse situations.

8–16 points You see yourself as moderate in Cultural Intelligence. A CQ personal development plan could help you to enhance your capabilities in areas where you see yourself as less capable of functioning effectively in culturally diverse situations.

17–20 points You see yourself as high in Cultural Intelligence. A CQ personal development plan could help you to build on your impressive CQ strengths and become even more capable of functioning effectively in culturally diverse situations.

Source: Cultural Intelligence Center, "Self-Assessment of Your CQ," http://www.culturalq.com/selfassess.html (accessed July 28, 2014).

The effective practice of cultural intelligence requires a manager to parcel out what actions are true of all people, those that are unique to a particular group or culture, or whether the action lies somewhere along this continuum.[4] A person with high CQ will be skilled at recognizing how one individual or group is influenced by national, professional, and organizational cultures. For example, there are multiple layers of cultural effects to manage when an Irish manufacturing process expert from a consulting firm works with a Croatian engineer for a government agency. The Irish expert would have to interpret and act according to Croatia's national culture, laws and governmental system, the agency's role and scope, the engineering profession's code of ethics, and the engineer's personality and values. Therefore, to achieve social responsibility in a global context, CQ is integral. Cognitively, employees are obliged to learn the rules, values and standards of different cultures. This entails studying the history, laws, symbols, customs, and related facets of a new culture. Motivationally, they should be willing and confident enough to adapt to these standards but also strong enough to resist adapting when a legal, ethical, or other social responsibility expectation is in jeopardy. Finally, employees must develop a keen capacity to mirror gestures, words, and other behaviors that demonstrate they have "entered the world" of their cultural counterparts.[5]

Finally, it is important to remember that even one country is not entirely homogeneous. The extent to which a country has experienced immigration, supported and encouraged diversity, and realized the "melting pot" effect determines the internal homogeneity or heterogeneity of the country. For example, Japan, Norway, Saudi Arabia, and Poland are relatively homogeneous when compared to India, Australia, Britain, the United States, and Canada. The world's 200 countries contain 5,000 different ethnic groups. Approximately two-thirds of all countries have at least one minority group that comprises 10 percent of the total population and therefore represents a distinct subculture.[6] In more heterogeneous countries, astute managers will need to recognize and respond to subcultures. This, of course, requires a higher commitment to the cognitive, motivational, and behavioral aspects of CQ amidst an array of stakeholder interests and influences.

GLOBAL STAKEHOLDERS

In Chapter 1, we defined stakeholders as those people and groups to whom an organization is responsible—including customers, investors and shareholders, employees, suppliers, governments, communities, and many others—because they have a "stake" or claim in some aspect of a company's products, operations, markets, industry, or outcomes. These groups not only are influenced by businesses, but they also have the ability to affect businesses. Table 12.1 describes stakeholder issues that are likely to be present when planning and conducting business outside of the home country. Note that these issues include economic, legal, ethical, and philanthropic considerations of other cultures and countries.

TABLE 12.1 Examples of Stakeholder Issues in a Global Environment

Stakeholder Groups	Potential Issues
Employees	Wages and benefits relative to home country standards
	Attitudes toward employees from different genders and ethnicities, especially in executive positions Existence of collective bargaining efforts Laws and regulations for employee rights, health and safety Norms of employee volunteering Availability and comfort with open-door policies and other management practices
Customers	Laws and regulations on product safety and liability
	Presence and power of consumer rights groups Respect for the product needs of subcultures and minority groups Attitudes and accommodations for customers with disabilities
Shareholders	Laws and regulations regarding ownership and corporate governance
	Stability and governance of stock exchanges Willingness and ability to participate in shareholder meetings
Suppliers	Ethical and social considerations in the supply chain
	Prices offered to suppliers in developed countries and developing countries in comparison to other suppliers Availability and attitudes toward minority suppliers
Community	Norms of community relations and dialogue
	Expectations of community service and/or philanthropy Rights of indigenous people Availability and quality of infrastructure (roads, utilities, schools, etc...)
Environmental Groups	Environmental law and regulations
	Availability of "green" electricity, recycled materials, and other environmentally friendly inputs Environmental expectations relative to those in home country Use of natural resources to achieve business goals

From an economic perspective, differences in the development of countries can easily pose new challenges with stakeholders. As more companies move manufacturing and customer service operations to less developed nations, critics speak out about job loss in the home country and the pay and working conditions in the offshore operation. While overseas outsourcing adds another layer of complexity for management, economic considerations for cost cutting typically trump social and political concerns. Some firms report significant savings in salary costs due to the eagerness and productivity of workers, allowing the salary dollar to go further in developing nations.[7]

Clearly, the legal and regulatory environment varies from country to country. Managers need to understand not only the written code but also the nuances of implementation and enforcement. One of the most widely discussed stakeholder issues in the global economy is the extent to which bribery is a common and expected practice. Some American multinational corporations claim the passage of the Foreign Corrupt Practices Act severely reduces their ability to compete in the global marketplace. French power and transportation company Alstom pled guilty to violating the Foreign Corrupt Practices Act with bribes to foreign officials in Indonesia, Saudi Arabia, Egypt, and the Bahamas. It paid $772 million to settle the charges. The number of bribery cases filed by civil and criminal investigators has increased in the United States over the last several years. This resurgence is supported by new efforts in the European Union and Japan to prosecute bribery cases.[8]

Beyond the complexities of the law lay the ethical standards of stakeholders around the world. As discussed in earlier chapters, there are several factors that influence the ethical decision-making process, with top management setting the tone and communicating expectations for all employees, suppliers, and business partners. For companies with operations in several countries, the code of conduct originating from the home office may not provide sufficient guidance. The United Parcel Service (UPS) published its first ethics code for domestic employees but realized an international version was needed. Instead of imposing the American version, the company established advisory panels in different regions and conducted 35 focus groups around the world. Using the domestic code as a starting point, UPS ultimately produced 28 codes of conduct for its overseas operations. The codes incorporated cultural differences that did not override key corporate values. For example, UPS managers in France knew that a policy prohibiting alcohol consumption during working hours would not work; in France, it is customary to have a glass of wine at lunch. When language experts started to translate antitrust law into other languages, it translated as "against trust" and needed to be revised. Executives at UPS acknowledge the tremendous resources expended on the process but are confident the culturally intelligent approach is most effective.[9]

Finally, the philanthropic expectations of stakeholders are also widely varied. The United States has a strong focus on building a culture of business philanthropy and employee volunteerism. However, this is not true around the world. In Latin America, for example, the roots of philanthropy extend to the Catholic Church, which provided education, healthcare, and social services. Later, wealthy families provided funds to "secular societies of social benefit" that implemented welfare and social projects. Corporate interest in philanthropy is more recent but has grown significantly as a way for business to become socially engaged. The Inter-American Development Bank hosts an annual conference for Latin American business leaders to learn more about social responsibility and philanthropy. Attendance has increased over the years and activities in corporate social investing, social reporting activities, and membership associations for philanthropy executives are being implemented.[10]

Shareholder Relations and Corporate Governance

While the prospect for global agreement on economic, legal, ethical, and philanthropic standards for business may seem beyond reach, existing efforts hold great promise. Whatever form it takes, a successful initiative must begin and end with the role of corporate governance and shareholder power in corporate decision-making. The board of directors must be committed to a system of oversight, accountability, and control that incorporates a social responsibility perspective. Without this commitment, checks and balances are not in place to limit opportunism and self-interest, advocate for stakeholder rights, or ensure a firm's corporate culture establishes integrity in all relationships. As discussed in Chapter 3, corporate governance reflects fundamental beliefs about the purpose of business organizations—ranging from maximizing shareholder value to a more collaborative and relational approach with multiple stakeholders.

The movement to write and implement widely accepted codes of conduct is several decades old. It began with social activists who derided apartheid in South Africa and urged companies to withdraw their investments and business interests from the country. Led by Reverend Leon Sullivan, who sat on the board of General Motors, interested citizens and other groups developed requirements any company should demand for its employees and workplace conditions. These standards covered non-segregation, equal and fair compensation, programs to move minorities into management ranks, and other measures that clearly conflicted with South African law permitting racial segregation and unequal rights. Eventually, the Sullivan Principles were adopted by over 100 companies in the United States that also withdrew existing operations and investments out of South Africa.[11]

The influence of the Sullivan Principles prompted several groups to develop codes of conduct or similar documents in an effort to build multicultural agreement on acceptable corporate governance and business practices. Perhaps the most successful initiative resulted in the Caux Round Table Principles for Business. The round table consists of business leaders from all regions of the world who have a strong desire and interest in promoting socially responsible capitalism. Frederick Phillips, former president of Phillips Electronics, and Olivier Giscard d'Estaing, former vice-chairman of INSEAD, a preeminent business school, founded the group in 1986. Although the original intent was to reduce trade tensions, the round table quickly turned to global corporate responsibility and established its principles. Today, the group's governing board includes executives from multinational corporations and governments.[12]

In addition to this fundamental guidance, the Caux Round Table publishes periodic opinions on a range of social responsibility issues, including executive compensation, environmental protection, and corruption. Table 12.2 provides an example of the type of principles often found in foundational statements such as the Caux Round Table.

TABLE 12.2 Global Principles for Ethical Business Conduct

Global principles are integrity statements about foundational beliefs that should remain constant as businesses operate globally. These principles address issues such as accountability, transparency, trust, natural environment, safety, treatment of employees, human rights, importance of property rights, and adherence to all legal requirements. The principles are designed to focus on areas that may present challenges to the ethical conduct of global business.

1. **Require accountability and transparency in all relationships.** Accountability requires accurate reporting to stakeholders, and transparency requires openness and truthfulness in all transactions and operations.

2. **Comply with the spirit and intent of all laws.** Laws, standards, and regulations must be respected in all countries as well as global conventions and agreements developed among nations.

3. **Build trust in all stakeholder relationships through a commitment to ethical conduct.** Trust is required to build the foundation for high integrity relationships. This requires organizational members to avoid major international risks such as bribery and conflicts of interest. Laws supporting this principle include the U.S. Foreign Corrupt Practices Act, the U.K. Bribery Act, OECD Convention, and UN Convention Against Corruption.

4. **Be mindful and responsible in relating to communities where there are operations.** The communities where businesses operate should be supported and improved as much as possible to benefit employees, suppliers, customers, and the community overall.

5. **Engage in sustainable practices to protect the natural environment.** This requires the protection of the long-term well-being of the natural environment including all biological entities as well as the interaction among nature, individuals, organizations, and business strategies.

6. **Provide equal opportunity, safety, and fair compensation for employees.** Employees should be treated fairly, not exploited or taken advantage of, especially in developing countries. Laws supporting this principle include equal opportunity legislation throughout the world.

7. **Provide safe products and create value for customers.** Product safety is a global issue as various governments and legal systems sometimes provide opportunities for firms to cut corners on safety. All products should provide their represented value and performance.

8. **Respect human rights as defined in the UN Global Compact.** Human rights are a major concern of the UN Global Compact and most other respected principles statements of international business.

9. **Support the economic viability of all stakeholders.** Economic viability supports all participants in business operations. Concerns such as fair trade and payment of a living wage are embedded in this principle.

10. **Respect the property of others.** Respect for property and those who own it is a broad concept that is an ethical foundation for the operation of economic systems. Property includes physical assets as well as the protection of intellectual property.

Source: O. C. Ferrell and Linda Ferrell, *Anderson School of Management*, University of New Mexico, Copyright © 2016.

Employee Relations

A critical consideration for companies conducting business around the world is how to manage differences that exist in employment standards and expectations. Modern corporations recognize the importance of tapping into global markets and talent pools in order to remain competitive.

Even in the best cases, building a dedicated, engaged, and satisfied workforce takes strategic planning and daily oversight by management. Executing this process in a new culture or across cultures takes more than merely transferring the policies and practices from the home country and home office. It must include consideration of the economic, legal, ethical, and philanthropic expectations of employee stakeholders in different countries. For example, Table 12.3 outlines key differences between employment law in Canada and the United States. There are important differences between these cultures, even though we often consider them to be similar.

Longitudinal research has affirmed what many global managers already know: employee attitudes and perceptions about work vary from country to country. As discussed in Chapter 7, employees typically value high ethical standards and volunteer activities and become more loyal and satisfied with their employer as a result. Thus, variations in employee attitudes and perceptions are integral to the successful implementation of social responsibility programs. For example, workers in France value a work-life balance more than any other national group. Japanese employees are often pleased with incentive compensation but lament relatively low base pay. Australians want a manager who acts as a coach and Chinese employees yearn for more training opportunities. In its annual survey, Mercer, an international research firm, identifies the factors most

TABLE 12.3 Differences in Employment Law: United States and Canada

Legal Issue	Canada	United States
Termination of Employment	Employers must give statutory notice of termination	Employment is "at will" and notice depends upon employment contracts or policies
Severance	Severance plans are uncommon and do not overrule statutory rights	Most severance plans require the employee to agree to a release of claims before receiving severance pay
Employment Litigation	Lawsuits against employers are generally settled quickly, and damage awards are predictable	Lawsuits against employers usually involve claims of human rights discrimination; litigation is costly, and damage awards are unpredictable
Compensation Disclosure	Despite new rules on disclosure, companies are not required to disclose the amounts of compensation actually received by executive officers from their exercise of options	Public companies must fully disclose the compensation of executives and board members in plain English, including the objectives and implementation of executive compensation programs
Healthcare Benefits	Single-payer universal healthcare system; hospital services are nonprofit, reducing administrative costs	Universal healthcare system involving many insurance companies and overhead; administrative costs very high

(Continued)

TABLE 12.3 *(Continued)*

Unions	No "right-to-work" laws that prohibit unions or for requiring employees covered by union contracts to pay; many provinces have bans on temporary or permanent striker replacement	Harder to get a union started; states beginning to pass "right-to-work" legislation which mandates that workers do not have to support a union even though they benefit from collective bargaining
Changes to Post-Retirement Benefits	Very difficult to decrease post-retirement benefits without providing notice; almost impossible to reduce benefits for existing retirees.	More flexibility in making changes to post-retirement benefits

Sources: Adapted from Christina Medland, "Ten Key Differences in Canadian and US Employment Law," *TLOMA Today*, April 22, 2008, http://tloma.com/docs/tloma-today/tloma-today-april-2008 (accessed June 22, 2016); Andrew MacDougall and Elizabeth Walker, "Trick or Treat? Changes to Canadian Executive Compensation Disclosure Rules Come into Effect October 31, 2011," Oslesr, August 3, 2011, http://www.osler.com/NewsResources/Details.aspx?id=3660 (accessed June 22, 2016); Adrienne Silnicki, "America, Want Freedom of Choice? Try Public Healthcare Like Canada," *The Guardian*, November 25, 2013, http://www.theguardian.com/commentisfree/2013/nov/25/america-canada-freedom-of-choice-public-healthcare (accessed June 22, 2016); Kris Warner, "The Real Reason for the Decline of American Unions," *Bloomberg*, January 23, 2013, http://www.bloombergview.com/articles/2013-01-23/the-real-reason-for-the-decline-of-american-unions (accessed June 22, 2016); Dave Jamieson, "Michigan Right To Work: Caught Off-Guard, Unions Hope To Stop Anti-Labor Law From Spreading," *Huffington Detroit,* December 11, 2012, http://www.huffingtonpost.com/2012/12/11/michigan-right-to-work-unions_n_2277900.html (accessed June 22, 2016).

employee engagement
The psychological state in which employees feel a vested interest in the company's success and are motivated to perform at levels that exceed job requirements.

important for **employee engagement**, the psychological state in which employees feel a vested interest in the company's success and are motivated to perform at levels that exceed job requirements. Table 12.4 depicts the results of Mercer's study of employees in different countries. The survey identifies four global drivers of employee engagement. Despite national differences, employees in different parts of the world are fairly consistent in noting the importance of (1) the work itself, including opportunities for development, (2) confidence and trust in leadership, (3) recognition and rewards, and (4) organizational communication. This information is valuable to managers, as it improves the cognitive nature of cultural intelligence and provides direction on motivational and behavioral competencies that should be impactful across nations. Understanding the four drivers enables human resource (HR) professionals to instill consistency across policies in a multinational firm.[13]

As discussed earlier in this chapter, cultural intelligence is an integral part of employees' ability to manage and succeed in a global economy. In the context of business ethics, CQ is especially critical. Applying the legal requirements of the host or home country to the problem may be a starting point. However, as we discussed in earlier chapters, legal standards are not sufficient for a firm dedicated to ethical business practices. Some industries operate under a set of values or principles, which may also serve a purpose in the international arena. For example, the tourism industry established

TABLE 12.4 Employee Engagement Factors in Six Countries

Brazil	Canada	China
• Sense of personal accomplishment • Confidence in senior management • Training opportunities • Fair pay based on performance • Good reputation for customer service • Comparable benefits for industry	• Being treated respectfully • Good work/life balance • Feeling they can provide good service to clients/customers	• Sense of personal accomplishment • Fair pay based on performance • Good reputation for customer service • Comparable benefits to industry • Confidence in senior management • IT systems support business needs • Training opportunities • Regular performance feedback
United States	**United Kingdom**	**Sweden**
• Confidence that career objectives can be met • Sense of personal accomplishment • Confident in organization's success • Quality is high priority • Opportunity for growth • Information and assistance to manage career • Flexibility to provide good customer service	• Sense of personal accomplishment • Confidence in senior management • Training opportunities • Fair pay based on performance • Good reputation for customer service • Comparable benefits to industry	• Respectful treatment • Type of work they are involved with • Sense of personal accomplishment

Source: Kathy Gurchiek, "Engagement Factors Vary by Country, Business, Function," *Society for Human Resource Management*, January 23, 2008, http://www.shrm.org/publications/hrnews/pages/engagementfactorsvary.aspx (accessed August 13, 2014).

a global code of ethics that enumerates the industry's obligation to build respect between societies, assist in sustainable development, maintain cultural heritage, treat employees well, and promote individual fulfillment.[14] In other cases, guidance from a broad set of guidelines, such as the Caux Round Table Principles for Business, could be utilized. However, broad principles are often less useful in day-to-day situations.

The ethical decision-making framework discussed in Chapter 5 is fully effective in the global environment, but cultural differences introduce new complexities to the process. For this reason, companies know that training rubrics are pivotal to an employee's ability to assess an ethical issue and determine the most appropriate decision and action. Organizations develop a fixed set of principles and values globally. While decisions have to comply with national and local laws, codes of conduct for the firm are implemented globally. There are usually adjustments in training approaches as well as certain ethical risks that may be more important to address in a particular country.

Consumer Relations

International trade leaves some members of the economy, whether independent or corporate, marginalized and vulnerable to economic exploitation. From some consumer perspectives, conventional trade interferes with the ability of many people, particularly those in poor nations, to secure basic, sustainable livelihoods. By contrast, **fair trade** is a trading partnership based on dialogue, transparency, and respect that seeks greater equity in international trade and contributes to sustainable development. Fair trade benefits those who have limited opportunities to begin with and are further stunted by market forces that identify them as negligible. Table 12.5 describes the five principles of fair trade organizations, including the rights and responsibilities of producers, intermediaries, business partners, resellers, and consumers.

fair trade
A trading partnership based on dialogue, transparency, and respect that seeks greater equity in international trade and contributes to sustainable development.

Products that meet fair trade standards are licensed to display the Fair Trade Certified label, signifying a producer's adherence to fair economic, social, and environmental practices in producing and selling products. There are nearly 12,000 fair trade certified products coming from approximately 1.2 million farmers and workers in 70 countries. Fair trade products are available in most grocery stores, restaurants, and cafes, all over the United States, contributing to the record volume growth year after year.[15]

As discussed in Chapter 8, consumers are increasingly concerned with the origins of products they purchase, including the working conditions, ethical standards, and related social responsibility practices of manufacturers. For example, low wages and substandard working conditions have marked

TABLE 12.5 Charter of Fair Trade Principles

Principle	Description
1. Market access for marginalized producers	Fair Trade helps producers realize the social benefits of traditional forms of production. It enables buyers to trade with producers who would otherwise be excluded from the markets. It helps shorten trade chains so that producers receive more from the final selling price of their goods than is the norm in conventional trade via multiple intermediaries.
2. Sustainable and equitable trading relationships	The economic basis of transactions within Fair Trade relationships takes account of all costs of production, both direct and indirect. Fair Trade buyers offer trading terms that enable producers and workers to maintain a sustainable livelihood. Prices and payment terms are determined by assessment of economic, social, and environmental factors rather than just reference to current market conditions. The commitment to long-term trading partnership found in Fair Trade enables both sides to cooperate through information sharing and planning.
3. Capacity building and empowerment	Fair Trade relationships assist producer organizations to understand more about market conditions and trends and to develop knowledge, skills, and resources to exert more control and influence over their lives.

(Continued)

TABLE 12.5 (*Continued*)

4. Consumer awareness raising and advocacy	Fair Trade relationships provide the basis for connecting producers with consumers and for informing consumers of the need for social justice and the opportunities for change. Consumer support enables Fair Trade organizations to be advocates and campaigners for wider reform of international trading rules and to achieve the ultimate goal of a just and equitable global trading system.
5. Fair trade as a "social contract"	Fair Trade transactions exist within an implicit "social contract" in which buyers agree to do more than is expected by the conventional market. In return, producers use the benefits of Fair Trade to improve their social and economic conditions, especially among the most disadvantaged members of the organization. Fair Trade is not charity but a partnership for change and development through trade.

Source: World Fair Trade Organization and Fairtrade Labelling Organizations International, *A Charter of Fair Trade Principles*, January 2009, http://www.wfto.com/sites/default/files/Charter-of-Fair-Trade-Principles-Final%20%28EN%29.PDF (accessed June 22, 2016).

the reputation of clothing manufacturers. In an effort to minimize these costs, Fair Trade USA began certifying apparel. PrAna, a yoga apparel company, is one of the first American firms to receive this certification. The certification comes from verification of sources of materials as well as a review of the company's books, systems, and pay scales.[16] Today, PrAna sells at least nine fair trade certified products.

Rice farming is present all over the world and is responsible for billions of jobs, making it an important aspect in the social well-being of numerous communities. Pesticides and chemicals used in rice farming initially increase production, but they eventually reduce production and negatively affect workers' health. A decline in global rice prices puts farmers in difficult situations. When prices fall, some farmers apply for loans that may carry high interest rates while others might lose their livelihoods. Areas particularly dense with rice farms are reported to have high suicide rates and incidents of children being sold for sex. Fair trade rice seeks to improve these conditions by providing stability in the market, seeking organic methods, and regulating the use of chemicals in production.[17]

The Fair Trade Certified label is not only recognized by 73 percent of American consumers but is also a trusted symbol among this group. There is a high level of durability among fair trade certified products even during times of economic downturn. This is due in large part to the system of standards of the Fair Trade organization. In order to continue to remain relevant, they are committed to revising these standards every five years. For example, Fair Trade USA announced it would revise the previously separate standards for farmers and independent growers by combining them to apply to both groups. Such a move reduces complexity and allows for consistency and relevance in the certification process. Table 12.6 shows some of the Fair Trade Certified brands currently on the market.[18]

TABLE 12.6 Fair Trade Certified Brands

Allegro Coffee Company	Appalachian Coffee Company	Arrowhead Mills
Barefoot & Chocolate LLC	Bhakti Inc.	Bigelow Tea
Celestial Seasonings	China Mist	Chocolate Alchemy
Clearly Kombucha	Dawn Food Products	Eco Lips INC
General Mills	Good & Fair Clothing	Green Mountain Coffee Roasters
Hershey Company	Honest Tea	Lundberg Family Farms
Naked Juice Company	Organic Spices	Traditional Medicinals

Source: "Products and Partners," *Fair Trade USA,* http://fairtradeusa.org/products-partners?partner_type=Brandholder#tabset-tab-2 (accessed June 22, 2016).

GLOBAL DEVELOPMENT

Companies are increasing efforts to enhance the infrastructure, human rights, and educational systems of a particular country, state, or city to further global development. Experts have concluded that political, social, and economic freedoms are fundamental to national competitiveness and development. Without widespread trust and the effective operations of different institutions, a given society will not be able to enhance and enrich the lives of its people. Political freedoms, such as free speech and elections, lead to economic security, and social freedoms such as education and healthcare lead to stronger economic participation. Finally, economic security frees people to participate in social and political activities.[19] Multinational corporations are increasingly interested in mechanisms for promoting freedom and development.

development
An improvement in the economic, environmental, educational, and health conditions of a country.

Development refers to improvement in the economic, environmental, educational, and health conditions of a country. Common issues in development include poverty, quality of healthcare, access to education, voting rights, water quality, governance and rule of law, domestic finance systems, and climate change. A major goal of the United Nations (UN) is to realize improvements in the development of countries around the world. While these improvements may be grounded in ethical concerns, they are critical to the stability of the global economy. The UN works from the philosophy that it is in the world's best interest to tackle problems that limit the capacity of some people to live healthy and prosperous lives. The UN's Millennium Development Goals are designed to meet these challenges and have established the following goals: (1) eradicate extreme poverty and hunger, (2) achieve universal primary education, (3) eliminate gender disparity in primary and secondary education, (4) reduce child mortality, (5) improve maternal health, (6) combat HIV/AIDS, malaria, and other diseases, (7) ensure environmental sustainability, and (8) develop a global partnership for development.[20] Meeting these goals and finding solutions to these problems progress the economy and improves the lives of individuals in areas heavily affected by these issues.

The UN also established the Global Compact, which encourages organizations to commit to common principles whereby effective and responsible business can be conducted on a global scale. The UN's Global Compact is a set of ten universally accepted principles (See Table 12.7) in the areas of human rights, labor, environment, and anti-corruption, to which approximately 10,000 organizations have officially declared their commitment. Corporate signatories attest to their willingness to integrate these principles into everyday business practices, publish examples of their commitment and projects on an annual basis, and commit to a stronger alignment between the objectives of the international community and those of the business world.[21]

Although the UN has been most progressive in gaining corporate support for global development and popularizing business partnerships, corporations have aligned themselves with non-business organizations to advance development for a number of years.[22] For example, a company interested in building an offshore call center may realize roadways and utilities need to be improved in the area. In another situation, a firm may know a natural resource is abundant in a developing country, yet realizes the people and government of the country do not have the economic and educational resources to market it worldwide. In both cases, the company may choose to invest resources by partnering with the local government, nonprofit agencies, and other nongovernmental organizations. Critics muse that while this approach certainly has a social component, the business case for making a profit is the overriding concern. An extensive review

TABLE 12.7 Ten Principles of the UN Global Compact

Human Rights
1. Support and respect the protection of internationally proclaimed human rights
2. Ensure nonparticipation in human rights abuses
Labor
3. Uphold the freedom of association and the effective recognition of the right to collective bargaining
4. Eliminate all forms of forced and compulsory labour
5. Abolition of child labour
6. Eliminate discrimination with respect to employment and occupation
Environment
7. Support a precautionary approach to environmental challenges
8. Undertake initiatives to promote greater environmental responsibility
9. Encourage the development and diffusion of environmentally friendly technologies
Anticorruption
10. Work against corruption in all its forms, including extortion and bribery

Source: "Ten Principles," United Nations Global Compact, http://www.unglobalcompact.org/AboutTheGC/TheTenPrinciples/index.html (accessed June 22, 2016).

of the outcomes of development partnerships between large oil companies and local governments in the Nigerian Delta region revealed (1) the linkage between improvement in social infrastructures and economic growth is nonexistent, (2) it is almost impossible for business investments to make significant gains because these communities have long been neglected, and (3) business-driven investment in social infrastructure has been unevenly distributed and failed to prioritize community needs.[23]

There are many diverse types of partnerships for development. While the partnership consists of at least one public entity and one private entity, the specific kinds of public and private entities involved vary to include a wide range of social and economic players. However, each partnership must confront two elements: (1) the level of social control via stakeholder influence they maintain and (2) the challenges they pose to conventional business management and goals. In lieu of these two points, partnerships for development may be categorized into four types: conventional business partnerships, corporate social responsibility partnerships, corporate accountability partnerships, and social economy partnerships. Table 12.8 provides a brief description of the four types.

TABLE 12.8 Partnerships for Development of Social Responsibility

Conventional business partnerships

These partnerships focus on efficient and effective decisions to carry out a business objective when there is limited competition. Social responsibility is not a strategic concern. Example: Tennessee Valley Authority

Corporate social responsibility partnerships

Businesses make a profit but also serve the public interest. Through voluntary cooperative relationships, businesses and their partners arrive at a win-win authentic partnership. They thrive and prosper for their stakeholders. Example: Starbucks supports coffee growers in receiving a fair wage.

Corporate accountability partnerships

These partnerships focus on rules and structure with an emphasis on ethics, compliance, and social responsibility. ISO 19600, based on the Australian standard for compliance management, is being adopted as an international benchmark. ISO 19600 standards provide an accountability audit to social responsibility.

Social economy partnerships

These are based on partnerships between nonprofit organizations and businesses. Both parties help to develop and institutionalize objectives to benefit society. Example: Home Depot partners with Habitat for Humanity

Sources: Ananya Mukherjee Reed and Darryl Reed, "Partnerships for Development: Four Models of Business Development," *Journal of Business Ethics* 90, supplement 1 (May 2009): 3-37; Maria May Seitanidi and Andrew Crane, "Implementing CSR Through Partnerships: Understanding the Selection, Design and Institutionalisation of Nonprofit-Business Partnerships," *Journal of Business Ethics* 85, supplement 2 (April 2008): 413-429; Scott James, "CSR Means True Partnerships," *Forbes*, July 30, 2011, http://www.forbes.com/sites/csr/2011/07/30/csr-means-true-partnerships/ (accessed June 22, 2016); CompliSpace, "A New Global Standard for Compliance: ISO 19600," September 15, 2014, http://complispace.wordpress.com/2014/09/15/a-new-global-standard-for-compliance-iso-19600/ (accessed June 22, 2016).

Conventional Business Partnerships

Conventional business partnerships (CBPs) for development may seem unlikely. However, in the case of some public services, such as utilities, they do sometimes emerge. The goal of these partnerships is to promote efficiency in markets where competition does not exist. This assumes that states are inefficient and that a business organization provides the best solution. The role of business is to increase efficiency, while the role of government is to make sure that the benefits of increased efficiency are delivered to consumers. Government also monitors access to and affordability of the public service. CBPs do not have to prove a specific effort toward social responsibility but are commonly recognized and supported by the United Nations, World Bank, and other supraregional organizations. Specifically, these organizations have sought privatization through conventional business partnerships.

Privatization occurs when public operations are sold to private entities. Public-private partnerships count as partial privatization. Full privatization further reduces the public element of the equation. Social services often attract privatization interest, particularly those in developing nations since privatization provides a point of entry into new markets for investors. But long-standing public provision of goods and services carries deeply imbedded interests in keeping the goods and services public.[24]

privatization
A process that occurs when public operations are sold to private entities. Public-private partnerships count as partial privatization.

The World Bank began advocating the privatization of public utilities in the early 1990s and eventually, this became a requirement for some countries seeking substantial loans. While there have been successes, water privatization efforts in Bolivia provides a stark reminder that CBPs may be fraught with difficulty. Protesters in El Alto, Bolivia demanded control of water be taken back from Suez, a French water company affiliated with the World Bank. Within three days, the President of Bolivia met the public's demand and cancelled the deal. Five years earlier, Bolivian citizens protested against the control of water by the Bechtel Corporation. That protest was much more dramatic and violent, with the government declaring martial law. At this time, however, the reluctance to cancel the foreign control of water service was due to financial and political pressure. Cancellation of this deal would have made foreign investors hesitant to pursue investment opportunities in the country, and Bolivia was forced to privatize in order to receive much needed aid from the World Bank. While many citizens did not agree with the principle of privatizing water service, their outrage came from the practical results that followed the change in service. Theoretically, privatization would bring investment and successful management to services traditionally run with little efficiency and much corruption. When implemented, however, investment translated to unaffordable, market rate pricing, and successful management translated into indifference to poor social conditions that were either introduced or exacerbated by privatization.[25] The World Bank eventually softened its position by becoming open to other options besides privatization, but the idea that poor governments need to increase their reliance on private agents for political and economic risks remains.

Corporate Social Responsibility Partnerships

Corporate social responsibility partnerships (CSRPs) are voluntary and business centered. Potential benefits alone compel individual businesses to enter into these partnerships, and success rests in the motivation causing corporate engagement. Such motivation may be philosophical or ethical, though it may be that pragmatic concerns are the major sources of motivation. CSRPs provide resources for social initiatives, such as job training and entrepreneurial development, that contribute to a citizen's livelihood. While these initiatives benefit members of society, they also provide for a stronger work force and economic contagion. Microcredit programs are part of CSRP's activity in resource provision, with the largest such partnership being the Global Microcredit Summit, a nonprofit organization dedicated to improving access to credit and financial self-sufficiency for the poorest people in the world.[26]

Microcredit activity began in Bangladesh. The initiative produced remarkable success to the extent that prominent figures of the endeavor, Grameen Bank and its founder Muhammad Yunus, received the Nobel Peace Prize. Microcredit works toward moving large populations out of poverty through financial assistance. Grameen Bank remains an influential model for microcredit institutions and partnerships all over the world. While microcredit allows borrowers to take action that directly improves their income, indirect improvements such as quality of life also result. Borrowers have access to better housing, food, sanitation, and education and are better able to take advantage of the improved options.[27]

Corporate Accountability Partnerships

The final two categories of partnerships for development take a distrust of corporate social responsibility models as a starting point for defining their framework. Corporate accountability partnerships (CAP) spring from the idea that corporate social responsibility partnerships are neither accountable nor effective and are only really interested in public relations. As the name implies, corporate accountability partnerships focus on accountability and the setting of requirements and standards based on what society expects.

For corporate accountability partnerships to be successful, they must gain and direct public support, maximize the limited resources they tend to have, plan for the long-term, and convince public institutions of the necessity and importance of enforcing socially demanded standards. Corporate accountability partnerships use legal and social means, ranging from policy and certification initiatives to protests and activism. Certification CAPs focus mainly on labor rights and the environment and try to achieve answerability, enforcement, and universality. CAPs seek to achieve corporate recognition of standards deemed appropriate by society and utilize third party audits and checks on the partnership.

A widely known certification CAP is the Fair Labor Association (FLA), which was organized after numerous media reports decrying child labor, poor working conditions, and low wages were released. Today, the FLA works to end sweatshop conditions for factory workers and organizes universities, social groups, and socially responsible organizations to protect workers' rights and insist on better working conditions all over the globe. Nestlé is an example of a corporation working with the FLA to ensure fair labor conditions. The cocoa industry is notorious for forced and child labor conditions, and as one of the world's largest food companies, Nestlé allowed the FLA to conduct a review of labor conditions throughout the entire supply chain. The FLA commented that this was the first such review of a multinational company. The findings concluded that, despite implementation of industry standards, many violations were still occurring. In the Ivory Coast, especially, both child and forced labor are culturally normal behaviors. Nestlé now knows that better communication of labor practices, along with stronger oversight, farther down the supply chain are needed in order to come closer to eliminating these undesirable labor practices.[28]

Social Economy Partnerships

Social economy partnerships (SEPs) pursue alternatives to conventional corporations and profit maximization. SEPs have a distinctly social purpose, use democratic governance, and cooperate with other social economy partnerships. Social economy organizations include nonprofits, community economic development corporations, cooperatives, and cooperative development organizations.

The SEP philosophy emphasizes cooperation and assistance rather than traditional business logic. These partnerships provide resources and support mostly in informal sectors of the urban poor. SEPs bring people together for recycling, street vending, and other work that many other citizens will not perform. Entrepreneurship is viewed collectively and the group stays connected to social and political movements. Social economy partnerships in these informal sectors provide economic profits as well as social benefits that are usually reserved for those with full-time jobs in the formal sector. The Self Employed Women's Association is a trade union in India for poor, self-employed women. These women compose the majority of the labor force but are part of the unorganized sector and are not provided with the regular salaries and benefits. The SEWA organizes cooperative arrangements to help women find regular employment, increase their incomes, become literate, access better healthcare, obtain child care, and increase their financial assets. Through various cooperatives, women obtain insurance, get assistance in marketing their goods worldwide, participate in leadership training, and access significant loans and banking products. Without SEWA and its extended partnerships, these women would be destined for a life of poverty.[29]

Ethical Responsibilities in Finance

Rabobank: Banking on Cooperatives

Cooperatives are organizations that seek a variety of benefits by approaching economics and entrepreneurship in social terms. Instead of investors, the co-op is developed by members who have one vote a piece in governance matters. The integration of business and social interests is made easier by the democratic governance of the co-op. Equality in voting also means accountability and transparency are requisite. A co-op may have individual people as members or it may have small business and organization members. While cooperatives are usually surprisingly successful financially, the traditional dynamics that motivate and relate owners, consumers, and workers are altered. However, cooperatives still have to operate in a sound business manner and try to produce a surplus similar to a profit.

The cooperative began to emerge in the beginning of the nineteenth century in Europe. First, owners of a cotton mill in Scotland came together in order to extend the distribution of profits to employees. A few years later, a group of English textile workers called the Rochdale Pioneers established a cooperative in 1844. This cooperative joined together weavers and other artisans who were facing poverty, yet decided they should pool their meager resources to open a store selling food they could no longer afford. They opened their store with a small number of items but quickly expanded their product range. Before long, the Rochdale Pioneers offered one of the best selections of food and household items in the area and was fully meeting its objective: *to form arrangements for the pecuniary benefit and the improvement of the social and domestic conditions of its members*. The concept spread to a variety of industries and countries.

Rabobank is a group of Dutch banks that has its origins in two rural cooperative banks founded in 1898. In 1972, the two banks merged to form Rabobank. Rabobank has 106 local member banks and is identified as one of the safest cooperative banks in the world. Rabobank's growth was made possible through the retention of its profits. It is owned and controlled by its members and works for its members. Rabobank has always had a commitment to corporate social responsibility and implements social responsibility in its lending practices. Accordingly, in making credit decisions, Rabobank assesses a company's strategy and track record for handling sensitive issues that call for corporate social responsibility.

Rabobank views companies that lack social responsibility as a credit risk and also a risk to the co-op's reputation. For this reason, it has an Ethics Committee that is tasked with assessing ethical issues, developing ethics policies, publishing recommendations, strengthening employee confidence in ethical decision-making, and discussing social issues in which the bank should take a stand. Rabobank also developed a CSR spectrum to describe how corporate social responsibility is integrated into daily activities:

- Ambition and Identity
  - CSR ambitions
  - CSR organization
- Client & financial services
  - CSR in client acceptance process
  - CSR client engagement
  - Sustainable products & services
- Social engagement
  - Social activities
  - Dialogue with stakeholders
- Business operations
  - Internal environment policy
  - Internal personnel policy

Sources: Kevin M. Blakely, "At Rabobank, It's All About the Customer," *The RMA Journal 91*, no. 10 (July/August 2000): 36–43 (accessed via ProQuest Database); Riccardo Lottie, Peter Mensing, and Davide Valenti, "A Cooperative Solution," *Strategy + Business 43* (Summer 2006); David Thompson, "Co-op Principles: Then and Now (Parts 1 and 2)," http://www.grocer.coop/articles/co-op-principles-then-and-now-parts-1-and-2 (accessed August 9, 2016); Rabobank, "The dynamics of ethics," https://www.rabobank.com/en/about-rabobank/in-society/ethics/index.html (accessed August 9, 2016); Peter Vos, "Water: The Need to Pay the Due," Rabobank, http://www.unep.org/resourceefficiency/Portals/24147/scp/water/documents/Presentations/Rabobank%20(Peter%20Vos).pdf (accessed August 9, 2016); Rabobank, "Rabobank members agree to new governance," December 2, 2015, https://www.rabobank.com/en/press/search/2015/Rabobank_governance%20.html (accessed August 9, 2016).

The four models of business involvement in development allow almost any firm the opportunity to engage in partnerships that improve health, education, economic, and other prospects for people around the world. In addition to corporate efforts, individual countries are also engaged in development efforts. The Center for Global Development produces a Commitment to Development Index (CDI) that ranks 27 developed nations by their contributions to and support of development in poorer, developing countries. While these contributions are considered the right thing to do and usually reflect national ideals and values, there are also benefits to global security and economic health. Countries included in the index are assessed based on governmental policy efforts in areas including aid, trade, investment, migration, the environment, security, and technology. Policy efforts are used as indicators partly to control for the varying sizes of economies among the countries ranked. For the CDI, policies of rich countries, particularly the coherence of those policies, are important to development. The CDI also shows evidence that development involves more than monetary aid and that partnerships can provide greater benefits than the individual partners can produce alone.[30]

GLOBAL REPORTING INITIATIVE

Regardless of the social responsibility activities a company pursues, it must also consider the best mechanisms for communicating its values and plans, highlighting successes, and gaining feedback for the future. In some cases, a firm may be a signatory to a set of standards, member of a particular association, or otherwise obligated to formally assess and document social responsibility outcomes. As stated earlier, companies that commit to the Global Compact are required to present an annual account of how they implement the ten principles and support the UN's development goals. This document, entitled the Communication on Progress, may be part of the company's annual report, sustainability report, or some other social reporting mechanism.

The Global Reporting Initiative (GRI) provides a framework for businesses and other organizations to assess their performance across an array of social responsibility indicators. A firm may use this as a self-audit, but others choose to formally share the audit results with stakeholders. One of the greatest benefits of the GRI is that it makes comparisons possible because it uses a globally applicable and well vetted framework. The GRI emphasizes consensus and continuous improvement in developing and maintaining the GRI Sustainability Reporting Framework, which seeks to provide transparency and accountability in sustainability reporting akin to that found in financial reporting. Diverse representatives contribute business, civil, academic, labor, and other professional perspectives in deciding which areas of sustainability are to be included in the framework and the appropriate measures to be used for determining performance in those areas. The framework is in perpetual draft form, with innovation in technologies and shifts in cultural attitudes accommodated by the GRI's continuous improvement approach.

The GRI Sustainability Reporting Framework includes three categories of core indicators: economic, environmental, and social performance. The social category of core indicators is further divided into labor practice, human rights, product responsibility, and society. Quantitative or qualitative performance indicators are used to evaluate different aspects of each category.

The economic category examines an organization's interaction with the economic system in which it operates by measuring economic performance, market presence, and indirect economic impact indicators. The environmental category covers an organization's energy use, both direct and indirect, as well as pollution. The category assumes a link between energy consumption and emissions that contribute to climate change, and thus emphasizes efficient energy use and an increasing reliance on renewable energy sources over fossil fuel.

The society category examines the organization as it functions in relation to market structures and social institutions. Measures include the impact on local communities, bribery and corruption, and public policy making. The human rights indicators consider the operation of an organization as it provides for basic human rights. Measures include incidents regarding human rights and provisions made for such rights in an organization's internal and external business relationships. The labor practices category is an extension of the human rights category that focuses specifically on the environment and practices to which workers are subject. An examination of workforce demographics, communications between the organization and its employees, and opportunities extended to workers for personal development comprise the category's measurements. Finally, the product responsibility category focuses on the products of an organization as they affect consumers. Considerations such as safety, product information, and privacy rights of customers are evaluated. Indicators appear in pairs with one addressing the relevant processes of the organization and the second addressing the compliance of the organization.[31]

SUMMARY

In this chapter, we discussed a variety of social responsibility issues and stakeholders from a global perspective. The expanding global marketplace requires that executives and managers develop the ability to conduct business effectively and in a socially responsible way the world over. The movement of people across cities and continents means that ideas, values, traditions, languages, and customs have also migrated and global employees need many skills. Cultural intelligence is the ability to interpret and adapt successfully to different national, organizational, and professional cultures. There are three components to the development and use of cultural intelligence, including cognitive, motivational and behavioral. Cultural intelligence is desired of all employees but is mandatory for those who work in different countries, manage diverse groups, and have responsibilities that require them to interpret unfamiliar behaviors and situations.

Cultural intelligence is critical for dealing effectively with stakeholders, including customers, investors and shareholders, employees, suppliers, governments, communities and others. Stakeholders in other countries and cultures will bring unique insights and attitudes to bear on the business relationship, including differences in economic, legal, ethical, and philanthropic expectations. We delved into a few trends related to stakeholders in the global economy, including the Caux Round Table Principles for Business, fair trade, employee engagement, and others.

The reflexive nature of the global economy means that the success of a particular company is a function of many factors, including the extent to which the firm's home country is comprised of trust-based institutions. Some nations have well-developed systems for ensuring economic, legal, and ethical standards in business activities. In other cases, corporations are interested in a particular market but know that fundamental institutions and standards are sorely underdeveloped and negatively affect market potential. The four models of business involvement in development allows almost any firm the opportunity to engage in partnerships that improve health, education, economic, and other prospects for people around the world. In addition to corporate efforts, individual countries are also engaged in development efforts.

Finally, the Global Reporting Initiative (GRI) provides a framework for businesses and other organizations to assess their performance across an array of social responsibility indicators. A firm may use this as a self-audit but others choose to formally share the audit results with stakeholders. One of the greatest benefits of the GRI is that it makes comparisons possible because it uses a globally applicable and well-vetted framework.

Responsible Business Debate

Europe's Wood Harvesting from the United States

Issue: *Is it ethical for the European Union to harvest wood from the United States to meet its energy goals?*

The European Union (EU) is known for their strict environmental goals for reducing greenhouse gas emissions. In 2007, the EU's environmental agency set the goal of incorporating renewable energy sources that will account for 20 percent of their overall power by the year 2020. While renewable sources such as wind and solar are being used, many of the EU's power plants run on coal energy. As a result, the EU has decided to power their plants with wood instead of coal. Wood is a cleaner fuel source than coal and is said to be renewable because trees can be replanted. However, this creates a significant challenge for the EU. The EU requires that loggers obtain permits before they begin cutting down trees, and there are many restrictions as to where and how many trees can be cut. Additionally, the amount of forests in the EU is significantly less than in the United States, and the United States does not have as many logging restrictions.

For these reasons the EU has contracted with logging companies in the southern United States to cut, press, and ship wood pellets. Many in the industry are happy about this new demand, since the closing of paper mills in the area have created unemployment. The EU states that they only take small trees and branches from these forests and only from forests that can successfully be reforested. Furthermore, it is said that newer trees absorb more carbon dioxide than older ones, so once trees have been cut, new trees are planted.

However, environmentalists are concerned that the scope of the demand will deteriorate the forests. There are not strict controls for cutting, and sometimes older trees constitute some of the material for the pellets. Cutting older trees could defeat the purpose for clean energy as the older trees harbor large amounts of carbon, which is released once it is burned.

Despite assurances, large-scale clear-cutting is taking place in these forests. Because this is a fairly new territory for renewable energy, there are no set guidelines nor is one entity officially held accountable for how the forests are being cut. Clear-cutting is mostly illegal in the EU with a few exceptions. Critics see the EU as going against their own environmental laws as a means of achieving energy goals. Environmentalists also fear that due to the demand and lack of strict controls, some U.S. wetlands and other sensitive areas are being logged.

In one year, Europe burned 6.7 million tons of wood pellets, and America supplied 1.9 million tons of those pellets. The European consumption of pellets is expected to double by 2020, and the American contribution has been exponentially growing. The EU is aware of the challenges between their laws and their practices in the United States, and they are making an effort to analyze the rules and influence the policy. As a general rule, suppliers adhere to state-recommended best-management practices, and customers are allowed to investigate operations as a means of control.

There Are Two Sides to Every Issue:

1. It is acceptable for the European Union to harvest American wood because wood is cleaner than coal and the harvesting is done as sustainably as possible.

2. It is unacceptable for the European Union to harvest American wood because it destroys American forests and will have negative long-term consequences.

Sources: Justin Scheck and Ianthe Jeanne Dugan, "Europe's Green-Fuel Search Turns to America's Forests," *The Wall Street Journal,* May 27, 2013, http://online.wsj.com/article/SB10001424127887324082604578485491298208114.html?mod=ITP_pageone_0 (accessed August 9, 2016); Michael Bastasch, "Europe Importing US Trees to Keep the Lights On," May 28, 2013, Daily Caller, http://dailycaller.com/2013/05/28/europe-importing-u-s-trees-to-keep-the-lights-on/ (accessed August 9, 2016); Sasha Lyutse's Blog, National Resources Defense Council (NRDC), "How European Power Companies Skirt Their Own Environmental Rules By Logging in the U.S. Forests For Fuel," *Switchboard,* May 29, 2013, http://switchboard.nrdc.org/blogs/slyutse/how_european_power_companies_s.html (accessed August 9, 2016).

KEY TERMS

cultural intelligence (p. 404)
employee engagement (p. 412)

fair trade (p. 414)
development (p. 416)

privatization (p. 419)

DISCUSSION QUESTIONS

1. Define *cultural intelligence* in your own terms. Compare your definition with the definition used in this chapter.
2. How are stakeholder relationships in a global context different from those in a domestic context? In what ways are they alike?
3. What is the likelihood that corporate leaders agree on a global set of social responsibility standards? What evidence do you have?
4. How can organizations create stronger engagement with employees? What would be the effects on social responsibility? How would social responsibility affect engagement?
5. Define *fair trade* in your own terms. In what ways should consumers consider fair trade issues when making purchases and investments?
6. Review the UN Global Compact principles in Table 12.7. In what ways are these principles and issues related to a successful global economy? What benefits and/or challenges do they present to multinational corporations?
7. What are some ways that a company can measure its progress to comply with global reporting initiative guidelines? Propose both quantitative and qualitative measures.

EXPERIENTIAL EXERCISE

Choose two multinational companies, each based in a different home country, and visit their respective websites. Peruse these sites for information that is directed at three company stakeholders: employees, customers, and the community. Make a list of the types of information that are on the site and indicate how the information might be used and perceived by these three stakeholder groups. What differences and similarities did you find between the two companies? How are the differences attributable to cultural nuances?

MANUFACTURING MISCONDUCT: WHAT WOULD YOU DO?

Jaime and Catherine looked at each other. Each was thinking, "How do we do this?," but offered no immediate suggestions. Both were mid-level executives with a multinational corporation that manufactured clothing, handbags, and accessories in developing countries, including Guatemala and Honduras. The company is a member of the Fair Labor Association and takes pride in its commitment to a safe, healthy, and equitable work environment for all employees. Jaime, a native of Mexico, had professional experience in Peru, Chile, and Mexico. Catherine, a native of the United States, spoke fluent Spanish and was being groomed to take international assignments. Two weeks ago, the Vice President of Latin American Operations called Jaime and Catherine, asking them to take on an internal consulting project.

The Vice President was concerned about rumors surrounding the company's largest manufacturing site in Honduras. This site employed over 1,000 people, the majority of whom worked in low-skilled

manufacturing roles. Although no employee had come forward, or used the firm's ethics hotline, the site's regional manager (RM) was concerned about management practices and workplace conditions. Each time the RM visited the site, he sensed that he was not experiencing the daily "reality" of the manufacturing site. So far, he had little proof but decided to share his concerns with other executives. Specifically, he was worried about (1) possible intimidation of union members and leaders, (2) discriminatory management tactics, and (3) forced overtime that was not properly compensated.

Two weeks later, Jaime and Catherine arrived at the site, tasked with determining whether management practices and workplace conditions were compatible with corporate standards and FLA principles. First, they need to develop a plan for gathering information from employees, including those who were either scared of retaliation or generally mistrusting of corporate management. What would you do?

Uber Faces Ethical and Regulatory Challenges[*]

Uber Technologies, Inc. (Uber) is a tech startup that provides ride-sharing services by facilitating a connection between independent contractors (drivers) and riders with the use of an app. Uber has expanded its operations to 300 cities around the world and is valued at around $60 billion. Because its services cost less than taking a traditional taxi, in the few years it has been in business, Uber and similar ride-sharing services have upended the taxi industry. The company has experienced resounding success and is looking toward expansion both domestically and abroad.

However, Uber's rapid success is creating ethical challenges in the form of legal and regulatory, social, and technical obstacles. The taxi industry, for instance, is arguing that Uber has an unfair advantage because it does not face the same licensing requirements as they do. Others accuse Uber of not vetting their drivers, creating potentially unsafe situations for their passengers. An accusation of rape in India brought this issue of safety to the forefront. Some major cities are banning ride-sharing services like Uber because of these various concerns. Other cities are making it increasingly difficult for Uber to operate. For instance, the firm left Austin, Texas because the city adopted unfavorable regulation that required fingerprint background checks. Additionally, Uber has faced various lawsuits, including a lawsuit filed by its independent contractors. Its presence in the market has influenced lawmakers to draft new regulations to govern these ride-sharing systems. Legislation can often hinder a company's expansion opportunities because of the resources it must expend to comply with regulatory requirements.

On the other hand, Uber is highly praised for giving independent contractors an opportunity to earn money as long as they have a car, while also offering convenient ways for consumers to get around at lower costs. Although its "Surge Pricing" technique has been criticized for charging higher fares during popular times, it is becoming a model for other companies. For instance, Zappos is adopting Uber's surge pricing strategy in how it compensates its call center employees. The biggest issues Uber faces include legal actions because drivers are not licensed, rider and driver safety, protection and security of customer and driver information, and a lack of adequate insurance coverage. To be successful Uber must address these issues so it can reduce resistance as it expands into other cities.

BACKGROUND

Uber is probably the most well-known company that operates in the sharing economy. The sharing economy refers to an economic model that involves the sharing of underutilized resources. Although Uber was not the first firm to operate in the sharing economy, it has largely popularized this new economic model, paving the way for other firms to begin offering services in other industries.

The story of Uber began in 2009 when co-founders Travis Kalanick and Garrett Camp developed a smartphone application to connect drivers-for-hire with people needing rides to a destination in their city. This innovative service was originally founded as UberCab, Inc., a privately held company. It was renamed Uber Technologies, Inc. in 2010. Co-founders Kalanick and Camp designed the mobile app for iPhone and Android smartphones, enabling customers to get an estimated time of arrival from the driver on their smartphone with the use of an integrated GPS system. Uber has been referred to as a "labor-broker," a firm that connects people who need transportation services with those willing to provide them.

Consumers liked the Uber app because of its convenience and ease-of-use. After the mobile app is downloaded to their smartphones, passengers can pay for the rides-for-hire service through a third party, known as a Transportation Network Company (TNC),

*This case was developed by Jennifer Sawayda under the direction of O.C. and Linda Ferrell. Noushin Laila Ansari, Lecia Weber, Sederick Hood, and Christian Otto developed an earlier version of this case under the direction of O. C. Ferrell and Linda Ferrell, Belmont University. This case was prepared for classroom discussion rather than to illustrate effective or ineffective handling of an administrative situation. ©O.C. Ferrell and Linda Ferrell, 2016.

using the UberX platform that scans or takes a picture of their credit card with the smartphone's camera. Uber does not maintain automobile inventory for drivers, such as a fleet of taxicabs or limousines. Instead, each driver-for-hire supplies his or her own personal automobile, gas, insurance, and maintenance of his or her own car. Drivers can drive their own cars where they want when they want, providing them with significant freedom to run their own small businesses. A surge pricing model is used during times of peak demand. While Uber initially charged about a 20 percent commission, it later introduced a tiered structure in some cities that charged different commission rates depending upon the number of hours worked. For instance, in San Francisco a driver pays Uber a 30 percent commission on the first 20 rides in the week, 25 percent on the next 20 rides, and 20 percent on rides after that.

Due to the increased demand in the rides-for-hire industry, Uber has an estimated total valuation of $60 billion. Uber recently relocated to new headquarters in San Francisco, providing office space for nearly 700 employees. In the near future, it plans to expand to two 10-story buildings, increasing its total square feet of office space utilization to more than 700,000 square feet.

Uber Technologies, Inc. provides rides-for-hire services to 300 cities worldwide. Uber maintains a presence in major U.S. cities including Los Angeles, San Francisco, New York City, Chicago, Washington D.C., and Boston. Uber technology-based products are available under these various brands: UberX, UberXL, UberPop, UberBlack, UberSUV, UberTaxi, UberLux, UberSelect, UberPool, and the logistics-request brands referred to as UberRush and UberEats. Uber has also upgraded its current navigation service (Google and Apple) with deCarta Mapping Company. This new mapping system will continue to improve Uber's navigation and location technologies.

UBER'S MARKETING STRATEGY

Like all companies, Uber must understand its target market and maintain a strong marketing mix to be successful. Due to its technology, Uber does not have as many constraints as taxicabs, although it has encountered regulatory obstacles and public resistance. The Uber business model takes advantage of the smartphone technology of consumers and links them with independent drivers as their cabs. This provides a more potentially efficient and less expensive way to purchase transportation.

PRODUCTS

Uber's service products are digitally mediated via a smartphone app that consumers download. When they want to request a ride, they can use the app to contact a driver in the near vicinity. The Uber app allows consumers to track the location of the car and alerts them to when the car arrives.

Uber offers a few different services to customers based upon their preferences. Its most used service is UberX, the low-budget option. Drivers use their own vehicles to transport passengers. UberTaxi is an app that connects licensed taxi drivers to passengers. UberBlack is for consumers who desire to have their own private driver in a high-end sedan. UberSelect costs twice as much as UberX but less than UberBlack. UberSelect uses vehicle brands like BMW and Lexus. UberSUV connects users with SUVs, while UberLux is the most expensive service with luxury vehicles. UberXL is similar to UberSUV but costs 50 percent less. Other low-cost options include UberPool, which allows passengers to share rides and split the costs, and UberPop, a service costing less than UberX because it utilizes nonprofessional drivers and smaller cars. Despite the opportunities UberPop provides, its use of nonprofessional drivers has led to regulatory issues in different countries.

Uber is also attempting to expand into other services. Its UberRush app, launched in New York., Chicago, and San Francisco, is used for package deliveries. Uber is marketing its UberRush service to businesses who want to provide on-demand delivery to their clients. UberEats is a meal delivery app that partners with local restaurants to offer meals to consumers within 10 minutes. These new services are allowing Uber to branch out and expand its services into different businesses.

DISTRIBUTION

One major reason Uber is so popular is because its app allows users to contact any drivers in the near vicinity. Drivers use the Uber app to provide them with directions. It is estimated that Uber has more than 450,000 drivers in the United States who make at least four trips. The number of drivers has doubled every 6 months for the past 2 years. Los Angeles, San Francisco, New York, Chicago, Washington D.C., and Boston have the most drivers in the United States. Most Uber drivers offer their ride-sharing services on a part-time basis.

To be successful, Uber engages in strategic partnerships with other companies. In the United States, it has partnered with American Express. Card members enrolled in American Express's Membership Rewards program can earn points with Uber for rides. Strategic partnerships with local firms are especially important as Uber expands internationally because it allows the company to utilize the resources and knowledge of domestic firms familiar with the country's culture. Uber has partnered with Times Internet in India, Baidu in China, and America Movil in Latin America.

PRICING

Uber uses its app to determine pricing. Once the passenger completes his or her ride with an Uber partner–driver, the person's credit card is charged automatically. Fees charged for speeds over 11 miles per hour are charged by the distance traveled. Uber operates on a cost leadership basis, claiming that it offers lower rates than taxis. However, the app OpenStreetCab suggests that Uber might be more cost-efficient only when the fare is more than $35.

Uber uses an algorithm to estimate fees charged when demand is high. Called surge pricing, Uber has even applied for a patent for this type of system. This "peak pricing" strategy is not too different than when utilities or flights charge higher prices when demand is high. Passengers are alerted during times where the price is higher. However, the extent of the pricing increase has been questioned, as some consumers believe Uber uses this high demand to "price gouge" passengers.

In some situations, Uber's surge pricing has led to considerable criticism. During one New Year's Eve, pricing surged up to seven times the normal price. During a hostage crisis in Sydney, Australia, Uber charged as much as four times the normal price as an influx of people struggled to evacuate. During ice storms and snowstorms, surge pricing may also be applied. Uber responded by claiming its price hikes encouraged more drivers to pick up passengers in the area, but consumers were outraged about the hostage crisis situation. Within an hour Uber agreed to refund users in the area who paid the higher prices. In extreme shortages, prices are sometimes hiked to as high as 6 to 8 percent. On the one hand, Uber argues that surge pricing increases the number of drivers during times of high demand. It is estimated that the number of drivers increases by 70 to 80 percent due to surge pricing. Still, some consumers believe this is a form of price gouging and that Uber capitalizes on emergency situations such as the Sydney hostage crisis. Uber has to reconcile these different situations to create a pricing strategy considered fair and ethical by its users.

PROMOTION

Uber has engaged in a number of promotional activities to make its brand known. Often it adopts buzz-marketing strategies to draw attention to its services. For instance, to celebrate National Ice Cream Month, Uber launched on-demand ice cream trucks in seven major cities. In one promotion, Uber partnered with General Electric to offer free DeLorean rides to San Francisco users reminiscent of the movie *Back to the Future*. Uber also uses promotion to portray its benefits compared to its rivals. For instance, Uber assumed a combative advertising approach to its major rival Lyft through a Facebook ad campaign. Uber advertising often stresses the convenience and low cost of its ride-sharing services.

However, like all companies, Uber must take care to ensure that its advertising could not be construed as misleading. A lawsuit was filed in the U.S. District Court in San Francisco stating that Uber violated the 1946 Lanham Act that prohibits false advertising. Taxi companies claimed, for instance, that Uber's drivers do not have to undergo fingerprinting in California as part of background checks, and yet it uses advertising such as "the safest ride on the road" and sets "the strictest safety standards possible," as well as Uber's $1 "Safe Rides Fee." According to the taxi drivers, these deceptive advertising practices take customers away from their services and are therefore leading to economic harm.

UBER FACES CHALLENGES

Uber faces a number of additional challenges including internal struggles, legal and regulatory challenges, and global issues. In the United States, major cities are considering regulating Uber. However, it faces more obstacles as it expands internationally. Some countries are opting to ban Uber or certain services altogether. Uber will have to adapt its marketing strategy to address both domestic challenges within the United States as well as to the various laws enforced in different countries.

INTERNAL CHALLENGES—DRIVER SATISFACTION

Uber operates in an industry where trust between strangers is vital. This trust ensures a safe and comfortable ride for both passenger and driver. Uber has developed a rating system to help assure this trust and reliability between passengers and drivers, called a rideshare ratings system. Rideshare rating systems pose a unique challenge for Uber because of the way they are set up and the level of rider objectivity. Uber's insistent policy of maintaining a five-star fleet can put drivers at a disadvantage. Uber rivals have similar policies; for instance, Lyft tells customers that anything less than five stars indicates unhappiness with the ride.

Low driver scores can mean drivers are forced to take remedial classes where they learn about safe driving techniques and driver etiquette. Those who fail to increase their scores risk suspension or permanent deactivation. Because consumers have different views of what constitutes quality, it can be argued that Uber drivers are placed at the mercy of the consumer's mood.

Drivers have also expressed unhappiness with Uber's pay. Uber will often lower fare rates in order to gain a competitive advantage in different markets, which cuts into driver earnings. Additionally, drivers are driving their own cars and spending their personal funds on upkeep and insurance. In 2014 drivers working with Teamsters Local 986 launched the California App-based Drivers Association (CADA), an Uber drivers' union. More cities have started their own unions.

Uber has begun to guarantee hourly earnings of $10 to $26 per hour for its drivers, but to qualify drivers have to comply with Uber's rules—including accepting 90 percent of ride requests, doing one ride per hour, and being online 50 out of 60 minutes. Critics say these restrictions effectively keep drivers from working for other ride-sharing services. Uber drivers are independent contractors and not employees of the company, so they have the option to work for competitors. However, these new criteria may be a way to keep drivers working for Uber and no one else.

This independent contractor status has created controversy for drivers. Drivers claim that Uber's requirements make them more like employees than independent contractors. For instance, Uber has certain rules about types of cars and soliciting business. Disgruntled drivers have staged protests and filed class-action lawsuits against the firm. Uber has lost class-action lawsuits in California and Massachusetts. According to the rulings in these states, Uber drivers qualified as employees. Therefore, Uber owed them money in the form of expense reimbursements and car maintenance. After losing the lawsuits in California and Massachusetts, Uber agreed to pay as much as $100 million, which will be distributed among the drivers in those areas. However, compensation will depend on time spent driving and mileage. Those who drove less than 750 miles will likely only receive about $24.

As a result of the settlement, Uber has announced changes that will apply to its drivers across the country. For instance, it will no longer deactivate Uber drivers from its app unless there is sufficient cause to do so. Drivers must be given two warnings beforehand (unless it involves fraud, discrimination, or other illegal conduct), and the reason must be stated in writing. Uber also agreed to provide more information to its drivers about how its rating system works, and it will fund a Drivers Association in the two states. These associations will enable Uber drivers in California and Massachusetts to elect a leader who will meet with Uber on a quarterly basis and discuss driver issues. Finally, Uber was required to clarify in its communications that drivers can request tips because tips are not included on Uber's app. These actions are an attempt on Uber's part to provide drivers with more freedom as independent contractors. The more control Uber exerts over drivers, the more likely they will be considered as employees rather than independent contractors. To ensure that it operates on the right side of employment law, Uber must carefully understand the line separating independent contractors from employees.

COMPETITOR SABOTAGE AND DATA LEAKS

Lyft, Uber's main competitor, claims that Uber employees and recruiters were ordering rides from Lyft and then cancelling them simply to put them at a disadvantage. This wasted the time of Lyft drivers and caused them to lose out on legitimate passengers. Lyft claims that one Uber recruiter opened up 29 accounts using the Lyft app. The recruiter booked and then cancelled 1,524 rides. Lyft also complained that when Uber employees did book and accept rides from Lyft, they only did so to try to convince the Lyft driver to work for Uber instead. Uber promised it would "tone down their sales tactics" and apologized for the misconduct. There is no evidence to suggest that competitor sabotage was ever sanctioned by Uber headquarters.

Additionally, in 2014 Uber experienced a data breach that exposed the data of 50,000 U.S. drivers. After Uber learned about the breach, it did not alert drivers in a timely manner. Another issue regarding driver privacy involves what has been termed Uber's "god view" tool. This tool reveals the locations of Uber cars and their drivers. The New York attorney general filed a lawsuit against Uber in regards to the data breach and for not alerting its drivers in a timely manner that their information might have been compromised. Uber paid $20,000 to settle.

LEGAL CHALLENGES

Regulation is a constant challenge for Uber. As it becomes more popular, Uber will become subject to more legal and regulatory requirements common to other big businesses. For instance, the Americans with Disabilities Act is becoming a challenge for Uber. Since the Uber service is usually operated within a driver's personal vehicle, many of the vehicles are not wheelchair friendly. The National Federation of the Blind also filed lawsuits against Uber because of instances where passengers were denied access to rides because they had service dogs. According to allegations, some drivers left passengers in extreme weather and then charged them cancellation fees afterward. A complaint filed in the Northern California District Court claims that a woman's service dog was placed in the trunk. Uber responded by claiming that according to its policy, drivers are terminated if they refuse to grant access to service dogs. However, the National Federation of the Blind claims that Uber had allegedly responded by saying they have no control over their drivers. The organization maintains that since Uber manages payments and services through its app and assesses customer feedback on driver performance, it has an obligation to ensure its drivers are not discriminating against the visually impaired. Uber claims that it is committed to equal access and has partnered with organizations such as the Lighthouse for the Blind in San Francisco to enable access to its technological services for those who are blind. The Uber app is compatible with VoiceOver iOS so that blind individuals are able to access and use its app.

Taxi lobbying groups are also pressuring local governments to block Uber in many cities. They claim that Uber hurts their business and has an unfair advantage, as Uber drivers are not subject to the same restrictions as licensed taxi drivers. For this reason, they do not have to pay taxes or licensing fees. Cities have taken action against Uber by blocking ordinances that provide a path to legalization for mobile ride-booking apps and issuing cease-and-desist orders. Several U.S. airports such as Salt Lake City have restrictions on Uber.

In addition to having an unfair competitive advantage, another accusation levied against Uber is that it does not adhere to proper safety standards. Allegedly, Uber drivers were involved in three rapes in Delhi, India; Chicago; and Boston. These rapes have harmed Uber's reputation and cast its safety into serious question. In India the rapist was convicted and sentenced to life in prison. The victim filed a lawsuit against Uber, which it settled out of court. Additionally, a lawsuit was filed against Uber in San Francisco for the wrongful death of a 6-year-old girl. The lawsuit alleged that a driver was distracted using the UberX app when he struck and killed the girl. Uber responded by claiming that the driver was not an agent for Uber and was not en route or transporting a passenger at the time of the accident. However, it settled with the family of the victim.

In 2016 a driver named Jeffrey Dalton in Kalamazoo, Michigan shot individuals in a rampage that lasted five hours. Six people were killed. It appears that Dalton picked up Uber passengers both before and after the shootings. It is important to note that Dalton did not have a criminal record, and even the FBI concedes that he did not raise any red flags. While it does not seem that Uber could have foreseen the attacks, the procedures it uses for background checks are increasingly questioned.

To reestablish its reputation for safety, Uber has added a "safe ride checklist" to its app that is a pre-pickup notification encouraging riders to confirm the license plate number and verify their driver's name and appearance before entering a vehicle. They have also added a team of safety and fraud experts to authenticate drivers and a dedicated incident-response team to address rider issues in India. However, Uber does not require fingerprint scans for its drivers, except in New York City and Houston. Uber has even threatened to exit the Houston market as it claims that the fingerprint scan requirements have resulted in a 35 percent increase in wait time for passengers. It already exited the market in Austin, Texas because of the government's mandatory fingerprinting.

Insurance is another criticism against Uber. Although Uber's website claims that it offers $1 million in liability insurance plans for its drivers, some states are issuing warnings stating that rideshare insurance may not cover them should there be an accident. Many states are reconsidering insurance requirements in light of this issue, and insurance firms such as GEICO and MetLife have begun offering insurance packages for ride-sharing services.

GLOBAL EXPANSION

Uber has adopted the motto "Available locally, expanding globally" to describe the opportunities it sees in global expansion. International expansion is a major part of Uber's marketing strategy, and it has thus far established the ride-sharing service in 300 global cities.

Uber is correct in assuming that consumers from other countries would also appreciate the low cost, convenience, and freedom that its app services offer.

Many countries have regulatory hurdles that have caused trouble for Uber to successfully operate in these areas. Several cities across the world have banned select Uber services. On the other hand, it is hard for countries and cities to ban Uber completely since so many of the activities are performed over the Internet. U.S. cities such as Portland, Oregon have accused Uber of aggressively trying to move into new territories in spite of legal opposition. In fact, Costa Rica maintains that Uber drivers are operating in the country illegally.

Many, if not all, of the instances involve banning Uber or Uber services due to the lack of professional licenses for drivers. In Taiwan authorities claimed that Uber services violated highway laws by not having transport-licenses to operate legally. The ministry of Economic Affairs has looked into the possibility of revoking Uber's business registration. In Spain, Uber shut down its ride-sharing service after a judge ruled that Uber drivers are not legally authorized to transport passengers by unfairly competing against licensed taxi drivers. In Australia, Victoria and New South Wales ruled Uber's app to be illegal due to safety concerns. Police in Cape Town, South Africa, impounded 33 cars operating with the Uber app because the drivers did not have a taxi license. Taxi driver protests against Uber have occurred frequently in the various countries in which Uber is trying to expand, sometimes resulting in driver injuries and vandalism.

FRANCE

In 2011 Paris became the first city outside of the United States where Uber set up operations. However, the government banned UberPop because drivers for this service do not need to be licensed. French police even raided Uber's Paris office. A French law was passed mandating that operating a service that connects passengers to nonlicensed drivers is punishable with fines over $300,000 and up to 2 years in prison. Hundreds of Uber drivers in France were issued fines for operating illegally, and two executives were arrested.

Uber challenged that law, claiming that it is unconstitutional because it hinders free enterprise. A French court decided against banning UberPop and sent the case to a higher court. This has generated strong criticism from taxicab officials in France as they claim that they have to license drivers while Uber is currently free from this restriction. In 2015 the Constitutional Council in France upheld the ban.

Taxi drivers have staged numerous protests in France, resulting in damaged vehicles and some incidents where Uber drivers were held against their will. One protest gained notable attention because it involved rocker Courtney Love, who was caught in the protest on her way from the airport. Love claims the car was vandalized and her driver was held hostage. The French government informed the public that violence was not justified and that UberPop continues to remain illegal. Violating the ban could subject drivers to fines, imprisonment, and vehicle seizures. However, according to government authorities, the Uber app itself cannot be banned without a court order.

INDIA

India is Uber's second largest market after the United States. India rejected Uber's application for a taxi license. In New Delhi a woman's rape allegation led to a ban against app-based services without radio-taxi permits in the capital. In response to the alleged rape, Uber began installing "panic button" and tracking features to its app. Uber also began offering its service in New Delhi without charging booking or service fees.

Despite these changes, Uber continued to run afoul of Indian authorities. India asked Internet service providers to block Uber's websites because it continued to operate in the city despite being banned. However, it did not ban the apps themselves because doing so would require it to institute the ban across the entire country. Uber must tread carefully to seize upon opportunities in India without violating regulatory requirements. This is more difficult as Uber drivers are independent contractors who set their own schedules and make their own decisions about whether to work.

GERMANY

Uber provides its ride-sharing service in Germany's five biggest cities, namely Frankfurt, Berlin, Hamburg, Munich, and Düsseldorf. In 2014 Frankfurt's court filed an injunction against Uber. A nationwide ban was instituted against Uber's UberPop services after taxicab operators asked for an emergency injunction, but it was overturned because the judge determined they waited too long to file the injunction.

However, in 2015 a German court banned Uber services if they used unlicensed drivers. Uber argued in court that the company itself is only an agent to connect driver and rider. Rules that apply to taxi services supposedly do not apply, and all services are deemed to be legal, according to Uber. The court ruled that Uber's business model clearly infringes the Personal Transportation Law, because drivers transport riders without a personal transportation license. The injunction includes a fine of more than $260,000 per ride for noncompliance. If the injunction is breached, drivers could go to jail for up to half a year, in addition to an imposition of fines. The German Taxi Association (Taxi Deutschland) was pleased with the outcome, claiming that taxi services will remain in the hands of qualified people and keep everyone safer.

Despite the ruling, an Uber spokesperson said that the company would not give up on Germany because UberBlack and UberTaxi services will remain unaffected by the District Court's verdict. UberBlack and UberTaxi use licensed taxis and limousine drivers. However, competitors have quickly risen to challenge Uber in the German market, and some question whether Uber has a future in Germany.

CONCLUSION

The long-term viability of Uber depends on managing future risks in six key areas:

- Ethics and Compliance: Uber does not communicate ethical values or a code of ethics for its independent contractors. Drivers are provided with various training modules to deal with issues such as safety. However, Uber does not require drivers to complete these modules before becoming an independent contractor for the firm. Most drivers indicate that they skip over these training modules; they simply have their car approved and undergo a background check. Independent contractors in the direct selling industry are provided with a comprehensive code of ethics to provide guidance for ethical behavior. Uber will continue to face ethical risks if it does not communicate required ethical standards to drivers.
- Drivers: The number of disgruntled drivers could get out of control if Uber increases its profit share deductions. With recent laws mandating healthcare insurance, drivers may require healthcare coverage. Training programs to improve driving skills could reduce risk from negligent drivers and decrease liability insurance costs.
- Competitors: Uber's business model can be found in similar rides-for-hire services, such as Lyft, Sidecar,

and Curb. More rides-for-hires could emerge, in addition to the everyday competition from taxicabs, limos, rental car businesses, air travel, trains, and city and chartered buses. In China Didi Chuxing seems to be gaining market share.

- Customer Base: Increasing the demand for rides-for-services is a continuous or future challenge that requires attention primarily to safety improvements and rates that have a cost/benefit to both passengers and drivers. Unpredictable demand is a future risk that could be met with product diversification. Currently, Uber offers technology-oriented products, and it must continue to be competitive in an industry where there is intense competition for rates.
- Technology: Customers are wary of downloading apps, and some online businesses have been hacked for credit card information. Uber itself experienced a data breach that resulted in the data of 50,000 drivers being hacked. Because Uber has responsibilities to protect the privacy of both its independent contractors and passengers, it must increase its security protocols and communicate any potential breaches in a timely fashion.
- Customer satisfaction: Some customers experience long waits, inexperienced drivers, and even sexual harassment. Better Business Bureau complaints mainly involve pricing and problems with service. Uber might use the Internet to check consumer complaints and address them to improve customer satisfaction.

The emergence of Uber has influenced many services to follow the Uber business model. There are similar firms that offer ride-sharing services, and there are firms that want to be an Uber-type business in the way they deliver goods and services. For example, Cargomatic has developed an app to help fill space on trucks. Cargomatic, which now operates in California and New York, has been called the Uber for truckers because it connect shippers with drivers who are looking for extra shipments to haul. This is signaling a shift in the industry in which people are the infrastructure rather than buildings or fleets of vehicles.

Uber faces a number of ethical challenges, including regulatory and legal issues both inside and outside of the United States. Laws that protect consumers specifically target taxi services, whereas Uber defines its services as "ride sharing" and Uber as an "agent" of their "individual contractors." However, many courts do not view its services in the same way and are forcing Uber to comply with licensing laws or stop business in certain areas.

Despite Uber's challenges, the company has become widely popular among consumers and independent contractors. Supporters claim that Uber is revolutionizing the transportation service industry. Investors clearly believe Uber is going to be a strong market player in the long run.

Uber has a bright future and expansion opportunities are great. It is therefore important for Uber to ensure the safety of their riders and the drivers. They should also adopt controls to ensure that independent contractors using their app obey relevant country laws. Uber has to address these issues to uphold the trust of their customers and achieve long-term market success.

Questions for Discussion

1. What are the ethical challenges that Uber faces in using app-based peer-to-peer sharing technology?
2. Since Uber is using a disruptive business model and marketing strategy, what are the threats that the company will have to overcome to be successful?
3. Because Uber is so popular and the business model is being expanded to other industries, should there be regulation to develop compliance with standards to protect competitors and consumers?

Sources

Chloe Albanesius, "Uber rolling out on-demand ice cream trucks," *PC Magazine*, July 12, 2012, http://www.pcmag.com/article2/0,2817,2407069,00.asp (accessed May 22, 2015).

American Express Company, "Frequently asked questions," https://sync.americanexpress.com/Uber/Faq\ (accessed May 22, 2015).

Erin Arvedlund, "Uber slapped with suit by 45 Phila. taxi companies," *Philly.com,* December 26, 2014, http://articles.philly.com/2014-12-26/business/57398500_1_taxi-medallion-travis-kalanick-uberx (accessed July 22, 2016).

Eric Auchard and Christoph Steitz, "German court bans Uber's unlicensed taxi services," *Reuters*, March 18, 2015, http://www.reuters.com/article/2015/03/18/us-uber-germany-ban-idUSKBN0ME1L820150318 (accessed May 21, 2015).

Emily Badger, "Now we know how many drivers Uber has – and have a better idea of what they're making," *Washington Post*, January 22, 2015, http://www.washingtonpost.com/blogs/wonkblog/wp/2015/01/22/now-we-know-many-drivers-uber-has-and-how-much-money-theyre-making%E2%80%8B/ (accessed May 22, 2015).

BBC, "India Uber driver given life term for Delhi rape," *BBC News*, November 3, 2015, http://www.bbc.com/news/world-asia-india-34707254 (accessed July 22, 2016).

BBC, "Judge overturns Uber ride-sharing ban in Germany," *BBC*, September 16, 2014, http://www.bbc.com/neThews/technology-29221372 (accessed May 22, 2015).

Nick Bilton, "Disruptions: Taxi supply and demand, priced by the mile," *New York Times*, January 8, 2012, http://bits.blogs.nytimes.com/2012/01/08/disruptions-taxi-supply-and-demand-priced-by-the-mile/ (accessed May 22, 2015).

Kristen V. Brown, "Uber shifts into mid-market headquarters," *SFGate, San Francisco Chronicle*, June 2, 2014, http://www.sfgate.com/technology/article/Uber-shifts-into-Mid-Market-headquarters-5521166.php (accessed May 21, 2015).

Rachel Botsman presentation, "The Shared Economy Lacks a Shared Definition," *Fast Company,* November 21, 2013, http://www.fastcoexist.com/3022028/the-sharing-economy-lacks-a-shared-definition (accessed February 16, 2016).

Joshua Brustein, "Uber's other legal mess: Drivers sue over missing tips," *Bloomberg*, August 29, 2013, http://www.bloomberg.com/bw/articles/2013-08-29/ubers-other-legal-mess-drivers-sue-over-missing-tips (accessed May 21, 2015).

Michael Carney, "Playing favorites: Uber adds new security features, but only in select crisis-riddled markets," *PandoDaily*, January 2, 2015, http://pando.com/2015/01/02/playing-favorites-uber-adds-new-security-features-but-only-in-select-crisis-riddled-markets/ (accessed May 21, 2015).

Chicago Tribune Staff, "UberSelect premium car option now available in Chicago," *The Chicago Tribune,* March 2, 2015, http://www.chicagotribune.com/business/ct-uber-select-0302-biz-20150302-story.html (accessed July 22, 2016).

Amit Chowdhry, "Uber is acquiring mapping company deCarta," *Forbes*, March 4, 2015, http://www.forbes.com/sites/amitchowdhry/2015/03/04/uber-acquires-decarta/ (accessed May 21, 2015).

Susan Decker and Serena Saitto, "Uber seeks to patent pricing surges that critics call gouging," *Bloomberg*, December 18, 2014, http://www.bloomberg.com/news/articles/2014-12-18/uber-seeks-to-patent-pricing-surges-that-critics-call-gouging (accessed May 22, 2015).

Cotton Delo, "In quest for ride-sharing supremacy, Uber takes on Lyft with Facebook ads," *Advertising Age*, January 17, 2014, http://adage.com/article/digital/uber-takes-lyft-facebook-attack-ads/291158/ (accessed May 22, 2015).

Karen Demato, "Uber and auto insurance: Regulators weigh in," *Wall Street Journal*, March 31, 2015, http://blogs.wsj.com/totalreturn/2015/03/31/uber-and-auto-insurance-regulators-weigh-in/ (accessed May 22, 2015).

Lydia DePillis, "No, driver lawsuits won't destroy the 'Uber for X' business model," *Forbes*, March 13, 2015, http://www.washingtonpost.com/blogs/wonkblog/wp/2015/03/13/no-driver-lawsuits-wont-destroy-the-uber-for-x-business-model/ (accessed May 22, 2015).

Dee-Ann Durbin and Tom Krishner, "Uber defends driver screening in wake of Kalamazoo shootings," *CBC News*, February 23, 2016, http://www.cbc.ca/news/business/uber-driver-screening-kalamazoo-1.3459572 (accessed July 22, 2016).

Economist staff, "The Rise of the Sharing Economy," *The Economist*, May 9, 2013, http://www.economist.com/news/leaders/21573104-internet-everything-hire-rise-sharing-economy (accessed February 16, 2016).

Erica Fink, "Uber's dirty tricks quantified: Rival counts 5,560 canceled rides," *CNN Money*, August 12, 2014, http://money.cnn.com/2014/08/11/technology/uber-fake-ride-requests-lyft/index.html (accessed July 22, 2016).

Matt Flegenheimer, "For now, taxi office says, cab-hailing apps aren't allowed," *New York Times*, September 6, 2012, http://www.nytimes.com/2012/09/07/nyregion/cab-hailing-apps-not-allowed-by-new-york-taxi-commission.html?_r=0 (accessed May 21, 2015).

Anja Floetenmeyer, "Taxi Deutschland - Taxi Deutschland app got Uber banned throughout Germany," *Taxi Deutschland*, http://www.taxi-deutschland.net/index.php/pressemitteilung/121-taxi-deutschland-app-got-uber-banned-throughout-germany (accessed May 21, 2015).

Anne Freier, "Uber usage statistics and revenue," *Business of Apps*, September 14, 2015, http://www.businessofapps.com/uber-usage-statistics-and-revenue/ (accessed July 18, 2016).

Anna Gallegos, "The four biggest legal problems facing Uber, Lyft and other ridesharing services | LXBN," *LXBN*, June 4, 2014, http://www.lxbn.com/2014/06/04/top-legal-problems-facing-uber-lyft-ridesharing-services/ (accessed May 21, 2015).

Jefferson Graham, "App greases the wheels," *USA Today*, May 27, 2015, p. 5B.

Steven Gursten, "What's the difference between Uber Black and UberX, and what are my rights if I am injured in an Uber car crash?" *Legal Examiner*, March 28, 2014, http://detroit.legalexaminer.com/automobile-accidents/uber-black-uberx-rights-if-injured/ (accessed May 21, 2015).

Felicitas Hackmann, "uberPOP, Uber's ride-sharing service, pops up in more EU cities," *VentureBeat*, April 15, 2014, http://venturebeat.com/2014/04/15/uberpop-ubers-peer-to-peer-service-pops-up-in-more-eu-cities/ (accessed May 22, 2015).

Ellen Huet, "Uber's clever, hidden move: How its latest fare cuts can actually lock in its drivers," *Forbes*, http://www.forbes.com/sites/ellenhuet/2015/01/09/ubers-clever-hidden-move-how-fare-cuts-actually-lock-in-its-drivers/ (accessed May 21, 2015).

Trevor Hughes, "Passengers flock to upstart car services," *USA Today*, July 10, 2014, 5B.

Ellen Huet, "Uber tests taking even more from its drivers with 30% commission," *Forbes*, May 18, 2015, http://www.forbes.com/sites/ellenhuet/2015/05/18/uber-new-uberx-tiered-commission-30-percent/ (accessed May 21, 2015).

Hanna Ingber, "Courtney Love Tweets Ordeal During Violent Uber Protests in Paris," *The New York Times*, June 25, 2015, http://www.nytimes.com/2015/06/26/world/europe/courtney-love-describes-ordeal-during-violent-uber-protests-in-paris.html?_r=0 (accessed July 22, 2016).

Kat Kane, "The big hidden problem with Uber? Insincere 5-star ratings," *Wired*, March 19, 2015, http://www.wired.com/2015/03/bogus-uber-reviews/ (accessed May 21, 2015).

Karun, "Times Internet and Uber enter into a strategic partnership," *Uber Blog*, March 22, 2015, http://blog.uber.com/times-internet (accessed May 22, 2015).

R. Jai Krishna and Joanna Sugden, "India asks Internet service providers to block Uber website in Delhi," *Wall Street Journal*, May 14, 2015, http://www.wsj.com/articles/india-asks-internet-service-providers-to-block-uber-website-in-delhi-1431606032 (accessed May 21, 2015).

Tracy Lien, "California taxis sue Uber, allege unfair advertising, unfair competition," *Los Angeles Times*, March 18, 2015, http://www.latimes.com/business/technology/la-fi-tn-taxi-uber-unfair-competition-lawsuit-20150318-story.html#page=1 (accessed May 22, 2015).

Douglas MacMillan, "The Fiercest Rivalry in Tech: Uber vs. Lyft," *The Wall Street Journal*, August 12, 2014, B1

Douglas MacMillan, Sam Schechner, and Lisa Fleisher, "Uber snags $41 billion valuation," *Wall Street Journal*, December 5, 2014, http://www.wsj.com/articles/ubers-new-funding-values-it-at-over-41-billion-1417715938 (accessed May 21, 2015).

Pamela MacLean, "Judges back drivers in lawsuits against Uber, others," *Boston Globe*, March 12, 2015, http://www.bostonglobe.com/business/2015/03/11/uber-lyft-drivers-are-roll-push-for-employee-status/XVOgSEkF6KlXM1VT35RcHL/story.html (accessed May 21, 2015).

Making Sen$e Editor, "What it's really like to be an Uber driver," *PBS*, October 6, 2014, http://www.pbs.org/newshour/making-sense/what-its-really-like-to-be-an-uber-driver/ (accessed May 21, 2015).

Devan McClaine, "Rider seeking taxi driver," *San Francisco Business Times*, February 3, 2012, http://www.bizjournals.com/sanfrancisco/print-edition/2012/02/03/rider-seeking-taxi-driver.html (accessed May 21, 2015).

Patrick McGroarty, "Cape Town impounds 33 Uber cars," *Wall Street Journal*, January 6, 2015, http://www.wsj.com/articles/cape-town-impounds-33-uber-cars-1420557450 (accessed May 22, 2015).

Christopher Mims, "At startups, people are 'new infrastructure'," *Wall Street Journal*, March 8, 2015, http://www.wsj.com/articles/at-startups-people-are-new-infrastructure-1425858978 (accessed May 21, 2015).

James Nash, "The Company Cities Love to Hate," *Bloomberg Businessweek*, July 3, 2014, pp. 31–33.

Eric Newcomer, "Cash burns fast for Uber-like startups that grow city by city," *Bloomberg*, March 12, 2015, http://www.bloomberg.com/news/articles/2015-03-12/cash-burns-fast-for-uber-like-startups-that-grow-city-by-city (accessed May 21, 2015).

"ObamaCare's individual mandate: What is the tax penalty for not having health insurance," *ObamaCare Facts*, http://obamacarefacts.com/obamacare-individual-mandate/ (accessed May 21, 2015).

Charlie Osborne, "Uber fined $20K in data breach, 'god view' probe," *CNET*, January 7, 2016, http://www.cnet.com/news/uber-fined-20k-in-surveillance-data-breach-probe/ (accessed July 22, 2016).

Krystal Peak, "Uber pulls in another $32M for app-based car service," *VatorNews*, December 7, 20111, http://vator.tv/news/2011-12-07-uber-pulls-in-another-32m-for-app-based-car-service (accessed May 22, 2015).

PricewaterhouseCoopers, *The Sharing Economy: Consumer Intelligence Series*, 2015, https://www.pwc.com/us/en/technology/publications/assets/pwc-consumer-intelligence-series-the-sharing-economy.pdf (accessed March 4, 2016).

Saritha Rai, "Uber gets serious about passenger safety in India, introduces panic button,' *Forbes*, February 12, 2015, http://www.forbes.com/sites/saritharai/2015/02/12/uber-gets-serious-about-passenger-safety-in-india-introduces-panic-button/ (accessed May 22, 2015).

Brad Reed, "Meet the brilliant app that neither Uber nor cab companies want you to know about," *BGR*, March 18, 2015, http://bgr.com/2015/03/18/uber-vs-taxi-cost/ (accessed May 22, 2015).

Reuters, "Uber driver attacked and cars stopped during Costa Rica launch," *Reuters*, August 23, 2015, http://www.reuters.com/article/costarica-uber-idUSL-1N10Y0LW20150823 (accessed July 22, 2016).

Reuters, "Uber sued over driver data breach, adding to legal woes," *Fortune*, March 13, 2015, http://fortune.com/2015/03/13/uber-sued-data-breach/ (accessed May 21, 2015).

Kate Rogers, "What the Uber, Lyft lawsuits mean for the economy," *CNBC*, March 16, 2015, http://www.cnbc.com/id/102503520 (accessed May 21, 2015).

Sam Schechner and Tom Fairless, "Europe steps up pressure on tech giants," *Wall Street Journal*, April 2, 2015, http://www.wsj.com/articles/europe-steps-up-pressure-on-technology-giants-1428020273 (accessed May 21, 2015).

Mark Scott, "As Uber Stumbles, German Rivals Prosper," *The New York Times,* January 4, 2016, http://bits.blogs.nytimes.com/2016/01/04/as-uber-stumbles-german-rivals-prosper/ (accessed July 22, 2016).

Mark Scott, "French Law that Banned UberPop Services Survives Legal Challenge," *The New York Times*, September 22, 2015, http://www.nytimes.com/2015/09/23/technology/french-law-that-banned-uberpop-service-survives-legal-challenge.html (accessed July 22, 2016).

Joana Sugden and Aditi Malhotra, "Indian officials drafting national rules for Uber, other taxi apps," *Wall Street Journal*, April 7, 2015, http://www.wsj.com/articles/indian-officials-drafting-national-rules-for-uber-other-taxi-apps-1428427528 (accessed May 21, 2015).

Taylor Sopper, "Uber for picture framing: Mountary launches service in Seattle, brings experts to your door," April 7, 2015, http://www.geekwire.com/2015/

uber-for-picture-framing-mountary-launches-service-in-seattle-brings-experts-to-your-door/ (accessed May 21, 2015).

Carolyn Said, "Taxis sue Uber for misleading ads on safety," *SFGate*, March 18, 2015, http://www.sfgate.com/business/article/Taxis-sue-Uber-for-misleading-ads-on-safety-6142760.php (accessed May 21, 2015).

Sam Schechner, "Uber wins French court reprieve over legality of low-cost service," *Wall Street Journal*, March 31, 2015, http://www.wsj.com/articles/uber-wins-french-court-reprieve-over-legality-of-low-cost-service-1427794312 (accessed May 22, 2015).

Samantha Shankman, "Uber gets into ride-sharing game in Paris," *Skift*, February 4, 2014, http://skift.com/2014/02/04/uber-gets-into-the-ride-sharing-game-in-paris/ (accessed May 21, 2015).

Aditi Shrivastava, "Uber resumes operations in Delhi post 1.5 months ban," *Economic Times*, January 23, 2015, http://articles.economictimes.indiatimes.com/2015-01-23/news/58382689_1_indian-taxi-market-radio-taxi-scheme-uber-spokesman (accessed May 22, 2015).

Spiegel, "Vermittlung Privater Fahrer: Gericht Verbietet Uber deutschlandweit," http://www.spiegel.de/wirtschaft/unternehmen/uber-urteil-gericht-verbietet-uber-deutschlandweit-a-1024214.html (accessed May 21, 2015).

Gail Sullivan, "Uber sued for allegedly refusing rides to the blind and putting a dog in the trunk," *The Washington Post*, September 10, 2014, https://www.washingtonpost.com/news/morning-mix/wp/2014/09/10/uber-sued-for-allegedly-refusing-rides-to-the-blind-and-putting-a-dog-in-the-trunk/ (accessed July 22, 2016).

Taxi Deutschland, "Uber legal problems worldwide," http://www.taxi-deutschland.net/images/presse/Infografik_Uber-legal-issues_EN_v12_2015-02-06_final.pdf (accessed May 21, 2015).

Uber website, https://www.uber.com/ (accessed July 22, 2016).

Uber, "Commitment to Innovation for the Blind and Low Vision Community," *Uber Newsroom*, July 8, 2015, https://newsroom.uber.com/commitment-to-innovation-for-the-blind-and-low-vision-community/ (accessed July 22, 2016).

Andrew Watts, "The Real Reason Uber and Lyft Left Austin," *The Huffington Post*, Mary 10, 2016, http://www.huffingtonpost.com/andrew-watts/the-real-reason-uber-and-lyft-left-austin_b_9889406.html (accessed July 18, 2016).

Karen Weise, "How Uber Rolls," June 29-July 5, 2015, *Bloomberg Businessweek*, 54–59.

Elizabeth Weise, "Most Uber drivers to get less than $25 from big settlement," *USA Today*, April 27, 2016, http://www.usatoday.com/story/tech/2016/04/26/most-uber-drivers-see-little-100-milion-payout/83546898/ (accessed July 22, 2016).

Kale Williams, "Uber denies fault in S.F. crash that killed girl," *SFGate*, May 7, 2014, http://www.sfgate.com/bayarea/article/Uber-denies-fault-in-S-F-crash-that-killed-girl-5458290.php (accessed May 22, 2015).

Kale Williams and Kurtis Alexander, "Uber sued over girl's death in S.F.," *SFGate*, January 28, 2014, http://www.sfgate.com/bayarea/article/Uber-sued-over-girl-s-death-in-S-F-5178921.php (accessed May 22, 2015).

CASE 2

The Mission of CVS: Corporate Social Responsibility and Pharmacy Innovation

INTRODUCTION

In 1963, brothers Stanley and Sidney Goldstein founded the first Consumer Value Store (CVS) with partner Ralph Hoagland in Lowell, Massachusetts. The store originally sold health and beauty supplies. It was widely successful, and grew to include 17 stores in one year. By 1967, CVS began offering in-store pharmacy departments, and in less than a decade it was acquired by the retail holding corporation Melville Corporation. This marked the beginning of CVS's expansion across the east coast through new store openings or mergers and acquisitions. It soon reached the milestone of exceeding $100 million in sales in 1974.

As the company grew, it faced intense competition, which it responded to through a differentiation strategy. CVS focused on its core offerings of health and beauty products, placing stores in shopping malls to generate more foot traffic. This strategy worked well for the company, allowing it to hit $1 billion in sales by 1985. The company celebrated its 25th year in 1988 with 750 stores and $1.6 billion in sales. The acquisition of People's Drug stores enabled CVS to establish its presence more widely along the coast and spurred the launch of PharmaCare, a pharmacy benefit management (PBM) company providing services to employers and insurers. In 1996 the Melville Corporation restructured, and CVS became independent as a publicly traded company on the New York Stock Exchange.

This new surge of investment allowed the company to expand widely across the nation into the Midwest and Southeast. CVS's acquisition of 2,500 Revco stores became the largest acquisition in U.S. retail pharmacy history. With the rise of the Internet, CVS seized upon the opportunity to launch CVS.com in 1999 (and Caremark.com after the 2007 acquisition). This became the first fully integrated online pharmacy in the United States. In another first for the U.S. pharmacy retail industry, the company introduced the ExtraCare Card loyalty program in 2001. The company's 40th anniversary in 2003 was marked with increasing westward expansion, 44 million loyalty card holders, and more than 4,000 stores in approximately 30 states. In the following five years, the company's acquisitions allowed CVS to gain leadership in key markets, begin a mail order business, and open its 7,000th retail location. It would also undergo a name change to CVS/Caremark after acquiring Caremark Rx, a prescription benefits management organization.

The two most important acquisitions in the history of CVS include MinuteClinic walk-in health clinics (in 2005) and Caremark Rx, Inc., (in 2007), a pharmacy benefits management company. To date, MinuteClinic has facilitated over 18 million patient visits in 800 clinics across 27 states, putting them in prime position to reach their 2017 goal of operating 1,500 clinics in 35 states. CVS/Caremark, as it was renamed after the acquisition, became the second largest pharmacy in the United States after Walgreen's, introducing new services such as online prescription refills. By 2011, the company had more than $100 billion in revenue, 7,500 retail pharmacies, 31 retail specialty pharmacies, 12 specialty mail order pharmacies, 18 onsite pharmacies, and a pharmacy benefit management business.

CVS sells products that meet the highest quality standards as well as its own line of products whose specifications and performance are annually tested and reviewed to ensure compliance with applicable consumer safety laws. In addition, the company has instituted its own Cosmetic Safety Policy that cosmetic products on the shelves must meet. CVS employs 243,000 people in over 9,600 locations across 49 states, the District of Columbia, Puerto Rico, Brazil, and Northern Ireland. Corporate headquarters are located in Woonsocket, Rhode Island. In one year, CVS filled and managed 1.9 billion prescriptions, provided services to 75 million PBM clients, and surpassed $139 billion in net revenues. The company is proud to note their number 10 spot on the Fortune 100 list. Today, CVS is one of the largest pharmacy health care providers and pharmacies in the

*This case was prepared by Yixing Chen, Christine Shields, and Michelle Urban for and under the direction of O. C. Ferrell and Linda Ferrell © 2014. It was prepared for classroom discussion rather than to illustrate either effective or ineffective handling of an administrative, ethical, or legal decision by management. All sources used for this case were obtained through publicly available material.

United States, and is comprised of four business functions: CVS/Caremark, MinuteClinic, PBM Services, and Retail Pharmacy. In 2014 CVS decided to change its name to CVS Health to reflect it emphasis on the health care industry. To further this goal, CVS made a deal to purchase Target's health services and clinics. Pharmacies in Target stores will be rebranded as CVS Pharmacies. CVS paid Target $1.9 billion for the pharmacy business and will pay Target $20 to $25 million in rent for the space.

The following case will explain some of the legal and ethical challenges CVS/Caremark has encountered, including a settlement with the Federal Trade Commission (FTC) and U.S. Department of Health & Human Services (HHS) regarding violations of the Health Insurance Portability and Accountability Act (HIPAA) Privacy Rule, deceptive business practices, and unseemly conduct by a manager resulting in a death. Our examination will also include how CVS/Caremark responded to such allegations, and how it has worked to redefine the company as a healthcare provider. We will analyze the company's ethical structure, including their recent decision to stop selling cigarettes, as well as an overview of some criticisms the company has received during their transition. The conclusion offers some insights into the future challenges CVS will likely experience.

ETHICAL CHALLENGES

Like most large companies, CVS must frequently address ethical risk areas and maintain socially responsible relationships with stakeholders. Although CVS has excelled in social responsibility, it has suffered from ethical lapses in the past. The next section addresses some of CVS's most notable ethical challenges, some of which resulted in legal repercussions.

HIPAA Privacy Case of 2009

As a company grows and achieves widespread influence, it also inherits a responsibility to act ethically and within the law. In 2009, CVS/Caremark was accused of improperly disposing of patients' health information. It was alleged that company employees threw prescription bottle labels and old prescriptions into the trash without destroying sensitive patient information, making it possible for the information to fall into public hands. This is a violation of the HIPAA Privacy

Rule, which requires companies operating in the health industry to properly safeguard the information of their patients. The allegations initiated investigations by the Office of Civil Rights (OCR) and the FTC, marking the first such collaborative investigation into a company's practices. These investigations revealed other issues as well, including a failure of company policies and procedures to completely address the safe handling of sensitive patient information, lack of proper employee training on disposal of sensitive information, and negligence in establishing repercussions for violations of proper disposal methods. This was in spite of the fact that CVS materials reassure clients that their privacy is a top priority for the pharmacy. This claim, in addition to the investigative findings, prompted the FTC to allege that CVS was making deceptive claims and had unfair security practices, both of which are violations of the FTC Act.

CVS settled the case with the U.S. Department of Health & Human Services (HHS), which oversees the enforcement of the HIPAA Privacy Rule, for $2.25 million regarding improper disposal of patients' health information. The settlement also mandated that the company implement a Corrective Action Plan with the following seven guidelines: (1) revise and distribute policies regarding disposal of protected health information; (2) discipline employees who violate them; (3) train workforce on new requirements; (4) conduct internal monitoring; (5) involve a qualified, independent third-party to assess company compliance with requirements and submit reports to HHS; (6) establish internal reporting procedures requiring employees to report all violations of these new privacy policies; and (7) submit compliance reports to HHS for three years. The company also settled with the FTC by signing a consent order, requiring the company to develop a comprehensive program that would ensure the security and confidentiality of information collected from customers. In so doing, the company agreed to a biennial audit from an independent third party. This audit is meant to ensure that CVS's program meets the FTC's standards for its security program. CVS is forbidden by law from misrepresenting its security practices.

Deceptive Business Practices

In addition to privacy challenges, CVS/Caremark has been accused of deceptive business practices. A 2008 civil lawsuit involving 28 states was filed against the personal benefits management division of

CVS/Caremark, which acts as the prescription drug claim intermediary between employers and employees. It also maintains relationships with drugstores and manufacturers. The allegations of the lawsuit included urging doctors to switch patients to name brand prescriptions under the notion that it would save them money. Furthermore, these switches were encouraged without informing doctors of the financial burden it would impose on patients, and employer healthcare plans were not informed that this activity would benefit CVS/Caremark. This could be seen as a conflict of interest at the expense of customers. Due to these allegations, the suit called for a revision in how the division gives information to consumers. In the end, CVS/Caremark signed a consent decree without admitting fault and paid a settlement of $38.5 million to reimburse states for the legal costs and patients overcharged due to the switch in prescription. In a similar matter, a multiyear-long FTC investigation concluded (in 2009) that the company had misled consumers regarding prices on certain prescriptions in one of its Medicare plans. The switch harmed elderly customers as they were billed for up to ten times the amount they anticipated. CVS/Caremark settled with the FTC for $5 million to reimburse customers for the change in price.

Overdistribution of Oxycodone

In 2012, CVS faced challenges with another federal agency—the Drug Enforcement Administration (DEA). The DEA suspended the company's license to sell controlled substances at two Florida locations, only a few miles apart from one another. These locations were found to have ordered a total of 3 million oxycodone pills in 2011. The average order for a U.S. pharmacy in the same year is 69,000 pills. Intensifying the matter, abuse of narcotics (pain pills) is prevalent in the area. Florida state legislation had been implemented in response to the issue as local clinics became known as "pill mills" for their liberal distribution of prescriptions for pain pills.

CVS responded to the DEA's investigation by notifying some of the area doctors that they would not fill prescriptions written for oxycodone (Schedule II narcotics). However, they also requested a temporary restraining order against the DEA, which would disable the temporary suspension of selling the drugs.

The DEA suspension decreased the amount of such narcotics being distributed to the two CVS locations by 80 percent in a period of three months, limiting their ability to make a profit. When the matter came before a federal judge, he ruled that the company was at fault for lack of proper oversight in distributing the drug and other narcotics. The ruling further implied company negligence as such a large amount of pills should have been noticed as a blatant abnormality.

Later that year, the DEA completely revoked the licenses of the two locations to sell controlled substances—the first time this has occurred with a national retail pharmacy chain. CVS claims that they have improved their procedures regarding its distribution of controlled substances; however, the DEA's claims explicitly included negligence on the part of pharmacists in light of obvious "questionable circumstances." These circumstances included the fact that several customers were coming to Florida from out of state to fill prescriptions. Many lacked insurance and paid in cash, a red flag that can suggest illegal use of drugs. This was in addition to the heavy pill problem in the area which had already prompted state legislation.

Testimonies from employees indicated company negligence as they had knowledge of the top prescribing doctors in the area and awareness that daily oxycodone quotas were being depleted—sometimes within 30 minutes of the pharmacy opening. Pharmacists also indicated that they set aside pills for those patients they considered to have a real need for them because they had strong suspicions that most of the people purchasing the pills were abusers. They did not feel at liberty to refuse prescriptions to customers, however, because they are not trained to diagnose illnesses. In 2013, CVS announced a review of its database of healthcare providers to find abnormalities in narcotic prescriptions. They found and notified at least 36 providers to whom they would no longer fill orders due to high prescription rates.

Another incident in 2014 involving the disappearance of 37,000 pain pills in four California stores brought the DEA and CVS together again. These stores have a history of not being able to account for several pain prescription drugs. This incident carries up to 2,973 violations of the Federal Controlled Substances Act and could cost the company up to $29 million in penalties. In 2012, the DEA investigated missing pills in a store wherein an employee admitted taking approximately 20,000 pills. This piqued the curiosity of investigators, who found three retail locations that each had thousands of pills missing.

Death of a Shoplifter

In 2010, a man accused of shoplifting toothpaste was chased out of a CVS store by a manager. Video surveillance footage showed an altercation between the two. Six bystanders came to the manager's assistance, one of whom was seen kicking and punching the perpetrator while the manager held him around the neck. Within seconds, the man was heard saying he could not breathe and died shortly thereafter. Police investigated the incident and have not filed charges despite the medical examiner's classification of the death as a homicide. The manager claimed that the shoplifter punched him, so he retaliated in self defense. The victim's mother is filing a civil lawsuit against the manager and claiming CVS is liable for her son's death. Whether or not CVS is found culpable, the tragedy cast a shadow over CVS and how it handles shoplifters.

MOVING TOWARD A HEALTHCARE COMPANY

Despite the ethical challenges CVS has experienced, it is trying to reposition itself as a socially responsible organization that places priority on consumer health. Being a quality healthcare company not only offers reputational benefits, but financial advantages as well. Changes in both the economic and healthcare landscape are creating new opportunities for CVS to provide different programs and redefine itself. Trends including the declining number of primary care physicians, the 16 million baby boomers who are becoming eligible for Medicare benefits, and the more than 30 million newly insured Americans under the Affordable Care Act (ACA) offer CVS an attractive market in which to expand. For example, CVS has refocused its efforts on supplying the growing need for chronic disease management that consumes costly resources when patients do not adhere to physician recommended medications and monitoring methods to maintain health. PBM services are being successfully implemented, including mail order, specialty pharmacy, plan design and administration, formulary management, discounted drug purchase arrangements, and disease management services.

Innovative programs such as Pharmacy Advisor and Maintenance Choice, developed in collaboration with researchers from Harvard University and Brigham and Women's Hospital, help patients stay on their medications. Research shows that regular interaction between patient and pharmacist increases the likelihood that patients will adhere to their medication regimen. Many patients who take regular prescriptions often think that they are well enough to cease taking their medication. However, when the symptoms of their ailments reappear, the costs are great, both financially and medically. CVS's programs allow the company to inform patients about the benefits and risks of these effects through education and awareness. The entire industry also benefits from this knowledge by preventing more costly medical procedures due to medication non-adherence, which occurs when patients skip or incorrectly take their dosage requirements. This is estimated to cost between $5 and $10 for every $1 spent on adherence programs. These services are key components of CVS's competitive advantage, allowing them to provide the best possible patient care. They were also proactive in preparing patients for Health Care Reform. For instance, CVS/Caremark partnered with the Centers for Medicare and Medicaid Services to raise awareness about new services available to Medicare patients under the ACA.

To help people keep up with these and other changes in healthcare, CVS has established its presence on social media and mobile devices. The company introduced a mobile application for customers to conveniently refill prescriptions, while their Facebook and Twitter pages provide helpful health tips. Customers benefit from using CVS's digital tools for savings and new user experience. CVS's iPad application allows individuals to have a 3D digital pharmacy experience reminiscent of shopping in a store. Those who are unable to physically visit the store, or prefer the convenience of shopping from home, are able to partake in the CVS experience through the company's technology. With over 10 million registered users, many are saving money and time filling and refilling prescriptions as well as having instant access to essential drug information.

MinuteClinics are one of the major contributors to CVS's rebranding efforts. These clinics are the first in healthcare retail history to be accredited by the Joint Commission, the national evaluation and certifying agency for healthcare organizations and programs in the United States. This accreditation signifies the clinic's commitment to and execution in providing safe, quality healthcare that meets nationally set standards.

In addition to healthcare services, MinuteClinics provide smoking cessation and weight loss programs that contribute positively to people's health. These clinics are also the first retail clinic provider to launch a partnership with the National Patient Safety Foundation for its health literacy program to help improve patient education and community health.

Under the ACA, healthcare organizations are eligible to become members of the Accountable Care Organizations (ACO) program. This program ensures that members are accountable in providing quality healthcare to the sick as well as meeting certain standards to provide health-conscious programs such as those related to smoking cessation and weight loss. Accountability is measured by positive outcomes, resulting in cost savings, which in turn is divided up among members to continue these effective programs and services. There are more than 700 ACOs covering 23.5 million patients, with 7.8 million a part of Medicare ACO programs.

REVEALING CVS'S NEW DIRECTION: TOBACCO-FREE CVS

In order to be consistent with their transition from pharmacy to healthcare company, CVS has made some landmark decisions aimed toward helping individuals lead healthier lives. In 2014, CVS announced that it would no longer sell tobacco products. The revenues generated from selling tobacco products are about $2 billion annually, so this bold decision sends a strong message to stakeholders regarding the values of the company. A company that is consistent in their actions will gain a good reputation, which will attract more customers and generate revenue. This decision also gives CVS an advantage in terms of the ACA. As the ACA changes the healthcare landscape, companies are racing to get a stronghold in the new system to be listed as a preferred pharmacy. CVS/Caremark's alignment in defining itself as a healthcare provider will likely result in stronger relationships with doctors and hospitals, creating an advantage of preference. The goal is that referrals for medication will be done through CVS and serve to boost reputation within all CVS segments. This, in conjunction with its status as an ACO, puts CVS in a competitive position to attract newly insured Americans.

This decision spurred 24 state attorneys general to send letters to other pharmacy retailers, including Walmart Stores, Inc., Walgreen Co., and Rite Aid Corp., highlighting the contradiction of selling deadly products and healthcare services simultaneously. The letter also noted that drug store sales make it easier for younger age groups to begin smoking and more difficult for those trying to quit smoking. Walmart and Walgreen acknowledged the letter, but made no indication that they would stop selling tobacco products. Rite Aid responded by saying they will continue to sell both tobacco products as well as smoking cessation services, as the practice is legal. While this letter does not seem to have much of an influence on retailers, some speculate that it increases the pressure on the $100 billion tobacco industry, which is already facing decreasing sales, rising taxes, and smoking bans. For CVS, the decision will affect their short-term profits and reduce each share by $0.06–$0.09 each. Investors do not seem worried, however, as the long-term benefits will make up the difference.

CRITICISM AGAINST CVS

CVS's new programs are encroaching on the medical industry by providing services to patients. As customers increasingly choose to visit local pharmacy clinics for aches, pains, or common illnesses, primary physicians are feeling the losses, especially since this sector's healthcare professionals are dwindling. Choosing a retail pharmacy clinic over a physician's office benefits the patient with lower costs and savings, which is a threat to traditional doctors' offices. Some groups are publicizing negative feedback on pharmacy care. For instance, the American Academy of Pediatrics issued a statement warning patients not to visit such clinics because they cannot offer the specialized care children need. Some groups argue that programs such as CVS's MinuteClinic do not offer the same caliber of service and care as a doctor. However, as stated above, CVS holds itself to a very high standard for care in trying to help patients be healthy. It continues to be accredited by the Joint Commission.

CVS MinuteClinics do recognize their limitations, however. Their website offers information to visitors regarding when they should and should not visit the clinics. For example, the website recommends that patients with severe symptoms such as chest pain, shortness of breath and difficulty breathing, poisoning, temperatures above 103 degrees Fahrenheit (for adults) and 104 (for children), and ailments requiring controlled substances should seek care elsewhere. MinuteClinics staff nurse practitioners and physician assistants who are able to provide services for minor wounds, common illnesses, wellness tests and physicals, etc. Other information regarding insurance and pricing are also available on the website.

STAKEHOLDER ORIENTATION

CVS's mission to be a pharmacy innovation company is guided by five values: innovation, collaboration, caring, integrity, and accountability. CVS uses these values to determine their actions and decisions, which offers a glimpse into their ethical culture. The company's goal is to use their assets to reinvent the pharmacy experience and offer innovative solutions that help people on a better path to health. This goal relays to stakeholders that the company cares about their health. CVS/Caremark's business is committed to fostering a culture that encourages creativity and innovation, recognizing that contributions from all members are a high priority. This commitment highlights their value of collaboration with partners and stakeholders, which also serves to hold them accountable for their operating activities—thus strengthening their integrity. Another important factor in their ethical culture is to address enhanced access to care while also lowering its cost.

CEO Larry J. Merlo emphasizes the long-term perspective the company is committed to with each decision and how it will affect each stakeholder group. He states that CVS's priorities remain in customer health, the sustainability of healthcare systems, good stewardship, positive contributions to their communities, and a meaningful workplace for employees. Such a statement from the top leader of the company sets the tone that creates the ethical culture behind CVS. The company's Code of Conduct includes ethical behavior expectations, and they are proud to have good relationships with employee unions who represent approximately 6 percent of their workforce. CVS employs a Chief Compliance Officer, offers regular compliance education and training, provides an ethics hotline for confidential reporting, and has developed a response and prevention guideline for addressing violations of CVS's policies or federal, state, or local laws. CVS's corporate governance includes a privacy program, information security, and a corporate framework that focuses on the company's values.

So far we have addressed how CVS meets the needs of its customer stakeholders. However, CVS tries to maintain a stakeholder orientation in which all stakeholder needs are addressed. The following sections will describe how they meet the needs of other stakeholders.

Employees

CVS implemented the Values in Action program for employees, giving them a chance to recognize colleagues through online reward systems. Peers can nominate each other across the company for leadership traits and other commendable accomplishments. Each nomination grants points, which can be redeemed for merchandise, travel, and more. Programs like these let employees know they are valued and empower them in their commitment to CVS. The Values in Action Breakthrough Awards is an annual company-wide broadcast that honors specific individuals exemplifying the company's values in innovation, collaboration, caring, integrity, and accountability.

CVS focuses strongly on compliance and integrity training for employees. The compliance and integrity training for employees is led by a Compliance Officer. Regular compliance education and training programs, a confidential 24/7 ethics hotline, and an efficient audit, response, and prevention process are components that make this program comprehensive. The company also supports the development of employees through professional development training sessions. The purpose of such training is not only to keep employees current on new technologies and processes but to help them advance in their careers within the company.

Shareholders

CVS seeks to protect shareholder interests while maintaining broad stakeholder engagement. As a result, CVS carefully designed a comprehensive corporate governance system ranging from board independence to executive compensation. Following a corporate governance framework, a variety of specialized committees has been established with different functions for shareholders. From an information governance standpoint, the oversight committee makes recommendations to enhance the ability of information security. On behalf of the board of directors, the audit committee is in charge of the risk oversight and is responsible for protecting the reputation and core interests of the company.

In order to balance the interests of different groups, senior management created a reformative executive compensation system. This system is based on financial performance as well as service quality and customer satisfaction. While a pay for performance compensation system is still utilized at CVS, a significant portion of annual executive compensation is delivered into long-term equity rather than short-term. In a move to further align the commitment of CVS to link pay with performance, total shareholder return is added on a three-year incentive plan. Each three-year period is known as a cycle that has a predetermined set of goals for the company/executive to accomplish. At the end of each term, performance is evaluated and the executive will receive compensation based on these results. For example, if the results surpass the goal by 25 percent, the executive pay will increase by a certain predetermined amount. The details will vary for each cycle, but the purpose of the plan is to pay only when the company and its shareholders are benefited from the performance of the executive.

Communities

CVS has grown its ethical culture not only to include the company's functions but the communities around them. Community engagement and philanthropic endeavors, for example, are long-standing commitments CVS has devoted time and resources in developing. Community partnerships have supported veteran hiring, scholarships to future pharmacists, and engaged high school, college, and post-graduate students' interest in science, technology, engineering, and math (STEM) careers. CVS believes that by helping to further advancements in the best health outcomes, they are investing in their current and future workforce.

CVS donated over $56 million to various organizations to support community needs and builds strategic partnerships with them to create an awareness of healthy behaviors and educate the community on ways to become insured under the ACA. The company also offers free health screenings and flu shots for the uninsured, prescription discount card programs, and other community programs to supply individuals with the medications they need to maintain health. The discount card program saves customers over 70 percent on medications, resulting in millions of dollars in savings every year. Volunteerism is also supported by CVS, as employees are encouraged to form groups and obtain sponsorship from the company to address needs within their community. The amount of time that CVS employees volunteered for their communities is valued at $1.5 million.

Suppliers

CVS has developed a commitment called Prescription for a Better World, which encompasses their Code of Conduct, Supplier Ethics Policy, Supplier Diversity, and Supplier Audit Program to promote integrity, accountability, and diversity. These programs work to ensure that human rights are respected throughout the entire supply chain. In developing these policies, CVS used principles initiated by the International Labor Organization and the United Nations' Universal Declaration of Human Rights. The human rights framework guides all suppliers of CVS to avoid unethical and illegal practices such as child labor, human trafficking, discrimination, and dangerous workplace conditions.

The Supplier Audit Program is a risk-based assessment conducted by more than one third party to evaluate workplace conditions, including labor, wages and hours, health and safety, management system and environment, as well as operational, financial and legal risks, to assure that employees' rights are not being violated. This program was fully expanded to factories in countries considered to be at high risk for such violations, and they are in the process of implementing full social audits for subcontractors in these areas. In addition, CVS works with globally recognized organizations including Worldwide Responsible Accredited Production (WRAP) and Social Accountability International (SAI) to ensure their measurements are relevant and effective. Finally, partnerships with Intertek's GSV program maintains the company's certification status with the U.S. Customs-Trade Partnership Against Terrorism (C-TPAT) program to ensure quality of products made in countries such as China.

Environmental Impact

Environmental impact is also important to CVS. They record their progress on this front in their annual Corporate Social Responsibility (CSR) Report. They have set a carbon intensity reduction goal of 15 percent by 2018, and through energy efficiency upgrades have been able to surpass this goal by reaching 16 percent in 2015. CVS opened their first Leadership in Energy and Environmental Design (LEED) Platinum store, which will serve as a test site to determine the most effective and relevant environmental innovations for the company's environmental operations goals. They will use this information to set best practices before constructing other stores.

CVS expanded their Energy Management System (EMS), which is designed to ISO (International Organization for Standardization) specifications. This digital system tracks and manages energy use, so that each store can be continually monitored and adjusted according to each location's condition. They are also in the process of upgrading lighting in the stores to more energy efficient bulbs. Increasing water use was identified as a significant inefficiency, and CVS has responded by eliminating irrigation at retail locations and opting for less water-intensive landscapes. Finally, CVS offers customers ways to recycle and properly dispose of expired, unused, or unwanted medications, which benefits both human and environmental well-being.

CONCLUSION

CVS is implementing strategies and allocating resources in the hope of achieving an ethical culture that benefits all stakeholder groups. This helps CVS to maximize ethical decision-making and remain sustainable for years to come. It seems they have learned from previous ethical lapses by being aware of addiction problems within their communities. In 2014, CVS voluntarily opted to stop selling some cold medications in West Virginia and surrounding areas as more methamphetamine labs and corresponding abuse became more prominent throughout the state. The company's impact on the environment is one of the next big challenges they will have to overcome. As one of the largest pharmacies in the United States, they have a long way to go to reduce their overall footprint. However, they are on the right track, having set goals and implementing action steps to achieve these goals. With the mission of helping people live healthier lives and innovating the pharmacy industry, CVS has a great responsibility in developing a business model allowing them to remain competitive while acting ethically at the same time.

Questions for Discussion

1. How has CVS handled its ethical challenges?
2. Evaluate CVS's decision to no longer sell tobacco products.
3. What is the future of CVS in positioning itself as a healthcare company based on its decision to be socially responsible?

Sources

Reed Abelson and Natasha Singer, "CVS Settles Prescription Price Case," *The New York Times*, January 12, 2012, http://www.nytimes.com/2012/01/13/business/cvs-caremark-settles-charges-over-prescription-prices.html (accessed August 9, 2016).

Devlin Barrett, "Judge Rules against CVS in Oxycodone Fight," *The Wall Street Journal*, March 13, 2012, http://online.wsj.com/news/articles/SB10001424052702303717304577279871365405382 (accessed August 9, 2016).

Nathan Bomey, "CVS launches rebranding of Target pharmacy," *USA Today*, February 3, 2016, http://www.usatoday.com/story/money/2016/02/03/target-cvs-health-pharmacy-store/79701130/ (accessed August 9, 2016).

Rebecca Borison, "CVS/Pharmacy iPad App Mimics in-store Experience," *Mobile Commerce Daily*, August 14, 2013, http://www.mobilecommercedaily.com/cvspharmacy-exec-offering-virtual-store-experience-via-ipad-app (accessed August 9, 2016).

Hank Cardello, "CVS and the Rise of Corporate Profitable Morality," *Forbes*, February 27, 2014, http://www.forbes.com/sites/forbesleadershipforum/2014/02/27/cvs-and-the-rise-of-profitable-corporate-morality/#2569f0383aca (accessed August 9, 2016).

"Corporate Social Responsibility Report," CVS Caremark, 2013, http://info.cvscaremark.com/CSR-Report/#1 (accessed August 9, 2016).

CVS Health, "History," https://cvshealth.com/about/company-history (accessed August 9, 2016).

"CVS Caremark Maintenance Choice Program Improves Medication Adherence for US Airways Employees and Dependents," *PR Newswire*, http://www.prnewswire.com/news-releases/cvs-caremark-maintenance-choice-program-improves-medication-adherence-for-us-airways-employees-and-dependents-102946359.html (accessed August 9, 2016).

"CVS Caremark Settles FTC Charges: Failed to Protect Medical and Financial Privacy of Customers and Employees; CVS Pharmacy Also Pays $2.25 Million to Settle Allegations of HIPAA Violations," The Federal Trade Commission, February 18, 2009, http://www.ftc.gov/news-events/press-releases/2009/02/cvs-caremark-settles-ftc-chargesfailed-protect-medical-financial (accessed August 2, 2014).

CVS Health, "CVS Health at a Glance," https://cvshealth.com/about/facts-and-company-information (accessed August 9, 2016).

CVS Health, "Our New Name," September 3, 2014, http://cvshealth.com/newsroom/our-new-name (accessed August 9, 2016).

CVS Health, *Prescription for a Better World: 2015 Corporate Social Responsibility Report*, 2016, http://cvshealth.com/sites/default/files/2015-csr-report.pdf (accessed August 9, 2016).

"CVS Pays $2.25 Million & Toughens Disposal Practices to Settle HIPAA Privacy Case," U.S. Department of Health and Human Services, http://www.hhs.gov/ocr/privacy/hipaa/enforcement/examples/cvsresolutionagreement.html (accessed August 9, 2016).

Mike Estrel, "States Urge Retailers to Drop Tobacco," *The Wall Street Journal*, March 18, 2014, p. B3.

"Everybody Loves a Quitter," CVS MinuteClinic, http://www.cvs.com/minuteclinic/resources/smoking-cessation (accessed August 9, 2016).

Joseph H. Harmison, "CVS Caremark Abuses Warrant through FTC Investigation and Remedies," *The Hill*, May 25, 2010, http://thehill.com/blogs/congress-blog/healthcare/99759-cvs-caremark-abuses-warrant-through-ftc-investigation-and-remedies (accessed August 9, 2016).

Chris Isidore, "Cigarette Sales: Walgreens, Rite-Aid, Wal-Mart, Kroger & Safeway Urged to Selling Tobacco," *CNN Money*, March 17, 2014, http://www.wptv.com/web/wptv/news/health/cigarette-sales-walgreens-rite-aid-wal-mart-kroger-safeway-urged-to-selling-tobacco (accessed August 6, 2014).

Bruce Japsen, "How Obamacare Helps CVS Kick The Habit," *Forbes,* February 2, 2014, http://www.forbes.com/sites/brucejapsen/2014/02/15/how-obamacare-helps-cvs-kick-the-habit/#4ef34990179b (accessed August 9, 2016).

Elisabeth Leamy, "Drug Discount Cards Help You Save on Prescription Meds," *ABC News*, August 20, 2012, http://abcnews.go.com/Business/drug-discount-cards-save-money-prescription-meds/story?id=17029498 (accessed August 9, 2016).

Donna Leinwand Leger, "DEA: Oxycodone Orders by Pharmacies 20 Times Average," *USA Today*, February 7, 2012, http://usatoday30.usatoday.com/money/industries/health/story/2012-02-06/dea-cvs-oxycodone-raid/52994168/1 (accessed August 9, 2016).

Natasha Leonard, "Homeless man Choked to Death After Shoplifting Toothpaste," *Salon*, January 18, 2013, http://www.salon.com/2013/01/18/homeless_man_choked_to_death_after_shoplifting_toothpaste/ (accessed August 9, 2016).

"The Long-Term Incentive Plan, CVS Caremark," March 24, 2009, http://www.wikinvest.com/stock/CVS_Caremark_Corporation_(CVS)/Long-term_Incentive_Plan (accessed August 9, 2016).

Kris Maher and Sara Germano, "CVS Takes Steps on Meth Abuse in West Virginia," *The Wall Street Journal*, July 8, 2014, p. A3.

Timothy W. Martin, "CVS to Kick Cigarette Habit," *The Wall Street Journal*, February 6, 2014, pp. B1–B2.

James P. Miller, "CVS Caremark Settles Deceptive-practices Complaint for $38.5 Million," *Chicago Tribune*, February 15, 2008, http://articles.chicagotribune.com/2008-02-15/business/0802140788_1_cvs-caremark-caremark-rx-pharmacy-benefits (accessed August 9, 2016).

Chris Morran, "CVS Being Investigated After 37,000 Pain Pills Go Missing," *The Consumerist*, March 11, 2014, http://consumerist.com/2014/03/11/cvs-being-investigated-after-37000-pain-pills-go-missing/ (accessed May 9, 2016).

Mark Morelli, "Healthy First: CVS Will Stop Selling Cigarettes," *The Motley Fool*, February 7, 2014, http://www.fool.com/investing/general/2014/02/07/healthy-first-cvs-will-stop-selling-cigarettes.aspx (accessed August 9, 2016).

David Muhlstein, "Growth and Dispersion of Accountable Care Organizations in 2015," *Health Affairs Blog*, March 31, 2015, http://healthaffairs.org/blog/2015/03/31/growth-and-dispersion-of-accountable-care-organizations-in-2015-2/ (accessed August 9, 2016).

"Pharmacy Advisor," *CVS Caremark*, http://info.cvscaremark.com/cvs-insights/our-pharmacy-advisor-program (accessed August 9, 2016).

Paul Edward Parker, "Rite Aid Responds to CVS Decision to Stop Selling Tobacco," *Providence Journal*, February 6, 2014, http://www.providencejournal.com/article/20140206/News/302069917 (accessed August 9, 2016).

Amy Pavuk, "Rx for Danger: DEA Blasts CVS for Ignoring 'Red Flags' at Sanford Stores," *Orlando Sentinel*, October 28, 2012, http://articles.orlandosentinel.com/2012-10-28/news/os-cvs-dea-oxycodone-ban-20121028_1_sanford-cvs-sanford-pharmacies-sanford-stores (accessed August 9, 2016).

Amy Pavuk, "Two Sanford Pharmacies Banned From Selling Oxycodone, Controlled Substances," *Orlando Sentinel*, September 12, 2012, http://articles.orlandosentinel.com/2012-09-12/news/os-sanford-cvs-caremark-revoke-drugs-20120912_1_revokes-prescription-drug-abuse-oxycodone-and-other-prescription (accessed August 9, 2016).

"Press Release: More Partnerships between Doctors and Hospitals Strengthen Coordinated Care for Medicare Beneficiaries," Centers for Medicare and Medicaid Services Press Release, December 23, 2013, https://www.cms.gov/Newsroom/MediaReleaseDatabase/Press-Releases/2013-Press-Releases-Items/2013-12-23.html (accessed August 9, 2016).

"Quality," CVS MinuteClinic, http://www.cvs.com/minuteclinic/visit/about-us/quality (accessed August 9, 2016).

"Services," CVS MinuteClinics, http://www.cvs.com/minuteclinic/services (accessed August 9, 2016).

Kyle Stock, "Pediatricians Seek Risk-to Kids and Themselves-in DrugStore Health Clinics," *Bloomberg*, February 24, 2014, http://www.bloomberg.com/news/articles/2014-02-24/apa-warns-parents-about-cvs-and-walgreens-child-health-clinics (accessed August 9, 2016).

Christopher Tkaczyk, "The 10 biggest companies of the Fortune 500," *Fortune*, June 4, 2015, http://fortune.com/2015/06/04/biggest-companies-fortune-500/ (accessed August 9, 2016).

"We're a Pharmacy Innovation Company and Every Day We're Working to Make Health Care Better," About CVS Caremark, http://info.cvscaremark.com/about-us/our-purpose-building-bridge-better-health (accessed August 5, 2014).

Jessica Wohl, "CVS Cuts Off Docs Who Prescribe Too Many Narcotics," *NBC News*, August 22, 2013, http://www.nbcnews.com/health/health-news/cvs-cuts-docs-who-prescribe-too-many-narcotics-f6C10975693 (accessed August 9, 2016).

Belle Meade Plantation: The First Nonprofit Winery Engages in Social Entrepreneurship

INTRODUCTION

Belle Mead Plantation, over 200 years old, is using social entrepreneurship to preserve the history of the nineteenth century. In 1807, John Harding founded the Belle Meade Plantation in Nashville, Tennessee. The plantation would become known for breeding some of the best-known thoroughbred horses in U.S. history. By the time of the U.S. Civil War, the Plantation had become famous as a 5,400-acre stud farm that was producing some of the best racehorses in the United States. Following the Civil War, much of the thoroughbred industry moved to the Lexington, Kentucky area. Kentucky remained in the Union and had the advantage during reconstruction. However, Belle Meade recovered, and various family members managed a successful thoroughbred breeding plantation that was among the best in the nation. After the plantation was sold early in the twentieth century, the grounds of Belle Meade Plantation were eventually converted into a museum focusing on its history. Today Belle Meade Plantation operates as a nonprofit to preserve its history and provide an opportunity to experience life in the nineteenth century. The plantation gives families the chance to have an educational experience. Guests can visit the plantation and tour the mansion, stables, and other buildings to experience 'stepping back in time.'

This case focuses on the challenges in 2004 when Alton Kelley, executive director of Belle Meade Plantation, and his wife, Sheree, were both facing the monumental task of securing adequate, long-term funding to maintain Belle Meade Plantation. At the time, the existing sources of funding for the operations of Belle Meade Plantation were (in descending revenue order): (1) ticket sales from visiting tourists, (2) hosting special events, (3) corporate and private donations, and (4) sales of items from the gift shop, including a line of private-labeled products, such as cheese, country ham, grits, and a variety of souvenirs. For the fifth consecutive year, donations from corporations and individuals had declined to the lowest levels in memory, and the couple believed they had little choice but to look for solutions that were well outside of the proverbial box. The organization and its board of directors could no longer rely solely on corporate donations for the ongoing operations of the Belle Meade Plantation.

After evaluating and discarding a variety of other alternatives, the Kelleys set about pursuing an ambitious plan to use social entrepreneurship to generate revenue for maintaining the nonprofit. Their solution was to build and operate a nonprofit winery on the historic site to help sustain current and future long term financing needs. The idea was bold, given that there were no other known nonprofit wineries in the United States. However, the Kelleys believed that if they could successfully navigate through the numerous legal and market-based challenges, this social enterprise would provide the necessary funding required for supporting the property's ongoing operations.

The first step was in 2009, when The Harding House Restaurant opened on the grounds, immediately adjacent to the mansion, to replace the popular "Martha's at the Plantation." The restaurant is an independent operation and pays rent to Belle Meade Plantation with all profits remaining in the restaurant.

This case will analyze the next step of Belle Meade's use of social entrepreneurship to create a sustainable organization. We begin by examining the history of Belle Meade Plantation. Next, background is provided on the challenges nonprofits encounter in trying to remain economically sustainable. Belle Meade recognized that the market for wine in Tennessee offered a major opportunity, leading them to adopt the nation's only nonprofit winery. We then discuss the different forms of promotion used to promote Belle Meade and its winery, including social media and events. We conclude with an examination of some of the challenges Belle Meade is likely to encounter as it continues to expand.

*Dr. Robert P. Lambert and Dr. Joe Alexander, Belmont University © 2014. Alton Kelley, Executive Director of Belle Meade Plantation, and Sheree Kelley, Belle Meade Winery Manager, participated in developing this case. Jennifer Sawayda assisted in editing a version of this case. It was prepared for classroom discussion rather than to illustrate either effective or ineffective handling of an administrative, ethical, or legal decision by management. All sources used for this case were obtained through personal interviews, publicly available material, and the Belle Meade website.

BRIEF HISTORY OF BELLE MEADE PLANTATION

The roots of Belle Meade extend back to its successful breeding of thoroughbreds. As early as 1816, founder John Harding was placing advertisements in Nashville newspapers to promote his horses. In 1820, he commissioned a brick home in the Federal style on his farm and officially named the estate "Belle Meade." By this time, he became interested in racing his horses locally. John registered his own racing silks with the Nashville Jockey Club in 1823 and was training horses on the track at another of his properties, McSpadden's Bend Farm. By the time John Harding's son, William Giles Harding, assumed management of the Belle Meade plantation, he already shared his father's interest in breeding and racing. Even though the Civil War interrupted both breeding and horse-racing in the southern United States, Belle Meade was large enough in acreage to elude Union troops by hiding the prized horses at various locations throughout the heavily wooded nearby hills.

After the Civil War, Harding became famous for winning more purses with his horses than any man living at that time in the United States—even though much of the thoroughbred industry had moved to Kentucky. He was also the first in Tennessee to use the auction system for selling thoroughbreds. With the auction system, he became the most successful thoroughbred breeding farm and distributor in the State of Tennessee. Belle Meade's breeding lineage has boasted some of the best-known thoroughbred horses in U.S. history, including *Bonnie Scotland*, *Secretariat*, *Seabiscuit*, *Barbaro*, and 2014 Kentucky Derby winner *California Chrome*. When General Harding died in 1886, *The Spirit of the Times* praised him as having done as much to promote breeding interests as any American in the nineteenth century.

After Harding's death, his son-in-law General William Hicks Jackson and oldest daughter assumed one-third ownership of the horse farm. General Jackson's flair for entertaining and his confident, outgoing nature helped the farm attract thousands of people to the yearling sales. He later modernized the mansion's interior. By the time the plantation was sold in the early twentieth century, it had hosted a number of American historical figures, including President Grover Cleveland, Robert Todd Lincoln, General Ulysses S. Grant, General William T. Sherman, General Winfield Scott Hancock, and Adlai E. Stevenson.

Today, the Greek revival-styled mansion is the centerpiece of the affluent Belle Meade region of Nashville, with the historic homestead surrounded by 30 acres of manicured lawns and shade trees. A long driveway leads uphill to the mansion, fronted by six columns and a wide veranda. Inside, the restored building is furnished with nineteenth-century antiques that illustrate the elegance and wealth that the Southern gentility enjoyed in the late 1800s. Tours are provided to the general public, with costumed guides following a theme that changes every three months with the seasons. These themed tours are intended to provide fascinating glimpses into the lives of the people who once lived at Belle Meade. During the tour, visitors are able to see the numerous historic facilities on the property, including a log cabin, smokehouse, and creamery. The tour makes the nineteenth century come alive and provides an opportunity to experience life in the nineteenth century. Belle Meade's park-like grounds has made it a popular site for festivals throughout the year.

NONPROFITS MOVE IN DIRECTION OF SOCIAL ENTREPRENEURSHIP

Recent decades have led to challenges for nonprofits like Belle Meade Plantation. Since the last economic downturn reduced household incomes and lowered investors' and consumers' confidence in the economy, nonprofit contributions plummeted. Most nonprofits' incomes dwindle during recessionary periods based on a variety of factors: (1) corporate and individual donations decrease, (2) federal, state, and local funding sources decline, and (3) earnings from endowments shrink with their capital market values. At the same time, economic downturns also put added demands on nonprofits' already dwindling resources, including: (1) a typical increase in the frequency of client requests for financial or service needs, and (2) a decrease in the number of individuals who, based on concerns regarding their own household incomes, are either unable or unwilling to volunteer their time in support of an organizational mission. As a result, nonprofits tend to focus their dollars more directly into client services. Charitable contributions to nonprofits bottomed out in 2009. The average rate of growth in charitable giving during 2010 and 2011 was at its lowest in 40 years. Even as the economy began to improve, many nonprofits continued to report that their contributions had either decreased or remained stable.

Belle Meade was faced with exactly these problems. Like other nonprofits, its leaders needed to look for innovative solutions toward increasing the long-term sustainability of their organizations. As leaders of the nonprofit sector plan for the future, understanding the economic climate and the actions taken as a result of challenging economic times can assist executive directors and other leaders in determining strategically the operational needs of their organization and how to best serve their communities.

Nonprofit organizations, facing cuts in donations from individuals and organizations, have been experimenting with new ways to strengthen their bottom lines. In addition to cutting costs and eliminating waste, nonprofit leaders such as the Kelleys had to think more creatively about their fundraising strategies and consider the role of nontraditional philanthropic organizations or individuals. Even at significant levels of visitor traffic at Belle Meade, base admission ticket revenues were not nearly enough to fully support the site's operation. According to the Kelleys, "Every time there is a new charity in Nashville, the 'giving pie' gets thinner." The Kelleys therefore began to consider the idea of social entrepreneurship. Social entrepreneurship occurs when an entrepreneur founds a business with the purpose of creating social value. In this case, Belle Meade could sell a product and then use the proceeds to support the nonprofit. Generating their own revenue would reduce the dependence on outside contributions and make the nonprofit less susceptible to economic downturns.

The Kelleys knew that management clearly had no choice but to consider substantive changes in their revenue model in order to ensure long-term survival. The question involved deciding upon what product would be appropriate to sell to generate revenue and align with Belle Meade's strong historical roots. Management knew from historical research that Muscadine grapes were grown on the plantation back into the 1800s. The Hardings, Belle Meade's nineteenth-century founders, actually produced wine from the vineyards on their property. Curator John Lamb confirmed the story: "There are numerous invoices from the 1800s that show the Hardings purchased and served fine wines and also purchased empty wine bottles—presumably to fill with wines made on the property."

The Kelleys became convinced that resurrecting wine production and sales on the property would provide a major source of revenue and self-sufficiency for the property. The winery at Belle Meade Plantation would become the only winery registered in Nashville and the only nonprofit winery in the United States. Although it would operate as a nonprofit—reinserting profits into the maintenance and operation of the museum—the winery would effectively develop a strategic business approach and implement a successful revenue model.

MARKET FOR WINE IN TENNESSEE

The wine industry in Tennessee was dealt a blow with Prohibition during the 1920s, so until 1975 the state had no formal modern wineries. In the late 1970s, Judge William O. Beach championed legislation that enabled the State's wine industry to move forward more rapidly. Another industry leader was Fay Wheeler, who was instrumental in assuring passage of the Wine and Grape Act of 1977. In 1980, she started Tennessee's first licensed winery, and to many, Wheeler is considered the founder of Tennessee's contemporary wine industry. By 1995 Tennessee had 15 wineries, and in the next 10 years this number would double to 27. As of 2010, Tennessee boasted 45 registered wineries, with the likelihood of continued growth. Belle Meade recognized that these strong growth opportunities would be beneficial toward their decision to open a nonprofit winery.

There are, at present, between 500 and 750 acres of wine grapes grown in Tennessee—a number that is on the rise. Many vineyards are small (i.e., less than five acres), which is a challenge to growers, since wineries juggle the decision to buy small quantities locally or purchase larger quantities from outside the state's borders.

Finally, it is worth noting that not all wines are produced from grapes. Several Tennessee fruit-bearing trees or bushes are commonly used to produce what are accordingly referred to as "fruit wines." The more common take advantage of fruits such as black raspberries, peaches, blackberries, strawberries, rhubarb, and apples—all of which grow well within a portion of the geographic areas included within the State. For example, one of the wines that Belle Meade offers is a blackberry wine.

BEGINNING OF THE WINERY

Belle Meade did understand the challenge of developing a successful winery. It was not enough just to sell wine with a Belle Meade label. To align with Belle Meade's mission, the product would have to fit with the organization's historical background. "There was a lot of brainstorming among staff to come up with new ideas," the Kelleys claim. "And as we continue to believe, it is important that everything we do is connected to the site's heritage. We just look for ways to modernize what the original owners did and make money to support the site."

With a desire to narrow viable possibilities to those that fit with the historical nature of the Plantation's roots, the seeds of a winery concept began to germinate. A decision was subsequently made to visit the Biltmore Estate's Winery in Ashville, North Carolina as it is the most visited winery in the United States. "We were looking for best practices," the Kelleys said. These practices would be used to establish their own winery to support its nonprofit mission.

While the Kelleys' initial concept for a winery in Nashville was relatively small compared to Biltmore's, they saw incredible potential for such an operation since there were currently no wineries in Nashville. They also learned that at Biltmore, one out of five guests to the Estate made a wine purchase before leaving the property. This further fueled their beliefs that a winery would generate the revenue needed to operate Belle Meade. Their next decision was to locate the winery *on* the Belle Meade property.

The Kelleys presented their proposal for a winery at the next meeting with the board of directors. Through their research, the Kelleys had determined that an existing building on the property built in 1998 as an education venue could be converted into the winery and a gift shop. However, this would not come without financial risk. In order to get the winery operational, an investment of $250,000 would be required. The Kelleys had determined that in the first year of operation, all of the bottling activities would be done by hand using employees of the historic plantation, the winery, and volunteers. If sales increased beyond $1,000,000, mobile bottling equipment would be used for the higher volume.

The Kelleys provided the board with projected revenues for the first five years, along with the planned operation's anticipated expenses. Two of the board members were presidents of local banks and were convinced that the proposed winery was a fairly low-risk investment. The remaining board members concurred, and ultimately a final vote yielded approval for the project.

The Winery at Belle Meade first opened to visitors touring the mansion in November 2009. The building housing the winery made it a reasonably good fit for serving as the initial start-up site. By 2009, the directors of the historic plantation renovated the building for use as a combination winery and tasting room, and Brian Hamm was appointed as the winemaker. The staff began to research which wines should be produced to meet plantation revenue objectives. Advice from the local wine-making community informed them that if their objective was 'status,' then dry wines should be the target. However, they advised Belle Meade to adopt sweeter wines if their objective was to make money. It is no secret that Belle Meade's current portfolio of wines leans heavily to the sweet end of the spectrum. This fits with their objectives to generate revenue for the plantation.

A major start-up hurdle for Belle Meade turned out to be the issue of where to store the bottled wine. Ideally, the location needed to be secure and near the point-of-sale as well as of sufficient size to accommodate growth in volume over time. It also needed to be "climate-friendly" to minimize significant variations in temperature to protect the product. The best solution turned out to be the historical dairy located right there on the property. It was a large building located relatively close to the mansion. Because it was made out of stone, it created an almost ideal environment for storing the cases of wine. This became Belle Meade's bonded storage facility.

When the idea of a winery was first conceived, the Kelleys immediately realized that the existing 250,000 annual visitors to the historic property were going to be the primary initial market for the wines produced at the winery. Property tours were redesigned to conclude with an opportunity for guests to be escorted to the tasting room for a complimentary tasting. Each wine would be presented to include the background on its composition and properties, along with any relevant historical facts that aligned with what had been presented on the earlier tour. Each bottle comes in Belle Meade-specific packaging with thoroughbred horse designer labels to connect it with the Plantation's past. Because of the unique vintages produced at the winery, tourists often purchase multiple bottles and sometimes take cases back to their family and friends.

According to Sheree Kelley, Belle Meade Winery Manager, "We are different because people come to see the plantation and then discover the winery." As with all

FIGURE 1 Illustration of Hand-Bottling—Year One of Operations

social entrepreneurships, the main purpose is to create social change. As the Belle Meade Plantation website explains, the site makes history real for visitors by educating them about their historical roots. The winery profits are used for historical preservation of the Plantation and educational initiatives on-site. One such educational initiative involves hosting summer camps for children. During the school year, the nonprofit also underwrites many school trips to the Plantation, enabling children to experience and learn about the history of the 1800s.

SUCCESS BEYOND EXPECTATIONS: TOURS, TASTINGS, AND SOCIAL MEDIA

An official tour of the Belle Meade Plantation begins as guests enter the front doors of the mansion. The mansion is maintained as closely as possible to how it is believed to have existed in the 1890s. Upon entering the mansion, visitors enter a dark, subdued foyer decorated with framed pictures of racing horses to emphasize the plantation's history in thoroughbred breeding and racing. Since the 1990s, every horse that has run the Kentucky Derby has been a blood descendent of Belle Meade Plantation. Many of these legendary horses grace the various Belle Meade labels on their wine bottles.

After touring the grounds, visitors are invited to wine tastings in Belle Meade's tasting room. The interior of the tasting room fits in with the historical roots of the plantation, from the medium dark wood supported by a stone base to a wood-burning fireplace to add ambience to the room. Glass windows allow visitors a direct view into the tank room where the wine is stored prior to bottling. To enhance its warmth and hospitality, the room also includes a dessert counter with Peanut Butter Pecans, artisanal chocolates, and other confectionaries. These desserts also serve as added revenue for the nonprofit. A wine garden is available outside the doorway for visitors who want to purchase a bottle of wine and enjoy it on the premises. Since opening in 2009, the winery has become an all-staff effort. The winery has been an overwhelming success, exceeding the first year's 10,000-bottle sales goal with sales topping 54,000 bottles. Figure 1 shows an illustration of the company's hand-bottling efforts during the first year of operation. Belle Meade ensures that everyone on their staff is knowledgeable about the winery process. "Some of the grapes are grown and crushed in Middle Tennessee, and the juice is brought to our tanks on site. Everyone on staff knows how to bottle wine—it's a great team-building exercise," the Kelleys explain.

The winery's annual revenues has grown to approximately $3.0 million, with an additional $200,000 in wine-related merchandise. Table 1 presents a pro forma income statement summarizing the Winery's first four years of operations. However, despite their success, the Kelleys are careful to note that "starting a winery is a monumental decision. It's not for the faint of heart!"

Promoting the Social Enterprise

Belle Meade's staff does not rest on their laurels. Like any business, they recognize the need to engage in marketing. The winery sells all of its output each year at current prices, with the ability to sell more if storage and warehousing becomes available. The primary means of marketing the winery is through the organization's own website (www.bellemeadewinery.com), tourist visits, local press/media, social media, and word of mouth. Because of current demand for its products, the Winery has not undertaken any traditional advertising. However, it does make extensive use of social media for no-cost promotions with a quick turn-around time.

"In 2011, we started a Groupon promotion in the third week of January," stated the Kelleys. "We offered two tours and two free wine tastings at half-price and

TABLE 1 Pro Forma Income Statement—Belle Meade Winery 2010–2015

	2010	2011	2012	2013	2014	2015
Revenue:						
Wine Sales	$456,485	$1,019,346	$1,536,865	$2,001,223	$3,050,000	$3,150,000*
Gift Shop Sales	31,500	42,478	45,650	53,275	60,100	112,500**
Total Revenue	$487,985	$1,061,824	$1,582,515	$2,054,498	$3,110,100	$3,262,500
Expenses:						
Cost of Sales	$165,212	$375,620	$566,552	$736,714	$915,000	$1,308,000
Other Expenses	91,234	122,925	173,500	195,800	298,595	$424,000
Total Expenses	$256,446	$498,545	$730,052	$932,514	$1,213,595	$1,732,000
Net Income	$231,539	$563,279	$852,463	$1,121,984	$1,896,505	$1,530,000

• WINE STORAGE CAPACITY HAS BEEN REACHED, SO PRODUCTION HAS BEEN CAPPED - Lobbying to change state laws to allow off-site storage of bonded wine

** Growth has come from increase of food and wine tastings, sale of foods and cheese inside store, wine by the glass sales and increase in Wine Club memberships (500 plus)

sold 1,300 tickets. That is 2,600 people who have 60 days to redeem their voucher." Groupon's success prompted another discount voucher promotion through Living Social. A Valentine's Day special resulted in the sale of 1,000 tickets. Even more impressive, these incentives generated record sales in Belle Meade's slowest months. The Winery also hosts several events for the local community, such as Jazz on the Lawn during the summer and Tennessee's largest Kentucky Derby Party.

The organization is also examining market trends to improve demand for their tours. "We were looking at travel trends, and we know that people want to be more involved than just taking a tour," said the Kelleys. As a result, Belle Meade is introducing a Southern culinary experience using graduate students from the University of Mississippi's *Southern Foodways* program to create the tour. The plan is to use the original kitchen to give visitors the chance to taste Southern biscuits, beaten biscuits, and cornbread. The experience includes a tour of the root cellar and smokehouse where visitors will learn why the South's heat and humidity created a need for food preservation techniques such as curing ham.

New tours are also being planned that further incorporate the winery. With help from Belmont University's MBA students, a marketing plan was developed suggesting an event called the Progressive Wine Tour. This event would provide guests with a tour of the historic Belle Meade Mansion and a personalized walking tour of historical points of interest on the plantation property. During the tour, guests would be treated to five of the Belle Meade premium wines paired with light appetizers at focal points throughout the property.

The winery has become exceedingly popular. Many local prominent restaurants in Nashville have requested that Belle Meade wines become the official wine of their restaurant. The Winery has been forced to decline to sell to restaurants due to limited supply. The Winery also sells its products online and is available in over 15 states.

APPROACHING CHALLENGES FACING BELLE MEADE PLANTATION

While the winery has experienced phenomenal success since opening, there are still significant risk factors that it must address. One of the major challenges involves managing future growth. The winery is constrained by liquor laws that require the production of wine be done on-site where the wine is sold. An off-site storage facility is not legal in the State of Tennessee. Because visitation to the Plantation has grown at a record pace and approached capacity limits, handling the growing crowds and staffing at Belle Meade has proven to be a challenge.

Currently, Belle Meade Winery is the only winery located in Nashville. However, like any entrepreneurial endeavor success tends to create more competition. Belle Meade must be on the lookout for rivals who might choose to establish themselves in Nashville. While the company has seen great success with social media, to date it has done little in the way of formal promotional spending. Its excellent sales staff, outstanding products, captive audience, social media marketing, and a lack of direct competition eliminates the need for formal spending on promotion, but this might change if competitors enter the same area. It is also possible that other historic properties in Nashville, such as The Hermitage or Belmont Mansion, might try to pursue similar social entrepreneurship opportunities. Belle Meade still faces competition from other historic sites that capture consumers' time and money. Finally, with Nashville as the epicenter of the food movement, Belle Meade is faced with more decisions regarding whether to pair local foods and wines within their operations. These challenges illustrate that Belle Meade must operate with the same business concepts as for-profit organizations. Social entrepreneurship rests on a sound business strategy.

Questions for Discussion

1. Analyze the strengths and weaknesses of the Belle Meade strategy and implementation of their nonprofit winery.
2. Given the success of the current Belle Meade Winery, how can Belle Meade effectively address the challenges facing the winery for future growth?
3. Understanding the success of the Belle Meade Winery, what could other nonprofit organizations learn in creating social entrepreneurship ventures to sustain their operations?

Sources

Robert Barro, *Crisis of governments: The ongoing global financial crisis and recession,* 2011, http://www.iea.org.uk/sites/default/files/publications/files/Crises%20of%20Government.pdf (accessed August 8, 2016).

Belle Meade, "The History of Belle Meade," bellemeade-plantation.com/history (accessed August 8, 2016).

Belle Meade, "The Winery at Belle Meade Plantation," bellemeadewinery.com (accessed August 8, 2016).

Woods Bowman, "Financial Capacity and Sustainability of Ordinary Nonprofits," *Nonprofit Management Leadership* 22, no. 1 (Fall 2011): 37–51.

Julianne Gassman, Norma A Dolch, Ann Marie Kinnell, Regan Harwell Schaffer, Sue Ann Strom, and Amy Costliow, "A Three Year Study of the Nonprofit Sector's Response to the Economic Challenges in Six Cities Across the Nation," *Center for Nonprofit Strategy and Management,* Baruch College, The City University of New York, June 2012.

GuideStar, "Late Fall 2011 Nonprofit Fundraising Study," 2014, http://www.guidestar.org/rxg/news/publications/nonprofits-and-economy-late-fall-2011.aspx (accessed August 8, 2016).

Michelle Nichols, "Charities Still Struggling in Wake of Recession," *The Fiscal Times,* June 19, 2012, http://www.thefiscaltimes.com/Articles/2012/06/19/Charities-Still-Struggling-in-Wake-of-Recession (accessed August 8, 2016).

Lisa M. Sontag-Padilla, Lynette Staplefoot, and Kristy Gonzalez Morganti, *Financial Sustainability for Nonprofit Organizations; A Review of the Literature,* 2012, Rand Corporation, 1200 South Hayes Street, Arlington, VA, p. 2.

Terry and Kathy Sullivan, "Tennessee," *Wine Trail Traveler,* http://winetrailtraveler.com/tennessee/tennessee.php (accessed August 8, 2016).

"Welcome to Tennessee Wine Country," *Tennessee Wines,* http://www.tennesseewines.com/ (accessed August 8, 2016).

Multilevel Marketing Under Fire: Herbalife Defends Its Business Model

INTRODUCTION

Herbalife International is the third largest direct-selling, multi-level marketing company in the world. Its product line consists of weight-management and nutrition products. These products are not sold in retail stores; rather, consumers interact with independent contractors to order the products. Herbalife's headquarters are located in Los Angeles, California, and they operate in several countries throughout the world. Herbalife is a publicly traded company that is both loved and hated by investors and consumers.

This case first discusses the history of the company from its founding to its present status, followed by a description of the types of products Herbalife offers. Then we will get into a discussion of multilevel marketing and the role of independent contractors in the direct-selling model. Next will be a discussion of pyramid schemes and why they are often confused with the multilevel marketing model. We then examine Herbalife to determine whether it is a pyramid scheme.

We will illuminate the role of hedge fund investor William Ackman in the backdrop of Herbalife's business model and show his contentions with the company and some of the criticisms against him. The case shows that while Ackman's accusations may be the most widely known, there are other accusations (mostly referring to pyramid schemes) that Herbalife has had to face over the course of its existence. The case ends with a brief overview of Herbalife's social responsibility program and conclusions.

HISTORY

Herbalife is a company that focuses on nutrition, weight-management, and personal care products with independent contractors in more than 90 countries. Mark Hughes founded the company in 1980 out of a desire to create a safe alternative to other weight-loss products. Herbalife's first sales were made from out of the trunk of Hughes' car in Los Angeles, California, and two years later the company reached $2 million in sales. Herbalife was taken public in 1986 on the NASDAQ stock exchange. Since then, Herbalife has become a multi-billion dollar global company.

In 1999, Hughes planned to take the company back to the private sector by purchasing all of its remaining shares, but this attempt was stopped as investors sought legal action. The next year, Mark Hughes died unexpectedly at the age of 44. Christopher Pair, who was Herbalife's former Chief Operating Officer (COO), then became President and Chief Executive Officer (CEO) of the company. His reign at Herbalife was cut short as he stepped down one year later.

An Internet retailer, Rbid.com, made a bid of $173 million to acquire Herbalife, but the Mark Hughes Family Trust rejected the offer. In 2002, the investment firm J.H. Whitney & Co. purchased the company along with another investor and took it back to the private sector. However, in 2004, Herbalife went public once again and was traded on the New York Stock Exchange. Michael O. Johnson has been Herbalife's CEO since 2003. The company currently employs 8,000 people and has almost three million independent contractors throughout the world.

PRODUCTS

Herbalife sells weight-management, targeted nutrition, energy and fitness, and personal care products, all intended to support a healthy lifestyle. Additionally, the firm offers a set of core products: Formula 1 Nutritional Shake Mix is a protein and fiber shake with several minerals, vitamins, and nutrients offered in seven flavors; Formula 2 Multivitamin Complex is a multivitamin that contains over 20 vitamins, minerals, and herbs

*This case was prepared by Michelle Urban, Katy Melloy, Carin Malm, and Emily McGowan for and under the direction of O.C. Ferrell and Linda Ferrell ©2014. Jennifer Sawayda provided editorial assistance. It was prepared for classroom discussion rather than to illustrate either effective or ineffective handling of an administrative, ethical, or legal decision by management. All sources used for this case were obtained through publicly available material.

essential to healthy living; and Formula 3 Cell Activator promotes absorption of minerals and vitamins while improving energy levels. These three core products are at the heart of the Herbalife product line and serve as the baseline for nutrition and weight management goals.

The weight-management line consists of a variety of Formula 1 protein shakes, supplements, weight-loss enhancers, protein bars, and snacks, all serving the purpose of helping customers attain their weight goals. There are three weight-management program sets, each with a combination of shakes, supplements, and enhancers designed for different types of weight management needs. Each component of this line can also be purchased separately. The Personalized Protein Powder and the Protein Drink Mix offer an alternative to traditional meals while providing energy and curbing hunger cravings, whether consumers just want to lose or maintain their weight or build muscle mass. The enhancers and supplements offer a mix of vitamins, minerals, herbs, and nutrients. For example, Prolessa Duo and Snack Defense work to stave off hunger in order to control weight gain and help the body process sugars more efficiently. Other enhancers, such as Total Control, boost metabolism, energy, and alertness, while Thermo-Bond helps the digestive system. Cell-U-Loss helps the body eliminate unnecessary water and rejuvenate skin with its combination of herbal extracts. An assortment of healthy snacks and beverages are also offered in this line, such as protein bars, soups, teas, and soy nuts.

Targeted nutrition products include dietary and nutritional supplements that contain herbs, vitamins, minerals, and other natural ingredients to strengthen specific areas of the body that tend to be problematic for most people. For example, Tri-Shield helps the heart stay healthy by maintaining good cholesterol levels and providing antioxidants; Ocular Defense Formula and Joint Defense Advanced offer support to the eyes and joints of aging adults; Active Fiber Complex and Aloe Vera Powder helps those with digestive issues; RoseGuard and Schizandra Plus strengthen the liver, immune system, and cells; and Relax Now and Sleep Now, which are part of the stress management line, serve to promote ease and rest. Herbalife also offers nutrition products specifically for women, men, and children.

Herbalife also provides energy and hydration drinks for those engaged in sports and fitness activities. Customers can choose from an assortment of beverages such as Liftoff, a fizzy drink mix that enhances clarity and rehydrates the body, or they can choose supplements such as N-R-G Nature's Raw Guarana Tablets, which also promote mental clarity. Herbalife24 is the sports drink line that includes formulas for hydration, prolonged endurance, restoration of strength, and recovery.

Personal care products include skin cleansers, moisturizers, lotions, shampoos, and conditioners from a variety of different lines. Herbal Aloe Strengthening Shampoo and Conditioner, hand and body wash, cream, soothing gel, and bath and body bar is claimed to improve the look and feel of hair and skin. The Multivitamin line is similar to taking a multivitamin every day and includes a cleanser, toner, moisturizer, sunscreen, eye gel, and cream infused with vitamins for skin. Radiant C scrub cleanser, skin booster, and body lotion claim to renew and rehydrate the skin with a concentration of vitamin C. Other items include anti-aging products and fragrances for men and women.

MULTILEVEL MARKETING

Direct selling is the marketing of products to ultimate consumers through person-to-person sales presentations at home or online. People are attracted to direct selling for many reasons. Some are passionate about the product and want to promote the company. Others want to receive a discount on their personal orders. Many find working as a direct seller to be a flexible, part-time opportunity for extra income. Additionally, some independent contractors simply enjoy the social aspect of direct selling. Within the direct selling model are two compensation models: single-level marketing and multilevel marketing. Single-level marketing is when a contractor makes a commission for arranging a sale or earns a margin as a reseller. Multilevel marketing, sometimes called network marketing, is a compensation wherein contractors earn income from their own sales of products as well as commissions from sales made by those they have recruited. Sales are never forced, as a legitimate company does not force downline sales.

However, it is not necessary for contractors to recruit other individuals in order to earn money. It is a choice made by the contractor if they want to increase their earnings by making a commission from the sales of their recruits. Approximately 71–72 percent of Herbalife members are single-level distributors, meaning they do not sponsor other Herbalife distributors. This means that these Herbalife members buy products from the company at a discount and have the complete

TABLE 1 Top Ten Direct Selling Companies

	Company Name and Product Line	2015 Revenue (USD Billions)
1	Amway Nutrition, Beauty, Bath and Body, Home, Jewelry, Food and Beverage, Fragrances	$9.5
2	Avon Cosmetics, Skin Care, Fragrance, Personal Care, Hair Care, Jewelry, Gifts	$6.16
3	Herbalife Nutrition, Weight-Loss Management, Personal Care	$4.47
4	Vorwerk Household Appliances and Cosmetics	$4.00
5	Infinitus Chinese supplements	$3.58
6	Mary Kay Cosmetics, Skin Care, Body and Sun, Men's Product's, Fragrance Gifts	$3.70
7	Perfect Health Food, Household, Beauty, and Skincare Products	$3.58
8	Natura Cosmetics	$2.41
9	Tupperware Food Storage and Preparation, Cookware, Serving Items, Cosmetics, Beauty	$2.28
10	Nu Skin Skin Care	$2.25

Source: Direct Selling News, "2016 DSN Global 100 List," *Direct Selling News,* 2016, http://directsellingnews.com/index.php/view/2016_dsn_global_100_list#.V2ri93kUVVJ (accessed June 22, 2016).

freedom to determine pricing as well as in all decisions involving their final customers. Since many of these members simply want a discount on these products, they may not be as interested in making profits but simply enjoy the opportunity to receive these discounts. Furthermore, rewards are not given simply for recruiting another contractor. See Table 1 for the top ten global direct selling companies.

Another aspect of multilevel marketing involves internal consumption, which is the purchasing of products at a discount from the firm for the contractor's own use. Most retailers provide internal consumption incentives by offering discounts to employees who purchase products. Department stores, automobile manufacturers, and airline companies provide incentives such as discounts that encourage internal consumption. Many people become resellers to get discounts on products for their own use. Therefore, the claim that internal consumption is unacceptable is refutable on the basis that the vast majority of companies selling consumer products encourage their employees or independent

contractors to purchase their products. Many individuals committed to these products believe in the brands for their own personal use and want to 'spread the word' by creating a broader sales and communication network. Some do not even necessarily care about making a profit from the business. This is a common and legal approach for direct selling products around the world. In fact, most direct selling companies use multilevel marketing. At Herbalife, there is no limit to the number of levels of recruits.

Despite the legitimacy of multilevel marketing, China has restricted direct selling to single-level marketing only. China believes multilevel marketing is linked to fraudulent activities such as pyramid schemes because of the assumption that discounts are used to force internal consumption. China allows direct selling companies to do business within their borders if they sign a contract saying they will not employ the multilevel marketing aspect of direct selling. Instead of having independent contractors recruit others, they sell their products from retail stores.

INDEPENDENT CONTRACTORS

There are nearly 3 million independent contractors of Herbalife products, and all of them personally use these products. Many are attracted to the low startup cost of selling Herbalife. The startup cost for a part-time contractor is $57.75 for a kit. For this price, they will receive the mini-International Business Pack, which includes forms, applications, a tote bag, and samples of various Herbalife products. Informational and training materials educate the contractor on using and retailing the products, business basics, and how to build a sales and marketing plan. Alternately, if a contractor wants to work full-time, they can purchase the full International Business Pack for $89.55. This pack comes with all of the materials that the mini-pack offers but with more product samples and information on how to run your business. There is no fee to join, and the only money spent is for the value of the kit.

Contractors enjoy discounts off products, ranging from 25–50 percent depending on the level of contractorship. Herbalife resellers often purchase the products themselves and then resell them directly to buyers; however, it is possible for the reseller to make the sale and get the product directly from Herbalife. Resellers can resell the products at any price they want. Each Herbalife product has a certain number of Value Points, and the number of Value Points a contractor accumulates determines what level of contractorship he or she has. Personally purchased Value Points are awarded based on the volume that a contractor purchases from Herbalife using his or her Herbalife identification number. Royalty Override Points are accumulated based on the Total Volume of products sold by personally sponsored supervisors that the reseller has recruited.

To go from basic distributor to the Senior Consultant level, a Herbalife member must have accumulated a minimum of 500 Volume Points in one month. To be promoted from Senior Consultant to Senior Contractor, a contractor must accumulate at least 1,000 personally purchased Value Points in one order. Levels after that include Qualified Producer (2,500 Volume Points accumulated in 1–3 months), Supervisor (4,000 Value Points in one month, 2,500 Value Points in each of two consecutive months, or 5,000 personally purchased Value Points within 12 months), and World Team (2,500 Value Points in each of 4 consecutive months, 10,000 Volume Points at 50 percent in one month, or 500 Royalty Override Points in 1 month). Once a contractor reaches the Supervisor level, the product discount is increased from 25 to 50 percent and a profit can be made on sales to other contractors, which can reach up to 5 percent.

In the event that a contractor no longer wants to sell Herbalife products, the company will buy back the remaining inventory the contractor has on hand. Herbalife goes beyond the Direct Selling Association's ethical guidelines for buying back products by reimbursing the distributor for everything that he or she paid for initially (100 percent buyback policy). The company also discourages contractors from inventory loading, which the Federal Trade Commission (FTC) has defined as a practice requiring a contractor to make a large purchase of a large amount of nonreturnable inventory. To renew their membership, contractors pay a $10 annual membership fee to Herbalife.

The Herbalife business model has succeeded due to their excellent products and customer support. Most independent contractors do not have a physical store location but practice direct selling from home. They are not employees but business people who choose how they want to operate. There are strict company policies and legal requirements that contractors must abide by that regulate product information, sales techniques, advertising, lead generation, social media, and related issues. For instance, members can sell online, but there are advertising restrictions for online sales. The products cannot be searchable online by their price, and the only way a potential buyer can get more information is by getting a password from the reseller. This facilitates a conversation between the buyer and reseller, allowing a relationship to develop even through online transactions. Contractors are not able to resell products on auction sites or in retail stores (excluding China).

Herbalife's selling policies are guided by the principles of the World Federation of Direct Selling Association (WFDSA) and the Direct Selling Association (DSA) in the United States. The WFDSA promotes ethical practices in direct selling globally through advocacy and strong relationships with government, consumers, and academia. The DSA also emphasizes ethics and requires that members adhere to their code of ethics (See Table 2). Herbalife is a member of the DSA and abides by their code of ethics. This code of ethics recognizes the importance of a fair and ethical approach to direct selling, since direct selling requires sensitive and personal one-on-one interaction that can lead to undue pressures placed upon consumers. The code has no tolerance for deceptive or unlawful practices regarding recruits and customers; requires that salespeople provide accurate and truthful information about the price, quality, promotion, etc. of the products; illuminates and enforces the need for a clear record of the sales made by contractors; necessitates that warranties and

TABLE 2 Direct Selling Association Code of Ethics

As a consumer you should expect salespeople to:

Tell you who they are, why they are approaching you, and what products they are selling.

Promptly end a demonstrations or presentation at your request.

Provide a receipt with a clearly stated cooling off period permitting the consumer to withdraw from a purchase order within a minimum of three days from the date of the purchase transaction and receive a full refund of the purchase price.

Explain how to return a product or cancel an order.

Provide you with promotional materials that contain the address and telephone number of the direct selling company.

Provide a written receipt that identifies the company and salesperson, including contact information for either.

Respect your privacy by calling at a time that is convenient for you.

Safeguard your private information.

Provide accurate and truthful information regarding the price, quality, quantity, performance, and availability of their product or service.

Offer a written receipt in language you can understand.

Offer a complete description of any warranty or guarantee.

As a salesperson, you should expect a DSA member company to:

Provide you with accurate information about the company's compensation plan, products, and sales methods.

Describe the relationship between you and the company in writing.

Be accurate in any comparisons about products, services or opportunities.

Refrain from any unlawful or unethical recruiting practice and exorbitant entrance or training fees.

Ensure that you are not just buying products solely to qualify for downline commissions.

Ensure that any materials marketed to you by others in the salesforce are consistent with the company's policies are reasonably priced and have the same return policy as the company's.

Require you to abide by the requirements of the Code of Ethics.

Safeguard your private information.

Provide adequate training to help you operate ethically.

Base all actual and potential sales and earning claims on documented facts.

Encourage you to purchase only the inventory you can sell in a reasonable amount of time.

Repurchase marketable inventory and sales aids you have purchased within the past 12 months at 90 percent or more of your original cost if you decide to leave the business.

Explain the repurchase option in writing.

Have reasonable start-up fees and costs.

Source: Direct Selling Association, "DSA Code of Ethics," MLM.com, 2016, http://mlm.com/summary-version-of-the-dsa-code-of-ethics/ (accessed June 22, 2016).

guarantees be fully acknowledged; requires salespeople to clearly identify themselves to customers and maintain the confidential information of their customers; has no tolerance for pyramid schemes; and provides guidelines on inventory purchases, earnings reporting, inventory loading, paying fees, and training.

A 2013 survey conducted by Nielsen, a reputable global information measuring company, showed (without interference from Herbalife) the number of end-consumers Herbalife serves. The study, which took place online over the course of two months, sampled 10,525 consumers and was balanced in terms of demographics, income, and geographic placement. The results indicated that 3.3 percent of the general population made a Herbalife purchase sometime over the last three months. This percentage of the population translates into 7.9 million customers, which does include Herbalife's contractors. According to the data, however, the number of contractors is approximately 550,000, indicating that the number of end users is higher than the number of independent contractors. Additionally, the study showed that those who made a purchase in the last three months tend to make Herbalife purchases consistently (approximately every two months), and that the most popular products are those having to deal with weight management (95 percent of those who made a purchase in the last three months).

One of the biggest arguments against Herbalife is its line commissions. Currently, Herbalife contractors can earn commissions on what every recruit below them buys or sells. There are no restrictions on the number of levels of recruits that contractors can earn a commission on, unlike some other multilevel marketing companies.

PYRAMID SCHEME

There are four defining characteristics of a pyramid scheme. The first, which is dictated by the FTC, is that consumers or investors are promised large profits based primarily on recruiting others to join their program. The promise is not based on profits from any real investment or real sale of goods. Second, according to the Securities and Exchange Commission (SEC), the promise of high profits rests on nothing more than a consumer or investor handing over their money and convincing others to do the same. Third, the Federal Bureau of Investigation (FBI) warns that pyramid schemes can be in the form of marketing and investment frauds when an individual is offered a contractorship or franchise to market a particular product. The real profit is earned not by the sale of the product but by the sale of new contractorships. Lastly, the California Department of Justice identifies the difference between a pyramid scheme and a legitimate multilevel marketing plan. In a multilevel marketing model, money is only made through the eventual retail sale of the product to an end user. In an illegal pyramid scheme, the participants at the top of the pyramid earn money when new members are recruited. Each new member is then required to recruit new participants. As this process goes on, the possible pool of participants shrinks, making it hard for those at the bottom to gain a return on their investment. A pyramid scheme will ultimately collapse due to a lack of new recruits and is therefore unsustainable. Another important point is that a pyramid scheme that seems to offer a product will have little to no market value. The recruits are being sold on an idea or a model.

Pyramid schemes can be hard to identify clearly, but the FTC has warned consumers about two red flags.

The first is inventory loading, which looks similar to internal consumption because it encourages large-scale purchases of nonrefundable products by a distributor. Not only is inventory loading a red flag but also illegal. The second is a lack of retail sales. If a supposed business has both of these characteristics, it is possible that it is a pyramid scheme and not a business at all. Another way of detecting a pyramid scheme is by examining the intention of the buyer. If the buyer purchased a product he or she really did not want just to participate, it is an indication that it could be a pyramid scheme. It is for these reasons that some direct selling businesses using the multilevel marketing compensation method can appear to be pyramid schemes. Because Herbalife sells not only their nutrition products but also a business opportunity, the firm has been accused of running a pyramid scheme.

IS HERBALIFE A PYRAMID SCHEME?

In 2012, Herbalife was accused of being an elaborate pyramid scheme by hedge fund manager William Ackman. Ackman had bet $1 billion in a short sale off Herbalife's stock. Short selling occurs when an investor sells shares borrowed from a lender (e.g. a broker) in the belief that the stock will decrease. The investor takes the money for the stock sale, but eventually must re-purchase the stock and return them to the lender. If the stock has gone down, the investor makes a profit. However, if it has gone up, the investor loses money because he or she is buying back the shares at a higher rate than the price at which they originally sold them.

Ackman's accusations against Herbalife included the following: 1) the majority of contractors for Herbalife lose money, 2) Herbalife pays more for recruiting new contractors than selling actual products, and 3) only the top 1 percent of contractors earn most of the money. The accusation is a result of the confusion that comes from the way their earning structure operates. Ackman argued that Herbalife recruits contractors under false beliefs that they can earn the income of those at the top by selling the product and that the real money comes not from selling products but from recruiting other contractors. His reasoning is that contractors earn rewards for every member they recruit, and every member the recruits recruit. However the term "rewards" is misleading. In a multilevel marketing compensation method, contractors earn a commission on the sales of their recruits.

The term "rewards" implies that there is some amount of money given for simply recruiting. However, this is not how Herbalife pays its contractors. Herbalife operates a little differently than other multilevel marketers in that most have a cut-off on what level of recruits a contractor can earn compensation from. Herbalife does not have a cut-off (although the average is approximately six levels downline). While this characteristic differs from other multilevel marketing companies, it is not enough to classify Herbalife as a pyramid scheme.

Another contention of Ackman's is that when an individual goes to purchase Herbalife products, distributors try to convince him or her to become a recruit rather than remain a customer. He argues that the only thing keeping the company running is new recruits, and it will soon run out of available people to recruit into the business. Ackman alleges that Herbalife enters new countries after the current pool of recruits in a particular country is exhausted.

On the other hand, many consumers and organizations buy and use Herbalife products and see them as high-quality and credible. For example, Los Angeles fire and police department officers use Herbalife products in their fitness centers. Herbalife products have even been adopted by some Chinese Olympic teams. Additionally, because the number of end users is larger than the number of independent contractors, supporters of Herbalife claim it cannot possibly be operating a pyramid scheme. This supports the fact that Herbalife uses a valid and successful business model, which is producing profits directly related to product sales and allowing them to expand globally.

Ackman, however, has made claims to invalidate these numbers. He claims that the survey measuring the number of contractors versus end consumers contradicts two others that were released by the company. He also states that Herbalife refuses to make the details of its recruiting process public knowledge so it can be scrutinized. Ackman's company has accused the survey sample of being too small, making the results overly optimistic. He takes issue with the fact that there are not enough specifics in the survey (prices consumers paid and an itemized breakdown of the products purchased).

Herbalife has also been accused of issuing false accounting statements. There has never been any legal accusation about the recording of sales. According to allegations, products are sold to contractors and are shown as retail sales on the company's revenue. The company does not always trace whether the product was consumed by the contractor (i.e., internal consumption) or to whom the contractor sold the product. The criticism is that the company should not be making money off the contractors but should only record revenues made from end users. Those who criticize internal consumption by contractors or employees within a company fail to recognize that this is an acceptable practice. Coca-Cola has 100 percent internal consumption because all of its products are sold to resellers. Costco also has 100 percent internal consumption because all of its products are sold to Costco members. This shows that the percentage of internal consumption is not by itself enough to indicate a pyramid scheme. There has never been major criticisms of companies encouraging internal consumption except with the direct selling, multilevel marketing compensation model.

Second, sometimes when new contractors are recruited, they need to buy products that they can consume themselves or sell to others. These practices have caused suspicion among Herbalife's critics. On the other hand, a contractor is only required to buy more products after the initial purchase if they want or need it for personal or business purposes. Once individuals sign up to be contractors, they indicate if they want the products for personal use or to make available for sale. If contractors have recruits under them, they have the opportunity to earn commissions based on the sales of those recruits. On the other hand, if the contractors do not care about the commission, they do not have to purchase anything more. In the case of Herbalife, the amount of products contractors are required to purchase is lower than many other multilevel marketing businesses.

There is also a criticism that a large number of contractors are not successful in selling their products. The ease of entry and extremely low cost of becoming a contractor makes it possible for those with little experience to enter the business. Even if they are not successful at direct selling, the cost of entry is less than $100 and they still have products that they can consume. Herbalife's records show that only 1 percent of its registered contractors will make $100,000 from the business in their lifetime. Ackman has argued that the numbers Herbalife reports are false. He estimates their retail sales to be only 3 percent of their revenue, while the rest is made by recruiting practices. Ackman also implied that Herbalife saturates markets, requiring it to get most of its sales from new, undeveloped markets.

These discrepancies can be explained when the types of contractors are analyzed. There are those that sign up only to get the contractor's discount on the product because they want the product for personal use; those who only want to sell the products as a source of additional income; and those that want to sell as a full-time business opportunity. Furthermore, every kind of direct selling business requires a large amount of effort to make a good profit. Even with businesses like Herbalife, if a contractor wants to make a living from distributing, relationships with customers must be maintained, and relationships with recruits must be maintained to encourage them to make as many sales and new recruits as possible. Many who begin in any direct selling business are either not willing or lack the business knowledge to put in that much effort. Those who sign up for this opportunity as a side job only work part-time or less, depending on how much extra money they want to make. In terms of market saturation, it would appear that Ackman is incorrect. Herbalife receives approximately 90 percent of its sales from markets in which it has done business for at least ten years, and growth in mature markets is growing by double digits.

Herbalife has defended itself against allegations of being a pyramid scheme. It responded to Ackman's charges in January 2013. However, the company's stock fell 43 percent four days after Ackman's accusations to $24.24, which was the largest drop the company had seen in several months. In response to Ackman's lobbying efforts, Herbalife hired a lobby team consisting of Glover Park Group and the Podesta Group.

CRITICISM AGAINST WILLIAM ACKMAN

As mentioned earlier, in accusing Herbalife of operating a pyramid scheme, William Ackman bet against their stock to the amount of $1 billion. Initially, the accusations caused Herbalife's stock to drop, benefiting Ackman's company because of his short sale. Ackman had pledged to give any profits from the short sale to charity, but to many people the short sale and subsequent accusations appeared to be a serious conflict of interest.

Another issue involved letters from supposed victims of Herbalife's deceptive practices. Because one of Ackman's contentions is that Herbalife targets minorities, Ackman's company has paid civil rights organizations $130,000 to collect names of people who were victims of Herbalife. However, the Nevada Attorney General found issues with some of these letters. Three of the letters from nonprofit groups signed by Hispanic community leaders were identical, and none of the leaders could identify any Herbalife victims by name. Other attorneys general have had similar experiences. Some of the leaders who had allegedly written the letters later denied they had written them. This could represent questionable conduct to encourage regulators to act.

Shortly after Ackman's accusations, another investor, Carl Icahn, came to the defense of Herbalife and became a majority shareholder and board member. This helped boost investor confidence in Herbalife, and their stock began to increase. This was bad news for Ackman when he was forced to cover his short sale. He took a loss on 8 million shares of stock. However, the state of Herbalife was still uncertain amid accusations, investor uncertainty, and Herbalife's strong stance that it was not operating a pyramid scheme. Pyramid schemes take some time to reveal themselves, so it was just a matter of waiting until Herbalife either crumbled or succeeded before anyone could be certain about the future of the company.

An article in the March 15, 2014, issue of the *Economist* as well as *The New York Times* provided a critical assessment of Ackman's attempts to use state-of-the-art lobbying in Washington to support his $1 billion short bet against Herbalife. Ackman has been at the heart of well-executed lobbying, although he claims to have spent only $264,000 on his lobbying campaign. On the other hand, Ackman's company's lobbying budget was seven times that much. According to the *Economist*, Ackman sees himself as a moral crusader against Herbalife, but his critics see him as simply a "greedy billionaire who is now exploiting America's newly laissez-faire attitude to political spending in pursuit of a big financial payday." Ackman has gained support from one U.S. senator and a U.S. Congressperson who have asked for the FTC to investigate Herbalife. The FTC did begin an investigation, and Herbalife claims that they welcome the opportunity to vet their business model and put these attacks behind them.

THE CONTROVERSY CONTINUES

Despite the company's recent success, the allegations continue. Special interest groups such as the Hispanic Federation and the National Consumers League are taking issue with the company and urging the FTC to investigate Herbalife's operations. Not only are they continuing the claim that Herbalife is operating a massive pyramid scheme but they are furthering the argument to say that the company is targeting vulnerable groups including low-income Hispanic immigrants and low-income African Americans. The allegations against Herbalife include aggressive recruiting techniques, promises of getting rich with minimal work, and taking advantage of people with little or no business experience.

The claims arose from the proliferation of nutrition clubs that have been established in Latino/Hispanic communities in Southern California. Nutrition clubs involve community members who pay a membership fee to discuss health issues and consume Herbalife products in a social setting. The popularity of these nutrition clubs originated in Mexico, which is where most of the immigrants in Southern California immigrated from. Herbalife claims that the nutrition clubs started arising in these areas because Hispanics saw how successful they were in Mexico and wanted to import the idea to the United States. Others claim that these clubs are harming the community because they turn out to be too costly for those who run them and end up losing more than they bargained for. Congresswoman Linda Sanchez, who represents Southern California, has written a letter to the FTC asking the agency to investigate Herbalife. She cited the intense media coverage and outreach from special interest groups and constituents as reasons for the FTC to investigate the company. Similar claims also abound in New York. New York City Councilwoman Julissa Ferreras has also written to the FTC advocating for an investigation.

Desmond Walsh, President of Herbalife, maintains that the company does not target specific demographics and that the rise of nutrition clubs in Latino/Hispanic communities is a result of immigrants seeing the business opportunity and importing the clubs from Mexico. Another issue with these clubs is that owners are operating them out of their homes and making and selling shakes. The Los Angeles Department of Health has closed some of these clubs as it is illegal to make and sell food items out of one's home. These clubs have to follow the same regulations as restaurants, requiring permits and other sorts of time-consuming and expensive governmental red tape. Critics claim that Herbalife does not adequately train their contractors in areas such as business and laws, so they are destined to fail. Herbalife, on the other hand, refutes those claims and states that they encourage their contractors to abide by their local laws.

In February 2013, it was reported that Hispanics make up 60 percent of Herbalife's customer base. One reason may be because they are good at direct selling due to their large network base and relationship building tendencies. The SEC is currently conducting an investigation into Herbalife's business operations.

One of their own former contractors filed a Class Action Complaint against Herbalife claiming, among other serious allegations, that the company is operating as a pyramid scheme. Some of the key allegations provided in this particular case include undisclosed facts, such as a large majority of all contractors (approximately 71 percent) make few, if any, retail sales and are forced to self-consume the Herbalife products. Herbalife will likely continue facing similar accusations in the future and must remain proactive in addressing them.

In 2014, Ackman profiled Herbalife's top distributors and continued his lobbying in Washington to have Herbalife investigated by the FTC. The FTC announced that it was initiating a probe into Herbalife's business practices. Herbalife responded by launching a new website, iamherbalife.com, that features dozens of positive testimonials from users of its products. One of Ackman's accusations is that the company sells a questionable product to gullible immigrants. Research shows that Herbalife sales continue to increase and that it has millions of customers who are not independent contractors or distributors using its products. While multilevel marketing compensation systems have been examined by the FTC in the past, the laws associated with pyramid schemes are considered ambiguous by some stakeholders. One of the key factors in a pyramid scheme is that there is no product sell-through, and in the case of Herbalife, they have definitively demonstrated that the sales are driven primarily by selling products to consumers. This seemed to be the conclusion reached by the FTC. The FTC did allege that Herbalife had not disclosed enough to distributors and that it promoted "get-rich-quick" promises that were not realistic. Herbalife paid $200 million and promised to improve disclosures with distributors. The FTC did not rule that Herbalife was a pyramid scheme. This refuted Ackman's accusations and meant that he will probably lose hundreds of million in his short sales of Herbalife stock.

However, the concept of internal consumption—although legitimate—continues to be questioned by regulators. The belief prevails that a large amount of internal consumption in direct selling companies indicates a pyramid scheme. In 2012 a U.S. judge ordered an organization called BurnLounge to disband and reimburse customers $17 million after the FTC deduced that the company was operating a pyramid scheme. BurnLounge marketed itself as a way for entrepreneurs to sell digital music and earn large incomes. Participants paid to enter the scheme. Very little sales were recorded, and 90 percent of participants did not act as independent distributors selling a product.

BurnLounge appealed. They stated that the FTC did not have enough evidence. The appeal in 2014 was held by the Ninth Circuit Court of Appeals. The implications of this case for the multilevel marketing direct selling industry were significant. In the initial judgment against BurnLounge, it was ruled that sales of products to ultimate users do not include sales to participants. It was feared that a legal decision could rule that the majority of products must be sold to people outside the company's network. In other words, a majority of sales would have to be made to end consumers, with sales to distributors not counted. This possibility could have put limitations on internal consumption. The 2016 FTC consent order with Herbalife dealt directly with the concept of internal consumption. Although this order does not apply to all companies, it requires Herbalife to carefully track the sales of products that are viewed as internal consumption and sales of products sold outside the network. This FTC requirement attempts to address the issue of inventory loading, or independent contractors who buy large amounts of the product in order to increase their commissions. The FTC is also severely limiting any commissions that can be made on products that independent contractors consume themselves.

The federal appeals court upheld the FTC's decision that BurnLounge was operating an illegal pyramid scheme. However, the ruling was viewed favorably by the direct selling industry overall because BurnLounge was determined to be a pyramid scheme due to the fact that participants had to pay to join the scheme and were mainly motivated by recruiting others into the scheme (versus selling an actual product). The biggest relief for organizations like Herbalife is that the court did not rule that commissions generated from goods sold to independent contractors were illegal. Internal consumption was defined as purchases made by distributors for personal consumption or resale, and not for buying products simply to qualify for bonuses or to get a discount. Like any other reseller, distributors purchasing products for internal consumption have the option of consuming the product or selling it to others. It would be impossible to know the exact percentage of the product being consumed by the independent contractor versus sales to consumers.

Rather than focusing upon the amount of consumption, the decision seemed to focus more upon whether the emphasis of the business involves sales of products or recruitment. Other areas of emphasis involve how these organizations calculate commissions and the importance of selling the product for the successful operation of the business. The intent for purchase is also a crucial component. If the purchases are driven by the product's value, instead of by money-making ventures, then it is most likely a legitimate operation.

Additionally, the BurnLounge decision described some tests that could indicate a pyramid scheme. Specifically, red flags include focusing more upon recruitment than merchandise, paying bonuses primarily on recruitment activity, promoting the program instead of selling the product, having participants purchase the right to earn profits through the recruitment of other individuals, developing strong incentives for recruitment, motivating package purchases by the opportunity to earn money, and making it unlikely that meaningful retail sales will occur.

Although some of these are not necessarily red flags by themselves, several of them taken together could indicate a pyramid scheme. For instance, the Court found that 95 percent of BurnLounge distributors brought premium products but only 35 percent of non-distributors did so. BurnLounge products had little value, and distributors were required to buy premium packages if they wanted to be eligible to receive additional commissions. Because Herbalife contractors sell products of value, participants do not have to pay simply to participate, and retail sales do occur, this legal decision lends more credence to Herbalife as a legitimate business model.

HERBALIFE'S SOCIAL RESPONSIBILITY

Herbalife is proud of its Corporate Social Responsibility program and believes it best sums up the company's top value of doing the right, honest, and ethical thing. These methods and policies relate to the directing and administering of short and long-term goals. They are put in place to ensure accountability and economic efficiency for Herbalife's stakeholders. Herbalife is proud that because of these policies they met independence criteria almost a year early and meet all NYSE-listed public company requirements for transparency.

Herbalife's business ethics allows it to uphold the highest ethical standards in the operation of the company. CEO Michael Johnson has said that its reputation is its greatest asset, and its Corporate Code of Business Conduct and Ethics reflects this. Herbalife encourages fair interactions and good judgment between any persons associated with the company and customers. There are guidelines set in place as to how contractors and employees of Herbalife should interact with suppliers, competitors, business partners, and the government. Herbalife encourages obedience to laws and sets boundaries on gifts and entertainment, describing the difference between small gifts for hospitality and bribes. The company discourages conflict of interest situations as well as insider trading and offers three methods of reporting unethical behavior through the company hotline, website, or by contacting the General Counsel. Individuals who do not comply are disciplined, suspended, or terminated. Herbalife also requires annual ethics training for all employees worldwide.

Another aspect of its Social Responsibility program includes its philanthropic efforts. The Herbalife Family Foundation (HFF) and the Casa Herbalife program, founded in 1994 by Mark Hughes, provide funding and volunteerism to charitable organizations taking care of children-at-risk around the world. HFF works to improve nutrition and help with disaster relief efforts. Herbalife has also partnered with the Global Alliance for Improved Nutrition (GAIN) and DSM Nutritional Products, a producer of vitamins and nutrition ingredients, to help deliver nutrients to women and children around the world. This partnership is under the umbrella of GAIN's Future Fortified campaign.

Lastly, as a part of Herbalife's Corporate Social Responsibility program, it engages in Employee Wellness and Live Green environmentally conscious initiatives. The company encourages and incentivizes employees to become and stay healthy and participate in fitness activities. Such incentives include complimentary products and lower individual health insurance costs. The company has even been recognized by *Men's Fitness* magazine as "One of the 15 Fittest Companies in America." Through environmentally conscious initiatives, Live Green and the 3Rs—reduce, reuse and recycle—Herbalife makes its impact on the environment a priority.

CONCLUSION

Herbalife battled Ackman's accusations from late 2012 until July 2016. During that time, Ackman was successful in getting the Federal Trade Commission to launch a major investigation into whether Herbalife was a pyramid scheme. After the long investigation, the Federal Trade Commission concluded that Herbalife was not a pyramid scheme but reached a consent order, which is a joint agreement, that Herbalife would change some of its business practices. Specifically, the company has to track the sales of its products to consumers outside of its network and sales that involve internal consumption. In addition, the company has to provide more training and monitoring of its independent contractors to make

sure they do not over-promise the financial opportunity in selling Herbalife products.

The products of Herbalife are exclusively sold by nearly 2.3 million independent contractors in 90 different countries It sponsors several professional athletes, teams, and sporting events. Additionally, the company is proud of its Corporate Social Responsibility initiatives. Herbalife is a successful company, but ethical issues will continue to ensue. Trust in business is at a low point in our society. Marketing is often seen as a part of business that is suspect. A direct selling firm receives additional scrutiny as it is focused on personal selling to distribute all of its products.

Herbalife contractors do not have the overhead expenses that a retail store with a building, fixtures, utilities, and other expenses requires. Therefore, the markup on products such as cosmetics, nutritional supplements, jewelry, and clothing may be similar in both the retail store and in direct selling. A direct selling company is a flat organization with low overhead and compensation systems for the network of sales contractors that make the product available to final consumers. The concept of internal consumption, which exists in nearly all businesses, is considered questionable by some critics who fail to understand that there is nothing illegal or unethical about internal consumption. However, the Federal Trade Commission has asked Herbalife to keep precise records, including the names of purchasers, to differentiate between internal consumption and sales to consumers outside the network.

On the other hand, some direct selling companies have been associated with inventory loading, sometimes called garage stuffing, when sales contractors are encouraged to buy more products than they can consume or sell. This ethical breach has nothing to do with a company being a pyramid scheme just because it uses a multilevel compensation method. All businesses have compensation methods that reward sales managers and higher-level managers, including the CEO, for performance. Every business has to produce revenue, and the marketing function is exclusively in charge of developing sales.

However, companies can fight against criticism of their operations by maintaining total transparency concerning how their sales incentive models work, and there should be due diligence to ensure that sales contractors are not exploited in any way. Herbalife continues to have many loyal contractors throughout the world, showing that the firm has many supporters who believe the company is a legitimate and successful business operation.

Questions for Discussion

1. Why has Herbalife's multilevel compensation model been confused with a pyramid scheme?
2. Describe the differences between a legitimate business model and a pyramid scheme.
3. How has Herbalife demonstrated social responsibility?

Sources

Amway website, http://www.amway.com/about-amway/campaigns-and-sponsorships/what-is-amway?cid=TC|22217|amway||S|e|14426411298&mkwid=sOYgfuJnr&pcrid=14426411298&pkw=amway&pmt=e&s_kwcid=TC|22217|amway||S|e|14426411298 (accessed August 8, 2016).

Avon website, https://www.avon.com/ (accessed August 8, 2016).

David Benoit, "Herbalife to Pay $200 Million Over Claims of Misrepresentation," *The Wall Street Journal*, July 15, 2016, http://www.wsj.com/articles/herbalife-to-pay-200-million-over-claims-of-misrepresentation-1468584397 (accessed July 15, 2016).

Belcorp website, http://www.belcorp.biz/en/index.html (accessed August 8, 2016).

Michelle Celarier, "NYC Pol: It's Herb-sploitation," *New York Post*, June 14, 2013, http://nypost.com/2013/06/14/nyc-pol-its-herb-sploitation/ (accessed August 8, 2016).

Juliet Chung, "In Herbalife Fight, Both Sides Prevail," *The Wall Street Journal,* March 31, 2013, http://online.wsj.com/article/SB10001424127887323361804578388682197247250.html (accessed August 8, 2016).

Anne T. Coughlan, "Assessing an MLM Business," Herbalife, July 2012, http://ir.herbalife.com/assessing-MLM.cfm (accessed August 8, 2016).

Javier E. David, "Herbalife CEO Casts Doubt on Ackman's Motives in Shorting Stock," *CNBC*, January 10, 2013, http://www.cnbc.com/id/100369698 (accessed August 8, 2016).

"Datamonitor the Home of Business Information," *Datamonitor the Home of Business Information*, http://www.datamonitor.com/ (accessed April 21, 2013).

"Direct Selling Methods: Single Level and Multilevel Marketing," More Business, March 26, 2007, http://www.morebusiness.com/running_your_business/management/Direct-Sales.brc (accessed August 8, 2016).

Economist staff, "The House of Cards Put," *The Economist,* March 15, 2014, http://www.economist.com/news/finance-and-economics/21599055-activist-investing-meets-activist-government-house-cards-put (accessed August 8, 2016).

Federal Trade Commission, "FTC Action Leads to Court Order Shutting Down Pyramid Scam Thousands of Consumers Burned by BurnLounge," March 14, 2012, https://www.ftc.gov/news-events/press-releases/2012/03/ftc-action-leads-court-order-shutting-down-pyramid-scamthousands (accessed August 8, 2016).

O. C. Ferrell and Linda Ferrell, "Defining a Pyramid Scheme," PowerPoint presentation, University of New Mexico, 2013.

Agustino Fontevecchia, "The Anti-Ackman Effect: Herbalife Surges Then Plunges As Hedge Fund Billie Omits It From Ira Sohn Speech," *Forbes,* May 8, 2013, http://www.forbes.com/sites/afontevecchia/2013/05/08/the-anti-ackman-effect-herbalife-surges-then-punges-as-hedge-fund-billie-omits-it-from-ira-sohn-speech/#f9193c43eb34 (accessed August 8, 2016).

Agustino Fontevecchia, "Investors Side with Carl Icahn: Herbalife Soars After Epic TV Battle with Ackman," *Forbes,* January 25, 2013, http://www.forbes.com/sites/afontevecchia/2013/01/25/investors-side-with-carl-icahn-herbalife-soars-after-epic-tv-battle-with-ackman/#7dc2564243c9 (accessed August 8, 2016).

"Frauds of the Century," in *Business Ethics: Ethical Decision Making and Cases*, 10th ed., ed. O.C. Ferrell, John Fraedrich, and Linda Ferrell (Mason, OH: South-Western Cengage Learning, 2015).

Karen Gullo, "BurnLounge Ruling in FTC Case Seen as Good for Herbalife," *Bloomberg,* June 2, 2014, http://www.bloomberg.com/news/articles/2014-06-02/burnlounge-shutdown-by-ftc-upheld-by-federal-appeals-court-1-.html (accessed August 8, 2016).

Herbalife, *Annual Report 2015*, http://files.shareholder.com/downloads/ABEA-48ZAJ9/2598590182x0x882574/93BF84C9-495D-4D9A-A06A-3C20F9294252/Herbalife_Ltd_2015_Annual_Report.pdf (accessed August 8, 2016).

Herbalife, United States—Official Site, http://www.herbalife.com/ (accessed August 8, 2016).

Herbalife, "International Business Pack (IBP)," http://www.beststarttoday.com/Herbalife_International_Business_Pack_p/5000.htm (accessed June 17, 2013).

Herbalife,"Mini International Business Pack (IBP)," http://www.beststarttoday.com/Herbalife_Mini_International_Business_Pack_IBP_p/5043.htm (accessed June 17, 2013).

Herbalife, "Product Catalogue," http://catalog.herbalife.com/Catalog/en-US (accessed August 8, 2016).

Herbalife, *Sales & Marketing Plan and Business Rules,* 2012, http://factsaboutherbalife.com/media/2012/12/

Marketing-Plan-and-Business-Rules-2012.pdf (accessed August 6, 2016).

Herbalife, "Social Responsibility," http://company.herbal-ife.com/social-responsibilty (accessed August 8, 2016).

Herbalife, "Statement of Average Gross Compensation Paid by Herbalife to United States Contractors in 2012," 2012, http://opportunity.herbalife.com/Content/en-US/pdf/business-opportunity/statement_average_gross_usen.pdf (accessed August 8, 2016).

"Herbalife Ltd.," Hoover's Company Records—In-depth Records, April 17, 2013.

"Herbalife Review," *Vital Health Partners RSS*, Web, April 23, 2013.

Tabinda Hussain, "Hispanic Federation Urges FTC To Investigate Herbalife," Value Walk, May 20, 2013, http://www.valuewalk.com/2013/05/hispanic-federation-urges-ftc-to-investigate-herbalife/ (accessed August 8, 2016).

Investopedia staff, "Short Selling: What Is Short Selling?" Investopedia, http://www.investopedia.com/university/shortselling/shortselling1.asp (accessed August 8, 2016).

Julia La Roche, "California Congresswoman Asks the FTC to Investigate Herbalife," *Business Insider,* June 13, 2013, http://www.businessinsider.com/sanchez-asks-ftc-to-probe-herbalife-2013-6 (accessed June 17, 2013).

Richard Lee and Jason D. Schloetzer, "The Activism of Carl Icahn and Bill Ackman," Director Notes: The Conference Board, May 2014, No. DN-V6N10.

Lehman, Lee, and Xu. "Direct Sale," Lehman Law, http://www.lehmanlaw.com/practices/direct-sale.html (accessed August 8, 2016).

Mary Kay website, http://www.marykay.com/awine/en-US/_layouts/MaryKayCoreCatalog/ProductsAndShop.aspx?dsNav=N:2000040 (accessed August 8, 2016).

Dan McCrum, "Herbalife Faces Challenge of Greater Transparency over Sales," *Financial Times,* June 17, 2013, http://www.ft.com/intl/cms/s/0/9289508c-d2e6-11e2-aac2-00144feab7de.html#axzz2a59tMxoo (accessed August 8, 2016).

Dan McCrum, "Keep an eye on the FTC vs Burnlounge," *Financial Times,* March 21, 2014, http://ftalphaville.ft.com/2014/03/21/1806772/keep-an-eye-on-the-ftc-vs-burnlounge/ (accessed May 30, 2014).

Natura website, http://www.natura.com.br/ (accessed August 8, 2016).

"New Pyramid Scheme Allegations against Herbalife That Might Just Stick | Shortzilla LLC," Shortzilla LLC, April 11, 2013, http://www.shortzilla.com/new-pyra-mid-scheme-allegations-against-herbalife-that-might-just-stick/ (accessed July 25, 2013).

Nu Skin website, http://www.nuskin.com/ (accessed August 8, 2016).

Oriflame website, http://oriflame.com/ (accessed August 8, 2016).

Stuart Pfiefer, "Consumer Group Urges FTC to Investigate Herbalife," *Los Angeles Times,* March 12, 2013, http://articles.latimes.com/2013/mar/12/business/la-fi-mo-consumer-group-urges-ftc-to-investigate-herbalife-20130312 (accessed August 8, 2016).

Stuart Pfeifer, "Herbalife Shares Surge Past Price When Ackman Made Allegations," *Los Angeles Times,* May 6, 2013, http://articles.latimes.com/2013/may/06/business/la-fi-mo-herbalife-stock-price-20130506 (accessed August 8, 2016).

Steven Pfiefer, "Latinos Crucial to Herbalife's Financial Health," *Los Angeles Times,* February 15, 2013, http://articles.latimes.com/2013/feb/15/business/la-fi-herbal-ife-latino-20130216 (accessed August 8, 2016).

Stuart Pfiefer, "Rep. Linda Sanchez Asks FTC to Investigate Herbalife," *Los Angeles Times,* June 14, 2013, http://articles.latimes.com/2013/jun/14/business/la-fi-herbalife-ftc-20130614 (accessed August 8, 2016).

William Pride and O.C. Ferrell, *Foundations of Marketing,* 5th ed. (Mason, OH: South-Western Cengage, 2013), p. 444.

Pyramid Scheme, "Funk & Wagnalls New World Encyclopedia," *EBSCOhost* (accessed April 20, 2013).

Pyramid Scheme Alert, "China Leads the World in Fighting the Global Scourge of Pyramid Schemes," September 2009, http://pyramidschemealert.org/PSAMain/news/ChinaLeadsPyramidFight.html (accessed August 8, 2016).

Martin Russell, "Herbalife Scam: Let's Review the Claims," Careful Cash RSS, March 4, 2011, http://www.carefulcash.com/herbalife-scam-lets-review-the-claims/ (accessed August 8, 2016).

Steve Schaefer, "Ackman Takes Ax to Herbalife, Company Says It Is 'Not An Illegal Pyramid Scheme'," *Forbes,* 2012, p. 4.

Steve Schaefer, "Herbalife Posts Record Results, Raises Guidance," *Forbes,* April 29, 2013, http://www.forbes.com/sites/steveschaefer/2013/04/29/herbalife-posts-record-results-raises-guidance/#515eac743a05 (accessed August 8, 2016).

Michael S. Schmidt, Eric Lipton, and Alexandra Stevenson, "After Big Bet, Hedge Fund Pulls the Levers of Power," *The New York Times,* March 9, 2014, http://www.nytimes.com/2014/03/10/business/staking-1-billion-that-herbalife-will-fail-then-ackman-lobbying-to-bring-it-down.html (accessed August 8, 2016).

Duane D. Stanford and Kelly Bit, "Herbalife Drops After Ackman Says He's Shorting Shares," *Bloomberg,* December 20, 2012, http://www.bloomberg.com/news/2012-12-19/herbalife-drops-after-cnbc-says-ackman-is-short-company.html (accessed August 8, 2016).

The Street Wire, "Herbalife, Ltd. Stock Buy Recommendation Reiterated," June 11, 2013, http://www.thestreet.mobi/story/11947125/1/herbalife-ltd-stock-buy-recommendation-reiterated-hlf.html?puc=yahoo&cm_ven=YAHOO (accessed August 8, 2016).

Nathalie Tadena, "Ackman: Herbalife Should Come Clean on Surveys," *The Wall Street Journal,* June 18, 2013, http://blogs.wsj.com/moneybeat/2013/06/18/ackman-herbalife-should-come-clean-on-surveys/ (accessed August 8, 2016).

Kevin Thompson, "The BurnLounge Court Decision Clears the Air on Many Issues," *Direct Selling News,* August 2014, pp. 64–66.

Kevin Thompson, "Inventory Loading: When Does a Company Cross the Line?" *Thompsonburton.com,* March 20, 2010, http://thompsonburton.com/mlmattorney/2010/03/20/inventory-loading-when-does-a-company-cross-the-line/ (accessed August 8, 2016).

Tupperware website, http://order.tupperware.com/coe/app/home (accessed August 8, 2016).

theflyonthewall.com, "Congresswoman asks FTC to Investigate Herbalife, NY Post Reports," June 13, 2013, http://finance.yahoo.com/news/congresswoman-asks-ftc-investigate-herbalife-101651927.html (accessed August 8, 2016).

Michelle Urban and Jennifer Sawayda, "The Network Marketing Controversy," Daniels Fund Ethics Initiative website, 2013, http://danielsethics.mgt.unm.edu/pdf/network-marketing-di.pdf (accessed August 8, 2016)

Nathan Vardi, "Carl Icahn and Herbalife are Crushing Bill Ackman," *Forbes,* May 21, 2013, http://www.forbes.com/sites/nathanvardi/2013/05/21/carl-icahn-and-herbalife-are-crushing-bill-ackman/ (accessed August 8, 2016).

"The Verge," *The Verge*, Web, April 21, 2013.

Vorwerk website, http://corporate.vorwerk.com/en/home/ (accessed August 8, 2016).

Miles Weiss, "Icahn Says No Respect for Bill Ackman After Herbalife Bet," *Bloomberg,* January 25, 2013, http://www.bloomberg.com/news/2013-01-24/icahn-says-no-respect-for-bill-ackman-after-herbalife-bet.html (accessed August 8, 2016).

World Federation of Direct Selling Association, "Objectives," http://www.wfdsa.org/about_wfdsa/?fa=objectives (accessed July 10, 2013).

Yahoo! Finance, "Herbalife Announces Results of Study on Contractors and End Users in the U.S.," June 11, 2013, http://finance.yahoo.com/news/herbalife-announces-results-study-contractors-214500826.html (accessed June 12, 2013).

Yahoo! Finance, "Herbalife Says Survey Indicates 7.9M Customers in the U.S.," June 12, 2013, http://finance.yahoo.com/news/herbalife-says-survey-indicates-7-103428808.html (accessed August 8, 2016).

Daniel Yi and Tom Petruno, "Herbalife Investor Bids for Rest of Firm," *Los Angeles Times,* February 3, 2007, http://articles.latimes.com/2007/feb/03/business/fi-herbalife3 (accessed August 8, 2016).

Hobby Lobby: Balancing Stakeholders and Religious Freedom in Business Decisions

INTRODUCTION

Ethical business and stakeholder management is complex by any standard. Business leaders must balance a variety of competing pressures and concerns and make the best decisions they can to produce quality products, satisfy customers, provide a favorable work experience for employees, consider the environmental and social impact of their business operations, potentially contribute independently to society through donations and public service, and more. All of this must be resolved in pursuit of the traditional overarching goal of bottom line (or, more recently, triple bottom line) profitability. How much, then, is this complexity multiplied when a company seeks not only to grow and remain profitable but also to accomplish a separate mission, such as to exemplify and adhere to the deeply held religious and personal values of its founders?

Hobby Lobby is such a company. Although on its face it is simply a successful arts, crafts, and home decorating retailer, the family that founded it and continues to own it privately does not see this as its overall mission. They established the company on a firm bedrock of biblical Christian principles, and an essential and enduring part of the firm's mission is to honor these values in its business choices. The company keeps its stores closed on Sundays; refuses to sell certain items such as shot glasses or contract out "back-haul" trucking space to transport beer; pays its lowest-level employees significantly more than the legal minimum wage; and donates half of its profits to ministries and charitable organizations. These decisions have cost it millions in potential earnings, but the owners consider it a cost of running a business the way they believe it should be done.

Whether this style constitutes ethical business practices and effective stakeholder management is in the eye of the beholder. Christian organizations such as the National Bible Association have bestowed Hobby Lobby and its leadership with ample praise. However, even non-Christians can find much to appreciate in the firm's high base wages, its focus on an employee work-life balance, charitable donations, and so on. The company has also steadily expanded and has experienced continued financial success.

On the other hand, conflicts have inevitably arisen between the company's Christian focus and the needs and desires of non-Christian employees, customers, and other stakeholders. At no time has this conflict been more starkly exhibited than in the company's 2012–2014 lawsuit against the government to strike down the 2010 Patient Protection and Affordable Care Act's requirement that most companies expand their employee health insurance coverage to pay for certain contraceptives the company's leadership considers "abortifascients"—causing the death of human life after it has begun. Hobby Lobby won the case—the U.S. Supreme Court struck down the requirement—but the legal battle has polarized public perception of the company, with many viewing its biblical foundation as nothing more than its owners attempting to force their religious beliefs upon customers, employees, and society at large. While the long-term effects of the Supreme Court's decision on the law of religious freedom and expression for closely held private companies—as well as on the future of Hobby Lobby itself—are still unknown, the situation serves as a striking landmark in the history of a company that has attempted, for better or worse, to hold to its own unique perception of what constitutes ethical business management.

This case describes the Supreme Court ruling in favor of Hobby Lobby and its implications. We begin by looking at how Hobby Lobby was developed. Its ethical and socially responsible business practices are based on biblical principles that the company uses to guide its decision-making. The second part of this case describes the ethical challenges Hobby Lobby has faced, including its refusal to offer certain contraceptives and its 401(k) plans.

*This case was prepared by RuthAnn Tibbetts, Mariah Maestas, and Isaac Emmanuel for and under the direction of O. C. and Linda Ferrell, © 2015. Jennifer Sawayda provided editorial assistance. It was prepared for classroom discussion rather than to illustrate either effective or ineffective handling of an administrative, ethical, or legal decision by management. All sources used for this case were obtained through publicly available material.

THE CRAFTING OF HOBBY LOBBY

Hobby Lobby opened its doors in Oklahoma City, Oklahoma in 1972, founded by David Green as an extension of a miniature picture frame company he originally ran out of his garage. The company has now grown to over 600 stores in more than 41 states and employs 28,000 employees.

Ethics, Corporate Social Responsibility, and Business Practices—Based on Biblical Principles

Hobby Lobby was founded on biblical Christian principles. As founder and current CEO David Green has written, "I've always said that the first two goals of our business are (1) to run our business in harmony with God's laws, and (2) to focus on people more than money." The company's current website states, "We believe that it is by God's grace and provision that Hobby Lobby has endured. He has been faithful in the past, and we trust Him for our future." The Hobby Lobby mission statement includes the following commitments:

- Honoring the Lord in all we do by operating the company in a manner consistent with biblical principles.

- Offering our customers exceptional selection and value in the crafts and home decor market.

- Serving our employees and their families by establishing a work environment and company policies that build character, strengthen individuals, and nurture families.

- Providing a return on the owner's investment, sharing the Lord's blessings with our employees, and investing in our community.

These commitments are based on the core Christian values that the Green family lives by, and company leaders deeply stress these values, along with a shared company vision that emphasizes a family culture. This overall viewpoint and focus greatly affects the company's practical business decisions, often in ways that forego profits. For example, the company gives a 10 percent discount to churches, schools, and national charitable organizations. The company also takes care of its employees through various benefits. As of July 2014, a full time hourly employee received $14.50 per hour, double the required national minimum wage. The company stresses a strong work-life balance; stores are closed on Sundays (costing the company an estimated $100 million or more in lost sales annually); and workdays are shorter than most other retailers to allow employees to spend quality time with their families and handle other needs. The company's healthcare plan is also very generous compared to most other retail companies, and it hires chaplains to attend to employees' emotional and spiritual needs.

Smaller business decisions are affected as well. As mentioned earlier, the company will not sell certain disapproved items such as shot glasses. It passes up free revenue by refusing to contract out excess "back-haul" trucking space to carry beer ("back-haul" meaning space in trucks returning from cargo deliveries who have to expend the same amount of gas and effort to drive back but often do not have much to transport). It stocks a significant amount of religious, mostly Christian, merchandise such as crosses and other decorations, plays Christian music in its stores, and does not allow violent or bloody Halloween decorations.

Both Hobby Lobby as a company and the Green family privately spend a significant amount of money promoting charitable, primarily Christian-focused, causes, and have been recognized for doing so. Over 10 percent of Hobby Lobby's yearly income, including 50 percent of profits, is donated to ministries and other nonprofits according to biblical principles (tithing a set portion of income to God's work). Some of that money has gone toward acquiring one of the world's largest private collections of Bibles and biblical artifacts, which will eventually be placed in a public Bible-themed museum planned in Washington, D.C. In 2010, David Green and his wife, Barbara, signed on to the Giving Pledge, a campaign begun by Bill Gates and Warren Buffet to encourage wealthy individuals and families to commit to giving half of their wealth over the course of their lives (or after death) to philanthropic causes. In 2013, Hobby Lobby president Steve Green was presented with the Templeton Award by the National Bible Association in recognition of his "outstanding example for business leaders across the country … his exemplary spiritual values and his continued commitment to the Bible."

Despite this focus on Christian values, beliefs, and causes, the Green family has stated that they welcome individuals with different religious backgrounds and beliefs into the company. The core values of their religion call for respect of all individuals, and therefore they do not hire on the basis of religion.

Hobby Lobby does not appear to have a formal ethics and compliance program. Although it is a private corporation, this may become an issue as the Federal Sentencing Guidelines for Organizations highly recommend having a formal ethics and compliance program—especially for larger companies. When company size increases, ethical risk areas become harder to detect without the internal controls provided by a formal ethics and compliance program. However, David Green has high-quality traits that he shares with each of his employees. Through these qualities Green believes that employees will act and live ethically in accordance with biblical principles. Most businesses today as well as the government would recommend additional training and due dialogue on ethical risk areas. Some ethical risks have legal ramifications that may require specialized compliance training. For example, many accounting and human resources decisions can have legal consequences. There are many ethical gray areas that may need to be resolved by those with experience or a legal background. Elements of an ethics program are not just principles but include codes of ethics, training, and opportunities for reporting misconduct.

ETHICAL CHALLENGES—BALANCING RELIGIOUS CONVICTION WITH STAKEHOLDER INTERESTS

Like all companies, Hobby Lobby has encountered a number of controversies over the years. These controversies are intensified by the fact that the beliefs of the company's leadership sometimes clash with those of other societal stakeholders.

Minor Controversies

Not all of Hobby Lobby's challenges have been major. Hobby Lobby has faced several minor controversies in relation to its Christian-based value structure. One such ethical challenge occurred in October 2013, when a customer shopping at a Hobby Lobby store asked why

they did not sell Hanukkah items. The Hobby Lobby employee allegedly responded, "We don't cater to you people." An online blogger heard about the story, called another store to ask the same question, and was told that Hobby Lobby does not carry Jewish merchandise because the owners are Christian. He subsequently wrote a blog post harshly criticizing Hobby Lobby's apparent refusal to sell Jewish items, and the post quickly went viral.

In response, Hobby Lobby released a statement officially apologizing for any inappropriate employee remarks and explaining that it has no problem selling items celebrating Jewish holidays. The firm claims they have sold Jewish holiday items in the past and will continue to do so in regions where there is a significant Jewish population. The statement also emphasized the company's respect for the Jewish faith and noted that Hobby Lobby contributes to several Jewish-focused charitable organizations. This was sufficient to defuse the situation, with the blogger and other offended parties accepting the apology and expressing appreciation for Hobby Lobby's prompt and concerned response.

When Chik-Fil-A came under fire for its owner publicly stating that the company opposed same-sex marriage based on biblical and Christian principles, Hobby Lobby received numerous requests to clarify its own stance, considering it was also a company founded on Christian values. In August 2012, Debra Love, president of Hobby Lobby International, released a comment to PR Newswire, stating:

> Our core values call for respect for each other, our customers and our suppliers and for us to treat others as we would best like to be treated ourselves. We believe that we must demonstrate love for our fellow man as we are called upon to do as Christians. We respect our employees by offering a workplace that is free of judgment and bias, and one that gives everyone an opportunity to succeed and grow.

Although these controversies ended up being of little practical consequence to Hobby Lobby, they effectively illustrate the difficulties the company necessarily faces in attempting to remain both true to Christian principles and accommodating to the needs of its diverse stakeholder base. This emphasizes the need for Hobby Lobby to ensure that its values are effectively communicated to all employees. A shared value system helps to avoid inconsistencies in employee behavior, such as what occurred with the employees who responded negatively to the questions of Jewish customers.

The Lawsuit: *Burwell v. Hobby Lobby*

In 2010, President Obama signed into enactment the Patient Protection and Affordable Care Act (ACA). The law requires that if a company with 50 or more employees offers them health insurance, that health insurance must provide "minimum essential coverage" as determined by the U.S. Department of Health and Human Services. Failure to meet this standard or failure to provide health insurance at all potentially subjects the company to significant daily and/or yearly fines.

Since August 2011, this required "minimum essential coverage" includes full coverage for 20 types of contraceptives. Four of these—two "morning after" emergency contraceptive pills and two intrauterine devices—are considered by some to be "abortifacients," meaning that they potentially take effect only after the egg has already been fertilized. For those who believe human life begins at fertilization, these contraceptives have the effect of ending life—something which they believe to be highly immoral. While there are numerous exceptions to which companies must comply with the contraception coverage requirement—such as exemptions for fully religious organizations like churches and religious nonprofit organizations—none of them cover a for-profit corporation with religious underpinnings such as Hobby Lobby.

The Green family has no objection to contraception as a general matter; in fact, before the contraception coverage requirement was enacted, Hobby Lobby was already voluntarily providing coverage for all 20 contraception methods as part of its generous benefits plan. However, the Green family was unaware that their offered coverage included the four "abortifascent" methods, which they are religiously against and believe violates biblical principles. After the ACA was enacted, Hobby Lobby was contacted by The Beckett Fund for Religious Liberty, a nonprofit public interest law firm dedicated to promoting religious freedom, who informed them of the new contraception coverage requirements and offered to represent them in fighting it. The Green family claimed that they were shocked that their company had been providing coverage of these contraception methods. They asked their insurer to discontinue covering them and then evaluated their options.

If it refused to comply with the requirement, Hobby Lobby would face a fine of $100 per employee per day, adding up to an enormous $475 million per year. If it refused to provide health insurance at all, it could be fined the still-hefty cost of up to $26 million yearly, as well as lose the competitive advantage of its above-average health insurance plans—not to mention cutting out a significant piece of its "people over profit" corporate culture. Caught between legal compliance, unsustainable financial and business consequences, and the Green family's refusal to be complicit in actions that violated their religious convictions, Hobby Lobby filed suit against the government in September 2012.

Over the next two years, the lawsuit went through the courts, from the federal district court (which ruled against Hobby Lobby, finding they were required to provide the coverage) to the circuit court of appeals (which reversed, finding Hobby Lobby could not be required to do so) and finally coming before the U.S. Supreme Court. As it did so, Hobby Lobby found itself at the center of a polarized public debate over the arguments and potential effects of the lawsuit. Some saw the case as a clear exercise of religious freedom—private owners running their company the way they saw fit. Others were outraged and saw it as quite the opposite—a single religious family using their company to impose their beliefs on thousands of women and thus trampling their employees' own religious freedom, reproductive freedom, freedom of choice, and more. Were for-profit corporations even capable of holding religious values that would enable them to be protected by the Constitution and/or laws promoting religious freedom? If Hobby Lobby won, would it unleash a number of lawsuits from companies attempting to claim religious exemptions to everything, from social security contributions to the minimum wage? On the other hand, if Hobby Lobby lost, what would it mean for the future of the company and for the claims of the many other companies (as of June 2014, at least 80) also challenging the contraceptive mandate?

On June 30, 2014, the U.S. Supreme Court issued a divided 5-4 decision in *Burwell v. Hobby Lobby*. Consolidating the Hobby Lobby claims with the essentially identical claims of two other companies, the majority of the Court found that none of them could be required to cover the four "abortifascent" contraception methods. This ruling was not based directly on the First Amendment's protection of religious free exercise but rather on a 1993 law called the Religious Freedom Restoration Act (RFRA), which proscribed limits on the federal government's ability to burden free exercise of religion. One of these limits was that the government's action must be "the least restrictive means" of accomplishing its goal. The Court found that the RFRA could be applied to protect private, closely held corporations; that such corporations were legally capable of "exercising religion" through religiously motivated business practices and the beliefs of their private owners; and that the contraception mandate was not the least restrictive means to provide contraceptive coverage to business employees, as clear alternatives existed such as the government allowing employers to opt out and then provide the coverage directly itself.

The Court emphasized that its holding was narrow, applying only to the contraceptive mandate, and claimed its holding should have little effect on whether employees can actually get contraceptive coverage. According to the Court, it only applies to whether employers must provide it under the ACA. Regardless of the details, however, the decision was a clear victory for the Green family. They would no longer be required to choose between endangering the future financial stability of their company and violating their Christian convictions, and—in this aspect at least—could continue to run Hobby Lobby the way they felt was right.

This could have major consequences for businesses. Essentially, the ruling states that Hobby Lobby employees can receive free contraceptive coverage through third parties, much as non-profits can. One issue is how to define a closely held corporation. The definition of a closely held corporation is important because it will determine whether a for-profit business has the same rights and exemptions as a nonprofit. The Department of Health and Human Services (HHS) has recommended that closely held corporations should include those that do not have publicly traded shares and where there is a limited or specified number of shareholders. HHS believes a solid definition is needed to protect the rights of closely held corporations to exercise their religious freedom while simultaneously giving women right to contraceptive care.

The future implications of this saga on Hobby Lobby's public reputation and business success remain to be seen. Many who were previously unaware of the company's religious underpinnings may now see the company in a different light, and choose accordingly. This is not helped by the large amount of misinformation that has circulated about the case, from what exactly Hobby Lobby was suing over (refusal to support what they saw as abortive measures, not contraception as a whole) to the true implications of the Supreme Court's ruling (much narrower and less wide-ranging than many have stated). The Green family made a choice as to which values to uphold, and only time will tell the consequences.

A Final Wrinkle—Hobby Lobby's 401(k) Plans

Some critics of Hobby Lobby's stance on the contraception mandate have noted that the 401(k) plans Hobby Lobby offers its employees allow investment in companies that are manufacturing the very contraceptive methods Hobby Lobby sued to be free of supporting. Being as Hobby Lobby holds over $73 million in mutual funds and 401(k) plans and contributes large matching funds to its employees' investments, these critics see contradiction and hypocrisy in the Green family's apparent decision to fight in one arena and let the other be. Does this exhibit complacent management? Is the company truly as deeply based on Christian principles as it claims?

Supporters of Hobby Lobby point to what they see as essentially important distinctions between providing insurance coverage of "abortifascent" contraception methods and contributing to 401(k) plans that include investments in the companies that make them. For example, employees choose what to invest their plans in; Hobby Lobby's involvement is completely passive, unlike a mandate to specifically pay for the contraception. Also, 401(k) funds necessarily involve diversified portfolios of investments in hundreds or even thousands of companies, making the link much more indirect and attenuated. Whether these arguments are satisfactory likely depends on the individual, but they again show the balance Hobby Lobby must attempt to achieve between its biblical foundations and the realities of its business operations and decision-making.

CONCLUSION

Although Hobby Lobby is founded on biblical principles, they have faced several ethical challenges and risks as a company. Their strong religious beliefs make them competitive, and they believe this has contributed to their continued success. The leadership of Hobby Lobby is committed to a greater good through corporate socially responsible behavior, such as donations to communities and giving back through other means. Another factor of their social responsibility is the fact that they have great benefits for their employees. Ethical leadership drives the benefits offered to their employees. Having wages above minimum wage, offering above normal healthcare coverage, being closed on Sundays, and having shorter than normal work days benefit the employees and create a favorable workplace. On the other hand, some of their customers would like to make purchases on Sunday, so Hobby Lobby does miss out on this opportunity for sales. In addition, some consumers may think Hobby Lobby closing on Sunday is an attempt to force the acceptance of their religious principles.

While there would almost be unanimous agreement that Hobby Lobby's ethical intentions are sound, some critics might argue that the principles, values, and beliefs of specific stakeholders such as consumers and employees should be respected. There are concerns about taking an individual's personal principles and being in a position of power to enforce those principles on others. However, in this case, employees and customers can analyze the facts and decide whether they want to work for Hobby Lobby or be a customer. The conflicts and controversies associated with the successful appeal to the Supreme Court to restrict the coverage of "abortifascients" will continue.

Although Hobby Lobby has been ethical in responding to the challenges they have faced in the past, the Affordable Care Act really brings their beliefs into view. The ruling of this case is at the forefront as some other companies in the future might be able to file similar lawsuits claiming religious beliefs for not offering benefits or certain rights to employees. The ruling was in favor of Hobby Lobby, and this could enable other companies to be exempt for at least some benefits to employees.

The challenge for Hobby Lobby will be to maintain a strong reputation as a religious organization while still accepting others' rights. Hobby Lobby is a positive example of a business and will demonstrate the character of their company through the future decisions they have to make. The lawsuit against the government is a display of their religious beliefs, and their success in obtaining the right to withhold certain medical benefits illustrates their commitment to principles. On the other hand, stakeholders may continue to question the Green family because there are firms in the 401(k) plans that are involved with the type of contraceptives they claim to be against. This might violate some of their principles.

The ethics of the Green family and the running of the for-profit company Hobby Lobby has been strong in the past. However, the Affordable Care Act has brought to light some ethical leadership challenges, and how Hobby Lobby faces them will determine the future of this company.

Questions for Discussion

1. Should the founders and owners of a private company that serves the public incorporate their religious values in the policies that impact the behavior of employees, consumers, and other stakeholders?
2. Evaluate the decision of Hobby Lobby to spend considerable resources in refusing to offer coverage of "abortifascient" birth control methods and taking their fight to the U.S. Supreme Court.
3. How will the U.S. Supreme Court decision in *Burwell v. Hobby Lobby* (divided 5-4 decision) impact Hobby Lobby's stakeholders and its future success?

Sources

Susan Berfield, "Does God Hate Obamacare? Hobby Lobby Takes Its Case to the Supreme Court," *Bloomberg Businessweek*, April 2014, pp. 76–79.

ChristiaNet, "Hobby Lobby CEO, David Green," *ChristiaNet*, 2012, http://christiannews.christianet. com/1096289115.htm (accessed August 10, 2016).

Forbes, "America's Largest Private Companies," http:// www.forbes.com/companies/hobby-lobby-stores/ (accessed August 10, 2016).

Jaime Fuller, "Here's What You Need to Know About the Hobby Lobby Case," *The Washington Post*, March 24, 2014, https://www.washingtonpost.com/news/the-fix/ wp/2014/03/24/heres-what-you-need-to-know-about-the-hobby-lobby-case/ (accessed August 10, 2016).

Billy Hallowell, "Hobby Lobby President Apologizes, Pledges to Carry Jewish Holiday Items After Blogger Claims Worker Said They Don't 'Cater to You People'," *The Blaze*, October 7, 2013, http://www.theblaze.com/ stories/2013/10/07/hobby-lobby-president-apologizes-pledges-to-carry-jewish-holiday-items-after-blogger-claims-worker-said-they-dont-cater-to-you-people/ (accessed August 10, 2016).

Hobby Lobby, *Customer Service: Frequently Asked Questions*, 2014, http://www.hobbylobby.com/customer_service/faq.cfm (accessed August 10, 2016).

Hobby Lobby, "Hobby Lobby Marks 40 Years of Helping Families Celebrate Life," *Business Wire*, September 8, 2010, http://www.businesswire.com/news/ home/20100908006739/en/Hobby-Lobby-Marks-40-Years-Helping-Families (accessed August 10, 2016).

"Hobby Lobby," Our Story, http://www.hobbylobby.com/ about-us/our-story (accessed August 10, 2016).

Hobby Lobby, Burwell v. Hobby Lobby: FAQ, http://www. hobbylobbycase.com/faq/ (accessed August 10, 2016).

Alex Murashko, "Hobby Lobby's President Honored for Practicing Biblical Values in the Marketplace," *The Christian Post*, February 5, 2013, http://www.christianpost.com/news/hobby-lobbys-president-honored-for-practicing-biblical-values-in-marketplace-89462/ (accessed August 10, 2016).

PR Newswire iReach, "Hobby Lobby comments on Chik-Fil-A," *PR Newswire*, August 5, 2012, http://www.prnewswire.com/news-releases/hobby-lobby-comments-on-chik-fil-a-165046896.html (accessed August 25, 2014).

Thomas Reese, "In the Hobby Lobby case before the Supreme Court, law is not the ethics," *National Catholic Reporter: The Independent News Source,* April 11, 2014, https://www.ncronline.org/blogs/faith-and-justice/hobby-lobby-case-supreme-court-law-not-ethics (accessed August 10, 2016).

The Seattle Times, "Hobby Lobby CEO Green joins Giving Pledge list," *The Seattle Times*, December 10, 2010, http://seattletimes.com/html/businesstechnology/2013642781_apusgivingbywealthyokla.html (accessed August 10, 2016).

Sanjeev Sriram, "My Faith Is Offended by Inequality, Not Birth Control," *Huff Post: Politics*, March 26, 2014, http://www.huffingtonpost.com/sanjeev-k-sriram/my-faith-is-offended-by-i_b_5031689.html (accessed August 10, 2016).

Nina Totenberg, "Hobby Lobby Contraceptive Case Goes Before Supreme Court," *NPR*, March 25, 2014, http://www.npr.org/2014/03/25/293956170/hobby-lobby-contraceptive-case-goes-before-supreme-court (accessed August 10, 2016).

Supreme Court of the United States, *Burwell, Secretary of Health and Human Services, et al. v. Hobby Lobby Stores, Inc., et al.: Certiorari to the United States Supreme Court of Appeals for the Tenth Circuit,* No. 13-354, June 30, 2014.

Ilya Shapiro, "Hobby Lobby: Government Can't Violate Religious Liberties Willy-Nilly," *The Federalist*, July 1, 2014, http://thefederalist.com/2014/07/01/hobby-lobby-government-cant-violate-religious-liberties-willy-nilly/ (accessed August 10, 2016).

Mark L. Russell, "A Candid Interview with David Green Founder and CEO of Hobby Lobby," *The High Calling,* October 25, 2014, http://www.thehighcalling.org/leadership/candid-interview-david-green-founder-and-ceo-hobby-lobby (accessed August 25, 2014).

Ryan Ellis, "Hobby Lobby Owners Can Have a 401(k) and First Amendment Rights," *Forbes,* July 1, 2014, http://www.forbes.com/sites/ryanellis/2014/07/01/hobby-lobby-owners-can-have-a-401k-and-first-amendment-rights/#909f6e35b54f (accessed August 10, 2016).

Alex Kocman, "Hobby Lobby Raises Minimum Wage to $14: What Happens When Govt Doesn't Tie Businesses' Hands," *Charisma News,* July 3, 2014, http://www.charismanews.com/marketplace/44543-hobby-lobby-raises-minimum-wage-to-14-what-happens-when-govt-doesn-t-tie-businesses-hands (accessed August 10, 2016).

Susan Thurston, "Hobby Lobby's Religious Convictions Aren't for Sale," *Tampa Bay Times,* January 10, 2014, http://www.tampabay.com/news/business/retail/hobby-lobbys-religious-convictions-arent-for-sale/2160568 (accessed August 10, 2016).

Glenn Kessler, "Hillary Clinton's Claim That Hobby Lobby Wanted to Stop Covering All Contraceptive Procedures," *Washington Post,* July 3, 2014, https://www.washingtonpost.com/news/fact-checker/wp/2014/07/03/hillary-clintons-claim-that-hobby-lobby-wanted-to-stop-covering-all-contraception-procedures/ (accessed August 10, 2016).

Maggie Fox, "Supreme Court on Birth Control: What Hobby Lobby Ruling Means," *NBC News,* June 30, 2014, http://www.nbcnews.com/health/health-care/supreme-court-birth-control-what-hobby-lobby-ruling-means-n144526 (accessed August 10, 2016).

Kent Hoover, "HHS Issues Contraception Workaround in Response to Hobby Lobby Ruling," *Columbus Business First,* August 22, 2014, http://www.bizjournals.com/columbus/news/news-wire/2014/08/22/hhs-issues-contraception-workaround-in-response-to.html?ana=e_abq_rdup&s=newsletter&ed=2014-08-25&u=38ahMxn8yHTkJb3pqpxi7Q091b98b0&t=1408977152 (accessed August 10, 2016).

Starbucks' Mission: Social Responsibility and Brand Strength

INTRODUCTION

Howard Schultz joined Starbucks in 1982 as director of retail operations and marketing. Returning from a trip to Milan, Italy, with its 1,500 coffee bars, Schultz recognized an opportunity to develop a similar retail coffee bar culture in Seattle.

In 1985, the company tested the first downtown Seattle coffeehouse, served the first Starbucks café latté, and introduced its Christmas Blend. Since then, Starbucks expanded across the United States and around the world, now operating over 24,000 stores in 70 countries. Historically, Starbucks grew at a rate of about three stores a day, although the company cut back on expansion in recent years. The company serves approximately 70 million customers per week and has revenues of approximately $19 billion a year. It is the largest coffeehouse company in the world.

Starbucks locates its retail stores in high-traffic, high-visibility locations. The stores are designed to provide an inviting coffee bar environment that is an important part of the Starbucks product and experience. It was the intention of Howard Schulz to make Starbucks into "the third place" for consumers to frequent, after home and work. Because the company is flexible regarding size and format, it locates stores in or near a variety of settings, including office buildings, bookstores, and university campuses. It can situate retail stores in select rural and off-highway locations to serve a broader array of customers outside major metropolitan markets and further expand brand awareness.

In addition to selling products through retail outlets, Starbucks sells coffee and tea products and licenses its trademark through other channels and its partners. For instance, its Frappuccino coffee drinks, Starbucks Doubleshot espresso drinks, super-premium ice creams, and VIA coffees can be purchased in grocery stores and through retailers like Walmart and Target. Starbucks partnered with Courtesy Products to create single-cup Starbucks packets marketed toward hotel rooms. Starbucks also partnered with Green Mountain Coffee Roasters to introduce Starbucks-branded coffee and tea pods to the market. These pods target consumers who own Keurig single-cup brewing machines. Although the two businesses would normally be rivals, this partnership is beneficial for both Green Mountain and Starbucks. Since Green Mountain owns Keurig's single-serve machines, the partnership enables Starbucks to access this technology to market a new product. Green Mountain benefits because the partnership generates new users of Keurig single-cup brewing machines attracted to the Starbucks name.

This partnership between Green Mountain and Starbucks did not stop Starbucks from launching its own line of single-serve machines. In 2012, Starbucks introduced its Verismo 580 Brewer that allows consumers to brew a cup of Starbucks coffee in their own homes (later versions include the Verismo 583 and 600). The coffee has the strong, bold flavor of a cup purchased in any Starbucks retail location. Starbucks offers a limited assortment of coffees to emphasize quality rather than quantity. Not to be outdone, Green Mountain released another type of single-serve coffee brewer called the Rivo. Unlike the Verismo, that uses powdered milk pods, the Rivo uses fresh milk. The race to conquer the single-serve coffee market is intensifying between the two companies.

A common criticism of Starbucks is the company's strategy for location and expansion. Its "clustering" strategy, placing a Starbucks literally on every corner in some cases, forced many smaller coffee shops out of business. This strategy dominated for most of the 1990s and 2000s and Starbucks became the butt of jokes. Many people began to wonder whether two Starbucks directly across the street from each other were really needed. The last recession brought a change in policy, however. Starbucks pulled back on expansion, closed hundreds of stores around the United States, and focused more on international markets. Now Starbucks is beginning to focus on U.S. expansion once more.

At the end of 2014, Starbucks opened a 15,000 square-foot Starbucks Reserve Roastery and Tasting Room in Seattle, a place where coffee is roasted, bagged, sold, and shipped internationally. Equipped with a Coffee Library and Coffee Experience Bar, the roastery is intended to redefine the coffee retail experience for customers. The roastery sells 28-30 different coffees and gets 1,000 to 2,000 customers daily. CEO Howard Schultz believes the roastery has the potential to redefine the Starbucks retail experience. Starbucks has also added local Mora ice cream to the product line at the roastery so consumers can create Affogato-style beverages (espresso poured over ice cream).

NEW PRODUCT OFFERINGS

Starbucks introduced a number of new products over the years to remain competitive. In 2008, Starbucks decided to return to its essentials with the introduction of its Pike Place Blend. The company hoped that the blend would return Starbucks to its roots of distinctive, expertly blended coffee. In order to get the flavor perfect, Starbucks enlisted the inputs of 1,000 customers over 1,500 hours. To kick off the new choice, Starbucks held the largest nationwide coffee tasting in history. To make the brew even more appealing, Starbucks joined forces with Conservation International to ensure the beans were sustainably harvested. Also, after feedback revealed many of its customers desired a lighter blend, Starbucks introduced Blonde Roast blend in 2011. In 2015 the company commercialized the Flat White based on a latte drink popular in Australia. Unlike previous new offerings, the company did not perform limited-market testing but instead introduced it nationwide in an attempt to remain competitive with rivals.

Starbucks executives believe the experience customers have in the stores should be consistent. Therefore, Starbucks began to refocus on the customer experience as one of the key competitive advantages of the Starbucks brand. To enhance the European coffee shop experience for which Starbucks is known, shops are replacing their old espresso machines with new, high-tech ones. To keep the drink-making operation running efficiently and accurately, Starbucks mandated baristas to make no more than two drinks at the same time. It is also introducing more lines of single-origin coffees to appeal to coffee enthusiasts interested in where their coffee comes from.

Additionally, Starbucks fosters brand loyalty by increasing repeat business. One of the ways it accomplishes this is through the Starbucks Card, a reloadable card introduced in 2001. For the tech-savvy visitor, Starbucks introduced the Starbucks Reward Mobile app. With the app customers are able to order or pre-order their coffee, and merely scan their phone for payment. Today the company has 12 million active users of its Starbucks Rewards mobile app –the third most popular digital payment app in the country. It is estimated that Starbucks processes 5 million mobile payments a week. Howard Schultz believes the future is digital and is placing more emphasis on digital marketing strategies.

STARBUCKS CULTURE

In 1990, Starbucks' senior executive team created a mission statement that specified the guiding principles for the company. They hoped the principles included in the mission statement would assist partners in determining the appropriateness of later decisions and actions. After drafting the mission statement, the executive team asked all Starbucks partners to review and comment on the document. Based on their feedback, the final statement put "people first and profits last." In fact, the number one guiding principle in Starbucks' mission statement is to create a great and respectable work environment for its employees.

Starbucks has done three things to keep the mission and guiding principles alive over the decades. First, it distributes the mission statement and comment cards for feedback during orientation to all new partners. Second, Starbucks continually relates decisions back to the guiding principle or principles it supports. These principles focus on coffee, partners, customers, stores, neighborhoods, and shareholders. And finally, the company formed a "Mission Review" system so partners can comment on a decision or action relative to its consistency with one of the six principles. These guiding principles and values have become the cornerstone of a strong ethical culture of predominately young and educated workers.

Starbucks founder and CEO Howard Schultz has long been a public advocate for increased awareness of ethics in business. In a 2007 speech at Notre Dame, he spoke to students about the importance of balancing "profitability and social consciousness." Schultz is a true believer that ethical companies do better in the long run, something that has been confirmed by research. Schultz maintains that, while it can be difficult to do the right thing at all times, in the long term it is better for a company to take short-term losses than lose sight of its core values.

The care the company shows its employees is a large part of what sets it apart. Starbucks offers all employees who work more than 20 hours per week a comprehensive benefits package that includes stock options as well as medical, dental, and vision benefits. In another effort to benefit employees, Starbucks partnered with Arizona State University (ASU) to offer tuition assistance to those who want to earn a degree from the university's online program. In 2014, it was voted as one of the most ethical companies on *Ethisphere*'s annual list for the eighth consecutive year.

Another key part of the Starbucks image involves its commitment to ethics and sustainability. To address concerns related to these issues, Starbucks launched the Shared Planet website. Shared Planet has three main goals: to achieve ethical sourcing, environmental stewardship, and greater community involvement. The website is a means of keeping customers current on initiatives within the company. It describes how well Starbucks fares on achieving its social responsibility goals, and it provides a means for customers to learn things like the nutrition data of Starbucks' offerings and other concerns related to Starbucks products.

Starbucks actively partners with nonprofits around the globe. Starbucks is one of the largest buyers of Fair Trade Certified as well as certified organic coffee. It also purchased 4.4 million pounds of certified organic coffee. Another organization Starbucks partnered with is the Foodservice Packaging Institute/Paper Recovery Alliance. The partnership addresses the issue of responsible foodservice packaging in terms of its use, recovery, and processing. Starbucks has invested over $70 million in programs for farmers around the world.

Conservation International joined with Starbucks in 1998 to promote sustainable agricultural practices, namely shade-grown coffee, and help prevent deforestation in endangered regions around the globe. The results of the partnership proved to be positive for both the environment and the farmers. For example, in Chiapas, Mexico, shade-grown coffee acreage (that reduces the need to cut down trees for coffee plantations) increased well over 220 percent, while farmers receive a price premium above the market price. Starbucks and Oprah, two of the biggest global brands, joined forces to create Oprah's Chai Tea in 2014. A specially created blend from the stores of Teavana, one of Starbucks' most recent acquisitions, these branded products contribute to youth education programs. All profits made from this tea go toward this cause.

Starbucks works with many other organizations as well, including the African Wildlife Foundation and Business for Social Responsibility. The company's efforts at transparency, the treatment of its workers, and its dozens of philanthropic commitments demonstrate how genuine Starbucks is in its mission to be an ethical and socially responsible company.

CORPORATE SOCIAL MISSION

Although Starbucks supported responsible business practices virtually since its inception, as the company has grown, so has the importance of defending its image. At the end of 1999, Starbucks created a Corporate Social Responsibility department, now known as the Global Responsibility Department. Global Responsibility releases an annual report in order for shareholders to keep track of its performance and can be accessed through the Shared Planet website. Starbucks is concerned about the environment, its employees, suppliers, customers, and communities. Howard Schultz has commented that achieving social change to improve society is an important part of the company's core identity.

Environment

In 1992, long before it became trendy to be "green," Starbucks developed an environmental mission statement to clearly articulate the company's environmental priorities and goals. This initiative created the Environmental Starbucks Coffee Company Affairs team, the purpose of which was to develop environmentally responsible policies and minimize the company's "footprint." As part of this effort, Starbucks began using environmental purchasing guidelines to reduce waste through recycling, conserving energy, and educating partners through the company's "Green Team" initiatives. Concerned stakeholders can now track the company's progress through its website that clearly outlines Starbucks' environmental goals and how the company fares in living up to those goals. Starbucks also began offering a $1 plastic cup for purchase that is good for a recommended 30 uses.

Employees

Growing up poor with a father whose life was nearly ruined by an unsympathetic employer who did not offer health benefits, Howard Schultz always considered the creation of a good work environment a top priority. He believes companies should value their workers. When forming Starbucks, he decided to build a company that provided opportunities his father did not have. The result is one of the best healthcare programs in the coffee shop industry. Schultz's key to maintaining a strong business is developing a shared vision among employees as well as an environment to which they can actively contribute. Understanding how vital employees are, Schultz is the first to admit his company centers on personal interactions: "We are not in the coffee business serving people, but in the people business serving coffee." Starbucks is known for its diversity, and 40 percent of its baristas are ethnic minorities.

However, being a great employer does take its toll on the company. In 2008, Starbucks closed 10 percent of stores in order to continue to provide employees with health insurance. This decision, based on its guiding principle of "people first, profits last," shows how much the company values its employees.

Employees have an opportunity to join Starbuck's stock-sharing program called Bean Stock. They have generated $1 billion in financial gains through stock options. In 2015 Starbucks gave employees a raise and increased starting pay rates across the country.

As a way to improve employee health, Starbucks established a program for employees called "Thrive Wellness" that offers various resources aimed at assisting employees in incorporating wellness into their lives. The program offers resources such as smoking cessation, weight loss, and exercise. Starbucks also estimates that 70 percent of employees are either currently in college or desire to earn a degree. The aforementioned partnership with ASU provides this opportunity as students can choose from 40 programs online or in-person with no obligation to remain as a Starbuck's employee while receiving or achieving their degree. More than 2,000 employees applied to the program when it was initially launched. The rising cost of education is an important issue that CEO Howard Schultz wants to help alleviate.

Suppliers

Even though it is one of the largest coffee brands in the world, Starbucks maintains a good reputation for social responsibility and business ethics throughout the international community of coffee growers. It builds positive relationships with small coffee suppliers while also working with governments and nonprofits wherever it operates. Starbucks practices conservation as well as Starbucks Coffee and Farmer Equity

Practices (C.A.F.E.), a set of socially responsible coffee buying guidelines that ensure preferential buying status for participants that receive high scores in best practices. Starbucks pays coffee farmers premium prices to help them make profits and support their families. More than 95 percent of total coffee purchases are C.A.F.E. verified, and the company is on track to have 100 percent of its coffee purchases verified by 2015.

The company is also involved in social development programs, investing in programs to build schools and health clinics, as well as other projects that benefit coffee-growing communities. Starbucks collaborates directly with some of its growers through Farmer Support Centers, located in Costa Rica, Rwanda, Tanzania, South America, and China. Farmer Support Centers provide technical support and training to ensure high-quality coffee into the future. In 2013, Starbucks donated approximately $11 million for loans and farmer support programs, with the goal of reaching $20 million for the 2015 year. It is a major purchaser of Fair Trade Certified, shade-grown, and certified organic beans that further support environmental and economic efforts. The purchase was one step toward Starbucks' goal of increasing its ethically sourced coffee to 100 percent by 2015.

Customers

Strengthening its brand and customer satisfaction is more important than ever as Starbucks seeks to regroup after the latest recession forced the company to rethink its strategy. Starbucks refocused the brand by upgrading its coffee-brewing machines, introducing new food and drink items for health and budget-conscious consumers, and refocusing on its core product. Recognizing the concern over the obesity epidemic, Starbucks ensures that its grab-and-go lunch items are under 500 calories and is involved in two sodium reduction programs: the National Salt Reduction Initiative in New York and the UK Food Standards Agency Salt Campaign. The company focuses more on the quality of the coffee, the atmosphere of the coffee shops, and the overall Starbucks experience, rather than continuing its rapid expansion of stores and products. Enhancing the customer experience in its stores became a high priority. As a way to encourage people to relax and spend time there, Starbucks offers free wireless Internet access in all its U.S. stores. They have also partnered with Duracell Powermat to install over 100,000 wireless phone chargers in Starbucks and Teavana locations across the United States.

Communities

Starbucks coffee shops have long sought to become the "instant gathering spot" wherever they locate, a "place that draws people together." The company established community stores, which not only serve as a meeting place for community programs and trainings but also as a source of funding to solve issues specific to the local community. There are currently five such locations (including one in Thailand), and Starbucks aims to establish a total of 50 by 2018. Schultz even used the advance and ongoing royalties from his book, *Pour Your Heart into It,* to create the Starbucks Foundation that provides opportunity grants to nonprofit literacy groups, sponsors young writers' programs, and partners with Jumpstart, an organization helping children prepare developmentally for school. The company announced its intention to hire 10,000 veterans by 2018.

Additionally, Starbucks takes a proactive approach to addressing employment opportunities and job training. The company has joined other firms to support the "100,000 Opportunities Initiative," with the goal to create 100,000 employment and internship opportunities for lower-income youth between 16 and 24 years of age. Howard Schultz helped spearhead the initiative and announced plans to hire 10,000 young workers over a three-year period. Starbucks also announced it was building 15 new store locations in lower-income, predominately minority neighborhoods in an attempt to improve communities through employment, education, and training. For instance, its location in Ferguson, Missouri acts as a coffee shop as well as a job training facility for community members. Starbucks also plans to partner with local organizations to sell their products in its stores.

BRAND EVOLUTION

Although Starbucks achieved massive success in the last four decades, the company realizes it must modify its brand to appeal to changing consumer tastes. All established companies, no matter how successful, must learn to adapt their products and image to appeal to the shifting demands of their target markets. Starbucks is no exception. The company is associated with premium coffee beverages, an association that served it well over the years. However, as competition in specialty coffee drinks increases, Starbucks recognized the need to expand its brand in the eyes of consumers.

One way it is doing this is through adopting more products. In addition to coffee, Starbucks stores sell coffee accessories, teas, muffins, CDs, water, grab-and-go products, Starbuck Petites, upscale food items, handcrafted sodas called Fizzios, as well as wine and beer in select locations. Food sales make up 20 percent of Starbucks' revenue. The rise in coffee prices has created an opportunity for expansion into consumer packaged goods that will protect Starbucks against the risks of relying solely on coffee. In order to remain competitive, Starbucks made a series of acquisitions to increase the value of its brand, including Bay Bread (a small artisan bakery), La Boulange (a bakery brand), Evolution Fresh (a juice brand), and Teavana (a tea brand). This allowed Starbucks to offer high quality breakfast sandwiches as well as Paninis and wraps for lunch.

To symbolize this shift into the consumer packaged goods business, Starbucks gave its logo a new look. Previously, the company's circular logo featured a mermaid with the words "Starbucks Coffee" encircling it. In 2011, Starbucks removed the words and enlarging the mermaid to signal to consumers Starbucks is more than just the average coffee retailer.

SUCCESS AND CHALLENGES

For decades, Starbucks revolutionized our leisure time. Starbucks is the most prominent brand of high-end coffee in the world but also one of the defining brands of our time. In most large cities, it is impossible to walk more than a few blocks without seeing the familiar mermaid logo.

In the past few decades, Starbucks achieved amazing levels of growth, creating financial success for shareholders. Starbucks' reputation is built on product quality, stakeholder concern, and a balanced approach to all of its business activities. Of course, Starbucks does receive criticism for putting other coffee shops out of business and creating a uniform retail culture in many cities. Yet the company excels in its relationship with its employees and is a role model for the fast-food industry in employee benefits. In addition, in an age of shifts in supply chain power, Starbucks is as concerned about its suppliers and meeting their needs as it is about any other primary stakeholder.

In spite of Starbucks' efforts to support sustainability and maintain high ethical standards, the company garnered harsh criticism in the past on issues such as a lack of fair trade coffee, hormone-added milk, and Howard Schultz's alleged financial links to the Israeli government. In an attempt to counter these criticisms, in 2002 Starbucks began offering Fair Trade Certified coffee, a menu item that was quickly made permanent. Approximately 95 percent of coffee in the United States is ethically sourced currently.

Starting in late 2008, Starbucks had something new to worry about. A global recession caused the market to bottom out for expensive coffee drinks. The company responded by slowing its global growth plans after years of expanding at a nonstop pace and instead refocused on strengthening its brand, satisfying customers, and building consumer loyalty. After Starbucks stock started to plummet, Howard Schultz returned as CEO to return the company to its former glory.

Schultz was successful, and Starbucks rebounded from the effects of the recession. The company is once again looking toward possibilities in international markets. This represents both new opportunities and challenges. When attempting to break into the U.K. market, for instance, Starbucks met with serious resistance. Realizing the homogenization of its stores did not work as well in the United Kingdom, Starbucks began to remodel its stores so they took on a more local feel. At the end of 2012, Starbucks came under public scrutiny for allegedly not paying taxes for the last 14 of the 15 years they were established in the United Kingdom. A protest group called UK Uncut began "sitting in" at the stores, encouraging coffee drinkers to buy their coffee elsewhere. Starbucks claims it did not pay taxes because it did not make a profit. However, the company said it would stop using certain accounting techniques that showed their profits overseas. Starbucks also agreed to pay 20 million pounds over the next two years, whether or not it makes a profit.

Starbucks is rapidly expanding in China, and the country set to become the company's second largest market behind the United States. Starbucks effectively overcame obstacles in tapping into the Chinese market and adapted its strategy to attract Chinese consumers. After the 2007 closure of the retail operation in the Forbidden City, resulting from cultural concerns of the presence of a Western staple in a sacred area, Starbucks became more sensitive to the specific needs and nuances of the country. Through educating Chinese consumers on coffee (because the beverage is not largely consumed there), they are now drinking as much coffee as Americans.

Another challenge Starbucks must address is despite the company's emphasis on sustainability, billions of disposable Starbucks cups are thrown into landfills each year. Although Starbucks has taken initiatives to make the cups more ecofriendly, such as changing from polyethylene No. 1 to the more ecofriendly polypropylene No. 5, the cup represents a serious waste problem for Starbucks. Starbucks encourages consumers to bring in reusables (such as the Starbucks tumblers it sells) for a 10-cent rebate, yet these account for less than 2 percent of drinks served. The company hopes to achieve less cup waste with its new $1 reusable cup. It remains to be seen whether Starbucks will achieve its goal of total recyclability in the short term.

CONCLUSION

Despite the setbacks it experienced during the recession, the future looks bright for Starbucks. In 2015 the company underwent a 2-for-1 stock split as its way of addressing record highs in the company's stock history. It is estimated the Starbucks shares have quadrupled four times over the past five years. The company continues to expand globally into markets such as Bangalore, India; San Jose, Costa Rica; Oslo, Norway; and Ho Chi Minh City, Vietnam. Schultz is hopeful that the new roastery in Seattle will continue to spread the Starbucks name and the distribution of its coffee globally. The challenges the company experienced and will continue to experience in the future have convinced the firm to focus on its strengths and embrace the opportunity to emphasize community involvement, outreach work, and its overall image and offerings. The company must continue to apply the balanced stakeholder orientation that is so crucial to its success.

Questions for Discussion

1. Why do you think Starbucks has been so concerned with social responsibility in its overall corporate strategy?
2. Is Starbucks unique in being able to provide a high level of benefits to its employees?
3. Do you think Starbucks has grown rapidly because of its ethical and socially responsible activities or because it provides products and an environment customers want?

Sources

Chris Barth, "Green Mountain Hopes to Beat Starbucks in the U.S. with One Simple Ingredient," *Forbes*, November 9, 2012, http://www.forbes.com/sites/chris-barth/2012/11/09/green-mountain-hopes-to-beat-star-bucks-in-the-u-s-with-one-simple-ingredient/ (accessed August 10, 2016).

Susan Berfield, "Starbucks' Food Fight," *Businessweek*, June 12, 2012, http://www.businessweek.com/articles/2012-06-12/starbucks-food-fight (accessed August 10, 2016).

Christine Birkner, "Taking Care of Their Own," *Marketing News*, February 2015, pp. 45–49.

Ilan Brat, "Starbucks Lines Up Delivery Options," *The Wall Street Journal*, March 19, 2015, B2.

Laurie Burkitt, "Starbuck Menu Expands in China," *The Wall Street Journal,* March 9, 2011, p. B7.

Peter Campbell, "Starbucks caves in to pressure and promises to hand the taxman £20m after public outcry," *dailymail.co.uk*, December 6, 2012, http://www.dailymail.co.uk/news/article-2244100/Starbucks-caves-pressure-promises-pay-20m-corporation-tax-2-years.html (accessed August 10, 2016).

CC, "Starbucks Brings Imported Coffee to a Land of Exported Coffee," *Fast Company*, May 2012, p. 30.

Geoff Colvin, "Questions for Starbucks' Chief Bean Counter," *Fortune*, December 9, 2013, pp. 78–82.

"Coffee Deal Has Stocks Soaring," *USA Today,* March 11, 2011, p. 5B.

Conservation International, "Follow Starbucks' 15 Year Journey to 100% Ethically Sourced Coffee," http://www.conservation.org/partners/pages/starbucks.aspx (accessed August 10, 2016).

Eartheasy.com, "Shade Grown Coffee," http://www.earth-easy.com/eat_shadegrown_coffee.htm (accessed August 7, 2014).

Eatocracy editors, "Starbucks Introduces $1 Reusable Cup to Cut Down on Waste," *Eatocracy*, January 3, 2013, http://eatocracy.cnn.com/2013/01/03/starbucks-introduces-1-reusable-cup-to-cut-down-on-waste/ (accessed August 7, 2014).

Roxanne Escobales and Tracy McVeigh, "Starbucks hit by UK Uncut Protests As Tax Row Boils Over," *guardian.co.uk*, December 8, 2012, http://www.guardian.co.uk/business/2012/dec/08/starbucks-uk-stores-protests-tax (accessed August 10, 2016).

Ethisphere Institute, "World's Most Ethical Companies - Honorees," *Ethisphere*, 2016, http://ethisphere.com/worlds-most-ethical/wme-honorees/ (accessed August 10, 2016).

Rana Foroohar, "Starbucks for America," *Time*, February 16, 2015, 18–23.

Bobbie Gossage, "Howard Schultz, on Getting a Second Shot," *Inc.*, April 2011, pp. 52–54.

Haley Geffen, "Starbucks: Howard Schultz on the Coffee Chain's Expansion Under His Leadership," *Bloomberg Businessweek*, December 8-14, 2014, p. 32.

Jason Groves and Peter Campbell, "Starbucks Set to Cave in and Pay More Tax After Threats of Boycott at its 'immoral' Financial Dealings," *dailymail.co.uk*, December 3, 2012, http://www.dailymail.co.uk/news/article-2242596/Starbucks-pay-tax-public-outcry-financial-dealings.html (accessed August 10, 2016).

Bruce Horovitz, "For Starbucks, a split and a jolt," *USA Today*, March 19, 2015, 2B.

Bruce Horovitz, ¡Handcrafted Sodas to Bubble Up At Starbucks,î *USA Today*, June 23, 2014, p. 4B.

Bruce Horovitz, "Starbucks Aims beyond Lattes to Extend Brand to Films, Music and Books," *USA Today,* May 19, 2006, pp. A1, A2.

Bruce Horovitz, "Starbucks Brews Wireless Charging," *USA Today*, June 12, 2014, Page 2B.

Bruce Horovitz, "Starbucks Remakes Its Future," *USA Today,* October 18, 2010, pp. 1B–2B.

Bruce Horovitz, "Starbucks Sales Pass BK, Wendy's," *USA Today,* April 27, 2011, p. 1A.

Bruce Horovitz, "Starbucks Serving Alcohol At More Sites," *USA Today*, March 21, 2014, p. 3B.

Bruce Horovitz, "Starbucks Shells Out Bread for Bakery," *USA Today*, June 5, 2012, p. 1B.

Bruce Horovitz, Bruce Horovitz, "Starbucks taps into tasting room fad," *USA Today*, December 5, 2014, 1B–2B.

Bruce Horovitz and Howard Schultz, "Starbucks Hits 40 Feeling Perky," *USA Today,* March 7, 2011, pp. 1B, 3B.

John Jannarone, "Green Mountain Eclipses Starbucks," *The Wall Street Journal,* March 9, 2011, p. C14.

John Jannarone, "Grounds for Concern at Starbucks," *The Wall Street Journal,* May 3, 2011, p. C10.

Julie Jargon, "At Starbucks, Baristas Told No More than Two Drinks," *The Wall Street Journal,* October 13, 2010, http://online.wsj.com/article/SB10001424052748704164004575548403514060736.html (accessed August 10, 2016).

Julie Jargon, "Coffee Talk: Starbucks Chief on Prices, McDonald's Rivalry," *The Wall Street Journal,* March 7, 2011, p. B6.

Julie Jargon, "Starbucks Brews Plan Catering to Aficionados," *The Wall Street Journal*, September 11, 2014, B7.

Julie Jargon, "Starbucks CEO to Focus on Digital," *The Wall Street Journal*, January 30, 2014, B6.

Julie Jargon, "Starbucks Logo Loses 'Coffee,' Expands Mermaid as Firm Moves to Build Packaged-Goods Business," *The Wall Street Journal,* January 6, 2011, p. B4.

Julie Jargon, "Starbucks in Pod Pact," *The Wall Street Journal,* March 11, 2011, p. B4.

Julie Jargon and Douglas Belkin, "Starbucks to Subsidize Online Degrees," *The Wall Street Journal,* June 16, 2014, p. B3.

Sarah Jones, "Starbucks Shows that Healthcare isn't a Job Killer by Adding 1,500 Cafes," *PoliticusUSA,* December 6, 2012, http://www.politicususa.com/2012/12/06/healthcare-providing-starbucks-expanding-1500-cafes.html (accessed August 10, 2016).

David Kesmodel and Ilan Brat, "Why Starbucks Takes On Social Issues," *The Wall Street Journal*, March 24, 2015, B3.

Beth Kowitt, "Coffee Shop, Contained," *Fortune*, May 20, 2013, p. 24.

Katie Lobosco, "Oprah Chai Tea Comes to Starbucks," *CNN Money*, March 19, 2014, http://money.cnn.com/2014/03/19/news/companies/oprah-starubucks-tea/ (accessed August 10, 2016).

Laura Lorenzetti, "Where Innovation Is Always Brewing," *Fortune*, November 17, 2014, p. 24.

Kate McClelland, "Starbucks Founder Speaks on Ethics," *Notre Dame Observer,* March 30, 2007, http://ndsmcobserver.com/2007/03/starbucks-founder-speaks-on-ethics/ (accessed August 8, 2014).

Adam Minter, "Why Starbucks Won't Recycle Your Cup," *Bloomberg View,* April 7, 2014, http://www.bloombergview.com/articles/2014-04-07/why-starbucks-won-t-recycle-your-cup (accessed August 10, 2016).

MSNBC.com, "Health Care Takes Its Toll on Starbucks," September 14, 2005 http://www.msnbc.msn.com/id/9344634/ (accessed August 10, 2016).

Reuters, "Starbucks to Open First Outlet in Vietnam in Early February," *Economic Times,* January 3, 2013, http://www.reuters.com/article/2013/01/03/starbucks-vietnam-idUSL4N0A815420130103 (accessed August 10, 2016).

Mariko Sanchanta, "Starbucks Plans Big Expansion in China," *The Wall Street Journal,* April 14, 2010, p. B10.

David Schorn, "Howard Schultz: The Star of Starbucks," *60 Minutes,* http://www.cbsnews.com/stories/2006/04/21/60minutes/main1532246.shtml (accessed August 10, 2016).

E. J. Schultz, "How VIA Steamed up the Instant Coffee Category," *Advertising Age,* January 24, 2011, http://adage.com/article?article_id=148403 (accessed August 10, 2016).

SCS Global Services, "Starbucks C.A.F.E. Practices," http://www.scsglobalservices.com/starbucks-cafe-practices (accessed August 10, 2016).

Starbucks, 2014 *Annual Meeting of Shareholders*, 2014, https://news.starbucks.com/2014annualmeeting (accessed August 10, 2016).

Starbucks, "Affogato Line-up at Starbucks Roastery in Seattle," June 27, 2016, https://news.starbucks.com/news/affogato-line-up-at-starbucks-roastery (accessed August 10, 2016).

"Starbucks: A Farm of Its Own," *Bloomberg Businessweek*, March 25–31, 2013, p. 23.

Starbucks, "Community Stores," http://www.starbucks.com/responsibility/community/community-stores (accessed August 10, 2016).

"Starbucks Corporation (SBUX)," *YAHOO! Finance,* http://finance.yahoo.com/q/is?s=SBUX+Income+Statement&annual (accessed August 10, 2016).

Starbucks, "Farming Communities," http://www.starbucks.com/responsibility/community/farmer-support (accessed August 10, 2016).

Starbucks, "Food," http://www.starbucks.com/food (accessed August 10, 2016).

Starbucks, "Goals & Progress: Cup Recycling," http://www.starbucks.com/responsibility/global-report/environmental-stewardship/cup-recycling (accessed August 10, 2016).

Starbucks, "Investing in Farmers," http://www.starbucks.com/responsibility/community/farmer-support/farmer-loan-programs (accessed August 10, 2016).

Starbucks, "Mobile Applications," http://www.starbucks.com/coffeehouse/mobile-apps (accessed August 8, 2014).

Starbucks, "Recycling & Reducing Waste," http://www.starbucks.com/responsibility/environment/recycling (accessed August 10, 2016).

Starbucks, "Starbucks Company Profile," September 2013, http://news.starbucks.com/uploads/documents/AboutUs-CompanyProfile-Q3-2013-9.18.13.pdf (accessed August 10, 2016).

"Starbucks to Enter China's Tea Drinks Market," *China Retail News,* March 11, 2010, www.chinaretailnews.com/2010/03/11/3423-starbucks-to-enter-chinas-tea-drinks-market (accessed August 10, 2016).

"Starbucks Unveils Minimalist New Logo," *USA Today,* January 6, 2011, p. 11B.

Starbucks, "Small Changes Add Up to a Big Impact," http://www.starbucks.com/promo/nutrition (August 10, 2016).

"Statistics and Facts on Starbucks," *Statista*, October 2013, http://www.statista.com/topics/1246/starbucks/ (accessed August 10, 2016).

Charlie Rose, "Charlie Rose Talks to Howard Schultz," *Bloomberg Businessweek*, April 7–13, 2014, p. 32.

Trefis Team, "Starbucks' Profits Surge Despite Sales Slowing Down," *Forbes*, January 30, 2014, http://www.forbes.com/sites/greatspeculations/2014/01/30/starbucks-profits-surge-despite-sales-slowing-down/ (accessed August 10, 2016).

David Teather, "Starbucks Legend Delivers Recovery by Thinking Smaller," *The Guardian,* January 21, 2010, https://www.theguardian.com/business/2010/jan/21/starbucks-howard-schultz (accessed August 10, 2016).

Jorge Velasquez, "Starbucks Debuts $1 Reusable Cup," *KRCA*, January 3, 2013, http://www.kcra.com/news/Starbucks-debuts-1-reusable-cup/-/11797728/17994788/-/5dbclr/-/index.html (accessed August 10, 2016).

Daisuke Wakabayashi, "Starbucks Drops Square App as Mobile-Payments Battle Intensifies," *The Wall Street Journal*, December 22, 2014, http://blogs.wsj.com/digits/2014/12/22/starbucks-drops-square-app-as-mobile-payments-battle-intensifies/ (accessed August 10, 2016).

Nicole Wakelin, "The New Starbucks Verismo Single-Serve Home Coffee Brewer," *Wired*, November 18, 2012, http://archive.wired.com/geekmom/2012/11/starbucks-verismo/ (accessed August 10, 2016).

Jonathan Watts, "Starbucks Faces Eviction From the Forbidden City," *www.guardian.co.uk*, January 18, 2007, http://www.guardian.co.uk/world/2007/jan/18/china.jonathanwatts (accessed August 10, 2016).

Dan Welch, "Fairtrade Beans Do Not Mean a Cup of Coffee is Entirely Ethical," *guardian.co.uk*, February 28, 2011, http://www.guardian.co.uk/environment/green-living-blog/2011/feb/28/coffee-chains-ethical (accessed August 10, 2016).

Venessa Wong, "Starbucks Serves Up 'Flat Whites,' Tries to Prove It Can Still Be Different," *Bloomberg Businessweek*, January 6, 2015, http://www.bloomberg.com/news/articles/2015-01-06/starbucks-serves-up-flat-whites-tries-to-prove-it-can-still-be-different (accessed August 10, 2016).

Aamer Madhani, "Starbucks to open stores in low-income areas," *USA Today*, July 16, 2015, http://www.usatoday.com/story/news/2015/07/16/starbucks-to-open-15-locations-in-low-income-minority-communities/30206071/ (accessed July 20, 2015); Julie Jargon, "Starbucks Leads Push to Boost Youth Jobs," *The Wall Street Journal*, July 14, 2015, B3; Micah Solomon, "Starbucks to Open Store, Customer Service Training Center in Ferguson, 14 Other Distressed Locations," *Forbes*, July 16, 2015, http://www.forbes.com/sites/micahsolomon/2015/07/16/starbucks-to-open-store-customer-service-training-center-in-ferguson-14-other-distressed-locations/ (accessed July 20, 2015).

Lululemon: Encouraging a Healthier Lifestyle

INTRODUCTION

Lululemon Athletica is an athletic apparel company intended for individuals with active lifestyles. The organization has deep roots in the yoga community and is one of the few businesses to offer apparel for this specific market. Lululemon is based in Vancouver, British Columbia, Canada, and operates its clothing stores in numerous countries throughout the world. The apparel store offers product lines that include fitness pants, shorts, tops, and jackets for activities such as yoga, running, and other fitness programs. It operates in three segments. These segments consist of corporate-owned and operated retail stores, a direct to consumer e-commerce website, and wholesale avenues. As of 2015, the company operates 354 stores predominantly in the United States, Canada, Australia, and New Zealand. With nearly 2,800 employees, Lululemon has grown rapidly in the last 20 years and is expected to continue its growth strategy well into the foreseeable future. It has also established a subsidiary geared toward youth called Ivivva Athletica.

Store growth and expansion into other countries has allowed Lululemon to achieve financial success. The organization has seen continuous increases in revenue, with its annual revenue over $2 billion. Over the past four years, Lululemon has consistently posted annual revenue increases of about $300 million. While financially stable, the organizational structure has seen changes with the hiring of a new CEO. Lululemon hired Laurent Potdevin in January of 2014 hoping to appoint a worthy and experienced industry professional. The company also hopes to distance itself from negative headlines circling former CEO Denis "Chip" Wilson. Potdevin was once the CEO at TOMS Shoes and has worked in the industry for over 20 years.

There is no question that Lululemon has seen great success in recent years. From its conception in 1998, the organization has grown tremendously in markets across the globe. However, Lululemon's success has also been tainted by controversy, negative publicity, and questionable ethical decisions. This case will detail the issues and controversies circling this organization and identify how Lululemon has managed these issues. In addition, we provide information regarding the positive ethical decisions that have been made throughout Lululemon's history.

BACKGROUND

Lululemon was founded by Denis "Chip" Wilson in 1998 in British Colombia, Canada. Prior to Lululemon, Wilson had spent two decades in the surf, skate, and snowboard business. He was looking for a change. After attending the first commercial yoga class offered in Vancouver, Wilson fell in love with the activity and felt incredible during and after the exercises. With a passion for technical athletic fabrics, Wilson realized that the current cotton clothing being used for power yoga was inappropriate and unpractical. Movements required breathability, flexibility, and a stretchiness that an individual could pour sweat into during exercise. With this in mind, Wilson created a design studio for his new clothing. Struggling to pay rent, the design studio became a yoga studio during the night hours. Yoga instructors who taught at the studio were asked to wear the new products and provided Wilson with useful insight and feedback on the clothing. In order to name the new company, Wilson surveyed 100 people and offered a list of 20 brand names as well as 20 logos. Lululemon is a created word that has neither roots nor meaning. It is believed that Wilson selected this name because he enjoys the sound of the 3 L's when the word is spoken. The logo, which is actually a stylized letter A, was a logo intended for the brand name Athletically Hip, which was not selected as the company's name.

The first store opened in November 2000, in the beach area of Vancouver, British Columbia. The store

*This case was prepared by Justus Adams, Kristen Bruner, Ivan Mora Juarez, and Jennifer Sawayda for and under the direction of O.C. Ferrell and Linda Ferrell ©2015. It was prepared for classroom discussion rather than to illustrate either effective or ineffective handling of an administrative, ethical, or legal decision by management. All sources used for this case were obtained through publicly available material.

was intended to be a community-gathering place for individuals to discuss health topics like dieting, exercise, and cycling. However, the store was so popular and busy that satisfying the customer became nearly impossible. The business grew quickly as products were popular among customers and the staff was eager to learn, expand, and challenge themselves.

From the beginning, Lululemon had a strong mission that embraced a healthy and active lifestyle. Inspired by author and philosopher Ayn Rand, Chip Wilson modeled Lululemon with the intent that involves "elevating the world from mediocrity to greatness." The company adopted the following mission statement: "Creating components for people to live longer, healthier, fun lives." Lululemon tries to reflect this in its corporate culture. Store managers, for instance, are provided with much control over the operations of their stores, and Lululemon operates with a decentralized corporate culture. Lululemon employees are recruited and hired based on their level of commitment and how well they fit into the corporate culture. To bring its mission statement to fruition, Lululemon refers to its employees as "educators" to acknowledge the crucial role they play in helping customers to obtain a healthy and active lifestyle.

Lululemon stores today are focused heavily on community involvement and interaction with local enthusiasts. Nearly all stores host in-house events on a nightly or weekly basis, with classes ranging from beginner and advanced yoga to goal setting and self-defense workshops. Events and workshops generally occur after store hours and occur on the saleroom floor after racks and products have been moved.

Unlike many stores, Lululemon does not offer discounts, but sells approximately 95 percent of its products at full price. It also sells its products at higher prices than its competitors, reflecting the value of Lululemon's products. Lululemon operates on the concept of scarcity to encourage customers to buy immediately. Its store shelves often have fewer products than the shelves can hold, and many products have quick life cycle times such as six-week life cycles. Customers are therefore encouraged to purchase the product before it is gone, which is thought to be a major influence in Lululemon's continued popularity and success with customers.

In order to anchor its mission statement, Lululemon has adopted seven core values: quality, product, integrity, balance, entrepreneurship, fun, and greatness. These values serve to motivate employees and guide their decisions.

ETHICAL RISKS AND CHALLENGES

Despite Lululemon's strong mission statement and core values, Lululemon has faced much controversy over its history. Founder and former CEO Chip Wilson has also been criticized for controversial statements he has made, which eventually helped lead to his ouster as CEO. There have also been questions regarding whether Lululemon's corporate culture—with its strong emphasis on greatness and competitiveness—is necessarily healthy for employees.

Founder Chip Wilson

Lululemon founder Chip Wilson is thought of by many as a man with unorthodox opinions. Although Wilson has not been CEO since 2005, he has been known to do things without informing top management, such as printing out Lululemon tote bags with the phrase "Who Is John Galt?" from Ayn Rand's *Atlas Shrugged*. A former CEO at Lululemon felt pressured by Wilson to attend the Landmark Forum, a leadership-development training program which Wilson highly supports. Wilson has performed other controversial actions that have generated concern from Lululemon's board.

Much of the controversy around Chip Wilson centers on his statements. For instance, in a 2009 interview with Canada's *National Post Business Magazine*, he admitted to having chosen the company name because "it's funny to watch [Japanese] say it." Wilson also stated on a blog his opinion that the rise in divorce rates and breast cancer among "Power Women" was due to a combination of smoking, taking birth control pills, and the additional stress which came from taking on the career responsibilities once held mostly by men. He attributed Lululemon's growth as stemming from the coming together of "female education levels, breast cancer, yoga/athletics and the desire to dress feminine."

Another highly controversial statement of Chip Wilson's involves his opinions regarding child labor laws. Wilson argues that "third-world children should be allowed to work in factories because it provides them with much-needed wages." He claims this can help lead citizens of these countries out of poverty. The practice of child labor is a hot-button issue in the Western world because of the poor working conditions and rampant abuse worldwide. This support of child labor has angered critics, who believe Lululemon might be exploiting children in developing countries. They argue that providing children with more education is much more likely to lift them out of poverty than having them earn low wages at a dangerous job. Lululemon founder Chip Wilson would continue to make controversial statements, eventually leading to his resignation as Chairman of the Board.

Chip Wilson later challenged the board, claiming that the current board was not aligned with Lululemon's core values. He released this statement at the June 2014 shareholders meeting and voted against the board's chairman and another director. Both men were re-elected. A few months later, Wilson sold half of his 27 percent stake to private equity organization Advent International, who in turn received two board seats on Lululemon's board. With less of a stake in the firm, Wilson's impact on decision-making at the organization may be reduced.

MISLEADING ADVERTISING

In 2007, the *New York Times* cast doubt on the authenticity of Lululemon's VitaSea line of products. Lululemon claimed that its VitaSea products were infused with seaweed, which had medicinal properties including stress relief. In November 2007, the *New York Times* released an article claiming that it had tested VitaSea products and could not find seaweed fiber in the product. This claim unleashed a storm of criticism.

Lululemon responded by refuting the claims of the *New York Times*. They cited independent tests performed the previous year. They also responded to the accusations by stating that a lab in Hong Kong had performed different tests on the product throughout the year, all of which confirmed that the products contained everything that they advertised.

However, Canada's Competition Bureau challenged Lululemon, not due to the content of the VitaSea product, but rather the company's claims about the product's health benefits. The bureau believed that these claims of health benefits from seaweed were unsubstantiated and ordered Lululemon to remove all such labeling.

Corporate Culture

As mentioned earlier, Wilson founded his company on the values of Ayn Rand. The notion of striving for greatness resonated with Wilson after having read Rand's book *Atlas Shrugged* at the age of 18. Since then, he has utilized the concept as a way to market his brand. This idea of "greatness" contributes to a competitive organizational culture. Wilson admits that the firm tries to hire employees with Type A personalities, or those with more competitive personalities who are concerned with achievement and personal improvement. New hires read books selected by Chip Wilson that he feels is critical to personal development. Employees are also required to write out their goals for the next ten years, which are then posted in Lululemon stores. Employees are encouraged to exercise regularly and remain close-knit.

Some have questioned how this competitive culture obsessed with greatness fits in with the yoga tradition based on Buddhist and Hindu philosophies. Both ideologies promote the notion of ridding one's self of the Ego. The Ego is seen as a source of suffering, and Buddhism is based on the absolution of suffering. Enlightenment is achieved when the Ego has been successfully removed. There are specific postures used to accomplish this, and it can take years of practice. On the other hand, one of the criticisms of Lululemon goes back to Ayn Rand's teachings and their promotion of "rugged individualism," the elevation of mediocrity to greatness, and the relentless pursuit of happiness. Despite it being a business, some believe that these "individual" teachings do not belong in the yoga clothing industry, because they directly contradict the Vedic philosophy that underlies yoga. Others have claimed that Lululemon's corporate culture is almost "cultish" in its style.

In March 2011, an employee of Lululemon located in Bethseda, Maryland was brutally murdered by her co-worker after hours. It is believed the employee had observed the co-worker trying to steal clothing from Lululemon. After the store closed, the co-worker lured the employee back into the store and brutally murdered her. She then attempted to make the scene look as if two masked men had broken in and harmed them. After the truth was revealed, the co-worker was sentenced to life in prison without parole.

Lululemon and many others attribute this brutality as a random act of violence. However, those who describe the corporate culture as "cultish" and "competitive" argue that the culture creates an environment where employees are pressured to live up to company standards. Although this in itself is certainly not the reason for the murder, critics have sometimes charged Lululemon with having an unethical corporate culture promoting competition over collaboration.

Too-Sheer Yoga Pants

A more recent ethical problem for Lululemon occurred in March 2013, when they released black Luon yoga pants that become sheer when the wearer bends over. They instituted a massive recall which comprised 17 percent of all the women's pants sold in their stores. The recall resulted in large shortages, which impacted financial results and drove the stock price down. The company lost $2 billion in market value. Afterward, investors attempted to sue Lululemon, claiming that they purposefully hid defects in the pants. However, the lawsuit was dismissed the next year.

The scandal resulted in the resignation of CEO Christine Day. A few months later, in November 2013, Chip Wilson defended his product by suggesting that women's bodies are to blame for the fabric's sheerness and their tendency for pilling. He also claims that many women buy pants that are too small for them, which wears them out. When questioned about whether Lululemon is truly a clothing retailer for everybody, Wilson stated that the product was appropriate for all sizes but that some people simply misuse the product. Critics viewed this as a sexist comment, exacerbating the issue at hand. In the midst of consumer outrage, Wilson stepped down as Chairman of the Board.

Customer Privacy

Lululemon is known for wanting to avoid collecting large amounts of customer information through big data techniques. Instead, they desire to have a close and open relationship with customers. One of the ways they do this is by listening to customers as they shop in the store. Lululemon takes customer complaints or concerns seriously and will attempt to make decisions based on this information.

Although this emphasis on listening to the customer is an important part of Lululemon's customer relations, some people believe Lululemon takes it too far. A less well-known ethical risk that the company practices is the training of retail employees to eavesdrop on their customers. Lululemon prefers this to spending money on marketing software that tracks purchases, or sending out survey requests. Christine Day, the former CEO, used to spend much of her time in retail stores, pretending to be a customer, in order to listen to complaints and observe shopping habits. When she was with the company, she had stores set up their clothes-folding tables next to the fitting rooms so employees could better overhear any complaints. Whether these practices are smart marketing techniques or infringements on employee privacy is ambiguous.

POSITIVE ETHICAL PRACTICES

Despite the criticisms launched against Lululemon, the mission to help customers live a better life continues. Lululemon defines having a better life as living healthier, leading to a longer and more adequate life. Its mission to elevate humanity from mediocrity to greatness demonstrates that it wants consumers and employees to achieve their maximum potential. This is not too different from Abraham Maslow's concept of self-actualization. Lululemon has developed a manifesto to describe their way of business: "We are passionate about sweating every day and we want the world to know it. Breathing deeply, drinking water and getting outside also tops the list of things we can't live without. Get to know our manifesto and learn a little more about what lights our fire."

This manifesto clearly shows the backbone of Lululemon and the way they do business. The manifesto strives toward providing greatness to the people that use Lululemon products. The higher prices Lululemon charges are a sign of excellence and the belief that they are selling more than just clothing to the customers. It is a belief that the customer is buying a lifestyle that comes with the Lululemon brand and the set of values that Lululemon is conveying in the manifesto. As a result, Lululemon has gained a large following and clientele that believe in their products.

Contributions to Communities

Lululemon takes its responsibilities to communities seriously. It recognizes that community involvement will not only help gain new customers, but will also promote their mission of creating a healthier lifestyle. For these reasons, Lululemon holds free weekly yoga classes taught by fitness professionals. Lululemon shoppers who have attended the free yoga classes can get a 15 percent discount on their purchases.

Additionally, while the practice of secretly observing customers might be controversial in some ways, it also demonstrates Lululemon's commitment toward meeting customer needs. Lululemon believes that customer relationships are not based on technology, but rather on more basic marketing techniques like simply talking with the customer. The Lululemon culture encourages employees to establish strong connections with their customers, which is why the company emphasizes that its employees are "educators." By listening carefully to customer concerns as they shop, Lululemon gets an immediate picture of problems that the company can address. For instance, one time when the CEO was in a Lululemon store she overheard many complaints that a certain type of knit sweater had sleeves that were too tight. Based on this information, she canceled future orders. It is clear that Lululemon is willing to make quick product changes in response to customer feedback.

Lululemon also contributes to local charities throughout their communities. In many communities, Lululemon empowers customers by offering the clientele the ability to suggest organizations and charities to receive donations. Lululemon's program allows for up to eight local charities to receive donations. This shows their commitment to their local communities and their willingness to give back as much as possible, while still maintaining a healthy bottom line. Lululemon's efforts display a stakeholder mindset as they make decisions that benefit their shareholders, clients, local neighborhoods, and nearby businesses.

RELATIONSHIPS WITH EMPLOYEES

Lululemon recognizes that customer satisfaction is only as good as the employees that provide it. Lululemon therefore strives to make its employees into ambassadors for the brand. This can only happen if employees are passionate and committed to company products and values. The hiring process at Lululemon is extensive as the firm only wants to hire those who it believes will be the right fit with its company culture. It is also costly. Applicants may go through more than one interview, and those that get farther in the process are often asked to attend yoga classes where the recruiters can see how they interact with others. When an applicant is chosen as an employee, he or she will undergo 30 hours of training. They also spend three weeks working on the floor.

As mentioned before, Lululemon strives to get employees inspired. Employees must develop their personal goals, which are then hung in the stores. To encourage healthy living and incentivize employees, the company offers staff free fitness classes. It also tries to help their employees find the right balance between family and work. Lululemon frequently sends merchandising tips to their sales employees and encourages them to take responsibility and ownership of the store.

Lululemon believes in hiring managers internally, which motivates lower-level employees because they know they have a good chance of becoming a leader. Approximately 70 percent of Lululemon managers are internal hires. Employee satisfaction at Lululemon appears to be high; in exit interviews, 90 percent of employees claim they would recommend for their friends to work at Lululemon.

Lululemon also offers its employees unique perks. It frequently sanctions events such as group hikes or exercise sessions to help its employees bond with one another. After a year of employment, Lululemon sends employees to the Landmark Forum, a three-day self-improvement program at a cost of approximately $500 per employee. (Some have criticized the Landmark Forum and Chip Wilson's endorsement of it, while others claim the experience transformed their lives.) Lululemon has also created the "Fund a Goal" program for high-performing employees. This incentive pays for these employees to achieve one of the goals on their list.

CONCLUSION

Lululemon focuses much of their efforts on the legacy that they will leave behind (the legacy they are creating now for future generations). Throughout the years, Lululemon has created a culture of promoting a healthy lifestyle, which can be achieved through healthy eating, yogi tradition, and in-store fitness classes. The company stresses a culture in which employees, customers, and other stakeholders can achieve greatness. As a result, the organization has seen rapid success and growth during the last decade. However, the company has been hit by a number of scandals, requiring them to rebuild their reputation and adopt new leadership.

The changes that Lululemon has implemented demonstrate that the organization is willing to make difficult decisions to do the right thing. If Lululemon continues to put stakeholders first and refuses to deviate from its values, it is likely to avoid similar ethical issues in the future. A strong values-based corporate culture will help Lululemon remain a successful company with a reputation for both ethical behavior and quality products. In addition, most companies the size of Lululemon have an effective ethics and compliance program to help build an ethical culture. Based on past issues that the company has faced, it appears that it is time to embrace a more proactive approach to managing ethics and social responsibility.

Questions for Discussion

1. How has Lululemon handled various ethical issues that it has faced over the last few years?
2. How has the ethical culture of Lululemon impacted its relationship with customers and employees?
3. To avoid negative publicity and ethical challenges, what steps should Lululemon take to improve its stakeholder relationships?

Sources

David Creelman, "Embracing the Unorthodox: Welcome to the High Commitment Workplace," *HR Voice,* January 26, 2012, http://www.hrvoice.org/embracing-the-unorthodox-welcome-to-the-high-commitment-workplace/ (accessed August 11, 2016).

Jim Edwards, "12 Utterly Bizarre Facts About The Rise Of Lululemon, The Cult-Like Yoga Brand," *Business Insider,* April 24, 2012, http://www.businessinsider.com/12-utterly-bizarre-facts-about-the-rise-of-lululemon-2012-4?op=1 (accessed August 11, 2016).

Amelia Hill, "I Thought I'd Be Brainwashed. But How Wrong Could I Be…" *The Guardian,* December 13, 2003, http://www.theguardian.com/uk/2003/dec/14/ameliahill.theobserver (accessed August 11, 2016).

"Hiring for Culture Fit at Lululemon Athletica," *Canadian HR Reporter,* http://www.hrreporter.com/videodisplay/190-hiring-for-culture-fit-at-lululemon-athletica (accessed August 11, 2016).

Chris Isidore, "See-through pants problem causes Lululemon recall," *CNN Money,* March 19, 2013, http://money.cnn.com/2013/03/19/news/companies/lululemon-pants/index.html?iid=EL (accessed August 11, 2016).

Sally Kempton, "Sophisticated Ego," *Ego,* http://www.yoga-journal.com/wisdom/2502 (accessed August 11, 2016).

Stewart J. Lawrence, "Murder At Lululemon: Yoga's 'Heart of Darkness'?" *The Huffington Post,* November 9, 2011, http://www.huffingtonpost.com/stewart-j-lawrence/when-yogis-kill-the-grisl_b_1077457.html (accessed August 11, 2016).

Colleen Leahy and Christine Day, "Lululemon CEO: How to Build Trust Inside Your Company," *CNN Money,* May 16, 2012, http://fortune.com/2012/03/16/lululemon-ceo-how-to-build-trust-inside-your-company/ (accessed August 11, 2016).

Lululemon Athletica website, http://www.lululemon.com/ (accessed August 11, 2016).

Lululemon Athletica, Inc., "lululemon athletica inc. Announces Third Quarter Fiscal 2015 Results," December 9, 2015, http://investor.lululemon.com/releasedetail.cfm?ReleaseID=946223 (accessed August 11, 2016).

"Lululemon to Remove Claims From Seaweed Product Line," *CBC News,* November 16, 2007, http://www.cbc.ca/news/business/lululemon-to-remove-claims-from-seaweed-clothing-line-1.655660 (accessed August 11, 2016).

Lululemon, *Global Code of Business Conduct and Ethics,* http://files.shareholder.com/downloads/LULU/0x0x186005/3c1b56bd-5468-433e-a3c6-681657524c3a/LULU_WebDoc_2420.pdf (accessed August 11, 2016).

Melissa Lustrin and Felicia Patinkin, "Lululemon Founder Chip Wilson Blames Women's Bodies for Yoga Pant Problems," *ABC News,* November 7, 2013, http://abcnews.go.com/US/lululemon-founder-chip-wilson-blames-womens-bodies-yoga/story?id=20815278 (accessed August 11, 2016).

Ashley Lutz, "Lululemon Spends $500 for Workers to Attend a Controversial Retreat Endorsed by Founder Chip Wilson," *Business Insider,* January 9, 2014, http://www.businessinsider.com/lululemons-landmark-retreat-for-workers-2014-1 (accessed May 16, 2014).

Ashley Lutz, "You Really Have to 'Drink the Kool-Aid' at Lululemon to Succeed at Lululemon," *Business Insider,* February 19, 2013, http://www.businessinsider.com/what-its-like-to-work-at-lululemon-2013-2# (accessed August 11, 2016).

Mary Mann, "Yoga, Spinning and a Murder: My strange Months at Lululemon," *Salon,* December 31, 2013, http://www.salon.com/2013/12/31/yoga_spinning_and_a_murder_my_strange_months_at_lululemon/ (accessed August 11, 2016).

Dana Mattioli, "Lululemon's Secret Sauce," *The Wall Street Journal*, March 22, 2012, http://online.wsj.com/news/articles/SB10001424052702303812904577295882632723066 (accessed August 11, 2016).

Laura McClure, "The Landmark Forum: 42 Hours, $500, 65 Breakdowns," *Mother Jones,* July/August 2009, http://www.motherjones.com/media/2009/07/landmark-42-hours-500-65-breakdowns (accessed August 11, 2016).

Market Watch, "lululemon athletica inc.," 2016, http://www.marketwatch.com/investing/stock/lulu/financials (accessed August 11, 2016).

Daniel Stashower, "The Yoga Store Murder: The Shocking True Account of the Lululemon Athletica Killing," *The Wall Street Journal.* November 29, 2013, http://www.washingtonpost.com/opinions/the-yoga-store-murder-the-shocking-true-account-of-the-lululemon-athletica-killing-by-dan-morse/2013/11/29/36493e46-51fc-11e3-a7f0-b790929232e1_story.html (accessed August 11, 2016).

Jonathan Stempel and Joseph Ax, "Lululemon Prevails in Lawsuit over Yoga Pants Recall," *Chicago Tribune,* April 4, 2014, http://articles.chicagotribune.com/2014-04-04/business/sns-rt-us-lululemon-lawsuit-yoga-pants-20140404_1_yoga-pants-dennis-chip-wilson-quality-control (accessed August 11, 2016).

Mark Walker, "Lululemon Athletica—Driving a Culture of Individual and Organizational Development, Accountability and Innovation," *HRM Today,* September 29, 2011, http://www.hrmtoday.com/featured-stories/lululemon-athletica-driving-a-culture-of-individual-and-organizational-development-account-ability-and-innovation/ (accessed May 16, 2014).

"Yoga and Buddhism: Similarities and Differences," June 13, 2012, http://www.vedanet.com/2012/06/yoga-and-buddhism-similarities-and-differences/ (accessed May 16, 2014).

Suzanne Kapner and Joann S. Lublin, "Lululemon Founder Shrinks Role, Clears Way for New CEO," *The Wall Street Journal*, December 10, 2013, pp. B1–B2.

Joann S. Lublin and Suzanne Kapner, "Lululemon Founder Sparks a Fight with Board," *The Wall Street Journal*, June 11, 2014, http://online.wsj.com/articles/lululemon-founder-votes-against-chairman-1402483176 (accessed August 11, 2016).

Samantha Sharf, "Lululemon and Billionaire Founder Chip Wilson Call a Truce," *Forbes,* August 7, 2014, http://www.forbes.com/sites/samantha-sharf/2014/08/07/lululemon-calls-a-truce-with-billion-aire-founder-chip-wilson/ (accessed August 11, 2016).

The Hershey Company and West African Cocoa Communities

INTRODUCTION

With over $7.4 billion dollars in sales every year, the Hershey Company is one of the world's largest producers of chocolate and candy products. Hershey's products are sold in more than 70 countries and include Hershey's Kisses and Hershey's Milk Chocolate Bars as well as brands such as Reese's, Whoppers, Almond Joy, and Twizzlers.

Although Hershey strives to be a model company and has several philanthropic, social, and environmental programs, the company has struggled with ethical issues related to the labor issues associated with West African cocoa communities, including child labor. Hershey has developed several initiatives to improve the lives of West African cocoa workers and is involved with a number of organizations that are involved in cocoa communities. However, critics argue that Hershey is not doing enough to stop labor exploitation on cocoa plantations. This case examines some of the issues related to the Hershey Chocolate Company and West African cocoa communities.

HERSHEY'S HISTORY

The Hershey Chocolate Company was founded in 1894 by candy-manufacturer Milton Hershey. Originally in the business of making caramel, Hershey began producing chocolate in 1893 after he purchased chocolate-making equipment. Hershey's chocolate business started off as a side project, a way to create sweet chocolate coatings for his caramels; however, the company soon began producing baking chocolate and cocoa and then selling the extra product to other confectioners. The successful sale of Hershey's excess products was enough to make the chocolate department its own separate entity.

Despite its immediate success, Milton Hershey still craved more chocolate, especially milk chocolate. At the time, milk chocolate was perceived as a treat only the wealthy could afford to enjoy. Hershey set out to find a less expensive way to produce milk chocolate while still maintaining its quality. Therefore, in 1896, Hershey bought a milk processing plant in Derry Township, Pennsylvania and began working day and night until 1899 when he created the perfect milk chocolate recipe—a recipe that could be manufactured cheaply and efficiently while maintaining a high level of quality. The company soon opened a factory and began introducing new chocolate treats; the most popular of these was the Hershey's Kiss, a small dollop-shaped chocolate candy wrapped in foil.

The Kiss was only the beginning; Hershey's soon came out with Mr. Goodbar and the Krackel bar, both of which remain popular today. In 1923 Hershey's began collaborating with another famous confectioner, Reese. H.B. Reese was a former employee at the Hershey Company who started his own candy company that focused on a single product, the peanut butter cup. Due to his ties with the Hershey Company, the chocolate coating for the Reese's peanut butter cups was supplied by Hershey.

Throughout the mid-20th century, the Hershey Chocolate Company continued to expand. The company's entrepreneurial spirit continued after Milton Hershey's death in 1945. The company acquired several other companies, including Reese's, and was renamed the Hershey Foods Corporation in 1968. From 1969 to 2004, the company grew from $334 million to $4.4 billion in net sales. The company changed its name to the Hershey Company in 2005.

Today, the Hershey Company is North America's largest producer of chocolate and candies. It plans to expand into other products such as cookies, beverages, and health foods. The company sells over 80 brands of

*This material was developed by Harper Baird, Nicole Guevara, and Aleksander Karpechenko under the direction of O.C. Ferrell and Linda Ferrell. Jennifer Sawayda provided updates. It is intended for classroom discussion rather than to illustrate effective or ineffective handling of administrative, ethical, or legal decisions by management. Users of this material are prohibited from claiming this material as their own, emailing it to others, or placing it on the Internet. (2016)

products in approximately 70 countries and generates annual sales of $7.4 billion.

ETHICS, VALUES, AND SOCIAL RESPONSIBILITY AT HERSHEY

Hershey's commitments to its stakeholders through ethical behavior are outlined in the Code of Ethical Business Conduct. The code covers issues from conflicts of interest and antitrust to fair trade, sustainable supply chain management, and workplace diversity. The company encourages ethics reporting through a variety of channels, including management, HR, executives, and third-party reporting. All employees go through ethics training and certify their adherence to the code every year. Hershey's Ethical Business Practices Committee provides oversight and guidance in all ethical issues at the company.

Hershey's Values

Hershey's four core values are centered on the idea of "One Hershey":

- Open to Possibilities: "We are open to possibilities by embracing diversity, seeking new approaches and striving for continuous improvement."
- Growing Together: "We are growing together by sharing knowledge and unwrapping human potential in an environment of mutual respect."
- Making a Difference: "We are making a difference by leading with integrity and determination to have a positive impact on everything we do."
- One Hershey: "We are One Hershey, winning together while accepting individual responsibility for our results."

Hershey's Social Responsibility Strategy

Hershey's corporate social responsibility (CSR) strategy centers on engagement with its stakeholders and continually improving its CSR performance. The company also incorporates its values into its programs and initiatives. The company believes that "The Hershey Company's commitment to corporate social responsibility is a direct reflection of our founder's life-affirming spirit." Hershey

uses its value chain to categorize its social responsibility activities into four groups: Marketplace, Environment, Workplace, and Community.

MARKETPLACE

Hershey strives to conduct business fairly and ethically by focusing on the integrity of its supply, consumer well-being, and alignment with customers.

For Hershey, the integrity of supply includes not only the ingredients but also the people and processes used to grow, process, and acquire those ingredients (the entire supply chain). Cocoa is of particular concern to Hershey, and it is involved in a number of cocoa-sector initiatives and partnerships to make progress in sustainable cocoa farming and fair labor. These issues are explored in greater detail later in this case.

The company sponsors several consumer health initiatives and programs, including Moderation Nation, a national consumer education initiative that promotes balanced lifestyles, which is sponsored by the Hershey Center for Health & Nutrition (HCHN) and the American Dietetic Association (ADA). The company also hosts Hershey's Track and Field Games across the U.S. to encourage children ages 9-14 to engage in sports and a healthy lifestyle.

ENVIRONMENT

Maintaining the environment is important to Hershey, and it is taking many steps to reduce its impact on the environment, including sustainable product designs, sustainable sourcing, and efficient business operations. Some specific programs include the following:

- Sustainable palm oil sourcing: Palm oil comes from the African oil palm tree and is used in a wide variety of products, include Hershey's chocolate. However, the production of palm oil is highly controversial because of its impact on ecosystems. To combat concerns, Hershey became a member of the Roundtable of Sustainable Palm Oil (RSPO) and purchases its palm oil only from suppliers that are also RSPO members.
- Sustainable paper: In 2011 Hershey began to purchase paper for its office from suppliers that use sustainable forestry practices and are Forest Stewardship Council or Sustainable Forestry Initiative certified.
- Recyclable packaging: More than 80 percent of Hershey's packaging is recyclable, including syrup

bottles, foil, paper wrappers, and boxes. Recycling helped Hershey to reduce its packaging waste by 1.75 million pounds in 2014.

- Zero-waste-to-landfill facility: In 2011, the Reese's plant became a zero-waste-to-landfill facility, meaning that none of the plant's routine manufacturing waste went to a landfill. Today six Hershey manufacturing plants and five other facilities have achieved zero-waste-to-landfill. The waste that is not recycled goes to an energy incinerator and is used as a source of fuel.

WORKPLACE

Hershey wants to provide value to its employees and make the company a desirable place to work by focusing on safety, wellness, openness, and inclusion. The company has strong diversity policies and focuses on continuous safety improvements in its manufacturing facilities. However, this does not mean that Hershey never faced workplace issues. In 2011, over 400 foreign students working for Hershey went on strike after Excel, one of the company's subcontractors, misled and underpaid them. OSHA later fined the sub-contractor $283,000 for health and safety violations.

Hershey has continued to improve its workplace practices. In 2013 it was listed in *Corporate Responsibility* magazine as one of America's "Best Corporate Citizens." It launched an initiative called "Manufacturing Apprenticeship Program" to recruit, train, and retain employees with physical or intellectual disabilities for its manufacturing plants. Hershey is also considered one of the best places to work for LGBT employees.

COMMUNITY

Hershey's biggest philanthropic contribution is through its Milton Hershey School. Milton Hershey and his wife, Catherine, started the school in 1909 to help orphan boys receive an education while living in a nurturing environment that included meals and clothes. The school was a cause dear to the couple's heart because they were unable to have children of their own. After his wife's death, Milton Hershey created the Hershey Trust Fund, to which he donated most of his money, to be used for the support of the school. To this day, the fund remains the company's biggest shareholder and largest beneficiary. It holds a 30 percent stake in Hershey.

Although the school is Hershey's biggest philanthropic contribution, the company also donates to and supports over 1,400 organizations including the American Red Cross, Habitat for Humanity, Junior Achievement, Dress for Success, and the Children's Miracle Network. The company has also designed a way to get their employees involved in the community. Hershey designed a program called "Dollars for Doers" in which employees who participate in 50 hours of community service over one year are rewarded $250, by the company, to donate to an organization of their choice.

Board changes

Despite its strong record of social responsibility, in 2016 Hershey experienced a board upheaval when the Hershey Trust Co. settled with the Pennsylvania attorney general's office. The attorney general's office had begun investigating concerns that board members were overpaid, received reimbursements for excessive travel expenses, and exceeded 10-year term limits. There were also questions about whether board members of the trust were acting in the best interests of the Milton Hershey School. The board had rejected different offers by other firms to acquire Hershey. The local community of Hershey, Pennsylvania encouraged Hershey to remain independent, but some believe that selling the company would be the most beneficial option for the school. The Hershey Trust holds 81 percent of the voting power, which gives it the power to control votes on mergers or acquisitions.

The allegations are serious enough that Hershey agreed to make corporate governance changes. Some of the board members resigned. Additionally, Hershey developed a legal document that caps board member terms as well as compensation. This lapse in corporate governance is a slight blow to Hershey's reputation, but it also offers the firm an opportunity to learn from its mistakes and develop more sound leadership for the future.

LABOR ISSUES IN THE COCOA INDUSTRY

Although the Hershey Company strives to engage in ethical and responsible behavior, the realities of the cocoa industry present several ethical challenges related to the fair and safe treatment of workers, especially children. Chocolate is one of the world's most popular confections, but few people consider the sources of the chocolate they consume.

The process of making chocolate spans several countries and companies even before the ingredients arrive at the manufacturing plant. It starts with the cocoa bean, which is found within the *Theodroma Cacao*, also known as the cocoa pod (fruit). The harvest process is labor intensive and starts when the seeds (cocoa beans) are extracted by splitting the pod with a machete. Each pod can contain anywhere from 20 to 50 beans, and around 400 beans are needed to produce one pound of chocolate. After the beans have been extracted, they are laid out to dry in the sun for several days in order to acquire the flavor needed for chocolate. The beans are then packed into bags and sent out for shipment.

Chocolate manufacturers rarely buy directly from cocoa bean companies. The actual process of procuring cocoa beans and other cocoa products is conducted through one of the two world exchanges, either the NYSE Euronext or the Intercontinental Exchange. The chocolate industry is valued at $100 billion.

The cocoa bean supply chain is extensive and elaborate; at times the cocoa bean can go through up to 12 different stages before getting to the chocolate manufacturers, and the price per pound of cocoa beans changes significantly throughout the supply chain. By the time the beans reach the chocolate manufacturers, they are a mix of beans from hundreds of cocoa plantations.

Although the process of manufacturing chocolate requires many steps before it can begin, most of the major ethical and legal issues are related to the source of the cocoa bean. Cocoa plantations are found in areas with rainy, hot, tropical climates and high amounts of vegetation. The global cocoa market is currently supplied by mostly poor nations, with 70 percent from Africa (Ivory Coast, Ghana, Nigeria, Cameroon), especially the Ivory Coast, which supplies 40 percent of the entire global market, and Ghana, which supplies 20 percent. This is followed by 19 percent from Asia and Oceania (Indonesia, Papua New Guinea, Malaysia),

and 11 percent from the Americas (Ecuador, Brazil, Colombia).

With the majority of the global cocoa supply coming from Africa, the need for workers on plantations never dwindles, which has brought about the thriving business of child labor, slavery, and human trafficking across African borders. Many cocoa farms do not own the cocoa plantation and pay the land owner 50-66 percent of each year's crop. To keep costs low, farmers often use their own family members as a source of labor.

Children who work on cocoa plantations are usually somewhere between 12 and 15 years old but some are as young as 5 years old. Many of them work in hazardous conditions on the plantations. Hazardous conditions include applying pesticides, working with sharp objects like knives and machetes, working without safety equipment, and working in environments full of snakes, insects, and other dangerous animals. Although governments and corporations are aware of this problem, no accurate information, aside from estimates, exists regarding the true number of children working on cocoa plantations. The difficulty of obtaining accurate data can be attributed to the immense quantity of cocoa plantations across Africa, totaling well over 1,000,000 small plantations (average size 2-4 hectares), with between 600,000 and 800,000 plantations located throughout the Ivory Coast.

Nonetheless, it is estimated that two-thirds of African farms use child labor. Research conducted by the International Labor Organization (ILO) stated that in 2007 there were 284,000 children who worked in hazardous conditions related to cocoa in the Ivory Coast. Furthermore, according to surveys conducted by both Tulane University and the Government of the Ivory Coast, an estimated 819,921 children in the Ivory Coast alone are working in some area of the cocoa business. According to an ILO investigation in 2002, an estimated 12,000 child laborers in the Ivory Coast had no relatives anywhere near the plantations, which suggests that they may have been trafficked.

In addition to child labor, many cocoa plantations engage in exploitation of other workers. While some non-family workers are paid, others may be enslaved or work in abusive conditions. They may have been trafficked from neighboring countries or tricked into owing large amounts of money to their employers. The workers are often threatened with physical punishment or death if they attempt to leave the plantation.

The number of victims of labor exploitation has increased. A recent survey has found that child labor has increased 21 percent from five years before. About 2.1 million children are employed in child labor in the Ivory Coast and Ghana. Most of the people working on cocoa farms live well below the poverty line. In Ghana the average income per day is 84 cents, while in the Ivory Coast it is 50 cents. According to the World Bank, $1.90 is the cutoff rate for extreme poverty. Demand for chocolate has increased with the rising middle class of consumers in places like China. In fact, prices of cocoa have increased by 13 percent. The Ivory Coast exports 1.8 million metric tons of cocoa a year, two-fifths of the world's production. Yet many farmers do not see any increase in additional compensation or standard of living.

Global Efforts to Improve Labor Conditions

The issues of child labor, human trafficking, and forced labor in West Africa have drawn the attention of many organizations as well as the companies who procure products from that region. They have implemented many different initiatives, laws, and other precautionary measures in order to reduce the use of children for cocoa farming in terms of manual labor. In Africa individuals under the age of 14 are not allowed by law to work within the business sector, which does not include family farms. This law seems to be effective, but in reality, it does almost nothing when considering the large amounts of family cocoa farms and the ease of hiding non-family laborers.

To help change labor practices without relying on governmental or legal support, several organizations are working to encourage the ethical sourcing of cocoa. Most of these organizations focus on the fair treatment and education of cocoa producers and raising voluntary support from companies. The following are some of the global organizations and programs that are working to combat the labor problem within the cocoa industry:

- World Cocoa Foundation (WCF): An organization devoted to improving cocoa farmers' lives through sustainable and responsible cocoa farming practices.
- Sustainable Tree Crops Program (STCP): Farmers learn to improve their cocoa crop yields and earn more money through nine-month field training courses.
- Harkin-Engel Protocol: An initiative enacted in 2001 to commit the chocolate industry to fighting the worst cases of child labor. The agreement was

signed by eight chocolate manufacturers, including The Hershey Company.
- International Cocoa Initiative (ICI): An independent foundation established in 2002 under the Harkin-Engel Protocol to address the worst forms of child labor and adult forced labor on cocoa farms in West Africa. The organization works to inform and educate communities on child labor and how to create community-based solutions.
- International Labor Organization (ILO): An organization working to combat the various child labor related problems within West Africa. The different programs initiated by the ILO have focused on creating sustainable ways of removing children from child labor in the cocoa business, improving community initiatives to fight child labor, and increasing overall income for the adult sector to prevent the need for child labor.

In addition, the fair trade movement encourages traders of chocolate and other products to move beyond ethical sourcing. The intent of the fair trade movement is to raise awareness about working conditions, culture, and identity of producers. Traders must meet several standards, including paying a sustainable price to producers that reflects the costs of production and living as well as paying a premium that producers can use to invest in business and social programs, make advance payments when requested, and sign long-term contracts to encourage planning. Products made using fair trade practices are usually certified and sold to consumers at a higher price. While the demand for fair trade products is growing, the market is currently small.

HERSHEY'S EFFORTS TO IMPROVE LABOR CONDITIONS

Hershey has made several commitments to help reduce labor issues in its own supply chain and in the chocolate industry. Hershey is involved in West Africa and the organizations that fight child labor in West African cocoa farming. The company is a member of the WCF, ICI, and is one of the eight corporations that signed the Harkin-Engel Protocol. Involvement in these programs and organizations requires Hershey to commit to certain standards and contribute to fighting child labor.

The Hershey Company is dedicated to sustainably and ethically supplying the cocoa needed for its products, as well as educating its suppliers. One program that integrates these two concepts is Hershey's "CocoaLink – Connecting Cocoa Communities" program. CocoaLink use mobile technology to share practical information with rural cocoa farmers. Farmers receive free text or voice messages that cover topics such as improving farming practices, farm safety, child labor, health, crop disease prevention, post-harvest production, and crop marketing. Farmers can also share information and receive answers to specific cocoa-farming questions.

In 2012 Hershey launched the Hershey Learn to Grow (LTG) farm program in Ghana, which provides local farmers with information on best practices in sustainable cocoa farming. Specifically, the program seeks to encourage ethical farming practices as well as leadership and empowerment. Both men and women are being trained on how to improve crop yields. Those who meet acceptable certification standards receive extra money. Hershey estimates that this program influenced over 31,000 farmers by 2015.

Hershey also produces some of its products using ethical and sustainable cocoa. Hershey Bliss, one of the company's specialty chocolates, is made with 100 percent Rainforest Alliance Certified cocoa. This means that the cocoa is grown using farming methods that are safe, sustainable, and that respect the rights of the workers.

By 2017 Hershey hopes to expand its cocoa community programs by investing in West Africa and working closely with agricultural experts and the government. Hershey also announced that over a five-year period, it will invest $10 million in West Africa in order to reduce child labor, improve the cocoa farming community, and directly benefit 750,000 African cocoa farmers.

In 2013 Hershey initiated the 21st Century Cocoa Plan with the intent to have all of its cocoa certified as sustainable by 2020. It has partnered with three certification organizations: UTZ, Fairtrade USA, and Rainforest Alliance. The company claims that by the end of 2015, it had achieved sustainable certification for 50 percent of its cocoa. In order to achieve sustainable certification, third-party auditors must examine farmers supplying the cocoa to see whether they are following best practices. One crucial practice analyzed is whether the farmers make use of child labor.

As part of its initiative toward sustainably-sourced cocoa, in 2014 Hershey helped co-found an industry approach with 10 other chocolate companies referred to as CocoaAction. Operated under the World Cocoa Foundation, CocoaAction has $500 million in funding, which is being used to improve the lives of farmers in the Ivory Coast and Ghana through training and educational opportunities.

Criticism of Hershey's Efforts

Some critics argue that Hershey is not doing enough to combat labor exploitation and improve communities in West Africa. Over the past few years, Mars, Mondelez, Nestlé, Cargill, and other competitors have worked to adopt fair trade certification and/or release information regarding their suppliers. Despite many requests for public disclosure of its cocoa suppliers, Hershey still declines to name them. It is well known that Hershey acquires most of its cocoa from West Africa, but the specific sources are more difficult to identify.

According to a 2010 report titled "Time to Raise the Bar: The Real Corporate Social Responsibility for the Hershey Company,"

> "Hershey has no policies in place to purchase cocoa that has been produced without the use of labor exploitation, and the company has consistently refused to provide public information about its cocoa sources…Finally, Hershey's efforts to further cut costs in its cocoa production has led to a reduction in good jobs in the United States."

The report, compiled by Global Exchange, Green America, the International Labor Rights Forum, and Oasis USA, accused Hershey of not embracing fair trade practices despite having a U.S. market share of over 40 percent. It also accused Hershey of greenwashing, or creating a false impression regarding its eco-friendly behavior, by donating to various programs without actually changing its policies to ensure that its cocoa is ethically produced. Green America even created a coalition called "Raise the Bar, Hershey!" to urge the company to address child labor and trafficking in the supply chain.

Since then relations between Hershey and Green America seem to have improved somewhat. The organization was pleased with Hershey's pledge to source 100 percent of its cocoa from sustainable sources (free from child labor) by 2020. However, the company has many obstacles to overcome, and Green America has ranked Hershey's competitors higher than Hershey in its approach to solving the child labor problem. Green America developed a "Big Chocolate Scorecard" to grade chocolate manufacturers on the sustainability of their supply chains. Hershey ranked behind its major competitors Nestlé, Mars, Mondelez, and Ghirardelli (owned by Lindt). Hershey received a C- according to the scorecard's ranking criteria. However, even Nestlé—the highest ranked among the top chocolate manufacturers—only scored a C+. A representative from Green America maintains that Hershey scored lower because it relies more on third-party certification rather than direct engagement. The organization believes that while third-party certification is a step in the right direction, it is only part of the solution to combatting child labor.

CONCLUSION

The labor issues in the chocolate industry are complex and are connected to the poverty within West Africa. The exploitation of cocoa communities is intertwined with the meager incomes for the majority of the population, a lack of education and opportunity, governmental corruption, and other conditions in the region. Improving the overall well-being of West Africa is an important part of any attempt to effectively fight the problems associated with labor cocoa plantations.

The Hershey Company recognizes the need to improve labor conditions in the supply chain and has developed several initiatives to help create positive change in the cocoa industry. However, despite the company's large financial contributions, the company trails behind competitors Nestlé, Mars, Mondelez, and Ghirardelli on efforts to address sustainability, poverty, and child labor. On the other hand, the company appears to have improved significantly in combatting child labor after initiating the 21st Century Cocoa Plan in 2013.

In the end, labor exploitation in the chocolate industry cannot be solved by one company alone. There are many possible solutions, and it will take many years and a large amount of investment from the chocolate industry before conditions change. However, by making small changes to West African cocoa communities, the quality of life for thousands of cocoa workers will slowly improve.

Questions for Discussion

1. Should Hershey be held ethically responsible for child labor conditions in the West African cocoa communities?

2. How can Hershey balance its ethical culture and concern for labor conditions in West Africa in relating to various stakeholders?

3. If it is not possible for Hershey to gain control of its supply chain for a required raw material (cocoa beans) in its final product, what are its alternatives?

Sources

Christian Alexandersen, "Hershey Co. a sweet place to work for LGBT community, report finds," *Penn Live,* November 18, 2015, http://www.pennlive.com/news/2015/11/hershey_co_a_sweet_place_to_wo.html (accessed July 27, 2016).

"'Bitter' Chocolate Report: Hershey Dominates U.S. Market, But Lags Behind Competitors in Avoiding Forced Labor, Human Trafficking, and Abusive Child Labor," September 13, 2010, http://www.prnewswire.com/news-releases/bitter-chocolate-report--hershey-dominates-us-market-but-lags-behind-competitors-in-avoiding-forced-labor-human-trafficking-and-abusive-child-labor-102803859.html (accessed July 21, 2016).

Business Wire, "Hershey '21st Century Cocoa Plan' Outlines Commitments to Sustainable Cocoa and Improving Cocoa Communities," *BusinessWire,* March 21, 2013, http://www.businesswire.com/news/home/20130321006184/en/Hershey-%E2%80%9821St-Century-Cocoa-Plan%E2%80%99-Outlines-Commitment (accessed July 21, 2016).

Business Wire, "The Hershey Company Recognized as One of America's '100 Best Corporate Citizens'," April 12, 2013, http://www.businesswire.com/news/home/20130412005450/en/Hershey-Company-Recognized-America%E2%80%99s-%E2%80%98100-Corporate-Citizens%E2%80%99 (accessed July 27, 2016).

"The Cocoa Industry in West Africa: A history of exploitation," Anti-Slavery International, 2004, http://www.antislavery.org/includes/documents/cm_docs/2008/c/cocoa_report_2004.pdf (accessed July 21, 2016).

"Cocoa Farming: An Overview," The European Chocolate & Cocoa Industry," http://www.cocoafarming.org.uk/cocoa_farming_bw_v8_uk.pdf (accessed July 21, 2016).

"Cocoa Market Update," World Cocoa Foundation, April 1, 2014, http://www.worldcocoafoundation.org/wp-content/uploads/Cocoa-Market-Update-as-of-4-1-2014.pdf (accessed July 21, 2016).

Annie Gasparro, "Hershey Trust to Reach Settlement with Pennsylvania Attorney General's Office," *The Wall Street Journal,* July 22, 2016, http://www.wsj.com/articles/hershey-trust-to-reach-settlement-with-pennsylvania-attorney-generals-office-1469224460 (accessed July 27, 2016).

Green America, "2016 Chocolate Scorecard," http://www.greenamerica.org/programs/fairtrade/whatyoucando/2010Scorecard.cfm (accessed July 21, 2016).

Green America, "Thank you, Hershey! Please keep your promise to address child labor in your supply chain," http://www.greenamerica.org/takeaction/hershey/ (accessed July 21, 2016).

The Hershey Company website, http://www.thehershey-company.com (accessed July 21, 2016).

Hershey, "Cocoa Sustainability Strategy," https://www.thehersheycompany.com/en_us/responsibility/good-business/creating-goodness/cocoa-sustainability.html (accessed July 21, 2016).

"Hershey Fudges Labor Relations Image," Forbes.com, August 26, 2011, http://www.forbes.com/sites/susan-adams/2011/08/26/hershey-fudges-labor-relations-image (accessed July 21, 2016).

"International Programme on the Elimination of Child Labour (IPEC)" International Labour Organization, http://www.ilo.org/public//english//standards/ipec/themes/cocoa/download/2005_02_cl_cocoa.pdf (accessed July 21, 2016).

"Name Change at Hershey," Prepared Foods Network, April 26, 2005, http://www.preparedfoods.com/articles/name-change-at-hershey (accessed July 21, 2016).

Jenara Nerenberg, "Hershey Gets a Not-So-Sweet Kiss for Fair Trade Month," *Fast Company*, October 5, 2010, http://www.fastcompany.com/1693089/hershey-gets-a-not-so-sweet-declaration-for-fair-trade-month (accessed July 21, 2016).

Brian O'Keefe, "Inside Big Chocolate's Child Labor Problem," *Fortune,* March 1, 2016, http://fortune.com/big-chocolate-child-labor/ (accessed July 21, 2016).

Brian O'Keefe, "Was Your Easter Chocolate Made with Child Labor?" *Fortune,* March 25, 2016, http://fortune.com/2016/03/25/easter-chocolate-child-labor/ (accessed July 21, 2016).

Payson Center for International Development and Technology Transfer, "Oversight of Public and Private Initiatives to Eliminate the Worst Forms of Child Labor in the Cocoa Sector in Cote d'Ivoire and Ghana," Tulane University, March 31, 2011, http://www.childlabor-payson.org/Tulane percent20Final percent20Report.pdf (accessed May 25, 2012).

Julia Preston, "Hershey's Packer Is Fined Over Its Safety Violations," February 21, 2012, http://www.nytimes.com/2012/02/22/us/hersheys-packer-fined-by-labor-department-for-safety-violations.html (accessed July 21, 2016).

"Protocol for the Growing and Processing of Cocoa Beans and Their Derivative Products in a Manner That Complies with ILO Convention 182 Concerning the Prohibition and Immediate Action for the Elimination of the Worst Forms of Child Labor," Chocolate Manufacturers Association, http://www.cocoainitiative.org/images/stories/pdf/harkin percent20engel percent20protocol.pdf (accessed May 25, 2012).

Sudarsan Raghavan and Sumana Chatterjee, "A Taste of Slavery," StopChocolateSlavery, http://vision.ucsd.edu/~kbranson/stopchocolateslavery/atasteofslavery.html (accessed July 21, 2016).

Paul Robson, "Ending Child Trafficking in West Africa," Anti-Slavery International, December 2010, http://www.antislavery.org/includes/documents/cm_docs/2011/c/cocoa_report_for_website.pdf (accessed July 21, 2016).

The Coca-Cola Company Struggles with Ethical Crises

INTRODUCTION

As one of the most valuable brand names worldwide, Coca-Cola has generally excelled as a business over its long history. However, in recent decades the company has had difficulty meeting its financial objectives and has been associated with a number of ethical crises. As a result, some investors have lost faith in the company. For example, Warren Buffet (board member and strong supporter of and investor in Coca-Cola) resigned from the board in 2006 after years of frustration over Coca-Cola's failure to overcome its challenges.

Since the 1990s, Coca-Cola has been accused of unethical behavior in a number of areas, including product safety, anti-competitiveness, racial discrimination, channel stuffing, distributor conflicts, intimidation of union workers, pollution, depletion of natural resources, and health concerns. The company has dealt with a number of these issues, some via private settlements and some via court battles, while others remain unresolved. Although its handling of different ethical situations has not always been lauded, Coca-Cola has generally responded by seeking to improve its detection and compliance systems. However, it remains to be seen whether the company can permanently rise above its ethical problems, learn from its mistakes, make necessary changes, avoid further problems, and still emerge as a leader among beverage companies.

HISTORY OF THE COCA-COLA COMPANY

Founded in 1886, the Coca-Cola Company is the world's largest beverage company. In addition to Coca-Cola and Diet Coke, it sells other profitable brands including Powerade, Minute Maid, and Dasani water. To service global demand, the company has the world's largest distribution system, which reaches customers and businesses in nearly every country on the planet.

Until the mid-twentieth century Coca-Cola focused on expanding market share within the United States. After World War II, however, the company began to recognize the opportunity in global sales. In the last part of the twentieth century, Coca-Cola extended this global push, taking advantage of international revenue opportunities and fierce soft drink competition in an effort to dominate the global soft drink industry. By the late 1990s, Coca-Cola had gained more than 50 percent global market share in the soft drink industry, while PepsiCo, the company's greatest rival, stood around 15–20 percent. Coca-Cola remains largely focused on beverages, while PepsiCo has diversified into snack and breakfast foods such as chips, dips, and oatmeal.

While PepsiCo has tended to focus more on American markets, the largest portion of Coca-Cola's profits (80 percent as of 2014) is generated from outside the United States. As the late Roberto Goizueta, former CEO of Coca-Cola, once said, "Coca-Cola used to be an American company with a large international business. Now we are a large international company with a sizable American business."

In spite of international presence and a strong recognition, Coca-Cola has run into numerous difficulties. The company's problems began in the late 1990s at the executive level. Doug Ivester, who was heralded for his ability to handle the company's complex finances and had been groomed for the CEO position by Goizueta, reached the title in 1997. However, his tenure was short-lived. Tough competition from PepsiCo combined with the many ethical disasters Coca-Cola faced throughout the 1990s served to be too burdensome for Ivester to handle. Ivester's departure in 1999 represented a high-profile aberration in a relatively strong 100-year record.

In 2000, Doug Daft, the company's former President and Chief Operating Officer (COO), replaced Ivester as CEO. Daft's tenure too was rocky, and the company continued to have problems throughout the first part of the decade. For example, the company was allegedly involved in racial discrimination, misrepresentations

*This material was developed by Jennifer Sawayda, Kevin Sample, and Rob Boostrum under the direction of Debbie Thorne, O.C. Ferrell, and Linda Ferrell ©2014. Julian Mathias provided crucial updates and editorial assistance for this case. It was prepared for classroom discussion rather than to illustrate either effective or ineffective handling of an administrative, ethical, or legal decision by management. All sources used for this case were obtained through publicly available material.

of market tests, manipulation of earnings, and the disruption of long-term contractual arrangements with distributors.

By 2004, Neville Isdell, former Chairman and CEO of Coca-Cola Beverages Plc. in Great Britain, was called out of retirement to improve Coca-Cola's reputation; however, the company continued to face ethical crises. Despite these challenges, Coca-Cola's overall performance seemed to improve under Isdell's tenure. In 2008, Isdell relinquished the role of CEO to then-President and COO Muhtar Kent. Isdell also decided to step down as Chairman of the Board in order to return to retirement. Under Kent's leadership, Coca-Cola is seeking to revise its strategy through social responsibility initiatives, brand expansion, and company diversity. When Kent took over as CEO in 2008, women held 23 percent of the senior management roles at Coca-Cola—that number has now risen to above 30 percent.

Coca-Cola has been a success for more than 120 years. In contrast, PepsiCo (founded at roughly the same time) did not become a serious competitor until after World War II, when it came up with the idea to sell its product in larger portions for the same price as Coca-Cola. The "cola wars" picked up speed in the mid-1960s and have not abated since. Today, the two American companies wage war primarily on international fronts. While the fight occasionally grows ugly, with accusations of anticompetitive behavior, generally the two companies remain civil.

For the first time in history, supermarket sales of PepsiCo overtook Coca-Cola's supermarket sales in 1979. It was not until early 2006, however, that PepsiCo enjoyed a market value greater than Coca-Cola for the first time. PepsiCo's strategy of focusing on snack foods and innovative approaches in the non-cola beverage market has helped the company gain market share and surpass Coca-Cola in overall performance. During the latest recession, PepsiCo's diversification strategy continued to pay off, which helped grow the company into the largest snack-maker in the world. On the other hand, some investors fear for Coca-Cola's long-term prospects because of the company's dependence on international sales and a strong dollar. Combined with a global economic downturn, these are liabilities that may hurt Coca-Cola's long-term profitability. Because PepsiCo does 60 percent of its business in North America, a strong dollar does not adversely affect the company as much as it does Coca-Cola. These factors may give PepsiCo more of an advantage over Coca-Cola in the future.

However, an important investment in Green Mountain Coffee Roasters (owner of Keurig brewing systems) will likely increase Coca-Cola's American presence. The companies signed a ten-year agreement to develop and sell cold beverages designed for the Keurig systems. Additionally, Coca-Cola is using their marketing savvy to appeal to Millennials—one of the largest growing demographics. The company is focusing on their Freestyle machine, which dispenses 146 flavors of soda at the touch of an icon. The modern touchscreen activated machine not only allows people to mix flavors of soda to create their own mix but also allows them to control the amount of soda they intake. Each touch of an icon dispenses small amounts of soda. The company also developed a mobile application so users can premix flavors and share them with their friends on social media.

COCA-COLA'S REPUTATION

Coca-Cola remains one of the most recognized brand names in the world today, with a market value of more than $193 billion in 2016. The company has always demonstrated strong market orientation, making strategic decisions and taking action to attract, satisfy, and retain customers. During World War II, for example, then-president Robert Woodruff distributed Coca-Cola around the world to sell to members of the armed services for a nickel a bottle. This strategy gave soldiers an affordable taste of home, created lifelong loyal customers, and increased global brand recognition. The presence of Coca-Cola products in almost every corner of the globe today shows how successful the company's international marketing strategy has been. Savvy marketing and a reputation for quality have always been hallmarks of Coca-Cola that have helped to make the product ubiquitous.

However, in the 1990s and 2000s poor decisions, mismanagement, and alleged misconduct cast a shadow over the company. In 2000, Coca-Cola failed to make the top ten of *Fortune*'s annual "America's Most Admired Companies" list for the first time in ten years. In 2001, the company disappeared from the top 100 of *Business Ethics* magazine's annual list of "100 Best Corporate Citizens." For a company that had been on both lists for years, this was disappointing but not unexpected given its record of ethical crises. However, there are signs that Coca-Cola is bouncing back. In 2015, Coca-Cola ranked 10 in *Fortune*'s "World's Most Admired Companies" and number 15 in *Corporate Responsibility* Magazine's "100 Best Corporate Citizens" list, while PepsiCo was number 55.

CRISIS SITUATIONS

In 1996, Coca-Cola traded just below $50 a share. In the first half of 2014 it ranged between $42 and $46. This may be attributed to various internal problems associated with top management turnover and departure of key investors, as well as external problems that have led to a loss of reputation. The following incidents exemplify some of the key crises Coca-Cola has faced in the last several years.

Contamination Scare

Perhaps the most damaging of Coca-Cola's crises—and a situation dreaded by every company—began in June 1999 when about 30 Belgian children became ill after consuming Coca-Cola products. Although the company issued an isolated product recall, the problem escalated. The Belgian government eventually ordered the recall of all Coca-Cola products, which prompted officials in Luxembourg and the Netherlands to do the same. Coca-Cola finally determined that the illnesses were the result of an improperly processed batch of carbon dioxide. Coca-Cola was slow to issue a response to the problem, taking several days to address the media. The company had initially judged the problem to be minor and did not immediately investigate the extent of the issue. The slow response time led to a public relations nightmare. France soon reported more than 100 people sick from bad Coca-Cola and temporarily banned all of the company's products as well. Soon thereafter, a shipment of Bonaqua, a new Coca-Cola water product, arrived in Poland contaminated with mold. In each of these instances, the company's slow responses and failure to acknowledge the severity of the situation harmed its reputation and cast doubt on then-CEO Ivester's ability to successfully lead.

The contamination crisis was exacerbated in December 1999 when Belgium ordered Coca-Cola to halt the "Restore" marketing campaign it had launched in order to regain consumer trust and sales in Belgium. A rival firm claimed that the campaign strategy—which included free cases of the product, discounts to wholesalers and retailers, and extra promotion personnel—was unlawful. The claim was upheld under Belgium's strict antitrust laws, and Coca-Cola was forced to abandon the campaign. This decision, following the previous crisis, further reduced Coca-Cola's market standing in Europe.

Allegations of Racial Discrimination

In 1999, Coca-Cola's reputation was dealt another blow when 1,500 African American employees sued for racial discrimination. The lawsuit, which eventually grew to include 2,000 current and former employees, accused the company of discriminating in areas of pay, promotion, and performance evaluation. Plaintiffs charged that the company grouped African American workers at the bottom of the pay scale, earning approximately $26,000 a year less than Caucasian employees in comparable jobs. The suit also alleged that top management had known about companywide discrimination since 1995 but had done nothing about it. In 1992, Coca-Cola pledged to spend $1 billion on goods and services from minority vendors, an action designed to show the public that Coca-Cola did not discriminate, but the lawsuit from its own employees painted a different picture. Although Coca-Cola strongly denied the allegations, the lawsuit provoked unrest within the company. In response, Coca-Cola created a diversity council and the company paid $193 million to settle the claims.

Inflated Earnings Related to Channel Stuffing

Coca-Cola was also accused of channel stuffing—the practice of shipping extra, unrequested inventory to wholesalers and retailers before the end of a quarter. A company counts the shipments as sales although the product often remains in warehouses or is later returned. Because the goods have been shipped, the company counts them as revenue at the end of the quarter. Channel stuffing creates the appearance of strong demand (or conceals declining demand), resulting in inflated financial statement earnings and the subsequent misleading of investors.

In 2004, Coca-Cola was accused of sending extra concentrate to Japanese bottlers between 1997 and 1999 in an effort to inflate its profits. The company was already under investigation for a 2000 lawsuit filed by a former employee regarding accusations of fraud and improper business practices. The company settled the channel stuffing allegations, but the Securities and Exchange Commission (SEC) did find that the violation had occurred. Coca-Cola had pressured bottlers into buying additional concentrate in exchange for extended credit.

Trouble with Distributors

In early 2006 Coca-Cola once again faced problems—this time on its home front. Fifty-four of its U.S. bottlers filed lawsuits against Coca-Cola and the company's largest bottler, Coca-Cola Enterprises (CCE). The suit sought to block both Atlanta-based entities from expanding delivery of Powerade sports drinks directly to Walmart warehouses instead of to individual stores. Bottlers alleged that the Powerade bottler contract did not permit warehouse delivery to large retailers. They claimed that Coca-Cola breached the agreement by committing to provide warehouse delivery of Powerade to Walmart and by proposing to use CCE as its agent for delivery. The main problem was that Coca-Cola was attempting to step away from the century-old tradition of direct-store delivery (DSD), in which bottlers deposit drinks at individual stores, stock shelves, and build merchandising displays. Bottlers claimed that if Coca-Cola and CCE went ahead with their plan, it would greatly diminish the value of their businesses.

In their defense, Coca-Cola and CCE asserted that they were simply trying to accommodate a request from Walmart for warehouse delivery (which is how PepsiCo distributes its Gatorade brand). CCE had also proposed making payments to other bottlers in return for taking over Powerade distribution in their territories. However, bottlers feared such an arrangement violated antitrust laws. The bottlers and Coca-Cola reached an undisclosed agreement in 2007. As part of the settlement, warehouse deliveries were deemed acceptable in some situations, and guidelines were developed for assessing those situations.

When addressing problems faced by Coca-Cola, the media tends to focus primarily on the company's reputation rather than on its relations with bottlers, distributors, suppliers, and other partners. Without these strategic partnerships, Coca-Cola would not be where it is today. Such partnerships involve sharing in risks and rewards. Issues such as the contamination scare and racial discrimination allegations, especially when handled poorly, can reflect on business relationships beyond the key company's business. When the reputation of one company suffers, all those within the supply chain suffer in some way. This is especially true because Coca-Cola adopted an enterprise-resource system that linked Coca-Cola's once highly secret information to a host of partners. The company's crises also harmed their partner companies, their stakeholders, and eventually their bottom lines.

Issues Regarding Water Usage, Pollution, and Supply Chain Oversight

Coca-Cola has also encountered trouble at its bottling plants in India, fielding accusations of both groundwater depletion and contamination. In 2003 the Centre for Science and Environment (CSE) tested soft drinks produced in India by Coca-Cola and other companies, and found extreme levels of pesticides from using contaminated groundwater. In 2004, the first set of standards for pesticides in soft drinks was developed and supported by an Indian parliamentary committee. Although Coca-Cola denied the allegations, stating that its water is filtered and its final products are tested before being released, sales dropped temporarily by 15 percent.

In the Indian city of Varanasi, Coca-Cola was also accused of contaminating the groundwater with wastewater. Officials at the company admitted that the plant did have a wastewater issue but insisted that a new pipeline had been built to eliminate the problem. However, during the early 2000s a number of tests were conducted regarding "sludge" produced at Coca-Cola's Indian plants. These tests, conducted by the Central Pollution Control Board of India and the British Broadcasting Corporation, came up with toxic results.

The company runs bottling plants in a handful of drought-plagued areas around India, and groups of officials blame the plants for a dramatic decline in available water. In 2004, local officials closed a Coca-Cola plant in the Indian state of Kerala; however, the closure was overturned by Kerala's court. Although the court agreed that Coca-Cola's presence contributed to water depletion, it stated the company was not solely to blame. Nonetheless, farmers and local residents, forced to vie with Coca-Cola for water, have protested the company's presence both there and throughout India.

As a result of these accusations, the University of Michigan requested that the Energy and Resources Institute in New Delhi research the issues. The university suspended its contracts with Coca-Cola until the company hired third parties to investigate the claims. The Energy and Resources Institute's findings indicated that Coca-Cola's soda did not contain higher-than-normal levels of pesticides. However, the report did indicate that the company's bottling plants were stressing water resources and suggested that the company do a better job of considering a plant's location based on resources and future impact.

In late 2013, Oxfam International, an international federation that investigates and fights against social injustice, poverty, and human rights violations, encouraged Coca-Cola to scrutinize its suppliers about the possibility that they engaged in "land grabs," a practice where local farmers and residents are forced off their land by large and influential institutions. Coca-Cola responded to the allegations by disclosing the names of its suppliers and agreeing to conduct independent assessments of its top sugar suppliers. The actions of Coca-Cola reflect the increased supply chain oversight expected from large, multinational corporations today.

Coca-Cola's Impact on Health

For years Coca-Cola has been battling consumer perceptions that its soft drinks contribute to obesity. The soda industry is worth $75 billion, and soda consists of 74 percent of Coca-Cola's business worldwide. Sales in the United States have fallen due to concerns over the health effects of soda. In 2016 soda consumption hit a 30-year low. Even demand for Diet Coke has dropped because of fears about aspartame. To deal with this lapse in demand, Coca-Cola has branched out into other beverages and is trying to reposition itself in the United States. For example, it is cutting back on supersized drinks and going back to older, smaller sizes. Coca-Cola has started to acknowledge the health problems of its soda drinks. However, this comes after a number of legal challenges regarding the health of its products.

In 2008, Coca-Cola launched a "Motherhood and Myth-Busting" campaign in Australia, attempting to convince the public that a diet including soda was healthy for children. The Australian Competition and Consumer Commission promptly took Coca-Cola to court after the Obesity Policy Coalition, the Parents' Jury, and the Australian Dental Association all filed complaints. As a result, in 2009 the company was forced to release new advertisements in a number of Australian newspapers correcting information such as the amount of caffeine found in Diet Coke. Coca-Cola admits that it did not supply consumers with detailed information during its campaign. Also in 2008 the FDA declared that the company violated the Federal Food, Drug, and Cosmetic Act when naming the Coca-Cola Diet Plus beverage. Using "plus" in the name indicated an unsubstantiated nutritional claim.

The next year Coca-Cola was sued by the Center for Science in the Public Interest regarding misleading marketing that concerned the contents of its VitaminWater. Although the beverage is marketed as healthy, it contains a high amount of sugar. (One television advertisement featured a woman describing how VitaminWater has allowed her to use so few sick days she could "play hooky" at home with her boyfriend.) Coca-Cola tried to have the lawsuit dismissed, but a judge ruled that it could continue after determining that VitaminWater lacked the nutritional requirements needed to make certain health claims. Coca-Cola also faced challenges in California with a proposed regulation that would make it mandatory to label genetically modified foods. Known as proposition 37, it was defeated in 2012. Coca-Cola and PepsiCo, among many others, contributed millions of dollars to help defeat the proposed law.

As concerns over obesity escalate, the U.S. government has considered imposing a tax on soft drinks. Coca-Cola and similar companies vehemently oppose such a tax and accuse the government of unfairly targeting its industry. Even local government officials such as former New York City Mayor Michael Bloomberg tried to address this issue by imposing a local sugar tax and banning the sale of large sodas. While legislation on the issue is still pending in the United States, Mexico has rapidly taken action. The country's population has surpassed the United States in terms of obesity, and diabetes is counted as the second-most common cause of death. In 2014, an 8 percent tax was instituted for sugary snacks and a 12 percent tax on sodas. This comes after a year of special-interest-group-inspired advertisements admonishing people to reconsider drinking sodas. Furthermore, Mexican education officials encourage vendors not to sell sodas in schools, and consumer protection agencies criticized a Coca-Cola advertisement depicting people drinking a smaller sized soda while engaging in activities that burned 149 calories as misleading. A decrease in Mexican consumption of Coca-Cola products would greatly affect the company, as the country is the second most profitable region. Coca-Cola is a staple in many Mexican homes as it has become a symbol of status. However, Coca-Cola—along with other companies such as Nestlé and PepsiCo—are not discouraged by the tax and have stated that they will continue to invest heavily in Mexico as it is a highly profitable market.

CEO Muhtar Kent believes the problem of obesity stems more from a "sedentary lifestyle" than from sugary beverages. He also points to the fact that the average caloric content in soft drinks has dropped 25 percent over the last two decades through the adoption of diet beverages. The trade group for Coca-Cola and other soft-drink makers is spending millions of dollars in lobbying efforts and has run advertisements encouraging consumers to oppose the tax. In 2013, Coca-Cola launched a new ad campaign in an effort to portray the obesity epidemic as a complex problem, requiring the cooperation of businesses, governments, and local communities to alleviate. One of the campaign advertisements titled "Coming Together" reminds viewers that reducing caloric intake, a major factor in reducing weight, may require more than simply eliminating Coca-Cola products. The campaign also includes programs aimed to encourage more physical activity in schools and communities.

Another possible challenge for Coca-Cola involves claims that certain ingredients in its products could contribute to cancer. In 2011, the Center for Science in the Public Interest (CSPI) wrote a letter to the Food and Drug Administration urging the agency to institute a ban against caramel coloring in soda drinks and other products. CSPI maintains that the caramel coloring contains two cancer-causing ingredients. The American Beverage Association has denied this view, claiming that there is no evidence that shows caramel coloring causes cancer in humans. However, California subsequently made plans to consider labeling products that contain caramel coloring. PepsiCo and Coca-Cola reformulated their products in California and adopted a caramel coloring that did not contain the problematic ingredients. Interestingly, a later study revealed that ten out of ten samples of PepsiCo products sold outside of California across the nation still contain a controversial ingredient, while only one out of ten Coca-Cola products did so. This suggests that Coca-Cola has gone beyond merely complying with state law and is taking action to address concerns across the nation.

Cola-Cola's Data Breach

In 2014, Coca-Cola announced that the information of more than 70,000 employees, vendors, and contractors was compromised when a former employee stole laptops from company headquarters. Employees were angered when they were told that the company had known about the breach for more than a month, but the company responded by saying they had to ensure that the information was not misused. They also noted that they complied with the law, which requires notification within 45 days of discovery. Even more surprising was the fact that the laptops had been missing for a period of several years. They were in the care of a former employee who had been charged with their disposal while still employed with the company.

Human resources employees used the laptops, so sensitive information including Social Security numbers, driver's license numbers, and other identifying details were readily available on the laptop. Company policy dictates that such information be encrypted. However, these laptops had not undergone that process. Coca-Cola assured employees that the information did not appear to have been used maliciously. To date, no arrest or full explanation has been made regarding the breach, but many are surprised by the incident, since Coca-Cola has a reputation for placing information security as a high priority.

POM Sues Coca-Cola

In 2008, POM Wonderful, a company that sells 100 percent pomegranate juice, filed a lawsuit against Coca-Cola alleging deceptive advertising and labeling. The allegations regard the labeling of one of Coca-Cola's Minute Maid juice offerings that claims to be real pomegranate blueberry juice. Both POM and Coca-Cola agree that more than 99 percent of the juice is comprised of apple and grape juices, while the rest is actual pomegranate and blueberry juice. The issue of debate is whether the claims are deceptive or misleading under the Lanham Act, which prohibits mischaracterization of products.

Coca-Cola maintains that the Food and Drug Administration (FDA) allows labeling products according to their lesser ingredients, and that their label depicts all fruits that are in the drink. POM Wonderful claims consumers were misled into believing they were purchasing pomegranate blueberry juice. They also claim their sales were harmed due to the labeling. Apple and grape juices are less expensive than pomegranate, so Coca-Cola was able to offer their juice at a lower price than POM Wonderful. In 2014, the Supreme Court gave POM Wonderful approval to go ahead with the lawsuit.

RECOVERY FROM ETHICAL CRISES

Following the health scare in Belgium, Belgian officials closed their investigation involving Coca-Cola and announced that no charges would be filed. A Belgian health report indicated that no toxic contamination had been found inside the bottles. There were small traces of carbonyl sulfide, producing a rotten-egg smell, but it was not nearly enough to be toxic. Officials also reported no structural problems within Coca-Cola's production plant.

The racial discrimination lawsuit, along with the threat of a boycott by the National Association for the Advancement of Colored People (NAACP), led Coca-Cola to address its diversity issues. When the company settled the racial discrimination lawsuit, the agreement stipulated that Coca-Cola would donate $50 million to a foundation supporting programs in minority communities, hire an ombudsman reporting directly to the CEO to investigate complaints of discrimination and harassment, and set aside $36 million to form a task force with authority to oversee the company's employment practices. The task force, which includes business and civil rights experts, has unprecedented power to dictate company policy regarding the hiring, compensation, and promotion of women and minorities.

In response to the SEC's findings regarding channel stuffing, Coca-Cola created an ethics and compliance office, and is required to verify that it has not altered the terms of payment or extended special credit on a quarterly basis. Additionally, the company agreed to work to reduce the amount of concentrate held by international bottlers.

Although Coca-Cola's issues in India did cause a temporary dip in sales and ongoing protests, the company insists that it has taken measures to ensure safety and quality. Coca-Cola has partnered with local governments, NGOs, schools, and communities to establish rainwater collection facilities across India. The goal is to work toward renewing and returning all groundwater. In addition, the company is strengthening its plant requirements and working with local communities to ensure the sustainability of local water resources. As a result, Coca-Cola has received several corporate social responsibility awards in areas such as water conservation, management, and community development initiatives.

Despite its global work in water sustainability, groundwater depletion issues continue to plague Coca-Cola in India. The state of Kerala passed a law that allows individuals to seek compensation from the company. The government claims that Coca-Cola "over-extracted" groundwater and improperly disposed of sludge, causing damages to the environment and local populations.

Coca-Cola has countered that the decision was not based on facts and claims that studies have failed to find a link between Coca-Cola's bottling operations and environmental damage. Nonetheless, government data show a drastic drop in groundwater levels at Kala Dera during the years Coca-Cola operated in the region. In 2013, Coca-Cola faced opposition from local villages when it sought to increase its groundwater usage five-fold at its bottling plant in Mehdiganj. This situation could partially undermine the company's sustainability image in India. In addition, Coca Cola's CEO, Muhtar Kent, publically stated in late 2013 that the company and its partners will invest $5 billion in India by 2020 as part of an expansion strategy into emerging markets. This expansion will likely present future challenges for Coca-Cola and India to reconcile.

Responding to health issues related to Coca-Cola's products is a more complex process. The company itself cannot be held responsible for how many sugary or artificially sweetened beverages the public consumes. Ultimately, Coca-Cola's responsibility is to disclose honest detailed information regarding its products so that consumers may make educated beverage choices. Coca-Cola has also begun researching healthier products, both as a way to enhance its reputation and increase profits. To make its soft drinks healthier, Coca-Cola is investigating no-calorie sweeteners like stevia as future product ingredients. Coca-Cola is also creating smaller-sized soft drinks. The "Coke Mini" product is only 7.5 ounces and contains 90 calories. Additionally, Coca-Cola is making an effort to encourage consumers to exercise and embrace a healthy lifestyle through nutritional education and partnerships with governments, NGOs, and public health representatives. For instance, the company awarded a grant to the American Academy of Family Physicians to create educational content regarding soft drinks and sweeteners on AAFP's health and wellness website. Although critics accuse AAFP of selling out, the AAFP assured the public that it will not endorse the brands or products of any of its partners. In 2015 the AAFP and Coca-Cola ended their partnership.

SOCIAL RESPONSIBILITY FOCUS

Because Coca-Cola is a globally recognized brand and has a strong history of market orientation, the company has developed a number of social responsibility initiatives to further enhance its business. These initiatives are guided by the company's core beliefs in marketplace, workplace, community, and environment. As stated in its Mission, Vision, and Values statements, Coca-Cola wants to "Inspire Moments of Optimism" through brands and actions as well as to create value and make a positive difference in the countries in which it does business.

For instance, Coca-Cola joined former U.S. Secretary of State Madeleine Albright and The Aspen Institute President and CEO Walter Isaacson on an initiative to provide assistance to entrepreneurs in Muslim-majority countries. The Partners for a New Beginning (PNB) is working to encourage businesses, universities, NGOs, and other organizations to help Muslim entrepreneurs through investments and/or contributions of technology and equipment. PNB also vowed to increase access to finance, education, and other areas of business for Muslim entrepreneurs. According to CEO Muhtar Kent, Coca-Cola's participation in this initiative will help to "build a strong bridge of understanding and respect between the U.S. and the Muslim world."

Coca-Cola also offers grants to various colleges and universities, both nationally and internationally. In addition to grants, Coca-Cola provides scholarships to hundreds of colleges, including 30 tribal colleges belonging to the American Indian College Fund. Such initiatives help enhance the Coca-Cola name and ultimately benefit shareholders. Through the Coca-Cola Scholars Foundation, 250 new Coca-Cola Scholars are named each year and brought to Atlanta for interviews. Fifty students are then designated National Scholars, receiving awards of $20,000 for college; the remaining 200 are designated Regional Scholars, receiving $10,000 awards.

Like many other companies, Coca-Cola is addressing the issues of recycling and climate change. In 2007, Coca-Cola signed the UN Global Compact's "Caring for Climate: The Business Leadership Platform." In doing so, the company pledged to increase energy efficiency and reduce emissions. In 2009 Coca-Cola released the PlantBottle™. This new bottle, made from 30 percent plant-based material, is fully recyclable and reduces use of nonrenewable resources and production of carbon emissions. Coca-Cola has partnered with the Heinz Co. to extend PlantBottle packaging to Heinz ketchup bottles. Coca-Cola also used the PlantBottle when it sponsored the 2010 Olympics in Vancouver. In fact, Coca-Cola vowed to produce zero waste during the games, one of the first times such a major marketer has embarked on this initiative. Some of the other ways that Coca-Cola went "green" during the Olympics included its use of diesel-electric hybrid delivery trucks, staff uniforms made out of recycled bottles, and carbon offsets for air travel.

Coca-Cola has also taken steps to accelerate the empowerment of women entrepreneurs that are part of its supply chain. The company's 5by20 program impacted nearly 300,000 women by 2012 and includes skills training, financing, networking, and other types of support. For example, the company hosted a women's business workshop in South Africa and partnered with TechnoServe to provide local farmers with information about pest and disease control. The company hopes to reach 5 million women entrepreneurs and be active in 100 countries by 2020.

Finally, Coca-Cola is taking action to improve communities, both nationally and on a global scale. For instance, Coca-Cola's Sprite business partnered with NBA basketball star LeBron James on the Sprite Spark Parks Project. Sprite announced plans to contribute $2 million into the building or restoration of over 150 basketball courts, athletic fields, community spaces, and playgrounds in a minimum of 40 cities. In terms of its global responsibilities, the company remains proactive on issues such as the HIV/AIDS epidemic in Africa. Coca-Cola has partnered with UNAIDS and other NGOs to put in place important initiatives and programs to help combat the threat of HIV/AIDS.

Coca-Cola excels at relationship marketing because consumers generally respect the company, trust its products, and have emotional attachments through brand recognition and product loyalty. At the same time, problems at the company can stir the negative emotions of stakeholders.

THE CURRENT SITUATION AT COCA-COLA

In the early part of the twenty-first century, Coca-Cola's financial performance was positive, with the company maintaining a sound balance sheet. However, earnings across the soft drink industry have been on a slow decline because of decreased consumption, increased competition, and the latest global recession. Nevertheless, Coca-Cola is confident of its long-term viability and remains strong in the belief that the company is well-positioned to succeed.

In an attempt to regain growth, Coca-Cola is expanding globally. With Coca-Cola reaching market saturation in developed countries, the company is looking to gain a foothold in emerging economies. In 2010, the company announced plans to undergo a major expansion in Africa, with plans to invest $12 billion into the continent within the next ten years. Such a plan has both positive and negative aspects. On the negative side, organizations like the World Health Organization are criticizing such an expansion as they believe it is unethical to introduce a product with no nutritional benefits into impoverished countries. On the other hand, Coca-Cola employs approximately 65,000 Africans and encourages entrepreneurship. Beyond its investment in Africa, Coca-Coca committed $30 billion toward growth in emerging markets such as China, Mexico, Brazil, Russia, and the Middle East. Success in emerging economies may be the push that Coca-Cola needs to jumpstart growth.

CONCLUSION

For more than a decade Coca-Cola has been fighting allegations of a lack of health and safety of its products, racial discrimination, channel stuffing, unfair distributor treatment, and the pollution and pillaging of natural resources. However, under Neville Isdell and Muhtar Kent's leadership, the company appears to have rebounded and has begun to take strides toward improving its image. The company is focusing more on environmental stewardship, for example. Yet the company's critics say that Coca-Cola is not doing enough—that its efforts are merely window dressing to hide its corruption. Case in point: although the company claims to have addressed all its issues in India and says it is making an effort to aid the country's population, both the government and the citizens of Kerala maintain that the company has decreased the area's groundwater. Shareholder reactions have altered many times over the company's history, but the company has retained a large loyal base. The company hopes that its current leadership is strong enough to move Coca-Cola past this focus on ethics and into a profitable start to the next decade of the twenty-first century.

Questions for Discussion

1. What role does corporate reputation play within organizational performance and social responsibility? Develop a list of factors or characteristics that different stakeholders may use in assessing corporate reputation. Are these factors consistent across stakeholders? Why or why not?
2. Assume you have just become CEO at Coca-Cola. Outline the strategic steps you would take to remedy the concerns emanating from the company's board of directors, consumers, employees, business partners, governments, and the media. What elements of social responsibility would you draw from in responding to these stakeholder issues?

3. What do you think of Coca-Cola's environmental initiatives? Are they just window dressing, or does the company seem to be sincere in its efforts?

Sources

AAFP, "Coca-Cola Grant Launches AAFP Consumer Alliance Program," October 6, 2009, http://www.aafp.org/media-center/releases-statements/all/2009/consumeralliance-cocacola.html (accessed August 11, 2016).

Paul Ames, "Case Closed on Coke Health Scare," *AP News Archive*, April 22, 2000, http://www.apnewsarchive.com/2000/Case-Closed-on-Coke-Health-Scare/id-defe7e86eca6b1bce9d723957456e9f9 (accessed August 11, 2016).

Katrina Brooker, "The Pepsi Machine," *Fortune*, February 6, 2006, pp. 68–72.

Kelly Burke, "Coca-Cola Busted for Big Fat Rotten Lies," *The Sydney Morning Herald*, April 2, 2009, http://www.smh.com.au/national/cocacolabusted-for-bigfat-rotten-lies-20090402-9kn6.html?page=1 (accessed August 12, 2016).

Randall Chase, "Judge Dismisses Shareholder Suit against Coca-Cola," Associated Press via SignonSanDiego.com, October 22, 2007, http://www.signonsandiego.com/news/business/20071022-1441-coca-cola-lawsuit.html (accessed August 12, 2016).

"Coca-Cola Appears to Have Settled Lawsuit over Distribution to Retail Distribution Centers," *Supply Chain Digest*, February 14, 2007, http://www.scdigest.com/assets/newsViews/07-02-14-2.cfm?cid=896&ctype=content (accessed August 12, 2016).

Coca-Cola Company website, http://www.thecoca-cola-company.com (accessed August 12, 2016).

T.C. Doyle, "Channel Stuffing Rears Its Ugly Head," *CRN*, May 6, 2003, http://business.highbeam.com/4553/article-1G1-101586134/channel-stuffing-rears-its-ugly-head-desperate-times (accessed August 12, 2016).

Kevin Drawbaugh, "Soda Pop, Sales Tax Targeted to Cut Deficit," *Reuters*, http://www.reuters.com/article/us-usa-deficit-domenici-rivlin-idUSTRE6AG31U20101117 (accessed August 12, 2016).

Emily Fredrix, "Coca-Cola Says Industry Must Fight Soda Taxes," *Manufacturing.Net*, June 14, 2010, http://www.manufacturing.net/News-Coca-Cola-Says-Industry-Must-Fight-Soda-Taxes-061410.aspx (accessed August 7, 2014).

Nicole Gaouette, "Clinton Says Intel, Coca-Cola Will Assist Muslim Entrepreneurs," *Bloomberg*, April 28, 2010, http://www.bloomberg.com/news/articles/2010-04-28/clinton-says-intel-coca-cola-will-assist-entrepreneurs-in-islamic-nations (accessed August 12, 2016).

David Glovin and Duane D. Stanford, "PepsiCo Sues Coca-Cola over Powerade Advertisements (Update3)," *Bloomberg,* April 13, 2009, http://www.bloomberg.com/apps/news?pid=20601110&sid=aYXG QIH6Hisk (accessed August 7, 2014).

"Grand Jury to Investigate Coke on Channel Stuffing Allegations," *Atlanta Business Chronicle,* May 3, 2004, atlanta.bizjournals.com/atlanta/stories/2004/05/03/daily2.html (accessed August 12, 2016).

"Heinz to Use Coca-Cola PlantBottle Technology," *Atlanta Business Chronicle,* February 23, 2011, http://www.bizjournals.com/atlanta/news/2011/02/23/heinz-to-use-coca-cola-plantbottle.html (accessed August 7, 2014).

Katherine Hobson, "What Do Jelly Beans Have to Do with Coke's VitaminWater?" *The Wall Street Journal,* July 26, 2010, http://blogs.wsj.com/health/2010/07/26/what-do-jelly-beans-have-to-do-with-cokes-vitaminwater/ (accessed August 12, 2016).

Andrew J. Hoffman and Sarah Howie, "Coke in the Cross Hairs: Water, India and the University of Michigan," *Globalens,* July 25, 2010, http://globalens.com/DocFiles/PDF/cases/inspection/GL1429098I.pdf (accessed August 7, 2014).

Marjorie Kelly, "100 Best Corporate Citizens," *Business Ethics* (Spring 2007): 23–24; Muhtar Kent, "Coke Didn't Make America Fat," *The Wall Street Journal,* October 7, 2009, http://online.wsj.com/article/SB10001424052748703298004574455464120581696.html (accessed August 11, 2016).

Chris Morran, "Consumers Group Asks FTC to Stop Misleading VitaminWater Marketing," *Consumerist,* February 2, 2011, http://consumerist.com/2011/02/consumers-group-asks-ftc-to-stop-misleading-vitamin-water-marketing.html (accessed August 12, 2016).

"Coca-Cola Unveils Sleek, New 90-Calorie Mini Can," *Reuters,* October 14, 2009, http://www.reuters.com/article/2009/10/14/idUS153812+14-Oct-2009+BW20091014 (accessed August 7, 2014).

Jyotsna Singh, "India Coca-Cola Compensation Law is Passed in Kerala," *BBC News,* February 24, 2011, http://www.bbc.com/news/world-south-asia-12567542 (accessed August 12, 2016).

"Sprite and LeBron James Pump New Life into Neighborhood Basketball Courts Around the Country," *Reuters,* February 18, 2011, http://www.reuters.com/article/2011/02/18/idUS202128+18-Feb-2011+BW20110218 (accessed August 7, 2014).

Amit Srivastava, "Reality Check for Coca-Cola's Public Relations," India Resource Center, April 16, 2009, http://www.indiaresource.org/campaigns/coke/2009/realitycheck.html (accessed August 12, 2016).

Duane D. Stanford, "Coke's Last Round," *Bloomberg Businessweek,* November 1–7, 2010, pp. 54–61.

Claire Suddath and Duane Stanford, "Coke Is Ready to Talk About Its Problem," *Bloomberg Businessweek,* July 31, 2014, pp. 38–43.

Chad Terhune, "Bottlers' Suit Challenges Coke Distribution Plan," *The Wall Street Journal,* February 18–19, 2006, p. A5.

Chad Terhune, "A Suit by Coke Bottlers Exposes Cracks in a Century-Old System," *The Wall Street Journal,* March 13, 2006, p. A1.

Amy Waldman, "India Tries to Contain Tempest over Soft Drink Safety," *The New York Times,* August 23, 2003, http://www.nytimes.com/2003/08/23/international/asia/23INDI.html (accessed August 12, 2016).

Elizabeth Weise, "Group Urges Caramel Coloring in Colas Be banned," *USA Today,* http://www.usatoday.com/money/industries/food/2011-02-21-colacolor21_ST_N.htm (accessed August 12, 2016).

Natalie Zmuda, "Big Red Goes Completely Green at Olympics," *Advertising Age,* February 1, 2010, p. 2.

Allison Aubrey, "Coke Changed Caramel Color to Avoid Cancer Warning; Pepsi in Transition," *NPR,* July 3, 2013, http://www.npr.org/blogs/the-salt/2013/07/03/198040172/coke-changed-caramel-color-to-avoid-cancer-warning- pepsi-in-transition (accessed August 12, 2016).

Coca-Cola Hellenic Bottling Company, "The Coca-Cola System," 2013, http://www.coca- colahellenic.com/aboutus/cocacolasystem/ (accessed August 7, 2014).

Susan Bulkeley Butler, "Why I'd Like to Buy Muhtar Kent a Coke," *The Huffington Post,* September 10, 2013, http://www.huffingtonpost.com/susan-bulkeley-butler/why-id-like-to-buy-muhtar-kent-a-coke_b_3893229.html (accessed August 12, 2016).

"50 Greatest Business Rivalries of All Time," *CNN Money,* 2013, http://money.cnn.com/gallery/news/companies/2013/03/21/greatest-business-rivalries.fortune/2.html (accessed August 12, 2016).

Bloomberg News, "Snack Foods Drive PepsiCo earnings in 3rd Quarter," *NJ.com,* October 16, 2013, http://www.nj.com/business/index.ssf/2013/10/snack_foods_drive_pepsico_earn.html (accessed August 11, 2016).

Howard Schneider, "Coke, Pressed by Oxfam, Pledges Zero Tolerance for Land Grabs In Sugar Supply Chain," *Washington Post,* November 8, 2013, http://www.washingtonpost.com/business/economy/

coke-pressed-by-oxfam-pledges-zero- tolerance-for-land-grabs-in-sugar-supply-chain/2013/11/08/cb6946e4-48b3-11e3-a196-3544a03c2351_story.html (accessed August 12, 2016).

"The Coca-Cola Company declares 'Zero Tolerance' for Land Grabs in Supply Chain," Oxfam International, November 8, 2013, https://www.oxfam.org/en/press-room/pressreleases/2014-03-18/pepsico-declares-zero-tolerance-land-grabs-supply-chain (accessed August 12, 2016).

"Who's Funding Prop 37, Labeling for Genetically Modified Foods?" KCET, 2012, http://www.kcet.org/news/ballotbrief/elections2012/propositions/prop-37-funding-genetically-engineered-food.html (accessed August 7, 2014).

Text of Proposed Laws, 2012, http://vig.cdn.sos.ca.gov/2012/general/pdf/text-proposed-laws-v2.pdf#nameddest=prop37, pp. 80-141.

Coca-Cola Company, "The Coca-Cola Company Reinforces Its Commitment to Help America in the Fight against Obesity," January 14, 2013, http://www.coca-colacompany.com/press-center/press-releases/the-coca-cola-company-reinforces-its-commitment-to-help-america-in-the-fight-against-obesity (accessed August 11, 2016).

India Resource Center, "Coca-Cola Extracts Groundwater Even as Farmers and Community Left Without Water," September 21, 2011, http://www.indiaresource.org/news/2011/1008.html (accessed August 12, 2016).

"Opposition Grows to Coca-Cola's Expansion Plans and Current Operations," India Resource Center, April 18, 2013, http://www.indiaresource.org/news/2013/1008.html (accessed August 11, 2016).

Nikhil Gulati and Rumman Ahmed, "India Has 1.2 Billion People but Not Enough Drink Coke," *The Wall Street Journal,* July 13, 2012, http://online.wsj.com/news/articles/SB10001424052702304870304577490092413939410 (accessed August 11, 2016).

Coca-Cola, #5by20 http://www.coca-colacompany.com/stories/5by20/ (accessed August 7, 2014).

Leon Stafford, "Coca-Cola to Spend $30 Billion to Grow Globally," *Atlanta-Journal Constitution,* September 9, 2012, http://www.ajc.com/news/business/coca-cola-to-spend-30-billion-to-grow-globally/nR6YS/ (accessed August 12, 2016).

Matthew J. Belvedere, "Coca-Cola CEO: We're Getting Our Momentum Back," *CNBC,* April 15, 2014, http://www.cnbc.com/id/101582022# (accessed August 12, 2016).

Amy Guthrie, "Mexico Finds A New Target: Soft Drinks," *The Wall Street Journal,* August 29, 2013, pp. B1, B2.

Dan D'Ambrosio, "Coke Buys Stake in Coffee Maker," *USA Today,* February 6, 2014, p. 2B.

Mike Esterl, "Coke's Employee Data Spill is Not Rare," *The Wall Street Journal,* January 27, 2014, p. B3.

Mike Esterl, "Coke Says Employee Data Was Exposed," *The Wall Street Journal,* January 25–26, 2014, pp. B1, B3.

Mike Esterl and John Revill, "Pepsi, Nestle Undeterred by Mexico's Fat Tax," *The Wall Street Journal,* January 25–26, 2014, p. B3.

Richard Wolfe, "Supreme Court Skeptical of Coke's 'Pomegranate Juice'," *USA Today,* April 22, 2014, p. 3A.

Brent Kendall, "Supreme Court Allows Pom to Sue Coca-Cola," *The Wall Street Journal,* June 13, 2014, p. B3.

Bruce Horovitz, "Coke Tries to Regain Its Fizz," *USA Today,* April 15, 2014, pp. 1B, 3B.

"CR's 100 Best Corporate Citizens 2015," *CR Magazine,* http://www.thecro.com/files/100%20Best%20List%202015.pdf (accessed August 11, 2016).

American Academy of Family Physicians, "AAFP, Coca-Cola End Consumer Alliance Agreement," June 26, 2015, http://www.aafp.org/news/inside-aafp/20150626tccc.html (accessed August 11, 2016).

John Kell, "Soda Consumption Falls to 30-Year Low to 30-Year Low in the U.S.," *Fortune,* March 29, 2016, http://fortune.com/2016/03/29/soda-sales-drop-11th-year/ (accessed August 11, 2016).

Enron: Questionable Accounting Leads to Collapse

INTRODUCTION

Once upon a time, there was a gleaming office tower in Houston, Texas. In front of that gleaming tower was a giant "E," slowly revolving, flashing in the hot Texas sun. But in 2001, the Enron Corporation, which once ranked among the top Fortune 500 companies, would collapse under a mountain of debt that had been concealed through a complex scheme of off-balance-sheet partnerships. Forced to declare bankruptcy, the energy firm laid off 4,000 employees; thousands more lost their retirement savings, which had been invested in Enron stock. The company's shareholders lost tens of billions of dollars after the stock price plummeted. The scandal surrounding Enron's demise engendered a global loss of confidence in corporate integrity that continues to plague markets today, and eventually it triggered tough new scrutiny of financial reporting practices. In an attempt to understand what went wrong, this case will examine the history, culture, and major players in the Enron scandal.

ENRON'S HISTORY

The Enron Corporation was created out of the merger of two major gas pipeline companies in 1985. Through its subsidiaries and numerous affiliates, the company provided goods and services related to natural gas, electricity, and communications for its wholesale and retail customers. Enron transported natural gas through pipelines to customers all over the United States. It generated, transmitted, and distributed electricity to the northwestern United States, and marketed natural gas, electricity, and other commodities globally. It was also involved in the development, construction, and operation of power plants, pipelines, and other energy-related projects all over the world, including the delivery and management of energy to retail customers in both the industrial and commercial business sectors.

Throughout the 1990s, Chairman Ken Lay, CEO Jeffrey Skilling, and CFO Andrew Fastow transformed Enron from an old-style electricity and gas company into a $150 billion energy company and Wall Street favorite that traded power contracts in the investment markets. From 1998 to 2000 alone, Enron's revenues grew from about $31 billion to more than $100 billion, making it the seventh-largest company in the Fortune 500. Enron's wholesale energy income represented about 93 percent of 2000 revenues, with another 4 percent derived from natural gas and electricity. The remaining 3 percent came from broadband services and exploration. However, a bankruptcy examiner later reported that although Enron had claimed a net income of $979 million in that year, it had really earned just $42 million. Moreover, the examiner found that despite Enron's claim of $3 billion in cash flow in 2000, the company actually had a cash flow of negative $154 million.

ENRON'S CORPORATE CULTURE

When describing the corporate culture of Enron, people like to use the word "arrogant," perhaps justifiably. A large banner in the lobby at corporate headquarters proclaimed Enron "The World's Leading Company," and Enron executives believed that competitors had no chance against it. Jeffrey Skilling even went so far as to tell utility executives at a conference that he was going to "eat their lunch." This overwhelming aura of pride was based on a deep-seated belief that Enron's employees could handle increased risk without danger. Enron's corporate culture reportedly encouraged flouting the rules in pursuit of profit. And Enron's executive compensation plans seemed less concerned with generating profits for shareholders than with enriching officer wealth.

Skilling appears to be the executive who created the system whereby Enron's employees were rated every

*This case was prepared by Harper Baird, Jennifer Jackson, and Neil Herndon for and under the direction of O. C. and Linda Ferrell © 2017. Michelle Urban provided editorial assistance. O.C. and Linda Ferrell conducted personal interviews with Ken Lay in 2006 in the development of this case. It was prepared for classroom discussion rather than to illustrate either effective or ineffective handling of an administrative, ethical, or legal decision by management. All sources used for this case were obtained through publicly available material.

six months, with those ranked in the bottom 20 percent forced out. This "rank and yank" system helped create a fierce environment in which employees competed against rivals not only outside the company but also at the next desk. The "rank and yank" system is still used at other companies. Delivering bad news could result in the "death" of the messenger, so problems in the trading operation, for example, were covered up rather than being communicated to management.

Ken Lay once said that he felt that one of the great successes at Enron was the creation of a corporate culture in which people could reach their full potential. He said that he wanted it to be a highly moral and ethical culture and that he tried to ensure that people honored the values of respect, integrity, and excellence. On his desk was an Enron paperweight with the slogan "Vision and Values." Despite such good intentions, however, ethical behavior was not put into practice. Instead, integrity was pushed aside at Enron, particularly by top managers. Some employees at the company believed that nearly anything could be turned into a financial product and, with the aid of complex statistical modeling, traded for profit. Short on assets and heavily reliant on intellectual capital, Enron's corporate culture rewarded innovation and punished employees deemed weak.

ENRON'S ACCOUNTING PROBLEMS

Enron's bankruptcy in 2001 was the largest in U.S. corporate history at the time. The bankruptcy filing came after a series of revelations that the giant energy trader had been using partnerships, called "special-purpose entities" or SPEs, to conceal losses. In a meeting with Enron's lawyers in August 2001, the company's then-CFO Fastow stated that Enron had established the SPEs to move assets and debt off its balance sheet and to increase cash flow by showing that funds were flowing through its books when it sold assets. Although these practices produced a very favorable financial picture, outside observers believed they constituted fraudulent financial reporting because they did not accurately represent the company's true financial condition. Most of the SPEs were entities in name only, and Enron funded them with its own stock and maintained control over them. When one of these partnerships was unable to meet its obligations, Enron covered the debt with its own stock. This arrangement worked as long as Enron's stock price was high, but when the stock price fell, cash was needed to meet the shortfall.

After Enron restated its financial statements for fiscal year 2000 and the first nine months of 2001, its cash flow from operations went from a positive $127 million in 2000 to a negative $753 million in 2001. With its stock price falling, Enron faced a critical cash shortage. In October 2001, after it was forced to cover some large shortfalls for its partnerships, Enron's stockholder equity fell by $1.2 billion. Already shaken by questions about lack of disclosure in Enron's financial statements and by reports that executives had profited personally from the partnership deals, investor confidence collapsed, taking Enron's stock price with it.

For a time, it appeared that Dynegy might save the day by providing $1.5 billion in cash, secured by Enron's premier pipeline Northern Natural Gas, and then purchasing Enron for about $10 billion. However, when Standard & Poor's downgraded Enron's debt to below investment grade on November 28, 2001, some $4 billion in off-balance-sheet debt came due, and Enron did not have the resources to pay. Dynegy terminated the deal. On December 2, 2001, Enron filed for bankruptcy. Enron now faced 22,000 claims totaling about $400 billion.

The Whistle-Blower

Assigned to work directly with Andrew Fastow in June 2001, Enron vice president Sherron Watkins, an eight-year Enron veteran, was given the task of finding some assets to sell off. With the high-tech bubble bursting and Enron's stock price slipping, Watkins was troubled to find unclear, off-the-books arrangements backed only by Enron's deflating stock. No one seemed to be able to explain to her what was going on. Knowing she faced difficult consequences if she confronted then-CEO Jeffrey Skilling, she began looking for another job, planning to confront Skilling just as she left for a new position. Skilling, however, suddenly quit on August 14, saying he wanted to spend more time with his family. Chair Ken Lay stepped back in as CEO and began inviting employees to express their concerns and put them into a box for later collection. Watkins prepared an anonymous memo and placed it into the box. When Lay held a companywide meeting shortly thereafter and did not mention her memo, however, she arranged a personal meeting with him.

On August 22, 2001, Watkins handed Lay a seven-page letter she had prepared outlining her concerns. She told him that Enron would "implode in a wave of accounting scandals" if nothing was done. Lay arranged to have Enron's law firm, Vinson & Elkins and Arthur Andersen, look into the questionable deals, although Watkins advised against having a party investigate that might be compromised by its own involvement in Enron's conduct. Lay maintained that both the law firm and accounting firm did not find merit in Watkins's accusations. Near the end of September, Lay sold some $1.5 million of personal stock options, while telling Enron employees that the company had never been stronger. By the middle of October, Enron was reporting a third-quarter loss of $618 million and a $1.2 billion write-off tied to the partnerships about which Watkins had warned Lay.

For her trouble, Watkins had her computer hard drive confiscated and was moved from her plush executive office suite on the top floor of the Houston headquarters tower to a sparse office on a lower level. Her new metal desk was no longer filled with the high-level projects that had once taken her all over the world on Enron business. Instead, now a vice president in name only, she faced meaningless "make work" projects. It is important to note that Watkins stayed in the company after warning Lay about the risks and did not become a public whistle-blower during this time. In February 2002 she testified before Congress about Enron's partnerships and resigned from Enron in November of that year.

The Chief Financial Officer

In 2002 the U.S. Justice Department indicted CFO Andrew Fastow –who had won the "CFO of the Year" award two years earlier from *CFO Magazine* –on 98 counts for his alleged efforts to inflate Enron's profits. The charges included fraud, money laundering, conspiracy, and one count of obstruction of justice. Fastow faced up to 140 years in jail and millions of dollars in fines if convicted on all counts. Federal officials attempted to recover all of the money Fastow had earned illegally, and seized some $37 million.

Federal prosecutors argued that Enron's case was not about exotic accounting practices but about fraud and theft. They contended that Fastow was the brain behind the partnerships used to conceal some $1 billion in Enron debt and that this debt led directly to Enron's bankruptcy. The federal complaints alleged that Fastow had defrauded Enron and its shareholders through off-balance-sheet partnerships that made Enron appear to be more profitable than it actually was. They also alleged that Fastow made about $30 million both by using these partnerships to get kickbacks that were disguised as gifts from family members, and by taking income himself that should have gone to other entities.

Fastow initially denied any wrongdoing and maintained that he was hired to arrange the off-balance-sheet financing and that Enron's board of directors, chair, and CEO had directed and praised his work. He also claimed that both lawyers and accountants had reviewed his work and approved what was being done, and that "at no time did he do anything he believed was a crime." Skilling, COO from 1997 to 2000 before becoming CEO, had reportedly championed Fastow's rise at Enron and supported his efforts to keep up Enron's stock prices.

Fastow eventually pleaded guilty to two counts of conspiracy, admitting to orchestrating myriad schemes to hide Enron debt and inflate profits while enriching himself with millions. He surrendered nearly $30 million in cash and property, and agreed to serve up to 10 years in prison once prosecutors no longer needed his cooperation. He was a key government witness against Lay and Skilling. His wife Lea Fastow, former assistant treasurer, quit Enron in 1997 and pleaded guilty to a felony tax crime, admitting to helping hide ill-gotten gains from her husband's schemes from the government. She later withdrew her plea, and then pleaded guilty to a newly filed misdemeanor tax crime. In 2005 she was released from a year-long prison sentence, and then had a year of supervised release.

In the end, Fastow received a lighter sentence than he otherwise might have because of his willingness to cooperate with investigators. In 2006 Fastow gave an eight-and-a-half-day deposition in his role as government witness. He helped to illuminate how Enron had managed to get away with what it did, including detailing how many major banks were complicit in helping Enron manipulate its financials to help it look better to investors. In exchange for his deposition, Fastow's sentence was lowered to six years from 10. Fastow has also stated that Enron did not have to go out of business if there had been better financial decisions made at the end.

The case against Fastow had been largely based on information provided by Michael Kopper, the company's managing director and a key player in the establishment and operation of several of the off-balance-sheet partnerships and the first Enron executive to plead guilty to a crime. Kopper, a chief aide to Fastow, pleaded guilty to money laundering and wire fraud. He faced up to 15 years in prison and agreed to surrender $12 million earned from illegal dealings with the partnerships. However, Kopper only had to serve three years and one month of jail time because of the crucial role he played in providing prosecutors with information. After his high-powered days at Enron, Kopper's next job was as a salaried grant writer for Legacy, a Houston-based clinic that provides services to HIV-positive and other chronically ill patients.

Today Andy Fastow has been released from prison and works as a document-review clerk at a law firm. He also speaks about business ethics at many different forums, including Leeds Business School at the University of Colorado, the University of New Mexico, the University of Texas at Austin, and the Association of Certified Fraud Examiners global conference. During his speaking engagements, Fastow has emphasized that a major problem companies encounter in business ethics is not using principles and overly relying on rules. He claims that laws and regulations technically allowed the risky transactions he made at Enron. He also cited General Motors, IBM, and the nation of Greece as more recent examples of companies (or nations) that faced hardship and/or bankruptcy because they took actions that were highly risky but technically allowable by law.

The main idea that Fastow tries to communicate in his lectures is that it is not enough to simply obey rules and regulations. It is also easy to rationalize questionable behaviors. Fastow claims that ethical decisions are rarely black-and-white, and sometimes unethical decisions seem more or less unethical depending upon the situation. For instance, he used Apple's tax evasion as an example of an action that seemed less unethical because it was less pronounced than what often occurs in other cases. There are always murky areas where regulations can be exploited. Instead, businesspeople must be able to recognize when issues are going too far and stop them before they snowball into an Enron-esque crisis. Fastow recommends that the best way to deal with questionable situations is to construct and examine a worst-case scenario analysis and look at the risks of questionable deals with more scrutiny.

The Chief Executive Officer

Former CEO Jeffrey Skilling, generally perceived as Enron's mastermind, was the most difficult to prosecute. At the time of the trial, he was so confident that he waived his right to avoid self-incrimination and testified before Congress, saying, "I was not aware of any inappropriate financial arrangements." However, Jeffrey McMahon, who took over as Enron's president and COO in February 2002, told a congressional subcommittee that he had informed Skilling about the company's off-balance-sheet partnerships in 2000, when he

was Enron's treasurer. McMahon said that Skilling had told him that "he would remedy the situation."

Calling the Enron collapse a "run on the bank" and a "liquidity crisis," Skilling said that he did not understand how Enron had gone bankrupt so quickly. He also said that the off-balance-sheet partnerships were Fastow's creation. However, the judge dealt a blow to Lay and Skilling when he instructed the jury that it could find the defendants guilty of consciously avoiding knowing about wrongdoing at the company.

Many former Enron employees refused to testify because they were not guaranteed that their testimony would not be used against them in future trials, and therefore questions about the company's accounting fraud remain. Skilling was found guilty of honest services fraud and sentenced to 24 years in prison, which he has been serving in Colorado. He maintains his innocence and has appealed his conviction. After his release from prison, Andy Fastow was quoted as saying that the bankruptcy of Enron was not Skillings' fault. In 2008 a panel of judges from the Fifth Circuit Court of Appeals in New Orleans rejected his request to overturn the convictions of fraud, conspiracy, misrepresentation, and insider trading. However, the judges did grant Skilling one concession. The three-judge panel determined that the original judge had applied flawed sentencing guidelines in determining Skilling's sentence. The Court ordered that Skilling be resentenced. The matter was taken to the Supreme Court.

In June 2010 the United States Supreme Court ruled that the honest services law could not be used to convict Skilling because the honest services law applies to bribes and kickbacks, not to conduct that is ambiguous or vague. The Supreme Court decision did not suggest that there had been no misconduct, only that Skilling's conduct was not in violation of a criminal fraud law. The court's decision did not overturn the conviction and sent the case back to a lower court for evaluation.

The Chair

Ken Lay became chair and CEO of the company that was to become Enron in 1986. A decade later, Lay promoted Jeffrey Skilling to president and chief operating officer, and then, as expected, Lay stepped down as CEO in 2001 to make way for Skilling. Lay remained as chair of the board. When Skilling resigned later that year, Lay resumed the role of CEO.

Lay, who held a doctorate in economics from the University of Houston, contended that he knew little of what was going on, even though he had participated in the board meetings that allowed the off-balance-sheet partnerships to be created. Lay said he believed the transactions were legal because attorneys and accountants had approved them. Only months before the bankruptcy in 2001, he reassured employees and investors that all was well at Enron, based on strong wholesale sales and physical volume delivered through the marketing channel. He had already been informed that there were problems with some of the investments that could eventually cost Enron hundreds of millions of dollars. In 2002, on the advice of his attorney, Lay invoked his Fifth Amendment right not to answer questions that could be incriminating.

Lay was expected to be charged with insider trading, and prosecutors investigated why he had begun selling about $80 million of his own stock beginning in late 2000, even as he encouraged employees to buy more shares of the company. It appears that Lay drew down his $4 million Enron credit line repeatedly and then repaid the company with Enron shares. These transactions, unlike usual stock sales, do not have to be reported to investors. Lay says that he sold the stock because of margin calls on loans he had secured with Enron stock and that he had no other source of liquidity. According to Lay, he was largely unaware of the ethical situation within the firm. He had relied on lawyers, accountants, and senior executives to inform him of issues such as misconduct. He felt that he had been protected from certain knowledge that would have been beneficial and would have enabled him to engage in early correction of the misconduct. Lay claims that all decisions he made related to financial transactions were approved by the company's lawyers, and the Enron board of directors. Lynn Brewer, a former Enron executive, states that Lay was not informed about alleged misconduct in her division. Additionally, Mike Ramsey, the lead attorney for Lay's defense, claimed that he was not aware of most of the items in the indictment. In the end Lay was convicted on 19 counts of fraud, conspiracy, and insider trading. However, the verdict was thrown out in 2005 after he died of heart failure at his home in Colorado. The ruling protected some $43.5 million of Lay's estate that the prosecution had claimed Lay stole from Enron.

The Lawyers

Enron was Houston law firm Vinson & Elkins' top client, accounting for about 7 percent of its $450 million revenue. Enron's general counsel and a number of members of Enron's legal department came from Vinson & Elkins. Vinson & Elkins seems to have dismissed Sherron Watkins's allegations of accounting fraud after making some inquiries, but this does not appear to leave the firm open to civil or criminal liability. Of greater concern are allegations that Vinson & Elkins helped structure some of Enron's special-purpose partnerships. In her letter to Lay, Watkins had indicated that the firm had written opinion letters supporting the legality of the deals. In fact, Enron could not have done many of the transactions without such opinion letters. The firm did not admit liability, but agreed to pay $30 million to Enron to settle claims that Vinson & Elkins had contributed to the firm's collapse.

Merrill Lynch

The brokerage and investment-banking firm Merrill Lynch also faced scrutiny by federal prosecutors and the SEC for its role in Enron's 1999 sale of Nigerian barges. The sale allowed Enron to improperly record about $12 million in earnings and thereby meet its earnings goals at the end of 1999. Merrill Lynch allegedly bought the barges for $28 million, of which Enron financed $21 million. Fastow gave his word that Enron would buy Merrill Lynch's investment out in six months with a 15 percent guaranteed rate of return. Merrill Lynch went ahead with the deal despite an internal document that suggested that the transaction might be construed as aiding and abetting Enron's fraudulent manipulation of its income statement. Merrill Lynch denies that the transaction was a sham and said that it never knowingly helped Enron to falsify its financial reports.

There are also allegations that Merrill Lynch replaced a research analyst after his coverage of Enron displeased Enron executives. Enron reportedly threatened to exclude Merrill Lynch from an upcoming $750 million stock offering in retaliation. The replacement analyst is reported to have then upgraded his report on Enron's stock rating. Merrill Lynch maintains that it did nothing improper in its dealings with Enron. However, the firm agreed to pay $80 million to settle SEC charges related to the questionable Nigerian barge deal.

Merrill Lynch continued to use risky investment practices, which contributed to severe financial losses for the company as the economy entered a recession in 2008. In 2008 Bank of America agreed to purchase the company for $50 billion, possibly after pressure from the federal government.

ARTHUR ANDERSEN LLP

In its role as Enron's auditor, Arthur Andersen was responsible for ensuring the accuracy of Enron's financial statements and internal bookkeeping. Investors used Andersen's reports to judge Enron's financial soundness and future potential, and expected that Andersen's certifications of accuracy and application of proper accounting procedures would be independent and free of any conflict of interest.

However, Andersen's independence was called into question. The accounting firm was one of Enron's major business partners, with more than 100 employees dedicated to its account, and it sold about $50 million a year in consulting services to Enron. Some Andersen executives even accepted jobs with the energy trader. In March 2002 Andersen was found guilty of obstruction of justice for destroying relevant auditing documents during an SEC investigation of Enron. As a result, Andersen was barred from performing audits. The damage to the firm was such that the company no longer operates, although it has not been dissolved formally.

It is still not clear why Andersen auditors failed to ask Enron to better explain its complex partnerships before certifying Enron's financial statements. Some observers believe that the large consulting fees Enron paid Andersen unduly influenced the company's decisions. An Andersen spokesperson said that the firm looked hard at all available information from Enron at the time. However, shortly after speaking to Lay Vice President Sherron Watkins took her concerns to an Andersen audit partner who reportedly conveyed her questions to senior Andersen management responsible for the Enron account. It is not clear what action, if any, Andersen took.

THE FALLOUT

Although Enron executives obviously engaged in misconduct, some people have questioned the tactics that federal investigators used against Enron. Many former Enron employees feel that it was almost impossible to obtain a fair trial for Lay and Skilling. The defense was informed that 130 of Enron's top managers, who could have served as witnesses for the defense, were considered unindicted co-conspirators with Lay and Skilling. Therefore, the defense could not obtain witnesses from Enron's top management teams under fear that the prosecution would indict the witnesses.

Enron's demise caused tens of billions of dollars of investor losses, triggered a collapse of electricity-trading markets, and ushered in an era of accounting scandals that precipitated a global loss of confidence in corporate integrity. Today companies must defend legitimate but complicated financing arrangements. Legislation like Sarbanes–Oxley, passed in the wake of Enron, has placed more restrictions on companies. Four thousand former Enron employees struggled to find jobs, and many retirees lost their entire retirement portfolios. One senior Enron executive committed suicide.

In 2003 Enron announced its intention to restructure and pay off its creditors. It was estimated that most creditors would receive between 14.4 and 18.3 cents for each dollar they were owed—more than most had expected. Under the plan, creditors would receive about two-thirds of the amount in cash and the rest in equity in three new companies, none of which would carry the tainted Enron name. The three companies were CrossCountry Energy Corporation, Prisma Energy International, Inc., and Portland General Electric.

CrossCountry Energy Corporation would retain Enron's interests in three North American natural gas pipelines. In 2004 Enron announced an agreement to sell CrossCountry Energy to CCE Holdings LLC for $2.45 billion. The money was to be used for debt repayment, and represented a substantial increase over a previous offer. Similarly, Prisma Energy International, Inc., which took over Enron's 19 international power and pipeline holdings, was sold to Ashmore Energy International Ltd. The proceeds from the sale were given out to creditors through cash distributions. The third company, Portland General Electric (PGE), Oregon's largest utility, emerged from bankruptcy as an independent company through a private stock offering to Enron creditors.

All remaining assets not related to CrossCountry, Prisma, or Portland General were liquidated. Although Enron emerged from Chapter 11 bankruptcy protection in 2004, the company was wound down once the recovery plan had been carried out. That year, all of Enron's outstanding common stock and preferred stock were cancelled. Each record holder of Enron Corporation stock on the day it was cancelled was allocated an uncertified, nontransferable interest in one of two trusts that held new shares of the Enron Corporation.

The Enron Creditors Recovery Corporation was formed to help Enron creditors. It states that its mission is "to reorganize and liquidate the remaining operations and assets of Enron following one of the largest and most complex bankruptcies in U.S. history." In the very unlikely event that the value of Enron's assets would exceed the amount of its allowed claims, distributions were to be made to the holders of these trust interests in the same order of priority of the stock they previously held.

In addition to trying to repay its shareholders, Enron also had to pay California for fraudulent activities it committed against the state's citizens. The company was investigated in California for allegedly colluding with at least two other power sellers in 2000 to obtain excess profits by submitting false information to the manager of California's electricity grid. In 2005 Enron agreed to pay California $47 million for taking advantage of California consumers during an energy shortage.

LEARNING FROM ENRON

Enron was the biggest business scandal of its time, and legislation like the Sarbanes–Oxley Act was passed to prevent future business fraud. But did the business world truly learn its lesson from Enron's collapse? Greed and corporate misconduct continued to be a problem throughout the first decade of the twenty-first century, culminating in the 2008–2009 global recession. Corporations praised high performance at any cost, even when employees cut ethical corners. In the mortgage market, companies like Countrywide rewarded their sales force for making risky subprime loans, even going so far as to turn their back on loans that they knew contained falsified information in order to make a quick profit. Other companies traded in risky financial instruments like credit default swaps (CDSs) when they knew that buyers did not have a clear understanding of the risks of such instruments. Although they promised to insure against default of these instruments, the companies did not have enough funds to cover the losses after the housing bubble burst. The resulting recession affected the entire world, bankrupting such established companies as Lehman Brothers and requiring government intervention in the amount of nearly $1 trillion in Troubled Asset Referendum Program (TARP) funds to salvage numerous financial firms. The economic meltdown inspired a new wave of legislation designed to prevent corporate misconduct, including the Dodd–Frank Wall Street Reform and Consumer Protection Act.

It is unfortunate that the Enron scandal did not hinder corporate misconduct. However, Enron still has lessons to teach us. Along with the business scandals of the financial crisis, Enron demonstrates that, first,

regulatory agencies must be improved so as to better detect corporate misconduct. Second, companies and regulatory authorities should pay attention to the warnings of concerned employees and "whistle-blowers" like Sherron Watkins. Third, executives should understand the risks and rewards of the financial instruments their companies use and maintain a thorough knowledge of the inner workings of their companies (something that Ken Lay claimed he did not have). These conditions are crucial to preventing similar business fraud in the future.

CONCLUSION

The example of Enron shows how an aggressive corporate culture that rewards high performance and gets rid of the "weak links" can backfire. Enron's culture encouraged intense competition, not only among employees from rival firms but also among Enron employees themselves. Such behavior creates a culture where loyalty and ethics are cast aside in favor of high performance. The arrogant tactics of Jeffrey Skilling and the apparent ignorance of Ken Lay further contributed to an unhealthy corporate culture that encouraged cutting corners and falsifying information to inflate earnings.

The allegations surrounding Merrill Lynch's and Arthur Andersen's involvement in the debacle demonstrate that rarely does any scandal of such magnitude involve only one company. Whether a company or regulatory body participates directly in a scandal or whether it refuses to act by looking the other way, the result can be further perpetuation of fraud. This fact was emphasized during the 2008–2009 financial crisis, in which the misconduct of several major companies and the failure of monitoring efforts by regulatory bodies contributed to the worst financial crisis since the Great Depression. With the country recovering from widespread corporate corruption, the story of Enron is once again at the forefront of people's minds. Andy Fastow has stated that businesspeople are falling into the same trap as he fell into at Enron and believes fraud is "ten times worse" today than it was during Enron's time.

The Enron scandal has become legendary. In 2005, four years after the scandal, a movie was made about the collapse of Enron called *Enron: The Smartest Guys in the Room*. To this day, Jeffrey Skilling continues to maintain his innocence and appeal his case. In April of 2012, the Supreme Court denied his appeal, claiming that any errors made in the trial were negligible. However, the following year a federal judge reduced Skilling's sentence to 14 years. Enron's auditor, Arthur Andersen, faced over 40 shareholder lawsuits claiming damages of more than $32 billion. In 2009, the defunct company agreed to pay $16 million to Enron creditors. Enron itself faced many civil actions, and a number of Enron executives faced federal investigations, criminal actions, and civil lawsuits. As for the giant tilted "E" logo so proudly displayed outside of corporate headquarters, it was auctioned off for $44,000.

Questions for Discussion

1. How did the corporate culture of Enron contribute to its bankruptcy?
2. Did Enron's bankers, auditors, and attorneys contribute to Enron's demise? If so, how?
3. What role did the company's chief financial officer play in creating the problems that led to Enron's financial problems?

Sources

Associated Press, "Ex-Enron CFO Fastow Indicted on 78 Counts," *The Los Angeles Times,* November 1, 2002, http://articles.latimes.com/2002/nov/01/business/fi-fastow1 (accessed August 9, 2016).

Associated Press, "Merrill Lynch Settles an Enron Lawsuit," *The New York Times,* July 7, 2006, http://www.nytimes.com/2006/07/07/business/07enron.html?scp=3&sq=%22merrill%20lynch%22%20enron&st=cse (accessed August 9, 2016).

Associated Press, "Two Enron Traders Avoid Prison Sentences," *The New York Times,* February 15, 2007, http://www.nytimes.com/2007/02/15/business/15enron.html?ex=1329195600&en=0f87e8ca83a557ed&ei=5090&partner=rssuserland&emc=rss (accessed August 9, 2016).

Alexei Barrionuevo, "Fastow Gets His Moment in the Sun," *The New York Times,* November 10, 2006, http://www.nytimes.com/2006/11/10/business/10fastow.html (accessed August 9, 2016).

Alexei Barrionuevo, Jonathan Weil, and John R. Wilke, "Enron's Fastow Charged with Fraud," *The Wall Street Journal,* October 3, 2002, pp. A3–A4.

Eric Berger, "Report Details Enron's Deception," *The Houston Chronicle,* March 6, 2003, pp. 1B, 11B.

Associated Press, "Enron Settles California Price-Gouging Claim," *USA Today,* July 15, 2005, http://usatoday30.usatoday.com/money/industries/energy/2005-07-15-enron-sate-settlement_x.htm (accessed August 9, 2016).

John Carney, "The Truth About Why Jeff Skilling's Sentence Got Downsized," *CNBC,* June 21, 2013, http://www.cnbc.com/id/100835443# (accessed August 9, 2016).

Christine Y. Chen, "When Good Firms Get Bad Chi," *Fortune,* November 11, 2002, p. 56.

Scott Cohn, "Fastow: Enron Didn't Have to Go Bankrupt," *CNBC,* June 26, 2013, http://www.cnbc.com/id/100847519 (accessed August 9, 2016).

Francesca Di Meglio, "Enron's Andrew Fastow: The Mistakes I Made," *Bloomberg Businessweek,* March 22, 2012, http://www.bloomberg.com/bw/articles/2012-03-22/enrons-andrew-fastow-the-mistakes-i-made (accessed August 9, 2016).

Kurt Eichenwald, "Enron Founder, Awaiting Prison, Dies in Colorado," *The New York Times,* July 6, 2006, http://www.nytimes.com/2006/07/06/business/06enron.html (accessed August 9, 2016).

Peter Elkind and Bethany McLean, "Feds Move up Enron Food Chain," *Fortune,* December 30, 2002, pp. 43–44.

Enron Creditors Recovery Co., "Enron Announces Completed Sale of Prisma Energy International, Inc.," September 7, 2006, http://www.enron.com/index_option_com_content_task_view_id_94_Itemid_34.htm (accessed August 8, 2014).

Enron Creditors Recovery Corp. website, http://www.enron.com/ (accessed August 8, 2014).

Greg Farrell, "Former Enron CFO Charged," *USA Today,* October 3, 2002, p. B1.

Greg Farrell, Edward Iwata, and Thor Valdmanis, "Prosecutors Are Far from Finished," *USA Today,* October 3, 2002, pp. 1–2B.

Mark Felsenthal and Lillia Zuill, "AIG Gets $150 Billion Government Bailout; Posts Huge Losses," *Reuters,* November 10, 2008, http://www.reuters.com/article/sppage012-n10464039-oisbn-idUSN1046403920081111 (accessed August 9, 2016).

O. C. Ferrell, "Ethics," *BizEd,* May/June 2002, pp. 43–45.

O. C. Ferrell and Linda Ferrell, "The Responsibility and Accountability of CEOs: The Last Interview with Ken Lay," *Journal of Business Ethics* 100 (2011): 209–219.

O. C. Ferrell and Linda Ferrell, *Examining Systemic Issues That Created Enron and the Latest Global Financial Industry Crisis* (2009), White paper.

O. C. Ferrell and Linda Ferrell, "Understanding the Importance of Business Ethics in the 2008–2009 Financial Crisis," in *Business Ethics,* 7th ed., ed. Ferrell, Fraedrich, and Ferrell (Boston: Houghton Mifflin, 2009).

Jeffrey Fick, "Report: Merrill Replaced Enron Analyst," *USA Today,* July 30, 2002, p. B1.

IBD's Washington Bureau, "Finger-Pointing Starts as Congress Examines Enron's Fast Collapse," *Investor's Business Daily,* February 8, 2002, p. A1.

Daren Fonda, "Enron: Picking over the Carcass," *Fortune,* December 30, 2002–January 6, 2003, p. 56.

Mike France, "One Big Client, One Big Hassle," *BusinessWeek,* January 28, 2002, pp. 38–39.

Bryan Gruley and Rebecca Smith, "Keys to Success Left Kenneth Lay Open to Disaster," *The Wall Street Journal,* April 26, 2002, pp. A1, A5.

Tom Hamburger, "Enron CEO Declines to Testify at Hearing," *The Wall Street Journal,* December 12, 2001, p. B2.

Daniel Kadlec, "Power Failure," *Time,* December 2, 2001, http://content.time.com/time/magazine/article/0,9171,1001395,00.html (accessed August 9, 2016).

Daniel Kadlec, "Enron: Who's Accountable?" *Time,* January 13, 2002, http://content.time.com/time/magazine/article/0,9171,1001636,00.html (accessed August 9, 2016).

Jeremy Kahn, "The Chief Freaked Out Officer," *Fortune,* December 9, 2002, pp. 197–198, 202.

Matthew Karnitschnig, Carrick Mollenkamp, and Dan Fitzpatrick, "Bank of America to Buy Merrill," *The Wall Street Journal,* September 15, 2008, http://online.wsj.com/article/SB122142278543033525.html?mod=special_coverage (accessed August 8, 2014).

Kathryn Kranhold and Rebecca Smith, "Two Other Firms in Enron Scheme, Documents Say," *The Wall Street Journal,* May 9, 2002, pp. C1, C12.

Scott Lanman and Craig Torres, "Republican Staff Says Fed Overstepped on Merrill Deal (Update 1)," *Bloomberg,* June 10, 2009, http://www.bloomberg.com/apps/news?pid=newsarchive&sid=a5A4F5W_PygQ (accessed August 8, 2014).

Juan A. Lozano, "U.S. Court Orders Skilling Resentenced," *The Washington Post,* January 7, 2009, http://www.washingtonpost.com/wp-dyn/content/article/2009/01/06/AR2009010603214.html (accessed August 9, 2016).

Bethany McLean, "Why Enron Went Bust," *Fortune,* December 24, 2001, pp. 58, 60–62, 66, 68.

Jodie Morse and Amanda Bower, "The Party Crasher," *Fortune,* December 30, 2002–January 6, 2003, pp. 53–56.

Belverd E. Needles, Jr. and Marian Powers, "Accounting for Enron," *Houghton Mifflin's Guide to the Enron Crisis* (Boston: Houghton Mifflin, 2003), pp. 3–6.

Floyd Norris, "Ruling Could Open Door to New Trial in Enron Case," *The New York Times,* January 6, 2009, http://www.nytimes.com/2009/01/07/business/07enron.html?scp=3&sq=skilling&st=nyt (accessed August 9, 2016).

"Playing the Blame Game," *Time,* January 20, 2002, http://content.time.com/time/interactive/0,31813,2013797,00.html (accessed August 9, 2016).

Brian Ross and Alice Gomstyn, "Lehman Brothers Boss Defends $484 Million in Salary, Bonus," *ABC News,* October 6, 2008, http://www.abcnews.go.com/Blotter/Story?id=5965360&page=1 (accessed August 9, 2016).

Miriam Schulman, "Enron: Whatever Happened to Going Down with the Ship?" Markkula Center for Applied Ethics, www.scu.edu/ethics/publications/ethicalperspectives/schulman0302.html (accessed August 8, 2014).

William Sigismond, "The Enron Case from a Legal Perspective," in *Houghton Mifflin's Guide to Enron,* an uncorrected proof (Boston, MA: Houghton Mifflin, 2003), pp. 11–13.

Rebecca Smith and Kathryn Kranhold, "Enron Knew Portfolio's Value," *The Wall Street Journal,* May 6, 2002, pp. C1, C20.

Rebecca Smith and Mitchell Pacelle, "Enron Plans Return to Its Roots," *The Wall Street Journal,* May 2, 2002, p. A1.

Andrew Ross Sorkin, "Ex-Enron Chief Skilling Appeals to Supreme Court," DealBook Blog, *The New York Times,* March 12, 2009, http://dealbook.blogs.nytimes.com/2009/05/12/former-enron-chiefskilling-appeals-to-supreme-court/?scp=1-b&sq=skilling&st=nyt (accessed September 7, 2009).

"Times Topics: Enron Creditors Recovery Corporation (Formerly Enron Corporation)," *The New York Times,* http://topics.nytimes.com/top/news/business/companies/enron/index.html?scp=1-spot&sq=Enron&st=cse (accessed August 9, 2016).

Jake Ulick, "Enron: A Year Later," *CNN Money,* December 2, 2002, http://money.cnn.com/2002/11/26/news/companies/enron_anniversary/index.htm (accessed August 9, 2016).

"The Other Side of the Enron Story," Ungagged.net, http://ungagged.net (accessed August 8, 2014).

Joseph Weber, "Can Andersen Survive?" *BusinessWeek,* January 28, 2002, pp. 39–40.

James Vicini, "Supreme Court Rejects Jeffrey Skilling's Appeal In Enron Case," *The Huffington Post,* April 16, 2012, http://www.huffingtonpost.com/2012/04/16/supreme-court-jeffrey-skilling_n_1428432.html (accessed August 9, 2016).

Thomas Weidlich, "Arthur Andersen Settles Enron Suit for $16 Million," Bloomberg.com, April 28, 2009, http://www.bloomberg.com/apps/news?pid=20601072&sid=avopmnT7eWjs (accessed August 8, 2014).

Winthrop Corporation, "Epigraph," *Houghton Mifflin's Guide to Enron,* p. 1.

Wendy Zellner, "A Hero—and a Smoking-Gun Letter," *Business Week,* January 28, 2002, pp. 34–35.

Selah Maya Zighelboim, "Former Enron CFO Andrew Fastow Reflects on Business Ethics," *McCombs Today,* February 18, 2015, http://www.today.mccombs.utexas.edu/2015/02/former-enron-cfo-andrew-fastow-ethics (accessed August 9, 2016).

CASE 11

The Complexity of Intellectual Property

INTRODUCTION

Intellectual property (IP) has existed since mankind began creating goods used in commerce. Records of IP law date back to medieval Europe in the 1500s when regulations were created to restrict the paper industry so the government could control what ideas were being printed and shared with the common people. Although the first IP laws were enacted for political and religious reasons, these laws were soon being designed to grant the first inventor of a product the rights of that product for a certain period of time. This concept has evolved into the complex structure of today's IP law.

IP refers to any creation that is tangible or intangible and used in commerce. There are two types of IP: (1) inventions with patents, designs, and trademarks and (2) copyrighted items including artwork, writing, music, and more. Both these types involve a person's or company's original work; however, the level of formality and protection differ greatly. Patents and registered trademarks go through a complex series of submissions and approvals before being provided with legal protection. Copyrighted items, on the other hand, are different. Any fixed form of writing or artwork that a person or company can call their own is copyrighted automatically, even if the owner is not aware of it. Those who wish to reproduce someone else's IP must normally secure permission from the creator before doing so.

There are exceptions to IP law, including fair use and public domain. Fair use refers to the ability to use part of another's copyrighted work without securing permission. For instance, certain parts of a work can be used for nonprofit educational purposes, such as for a classroom assignment, under terms of fair use. Fair use for works of parody will be discussed later in the analysis. Some factors to consider when determining whether a use of copyrighted material falls within fair use are: the length of the copyrighted work to be reproduced, whether the work will be used for commercial purposes, and whether the use will substantially impact the copyright holder's profits or the value of the work. It is important to give attribution to the creator even if used under fair use. Public domain refers to works that are no longer protected under IP laws or that do not qualify for IP protection. Government works and works created before 1924 are not protected under IP law. Some creators of original material might also choose to grant a license for the general public to use their materials.

This case will begin by examining three of the major IP laws with which businesses are most concerned: patents, trademarks, and copyrights. We then examine some of the major ethical issues involved with IP. The Internet in particular has made it easier to violate IP laws through the downloading and/or sharing of content. In addition, a lack of knowledge of IP law has significantly contributed to violations. IP violations are not limited to individuals or unethical companies, however. Even established firms accuse or are accused of IP violations. To illustrate this point, we discuss the multi-chaptered, international legal battle that has been raging between Apple and Samsung since 2011 involving various claims of mutual IP infringement. We then examine some of the objections to IP law. We conclude by examining how collaborations such as the COUNTER Project are working to provide information and recommendations to help countries standardize IP law, clarify IP regulations over the Internet, and use effective policymaking to keep IP protected.

TYPES OF INTELLECTUAL PROPERTY PROTECTION

Consider the following scenario. A popular company wants to enter another country. However, a domestic organization has legally obtained trademark rights to the company's name. It agrees to drop its trademark rights for a significant fee. Should the company pay the money to use its own name? This scenario demonstrates the complexity of IP law. On the one hand, the domestic entity legally obtained rights to use the name in that particular country. On the other hand, the entity did so in the hopes of forcing the well-known company to pay to obtain the rights to use its own name.

This scenario is exactly what Starbucks faced when entering Russia. Although Starbucks had filed a trademark for its company name in Russia in the 1990s, it refrained from opening stores in Russia for years. In the meantime, a Russian lawyer convinced the government to annul the trademark registration because Starbucks was not conducting commerce in the country. He then registered the name "Starbucks" on behalf of a company he represented. He agreed to abandon his registration if Starbucks paid him $600,000. Starbucks refused, and for three years the dispute prevented Starbucks from opening stores in the country. While authorities eventually ruled in favor of Starbucks, the obstacles it faced are similar to the situations of other well-known companies operating globally in areas with different IP laws.

It is important for firms to have a strong understanding of IP law. The next three sections will discuss some of the rules governing different types of IP protection.

Patents

One of the most publicized forms of IP, especially within technology companies, is the patent. The patent submission process can be complex and expensive, but in the competitive field of technology, electronics, and programming, owning a patent could mean the rise or fall of a company. Patents are used to drive innovation by giving the owner recognition for his or her creativity. The types of new inventions that can be patented are not limited to tangible items; they also include processes, machines, articles of manufacturing, compositions of matter, and improvements to any of the items mentioned.

Although there are different types of patent documents available, the three most common are utility, plant, and design patents. Utility patents are awarded for new and useful or significantly improved products, machines, processes, and other compositions of matter. Plant patents are awarded to investors who have developed or reproduced an entirely new type of plant. Monsanto's genetically modified seeds have plant patent protection. Design patents are awarded to inventors of "new, original, and ornamental design for an article of manufacture." In the U.S., utility and

plant patents remain valid for 20 years after the official application date, while design patents remain valid for 14 years. After a patent expires, other companies can reproduce the same or similar items.

Not everything is easily patentable. For instance, the programming of software can sometimes be patented, but there has been much discussion on whether such a patent is worth it in the long run considering the time frame of getting a patent filed (which takes at least a year) and the ever-changing world of software; by the time the patent is issued, it might already be irrelevant. Other items cannot be patented at all, including laws of nature, physical phenomena, abstract ideas, literary and artistic works, or items that are not useful or that are offensive. Yet there may be exceptions even to these rules. For instance, human genes cannot be patented as they are a natural phenomenon. However, what happens if a firm genetically engineers a human gene in a laboratory, putting great time and effort into the process, to create a useful contribution to society? Is this patentable despite the fact that a gene would not normally qualify for patent protection? This issue was taken up by the U.S. Supreme Court. It ruled that companies cannot patent genes they discover even if they have succeeded in separating the gene from surrounding material. The Court decided that in this instance, the company does not actually create anything. However, the Court did find that synthesized DNA can be patented.

Copyrights

While literary and artistic works are not covered by patents, they are protected under copyright. Copyright is a form of protection that keeps other people from infringing on a person's original and creative work. Items that are commonly copyrighted include books, art, music, movies, and any other artistic work that is fixed or stable. In the United States, unlike patents, copyrights do not require the owner to submit any form of registration in order to be protected. All copyrights are protected for 70 years after the death of the owner. If there are multiple owners, then the copyright exists 70 years after the last surviving owner dies. The © symbol indicates copyright ownership.

Since the copyright process is simpler than the patent or trademark protection process, people tend to think of copyright laws as being more relaxed and not as strict. Many people think that copyright violations are not serious as long as the original source is cited. Yet such an assumption is incorrect. Copyright violations can result in serious penalties for violators. However, it is not always easy to prove infringement. If a copyright is not filed, it might be harder for an owner to prove that he or she was the original developer of the copyrighted work. Technically, two people could develop identical works at the same time without infringement. Because copyright protection is easier to attain, this makes it easier to violate by others. For these reasons, many copyright owners choose to file a copyright registration. These registrations are important for the copyright holder to prove infringement in a court of law.

One common misconception of copyright law is that changing the original work or basing a new piece on an original copyrighted work does not violate copyright. Unfortunately, such an assumption is false. Derivatives are works derived from another source or work. Under copyright law, derivatives cannot be sold without the permission of the copyright holder. One famous example of copyright infringement involving a derivative is artist Shepard Fairey's "Hope" poster of President Obama distributed before the 2008 election. The likeness of President Obama was found to have been taken from an Associated Press photograph of Obama when he was a Senator. This act was considered an infringement of copyright, and Fairey eventually pled guilty to criminal charges—not for copyright infringement but for attempting to cover up the infringement through the fabrication of false information.

There are exceptions to copyright permissions. When a person purchases a copyrighted work, he or she has the ability to resell it without paying a fee or securing permission. However, if the person makes copies of the work (e.g. copies of book pages) the person may be infringing a copyright.

Additionally, works of parody are an exception to the rule. Parody is a creation that imitates the characteristic style of an author or a work for comic effect or ridicule. Whereas copyright holders often give permission for others to use or reproduce their works for a fee, they are not likely to give permission to those who desire to make fun of their work. Therefore, parody is an exception to the rule. However, even creators of parody pieces must exert caution because there are often not clear guidelines for what officially constitutes parody.

Trademarks

The trademark is somewhat of an extension of copyright law and gives protection to the owner of a "mark" that identifies the good or service that is produced. The purpose of a trademark is to provide a way to recognize a company or brand from other competitors. A trademark can consist of any combination of words, letters, numbers, drawings, symbols, 3D graphics, packaging, audio sounds, fragrances, or colors. The McDonald's golden arches, the Google name, and the Apple Inc. symbol are trademarks protected under law. A majority of countries in the world allow trademarks to be registered and protected. However, trademarks do not have to be registered in order to be acquired. Trademarks can be renewed for as long as the company continues to use them. They are meant to prevent counterfeiters from selling goods or services under a similar name or mark, which would create confusion among consumers.

A trademark has two possible symbols. The TM symbol indicates that the mark is a trademark but is not registered. The ® symbol indicates a registered trademark. (Another symbol SM is used to indicate an unregistered trademark of a service.) A registered trademark acts as a public declaration that a person claims ownership of a brand and can seek legal action against infringers. In the United States, trademarks can be registered in each state and in the federal system. An unregistered trademark does not offer as much protection but can be recognized and protected in some cases. Trademarks only apply to the country in which they were awarded; a global organization must register their trademarks in the different countries in which they do business if they hope to retain rights to their brand. As demonstrated by the Starbucks case, it is not uncommon for individuals in different countries to register a brand name of a foreign company and then attempt to sell the rights to the business when it enters their country. Cybersquatting, in which an entity registers the Internet domain name of a company before they are able to do so, is also becoming more common. It is therefore important that multinational firms take immediate action to register trademarks.

As already mentioned, trademarks can continue to be registered so that the individual or organization retains constant rights to the mark. However, businesses must be careful to ensure that their trademarks do not become common terms. If a trademark becomes synonymous with a general product or a verb, then the company can lose rights to that trademark. When this occurs, the trademark is referred to as a generic trademark. Aspirin, margarine, videotape, kerosene, and cellophane used to have trademark protection but became such a part of the vernacular that they have become generic. Google is in danger of becoming a generic trademark because people so often use the term to describe "search" on the Internet. A good way to try and prevent a trademark from becoming generic is to put the word "brand" behind the name as well as capitalizing the brand name.

WORKS MADE FOR HIRE

Works made for hire are creative works developed under the scope of employment. An engineer is commissioned to make a new product for his or her company. A technical writer develops technical documents for an organization. A graphic artist at an advertising firm creates an original advertisement for a marketing campaign. All of these situations are works made for hire because they were done in the scope of employment. Because they are works made for hire, IP protection for the original work or invention goes to the employer. In other words, the employer owns the creation. The employee that created the work is compensated through wages, benefits, and/or other forms of remuneration.

Works made for hire are important to understand because some creators, such as artists, might be shocked to learn that they do not have ownership of the material they created. To determine whether the creator has developed a work under the scope of employment, three criteria can be used: (1) the amount of control the employer has over the work; (2) the amount of control the employer has over the employee; and (3) the standard and conduct of the creator. For instance, if the creator of a work develops an original creation at the employer's location or by using the employer's equipment, then the creation is often viewed as a work made for hire. On the other hand, an original creation developed during the creator's own time without the use of employer resources would most likely belong to the creator. Yet it is important to carefully monitor the relationship between the employee and employer to determine whether a creation could qualify as a work made for hire. This was the major issue in the 2004 lawsuit between Mattel and MGA Entertainment over the product line known as the "Bratz" dolls. Mattel claimed that the designer of the Bratz dolls developed the dolls when he was still under contract with Mattel. Mattel argued that it owned the rights for Bratz and that MGA was infringing on its copyright. After eight years of litigation and hundreds of millions spent by both companies, the suit ended inconclusively in 2013 with no damages awarded for infringement on either side, although Mattel was ordered to pay a large portion of MGA's legal fees. However, the battle is not over, as MGA in 2014 filed another related lawsuit against Mattel. MGA claimed Mattel engaged in anticompetitive practices, such as the

theft of information from MGA. Mattel's attempt to have MGA's bid denied was unsuccessful. This serves as a good illustration of the importance of these IP issues and how much they can potentially cost companies.

ETHICAL ISSUES

The large number of laws that comprise IP protection do not deter some people from finding loopholes within the system and capitalizing on an established brand, patent, or copyright. Most unethical activities that involve IP take place within the areas of copyrights and patents, although as the Starbuck case demonstrates, trademark infringement is also a problem. The proliferation of information on the Internet as well as looser laws have made the infringement of copyrighted items difficult to control. Much information published on the Internet is copyrighted, although government materials and facts are not protected under copyright law. All Internet users must abide by copyright rules, but not everyone is aware of this, making infringement easier. Whereas most infringements are small, others can be large and intentional. For instance, the website Pirate Bay was founded on the premise of peer-to-peer file sharing. However, much of the downloadable content was protected under copyright. The founders of the site later faced jail time for promoting downloads of copyrighted material.

It is no mystery that the increase in patent lawyers in the United States can be attributed to demand for those who can understand and decipher the complex rules of patent law. Through the last decade, the patent filing system has been criticized due to its tendency to be vague and unclear. This has allowed owners to file patents for inventions that should not have been submitted or that the owners have no intention of actually creating or using. A new term has been invented to account for these situations: patent troll. Patent trolls are companies that file patents for products or processes they do not actually manufacture, market, or use. Their purpose is to use their patents to force companies who later choose to make the product or use the patented process or machine to pay them royalties. Often patent trolls go after small companies who do not have the resources to take the patent troll to court—at court only about 10 percent of patent trolls win their cases. One of the recommended ways to combat such questionable behavior is to have better controls in place so that the U.S. Patent and Trademark Office does not award IP protections to those who are not involved in creating a new and innovative product, design, or process.

Due to the complexity of patent law, the U.S. government passed the America Invents Act (AIA), which took effect on March 16, 2013, with the intent to simplify the patent process and bring it more in line with the patent procedures of other countries. The new law will change the "first-to-invent" rule to a "first-to-file" rule. Under the previous law, if two people filed for patents for the same invention, then the person who invented the product first received patent rights. However, under the new law the person that files the patent first will receive the rights. Exceptions to this rule would be if the inventor publicly made the invention known so that others should have been aware. While this is meant to simplify the patent process, critics believe this will prove to be more costly and unfair in the long-run.

The following section discusses some common issues in IP infringement. These issues are particularly significant as many people do not understand that engaging in these activities could qualify as IP infringement.

Music and Movie Downloads

The music and movie industry has endured large losses from pirated illegal downloads. Record labels and production companies are on a long hunt to catch those who are using file-sharing websites such as Pirate Bay to download protected material. Many people have been fined for entertainment they have downloaded. The music industry has taken an especially large hit from file sharing because of the simplicity of downloading a 5-minute song compared to a video or movie that has both animation and a sound track.

The music industry recorded its all-time highest sales in 1999, with $14.6 billion. Since then they have faced a dramatic fall. A decade later, their revenues from music sales totaled $6.3 billion, less than 50 percent of their peak. Although the loss is due to many different factors including new technology such as streaming, illegal downloading has been a major problem for the music industry.

The music industry encountered problems even during its record year of sales. In 1999, an 18-year-old student at the University of Southern California created a file-sharing website called Napster. Napster quickly became viral and saw huge increases in its subscribers each day. The website allowed users to upload digital files for music, photos, movies, games, and computer programs. Once the file was uploaded, other users could download it to their computer and enjoy it.

Napster was sued in December 1999 by the music industry. In February 2001, the court ruled that Napster was required to implement a new technology within their site that would weed out copyrighted material, preventing it from being uploaded and traded. It also forced Napster to be a for-pay service website. Napster argued that the new technology was not possible to implement for several reasons. The firm claimed that the technology did not exist to track and take down all copyrighted works. The company also pointed out that even if the technology did exist, it would slow the site down, rendering it useless or completely crashing it altogether. Napster decided the only possibility was to make it a pay site. After that ruling, many other cases have also been addressed. In 2012, the file hosting service Megaupload was shut down and its founder arrested on charges that the site encouraged massive illegal downloading and copyright infringements.

In 2012, an attempt was made to pass laws to discourage copyright infringement on the Internet. The proposed laws were called the Stop Online Piracy Act (SOPA) and the Protect Intellectual Property Act (PIPA). Some of the ways these laws proposed to deter IP infringement on the Internet included blocking websites that violated IP laws from U.S.-based funding sources, payment processors, search engine listings, and web browser visibility. Platforms or websites that contained unauthorized content would be required to remove it. One way that the laws would have enforced these provisions was to alter the DNS system, which is an important part of the Internet. Under the laws, Internet sites found in violation could theoretically be shut down. The proposed laws were supported by the entertainment industry but were largely opposed by Internet companies. On January 18, 2012, Wikipedia and many other sites went offline for the day, and Google blacked out its letters on its search engine, to protest the laws. The pressure eventually resulted in the proposed laws being abandoned. The struggle to control IP violations over the Internet continues.

Education

Some copyright infringements occur in a profession where it might be least expected—education. It is not unheard of for teachers to have websites where they post what they are planning to teach, and in doing so use other teachers' lesson plans that they pass off as their own without giving credit to the original teacher. Other potentially infringing activities are not so clear. For instance, is it acceptable to scan a piece of a document and place it on a class website if credit is acknowledged to the original source? How about hyperlinks to webpages? These different scenarios can be confusing, and many teachers will try to avoid any potential legal difficulties by contacting the copyright holders for permission.

Another infringement that both teachers and students are guilty of is making copies for the classroom. For instance, when professors have only one or a few copies of a particular material, they will often make more copies for everyone to have rather than buying additional copies. Choir directors do this frequently with sheet music. Students might make copies of an entire textbook from the library to avoid paying for a book or they might make copies for their friends in the classroom. Because this involves education, many fair use doctrines apply. For instance, students can make copies from a library book, although restrictions apply to the amount (not the entire book) and the intent (making many copies to provide to classmates is unacceptable). Professors or teachers can pass out spontaneous handouts of copyrighted material for one-time use if it was not planned far in advance. In terms of showing movies in class, teachers are allowed to show movies for instructional purposes as long as it involves face-to-face interaction and is in a physical classroom.

What happens if you buy many copies of an item legally and then choose to resell them? Normally, the right of first sale would apply. However, a controversy arose after a Thai student was sued for purchasing less expensive foreign editions of textbooks and reselling them to U.S. students through eBay. The foreign textbooks specifically stated that the books were only intended for certain regions. Publisher John Wiley & Sons initially won a $600,000 judgment against the student, Supap Kirtsaeng. Kirtsaeng maintained that the right of first sale should apply to foreign markets as well, and the issue was taken to the U.S. Supreme Court. The Supreme Court ruled in the student's favor, saying that such restrictions could be damaging. It found that publishers did not have special rights under copyright law to impose such restrictions.

APPLE VS. SAMSUNG

Sometimes IP violations create major conflicts between large companies. This is particularly true in the technology industry, where an important piece of IP can provide a significant competitive advantage and be worth protecting even at the cost of hundreds of millions of dollars and years of litigation. Since 2009,

Apple has sued a variety of Android smartphone manufacturers, including Nokia, HTC, and Motorola, over alleged infringements on patents and other IP relating to Apple's iOS operating system and its popular iPhone, iPad, and other mobile devices. The lawsuits have claimed infringement by both the Android operating system itself and the companies' individual design decisions (device appearance and functionality, operating system customizations, and even the boxes the devices are sold in). These suits are Apple's attempt to use its IP as legal leverage against the stiff competition that Android represents, as well as combat what its founder, Steve Jobs, considered to be blatant and unethical stealing of Apple's original ideas (of course, as is often true in IP, many would disagree with Jobs' viewpoint on where these ideas truly originated, what constitutes theft as opposed to fair and legal competition, etc.).

In April 2011, Apple sued Samsung Electronics for a variety of alleged IP infringements, including patent, trademark, and trade dress (another, less well-known form of IP). The lawsuit drew special attention because Apple and Samsung are the world's two largest smartphone manufacturers, making up more than 50 percent of the market as of 2012. Therefore, the outcome of their legal battle would likely define the future of Apple's ability to leverage its IP against other smartphone manufacturers. Furthermore, Samsung was not only one of Apple's biggest competitors but also one of its most important business partners, supplying a variety of key hardware pieces such as chips and screens for its mobile devices. This indicated that Apple found protection of its IP to be important enough to possibly jeopardize a key business relationship.

However, Samsung was not going down without a fight. It countersued Apple, claiming infringement on several of its own patents relating to mobile communications technologies. It also filed similar IP infringement suits against Apple in several other countries, including South Korea (Samsung's home country), Germany, Japan, Australia, and the UK. By 2012, the two companies were in a full-blown IP war, battling in over 50 lawsuits around the globe and claiming billions of dollars in damages. Who would win, and what would the result mean for the future of the two companies and of the smartphone industry as a whole?

Apple's Claim

Apple's essential claim was that many of Samsung's devices, as well as its "TouchWiz" Android customization, directly copied or imitated Apple's legally protected creations. These imitations included device design such as shape, color, bezel placement, and material; software design such as icon layout and appearance and features like tap to zoom, flip to rotate, and slide to scroll; marketing design such as key details of the boxes the devices were sold in; and more. Some of these alleged infringements were based on specific patents and trademarks owned by Apple; others were not about the specifics but were based on the argument that taken as a whole, their effect was to confuse customers and make them feel like they were buying Apple-like products. Apple sought monetary damages as reimbursement for the infringements, legal judgments that would serve as leverage for the future (such as requiring that Samsung, and potentially all Android manufacturers, seek and pay for licensing from Apple to use these features), and ideally, injunctions from the courts barring Samsung from selling their products and thus effectively removing them as competition for Apple in those markets.

Samsung's Claim

Samsung defended itself with many of the common counter-IP arguments. It argued, for example, that all it had done was compete in a legal fashion—which often involves a level of acceptable imitation—and Apple's true purpose was to curtail fair and honest competition, which is beneficial for consumers and the market. Samsung also argued that many of Apple's alleged inventions were actually themselves taken from earlier ideas by other companies, and therefore Apple could not claim to have created or own them. Furthermore, Samsung brought its own IP protections into the lawsuit, specifically alleging that Apple was in violation of several patents relating to use of the "3G" network.

Samsung's decision to countersue Apple in countries other than the United States was also a strategic one. Other countries have different and sometimes stricter policies over patents than the United States. Samsung probably calculated it was more likely to prevail in those other countries according to their patent laws. Also, some commentators have noted that U.S. juries often seem to favor domestic companies over foreign ones. Samsung, as a South Korean company, may have felt it had better odds against California-based Apple in non-U.S. courts.

Results, Aftermath, and Implications

Although both Apple and Samsung won apparently decisive victories in different countries, commentators seem to agree that the IP war has done little for either company other than waste time and hundreds of millions in legal fees. The original U.S. lawsuit went overwhelmingly to Apple, with the jury finding that Samsung had intentionally and deliberately infringed on several of Apple's claimed patents and other IP protections and awarding Apple over $1 billion in damages. (Although this was eventually reduced to $929 million due to jury errors requiring the judge's intervention and a damages-only retrial. This amount is still unsettled pending Samsung's appeal.) In contrast, the UK lawsuit resulted in Apple being required to post a public notice on its website for six months stating that Samsung had not copied the iPad in designing its Galaxy tablets.

In February 2012, Apple filed a second U.S. lawsuit against Samsung alleging violation of five additional patents. The jury in May 2014 awarded Apple $119 million, finding violation of two patents, as well as awarding Samsung $158,400 for Apple's violation of one of its patents. Although this again seems to be a clear Apple victory, commentators are calling it a disappointing one, as the damages awarded were a fraction of the $2.2 billion that Apple claimed. More importantly, neither U.S. lawsuit has enabled Apple to secure any sort of injunction against Samsung selling its products in the future, meaning that although Apple will be receiving several large one-time sums and has forced Samsung to develop alternatives or workarounds to the infringing parts of its products, the ruling may have little long-term effect on Samsung's ability to continue competing fiercely against Apple in the United States.

The lawsuits in other countries have been largely inconclusive. For example, South Korea found infringement on both sides and awarded nominal damages to both companies. Perhaps recognizing this, as of August 2014 the companies have agreed to jointly abandon all of the non-U.S. lawsuits. Therefore, the Apple-Samsung IP war seems to have largely ended as quickly and dramatically as it began.

The long-term implications of this IP battle are still unclear. The cost of the litigation itself, and even the $1 billion or so in damages awarded to Apple in the United States, will likely have little effect on the very deep pockets of either company. It is possible that Samsung and other smartphone manufacturers will be more careful to distinguish their designs from Apple's, now that they know there is a possibility for courts to rule in Apple's favor (and that Apple is not afraid to take them to court to prove it). The saga may also have made the industry in general more IP-aware, with companies being sure to protect their investments with patents and trademarks as well as keep a close eye on the IP protections their competitors have filed for. Interestingly, in 2012, Google increased the number of patents they owned by 170 percent. While Apple and other companies also added to their patents during this time, Google may be reacting to the Apple-Samsung battle by acquiring significantly more patents, pre-emptively seeking greater protection for their own phones and the Android operating system itself (which they developed and license out to smartphone manufacturers such as Samsung).

The consumer may be the one who is most affected by this proceeding. Applying for and keeping track of IP protections, litigating them in court, and being generally more concerned about avoiding any appearance of copying all costs money, and these costs may be passed on to consumers as the new norm for doing business in the smartphone world. Any company that wins a decisive IP victory might also gain a great competitive advantage over others, which could lead to fewer choices for consumers.

By aggressively defending its IP, Apple may have given itself an advantage over its competitors, although the size of that advantage is likely much smaller than it had hoped for. On the other hand, the result could spur further patent wars. To protect their IP, companies will need to file for patents and other protections quickly, even before they have worked out all the details of the product. Technology companies have to carefully examine features as simple as shape or color because of the possibility of IP infringement.

ANTI-INTELLECTUAL PROPERTY GROUPS

Critics point out that IP laws could become too restrictive and hinder innovation. With stricter and broader patent protection, some companies may become discouraged when trying to improve upon technologies because of the fear that they will commit patent infringement. Google has been a major advocate of limiting the effects of patent laws. In 2011, Google

took center stage with its complaint that patent owners are attempting to use IP laws in unfair ways to restrict the company from developing new technologies. It has often advocated for open source technology, in which product designs and blueprints are available for other companies to build upon. Supporters of open source believe this allows for greater innovation and improved technology development.

More and more detractors are criticizing the use of copyrights, patents, and trademarks. Anti-copyright groups are becoming increasingly common. Companies such as Pirate Bay have clearly displayed an antagonism toward copyright laws. Rasmus Fleischer, one of the founders of Piracy Bureau—an organization against copyrights for digital media—believes that copyrighting content on the Internet makes no sense and that copyright laws are a form of control and censorship. Other criticisms from anti-copyright groups include that IP laws restrict freedom of expression and the distribution of knowledge.

However, even Google uses a wide range of copyrighted content in its own search engine. Google may be taking a step back on its stance after realizing the need to protect its own property. IP protections provide great benefits and give people with incentives to create and protect their innovations. While it is certainly essential to protect IP, the debate over whether IP laws go too far continues to rage. The ease of infringing on IP has also complicated this issue, leading to the proposal of laws that are criticized by detractors as being too restrictive. In addition, because IP laws vary from country to country, multinational firms face major obstacles when trying to protect their brands and products in other countries. Finding the right balance to protect both freedom of expression and IP is challenging.

THE COUNTER PROJECT

In response to the complexity and challenges of IP, governments have begun researching ways to clarify laws and create more uniform standards. Before this task can be completed, however, it is important to determine the extent of global piracy and gather further research on its causes, possible solutions, what has and has not worked to curtail it, and so on. From 2008–2011, the European Commission funded the COUNTER Project, led by professors at the University of Central Lancashire, to gain a better understanding of the practice of pirating, counterfeiting, and illegal file-sharing from a variety of viewpoints including legal, social, business, cultural, and psychological. The Project's research and conclusions were then made available through papers, conferences, and other initiatives so they could be used to help formulate the public policy of European and other countries in this area.

One area of investigation for the COUNTER Project concerned user-generated content. User-generated content that consists of copyrighted material is a major issue on websites such as YouTube. The COUNTER Project found that most copyright holders tend to sue web platforms and websites that host copyrighted content rather than users who download the content because suing individual users would not be feasible. This type of research has led the COUNTER project to develop recommendations for standardizing IP laws and holding stakeholders accountable. For instance, COUNTER found that browse wrap agreements, the part of the website that informs the user of the terms and conditions for using that website, are often inadequate. By using a site with a browse wrap agreement, the user is implicitly entering into a contract agreeing to the terms and conditions of the site. However, penalties are not often enforced when users violate the agreement. This is at least partly because courts have determined that many of the links to these agreements are not conspicuous enough for users to notice or access. The COUNTER Project therefore recommends creating a standardized and transparent method for websites to display these browse wrap agreements so that they meet all relevant conditions. These findings and recommendations could have significant implications for global public policy on protecting IP over the Internet.

CONCLUSIONS

The controversy over IP is far from over. Due to the proliferation of technology, both individuals and companies are exposed to more information than ever before. With this greater access to information and technology comes a greater ability to infringe upon copyrighted material. Unfortunately, many consumers and companies are unaware that simple activities, such as making copies of copyrighted materials or copying software onto multiple computers, can be violations. Companies are trying to combat piracy of their products by filing for more IP protections as well as filing lawsuits against those they believe could be infringing on their property. As a result, an increasing amount of cases are being brought to court, particularly among technology firms. However, even the legal system has trouble determining

what can constitute as a violation, as evidenced by the various lawsuits previously mentioned (between Mattel and MGA, between textbook publisher John Wiley & Sons and student Supap Kirtsaeng, and between Apple and Samsung).

To try and standardize IP protections, collaborations such as the COUNTER Project are working to gain a better understanding of piracy and ways to combat it. However, although it is widely acknowledged that creators should have some protection for their creations, critics of IP laws believe these laws often give too much power to organizations and feel that the current system of laws stifles creativity and innovation. Businesses must decide whether and how to protect their brands or products. It is necessary for businesses to be familiar with IP laws so they can understand both how to protect themselves against infringement and how to keep themselves from infringing on the IP of others. The more that consumers and organizations understand IP regulation, the more equipped they will be to navigate this complex area of law.

Questions for Discussion

1. Why are intellectual property protections necessary?
2. Why do consumers and companies often violate intellectual property laws?
3. What are some of the objections that critics of intellectual property laws maintain? Do you agree with some of the objections?

Sources

American Library Association, "Performance of or Showing Films in the Classroom," http://www.ala.org/advocacy/sites/ala.org.advocacy/files/content/copyright/fairuse/web- digital%20delivery%20in%20classroom-rev3psa.pdf (accessed June 14, 2013).

Maurizio Borghi, Indranath Gupta, and Eva Hemmungs Wirtén, *Deliverable D26: Reusing Copyrighted Material in User-Generated Content,* Counter© Counterfeiting and Piracy Research, March 5, 2010.

Maurizio Borghi, Maria Lillà Montagnani, and Indranath Gupta, *Deliverable D27: Evaluating Scenarios For Managing Copyright Online,* Counter© Counterfeiting and Piracy Research, May 30, 2010.

Kit Chellel, "Samsung Wins U.K. Apple Ruling Over 'Not as Cool' Galaxy Tab," *Bloomberg,* July 9, 2012, http://www.bloomberg.com/news/2012-07-09/samsung-wins-u-k-apple-ruling-over-not-as-cool-galaxy-tablet.html (accessed August 15, 2016).

Eric Clemons, "Innovation and Google's Attack on the Patent System," *Business Insider,* August 16, 2011, http://www.businessinsider.com/innovation-and-googles-attack-on-the-patent-system-2011-8 (accessed August 15, 2016).

Copyright Clearance Center, *Copyright Basics Video*, http://www.copyright.com/content/cc3/en/toolbar/education/resources/copyright_basics1.html (accessed August 15, 2016).

Copyright Clearance Center, Inc., "Using Content: Photocopies," 2005, http://www.copyright.com/Services/copyrightoncampus/content/ (accessed June 14, 2013).

Creative Commons, "About CC0—'No Rights Reserved'," http://creativecommons.org/about/cc0 (accessed August 15, 2016).

Paul Elias, "Apple's Samsung Verdict Nearly Cut in Half by Federal Judge," *The Huffington Post,* March 1, 2013, http://www.huffingtonpost.com/2013/03/01/half-of-billion-apple-samsung-settlement-invalidated_n_2792624.html (accessed June 7, 2013).

Tim Cushing, "It's Finally Over: 8 Years of Mattel vs. Bratz and No One's Getting Paid But the Lawyers," *Tech Dirt,* January 29, 2013, https://www.techdirt.com/articles/20121019/17344420768/its-finally-over-8-years-mattel-vs-bratz-no-ones-getting-paid-lawyers.shtml (accessed August 15, 2016).

Seth Fiegerman, "A UK Judge Is Forcing Apple to Publish on Its Website That Samsung Didn't Copy Apple," *Business Insider,* July 18, 2012, http://www.businessinsider.com/bloomberg-apple-must-post-notice-online-in-uk-saying-samsung-didnt-copy-ipad-2012-7 (accessed August 15, 2016).

Rasmus Fleischer, "The Future of Copyright," Cato Unbound, June 8, 2008, http://www.cato-unbound.org/2008/06/09/rasmus-fleischer/future-copyright (accessed August 15, 2016).

Tom Gara, "In the Mobile Patent Wars, Google Armed up in 2012," *The Wall Street Journal,* January 10, 2013, http://blogs.wsj.com/corporate-intelligence/2013/01/10/in-the-mobile-patent-wars-google-armed-up-in-2012/ (accessed August 15, 2016).

David Goldman, "Music's Lost Decade: Sales Cut In Half," *CNN Money,* February 3, 2010, http://money.cnn.com/2010/02/02/news/companies/napster_music_industry/ (accessed August 15, 2016).

Dino Grandoni, "How the Apple Samsung Lawsuit Hurt Consumers," *The Huffington Post,* July 31, 2012, http://www.huffingtonpost.com/2012/07/31/apple-samsung-lawsuit-consumers_n_1721623.html (accessed August 15, 2016).

Parker E. Howell, "Whose Invention Is It Anyway? Employee Invention-Assignment Agreements and Their Limits," *Washington Journal of Law, Technology & Arts* 8, no. 2 (Fall 2012), pp. 237–264.

International Trademark Association, "Fact Sheets Types of Protection," 2016, http://www.inta.org/TrademarkBasics/FactSheets/Pages/TrademarksvsGenericTermsFactSheet.aspx (accessed August 15, 2016).

John Kell, "Bratz Doll Maker MGA Entertainment Sues Mattel," *The Wall Street Journal,* January 13, 2014, http://online.wsj.com/news/articles/SB10001424052702303595404579318680190603384 (accessed August 15, 2016).

Brett Kendall, "High Court Rules in Favor of Book Reseller," *The Wall Street Journal,* March 19, 2013, http://online.wsj.com/article/SB10001424127887324323904578370263406999592.html (accessed August 15, 2016).

Jessica E. Lessin, Lorraine Luk, and Juro Osawa, "Apple Finds It Difficult to Divorce Samsung," *The Wall Street Journal,* July 1, 2013, http://online.wsj.com/news/articles/SB10001424127887324682204578513882349940500 (accessed August 15, 2016).

Florian Mueller, "Apple Wins $119 Million in Patent Damages from Samsung, Wanted $2.2 Billion: Mixed Verdict," *Foss Patents,* May 2, 2014, http://www.fosspatents.com/2014/05/apple-wins-119-million-in-patent.html (accessed August 15, 2016).

Florian Mueller, "Judge Denies Apple Bid for Sales Ban Against Samsung in Second California Patent Case," *Foss Patents,* August 27, 2014, http://www.fosspatents.com/2014/08/judge-denies-apple-bid-for-sales-ban.html (accessed August 15, 2016).

Florian Mueller, "The Truth is Neither the Courts Nor the Parties *Really* Wanted Today's Apple-Samsung Damages Retrial," *Foss Patents,* November 12, 2013, http://www.fosspatents.com/2013/11/the-truth-is-neither-court-nor-parties.html (accessed August 15, 2016).

Nash Information Services, LLC, "Total Box Office Records," The Numbers, http://www.the-numbers.com/movies/records/ (accessed April 25, 2013).

National Paralegal College, "History and Sources of Intellectual Property Law," National Paralegal College, http://nationalparalegal.edu/public_documents/courseware_asp_files/patents/IntroIP/History.asp (accessed August 15, 2016).

OECD, *The Economic Impact of Counterfeiting and Piracy* (Paris, France: OECD Publications, 2008).

Christopher Parsons, "Thoughts on COUNTER: Counterfeiting and Piracy Research Conference," *Technology, Thoughts & Trinkets,* April 1, 2010, http://www.christopher-parsons.com/thoughts-on-counter-counterfeiting-and-piracy-research-conference/ (accessed September 2, 2014).

Nilay Patel, "Apple Sues Samsung: a Complete Lawsuit Analysis," *The Verge,* April 19, 2011, http://www.theverge.com/2011/04/19/apple-sues-samsung-analysis (accessed August 15, 2016).

Evan Ramstad, "Award to Apple Isn't Raised," *The Wall Street Journal,* June 30, 2012, http://online.wsj.com/article/SB100014241278873243292045782728704 32069736.html?KEYWORDS=apple+samsungKEYWO RD S%3Dapple+samsung (accessed August 15, 2016).

Reuters, "Jury Rules for Mattel in Bratz Doll Case," *The New York Times,* July 18, 2008, http://www.nytimes.com/2008/07/18/business/18toy.html?_r=2&ref=business&oref=slogin (accessed August 15, 2016).

Reuters, "Megaupload Founder Kim Dotcom Granted Access to Police Evidence," *The Guardian,* May 31, 2013, http://www.guardian.co.uk/technology/2013/may/31/megaupload-kim-dotcom-access-evidence (accessed June 7, 2013).

Matt Richtell, "The Napster Decision: The Overview; Appellate Judges Back Limitations on Copying Music," *The New York Times,* February 13, 2001, http://www.nytimes.com/2001/02/13/business/napster-decision-overview-appellate-judges-back-limitations-copying-music.html?pagewanted=all&src=pm (accessed August 15, 2016).

"The Right to Share: Principles on Freedom of Expression and Copyright in Digital Age," Article 19, April 25, 2013, http://www.article19.org/resources.php/resource/3716/en/ (accessed August 15, 2016).

Adam Santariano and Joel Rosenblatt, "Apple, Samsung Agree to End Patent Suits Outside U.S.," *Bloomberg,* August 5, 2014, http://www.bloomberg.com/news/articles/2014-08-05/apple-samsung-agree-to-end-patent-suits-outside-u-s- (accessed August 15, 2016).

Ian Scerr, "Apple, Samsung Square Off over Patent Damages," *The Wall Street Journal,* December 6, 2012, http://online.wsj.com/article/SB100014241278873235 01404578164021886466686.html?mod=WSJ_article_comments#articleTab s%3Darticle (accessed August 15, 2016).

Mark Scott, "Pirate Bay's Weird New Business Plan," *Bloomberg Businessweek,* July 1, 2009, http://www.businessweek.com/globalbiz/content/jul2009/gb2009071_378545.htm (accessed June 7, 2013).

Scott Shane, "How to Neuter Patent Trolls," *Bloomberg Businessweek,* March 26, 2013, http://www.businessweek.com/articles/2013-03-26/how-to-neuter-patent-trolls (accessed August 15, 2016).

Daniel Siegal, "Mattel Can't Shake MGA's $1B Bratz Trade Secrets Suit," *Law 360,* http://www.law360.com/articles/596114/mattel-can-t-shake-mga-s-1b-bratz-trade-secrets-suit (accessed August 15, 2016).

Bill Singer, "Obama Hope and Progress Photo Ends with Artist's Criminal Plea," *Forbes,* September 7, 2012, http://www.forbes.com/sites/billsinger/2012/09/07/obama-hope-and-progress-photo-ends-with-artists-criminal-plea/#6fe124307e58 (accessed August 15, 2016).

Sean Stonefield, "The 10 Most Valuable Trademarks," *Forbes,* June 15, 2011, http://www.forbes.com/sites/seanstonefield/2011/06/15/the-10-most-valuable-trademarks/ (accessed August 15, 2016).

The United States Patent and Trademark Office, "Patents," http://www.uspto.gov/inventors/patents.jsp#heading-1 (accessed June 7, 2013).

University of Central Lancashire, "COUNTER Project: EU FP7—217514," *University of Central Lancashire,* http://www.uclan.ac.uk/research/explore/projects/counter_project.php (accessed August 15, 2016).

U.S. Patent and Trademark Office, "Frequently Asked Questions about Trademarks," April 23, 2013, http://www.uspto.gov/faq/trademarks.jsp#_Toc275426680 (accessed June 7, 2013).

Richard Wolf, "Justices Rule Human Genes Cannot Be Patented," *USA Today,* June 13, 2013, http://www.usatoday.com/story/news/nation/2013/06/13/supreme-court-gene-breast-ovarian-cancer-patent/2382053/ (accessed August 15, 2016).

World Intellectual Property Organization, "About Trademarks," http://www.wipo.int/trademarks/en/about_trademarks.html#function (accessed August 15, 2016).

World Intellectual Property Organization, "What is Intellectual Property?" http://www.wipo.int/about-ip/en/ (accessed August 15, 2016).

Jun Yang, "Samsung Sues Apple on Patent-Infringement Claims as Legal Dispute Deepens," *Bloomberg,* April 21, 2011, http://www.bloomberg.com/news/2011-04-22/samsung-sues-apple-on-patent-infringement-claims-as-legal-dispute-deepens.html (accessed September 2, 2014).

Salesforce.com: Responsible Cloud Computing

INTRODUCTION

Salesforce.com is a cloud computing company and customer relationship vendor. It distributes cloud computing software to businesses to help them manage their sales. Companies can use Salesforce.com's subscription service to purchase products that will help them record, store, analyze, share, and act upon business data. In doing so, businesses are able to efficiently manage customer accounts, track sales leads, evaluate marketing campaigns, and provide post-sales service. Salesforce.com has recently developed new and innovative products to help businesses understand their customers. Salesforce1, for instance, makes it easier for salespeople to interact with clients using Saleforce.com tools through apps on their mobile devices.

Salesforce.com is currently the business leader in the industry and has expanded greatly since 2006. Unlike so many companies, Salesforce.com grew during the recession. In a time when companies needed to focus on their customers, Salesforce.com responded with quality Customer Relationship Management (CRM) products to offer a valuable solution. Today, Salesforce.com has over 100,000 customers.

While Salesforce.com is admired for its products, it is also viewed positively from an ethical standpoint. Due to a concern for their voluntary responsibilities and their workforce, Salesforce.com has been nominated onto *Fortune* magazine's "100 Best Companies to Work For" for the past eight consecutive years. Additionally, the Ethisphere Institute has selected Salesforce.com as one of its "World's Most Ethical" for eight years

This case will provide a brief history of Salesforce.com, including describing some of the products they offer as well as ways in which they incentivize their sales force. Additionally, we examine Salesforce.com's corporate social responsibility initiatives and the impact they have had upon stakeholders. Finally, we look at issues facing Salesforce.com as well as its future plans.

HISTORY

In 1999 partners Parker Harris, Dave Moellenhoff, Frank Dominguez, and former Oracle executive Marc Benioff founded Salesforce.com as a company that offered software as a service; it has now grown to a company leading the cloud computing software industry. In 2000, it opened headquarters in San Francisco, with regional headquarters in Dublin (covering Europe, the Middle East, and Africa), Singapore (covering the Asia Pacific), and Tokyo (covering Japan). Other major offices are located in Toronto, New York, London, Sydney, and San Mateo, California. Salesforce.com's services have been translated into 16 different languages. Within a year of business, the company attained 1,500 customers and 2,100,000 subscribers. Each year in business brought an average of 10,500 customers into the cloud computing market.

Salesforce.com software is comprised of a number of products, including Sales Cloud, Service Cloud, Data.com, Desk.com, Chatter, and Function.com. The Sales Cloud allows for sales representatives to focus on selling instead of worrying so much about the administrative side of business. The Service Cloud allows companies to provide faster and more responsive service across every channel, which makes it easy to connect service applications with popular Web communities such as Twitter and Facebook. Data.com helps businesses with the prospecting process of personal selling. It also helps clean up data. Desk.com is used to provide customer support for small businesses. Employees can work more efficiently and closely with colleagues on their own private and secure social network—Chatter. Chatter automatically pushes updates on the people, projects, and data that matter most to employees. Businesses use Force.com to build apps and create websites easily and quickly. Salesforce.com is also coming out with new products to address its customers' changing needs. For instance, its IOT Cloud connects multiple devices and data from the Internet of Things.

---

*This case was prepared by Melanie Martinez, Veronica Vigil, and Danielle Jolley for and under the direction of O.C. and Linda Ferrell ©2017. It was prepared for classroom discussion rather than to illustrate either effective or ineffective handling of an administrative, ethical, or legal decision by management. All sources used for this case were obtained through publicly available material.

One client of Salesforce.com that has benefited from its services is General Electric (GE) Aviation. GE Aviation uses Salesforce.com tools to connect with customers and collaborate with one another. For instance, GE Aviation uses Chatter to connect sales and marketing people, enabling them to provide quick feedback and share information quickly and efficiently. The chief marketing officer of GE has praised the ability the firm has with Salesforce.com technology to gather real-time information.

In addition to offering superior products that help companies better manage their sales forces, Salesforce.com also offers many incentives to their employees. On average, Salesforce.com pays their employees competitively and provides lucrative benefits to employees to ensure satisfaction. Some of the substantial benefits include paid holidays, a wellness allowance, education reimbursement, and volunteer time off. One of its newest perks include a communal workspace where up to six employees can bring their dogs to work. Salesforce.com adopted a separate workspace to balance the needs of employees who are allergic to dogs.

Along the way, Salesforce.com has developed partnerships and embarked upon multiple acquisitions in order to increase their market share. The company has acquired many other companies, including GroupSwim (2009, now part of Chatter), Jigsaw Data Corp. (2010, later renamed Data.com), Radian 6 (2011), and ExactTarget (2013). These acquisitions have enabled Saleforce.com to offer more diversified CRM software. Customers can now manage finances, customer accounts, call logs, emails, and much more through one system, which makes business operations more organized and functional.

ETHICAL CONDUCT

Salesforce.org is based on a simple idea: donate 1 percent of Salesforce's resources to support organizations that are working to make the world a better place. The organization takes just a fraction of Salesforce.com's time, product, and equity and gives it to social-change organizations so these organizations can amplify their impact. From the beginning, Marc Benioff wanted to incorporate a philanthropic aspect to his company. He decided to implement the 1-1-1 initiative to extend the reach of Salesforce.com and provide a vision Salesforce.org. Thanks to Salesforce.com's impact, many other companies, including LiveOps and NewVoiceMedia, are also incorporating the 1-1-1 model into their business operations.

One Percent Time

Every year Salesforce.com employees receive six paid volunteer days off in order to respond to community needs around the globe. The company believes that through doing this they can promote a culture of care and help. Each employee is encouraged to contribute to nonprofits that they are passionate about and help those organizations grow and prosper. To date, volunteers have supported nonprofits across the country and around the world with 1.3 million volunteer hours of service. In addition to volunteering in their communities, some employees also volunteer their technical skills by offering to help organizations in the Power of Us program learn how to use Salesforce.com technology. By implementing this business practice, employees at Salesforce.com became more satisfied at work.

One Percent Equity

Salesforce.com donates 1 percent of its capital to Salesforce.org. Its annual granting program focuses on empowering organizations that have a proven commitment to the 1-1-1 model and that are using technology in innovative ways. Founding stock from Salesforce.com provides funds for grants, with a specific focus on supporting youth, technology innovation, and employee-inspired volunteer projects. Salesforce.org has given more than $100 million in grants since its inception in 2000. Nonprofits currently using Salesforce.com's CRM are eligible for these grants, which fund customizations that will provide measurable benefits to the organization and other nonprofits. Salesforce.com donates in other ways as well. It donated $200 million to a children's hospital named after the firm.

Additionally, employees are rewarded for volunteering. They receive seven days of volunteer time off each year, and the top 100 volunteers receive $10,000 grants to give to the nonprofit of their choice.

One Percent Product

More than 28,000 nonprofits and higher education institutions of all shapes and sizes are using Salesforce.com to take their organization's impact to a new level. It has created a program called the Power of Us with an emphasis on nonprofit organizations and higher education institutions. The company provides the organizations with product donations of the initial ten licenses and steep discounts on all future licenses and products to fuel this transformation. The company donates Salesforce.com CRM licenses to help nonprofits increase their efficiency so they can focus their time and resources on the organization's core mission.

Salesforce.com has also formed a global coalition with its customers and partners that are working to make a positive impact on the environment. Salesforce.com encourages companies to use its products in order to reduce the company's environmental impact; it claims that operating with the cloud is 95 percent more efficient than on premises technology. Through tests, Salesforce.com has found that on average 95 percent less carbon is released and consequently fewer greenhouse gas emissions. Salesforce.com has architecture that is multitenant, which means it is a shared utility in order to optimize computing resources across all its customers. Because of this, using a remarkably small number of servers saves energy in the following ways:

- Optimized runtime processing
- Optimized storage
- Predictable load balancing
- Continual analysis and energy improvement
- Energy efficient servers
- Micro-energy management
- Optimized power consumption
- Standardized architecture

AWARDS

Salesforce.com has received many awards for their social contributions and ethical business practices. In receiving these awards, Salesforce.com has proven that conducting their business in an ethical manner has proven beneficial not only to their company but to their shareholders and customers as well. Listed below are some of the awards Salesforce.com has received:

Stevie Awards: Data.com Best New Marketing Solution, 2012

CRM Excellence Award: Best Enterprise Suite CRM, 2011

CRM Market Award: Service Leader, 2011

eWeek Product of the year: Chatter, 2010

Fortune: The 100 Best Companies to Work For

Ethisphere: World's Most Ethical Companies

Forbes: World's Most Innovative Companies, 2011, 2012, 2013, 2014, 2015, 2016

CHALLENGES

Because Salesforce.com is a completely online based system, it could face significant challenges. Unlike traditional business computing systems, which are local to an organization's network and the individual employee's computer, Salesforce.com requires the use of the Internet. Internet crashes and even wide-scale hacking is a risk for all Internet companies and programs. Because Salesforce.com relies so heavily on the Internet, problems with the Internet or from outside forces could be damaging.

However, since its inception in 1999, Salesforce.com has improved its ability to stay online. When first developed, loss of connectivity was a weekly problem. Yet it seems that since 2005, Salesforce.com has had only a few incidents per year pertaining to major network issues. As Salesforce.com continues to grow and accumulate more customers, the issue of being offline, even for a few hours, could yield catastrophic effects. As recently as January 2011, Salesforce.com had what it called "availability" issues. While it seems that these issues lasted just over two hours, it left countless people unable to do their jobs. Furthermore, there is no way to track how often individuals lose their connectivity and are left out of work. This is a risk that people who choose Salesforce.com must face—and a risk that Salesforce.com must continue to address in order to reassure its clients.

On top of a total loss of connectivity, there are cases in which customers have had issues with Salesforce.com. These issues are typically accompanied by slowness in the general system, along with some applications not functioning. This is yet another risk that comes with cloud computing.

Some investors are also worried about Salesforce.com's many acquisitions. For instance, Salesforce acquired ExactTarget for $2.5 billion. After the announcement, Salesforce stock fell, signaling investors' concerns about the benefits of the acquisition. Acquisitions can be tricky because of the costs involved as well as whether the acquired company will fit into the acquiring company's strategy. Many companies lose money on their acquisitions, which harms shareholders because they lose value on the deal. According to some investors, Salesforce.com has had inconsistent profitability, which places into question their wisdom of acquiring a variety of companies in a short period of time. Only time will tell whether Salesforce.com's acquisitions will benefit stakeholders in the long-term.

Another challenge that Salesforce.com has encountered along the way has come in the form of stock options. Many, specifically within the industry, have speculated about this ethical dilemma. Since the beginning, Salesforce.com has predominantly maintained a high stock price, and many attribute it to institutional ownership. It has been said that the market has not been able to access the stock, which has created an inflated price. This has led many to question whether this action is ethical due to the potential of overvaluing the company.

CONCLUSION

Cloud computing has proven to be a highly successful industry. As Salesforce.com is at the top of the totem pole among its peers, the natural question must be what's next for this heavyweight? There are numerous opportunities Salesforce.com is examining. The U.S. government is currently considering cloud computing, along with other large organizations. This could represent a major opportunity for Salesforce.com.

Salesforce.com is a remarkable company which has proven to be not only a successful business but also an organization that reaches beyond their doors to the community. It has become so successful that it announced its intention to lease the tallest building in San Francisco with rent at approximately $83 per square foot! While Salesforce.com's future forecast has a positive outlook, the challenge now will be to show people that they have a solidified core competency. Although Salesforce.com may have few competitors, their consistent customer service, positive community outreach, and diversification of services has propelled Salesforce.com into becoming the dominating company within the cloud industry.

Questions for Discussion

1. How has Salesforce.com created an ethical culture?

2. What are some of the ethical challenges that Salesforce.com faces?

3. How has Salesforce.com integrated philanthropy into its operations?

Sources

"100 Best Companies to Work For," *Fortune*, http://fortune.com/best-companies/salesforce-23/ (accessed August 15, 2016).

"2010 World's Most Ethical Companies—Company Profile: Salesforce.com," *Ethisphere*, Q1 (2010): 32–33.

Ethisphere Institute, "World's Most Ethical Companies® Honorees," 2014, http://worldsmostethicalcompanies.ethisphere.com/honorees/ (accessed August 15, 2016).

"Adoption of Salesforce.com's 1/1/1 Model Accelerates Around the World," *PR Newswire*, http://www.prnewswire.com/news-releases/adoption-of-salesforcecoms-111-model-accelerates-around-the-world-85034902.html (accessed August 15, 2016).

Brett Arends, "The Truth Behind the Salesforce.com Hype," *The Wall Street Journal*, February 25, 2011, http://online.wsj.com/article/SB10001424052748704150604576166280156761902.html (accessed August 15, 2016).

Tim Brugger, "Not All Wine and Roses for Salesforce.com," *www.beta.fool.com*, February 24, 2012, http://beta.fool.com/timbrugger/2012/02/24/not-all-wine-and-roses-salesforcecom/2328/ (accessed August 27, 2014).

"Building Enterprise, Vertical CRM Applications on Salesforce," *RoundCorner*, March 27, 2014, http://roundcorner.com/building-enterprise-vertical-crm-applications-salesforce/ (accessed August 15, 2016).

Rosemary Cafasso, "CEO Benioff Outlines Priorities for Salesforce.com," *Search Cloud Applications*, September 4, 2011, http://searchcloudapplications.techtarget.com/news/2240078855/CEO-Benioff-outlines-priorities-for-Salesforcecom (accessed August 15, 2016).

Alison Diana, "Salesforce.com Launches Chatter Collaboration Tool," *Information Week*, June 22, 2010, http://www.informationweek.com/news/storage/disaster_recovery/225700975 (accessed August 15, 2016).

Dan Farber, "Salesforce.com's Marc Benioff Preaches the Social Enterprise Gospel," *www.cnet.com*, September 19, 2012, http://news.cnet.com/8301-1001_3-57515986-92/salesforce.coms-marc-benioff-preaches-the-social-enterprise-gospel/ (accessed August 15, 2016).

Carmine Gallo, "Storytelling Tips from Salesforce's Marc Benioff," *Businessweek,* November 3, 2009, http://www.businessweek.com/smallbiz/content/nov2009/sb2009112_279472.htm (accessed August 27, 2014).

Tim Gibbon, "Salesforce.com Hooks Up to Twitter Firehose," *Technorati,* June 14, 2012, http://technorati.com/business/article/salesforcecom-hooks-up-to-twitter-firehose/ (accessed November 26, 2012).

Doug Henschen, "Salesforce.com's Next Steps to Become the Next Oracle," *Information Week,* September 24, 2012, http://www.informationweek.com/software/enterprise-applications/salesforcecoms-next-steps-to-become-the/240007810 (accessed August 15, 2016).

"History of Salesforce," *SalesforceProGrammers,* 2010, http://salesforceprogrammers.com/article467-History_of_Salesforce_.html (accessed August 7, 2014).

Steven D. Jones, "Salesforce.com Shares Weaken on Concern About Billings Growth," *The Wall Street Journal,* November 18, 2011, http://online.wsj.com/article/BT-CO-20111118-712216.html (accessed December 13, 2011).

Chris Kanaracus, "Five Questions for Salesforce.com at Dreamforce," *Computer World,* September 17, 2012, http://www.computerworld.com/s/article/9231362/Five_questions_for_Salesforce.com_at_Dreamforce (accessed August 15, 2016).

Chris Kanaracus, "Salesforce.Com's Benioff Talks Growth, Microsoft," *CIO,* June 6, 2011, http://www.cio.com/article/683621/Salesforce.Com_s_Benioff_Talks_Growth_Microsoft (accessed August 15, 2016).

Michael Kigsman, "Salesforce.com: Pushing Social Business into the Mainstream," *ZDNet,* September 24, 2012, http://www.zdnet.com/salesforce-com-pushing-social-business-into-the-mainstream-7000004642/ (accessed August 15, 2016).

Paul R. La Monica, "No Clouds for Salesforce, Stock Up 8%," *CNN,* November 21, 2012, http://buzz.money.cnn.com/2012/11/21/salesforce-earnings-stock/ (accessed August 15, 2016).

Marshall Lager, "Salesforce.com Expands the Cloud to Sales," February 10, 2009, http://www.destinationcrm.com/Articles/CRM-News/Daily-News/Salesforce.com-Expands-the-Cloud-to-Sales-52602.aspx (accessed August 15, 2016).

Dan Levy, "Salesforce $1 Billion Deal Sets San Francisco Office Rent Record," *Bloomberg Businessweek,* April 12, 2014, http://www.bloomberg.com/news/articles/2014-04-11/salesforce-tower-rents-said-to-set-san-francisco-record (accessed August 15, 2016).

Eric Martin, "Salesforce.com, Fastenal to Replace Fannie, Freddie in S&P 500," *Bloomberg,* September 9, 2008, http://www.bloomberg.com/apps/news?pid=newsarchive&sid=abSHUiBFprac&refer=us (accessed August 27, 2014).

Rich Miller, "Major Outage for Salesforce.com," *Data Center Knowledge,* July 10, 2012, http://www.datacenterknowledge.com/archives/2012/07/10/major-outage-salesforce-com/ (accessed August 15, 2016).

Erika Morphy, "Salesforce.com Reaches for Bigger Slice of Government Cloud Pie," *CRM Buyer,* April 25, 2012, http://www.crmbuyer.com/story/74950.html (accessed August 15, 2016).

Milton Moskowitz and Charles Kapelke, "25 Top-paying Companies," CNNMoney, January 26, 2011, http://money.cnn.com/galleries/2011/pf/jobs/1101/gallery.best_companies_top_paying.fortune/index.html (accessed August 15, 2016).

Matt Phillips, "Salesforce.com: Getting its Mo-mo Back?" *Wall Street Journal,* April 20, 2011, http://blogs.wsj.com/marketbeat/2011/04/20/salesforce-com-getting-its-mo-mo-back/ (accessed August 27, 2014).

Raj Sabhlok, "Are You Getting Screwed by Salesforce's $2.5 Billion Deal," *Forbes,* June 5, 2013, http://www.forbes.com/sites/rajsabhlok/2013/06/05/salesforces-2-5-billion-deal-customers-will-pay-one-way-or-another/ (accessed August 15, 2016).

Salesforce.com website, http://www.salesforce.com/ (accessed August 15, 2016).

Salesforce.com, "Recognition," http://www.salesforce.com/company/awards/ (accessed August 15, 2016).

Salesforce.com, "GE," http://www.salesforce.com/customers/stories/ge.jsp (accessed August 15, 2016).

Salesforce.com, "Grants and Programs," http://www.salesforce.org/grants/ (accessed August 15, 2016).

Salesforce.com, "Salesforce.com Foundation Announces $10 Million in Grants for San Francisco's District 10 in Celebration of the Tenth Annual Dreamforce," September 17, 2012, http://www.salesforce.com/company/news-press/press-releases/2012/09/120917-2.jsp (accessed August 15, 2016).

Salesforce.com, "Salesforce Touch is Upgrading to Salesforce1," https://releasenotes.docs.salesforce.com/en-us/winter14/release-notes/rn_186_mobile_touch.htm (accessed August 15, 2016).

"Salesforce.com Inc.," *The New York Times,* http://topics.nytimes.com/top/news/business/companies/salesforce-com-inc/index.html (accessed August 15, 2016).

"Salesforce.com Named One of the 'World's Most Ethical Companies' in 2010 for the Fourth Consecutive Year," Salesforce.com, March 29, 2010, http://www.salesforce.com/company/news-press/press-releases/2010/03/100329.jsp (accessed August 15, 2016).

"Salesforce Takes on Dropbox with Cloud Storage and File Sharing," *Forbes*, September 14, 2012, http://www.forbes.com/sites/greatspeculations/2012/09/14/salesforce-takes-on-dropbox-with-cloud-storage-and-file-sharing-services/ (accessed August 27, 2014).

Salesforce.com, "Transform Your Organization with Salesforce CRM," Salesforce.com Foundation, http://www.salesforcefoundation.org/get-started/ (accessed August 7, 2014).

Salesforce.org, "Integrated Philanthropy," http://www.salesforce.com/company/salesforceorg/ (accessed August 15, 2016).

Salesforce.org, "The Power of Us Program," http://www.salesforce.org/nonprofit/power-of-us/ (accessed August 15, 2016).

Salesforce.org, "Pro Bono Support," http://www.salesforce.org/volunteers/probono/ (accessed August 15, 2016).

Tracey E. Schelmetic, "Mixed Fiscal News for Salesforce.com," *www.tmcnet.com*, August 24, 2012, http://salesforce-news.tmcnet.com/salesforce/articles/304715-mixed-fiscal-news-salesforcecom.htm (accessed August 15, 2016).

Tom Taulli, "Salesforce.com Puts a $400 Million Small Business Project—Into the Cloud," *Forbes*, April 21, 2011, http://www.forbes.com/sites/tomtaulli/2011/04/21/salesforce-com-puts-a-400-million-small-biz-project-into-the-cloud/#4518c46f600b (accessed August 15, 2016).

Christpher Tkaczyk, "Bring Your Best Friend to Work," *Fortune*, August 11, 2014, p. 26.

Maria Verlengia, "Salesforce.com Gears Up for a Social, Transparent World, *www.crmbuyer*.com, May 2, 2011, http://www.crmbuyer.com/story/Salesforcecom-Gears-Up-for-a-Social-Transparent-World-72341.html?wlc=1304361793 (accessed August 15, 2016).

Rick Whitig, "Salesforce Adds Business Process Development to Force.com," *CRN*, February 3, 2010, http://www.crn.com/news/applications-os/222600988/salesforce-adds-business-process-development-to-force-com.htm;jsessionid=03xBP7Xtm2jGexbN9GQZ7Q**.ecappj01 (accessed November 19, 2012).

Mattel Responds to Ethical Challenges

INTRODUCTION

Mattel, Inc. is a global leader in designing and manufacturing toys and family products. Well-known for brands such as Barbie, Fisher-Price, Disney, Hot Wheels, Matchbox, Cabbage Patch Dolls, and board games, the company boasts nearly $5.7 billion in annual revenue. Headquartered in El Segundo, California, Mattel is the second largest toymaker in the world. Today, approximately 46 percent of its sales are from international customers.

It all started in a California garage workshop when Ruth and Elliot Handler and Matt Matson founded Mattel in 1945. The company started out making picture frames, but the founders soon recognized the profitability of the toy industry and switched their emphasis to toys. Mattel became a publicly owned company in 1960, with sales exceeding $100 million by 1965. Over the next 50 years, Mattel went on to become the world's largest toy company in terms of revenue.

In spite of its overall success, Mattel has had its share of losses over its history. During the mid- to late 1990s, Mattel lost millions to declining sales and bad business acquisitions. In January 1997, Jill Barad took over as Mattel's CEO. Barad's management-style was characterized as strict and her tenure at the helm proved challenging for many employees. While Barad had been successful in building the Barbie brand to $2 billion by the end of the twentieth century, growth slowed in the early twenty-first. Declining sales at outlets such as Toys "R" Us marked the start of some difficulties for the retailer, responsibilities for which Barad accepted and resigned in 2000.

Robert Eckert replaced Barad as CEO. Aiming to turn things around, Eckert sold unprofitable units and cut hundreds of jobs. In 2000, under Eckert, Mattel was granted the highly sought-after licensing agreement for products related to the *Harry Potter* series of books and movies. The company continued to flourish and build its reputation, even earning the Corporate Responsibility Award from UNICEF

in 2003. Mattel released its first Annual Corporate Responsibility Report the following year. Eckert retired as CEO in 2011, and he was replaced by former COO Bryan Stockton. In 2015, amid declining sales, Stockton was replaced with former chief executive of PepsiCo Christopher Sinclair.

MATTEL'S CORE PRODUCTS

Mattel has a number of well-known brands under the Mattel and Fisher-Price names. Fisher-Price focuses more on toys for infants and has been a subsidiary of Mattel since 1993. Some of Mattel's more popular brands through the years have included Barbie, Hot Wheels, and Cabbage Patch dolls. This section will briefly describe these brands and their major influence on the success of Mattel.

Barbie and American Girl

Among its many lines of popular toy products, Mattel is famous for owning top girls' brands. In 1959, Mattel introduced a product that would change its future forever: the Barbie doll. One of the founders, Ruth Handler, had noticed how her daughter loved playing with paper cutout dolls. She decided to create a doll based on an adult rather than on a baby. Barbie took off to become one of Mattel's critical product lines and the number one girls' brand in the world. Annual sales of Barbie net approximately $1 billion, and one doll is sold approximately every three seconds. The Barbie line today includes dolls, accessories, Barbie software, and a broad assortment of licensed products such as books, apparel, food, home furnishings, home electronics, and movies.

The popularity of Barbie has allowed Mattel to introduce many different versions of the iconic doll. Barbie has had at least 40 different nationalities, and the company has partnered with 75 different fashion designers throughout the years to design Barbie's outfits. Mattel has also found that while Barbie is popular with children, many adults enjoy collecting special-

*This case was prepared by Debbie Thorne, John Fraedrich, and O.C. Ferrell © 2017. Jennifer Sawayda and Jennifer Jackson provided editorial assistance. This case is meant for classroom discussion and is not meant to illustrate either effective or ineffective handling of an administrative, ethical, or legal decision by management. All sources used for this case were obtained through publicly available materials.

edition Barbie dolls as a pastime. Mattel often releases limited-edition Barbie dolls at a more expensive price geared toward adult collectors.

Despite Barbie's longstanding popularity, in recent years sales of the Barbie brand have plummeted. Barbie appears to have reached the maturity stage of the product life cycle. Mattel needed to find a way to reignite interest in its Barbie brand.

The company decided that it wanted young girls to be able to see themselves in the Barbie brand. For years Mattel has withstood criticism that Barbie's thin body shape was unrealistic and set unhealthy standards for girls. To reposition the Barbie brand, Mattel introduced Barbie in three body types: petite, curvy, and tall. These new Barbie dolls will come in a variety of ethnicities and hair styles, reflecting the multicultural nature of the girls that play with them. Mattel is hoping these new versions will resonate with its target market and push Barbie back into the growth stage.

To supplement the Barbie line, in 1998 Mattel acquired a popular younger type of doll. Mattel announced it would pay $700 million to Pleasant Co. for its high-end American Girl collection. American Girl dolls are sold with books about their lives, which take place during important periods of U.S. history. The American Girls brand includes several book series, accessories, clothing for dolls and girls, and a magazine that ranks in the top ten American children's magazines.

Hot Wheels

Hot Wheels roared into the toy world in 1968. Co-founder Elliot Handler recognized the potential demand for die-cast cars among boys and decided to create a toy that would compete with British company Lesney's Matchbox toys (Lesney was later acquired by Mattel). The original hot wheels were 1:64 scale, but in 1970 they were expanded to include cars that were 1:43 scale. More than 40 years later, the brand is hotter than ever and includes high-end collectibles, NASCAR (National Association for Stock Car Auto Racing) and Formula One models for adults, high-performance cars, track sets, and play sets for children of all ages. The brand is connected with racing circuits worldwide. More than 15 million boys aged five to 15 are avid collectors, each owning 41 cars on average. Two Hot Wheels cars are sold every second of every day, and annual sales total approximately $1 billion. The brand began with cars designed to run on a track and

has evolved into a "lifestyle" brand with licensed Hot Wheels shirts, caps, lunch boxes, backpacks, and more.

Much like Barbie, there are many adult collectors of Hot Wheels. Many of these collectors were avid fans of Hot Wheels as children and continue to hold a favorable view of the toys as adults. Adult collectors are estimated to have about 1,550 cars on average. As a result, Mattel has created a Hot Wheels website for collectors. The website discusses upcoming Hot Wheel releases, special events, and other Hot Wheels news. Together, Hot Wheels and Barbie generate 25 percent of Mattel's revenue in North America.

Cabbage Patch Kids

Since the introduction of mass-produced Cabbage Patch Kids in 1982, more than 90 million dolls have been sold worldwide. In 1994, Mattel took over selling these beloved dolls after purchasing production rights from Hasbro. In 1996, Mattel created a new line of Cabbage Patch doll, called Snacktime Kids, which was expected to meet with immense success. The Snacktime Kids had moving mouths that enabled children to "feed" them plastic snacks. However, the product backfired. The toy had no on/off switch and reports of children getting their fingers or hair caught in the dolls' mouths surfaced during the 1996 holiday season. Mattel voluntarily pulled the dolls from store shelves by January 1997, and offered consumers a cash refund of $40 on returned dolls. The U.S. Consumer Product Safety Commission applauded Mattel's handling of the Snacktime Kids situation. Mattel effectively managed a situation that could easily have created bad publicity or a crisis situation. Mattel stopped producing Cabbage Patch Kids in 2000.

MATTEL'S COMMITMENT TO ETHICS AND SOCIAL RESPONSIBILITY

Mattel's core products and business environment create many ethical issues. Because the company's products are designed primarily for children, it must be sensitive to social concerns about children's rights. It must also be aware that the international environment often complicates business transactions. Different legal systems and cultural expectations about business can create ethical conflicts.

Finally, the use of technology may present ethical dilemmas, especially regarding consumer privacy.

Mattel has recognized these potential issues and taken steps to strengthen its commitment to business ethics. The company also purports to take a stand on social responsibility, encouraging its employees and consumers to do the same. Although it has faced challenges in the past, Mattel has been recognized as an ethical company. In 2015 it was nominated as one of the World's Most Ethical companies by the Ethisphere Institute.

Privacy and Marketing Technology

One issue Mattel has tried to address repeatedly is that of privacy and online technology. Advances in technology have created special marketing issues for Mattel. The company recognizes that, because it markets to children, it must communicate with parents regarding its corporate marketing strategy. Mattel has taken steps to inform both children and adults about its philosophy regarding Internet-based marketing tools. The privacy policy on the Mattel websites describes how Mattel does not collect online information from children under the age of 13 without parental consent. The policy also discusses the use of cookies and describes how users can opt out of some of the tracking features. In 2013, Mattel updated its privacy policy on the website to make the site more informative. For instance, the policy discusses mobile applications, pixel tags, social media platforms, and targeted advertising. To increase understanding Mattel also developed answers for some of the most frequently asked Internet privacy questions. By assuring parents that their children's privacy will be respected, Mattel demonstrates that it takes its responsibility of marketing to children seriously.

Expectations of Mattel's Business Partners

Mattel, Inc. is also making a serious commitment to business ethics in its dealings with other industries. In late 1997, the company completed its first full ethics audit of each of its manufacturing sites as well as the facilities of its primary contractors. The audit revealed that the company was not using any child labor or forced labor, a problem plaguing other overseas manufacturers. However, several contractors were found to be in violation of Mattel's safety and human rights standards and were asked to change their operations or risk losing Mattel's business. The company now conducts unannounced audits in manufacturing facilities periodically.

In an effort to continue its strong record on human rights and related ethical standards, Mattel instituted a code of conduct entitled Global Manufacturing Principles in 1997. One of these principles requires all Mattel-owned and contracted manufacturing facilities to favor business partners committed to ethical standards comparable with those of Mattel. Other principles relate to safety, wages, and adherence to local laws. Mattel's audits and subsequent code of conduct were designed as preventative, not punitive, measures. The company is dedicated to creating and encouraging responsible business practices throughout the world.

Mattel also claims to be committed to its workforce. Mattel cares deeply about increasing its employees' skill sets and providing opportunities to excel. This reflects Mattel's concern for relationships between and with employees and business partners. The company's code is a signal to potential partners, customers, and other stakeholders that Mattel has made a commitment to fostering and upholding ethical values.

Legal and Ethical Business Practices

Mattel prefers to partner with businesses similarly committed to high ethical standards. At a minimum, partners must comply with the local and national laws of the countries in which they operate. In addition, all partners must respect the intellectual property of the company, and support Mattel in the protection of assets such as patents, trademarks, or copyrights. They are also responsible for product safety and quality, protecting the environment, customs, evaluation and monitoring, and compliance.

Mattel's business partners must have high standards for product safety and quality, adhering to practices that meet Mattel's safety and quality standards. In recent years, however, safety standards have been seriously violated, which will be discussed in more detail later. Also, because of the global nature of Mattel's business and its history of leadership in this area, the company insists that business partners strictly adhere to local and international customs laws. Partners must also comply with all import and export regulations. To assist in compliance with standards, Mattel's 1997 Global Manufacturing Principles insists that all manufacturing facilities provide the following:

- Full access for on-site inspections by Mattel or parties designated by Mattel
- Full access to those records that will enable Mattel to determine compliance with its principles
- An annual statement of compliance with Mattel's Global Manufacturing Principles, signed by an officer of the manufacturer or manufacturing facility

Source: Quoted in S. Prakash Sethi, Emre A. Veral, H. Jack Shapiro, and Olga Emelianova, *Journal of Business Ethics* 99 (2011): 483–517.

With the creation of the Mattel Independent Monitoring Council (MIMCO), Mattel became the first global consumer products company to apply such a system to facilities and core contractors worldwide. The company seeks to maintain an independent monitoring system that provides checks and balances to help ensure that standards are met.

If certain aspects of Mattel's manufacturing principles are not being met, Mattel will try to work with them to help them fix their problems. New partners will not be hired unless they meet Mattel's standards. If corrective action is advised but not taken, Mattel will terminate its relationship with the partner in question. Overall, Mattel is committed to both business success and ethical standards, and it recognizes that it is part of a continuous improvement process.

Mattel Children's Foundation

Mattel takes its social responsibilities very seriously. Through the Mattel Children's Foundation, established in 1978, the company promotes philanthropy and community involvement among its employees and makes charitable investments to better the lives of children in need. Funding priorities have included building a new Mattel Children's Hospital at the University of California, Los Angeles (UCLA), sustaining the Mattel Family Learning Program, and promoting giving among Mattel employees.

In November 1998, Mattel donated a multiyear, $25 million gift to the UCLA Children's Hospital. The gift was meant to support the existing hospital and provide for a new state-of-the-art facility. In honor of Mattel's donation, the hospital was renamed Mattel Children's Hospital at UCLA.

The Mattel Family Learning Program utilizes computer learning labs as a way to advance children's basic skills. Now numbering more than 80 throughout the United States, Hong Kong, Canada, and Mexico, the labs offer software and technology designed to help children with special needs or limited English proficiency.

Mattel employees are also encouraged to participate in a wide range of volunteer activities. Employees serving on boards of local nonprofit organizations or helping with ongoing nonprofit programs are eligible to apply for volunteer grants supporting their organizations. Mattel employees contributing to higher education or to nonprofit organizations serving children in need are eligible to have their personal donations matched dollar for dollar up to $5,000 annually.

International Manufacturing Principles

As a U.S.-based multinational company owning and operating facilities and contracting worldwide, Mattel's Global Manufacturing Principles reflect not only its need to conduct manufacturing responsibly but also to respect the cultural, ethical, and philosophical differences of the countries in which it operates. These principles set uniform standards across Mattel manufacturers and attempt to benefit both employees and consumers.

Mattel's principles cover issues such as wages, work hours, child labor, forced labor, discrimination, freedom of association, and working conditions. Workers must be paid at least minimum wage or a wage that meets local industry standards (whichever is greater). No one under the age of 16 or the local age limit (whichever is higher) may be allowed to work for Mattel facilities. Mattel refuses to work with facilities that use forced or prison labor, or to use these types of labor itself. Additionally, Mattel does not tolerate discrimination. The company states that an individual should be hired and employed based on his or her ability—not on individual characteristics or beliefs. Mattel recognizes all employees' rights to choose to associate with organizations without interference. Regarding working conditions, all Mattel facilities and its business partners must provide safe working environments for their employees. In 2015, when China Labor Watch reported concerns that workers were being overworked and underpaid in Chinese factories making Mattel toys, Mattel launched an investigation to determine whether the allegations were true.

OVERSEAS MANUFACTURING

Despite Mattel's best efforts, not all overseas manufacturers have faithfully adhered to its high standards. Mattel has come under scrutiny over its sale of unsafe products. In September 2007, Mattel announced recalls of toys containing lead paint. The problem surfaced when a European retailer discovered lead paint on a toy. An estimated 10 million individual toys produced in China were affected. Mattel quickly stopped production at Lee Der, the company officially producing the recalled toys, after it was discovered that Lee Der had purchased lead-tainted paint to be used on the toys. Mattel blamed the fiasco on the manufacturers' desire to save money in the face of increasing prices. Mattel CEO Robert Eckert indicated that rising labor and raw material costs and the resulting pressure it created likely caused manufacturers to cut corners in order to save money.

The situation began when Early Light Industrial Co., a subcontractor for Mattel owned by Hong Kong toy tycoon Choi Chee Ming, subcontracted the painting of parts of *Cars* toys to another China-based vendor. The vendor, named Hong Li Da, decided to source paint from a non-authorized third-party supplier—a violation of Mattel's requirement to use paint supplied directly by Early Light. The products were found to contain "impermissible levels of lead."

On August 2, 2007, it was announced that another of Early Light's subcontractors, Lee Der Industrial Co., used the same lead paint found on *Cars* products. China immediately suspended the company's export license. Afterward, Mattel pinpointed three paint suppliers working for Lee Der—Dongxin, Zhongxin, and Mingdai. This paint was used by Lee Der to produce Mattel's line of Fisher-Price products. It is said that Lee Der purchased the paint from Mingdai due to an intimate friendship between the two company's owners. On August 11, 2007, Zhang Shuhong, operator of Lee Der, hung himself after paying his 5,000 staff members.

Later that month, Mattel was forced to recall several more toys because of powerful magnets in the toys that could come loose and pose a choking hazard for young children. If more than one magnet is swallowed, the magnets can attract each other inside the child's stomach, causing potentially fatal complications. Over 21 million Mattel toys were recalled in all, and parents filed several lawsuits claiming that these Mattel products harmed their children.

At first, Mattel blamed Chinese subcontractors for the huge toy recalls, but the company later accepted a portion of the blame for its troubles, while maintaining that Chinese manufacturers were largely at fault. The Chinese view the situation quite differently. As reported by the state-run Xinhua news agency, the spokesman for China's General Administration of Quality Supervision and Inspection and Quarantine (AQSIQ) stated that the importers were simply doing their jobs and that the toys conformed to the necessary regulations when created. The spokesman placed the blame on Mattel's quality control. Mattel also faced criticism from many of its consumers, who believed Mattel was denying culpability by placing much of the blame on China. Mattel was later awarded the 2007 "Bad Product" Award by Consumers International.

How did this crisis occur under the watch of a company praised for its ethics and high safety standards? Although Mattel had investigated its contractors, it did not audit the entire supply chain, including subcontractors. Such oversights left room for these violations. Mattel has also moved to enforce a rule that subcontractors cannot hire suppliers two or three tiers down. In a statement, Mattel says it has spent more than 50,000 hours investigating its vendors and testing its toys. Mattel also announced a three-point plan. This plan aims to tighten Mattel's control of production, discover and prevent the unauthorized use of subcontractors, and test the products itself rather than depending on contractors.

THE CHINESE GOVERNMENT'S REACTION

Chinese officials eventually did admit the government's failure to properly protect the public. The Chinese government promised to tighten supervision of exported products, but effective supervision is challenging in such a large country that is so burdened with corruption. In January 2008, the Chinese government launched a four-month-long nationwide product quality campaign, offering intensive training courses to domestic toy manufacturers to help them brush up on their knowledge of international product standards and safety awareness. As a result of the crackdown, AQSIQ announced that it had revoked the licenses of more than 600 Chinese toymakers. As of 2008, the State Administration for Commerce and Industry (SACI) released a report claiming that 87.5 percent of China's newly manufactured toys met quality requirements. While this represents an improvement, the temptation to cut corners remains strong in a country that uses price, not quality, as its main competitive advantage. Where there is demand, there will be people trying to turn a quick profit.

MATTEL VERSUS FORMER EMPLOYEE AND MGA

In 2004, Mattel became embroiled in a bitter intellectual property rights battle with former employee Carter Bryant and MGA Entertainment Inc. over rights to MGA's popular Bratz dolls. Carter Bryant, an on-again/off-again Mattel employee, designed the Bratz dolls and pitched them to MGA. A few months after the pitch, Bryant left Mattel to work at MGA, which began producing Bratz in 2001. In 2002, Mattel launched an investigation into whether Bryant had designed the Bratz dolls while employed with Mattel. After two years of investigation, Mattel sued Bryant. A year later MGA fired off a suit of its own, claiming that Mattel was creating Barbies with looks similar to those of Bratz in an effort to eliminate the competition. Mattel answered by expanding its own suit to include MGA and its CEO, Isaac Larian.

For decades, Barbie has reigned supreme on the doll market. However, Bratz dolls gave Barbie a run for her money. In 2005, four years after the brand's debut, Bratz sales were at $2 billion. At the same time, Barbie was suffering from declining sales. Although still widely popular, many analysts believe that Barbie has reached the maturity stage of its product life cycle. Concerns have increased in recent years as Barbie sales continue to drop significantly. This is requiring Mattel to try and popularize Barbie in other markets, such as China.

Four years after the initial suit was filed, Bryant settled with Mattel under an undisclosed set of terms. In July 2008, a jury deemed MGA and its CEO liable for what it termed "intentional interference" regarding Bryant's contract with Mattel. In August 2008, Mattel received damages in the range of $100 million. Although Mattel first requested damages of $1.8 billion, the company seemed pleased with the principle behind the victory.

In December 2008, Mattel appeared to win another victory when a California judge banned MGA from issuing or selling any more Bratz dolls. However, the tide soon turned on Mattel's victory. In July 2010, the Ninth U.S. Circuit Court of Appeals threw out the ruling. Eventually, the case came down to whether Mattel owned Bryant's ideas under the contract he had with the company. In April 2011, a California federal jury rejected Mattel's claims to ownership. In another blow to Mattel, the jury also ruled that the company had stolen trade secrets from MGA. According to the allegations, Mattel employees used fake business cards to get into MGA showrooms during toy fairs. Mattel was ordered to pay $85 million in liabilities, plus an additional $225 million in damages and legal fees. MGA CEO Isaac Larian also announced that he was filing an antitrust case against Mattel. Mattel continues to claim that Bryant violated his contract when he was working for the company.

Although the conflict appeared to be settled, the fight between MGA and Mattel continued. The antitrust suit against Mattel was dismissed, and in January 2013 the U.S Court of Appeals overturned MGA's victory over Mattel concerning the theft of trade secrets. However, the court maintains that Mattel is responsible for paying MGA's legal fines totaling $137.2 million. MGA CEO Isaac Larian was determined to contest this issue in court again and has referred to the people at Mattel as "crooks." MGA filed a lawsuit against Mattel claiming that the firm stole its trade secrets. Mattel attempted to get the court's permission to have MGA's lawsuit blocked, but a district court in California ruled that the trade theft lawsuit could proceed.

MATTEL LOOKS TOWARD THE FUTURE

Like all major companies, Mattel has weathered its share of storms. The company has faced a series of difficult and potentially crippling challenges, including the lawsuits with MGA regarding ownership of the Bratz dolls. During the wave of toy recalls, some analysts suggested that the company's reputation was battered beyond repair. Mattel, however, has refused to go quietly. Although the company admits to poorly handling past affairs, it is attempting to rectify its mistakes and to prevent future mistakes as well.

Until recently, Mattel was the world's largest toymaker. However, in 2014 Lego surpassed Mattel. The competition between toymakers is intensifying. To meet the competition, Mattel acquired Canada's Mega

Brands Inc.—also popular for its construction blocks—for $366.4 million. It is adapting its Barbie brands to different countries as well. In China it started introducing Barbie dolls with an education theme, such 'Violin Soloist' Barbie, to appeal to Chinese parents' values for education. However, with sales of its most popular brands decreasing, Mattel may have to start looking for other blockbuster products. Mattel is hard at work restoring goodwill and faith in its brands, even as it continues to be plagued with residual distrust over the lead paint scandal and its alleged theft of trade secrets. Reputations are hard won and easily lost, but Mattel appears to be steadfast in its commitment to restoring its reputation.

Questions for Discussion

1. Do manufacturers of products for children have special obligations to consumers and society? If so, what are these responsibilities?
2. How effective has Mattel been at encouraging ethical and legal conduct by its manufacturers? What changes and additions would you make to the company's Global Manufacturing Principles?
3. To what extent is Mattel responsible for issues related to its production of toys in China? How might Mattel have avoided these issues?

Sources

American Girl, www.americangirl.com (accessed August 16, 2016).

Lisa Bannon and Carlta Vitzhum, "One-Toy-Fits-All: How Industry Learned to Love the Global Kid," *Wall Street Journal*, April 29, 2003, http://online.wsj.com/article/SB105156578439799000.html (accessed August 16, 2016).

David Barboza, "Scandal and Suicide in China: a Dark Side of Toys," *New York Times*, August 23, 2007, http://www.nytimes.com/2007/08/23/business/worldbusiness/23suicide.html?pagewanted=all (accessed August 16, 2016).

David Barboza and Louise Story, "Toymaking in China, Mattel'S Way," *New York Times*, July 26, 2007, http://www.nytimes.com/2007/07/26/business/26toy.html?pagewanted=1&_r=3&hp (accessed August 16, 2016).

Brooks Barnes, "Thomas the Tank Engine to Receive a Multimillion Dollar Sheen," *The New York Times*, December 30, 2012, http://www.nytimes.com/2012/12/31/business/media/mattel-to-give-thomas-the-tank-engine-a-multimillion-dollar-sheen.html (accessed August 16, 2016).

"Bratz Loses Battle of the Dolls," *BBC News*, December 5, 2008, http://news.bbc.co.uk/2/hi/business/7767270.stm (accessed August 15, 2014).

Adam Bryant, "Mattel CEO Jill Barad and a Toyshop That Doesn't Forget to Play," *New York Times*, October 11, 1998.

Laurie Burkitt, "In China, Mattel Tries 'Violin Soloist' Barbie," *The Wall Street Journal*, November 8, 2013, p. B3.

Laurie Burkitt, "Mattel Plants Face Scrutiny in China," *The Wall Street Journal*, October 17, 2013, p. B3.

Nicholas Casey, "Mattel Prevails Over MGA in Bratz-Doll Trial," *The Wall Street Journal*, July 18, 2008, pp. B18, B19.

Nicholas Casey, "Mattel to Get Up to $100 Million in Bratz Case," *The Wall Street Journal*, August 27, 2008, http://online.wsj.com/news/articles/SB121978263398273857 (accessed August 16, 2016).

Andrea Chang, "Mattel Must Pay MGA $310 Million in Bratz Case," *Los Angeles Times*, August 5, 2011, http://articles.latimes.com/2011/aug/05/business/la-fi-mattel-bratz-20110805 (accessed August 15, 2014).

Shu-Ching Chen, "A Blow to Hong Kong's Toy King," *Forbes*, August 15, 2007, http://www.forbes.com/2007/08/15/mattel-china-choi-face-markets-cx_jc_0815autofacescan01.html (accessed August 16, 2016).

Consumers International, *International Bad Product Awards 2007*, http://marketing.by/webroot/delivery/files/InternationalBadProductsAwards-pressbriefing.pdf (accessed August 15, 2014).

Bill Duryea, "Barbie-holics: They're Devoted to the Doll," *St. Petersburg Times*, August 7, 1998.

Rachel Engers, "Mattel Board Members Buy $30 Million in Stock: Insider Focus," *Bloomberg*, December 22, 2000.

The Ethisphere Institute, "World's Most Ethical Companies—Honorees," *Ethisphere*, http://ethisphere.com/worlds-most-ethical/wme-honorees/ (accessed August 16, 2016).

Miranda Hitti, "9 Million Mattel Toys Recalled," *WebMD*, August 14, 2007, http://children.webmd.com/news/20070814/9_million_mattel_toys_recalled (accessed August 16, 2016).

Gina Keating, "MGA 'Still Accessing' Impact of Bratz Ruling: CEO," *Yahoo! News*, December 4, 2008, http://www.reuters.com/article/2008/12/05/us-mattel-larian-idUSTRE4B405820081205 (accessed August 16, 2016).

"Learning from Mattel," Tuck School of Business at Dartmouth, http://mba.tuck.dartmouth.edu/pdf/2002-1-0072.pdf (accessed August 16, 2016).

Judith Levy, "Third Toy Recall by Mattel in Five Weeks," *Business Standard,* September 5, 2007, http://seekingalpha.com/article/46374-mattel-announces-third-toy-recall (accessed August 16, 2016).

Shan Li, "Mattel CEO Robert Eckert to be Replaced by COO Bryan Stockton," *Los Angeles Times,* November 21, 2011, http://latimesblogs.latimes.com/money_co/2011/11/mattel-ceo-robert-eckert-steps-down-bryan-stockton.html (accessed August 16, 2016).

"Mattel and U.S. Consumer Product Safety Commission Announce Voluntary Refund Program for Cabbage Patch Kids Snacktime Kids Dolls," U.S. Consumer Product Safety Commission, Office of Information and Public Affairs, Release No. 97-055, January 6, 1997.

"Mattel Awarded $100M in Doll Lawsuit," *USA Today*, August 27, 2008, p. B1.

Mattel, Inc., *2014 Annual Report,* http://files.shareholder.com/downloads/MAT/0x0x820303/68C602DD-88F3-47F8-ABB5-46635E8495D8/Mattel_-_Bookmarked_2014_Annual_Report_Final_.PDF (accessed August 16, 2016).

Mattel, Inc., "About Us," Mattel, http://corporate.mattel.com/about-us/ (accessed February 19, 2013).

Mattel, Inc., *Annual Report 2011*, http://files.shareholder.com/downloads/MAT/2319434112x0x555821/3C654248-30D8-4A8D-A8FC-53A89560A3C3/2011_Mattel_Annual_Report.pdf (accessed August 16, 2016).

Mattel, Inc., "Barbie," http://www.barbie.com/ (accessed August 16, 2016).

Mattel, Inc., "Hot Wheels," www.hotwheels.com/ (accessed August 16, 2016).

Mattel, Inc., "Independent Monitoring Council Completes Audits of Mattel Plants in China and Mexico," May 7, 2001, http://investor.shareholder.com/mattel/releasedetail.cfm?releaseid=43066 (accessed August 16, 2016).

Mattel Inc., *Mattel Annual Report 2008*, 2009, http://files.shareholder.com/downloads/MAT/2328843115x0x283677/D4E18CB7-C8B4-4A28-BCE9-C114B248A26D/MattelAnnualReport2008.pdf (accessed August 16, 2016).

Mattel, Inc., "Mattel Children's Foundation," http://corporate.mattel.com/about-us/philanthropy/children-foundation.aspx (accessed August 16, 2016).

Mattel, Inc., "Mattel, Inc. Online Privacy Statement," 2013, http://corporate.mattel.com/privacy-statement.aspx (accessed August 16, 2016).

Marla Matzer, "Deals on Hot Wheels," *Los Angeles Times,* July 22, 1998.

Nasdaq, "MAT Company Financials," http://www.nasdaq.com/symbol/mat/financials?query=income-statement (accessed August 16, 2016).

Benjamin B. Olshin, "China, Culture, and Product Recalls," *S2R*, August 20, 2007, http://www.s2r.biz/s2rpapers/papers-Chinese_Product.pdf (accessed August 15, 2014).

Kim Peterson, "As Sales Plunge, Can Barbie Stay Relevant?" *CBS News,* February 3, 2014, http://www.cbsnews.com/news/as-sales-plunge-can-barbie-stay-relevant/ (accessed August 16, 2016)

Edvard Pettersson, "Mattel Wins Dismissal of MGA Entertainment's $1 Billion Antitrust Lawsuit," *Bloomberg,* February 22, 2012, http://www.bloomberg.com/news/articles/2012-02-22/mattel-wins-dismissal-of-mga-entertainment-s-1-billion-antitrust-lawsuit (accessed August 16, 2016).

Edvard Petterssen and Karen Gullo, "MGA Bratz Win Over Mattel Partly Erased by Appeals Court," *Bloomberg*, January 24, 2013, http://www.bloomberg.com/news/articles/2013-01-24/mga-bratz-win-over-mattel-partly-erased-by-appeals-court (accessed August 16, 2016).

PR Newswire, "Independent Monitoring Council Completes Audits of Mattel Manufacturing Facilities in Indonesia, Malaysia and Thailand," November 15, 2002, http://www.prnewswire.com/news-releases/independent-monitoring-council-completes-audits-of-mattel-manufacturing-facilities-in-indonesia-malaysia-and-thailand-76850522.html (accessed August 16, 2016).

PR Newswire, "Mattel, Inc., Launches Global Code of Conduct Intended to Improve Workplace, Workers' Standard of Living," November 20, 1997, http://www.prnewswire.com/news-releases/mattel-inc-launches-global-code-of-conduct-intended-to-improve-workplace-workers-standard-of-living-77630507.html (accessed August 16, 2016).

PR Newswire, "Mattel Reports Fourth Quarter and Full Year 2015 Financial Results and Declares Quarterly Dividend," February 1, 2016, http://www.prnewswire.com/news-releases/mattel-reports-fourth-quarter-and-full-year-2015-financial-results-and-declares-quarterly-dividend-300213040.html (accessed August 16, 2016).

S. Prakash Sethi, Emre A. Veral, H. Jack Shapiro, and Olga Emelianova, *Journal of Business Ethics* 99 (2011): 483–517.

Jack A. Raisner, "Using the 'Ethical Environment' Paradigm to Teach Business Ethics: The Case of the Maquiladoras," *Journal of Business Ethics* 16 (1997): 1331–1346.

Patricia Sellers, "The 50 Most Powerful Women in American Business," *Fortune,* October 12, 1998.

Frank Shyong and Andrea Chang, "Award is Tossed in Bratz Lawsuit," *Los Angeles Times*, January 25, 2013, http://articles.latimes.com/2013/jan/25/business/la-fi-bratz-mattel-20130125 (accessed August 16, 2016).

Laura S. Spark, "Chinese Product Scares Prompt US Fears," *BBC News*, July 10, 2007, http://news.bbc.co.uk/2/hi/americas/6275758.stm (accessed August 16, 2016).

Staff Reports, "A History of Hot Wheels," *Albert Lea Tribune,* February 3, 2008, http://www.albertleatribune.com/2008/02/03/a-history-of-hot-wheels/ (accessed August 16, 2016).

"Toymaker Mattel Bans Child Labor," *Denver Post,* November 21, 1998.

United States Government Accountability Office, "The United States Has Not Restricted Imports Under the China Safeguard," September 2005, http://www.gao.gov/new.items/d051056.pdf (accessed August 16, 2016).

U.S. Consumer Products Safety Commission, *Mattel Recalls Batman™ and One Piece™ Magnetic Action Figure Sets*, August 14, 2007, http://service.mattel.com/us/recall/J1944CPSC.pdf (accessed August 16, 2016).

Mandy Velez, "Mattel Agrees to Produce More Bald Barbie 'Ella' for Little Kids with Cancer," *The Huffington Post,* July 1, 2014, http://www.huffingtonpost.com/2014/07/01/mattel-to-continue-bald-ella-doll_n_5548672.html (accessed August 16, 2016).

Phil Wahba, "So much for Mattel ex-CEO resigning. He was fired," Fortune, April 9, 2015, http://fortune.com/2015/04/09/mattel-ceo-fired/ (accessed August 16, 2016).

Parker Waichman LLP, "Magnetic Toy Sets Defective Project Injury Lawsuits," http://www.yourlawyer.com/topics/overview/magnetic_toy_sets (accessed August 15, 2014).

Karen Weise, "Briefs: Mattel—Must Pay for Stealing Bratz Secrets," *Bloomberg Businessweek,* August 15–28, 2011, p. 22.

Michael White, "Barbie Will Lose Some Curves When Mattel Modernizes Icon," *Detroit News,* November 18, 1997.

Ann Zimmerman, "Mattel Loses in Bratz Spat," *The Wall Street Journal,* April 22, 2011, http://online.wsj.com/article/SB10001424052748703983704576276984087591872.html (accessed August 16, 2016).

Paul Ziobro, "Mattel Puts a Target on Lego," *The Wall Street Journal*, March 1–2, 2014, p. B3.

Abram Brown, "Toy Wars," *Forbes,* November 18, 2013, pp. 82–88.

Paul Ziobro, "Mattel Revenue Grows as Barbie Sales Increase," *The Wall Street Journal*, February 1, 2016, http://www.wsj.com/articles/mattel-says-barbie-sales-edge-higher-1454364171 (accessed August 16, 2016).

Rachel Abrams, "Barbie Adds Curvy and Tall to Body Shapes," *The New York Times*, January 28, 2016, http://www.nytimes.com/2016/01/29/business/barbie-now-in-more-shapes.html?_r=0 (accessed August 16, 2016).

Matthew Townsend, "Hello Barbie Pleads 'Buy Me' as Mattel Doll Fails to Catch Fire," *Bloomberg,* April 20, 2016, http://www.bloomberg.com/news/articles/2016-04-20/hello-barbie-pleads-buy-me-as-mattel-doll-fails-to-catch-fire (accessed August 16, 2016).

PR Newswire, "2nd District Court of Appeal Denies Mattel's Petition - MGA's $1 Billion Trade Secret Theft Case Against Mattel Will Continue," May 16, 2016, http://www.prnewswire.com/news-releases/2nd-district-court-of-appeal-denies-mattels-petition--mgas-1-billion-trade-secret-theft-case-against-mattel-will-continue-300269020.html (accessed August 16, 2016).

Claire Groden, "Hasbro, Mattel Toy Suppliers Slammed in Labor Report," *Fortune,* November 22, 2015, http://fortune.com/2015/11/22/hasbro-mattel-china-labor/ (accessed August 16, 2016).

Home Depot Implements Stakeholder Orientation

INTRODUCTION

When Bernie Marcus and Arthur Blank opened the first Home Depot store in Atlanta in 1979, they forever changed the hardware and home-improvement retailing industry. Marcus and Blank envisioned huge warehouse-style stores stocked with an extensive selection of products offered at the lowest prices. Do-it-yourselfers and building contractors can browse among 40,000 different products for the home and yard, from kitchen and bathroom fixtures to carpeting, lumber, paint, tools, and plant and landscaping items. If a product is not provided in one of the stores, Home Depot offers 250,000 products that can be special ordered. Some Home Depot stores are open 24 hours a day, but customers can also order products online. Additionally, the company offers free home-improvement clinics to teach customers how to tackle everyday projects like tiling a bathroom. For those customers who prefer not to "do it yourself," most stores offer installation services. Knowledgeable employees, recognizable by their orange aprons, are on hand to help customers find items or to demonstrate the proper use of a particular tool.

Currently, Home Depot employs more than 385,000 people and operates over 2,274 Home Depot stores in the United States, Mexico, Puerto Rico, the Virgin Islands, Guam, and Canada. In 2015 the company acquired Interline Brands, a repair and maintenance products seller, as a subsidiary for $1.6 billion. Home Depot is the largest home-improvement retailer in the world, with over $88 billion in revenues and approximately $7 billion in net income. Home Depot continues to do things on a grand scale, including putting its corporate muscle behind a tightly focused social responsibility agenda and international expansion.

MANAGING CUSTOMER RELATIONSHIPS

Back in 2006, John Costello was the Chief Marketing Officer, or "Chief Customer Officer," as he refers to the position. Costello consolidated marketing and merchandising functions to help consumers achieve their goals in home-improvement projects more effectively and efficiently. According to Costello, "Above all else, a brand is a promise. It says here's what you can expect if you do business with us. Our mission is to empower our customers to achieve the home or condo of their dreams." When Costello arrived in 2002 Home Depot's reputation was faltering. His plan called for overhauling the Home Depot website as well as integrating mass marketing and direct marketing with in-store experience. The new philosophy was expressed by the new Home Depot mantra: "You can do it. We can help." Teams of people from merchandising, marketing, visual merchandising, and operations attempted to provide the very best shopping experience. The idea was simple. Home Depot believed that customers should be able to read and understand how one ceiling fan is different from another, and associates (employees) should be able to offer installation and design advice.

In 2008 Frank Bifulco took over as new Chief Marketing Officer and Senior Vice President. It was a tough time for Home Depot. Because of the 2008–2009 recession, consumers were spending less on their homes. Home Depot's new marketing strategy was to emphasize the store's everyday low prices, high product value, and quality energy-saving products. At the same time, the company cut back on special offers like discounts and promotions.

Despite Home Depot's proactive approach to customer issues, the company has had its share of challenges, even before the onset of the recession. The company was forced to deal with negative publicity

*This case was developed by Jennifer Sawayda, Michelle Urban, and Melanie Drever for and under the direction of O. C. Ferrell and Linda Ferrell © 2017. We appreciate the previous editorial assistance of Jennifer Jackson. This case was prepared for classroom discussion rather than to illustrate either effective or ineffective handling of an administrative, ethical, or legal decision by management. All sources used for this case were obtained through publicly available material.

associated with customer-satisfaction measures published by outside sources. The University of Michigan's annual American Customer Satisfaction Index in 2006 showed Home Depot slipping to last place among major U.S. retailers.

Some former managers at Home Depot have blamed the company's service issues on a culture that operated under principles reminiscent of the military. Under former CEO Robert Nardelli, some employees feared being terminated unless they followed directions to a tee. Harris Interactive's 2005 Reputation Quotient Survey ranked Home Depot number 12 among major companies and said that customers appreciated Home Depot's quality services. However, two years later the company had fallen to number 27 on the list. Nardelli was ousted and replaced by Frank Blake in January 2007. The start of 2008 seemed more auspicious for Home Depot as it was listed as number six on *Fortune*'s Most Admired Companies (still trailing behind Lowe's), up from 13 in 2006. Home Depot also bounced back up on the American Customer Satisfaction Index.

The increase of customer satisfaction was due to several efforts on the part of Frank Blake. The company's Twitter feed was inundated with comments from dissatisfied customers about the customer service they encountered in the stores. Blake quickly admitted to the customer service problems the company was facing, apologized for the inconvenience it caused the customers, and encouraged them to continue to leave their feedback so that they could make improvements. Each one of the complaints was addressed; some angry followers were appeased by phone calls from store managers and personal emails responding to their specific issues. The responsiveness of Blake and his Senior Manager of Social Media, Sarah Molinari, not only transformed angry protesters into enthusiastic fans but also resulted in a strategic advantage for the company in terms of how they deal with customer feedback.

Inside the stores, self-checkout lanes were installed so that customers do not have to spend time waiting in line. However, at peak hours, waiting in line cannot be avoided. During such situations, Home Depot Associates can scan items in customers' baskets while they are in line and hand them a card that holds all their purchases. When the customer reaches the cashier, they simply scan the card and pay the total they owe. Home Depot was also the first to partner with PayPal, making it easier for customers who do not want to carry their wallet or cash with them to be able to pay more conveniently. Many of the Home Depot Associates are given devices called "First Phone," which is a phone/walkie-talkie/scanner. This device allows associates to quickly help customers by being able to call or page fellow associates who can answer customers' questions and have immediate access to the price of an item by scanning it right where they stand.

Another way in which Home Depot attempts to practice good customer service and simultaneously act in a socially responsible manner is through its program designed to teach children basic carpentry skills. Home Depot provides a free program called the Kids Workshop available at all its stores. During the workshops, children learn to create objects that can be used around their homes or neighborhoods. Projects include toolboxes, mail organizers, and window birdhouses and bughouses. More than 1 million children have built toolboxes through Kids Workshops. Home Depot also offers free workshops especially designed for women, do-it-yourselfers, and new homeowners.

These efforts have paid off for Home Depot. Boosted by the rising housing market, Home Depot is outperforming the retail market at a time when retail sales are slipping. Home Depot has successfully transformed itself into a firm with strong service, offering great value to consumers.

ENVIRONMENTAL INITIATIVES

Cofounders Marcus and Blank nurtured a corporate culture that emphasizes social responsibility, especially with regard to the company's impact on the natural environment. Home Depot began its environmental program on the twentieth anniversary of Earth Day in 1990 by adopting a set of Environmental Principles (see Table 1). These principles have since been adopted by the National Retail Hardware Association and Home Center Institute, which represents more than 46,000 retail hardware stores and home centers.

Guided by these principles, Home Depot has initiated a number of programs to minimize the firm's—and its customers'—impact on the environment. In 1991, the retailer began using store and office supplies, advertising, signs, and shopping bags made with recycled content. It also established a process for evaluating the environmental claims made by suppliers. The following year, the firm launched a program to recycle wallboard shipping packaging, which became the industry's first "reverse distribution" program. In addition, it was the first retailer in the world to combine a drive-through recycling center with one of its Georgia stores in 1993. One year later Home Depot

TABLE 1 Home Depot's Environmental Principles

- We are committed to selling products that are manufactured, packaged and labeled in an environmentally responsible manner to preserve raw materials and eliminate unnecessary waste.

- We will support efforts to enforce accurate, informative labeling of products with environmental marketing claims.

- We will recycle and encourage the use of materials and products with recycled content.

- We will conserve natural resources by using energy and water wisely and seek further opportunities to reduce resource consumption and improve the efficiency of our stores, offices, and distribution network.

- We will comply with environmental laws and will maintain programs and procedures to ensure compliance.

- We are committed to minimizing the environmental health and safety risk for our associates and our customers.

- We will train our employees accordingly to enhance understanding of environmental issues, policies, and green products offered in our stores.

- We will encourage our customers to become environmentally conscious shoppers.

Source: Home Depot, "The Home Depot Environmental Principles," https://corporate.homedepot.com/CorporateResponsibility/Environment/Pages/Principals.aspx (accessed September 10, 2014).

became the first home-improvement retailer to offer wood products from tropical and temperate forests that were certified as "well-managed" by the Scientific Certification System's Forest Conservation Program. The company also began to replace its hardwood wooden shipping pallets with reusable "slip sheets" to minimize waste and energy usage and to decrease pressure on hardwood resources.

In 1999, Home Depot joined the Certified Forests Products Council, a nonprofit organization that promotes responsible forest product buying practices and the sale of wood from Certified Well-Managed Forests. Yet the company continued to sell products made from wood harvested from old growth forests. Protesters led by the Rainforest Action Network, an environmental group, had picketed Home Depot and other home center stores for years in an effort to stop the destruction of old growth forests, of which less than 20 percent still survive. Later that year, during Home Depot's twentieth anniversary celebration, Arthur Blank announced that Home Depot would stop selling products made from wood harvested in environmentally sensitive areas.

To be certified by the Forest Stewardship Council (FSC), a supplier's wood products must be tracked from the forest, through manufacturing and distribution, to the customer. Harvesting, manufacturing, and distribution practices must ensure a balance of social, economic, and environmental factors. Blank challenged competitors to follow Home Depot's lead, and within two years several had met that challenge, including Lowe's, the number-two home-improvement retailer; Wickes, a lumber company; and Andersen Corporation, a window manufacturer. By 2003, Home Depot reported that it

had reduced its purchases of Indonesian lauan, a tropical rainforest hardwood used in door components, by 70 percent, and it continued to increase its purchases of certified sustainable wood products. Over the course of 2010–2011, Home Depot installed solar panels on 62 of its retail stores, making it the largest retailer to host solar programs. The company set the goal of reducing its energy usage 20 percent by 2015. It exceeded this goal, reducing its energy usage 32 percent in that time frame. The firm also announced its intention to power 10 percent of its stores with Bloom Energy fuel cells by the end of 2016. These fuel cells placed on-site use a chemical reaction to produce electricity. It is estimated that 15 percent of electricity coming from power lines is lost. Producing electricity on-site will significantly decrease this amount of wasted electricity, allowing Home Depot to operate more efficiently and sustainably.

For these efforts and more, the company was honored by being ranked as one of the top 25 Socially Responsible Dividend Stocks, which means that it is recognized as being a socially responsible investment. Being a responsible investment is determined not only through its environmental initiatives, but also through its social impact.

These efforts have yielded many rewards in addition to improved relations with environmental stakeholders. Home Depot's environmental programs have earned the company an A on the Council on Economic Priorities Corporate Report Card, a Vision of America Award from Keep America Beautiful, and a President's Council for Sustainable Development Award. The company has also been recognized by the U.S. Environmental Protection Agency with its Energy Star Award for

Excellence. In 2015 Home Depot was named the 2015 Partner of the Year for Sustained Excellence.

CORPORATE PHILANTHROPY

In addition to its environmental initiatives, Home Depot focuses corporate social responsibility efforts on affordable housing and disaster relief. For instance, Home Depot believes that it has a philanthropic responsibility to improve the communities in which it operates. In 2002, the company founded the Home Depot Foundation, which provides additional resources to assist nonprofits in the United States and Canada. The Foundation awards grants to eligible nonprofits and partners with innovative nonprofits across the country that are working to increase awareness and successfully demonstrate the connection between housing, the urban forest, and the overall health and economic success of their communities. Since its inception, the Foundation has invested $300 million in building and renovating affordable, sustainable homes, improving local parks and playgrounds, and repairing community facilities in communities nationwide. In addition, the company has invested in transforming veteran houses. It estimates it has transformed 25,000 veteran homes since 2011. It is also a strong supporter of Habitat for Humanity International, donating $6.2 million for Habitat's Repair Corp. Program. In 2015 it announced it was partnering with seven nonprofits, including Habitat for Humanity, to make repairs on the homes of 400 veterans in the Atlanta area.

Additionally, Home Depot addresses the growing needs for relief from disasters such as hurricanes, tornadoes, and earthquakes. Not only are they one of the first entities on scene to help rebuild communities in times of disaster, but they also make an annual donation of $1 million to the American Red Cross Annual Disaster Giving Program (ADGP), which enables them to respond quickly in times of need. After the 9/11 terrorist attacks in 2001, the company set up three command centers with more than 200 associates to help coordinate relief supplies such as dust masks, gloves, batteries, and tools to victims and rescue workers. After the 2010 Haitian earthquake, Home Depot Mexico donated $30,000 to Habitat for Humanity to assist in Haiti's recovery efforts, in addition to launching a fundraising program for its Mexican associates. Home Depot pledged to double the resources that its Mexican associates raised to aid in the relief effort. When Hurricane Sandy hit the American East Coast in 2012, Home Depot responded with $1 million in donations in gift cards, supplies, and contributions to organizations that provided food, clothing, shelter, and volunteer efforts. Members of their own volunteer team, Team Depot, helped with rebuilding efforts.

EMPLOYEE AND SUPPLIER RELATIONS

Home Depot encourages employees to become involved in the community through volunteer and civic activities. Home Depot also strives to apply social responsibility to its employment practices, with the goal of assembling a diverse workforce that reflects the population of the markets it serves. However, in 1997 the company settled a class-action lawsuit brought by female employees who alleged that they were paid less than male employees, awarded fewer pay raises, and promoted less often. The $87.5 million settlement represented one of the largest settlements in a gender discrimination lawsuit in U.S. history at the time. In announcing the settlement, the company emphasized that it was not admitting to wrongdoing and defended its record, saying that it provides equal opportunities for all and has a reputation of supporting women in professional positions.

Since the lawsuit, Home Depot has worked to show that it appreciates workforce diversity and seeks to give all its associates an equal chance to be employed and advance. In 2005, Home Depot formed partnerships with the ASPIRA Association, Inc., the Hispanic Association of Colleges and Universities, and the National Council of La Raza to recruit Hispanic candidates for part-time and full-time positions. Also in 2005, Home Depot became a major member of the American Association of Retired Persons' (AARP) Featured Retirement Program, which helps connect employees 50 years or older with companies that value their experience. Home Depot also has a strong diversity supplier program. As a member of the Women's Business Enterprise National Council and the National Minority Suppliers Development Council, Home Depot has come into contact and done business with a diverse range of suppliers, including many minority- and women-owned businesses. In 2005, the company became a founding member of The Resource Institute, whose mission is to help small minority- and women-owned businesses by providing them with resources and training. Home Depot's supplier diversity program has won it numerous recognitions. It ranked number 32 for the Top 50 American Organizations for Multicultural Business Opportunities in 2015.

NEW TECHNOLOGY INITIATIVES

While Home Depot has begun to slow its rate of expansion, the company is turning toward technology to improve customer service and become more efficient. Compared to its rivals, Home Depot has lagged behind technologically. For instance, employees were using computers powered by motorboard batteries and stocking shelves in the same way as they had done for the past 15 years. Unlike its rival Lowe's, Home Depot did not allow customers to order products online and then pick them up at the stores. As more and more consumers choose to complete their transactions on the Web, this represented a weakness for Home Depot. In 2010 Home Depot's online sales constituted only 1.5 percent of overall sales. Although its rapid expansion had increased its reach, Home Depot was not adapting as quickly to the fast-paced world of technology.

After recognizing its limitations in this field, Home Depot has embarked upon several technology initiatives. These initiatives are intended to improve both its customer service and Home Depot's daily operations. One small victory that Home Depot has achieved is beating Lowe's in unleashing a mobile app that enables consumers to order Home Depot products. Home Depot distributed 30,000 of its First Phone devices in over 1,900 of its stores to replace old computers in associates' carts. The device allows associates to communicate with other associates, print labels, process credit and debit card transactions, and manage inventory, among other functions. According to then-CEO Frank Blake, the purpose of First Phone is to help associates spend less time on routine tasks and more on customer service. Home Depot also redesigned its website to improve navigation and communication channels. The company provided upgrades such as live chat and developed a buy online pickup option. Home Depot has managed to reduce response time to customer emails from 24 hours to one hour or less.

In 2011, a special component of the Home Depot website was launched for "Pros" (Professional and Contractor Services). This website is intended to decrease the time it takes for professionals and contractors to get in and out of the store, allow them to order online and pick up their goods within a couple of hours, and enable delivery for certain products when ordered in bulk. Home Depot recognizes that professionals should spend less time in the store and more on the job. After this website was implemented, the speed with which this target market was able to get in and out of the store was increased by 27 percent from the previous year. Three percent of the customers identified as Pros make up 30 percent of Home Depot's annual revenue, making this a very important market for the retailer. Additionally, Home Depot is improving its logistics. Whereas before the company had its suppliers send trucks of merchandise directly to the stores, where associates would then unload them, Home Depot has created distribution centers to make operations run more smoothly. This change will also enable its associates to devote more time to customer service.

These are just a few of the steps that Home Depot is taking to adopt a more proactive stance toward technological innovation. By concentrating on innovations that will increase customer service, the retailer is attempting to advance its stakeholder orientation into all aspects of its operations. In 2014, Home Depot invested $1.5 billion in technological upgrades with a focus on the digital connectedness of their supply chain, fulfillment centers, and retail locations. This enabled the home improvement retailer to offer same day shipping, allowing it remain competitive online.

A STRATEGIC COMMITMENT TO SOCIAL RESPONSIBILITY

Home Depot strives to secure a socially responsible reputation with stakeholders. Although it received low scores in the past on customer surveys and the American Customer Satisfaction Index, it has worked hard to bring those scores back up. It has responded to concerns about its environmental impact by creating new standards and principles to govern its relationship with its suppliers. Despite Home Depot's success, however, the company does face challenges in the future. Though it remains the world's largest home retailer, its main competitor Lowe's is picking up the pace. Still, Home Depot's philanthropic endeavors and its promotion of its products' low prices and high value continue to make it a popular shopping destination.

Knowing that stakeholders, especially customers, feel good about a company that actively commits its resources to environmental and social issues, Home Depot executives have committed to social responsibility as a strategic component of the company's business operations. The company should remain committed to its focused strategy of philanthropy, volunteerism, and environmental initiatives. Customers' concerns over social responsibility and green products have not abated, and Home Depot's sales of green products are strong. Its commitment to social responsibility extends throughout the company, fueled by top-level support from its cofounders and reinforced by a corporate culture that places great value on playing a responsible role within the communities it serves.

CONCLUSION

Home Depot's strategic commitment to customer service and social responsibility is paying off for all stakeholders. Sales, revenues, and dividends have increased over the last five years. By 2014 Home Depot stock had reached an all-time high approaching $100 per share. There is a blurring between online and brick-and-mortar stores, with 30 percent of online sales picked up in a store. The company invests heavily in its employee training and success.

Home Depot continues to engage its employees and communities in volunteer efforts. The company responds quickly to aid employees and consumers in disaster situations such as floods, earthquakes, and hurricanes. Home Depot also supports Habitat for Humanity that has approximately 150,000 volunteers building and restoring homes for those in need. While any company this large will face legal and ethical challenges, Home Depot has established strong principles and values to be a responsible corporate citizen.

Team Depot, Home Depot's associate-led volunteer force, takes great strides to meet the needs of its stakeholders. After a series of spring storms damaged a number of communities in 2014, Home Depot provided relief and recovery efforts for 20 of the affected communities. Veterans and those in the military are also crucial stakeholders in Home Depot's corporate social responsibility program. Home Depot has donated $138 million to veteran causes. Home Depot also partners with another organization to honor military children who have overcome the challenges of having parents in the military to become strong citizens in their communities.

Home Depot has had great success in its adoption of a stakeholder orientation. It has rebounded from having low customer satisfaction into a company that is respected because of its strong performance and commitment to employees, customers, and communities.

Questions for Discussion

1. On the basis of Home Depot's response to environmental issues, describe the attributes of this stakeholder. Assess the company's strategy and performance with environmental and employee stakeholders.

2. As a publicly traded corporation, how can Home Depot justify budgeting so much money for philanthropy? What areas other than the environment, disaster relief, and affordable housing might be appropriate for strategic philanthropy by Home Depot?

3. How does Home Depot's desire to be passionate about customer service relate to their social responsibility?

Sources

American Red Cross, "Red Cross Responded to 176 Large U.S. Disasters in 2015," December 28, 2015, http://www.redcross.org/news/press-release/Red-Cross-Responded-to-176-Large-US-Disasters-in-2015 (accessed August 17, 2016).

Adam Blair, "Home Depot's $64 Million Mobile Investment Rolls Out to 1,970 Stores," *RIS*, December 7, 2010, http://risnews.edgl.com/store-systems/Home-Depot-s-$64-Million-Mobile-Investment-Rolls-Out-to-1,600-Stores56966 (accessed August 17, 2016).

Associated Press, "Home Depot CEO Nardelli Quits," *MSNBC*, January 3, 2007, http://www.msnbc.msn.com/id/16451112/ (accessed August 17, 2016).

Tom Brennan, "Home Depot vs. Lowe's," *CNBC*, August 26, 2008, http://www.cnbc.com/id/26406040/?__source=aollheadline|quote|text|&par=aol (accessed August 17, 2016).

Chris Burritt, "Home Depot's Fix-It Lady," *Bloomberg BusinessWeek*, January 17–23, 2011, pp. 65–67.

Miguel Bustillo, "For Lowe's, Landscape Begins to Shift," *The Wall Street Journal*, February 24, 2011, p. B3.

Jim Carlton, "How Home Depot and Activists Joined to Cut Logging Abuse," *The Wall Street Journal*, September 26, 2000, p. A1.

Cora Daniels, "To Hire a Lumber Expert, Click Here," *Fortune*, April 3, 2000, pp. 267–270.

Sarah Demaster, "Use Proper Lumber, Demand Protesters," *BNet*, April 5, 1999, http://findarticles.com/p/articles/mi_m0VCW/is_7_25/ai_54373184/ (accessed September 8, 2009).

DiversityBusiness.com, *America's Top Organizations for Multicultural Business Opportunities*, 2015, http://www.diversitybusiness.com/Resources/DivLists/2015/DivTop50/2015Div50C.htm (accessed August 17, 2016).

Kirsteny Downey Grimsley, "Home Depot Settles Gender Bias Lawsuit," *The Washington Post*, September 20, 1997, p. D1.

Shelly DuBois, "Home Depot Knows When to Call It Quits," *CNN Money*, October 26, 2012, http://management.fortune.cnn.com/2012/10/26/home-depot-knows-when-to-call-it-quits/ (accessed August 17, 2016).

Brian Grow, Diane Brady, and Michael Arndt, "Renovating Home Depot," *Businessweek,* March 6, 2006, http://www.bloomberg.com/news/articles/2006-03-05/renovating-home-depot (accessed August 17, 2016).

Habitat for Humanity, "Habitat for Humanity and the Home Depot Foundation Announce National Green Building Effort," March 20, 2008, http://www.habitat.org/newsroom/2011archive/09_26_2011_hfh_and_home_depot_partner.aspx (accessed August 17, 2016).

Habitat for Humanity, "Habitat for Humanity and the Home Depot Mexico partner to Help Rebuild Haiti," February 8, 2010, http://www.habitat.org/lac_eng/newsroom/2010/02_08_2010_homedepot_eng.aspx?tgs=Mi81LzIwMTEgMTI6NDg6NTYgUE0%3d (accessed September 15, 2014).

Harris Interactive, "The Annual RQ 2007: The Reputations of the Most Visible Companies," *Marketing Charts*, http://www.marketingcharts.com/direct/corporate-reputation-in-decline-but-top-companies-buck-trend-5129/harris-corporate-reputation-2007-most-visible-companiesjpg/ (August 17, 2016).

Ashley M. Heher, "Home Depot Reports Loss of $54M, but Beats Estimates," *USA Today,* February 24, 2009, http://www.usatoday.com/money/companies/earnings/2009-02-24-home-depot_N.htm (accessed August 17, 2016). Melissa Hincha-Ownby, "Home Depot Shrinks Energy Bill," *Forbes,* March 11, 2010, http://www.forbes.com/2010/03/10/energy-efficiency-lighting-technology-ecotech-home-depot.html (accessed August 17, 2016).

Home Depot website," http://www.homedepot.com/?cm_mmc=SEM%7cB%7cBT1&gclid=CJS4_YWByc4CFfRTMgodqf0K-Q&gclsrc=ds (accessed August 17, 2016).

"Home Depot: A Customer Success Story," *Social Link Media*, August 30, 2011, http://www.socialinkmedia.com/2011/08/the-home-depot-a-customer-service-success-story/ (accessed January 29, 2013).

Home Depot, "Eco Options Program," http://www.ecooptions.homedepot.com/ (accessed August 17, 2016).

Home Depot, "Responding to Natural Disasters," *Home Depot Foundation*, 2016, https://corporate.homedepot.com/community/disaster-relief (accessed August 17, 2016).

Home Depot, "Eco Success," April 20, 2015, https://corporate.homedepot.com/newsroom/turning-environmental-challenges-eco-success (accessed August 17, 2016).

Home Depot, "Giving Back," https://corporate.homedepot.com/community/partnerships/community/partnerships/home-depot-foundation-partnerships (accessed August 17, 2016).

"Home Depot Builds Out Its Online Customer Service," Internet Retailer, June 4, 2010, www.internetretailer.com/2010/06/04/home-depot-builds-out-its-online-customer-service (accessed September 15, 2014).

Home Depot, "The Home Depot Foundation Responds to Superstorm Sandy," *Home Depot Foundation*, 2012, http://homedepotfoundation.org/page/the-home-depot-foundation-responds-to-superstorm-sandy (accessed September 15, 2014).

Home Depot, "Supplier Diversity," https://corporate.homedepot.com/responsibility/people/supplier-diversity (accessed August 17, 2016)

Home Depot, "Through the Years: Doing the Right Thing for Our Environment," March 3, 2016, https://corporate.homedepot.com/newsroom/home-depot-environmental-milestones-2015 (accessed August 17, 2016).

"Home Depot Announces Commitment to Stop Selling Old Growth Wood; Announcement Validates Two-Year Grassroots Environmental Campaign," *Common Dreams Newswire*, August 26, 1999, http://www.commondreams.org/pressreleases/august99/082699c.htm (accessed August 17, 2016).

"Home Depot Retools Timber Policy," *Memphis Business Journal*, January 2, 2003, www.bizjournals.com/memphis/stories/2002/12/30/daily12.html (accessed August 17, 2016).

Home Depot Foundation, "Habitat for Humanity International and the Home Depot Foundation Announce 2014 Repair Corps Program," January 14, 2014, http://www.homedepotfoundation.org/page/repaircorps2014 (accessed September 15, 2014).

Home Depot Foundation, "Team Depot Blog," http://www.homedepotfoundation.org/blog/ (accessed September 15, 2014).

Hoovers Inc., "The Home Depot, Inc., Profile," http://www.hoovers.com/company-information/cs/company-profile.the_home_depot_inc.fbb298e093e95785.html (accessed August 17, 2016).

Susan Jackson and Tim Smart, "Mom and Pop Fight Back," *BusinessWeek*, April 14, 1997, p. 46.

Karen Jacobs, "Home Depot Pushes Low Prices, Energy Savings," *Reuters,* September 10, 2008, http://www.reuters.com/article/ousiv/idUSN1051947020080910 (accessed August 17, 2016).

Neil Janowitz, "Rolling in the Depot," *Fast Company*, May 2012, p. 38.

Mary Ellen Lloyd, "Home Improvement Spending Remains Tight," *The Wall Street Journal,* May 6, 2009, http://online.wsj.com/article/SB124162405957992133.html (accessed August 17, 2016).

Gene Marcial, "Inside Wall Street: Home Depot is a Home Run," *MSN Money,* October 9, 2012, http://money.msn.com/top-stocks/post.aspx?post=3cc1894a-1bd3-4fe5-a9a2-876512fd4344 (accessed September 15, 2014).

Jena McGregor, "Home Depot Sheds Units," *Bloomberg,* January 26, 2009, http://www.bloomberg.com/news/articles/2009-01-26/home-depot-sheds-units (accessed August 17, 2016).

PR Newswire, "The Home Depot Forms Unprecedented Partnership with Four Leading National Hispanic Organizations," *HispanicBusiness.com,* February 15, 2005, http://www.prnewswire.com/news-releases/the-home-depot-forms-unprecedented-hiring-partnership-with-four-leading-national-hispanic-organizations-54053897.html (accessed August 17, 2016).

PR Newswire, "The Home Depot Foundation Pledges $5 Million to Complete Critical Home Repairs for 400 Atlanta Senior Veterans in Partnership with Area Nonprofits," November 11, 2015, http://www.prnewswire.com/news-releases/the-home-depot-foundation-pledges-5-million-to-complete-critical-home-repairs-for-400-atlanta-senior-veterans-in-partnership-with-area-nonprofits-300176594.html (accessed August 17, 2016).

PR Newswire, "The Home Depot Launches Environmental Wood Purchasing Policy," August 26, 1999, http://www.prnewswire.com/cgi-bin/stories.pl?ACCT=104&STORY=/www/story/08-26-1999/0001010227&EDATE= (accessed August 17, 2016).

Reuters, "Home Depot Earnings Q3 2012: Improved Housing Market Boosts Retailer's Sales, Profits," *The Huffington Post,* November 11, 2012, http://www.huffingtonpost.com/2012/11/13/home-depot-earnings-q3-2012_n_2121025.html (accessed August 17, 2016).

Reuters, "Home Depot's Do-It-Yourself Model Fails in China's Do-It-For-Me Market," *Reuters,* September 14, 2012, http://www.reuters.com/article/2012/09/14/us-homedepot-chinastoreclosure-idUSBRE88D02W20120914 (accessed September 12, 2014).

Reuters, "Profile: Home Depot, Inc. (HD.N)," *Reuters,* http://www.reuters.com/finance/stocks/companyProfile?symbol=HD.N (accessed August 17, 2016).

Reuters and Fortune, "Home Depot just made its biggest acquisition in nearly a decade," *Fortune,* July 22, 2015, http://fortune.com/2015/07/22/home-depot-interline-brands-deal/ (accessed August 17, 2016).

Julie Scelfo, "The Meltdown in Home Furnishings," *The New York Times,* January 28, 2009, http://www.nytimes.com/2009/01/29/garden/29industry.html (accessed August 17, 2016).

Kelsey Swanekamp, "Home Depot Cuts Jobs," *Forbes,* January 26, 2010, http://www.forbes.com/2010/01/26/home-depot-jobs-markets-equities-cuts.html (accessed August 17, 2016).

Louis Uchitelle, "Home Depot Girds for Continued Weakness," *The New York Times,* May 18, 2009, http://www.nytimes.com/2009/05/19/business/19depot.html?pagewanted=all (accessed August 17, 2016).

Craig Webb, "Home Depot Exec Reveals New Initiatives to Serve Pros," *ProSales,* August 21, 2012, http://www.prosalesmagazine.com/business/sales/home-depot-exec-reveals-new-initiatives-to-serve-pros_o (accessed August 17, 2016).

Marianne Wilson, "Report: Home Depot to Spend $1.3 Billion on Technology and $700 Million on New Stores," *Chain Store Age,* June 20, 2012, http://www.chainstoreage.com/article/report-home-depot-spend-13-billion-technology-and-700-million-new-stores (accessed August 17, 2016).

"World's Most Admired Companies: Home Depot," *CNN Money,* http://money.cnn.com/magazines/fortune/globalmostadmired/2008/snapshots/2968.html (accessed August 17, 2016).

Yahoo Finance, "The Home Depot, Inc. (HD)," https://finance.yahoo.com/quote/HD/financials?p=HD (accessed August 17, 2016).

Paul Ziobro, "Home Depot, TJX Cos. Buck Retail Trends," *The Wall Street Journal,* August 16, 2016, http://www.wsj.com/articles/home-depot-t-j-maxx-buck-retail-trends-1471379637 (accessed August 17, 2016).

New Belgium Brewing: Engaging in Sustainable Social Responsibility

INTRODUCTION

Although most of the companies frequently cited as examples of ethical and socially responsible firms are large corporations, it is the social responsibility initiatives of small businesses that often have the greatest impact on local communities. These businesses create jobs and provide goods and services for customers in smaller markets that larger corporations are often not interested in serving. Moreover, they also contribute money, resources, and volunteer time to local causes. Their owners often serve as community leaders, and many choose to apply their skills and resources to tackling local problems and issues that benefit the whole community. Managers and employees become role models for ethical and socially responsible actions. One such small business is the New Belgium Brewing Company, Inc., based in Fort Collins, Colorado.

HISTORY OF THE NEW BELGIUM BREWING COMPANY

The idea for the New Belgium Brewing Company began with a bicycling trip through Belgium. Belgium is arguably the home of some of the world's finest ales, some of which have been brewed for centuries in that country's monasteries. As Jeff Lebesch, an American electrical engineer, cruised around that country on his mountain bike, he wondered whether he could produce such high-quality beers back home in Colorado. After acquiring the special strain of yeast used to brew Belgian-style ales, Lebesch returned home and began to experiment in his Colorado basement. When his beers earned thumbs up from friends, Lebesch decided to market them.

The New Belgium Brewing Company (NBB) opened for business in 1991 as a tiny basement operation in Lebesch's home in Fort Collins. Lebesch's wife

at the time, Kim Jordan, became the firm's marketing director. They named their first brew Fat Tire Amber Ale in honor of Lebesch's bike ride through Belgium. Initially, getting New Belgium beer onto store shelves was not easy. Jordan often delivered the beer to stores in the back of her Toyota station wagon. However, New Belgium beers quickly developed a small but devoted customer base, first in Fort Collins and then throughout Colorado. The brewery soon outgrew the couple's basement and moved into an old railroad depot before settling into its present custom-built facility in 1995. The brewery includes two brew houses, four quality assurance labs, a wastewater treatment facility, a canning and bottling line, and numerous technological innovations for which New Belgium has become nationally recognized as a "paradigm of environmental efficiencies."

Under the leadership of Kim Jordan, who acted as CEO for 15 years, NBB currently offers a variety of permanent and seasonal ales and pilsners. The company's standard line includes Sunshine Wheat, Ranger, Blue Paddle, 1554, Snapshot Wheat, Citradelic, Slow Ride, Rampant, Shift, Abbey, Trippel, and the original Fat Tire Amber Ale, still the firm's bestseller. Some customers even refer to the company as the Fat Tire Brewery. In 2016 the firm also released its line of "Glütiny," or reduced gluten, beers. Glütiny Pale Ale and Glütiny Golden Ale became a part of NBB's year-round beers. The brewery also has its seasonal ales Pumpkick, Hoppy Blonde, and Heavy Melon. The firm also started a Lips of Faith program, where small batch brews like La Folie, Pluot, and Chocolate Stout are created for internal celebrations or landmark events. Additionally, New Belgium is working in collaboration with other craft brewers to come up with new products. Through this, they hope to create improved efficiency and experimentation along with taking collaborative strides toward the future of American craft beer making. NBB teamed up with Maine-based Allagash Brewing for its

*This case was prepared by Jennifer Sawayda and Jennifer Jackson for and under the direction of O.C. Ferrell and Linda Ferrell © 2015. We appreciate the input and assistance of Greg Owsley, New Belgium Brewing, in developing this case. It was prepared for classroom discussion rather than to illustrate either effective or ineffective handling of an administrative, ethical, or legal decision by management. All sources used for this case were obtained through publicly available material and the New Belgium Brewing website.

25th anniversary to develop a pack of beers called "Fat Tire & Friends Collabeeration Pack." The pack contains six types of beers, including Fat Tire Ale, Allagash Fat Funk Ale, and Firestone Walker Fat Hoppy Ale.

NBB's most effective form of advertising has always been its customers' word of mouth, especially in the early days. Indeed, before New Belgium beers were widely distributed throughout Colorado, one liquor-store owner in Telluride is purported to have offered people gas money if they would stop by and pick up New Belgium beer on their way through Fort Collins. Although New Belgium has expanded distribution to a good portion of the U.S. market, the brewery receives numerous e-mails and phone calls every day inquiring when its beers will be available in other parts of the country.

Although still a small brewery when compared to many beer companies, like fellow Coloradan Coors, NBB has consistently experienced strong growth with estimated sales of more than $100 million (NBB being a private firm, detailed sales and revenue numbers are not available). It now has its own blog, Twitter, and Facebook pages. The organization sells more than 800,000 barrels of beer per year and has many opportunities for continued growth. For instance, while total beer consumption has remained flat, the market share of the craft beer industry is now at 6 percent. Growth for craft beer is likely to continue as new generations of beer drinkers appear to favor beers that are locally brewed.

Currently, New Belgium's products are distributed in 44 states plus the District of Columbia, British Columbia, and Alberta. Beer connoisseurs that appreciate the high quality of NBB's products, as well as the company's environmental and ethical business practices, have driven this growth. For example, when the company began distribution in Minnesota, the beers were so popular that a liquor store had to open early and make other accommodations for the large amount of customers. The store sold 400 cases of Fat Tire in the first hour it was open.

With expanding distribution, however, the brewery recognized a need to increase its opportunities for reaching its far-flung customers. It consulted with Dr. Douglas Holt, an Oxford professor and cultural branding expert. After studying the company, Holt, together with former Marketing Director Greg Owsley, drafted a 70-page "manifesto" describing the brand's attributes, character, cultural relevancy, and promise. In particular, Holt identified in New Belgium an ethos of pursuing creative activities simply for the joy of doing them well and in harmony with the natural environment.

With the brand thus defined, NBB worked with New York advertising agency Amalgamated to create a $10 million advertising campaign. The campaign would target high-end beer drinkers, men aged from 25 to 44, and highlight the brewery's down-to-earth image. The grainy ads focused on a man, Charles the Tinkerer, rebuilding a cruiser bike out of used parts and then riding it along pastoral country roads. The product appeared in just five seconds of each ad between the tag lines, "Follow Your Folly … Ours Is Beer." With nostalgic music playing in the background, the ads helped position the growing brand as whimsical, thoughtful, and reflective. NBB later re-released its Tinkerer commercial during the U.S. Pro Challenge. The re-released commercial had an additional scene with the Tinkerer riding part way next to a professional cyclist contestant, with music from songwriter and Tour de Fat enthusiast Sean Hayes. The commercial was featured on NBC.

It would be eight more years before NBB would develop its next television advertising campaign. In 2013 NBB developed a campaign called "Pairs Well with People" that included a 30-second television advertisement. The television ad described the unique qualities of NBB as an organization, including its environmental consciousness and 100 percent employee ownership. The advertisement was launched on four major networks in large cities across the United States. Because the primary purpose of the campaign was to create awareness in areas not as familiar with the brand (such as Raleigh-Durham and Minneapolis), NBB did not air the commercial in Colorado and states where the brand is well-known. The campaign also featured four 15-second online videos of how its beer "pairs well with people." Bar patrons featured in the 15-second digital ads were NBB employees.

In addition to the ad campaign, the company maintains its strategy of promotion through event sponsorships and digital media. To launch its Ranger IPA beer, New Belgium created a microsite and an online video of its NBB sales force dressed as rangers performing a hip-hop dance number to promote the beer. The only difference was that instead of horses, the NBB rangers rode bicycles. The purpose of the video was to create a hip, fun brand image for its new beer, with the campaign theme "To Protect. To Pour. To Partake." The company's Beer Mode mobile app gives users who download it access to exclusive content, preselects messages to post on the users' social media sites when they are spending time enjoying their beers, and provides users with the locations of retailers that sell NBB products. The company offers rewards to users for downloading the Beer

Mode app, visiting the NBB website, sharing the website on social media networks, and attending NBB events.

NEW BELGIUM ETHICAL CULTURE

According to New Belgium, the company places great importance on the ethical culture of the brand. The company is aware that if it embraces citizenship in the communities it serves, it can forge enduring bonds with customers. More than ever before, what a brand says and what a company does must be synchronized. NBB believes that as the mandate for corporate social responsibility gains momentum, business managers must realize that business ethics is not so much about the installation of compliance codes and standards as it is about the spirit in which such codes and standards are integrated. The modern-day brand steward—usually the most externally focused of the business management team—must prepare to be the internal champion of the bottom-line necessity for ethical, values-driven company behavior.

At New Belgium, a synergy of brand and values occurred naturally because the firm's ethical culture (in the form of core values and beliefs) was in place long before NBB had a marketing department. Back in early 1991, when New Belgium was just a fledgling home-brewed business, Jeff Lebesch and Kim Jordan took a hike into Rocky Mountain National Park armed with a pen and a notebook. There they took the first stab at what the company's core purpose would be. If they were going forward with this venture, what were their aspirations beyond profitability? What was at the heart of their dream? What they wrote down that spring day, give or take a little editing, are the core values and beliefs you can read on the NBB website today.

Since its inception, NBB adopted a triple bottom line (TBL) approach to business. Whereas the traditional bottom line approach for measuring business success is economic, TBL incorporates economic, social, and environmental factors. In other words, rather than just looking at financial data to evaluate company success, NBB looks at its impact upon profits, people, and the planet. One way that the company is advancing the TBL approach is through the creation of a high-involvement corporate culture. All employees at NBB are expected to contribute to the company vision, and accountability is spread throughout the organization. Just about any New Belgium worker can list many, if not all, of these shared values. For NBB, branding strategies are rooted in its company values.

New Belgium's Purpose and Core Beliefs

New Belgium's dedication to quality, the environment, its employees, and its customers is expressed in its mission statement: "To operate a profitable brewery which makes our love and talent manifest." The company's stated core values and beliefs about its role as an environmentally concerned and socially responsible brewer include the following:

1. Remembering that we are incredibly lucky to create something fine that enhances people's lives while surpassing our consumers' expectations
2. Producing world-class beers
3. Promoting beer culture and the responsible enjoyment of beer
4. Kindling social, environmental, and cultural change as a business role model
5. Environmental stewardship: minimizing resource consumption, maximizing energy efficiency, and recycling
6. Cultivating potential through learning, participative management, and the pursuit of opportunities
7. Balancing the myriad needs of the company, staff, and their families
8. Trusting each other and committing ourselves to authentic relationships, communications, and promises
9. Continuous, innovative quality and efficiency improvements
10. Having Fun

Employees believe that these statements help communicate to customers and other stakeholders what New Belgium, as a company, is about. These simple values—developed roughly 20 years ago—are just as meaningful to the company and its customers today, even though there has been much growth.

Employee Concerns

Recognizing employees' role in the company's success, New Belgium provides many generous benefits for its employees. In addition to the usual paid health and dental insurance and retirement plans, employees get a catered lunch every month to celebrate employees' birthdays as well as a free massage once a year, and they can bring their children and dogs to work. Employees who stay with the company for five years earn an all-expenses paid trip to Belgium to "study beer culture." Employees are also reimbursed for one hour of paid time off for every two hours of volunteer work that they perform. Perhaps most importantly, employees can also earn stock in the privately held corporation, which grants them a vote in company decisions. Employees currently own 100 percent of company stock. Open book management also allows employees to see the financial costs and performance of the company. Employees are provided with financial training so they can understand the books and ask questions about the numbers.

New Belgium also wishes to get its employees involved not only in the company but in its sustainability efforts as well. To help their own sustainability efforts, employees are given a fat-tired cruiser bike after one year's employment so they can ride to work instead of drive. An onsite recycling center is also provided for employees. Additionally, each summer New Belgium hosts the Tour de Fat, where employees can dress in costumes and lead locals on a bike tour. Other company perks include inexpensive yoga classes, free beer at quitting time, and a climbing wall. To ensure that workers' voices are heard, NBB has a democratically elected group of coworkers called POSSE. POSSE acts as a liaison between the board, managers, and employees.

Sustainability Concerns

New Belgium's marketing strategy involves linking the quality of its products, as well as its brand, with the company's philosophy of environmental friendliness. As chair of the sustainability subcommittee for its trade group the Brewers Association, NBB is at the forefront in advancing eco-friendly business processes among companies in its industry. Co-workers and managers from all areas of the organization meet monthly to discuss sustainability ideas as part of NBB's natural resource management team. From leading-edge environmental gadgets and high-tech industry advancements to employee-ownership programs and a strong belief in giving back to the community, New Belgium demonstrates its desire to create a living, learning community.

NBB strives for cost-efficient energy-saving alternatives for conducting its business and reducing its impact on the environment. In staying true to the company's core values and beliefs, the brewery's employee–owners unanimously agreed to invest in a wind turbine, making New Belgium the first fully wind-powered brewery in the United States. NBB has also invested in the following energy-saving technologies:

- A smart grid installation that allows NBB to communicate with its electricity provider to conserve energy. For example, the smart grid will alert NBB to non-essential operational functions, allowing the company to turn them off and save power.
- The installation of a 20 KW photovoltaic array on top of the packaging hall. The array produces 3 percent of the company's electricity.
- A brew kettle, the second of its kind installed in the nation, which heats wort sheets instead of the whole kettle at once. This kettle heating method conserves energy more than standard kettles do.
- Sun tubes, which provide natural daytime lighting throughout the brew house all year long.
- A system to capture its waste water and extract methane from it. This can contribute up to 15 percent of the brewery's power needs while reducing the strain on the local municipal water treatment facility.
- A steam condenser that captures and reuses the hot water that boils the barley and hops in the production process to start the next brew. The steam is redirected to heat the floor tiles and de-ice the loading docks in cold weather.

In April 2014, New Belgium was featured in a half-page advertisement supporting the EPA clean water rule that was introduced March 26, 2014. Andrew Lemley, New Belgium's Government Relations Director, was quoted in an EPA news release championing continued support for the Clean Water Act while also associating quality water with quality beer.

In addition to voicing political support for environmental protections, New Belgium also takes pride in reducing waste through recycling and creative reuse strategies. The company strives to recycle as many supplies as possible, including cardboard boxes, keg caps, office materials, and the amber glass used in bottling. The brewery also stores spent barley and hop grains in an on-premise silo and invites local farmers to pick up the grains, free of charge, to feed their pigs. Beyond the normal products that are recycled back into the food chain, NBB is working with partners to take the same bacteria that creates methane from NBB wastewater and convert it into a harvestable, high-protein fish food. NBB also buys recycled products when it can, and even encourages its employees to reduce air pollution by using alternative transportation. Reduce, Reuse, Recycle—the three R's of environmental stewardship—are taken seriously at NBB. The company has been a proud member of the environmental group Business for Innovative Climate & Energy Policy (BICEP), and it signed BICEP's Climate

Declaration in 2013 which calls for American businesses, stakeholders, and regulators to address climate change.

Additionally, New Belgium has been a long-time participant in green building techniques. With each expansion of its facility, the company has incorporated new technologies and learned a few lessons along the way. In 2002, NBB agreed to participate in the United States Green Building Council's Leadership in Energy and Environment Design for Existing Buildings (LEED-EB) pilot program. From sun tubes and day lighting throughout the facility to reusing heat in the brew house, NBB continues to search for new ways to close loops and conserve resources.

New Belgium has made significant achievements in sustainability, particularly compared to other companies in the industry. For instance, New Belgium uses only 3.9 gallons of water to make 1 gallon of beer, which is 20 percent less than most other companies. The company is attempting to create a closed-loop wastewater system with its own Process Water Treatment Plant, in which microbes are used to clean the wastewater. NBB recycles over 95 percent of its waste, and today 100 percent of its electricity comes from renewable energy sources. Despite these achievements, it has no intention of halting its sustainability efforts. The company hopes to reduce the amount of water used to make its beer by 10 percent through better production processes as well as decrease its carbon footprint by 25 percent per barrel. To encourage sustainability throughout the supply chain, NBB adopted Sustainable Purchasing Guidelines. The Guidelines allow them to pinpoint and work closely with eco-friendly suppliers to create sustainability throughout the entire value chain. For its part, NBB conducts life-cycle analysis on its packaging components while continually seeking more efficient refrigeration and transportation technology that can be incorporated into its supply chain.

Social Concerns

Beyond its use of environmentally friendly technologies and innovations, New Belgium also strives to improve communities and enhance people's lives through corporate giving, event sponsorship, and philanthropic involvement. Since its inception, NBB has donated more than $8 million to philanthropic causes. For every barrel of beer sold the prior year, NBB donates $1 to philanthropic causes within its distribution territories. The donations are divided between states in proportion to their percentage of overall sales. This is the company's way of staying local and giving back to the communities that support and purchase NBB products. NBB also participates in One Percent for the Planet, a philanthropic network to which the company donates one percent of its sales. In addition, NBB employees also partnered with Habitat for Humanity to build a house for a family who had lost their home to a fire.

Funding decisions are made by NBB's Philanthropy Committee, which is comprised of employees throughout the brewery, including owners, employee–owners, area leaders, and production workers. NBB looks for nonprofit organizations that demonstrate creativity, diversity, and an innovative approach to their mission and objectives. The Philanthropy Committee also looks for groups that incorporate community involvement in their operations.

Additionally, NBB maintains a community bulletin board in its facility and posts an array of community involvement activities and proposals. This community board allows tourists and employees to see the various opportunities to help out in the community, and it gives nonprofit organizations a chance to make their needs known. The NBB website also has a dedicated link where organizations can apply for grants. The company donates to causes with a particular emphasis on water conservation, sensible transportation and bike advocacy, sustainable agriculture, and youth environmental education, among other areas.

NBB also sponsors a number of events, with a special focus on those that involve "human-powered" sports that cause minimal damage to the natural environment. Through event sponsorships, such as the Tour de Fat, NBB supports various environmental, social, and cycling nonprofit organizations. In the Tour de Fat, one participant hands over his or her car keys and vehicle title in exchange for an NBB commuter bike and trailer. The participant is then filmed for the world to see as he or she promotes sustainable transportation over driving. In the course of one year, New Belgium can be found at anywhere from 150 to 200 festivals and events across the nation.

Organizational Success

New Belgium Brewing Company's efforts to embody a sustainability-oriented business has paid off with a very loyal following—in fact, the company expanded the number of tours it offers of its facilities due to such high demand. The company has also been the recipient of numerous awards. Past awards for NBB include the *Business Ethics Magazine*'s Business Ethics Award for its "dedication to environmental excellence in every part of its innovative brewing process," its inclusion in *The Wall Street Journal*'s 15 best small workplaces, and the award for "best mid-sized brewing company of the year" and best mid-sized brewmaster at the Great American Beer Festival. New Belgium has been awarded medals for three different brews: Abbey Belgian Style Ale, Blue Paddle Pilsner, and La Folie specialty ale.

Many applaud New Belgium Brewing Company's sustainability and philanthropic initiatives. According to David Edgar, former director of the Institute for Brewing Studies at the Brewers Association in Boulder, Colorado, "They've created a very positive image for their company in the beer-consuming public with smart decision-making." Although some members of society do not believe that a company whose major product is alcohol can be socially responsible, NBB has set out to prove that for those who make a choice to drink responsibly, the company can do everything possible to contribute to society. NBB also promotes the responsible appreciation of beer through its participation in and support of the culinary arts. For instance, it frequently hosts New Belgium Beer Dinners, in which every course of the meal is served with a complementary culinary treat.

Although NBB has made great strides in creating a socially responsible brand image, its work is not done. It must continually reexamine its ethical, social, and environmental responsibilities. In 2004, it received the Environmental Protection Agency's regional Environmental Achievement Award. It was both an honor and a motivator for the company to continue its socially responsible goals. After all, there are still many ways for NBB to improve as a corporate citizen. For example, although all electric power comes from renewable sources, the NBB plant is still heated in part by using natural gas. Furthermore, continued expansion requires longer travel distances to distribute its products, which increases the use of fossil fuels. In addition to addressing logistical challenges, NBB is part of an industry where there is always a need for more public dialogue on avoiding alcohol abuse. Practically speaking, the company has a never-ending to-do list.

NBB executives acknowledge that as its annual sales increase, the company will face increasing challenges to remain committed on a human level while also being culturally authentic. Indeed, how to boldly grow the brand while maintaining its perceptions of a humble feel has always been a challenge. Additionally, reducing waste to an even greater extent will require more effort on behalf of managers and employees, creating the need for a collaborative process that will require the dedication of both parties toward sustainability.

Perhaps as a way to deal with the long transportation distances necessary for national distribution as well as to expand production capacity, NBB opened a second brewery in Asheville, North Carolina, in 2015. Like Sierra Nevada, who already operates a brewery in Asheville, NBB is hoping to use its new $175 million facility as a hub for product distribution to eastern states—Asheville has legislation in place that makes regional distribution easier. However, opening its second brewery is more than just about increasing production capacity; NBB, along with hundreds of other craft brewers, are attracted to Asheville for its local culture that values sustainability and locally produced products. Asheville is surrounded by mountains, is near protected water sources, and is inhabited by many outdoor enthusiasts. Indeed, NBB is not the only craft brewery to recognize the potential of positive tourist exposure and local support by operating in the Asheville area. Sierra Nevada is planning to add regular tours of its brewery to emphasize its history and sustainable brewing practices. Additionally, other Asheville breweries have spent millions expanding their current operations in anticipation of NBB's entrance to the area.

NBB also faces increased competition from larger craft breweries. It still remains behind Boston Beer Co. (maker of Samuel Adams beer) and Sierra Nevada in market share. Like NBB, Boston Beer Co. and Sierra Nevada have plans to expand. Boston Beer allocated $35 million for capital investment projects at breweries in Massachusetts, Pennsylvania, and Ohio in 2012. NBB must also compete against craft beer alternatives released by traditional breweries, such as MillerCoor's New Moon Belgian White. It must constantly engage in environmental scanning and competitive analysis to compete in this increasingly competitive environment.

Every six-pack of New Belgium Beer displays the phrase "In this box is our labor of love. We feel incredibly lucky to be creating something fine that enhances people's lives." Although Jeff Lebesch and Kim Jordan are divorced and Lebesch has left the company to focus on other interests, the founders of New Belgium hope this statement captures the spirit of the company. In 2015 Kim Jordan announced she was turning the CEO position over to Chief Operations Officer and President Christine Perich so she could transition into becoming the Executive Chair of NBB's board of directors. This will allow Jordan to focus more on the long-term strategy and vision of the firm.

According to employee Dave Kemp, NBB's social responsibilities give the company a competitive advantage because consumers want to believe in and feel good about the products they purchase. NBB's most important asset is its image—a corporate brand that stands for quality, responsibility, and concern for society. Defining itself as more than a beer company, the brewer also sees itself as a caring organization that is concerned for all stakeholders.

Questions for Discussion

1. What environmental issues does the New Belgium Brewing Company work to address? How has NBB taken a strategic approach to addressing these issues? Why do you think the company has taken such a strong stance toward sustainability?
2. Do you agree that New Belgium's focus on social responsibility provides a key competitive advantage for the company? Why or why not?
3. Some segments of society contend that companies that sell alcoholic beverages and tobacco products cannot be socially responsible organizations because of the nature of their primary products. Do you believe that New Belgium's actions and initiatives are indicative of a socially responsible corporation? Why or why not?

Sources

"The 2011 World's Most Ethical Companies," *Ethisphere,* Q1 2011, 37–43.

The facts of this case are from Peter Asmus, "Goodbye Coal, Hello Wind," *Business Ethics* 13 (July/August 1999): 10–11.

"A Tour of the New Belgium Brewery—Act One," LiveGreen Blog, April 9, 2007, http://www.livegreensd.com/2007/04/tour-of-new-belgium-brewery-act-one.html (accessed April 13, 2012).

Robert Baun, "What's in a Name? Ask the Makers of Fat Tire," [Fort Collins] *Coloradoan.com*, October 8, 2000, pp. E1, E3.

Beerpulse.com, "New Belgium 2014 Update: Groundbreaking Hawaii, Kentucky, 3 Floyds Grätzer, FOCOIIab," March 25, 2014, http://beerpulse.com/2014/03/new-belgium-2014-update-hawaii-kentucky-2745/ (accessed August 10, 2016).

Carrie C. Causey, "Craft beer growing in popularity," *The Herald Weekly,* September 16, 2014, http://www.huntersvilleherald.com/news/2014/9/11/9914/craft-beer-growing-in-popularity (accessed September 16, 2014).

Karen Crofton, "How New Belgium Brewery Leads Colorado's Craft Brewers in Energy," *GreenBiz* August 1, 2014, http://www.greenbiz.com/blog/2014/08/01/how-new-belgium-brewery-leads-colorados-craft-brewers-energy (accessed August 10, 2016).

Robert F. Dwyer and John F. Tanner, Jr., *Business Marketing* (Burr Ridge, IL: Irwin McGraw-Hill, 1999), p. 104.

Environmental Protection Agency, "Here's What They're Saying About the Clean Water Act Proposed Rule," March 26, 2014, http://yosemite.epa.gov/opa/admpress.nsf/d0cf6618525a9efb85257359003fb69d/3f954c179cf0720985257ca7004920fa!OpenDocument (accessed August 18, 2014).

Mike Esterl, "Craft Brewers Tap Big Expansion," *The Wall Street Journal,* December 28, 2011, http://online.wsj.com/article/SB10001424052970203686204577114291721661070.html (accessed August 10, 2016).

Julie Gordon, "Lebesch Balances Interests in Business, Community," *Coloradoan.com*, February 26, 2003.

Del I. Hawkins, Roger J. Best, and Kenneth A. Coney, *Consumer Behavior: Building Marketing Strategy*, 8th ed. (Burr Ridge, IL: Irwin McGraw-Hill, 2001).

"How New Belgium Brewing is Positioning Itself to Remain Independent," *Denver Post,* January 15, 2013, http://blogs.denverpost.com/beer/2013/01/15/new-belgium-positio/7872/ (accessed August 10, 2016).

"Industry Profile: Breweries," *First Research,* October 17, 2011, http://www.firstresearch.com (accessed February 17, 2012).

David Kemp, Tour Connoisseur, New Belgium Brewing Company, personal interview by Nikole Haiar, November 21, 2000.

Tony Kiss, "Area breweries investing millions, adding staff," *The State,* September 14, 2014, http://www.thestate.com/news/business/article13882985.html (accessed August 10, 2016).

Dick Kreck, "Strange Brewing Standing Out," *Denver Post,* June 2, 2010, http://www.denverpost.com/2010/05/31/strange-brewing-standing-out/ (accessed August 10, 2016).

Devin Leonard, "New Belgium and the Battle of the Microbrews," *Bloomberg Businessweek,* December 1, 2011, http://www.bloomberg.com/news/articles/2011-12-01/new-belgium-and-the-battle-of-the-microbrews (accessed August 10, 2016).

Karlene Lukovitz, "New Belgium Brewing Gets 'Hopped Up'," *Media Post News,* February 3, 2010, http://www.mediapost.com/publications/article/121806/new-belgium-brewing-gets-hopped-up.html (accessed August 10, 2016).

NBB Films, "NBBspotsonNBC," NBB Films, YouTube, http://www.youtube.com/watch?v=KCnzyX-x-WQ (accessed August 10, 2016).

New Belgium Brewing website, http://www.newbelgium.com (accessed August 10, 2016).

"New Belgium Brewing Announces Asheville as Site for Second Brewery," *Denver Post*, April 5, 2012, http://marketwire.denverpost.com/client/denver_post/release.jsp?actionFor=1595119 (accessed April 19, 2012).

"New Belgium Brewing Company, Inc.," *Businessweek*, http://investing.businessweek.com/research/stocks/private/snapshot.asp?privcapId=919332 (accessed August 11, 2016).

New Belgium Brewing, *Corporate Sustainability Report*, New Belgium Brewing website, http://www.newbelgium.com/culture/alternatively_empowered/sustainable-business-story.aspx (accessed April 13, 2012).

New Belgium Brewing, *New Belgium Brewing: Follow Your Folly*, May 9, 2007, http://www.newbelgium.com/Files/NBB_student-info-packet.pdf (accessed August 11, 2016).

New Belgium Brewing, "Philanthropy," http://www.newbelgium.com/sustainability/Community/Philanthropy.aspx (accessed August 11, 2016).

"New Belgium Brewing Wins Ethics Award," *Denver Business Journal*, January 2, 2003, http://www.bizjournals.com/denver/stories/2002/12/30/daily21.html (accessed August 11, 2016).

One Percent for the Planet, "FAQ," http://onepercentfortheplanet.org/about/faq-about-1ftp/ (accessed August 11, 2016).

Greg Owsley, "The Necessity For Aligning Brand with Corporate Ethics," in *Fulfilling Our Obligation, Perspectives on Teaching Business Ethics*, ed. Sheb L. True, Linda Ferrell, and O. C. Ferrell (Atlanta, GA: Kennesaw State University Press, 2005), pp. 128–132.

Steve Raabe, "New Belgium Brewing Turns to Cans," *Denver Post*, May 15, 2008, http://www.denverpost.com/breakingnews/ci_9262005 (accessed August 11, 2016).

Steve Raabe, "Plans Brewing for New Belgium Facility on East Coast," *Denver Post*, December 22, 2011, http://www.denverpost.com/business/ci_19597528 (accessed August 18, 2014).

Bryan Simpson, "New Belgium Brewing: Brand Building through Advertising and Public Relations," http://fba.aiub.edu/Files/Uploads/INB110005.pdf (accesed August 11, 2016).

Mike Snider, "Big Brewers Happy to Go Hoppy," *USA Today*, October 30, 2013, p. 4B.

Mike Snider, "Sales of Craft beer Are Still Bubbling Up," *USA Today*, April 3, 2014, p. 3B.

Kelly K. Spors, "Top Small Workplaces 2008," *The Wall Street Journal*, February 22, 2009, http://online.wsj.com/article/SB122347733961315417.html (accessed August 18, 2014).

"Tour de New Belgium," Brew Public, November 23, 2010, http://brewpublic.com/places-to-drink-beer/tour-de-new-belgium/ (accessed April 16, 2013).

Tyghe Trimble, "Why Asheville Is the Next Craft Beer Capital," *Men's Journal*, http://www.mensjournal.com/food-drink/drinks/why-asheville-is-the-next-craft-beer-capital-20140804 (accessed August 11, 2016).

The Brewer's Association, "Craft Brewer Volume Share of U.S. Beer Market Reaches Double Digits in 2014," March 16, 2015, http://www.brewersassociation.org/press-releases/craft-brewer-volume-share-of-u-s-beer-market-reaches-double-digits-in-2014/ (accessed April 7, 2015).

Leigh Buchanan, "It's All About Ownership," *Inc.*, April 18, 2013, http://www.inc.com/audacious-companies/leigh-buchanan/new-belgium-brewing.html (accessed April 7, 2015).

The Egotist Network, "New Belgium Pairs Well With People in New Campaign from Denver's Cultivator," *The Denver Egotist*, May 20, 2013, http://www.thedenveregotist.com/news/local/2013/may/20/new-belgium-pairs-well-people-new-campaign-denvers-cultivator (accessed May 6, 2015).

New Belgium Brewing, "Beer Mode," http://www.newbelgium.com/app.aspx (accessed May 6, 2015).

New Belgium Brewing, "Beer Mode: A Brand (Spanking) New Mobile App! For Your Consideration...," April 23, 2013, http://www.newbelgium.com/community/Blog/13-04-23/Beer-Mode-a-brand-spanking-new-mobile-app-For-your-consideration.aspx (accessed May 6, 2015).

New Belgium Brewing, *New Belgium Brewing Packaging Reduction Goals*, 2014, http://www.newbelgium.com/files/sustainability/NBBPackagingReductionGoals2014.pdf (accessed April 7, 2015).

New Belgium Brewing, *Our Sustainable Success Story*, http://www.newbelgium.com/files/sustainability/New_Belgium_Sustainability_Brochure.pdf?pdf=sustainabilityreport (accessed April 7, 2015).

Jonathan Shikes, "New Belgium Airs TV Commercials for the First Time in Eight Years, but Not in Colorado," *Westword*, May 21, 2013, http://www.westword.com/restaurants/new-belgium-airs-tv-commercials-for-the-first-time-in-eight-years-but-not-in-colorado-5728121 (accessed May 6, 2015).

New Belgium Brewing, "New Belgium President and COO Christine Perich to Assume CEO Position," August 10, 2015, http://www.newbelgium.com/community/Blog/new-belgium-brewing/2015/08/10/New-Belgium-President-and-COO-Christine-Perich-to-assume-CEO-position (accessed August 10, 2016).

NOTES

Chapter 1

1. Philip Van Doorn, "2015 year in review: The S&P 500's winners and losers," *The Wall Street Journal*, December 31, 2015, http://www.marketwatch.com/story/2015-year-in-review-the-sp-500-2015-12-28 (accessed June 24, 2016).
2. National Consumers League, "Social responsibility about about worker welfare, survey says," May 2006, http://www.nclnet.org/social_responsibility_all_about_worker_welfare_survey_says (accessed June 24, 2016).
3. UNM Daniels Fund Ethics Initiative, "VW Cheats Environmental Expectations," 2015, https://danielsethics.mgt.unm.edu/pdf/vw-mini-case.pdf (accessed June 24, 2016); William Boston and William Wilkes, "Volkswagen's Ex-CEO Martin Winterkorn Faces Probe over Emissions Scandal," *The Wall Street Journal*, June 18, 2016, http://www.wsj.com/articles/former-volkswagen-ceo-martin-winterkorn-faces-market-manipulation-probe-in-germany-1466432926 (accessed June 24, 2016).
4. Shoko Oda, "Hackers Harpoon Japan Tax Agency Website in Whaling Protest," *Bloomberg, February 9*, 2016 (accessed June 24, 2016).
5. David Streitfeld, "Accusing Amazon of Antitrust Violations, Authors and Booksellers Demand Inquiry," *The New York Times*, July 13, 2015, http://www.nytimes.com/2015/07/14/technology/accusing-amazon-of-antitrust-violations-authors-and-booksellers-demand-us-inquiry.html?_r=0 (accessed June 24, 2016).
6. Luke Rosiak, "The Scooter Store Files for Bankruptcy While Under Investigation for Overbilling Medicare, Medicaid," *The Washington Times*, April 17, 2014, http://www.washingtontimes.com/news/2013/apr/17/the-scooter-store-files-for-bankruptcy-while-under/ (accessed June 24, 2016).
7. BusinessWire, "Ethisphere Announces 2011 World's Most Ethical Companies," *Ethisphere*, March 15, 2011, http://www.businesswire.com/news/home/20110315006776/en/Ethisphere-Announces-2011-World%E2%80%99s-Ethical-Companies#.U5iTXKLb4R4 (accessed June 24, 2016).
8. O. C. Ferrell, Linda Ferrell, and Jennifer Sawayda, "The Domain of Corporate Social Responsibility and Marketing," in *Handbook of Research on Marketing and Corporate Responsibility,* ed. Ronald Hill and Ryan Langan (Northampton, MA: Edward Elgan Publishing, Ltd., 2014).
9. Milton Friedman, *Capitalism and Freedom* (Chicago: University of Chicago Press, 1962).
10. Clive Crook, "Why Good Corporate Citizens Are a Public Menace," *National Journal,* April 24, 1999, p. 1087; Charles Handy, "What's a Business for?" *Harvard Business Review* 80 (December 2002): 49–55.
11. Altered Seasons, "About Us," http://www.alteredseasons.com/about-us (accessed June 2, 2014).
12. Associated Press, "BBB Expels Largest Bureau Over Pay-to-Play Charges," Fox News, March 12, 2013, http://www.foxnews.com/us/2013/03/12/bbb-expels-largest-bureau-over-pay-to-play-charges.html (accessed June 24, 2016).
13. Nancy J. Miller and Terry L. Besser, "The Importance of Community Values in Small Business Strategy Formation: Evidence from Rural Iowa," *Journal of Small Business Management* 38 (January 2000): 68–85; James Knight and Mary Kate O'Riley, "Local Heroes," *Director* 55 (February 2002): 28.
14. "The Small Business Economy: A Report to the President 2005," U.S. Small Business Administration, https://www.sba.gov/sites/default/files/files/sb_econ2005.pdf (accessed June 24, 2016).
15. Hershey, "About Hershey: Corporate Social Responsibility," http://www.hersheypa.com/about_hershey/about_csr.php (accessed June 24, 2016).
16. Herman Miller, "Our Values in Action," http://www.hermanmiller.com/about-us/our-values-in-action.html (accessed June 24, 2016).
17. "Press—Awards," Herman Miller Inc., http://www.hermanmiller.com/about-us/press.html (accessed June 3, 2014).
18. "The 1997 Cone/Roper Cause-Related Marketing Trends Report," *Business Ethics* 11 (March–April 1997): 14–16; Ronald Alsop, "Corporate Reputations Are Earned with Trust, Reliability, Study Shows," *Wall Street Journal*, September 23, 1999; Dale Kurschner, "5 Ways Ethical Busine$$ Creates Fatter Profit$," *Business Ethics* 10 (March–April 1996): 21.
19. Jim Carlton, "New Leaf: Once Targeted by Protestors, Home Depot Plays Green Role," *Wall Street Journal*, August 6, 2004, p. A1.
20. Case prepared by Michelle Urban and Jennifer Sawayda, "Starbucks' Mission: Social Responsibility and Brand Strength," in *Business Ethics: Ethical Decision Making and Cases*, ed. O. C. Ferrell, John Fraedrich, and Linda Ferrell, 10th ed. (Mason, OH: South-Western Cengage Learning, 2015), pp. 396–406.
21. Archie Carroll, "The Four Faces of Corporate Citizenship," *Business and Society Review* (January 1, 1998): p. 1; Naomi Gardberg and Charles Fombrun, "Corporate Citizenship: Creating Intangible Assets Across Institutional Environments," *Academy of Management Review* 31 (April 2006): 329–336.
22. Transparency International, "Corruption Perceptions Index 2013," http://cpi.transparency.org/cpi2013/results/ (accessed June 24, 2016).
23. Aruna Viswanatha, "Sandwich Chain Jimmy John's to Drop Noncompete Clauses from Hiring Packets," *The Wall Street Journal*, June 21, 2016, http://www.wsj.com/articles/sandwich-

chain-jimmy-johns-to-drop-noncompete-clauses-from-hiring-packets-1466557202 (accessed June 24, 2016).

24. Marriott, "Core Values and Heritage," http://www.marriott.com/culture-and-values/core-values.mi (accessed June 24, 2016).

25. "Code of Ethics," Direct Selling Association, http://www.dsa.org/consumerprotection/code-of-ethics (accessed June 24, 2016); "World Codes of Conduct for Direct Selling," World Federation of Direct Selling Associations, http://www.wfdsa.org/world_codes/ (accessed June 24, 2016).

26. UPS, "UPS Foundation—Our Mission," https://sustainability.ups.com/the-ups-foundation/ (accessed June 24, 2016).

27. Barbara W. Altman, "Transformed Corporate Community Relations: A Management Tool for Achieving Corporate Citizenship," *Business & Society Review* 102/103, no. 1 (March 1999): 43; Carroll, "Four Faces of Corporate Citizenship," p. 1.

28. Christopher N. Osher and Jennifer Brown, "Drug Firms Have Used Dangerous Tactics to Drive Sales to Treat Kids," *The Denver Post*, April 14, 2014, http://www.denverpost.com/investigations/ci_25561024/drug-firms-have-used-dangerous-tactics-drive-sales (accessed June 24, 2016).

29. BT, "Purposeful Business," http://www.btplc.com/Purposeful-business/ (accessed June 24, 2016).

30. Malcolm McIntosh, Deborah Leipziger, Keith Jones, and Gill Coleman, *Corporate Citizenship: Successful Strategies for Responsible Companies* (London: Financial Times Management, 2000); Linda S. Munilla and Morgan P. Miles, "The Corporate Social Responsibility Continuum as a Component of Stakeholder Theory," *Business and Society Review* 110 (December 2005): 371–387.

31. CRO Magazine, CR's 100 *Best Corporate Citizens 2016,* http://www.thecro.com/files/100%20Best%20List%202015.pdf (accessed June 24, 2016); ConocoPhillips Company, *ConocoPhillips: Sustainable Development,* 2013, http://www.conocophillips.com/sustainable-development/Documents/2013.11.7%201200%20Our%20Approach%20Section%20Final.pdf (accessed June 24, 2016).

32. R. Edward Freeman, *Strategic Management: A Stakeholder Approach* (Boston: Pitman, 1984).

33. Kingfisher, "Delivering Value," http://www.kingfisher.com/files/reports/annual_report_2012/business_review/delivering_value/ (accessed June 24, 2016); Kingfisher, "Net Positive," http://www.kingfisher.com/netpositive/index.asp?pageid=1 (accessed June 24, 2016).

34. Edward S. Mason, "Introduction," in *The Corporation in Modern Society,* ed. Edward S. Mason (Cambridge, MA: Harvard University Press, 1959), pp. 1–24.

35. Isabelle Maignan and O. C. Ferrell, "Measuring Corporate Citizenship in Two Countries: The Case of the United States and France," *Journal of Business Ethics* 23 (February 2000): 283; Robert J. Samuelson, "R.I.P.: The Good Corporation," *Newsweek,* July 5, 1993, p. 41.

36. Charles W. Wooten and Christie L. Roszkowski, "Legal Aspects of Corporate Governance in Early American Railroads," *Business and Economic History* 28 (Winter 1999): 325–326.

37. Ralph Estes, *Tyranny of the Bottom Line* (San Francisco: Berrett-Koehler, 1996); David Finn, *The Corporate Oligarch* (New York: Simon & Schuster, 1969).

38. Marina v. N. Whitman, *New World, New Rules* (Boston: Harvard Business School Press, 1999).

39. Mason, "Introduction."

40. Carl Kaysen, "The Corporation: How Much Power? What Scope?" in *The Corporation in Modern Society*, ed. Mason, pp. 85–105.

41. David M. Gordon, *Fat and Mean: The Corporate Squeeze of Working Americans and the Myth of Managerial "Downsizing"* (New York: Free Press, 1996).

42. Richard Leider, *The Power of Purpose: Creating Meaning in Your Life and Work* (San Francisco: Barrett-Koehler, 1997).

43. David J. Lynch, "Big Banks: Now Even Too Bigger to Fail," *Businessweek,* April 19, 2012, http://www.businessweek.com/articles/2012-04-19/big-banks-now-even-too-bigger-to-fail (accessed June 24, 2016).

44. Martin Wolf, "Comment and Analysis: The Big Lie of Global Inequality," *Financial Times,* February 9, 2000, p. 25.

45. Edelman, *2016 Edelman Trust Barometer Global Report,* http://www.edelman.com/insights/intellectual-property/2016-edelman-trust-barometer/global-results/ (accessed June 24, 2016).

46. M. N. Graham Dukes, "Accountability of the Pharmaceutical Industry," *The Lancet,* November 23, 2002, pp. 1682–1684; Elizabeth Olson, "Global Trade Negotiations Are Making Little Progress," *New York Times*, December 7, 2002, p. C3; Robert Pear, "Investigators Find Repeated Deception in Ads for Drugs," *New York Times*, December 4, 2002, p. A22.

47. John Dalla Costa, *The Ethical Imperative: Why Moral Leadership Is Good Business* (Reading, MA: Addison-Wesley, 1998).

48. Nestlé, "Nestlé's Corporate Business Principles," http://www.nestle.com/investors/corporate-governance/businessprinciples (accessed June 24, 2016).

49. The Coca-Cola Company, "Regional Sustainability Reports," October 23, 2013, http://www.coca-colacompany.com/sustainability/regional-sustainability-reports (accessed June 3, 2014).

50. S. A. Anwar, "APEC: Evidence and Policy Scenarios," *Journal of International Marketing and Marketing Research* 27 (October 2002): 141–153; Richard Feinberg, "Two Leading Lights of Humane Globalisation," *Singapore Straits Times,* February 21, 2000, p. 50.

51. Nicole Fallon, "15 Great Examples of Socially Responsible Businesses," *Business News Daily,* November 21, 2013, http://www.businessnewsdaily.com/5499-examples-socially-responsible-businesses.html (accessed June 24, 2016; SurveyMonky, "SurveyMonkey Contribute," http://help.surveymonkey.com/articles/en_US/kb/SurveyMonkey-Contribute (accessed June 24, 2016).)

52. Ibid.

53. Andreas Georg Scherer and Guido Palzaao, *Handbook of Research on Global Corporate Citizenship* (Cheltenham, UK: Edward Elgar, 2008).

54. Nielsen, "Nielsen Identifies Attributes of the Global, Socially-Conscious Consumer," March 27, 2012, http://www.nielsen.com/us/en/press-room/2012/nielsen-identifies-attributes-of-the-global--socially-conscious-.html (accessed June 24, 2016).

55. Frederick Reichheld, *The Loyalty Effect* (Cambridge, MA: Harvard Business School, 1996); Jeffrey S. Harrison and R. Edward Freeman, "Stakeholders, Social Responsibility, and Performance: Empirical Evidence and Theoretical Perspectives," *Academy of Management Journal* 42 (October 1999): 479.

56. Stephen R. Covey, "Is Your Company's Bottom Line Taking a Hit?" *PRNewswire,* June 4, 1998, http://www.prnewswire.

com; Terry W. Loe, "The Role of Ethical Climate in Developing Trust, Market Orientation and Commitment to Quality," unpublished Ph.D. dissertation, University of Memphis, 1996.

57. Ethics Resource Center, *National Business Ethics Survey of the U.S. Workforce* (Arlington, VA: Ethics Resource Center, 2014).

58. Cone Communications, *2013 Cone Communication Social Impact Study* (Boston: Cone Communications Public Relations and Marketing, 2013), p. 15.

59. Ibid.

60. Alsop, "Corporate Reputations Are Earned with Trust, Reliability, Study Shows," http://interactive.wsj.com.

61. "Richard Branson Reveals His Customer Service Secrets," *Forbes,* May 8, 2013, http://www.youtube.com/watch?v=Fy4lYDN1gz4 (accessed July 6, 2016).

62. Rachel W. Y. Yee, Andy C. L. Yeung, and T. C. Edwin Cheng, "An Empirical Study of Employee Loyalty, Service Quality and Firm Performance in the Service Industry," *International Journal of Performance Economics* 124, no. 1 (March 2010): 109–120.

63. C. B. Bhattacharya, Sankar Sen, and Daniel Korschun, "Using Corporate Social Responsibility to Win the War for Talent," MIT Sloan, Winter 2008, http://sloanreview.mit.edu/article/using-corporate-social-responsibility-to-win-the-war-for-talent/ (accessed July 6, 2016).

64. Tony Schwartz and Christine Porath, "Why You Hate Work," *The New York Times,* May 30, 2014, http://www.nytimes.com/2014/06/01/opinion/sunday/why-you-hate-work.html?_r=0 (accessed July 6, 2016).

65. John Galvin, "The New Business Ethics," *SmartBusinessMag.com,* June 2000, p. 97.

66. Paul Ziobro, "Target Earnings Slide 46% After Data Breach," *The Wall Street Journal,* February 26, 2014, http://online.wsj.com/news/articles/SB10001424052702304255604579406694182132568 (accessed July 6, 2016).

67. Dan Burrows, "Warren Buffett Buys a Stake in Verizon, Sells a Chunk of GM," *Investor Place,* May 16, 2014, http://investorplace.com/2014/05/warren-buffett-verizon-vz-stock-gm/#.V32MCnkUVVI (accessed July 6, 2016).

68. David Rynecki, "Here Are 8 Easy Ways to Lose Your Shirt in Stocks," *USA Today,* June 26, 1998, p. 3B.

69. "Investment Club Numbers Decline; Crisis of Confidence Caused Many to Take Their Money and Run," *Investor Relations Business,* September 23, 2002, p. 1; Charles Jaffe, "Securities Industry Aims to Renew Trust; Leaders Face Challenge of Rebuilding Investor Confidence Amid Slump," *Boston Globe,* November 8, 2002, p. E1.

70. Isabelle Maignan, O. C. Ferrell, and G. Tomas Hult, "Corporate Citizenship: Antecedents and Business Benefits," *Journal of the Academy of Marketing Science* 24, no. 4 (1999): 455–469.

71. S. B. Graves and S. A. Waddock, "Institutional Owners and Corporate Social Performance: Maybe Not So Myopic After All," *Proceedings of the International Association for Business and Society,* San Diego, CA, 1993; Ronald M. Roman, Sefa Hayibor, and Bradley R. Agle, "The Relationship between Social and Financial Performance," *Business and Society* 38 (March 1999); W. Gary Simpson and Theodor Kohers, "The Link between Corporate Social and Financial Performance: Evidence from the Banking Industry," *Journal of Business Ethics* 35 (January 2002): 97–109; Curtis Verschoor and Elizabeth A. Murphy, "The Financial Performance of U.S. Firms and Those with Global Prominence: How Do the Best

Corporate Citizens Rate?" *Business and Society Review* 197 (Fall 2002): 371–380; S. Waddock and S. Graves, "The Corporate Social Performance-Financial Performance Link," *Strategic Management Journal* 18 (1997): 303–319.

72. Chris C. Verschoor, "A Study of the Link between a Corporation's Financial Performance and Its Commitment to Ethics," *Journal of Business Ethics* 31 (October 1998): 1509.

73. Shawn L. Berman, Andrew C. Wicks, Suresh Kotha, and Thomas M. Jones, "Does Stakeholder Orientation Matter? The Relationship between Stakeholder Management Models and Firm Financial Performance," *Academy of Management Journal* 42 (October 1999): 502–503.

74. Roman, Hayibor, and Agle, "The Relationship between Social and Financial Performance."

75. Melissa A. Baucus and David A. Baucus, "Paying the Payer: An Empirical Examination of Longer Term Financial Consequences of Illegal Corporate Behavior," *Academy of Management Journal* 40 (1997): 129–151.

76. Marc Orlitzky and Diane L. Swanson, *Toward Integrative Corporate Citizenship: Research Advances in Corporate Social Performance* (New York: Palgrave Macmillan, 2008).

77. K. J. Arrow, *The Limits of Organizational* (New York: W. W. Norton, 1974), pp. 23, 26; D. C. North, *Institutions: Institutional Change, and Economic Performance* (Cambridge: Cambridge University Press, 1990).

78. Shelby D. Hunt, "Resource-Advantage Theory and the Wealth of Nations: Developing the Socio-Economic Research Tradition," *Journal of Socio-Economics* 26 (1997): 335–357.

79. North, *Institutions,* p. 9.

80. L. E. Harrison, *Who Prospers? How Cultural Values Shape Economic and Political Success* (New York: Basic Books, 1992), p. 16.

81. Edelman, "2014 Edelman Trust Barometer Global Survey," http://www.edelman.com/insights/intellectual-property/2014-edelman-trust-barometer/ (accessed July 6, 2016).

82. Hunt, "Resource-Advantage Theory and the Wealth of Nations," pp. 351–352.

83. © Transparency International, *Corruption Perceptions Index 2015* (Berlin, Germany, 2016). All rights reserved.

84. Transparency International, "Global Corruption Report 2006," http://www.transparency.org/whatwedo/pub/global_corruption_report_2006_corruption_and_health (accessed July 6, 2016).

85. Cummins, "Sustainability at Cummins," http://www.cummins.com/global-impact/sustainability (accessed July 6, 2016); Ethisphere Institute, "World's Most Ethical Companies® Honorees," 2016, http://worldsmostethicalcompanies.ethisphere.com/honorees/ (accessed July 6, 2016) Cummins, Cummins Engines website, https://cumminsengines.com/ (accessed July 6, 2016).

86. Better Business Bureau, "BBB Expels 5 Firms for Accreditation Violations," April 2, 2015, http://www.bbb.org/stlouis/news-events/news-releases/2015/04/bbb-revokes-accreditation-for-5-firms/ (accessed July 6, 2016).

87. "19th Annual Technical Excellence Awards," *PC Magazine,* November 19, 2002, http://www.pcmag.com (accessed December 20, 2002); Glenn R. Simpson, "Raytheon Offers Office Software for Snooping," *Wall Street Journal,* June 14, 2000, p. B1.

88. Robin Sidel, "Cyberthieves' Latest Target: Your Tax Forms," The Wall Street Journal, April 3, 2016, http://www.wsj.com/articles/

online-thieves-target-employee-tax-information-1459715329 (accessed July 6, 2016).

89. S&P Dow Jones Indices, "Dow Jones Sustainability World Index," 2014, http://eu.spindices.com/indices/equity/dow-jones-sustainability-world-index (accessed June 4, 2014); Dow Jones Sustainability Indices, "Overview," http://www.sustainability-indices.com/index-family-overview/djsi-diversi-fied-family-overview/index.jsp (accessed June 4, 2014).

90. William B. Werther and David Chandler, "Strategic Corporate Social Responsibility as Global Brand Insurance," *Business Horizons* 48 (July–August 2005): 317–324.

Chapter 2

1. Better Business Bureau, "The Children's Food and Beverage Industry Advertising Initiative in Action," http://www.bbb.org/us/storage/16/documents/CFBAI/ChildrenF&BInit_Sept21.pdf (accessed July 7, 2016); "Kaiser Family Foundation Releases New Report on Role of Media in Childhood Obesity," Washington Panel Discussion to Explore Role of Media/Policy Options, http://www.kff.org/entmedia/entmedia022404nr.cfm (accessed April 15, 2009); "More 'Healthy' Junk Food on the Horizon?" *CNNMoney.com*, http://money.cnn.com/2005/09/16/news/fortune500/healthy_food/index.htm (accessed July 7, 2016); Let's Move! http://www.letsmove.gov/ (accessed July 7, 2016); Michelle Healy, "Price Tag for Childhood Obesity $19,000 Per Kid," *USA Today*, April 7, 2014, http://www.usatoday.com/story/news/nation/2014/04/07/childhood-obesity-costs/7298461/ (accessed July 7, 2016); Stephanie Strom, "Food Companies Have Cut Back on Calories, Study Says," *The New York Times*, January 9, 2014, http://www.nytimes.com/2014/01/09/health/food-companies-have-cut-back-on-calories-study-says.html (accessed July 7, 2016); Dale Buss, "Coca-Cola Pledges to Cut Ads to Kids, Display More Calorie Information," *Brand Channel*, May 9, 2013, http://brandchannel.com/2013/05/09/coca-cola-pledges-to-cut-ads-to-kids-display-more-calorie-information/ (accessed July 7, 2016); Michael Castillo, "Disney to Cut Junk Food Advertising from Its Platforms," *CBS News*, June 5, 2012, http://www.cbsnews.com/news/disney-to-cut-junk-food-advertising-from-its-platforms/ (accessed July 7, 2016).

2. Scott J. Reynolds, Frank C. Schultz, and David R. Hekman, "Stakeholder Theory and Managerial Decision-Making: Constraints and Implications of Balancing Stakeholder Interests," *Journal of Business Ethics* 64, no. 3 (March 2006): 285–301.

3. Vikas Anand, Blake E. Ashforth, and Mahendra Joshi, "Business as Usual: The Acceptance and Perpetuation of Corruption in Organizations," *Academy of Management Executive* 18, no. 2 (2004): 39–53.

4. Chris Marsden, "The New Corporate Citizenship of Big Business: Part of the Solution to Sustainability?" *Business and Society Review* 105 (Spring 2000): 9–25; James E. Post, Lee E. Preston, and Sybille Sachs, *Redefining the Corporation: Stakeholder Management and Organizational Wealth* (Stanford, CA: Stanford University Press, 2002).

5. D. L. Swanson and W. C. Frederick, "Denial and Leadership in Business Ethics Education," in *Business Ethics: New Challenges for Business Schools and Corporate Leaders*, ed. R. A. Peterson and O. C. Ferrell (New York: M. E. Sharpe, 2004).

6. American Productivity & Quality Center, *Community Relations: Unleashing the Power of Corporate Citizenship* (Houston, TX: American Productivity & Quality Center, 1998); Thomas Donaldson and Lee E. Preston, "The Stakeholder Theory of the Corporation: Concepts, Evidence and Implications," *Academy of Management Review* 29 (January 1995): 65–91; Jaan Elias and J. Gregory Dees, "The Normative Foundations of Business," Harvard Business School Publishing, June 10, 1997.

7. G. A. Steiner and J. F. Steiner, *Business, Government, and Society* (New York: Random House, 1988).

8. Milton Friedman, "Social Responsibility of Business Is to Increase Its Profits," *New York Times Magazine*, September 13, 1970, pp. 122–126.

9. "Business Leaders, Politicians and Academics Dub Corporate Irresponsibility 'An Attack on America from Within,'" Business Wire, November 7, 2002, via America Online.

10. Adam Smith, *The Theory of Moral Sentiments*, Vol. 2 (New York: Prometheus, 2000).

11. Theodore Levitt, *The Marketing Imagination* (New York: Free Press, 1983).

12. Norman Bowie, "Empowering People as an End for Business," in *People in Corporations: Ethical Responsibilities and Corporate Effectiveness*, ed. Georges Enderle, Brenda Almond, and Antonio Argandona (Dordrecht, The Netherlands: Kluwer Academic Press, 1990), pp. 105–112.

13. Nielson, "Do Consumers Care About Social Impact?" August 6, 2013, http://www.nielsen.com/us/en/newswire/2013/do-consumers-care-about-social-impact-.html (accessed July 7, 2016).

14. Isabelle Maignan, "Antecedents and Benefits of Corporate Citizenship: A Comparison of U.S. and French Businesses," unpublished Ph.D. dissertation, University of Memphis, 1997.

15. Adapted from Isabelle Maignan, O. C. Ferrell, and Linda Ferrell, "A Stakeholder Model for Implementing Social Responsibility in Marketing," *European Journal of Marketing* 39 (September–October 2005), pp. 956–977.

16. Ibid.

17. Ibid.

18. MetLife, "Insights from MetLife's 12th Annual U.S. Employee Benefits Trends Study," 2014, https://benefit-trends.metlife.com/assets/downloads/benefits-breakthrough-summaries-2014.pdf (accessed July 7, 2016).

19. Isabelle Maignan and O. C. Ferrell, "Corporate Social Responsibility: Toward a Marketing Conceptualization," *Journal of the Academy of Marketing Science* 32 (2004): 3–19.

20. Ibid.

21. David L. Schwartzkopf, "Stakeholder Perspectives and Business Risk Perception," *Journal of Business Ethics* 64, no. 4 (April 2006): 327–342.

22. Maignan and Ferrell, "Corporate Social Responsibility."

23. Cloetta, "Corporate Responsibility," http://www.cloetta.com/en/corporate-responsibility/ (accessed July 7, 2016).

24. Ibid.

25. This section is adapted from Isabelle Maignan, Bas Hillebrand, and Debbie Thorne McAlister, "Managing Socially Responsible Buying: How to Integrate Non-economic Criteria into the Purchasing Process," *European Management Journal* 20 (December 2002): 641–648.

26. Andrew L. Friedman and Samantha Miles, "Developing Stakeholder Theory," *Journal of Management Studies* 39 (January 2002): 1–21; Ronald K. Mitchell, Bradley R. Agle, and Donna J. Wood, "Toward a Theory of Stakeholder

Identification and Salience: Defining the Principle of Who and What Really Counts," *Academy of Management Review* 22 (October 1997): 853–886.

27. Will Burns, "Walmart Brand Doubles Down On 'Live Better' With Commitment to American Manufacturing," *Forbes,* February 19, 2014, http://www.forbes.com/sites/will-burns/2014/02/19/walmart-brand-doubles-down-on-live-bet-ter-with-commitment-to-american-manufacturing/ (accessed July 7, 2016); Jason Furman, "The Fifth Anniversary of the American Recovery and Reinvestment Act," *The White House,* February 17, 2014, https://www.whitehouse.gov/blog/2014/02/17/fifth-anniversary-american-recovery-and-reinvestment-act (accessed July 7, 2016).

28. Amitai Etzioni, *Modern Organizations* (Upper Saddle River, NJ: Prentice Hall, 1964).

29. Treasury Advisory Committee on International Child Labor Enforcement, "Notices," *Federal Register*, March 6, 2000, 65 FR 11831.

30. Brian Scott, "3 Arrested in Denton Fracking Protest," *NBC,* June 1, 2015, http://www.nbcdfw.com/news/local/3-Arrested-in-Denton-Fracking-Protest-305759361.html (accessed July 7, 2016).

31. Mark C. Suchman, "Managing Legitimacy: Strategic and Institutional Approaches," *Academy of Management Review* 20 (July 1995): 571–610.

32. Brad Knickerbock, "Activists Step Up War to 'Liberate' Nature," *Christian Science Monitor*, January 20, 1999, p. 4.

33. Sharon Kelly, "Responding to Investor Pressure, ExxonMobil Agrees to Disclose Fracking Risks," *DeSmog Blog*, April 6, 2014, http://www.desmogblog.com/2014/04/06/exxonmobil-agrees-disclose-fracking-risks-investors (accessed July 7, 2016); Sharon Kelly, "Risks of Fracking Boom Draw Renewed Attention from Investors," *DeSomg Blog*, February 4, 2014, http://www.des-mogblog.com/2014/02/04/risks-fracking-boom-draw-renewed-attention-investors (accessed July 7, 2016).

34. Ruma Paul, "Protests Rage over Bangladesh Factory Fire, Supervisors Arrested," *Reuters*, November 28, 2012, http://www.reuters.com/article/us-bangladesh-fire-idUS-BRE8AQ0WE20121128 (accessed July 7, 2016); Joanne Chiu and Tripti Lahiri, "Factory Fire Draws Protests in Bangla-desh," *The Wall Street Journal*, November 26, 2012, http://online.wsj.com/news/articles/SB1000142412788732446930 4578142053199783698 (accessed July 7, 2016).

35. Hiroko Tabuchi, "Boeing Pitches Its Solution for Dreamliner Problems," *The New York Times*, March 15, 2013, http://www.nytimes.com/2013/03/15/business/boeing-presents-fix-for-787s-battery-problems.html (accessed July 7, 2016); Ben W. Heineman, Jr., "From BP to Boeing, Supplier Safety Is the CEO's Problem," *HBR Blog Network*, March 4, 2013, http://blogs.hbr.org/2013/03/bp-and-boeing-leadership-lesso/ (accessed July 7, 2016).

36. UNM Daniels Fund Ethics Initiative, "Should Pharmacies Sell Harmful Products?" https://danielsethics.mgt.unm.edu/pdf/cvs-debate-issue.pdf (accessed July 7, 2016).

37. Ronald Alsop, "Corporate Reputations Are Earned with Trust, Reliability, Study Shows," *Wall Street Journal*, September 23, 1999, http://interactive.wsj.com; John F. Mahon, "Corporate Reputation: A Research Agenda Using Strategy and Stakeholder Literature," *Business and Society* 41 (December 2002): 415–445.

38. The Nielson Company, "The Harris Poll 2014 RQ Summary Report," April 2014, http://www.nielsen.com/content/dam/corporate/us/en/reports-downloads/2014%20Reports/harris-poll-2014-rq-summary-report.pdf (accessed July 7, 2016).

39. Manto Gotsi and Alan Wilson, "Corporate Reputation Management: 'Living the Brand,'" *Management Decision* 39, no. 2 (2001): 99–105; Jim Kartalia, "Technology Safeguards for a Good Corporate Reputation," *Information Executive* 3 (September 1999): 4; Prema Nakra, "Corporate Reputation Management: 'CRM' with a Strategic Twist?" *Public Rela-tions Quarterly* 45 (Summer 2000): 35–42.

40. Jeanne Logsdon and Donna J. Wood, "Reputation as an Emerg-ing Construct in the Business and Society Field: An Introduc-tion," *Business and Society* 41 (December 2002): 265–270; "Putting a Price Tag to Reputation," Council of Public Relations Firms, http://www.prfirms.org (accessed December 20, 2002); Allen M. Weiss, Erin Anderson, and Deborah J. MacInnis, "Reputation Management as a Motivation for Sales Structure Decisions," *Journal of Marketing* 63 (October 1999): 74–89.

41. Christy Eidson and Melissa Master, "Who Makes the Call?" *Across the Board* 37 (March 2000): 16; Logsdon and Wood, "Reputation as an Emerging Construct in the Business and Society Field."

42. Alison Rankin Frost, "Brand vs. Reputation," *Communica-tion World* 16 (February-March 1999): 22–25.

43. Glen Peters, *Waltzing with the Raptors: A Practical Roadmap to Protecting Your Company's Reputation* (New York: Wiley, 1999).

44. AT&T, "Connect to Good: External Recognition," http://about.att.com/content/csr/home/frequently-requested-info/external-recognition.html (accessed July 7, 2016); It Can Wait website, http://about.att.com/content/csr/home/frequently-requested-info/external-recognition.html (accessed July 7, 2016); AT&T, "Connect to Good: The AT&T Issue Brief Library," http://about.att.com/content/csr/home/issue-brief-builder/environment/water-management.html (accessed July 7, 2016); Communities in Schools, "AT&T Invests $4.5 Million in the Future of Education for At-Risk Students," October 28, 2015, https://www.communitiesinschools.org/press-room/resource/t-invests-45-million-future-education-risk-students/ (accessed July 7, 2016).

45. "2014 Edelman Trust Barometer Global Results," *Edelman*, 2014, http://www.edelman.com/insights/intellectual-property/2014-edelman-trust-barometer/ (accessed July 7, 2016). "FDI Reputation," *Germany Trade & Invest*, 2016, https://www.gtai.de/GTAI/Navigation/EN/Invest/Business-location-germany/FDI/fdi-reputation.html (accessed July 7, 2016); "MBA—Reputation Management," European Univer-sity Business School Munich, https://www.euruni.edu/euruni/Programs/Graduate-MBA/MBA-Reputation-Management/Overview/MBA-Reputation-Management-Overview.html (accessed July 7, 2016).

46. Much of this section is adapted from Lisa A. Mainiero, "Action or Reaction? Handling Businesses in Crisis After September 11," *Business Horizons* 45 (September–October 2002): 2–10; Robert R. Ulmer and Timothy L. Sellnow, "Consistent Questions of Ambiguity in Organizational Crisis Communication: Jack in the Box as a Case Study," *Journal of Business Ethics* 25 (May 2000): 143–155; Robert R. Ulmer and Timothy L. Sellnow, "Strategic Ambiguity and the Ethic of Significant Choices in the Tobacco Industry's Crisis Communication," *Communication Studies* 48, no. 3 (1997):

215–233; Timothy L. Sellnow and Robert R. Ulmer, "Ambiguous Argument as Advocacy in Organizational Crisis Communication," *Argumentation and Advocacy* 31, no. 3 (1995): 138–150; Peter V. Stanton, "Ten Communication Mistakes You Can Avoid When Managing a Crisis," *Public Relations Quarterly* 47 (Summer 2002): 19–22.

47. Joanne Muller, "Exclusive Q&A: GM CEO Mary Barra On Crisis Management, Culture Change And The Future of GM," *Forbes*, May 29, 2014, http://www.forbes.com/sites/joannmuller/2014/05/29/exclusive-qa-gm-ceo-mary-barra-on-crisis-management-culture-change-and-the-future-of-gm/#3bfbea2b684d (accessed July 7, 2016); Mark Athitakis, "Three Lessons from Mary T. Barra's Crisis At GM," *Associations Now*, March 2014, http://associationsnow.com/2014/03/three-lessons-from-mary-t-barras-crisis-at-gm/ (accessed July 7, 2016).

48. Lynn Brewer, Robert Chandler, and O. C. Ferrell, *Managing Risks for Corporate Integrity: How to Survive an Ethical Misconduct Disaster* (Mason, OH: Texere/Thomson, 2006), pp. 2–3.

49. Michael Muskal, "BP Guilty of Criminal Misconduct, Negligence in Gulf Oil Spill," *The Los Angeles Times*, November 15, 2012, http://articles.latimes.com/2012/nov/15/nation/la-na-nn-bp-criminal-penalty-gulf-oil-spill-20121115 (accessed June 7, 2016); Jonathan L. Ramseur and Curry L. Hagerty, "Deepwater Horizon Oil Spill: Recent Activities and Ongoing Developments," *Congressional Research Service*, April 17, 2015, http://www.fas.org/sgp/crs/misc/R42942.pdf (accessed July 7, 2016); Associated Press, "Investigation into 2010 BP Oil Spill Finds Failures, Poor Testing and Ongoing Risks," *The Guardian*, June 5, 2014, https://www.theguardian.com/environment/2014/jun/05/bp-deepwater-horizon-spill-report-failures-risks (accessed July 7, 2016). (accessed June 5, 2014).

50. Sarah Kent and Christopher M. Matthews, "Huge 2010 Oil Spill Still Shadows BP," *The Wall Street Journal*, April 27, 2016, A1, A11.

51. Krystina Gustafson, "Lord & Taylor settles deceptive advertising charges," *CNBC*, March 15, 2016, http://www.cnbc.com/2016/03/15/ (accessed July 7, 2016).

52. Paul Argenti, "Crisis Communication: Lessons from 9/11," *Harvard Business Review* 80 (December 2002): 103–109; L. Paul Bremer, "Corporate Governance and Crisis Management," *Directors and Boards* 26 (Winter 2002): 16–20; Christine M. Pearson and Judith A. Clair, "Reframing Crisis Management," *Academy of Management Review* 23 (January 1998): 59–76.

53. Ben DiPietro, "Crisis of the Week: Disney Responds to Alligator Killing Boy," *The Wall Street Journal*, June 28, 2016, http://blogs.wsj.com/riskandcompliance/2016/06/28/crisis-of-the-week-disney-responds-to-alligator-killing-boy/ (accessed July 7, 2016).

54. Ibid.

55. Michael John Harker, "Relationship Marketing Defined?" *Marketing Intelligence and Planning* 17 (January 1999): 13–20; Robert M. Morgan and Shelby D. Hunt, "The Commitment-Trust Theory of Relationship Marketing," *Journal of Marketing* 58 (July 1994): 20–38.

56. Jordan Kahn, "Apple kicks off its big in-store iPhone upgrade event," 2014, *9to5Mac*, http://9to5mac.com/2014/05/09/apple-kicks-off-its-big-in-store-iphone-upgrade-event/ (accessed July 7, 2016).

57. Paula Andruss, "Secrets of the 10 Most-Trusted Brands," *Entrepreneur*, March 20, 2012, http://www.entrepreneur.com/article/223125 (accessed July 7, 2016).

58. Jörg Andriof and Sandra Waddock, "Unfolding Stakeholder Engagement," in *Unfolding Stakeholder Thinking: Theory, Responsibility and Engagement*, ed. Jörg Andriof, Sandra Waddock, Bryan Husted, and Sandra S. Rahman (Sheffield, UK: Greenleaf Publishing, 2002), pp. 19–42; James Coleman, "Social Capital in the Creation of Human Capital," *American Journal of Sociology* 94 (1988): S95–S120; Carrie R. Leana and Harry J. Van Buren III, "Organizational Social Capital and Employment Practices," *Academy of Management Review* 24 (July 1999): 538–555.

59. Barbara Gray, "Social Capital: The Secret Behind Airbnb and Uber," *BrandyCap*, June 4, 2014, http://bradycap.com/social-capital-the-secret-behind-airbnb-and-uber/ (accessed July 7, 2016).

60. Adapted from Maignan, Ferrell, and Ferrell, "A Stakeholder Model for Implementing Social Responsibility in Marketing," pp. 956–977.

61. Jacqueline Smith, "America's 100 Best Corporate Citizens," *Forbes*, April 11, 2013, http://www.forbes.com/sites/jacquelynsmith/2013/04/11/americas-100-best-corporate-citizens/2/ (accessed July 7, 2016); Marc Gunther, "Trouble Brewing: Has Success Spoiled Green Mountain?" *The Guardian*, May 28, 2014, http://www.theguardian.com/sustainable-business/green-mountain-keurig-coffee-pods-waste-recycling (accessed July 7, 2016).

62. Andrew M. Seaman, "U.S. Childhood Obesity Rates Have Actually Increased Over the Past 14 Years (STUDY)," *The Huffington Post*, April 8, 2014, http://www.huffingtonpost.com/2014/04/08/childhood-obesity-rates-increased_n_5111922.html (accessed July 7, 2016); "New CDC Data Show Encouraging Development in Obesity Rates among 2 to 5 Year Olds," *Centers for Disease Control*, February 25, 2014, http://www.cdc.gov/media/releases/2014/p0225-child-obesity.html (accessed July 7, 2016).

63. Corporate Social Responsibility at Starbucks, http://www.starbucks.com/aboutus/csr.asp (accessed July 7, 2016).

64. Maria Godoy, "New Rules Would Curb How Kids Are Sold Junk Food at School," *NPR*, February 25, 2014, http://www.npr.org/blogs/thesalt/2014/02/25/282507974/new-rules-would-curb-how-kids-are-sold-junk-food-at-school (accessed July 7, 2016); Eryn Brown and Teresa Watanabe, "Laws against junk food in schools help rich students more than poor ones," Los Angeles Times, May 4, 2015, http://www.latimes.com/science/sciencenow/la-sci-sn-school-junk-food-child-obesity-20150504-story.html (accessed July 7, 2016).

65. Dave Lieber, "Texas Business Owners Say Negative Comments on Yelp Hurt Bottom Line," *Dallas News*, November 7, 2013, http://www.dallasnews.com/investigations/watchdog/20131107-watchdog-texas-business-owners-say-negative-comments-on-yelp-hurt-bottom-line.ece (accessed June 6, 2014).

66. Michael Pirson and Deepak Malhotra, "Unconventional Insights for Managing Stakeholder Trust," *Sloan Management Review* 49 (Summer 2008): 42–50.

67. Taylor Ray, "World Watches as Coca-Cola Launches Flagship EKOCENTER in Rwanda," *Coca-Cola Journey,* June 24, 2016, http://www.coca-colacompany.com/coca-cola-unbottled/world-watches-as-coca-cola-launches-flagship-ekocenter-in-rwanda (accessed July 7, 2016); Adeline Chong, "Coke Combats Sustainability and Nutrition Critics with Rural

Ekocenters," *BrandChannel*, October 8, 2013, http://brand-channel.com/2013/10/08/coke-combats-sustainability-and-nutrition-critics-with-rural-ekocenters/ (accessed July 7, 2016).

68. Max B. E. Clarkson, "A Stakeholder Framework for Analyzing and Evaluating Corporate Social Performance," *Academy of Management Review* 20 (January 1995): 92–117.
69. Ibid.
70. Ibid.
71. Ibid.
72. Ibid.
73. Jörg Andriof, "Managing Social Risk Through Stakeholder Partnership Building," unpublished Ph.D. dissertation, Warwick Business School, 2000; Andriof, "Patterns of Stakeholder Partnership Building," pp. 215–238.
74. Nick Chaloner and David Brontzen, "How SABMiller Protects Its Biggest Asset—Its Reputation," *Strategic Communication Management* 6 (October–November 2002): 12–15.

Chapter 3

1. Devlin Barrett, "Credit Suisse to Pay $2.5 Billion in Pact," *The Wall Street Journal*, May 16, 2014, pp. C1–C2; Ben Protess and Jessica Silver-Greenberg, "Credit Suisse Pleads Guilty in Felony Case," *The New York Times*, May 19, 2014, http://dealbook.nytimes.com/2014/05/19/credit-suisse-set-to-plead-guilty-in-tax-evasion-case/?_php=true&_type=blogs&ref=business&_r=0 (accessed July 8, 2016); Dominic Rushe, "Credit Suisse Pleads Guilty to Criminal Charges in US Tax Evasion Settlement," *The Guardian*, May 19, 2014, http://www.theguardian.com/business/2014/may/19/credit-suisse-plead-guilty-criminal-charges-us-tax-evasion (accessed July 8, 2016); Jenny Anderson and Peter Eavis, "Credit Suisse's C.E.O. Is Called the Teflon Man," *The New York Times*, May 19, 2014, http://dealbook.nytimes.com/2014/05/19/credit-suisses-guilty-plea-casts-a-spotlight-on-the-banks-teflon-leader/ (accessed July 8, 2016); Frances Coppola, "Credit Suisse Is Too Big To Go To Jail," *Forbes*, May 24, 2014, http://www.forbes.com/sites/francescoppola/2014/05/24/credit-suisse-is-too-big-to-jail/#16c31ea5735f (accessed July 8, 2016). Sneha Shankar, "Credit Suisse Helped Rich Americans Evade Billions in Taxes: Senate Subcommittee Report," *International Business Times*, February 26, 2014, http://www.ibtimes.com/credit-suisse-helped-rich-americans-evade-billions-taxes-senate-subcommittee-report-1557956 (accessed July 8, 2016). Jenny Anderson, "Credit Suisse Investors Shrug Off Tax Plea," *The New York Times*, May 20, 2014, http://dealbook.nytimes.com/2014/05/20/credit-suisse-chief-sees-little-impact-from-tax-evasion-plea/ (accessed July 8, 2016).
2. Rafael LaPorta and Florencio Lopez-de-Silanes, "Investor Protection and Corporate Governance," *Journal of Financial Economics* 58 (October–November 2000): 3–38.
3. Gretchen Morgenson, "Directors Disappoint by What They Don't Do," *The New York Times*, May 11, 2013, http://www.nytimes.com/2013/05/12/business/board-directors-disappoint.html (accessed July 8, 2016).
4. *Dodge v. Ford Motor Co.*, 204 Mich. 459, 179 N.W. 668, 3 A.L.R. 413 (1919).

5. Jordan Owen, "Manager of Schaumburg health company convicted of Medicare fraud," *Chicago Sun Times*, April 18, 2016, http://chicago.suntimes.com/news/head-of-schaumburg-health-care-company-convicted-of-fraud/ (accessed July 8, 2016).
6. Alfred Marcus and Sheryl Kaiser, *Managing Beyond Compliance: The Ethical and Legal Dimensions of Corporate Responsibility* (Garfield Heights, OH: North Coast Publishers, 2006), p. 79.
7. Jeffrey Dastin and Alwyn Scott, "Activist investors question United Airlines CEO's board role, pay," *Reuters*, March 14, 2016, http://www.reuters.com/article/us-ual-board-idUSKC-N0WF0EA (accessed July 8, 2016).
8. Min-Jeong Lee, "Samsung Insider-Trading Probe Involves President-Level Executives," *The Wall Street Journal*, December 7, 2015, http://www.wsj.com/articles/samsung-insider-trading-probe-involves-president-level-executives-1449478252 (accessed July 8, 2016).
9. Ben W. Heineman Jr., "Are You a Good Corporate Citizen?" *Wall Street Journal*, June 28, 2005, http://online.wsj.com/article/0,,SB111991936947571125,00-search.html (accessed July 8, 2016).
10. Joann S. Lublin, "McKesson Makes Corporate-Governance Changes," *The Wall Street Journal*, January 21, 2014, http://online.wsj.com/news/articles/SB10001424052702304027204579335081375388634 (accessed July 8, 2016).
11. Erik Berglöf and Stijn Claessens, "Enforcement and Good Corporate Governance in Developing Countries and Transition Economies," *The World Bank Research Observer*, February 21, 2006, http://wbro.oxfordjournals.org/cgi/content/full/21/1/123 (accessed July 8, 2016); Darryl Reed, "Corporate Governance Reforms in Developing Countries," *Journal of Business Ethics* 37 (May 2002): 223–247.
12. Bryan W. Husted and Carlos Serrano, "Corporate Governance in Mexico," *Journal of Business Ethics* 37 (May 2002): 337–348.
13. Robert A. G. Monks, *Corporate Governance in the Twenty-First Century: A Preliminary Outline* (Portland, ME: LENS, 1996), http://www.lens-library.com/info/cg21.html.
14. McRitchie, "Ending the Wall Street Walk: Why Corporate Governance Now?" *Corporate Governance*, http://www.corp-gov.net/library/papers-references/ending-the-wall-street-walk-why-corporate-governance-now/ (accessed July 8, 2016).
15. David A. Cifrino and Garrison R. Smith, "NYSE and NASDAQ Propose to Review Corporate Governance Listing Standards," *Corporate Governance Advisor* 10 (November–December 2002): 18–25.
16. Timothy Devinney, "Is the Socially Responsible Corporation a Myth? The Good, the Bad, and the Ugly of Corporate Social Responsibility," *Academy of Management Perspectives* 23, no. 2 (May 2009): 44–56; Luke Mullins, "Obama's Financial Regulation Reform: 7 Things You Need to Know," *U.S. News*, June 17, 2009, http://money.usnews.com/money/blogs/the-home-front/2009/06/17/obamas-financial-regulation-reform-7-things-you-need-to-know (accessed July 8, 2016).
17. Ada Demb and Franz-Friedrich Neubauer, *The Corporate Board: Confronting the Paradoxes* (Oxford: Oxford University Press, 1992).
18. Jenny Strasburg, Giles Turner, and Eyk Henning, "Banker In Suicide Anxious on Probes," *The Wall Street Journal*, March 26, 2014, pp. C1, C2; Chad Bray, "Deutsche Bank Warns Investors on Currency Investigation," *The New York Times*, June 5, 2014, http://dealbook.nytimes.

com/2014/06/05/deutsche-bank-warns-investors-on-cur-rency-investigation/ (accessed July 8, 2016). Kathrin Jones and Thomas Atkins, "No End In Sight for Deutsche Bank Libor Probe: Sources," *Reuters*, May 12, 2014, http://www.reuters.com/article/2014/05/12/us-deutsche-bank-libor-idUSBREA4B09220140512 (accessed July 8, 2016).

19. Organisation for Economic Co-operation and Development, *The OECD Principles of Corporate Governance* (Paris: Organisation for Economic Co-operation and Development, 1999).

20. John Kester and Maxwell Murphy, "New Details on Conflict Minerals," *The Wall Street Journal*, June 3, 2014, pp. B1, B4.

21. "Corporate Governance," *International Finance Corporation: World Bank Group*, http://www.ifc.org/corporategovernance (accessed July 8, 2016).

22. Clive Crook, "Why Good Corporate Citizens Are a Public Menace," *National Journal*, April 24, 1999, p. 1087.

23. Joseph Major, "Citi's Board Seeks Revamp with ex-Finance Chiefs, Fed Official," *International Business Times*, http://www.ibtimes.com/articles/20090316/citi-calls-on-ex-finance-chiefs-former-fed-official-board.htm (accessed June 6, 2014).

24. Melvin A. Eisenberg, "Corporate Governance: The Board of Directors and Internal Control," *Cordoza Law Review* 19 (September–November 1997): 237.

25. Halah Touryalai, "Jamie Dimon's Power Struggle: Loses Bank Chairman Role, A Bigger Blow May Come Next," *Forbes*, October 4, 2013, http://www.forbes.com/sites/halahtouryalai/2013/10/04/jamie-dimons-power-struggle-loses-bank-chairman-role-a-bigger-blow-may-come-next/#43b1afa84729 (accessed July 12, 2016).

26. NYSE, "303A.01 Independent Directors," *NYSE Manual*, http://nysemanual.nyse.com/lcm/Help/mapContent.asp?sec=lcm-sections&title=sx-ruling-nyse-policymanual_303A.01&id=chp_1_4_3_2 (accessed July 12, 2016).

27. NYSE, "303A.00 Corporate Governance Standards," *NYSE Manual*, http://nysemanual.nyse.com/lcm/sections/lcm-sections/chp_1_4/default.asp (accessed July 12, 2016).

28. Louis Lavelle, "The Best and Worst Boards," *Business Week*, October 7, 2002, p. 104.

29. Harvey L. Pitt, "Retaining Ethical Cultures During a Week Economy," *Compliance Week*, June 30, 2009, https://www.complianceweek.com/blogs/harvey-l-pitt/retaining-ethical-cultures-during-a-weak-economy#.V4V9_LgrLIU (accessed July 12, 2016).

30. "Biz Deans Talk-Business Management Education Blog," January 2, 2009, http://www.deanstalk.net/deanstalk/2009/01/warren-buffetts.html (accessed June 7, 2014); "Volcker Rule Resource Center," *Securities Industry and Financial Markets Association*, http://www.sifma.org/issues/regulatory-reform/volcker-rule/overview/ (accessed July 12, 2016).

31. Adrian Cadbury, "What Are the Trends in Corporate Governance? How Will They Impact Your Company?" *Long Range Planning* 32 (January 1999): 12–19.

32. "How Shareholder Proposals Work," *The Equality Project*, http://www.equalityproject.org (accessed June 7, 2014); Barry Burr, "Shareholder Activism Hot in Poor Business Climate," *Pensions & Investments*, July 8, 2002, pp. 4, 32; Chuck Collins and Sam Pizzigati, "What Happened to the Crackdown on Executive Pay?" *The Baltimore Sun*, June 24, 2009, http://www.commondreams.org/view/2009/06/24-6 (accessed July 12, 2016).

33. Lauren Tara LaCapra, "BofA's Board Shuffle an Ode to Stakeholders," *The Street*, June 22, 2009, http://www.thestreet.com/story/10523721/1/bofas-board-shuffle-an-ode-to-shareholders.html?cm_ven=GOOGLEFI (accessed July 12. 2016).

34. "Internal Auditors: Integral to Good Corporate Governance," *Internal Auditor* 59 (August 2002): 44–49.

35. Donna Kardos, "KPMG Is Sued Over New Century," *Wall Street Journal*, April 2, 2009, http://online.wsj.com/news/articles/SB123860415462378767 (accessed July 12, 2016).

36. Eisenberg, "Corporate Governance."

37. Tom Hamburger, "Car Company with Ties to Terry McAuliffe Probed by SEC," *The Washington Post*, August 2, 2013, http://www.washingtonpost.com/politics/company-with-ties-to-terry-mcauliffe-is-under-sec-investigation/2013/08/02/da483b36-f956-11e2-b018-5b8251f0c56e_story.html (accessed July 12, 2016).

38. Lynn Brewer, Robert Chandler, and O. C. Ferrell, *Managing Risks for Corporate Integrity: How to Survive an Ethical Misconduct Disaster* (Mason, OH: Texere/Thomson, 2006), p. 72.

39. Ray A. Goldberg, *Kraft General Foods: Risk Management Philosophy* (Boston: Harvard Business School Press, 1994).

40. Heather Timmons, "Financial Scandal at Outsourcing Company Rattles a Developing Country," *New York Times*, January 7, 2009, http://www.nytimes.com/2009/01/08/business/worldbusiness/08outsource.html (accessed July 12, 2016).

41. Brewer, Chandler, and Ferrell, *Managing Risks for Corporate Integrity*, p. 75; John Browne and Robin Nuttall, "Beyond Corporate Social Responsibility: Integrated External Engagement," *McKinsey & Company*, March 2013, http://www.mckinsey.com/insights/strategy/beyond_corporate_social_responsibility_integrated_external_engagement (accessed July 12, 2016).

42. Brewer, Chandler, and Ferrell, *Managing Risks for Corporate Integrity*, p. 75.

43. Jim Billington, "A Few Things Every Manager Ought to Know About Risk," *Harvard Management Update*, March 1997, pp. 10–11; Lee Puschaver and Robert G. Eccles, "In Pursuit of the Upside: The New Opportunity in Risk Management," *PW Review*, December 1996.

44. Scott Alexander, "Achieving Enterprisewide Privacy Compliance," *Insurance & Technology* 25 (November 2000): 53; M. Joseph Sirgy and Chenting Su, "The Ethics of Consumer Sovereignty in an Age of High Tech," *Journal of Business Ethics* 28 (November 2000): 1–14.

45. Ed Silverstein, "CEO 'Pay' Definition Remains Unclear as SEC Struggles to Meet Dodd-Frank Deadlines," *Inside Counsel*, May 2, 2014, http://www.insidecounsel.com/2014/05/02/ceo-pay-definition-remains-unclear-as-sec-struggle (accessed July 12, 2016); Alyce Lomax, "Is Shareholder 'Say on Pay' Working?" *The Motley Fool*, April 3, 2014, http://www.fool.com/investing/general/2014/04/03/is-shareholder-say-on-pay-working.aspx (accessed July 12, 2016).

46. Sarah Anderson, John Cavanaugh, Scott Kinger, and Liz Stanton, "Executive Excess 2008. How Average Taxpayers Subsidize Runaway Pay," *Institute for Policy Studies, United for a Fair Economy*, http://faireconomy.org/files/executive_excess_2008.pdf (accessed July 12, 2016).

47. "Executive Paywatch," *AFL-CIO*, http://www.aflcio.org/Corporate-Watch/Paywatch-2015 (accessed July 12, 2016).

48. Kara Scanell, "SEC Ready to Require More Pay Disclosures," *The Wall Street Journal*, June 3, 2009, http://online.

wsj.com/article/SB124397831899078781.html (accessed July 12, 2016); "Food Security Catastrophe Bonds," *Sustainable Investing Challenge,* April 26, 2013, http://sustainableinvestingchallenge.org/wp-content/uploads/2013/03/FSC-Bonds.pdf (accessed July 12, 2016); "From SRI to ESG: The Changing World of Responsible Investing," *Commonfund Institute,* September 2013, https://www.commonfund.org/investorresources/publications/white%20papers/whitepaper_sri%20to%20esg%202013%200901.pdf (accessed June 7, 2014).

49. Gary Strauss, "America's Corporate Meltdown," *USA Today,* June 27, 2002, pp. 1A, 2A.

50. Louis Lavelle, "CEO Pay, the More Things Change….," *BusinessWeek,* October 16, 2000, http://www.businessweek.com/2000/00_42/b3703102.htm (accessed June 7, 2014).

51. Ted Mann, "GE's Immelt Misses Part of Five-Year Performance Target," *The Wall Street Journal,* February 17, 2016, http://www.wsj.com/articles/ges-immelt-misses-part-of-five-year-performance-target-1455753884 (accessed July 12, 2016).

52. Stephen Gandel, "The Only Thing Up on Wall Street Is Pay," *Fortune,* March 22, 2016, http://fortune.com/2016/03/22/wall-street-ceo-pay/ (accessed July 12, 2016).

53. "Measuring Corporate Governance Standards," *Asiamoney* 11 (December 2000–January 2001): 94–95.

54. Barbara Crutchfield George, Kathleen A. Lacey, and Jotta Birmele, "The 1998 OECD Convention," *American Business Law Journal* 37 (Spring 2000): 485–525; Ira Millstein, "Corporate Governance: The Role of Market Forces," *OECD Observer* (Summer 2000): 27–28; "About OECD," *Organisation for Economic Co-operation and Development,* http://www.oecd.org/pages/0,3417,en_36734052_36734103_1_1_1_1,00.html (accessed June 7, 2014).

55. Sean Mclain, Shefali Anand, and Biman Mukherji, "Frustrated by Indian Policy, Foreign Investors Pull Back," *The Wall Street Journal,* July 19, 2013, http://online.wsj.com/news/articles/SB10001424127887323993804578613730684912770 (accessed July 12, 2016).

56. Fareed Zakaria, "A Capitalist Manifesto: Greed is Good (to a point)," *Newsweek,* June 13, 2009, http://www.newsweek.com/id/201935 (accessed July 12, 2016).

57. Adam M. Brandenburger and Barry J. Nalebuff, *Co-opetition: 1. A Revolutionary Mindset That Redefines Competition and Cooperation; 2. The Game Theory Strategy That's Changing the Game of Business* (New York: Doubleday, 1997); Tom Hamburger and Ben Pershing, "Car Company with Ties to Terry McAuliffe is Under SEC Investigation," *The Washington Post,* August 2, 2013, http://www.washingtonpost.com/politics/company-with-ties-to-terry-mcauliffe-is-under-sec-investigation/2013/08/02/da483b36-f956-11e2-b018-5b8251f0c56e_story.html (accessed July 12, 2016).

58. Maher and Anderson, *Corporate Governance.*

59. Monks, *Corporate Governance in the Twenty-First Century.*

60. "Three Skills for Today's Leaders," *Harvard Management Update* 4 (November 1999): 11.

61. Catherine M. Daily, Dan R. Dalton, and Albert A. Cannella Jr., "Corporate Governance: A Decade of Dialogue and Data," *Academy of Management Review* 28 (July 2003): 371–382.

62. Carol Hymowitz, "How to Fix a Broken System," *Wall Street Journal,* February 24, 2003, pp. R1–R3.

63. Monks, *Corporate Governance in the Twenty-First Century.*

Chapter 4

1. Kurt Eichenwald, "The Great Smartphone War," *Vanity Fair,* June 2014, http://www.vanityfair.com/business/2014/06/apple-samsung-smartphone-patent-war (accessed July 15, 2016); "Samsung Ordered to Pay Apple $120m for Patent Violation," *The Guardian,* May 2, 2014, https://www.theguardian.com/technology/2014/may/03/samsung-ordered-to-pay-apple-120m-for-patent-violation (accessed July 15, 2016). Dan Levine, "Apple, Google Agree to Settle Lawsuit Alleging Hiring Conspiracy," *Reuters,* April 24, 2014, http://www.reuters.com/article/2014/04/24/us-apple-google-settlement-idUSBREA3N1Y120140424 (accessed July 15, 2016); Ian Scerr, "Apple, Samsung Square off over Patent Damages," *The Wall Street Journal,* December 6, 2012, http://online.wsj.com/article/SB10001424127887323501404578164021886466686.html?mod=WSJ_article_comments#articleTabs%3Darticle (accessed July 15, 2016); Evan Ramstad, "Award to Apple Isn't Raised," *The Wall Street Journal,* June 30, 2012, http://online.wsj.com/article/SB10001424127887324329204578272870432069736.html?KEYWORDS=apple+samsungKEYWORDS%3Dapple+samsung (accessed July 15, 2016); Dino Grandoni, "How the Apple Samsung Lawsuit Hurt Consumers," *The Huffington Post,* July 31, 2012, http://www.huffingtonpost.com/2012/07/31/apple-samsung-lawsuit-consumers_n_1721623.html (accessed June 7, 2013); Paul Elias, "Apple's Samsung Verdict Nearly Cut in Half by Federal Judge," *The Huffington Post,* March 1, 2013, http://www.huffingtonpost.com/2013/03/01/half-of-billion-apple-samsung-settlement-invalidated_n_2792624.html (accessed June 7, 2013).

2. David Goldman, "Obama Vows Antitrust Crackdown," *CNN Money,* May 11, 2009, http://money.cnn.com/2009/05/11/news/economy/antitrust/index.htm (accessed July 15, 2016).

3. Steve Lohr, "High-Tech Antitrust Cases: The Road Ahead," *The New York Times,* May 13, 2009, http://bits.blogs.nytimes.com/2009/05/13/high-tech-antitrust-the-road-ahead/ (accessed July 15, 2016).

4. Natalia Drozdiak and Sam Schechner, "EU Files Additional Formal Charges Against Google," *The Wall Street Journal,* July 14, 2016, http://www.wsj.com/articles/google-set-to-face-more-eu-antitrust-charges-1468479516 (accessed July 15, 2016).

5. Danielle Douglas, "Second-largest Swiss Bank Pleads Guilty to Tax Evasion," *The Washington Post,* May 19, 2014, http://www.washingtonpost.com/business/economy/credit-suisse-charged-in-tax-evasion-case/2014/05/19/772afeb2-dfb0-11e3-9743-bb9b59cde7b9_story.html (accessed June 9, 2014).

6. "Welcome to BBB*Online*'s Consumer Safe Shopping Site," *BBB,* http://www.bbb.org/online/consumer/default.aspx (accessed June 10, 2014).

7. "BBBOnline: Why Your Business Should Participate," *BBB,* http://www.bbb.org/us/bbb-online-business-accreditation/ (accessed June 10, 2014).

8. Alan S. Blinder, "Keynesian Economics," Library of Economics and Liberty, http://www.econlib.org/library/Enc/KeynesianEconomics.html (accessed July 15, 2016).

9. Robert L. Formaini, "Milton Friedman—Economist as Public Intellectual," *Economic Insights* 7, no. 2 (2002).

10. Lisa Rein, "Electric Rates No Bright Spot for O'Malley as Election Nears," *The Washington Post,* July 6, 2009, http://

www.washingtonpost.com/wp-dyn/content/article/2009/07/05/AR2009070502697.html (accessed July 15, 2016).

11. Joseph Walker, "Drugmakers' Pricing Power Remains Strong," *The Wall Street Journal*, July 14, 2016, http://www.wsj.com/articles/drugmakers-pricing-power-remains-strong-1468488601 (accessed July 15, 2016); Luke Timmerman, "A Timeline of the Turing Pharma Controversy," September 23, 2015, http://www.forbes.com/sites/luketimmerman/2015/09/23/a-timeline-of-the-turing-pharma-controversy/#30c633297b94 (accessed July 15, 2016).

12. Stephen Fottrell, "FlyDubai crash pilot 'was due to leave job over fatigue," *BBC*, March 26, 2016, http://www.bbc.com/news/world-europe-35855678 (accessed July 15, 2016).

13. "SOPA (Stop Online Piracy Act) Debate: Why Are Google and Facebook Against It?" *Washington Post*, November 17, 2011, http://www.washingtonpost.com/business/sopa-stop-online-piracy-act-debate-why-are-google-and-facebook-against-it/2011/11/17/gIQAvLubVN_story.html?tid=pm_business_pop (accessed July 15, 2016).

14. S. Bono, A. Rubin, A. Stubblefield, and M. Green, "Security Through Legality," *Communications of the ACM* 49 (June 2006): 41–43.

15. Federal Trade Commission, "Mobile Advertising Network InMobi Settles FTC Charges It Tracked Hundreds of Millions of Consumers' Locations Without Permission," June 22, 2016, https://www.ftc.gov/news-events/press-releases/2016/06/mobile-advertising-network-inmobi-settles-ftc-charges-it-tracked (accessed July 15, 2016).

16. Leslie Meredith, "Internet Safety for Kids: Almost all Children Under 2 Have a Digital Footprint," *The Huffington Post*, January 10, 2013, http://www.huffingtonpost.com/2013/01/10/children-internet-safety_n_2449721.html (accessed July 15, 2016).

17. Douglas Bonderund, "Online Fraud Hits New High in 2015-and It's Going for Broke," *Security Intelligence*, October 30, 2015, https://securityintelligence.com/online-fraud-hits-new-high-in-2015-and-its-going-for-broke/ (accessed July 15, 2016).

18. "The Sherman Antitrust Act," *Antitrust Case Browser*, http://www.stolaf.edu/people/becker/antitrust/statutes/sherman.html (accessed July 15, 2016).

19. Ibid.

20. U.S. Department of Justice, "Antitrust Enforcement and the Consumer," http://www.justice.gov/atr/public/div_stats/antitrust-enfor-consumer.pdf (accessed July 15, 2016).

21. Federal Trade Commission, "Marketers of Dietary Supplement Amberen Settle FTC Charges Regarding Misleading Weight-Loss and Menopause Relief Claims," May 20, 2016, https://www.ftc.gov/news-events/press-releases/2016/05/marketers-dietary-supplement-amberen-settle-ftc-charges-regarding (accessed July 15, 2016).

22. Manatt Phelps & Phillips LLP, "LASIK providers need corrective advertising," *Lexology*, January 18, 2013, http://www.lexology.com/library/detail.aspx?g=1cfa731f-3821-4e40-b270-bc5b9d8d813d (accessed July 15, 2016).

23. Alicia Mundy, "FTC Bars Pom Juice's Health Claims," *The Wall Street Journal*, January 16, 2013, http://online.wsj.com/news/articles/SB10001424127887323468604578245740405648024 (accessed July 15, 2016).

24. Jamie Dimon, "A Unified Bank Regulator Is a Good Start," *The Wall Street Journal*, June 29, 2009, http://www.wsj.com/articles/SB124605726587563517 (accessed July 15, 2016).

25. Jane J. Kim and Aaron Lucchetti, "Big Change in Store for Brokers in Obama's Oversight Overhaul," *The Wall Street Journal*, June 19, 2009, http://online.wsj.com/article/SB124536973514629609.html?mod=googlenews_wsj (accessed July 15, 2016).

26. Joe Flint, "Justice Department Sides with Broadcasters in Fight Against Aereo," March 3, 2013, http://articles.latimes.com/2014/mar/03/entertainment/la-et-ct-justice-department-aereo-supreme-court-brief-20140303 (accessed July 15, 2016). (accessed June 26, 2014); Keach Hagey, "Supreme Court Ruling a Likely Death Knell for Aereo," *The Wall Street Journal*, June 25, 2014, http://www.wsj.com/articles/supreme-court-ruling-a-likely-death-knell-for-aereo-1403707884 (accessed July 15, 2016).

27. Don Reisinger, "Here's How Much Cash You'll Collect From Apple's Price-Fixing Case," *Fortune*, June 21, 2016, http://fortune.com/2016/06/21/apple-lawsuit-price-fixing/ (accessed July 15, 2016).

28. *European Union*, "EU Member Countries," http://europa.eu/about-eu/countries/member-countries/index_en.htm (accessed July 15, 2016).

29. Europa, "Structural Reform of the EU Banking Sector," January 29, 2014, http://europa.eu/rapid/press-release_IP-14-85_en.htm?locale=en (accessed July 15, 2016); Europa, "Commission Roadmap to Meet the Long-term Financing Needs of the European Economy," March 27, 2014, http://europa.eu/rapid/press-release_IP-14-320_en.htm?locale=en (accessed July 15, 2016); Europa, "New Measures to Restore Confidence in Benchmarks Following LIBOR and EURIBOR Scandals," September 18, 2013, http://europa.eu/rapid/press-release_IP-13-841_en.htm?locale=en (accessed July 15, 2016).

30. FT reporters, "Why did we leave the EU? and other Brexit FAQs," *Financial Times*, June 28, 2016, http://www.ft.com/cms/s/0/f1300fb4-3c5a-11e6-8716-a4a71e8140b0.html#axzz4EUqkbcax (accessed July 15, 2016).

31. James Kanter, "E.U. Objects to U.S. Regulations on Capital Requirements," *The New York Times*, April 22, 2013, http://www.nytimes.com/2013/04/23/business/global/eu-objects-to-us-regulations-on-capital-requirements.html (accessed July 15, 2016).

32. Brandon Mitchener, "Global Antitrust Process May Get Simpler," *Wall Street Journal*, October 27, 2000, p. A17; Debbie Thorne LeClair, O. C. Ferrell, and Linda Ferrell, "Federal Sentencing Guidelines for Organizations: Legal, Ethical, and Public Policy Issues for International Marketing," *Journal of Public Policy and Marketing* 16 (Spring 1997): 30.

33. Susan Dudley and Melinda Warren, "Growth in Regulators' Budget Slowed by Fiscal Stalemate: An Analysis of the U.S. Budget for Fiscal Years 2012 and 2013," Washington University in St. Louis and The George Washington University, July 2012, http://wc.wustl.edu/files/wc/imce/2013regreport.pdf (accessed July 15, 2016).

34. "DMA Expels PPI Nuisance Callers from Membership," Direct Marketing Association, http://www.dma.org.uk/news/dma-expels-ppi-nuisance-callers-membership (accessed July 15, 2016).

35. William M. Pride and O. C. Ferrell, *Marketing: Concepts and Strategies*, 12th ed. (Boston: Houghton Mifflin, 2003), pp. 54–55; "2012 Annual Report," *The Council of Better Business Bureaus*, 2012, http://www.bbb.org/us/storage/113/documents/CBBB_AR_2012.pdf (accessed July 15, 2016).

36. Better Business Bureau, "Accreditation Revoked," April 22, 2016, http://www.bbb.org/southeast-texas/news-events/bbb-in-the-news/2016/04/revocation/ (accessed July 15, 2016).

37. National Archives, "Chapter 23. Records of the Joint Committees of Congress 1789–1968 (Record Group 128)," 1989, http://www.archives.gov/legislative/guide/house/chapter-23-joint-organization-of-congress-1944-1946.html (accessed June 11, 2014); National Archives, "Congressional Records," http://www.archives.gov/legislative/research/ (accessed June 11, 2014); "Driving Mr. Gephardt," *Newsweek,* August 21, 2000, p. 48.

38. "About the FEC," *Federal Election Commission*, http://www.fec.gov/about.shtml (accessed July 15, 2016).

39. "A Brief History of Money and Politics," *The Campaign Legal Center*, http://www.campaignlegalcenter.org/attachments/BCRA_MCCAIN_FEINGOLD/BCRA_REGULATIONS/1223.pdf (accessed June 11, 2014).

40. Gregory J. Krieg, "What Is a Super PAC? A Short History," *ABC News,* August 9, 2012, http://abcnews.go.com/Politics/OTUS/super-pac-short-history/story?id=16960267 (accessed July 15, 2016).

41. Tom Hamburger and Matea Gold, "Google, Once Disdainful of Lobbying, Now a Master of Washington Influence," *The Washington Post*, April 12, 2014, http://www.washingtonpost.com/politics/how-google-is-transforming-power-and-politicsgoogle-once-disdainful-of-lobbying-now-a-master-of-washington-influence/2014/04/12/51648b92-b4d3-11e3-8cb6-284052554d74_story.html (accessed July 15, 2016).

42. Peter Eavis, "U.S. Reforms No Pushover for Banks," *The Wall Street Journal*, June 22, 2009, http://online.wsj.com/article/SB124563161642335927.html (accessed July 15, 2016); Deborah Solomon and Damian Paletta, "U.S. Eyes Bank Pay Overhaul," *The Wall Street Journal*, May 13, 2009, http://online.wsj.com/article/SB124215896684211987.html (accessed July 15, 2016); Silla Brush, "Top 10 Lobbying Fights Over Financial Reform Overhaul Legislation," *The Hill*, March 16, 2010, http://thehill.com/business-a-lobbying/87225-top-10-lobbying-fights-over-financial-reform-overhaul (accessed July 15, 2016) Larry D. Wall, "Supervising Bank Compensation Policies," *Federal Reserve Bank of Atlanta*, November 2013, http://www.frbatlanta.org/cenfis/pubscf/nftv_1311.cfm (accessed July 15, 2016).

43. Jake Sherman, "Legislators Framing Climate Bills Hold Energy Stock," *The Wall Street Journal*, June 17, 2009, http://online.wsj.com/news/articles/SB124519704993421187 (accessed July 15, 2016).

44. Sandra Day O'Connor, "Judicial Independence and 21st Century Challenges," *The Bencher: The Magazine for the American Inns of Court*, July/August 2012, p. 14. Used information from the Annenberg Public Policy Institute; Richard H. Levenstein, "Making a Difference: Educating the Public About the Importance of a Fair, Impartial, and Independent Judiciary One Judge and One Lawyer at a Time," *The Bencher: The Magazine for the American Inns of Court*, July/August 2012, p. 22. Used information from a Harris Interactive Poll of Florida's adult population commissioned by the Florida Bar in December 2005; Doug Schuler, *Business and Government: Some Introductory Thoughts*, Rice University, Washington Campus PowerPoint © 2013; Jeffrey Toobin, "Money Unlimited: How Chief Justice John Roberts Orchestrated the Citizens United decision," *The New Yorker*, May 21, 2012, http://www.newyorker.com/reporting/2012/05/21/120521fa_fact_toobin?currentPage=all (accessed July 15, 2016).

45. Richard P. Conaboy, "Corporate Crime in America: Strengthening the Good Citizen Corporation," in *Corporate Crime in America: Strengthening the "Good Citizenship" Corporation* (Washington, DC: U.S. Sentencing Commission, 1995), pp. 1–2.

46. Win Swenson, "The Organizational Guidelines' 'Carrot and Stick' Philosophy, and Their Focus on 'Effective' Compliance," in *Corporate Crime in America: Strengthening the "Good Citizenship"-Corporation* (Washington, DC: U.S. Sentencing Commission, 1995), pp. 17–26.

47. Peter Lattman, "Ralph Lauren Corp. Agrees to Pay Fine in Bribery Case," *The New York Times*, April 22, 2013, http://dealbook.nytimes.com/2013/04/22/ralph-lauren-pays-1-6-million-to-resolve-bribery-case/?_php=true&_type=blogs&_r=0 (accessed July 15, 2016).

48. O. C Ferrell and Linda Ferrell, "Current Developments in Managing Organizational Ethics and Compliance Initiatives," University of Wyoming, white paper, Bill Daniels Business Ethics Initiative 2006.

49. Open Compliance Ethics Group 2005 Benchmarking Study Key Findings, file:///C:/Users/Linda%20Ferrell/Downloads/OCEG-200.PDF (accessed June 12, 2014).

50. "US Sentences Guidelines Changes Become Effective November 1," *FCPA Compliance and Ethics Blog*, November 2, 2010, http://tfoxlaw.wordpress.com/2010/11/02/us-sentencing-guidelines-changes-become-effective-november-1/ (accessed June 12, 2014).

51. Paula Desio, Deputy General Counsel, *An Overview of the Organizational Guidelines*, http://www.ussc.gov/sites/default/files/pdf/training/organizational-guidelines/ORGOVERVIEW.pdf (accessed February 25, 2015).

52. Ferrell and Ferrell, "Current Developments in Managing Organizational Ethics and Compliance Initiatives."

53. Protiviti, "2012 Sarbanes-Oxley Compliance Survey," 2012, http://www.protiviti.com/en-US/Documents/Surveys/2012-SOX-Compliance-Survey-Protiviti.pdf (accessed July 15, 2016).

54. National Whistleblowers Center, "Changing Corporate Culture," http://whistleblowers.nonprofitsoapbox.com/index.php?option=com_advancedtags&view=tag&id=80&Itemid=102 (accessed July 15, 2016).

55. President Barack Obama, "Remarks by the President on 21st Century Financial Regulatory Reform," *The White House*, June 17, 2009, https://www.whitehouse.gov/the-press-office/remarks-president-regulatory-reform (accessed July 15, 2016).

56. Ibid.

57. Joshua Gallu, "Dodd-Frank May Cost $6.5 Billion and 5,000 Workers," *Bloomberg*, February 14, 2011, http://www.bloomberg.com/news/articles/2011-02-14/dodd-frank-s-implementation-calls-for-6-5-billion-5-000-staff-in-budget (accessed July 15, 2016); Binyamin Appelbaum and Brady Dennis, "Dodd's Overhaul Goes Well Beyond Other Plans," *The Washington Post*, November 11, 2009, http://www.washingtonpost.com/wp-dyn/content/article/2009/11/09/AR2009110901935.html?hpid=topnews&sid=ST2009111003729 (accessed July 15, 2016).

58. Maria Bartiromo, "JPMorgan CEO Jamie Dimon Sees Good Times in 2011," *USA Today*, February 21, 2011, http://www.usatoday.com/money/companies/management/bartiromo/2011-02-21-bartiromo21_CV_N.htm (accessed July 15, 2016).

59. "Office of Financial Research," *U.S. Department of Treasury*, http://www.treasury.gov/initiatives/ofr/Pages/default.aspx (accessed July 15, 2016).

60. "Initiatives: Financial Stability Oversight Council," *U.S. Department of Treasury*, http://www.treasury.gov/initiatives/Pages/FSOC-index.aspx (accessed July 15, 2016).

61. "Financial Stability Oversight Council Created Under the Dodd-Frank Wall Street Reform and Consumer Protection Act: Frequently Asked Questions," October 2010, http://www.treasury.gov/initiatives/wsr/Documents/FAQs%20-%20Financial%20Stability%20Oversight%20Council%20-%20October%202010%20FINAL%20v2.pdf (accessed July 15, 2016).

62. "Subtitle A—Bureau of Consumer Financial Protection," *One Hundred Eleventh Congress of the United States of America*, p. 589.

63. "Wall Street Reform: Bureau of Consumer Financial Protection (CFPB)," *U.S. Treasury*, http://www.consumerfinance.gov/ (accessed July 15, 2016).

64. Ibid.; Sudeep Reddy, "Elizabeth Warren's Early Words on a Consumer Financial Protection Bureau," *The Wall Street Journal*, September 17, 2010, http://blogs.wsj.com/economics/2010/09/17/elizabeth-warrens-early-words-on-a-consumer-financial-protection-bureau/ (accessed July 15, 2016); Jennifer Liberto and David Ellis, "Wall Street Reform: What's in the Bill," *CNN*, June 30, 2010, http://money.cnn.com/2010/06/25/news/economy/whats_in_the_reform_bill/index.htm (accessed July 15, 2016).

65. Jean Eaglesham, "Warning Shot on Financial Protection," *The Wall Street Journal*, February 9, 2011, http://online.wsj.com/article/SB10001424052748703507804576130370862263258.html?mod=googlenews_wsj (accessed July 15, 2016).

66. Liz Rappaport, Liz Moyer, and Anupreeta Das, "Goldman Sets Funds for 'Volcker'," *The Wall Street Journal*, February 8, 2013, pp. C1–C2.

67. Jean Eaglesham, "Warning Shot on Financial Protection."

68. Jean Eaglesham and Ashby Jones, "Whistle-blower Bounties Pose Challenges," *The Wall Street Journal*, December 13, 2010, pp. C1, C3.

69. "SEC announces First Whistleblower Payout Under Dodd-Frank Bounty Program," *Compliance Corner*, August 2012, http://compliancecorner.wnj.com/?p=177 (accessed July 15, 2016).

Chapter 5

1. NiSource website, https://www.nisource.com/ (accessed June 24, 2016); BNK Invest, "NiSource a Top Socially Responsible Dividend Stock With 2.9% Yield," Nasdaq, May 14, 2014, http://www.nasdaq.com/article/nisource-a-top-socially-responsible-dividend-stock-with-29-yield-ni-cm352928 (accessed June 24, 2016); NiSource, Inc., *The NiSource Code of Business Conduct* (Merrillville, IN: NiSource Inc., 2014), p. 5; NiSource, Inc., "NiSource 2015 Sustainability Report," https://www.nisource.com/docs/default-source/2015-sustainability/2015-sustainability-report.pdf (accessed June 24, 2016);

1. "Walmart's Mexican Morass," *The Economist*, April 28, 2012, p. 71; Jack and Suzy Welch, "Whistleblowers: Why You Should Heed Their Warnings," *Fortune*, June 11, 2012, p. 86; Jonathan Stempel, "U.S. Judge Says Wal-Mart Should Face Lawsuit Over Alleged Mexico Bribery," *Reuters*, May 9, 2014, http://www.reuters.com/article/2014/05/09/us-walmart-mexico-lawsuit-idUSBREA480F620140509 (accessed June 27, 2014); "Walmart CEO Knew of Bribery Allegations in 2005: Lawmakers," *Huffington Post*, http://www.huffingtonpost.com/2013/01/10/walmart-bribery-allegations_n_2448403.html (accessed June 27, 2014); Walmart, "Walmart Statement in Response to December 17 New York Times Article About Allegations of Corruption in Mexico," http://news.walmart.com/news-archive/2012/12/17/walmart-statement-in-response-to-new-york-times-article-about-allegations-of-corruption-in-mexico (accessed June 27, 2014); Miguel Bustillo, "Wal-Mart Faces Risk in Mexican Bribe Probe," *The Wall Street Journal*, April 23, 2012, http://online.wsj.com/article/SB10001424052702303978104577360283629622556.html (accessed June 27, 2014); Abram Brown, "Wal-Mart Bribery Probe Expands Past Mexico to Brazil, China, and India," *Forbes*, November 15, 2012, http://www.forbes.com/sites/abrambrown/2012/11/15/probe-into-wal-mart-bribery-past-mexico-to-brazil-china-and-india/ (accessed June 27, 2014); David Barstow, "Vast Mexico Bribery Case Hushed Up by Wal-Mart After Top-Level Struggle," *The New York Times*, April 21, 2012, http://www.nytimes.com/2012/04/22/business/at-wal-mart-in-mexico-a-bribe-inquiry-silenced.html?pagewanted=all (accessed June 27, 2014); Shelly Banjo, "Wal-Mart Will Tie Executive Pay to Compliance Overhaul," *The Wall Street Journal*, April 23, 2013, p. B8; Shelly Banjo, "Wal-Mart Cheer: I-n-t-e-g-r-i-t-y," *The Wall Street Journal*, May 31, 2012, p. B3; Elizabeth A. Harris, "After Bribery Scandals, High-Level Departures at Walmart," *The New York Times*, June 4, 2014, http://www.nytimes.com/2014/06/05/business/after-walmart-bribery-scandals-a-pattern-of-quiet-departures.html?_r=0 (accessed June 27, 2014); David Barstow and Xanic von Bertrab, "The Bribery Aisle: How Wal-Mart Got Its Way in Mexico," *The New York Times*, December 17, 2012, http://www.nytimes.com/2012/12/18/business/walmart-bribes-teotihuacan.html?pagewanted=all (accessed June 27, 2014); Emily Jane Fox, "Wal-Mart Knew About Mexico Bribery in 2005, Say Lawmakers," *CNN*, January 10, 2013, http://money.cnn.com/2013/01/10/news/companies/walmart-investigation/ (accessed June 27, 2014); "Wal-Mart Says Bribe Probe Cost $439 Million in Two Years," *Bloomberg*, March 26, 2014, http://www.bloomberg.com/news/2014-03-26/wal-mart-says-bribery-probe-cost-439-million-in-past-two-years.html (accessed June 27, 2014).

2. Edelman, "2016 Edelman Trust Barometer," 2016, http://www.edelman.com/insights/intellectual-property/2016-edelman-trust-barometer/ (accessed August 3, 2016).

3. "Program Overview," *Raytheon*, http://www.raytheon.com/ourcompany/ourculture/ethics/ethics_over/index.html (accessed June 12, 2014).

4. Devin Thorpe, "Why CSR? The Benefits of Corporate Social Responsibility Will Move You to Act," *Forbes*, May 18, 2013, http://www.forbes.com/sites/devinthorpe/2013/05/18/why-csr-the-benefits-of-corporate-social-responsibility-will-move-you-to-act/#108178db5e1c (accessed August 3, 2016).

5. Anthony Shields, "Good Business: 10 Companies with Ethical Corporate Policies," *Minyanville*, February 16, 2013, http://www.minyanville.com/sectors/consumer/articles/Good-Business253A-Corporations-with-Great-Ethical/2/16/2013/id/48045?refresh=1 (accessed August 3, 2016).

6. Wendy Koch, "FDA Announces Rules Restricting E-cigarettes and Cigars," *USA Today*, April 24, 2014, http://www.

usatoday.com/story/news/nation/2014/04/24/fda-e-cigarette-rules/8050875/ (accessed August 3, 2016).

7. Tripp Mickle, "FDA to Regulate E-Cigarette Industry," *The Wall Street Journal*, May 6, 2016, B1-B2.

8. Debbie Thorne McAlister and Robert Erffmeyer, "A Content Analysis of Outcomes and Responsibilities for Consumer Complaints to Third Party Organizations," *Journal of Business Research* 56 (April 2003): 341–352.

9. Jeff Elder, "Silicon Valley Tech Giants Struck Deals on Hiring, Say Documents," *The Wall Street Journal*, April 20, 2014, http://www.wsj.com/articles/SB10001424052702304626304579509700352730842 (accessed August 3, 2016); Lance Whitney, "Apple, Google, others settle antipoaching lawsuit for $415 million," CNET, September 3, 2015, http://www.cnet.com/news/apple-google-others-settle-anti-poaching-lawsuit-for-415-million/ (accessed August 3, 2016).

10. "Biz Deans Talk-Business Management Education Blog," January 2, 2009, http://www.deanstalk.net/deanstalk/2009/01/warren-buffetts.html (accessed August 3, 2016).

11. Barry Newman, "An Ad Professor Huffs against Puffs, but It's a Quixotic Enterprise," *Wall Street Journal,* January 24, 2003, p. A1.

12. Shirley S. Wang, "Doctors, Device Makers: Close Ties," *The Wall Street Journal*, March 14, 2014, p. B7.

13. Mars Hill Church, "These Stats on Stealing Might Surprise You," *Mars Hill Church*, November 8, 2013, http://marshill.se/marshill/2013/11/08/these-stats-on-stealing-might-surprise-you (accessed August 3, 2016).

14. Boeing, *Ethical Business Conduct Guidelines,* April 8, 2011, http://www.boeing.com/assets/pdf/companyoffices/aboutus/ethics/ethics_booklet.pdf (accessed August 3, 2016).

15. Reuters, "BlackRock to pay $12 million in SEC conflict of interest case," *Fortune*, April 20, 2015, http://fortune.com/2015/04/20/blackrock-to-pay-12-million-in-sec-conflict-of-interest-case/ (accessed August 3, 2016).

16. Kate Sheppard, "Keystone XL Contractor's Potential Conflicts of Interest Not Mentioned in State Department Documents," *The Huffington Post*, October 25, 2013, http://www.huffingtonpost.com/2013/10/25/keystone-xl-contractor_n_4159685.html (accessed August 3, 2016).

17. Ed Silverman, "Novartis agrees to $25m settlement over bribery charges in China," *Stat*, March 23, 2016, https://www.statnews.com/pharmalot/2016/03/23/novartis-bribes-china/ (accessed August 3, 2016).

18. Leslie Wayne, "Hits, and Misses, in a War on Bribery," *The New York Times*, March 10, 2012, http://www.nytimes.com/2012/03/11/business/corporate-bribery-war-has-hits-and-a-few-misses.html (accessed August 3, 2016).

19. United States Department of Justice, "Foreign Corrupt Practices Act Antibribery Provisions," http://www.justice.gov/criminal/fraud/fcpa/ (accessed August 3, 2016).

20. Ashley Broughton, "Minorities Expected to be Majority in 2050," CNN, August 13, 2008, http://www.cnn.com/2008/US/08/13/census.minorities/index.html?iref=hpmostpop (accessed August 3, 2016); Eric Kanye, "Census: White Majority in U.S. Gone by 2043," *NBC News*, June 13, 2013, http://usnews.nbc-news.com/_news/2013/06/13/18934111-census-white-majority-in-us-gone-by-2043?lite (accessed August 3, 2016).

21. Mark H. Anderson, "Business Gets Stronger Hand in Age Cases," *The Wall Street Journal,* June 18, 2009, http://online.wsj.com/article/SB124535060326328507.html (accessed August 3, 2016).

22. Mitra Toossi, "Employment Outlook: 2010–2020," *Bureau of Labor Statistics*, January 2012, http://www.bls.gov/opub/mlr/2012/01/art3full.pdf (accessed August 3, 2016).

23. Paula N. Rubin, "Civil Rights and Criminal Justice: Primer on Sexual Harassment Series: NIJ Research in Action," October 1995, https://www.ncjrs.gov/txtfiles/harass.txt (accessed August 3, 2016).

24. "Sexual Harassment Charges FY 2010–FY 2013," *U.S. Equal Employment Opportunity Commission*, 2013, http://www.eeoc.gov/eeoc/statistics/enforcement/sexual_harassment_new.cfm (accessed June 19, 2014).

25. *Zabkowicz v. West Bend Co.*, 589 F. Supp. 780, 784, 35 EPD Par.34, 766 (E.D. Wis.1984).

26. Business Wire, "Expense Fraud Costs U.S. Employers $2.8 Billion Per Year, Shows Chrome River Survey," March 29, 2016, http://www.businesswire.com/news/home/20160329005218/en/Expense-Fraud-Costs-U.S.-Employers-2.8-Billion (accessed August 4, 2016).

27. Walter Pavlo, "Association of Certified Fraud Examiners Release 2014 Report on Fraud," *Forbes*, May 21, 2014, http://www.forbes.com/sites/walterpavlo/2014/05/21/association-of-certified-fraud-examiners-release-2014-report-on-fraud/#4410d88a5238 (accessed August 4, 2016).

28. "2013 Internet Crime Report," *Federal Bureau of Investigation*, 2013, http://www.ic3.gov/media/annualreport/2013_IC3Report.pdf (accessed August 4, 2016).

29. Nora J. Rifon, Robert LaRose, and Sejung Marina Choi, "Your Privacy Is Sealed: Effects of Web Privacy Seals on Trust and Personal Disclosures," *Journal of Consumer Affairs* 39, no. 2 (2002): 339–362.

30. Mitch Wagner, "Google's Pixie Dust," *InformationWeek,* no. 1061 (2005): 98.

31. Stephenie Steitzer, "Commercial Web Sites Cut Back on Collections of Personal Data," *Wall Street Journal*, March 28, 2002, http://online.wsj.com/article/SB1017247161553469240.html?mod=googlewsj (accessed August 4, 2016).

32. Kate Rogers, "One New Identity Theft Victim Every 3 Seconds in 2012," *Fox Business*, February 20, 2013, http://http://www.foxbusiness.com/features/2013/02/20/one-new-identity-theft-victim-every-3-seconds-in-2012.html (accessed August 4, 2016).

33. HM Government, 2015 Information Security Breaches Survey, http://www.pwc.co.uk/assets/pdf/2015-isbs-executive-summary-digital.pdf (accessed August 4, 2016).

34. "2012 Report Card on the Ethics of American Youth," *Josephson Institute Center for Youth Ethics*, 2012, http://charactercounts.org/pdf/reportcard/2012/ReportCard-2012-DataTables.pdf (accessed June 20, 2014); "For The First Time In A Decade, Lying, Cheating And Stealing Among American Students Drops," *Josephson Institute Center for Youth Ethics,* November 21, 2012, http://charactercounts.org/programs/reportcard/2012/installment_report-card_honesty-integrity.html (accessed June 20, 2014).

35. Immanuel Kant, "Fundamental Principles of the Metaphysics of Morals," in *Problems of Moral Philosophy: An Introduction,* 2nd ed., ed. Paul W. Taylor (Encino, CA: Dickenson, 1972), p. 229.

36. Stefanie E. Naumann and Nathan Bennett, "A Case for Procedural Justice Climate: Development and Test of a Multilevel Model," *Academy of Management Journal* 43 (October 2000): 881–889.

37. Joel Brockner and P. A. Siegel, "Understanding the Interaction between Procedural and Distributive Justice: The Role

of Trust," in *Trust in Organizations: Frontiers of Theory and Research,* ed. R. M. Kramer and T. R. Tyler (Thousand Oaks, CA: Sage, 1995), pp. 390–413.

38. Debbie Thorne LeClair, O. C. Ferrell, and John Fraedrich, *Integrity Management: A Guide to Managing Legal and Ethical Issues in the Workplace* (Tampa, FL: University of Tampa Press, 1998), p. 37.

39. John Fraedrich and O. C. Ferrell, "Cognitive Consistency of Marketing Managers in Ethical Situations," *Journal of the Academy of Marketing Science* 20 (1992): 242–252.

40. Shalom H. Schwartz, "Cultural Value Differences: Some Implications for Work," *Applied Psychology: An International Review* 48 (1999): 23–47.

41. Michel Callon, Pierrre Lascoumes, and Yannick Barthe, *Acting in an Uncertain World: An Essay on Technical Democracy* (Cambridge, MA: MIT Press, 2009).

42. Joel Gehman, Linda K. Treviño, and Raghu Garud, "Values Work: A Process Study of the Emergence and Performance of Organizational Values Practices," *Academy of Management Journal* 56, no. 1 (2013): 84–112.

43. Joseph W. Weiss, *Business Ethics: A Managerial, Stakeholder Approach* (Belmont, CA: Wadsworth, 1994), p. 13.

44. Carol Loomis, "Derivatives: The Risk That Still Won't Go Away," *Fortune,* June 6, 2009, pp. 55–60.

45. Ethics Resource Center, *2013 National Business Ethics Survey® of the U.S. Workforce* (Arlington, VA: Ethics Resource Center, 2014).

46. O. C. Ferrell, Larry G. Gresham, and John Fraedrich, "A Synthesis of Ethical Decision Models for Marketing," *Journal of Macromarketing* 9 (Fall 1989): 58–59.

47. Robert Gatewood, Robert Taylor, and O. C. Ferrell, *Management* (Homewood, IL: Richard D. Irwin, Inc., 1995).

48. Ethics & Compliance Initiative, 2016 Global Business Ethics SurveyTM: Measuring Risk and Promoting Workplace Integrity (Arlington, VA: Ethics & Compliance Initiative, 2016), p. 43.

49. "Employee Theft No Longer An If—Now It Is How Much!," *Kessler International,* April 26, 2013, http://www.investigation.com/press/press118.htm (accessed August 4, 2016).

50. Jeffrey L. Seglin, "Forewarned Is Forearmed? Not Always," *New York Times,* February 16, 2003, www.nytimes.com/2003/02/16/business/yourmoney/16ETHI.html (accessed August 4, 2016); Barbara Ley Toffler, *Final Accounting: Ambition, Greed and the Fall of Arthur Andersen* (New York: Broadway Books, 2003).

51. General Electric, "Ecomagination," http://www.ge.com/about-us/ecomagination (accessed June 30, 2014); General Electric, "Healthymagination," http://www.ge.com/about-us/ecomagination (accessed August 4, 2016); Business Wire, "GE Releases 2013 Progress against Sustainability Commitments," June 30, 2014, http://www.businesswire.com/news/home/20140630006140/en/GE-Releases-2013-Progress-Sustainability-Commitments (accessed August 4, 2016)

52. Amanda Hess, "Dov Charney Was Fired for Losing, Not Sexual Harassment," *Slate,* June 27, 2014, http://www.slate.com/blogs/xx_factor/2014/06/27/dov_charney_firing_american_apparel_ceo_was_fired_for_financial_reasons.html (accessed August 4, 2016).

53. Ferrell, Gresham, and Fraedrich, "A Synthesis of Ethical Decision Models for Marketing."

54. Muel Kaptein, "From Inaction to External Whistleblowering: The Influence of the Ethical Culture of Organizations on Employee Responses to Observed Wrongdoing," *Journal of Business Ethics* 98 (2011): 513–530.

55. Gehman, Treviño, and Garud, "Values Work."

56. Bert Scholtens and Lammertjan Dam, "Cultural Values and International Differences in Business Ethics," *Journal of Business Ethics* 75 (2007): 273–284.

57. "2011 Annual Report," *Marriott,* 2011, http://investor.shareholder.com/mar/marriottAR11/pdf/marriott11ar.pdf (accessed August 4, 2016).

58. Gary R. Weaver and Linda K. Trevino, "Compliance and Values Oriented Ethics Programs: Influences on Employees' Attitudes and Behavior," *Business Ethics Quarterly* 9, no. 2 (1999): 315–335.

59. Fraedrich and Ferrell, "Cognitive Consistency of Marketing Managers in Ethical Situations," 243–252.

Chapter 6

1. Traci Watson, "Eco-friendly Claims Go Unchecked," *USA Today,* June 22, 2009, p. A1; "The Seven Sins of Greenwashing," *Terrachoice,* http://sinsofgreenwashing.org/findings/the-seven-sins/ (accessed August 4, 2016); Matthew Knight, "It's Not Easy Being Green," *CNN,* July 23, 2008, http://www.cnn.com/2008/TECH/science/07/16/greenwash/index.html (accessed August 4, 2016); Elise Hunter, "How to Fight Greenwashing: The Value of Third-Party Certification in Green Building," *Triple Pundit,* June 13, 2014, http://www.triplepundit.com/2014/06/fight-greenwashing-value-third-party-certification-green-building/ (accessed July 1, 2014); Federal Trade Commission, "FTC Cracking Down on Misleading and Unsubstantiated Environmental Marketing Claims," October 29, 2013, http://www.ftc.gov/news-events/press-releases/2013/10/ftc-cracks-down-misleading-unsubstantiated-environmental (accessed August 4, 2016); Federal Trade Commission, "FTC Issues Revised 'Green Guides'," October 1, 2012, https://www.ftc.gov/news-events/press-releases/2012/10/ftc-issues-revised-green-guides (accessed August 4, 2016); "PepsiCo to no longer call Naked juices 'natural'," USA Today, July 26, 2013, http://www.usatoday.com/story/money/business/2013/07/26/pepsi-co-naked-juice-not-natural/2589717/ (accessed August 4, 2016); Claudia M. Vetesi and Michael Steel, "United States: Red Light for Green Claims: FTC Sends Warning Letters to Green Certifiers," Mondaq, December 9, 2015, http://www.mondaq.com/unitedstates/x/450178/advertising+marketing+branding/Red+Light+For+Green+Claims+FTC+Sends+Warning+Letters+To+Green+Certifiers (accessed August 4, 2016); John Askins, "FTC Cracks Down on False 'Green' Claims," har.com, November 2, 2015, http://www.har.com/blog_30928_ftc-cracks-down-on-false-green-claims- (accessed August 4, 2016).

2. Kevin Mitchell, "Maria Sharapova receives two-year ban for failing drug test," *The Guardian,* June 8, 2016, https://www.theguardian.com/sport/2016/jun/08/maria-sharapova-banned-two-years-failing-drugs-test-meldonium (accessed August 4, 2016).

3. Andy Adkins, "How Leaders Build Trust," *Fast Company,* August 7, 2012, http://www.fastcompany.com/3000204/how-leaders-build-trust (accessed August 4, 2016).

4. Reuters, "Priceline's CEO Is Resigning Over an Improper Relationship With an Employee," *Fortune,* April 28, 2016, http://fortune.com/2016/04/28/priceline-ceo-huston-resigns/ (accessed August 4, 2016).

5. "Integrity Survey 2013," *KPMG,* 2013, p. 1, http://www.kpmg.com/CN/en/IssuesAndInsights/ArticlesPublications/Documents/Integrity-Survey-2013-O-201307.pdf (accessed August 4, 2016).

6. "How Am I Doing?" *Business Ethics*, Fall 2005, p. 11.

7. "The Values and Ethics of TI," *Texas Instruments*, November 2010, http://www.ti.com/corp/docs/csr/downloads/ethics.pdf?DCMP=TI-Ethics&HQS=Brochure+OT+values-ethics-atti (accessed June 23, 2014).

8. "The TI Ethics Quick Test," *Texas Instruments*, http://www.ti.com/corp/docs/company/citizen/ethics/quicktest.shtml (accessed August 4, 2016).

9. Mark S. Schwartz, "A Code of Ethics for Corporate Code of Ethics," *Journal of Business Ethics* 41 (2002): 37

10. "National Business Ethics Survey of the U.S. Workforce," *Ethics Resource Center*, 2013, http://www.ethics.org/downloads/2013NBESFinalWeb.pdf (accessed June 23, 2014).

11. "Wells Fargo Team Member Code of Ethics and Business Conduct," www.wellsfargo.com/downloads/pdf/about/team_member_code_of_ethics.pdf (accessed June 23, 2014).

12. "ECOA Sponsoring Partner Member L'Oreal Sponsors the First Law and Business Ethics Masters Degree," CSRwire, October 6, 2008, http://www.csrwire.com/press/press_release/19336-ECOA-Sponsoring-Partner-member-L-Oreal-Sponsors-the-first-Law-and-Business-Ethics-Masters-Degree (accessed August 4, 2016); "About ECOA," ECOA, http://www.theecoa.org/imis15/ECOAPublic/ABOUT/ECOAPublic/AboutContent/ABOUT_THE_ECOA.aspx?hkey=e446751b-96ae-49ae-8b9d-aa387ef8a83b (accessed July 3, 2014).

13. Alynda Wheat, "Keeping an Eye on Corporate America," *Fortune,* November 25, 2002, pp. 44–45.

14. Debbie Thorne LeClair and Linda Ferrell, "Innovation in Experiential Business Ethics Training," *Journal of Business Ethics* 23 (2000): 313–322.

15. "Ethics," *Boeing*, http://www.boeing.com/boeing/companyoffices/aboutus/ethics/index.page (accessed August 4, 2016). Courtesy of Boeing Business Services Company.

16. "The 2013 Ethics and Compliance Hotline Benchmark Report," *Navex Global*, 2013, http://www.jdsupra.com/legalnews/the-2013-ethics-and-compliance-hotline-b-34059/ (accessed August 4, 2016).

17. Ibid.

18. U.S. Securities and Exchange Commission, "SEC Issues $17 Million Whistleblower Award," June 9, 2016, https://www.sec.gov/news/pressrelease/2016-114.html (accessed August 4, 2016).

19. Portfolio Media, Inc., "What CFTC's Record-Breaking Whistleblower Bounty Tells Us," Law360, April 21, 2016, http://www.law360.com/articles/785829/what-cftc-s-record-breaking-whistleblower-bounty-tells-us (accessed August 4, 2016).

20. Ethics Resource Center, *National Business Ethics Survey of the U.S. Workforce* (Arlington, VA: Ethics Resource Center, 2013), p. 34.

21. Darren Dahl, "Learning to Love Whistleblowers," *Inc.,* March 2006, pp. 21–23.

22. O. C. Ferrell, John Fraedrich, and Ferrell, *Business Ethics: Ethical Decision Making and Cases,*10th ed. (Mason, OH: South-Western Cengage Learning, 2015), p. 94.

23. Ibid., pp. 94–97.

24. Paul K. Shum and Sharon L. Yam, "Ethics and Law: Guiding the Invisible Had to Correct Corporate Social Responsibility Externalities," *Journal of Business Ethics* 98 (2011): 549–571.

25. Cornell University School of Hotel Administration, "Best Practices in US Lodging Industry Introduction," 2014, https://www.hotelschool.cornell.edu/research/chr/pubs/best/project/intro.html (accessed July 2, 2014).

26. Ferrell, Fraedrich, and Ferrell, "Business Ethics," pp. 311–313.

27. R. Eric Reidenbach and Donald P. Robin, *Ethics and Profits* (Englewood Cliffs, NJ: Prentice-Hall, 1989), p. 92.

28. Chris Golis, "Emotional Intelligence: Did Myers-Brigg Destroy Arthur Andersen?" *CBS*, April 16, 2011, http://www.cbsnews.com/news/emotional-intelligence-did-myers-briggs-destroy-arthur-andersen/ (accessed August 4, 2016).

29. R. Edward Freeman and Lisa Stewart, "Developing Ethical Leadership," *Business Roundtable Institute for Corporate Ethics*, 2006,http:// www.corporate-ethics.org.

30. James B. Avey, Michael E. Palanski, and Fred O. Walumbwa, "When Leadership Goes Unnoticed: The Moderating Role of Follower Self-Esteem on the Relationship between Ethical Leadership and Follower Behavior," *Journal of Business Ethics* 98 (2011): 573–582.

31. Constance E. Bagley, "The Ethical Leader's Decision Tree," *Harvard Business Review*, January–February 2003, p. 18.

32. O. C. Ferrell and Larry G. Gresham, "A Contingency Framework for Understanding Ethical Decision Making in Marketing," *Journal of Marketing* 49 (1985): 90–91.

33. Reuters, "Fear and respect: VW's culture under Winterkorn," *CNBC*, October 11, 2015, http://www.cnbc.com/2015/10/11/ (accessed August 5, 2016).

34. "Integrity Survey 2013," *KPMG*, http://www.kpmg.com/CN/en/IssuesAndInsights/ArticlesPublications/Documents/Integrity-Survey-2013-O-201307.pdf (accessed August 4, 2016).

35. John R. P. French and Bertram Ravin, "The Bases of Social Power," in *Group Dynamics: Research and Theory,* ed. Dorwin Cartwright (Evanston, IL: Row, Peterson, 1962), pp. 607–623.

36. Lynn Brewer, Robert Chandler, and O. C. Ferrell, *Managing Risks for Corporate Integrity: How to Survive an Ethical Misconduct Disaster* (Mason, OH: Texere/Thomson, 2006), p. 35.

37. Susan Pulliam, "How Following Orders Can Harm Your Career," *CFO Magazine*, October 3, 2003, http://ww2.cfo.com/human-capital-careers/2003/10/how-following-orders-can-harm-your-career/ (accessed August 4, 2016).

38. Southwest Airlines, "Welcome to Adopt-A-Pilot," http://www.southwest.com/adoptapilot/ (accessed August 4, 2016).

39. Ferrell and Gresham, "A Contingency Framework for Understanding Ethical Decision-Making in Marketing."

40. Janet Wiscombe, "Don't Fear Whistle-Blower: With HR's Help, Principled Whistle-Blowers Can Be a Company's Salvation," *Workforce,* July 2002, pp. 26–32.

41. Ferrell, Fraedrich, and Ferrell, "Business Ethics," pp. 313–315.

42. Freeman and Lisa Stewart, "Developing Ethical Leadership."

43. James M. Burns, *Leadership* (New York, NY: Harper & Row, 1985).

44. John P. Kotter, "What Leaders Really Do," *Harvard Business Review*, December 2001, https://hbr.org/2001/12/what-leaders-really-do (accessed August 4, 2016).

45. Stephen R. Covey, *The 7 Habits of Highly Effective People* (New York: Simon & Schuster, 1989).

46. Archie B. Carroll, "Ethical Leadership: From Moral Managers to Moral Leaders," in *Rights, Relationships and Responsibilities*, vol. 1, ed. O. C. Ferrell, Sheb True, and Lou Pelton (Kennesaw, GA: Kennesaw State University, 2003), pp. 7–17.

47. Jim Collins, "Leadership Lessons," *Leadership Excellence* 29, no. 2 (February 2012): 10.

48. Kotter, "What Leaders Really Do."

49. Carroll, "Ethical Leadership," p. 11.

50. Fortune, "100 Best Companies to Work for: NetApp," *CNNMoney*, 2013, http://archive.fortune.com/magazines/fortune/best-companies/2013/snapshots/6.html (accessed August 4, 2016).

51. Michael W. Grojean, Christian J. Resick, Marcus W. Dickson, and Brent D. Smith, "Leaders, Values and Organizational Climate Regarding Ethics," *Journal of Business Ethics* 55, no. 3 (December 2004): 223–241.

52. Whole Foods, "Our Core Values," http://www.wholefoodsmarket.com/mission-values/core-values (accessed August 4, 2016).

53. Ferrell, Fraedrich, and Ferrell, "Business Ethics," pp. 315–316.

54. Daniel J. Brass, Kenneth D Butterfield, and Bruce C. Skaggs, "Relationship and Unethical Behavior: A Social Science Perspective," *Academy of Management Review* 23 (January 1998): 14–31.

55. Linda Klebe Trevino, Gary R. Weaver, David G. Gibson, and Barbara Lay Toffler, "Managing Ethics and Legal Compliance: What Works and What Hurts," *California Management Review* 41 (1999): 131–151; Michael E. Brown and Linda K. Trevino, "Ethical Leadership: A Review and Future Directions," *The Leadership Quarterly* 17, no. 6 (December 2006): 595–616.

56. Mitchell J. Neubert, Dawn S. Carlson, K. Michele Kacmar, James A. Roberts, and Lawrence B. Chonko, "The Virtuous Influence of Ethical Leadership Behavior: Evidence from the Field," *Journal of Business Ethics* 90 (2009): 157–170.

57. Sean Valentine, Lynn Godkin, Gary M. Fleischman, Roland E. Kidwell, and Karen Page, "Corporate Ethical Values, Group Creativity, Job Satisfaction and Turnover Intention: The Impact of Work Context on Work Response," *Journal of Business Ethics* 98 (2011): 353–372.

58. Fortune, "100 Best Companies to Work For 2009," *CNNMoney*, http://money.cnn.com/magazines/fortune/best-companies/2009/snapshots/32.html (accessed August 4, 2016); "The Container Store: An Employee-Centric Retailer," *UNM Daniels Fund Business Ethics Initiative*, http://danielsethics.mgt.unm.edu/pdf/Container%20Store%20Case.pdf (accessed August 4, 2016).

59. Remi Trudel and June Cotte, "Does It Pay to Be Good?" *MIT Sloan Management Review* 50, no. 2 (2009): 60–68.

60. Tae Hee Choi and Jinchul Jung, "Ethical Commitment, Financial Performance, and Valuation: An Empirical Investigation of Korean Companies," *Journal of Business Ethics* 81, no. 2 (2008): 447–463.

61. Jin-Woo Kim, "Assessing the Long-term Financial Performance of Ethical Companies," *Journal of Targeting, Measurement and Analysis for Marketing* 18, no. 3/4 (2010): 199–208.

62. Win Swenson, "The Organizational Guidelines' Carrot and Stick' Philosophy, and Their Focus on 'Effective' Compliance," in *Corporate Crime in America: Strengthening the "Good Citizenship" Corporation* (Washington, DC: U.S. Sentencing Commission, 1995), pp. 17–26.

63. Ferrell, Fraedrich, and Ferrell, "Business Ethics," pp. 329–332.

64. Brass, Butterfield, and Skaggs, "Relationship and Unethical Behavior."

65. Cam Caldwell, Linda A. Hayes, and Do Tien Long, "Leadership, Trustworthiness, and Ethical Stewardship," *Journal of Business Ethics* 96 (2010): 497–512.

66. Al Lewis, "Lewis: A Good Man Who Did a Bad Thing," *The Denver Post*, October 25, 2012, http://www.denverpost.com/2012/10/25/lewis-a-good-man-who-did-a-bad-thing/ (accessed August 4, 2016).

67. Jim Collins, "Be Great Now." *Inc.*, June 2012, pp. 72–73

68. Robert Kerr, John Garvin, Norma Heaton, and Emily Boyle, "Emotional Intelligence and Leadership Effectiveness," *Leadership & Organizational Development Journal* 27, no.(4 (2006): 265–279.

69. "Seventy-One Percent of Employers Say They Value Emotional Intelligence Over IQ, According to CareerBuilder Survey," *CareerBuilder*, August 18, 2011, http://www.careerbuilder.com/share/aboutus/pressreleasesdetail.aspx?id=pr652&sd=8/18/2011&ed=8/18/2099 (accessed August 4, 2016).

70. Brewer, Chandler, and Ferrell, *Managing Risks for Corporate Integrity*.

71. Richard Boyatzis and Annie McKee, *Resonant Leadership: Renewing Yourself and Connecting with Others Through Mindfulness, Hope and Compassion* (Boston, MA: Harvard Business Review Press, 2005); Bruce Rosenstein, "Resonant Leader Is One In Tune with Himself, Others," *USA Today*, November 27, 2005, http://usatoday30.usatoday.com/money/books/reviews/2005-11-27-resonant-book-usat_x.htm (accessed August 4, 2016).

72. Peter Ubel, "Do Starbucks Employees Have More Emotional Intelligence than Your Physician?" *Forbes*, November 2, 2012, http://www.forbes.com/sites/peterubel/2012/11/02/do-starbucks-employees-have-more-emotional-intelligence-than-your-physician/#65a9b2a96beb (accessed August 4, 2016).

73. Burns, *Leadership*.

74. Royston Greenwood, Roy Suddaby, and C. R. Hinings, "Theorizing Change: The Role of Professional Associations in the Transformation of Institutionalized Fields," *Academy of Management Journal* 45 (January 2002): 58–80.

75. Shuili Du, Valérie Swaen, Adam Lindgreen, and Sankar Sen, "The Roles of Leadership Styles in Corporate Social Responsibility," *Journal of Business Ethics* 114 (2013): 155–169.

76. Eric Pillmore, "How Tyco International Remade Its Corporate Governance," speech at Wharton Business School, September 2006.

77. New Belgium Brewing, "Culture," http://www.newbelgium.com/Brewery/company/history.aspx (accessed August 4, 2016).

78. Bill George, Peter Sims, Andrew M. McLean, and Diana Mayer, "Discovering Your Authentic Leadership," *Harvard Business Review*, February 2007, https://hbr.org/2007/02/discovering-your-authentic-leadership (accessed August 4, 2016).

79. Stephen R. Covey, *Principle-Centered Leadership* (New York, NY: Franklin Covey Co., 1991), pp. 102–105.

80. Ferrell, Fraedrich, and Ferrell, "Business Ethics," pp. 326–327.

81. S. K. Collins and K. S. Collins, "Micromanagement—A Costly Management Style," *Radiology Management* 24, no. 6 (2002): 32–35.

82. Gary Yukl, "Managerial Leadership: A Review of Theory and Research," *Journal of Management* 15 (June 1989): 251–289.

83. Ryan S. Bisel, Katherine M. Kelley, Nicole A. Ploeger, and Jake Messersmith, "Workers' Moral Mum Effect: On Facework and Unethical Behavior in the Workplace," *Communication Studies* 62, no. 2 (2011): 153–170.

84. Ferrell, Fraedrich, and Ferrell, "Business Ethics," pp. 322–326.

85. Gary T. Hunt, *Communication Skills in the Organization* (Upper Saddle-River, NJ: Prentice-Hall, February 1989).

86. Ibid.

87. Robert Gatewood, Robert Taylor, and O. C. Ferrell, *Management* (Homewood, IL: Richard D. Irwin, Inc., 1995).

88. Sally Planalp and Julie Fitness, "Interpersonal Communication Ethics," in *The Handbook of Communication Ethics*, ed. George Cheney, Steve May, and Debashish Munshi (New York, NY: Taylor and Francis, 2011), pp. 135–147.

89. Jack R. Gibb, "Defensive Communication," *Journal of Communication* 11, no. 3 (September 1961): 141–148.

90. Hunt, *Communication Skills in the Organization*.

91. Mary Ellen Guffey, Kathleen Rhodes, and Patricia Rogen, *Business Communication: Process and Product* (Toronto, Canada: Nelson Education Ltd., 2010).

92. Cass R. Sunstein, "The Law of Group Polarization," John M. Olin Law & Economics Working Paper No. 91(1999) (2D Series), http://www.law.uchicago.edu/files/files/91.CRS_.Polarization.pdf (accessed August 4, 2016).

93. Gatewood, Taylor, and Ferrell, *Management*, p. 530.

94. Hunt, *Communication Skills in the Organization*.

95. Susan M. Heathfield, "Top Ten Employee Complaints," *About.com*, http://humanresources.about.com/od/retention/a/emplo_complaint.htm (accessed August 4, 2016).

96. Ibid.

Chapter 7

1. Erika Fry, "How CarMax Cares," *Fortune*, April 8, 2013, p. 21; CarMax website, "CarMax Culture and Values," http://www.carmax.com/enUS/company-info/culture.html (accessed July 15, 2016); Michael Myser, "The Wal-Mart of Used Cars," *CNN Money*, October 2, 2006, http://money.cnn.com/magazines/business2/business2_archive/2006/09/01/8384327/ (accessed July 15, 2016); Great Place to Work® Guides LLC dba Great Rated!™, "Inside Story at CarMax," http://us.greatrated.com/carmax (accessed July 15, 2016); CarMax, "CarMax Strategy Teams," http://ieee.illinois.edu/wordpress/wp-content/uploads/2013/02/CarMax-Strategy-Group-Teams.pdf (accessed July 7, 2014); CarMax, "CarMax Celebrates a Decade as One of FORTUNE Magazine's '100 Best Companies to Work For'," *The Wall Street Journal*, January 16, 2014, http://online.wsj.com/article/PR-CO-20140116-908916.html (accessed July 7, 2014) http://investors.carmax.com/news-releases/news-releases-details/2014/CarMax-Celebrates-a-Decade-as-One-of-FORTUNE-Magazines-100-Best-Companies-to-Work-For/default.aspx (accessed July 18, 2016); Fortune, "CarMax: 100 Best Companies to Work For," 2016, http://fortune.com/best-companies/carmax-85/ (accessed July 15, 2016); " About CarMax," http://fortune.com/best-companies/carmax-85/ (accessed July 15, 2016).

2. Joanne B. Ciulla, *The Working Life: The Promise and Betrayal of Modern Work* (New York: Times Books, 2000).

3. Ibid.; Adriano Tilgher, *Work: What It Has Meant to Men Through the Ages*, trans. Dorothy Canfield Fisher (New York: Harcourt, Brace & World, 1958).

4. These facts are derived from Brenda Paik Sunoo, "Relying on Faith to Rebuild a Business," *Workforce* 78 (March 1999): 54–59.

5. Polartec LLC, "About Polartec®/FAQ," http://polartec.com/about/faq.aspx (accessed July 15, 2016); "Polartec LLC," *Bloomberg Businessweek*, http://investing.businessweek.com/research/stocks/private/snapshot.asp?privcapId=728315 (accessed July 15, 2016); Sunoo, "Relying on Faith to Rebuild a Business"; Justin Pope, "Malden Mills Emerges from the Bankruptcy, Still Under Financial Cloud," *Houston Chronicle*,

August 15, 2003, p. B1. Janet B. Rodie, "Textile World News," *Textile World* 152 (January 2002): 12.

6. "Worldatwork Finds One-Third of Companies Downsized After 9/11," *Report on Salary Surveys* 2 (December 2002): 12; Stephanie Armour, "Companies Chisel Away at Workers' Benefits," *USA Today*, November 18, 2002, pp. 1B–3B; Lynn Gresham, "Winning the Talent War Requires a Fresh Benefits Approach," *Employee Benefit News*, April 15, 2006, p. 9.

7. Neil Conway and Rob B. Briner, *Understanding Psychological Contracts at Work* (London: Oxford University Press, 2006); Denise M. Rousseau, *Psychological Contracts in Organizations: Understanding Written and Unwritten Agreements* (Thousand Oaks, CA: Sage, 1995).

8. Jacqueline Coyle-Shapiro, "A Psychological Contract Perspective on Organizational Citizenship Behavior," *Journal of Organizational Behavior* 23 (December 2002): 927–946; William H. Turnley and Daniel C. Feldman, "The Impact of Psychological Contract Violations on Exit, Voice, Loyalty, and Neglect," *Human Relations* 52 (July 1999): 895–922.

9. Ibid.

10. Ans De Vos and Annelies Meganck, "What HR Managers Do Versus What Employees Value," *Personnel Review* 38 (2009): 45–60.

11. Kimberly D. Elsbach and Greg Elafson, "How the Packaging of Decision Explanations Affects Perceptions of Trustworthiness," *Academy of Management Journal* 43 (February 2000): 80–89; David E. Guest and Neil Conway, "Communicating the Psychological Contract: An Employer Perspective," *Human Resource Management Journal* 12, no. 2 (2002): 22–38.

12. Gillian Flynn, "Looking Back on 100 Years of Employment Law," *Workforce* 78 (November 1999): 74–77.

13. "A Guru Ahead of Her Time," *Nation's Business* 85 (May 1997): 24.

14. Steve Sayer, "Cleaning Up the Jungle," *Occupational Health and Safety* 66 (May 1997): 22.

15. Flynn, "Looking Back on 100 Years of Employment Law."

16. "Employee Relations in America," *IRS Employment Review* (March 1997): E7–E12; Roger LeRoy Miller and Gaylord A. Jentz, *Business Law Today* (Cincinnati, OH: West Legal Studies in Business, 2000).

17. C. Wright Mills, *White Collar: The American Middle Classes* (New York: Oxford University Press, 1951).

18. Ciulla, *The Working Life*; William H. Whyte, *The Organization Man* (New York: Simon & Schuster, 1956).

19. *Work in America: Report of a Special Task Force to the Secretary of Health, Education, and Welfare* (Cambridge, MA: MIT Press, 1973).

20. Ciulla, *The Working Life*.

21. Taina Savolainen, "Leadership Strategies for Gaining Business Excellence Through Total Quality Management: A Finnish Case Study," *Total Quality Management* 11 (March 2000): 211–226.

22. "Younger Employees Want Security," *USA Today*, October 3, 2001, p. 1B.

23. United States Department of Labor, "Labor Force Statistics from the Current Population Survey," July 15, 2016, http://data.bls.gov/timeseries/LNS14000000 (accessed July 15, 2016).

24. United States Department of Labor, "Employment and Unemployment among Youth Summary," *Bureau of Labor Statistics*, August 18, 2015, http://www.bls.gov/news.release/youth.nr0.htm (accessed July 15, 2016).

25. This section is adapted from Debbie Thorne LeClair, "The Ups and Downs of Rightsizing the Workplace," *ABACA Profile,* November–December 1999, p. 25.

26. Priti Pradhan Shah, "Network Destruction: The Structural Implications of Downsizing," *Academy of Management Journal* 43 (February 2000): 101–112; Steve Lohr, "Cutting Here, but Hiring Over There," *New York Times,* June 24, 2005, p. C3.

27. Elizabeth Weise, "Intel to lay off 11% of workforce in big shift from PCs," *USA Today,* April 20, 2016, http://www.usatoday.com/story/tech/2016/04/19/intel-lay-offs-12000-11/83242832/ (accessed July 18, 2016).

28. Colum Wood, "GM Says it Needs $16.6 Billion MORE: Will Cut 47,000 Jobs and Close 5 U.S. Plants to Get it," *Auto Guide,* February 17, 2009, http://www.autoguide.com/auto-news/2009/02/gm-says-it-needs-166-billion-more-will-cut-47000-jobs-and-close-5-us-plants-to-get-it.html (accessed June 28, 2014); *New York Times Special Report: The Downsizing of America* (New York: Times Books, 1996); Victor B. Wayhan and Steve Werner, "The Impact of Workforce Reductions on Financial Performance: A Longitudinal Perspective," *Journal of Management* 26 (2000): 341–363.

29. Thomas G. Cummings and Christopher G. Worley, *Organization Development and Change* (Cincinnati, OH: South-Western Cengage Learning, 2009).

30. Harry J. Van Buren III, "The Bindingness of Social and Psychological Contracts: Toward a Theory of Social Responsibility in Downsizing," *Journal of Business Ethics* 25 (January 2000): 205–219; Davis J. Flanagan and K. C. O'Saughnessy, "The Effects of Layoffs on Firm Reputation," *Journal of Management* (June 2005): 445.

31. Geoff Colvin, "Layoffs Cost More Than You Think," *Fortune,* March 30, 2009, p. 24.

32. Steve Beigbeder, "Easing Workforce Reduction," *Risk Management* 47 (May 2000): 26–30; Matthew Camardella, "Legal Considerations of Workforce Reduction," *Employment Relations Today* 29 (Autumn 2002): 101–106.

33. U.S. Department of Labor, "The Worker Adjustment and Retraining Notification Act," http://www.doleta.gov/programs/factsht/warn.htm (accessed July 18, 2016).

34. Pure Michigan, CV Marketing Sheet, http://www.mitalent.org/Media/Default/Files/JobSeeker/CV%20Market%20Sheet.pdf (accessed July 18, 2016).

35. Angelo J. Kinicki, Gregory E. Prussia, and Francis M. McKee-Ryan, "A Panel Study of Coping with Involuntary Job Loss," *Academy of Management Journal* 43 (February 2000): 90–100.

36. Wayhan and Werner, "The Impact of Workforce Reductions on Financial Performance."

37. Nicholas Stein, "Winning the War to Keep Top Talent," *Fortune,* May 29, 2000, pp. 132–138.

38. Carlyn Kolker, "Survivor Blues," *American Lawyer* 24 (October 2002): 116–118; Susan Reynolds Fisher and Margaret A. White, "Downsizing in a Learning Organization," *Academy of Management Review* 25 (January 2000): 244–251.

39. Susan Beck, "What to Do before You Say 'You're Outta Here,'" *Business Week,* December 8, 1997, p. 6.

40. U.S. Department of Labor, Employment Law Guide, http://www.dol.gov/compliance/guide/ (accessed July 18, 2016).

41. Robert Harding, "Minimum Wage Debate: What Supporters, Opponents Say About Effects of Raising the Minimum Wage," *Auburn Citizen,* May 14, 2014, http://auburnpub.com/news/local/minimum-wage-debate-what-supporters-opponents-say-about-effects-of/article_102e4516-f582-552d-a02e-3b71896c76aa.html (accessed July 18, 2016).

42. Wesley Lowery, "Senate Republicans Block Minimum Wage Increase Bill," *The Washington Post,* April 30, 2014, http://www.washingtonpost.com/blogs/post-politics/wp/2014/04/30/senate-republicans-block-minimum-wage-increase-bill/ (accessed July 18, 2016); Catherine Rampell and Steven Greenhouse, "$10 Minimum Wage Proposal Has Growing Support From White House," *The New York Times,* November 7, 2013, http://www.nytimes.com/2013/11/08/business/10-minimum-wage-proposal-has-obamas-backing.html?_r=0 (accessed July 18, 2016).

43. "Minimum Wage Laws in the States," U.S. Department of Labor, https://www.dol.gov/general/topic/wages/minimumwage (accessed July 18, 2016); "History of Federal Minimum Wage Rates Under the Fair Labor Standards Act, 1938–2009," U.S. Department of Labor, http://www.dol.gov/whd/minwage/chart.htm (accessed July 18, 2016); Miller and Jentz, *Business Law Today.*

44. Flynn, "Looking Back on 100 Years of Employment Law."

45. Robert J. Nobile, "HR's Top 10 Legal Issues," *HR Focus* 74 (April 1997): 19–20.

46. Miller and Jentz, *Business Law Today.*

47. Flynn, "Looking Back on 100 Years of Employment Law."

48. *The New OSHA: Reinventing Worker Safety and Health* (Washington, DC: U.S. Department of Labor, Occupational Safety and Health Administration, 1995), http://www.osha.gov/doc/outreachtraining/htmlfiles/newosha.html (accessed June 28, 2014); Dana E. Corbin, "Speaking Their Language," *Occupational Health & Safety* 71 (July 2002): 32; "Commonly Used Statistics," U.S. Department of Labor, https://www.osha.gov/oshstats/commonstats.html (accessed July 18, 2016).

49. Judith N. Mottl, "Industry Fights OSHA's Proposed Ergonomic Rule," *Informationweek,* June 19, 2000, p. 122; Daniel R. Miller, "OSHA Goes Too Far with Ergonomics Rules," *National Underwriter,* May 8, 2000, p. 59; John D. Schulz, "Trucking Wants Out," *Traffic World,* May 29, 2000, pp. 21–22; Robin Suttell, "Healthy Work," *Buildings* 96 (October 2002): 56–58; "Enforcement," U.S. Department of Labor, https://www.osha.gov/SLTC/ergonomics/faqs.html (accessed July 18, 2016).

50. Gildan Activewear Inc., "Ergonomics Program," http://www.genuinegildan.com/en/people/working-conditions/ergonomics-program/ (accessed July 18, 2016).

51. "Workplace Violence," Occupational Safety and Health Administration, http://www.osha.gov/SLTC/workplaceviolence/index.html (accessed July 18, 2016).

52. Karen Sarkis, "Workplace Violence Top Concern for Employers," *Occupational Hazards* 62 (June 2000): 23; Sarah J. Smith, "Workplace Violence," *Professional Safety* 47 (November 2002): 34–43; "Workplace Violence," Occupational Safety and Health Administration, http://www.osha.gov/SLTC/workplaceviolence/index.html (accessed July 18, 2016); Mark Haynes, "Workplace Violence: Why Every State Must Adopt a Comprehensive Workplace Violence Prevention Law," *Cornell HR Review,* April 13, 2013, http://www.cornellhrreview.org/workplace-

violence-why-every-state-must-adopt-a-comprehensive-workplace-violence-prevention-law/.

53. "Dealing with Violence in the Workplace," Society for Human Resource Management, October 3, 2012, http://www.shrm.org/templatestools/toolkits/pages/dealingwithviolencein-theworkplace.aspx (accessed June 30, 2014).

54. Joshua Berlinger and Dana Ford, "Kansas shooting: Gunman kills 3, wounds 14 at lawn care company," *CNN*, February 26, 2016, http://www.cnn.com/2016/02/25/us/kansas-shooting/ (accessed July 18, 2016).

55. Carrie Coolidge, "Risky Business," *Forbes*, January 6, 2003, p. 54; Todd Henneman, "Ignoring Signs of Violence Can Be Fatal, Costly Mistake," *Workforce Management*, February 27, 2006, p.10; John Leming, "New Product Covers Losses Related to Workplace Violence," *Journal of Commerce*, April 6, 2000, p. 15.

56. U.S. Equal Employment Opportunity Commission, "Pregnancy Discrimination Charges FY 2010–FY 2015," https://www.eeoc.gov/eeoc/statistics/enforcement/pregnancy_new.cfm (accessed July 18, 2016).

57. Judy Greenwald, "Employers Confront AIDS in Africa," *Business Insurance* 35 (July 23, 2001): 15; Michael T. Parker, "Fighting AIDS Stigma in the Workplace," *Business Mexico* 15 (August 2005): 43–44.

58. "Global Diversity Mission," Coca-Cola, http://www.coca-colacompany.com/our-company/diversity/global-diversity-mission (accessed July 18, 2016).

59. U.S. Equal Employment Opportunity Commission, "Facts About Sexual Harassment," http://www.eeoc.gov/eeoc/publications/fs-sex.cfm (accessed July 18, 2016).

60. Donald J. Petersen and Douglas P. Massengill, "Sexual Harassment Cases Five Years After *Meritor Savings Bank v. Vinson*," *Employee Relations Law Journal* 18 (Winter 1992–1993): 489–516.

61. Maria E. Conway, "Sexual Harassment Abroad," *Workforce* 77 (September 1998): 8–9; Javiera Medina Reza and Matthew Capelle, "Mexico Develops Steps to Take Seriously Sexual Harassment in the Workplace," *Littler*, September 13, 2012, https://www.littler.com/files/press/pdf/2012_09_ASAP_Mexico_Develops_Steps_Sexual_Harassment_Workplace.pdf (accessed July 18, 2016).

62. "Code of Practice to Clamp Down on Sexual Harassment at Work," European Commission, http://europa.eu/legislation_summaries/employment_and_social_policy/equality_between_men_and_women/c10917b_en.htm (accessed July 18, 2016).

63. Robert D. Lee and Paul S. Greenlaw, "The Legal Evolution of Sexual Harassment," *Public Administration Review* 55 (July 1995): 357–364.

64. Ibid.

65. George D. Mesritz, "Hostile Environment Sexual Harassment Claims: When Once Is Enough," *Employee Relations Law Journal* 22 (Spring 1997): 79–85; Laura Hoffman Roppe, "*Harris v. Forklift Systems, Inc.*: Victory or Defeat?" *San Diego Law Review* 32 (Winter 1996): 321–342.

66. Susan Antilla, "Women Charge Bias and Harassment in Suit against Sterling Jewelers," *The New York Times*, March 28, 2014, http://www.nytimes.com/2014/03/29/business/women-charge-bias-and-harassment-in-suit-against-sterling-jewelers.html (accessed July 18, 2016).

67. "Ashley Alford's Verdict: $95M for Sex Harassment," *Reuters*, June 14, 2011, http://www.reuters.com/article/tagblogs-findlawcom2011-freeenterprise-idUS71042601620110614 (accessed July 18, 2016).

68. Jonathan W. Dion, "Putting Employers on the Defense: The Supreme Court Develops a Consistent Standard Regarding an Employer's Liability for a Supervisor's Hostile Work Environment Sexual Harassment," *Wake Forest Law Review* 34 (Spring 1999): 199–227; Darlene Orlov and Michael T. Roumell, *What Every Manager Needs to Know About Sexual Harassment* (New York: AMACOM, 1999).

69. Joann Lublin, "Retaliation over Harassment Claims Takes Focus," *Wall Street Journal*, April 17, 2006, p. B4.

70. Howard Koplowitz, "Texas Man Wins Sexual Harassment Case against Female Boss: Jury Awards James Gist $567K in Pam Matranga Case," *International Business Times*, March 24, 2014, http://www.ibtimes.com/texas-man-wins-sexual-harassment-case-against-female-boss-jury-awards-james-gist-567k-pam-matranga (accessed July 18, 2016).

71. Janet P. Near and Marcia P. Miceli, "Organizational Dissidence: The Case of Whistleblowing," *Journal of Business Ethics* 4 (January 1985): 1–16.

72. This section is adapted from Randy Chiu, Richard Tansey, Debbie Thorne, and Michael White, "Is Procedural Justice the Dominant Whistleblowing Motive Among Employees?" unpublished manuscript.

73. Phaedra Haywood, "County Whistleblower Doesn't Regret Standing 'Up for What Is right'," *The Santa Fe New Mexican*, June 28, 2014, http://www.santafenewmexican.com/news/local_news/county-whistleblower-doesn-t-regret-standing-up-for-what-is/article_b5c02633-8e86-52d3-b5e5-2a2e09b11e1a.html (accessed July 18, 2016).

74. Lorri Freifeld, "Jiffy Lube Revs Up to No. 1," *Training Magazine*, https://trainingmag.com/trgmag-article/jiffy-lube-revs-no-1 (accessed July 18, 2016).

75. "Helping Employees Develop Professionally," University of California, Berkeley, http://hrweb.berkeley.edu/toolkits/managers-supervisors/helping-employees-develop (accessed June 30, 2014).

76. Scott Westcott, "Good Bye and Good Luck," *Inc* 28 (April 2006): 40–41.

77. Betsy Cummings, "Training's Top Five," *Successful Meetings* 49 (October 2000): 67–73; Adam J. Grossberg, "The Effect of Formal Training on Employment Duration," *Industrial Relations* 39 (October 2000): 578–599; Kathryn Tyler, "Extending the Olive Branch," *HR Magazine* 47 (November 2002): 85–89.

78. Laurie Miller, "ASTD 2012 State of the Industry Report: Organizations Continue to Invest in Workplace Learning," Association for Talent Development, November 8, 2012, https://www.td.org/Publications/Magazines/TD/TD-Archive/2012/11/ASTD-2012-State-of-the-Industry-Report (accessed July 18, 2016).

79. Starbucks, "Starbucks College Achievement Plan," http://www.starbucks.com/careers/college-plan (accessed July 18, 2016).

80. "Diversity: A 'New' Tool for Retention," *HR Focus* 77 (June 2000): 1, 14.

81. David Pollitt, "Diversity Is About More Than Observing the Letter of the Law," *Human Resource Management International Digest* 13 (2005): 37–40.

82. David P. Schulz, "Different Approaches to Approaching Differences," *Stores* 87 (April 2005): 98.

83. Marilyn Loden and Judith B. Rosener, *Workforce America! Managing Employee Diversity as a Vital Resource* (Burr Ridge, IL: Irwin/McGraw-Hill, 1991).

84. DiversityInc, "Kaiser Permanente: No. 4 in the DiversityInc Top 50," http://www.diversityinc.com/kaiser-permanente/ (accessed July 8, 2014); Lincoln Cushing, "Alva Wheatley: Champion of Kaiser Permanente Diversity," Kaiser Permanente, February 18, 2014, http://kaiserpermanentehistory.org/latest/alva-wheatley-champion-of-kaiser-permanente-diversity/ (accessed July 8, 2014).

85. Ira Teinowitz, "Courting Change," *Advertising Age* 72 (May 14, 2001): 16–20; Michelle Saettler, "General Mills, Clorox Target Hispanic Mobile Shoppers Via Bilingual Promotions Ap," *Mobile Marketer*, April 14, 2014, http://www.mobilemarketer.com/cms/news/strategy/17575.html (accessed July 18, 2016).

86. New York Life Insurance Company, "New York Life appoints Kathleen Navarro as chief diversity officer," December 15, 2014, http://www.newyorklife.com/about/about/nyl-appoints-kathleen-navarro-chief-diversity-officer

87. "Employers of the Year," *Equal Opportunity Publications,* 2014, http://www.eop.com/awards-CD-employers.php (accessed July 18, 2016).

88. Phil Gorman, Teresa Nelson, and Alan Glassman, "The Millennial Generation: A Strategic Opportunity," *Organizational Analysis* 12, no. 3 (2004): 255–270; Ron Zemke, Claire Raines, and Bob Filipczak, *Generations at Work: Managing the Clash of Veterans, Boomers, Xers, and Nexters in Your Workplace* (New York: AMACOM, 2000).

89. Arthur P. Brief, Elizabeth Umphress, Joerg Dietz, Rebecca Butz, John Burrows, and Lotte Scholten, "Community Matters: Realistic Group Conflict Theory and the Impact of Diversity," *Academy of Management Journal* 48 (October 2005): 830–844.

90. Cora Daniels, "To Hire a Lumber Expert, Click Here," *Fortune,* April 3, 2000, pp. 267–270.

91. Georgia Wells, "Facebook Blames Lack of Available Talent for Diversity Problem," *The Wall Street Journal*, July 14, 2016, http://www.wsj.com/articles/facebook-blames-lack-of-available-talent-for-diversity-problem-1468526303 (accessed July 15, 2016).

92. Tyrone A. Holmes, "How to Connect Diversity to Performance," *Performance Improvement* 44 (May–June 2005): 13–17.

93. Jeffrey R. Edwards and Nancy P. Rothbard, "Mechanisms Linking Work and Family," *Academy of Management Review* 25 (January 2000): 178–199.

94. Dalton Conley, *Elsewhere, USA: How We Got From the Company Man, Family Dinners, and the Affluent Society to the Home Office, Blackberry Moms, and Economic Anxiety*, 2009.

95. Douglas M. McCracken, "Winning the Talent War for Women: Sometimes It Takes a Revolution," *Harvard Business Review* 78 (November–December 2000): 159–167; Sally Roberts, "Work/Life Programs No Longer a 'Woman's Issue,'" *Business Insurance*, August 8, 2005, pp. 3–4; Stephanie Pappas, "Work-Life Balance Affects Men And Women Alike, Study Finds," *The Huffington Post*, March 15, 2013, http://www.huffingtonpost.com/2013/03/15/work-life-balance-affects-men-women-alike-same_n_2884315.html (accessed July 18, 2016).

96. Mark C. Crowley, "How SAS Became the World's Best Place to Work," *Fast Company*, January 22, 2013, http://www.fastcompany.com/3004953/how-sas-became-worlds-best-place-work (accessed July 18, 2016).

97. "Work Stress On the Rise: 8 In 10 Americans Are Stressed About Their Jobs, Survey Finds," *The Huffington Post*, April 10, 2013, http://www.huffingtonpost.com/2013/04/10/work-stress-jobs-americans_n_3053428.html (accessed July 18, 2016).

98. Bruce Horovitz, "All Stressed Out? Businesses Will Sell You Some Peace," *USA Today*, August 5, 2013, http://www.usatoday.com/story/money/business/2013/08/04/stress-deepak-chopra-dreamweaver-relaxation-drinks-american-psychological-association/2513655/ (accessed July 18, 2016).

99. Shai Oster, "They're Dying at Their Desks in China as Epidemic of Stress Proves Fatal," *Bloomberg*, http://www.bloomberg.com/news/articles/2014-06-29/is-work-killing-you-in-china-workers-die-at-their-desks (accessed July 18, 2016).

100. Charles R. Stoner, Jennifer Robin, and Lori Russell-Chapin, "On the Edge: Perceptions and Responses to Life Imbalance," *Business Horizons* (July–August 2005): 48–54.

101. SAS, Annual Report, http://www.sas.com/content/dam/SAS/en_us/doc/other1/2013-annual-report.pdf (accessed July 18, 2016); Thomas Watson, "Goodnight, Sweet Prince," *Canadian Business,* May 27, 2002, pp. 77–78; Mark C. Crowley, "How SAS Became the World's Best Place to Work," *Fast Company*, January 22, 2013, http://www.fastcompany.com/3004953/how-sas-became-worlds-best-place-work (accessed July 18, 2016).

102. E. Jeffrey Hill, Andrea Jackson, and Giuseppe Martinengo, "Twenty Years of Work and Family at International Business Machines Corporation," *American Behavioral Scientist* 49 (May 2006): 1165–1183.

103. Jessica Leong, "What Candidates Want: Improving the Applicant Screening Process," *Findly*, September 18, 2013, http://www.findly.com/blog/what-candidates-want-improving-the-applicant-screening-process/ (accessed July 18, 2016).

104. Selena Maranjian, "These Companies Do Work-Life Balance Right," *Daily Finance*, July 24, 2013, http://www.dailyfinance.com/2013/07/24/glassdoor-work-life-balance-report/ (accessed July 18, 2016).

105. Ibid.

106. Ryan Scott, "How Corporate Volunteer Programs Increase Employee Engagement," *Cause Cast*, February 16, 2012, http://www.causecast.com/blog/how-corporate-volunteer-programs-increase-employee-engagement (accessed July 18, 2016).

107. Blue Cross, Blue Shield, "Blue Cross and Blue Shield Companies Host Seventh Annual National Walk@Lunch Day™," April 24, 2013, http://www.bcbs.com/healthcare-news/bcbsa/bcbs-companies-host-seventh-annual-nwld.html (accessed July 8, 2014).

108. CA Technologies, "CA Technologies Holds Eighth Annual Worldwide Volunteer Month," September 30, 2013, http://investor.ca.com/releasedetail.cfm?releaseid=793863 (accessed July 18, 2016).

109. Sammi Caramela, "15 Cool Job Perks that Keep Employees Happy," *Business News Daily*, June 8, 2016, http://www.businessnewsdaily.com/5134-cool-job-benefits.html (accessed July 18, 2016).

110. ENSR, "An Employer of Choice," http://www.aecom.com/Careers/Our+People+and+Culture (accessed July 1, 2014); Roger E. Herman and Joyce L. Gioia, *How to Become an Employer of Choice* (Winchester, VA: Oakhill Press, 2000).

111. Ibid.; Da Joseph Kornik, "The Morale Majority," *Training* 43 (January 2006): 4.

112. "The Employee Ownership 100: America's Largest Majority Employee-Owned Companies," The National Center for Employee Ownership, June 2014, http://www.nceo.org/articles/employee-ownership-100 (accessed July 18, 2016).

113. "ESOP (Employee Stock Ownership Plan) Facts," The National Center for Employee Ownership, 2014, http://www.esop.org (accessed July 18, 2016).

114. Kris Frieswick, "ESOPs: Split Personality," *CFO,* July 7, 2003, p. 1; Ronald Mano and E. Devon Deppe, "We Told You So: ESOPs Are Risky," *Ohio CPA Journal* 61 (July–September 2002): 67–68; Matthew Mouritsen, Ronald Mano, and E. Devon Deppe, "The ESOP Fable Revisited: Employees' Exposure to ESOPs and Enron's Exit," *Personal Financial Planning Monthly* 2 (May 2002): 27–31.

115. Lara Moroko and Mark D. Uncles, "Employer Branding and Market Segmentation," *Sloan Management Review,* March 23, 2009, http://www.researchgate.net/publication/247478730_Employer_branding_and_market_segmentation (accessed July 18, 2016).

116. "The Nike Case and Corporate Self-Censorship," *Business & the Environment with ISO 14000 Updates* 15 (March 2004): 6–7; Isabelle Maignan, Bas Hillebrand, and Debbie Thorne McAlister, "Managing Socially Responsible Buying: How to Integrate Non-economic Criteria into the Purchasing Process," *European Management Journal* 20 (December 2002): 641–648.

117. Nike, Inc., "Awards & Recognition," http://nikeinc.com/pages/awards-recognition (accessed July 22, 2014).

Chapter 8

1. Peter Frost, "Protein Bar founder goes all-in on 'performance' coffee," *Crain's,* April 19, 2016, http://www.chicagobusiness.com/article/20160419/NEWS07/160419844/protein-bar-founder-goes-all-in-on-performance-coffee (accessed July 18, 2016).

2. Mark Brandau, "Protein Bar," *Nation's Restaurant News,* June 27, 2011, http://nrn.com/nrn-50/breakout-brands-protein-bar (accessed July 18, 2016); *The Protein Bar website,* http://www.theproteinbar.com/ (accessed July 18, 2016).

3. Whole Foods, "Whole Foods Market Reports Second Quarter Results," May 4, 2016, http://investor.wholefoodsmarket.com/investors/press-releases/press-release-details/2016/Whole-Foods-Market-Reports-Second-Quarter-Results-542016/default.aspx (accessed July 18, 2016); Sarah Halzack, "Why supermarkets are in trouble," *The Washington Post,* October 3, 2014, https://www.washingtonpost.com/news/business/wp/2014/10/03/why-supermarkets-are-in-trouble/ (accessed July 18, 2016).

4. "Whole Foods Market Reminds Consumers That How Their Food Tastes Has Everything to Do with How It Is Grown," *PR Newswire,* January 3, 2003, http://www.prnewswire.com/news-releases/whole-foods-marketr-reminds-consumers-that-how-their-food-tastes-has-everything-to-do-with-how-it-is-grown-73651002.html (accessed July 18, 2016); "Our Core Values," *Whole Foods Market,* http://www.wholefoodsmarket.com/mission-values/core-values (accessed July 18, 2015); "Whole Foods Market Reports First Quarter Results," *Whole Foods Market,* February 12, 2014, http://www.wholefoods-market.com/sites/default/files/media/Global/Company%20Info/PDFs/WFM-2014-Q1-financial.pdf (accessed July 18, 2016).

5. "International Buy Nothing Day," http://ecoplan.org/ibnd/ (accessed July 18, 2016).

6. "The Aggro of the Agora," *Economist,* January 14, 2006, p. 76; F. Knox, "The Doctrine of Consumer Sovereignty," *Review of Social Economy* 63 (September 2005): 383–394.

7. Duncan Graham and Andreas D. Arditya, "Heading to the Mall? Let the Buyer Beware," *Jakarta Post,* August 25, 2013, http://www.thejakartapost.com/news/2013/08/25/heading-mall-let-buyer-beware.html (accessed July 18, 2016).

8. Lee E. Norrgard and Julia M. Norrgard, *Consumer Fraud: A Reference Handbook* (New York: ABC-Clio, 1998).

9. David M. Gardner, Jim Harris, and Junyong Kim, "The Fraudulent Consumer," in *Marketing and Public Policy Conference Proceedings,* ed. Gregory Gundlach, William Wilkie, and Patrick Murphy (Chicago: American Marketing Association, 1999), pp. 48–54.

10. Ana Serafin Smith, "Retail Inventory Shrinkage Increased to $45.2 Billion in 2015," *National Retail Federation,* June 13, 2016, https://nrf.com/media/press-releases/retail-inventory-shrinkage-increased-452-billion-2015 (accessed July 18, 2016).

11. "ASA Bans Boots Anti-Cellulite Ads," *Soap, Perfumery & Cosmetics* 78 (October 2005): 5; Lisa McLaughlin, "Cloaking Cellulite," *Time,* May 24, 2004, p. 90; Christine Doyle, "How to Beat Cellulite—Part Two: Do Anti-Cellulite Creams, Lotions and Massage Really Work, or Do Women Just Like to Think They Do?" *Ottawa Citizen,* May 23, 2000, p. D8.

12. Federal Trade Commission, "FTC Announces Top National Consumer Complaints for 2013," February 27, 2014, http://www.ftc.gov/news-events/press-releases/2014/02/ftc-announces-top-national-consumer-complaints-2013 (accessed July 10, 2014).

13. "Bureau of Consumer Protection," Federal Trade Commission, http://www.ftc.gov/bcp/index.shtml (accessed July 20, 2016).

14. Paula Span, "F.T.C.'s Lumosity Penalty Doesn't End Brain Training Debate," *The New York Times,* January 15, 2016, http://www.nytimes.com/2016/01/19/health/ftcs-lumosity-penalty-doesnt-end-brain-training-debate.html?_r=0 (accessed July 20, 2016).

15. "Consumer Affairs and Outreach Division," Federal Communications Commission, http://transition.fcc.gov/cgb/cgb_offices.html (accessed July 20, 2016).

16. "Consumer Protection," Montana Department of Justice, https://doj.mt.gov/consumer/ (accessed July 20, 2016).

17. State of Texas, Business & Commerce Code, "Chapter 17: Deceptive Trade Practices," http://www.statutes.legis.state.tx.us/SOTWDocs/BC/htm/BC.17.htm (accessed July 2, 2014).

18. Robert B. Downs, "Afterword, in Upton Sinclair," *The Jungle* (New York: New American Library, 1960).

19. Abby W. Schachter, "Deconstructing the IKEA Dresser Recall," *The Wall Street Journal,* July 13, 2016, http://www.wsj.com/articles/deconstructing-the-ikea-dresser-recall-1468449602 (accessed July 20, 2016).

20. Rene Lynch, "Sketchers Lawsuit: How to Get Your Piece of the $40-Million Payout," *Los Angeles Times*, May 17, 2012, http://articles.latimes.com/2012/may/17/nation/la-na-nn-skechers-20120517 (accessed July 20, 2016). Federal Trade Commission, "Reebok to Pay $25 Million in Customer Refunds to Settle FTC Charges of Deceptive Advertising of EasyTone and RunTone Shoes," September 28, 2011, http://www.ftc.gov/news-events/press-releases/2011/09/reebok-pay-25-million-customer-refunds-settle-ftc-charges (accessed July 20, 2016).

21. "Sensa and Three Other Marketers of Fad Weight-Loss Products Settle FTC Charges in Crackdown on Deceptive Advertising," Federal Trade Commission, January 7, 2014, http://www.ftc.gov/news-events/press-releases/2014/01/sensa-three-other-marketers-fad-weight-loss-products-settle-ftc (accessed July 2, 2014).

22. Wine Institute, "Direct Wine Shipments," http://www.wineinstitute.org/programs/shipwine/main.htm (accessed July 20, 2016).

23. "Lemon Law Information and Sites," http://autopedia.com/html/HotLinks_LemonLaw.html (accessed July 20, 2016).

24. Peter Neumann and Calvin Ding, "China's New Tort Law: Dawn of the Product Liability Era," *China Business Review*, March 1, 2010, http://www.chinabusinessreview.com/chinas-new-tort-law-dawn-of-the-product-liability-era/ (accessed July 20, 2016).

25. Jennifer Levitz, "J&J Settles Many Surgical-Tool Lawsuits," *The Wall Street Journal*, March 19-20, 2016, A3.

26. "Regulatory Watch," *Business China*, February 27, 2006, p. 11.

27. Sandra N. Hurd, Peter Shears, and Frances E. Zollers, "Consumer Law," *Journal of Business Law* (May 2000): 262–277.

28. Irene M. Kunii, "Stand Up and Fight," *Business Week*, September 11, 2000, pp. 54–55.

29. Suk-ching Ho, "Executive Insights: Growing Consumer Power in China," *Journal of International Marketing* 9 (Spring 2001): 64–84.

30. Kenneth J. Meier, E. Thomas Garman, and Lael R. Keiser, *Regulation and Consumer Protection: Politics, Bureaucracy and Economics* (Houston, TX: Dame Publications, 1998).

31. Allan Asher, "Going Global: A New Paradigm for Consumer Protection," *Journal of Consumer Affairs* 32 (Winter 1998): 183–203; Benet Middleton, "Consumerism: A Pragmatic Ideology," *Consumer Policy Review* 8 (November–December 1998): 213–217; Audhesh Paswan and Jhinuk Chowdhury, "Consumer Protection Issues and Non-governmental Organizations in a Developing Market," in *Developments in Marketing Science*, ed. Harlan E. Spotts and H. Lee Meadow (Coral Gables, FL: Academy of Marketing Science, 2000), pp. 171–176.

32. Paul N. Bloom and Stephen A. Greyser, "The Maturing of Consumerism," *Harvard Business Review* 59 (November–December 1981): 130–139.

33. Consumers Union, www.consumersunion.org (accessed July 20, 2016); Rhoda H. Karpatkin, "Toward a Fair and Just Marketplace for All Consumers: The Responsibilities of Marketing Professionals," *Journal of Public Policy and Marketing* 18 (Spring 1999): 118–123.

34. "Empowerment to the Consumer," *Marketing Week*, October 21, 1999, p. 3; Pierre M. Loewe and Mark S. Bonchek, "The Retail Revolution," *Management Review* 88 (April 1999): 38–44.

35. Jim Guest, "Grassroots Advocacy Is Still in Style," *Consumer Reports* 70 (August 2005): 5; "About Us," Consumers Union, http://consumersunion.org/about/ (accessed July 20, 2016).

36. "Consumer Bill of Rights and Responsibilities: Report to the President of the United States," Advisory Commission on Consumer Protection and Quality in the Health Care Industry, November 1997, http://www.hcqualitycommission.gov/cborr/ (accessed July 2, 2014); Mary Jane Fisher, "Pressure Mounts for Patient Rights Agreement," *National Underwriter/Life & Health Financial Services*, May 22, 2000, pp. 3–4; Michael Pretzer, "New Mind 'Patient Relations': Get Ready for 'Consumer Rights,'" *Medical Economics*, February 23, 1998, pp. 47–55.

37. "Comprehensive Consumer Rights Bill Addresses Bank Fees, Identity Theft," *Consumer Financial Services Law Report*, May 15, 2000, p. 2.

38. Lori Sandoval, "Google Deletes Search Results in Europe, Abides by 'Right to be Forgotten' Rule," *Tech Times*, June 30, 2014, http://www.techtimes.com/articles/9370/20140630/google-deletes-search-results-in-europe-abides-by-right-to-be-forgotten-rule.htm (accessed July 20, 2016).

39. Helena Bottemiller, "McDonald's Apologizes to Chinese Consumers for Food Safety Violations," *Food Safety News*, March 19, 2012, http://www.foodsafetynews.com/2012/03/mcdonalds-apologizes-to-chinese-consumers-for-food-safety-violations/#.U7RqrZRdVc8 (accessed July 2, 2014).

40. Roger Yu, "FCC to fine AT&T $100M for slowing speeds," *USA Today*, June 17, 2015, http://www.usatoday.com/story/money/2015/06/17/fcc-fines-att-100-million/28863455/ (accessed July 20, 2016)

41. WebMD LLC, "URAC Health Website Accreditation," *WebMD*, http://www.webmd.com/about-webmd-policies/urac-center (accessed July 20, 2016).

42. "Dispute Resolution Services," Better Business Bureau, http://www.bbb.org/council/programs-services/dispute-handling-and-resolution/ (accessed July 2, 2014).

43. Federal Trade Commission, *Privacy Online: Fair Information Practices in the Electronic Marketplace: A Federal Trade Commission Report to Congress* (Washington, DC: FTC, May 2000), also available at www.ftc.gov/reports/privacy2000/privacy2000.pdf (accessed July 20, 2016).

44. PR Newswire, "Service Line Warranties of America Named the 2013 Winner of the Western Pennsylvania Torch Award for Marketplace Ethics," *The Business Journals*, January 15, 2014, http://www.prnewswire.com/news-releases/service-line-warranties-of-america-named-the-2013-winner-of-the-western-pennsylvania-torch-award-for-marketplace-ethics-240310951.html (accessed July 20, 2016); "About Us," Service Line Warranties, http://www.slwofa.com/slw-about.html (accessed July 20, 2016).

45. "Wal-Mart Bucks for Education," *Home Textiles Today*, June 5, 2000, p. 11; Mike France and Joann Muller, "A Site for Soreheads," *Business Week*, April 12, 1999, p. 86; Wendy Zellner, "Wal-Mart: Why an Apology Made Sense," *Business Week*, July 3, 2000, pp. 65–66; Wendy Zellner and Aaron Bernstein, "Up Against the Wal-Mart," *Business Week*, March 13, 2000, p. 76.

46. Michael Peel, "Wealthy Thais Vent Anger Over Sanction with European Goods Boycott," *Financial Times*, June 27, 2014, http://www.ft.com/cms/s/0/0f6e80b8-fdde-11e3-bd0e-00144feab7de.html#axzz38Ea1c4Xc (accessed July 20, 2016).

47. Andrea Seikaly, "Kim Kardashian Weighs in on Beverly Hills Hotel Boycott," *Variety,* June 23, 2014, http://variety.com/2014/biz/news/kim-kardashian-weighs-in-on-beverly-hills-hotel-boycott-1201243471/ (accessed July 20, 2016).

48. "David Lansky to Join the Markle Foundation," Markle Foundation, September 28, 2004, http://www.markle.org/news-events/media-releases/david-lansky-join-markle-foundation (accessed July 20, 2016); Foundation for Accountability, "FACCT Legacy Documents," http://www.policyarchive.org/collections/markle/index?section=8 (accessed July 20, 2016).

49. Adam Wooten, "Top 10 intercultural blunders of 2011," *Deseret News,* December 16, 2011, http://www.deseretnews.com/top/326/3/PUMA-shoe-design-disrespects-UAE-flag-Top-10-intercultural-blunders-of-2011.html (accessed July 20, 2016).

Chapter 9

1. Athima Chansanchai, "Happy Feet: Buy a Pair of TOMS Shoes and a Pair Will Be Donated to a Poor Child Abroad," *Seattle Pi,* June 11, 2007, http://www.seattlepi.com/default/article/Happy-feet-Buy-a-pair-of-TOMS-shoes-and-a-pair-1240201.php (accessed July 20, 2015); TOMS website, http://www.toms.com/ (accessed July 20, 2016); Booth Moore, "Toms Shoes' Model Is Sell a Pair, Give a Pair Away," *Los Angeles Times,* April 19, 2009, http://www.latimes.com/fashion/alltherage/la-ig-greentoms19-2009apr19-story.html (accessed July 20, 2016); Stacy Perman, "Making a Do-Gooder's Business Model Work," *Bloomberg Businessweek,* January 23, 2009, www.businessweek.com/smallbiz/content/jan2009/sb20090123_264702.htm (accessed July 14, 2014); Michelle Prasad, "TOMS Shoes Always Feels Good," *KENTON Magazine,* March 19, 2011, http://kentonmagazine.com/toms-shoes-always-feel-good (accessed July 14, 2014); Craig Sharkton, "Toms Shoes—Philanthropy as a Business Model," *sufac.com,* August 23, 2008, http://sufac.com/2008/08/toms-shoes-philanthropy-as-a-business-model (accessed June 3, 2011); *TOMS Campus Club Program,* http://images.toms.com/media/content/images/campus-clubs-assets/TOMSCampushandbook_082510_International_final.pdf (accessed July 14, 2014); "TOMS Company Overview," *TOMS,* http://www.toms.com/corporate-responsibility#companyInfo (accessed July14, 2014); *TOMS One for One Giving Report,* http://images.toms.com/media/content/images/giving-report/TOMS-Giving-Report-2010.pdf (accessed July 14, 2014); Mike Zimmerman, "The Business of Giving: TOMS Shoes," *Success Magazine,* September 30, 2009, www.successmagazine.com/the-business-of-giving/PARAMS/article/852 (accessed June 3, 2011); "TOMS Eyewear," www.toms.com/eyewear (accessed March 5, 2012); "TOMS Founder Shares Sole-ful Tale," *North Texas Daily,* April 14, 2011, www.ntdaily.com/?p=53882 (accessed March 5, 2012) TOMS, "Coffee," http://www.toms.com/coffee (accessed July 20, 2016)..

2. "Initiatives and Sponsorships," JPMorgan Chase & Co., http://www.jpmorganchase.com/corporate/Corporate-Responsibility/sponsorships (accessed July 28, 2016); J.P. Morgan Chase, "As always, the corporate challenge is open for healthy competition," July 21, 2016, https://www.jpmorganchasecc.com/events.php?city_id=10&page=events072116 (accessed July 28, 2016).

3. American Productivity and Quality Center, *Community Relations: Unleashing the Power of Corporate Citizenship* (Houston, TX: American Productivity and Quality Center, 1998); Edmund M. Burke, *Corporate Community Relations: The Principle of the Neighbor of Choice* (Westport, CT: Praeger, 1999).

4. Bradley K. Googins, "Why Community Relations Is a Strategic Imperative," *Strategy & Business* (Third Quarter 1997): 14–16.

5. "Community," *Merck,* http://www.merckresponsibility.com/giving-at-merck/community/ (accessed July 28, 2016).

6. "Academic Collaborations," *Dow,* http://www.dow.com/en-us/science-and-sustainability/collaborations/academic-collaborations/ (accessed July 28, 2016).

7. Business for Social Responsibility, "Community Involvement," www.bsr.org/resourcecenter/, (accessed December 4, 2000); Sandra A. Waddock and Mary-Ellen Boyle, "The Dynamics of Change in Corporate Community Relations," *California Management Review* 37 (Summer 1995): 125–138; Barron Wells and Nelda Spinks, "Communicating with the Community," *Career Development International* 4, no. 2 (1999): 108–116.

8. "CECP Presents 2014 Excellence Award to Direct Relief for Exemplary Collaboration with FedEx," CECP, May 20, 2014, http://cecp.co/pdfs/2014summit/EA_PR_May20_Final.pdf (accessed July 28, 2016).

9. Giving USA, "Giving USA: 2015 Was America's Most-Generous Year Ever," June 13, 2016, http://givingusa.org/giving-usa-2016/ (accessed July 28, 2016); PepsiCo, "Strategic Grants," http://www.pepsico.com/Purpose/Global-Citizenship/Strategic-Grants (accessed July 28, 2016).

10. Alyson Warhurst, "The Future of Corporate Philanthropy," *Business Week*, December 9, 2008, p. 16.

11. Takeda, *Community Involvement and Development,* 2013, https://www.takeda.com/investor-information/annual/files/ar2013_d11_en.pdf (accessed July 28, 2016).

12. "Community Needs Assessment Survey Guide," *Utah State University Extension,* http://extension.usu.edu/files/uploads/surveyguide.pdf (accessed July 28, 2016).

13. Target Sucks, http://www.ihatetarget.net (accessed July 28, 2016); I HATE Ryan Air…, http://ihateryanair.co.uk/ (accessed July 28, 2016).

14. Global Exchange, "Top Ten Corporate Criminals Alumni," http://www.globalexchange.org/corporateHRviolators/alums (accessed July 28, 2016).

15. Julie Jargon, "Starbucks Tries Franchising to Perk Up Europe Business," *The Wall Street Journal,* November 29, 2013, http://online.wsj.com/news/articles/SB10001424052702304607104579209971318755960 (accessed July 28, 2016).

16. "Winning Weekend," *AT&T,* February 12, 2014, http://about.att.com/newsroom/pebble_beach_winning_weekend_feb.html (accessed July 28, 2016).

17. "Quad/Graphics Closing Plant in Woodstock, Cutting 540 Jobs," *Chicago Tribune,* July 8, 2014, http://articles.chicagotribune.com/2014-07-08/business/chi-illinois-lay-offs-20140708_1_quad-graphics-illinois-employers-unemployment-rate (accessed July 28, 2016).

18. Lauren Sage Reinlie, "Construction Company Cited for Serious Safety Violations," *News and Information for the Emerald Coast,* June 20, 2014, http://www.nwfdailynews.com/business/local-business-news/construction-company-cited-for-serious-safety-violations-1.335694 (accessed July 5, 2014).

19. Wendy Zellner and Aaron Bernstein, "Up Against the Wal-Mart," *Bloomberg Businessweek,* March 13, 2000, pp. 76–78.

20. Rebecca Hiscott, "7 Companies That Aren't Waiting For Congress to Raise the Minimum Wage," *The Huffingtom Post*, June 26, 2014, http://www.huffingtonpost.com/2014/06/26/companies-minimum-wage_n_5530835.html (accessed July 28, 2016).

21. Walmart, "More than One Million Walmart Associates to Receive Pay Increase in 2016," January 20, 2016, http://news.walmart.com/news-archive/2016/01/20/more-than-one-million-walmart-associates-receive-pay-increase-in-2016 (accessed June 23, 2016).

22. "Daniels Fund Grants Program," http://danielsfund.org/Grants/index.asp (accessed July 28, 2016).

23. *New Belgium Brewing Company, Inc.,* www.newbelgium.com (accessed July 28, 2016).

24. Corporation for National & Community Service, "Volunteering and Civic Life in America 2015," https://www.volunteeringinamerica.gov/ (accessed July 28, 2016).

25. Corporate for National and Community Service, "Benefits of Volunteering," http://www.nationalservice.gov/about/volunteering/benefits.asp (accessed July 5, 2014).

26. "About Employee Volunteering," *National Centre for Volunteering,* http://www.ncvo.org.uk (accessed July 5, 2014).

27. Exelon, "Giving," http://www.exeloncorp.com/community/giving (accessed July 28, 2016).

28. "Corporate Opportunities," *WorldVision,* http://www.worldvision.org/get-involved/partners/ (accessed July 28, 2016).

29. Ingrid Murro Botero, "Charitable Giving Has 4 Big Benefits," *Business Journal of Phoenix,* January 1, 1999, www.bizjournals.com/phoenix/stories/1999/01/04/smallb3.html (accessed July 28, 2016).

30. Suzanne Perry, "The Stubborn 2% Giving Rate," *The Chronicle of Philanthropy*, June 17, 2013, http://philanthropy.com/article/The-Stubborn-2-Giving-Rate/139811/ (accessed July 28, 2016).

31. "Giving Statistics," *Charity Navigator,* 2016, http://www.charitynavigator.org/index.cfm?bay=content.view&cpid=42#.U7q_BhZX9g0 (accessed July 7, 2014).

32. Shalene Gupta, "When Marriages between Nonprofits and Corporations Sour," *Fortune,* June 26, 2014, http://fortune.com/2014/06/26/rocky-marriage-non-profits-corporations/ (accessed July 28, 2016).

33. Leon Kaye, "The Business Case for Strategic Philanthropy," *Triple Pundit,* August 8, 2013, http://www.triplepundit.com/2013/08/business-case-strategic-philanthropy/ (accessed July 28, 2016).

34. Michael E. Porter and Mark R. Kramer, "The Competitive Advantage of Corporate Philanthropy," *Harvard Business Review* 80 (December 2002): 56–68; Robbie Shell, "Breaking the Stereotypes of Corporate Philanthropy," *Wall Street Journal,* November 26, 2002, p. B2.

35. Jennifer Keishin Armstrong, "Setting a High Bar," *Fast Company,* February 2014, pp. 40–42; Nicole Goodkind, "KIND CEO: How we became the fastest growing nutrition bar in America," *Yahoo! Finance,* April 6, 2015, http://finance.yahoo.com/news/kind-bar-ceo--our-social-impact-doesn-t-persuade-customers-133322809.html (accessed July 28, 2016).

36. Noel M. Tichy, Andrew R. McGill, and Lynda St. Clair (eds.), *Corporate Global Citizenship: Doing Business in the Public Eye* (San Francisco: New Lexington Press, 1997).

37. Jessica Stannard and Tamara Backer, "How Employee Volunteers Multiply Your Community Impact PART 2," *OnPhilanthropy.com,* December 29, 2005, http://cwop.convio.net/site/News2?page=NewsArticle&id=5470 (accessed July 5, 2014).

38. J.P. Morgan Chase, "Generating Positive Impact Alongside Financial Return," https://www.jpmorganchase.com/corporate/Corporate-Responsibility/social-finance.htm (accessed July 28, 2016).

39. Paula Caligiuri, "When Unilever Bought Ben & Jerry's: A Story of CEO Adaptability," *Fast Company*, August 14, 2012, http://www.fastcompany.com/3000398/when-unilever-bought-ben-jerrys-story-ceo-adaptability (accessed July 28, 2016); David Gelles, "How the Social Mission of Ben & Jerry's Survived Being Gobbled Up," *The New York Times,* August 21, 2015, http://www.nytimes.com/2015/08/23/business/how-ben-jerrys-social-mission-survived-being-gobbled-up.html?_r=0 (accessed July 28, 2016).

40. Curt Weeden, *Corporate Social Investing* (San Francisco: Berrett-Koehler, 1998), pp. 116–123.

41. Avon, "Avon Breast Cancer Crusade," *Avon Foundation for Women*, https://www.avonfoundation.org/programs/breast-cancer/ (accessed July 28, 2016).

42. Tichy, McGill, and St. Clair, *Corporate Global Citizenship.*

43. Katharine M. Howie, Lifeng Yeng, Scott J. Vitell, Victoria Bush, and Doug Vorhies, "Consumer Participation in Cause-Related Marketing: An Examination of Effort Demands and Defensive Denial," *Journal of Business Ethics,* 2015, http://link.springer.com/article/10.1007%2Fs10551-015-2961-1 (accessed July 28, 2016).

44. Kevin T. Higgins, "Marketing with a Conscience," *Marketing Management* 11 (July–August 2002): 12–15; P. Rajan Varadarajan and Anil Menon, "Cause-Related Marketing: A Coalignment of Marketing Strategy and Corporate Philanthropy," *Journal of Marketing* 52 (July 1988): 58–74.

45. Erwann Michel-Kerjan, "Creating Value through Cause-Related Marketing and Celebrity Advocacy: The Case of YouthAIDS & PSI," January 2012, http://opim.wharton.upenn.edu/risk/library/WP2012-02_RiskCtr_YouthAIDS-PSI.pdf (accessed July 28, 2016); "Where We Work," PSI, http://www.psi.org/where-we-work/countries (accessed July 28, 2016).

46. Steve Hoeffler and Kevin Lane Keller, "Building Brand Equity Through Corporate Societal Marketing," *Journal of Public Policy & Marketing* 21 (Spring 2002): 78–89; Sue Adkins and Nina Kowalska, "Consumers Put 'Causes' on the Shopping List," *M2 PressWire,* November 17, 1997; Matt Carmichael, "Stat of the Day: 83% Want Brands to Support Causes," *Ad Age,* January 18, 2012, http://adage.com/article/adagestat/stat-day-83-brands-support/232141/ (accessed July 28, 2016).

47. Jennifer Mullen, "Performance-Based Corporate Philanthropy: How 'Giving Smart' Can Further Corporate Goals," *Public Relations Quarterly* 42 (June 22, 1997): p. 42; Michal Strahilevitz, "The Effects of Prior Impressions of a Firm's Ethics on the Success of a Cause-Related Marketing Campaign," *Journal of Nonprofit & Public Sector Marketing* 11, no. 1 (2003): 77–92.

48. Stan Friedman and Charles Kouns, "Charitable Contribution: Reinventing Cause Marketing," *Brand Week,* October 27, 1997.

49. "Nonprofit Corporation," *Entrepreneur,* http://www.entrepreneur.com/encyclopedia/nonprofit-corporation (accessed July 28, 2016).

50. Samer Abu-Saifan, "Social Entrepreneurship: Definition and Boundaries," *Technology Innovation Management Review*, February 2012, pp. 22–27.

51. H. Haugh, "Social Enterprise: Beyond Economic Outcomes and Individual Returns," in *Social Entrepreneurship*, ed. J. Mair, J. Robinson, and K. Hockerts (Basingstoke, UK: Palgrave Macmillan, 2006).

52. Raymond Dart, "The Legitimacy of Social Enterprise," *Nonprofit Management & Leadership* 14, no. 4 (Summer 2004): 411–424.

53. Oregon Public Broadcasting, "The New Heroes," PBS, 2005, http://www.pbs.org/opb/thenewheroes/whatis/ (accessed July 28, 2014).

54. The Institute for Social Entrepreneurs, *Evolution of the Social Enterprise industry: A Chronology of Key events*, August 1, 2008, http://socialent.org/documents/EVOLUTIONOFTHE-SOCIALENTERPRISEINDUSTRY--ACHRONOLOGY-OFKEYEVENTS.pdf (accessed July 28, 2016).

55. Oregon Public Broadcasting, "The New Heroes".

56. Adam Ludwig, "Ashoka Chairman Bill Drayton on the Power of Social Entrepreneurship," *Forbes*, March 12, 2012, http://www.forbes.com/sites/techonomy/2012/03/12/ashoka-chairman-bill-drayton-on-the-power-of-social-entrepreneurship/#8add3bc3d34c (accessed July 28, 2016); Yonatan Gordis, "On the Value or Values of Jewish Social Entrepreneurship," *Journal of Jewish Communal Service* 84, no. 1/2 (Winter/Spring 2009): 37–44.

57. Anand Giridharadas and Keith Bradsher, "Microloan Pioneer and His Bank Won Nobel Peace Prize," *The New York Times*, October 13, 2006, http://www.nytimes.com/2006/10/13/business/14nobelcnd.html?_r=0&adxnnl=1&pagewanted=1&adxnnlx=1406646197-P8A97M3K4GY-HoZx4UHWYWA (accessed July 29, 2014); Grameen Bank website, http://www.grameen-info.net/ (accessed July 28, 2016).

58. Giridharadas and Bradsher, "Microloan Pioneer and His Bank Won Nobel Peace Prize."

59. Ibid.; Grameen Bank, "Credit Delivery System," http://www.grameen.com/index.php?option=com_content&task=view&id=24&Itemid=169 (accessed July 28, 2016).

60. Muhammed Yunus, "Is Grameen Bank Different from Conventional Banks?," *Yunus Centre*, April 2009, http://www.muhammadyunus.org/index.php/design-lab/previous-design-labs/43-news-a-media/books-a-articles/232-is-grameen-bank-different-from-conventional-banks (accessed July 28, 2016); New Internationalist, "Microcredit and Grameen Bank," *New Internationalist*, https://newint.org/books/reference/world-development/case-studies/poverty-microcredit-grameen-bank/ (accessed July 28, 2016).

61. "Grameen Bank at a Glance," *Yunus Centre*, http://www.muhammadyunus.org/index.php/design-lab/previous-design-labs/37-about/about/371-grameen-bank-at-a-glance (accessed July 28, 2016).

62. Giridharadas and Bradsher, "Microloan Pioneer and His Bank Won Nobel Peace Prize.".

63. Grameen Bank, "General Questions on Grameen Bank FAQ," http://www.grameen.com/index.php?option=com_easyfaq&task=cat&catid=80&Itemid=524 (accessed July 28, 2016).

64. Oregon Public Broadcasting, "Meet the New Heroes: Mimi Silbert," PBS, 2005, http://www.pbs.org/opb/thenewheroes/meet/silbert.html (accessed July 29, 2014); Delancey Street Foundation, "Who are the Constituents?" http://www.pbs.org/opb/thenewheroes/meet/silbert.html (accessed July 29, 2014).

65. Sean Stannard-Stockton, "The Effective Strategic Philanthropist," *Tactical Philanthropy*, March 16, 2011, http://www.tacticalphilanthropy.com/2011/03/the-effective-strategic-philanthropist/ (accessed); Sean Stannard-Stockton, "The Social Entrepreneur," *Tactical Philanthropy*, March 15, 2011, http://www.tacticalphilanthropy.com/2011/03/the-effective-social-entrepreneur/ (accessed July 29, 2014).

66. Ruth McCambridge, "WSJ Chart on 2014 Corporate Giving Explains Some Things," *Nonprofit Quarterly*, June 25, 2015, https://nonprofitquarterly.org/2015/06/25/wall-street-journal-chart-on-2014-corporate-giving-explains-some-things/ (accessed July 28, 2016).

67. Walker Information, *Corporate Philanthropy National Benchmark Study, Employee Report* (Chicago: Walker Information, 2002).

68. Robert J. Williams and J. Douglas Barrett, "Corporate Philanthropy, Criminal Activity, and Firm Reputation: Is There a Link?" *Journal of Business Ethics* 26 (2000): 341–350.

69. Roger Bennett, "Corporate Philanthropy in France, Germany, and the UK," *International Marketing Review* 15 (June 1998): 469.

70. American Productivity and Quality Center, *Community Relations: Unleashing the Power of Corporate Citizenship*.

71. "BNP Paribas Foundation," *BNP Paribas*, http://www.bnpparibas.com/en/bnp-paribas-foundation/objectives (accessed July 28, 2016); Forbes Corporate Communications Staff, "BNP Paribas Wealth Management publishes BNP Paribas Individual Philanthropy Index by Forbes Insights," *Forbes*, February 11, 2014, http://www.forbes.com/sites/forbespr/2014/02/11/bnp-paribas-wealth-management-publishes-bnp-paribas-individual-philanthropy-index-by-forbes-insights/#f24078c63c54 (accessed July 28, 2016).

72. Weeden, *Corporate Social Investing*.

73. Reprinted with permission of the publisher. From *Corporate Social Investing*, copyright ©1998 by Curt Weeden, Berrett-Koehler Publishers, Inc., San Francisco, CA. All rights reserved. www.bkconnection.com.

74. Walter W. Wymer Jr. and Sridhar Samu, "Dimensions of Business and Nonprofit Collaborative Relationships," *Journal of Nonprofit & Public Sector Marketing* 11, no. 1 (2003): 3–22.

75. John A. Byrne, "The New Face of Philanthropy," *Business Week*, December 2, 2002, pp. 82–86; Stephanie Strom, "Ground Zero: Charity; a Flood of Money, Then a Deluge of Scrutiny for Those Handing It Out," *New York Times*, September 11, 2002, p. B5; Panel on the Nonprofit Sector, "Principles for Good Governance and Ethical Practice: A Guide for Charities and Foundations," http://www.nonprofitpanel.org/Report/principles/Principles_Executive_Summary.pdf, (accessed July 12, 2009).

76. Marc Holley, "The Role of Evaluation in Strategic Philanthropy," *Nonprofit Quarterly*, March 7, 2013, http://nonprofitquarterly.org/philanthropy/23808-the-role-of-evaluation-in-strategic-philanthropy.html (accessed April 28, 2016).

Chapter 10

1. Douglas MacMillan, "The Fiercest Rivalry in Tech: Uber vs. Lyft," *The Wall Street Journal*, August 12, 2014, B1; Trevor Hughes, "Passengers flock to upstart car services," *USA*

Today, July 10, 2014, 5B; James Nash, "The Company Cities Love to Hate," *Bloomberg Businessweek*, July 3, 2014, pp. 31–33; Sam Schechner, "Uber Tries to Thwart Ban in French Court," *The Wall Street Journal*, November 29–30, 2014, B4; Joanna Sugden, Aditi Malhotra, and Douglas Mac-Millan, "Uber Under Attack Around Globe," *The Wall Street Journal*, December 10, 2014, B1, B4; Karen Weise, "How Uber Rolls," June 29-July 5, 2015, *Bloomberg Businessweek*, 54–59; UNM Daniels Fund Ethics Initiative, "Truth, Transparency, and Trust: Uber Important in the Sharing Economy," PPT presentation, https://danielsethics.mgt.unm.edu/teaching-resources/presentations.asp (accessed July 18, 2016); Anne Freier, "Uber usage statistics and revenue," *Business of Apps*, September 14, 2015, http://www.businessofapps.com/uber-usage-statistics-and-revenue/ (accessed July 18, 2016); Andrew Watts, "The Real Reason Uber and Lyft Left Austin," *The Huffington Post*, Mary 10, 2016, http://www.huffing-tonpost.com/andrew-watts/the-real-reason-uber-and-lyft-left-austin_b_9889406.html (accessed July 18, 2016).

2. Andrea Peterson, "China Has Almost Twice As Many Internet Users As the U.S. Has People," *The Washington Post*, January 31, 2014, https://www.washingtonpost.com/news/the-switch/wp/2014/01/31/china-has-almost-twice-as-many-internet-users-as-the-u-s-has-people/ (accessed August 4, 2016); Reported by Yang Fan and Bi Zimo, translated and written in English by Luisetta Mudie, "China Blocks Chat Apps, Deletes Social Media Accounts," *Radio Free Asia*, July 2, 2014, http://www.rfa.org/english/news/china/blocks-07022014152248.html (accessed August 4, 2016).

3. Robert Valdes, "How Broadband Over Powerlines Works," http://computer.howstuffworks.com/bpl.htm (accessed August 4, 2016); Angela Moscaritolo, "Google Fiber Gets Greenlight in Overland Park, Kansas," *PC Mag*, July 8, 2014, http://www.pcmag.com/article2/0,2817,2460601,00.asp (accessed August 4, 2016); Stephen Shankland, "Fast Fiber-optic Broadband Spreads Across Developed World," *CNET*, January 11, 2014, http://www.cnet.com/news/fast-fiber-optic-broadband-spreads-across-developed-world/#! (accessed August 4, 2016).

4. Ernest Tucker, "Researchers Developing Supercomputer to Tackle Grid Challenges," *Renewable Energy World*, July 7, 2014, http://www.renewableenergyworld.com/articles/2014/07/researchers-developing-supercomputer-to-tackle-grid-challenges.html (accessed August 4, 2016); Peerzada Abrar, "Russia Offers to Develop Supercomputer with India to Counter Chinese Supremacy," *The Economic Times*, April 8, 2014, http://articles.economictimes.indiatimes.com/2014-04-08/news/48971401_1_us-supercomputer-tianhe-2-indian-institute (accessed August 4, 2016); "Big Data," *SAS*, http://www.sas.com/en_us/insights/big-data/what-is-big-data.html (accessed August 4, 2016).

5. Gyln Taylor, "The Future is Coming Much Faster than we Think, Here's Why," *That's Really Possible*, July 4, 2014, http://www.thatsreallypossible.com/exponential-growth/ (accessed August 4, 2016).

6. Charles Graeber, "Ten Days in Kenya with No Cash, Only a Phone," *Bloomberg Businessweek*, June 5, 2014, http://www.businessweek.com/articles/2014-06-05/safaricoms-m-pesa-turns-kenya-into-a-mobile-payment-paradise (accessed July 11, 2014).

7. Josh Gottheimer and Jordan Usdan, "Low-Cost Broadband and Computers for Students and Families," *Federal Communications Commission*, November 10, 2011, https://www.fcc.gov/news-events/blog/2011/12/14/low-cost-broadband-computers-millions-students-families (accessed August 4, 2016); "Cheap Internet Service Providers Offer High-speed Broadband Internet to Americans at $9.95/month," *Cheap Internet*, http://www.cheapinternet.com (accessed August 4, 2016).

8. Dwight Silverman, "Comcast offering $10 Internet for Low-income Families Who Qualify," *The Chron*, August 8, 2011, http://blog.chron.com/techblog/2011/08/comcast-offering-10-internet-for-low-income-families-who-qualify/ (accessed August 4, 2016).

9. "Charting the Future of the Net," MSNBC, July 7, 2000, www.msnbc.com (accessed August 8, 2006).

10. "Technology and Economic Growth: Producing Real Results for the American People," The White House, http://clinton3.nara.gov/WH/EOP/OSTP/html/techgrow.html (accessed August 4, 2016); Nicholas Bloom and Josh Lerner, "The NBER Productivity, Innovation, and Entrepreneurship Program," The National Bureau of Economic Research, 2013, http://www.nber.org/programs/pr/pr.html (accessed August 4, 2016).

11. Alan Greenspan, "Remarks to the Economic Club of New York," Federal Reserve Board, New York, January 13, 2000; Nicholas Bloom and Josh Lerner, "The NBER Productivity, Innovation, and Entrepreneurship Program," The National Bureau of Economic Research, 2013, http://www.nber.org/programs/pr/pr.html (accessed August 4, 2016).

12. Elana Varon, "B2B E-Commerce: What You Need to Know About Public and Private Exchanges," CIO.com, http://www.cio.com/article/30483/B_B_E_Commerce_What_You_Need_to_Know_about_Public_and_Private_Exchanges (accessed August 4, 2016); Elana Varon, "The ABCs of B2B," http://www.cchristopherlee.com/news/2001/010820b.htm (accessed August 4, 2016); Allison Enright, "B2b e-Commerce is Poised for Growth," *Internet Retailer*, May 31, 2013, https://www.internetretailer.com/2013/05/31/b2b-e-commerce-poised-growth (accessed August 4, 2016).

13. Kelly Thomas, "Supply Chain Segmentation: Ten Steps to Greater Profits," *Supply Chain Quarterly*, Quarter 1, 2012, http://www.supplychainquarterly.com/topics/Strategy/201201segmentation/#fnr1 (accessed August 4, 2016); University Alliance, "Walmart: Keys to Successful Supply Chain Management," University of San Francisco, http://www.usanfranonline.com/resources/supply-chain-management/walmart-keys-to-successful-supply-chain-management/#.U8HAtVaWsds (accessed August 4, 2016); Danielle Kucera, "Amazon Ramps Up $13.9 Billion Warehouse Building Spree," *Bloomberg*, August 21, 2013, http://www.bloomberg.com/news/articles/2013-08-20/amazon-ramps-up-13-9-billion-warehouse-building-spree (accessed August 4, 2016); "Amazon Global Fulfillment Center Network," *MWPVL*, 2014, http://www.mwpvl.com/html/amazon_com.html (accessed August 4, 2016).

14. "IT Failing One in Four Small Businesses," http://smallbiztechnology.com/archive/2009/08/it-failing-one-in-four-small-b.html (accessed August 4, 2016).

15. Norris Dickard and Diana Schneider, "The Digital Divide: Where We Are," *Edutopia*, July 1, 2002, http://www.edutopia.org/digital-divide-where-we-are-today (accessed August 4, 2016).

16. Greenspan, "Remarks to the Economic Club of New York."

17. Center for Advanced Purchasing Studies, "The Future of Purchasing and Supply: A Five and Ten Year Forecast,"

http://http://onlinelibrary.wiley.com/doi/10.1111/j.1745-493X.2000.tb00066.x/abstract?userIsAuthenticated=false&deniedAccessCustomisedMessage= (accessed August 5, 2016).

18. David Field, "Some E-ticket Fliers Can Print Boarding Passes on PC," *USA Today,* December 5, 2000, p. 12B.

19. Glenda Chui, "Mapping Goes Deep: Technology Points the Way to a Revolution in Cartography," *San Jose Mercury News,* September 12, 2000, p. 1F.

20. "Internet Users by Country (2016)," Internet Live Stats, 2016, http://www.internetlivestats.com/internet-users-by-country/ (accessed June 22, 2016).

21. Lauren O'Neil, "1,000+ New Domain Suffixes Set to Expand the Internet," *Your Community Blog,* January 2, 2014, http://www.cbc.ca/newsblogs/yourcommunity/2014/01/1000-new-domain-suffixes-set-to-expand-the-internet.html (accessed August 5, 2016). "New Generic Top-Level Domains," Internet Corporation for Assigned Names and Numbers (ICAAN), http://newgtlds.icann.org/en/ (accessed August 5, 2016).

22. William M. Pride and O. C. Ferrell, *Marketing: Concepts and Strategies,* 12th ed. (Boston: Houghton Mifflin, 2003), p. 493.

23. PYMNTS, "2014 Fraud Spike Cost US Retailers $32 Billion," February 17, 2015, http://www.pymnts.com/news/2015/2014-fraud-spike-cost-u-s-retailers-32-billion/ (accessed August 9, 2016).

24. Kimberly Palmer, "How Credit Card Companies Spot Fraud before You Do," *USA News,* July 10, 2013, http://money.usnews.com/money/personal-finance/articles/2013/07/10/how-credit-card-companies-spot-fraud-before-you-do (accessed August 5, 2016).

25. Michael Riley, Ben Elgin, Dune Lawrence, and Carol Matlack, "Missed Alarms and 40 Million Stolen Credit Card Numbers: How Target Blew It," *Bloomberg Businessweek,* March 13, 2014, http://www.businessweek.com/articles/2014-03-13/target-missed-alarms-in-epic-hack-of-credit-card-data (accessed August 5, 2016).

26. "Online Auction Fraud," http://www.fbi.gov/page2/june09/auctionfraud_063009.html (accessed July 14, 2014).

27. Economist staff, "Home, Hacked Home," *The Economist: Special Report on Cyber-Security,* July 12, 2014, pp. 14–15; Economist staff, "Prevention is better than cure," *The Economist: Special Report on Cyber-Security,* July 12, 2014, p. 16.

28. "Protecting Consumer Privacy," Federal Trade Commission, https://www.ftc.gov/news-events/media-resources/protecting-consumer-privacy (accessed August 5, 2016).

29. Pride and Ferrell, *Marketing: Concepts and Strategies,* pp. 600–601.

30. "Consumer Sentinel Network Data Book for January–December 2013," Federal Trade Commission, February 2014, https://www.ftc.gov/system/files/documents/reports/consumer-sentinel-network-data-book-january-december-2013/sentinel-cy2013.pdf (accessed August 5, 2016)

31. Blake Ellis, "Identity Fraud Hits New Victim Every Two Seconds," *CNN Money,* February 6, 2014, http://money.cnn.com/2014/02/06/pf/identity-fraud/ (accessed July 20, 2016); Roger Parloff, "Spy Tech That Reads Your Mind," *Fortune,* July 1, 2016, 72–77.

32. Rupert Jones, "Barclays to Sell Customer Data," *The Guardian,* June 24, 2013, http://www.theguardian.com/business/2013/jun/24/barclays-bank-sell-customer-data (accessed August 5, 2016); Daniel Bates, "New Privacy Fears as Facebook Begins Selling Personal Access to Companies to Boost Ailing Profits," *Mail Online,* October 3, 2012, http://www.dailymail.co.uk/news/article-2212178/New-privacy-row-Facebook-begins-selling-access-users-boost-ailing-profits.html (accessed August 5, 2016); Olga Kharif and Scott Moritz, "Carriers Sell Users' Tracking Data in $5.5 Billion Market," *Bloomberg,* June 6, 2013, http://www.bloomberg.com/news/2013-06-06/carriers-sell-users-tracking-data-in-5-5-billion-market.html (accessed August 5, 2016).

33. "Snapchat Settles FTC Charges That Promises of Disappearing Messages Were False," Federal Trade Commission, May 8, 2014, https://www.ftc.gov/news-events/press-releases/2014/05/snapchat-settles-ftc-charges-promises-disappearing-messages-were (accessed August 5, 2016).

34. "Children's Online Privacy Protection Act of 1998," www.ftc.gov/ogc/coppa1.htm (accessed August 5, 2016).

35. Cecilia Kang, "Preteens' Use of Instagram Creates Privacy Issue, Child Advocates Say," *The Washington Post,* May 15, 2013, http://www.washingtonpost.com/business/technology/preteens-use-of-instagram-creates-privacy-issue-child-advocates-say/2013/05/15/9c09d68c-b1a2-11e2-baf7-5bc2a9dc6f44_story.html (accessed August 5, 2016).

36. Senator Al Franken, "The Location Privacy Protection Act of 2014—Summary," 2014, http://www.franken.senate.gov/files/documents/140327Locationprivacy.pdf (accessed August 5, 2016).

37. "Mobile Privacy Disclosures: Building Trust Through Transparency," *Federal Trade Commission,* February 2013, https://www.ftc.gov/reports/mobile-privacy-disclosures-building-trust-through-transparency-federal-trade-commission (accessed August 5, 2016).

38. "Federal Trade Commission 2014 Privacy and Data Security Update," *Federal Trade Commission,* 2014, https://www.ftc.gov/system/files/documents/reports/privacy-data-security-update-2014/privacydatasecurityupdate_2014.pdf (accessed August 5, 2016).

39. "European Union Directive on Privacy," *Banking & Financial Services Policy Report,* December 2002.

40. "Europe Moves Ahead on Privacy," *The New York Times,* February 3, 2013, http://www.nytimes.com/2013/02/04/opinion/europe-moves-ahead-on-privacy-laws.html?_r=0 (accessed August 5, 2016).

41. "An Overview of Canada's New Private Sector Privacy Law: The Personal Information Protection and Electronic Documents Act," *Privacy Commissioner of Canada,* http://www.priv.gc.ca/speech/2004/vs/vs_sp-d_040331_e.cfm (accessed July 8, 2014).

42. "Electronic Network Consortium," http://www.nmda.or.jp/enc/index-english.html (accessed August 5, 2016).

43. "Privacy Information Management System P3P is Now Available on the Internet Toward User-Oriented E-Commerce," *Electronic Network Consortium,* July 16, 1999, http://www.nmda.or.jp/enc/privacy/p3p-press-en.html (accessed August 5, 2016).

44. John Ribeiro, "Google Says IE Privacy Policy Is Impractical in Modern Web," *PC World,* February 21, 2012, http://www.pcworld.com/article/250336/google_says_ie_privacy_policy_is_impractical_in_modern_web.html (accessed August 5, 2016); Riva Richmond, "A Loophole Big Enough for a Cookie to Fit Through," *The New York Times,* September 17, 2010, http://bits.blogs.nytimes.com/2010/09/17/a-loophole-big-enough-for-a-cookie-to-fit-through/ (accessed August 5, 2016).

45. Neil MacFarquhar, "Russia Quietly Tightens Reins on Web With 'Bloggers Law'," *The New York Times,* May 6, 2014,

http://www.nytimes.com/2014/05/07/world/europe/russia-quietly-tightens-reins-on-web-with-bloggers-law.html (accessed August 5, 2016); Mike Butcher, "Russia Moves To Ban Online Services That Don't Store Personal Data In Russia," *Tech Crunch*, July 2, 2014, https://techcrunch.com/2014/07/02/russia-moves-to-ban-online-services-that-dont-store-personal-data-in-russia/ (accessed August 5, 2016).

46. *TRUSTe.com*, www.truste.com (accessed August 5, 2016); Chris Connelly, "Trustmark Schemes Struggle to Protect Privacy," *Galexia*, 2008, http://www.galexia.com/public/research/assets/trustmarks_struggle_20080926/trustmarks_struggle_public.pdf (accessed August 5, 2016).

47. Guardian eCommerce, http://www.guardianecommerce.net/about.php (accessed August 5, 2016).

48. Erik Larson, "American Airlines Drops Google Trademark Lawsuit (Update 1)," *Bloomberg*, July 18, 2008, http://www.bloomberg.com/apps/news?pid=newsarchive&sid=aNtnl9vC6QLc (accessed July 22, 2014); Terry Baynes, "Rosetta Stone and Google Settle Trademark Lawsuit," *Reuters*, October 31, 2012, http://www.reuters.com/article/2012/10/31/us-usa-court-rosettastone-google-idUSBRE89U1GE20121031 (accessed August 5, 2016).

49. The National Bureau of Asian Research. "The IP Commission Report: The Report of the Commission on the Theft of American Intellectual Property," May 2013, http://www.ipcommission.org/report/IP_Commission_Report_052213.pdf (accessed August 5, 2016).

50. "Trends in Proprietary Information Loss," *ASIS International*, June 2007, https://foundation.asisonline.org/FoundationResearch/Publications/Documents/trendsinproprietaryinformationloss.pdf (accessed August 5, 2016).

51. The National Bureau of Asian Research. "The IP Commission Report: The Report of the Commission on the Theft of American Intellectual Property," May 2013, http://www.ipcommission.org/report/IP_Commission_Report_052213.pdf (accessed August 5, 2016).

52. McDonough, "But Can the WTO Really Sock It to Software Pirates?"; "The Compliance Gap: BA Global Compliance Survey," June 2014, http://globalstudy.bsa.org/2013/downloads/studies/2013GlobalSurvey_Study_en.pdf (accessed August 5, 2016); Business Software Alliance, "Seizing Opportunity Through License Compliance," 2016, http://globalstudy.bsa.org/2013/downloads/studies/2013GlobalSurvey_Study_en.pdf (accessed August 5, 2016).

53. Devlin Barrett and Siobhan Gorman, "U.S. Charges Five in Chinese Army with Hacking," *The Wall Street Journal*, May 19, 2014, http://online.wsj.com/news/articles/SB10001424052702304422704579571604060696532 (accessed August 5, 2016).

54. "Microsoft Settles 3,265 Software Piracy Cases in US and Abroad," *Press Release*, July 9, 2013, http://www.microsoft.com/en-us/news/press/2013/jul13/07-09caseapr.aspx (accessed August 5, 2016).

55. Chester Davis, "Microsoft Corporation Launches Cheaper Office Software," *Liberty Voice*, March 16, 2014, http://guardianlv.com/2014/03/microsoft-corporation-launches-cheaper-office-software/ (accessed August 5, 2016).

56. "The Digital Millennium Copyright Act Of 1998, U.S. Copyright Office," December 1998, http://www.copyright.gov/legislation/dmca.pdf (accessed August 5, 2016).

57. Brent Kendall and Keach Hagey, "Supreme Court Rules Aereo Violates Broadcasters' Copyrights," *The Wall Street Journal*, June 25, 2014, http://www.wsj.com/articles/supreme-court-rules-against-aereo-sides-with-broadcasters-in-copyright-case-1403705891 (accessed August 5, 2016); Jonathan Berr, "Supreme Court Deals Severe Blow to Aereo," *CBS*, June 25, 2014, http://www.cbsnews.com/news/supreme-court-deals-severe-blow-to-aereo/ (accessed August 5, 2016).

58. William T. Neese and Charles R. McManis, "Summary Brief: Law, Ethics and the Internet: How Recent Federal Trademark Law Prohibits a Remedy Against 'Cyber-Squatters,'" *Proceedings from the Society of Marketing Advances*, November 4–7, 1998.

59. Neese and McManis, "Summary Brief: Law, Ethics and the Internet."

60. Alex Rodriguez, "Crafty Russian Seeks Venti of Cash From Starbucks," *Chicago Tribune*, November 1, 2005, http://articles.chicagotribune.com/2005-11-01/news/0511010141_1_starbucks-international-starbucks-coffee-russian-rights (accessed August 5, 2016); New York Times Company, "World Business Briefing Asia: China: Starbucks Wins Trademark Infringement Suit," *The New York Times*, January 4, 2009, http://query.nytimes.com/gst/fullpage.html?res=9A07E5DB1130F937A35752C0A9609C8B63 (accessed August 5, 2016).

61. Martyn Williams, "Update: ICANN President Calls for Major Overhaul," *IDG News Service*, February 25, 2002, (accessed via Lexis-Nexis Academic Database).

62. Thomas A. Guida and Gerald J. Ferguson, "Strategy ICANN Arbitration vs. Federal Court: Choosing the Right Forum for Trademark Disputes," *Internet Newsletter*, November 7, 2002.

63. XDnet Web Services, ".XXX—What's It All About?" *XDnet.co.uk*, July 27, 2011, http://xdnet.co.uk/blog/2011/07/27/xxx-whats-it-all-about/ (accessed July 23, 2014).

64. "ICANN Hears Concerns About Accountability, Control," http://www.pcworld.com/businesscenter/article/151736/icann_hears_concerns_about_accountability_control.html (accessed August 5, 2016); Rana Foroohar, "The Internet Splits Up; The Web Changed the World. Politics Is Now Changing It Back," *Newsweek*, May 15, 2006, p. 1.

65. Arthur L. Caplan and Glenn McGee, "An Introduction to Bioethics," *Bioethics.net*, http://www.bioethics.net/bioethics-resources/bioethics-glossary/introduction/ (accessed August 5, 2016).

66. Lucette Lagundo, "Drug Companies Face Assault on Prices," *Wall Street Journal*, May 11, 2000, p. B1.

67. David Voreacos, "Florida Pharmacists Win $597 Million Blowing Whistle on Scheme," *Bloomberg*, August 12, 2013, http://www.bloomberg.com/news/2013-08-13/florida-pharmacists-win-597-million-blowing-whistle-on-scheme.html (accessed August 5, 2016).

68. "Persuading the Prescribers: Pharmaceutical Industry Marketing and its Influence on Physicians and Patients," *Pew Charitable Trusts*, November 11, 2013, http://www.pewtrusts.org/en/research-and-analysis/fact-sheets/2013/11/11/persuading-the-prescribers-pharmaceutical-industry-marketing-and-its-influence-on-physicians-and-patients (accessed August 5, 2016); Pharma Marketing Network, "Annual Spending on Direct-to-Consumer Advertising Ties an All-Time High," *Pharma Marketing Blog*, March 3, 2016, http://pharmamkting.blogspot.com/2016/03/annual-spending-on-direct-to-consumer.html (accessed August 5, 2016).

69. Biotechnology Industry Association, "Biotechnology Industry Facts," http://www.bio.org/articles/what-biotechnology (accessed August 5, 2016); Heidi Chial, Ph.D., "DNA

Sequencing Technologies Key to the Human Genome Project," *Scitable by Nature Education*, http://www.nature.com/scitable/topicpage/dna-sequencing-technologies-key-to-the-human-828 (accessed August 5, 2016).

70. "The Biotechnology Industry in the United States," Select USA, http://selectusa.commerce.gov/industry-snapshots/biotechnology-industry-united-states (accessed July 16, 2014).

71. Ben Weiss, "Biotech Industry R&D Spending Jumps Five Percent In 2011, BDO Study Finds," *Fierce Biotech*, September 19, 2012, http://www.fiercebiotech.com/press-releases/biotech-industry-rd-spending-jumps-five-percent-2011-bdo-study-finds (accessed July 16, 2014).

72. "Avon Breast Cancer Crusade: 20 Years of Progress," *Avon*, 2013, http://www.avon.hu/PRSuite/static/downloads/20th_anniversary.pdf (accessed August 5, 2016); Avon Foundation, "Breast Cancer," https://www.avonfoundation.org/programs/breast-cancer/ (accessed August 5, 2016).

73. Marilynn Marchione, "Study Suggests Setback in Effort to Morph Stem Cells into Insulin-Producing Pancreas Cells," *Milwaukee Journal Sentinel*, January 17, 2003, p. B8.

74. "Recent Advances in Embryonic Stem Cell Research," Genetics Policy Institute, http://www.genpol.org/stem_cell_research.html (accessed July 16, 2014).

75. John Leavitt, "What Will Human Clones Be Like?" *Connecticut Law Tribune*, January 24, 2003, p. 5.

76. Sarah Knapton, "Breakthrough in Human Cloning Offers New Transplant Hope," *The Telegraph*, April 17, 2014, http://www.telegraph.co.uk/science/science-news/10774097/Breakthrough-in-human-cloning-offers-new-transplant-hope.html (accessed July 16, 2014); Laura Ungar, "Stem-cell Advances May Quell Ethics Debate," *USA Today*, June 22, 2014, http://www.usatoday.com/story/news/nation/2014/06/22/stem-cell-advances-may-quell-ethics-debate/11222721/ (accessed August 5, 2016).).

77. Andy Coghlan, "Cloning Special Report: Cloning Without Embryos," *New Scientist*, January 29, 2000, p. 4.

78. Ibid.

79. Natasha McDowell, "Mini-pig Clone Raises Transplant Hope," http://www.newscientist.com/article/dn3257 (accessed August 5, 2016).

80. Rachel Nowak, "Australia OKs Human Embryo Research," http://www.newscientist.com/article/dn3149 (accessed July 16, 2014); "Stem Cell Research FAQs," *Research America*, http://www.researchamerica.org/stemcell_faqs (accessed August 5, 2016).

81. Ricki Lewis, PhD, "A Brief History of DNA Patents," *PLOS Blogs*, June 20, 2013, http://blogs.plos.org/dnascience/2013/06/20/a-brief-history-of-dna-patents/ (accessed August 5, 2016); Maggie Koerth-Baker, "Making Sense of the Confusing Supreme Court DNA Patent Ruling," *BoingBoing*, June 17, 2013, http://boingboing.net/2013/06/17/making-sense-of-the-confusing.html (accessed August 5, 2016).

82. Sarah Lueck, "New Kits Let You Test Your Own Genes, But Interpreting Results Can Be Tricky," *Wall Street Journal*, May 24, 2005, p. D1; Steve Johnson, "23 and Me Ordered by FDA To Stop Selling Genetic Tests," *San Jose Mercury News*, November 25, 2013, http://www.mercurynews.com/business/ci_24596362/fda-23andme-must-stop-selling-dna-test-kits (accessed August 5, 2016).

83. Garry Peterson, Saul Cunningham, Lisa Deutsch, Jon Erickson, Allyson Quinlan, Ernesto Raez-Luna, Robert Tinch, Max Troell, Peter Woodbury, and Scot Zens, "The Risks and Benefits of Genetically Modified Crops: A Multidisciplinary Perspective," *Conservation Ecology*, 4(1), 2000, p. 13.

84. Bill Gates, "Will Frankenfood Feed the World?" June 11, 2000, http://www.microsoft.com/presspass/ofnote/06-11time.mspx (accessed August 5, 2016); Natasha Gilbert and Nature magazine, "A Hard Look at 3 Myths About Genetically Modified Crops," *Scientific American*, May 1, 2013, http://www.scientificamerican.com/article/a-hard-look-at-3-myths-about-genetically-modified-crops/ (accessed August 5, 2016).

85. John Robbins, "Can GMOs Help End World Hunger?" *The Food Revolution Network*, December 10, 2012, http://foodrevolution.org/blog/gmos-world-hunger/ (accessed August 5, 2016); Joel Dunn, "Genetically Modified Crops and Hunger—Another Look at the Evidence," *The Permaculture Research Institute*, May 31, 2013, http://permaculturenews.org/2013/05/31/genetically-modified-crops-and-hunger-another-look-at-the-evidence/ (accessed August 5, 2016).

86. David Baulcombe, "It's Time to Rethink Europe's Outdated GM Crop Regulations," *The Guardian*, March 14, 2014, http://www.theguardian.com/environment/2014/mar/14/europe-gm-crop-regulations (accessed August 5, 2016); "GM Crops and Foods in Britain and Europe," *Gene Watch*, http://www.genewatch.org/sub-568547 (accessed August 5, 2016).

87. Peterson et al., "The Risks and Benefits of Genetically Modified Crops: A Multidisciplinary Perspective," *Conservation Ecology*, 4(1), 2000, p. 13.

88. Paul Magnusson, Ann Therese, and Kerry Capell, "Furor Over Frankenfood," *Business Week*, October 18, 1999, pp. 50, 51; "Japan Asks That Imports of Corn Be StarLink-Free," *Wall Street Journal*, October 30, 2000, p. A26; Naveen Thukral and Risa Maeda, "Japan Cancels GMO Wheat Order After Concerns Over U.S. Grain Developed By Monsanto," *The Huffington Post*, May 30, 2013, http://www.huffingtonpost.com/2013/05/30/japan-gmo-wheat-food-concerns_n_3357240.html (accessed August 5, 2016).

89. Heather Haddon, "Congress Passes GMO Labeling that Supersede Tough State Measures," *The Wall Street Journal*, July 14, 2016, http://www.wsj.com/articles/congress-passes-gmo-labeling-rules-that-supercede-tough-state-measures-1468516761 (accessed July 15, 2016).

90. "Pocket K No. 16: Global Status of Commercialized Biotech/GM Crops in 2013," *International Service for the Acquisition of Agri-Biotech Applications*, 2013, http://www.isaaa.org/resources/publications/pocketk/16/ (accessed August 5, 2016).

91. Carey Polis, "Whole Foods GMO Labeling To Be Mandatory By 2018," *The Huffington Post*, March 8, 2013, http://www.huffingtonpost.com/2013/03/08/whole-foods-gmo-labeling-2018_n_2837754.html (accessed August 5, 2016); "All Products for Allegro Coffee Company," *Non-GMO Project*, http://www.nongmoproject.org/find-non-gmo/search-participating-products/search/?brandId=1202 (accessed August 5, 2016); "On GMOs," *General Mills*, https://www.generalmills.com/en/ChannelG/Issues/on_biotechnology.aspx (accessed August 5, 2016); "Genetically Modified Crops," *Unilever*, http://www.unilever.com/sustainable-living-2014/our-approach-to-sustainability/responding-to-stakeholder-concerns/genetically-modified-crops/ (accessed July 16, 2014).

92. "'Terminator' Victory a Small Step in Long War," *CNN*, October 7, 1999, www.cnn.com/NATURE/9910/07/terminator.victory.enn/index.html (accessed August 5, 2016).

93. Adam Liptak, "Supreme Court Supports Monsanto in Seed-Replication Case," *The New York Times*, May 13, 2013, http://www.nytimes.com/2013/05/14/business/monsanto-victorious-in-genetic-seed-case.html (accessed August 5, 2016).

94. "Viewpoints: Is Genetically Modified Food Safe to Eat?" *PBS.org*, http://www.pbs.org/wgbh/harvest/viewpoints/issafe.html (accessed August 5, 2016).

95. Katy Canada, "GMOs Now 90 Percent of Corn, Beets and Soy in US," *The Pendulum*, February 2014, http://www.elonpendulum.com/2014/02/gmos-now-90-percent-corn-beets-soy-us/ (accessed July 16, 2014).

96. "Monsanto Attempts to Balance Stakeholder Interests," in *Business Ethics: Ethical Decision Making and Cases*, 9th ed. (pp. 308-318),ed. O.C. Ferrell, John Fraedrich, and Linda Ferrell (Mason, OH: South-Western Cengage Learning, 2013); Ian Berry, "Pesticides Make a Comeback," *The Wall Street Journal*, May 21, 2013, http://online.wsj.com/article/SB10001424127887323463704578496923254944066.html (accessed August 5, 2016); "The Perils of Always Ignoring the Bright Side," *The Wall Street Journal*, http://online.wsj.com/article/SB10000872396390444004704578030340322277954.html (accessed August 5, 2016).

97. Greg Farrell, "Police Have Few Weapons Against Cyber-Criminals," *USA Today*, December 6, 2000, p. 5B; Edward Iwata and Kevin Johnson, "Computer Crime Outpacing Cybercops," *USA Today*, June 7, 2000, p. 1A.

98. Siobhan Gorman and Julian E. Barnes, "Cyber Combat: Act of War," *The Wall Street Journal*, May 31, 2011, http://online.wsj.com/news/articles/SB10001424052702304563104576355623135782718 (accessed August 5, 2016); David E. Sanger and Elisabeth Bumiller, "Pentagon to Consider Cyberattacks Acts of War," *The New York Times*, http://www.nytimes.com/2011/06/01/us/politics/01cyber.html (accessed August 5, 2016).

99. Sheila M. J. Bonini, Lenny T. Mendonca, and Jeremy M. Oppenheim, "When Social Issues Become Strategic," *The McKinsey Quarterly* 2 (2006): 20.

Chapter 11

1. "Fracking: Energy Revolution or Environmental Catastrophe," Case prepared by Danielle Jolley, Kenny Leseberg, Max Ebnother, and Matthew Anton for the UNM Daniels Fund Ethics Initiative, http://danielsethics.mgt.unm.edu/pdf/fracking-.pdf (accessed August 5, 2016); Bryan Walsh, "The Gas Dilemma," *Time*, April 11, 2011, pp. 40–48; Jim Efstathiou Jr. and Kim Chipman, "The Great Shale Gas Rush," *Bloomberg Businessweek*, March 7–13, 2011, pp. 25–28; Sharon Begley, "Study Raises New Concern About Earthquakes and Fracking Fluids," *Reuters*, July 11, 2013, http://www.reuters.com/article/us-science-fracking-earthquakes-idUSBRE96A0TZ20130711 (accessed August 5, 2016). Russell Gold, "How to Make Fracking Safer," *The Wall Street Journal*, http://online.wsj.com/news/articles/SB10001424052702303532704579477931878610414 (accessed August 5, 2016); Alison Sider and Nicole Friedman, "Oil From U.S. Fracking Is More Volatile Than Expected," *The Wall Street Journal*, June 24, 2014, http://online.wsj.com/articles/oil-from-u-s-fracking-is-more-volatile-than-expected-1403653344 (accessed August 5, 2016).

2. PR Newswire, "American Consumers Take Sustainability to the Next Level," September 23, 2015, http://www.prnewswire.com/news-releases/american-consumers-take-sustain-

ability-to-the-next-level-300147756.html (accessed August 5, 2016).

3. Environmental Protection Agency, "Fortune 500® Partners List," June 25, 2016, https://www.epa.gov/sites/production/files/2016-02/documents/fortune500_jan2016.pdf (accessed August 5, 2016).

4. Ferrell, Fraedrich, Ferrell, *Business Ethics: Ethical Decision Making and Cases*, 10th ed. (Mason, OH: South-Western Cengage Learning, 2015), p. 347.

5. Kevin Gibson, "Stakeholders and Sustainability: An Evolving Theory," *Journal of Business Ethics* 109, no. 1 (2012): 15–25.

6. Ferrell, Fraedrich, Ferrell, *Business Ethics*..

7. Ibid.

8. Patrick E. Murphy, Magdalena Öberseder, and Gene R. Laczniak, "Corporate Societal Responsibility in Marketing: Normatively Broadening the Concept," *AMS Review* 3, no. 2 (2013).

9. Terry Macalister, "Green really is the new black as Big Oil gets a taste for renewables," *The Guardian*, May 21, 2016, https://www.theguardian.com/business/2016/may/21/oil-majors-investments-renewable-energy-solar-wind (accessed August 5, 2016).

10. "Air Quality," Office of Air Quality Planning and Standards, Environmental Protection Agency, https://www3.epa.gov/airquality/cleanair.html (accessed August 5, 2016).

11. Chelsea Harvey, "Air pollution in India is so bad that it kills half a million people every year," *The Washington Post*, May 11, 2016, https://www.washingtonpost.com/news/energy-environment/wp/2016/05/11/air-pollution-in-india-is-so-bad-that-it-kills-half-a-million-people-every-year/?utm_term=.fa198a78c6c3 (accessed August 5, 2016).

12. Environmental Protection Agency, "Overview of the Clean Air Act and Air Pollution," https://www.epa.gov/clean-air-act-overview (accessed August 5, 2016).

13. Sophia Yan, "China Declares 'War' on Pollution," *CNN Money*, March 6, 2014, http://money.cnn.com/2014/03/06/news/economy/china-pollution/ (accessed August 5, 2016).

14. Environmental Protection Agency, "Effects of Acid Rain," https://www.epa.gov/acidrain/effects-acid-rain (accessed August 5, 2016).

15. Dan Bobkoff, "Acid Rain Aftermath: Damaged Ecology, Damaged Politics," *Marketplace*, July 16, 2014, http://www.marketplace.org/2014/07/16/sustainability/we-used-be-china/acid-rain-aftermath-damaged-ecology-damaged-politics (accessed August 5, 2016).

16. Adam Mann, "Hole Found in Natural Protective Layer of Earth's Atmosphere," *Wired*, April 7, 2014, http://www.wired.com/2014/04/oh-hole-washing-machine/ (accessed August 5, 2016); "Is There a Connection between the Ozone Hole and Global Warming?" *Union of Concerned Scientists*, http://www.ucsusa.org/global_warming/science_and_impacts/science/ozone-hole-and-gw-faq.html (accessed August 5, 2016).

17. U.S. Energy Information Administration, International Energy Outlook 2016, May 11, 2016, http://www.eia.gov/forecasts/ieo/exec_summ.cfm (accessed August 5, 2016).

18. "The Largest Producers of CO2 Emissions Worldwide in 2015, Based on Their Share of Global CO2 Emissions," *Statista*, 2015, http://www.statista.com/statistics/271748/the-largest-emitters-of-co2-in-the-world/ (accessed August 5, 2016).

19. Peter Baker and Coral Davenport, "Obama Orders New Efficiency for Big Trucks," *The New York Times*, February 18, 2014, http://www.nytimes.com/2014/02/19/us/politics/

obama-to-request-new-rules-for-cutting-truck-pollution.html (accessed August 5, 2016); Coral Davenport, "Obama to Take Action to Slash Coal Pollution," *The New York Times*, June 1, 2014, http://www.nytimes.com/2014/06/02/us/politics/epa-to-seek-30-percent-cut-in-carbon-emissions.html (accessed August 5, 2016).

20. National Centers for Environmental Information, "Global Analysis - Annual 2015," https://www.ncdc.noaa.gov/sotc/global/201513 (accessed August 9, 2016).

21. "Climate Change Indicators in the United States," Environmental Protection Agency, 2015, https://www.epa.gov/climate-indicators/us-and-global-temperature (accessed August 5, 2016).

22. "Climate Change Moves Border," Planet Ski, June 28, 2009, http://www.planetski.eu/news/535 (accessed August 5, 2016).

23. Andrew Freedman, "How Global Warming Made Hurricane Sandy Worse," *Climate Central*, November 1, 2012, http://www.climatecentral.org/news/how-global-warming-made-hurricane-sandy-worse-15190 (accessed August 5, 2016); "Extreme Weather: Impacts of Climate Change," *Natural Resources Defense Council*, January 15, 2014, http://www.nrdc.org/globalwarming/climate-change-impacts/ (accessed August 5, 2016).

24. Andrew Childers, "EPA Underestimates Fracking's Impact on Climate Change," *Bloomberg*, May 9, 2014, http://www.bloomberg.com/news/2014-05-09/epa-underestimates-fracking-s-impact-on-climate-change.html (accessed July 18, 2014); Emily Gosden, "Fracking Can Be Part of the Solution to Global Warming, Say UN Climate Change Experts," *The Telegraph*, April 13, 2014, http://www.telegraph.co.uk/news/earth/environment/climatechange/10763844/Fracking-can-be-part-of-the-solution-to-global-warming-say-UN-climate-change-experts.html (accessed August 5, 2016); Bobby Magill, "Fracking Hurts US Climate Change Credibility, Say Scientists," *The Guardian*, October 11, 2013, http://www.theguardian.com/environment/2013/oct/11/fracking-us-climate-credibility-shale-gas (accessed July 18, 2014); Fred Pierce, "Fracking Could Accelerate Global Warming," *New Scientist*, August 12, 2013, http://www.newscientist.com/article/dn24029-fracking-could-accelerate-global-warming.html#.U80ba5RdVc- (accessed August 5, 2016).

25. Mark Alpert, "Protections for the Earth's Climate," *Scientific American* 293 (December 2005): 55.

26. "Status of Ratification of the Kyoto Protocol," United Nations Framework Convention on Climate Change, http://unfccc.int/kyoto_protocol/status_of_ratification/items/2613.php (accessed August 5, 2016); "Kyoto Protocol," United Nations Framework Convention on Climate Change, http://unfccc.int/kyoto_protocol/items/2830.php (accessed August 5, 2016).

27. Fiona Harvey, "Doha Climate Gateway: the Reaction," *The Guardian*, December 10, 2012, https://www.theguardian.com/environment/2012/dec/10/doha-climate-gateway-reaction (accessed August 5, 2016); United Nations Framework Convention on Climate Change, "Status of the Doha Amendment," July 2016, http://unfccc.int/kyoto_protocol/doha_amendment/items/7362.php (accessed August 5, 2016).

28. Jim Tankersley, "EPA Gives California Emissions Waiver," *The Los Angeles Times*, June 30, 2009, http://articles.latimes.com/2009/jun/30/nation/na-california-waiver30 (accessed August 5, 2016).

29. "About Energy Star," http://www.energystar.gov/about/ (accessed August 5, 2016).

30. Ferrell, Fraedrich, Ferrell, *Business Ethics*, p. 352.

31. Richard Harris, "Climate Change Bill Heads for House Vote," *NPR*, May 22, 2009, http://www.npr.org/templates/story/story.php?storyId=104436991 (accessed August 5, 2016).

32. United State Environmental Protection Agency, "Acid Rain Program," http://www.epa.gov/airmarkets/progsregs/arp/basic.html (accessed August 11, 2014).

33. Gloria Gonzalez and Ben McCarthy, "US EPA Gives Major Boost to Cap-and-Trade, But Not Offsets," *Ecosystem Marketplace*, June 2, 2014, http://www.ecosystemmarketplace.com/pages/dynamic/article.page.php?page_id=10379&section=news_articles&eod=1 (accessed August 5, 2016).

34. Ben Winkley, "Obama to Hit Coal in Search for Green Legacy," *The Wall Street Journal*, June 2, 2014, http://blogs.wsj.com/moneybeat/2014/06/02/obama-to-hit-coal-in-search-for-green-legacy/ (accessed August 5, 2016); Rebecca Smith, "EPA's New Emissions Rule to Alter Energy Landscape," *The Wall Street Journal*, August 2, 2015, http://www.wsj.com/articles/epas-new-emissions-rule-to-alter-energy-landscape-1438550219 (accessed August 5, 2016).

35. "Buildings and Emissions: Making the Connection," *Center for Climate and Energy Solutions*, http://www.c2es.org/technology/overview/buildings (accessed August 5, 2016).

36. "GHGRP 2012: Reported Data," Environmental Protection Agency, 2012, https://www.epa.gov/ghgreporting/ghgrp-2012-reported-data (accessed August 5, 2016).

37. "UN-Water Thematic Factsheets," *UN Water*, 2013, http://www.unwater.org/statistics/thematic-factsheets/en/ (accessed June 5, 2016).

38. Kevin Begos, "4 States Confirm Water Pollution From Drilling," *USA Today*, January 5, 2014, http://www.usatoday.com/story/money/business/2014/01/05/some-states-confirm-water-pollution-from-drilling/4328859/ (accessed August 5, 2016).

39. Water.org, http://water.org/ (accessed August 8, 2016).

40. Annmargaret Warner, "The 11 Most Polluted Beaches in the US," *Business Insider*, June 28, 2013, http://www.businessinsider.com/most-polluted-beaches-in-us-2013-6?op=1 (accessed August 8, 2016); Natasha Geiling, "America's Cleanest-and Most-Polluted Beaches," *Smithsonian*, June 27, 2014, http://www.smithsonianmag.com/travel/cleanest-and-dirtiest-beaches-America-180951869/?no-ist (accessed August 8, 2016).

41. "Water Quality Facts," Environmental Protection Agency, http://water.epa.gov/aboutow/owow/waterqualityfacts.cfm (accessed July 22, 2014).

42. Dina Gusovsky, "America's water crisis goes beyond Flint, Michigan," *CNBC*, March 24, 2016, http://www.cnbc.com/2016/03/24/americas-water-crisis-goes-beyond-flint-michigan.html (accessed August 8, 2016); Sara Ganim and Linh Tran, "How tap water became toxic in Flint, Michigan," *CNN*, January 13, 2016, http://www.cnn.com/2016/01/11/health/toxic-tap-water-flint-michigan/index.html (accessed August 8, 2016).

43. Dawn Fallik, "This New Study Found More Drugs in Our Drinking Water than Anybody Knew," *New Republic*, December 11, 2013, http://www.newrepublic.com/article/115883/drugs-drinking-water-new-epa-study-finds-more-we-knew (accessed August 8, 2016).

44. Lorna Thorpe, "Levi Strauss & Co—the Levi Style with a Lot Less Water," *The Guardian*, https://www.theguardian.com/sustainable-business/levi-rethinking-traditional-process-water (accessed August 8, 2016); Alexandra Alter, "Yet Another 'Footprint' to Worry About: Water," *The Wall Street Journal*,

February 17, 2009, http://online.wsj.com/news/articles/SB123483638138996305 (accessed August 8, 2016).

45. Susan Berfield, "There Will Be Water," *Business Week*, June 23, 2008, p. 40; "U.S. Drought Monitor Update for July 15, 2014," *National Climatic Data Center*, July 15, 2014, http://www.ncdc.noaa.gov/news/us-drought-monitor-update-july-15-2014 (accessed July 22, 2014); "Statistics & Facts," *Water Sense*, http://www.epa.gov/watersense/about_us/facts.html (accessed August 8, 2016); NOAA National Centers for Environmental Information, State of the Climate: Drought for June 2016, July 2016, http://www.ncdc.noaa.gov/sotc/drought/201606 (accessed August 8, 2016).

46. Ferrell, Fraedrich, Ferrell, *Business Ethics*, p. 354.

47. Josh Chin and Brian Spegele, "China Details Vast Extent of Soil Pollution," *The Wall Street Journal*, April 17, 2014, http://online.wsj.com/news/articles/SB10001424052702304626304579507040557046288 (accessed July 22, 2014).

48. Howard Mustoe, "Shell being sued in two claims over oil spill in Nigeria," *BBC News*, March 2, 2016, http://www.bbc.com/news/business-35701607 (accessed August 8, 2016).

49. Larry Neumeister, "US Court Rules for Chevron in Ecuador Rainforest-Damage Case," *ABC News*, August 8, 2016, http://abcnews.go.com/US/wireStory/us-court-rules-chevron-ecuador-rainforest-case-41207586 (accessed August 8, 2016).

50. "The Costs of Fracking," Environment America Research and Policy Center, September 20, 2012, http://www.environmentamerica.org/reports/ame/costs-fracking (accessed August 8, 2016); Hans Asfeldt, " 'This Land is Everything to Us': A Story of Fracking in Alberta," *Resilience*, September 26, 2013, http://www.resilience.org/stories/2013-09-26/this-land-is-everything-to-us-a-story-of-fracking-in-alberta (accessed August 8, 2016).

51. Environmental Protection Agency, "Advancing Sustainable Materials Management: Facts and Figures," April 11, 2016, https://www.epa.gov/smm/advancing-sustainable-materials-management-facts-and-figures (accessed August 8, 2016); "Landfills: Hazardous to the Environment," http://www.zerowasteamerica.org/landfills.htm (accessed August 8, 2016).

52. Matthew Dalton, "European Farmers Turn to Biogas Plants," *The Wall Street Journal,* June 18, 2009, http://online.wsj.com/article/SB124527861144324987.html (accessed August 8, 2016); Heijo Scharff, "Untapped Potential Achieving Adequate Control of Landfill Gas in Europe," *Waste Management World*, https://waste-management-world.com/a/untapped-potential-achieving-adequate-control-of-landfill-gas-in-europe (accessed August 8, 2016); "About LMOP," Environmental Protection Agency, https://www3.epa.gov/lmop/ (accessed August 8, 2016); "Recycling Facts & Statistics Infographic," *Harmony Enterprises*, February 2, 2012, http://harmony1.com/recycling-infographic/ (accessed August 8, 2016).

53. National Conference of State Legislatures, "Fees, Taxes and Bans: Recycling and Reuse," June 29, 2016, http://www.ncsl.org/research/environment-and-natural-resources/plastic-bag-legislation.aspx (accessed August 8, 2016); Economist staff, "In the Bin," *The Economist*, April 22, 2015, http://www.economist.com/blogs/democracyinamerica/2015/04/recycling-america (accessed August 8, 2016).

54. Tom Risen, "America's Toxic Electronics Waste Trade," *U.S. News*, April 22, 2016, http://www.usnews.com/news/articles/2016-04-22/the-rising-cost-of-recycling-not-exporting-electronic-waste (accessed August 8, 2016).

55. "11 Facts About E-Waste," *Dosomething.org*, https://www.dosomething.org/facts/11-facts-about-e-waste (accessed August 8, 2016).

56. Philip Fava, "Recycling E-Waste: How One Company Gets It Right," *Forbes*, November 13, 2012, http://www.forbes.com/sites/philfava/2012/11/13/recycling-e-waste-how-one-company-gets-it-right/#4f17468b2ed1 (accessed August 8, 2016).

57. Wendy Koch, "More States Ban Disposal of Electronics in Landfills," *USA Today,* December 18, 2011, http://usatoday30.usatoday.com/tech/news/story/2011-12-18/electronics-recycling/52055158/1 (accessed August 8, 2016).

58. "Rainforests," *The Nature Conservancy*, http://www.nature.org/ourinitiatives/urgentissues/rainforests/rainforests-facts.xml (accessed August 8, 2016); Justin Worland, "Here's How Many Trees Humans Cut Down Each Year," September 2, 2015, http://time.com/4019277/trees-humans-deforestation/ (accessed August 8, 2016).

59. Dom Phillips and Nick Miroff, "Brazil's new government may be less likely to protect the Amazon, critics say," *The Washington Post*, May 22, 2016, https://www.washingtonpost.com/world/the_americas/brazils-new-government-may-be-less-likely-to-protect-the-amazon-critics-say/2016/05/21/22cbce08-1c7d-11e6-82c2-a7dcb313287d_story.html (accessed August 8, 2016).

60. Bryan Walsh, "Study: Economic Boost of Deforestation is Short-Lived," *Time,* June 12, 2009, http://www.time.com/time/health/article/0,8599,1904174,00.html?iid=tsmodule (accessed August 8, 2016).

61. Martha Cuba, "Deforestation Now Driven by Profit, not Poverty," *Forest News*, August 2, 2012, http://blog.cifor.org/10382/deforestation-now-driven-by-profit-not-poverty#.U8-x6laWsds (accessed August 8, 2016).

62. Paul Brown, "An unnatural disaster," *The Guardian*, January 7, 2004, http://www.theguardian.com/science/2004/jan/08/biodiversity.sciencenews (accessed August 8, 2016).

63. Samantha Jakuboski, "Global Crisis: Honeybee Population on the Decline," *Green Science*, June 24, 2013, http://www.nature.com/scitable/blog/green-science/global_crisis_honeybee_population_on (accessed August 8, 2016).

64. David Biello, "It's Official: Fungus Causes Bat-Killing White-Nose Syndrome," *Scientific American*, October 26, 2011, http://www.scientificamerican.com/article/fungus-causes-bat-killing-white-nose-syndrome/ (accessed August 8, 2016); Lucie Couillard, "Shaver's Creek Sees 99 Percent Decrease in Bat Population," *The Daily Collegian*, June 26, 2013, http://www.collegian.psu.edu/news/borough/article_071184e5-6313-5959-a691-6a5426ac38b0.html (accessed August 8, 2016).

65. Eileen Campbell, "Why Are Frog Populations Declining?" *Mother Nature Network*, November 25, 2011, http://www.mnn.com/local-reports/illinois/local-blog/why-are-frog-populations-declining (accessed July 23, 2014); Daniel Fears, "Frog, Toad and Salamander Populations Plummeting, U.S. Survey Finds," *The Washington Post*, May 22, 2013, https://www.washingtonpost.com/national/health-science/frog-toad-and-salamander-populations-plummeting-us-survey-finds/2013/05/22/459c1c9e-c2f3-11e2-914f-a7aba60512a7_story.html (accessed August 8, 2016); Bruce Finley, "Study: Number of Frogs, Toads Declining at Alarming Rate," *The Denver Post*, May 22, 2013, http://www.denverpost.com/2013/05/22/study-number-of-frogs-toads-declining-at-alarming-rate/ (accessed August 8, 2016).

66. Ian Berry, "Pesticides Make a Comeback," *The Wall Street Journal,* May 21, 2013, http://online.wsj.com/article/SB10001

424127887323463704578496923254944066.html (accessed August 8 2016).

67. "Genuity DroughtGard Hybrids," *Monsanto*, http://www. monsanto.com/products/pages/droughtgard-hybrids.aspx (accessed August 8 2016).

68. "FDA Approves Orphan Drug ATryn to Treat Rare Clotting Disorder," FDA, February 6, 2009, http://www.fda. gov/NewsEvents/Newsroom/PressAnnouncements/2009/ ucm109074.htm (accessed August 8, 2016).

69. "About Genetically Engineered Foods," *Center for Food Safety*, http://www.centerforfoodsafety.org/issues/311/ge-foods/about-ge-foods (accessed August 8, 2016).

70. "Wal-Mart Says No to Milk from 'Juiced' Cows," Triple Pundit, March 28, 2008, http://www.triplepundit. com/2008/03/walmart-says-no-to-milk-from-juiced-cows/ (accessed August 8, 2016).

71. Maggie Caldwell, "5 Surprising Genetically Modified Foods," *Mother Jones*, August 5, 2013, http://www.motherjones.com/ environment/2013/08/what-are-gmos-and-why-should-i-care (accessed August 8, 2016).

72. "GMO Facts," *The NonGMO Project*, http://www. nongmoproject.org/learn-more/ (accessed August 8, 2016).

73. Charlie Dunmore and Olivia Kumwenda, "As Health Fears Ebb, Africa Looks at Easing GM Crop Bans," *Reuters*, June 6, 2013, http://www.reuters.com/article/2013/06/06/eu-africa-gmo-idUSL5N0EG3K520130606 (accessed August 8, 2016); Reuters, "South Africa to ease some GM crop rules to avert food crisis," *The Guardian*, February 23, 2016, https://www. theguardian.com/environment/2016/feb/23/south-africa-to-ease-some-gm-crop-rules-to-avert-food-crisis (accessed August 8, 2016); Utibe Effiong, "GMO Food for Dinner: What Has Nigeria Learned from the West?" *The Huffington* Post, June 18, 2016, http://www.huffingtonpost.com/utibe-effiong/gmo-food-for-dinner-what-_b_7477132.html (accessed August 8, 2016).

74. James Owen, "Bulging Mutant Trout Created: More Muscle, More Meat," *National Geographic*, March 29, 2010, http:// news.nationalgeographic.com/news/2010/03/100329-six-pack-mutant-trout-genetically-engineered-modified-gm/ (accessed August 8, 2016).

75. Chris D'Angelo, "FDA Sued Over Approval of Genetically Engineered Salmon," *The Huffington Post*, March 31, 2016, http://www.huffingtonpost.com/entry/fda-sued-over-genetically-engineered-salmon_us_56fd75f7e4b083f5c60730bc (accessed August 8, 2016).

76. "Supreme Court Hands Monsanto Victory Over Farmers on GMO Seed Patents, Ability to Sue," *RT Question More*, http://rt.com/usa/monsanto-patents-sue-farmers-547/ (accessed August 8, 2016); John Entine, " 'No Such Thing As GMO Contamination' Rules Australian Court in Landmark Decision, Rebuffing Organic Activists," *Forbes*, May 28, 2014, http://www.forbes.com/sites/jonentine/2014/05/28/no-such-thing-as-gmo-contamination-rules-australian-court-in-landmark-decision-rebuffing-organic-activists/#5de7d56522cb (accessed August 8, 2016); Wood Prairie Farm, "Organic Farmers vs. Monsanto: Final Appeal to U.S. Supreme Court to Protect Crops from GMO Contamination," *Eco Watch*, December 24, 2013, http://ecowatch.com/2013/12/24/farmers-monsanto-gmo-contamination/ (accessed August 8, 2016).

77. "Our Mission and What We Do," Environmental Protection Agency, https://www.epa.gov/aboutepa/our-mission-and-what-we-do (accessed August 8, 2016).

78. "FY 2011-2015 EPA Strategic Plan," Environmental Protection Agency, http://nepis.epa.gov/Exe/ZyPDF. cgi?Dockey=P1008YOS.PDF (accessed August 8, 2016).

79. "EPA Publishes Notice Identifying Hardrock Mining Industry for Financial Responsibility Requirements," EPA Newsroom, July 13, 2008, http://yosemite.epa.gov/opa/ admpress.nsf/d0cf6618525a9efb85257359003fb69d/ 90a65f473216e941852575f2004807eb!OpenDocument (accessed August 8, 2016).

80. James R. Healey, "The Big Squeeze Has Begun," *USA Today*, August 29, 2012, pp. 1B–2B.

81. Chris Woodyard and James Healey, "Ford Looking to Aluminum for Pickups?" *USA Today*, July 26, 2012, http://www. usatoday.com/money/autos/story/2012-07-26/aluminum-ford-f-150/56515524/1 (accessed August 8, 2016).

82. "The Plain English Guide to the Clean Air Act," https://www. epa.gov/clean-air-act-overview/plain-english-guide-clean-air-act (accessed August 8, 2016).

83. The Economist Staff, "Breathing Room," *The Economist*, September 8, 2012, http://www.economist.com/node/21562248 (accessed August 8, 2016).

84. Ferrell, Fraedrich, Ferrell, *Business Ethics*, p. 361.

85. "Summary of the Endangered Species Act," Environmental Protection Agency, http://www2.epa.gov/laws-regulations/ summary-endangered-species-act (accessed August 8, 2016).

86. U.S. Fish and Wildlife Service, "Environmental Conservation Online System: Listed Species Summary (Boxscore)," http:// ecos.fws.gov/ecp0/reports/box-score-report (accessed August 8, 2016)

87. Tiffany Gabbay, "Man Faces Two Years in Prison for Shooting Grizzly While Defending Family," *The Blaze*, August 26, 2011, http://www.theblaze.com/stories/2011/08/25/man-faces-2-years-in-prison-for-shooting-grizzly-while-defending-family/ (accessed August 8, 2016).

88. "Summary of the Toxic Substances Control Act," Environmental Protection Agency, http://www2.epa.gov/laws-regulations/summary-toxic-substances-control-act (accessed August 8, 2016).

89. Sabrina Tavernise, "F.D.A. Makes It Official: BPA Can't Be Used in Baby Bottles and Cups," *The New York Times*, July 17, 2012, http://www.nytimes.com/2012/07/18/science/ fda-bans-bpa-from-baby-bottles-and-sippy-cups.html?_r=0 (accessed August 8, 2016).

90. "Summary of the Clean Water Act," Environmental Protection Agency, http://www2.epa.gov/laws-regulations/ summary-clean-water-act (accessed August 8, 2016).

91. David Zucchino, "Duke Energy fined $102 million for polluting rivers with coal ash," *Los Angeles Times*, May 14, 2015, http://www.latimes.com/nation/la-na-duke-energy-coal-ash-20150514-story.html (accessed August 8, 2016).

92. "Summary of the Food Quality Protection Act (FQPA)," Environmental Protection Agency, https://www.epa.gov/laws-regulations/summary-food-quality-protection-act (accessed August 8, 2016).

93. Nicolas Loris and David W. Kreutzer, "Economic Realities of the Electric Car," *The Heritage Foundation*, January 24, 2011, http://www.heritage.org/research/ reports/2011/01/economic-realities-of-the-electric-car (accessed August 8, 2016).

94. Associated Press, "Bush Signs $12.3 Billion Energy Bill Into Law," *MSNBC*, August 8, 2005, http://www.msnbc.msn.com/ id/8870039// (accessed August 8, 2016).

95. U.S. Energy Information Administration, "Frequently Asked Questions," http://www.eia.gov/tools/faqs/faq.cfm?id=32&t=6 (accessed August 8, 2016).

96. Wind Energy Foundation, "Wind Energy FAQs," http://windenergyfoundation.org/about-wind-energy/faqs/ (accessed August 8, 2016).

97. Alyssa Danigelis, "Top 10 Countries on Wind Power," *Discovery*, January 25, 2013, http://news.discovery.com/tech/alternative-power-sources/top-10-countries-wind-power-130130.htm (accessed July 28, 2014).

98. "Local Press Release No. 2/2009 from Vestas Americas," *Vestas*, March 25, 2009, https://www.vestas.com/en/media/~/media/985ce1337cce4156a0872781385abc0f.ashx (accessed August 8, 2016); "Wind as a modern energy source: the Vestas view," *PES: Europe*, 50–52); "About," Vestas, http://www.vestas.com/en/about/profile#! (accessed August 8, 2016); American Wind Energy Association, "Turbines Manufacturers & Rankings," http://www.awea.org/AnnualMarket-Report.aspx?ItemNumber=6313 (accessed August 8, 2016).

99. "Wind Power Set to Boom in Mexico," Global Wind Energy Council, February 28, 2014, http://www.gwec.net/wind-power-set-boom-mexico/ (accessed August 8, 2016).

100. Jen Wilton, "Cancellation of Mexican Wind Farm Highlights Flaw in Green Transition," *New Internationalist,* April 4, 2014, https://newint.org/blog/2014/04/04/mexico-wind-farm/ (accessed August 8, 2016).

101. "Sustainable Construction Continues at Lipscomb with Second LEED-registered Project," Lipscomb University, http://www.lipscomb.edu/news/filter/item/0/22911 (accessed August 8, 2016).

102. "Geothermal Energy Facts," Conserve Energy Future, 2016, http://www.conserve-energy-future.com/GeothermalEnergy-Facts.php (accessed August 8, 2016).

103. Peter W. Davidson, "Celebrating the Completion of the World's Largest Concentrating Solar Power Plant," U.S. Department of Energy, February 13, 2014, http://www.energy.gov/articles/celebrating-completion-worlds-largest-concentrating-solar-power-plant (accessed August 8, 2016).

104. Rebecca Grant, "2013 is a 'Record-shattering' Year for Solar Power in America," *Venture Beat*, December 11, 2013, http://venturebeat.com/2013/12/11/2013-is-a-record-shattering-year-for-solar-power-in-america/ (accessed August 8, 2016).

105. "US Nuclear Power Policy," World Nuclear Association, July 2016, http://www.world-nuclear.org/information-library/country-profiles/countries-t-z/usa-nuclear-power-policy.aspx (accessed August 8, 2016).

106. Chris Cooper, Kiyotaka Matsuda, and Chisaki Watanabe, "ANA to Use Euglena Jet Fuel Made from Green Algae at Japan Plant," *Bloomberg*, December 1, 2015, http://www.bloomberg.com/news/articles/2015-12-01/ana-to-use-euglena-jet-fuel-made-from-green-algae-at-japan-plant (accessed August 8, 2016).

107. "Hydroelectric Power Water Use," *USGS*, May 13, 2009, http://ga.water.usgs.gov/edu/wuhy.html (accessed August 8, 2016); Institute for Energy Research, "Hydroelectric," http://instituteforenergyresearch.org/topics/encyclopedia/hydroelectric/ (accessed August 8, 2016).

108. Stefan Ambec and Paul Lanoie, "Does It Pay to Be Green? A Systematic Overview," *The Academy of Management Perspectives* 22, no. 4 (November 2008): 45–62.

109. Walmart, "Sustainability Leaders," http://corporate.walmart.com/global-responsibility/environment-sustainability/sustainability-index-leaders-shop (accessed August 8, 2016).

110. Miguel Bustillo, "Wal-Mart Plans Environmental Labels for Products," *The Wall Street Journal,* July 16, 2009, http://online.wsj.com/article/SB124766892562645475.html#mod=testMod (accessed August 8, 2016).

111. "Values and Stories," New Belgium Brewing, http://www.newbelgium.com/sustainability (accessed August 8, 2016).

112. "The EU Eco-label," http://ec.europa.eu/environment/ecolabel/ (accessed August 8, 2016).

113. Ferrell, Fraedrich, Ferrell, *Business Ethics*, p. 369.

114. "The Seven Sins of Greenwashing," Terra Choice, http://sinsofgreenwashing.org/ (accessed August 8, 2016).

115. Paul Hawken and William McDonough, "Seven Steps to Doing Good Business," *Inc.,* November 1993, pp. 79–90.

116. Timothy N. Carson and Lata Gangadharan, "Environmental Labeling and Incomplete Consumer Information in Laboratory Markets," *Journal of Environmental Economics and Management* 43, no. 1 (January 2002): 113–134.

117. Kent Walker and Fang Wan, "The Harm of Symbolic Actions and Green-Washing: Corporate Actions and Communications on Environmental Performance and Their Financial Implications," *Journal of Business Ethics* 109 (2012): 227–242.

118. "FTC Issues Revised 'Green Guides,' " Federal Trade Commission, October 1, 2012, http://www.ftc.gov/news-events/press-releases/2012/10/ftc-issues-revised-green-guides (accessed August 8, 2016).

119. United States Environmental Protection Agency, "Wastes - Resource Conservation - Common Wastes & Materials - Paper Recycling: Frequent Questions," https://archive.epa.gov/wastes/conserve/materials/paper/web/html/faqs.html#recycle (accessed August 8, 2016).

120. "About WasteWise," https://www.epa.gov/smm/wastewise (accessed August 8, 2016).

121. Ana Campoy, "'Water Hog' Label Haunts Dallas," *The Wall Street Journal*, July 15, 2009, http://online.wsj.com/article/SB124762034777142623.html (accessed August 8, 2016).

122. Green Globes website, http://greenglobe.com/ (accessed August 8, 2016).

Chapter 12

1. Economist staff, "Relentless.com," *The Economist,* June 21, 2014, pp. 23–26; Sarah Sloat, "Amazon Workers In Germany Extend Strike Action," *The Wall Street Journal*, June 2, 2014, http://online.wsj.com/articles/amazon-workers-in-germany-extend-strike-action-1401725008 (accessed August 9, 2016); "Amazon Workers Strike in Germany Over Pay," *BBC News,* December 16, 2013, http://www.bbc.com/news/business-25397316 (accessed August 9, 2016); Dan Kedmey, "Amazon Charges a Penny After France Bans Free Shipping," *Time,* July 11, 2014, http://time.com/2976723/amazon-france-free-shipping/ (accessed August 9, 2016); Bloomberg News, "Bezos' Kindle-Less Amazon Mashed in China by Ma's Alibaba," *Bloomberg,* February 8, 2013, http://www.bloomberg.com/news/articles/2013-02-07/kindle-less-amazon-in-china-doomed-to-1-market-share (accessed August 9, 2016); Carol Kopp, "Amazon Faces Hurdles in Chinese e-Reader

Market," *USA Today,* June 11, 2013, http://www.usatoday.com/story/tech/2013/06/11/amazon-china-kindle-yahoo-tmall/2411259/ (accessed August 9, 2016).

2. Paul Grey, "(2015) How Many Products Does Amazon Sell?" *ExportX,* December 2015, https://export-x.com/2015/12/11/how-many-products-does-amazon-sell-2015/ (accessed August 9, 2016); Lauren Gensler, "The World's Largest Retailers 2016: Wal-Mart Dominates but Amazon Is Catching Up," *Forbes,* May 27, 2016, http://www.forbes.com/sites/laurengensler/2016/05/27/global-2000-worlds-largest-retailers/#5dec764429a9 (accessed August 9, 2016).

2. Center for Cultural Intelligence, "What is Cultural Intelligence (CQ)?" http://www.cci.ntu.edu.sg/ (accessed August 9, 2016).

3. Mary Lou Egan and Marc Bendick, "Combining Multicultural Management and Diversity Into One Course on Cultural Competence," *Academy of Management Learning and Education* 7, no. 3 (2008): 387–393.

4. P. Christopher Early and Elaine Mosakowski, "Cultural Intelligence," *Harvard Business Review* 82 (October 2004): 1–9.

5. Ibid.

6. Marieke K. de Mooj, *Consumer Behavior and Culture* (Thousand Oaks, CA: Sage, 2003).

7. Business Knowledge Source, "Overseas Manufacturing Pros and Cons," www.businessknowledgesource.com (accessed July 28, 2014).

8. Carrie Johnson, "U.S. targets Overseas Bribery," *The Washington Post*, December 5, 2007, p. D1; The United States Department of Justice, "Alstom Pleads Guilty and Agrees to Pay $772 Million Criminal Penalty to Resolve Foreign Bribery Charges," December 22, 2014, https://www.justice.gov/opa/pr/alstom-pleads-guilty-and-agrees-pay-772-million-criminal-penalty-resolve-foreign-bribery (accessed August 9, 2016).

9. Andrew Singer, "United Parcel Service Translates and Transports an Ethics Code Overseas," *Ethikos and Corporate Conduct Quarterly*, May/June 2001, http://www.singerpubs.com/ethikos/html/ups.html (accessed August 9, 2016).

10. Susan Raymond, "Global Philanthropy Part 2: Philanthropy in Latin America," March 6, 2008, www.onphilanthropy.com (accessed July 29, 2014).

11. "Global Sullivan Principles of Social Responsibility," www.thesullivanfoundation.org/gsp/default.asp (accessed August 9, 2016).

12. Caux Round Table, "Global Governing Board," http://www.cauxroundtable.org/index.cfm?&menuid=11&parentid=9 (accessed August 9, 2016).

13. Mercer, *Engaging Employees to Drive Global Business Success*, 2007, https://www.dgfp.de/wissen/personalwissen-direkt/dokument/86227/herunterladen (accessed August 9, 2016).

14. "Global Code of Ethics for Tourism," World Tourism Organization, http://ethics.unwto.org/en/content/global-code-ethics-tourism (accessed August 9, 2016).

15. "2012 Almanac," *Fair Trade USA,* http://fairtradeusa.org/sites/default/files/2012_Fair-Trade-USA_Almanac.pdf (accessed August 9, 2016).

16. Stephanie Clifford, "Some Retailers Say More About Their Clothing's Origins," *The New York Times*, May 8, 2013, http://www.nytimes.com/2013/05/09/business/global/fair-trade-movement-extends-to-clothing.html (accessed August 9, 2016)

17. "Fair Trade," *GreenAmerica,* http://www.greenamerica.org/programs/fairtrade/ (accessed August 9, 2016).

18. "New Standard Development Project Plan: Agricultural Production Standard," *Fair Trade USA,* May 2014, http://fairtradeusa.org/sites/all/files/wysiwyg/filemanager/standards/Public_Summary_APS_Project_Plan_May2014.pdf (accessed August 9, 2016).

19. Amartya Sen, *Development as Freedom* (Random House: New York, 1999).

20. "News on Millennium Development Goals," United Nations, http://www.un.org/millenniumgoals/ (accessed August 9, 2016).

21. United Nations Global Compact, http://www.unglobalcompact.org/ (accessed August 9, 2016).

22. Ananya Mukherjee Reed and Darryl Reed, "Partnerships for Development: Four Models of Business Involvement," *Journal of Business Ethics* 90, supplement 1 (May 2009): 3–37.

23. Uwafiokun Idemudia, "Oil Extraction and Poverty Reduction in the Niger Delta: A Critical Examination of Partnership Initiatives," *Journal of Business Ethics* 90, supplement 1 (May 2009): 91–116.

24. "Socialism in Reverse," *Wall Street Journal*, July 29, 2006, http://online.wsj.com/news/articles/SB115412585898220871 (accessed August 9, 2016); Arijit Mukherjee and Kullapat Seutrong, "Privatization, Strategic Foreign Direct Investment and Host-Country Welfare," *European Economic Review* 53(7), 2009, 775-785.

25. William Finnegan, "Leasing the Rain," *The New Yorker*, April 8, 2002, http://www.newyorker.com/archive/2002/04/08/020408fa_FACT1?printable=true (accessed August 9, 2016); Jim Shultz, "The Politics of Water in Bolivia," *The Nation*, January 28, 2005, http://www.thenation.com/article/politics-water-bolivia (accessed August 9, 2016).

26. "About the Microcredit Summit Campaign," http://www.microcreditsummit.org/about-the-campaign2.html (accessed August 9, 2016).

27. Grameen Bank, "The Nobel Peace Prize 2006," http://www.grameen-info.org/index.php?option=com_content&task=view&id=197&Itemid=197 (accessed July 30, 2014); World Bank, "10 Years of World Bank Support for Microcredit in Bangladesh," http://web.worldbank.org/WBSITE/EXTERNAL/COUNTRIES/SOUTHASIAEXT/0,,contentMDK:21153910~pagePK:2865106~piPK:2865128~theSitePK:223547,00.html (accessed July 30, 2014).

28. "FLA Highlights Underlying Challenges of Child Labor After Extensive Investigation of Nestle Cocoa Supply Chain," June 29, 2012, http://www.fairlabor.org/blog/entry/fla-highlights-underlying-challenges-child-labor-after-extensive-investigation-nestl%C3%A9 (accessed August 9, 2016).

29. "Self Employed Women's Association," http://www.sewa.org (accessed August 9, 2016).

30. Center for Global Development, "The Commitment to Development Index," 2015, http://www.cgdev.org/cdi-2015 (accessed August 9, 2016).

31. Global Reporting Initiative website, https://www.globalreporting.org/Pages/default.aspx (accessed August 9, 2016).

GLOSSARY

bioethics   Refers to the study of ethical issues in the fields of medical treatment and research, including medicine, nursing, law, philosophy, and theology.

boycott   A form of consumer action in which consumers abstain from using, purchasing, or dealing with an organization.

bribery   The practice of offering something, such as money, gifts, entertainment, and travel, in order to gain an illicit advantage from someone in authority.

business ethics   The principles and standards that guide the behavior of individuals and groups in the world of business.

cause-related marketing   Ties an organization's product(s) directly to a social concern.

codes of conduct   Formal statements that describe what an organization expects of its employees; also called codes of ethics.

community   Members of society who are aware of, concerned with, or in some way affected by the operations and output of an organization.

community relations   The organizational function dedicated to building and maintaining relationships and trust with the community.

conflict of interest   An issue that arises when an individual must choose whether to advance his or her own interests, those of his or her organization, or those of some other group.

consequentialism   A class of moral philosophy that considers a decision right or acceptable if it accomplishes a desired result, such as career growth, the realization of self-interest, or utility in a decision.

Consumer Financial Protection Bureau (CFPB)   Established by the Dodd–Frank Act to regulate banks and other financial institutions by monitoring financial instruments like subprime mortgages and high-risk lending practices.

consumer fraud   Intentional deception to derive an unfair economic advantage over an organization.

consumerism   The movement to protect consumers from an imbalance of power on the side of business and to maximize consumer welfare in the marketplace.

consumers   Those individuals who purchase, use, and dispose of products for themselves and their homes.

core practices   Recognized best practices that are often encouraged by regulatory forces and industry trade associations.

corporate governance   Formal system of oversight, accountability, and control for organizational decisions and resources.

crisis management   The process of handling a high-impact event characterized by ambiguity and the need for swift action.

cultural intelligence   (CQ) The ability to interpret and adapt successfully to different national, organizational, and professional cultures.

deregulation   Removal of all regulatory authority.

development   An improvement in the economic, environmental, educational, and health conditions of a country.

Dodd–Frank Wall Street Reform and Consumer Protection Act   Passed in 2010 to prevent financial crisis by increased financial deregulation, additional oversight of the industry, and preventative measures against unhealthy risk-taking and deceptive practices.

egoism   A philosophy that defines right or acceptable conduct in terms of the consequences for the individual.

emotional intelligence   An important characteristic possessed by ethical leaders referring to the skills to manage themselves and their relationships with others effectively.

employee engagement   The psychological state in which employees feel a vested interest in the company's success and are motivated to perform at levels that exceed job requirements.

employer of choice   An organization of any size in any industry that is able to attract, optimize, and retain the best employee talent over the long term.

employment at will   A common-law doctrine until the early 1900s that allows either the employer or the employee to terminate the relationship at any time as long as it does not violate an employment contract.

Environmental Protection Agency (EPA)   The most influential regulatory agency that deals with environmental issues and enforces environmental legislation in the United States.

ergonomics   The design, arrangement, and use of equipment to maximize productivity and minimize fatigue and physical discomfort.

ethical climate   That part of the firm's culture that focuses specifically on issues of right and wrong.

ethical culture   Refers to the character of the decision-making process employees use to determine if their responses to ethical issues are right or wrong.

ethical diversity   Refers to the fact that employee values often differ from person to person.

ethical formalism   A class of moral philosophy that focuses on the rights of individuals and on the intentions associated with a particular behavior rather than on its consequences.

ethical issue   A problem, situation, or opportunity requiring an individual, group, or organization to choose among several actions that must be evaluated as right or wrong, ethical or unethical.

ethics officer   A high-ranking person known to respect and understand legal and ethical standards.

fair trade   A trading partnership based on dialogue, transparency, and respect that seeks greater equity in international trade and contributes to sustainable development.

Federal Sentencing Guidelines for Organizations (FSGO)   Developed by the U.S. Sentencing Commission and approved by Congress in November 1991 to streamline sentencing and punishment for organizational crimes and holds companies and employees responsible for misconduct.

fraud   Any false communication that deceives, manipulates, or conceals facts to create a false impression when others are damaged or denied a benefit.

genetically modified (GM) organisms   Organisms created through manipulating plant and animal DNA so as to produce a desired effect like resistance to pests and viruses, drought resistance, or high crop yield.

green marketing   A strategic process involving stakeholder assessment to create meaningful long-term relationships with customers while maintaining, supporting, and enhancing the natural environment.

greenwashing   Misleading a consumer into thinking that a product is more environmentally friendly than it is.

hostile work environment   A kind of work environment where the conduct is: unwelcome; severe and hostile as to affect conditions of employment; and offensive to a reasonable person.

hostile work environment sexual harassment   Less direct than quid pro quo harassment, it involves epithets, slurs, negative stereotyping, intimidating acts, graphic materials that show hostility toward an individual or group, and other types of conduct that affect the employment situation.

Intellectual property   (IP) Consists of the ideas and creative materials developed to solve problems, carry out applications, educate, and entertain others.

ISO 14000   A comprehensive set of environmental standards that encourage a cleaner, safer, and healthier world developed by the International Organization for Standardization.

justice theory   A class of moral philosophy that relates to evaluations of fairness, or the disposition to deal with perceived injustices of others.

Kyoto Protocol   A treaty among industrialized nations aimed at slowing global warming.

legitimacy   The perception or belief that a stakeholder's actions are proper, desirable, or appropriate within a given context.

lobbying   The process of working to persuade public and/or government officials to favor a particular position in decision-making.

mandated boundaries   Externally imposed boundaries of conduct, such as laws, rules, regulations, and other requirements.

monopoly   A market type in which just one business provides a good or service in a given market.

moral philosophies   Principles, or rules, which individuals apply in deciding what is right or wrong; morals refers to the individuals' philosophies about what is right or wrong.

neighbor of choice   An organization that builds and sustains trust with the community through employment opportunities, economic development, and financial contribution to education, health, artistic, and recreational activities of the community.

normative approaches   Provide a vision and recommendations for improving ethical decision-making; they are concerned with how organizational decision-makers should approach an ethical issue.

opportunity   A set of conditions that limits barriers or provides rewards.

organizational, or corporate, culture   A set of values, beliefs, and artifacts shared by members or employees of an organization.

philanthropy   The act of businesses giving back to communities and causes. Acts such as donations to charitable organizations to improve the quality of life, reduce government involvement, develop employee leadership skills, and create an ethical culture to act as buffer to organizational misconduct.

political action committees (PACs)   Organizations that solicit donations from individuals and contribute these funds to candidates running for political office.

power   The extent to which a stakeholder can gain access to coercive, utilitarian, or symbolic means to impose or communicate its views to an organization.

primary stakeholders   They are fundamental to a company's operations and survival; these include shareholders and investors, employees, customers, suppliers, and public stakeholders, such as government and the community.

principles   Specific and pervasive boundaries for behavior that are universal and absolute and often form the basis for rules.

privacy issues   Issues that businesses must address that include the monitoring of employees' use of available technology, consumer privacy, and online marketing.

privatization   A process that occurs when public operations are sold to private entities. Public-private partnerships count as partial privatization.

product liability   A business's legal responsibility for the performance of its products.

psychological contract   Largely unwritten, it includes beliefs, perceptions, expectations, and obligations that make up the agreement between individuals and the organizations that employ them.

quid pro quo sexual harassment   A type of sexual extortion where there is a proposed or explicit exchange of job benefits for sexual favors.

recycling   The reprocessing of materials, especially steel, aluminum, paper, glass, rubber, and some plastics, by many organizations for reuse.

reputation management   The process of building and sustaining a company's good name and generating positive feedback from stakeholders.

Sarbanes-Oxley Act   Enacted to restore stakeholder confidence and provide a new standard of ethical behavior for U.S. businesses in the wake of Enron and WorldCom in the early 2000s.

secondary stakeholders   They do not typically engage in direct transactions with a company and thus are not essential for its survival; these include the media, trade associations, and special-interest groups.

sexual harassment   Any repeated, unwanted behavior of a sexual nature perpetrated upon one individual by another; it may be verbal, visual, written, or physical and can occur between people of different genders or those of the same gender.

Unwelcome sexual advances, requests for sexual favors, and other verbal or physical conduct of a sexual nature which when submitted to or rejected explicitly or implicitly affects an individual's employment, unreasonably interferes with an individual's work performance, or creates an intimidating, hostile, or offensive work environment.

shareholder model of corporate governance   Founded in classic economic precepts, it focuses on improving the formal system of performance accountability between the top management and the shareholders.

significant others   Include superiors, peers, and subordinates in the organization who influence the ethical decision-making process.

social audit   The process of assessing and reporting a firm's performance in adopting a strategic focus for fulfilling the economic, legal, ethical, and philanthropic social responsibilities expected of it by its stakeholders.

social capital   An asset that resides in relationships and is characterized by mutual goals and trust.

social entrepreneurship   When an entrepreneur founds a business with the purpose of creating social value.

social responsibility   The adoption by a business of a strategic focus for fulfilling the economic, legal, ethical, and philanthropic responsibilities expected of it by its stakeholders.

stakeholder interaction model A model that conceptualizes the two-way relationships between a firm and a host of stakeholders.

stakeholder model of corporate governance A model where the business is accountable to all its stakeholders, not just the shareholders.

stakeholder orientation The degree to which a firm understands and addresses stakeholder demands.

stakeholders Constituents who have an interest or stake in a company's products, industry, markets, and outcomes.

strategic philanthropy The synergistic use of an organization's core competencies and resources to address key stakeholders' interests and to achieve both organizational and social benefits.

sustainability The potential for long-term well-being of the natural environment, including all biological entities, as well as the interaction among nature and individuals, organizations, and business strategies.

technology Relates to the application of knowledge, including the processes and applications to solve problems, perform tasks, and create new methods to obtain desired outcomes.

technology assessment A procedure used by companies to calculate the effects of new technologies by foreseeing the effects new products and processes will have on their firm's operations, on other business organizations, and on society in general.

trusts Organizations established to gain control of a product market or industry by eliminating competition.

urgency The time sensitivity and the importance of the claim to the stakeholder.

utilitarianism A consequentialist philosophy that is concerned with seeking the greatest good for the greatest number of people.

values Norms that are socially enforced, such as integrity, accountability, and trust.

vesting The legal right to pension plan benefits.

voluntary practices The beliefs, values, and voluntary responsibilities of an organization.

volunteerism When employees spend company-supported time in support of social causes.

whistle-blowing Exposing an employer's wrongdoing to outsiders such as the media or government regulatory agencies.

work/life programs Assist employees in balancing work responsibilities with personal and family responsibilities.

workforce reduction The process of eliminating employment positions.

workplace diversity Focuses on recruiting and retaining a diverse workforce as a business imperative.

INDEX